W9-BOD-667

International Economics
Theory and Policy

Paul R. Krugman
Massachusetts Institute of Technology

Maurice Obstfeld
University of California, Berkeley

International Economics

Theory and Policy

Third Edition

HarperCollinsCollegePublishers

Sponsoring Editor: Bruce Kaplan
Development Editor: Jane Tufts
Project Coordination, Text and Cover Design: Ruttle, Shaw & Wetherill, Inc.
Compositor: Ruttle, Shaw & Wetherill, Inc.
Printer and Binder: R.R. Donnelley & Sons Company
Cover Printer: The Lehigh Press, Inc.

Library of Congress Cataloging-in-Publication Data

Krugman, Paul R.
International economics: theory and policy / Paul R. Krugman, Maurice Obstfeld. —3rd ed.
p. cm.
Includes bibliographical references and index.
ISBN 0-673-52300-4
1. International economic relations. 2. International finance.
I. Obstfeld, Maurice. II. Title.
HF1359.K78 1994
337–dc20 93-44912
CIP

ISBN 0–673–52186–9

94 95 96 9 8 7 6 5 4 3 2

For Robin and Leslie Ann

Contents

* will appear in all subsequent chapters

Preface

The years since 1980 have brought a steady sequence of upheavals in economic relations among countries. Newly industrializing developing countries have seized from developed countries an important share of the world market for manufactured exports; a booming international capital market has forged new links among the world's financial centers but also raised new unease about global financial stability; wide swings in exchange rates and structural shifts in trade patterns have generated political pressures that gravely threaten the open international trading system built up so painstakingly after World War II; and, most recently, the countries of the former Soviet bloc have shaken off Communist rule in the hope of establishing market economies open to international flows of commodities and capital. Even in the United States, which is more self-sufficient than nations with smaller economies, problems of international economic policy have assumed primacy and moved decisively to the newspapers' front pages.

Recent general developments in the world economy raise concerns that have preoccupied international economists for more than two centuries, such as the nature of the international adjustment mechanism and the merits of free trade compared with protection. As always in international economics, however, the interplay of events and ideas has led to new modes of analysis. Three notable examples of recent progress are the asset market approach to exchange rates; new theories of foreign trade and industrial location based on increasing returns and market structure rather than comparative advantage; and the intertemporal analysis of international capital flows, which has been useful both in refining the concept of "external balance" and in examining the determinants of developing country borrowing and default.

The idea of writing this book came out of our experience in teaching international economics to undergraduates and business students over the past fifteen years. We perceived two main challenges in teaching. The first was to communicate to students the exciting intellectual advances in this dynamic field. The second was to show how the development of international economic theory has traditionally been shaped by the need to understand the changing world economy and analyze actual problems in international economic policy.

We found that published textbooks did not adequately meet these challenges. Too often, international economics textbooks confront students with a bewildering array of special models and assumptions from which basic lessons are difficult to extract. Because many of these special models are outmoded, students are left puzzled about the real-world relevance of the analysis. As a result, current textbooks typically leave a gap between the somewhat antiquated material to be covered in class and the exciting issues that dominate current research and policy debates. This gap has widened dramatically as the importance of international economic problems—and enrollments in international economics courses—have grown.

This book is our attempt to provide an up-to-date and understandable analytical framework for illuminating current events and bringing the excitement of international economics into the classroom. In analyzing both the real and the monetary sides of the subject, our approach has been to build up, step by step, a simple, unified framework for communicating the grand traditional insights as well as the newest findings and approaches. To help the student grasp and retain the underlying logic of international economics, we motivate the theoretical development at each stage by pertinent data or policy questions.

The Place of this Book in the Economics Curriculum

Students assimilate international economics most readily when it is presented as a method of analysis vitally linked to events in the world economy, rather than as a body of abstract theorems about abstract models. Our goal has therefore been to stress concepts and their application rather than theoretical formalism. Accordingly, the book does not presuppose an extensive background in economics. Students who have had a course in economic principles will find the book accessible, but students who have taken further courses in microeconomics or macroeconomics will find an abundant supply of new material. Specialized chapter appendices and mathematical postscripts have been included to challenge the most advanced students.

We follow the standard practice of dividing the book into two halves, devoted to trade and to monetary questions. Although the trade and monetary portions of international economics are often treated as unrelated subjects, even within one textbook, similar themes and methods recur in both subfields. One example is the idea of gains from trade, which is important in understanding the effects of free trade in assets as well as free trade in goods. International borrowing and lending provide another example. The process by which countries trade present for future consumption is best understood in terms of comparative advantage (which is why we introduce it in the book's first half), but the resulting insights deepen understanding of the external macroeconomic problems of developing and developed economies alike. We have made it a point to illuminate connections between the trade and monetary areas when they arise.

At the same time, we have made sure that the book's two halves are completely self-contained. Thus, a one-semester course on trade theory can be based on Chapters 2 through 12 and a one-semester course on international monetary economics can be based on Chapters 13 through 24. If you adopt the book for a full-year course covering both subjects, however, you will find a treatment that does not leave students wondering why the principles underlying their work on trade theory have been discarded over the winter break.

Some Distinctive Features of *International Economics: Theory and Policy*

This book covers the most important recent developments in international economics without shortchanging the enduring theoretical and historical insights that have traditionally formed the core of the subject. We have achieved this comprehensiveness by stressing how recent theories have evolved from earlier findings in response to an evolving world economy. Both the real trade portion of the book (Chapters 2 through 12) and the monetary portion (Chapters 13 throught 24) are divided into a core of chapters focused on theory, followed by chapters applying the theory to major policy questions, past and current.

In Chapter 1 we describe in some detail how this book addresses the major themes of international economics. Here we emphasize several of the newer topics that previous authors failed to treat in a systematic way.

ASSET MARKET APPROACH TO EXCHANGE RATE DETERMINATION

The modern foreign exchange market and the determination of exchange rates by national interest rates and expectations are at the center of our account of open-economy macroeconomics. The main ingredient of the macroeconomic model we develop is the interest parity relation (augmented later by risk premiums). Among the topics we address using the model are exchange rate ''overshooting''; behavior of real exchange rates; balance-of-payments crises under fixed exchange rates; and the causes and effects of central bank intervention in the foreign exchange market.

INCREASING RETURNS AND MARKET STRUCTURE

After discussing the role of comparative advantage in promoting trade and gains from trade, we move to the frontier of recent research (in Chapter 6) by explaining how increasing returns and product differentiation affect trade and welfare. The models explored in this discussion capture significant aspects of reality, such as intra-industry trade and shifts in trade patterns due to dynamic scale economies. The models show, too, that mutually beneficial trade need not be based on comparative advantage. The role of economies of scale is probed further in Chapter 8, which studies regional specialization within national economies.

POLITICS OF TRADE POLICY AND INDUSTRIAL POLICY

Starting in Chapter 3, we stress the effect of trade on income distribution as the key political factor behind restrictions on free trade. This emphasis makes it clear to students why the prescriptions of the standard welfare analysis of trade policy seldom prevail in practice. Chapter 12 is focused on the currently popular notion that governments should adopt ''industrial policies'' aimed at encouraging sectors of the economy seen as crucial. The chapter also includes a discussion of strategic trade policy based on simple ideas from game theory.

INTERNATIONAL MACROECONOMIC POLICY COORDINATION

Our discussion of international monetary experience (Chapters 19, 20, and 21) stresses the theme that different exchange rate systems have led to different *policy coordination* problems for their members. Just as the competitive currency depreciations of the interwar years showed how beggar-thy-neighbor policies can be self-defeating, the current float challenges national policy makers to recognize their interdependence and formulate policies cooperatively. Chapter 20 presents a detailed discussion of this very topical problem in the current system.

THE WORLD CAPITAL MARKET AND DEVELOPING COUNTRY DEBT

A broad discussion of the world capital market is given in Chapter 22, which takes up the welfare implications of international portfolio diversification as well as recent problems of prudential supervision of offshore financial institutions. Chapter 23 is devoted to the specific macroeconomic stabilization and liberalization problems of developing countries. The chapter places in historical perspective the interactions among developing country borrowers, developed country lenders, and official financial institutions such as the International Monetary Fund. In addition, students will find a structured approach to the recent developing country debt crisis. That problem is treated only vaguely in other textbooks despite its prominence on the international scene during the 1980s, the continuing debt problems of a number of countries, and the very real possibility of a relapse.

INTERNATIONAL FACTOR MOVEMENTS

In Chapter 7 we emphasize the potential substitutability of international trade and international movements of factors of production. A feature in the chapter is our analysis of international borrowing and lending as *intertemporal trade,* that is, the exchange of present consumption for future consumption. We draw on the results of this analysis in the book's second half to throw light on the macroeconomic implications of the current account.

New to the Third Edition

For this third edition of *International Economics: Theory and Policy,* we have extensively redesigned several chapters and written three new ones. These changes respond both to users' suggestions and to some important developments on the theoretical and practical sides of international economics. The most far-reaching changes are the following:

Chapter 8 The relevance of the distinction between international trade and *interregional trade* is the subject of this new chapter. After examining why political boundaries tend to separate national markets, the chapter reviews current plans for greater economic integration in Europe and in North America. The chapter's theoretical analysis shows how integrated markets allow greater specialization due to external economies. Also studied are the implications of high interregional factor mobility and the causes of regional decline.

Chapter 16 This chapter features a simplified and more intuitive treatment of long-run nominal and real exchange rates. After introducing the idea of purchasing power parity (PPP), Chapter 16 builds on PPP to develop the monetary approach to exchange rates. It then sketches the major factors influencing real exchange rates in the long run and shows how the monetary approach must be modified to account for shifts in those factors.

Chapter 21 Europe's drive toward monetary union provides the empirical background for this new chapter's theoretical analysis of optimum currency areas. After explaining the European Community's reasons for preferring fixed exchange rates, we describe the history and institutions of the European Monetary System (EMS). A model of optimum currency areas is developed next, and applied immediately to see if Europe itself is an optimum currency area. The chapter concludes by analyzing the Maastricht Treaty on European union and the dramatic EMS currency crisis that erupted in September 1992 and eventually led to a drastic widening of the system's exchange rate fluctuation bands.

Chapter 23 The partial easing of the debt crisis and the initial impact of the Brady Plan both are reflected in our updating of this chapter. Moves toward stabilization, economic opening, and reform in indebted developing countries receive more atention. The chapter's analytical focus is on the intertemporal rationale for developing country borrowing and the problem of sovereign default. Included in Chapter 23 is updated coverage of the foreign debt problems of Eastern Europe and the former Soviet Union.

Chapter 24 This new chapter is entirely devoted to the special problems of former Soviet bloc countries as they establish market economies open to world trade. The chapter explains how the centrally planned pattern of intra-bloc trade established under Soviet hegemony suddenly collapsed in the early 1990s, plunging the region into a deep recession. The chapter also looks at the disruption of trade relations within the former Soviet Union and the monetary problems arising from the continuing use of the ruble by the former Soviet republics.

In addition to these structural changes, we have updated the book in other ways to maintain current relevance. Thus, we analyze environmental issues in trade policy (Chapters 4 and 10); we examine the protective roles of anti-dumping actions (Chapter 6) and domestic content requirements (Chapter 9); we discuss the net foreign asset position of the United States and the country's new role as the world's biggest debtor (Chapter 13); and we look at how gaps in international bank supervision led to the BCCI scandal (Chapter 22).

Learning Features

This book incorporates a number of special learning features that will maintain students' interest in the presentation and help them master its lessons.

CASE STUDIES

Theoretical discussions are often accompanied by case studies that perform the threefold role of reinforcing material covered earlier, illustrating its applicability in the real world, and providing important historical information.

SPECIAL BOXES

Less central topics that nonetheless offer particularly vivid illustrations of points made in the text are treated in boxes. Among these are the political backdrops of Ricardo's and Hume's theories (pp. 56 and 532); industrial policy in the case of high-definition television (p. 290); the story of the Bolivian hyperinflation (p. 390); and China's growth into an exporter of manufactures (p. 263).

CAPTIONED DIAGRAMS

More than 200 diagrams are accompanied by descriptive captions that reinforce the discussion in the text and will help the student in reviewing the material.

SUMMARY AND KEY TERMS

Each chapter closes with a summary recapitulating the major points. Key terms or phrases appear in boldface type when they are introduced in the chapter and are listed at the end of each chapter. To further aid student review of the material, key terms are italicized when they appear in the chapter summary.

PROBLEMS

Each chapter is followed by problems intended to test and solidify students' comprehension. The problems range from routine computational drills to "big picture" questions suitable for classroom discussion. In many problems we ask students to apply what they've learned to real-world data or policy questions.

FURTHER READING

For instructors who prefer to supplement the textbook with outside readings, and for students who wish to probe more deeply on their own, each chapter has an annotated bibliography which includes established classics as well as up-to-date examinations of recent issues.

Study Guide, Instructor's Manual, and Reader

International Economics: Theory and Policy is accompanied by a Study Guide written by Linda S. Goldberg of New York University and Michael W. Klein of Tufts University. The Study Guide aids students by providing a review of central concepts from the text, further illustrative examples, and additional practice problems. An Instructor's Manual, also by Linda S. Goldberg and Michael W. Klein, includes chapter overviews, answers to the end-of-chapter problems, and suggestions for classroom presentation of the book's contents. The Study Guide and Instructor's Manual have been updated to reflect the changes in the third edition.

Also recommended for use with *International Economics: Theory and Policy* is *Current Issues in the International Economy: A Reader,* compiled by Professors Goldberg and Klein. Along with topical readings in trade and finance, this reader includes a valuable supplementary section that contains information on the Uruguay Round negotiations and international data on key macroeconomic variables.

Acknowledgments

Our primary debts are to Jane E. Tufts, the development editor, and Bruce Kaplan, the economics editor in charge of the project. Jane's judgment and skill have been reflected in all three editions of this book; we cannot thank her enough for her contributions. Bruce has been a valued adviser and advocate through two editions. Peg Markow's efforts as project manager are greatly appreciated. We thank the other editors who helped make the first two editions as good as they were.

We owe a special debt of gratitude to Matthew Jones, who painstakingly updated data, critiqued chapters, and checked galley proofs. Thanks to Matthew's unrelenting diligence, readers of this third edition will find far fewer errors and anachronisms than otherwise would have been present.

Very helpful comments were received from the following reviewers:

Richard Ault	Auburn University
George H. Borts	Brown University
Francisco Carrada-Bravo	American Graduate School of International Management
Ann Davis	Marist College
Gopal C. Dorai	William Paterson College
Gerald Epstein	University of Massachusetts at Amherst
JoAnne Feeney	University of Colorado, Boulder
Byron Gangnes	University of Hawaii at Manoa
Henk Jager	University of Amsterdam
Mark Jelavich	Northwest Missouri State University
Patrice Franko Jones	Colby College
Maureen Kilkenny	Pennsylvania State University
Bun Song Lee	University of Nebraska, Omaha
Shannon Mitchell	Virginia Commonwealth University
Kaz Miyagiwa	University of Washington
E. Wayne Nafziger	Kansas State University
Donald Schilling	University of Missouri, Columbia
Craig T. Schulman	University of Arkansas
Margaret Simpson	The College of William and Mary
Robert M. Stern	University of Michigan
Sarah Tinkler	Weber State University
Arja H. Turunen-Red	University of Texas, Austin
Dick vander Wal	Free University of Amsterdam

Although we have not been able to make each and every suggested change, we found reviewers' observations invaluable in revising the book. Obviously, we bear sole responsibility for its remaining shortcomings.

Introduction
Chapter 1

The study of international trade and money has always been an especially lively and controversial part of economics. Many of the key insights of modern economic analysis first emerged in eighteenth- and nineteenth-century debates over international trade and monetary policy. Yet there was never a time when the study of international economics was as important as it is today. Through international trade in goods and services, and international flows of money, the economies of different countries are more closely linked to one another now than ever before. At the same time, the world economy is more turbulent than it has been in many decades. Keeping up with the shifting international environment has become a central concern of both business strategy and national economic policy.

A look at some basic trade statistics gives a first view of the increasing importance of international economics to the United States. Figure 1-1 shows the levels of U.S. exports and imports as shares of gross national product from 1965 to 1991. Two points are apparent from the figure. First, the United States exports much more of what it produces and imports much more of what it consumes than it used to: from 1965 to 1980 the share of both exports and imports in GNP more than doubled. Second, U.S. trade has gone through sharp fluctuations since 1980. From 1980 to 1987, exports plunged relative to GNP while imports did not. From 1987 to 1991 there was, by contrast, an export boom. Both the long-term trend toward increasing trade and the fluctuations in U.S. exports relative to imports have been crucial developments for the U.S. economy. By 1980, hardly any discussion of domestic economic policy, be it

FIGURE 1-1
Exports and imports as a percentage of U.S. national income.
From the 1960s to 1980, both exports and imports rose steadily as shares of U.S. income. Since 1980, exports have fluctuated sharply.

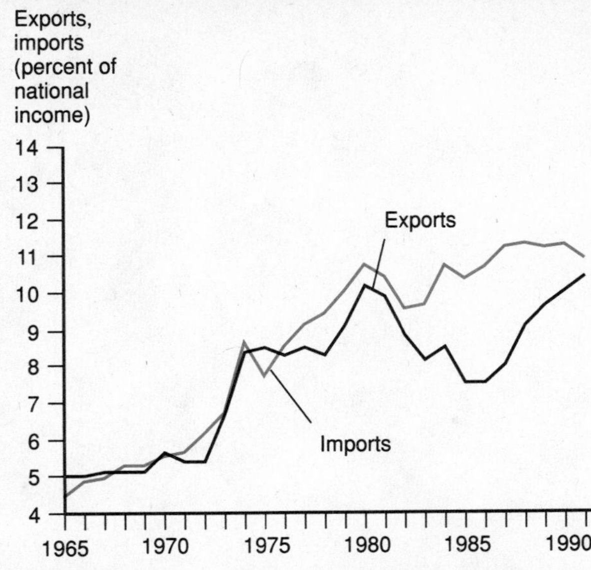

antitrust, regulation, taxation, or labor issues, could ignore the role of international trade. Since 1980, the gap between imports and exports has been one of the most heated issues of U.S. economic controversy.

If international economics has become crucial to the United States, it is even more crucial to other nations. Figure 1-2 shows the 1990 shares of imports and exports in GNP for a sample of countries. The United States, by virtue of its size and diversity

FIGURE 1-2
Exports and imports as percentages of national income in 1990.
International trade is even more important to most other countries than it is to the United States.

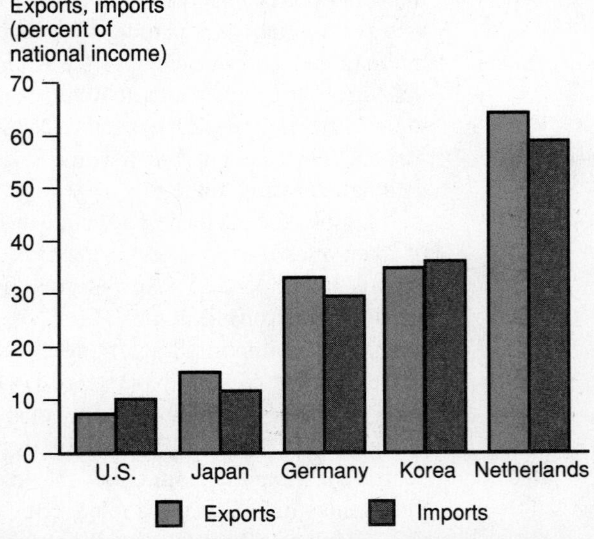

of its resources, actually relies less on international trade than almost any other country. This means that for the rest of the world, international economics is even more important than it is for the United States.

This book introduces the main concepts and methods of international economics and illustrates them with applications drawn from the real world. It is in large part devoted to the grand tradition of international economics; the nineteenth-century trade theory of David Ricardo and the even earlier international monetary analysis of David Hume remain quite relevant to the modern world. At the same time, we have made a special effort to bring the analysis up to date. The field of international economics has been in a creative ferment in recent years, with new views emerging on such issues as the political economy of trade policy, strategic trade policy, exchange rate determination, and the international coordination of macroeconomic policies. We have attempted to convey the key ideas of these new approaches while stressing the continuing usefulness of older ideas.

What Is International Economics About?

International economics uses the same fundamental methods of analysis as other branches of economics, because the motives and behavior of individuals and firms are the same in international trade as they are in domestic transactions. When a bottle of Spanish wine appears on a London table, the sequence of events that brought it there is not very different from the sequence that brings a California bottle to a table in New York—and the distance traveled is much less! Yet international economics involves new and different concerns, because international trade and investment occur between independent nations.[1] Spain and the United Kingdom are sovereign states; California and New York are not. Spain's wine shipments to the United Kingdom can be disrupted if the British government sets a quota that limits imports; Spanish wine can become suddenly cheaper to British wine drinkers if the foreign exchange value of Spain's peseta falls against that of Britain's pound sterling. Neither of these events can happen within the United States, where the Constitution forbids restraints on interstate trade and there is only one currency.

The subject matter of international economics, then, consists of issues raised by the special problems of economic interaction between sovereign states. Seven themes recur throughout the subject: the gains from trade, the pattern of trade, protectionism, the balance of payments, exchange rate determination, international policy coordination, and the international capital market.

THE GAINS FROM TRADE

Everyone knows that some international trade is beneficial—nobody would suggest that Norway should grow its own oranges. Many people, however, are skeptical about the benefits of trading for goods that a country could produce for itself. Shouldn't Americans buy American goods whenever possible to help save U.S. jobs? Probably

[1] Recent political events have, in some cases, blurred the line between international and interregional economics. We discuss regional issues in Chapter 8.

the most important insight in all of international economics is the idea that there are *gains from trade*—that is, that when countries sell goods and services to one another, this is almost always to their mutual benefit. The range of circumstances under which international trade is beneficial is much wider than most people appreciate. For example, many U.S. businesspeople fear that if Japanese productivity overtakes that of the United States, trade with Japan will damage the U.S. economy because none of our industries will be able to compete. U.S. labor leaders charge that the United States is hurt by trade with less advanced countries, whose industries are less efficient than ours but who can sometimes undersell U.S. producers because they pay much lower wages. Yet the first model of trade in this book (Chapter 2) demonstrates that two countries can trade to their mutual advantage even when one of them is more efficient than the other at producing everything and producers in the less efficient economy can compete only by paying lower wages. Trade provides benefits by allowing countries to export goods whose production makes relatively heavy use of resources that are locally abundant while importing goods whose production makes heavy use of resources that are locally scarce (Chapter 4). International trade also allows countries to specialize in producing narrower ranges of goods, allowing them to gain greater efficiencies of large-scale production (Chapter 6). Nor are the benefits limited to trade in tangible goods: international migration and international borrowing and lending are also forms of mutually beneficial trade, the first a trade of labor for goods and services, the second a trade of current goods for the promise of future goods (Chapter 7). Finally, international exchanges of risky assets such as stocks and bonds can benefit all countries by allowing each country to diversify its wealth and reduce the variability of its income (Chapter 22). These invisible forms of trade yield gains as real as the trade that puts fresh fruit from Latin America in Toronto markets in February.

THE PATTERN OF TRADE

Economists cannot discuss the effects of international trade or recommend changes in government policies toward trade with any confidence unless they know their theory is good enough to explain the international trade that is actually observed. Thus attempts to explain the pattern of international trade—who sells what to whom—have been a major preoccupation of international economists.

Some aspects of the pattern of trade are easy to understand. Climate and resources clearly explain why Brazil exports coffee and Saudi Arabia exports oil. Much of the pattern of trade is more subtle, however. Why does Japan export automobiles, while the United States exports aircraft? In the early nineteenth century English economist David Ricardo offered an explanation of trade in terms of international differences in labor productivity, an explanation that remains a powerful insight (Chapter 2). In the twentieth century, however, alternative explanations have also been proposed. One of the most influential, but still controversial, views links trade patterns to an interaction between the relative supplies of national resources such as capital, labor, and land on one side and the relative use of these factors in the production of different goods on the other. We present this theory in Chapter 4. Recent efforts to test the implications of this theory, however, appear to show that it is less valid than many had previously thought. More recently still, some international economists have proposed theories that suggest a substantial random component in the pattern of international trade, theories that are developed in Chapter 6.

PROTECTIONISM

If the idea of gains from trade is the most important theoretical concept in international economics, the seemingly eternal battle between free trade and protection is its most important policy theme. Since the emergence of modern nation-states in the sixteenth century, governments have worried about the effect of international competition on the prosperity of domestic industries and have tried either to shield industries from foreign competition by placing limits on imports or to help them in world competition by subsidizing exports. The single most consistent mission of international economics has been to analyze the effects of these so-called protectionist policies—and usually, though not always, to criticize protectionism and show the advantages of freer international trade.

The protectionist issue is especially intense in the United States because of the trends illustrated by Figure 1-1. Since World War II the United States has advocated free trade in the world economy, viewing international trade as a force not only for prosperity but also for world peace. With the growing role of trade in the U.S. economy from 1965 to 1980, however, many industries found that for the first time they were facing foreign competition in their home markets. Some of them found the foreign competition too much to handle and appealed for protection. During the 1970s these demands were opposed by other U.S. industries that were benefiting from increased export sales. In the 1980s, however, as exports plunged, the mood of Congress shifted toward protectionism. The Reagan and Bush administrations resisted this political pressure but made a series of concessions, limiting imports of Japanese automobiles, European steel, Canadian lumber, and many other goods. Congress recently passed a major new piece of legislation, the Omnibus Trade and Competitiveness Act of 1988, which significantly toughens U.S. trade policy. Although the opposition of most international economists to protection remains as strong as ever, there seems to be a real possibility that over the next few years the United States will move sharply away from its four-decade-long commitment to the principle of free trade.

As befits both the historical importance and the current relevance of the protectionist issue, roughly a quarter of this book is devoted to this subject. Over the years, international economists have developed a simple yet powerful analytical framework for determining the effects of government policies that affect international trade. This framework not only predicts the effects of trade policies, it allows cost-benefit analysis and defines criteria for determining when government intervention is good for the economy. We present this framework in Chapters 9 and 10 and use it to discuss a number of policy issues in those chapters and in the following two.

In the real world, however, governments do not necessarily do what the cost-benefit analysis of economists tells them they should. This does not mean that analysis is useless. Economic analysis can help make sense of the politics of international trade policy, by showing who benefits and who loses from such government actions as quotas on imports and subsidies to exports. The key insight of this analysis is that conflicts of interest *within* nations are usually more important in determining trade policy than conflicts of interest *between* nations. Chapters 3 and 4 show that trade usually has very strong effects on income distribution within countries, while Chapters 10, 11, and 12 reveal that the relative power of different interest groups within countries, rather than some measure of overall national interest, is often the main determining factor in government policies toward international trade.

THE BALANCE OF PAYMENTS

In 1990 both Japan and Brazil ran large trade surpluses—that is, each sold more goods to the rest of the world than it bought in return. Japan's surplus of $56 billion brought complaints from many other countries that Japan was gaining at their expense; Brazil's surplus of $9 billion (which represented a much larger fraction of the country's national income) brought complaints from the Brazilians that *they* were being unfairly treated. What does it mean when a country runs a trade surplus or a trade deficit? To make sense of numbers like the trade deficit, it is essential to place them in the broader context of the whole of a nation's international transactions.

The record of a country's transactions with the rest of the world is called the balance of payments. Explaining the balance of payments, and diagnosing its significance, is a main theme of international economics. It emerges in a variety of specific contexts: in discussing international capital movements (Chapter 7), in relating international transactions to national income accounting (Chapter 13), and in discussing virtually every aspect of international monetary policy (Chapters 17 through 23). Like the problem of protectionism, the balance of payments has become a central issue for the United States because the nation has run huge trade deficits in every year since 1982.

EXCHANGE RATE DETERMINATION

In February 1985, one U.S. dollar traded on international markets for 260 Japanese yen; in January 1988, a dollar was worth only 123 yen. This change had effects that reached far beyond financial markets. In February 1985, the average Japanese worker in manufacturing was paid a wage in yen that, converted into dollars at the prevailing rate of exchange, was only about half that of his or her U.S. counterpart. Three years later Japanese wages were about the same as U.S. wages. With their labor cost advantage vis-à-vis the United States gone, and in the face of competition from low-wage competitors like Korea and Taiwan, Japanese manufacturers were initially forced into layoffs that drove the Japanese unemployment rate to its highest level since the 1950s, after which they began investing heavily in acquiring production facilities in other countries—especially in the United States.

One of the key differences between international economics and other areas of economics is that countries have different currencies. It is usually possible to convert one currency into another (though even this is illegal in some countries), but as the example of the dollar-yen exchange rate indicates, relative prices of currencies may change over time, sometimes drastically.

The study of exchange rate determination is a relatively new part of international economics, for historical reasons. For most of the twentieth century, exchange rates have been fixed by government action rather than determined in the marketplace. Before World War I the values of the world's major currencies were fixed in terms of gold, while for a generation after World War II the values of most currencies were fixed in terms of the U.S. dollar. The analysis of international monetary systems that fix exchange rates remains an important subject, especially since European nations have made a major effort to create a fixed-rate system in Europe. Chapters 18 and 19 are devoted to the working of fixed-rate systems, Chapter 20 to the debate over which system, fixed or floating rates, is better, and Chapter 21 to the workings of the European monetary system. For the time being, however, some of the world's most important exchange rates fluctuate minute by minute and the role of changing exchange rates remains at the center of the international economics story. Chapters 14 through 17 focus on the modern theory of floating exchange rates.

INTERNATIONAL POLICY COORDINATION

The international economy comprises sovereign nations, each free to choose its own economic policies. Unfortunately, in an integrated world economy one country's economic policies usually affect other countries as well. When West Germany raised taxes and interest rates in 1981, all of Europe went into a recession; when the United States imposed a tariff on imports of lumber during 1986, the Canadian lumber industry experienced a crisis. Differences in goals between countries often lead to conflicts of interest. Even when countries have similar goals, they may suffer losses if they fail to coordinate their policies. A fundamental problem in international economics is how to produce an acceptable degree of harmony among the international trade and monetary policies of different countries without a world government that tells countries what to do.

For the last forty-five years international trade policies have been governed by an international treaty known as the General Agreement on Tariffs and Trade, and massive international negotiations involving dozens of countries at a time have been held. We discuss the rationale for this system in Chapter 10 and look at whether the current rules of the game for international trade in the world economy can or should survive.

While cooperation on international trade policies is a well-established tradition, coordination of international macroeconomic policies is a newer and more uncertain topic. Only in the last few years have economists formulated at all precisely the case for macroeconomic policy coordination. Nonetheless, attempts at international macroeconomic coordination are occurring with growing frequency in the real world. Both the theory of international macroeconomic coordination and the developing experience are reviewed in Chapters 19 and 20.

THE INTERNATIONAL CAPITAL MARKET

During the 1970s banks in advanced countries lent tens of billions of dollars to firms and governments in poorer nations, especially in Latin America. In 1982, Mexico announced it could no longer pay the money it owed without special arrangements that allowed it to postpone payments and borrow back part of its interest; soon afterward Brazil, Argentina, and a number of smaller countries found themselves in the same situation. While combined efforts of banks, governments, and countries avoided a world financial crisis in 1982, the debt difficulties of less-developed countries remained in a state of periodic crisis through 1990. The debt problem brought to the public's attention the growing importance of the international capital market.

In any sophisticated economy there is an extensive capital market: a set of arrangements by which individuals and firms exchange money now for promises to pay in the future. The growing importance of international trade since the 1960s has been accompanied by a growth in the *international* capital market, which links the capital markets of individual countries. Thus in the 1970s oil-rich Middle Eastern nations placed their oil revenues in banks in London or New York, and these banks in turn lent money to governments and corporations in Asia and Latin America. During the 1980s Japan converted much of the money it earned from its booming exports into investments in the United States, including the establishment of a growing number of U.S. subsidiaries of Japanese corporations.

International capital markets differ in important ways from domestic capital markets. They must cope with special regulations that many countries impose on foreign investment; they also sometimes offer opportunities to evade regulations placed on domestic markets. Since the 1960s, huge international capital markets have arisen, most notably the remarkable London Eurodollar market, in which billions of dollars are exchanged each day without ever touching the United States.

Some special risks are also associated with international capital markets. One risk is that of currency fluctuations: if the dollar falls suddenly against the Japanese yen, Japanese investors who bought U.S. bonds suffer a capital loss—as many discovered in 1985–1988. Another risk is that of national default: a nation may simply refuse to pay its debts (perhaps because it cannot), and there may be no effective way for its creditor to bring it to court. This remains a real possibility for the nations of Latin America; if all of them were to refuse payment, major U.S. banks would lose heavily.

The growing importance of international capital markets and their new problems demand greater attention than ever before. This book devotes two chapters to issues arising from international capital markets: one on the functioning of global asset markets (Chapter 22) and one on the international debt problem (Chapter 23).

International Economics: Trade and Money

The economics of the international economy can be divided into two broad subfields: the study of *international trade* and the study of *international money.* International trade analysis focuses primarily on the *real* transactions in the international economy, that is, on those transactions that involve a physical movement of goods or a tangible commitment of economic resources. International monetary analysis focuses on the *monetary* side of the international economy, that is, on financial transactions such as foreign purchases of U.S. dollars. An example of an international trade issue is the conflict between the United States and Europe over Europe's subsidized exports of agricultural products; an example of an international monetary issue is the dispute over whether the foreign exchange value of the dollar should be allowed to float freely or be stabilized by government action.

In the real world there is no simple dividing line between trade and monetary issues. Most international trade involves monetary transactions, while, as the examples in this chapter already suggest, many monetary events have important consequences for trade. Nonetheless, the distinction between international trade and international money is useful. The first half of this book covers international trade issues. Part One (Chapters 2 through 8) develops the analytical theory of international trade, and Part Two (Chapters 9 through 12) applies trade theory to the analysis of government policies toward trade. The second half of the book is devoted to international monetary issues. Part Three (Chapters 13 through 18) develops international monetary theory, and Part Four (Chapters 19 through 24) applies this analysis to international monetary policy.

Part One
International Trade Theory

Labor Productivity and Comparative Advantage: The Ricardian Model

Chapter 2

Countries engage in international trade for two basic reasons, each of which contributes to their gain from trade. First, countries trade because they are different from each other. Nations, like individuals, can benefit from their differences by reaching an arrangement in which each does the things it does relatively well. Second, countries trade to achieve economies of scale in production. That is, if each country produces only a limited range of goods, it can produce each of these goods at a larger scale and hence more efficiently than if it tried to produce everything. In the real world, patterns of international trade reflect the interaction of both these motives. As a first step toward understanding the causes and effects of trade, however, it is useful to look at simplified models in which only one of these motives is present.

The next four chapters develop tools to help us to understand how differences between countries give rise to trade between them and why this trade is mutually beneficial. The essential concept in this analysis is that of **comparative advantage.**

Although the idea of comparative advantage is simple, it can be somewhat confusing if stated in the abstract. The best way to grasp the concept properly is to examine a series of examples and models that demonstrate it. This chapter provides examples in which comparative advantage is solely the result of international differences in the productivity of labor. A model of comparative advantage resting on differences in labor productivity was first introduced in the early nineteenth century by the economist David Ricardo[1] and is therefore referred to as the **Ricardian model.**

A One-Factor Economy

To introduce the role of comparative advantage in determining the pattern of international trade, we begin by imagining that we are dealing with an economy—which we call Home—that has only one factor of production. (In later chapters we extend the analysis to models in which there are several factors.) Also we imagine that only two goods, wine and cheese, are produced. The technology of Home's economy can be summarized by the productivity of labor in each industry. It is convenient to express productivity in terms of the **unit labor requirement,** the number of hours of labor required to produce a pound of cheese or a gallon of wine. For future reference, let us define a_{LW} and a_{LC} as the unit labor requirements in wine and cheese production, respectively. Also, the economy's total resources may be defined as L, the total labor supply.

PRODUCTION POSSIBILITIES

Because any economy has limited resources, there are limits on what it can produce, and there are always trade-offs; to produce more of one good the economy must sacrifice some production of another good. These trade-offs are illustrated graphically by a **production possibility frontier** (line PF in Figure 2-1), which shows the maximum amount of wine that can be produced once the decision has been made to produce any given amount of cheese, and vice versa.

When there is only one factor of production the production possibility frontier of an economy is simply a straight line. We can derive this line as follows: Let Q_W be the economy's production of wine and Q_C its production of cheese. Then the labor used in producing wine will be $a_{LW}Q_W$, the labor used in producing cheese $a_{LC}Q_C$. The production possibility frontier is determined by the limits on the economy's resources—in this case, labor. The economy's total labor supply is L. So the limits on production are defined by the inequality

$$a_{LC}Q_C + a_{LW}Q_W \leq L. \tag{2-1}$$

When the production possibility frontier is a straight line, the **opportunity cost** of cheese in terms of wine is constant. The opportunity cost is the number of gallons of wine the economy would have to give up in order to produce an extra pound of cheese. In this case, to produce another pound would require a_{LC} person-hours. Each of these person-hours could in turn have been used to produce $1/a_{LW}$ gallons of wine. Thus the opportunity cost of cheese in terms of wine is a_{LC}/a_{LW}. This is equal to minus the slope

[1] The classic reference is David Ricardo, *The Principles of Political Economy and Taxation,* first published in 1817.

FIGURE 2-1
Home's production possibility frontier.
The line *PF* shows the maximum amount of cheese that can be produced given any production of wine, and vice versa.

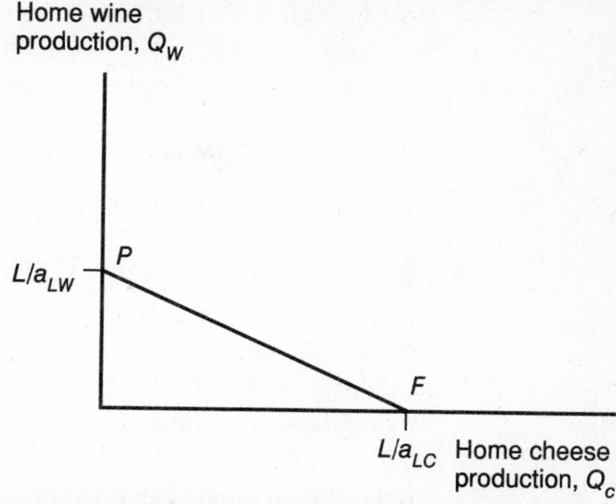

of the production possibility frontier, which itself is equal to the unit labor requirement in cheese (a_{LC} hours per pound) relative to that in wine (a_{LW} hours per gallon).

RELATIVE PRICES AND SUPPLY

The production possibility frontier illustrates the different mixes of goods the economy *can* produce. To determine what the economy will actually produce, however, we need to look at prices. Specifically, we need to know the relative price of the economy's two goods, that is, the price of one good in terms of the other.

In a competitive economy, supply is determined by the attempts of individuals to maximize their earnings. In our simplified economy, since labor is the only factor of production, the supply of cheese and wine will be determined by the movement of labor to whichever sector pays the higher wage.

Let P_C and P_W be the prices of cheese and wine, respectively. It takes a_{LC} person-hours to produce a pound of cheese; since there are no profits in our one-factor model, the hourly wage rate in the cheese sector will be equal to the value of what a worker can produce in an hour, P_C/a_{LC}. Since it takes a_{LW} person-hours to produce a gallon of wine, the hourly wage rate in the wine sector will correspondingly be equal to P_W/a_{LW}. Wages in the cheese sector will be higher if $P_C/P_W > a_{LC}/a_{LW}$; wages in the wine sector will be higher if $P_C/P_W < a_{LC}/a_{LW}$. But everyone will want to work in whichever industry offers the higher wage. The economy will therefore specialize in the production of cheese if $P_C/P_W > a_{LC}/a_{LW}$; it will specialize in the production of wine if $P_C/P_W < a_{LC}/a_{LW}$. Only when P_C/P_W is equal to a_{LC}/a_{LW} will both goods be produced.

What is the significance of the number a_{LC}/a_{LW}? We just saw that it is the oppportunity cost of cheese in terms of wine. The general point, then, is the following: *The economy will specialize in the production of cheese if the relative price of cheese exceeds its opportunity cost; it will specialize in the production of wine if the relative price of cheese is less than its opportunity cost.*

In the absence of international trade, Home would have to produce both goods for itself. But it will produce both goods only if the relative price of cheese is just equal to its opportunity cost. Since opportunity cost equals the ratio of unit labor requirements in cheese and wine, we can summarize with a simple labor theory of value: *In the absence of international trade, the relative prices of goods are equal to their relative unit labor requirements.*

Trade in a One-Factor World

To describe the pattern and effects of trade between two countries when each country has only one factor of production is simple. Yet the implications of this analysis can be surprising, and indeed often seem to those who have not thought about international trade to conflict with common sense. Even this simplest of trade models can offer some important guidance on real-world issues, such as what constitutes fair international competition and fair international exchange.

Before we get to these issues, however, let us get the model stated. Suppose that there are two countries. One of them we again call Home and the other we call Foreign. Each of these countries has one factor of production (labor) and can produce two goods, wine and cheese. As before, we denote Home's labor force by L and Home's unit labor requirements in wine and cheese production by a_{LW} and a_{LC}, respectively. For Foreign we will use a convenient notation throughout this book: when we refer to some aspect of Foreign, we will use the same symbol that we use for Home, but with an asterisk. Thus Foreign's labor force will be denoted by L^*; Foreign's unit labor requirements in wine and cheese will be denoted by a^*_{LW} and a^*_{LC}, respectively, and so on.

In general the unit labor requirements can follow any pattern. For example, Home could be less productive than Foreign in wine but more productive in cheese, or vice versa. For the moment, we make only one arbitrary assumption: that

$$a_{LC}/a_{LW} < a^*_{LC}/a^*_{LW} \tag{2-2}$$

or, equivalently, that

$$a_{LC}/a^*_{LC} < a_{LW}/a^*_{LW} \tag{2-3}$$

In words, we are assuming that the ratio of the unit labor requirement in cheese to that in wine is lower in Home than it is in Foreign. More briefly still, we can say that Home's relative productivity in cheese is higher than it is in wine. In this case we will say that *Home has a comparative advantage in cheese production.* The significance of this will become apparent shortly.

One point should be noted immediately, however: the definition of comparative advantage involves all four unit labor requirements, not just two. You might think that to determine who will produce cheese, all you need to do is compare the two countries' unit labor requirements in cheese production, a_{LC} and a^*_{LC}. If $a_{LC} < a^*_{LC}$, Home labor is more efficient than Foreign in producing cheese. This is a situation where Home has an **absolute advantage** in cheese production. What we will see in a moment, however, is that we cannot determine the pattern of trade from absolute advantage alone. One of the most important sources of error in discussions of international trade is to confuse comparative advantage with absolute advantage.

Given the labor forces and the unit labor requirements in the two countries, we can draw the production possibility frontier for each country. We have already done this for Home, by drawing *PF* in Figure 2-1. The production possibility frontier for Foreign is shown as F^*P^* in Figure 2-2. Given our assumption about relative unit labor requirements, the Foreign production possibility frontier is steeper than Home's.

In the absence of trade the relative prices of cheese and wine in each country would be determined by the relative unit labor requirements. Thus in Home the relative price of cheese would be a_{LC}/a_{LW}; in Foreign it would be a^*_{LC}/a^*_{LW}.

Once we allow for the possibility of international trade, however, prices will no longer be determined purely by domestic considerations. If the relative price of cheese is higher in Foreign than in Home, it will be profitable to ship cheese from Home to Foreign and to ship wine from Foreign to Home. This cannot go on indefinitely; Home will export enough cheese, and Foreign enough wine, so as to equalize the relative price. So what we need to determine is the world relative price of cheese after trade.

DETERMINING THE RELATIVE PRICE AFTER TRADE

Prices of internationally traded goods, like other prices, are determined by supply and demand. In discussing comparative advantage, however, we must apply supply-and-demand analysis carefully. In some contexts, such as some of the trade policy analysis in Chapters 9 through 12, it is acceptable to focus only on supply and demand in a single market. In assessing the effects of U.S. import quotas on sugar, for example, it is reasonable to use **partial equilibrium analysis,** that is, to study a single market, the sugar market. When we study comparative advantage, however, it is crucial to keep track of the relationships between markets (in our example the markets for wine and cheese). Since Home exports cheese only in return for imports of wine, and Foreign exports wine in return for cheese, it can be misleading to look at the cheese and wine markets in isolation. What is needed is **general equilibrium analysis** that takes account of the linkages between the two markets.

FIGURE 2-2
Foreign's production possibility frontier.
Because Foreign's relative unit labor requirement in cheese is higher than Home's, its production possibility frontier is steeper.

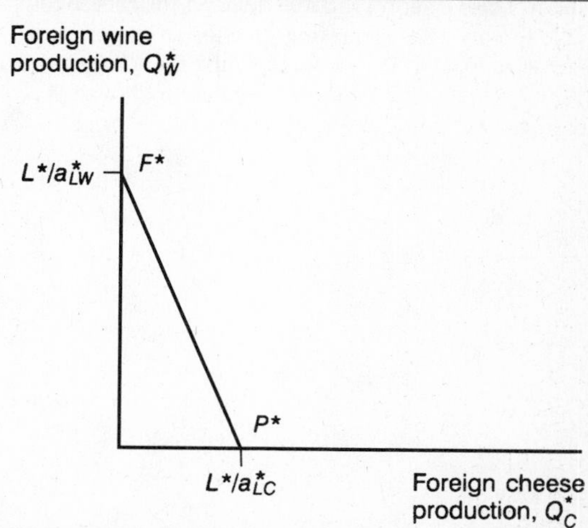

One useful way to keep track of two markets at once is to focus not just on the quantities of cheese and wine supplied and demanded but also on the *relative* supply and demand, that is, on the number of pounds of cheese supplied or demanded divided by the number of gallons of wine supplied or demanded.

Figure 2-3 shows world supply and demand for cheese relative to wine as functions of the price of cheese relative to that of wine. The **relative demand curve** is indicated by *RD;* the **relative supply curve** is indicated by *RS.* World general equilibrium requires that relative supply equal relative demand, and thus the world relative price is determined by the intersection of *RD* and *RS.*

The striking feature of Figure 2-3 is the funny shape of the relative supply curve *RS:* a "step" with flat sections linked by a vertical section. Once we understand the derivation of the *RS* curve, we will be almost home free in understanding the whole model.

First, as drawn, the *RS* curve shows that there is no supply of cheese if the world price drops below a_{LC}/a_{LW}. To see why, recall that we showed that Home will specialize in the production of wine whenever $P_C/P_W < a_{LC}/a_{LW}$. Similarly, Foreign will specialize in wine production whenever $P_C/P_W < a^*_{LC}/a^*_{LW}$, which is by assumption greater than a_{LC}/a_{LW}. So at relative prices of cheese below a_{LC}/a_{LW}, there will be no world cheese production.

Next, when the relative price of cheese is exactly a_{LC}/a_{LW}, we know that workers in Home can earn exactly the same amount making either cheese or wine. So Home will be willing to supply any relative amount of the two goods, producing a flat section to the supply curve.

We have already seen that if P_C/P_W is above a_{LC}/a_{LW}, Home will specialize in the production of cheese. As long as $P_C/P_W < a^*_{LC}/a^*_{LW}$, however, Foreign will continue to specialize in producing wine. When Home specializes in cheese production, it

FIGURE 2-3
World relative supply and demand.
The *RD* curve shows that the demand for cheese relative to wine is a decreasing function of the price of cheese relative to that of wine, while the *RS* curve shows that the supply of cheese relative to wine is an increasing function of the same relative price.

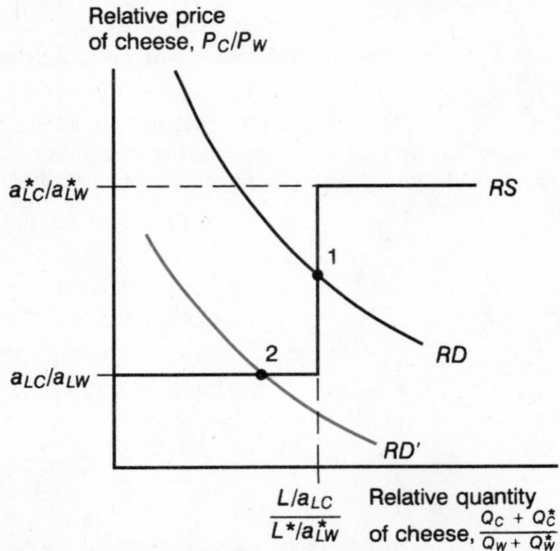

produces L/a_{LC} pounds. Similarly, when Foreign specializes in wine it produces L^*/a^*_{LW} gallons. So for any relative price of cheese between a_{LC}/a_{LW} and a^*_{LC}/a^*_{LW} the relative supply of cheese is

$$(L/a_{LC})/(L^*/a^*_{LW}). \qquad \textbf{(2-4)}$$

At $P_C/P_W = a^*_{LC}/a^*_{LW}$, we know that Foreign workers are indifferent between producing cheese and wine. Thus here we again have a flat section of the supply curve.

Finally, for $P_C/P_W > a^*_{LC}/a^*_{LW}$, both Home and Foreign will specialize in cheese production. There will be no wine production, so that the relative supply of cheese will become infinite.

The relative demand curve *RD* does not require such exhaustive analysis. The downward slope of *RD* reflects substitution effects. As the relative price of cheese rises, consumers will tend to purchase less cheese and more wine, so the relative demand for cheese falls.

The equilibrium relative price of cheese is determined by the intersection of the relative supply and relative demand curves. Figure 2-3 shows a relative demand curve *RD* that intersects the *RS* curve at point 1, where the relative price of cheese is between the two countries' pretrade prices. In this case each country specializes in the production of the good in which it has a comparative advantage: Home produces only cheese, Foreign only wine.

This is not, however, the only possible outcome. If the relevant *RD* curve were *RD'*, for example, relative supply and relative demand would intersect on one of the horizontal sections of *RS.* At point 2 the world relative price of cheese after trade is a_{LC}/a_{LW}, the same as the opportunity cost of cheese in tems of wine in Home.

What is the significance of this outcome? If the relative price of cheese is equal to its opportunity cost in Home, the Home economy need not specialize in producing either cheese or wine. In fact, at point 2 Home must be producing both some wine and some cheese; we can infer this from the fact that the relative supply of cheese is less than it would be if Home were in fact completely specialized. Since P_C/P_W is below the opportunity cost of cheese in terms of wine in Foreign, however, Foreign does specialize completely in producing wine. It therefore remains true that if a country does specialize, it will do so in the good in which it has a comparative advantage.

Let us for the moment leave aside the possibility that one of the two countries does not completely specialize. Except in this case, the normal result of trade is that the price of a traded good (e.g., cheese) relative to that of another good (wine) ends up somewhere in between its pretrade levels in the two countries.

The effect of this convergence in relative prices is that each country specializes in the production of that good in which it has the relatively lower unit labor requirement. The rise in the relative price of cheese in Home will lead Home to specialize in the production of cheese, producing at point *F* in Figure 2-1. The fall in the relative price of cheese in Foreign will lead Foreign to specialize in the production of wine, producing at point *F** in Figure 2-2.

THE GAINS FROM TRADE

We have now seen that countries whose relative labor productivities differ across industries will specialize in the production of different goods. We next show that both countries derive **gains from trade** from this specialization. This mutual gain can be demonstrated in two alternative ways.

The first way to show that specialization and trade are beneficial is to think of trade as an indirect method of production. Home could produce wine directly, but trade with Foreign allows it to ''produce'' wine by producing cheese and then trading the cheese for wine. This indirect method of ''producing'' a gallon of wine is a more efficient method than direct production. Consider two alternative ways of using an hour of labor. On one side, Home could use the hour directly to produce $1/a_{LW}$ gallons of wine. Alternatively, Home could use the hour to produce $1/a_{LC}$ pounds of cheese. This cheese could then be traded for wine, with each pound trading for P_C/P_W gallons, so our original hour of labor yields $(1/a_{LC})(P_C/P_W)$ gallons of wine. This will be more wine than the hour could have produced directly as long as

$$(1/a_{LC})(P_C/P_W) > 1/a_{LW}, \tag{2-5}$$

or

$$P_C/P_W > a_{LC}/a_{LW}.$$

But we just saw that in international equilibrium, if neither country produces both goods, we must have $P_C/P_W > a_{LC}/a_{LW}$. This shows that Home can ''produce'' wine more efficiently by making cheese and trading it than by producing wine directly for itself. Similarly, Foreign can ''produce'' cheese more efficiently by making wine and trading it. This is one way of seeing that both countries gain.

Another way to see the mutual gains from trade is to examine how trade affects each country's possibilities for consumption. In the absence of trade, consumption possibilities are the same as production possibilities (the solid lines *PF* and *F*P** in Figure 2-4). Once trade is allowed, however, each economy can consume a different mix of cheese and wine from the mix it produces. Home's consumption possibilities are indicated by the colored line *TF* in Figure 2-4a, while Foreign's consumption possibilities are indicated by *F*T** in Figure 2-4b. In each case trade has enlarged the range of choice, and therefore it must make residents of each country better off.

A NUMERICAL EXAMPLE

To solidify understanding of the points we have just made, it is useful to consider a numerical example. Suppose, then, that Home and Foreign have the unit labor requirements illustrated in Table 2-1.

A striking feature of this table is that Home has lower unit labor requirements, that is, has higher labor productivity, in both industries. Let us leave this observation for a moment, however, and focus on the pattern of trade.

The first thing we need to do is determine the relative price of cheese P_C/P_W. This depends on demand; however, we know that it must lie between the opportunity cost of cheese in the two countries. In Home, we have $a_{LC} = 1$, $a_{LW} = 2$; so the opportunity cost of cheese in terms of wine is $a_{LC}/a_{LW} = 1/2$. In Foreign, $a^*_{LC} = 6$, $a^*_{LW} = 3$; so the opportunity cost of cheese is 2. In world equilibrium, the relative price of cheese must lie between these values. For the sake of the example, let us assume that in world equilibrium $P_C/P_W = 1$: a pound of cheese trades for a gallon of wine on world markets.

FIGURE 2-4
Trade expands consumption possibilities.
International trade allows Home and Foreign to consume anywhere within the colored lines, which lie outside the countries' production possibility frontiers.

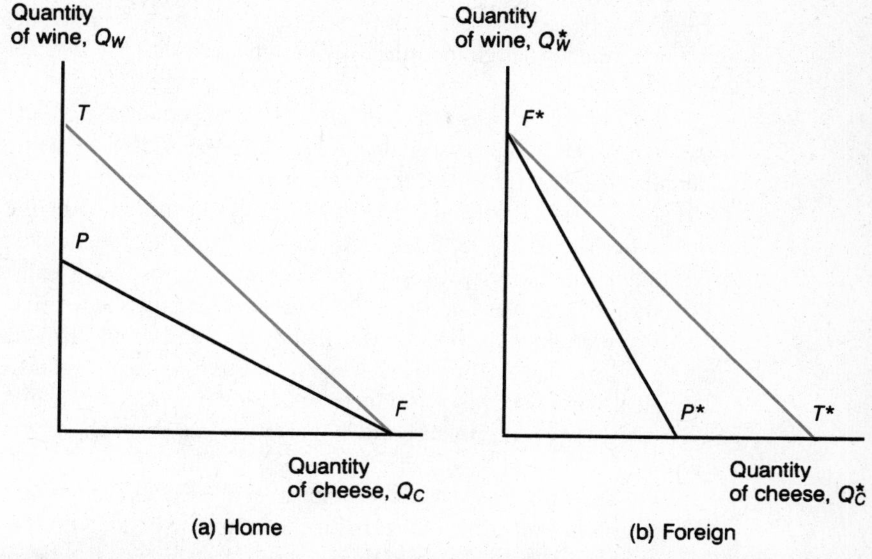

At this relative price of cheese, we can immediately see that each country will specialize, Home in cheese and Foreign in wine. To check this, notice that a worker in Home would earn only half as much producing wine as producing cheese, while the reverse is true for a worker in Foreign.

We can now check for gains from trade. First, we want to show that Home can "produce" wine more efficiently by making cheese and trading it for wine than by direct production. This is easy: in direct production, an hour of Home labor produces only 1/2 gallon of wine. The same hour could be used to produce 1 pound of cheese, which can then be traded for 1 gallon of wine. This shows that Home does indeed gain from trade. Similarly, Foreign could use 1 hour of labor to produce 1/6 pound of cheese; but it can instead use the hour to produce 1/3 gallon of wine and trade the wine for 1/3 pound of cheese. In this example, each country can use labor twice as efficiently to trade for what it needs instead of producing its imports for itself.

TABLE 2-1 Unit labor requirements

	Cheese	*Wine*
Home	$a_{LC} = 1$	$a_{LW} = 2$
Foreign	$a^*_{LC} = 6$	$a^*_{LW} = 3$

Although it is not essential for analyzing the effect of trade on the welfare of either country, it is interesting to notice the implications of trade for the ratio of wage rates in the two countries. To determine the ratio of wage rates, first note what the wage rate of each country must be in terms of the good it produces. After trade, Home produces cheese; since it takes 1 hour of labor to produce 1 pound of cheese, the wage rate in Home is 1 pound of cheese per person-hour. Similarly, Foreign produces wine, needing 3 hours of labor per gallon; thus the foreign wage rate is 1/3 gallon of wine per person-hour.

To make these wage rates in terms of wine and cheese comparable, we must make use of the relative prices of the two goods. If 1 gallon of wine costs the same as 1 pound of cheese, then the wage rate in Foreign must be one-third the wage rate in Home. The ratio of the wage rates lies between the ratios of the two countries' productivities in the two industries. Home is six times as productive as Foreign in cheese, but only one-and-a-half times as productive in wine, and it ends up with a wage rate three times as high as Foreign's. It is precisely because the relative wage is intermediate between the relative productivities that each country ends up with a *cost* advantage in one good. Because of its lower wage rate, Foreign has a cost advantage in wine, even though it has lower labor productivity. Home has a cost advantage in cheese despite its higher wage rate, because the higher wage is more than offset by its higher productivity.

We have now developed the simplest of all models of international trade. Obviously the Ricardian one-factor model is far too simple to be a complete analysis of either the causes or the effects of international trade. Yet a focus on relative labor productivities can be a very useful tool for thinking about international trade. In particular, the simple one-factor model is a good way to deal with several common misconceptions about the meaning of comparative advantage and the nature of the gains from free trade. These misconceptions appear so frequently in public debate about international economic policy, and even in statements by those who regard themselves as experts, that in the next section we take time out to discuss some of the most common misunderstandings about comparative advantage in the light of our model.

Misconceptions about Comparative Advantage

There is no shortage of muddled ideas in economics. Politicians, business leaders, and even economists frequently make statements that do not stand up to careful economic analysis. For some reason this seems to be especially true in international economics. Open the business section of any Sunday newspaper or weekly news magazine and you will probably find at least one article that makes foolish statements about international trade. Three misconceptions in particular have proved highly persistent, and our simple model of comparative advantage can be used to see why they are incorrect.

PRODUCTIVITY AND COMPETITIVENESS

Myth 1: Free trade is beneficial only if your country is productive enough to stand up to international competition. This argument, most often used with regard to less-developed countries, implies that poor countries should isolate themselves from the international economy until they are strong enough to compete. In 1983, for example, a columnist in the *Wall Street Journal* asserted that "Many small countries have no comparative advantage in anything."[2] This fallacy has been given a new lease on life by Japan's technological challenge to the United States. This challenge has produced fears that a failure of the United States to keep its technological lead will mean that trade will become a source of harm instead of gain.

To see the fallacy in this reasoning, we need look no further than our simple numerical example of trade. In that example, Home has lower unit labor requirements and thus higher productivity in both the cheese and wine sectors. Yet, as we saw, both countries gain from trade. It is always tempting to suppose that the ability to export a good depends on an *absolute* advantage in productivity: what the *Wall Street Journal* columnist must have meant is that "many small countries have no absolute productivity advantage over other countries in anything." What he failed to understand is that an absolute productivity advantage over other countries in producing a good is neither a necessary nor a sufficient condition for having a *comparative* advantage in that good. In our one-factor model the reason why absolute productivity advantage in an industry is neither necessary nor sufficient to yield competitive advantage is clear: *The competitive advantage of an industry depends not only on its productivity relative to the foreign industry, but also on the domestic wage rate relative to the foreign wage rate.* A country's wage rate, in turn, depends on relative productivity in its other industries. In our numerical example, Foreign is less efficient than Home in the manufacture of wine, but at even a greater relative productivity disadvantage in cheese. Because of its overall lower productivity, Foreign must pay lower wages than Home, sufficiently lower that it ends up with lower costs in wine production. Similarly, in the real world Portugal has low productivity in producing, say, clothing as compared with the United States, but because Portugal's productivity disadvantage is even greater in other industries it pays low enough wages to have a comparative advantage in clothing all the same.

But isn't a competitive advantage based on low wages somehow unfair? Many people think so; their beliefs are summarized by our second misconception.

THE SWEATSHOP LABOR ARGUMENT

Myth 2: Foreign competition is unfair and hurts other countries when it is based on low wages. This argument, sometimes referred to as the **sweatshop labor argument,** is a particular favorite of labor unions seeking protection from foreign competition. People who adhere to this belief argue that industries should not have to cope with foreign industries that are less efficient but pay lower wages. This view is widespread and taken seriously by respectable opinion: during 1986 the *New York Times* printed three articles by Professor John Culbertson of the University of Wisconsin, arguing that foreign competition based on low wages is destructive to the United States.

Again, our simple example reveals the fallacy of this argument. In the example, Home is more productive than Foreign in both industries, and Foreign's lower cost of wine production is entirely due to its much lower wage rate. Foreign's lower wage rate

[2] B. Bruce-Biggs, "The Coming Overthrow of Free Trade," *Wall Street Journal,* February 28, 1983.

is, however, irrelevant to the question of whether Home gains from trade. Whether the lower cost of wine produced in Foreign is due to high productivity or low wages does not matter. All that matters to Home is that it is cheaper in terms of its own labor for Home to produce cheese and trade it for wine than to produce wine for itself.

This is fine for Home, but what about Foreign? Isn't there something wrong with basing one's exports on low wages? Certainly it is not an attractive position to be in, but the idea that trade is good only if you receive high wages is our final fallacy.

UNEQUAL EXCHANGE

Myth 3: Trade exploits a country and makes it worse off if the country uses more labor to produce the goods it exports than other countries use to produce the goods it receives in return. This argument, sometimes called the doctrine of **unequal exchange,** has its roots in the Marxist idea that value is created only by labor and tends to be favored by third-world advocates of a redistribution of income from rich countries to poor.[3]

While there is a certain plausibility to the idea that a country is being exploited if its exports embody more labor than its imports, unequal exchange does not mean that the low-wage country loses from trade. In the numerical example, Foreign exchanges 1 gallon of wine for each pound of cheese it receives; it exchanges something it took 3 hours of labor to produce for something that Home produced with only 1 hour of labor. This inequality of labor input is, however, irrelevant to the conclusion that Foreign gains from trade. In asking whether trade is beneficial, you should not compare the domestic labor used to produce your exports with the foreign labor used to produce your imports. Rather, you should compare the labor used to produce your exports with the amount of labor it would have taken to produce your imports yourself. Through trade, Foreign is able to get 1 pound of cheese from 3 hours of labor, when it would have taken 6 hours to produce that pound domestically. If another country can produce your imports with much less labor than would have been required in your country, good for them; this fact does not reduce your own benefit from trade.

Comparative Advantage with Many Goods

In our discussion so far we have relied on a model in which only two goods are produced and consumed. This simplified analysis allows us to capture many essential points about comparative advantage and trade and, as we saw in the last section, gives us a surprising amount of mileage as a tool for discussing policy issues. To move closer to reality, however, it is necessary to understand how comparative advantage functions in a model with a larger number of goods.

SETTING UP THE MODEL

Again, imagine a world of two countries, Home and Foreign. As before, each country has only one factor of production, labor. Each of these countries will now, however,

[3] As an example, see Arghiri Emmanuel, *Unequal Exchange* (New York: Monthly Review Press, 1972).

be assumed to consume and to be able to produce a large number of goods—say, N different goods altogether. We assign each of the goods a number from 1 to N.

The technology of each country can be described by its unit labor requirement for each good, that is, the number of hours of labor it takes to produce one unit of each. We label Home's unit labor requirement for a particular good as a_{Li}, where i is the number we have assigned to that good. If cheese is now good number 7, a_{L7} will mean the unit labor requirement in cheese production. Following our usual rule, we label the corresponding Foreign unit labor requirements a^*_{Li}.

To analyze trade, we next pull one more trick. For any good we can calculate a_{Li}/a^*_{Li}, the ratio of Home's unit labor requirement to Foreign's. The trick is to relabel the goods so that the lower the number, the lower this ratio. That is, we reshuffle the order in which we number goods in such a way that

$$a_{L1}/a^*_{L1} < a_{L2}/a^*_{L2} < a_{L3}/a^*_{L3} < \ldots < a_{LN}/a^*_{LN}. \quad \textbf{(2-6)}$$

RELATIVE WAGES AND SPECIALIZATION

We are now prepared to look at the pattern of trade. This depends on only one thing: the ratio of Home to Foreign wages. Once we know this ratio, we can determine who produces what.

Let w be the wage rate per hour in Home and w^* be the wage rate in Foreign. The ratio of wage rates, which is all that will concern us, is then w/w^*. The rule for allocating world production, then, is simply this: any good for which $a^*_{Li}/a_{Li} > w/w^*$ will be produced in Home, while any good for which $a^*_{Li}/a_{Li} < w/w^*$ will be produced in Foreign.

The reason is that goods will always be produced where it is cheapest to make them. The cost of making some good, say good i, is the unit labor requirement times the wage rate. To produce good i in Home will cost wa_{Li}. To produce the same good in Foreign will cost $w^*a^*_{Li}$. It will be cheaper to produce the good in Home if

$$wa_{Li} < w^*a^*_{Li},$$

which can be rearranged to yield

$$a^*_{Li}/a_{Li} > w/w^*.$$

On the other hand, it will be cheaper to produce the good in Foreign if

$$wa_{Li} > w^*a^*_{Li},$$

which can be rearranged to yield

$$a^*_{Li}/a_{Li} < w/w^*.$$

We have already lined up the goods in increasing order of a_{Li}/a^*_{Li}. This criterion for specialization tells us that what happens is a ''cut'' in that lineup, determined by the ratio of the two countries' wage rates, w^*/w. All the goods to the left of the cut end up being produced in Home; all the goods to the right end up being produced in Foreign. (It is possible, as we will see in a moment, that the ratio of wage rates is exactly equal to the ratio of unit labor requirements for one good. In that case this borderline good may be produced in both countries.)

Table 2-2 offers a numerical example in which Home and Foreign both consume and are able to produce *five* goods: apples, bananas, caviar, dates, and enchiladas.

The first two columns of this table are self-explanatory. The third column is the ratio of the Foreign unit labor requirement to the Home unit labor requirement for each good—or, stated differently, the relative Home productivity advantage in each good. We have labeled the goods in order of Home productivity advantage, with the Home advantage greatest for apples and least for enchiladas.

Which country produces which goods depends on the ratio of Home and Foreign wage rates. Home will have a cost advantage in any good for which its relative productivity is higher than its relative wage, and Foreign will have the advantage in the others. If, for example, the Home wage rate is 5 times that of Foreign, apples and bananas will be produced in Home and caviar, dates, and enchiladas in Foreign. If the Home wage rate is only 3 times that of Foreign, Home will produce apples, bananas, and caviar, while Foreign will produce only dates and enchiladas.

Is such a pattern of specialization beneficial to both countries? We can see that it is by using the same method we used earlier: comparing the labor cost of producing a good directly in a country with that of indirectly ''producing'' it by producing another good and trading for the desired good. If the Home wage rate is 3 times the Foreign wage. Home will import dates and enchiladas. A unit of dates requires 12 units of Foreign labor to produce, but its cost in Home labor, given the difference in wages, is only 4 person-hours—less than the 6 person-hours it would take to produce it at Home. For enchiladas, Foreign actually has higher productivity along with lower wages; it will cost Home only 3 person-hours to acquire a unit of enchiladas through trade, compared with the 12 person-hours it would take to produce it domestically. A similar calculation will show that Foreign also gains; for each of the goods Foreign imports it turns out to be cheaper in terms of domestic labor to trade for the good rather than produce the good domestically.

One piece is missing from this account, however: we have not yet explained how to determine the relative wage rate. This is the task to which we now turn.

DETERMINING THE RELATIVE WAGE IN THE MULTIGOOD MODEL

In the two-good model we determined relative wages by first calculating Home wages in terms of cheese and Foreign wages in terms of wine, then using the price of cheese relative to that of wine to deduce the ratio of the two countries' wage rates. We could do this because we knew that Home would produce cheese and Foreign wine. In the many-good case, who produces what can be determined only after we know the relative wage rate, so this procedure is unworkable. Instead, to determine relative wages in a multigood economy we must look behind the relative demand for goods to the implied relative demand for labor. This is not a direct demand on the part of consumers; rather, it is a **derived demand** that results from the demand for goods produced with each country's labor.

The relative derived demand for Home labor will fall when the ratio of Home to Foreign wages rises, for two reasons. First, as Home labor becomes more expensive relative to Foreign labor, goods produced in Home also become relatively more expensive, and world demand for these goods falls. Second, as Home wages rise, fewer

TABLE 2-2 Home and Foreign unit labor requirements

Good	*Home unit labor requirement* (a_{Li})	*Foreign unit labor requirement* (a^*_{Li})	*Relative Home productivity advantage* (a^*_{Li}/a_{Li})
Apples	1	10	10
Bananas	5	40	8
Caviar	3	12	4
Dates	6	12	2
Enchiladas	12	9	0.75

goods will be produced in Home and more in Foreign, further reducing the demand for Home labor.

We can illustrate these two effects using our numerical example. Suppose we start with the following situation: the Home wage is initially 3.5 times the Foreign wage. At that level, Home would produce apples, bananas, and caviar while Foreign would produce dates and enchiladas. If the relative Home wage were to increase from 3.5 to just under 4, say 3.99, the pattern of specialization would not change, but as the goods produced in Home became relatively more expensive, the relative demand for these goods would decline and the relative demand for Home labor would decline with it.

Suppose now that the relative wage were to increase slightly from 3.99 to 4.01. This small further increase in the relative Home wage would bring about a shift in the pattern of specialization. Because it is now cheaper to produce caviar in Foreign than in Home, the production of caviar shifts from Home to Foreign. What does this imply for the relative demand for Home labor? Clearly it implies that as the relative wage rises from a little less than 4 to a little more than 4 there is an abrupt drop-off in the relative demand, as Home production of caviar falls to zero and Foreign acquires a new industry. If the relative wage continues to rise, relative demand for Home labor will gradually decline, then drop off abruptly at a relative wage of 8, at which wage production of bananas shifts to Foreign.

We can illustrate the determination of relative wages with a diagram like Figure 2-5. Unlike Figure 2-3, this diagram does not have relative quantities of goods or relative prices of goods on its axes. Instead it shows the relative quantity of labor and the relative wage rate. The world demand for Home labor relative to its demand for Foreign labor is shown by the curve *RD*. The world supply of Home labor relative to Foreign labor is shown by the line *RS*.

The relative supply of labor is determined simply by the relative size of Home and Foreign labor forces. Assuming that the number of person-hours available does not vary with the wage, the relative wage has no effect on relative labor supply and thus *RS* is simply a vertical line.

Our discussion of the relative demand for labor explains the ''stepped'' shape of *RD*. Whenever we increase the wage rate of Home workers relative to Foreign workers, the relative demand for goods produced in Home will decline and the demand for

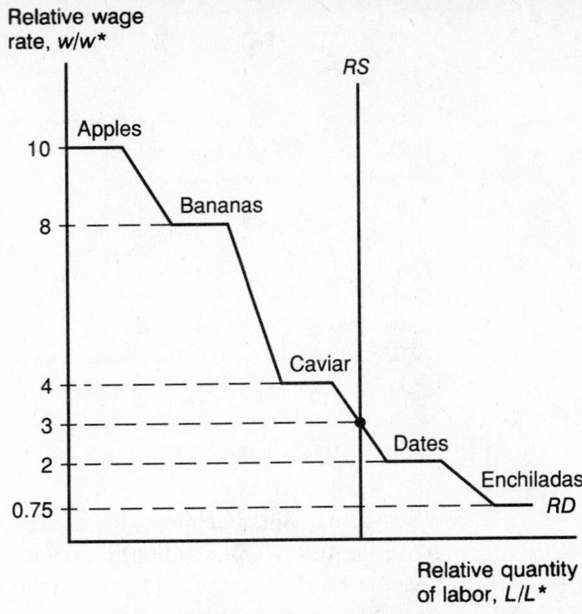

FIGURE 2-5
Determination of relative wages.
In a many-good Ricardian model, relative wages are determined by the intersection of the derived relative demand curve for labor *RD* with the relative supply *RS*.

Home labor will decline with it. In addition, the relative demand for Home labor will drop off abruptly whenever an increase in the relative Home wage makes a good cheaper to produce in Foreign. So the curve alternates between smoothly downward-sloping sections where the pattern of specialization does not change and "flats" where the relative demand shifts abruptly because of shifts in the pattern of specialization. As shown in the figure, these "flats" correspond to relative wages that equal the ratio of Home to Foreign productivity for each of the five goods.

The equilibrium relative wage is determined by the intersection of *RD* and *RS*. As drawn, the equilibrium relative wage is 3. At this wage, Home produces apples, bananas, and caviar while Foreign produces dates and enchiladas. The outcome depends on the relative size of the countries (which determines the position of *RS*) and the relative demand for the goods (which determines the shape and position of *RD*).

If the intersection of *RD* and *RS* happens to lie on one of the flats, both countries produce the good to which the flat applies.

Adding Transport Costs and Nontraded Goods

We now extend our model another step closer to reality by considering the effects of transport costs. Transportation costs do not change the fundamental principles of comparative advantage or the gains from trade. Because transport costs pose obstacles to the movement of goods and services, however, they have important implications for the way a trading world economy is affected by a variety of factors such as foreign aid, international investment, and balance of payments problems. While we will not deal with the effects of these factors yet, the multigood one-factor model is a good place to introduce the effects of transport costs.

First, notice that the world economy described by the model of the last section is marked by very extreme international specialization. At most there is one good that both countries produce; all other goods are produced either in Home or in Foreign, not in both.

There are three main reasons why specialization in the real international economy is not this extreme.

1. The existence of more than one factor of production reduces the tendency toward specialization (see the next two chapters).
2. Countries sometimes protect industries from foreign competition (discussed at length in Chapters 9 through 12).
3. It is costly to transport goods and services, and in some cases the cost of transportation is enough to lead countries into self-sufficiency in certain sectors.

In the multigood example of the last section we found that at a relative Home wage of 3, Home could produce apples, bananas, and caviar more cheaply than Foreign, while Foreign could produce dates and enchiladas more cheaply than Home. *In the absence of transport costs,* then, Home will export the first three goods and import the last two.

Now suppose there is a cost to transporting goods, and that this transport cost is a uniform fraction of production cost, say 100 percent. This transportation cost will discourage trade. Consider, for example, dates. One unit of this good requires 6 hours of Home labor or 12 hours of Foreign labor to produce. At a relative wage of 3, 12 hours of Foreign labor cost only as much as 4 hours of Home labor; so in the absence of transport costs Home imports dates. With a 100 percent transport cost, however, importing dates would cost the equivalent of 8 hours of Home labor, so Home will produce the good for itself instead.

A similar cost comparison shows that Foreign will find it cheaper to produce its own caviar than import it. A unit of caviar requires 3 hours of Home labor to produce. Even at a relative Home wage of 3, which makes this the equivalent of 9 hours of Foreign labor, this is cheaper than the 12 hours Foreign would need to produce caviar for itself. In the absence of transport costs, then, Foreign would find it cheaper to import caviar than to make it domestically. With a 100 percent cost of transportation, however, imported caviar would cost the equivalent of 18 hours of Foreign labor and would therefore be produced locally instead.

The result of introducing transport costs in this example, then, is that while Home still exports apples and bananas and imports enchiladas, caviar and dates become **nontraded goods,** which each country produces for itself.

In this example we have assumed that transport costs are the same fraction of production cost in all sectors. In practice there is a wide range of transportation costs. In some cases transportation is virtually impossible: services such as haircuts and auto repair cannot be traded internationally (except where there is a metropolitan area that straddles a border, like Detroit-Windsor). There is also little international trade in goods with high weight-to-value ratios, like cement. (It is simply not worth the transport cost of importing cement, even if it can be produced much more cheaply abroad.) Many goods end up being nontraded either because of the absence of strong national cost advantages or because of high transportation costs.

The important point is that nations spend a large share of their income on nontraded goods. This observation is of surprising importance in our later discussion of international transfers of income (Chapter 5) and in international monetary economics.

Empirical Evidence on the Ricardian Model

The Ricardian model of international trade is an extremely useful tool for thinking about the reasons why trade may happen and about the effects of international trade on national welfare. But is the model a good fit to the real world? Does the Ricardian model make accurate predictions about actual international trade flows?

The answer is a heavily qualified yes. Clearly there are a number of ways in which the Ricardian model makes misleading predictions. First, as was mentioned in our discussion of nontraded goods in the previous section, the simple Ricardian model predicts an extreme degree of specialization that we do not observe in the real world. Second, the Ricardian model assumes away effects of international trade on the distribution of income *within* countries, and thus predicts that countries as a whole will always gain from trade; in practice, international trade has strong effects on income distribution, which are the focus of Chapter 3. Third, the Ricardian model allows no role for differences in resources among countries as a cause of trade, thus missing an important aspect of the trading system (the focus of Chapter 4). Finally, the Ricardian model neglects the possible role of economies of scale as a cause of trade, which leaves it unable to explain the large trade flows between apparently similar nations—an issue discussed in Chapter 6.

In spite of these failings, however, the basic prediction of the Ricardian model—that countries should tend to export those goods in which their productivity is relatively high—has been strongly confirmed by a number of studies over the years.[4]

Figure 2-6 illustrates the evidence in favor of the Ricardian model, using data presented in a paper by the Hungarian economist Bela Balassa in 1963. The figure compares the ratio of U.S. to British exports in 1951 with the ratio of U.S. to British labor productivity, for twenty-six manufacturing industries. The productivity ratio is measured on the horizontal axis, the export ratio on the vertical axis. Both axes are given a logarithmic scale; this is not of any basic importance, but turns out to produce a clearer picture.

Ricardian theory would lead us broadly to expect that the higher the relative productivity in the U.S. industry, the more likely U.S. rather than U.K. firms would export in that industry. And that is what Figure 2-6 shows. In fact, the scatterplot lies quite close to an upward sloping line, also shown in the figure. Bearing in mind that the data used for this comparison are, like all economic data, subject to substantial measurement errors, the fit is remarkably close.

[4] The pioneering study by G. D. A. MacDougall is listed in Further Reading at the end of the chapter. A well-known follow-up study, on which we draw here, was Bela Balassa, "An Empirical Demonstration of Classical Comparative Cost Theory," *Review of Economics and Statistics* 4 (August 1963), pp. 231–238; we use Balassa's numbers as an illustration.

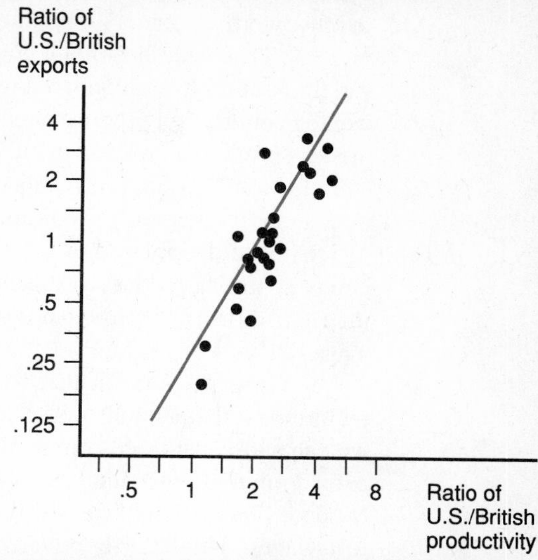

FIGURE 2-6
Productivity and exports.
A comparative study showed that U.S. exports were high relative to British exports in industries in which the U.S. had high relative labor productivity.

It is also interesting that the evidence in Figure 2-6 confirms the basic insight that trade depends on *comparative,* not *absolute* advantage. At the time to which the data refer, U.S. industry had much higher labor productivity than British industry—on average about twice as high. The commonly held misconception that a country can be competitive only if it can match other countries' productivity, which we discussed earlier in this chapter, would have led one to predict a U.S. export advantage across the board. The Ricardian model tells us, however, that having high productivity in an industry compared with foreigners is not enough to ensure that a country will export that industry's products; the relative productivity must be high compared with relative productivity in other sectors. As it happens, U.S. productivity exceeded British in all twenty-six sectors shown in Figure 2-6, by margins ranging from 11 to 366 percent. In 12 of the sectors, however, Britain actually had larger exports than the United States. A glance at the figure shows that in general, U.S. exports were larger than U.K. exports only in industries where the U.S. productivity advantage was somewhat more than two to one.

So in a rough way, at least, the Ricardian model is borne out by the evidence. As we will see later, the same cannot be said of all widely used models of international trade.

Summary

1. We examined the *Ricardian model,* the simplest model that shows how differences between countries give rise to trade and *gains from trade.* In this model labor is the only factor of production and countries differ only in the productivity of labor in different industries.
2. In the Ricardian model, countries will export goods that their labor produces

relatively efficiently and import goods that their labor produces relatively inefficiently. In other words, a country's production pattern is determined by *comparative advantage.*

3. That trade benefits a country can be shown in either of two ways. First, we can think of trade as an indirect method of production. Instead of producing a good for itself, a country can produce another good and trade it for the desired good. The simple model shows that whenever a good is imported it must be true that this indirect "production" requires less labor than direct production. Second, we can show that trade enlarges a country's consumption possibilities, implying gains from trade.

4. The distribution of the gains from trade depends on the relative prices of the goods countries produce. To determine these relative prices it is necessary to look at the *relative world supply and demand* for goods. The relative price implies a relative wage rate as well.

5. The proposition that trade is beneficial is unqualified. That is, there is no requirement that a country be "competitive" or that the trade be "fair." In particular, we can show that three commonly held beliefs about trade are wrong. First, a country gains from trade even if it has lower productivity than its trading partner in all industries. Second, trade is beneficial even if foreign industries are competitive only because of low wages. Third, trade is beneficial even if a country's exports embody more labor than its imports.

6. Extending the one-factor, two-good model to a world of many commodities does not alter these conclusions. The only difference is that it becomes necessary to focus directly on the relative demand for labor to determine relative wages rather than to work via relative demand for goods. Also, a many-commodity model can be used to illustrate the important point that transportation costs can give rise to a situation in which some *nontraded goods* exist.

7. While some of the predictions of the Ricardian model are clearly unrealistic, its basic prediction—that countries will tend to export goods in which they have relatively high productivity—has been confirmed by a number of studies.

Key Terms

comparative advantage
Ricardian model
unit labor requirement
production possibility frontier
opportunity cost
absolute advantage
partial equilibrium analysis
general equilibrium analysis
relative demand curve
relative supply curve
gains from trade
sweatshop labor argument
unequal exchange
derived demand
nontraded goods

Problems

1. Home has 1200 units of labor available. It can produce two goods, apples and bananas. The unit labor requirement in apple production is 3, while in banana production it is 2.

a. Graph Home's production possibility frontier.

b. What is the opportunity cost of apples in terms of bananas?

c. In the absence of trade, what would the price of apples in terms of bananas be? Why?

2. Home is as described in problem 1. There is now also another country, Foreign, with a labor force of 800. Foreign's unit labor requirement in apple production is 5, while in banana production it is 1.

a. Graph Foreign's production possibility frontier.

b. Construct the world relative supply curve.

3. Now suppose world relative demand takes the following form:
Demand for apples/demand for bananas = price of bananas/price of apples

a. Graph the relative demand curve along with the relative supply curve.

b. What is the equilibrium relative price of apples?

c. Describe the pattern of trade.

d. Show that both Home and Foreign gain from trade.

4. Suppose that instead of 1200 workers, Home had 2400. Find the equilibrium relative price. What can you say about the division of the gains from trade between Home and Foreign in this case?

5. Suppose that Home has 2400 workers, but they are only half as productive in both industries as we have been assuming. Construct the world relative supply curve and determine the equilibrium relative price. How do the gains from trade compare with those in the case described in problem 3?

6. "Korean workers earn only $2.50 an hour; if we allow Korea to export as much as it likes to the United States, our workers will be forced down to the same level. You can't import a $5 shirt without importing the $2.50 wage that goes with it." Discuss.

7. Japanese labor productivity is roughly the same as that of the United States in the manufacturing sector (higher in some industries, lower in others), while the United States is still considerably more productive in the service sector. But most services are nontraded. Some analysts have argued that this poses a problem for the United States, because our comparative advantage lies in things we cannot sell on world markets. What is wrong with this argument?

8. Anyone who has visited Japan knows it is an incredibly expensive place; although Japanese workers earn about the same as their U.S. counterparts, the purchasing power of their incomes is about one-third less. Extend your discussion from question 7 to explain this observation. (Hint: Think about wages and the implied prices of nontraded goods.)

9. How does the fact that many goods are nontraded affect the extent of possible gains from trade?

10. We have focused on the case of trade involving only two countries. Suppose that there are many countries capable of producing two goods, and that each country has only one factor of production, labor. What could we say about the pattern of production and trade in this case? (Hint: Try constructing the world relative supply curve.)

Further Reading

Donald Davis. "Intraindustry Trade: A Heckscher-Ohlin-Ricardo Approach" (working paper, Harvard University). A recent revival of the Ricardian approach to explain trade between countries with similar resources.

Rudiger Dornbusch, Stanley Fischer, and Paul Samuelson. "Comparative Advantage, Trade and Payments in a Ricardian Model with a Continuum of Goods." *American Economic Review* 67 (December 1977), pp. 823–839. More recent theoretical modeling in the Ricardian mode, developing the idea of simplifying the many-good Ricardian model by assuming that the number of goods is so large as to form a smooth continuum.

Giovanni Dosi, Keith Pavitt, and Luc Soete. *The Economics of Technical Change and International Trade.* Brighton: Wheatsheaf, 1988. An empirical examination that suggests that international trade in manufactured goods is largely driven by differences in national technological competences.

G. D. A. MacDougall. "British and American Exports: A Study Suggested by the Theory of Comparative Costs." *Economic Journal* 61 (December 1951), pp. 697–724; 62 (September 1952), pp. 487–521. In this famous study, MacDougall used comparative data on U.S. and U.K. productivity to test the predictions of the Ricardian model.

John Stuart Mill. *Principles of Political Economy.* London: Longmans, Green, 1917. Mill's 1848 treatise extended Ricardo's work into a full-fledged model of international trade.

David Ricardo. *The Principles of Political Economy and Taxation.* Homewood, IL: Irwin, 1963. The basic source for the Ricardian model is Ricardo himself in this book, first published in 1817.

Appendix to Chapter 2 ● A Ricardian Model with Very Many Goods

In this chapter our analysis became somewhat more complicated when we went from a model with only two goods to a model with a number of goods. Trade theorists have, however, noticed something surprising: if the number of goods becomes *very* large, so that one can think of them as virtually uncountable, the model actually becomes simpler again. A well-known 1977 article by Rudiger Dornbusch, Stanley Fischer, and Paul Samuelson of the Massachusetts Institute of Technology (see Further Reading) develops a Ricardian model with a very large number of goods that illustrates the points made in this chapter in a particularly clear way.

TECHNOLOGY AND SPECIALIZATION

Suppose that Home and Foreign still have only one factor of production, labor, available in quantities L and L^* in each country. Each country, however, consumes and is able to produce an extremely large number of goods. We label each of these goods with a number. We will explain in a moment the way these numbers will be assigned.

For each good both Home and Foreign will have a unit labor requirement in production. For good number z, let $a(z)$ be the unit labor requirement in Home and $a^*(z)$ be the unit labor requirement in Foreign. Then $a^*(z)/a(z)$ is the ratio of Home's productivity in that good to Foreign's. We define $A(z) = a^*(z)/a(z)$.

In labeling the goods we use the following rule: number the good with the highest A as good 1, the good with the next highest A as 2, and so on, so that

$$A(1) > A(2) > A(3) > \dots$$

That is, we order the goods in decreasing order of Home's comparative advantage.

Now we graph $A(z)$ against z (Figure 2A-1). Here we use the assumption that there is a very large number of goods. In reality, z can take on only whole-number values, so that the curve $A(z)$ should be a series of discrete points at $z = 1$, $z = 2$, and so on. If there are thousands or millions of goods, however, any graph that compresses the z axis onto a single page will show an $A(z)$ that is indistinguishable from a solid curve. We ignore the tiny holes that we know are there and treat $A(z)$ as if it were in fact a smooth, continuous mathematical relationship. It is, of course, downward-sloping, because we numbered the goods that way.

Which goods will be produced in Home and which in Foreign? This depends on the ratio of the Home and Foreign wage rates. The cost of producing good z in Home is $wa(z)$, where w is the wage rate of Home workers. The cost of producing the same good in Foreign is $w^*a^*(z)$. The good will therefore be cheaper to produce in Home if

$$wa(z) < w^*a^*(z)$$

or, equivalently,

$$w/w^* < a^*(z)/a(z)$$

or, finally,

$$A(z) > w/w^*.$$

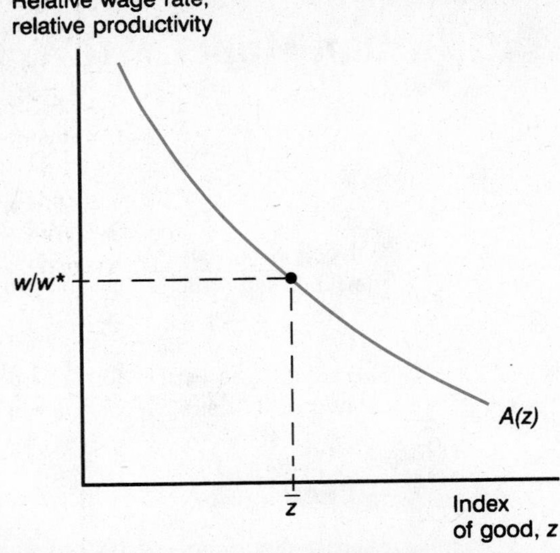

FIGURE 2A-1
Relative Home productivity.
Goods are numbered in order of the ratio of Foreign to Home unit labor requirement, so that the curve $A(z)$ is downward-sloping.

Given the ratio of Home to Foreign wages w/w^*, then, we can establish the pattern of international specialization. There is a marginal good $\bar{z}$ for which $w/w^* = A(\bar{z})$ (see Figure 2A-1). All goods with lower numbers than $\bar{z}$ will be produced in Home, all goods with higher numbers in Foreign.

DEMAND AND EQUILIBRIUM

Next we turn to the determination of the relative wage. To do this we need to specify demand. A simple assumption about demand that is popular in international economics is that everyone in the world spends a constant share of his or her income on each good. For example, it might be the case that everyone spends 20 percent of income on food, 25 percent on housing, 15 percent on transportation, and so on. In our case, we assume that a fraction $b(z)$ of world income is spent on each good z.

Next we need to know the fraction of world income spent on all goods manufactured in Home. This depends on which goods are made there—but we know that this will consist of all goods with numbers less than $\bar{z}$. Let $G(\bar{z})$ be the fraction of income spent on Home-made goods; it is equal to

$$G(\bar{z}) = b(1) + b(2) + \ldots + b(\bar{z}). \qquad \textbf{(2A-1)}$$

Clearly $G(\bar{z})$ will be larger the larger $\bar{z}$ is. Like $A(z)$, $G(z)$ describes a set of discrete points rather than a continuous curve, but with a very large number of goods we can ignore the holes.

Now we turn to the derived demand for Home labor. The total value of spending on Home goods will be $G(\bar{z})$ times world income. All this spending will accrue to Home workers as wages, thus we have

$$wL = G(\bar{z}) \times \text{world income}. \qquad \textbf{(2A-2)}$$

World income, however, is the sum of the total wages earned in Home and Foreign, $wL + w^*L^*$. Thus we have

$$wL = G(\bar{z})\,(wL + w^*L^*), \qquad \textbf{(2A-3)}$$

which can be rearranged as

$$w/w^* = \frac{G(\bar{z})}{1\text{-}G(\bar{z})} \times \frac{L^*}{L} \qquad \text{(2A-4)}$$
$$= B(\bar{z})L^*/L.$$

The numerator of $B(z)$ is higher, the higher z is, while the denominator is less; therefore, $B(z)$ must rise when z rises. The intuition is that the more goods Home produces (and therefore the fewer Foreign produces), the higher the relative demand for Home labor and thus the higher Home's relative wage.

We have now established a relationship between the relative wage and the pattern of specialization, on one hand, and between the pattern of specialization and the relative wage, on the other. We can put these together on a single diagram (Figure 2A-2) to see how specialization and relative wages are simultaneously determined.

THE GAINS FROM TRADE

We can use this model to establish in a particularly neat way that trade is mutually beneficial to Home and Foreign. First, we ask what the prices of goods in international trade are. In a Ricardian one-factor economy, the price of a good will simply be the labor cost of production. Let $p(z)$ be the price of good z; then

$$p(z) = wa(z) \qquad \text{if the good is produced in Home}$$
$$= w^*a^*(z) \qquad \text{if the good is produced in Foreign.}$$

Now we ask: is it more efficient for Home to trade for its imports rather than to produce them directly?

For Home to produce one unit of good z directly requires $a(z)$ person-hours. These person-hours earn an income $wa(z)$. If the good is imported, the income from the labor that would have been used to produce one unit of good z at Home can purchase $wa(z)/p(z)$ units of imports of z, where $p(z) = w^*a^*(z)$. It is cheaper for Home to import good z if the labor that could produce

FIGURE 2A-2
Determining relative wages and the pattern of specialization.
The ratio of Home to Foreign wage rates, and which country produces which goods, are determined simultaneously by the intersection of the relative productivity curve and the relative labor demand curve.

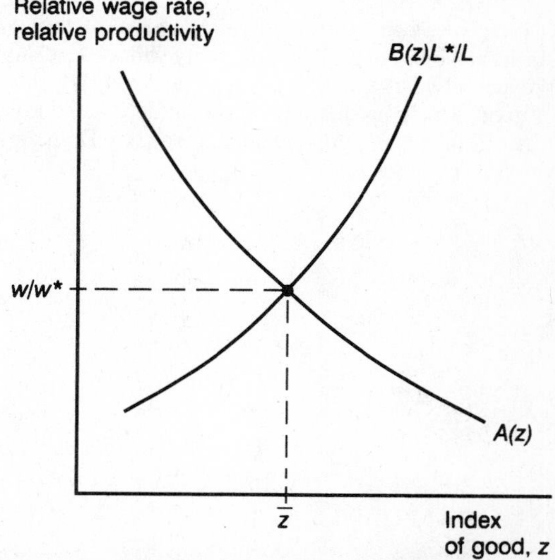

a unit of z directly can indirectly generate more than one unit by producing instead exports to be traded; that is, if

$$wa(z)/p(z) = wa(z)/w^*a^*(z) > 1.$$

This is equivalent to

$$a^*(z)/a(z) = A(z) < w/w^*.$$

But we saw that the pattern of specialization is determined precisely by the requirement that Home produce all goods with $A(z) > w/w^*$, while Foreign produces all goods with $A(z) < w/w^*$. Gains from trade are therefore assured.

AN APPLICATION: PRODUCTIVITY GROWTH

An interesting application of this very-many-good model, one that is relevant to our discussion of misconceptions about international trade, is to ask what happens when one country's productivity increases. Is this good or bad for the other country?

Suppose that Foreign's productivity increases by 10 percent. We assume that this productivity increase takes place across the board, so that Foreign's unit labor requirement falls by 10 percent in every industry (if we didn't assume this, we would have to renumber the goods—can you see why?). Since $a^*(z)$ has fallen by 10 percent in all industries, $A(z)$ shifts down by 10 percent, a shift illustrated by the movement from $A^1(z)$ to $A^2(z)$ in Figure 2A-3. As the figure shows, Home's relative wage w/w^* falls. So does $\bar{z}$: the range of goods that Home produces also becomes narrower.

You might be tempted, looking at these results, to conclude that Home is worse off as a result of competition with Foreign. But this conclusion is wrong. In fact, Home is clearly better off.

To see why, look at Home's real wage, the wage rate divided by the price, in terms of each of the goods. If all real wages either stay the same or rise, Home is better off, and that is what happens. Even though Home's relative wage falls, it falls by *less* than the 10 percent decline in

FIGURE 2A-3
Effects of an increase in Foreign productivity.
An increase in Foreign's productivity shifts the relative productivity curve down from $A^1(z)$ to $A^2(z)$. The range of goods Home produces falls, and so does its relative wage. Nonetheless, the *real* wage earned by Home's workers increases.

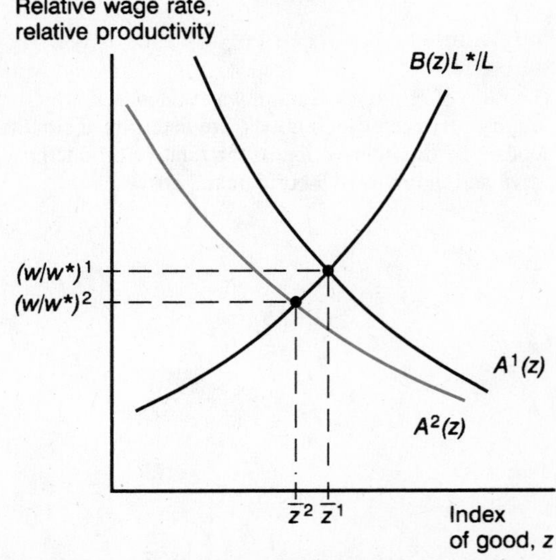

Foreign unit labor requirements. This means that Foreign goods get cheaper in terms of Home labor.

Figure 2A-3 divides the goods into three groups: consistent Home exports, consistent imports, and transitional goods that shift from exports to imports. Let's examine what happens to Home's real wages in terms of each group.

The prices of goods that Home exports both before and after the change—goods with an index $z < \bar{z}^2$—are proportional to the Home wage rate: $p(z) = wa(z)$; so the real wage rate $w/p(z)$ in terms of these goods does not change.

The prices of goods that Home consistently imports—goods with $z > \bar{z}^1$—depend on both Foreign wages and Foreign unit labor requirements:

$$p(z) = w^*a^*(z),$$

implying

$$w/p(z) = (w/w^*) \times [1/a^*(z)].$$

We know that w/w^* falls—but we also know that it falls proportionally less than $a^*(z)$, implying that for these consistent imports the Home real wage rises.

Finally, the transitional goods—goods with $\bar{z}^1 < z < \bar{z}^2$—were produced in Home but are now produced in Foreign. Before the change Home's real wage in terms of each such good was $1/a(z)$, the inverse of the unit labor requirement. Home will abandon production of a good only if its price falls below production cost:

$$p(z) < wa(z),$$

or

$$w/p(z) > 1/a(z).$$

This says, however, that on transitional goods Home's real wage must also have risen.

On two of three kinds of good, then, Home's real wage rises, while on the third there is no change. Home is unambiguously better off.

This example shows that the common belief that it is always bad when someone gains on you technologically is wrong.

Specific Factors and Income Distribution

Chapter 3

As we saw in Chapter 2, international trade can be mutually beneficial to the nations engaged in it. Yet throughout history, governments have protected sectors of the economy from import competition. For example, despite its commitment in principle to free trade, the United States limits imports of steel, textiles, sugar, and other commodities. If trade is such a good thing for the economy, why is there opposition to its effects? To understand the politics of trade, it is necessary to look at the effects of trade, not just on a country as a whole but on the distribution of income within that country.

The Ricardian model of international trade developed in Chapter 2 illustrates the potential benefits from trade. In that model trade leads to international specialization, with each country shifting its labor force from industries in which that labor is relatively inefficient to industries in which it is relatively more efficient. Because labor is the only factor of production in the model, and it is assumed to be able to move freely from one industry to another, there is no possibility that individuals will be hurt by trade. The Ricardian model thus suggests not only that all countries gain from trade, but that every *individual* is made better off as a result of international trade, because trade does not affect the distribution of income. In the real world, however, trade has substantial effects on the income distribution within each trading nation, so that in practice the benefits of trade are often distributed very unevenly.

There are two main reasons why international trade has strong effects on the distribution of income. First, resources cannot move immediately or costlessly from one industry to another. Second, industries differ in the factors of production they demand: a shift in the mix of goods that a country produces will ordinarily reduce the demand for some factors of production, while raising the demand for others. For both of these reasons, international trade is not as unambiguously beneficial as it appeared to be in Chapter 2. While trade may benefit a nation as a whole, it often hurts significant groups within the country, at least in the short run.

Consider the effects of Japan's rice policy. Japan allows very little rice to be imported, even though the scarcity of land means that rice is much more expensive to produce in Japan than in other countries (including the United States). There is little question that Japan as a whole would have a higher standard of living if free imports of rice were allowed. Japanese rice farmers, however, would be hurt by free trade. While the farmers displaced by imports could probably find jobs in manufacturing or services in Japan's full employment economy, they would find changing employment costly and inconvenient. Furthermore, the value of the land that the farmers own would fall along with the price of rice. Not surprisingly, Japanese rice farmers are vehemently opposed to free trade in rice, and their organized political opposition has counted for more than the potential gains from trade for the nation as a whole.

A realistic analysis of trade must go beyond the Ricardian model to models in which trade can affect income distribution. This chapter concentrates on a particular model, known as the specific factors model, that brings income distribution into the story in a particularly clear way.

The Specific Factors Model

The **specific factors model** was developed by Paul Samuelson and Ronald Jones.[1] Like the simple Ricardian model, it assumes an economy that produces two goods and that can allocate its labor supply between the two sectors. Unlike the Ricardian model, however, the specific factors model allows for the existence of factors of production besides labor. Whereas labor is a **mobile factor** that can move between sectors, these other factors are assumed to be **specific.** That is, they can be used only in the production of particular goods.

ASSUMPTIONS OF THE MODEL

Imagine an economy that can produce two goods, manufactures and food. Instead of one factor of production, however, the country has *three:* labor (L), capital (K), and land (T for *terrain*). Manufactures are produced using capital and labor (but not land), while food is produced using land and labor (but not capital). Labor is therefore a *mobile* factor that can be used in either sector, while land and capital are both *specific* factors that can be used only in the production of one good.

How much of each good does the economy produce? The economy's output of manufactures depends on how much capital and labor are used in that sector. This relationship is summarized by a **production function** that tells us how much manufac-

[1] Paul Samuelson, "Ohlin Was Right," *Swedish Journal of Economics* 73 (1971), pp. 365–384; and Ronald W. Jones, "A Three-Factor Model in Theory, Trade, and History," in Jagdish Bhagwati et al., eds., *Trade, Balance of Payments, and Growth* (Amsterdam: North-Holland, 1971), pp. 3–21.

tures output can be produced given any input of capital and labor. The production function for manufactures can be summarized algebraically as

$$Q_M = Q_M(K, L_M), \tag{3-1}$$

where Q_M is the economy's output of manufactures, K is the economy's capital stock, and L_M is the labor force employed in manufactures. Similarly, for food we can write the production function

$$Q_F = Q_F(T, L_F), \tag{3-2}$$

where Q_F is the economy's output of food, T is the economy's supply of land, and L_F is the labor force devoted to food production. For the economy as a whole, the labor employed must equal the total labor supply L:

$$L_M + L_F = L. \tag{3-3}$$

PRODUCTION POSSIBILITIES

The specific factors model assumes that each of the specific factors capital and land can be used in only one sector, manufactures and food, respectively. Only labor can be used in either sector. Thus to analyze the economy's production possibilities, we need only to ask how the economy's mix of output changes as labor is shifted from one sector to the other. This can be done graphically, first by representing the production functions (3-1) and (3-2), then by putting them together to derive the production possibility frontier.

Figure 3-1 illustrates the relationship between labor intput and output of manufactures. The larger the input of labor, for a given capital supply, the larger will be output. In Figure 3-1, the slope of $Q_M(K,L_M)$ represents the **marginal product of labor,** that is, the addition to output generated by adding one more person-hour. However, if labor input is increased without increasing capital as well, there will normally be **diminishing returns:** because adding a worker means that each worker has less capital to work

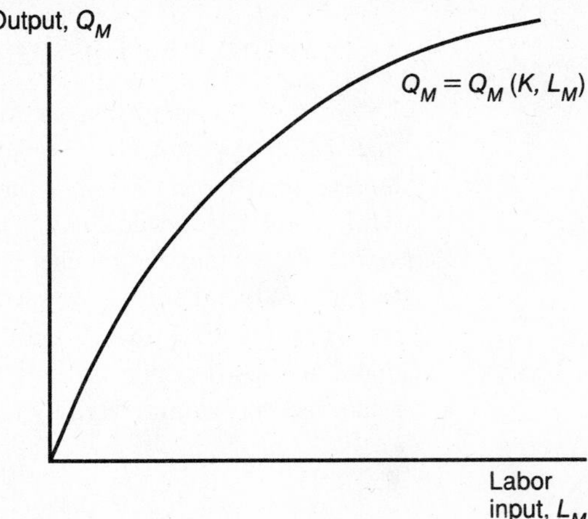

FIGURE 3-1
The production function for manufactures.
The more labor that is employed in the production of manufactures, the larger the output. As a result of diminishing returns, however, each successive person-hour increases output by less than the previous one; this is shown by the fact that the curve relating labor input to output gets flatter at higher levels of employment.

with, each successive increment of labor will add less to production than the last. Diminishing returns are shown by the fact that $Q_M(K,L_M)$ gets flatter as we move to the right, so that the marginal product of labor declines as more labor is used.

Figure 3-2 shows the same information a different way: in this figure we directly plot the marginal product of labor as a function of the labor employed. In the appendix to this chapter we show that the area under the marginal product curve represents the total output of manufactures.

A similar pair of diagrams can represent the production function for food. These diagrams can then be combined to derive the production possibility frontier for the economy, as illustrated in Figure 3-3.

Figure 3-3 is a four-quadrant diagram. In the lower right quadrant we show the production function for manufactures illustrated in Figure 3-1. This time, however, we turn the figure on its side: a movement downward along the vertical axis represents an increase in the labor input to the manufactures sector, while a movement to the right along the horizontal axis represents an increase in the output of manufactures. In the upper left quadrant we show the corresponding production function for food; this part of the figure is also flipped around, so that a movement to the left along the horizontal axis indicates an increase in labor input to the food sector, while an upward movement along the vertical axis indicates an increase in food output.

The lower left quadrant represents the economy's allocation of labor. Both quantities are measured in the reverse of the usual direction: a downward movement along the vertical axis indicates an increase in the labor employed in manufactures, a leftward movement along the horizontal axis indicates an increase in labor employed in food. Since an increase in employment in one sector must mean that less labor is available for the other, the possible allocations are indicated by a downward sloping line. This line, labeled *AA,* slopes downward at a 45-degree angle, that is, with a slope of -1. To see why this line represents the possible allocations, notice that if all labor were employed in food production, L_F would equal L, while L_M would equal 0. If one were

FIGURE 3-2
The marginal product of labor.
The marginal product of labor in the manufactures sector, equal to the slope of the production function shown in Figure 3-1, is lower the more labor the sector employs. Total output of manufactures is measured by the area under the curve up to the level of employment.

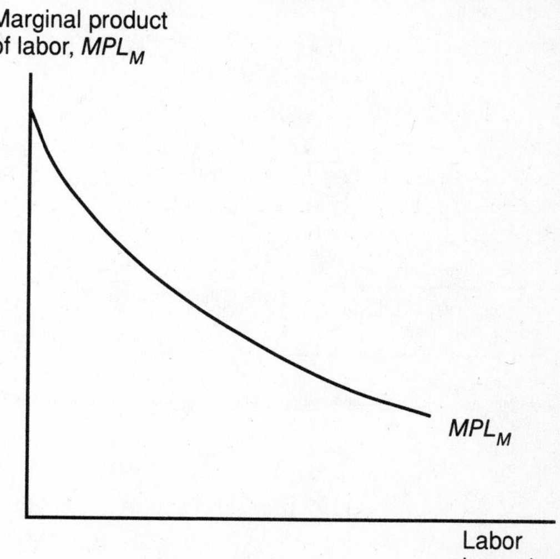

FIGURE 3-3
The production possibility frontier in the specific factors model. Production of manufactures and food is determined by the allocation of labor. In the lower left quadrant, the allocation of labor between sectors can be illustrated by a point on the line *AA*, which represents all combinations of labor input to manufactures and food that sum up to the total labor supply *L*. Corresponding to any particular point on *AA*, such as point 2, is a labor input to manufactures (L_M^2) and a labor input to food (L_F^2). The curves in the lower right and upper left quadrants represent the production functions for manufactures and food respectively; these allow determination of output (Q_M^2, Q_F^2) given labor input. Then in the upper right quadrant the curve *TT* shows how the output of the two goods varies as the allocation of labor is shifted from food to manufactures, with the output points 1′, 2′, 3′ corresponding to the labor allocations 1, 2, 3. Because of diminishing returns, *TT* is a bowed-out curve instead of a straight line.

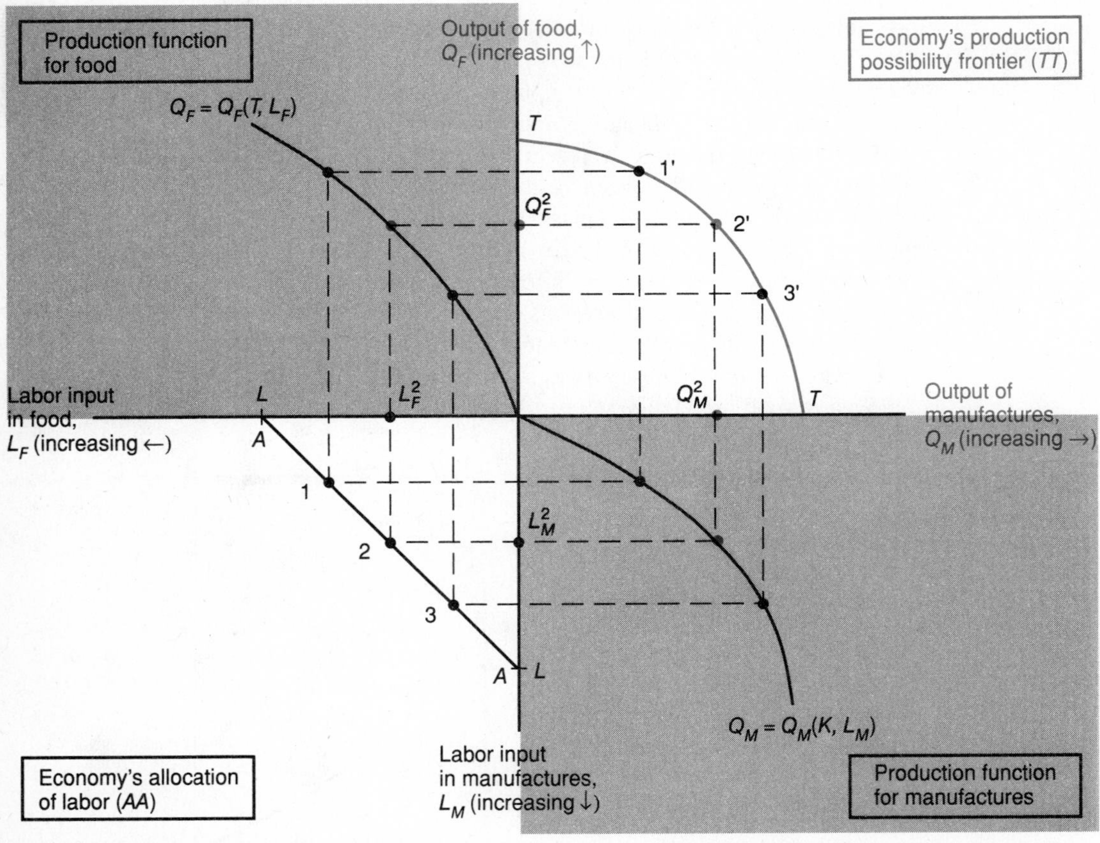

then to move labor gradually into the manufacturing sector, each person-hour moved would increase L_M by one unit while reducing L_F by one unit, tracing a line with a slope of -1, until all the entire labor supply *L* was employed in manufactures. Any particular allocation of labor between the two sectors can then be represented by a point on *AA*, such as point 2.

We can now see how to determine production given any particular allocation of labor between the two sectors. Suppose that the allocation of labor were represented by point 2 in the lower left quadrant, that is, with L_M^2 hours in manufacturing and L_F^2 hours in food. Then we can use the production function for each sector to determine output: Q_M^2 units are produced in manufacturing, Q_F^2 in food. Using these coordinates Q_M^2, Q_F^2, point 2′ in the upper right quadrant of Figure 3-3 shows the resulting output of manufactures and food.

To trace the whole production possibility frontier, we simply imagine repeating this exercise for many alternative allocations of labor. We might start with most of the labor allocated to food production, as at point 1 in the lower left quadrant, then gradually increase the amount of labor used in manufactures until very few workers are employed in food, as at point 3; the corresponding points in the upper right quadrant will trace out the curve running from 1′ to 3′. Thus *TT* in the upper right quadrant shows the economy's production possibilities for given supplies of land, labor, and capital.

In the Ricardian model, where labor is the only factor of production, the production possibility frontier is a straight line: the opportunity cost of manufactures in terms of food is constant. In the specific factors model, however, the addition of other factors of production changes the shape of the production possibility frontier *TT* to a curve. The curvature of *TT* reflects diminishing returns to labor in each sector; these diminishing returns are the crucial difference between the specific factors and the Ricardian models.

Notice that when tracing *TT* we shift labor from the food to the manufacturing sector. If we shift one person-hour of labor from food to manufactures, however, this extra input will increase output in that sector by the marginal product of labor in manufactures, MPL_M. To increase manufactures output by one unit, then, we must increase labor intput by $1/MPL_M$ hours. Meanwhile, each unit of labor input shifted out of food production will lower output in that sector by the marginal product of labor in food, MPL_F. To increase output of manufactures by one unit, then, the economy must reduce output of food by MPL_F/MPL_M units. The slope of *TT,* which measures the opportunity cost of manufactures in terms of food—that is, the number of units of food output that must be sacrificed to increase manufactures output by one unit—is therefore

$$\text{Slope} = -MPL_F/MPL_M$$

We can now see why *TT* has the bowed shape it does. As we move from 1′ to 3′, L_M rises and L_F falls. We saw in Figure 3-2, however, that as L_M rises, the marginal product of labor in manufactures falls; correspondingly, as L_F falls, the marginal product of labor in food rises. So *TT* gets steeper as we move down it to the right.

We have now shown how output is determined, given the allocation of labor. The next step is to ask how a market economy determines the allocation of labor.

PRICES, WAGES, AND LABOR ALLOCATION

How much labor will be employed in each sector? To answer this look at supply and demand in the labor market. The demand for labor in each sector depends on the price of output and the wage rate. In turn, the wage rate depends on the combined demand for labor by food and manufactures. Given the prices of manufactures and food together with the wage rate, we can determine each sector's employment and output.

First, let us focus on the demand for labor. In each sector, profit-maximizing employers will demand labor up to the point where the value produced by an additional person-hour equals the cost of employing that hour. In the manufacturing sector, for example, the value of an additional person-hour is the marginal product of labor in manufacturing multiplied by the price of one unit of manufactures: $MPL_M \times P_M$. If w is the wage rate of labor, employers will therefore hire workers up to the point where

$$MPL_M \times P_M = w. \tag{3-4}$$

But the marginal product of labor in manufacturing, already illustrated in Figure 3-2, slopes downward because of diminishing returns. So for any given price of manufactures P_M, the value of that marginal product, $MPL_M \times P_M$, will also slope down. We can therefore think of equation (3-4) as defining the demand curve for labor in manufactures: if the wage rate falls, other things equal, employers in the manufacturing sector will want to hire more workers.

Similarly, the value of an additional person-hour in food is $MPL_F \times P_F$. The demand curve for labor in the food sector may therefore be written

$$MPL_F \times P_F = w. \tag{3-5}$$

The wage rate w must be the same in both sectors, because of the assumption that labor is freely mobile between sectors. That is, since labor is a mobile factor, it will move from the low-wage sector to the high-wage sector until wages are equalized. The wage rate, in turn, is determined by the requirement that total employment equal total labor supply:

$$L_M + L_F = L. \tag{3-6}$$

By representing these three equations in a diagram (Figure 3-4), we can see how the wage rate and employment in each sector are determined given the prices of food and

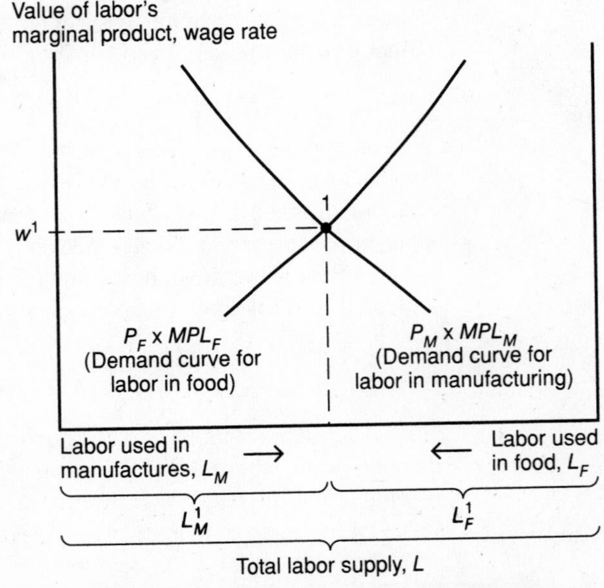

FIGURE 3-4
The allocation of labor.
Labor is allocated so that the value of its marginal product is the same in manufactures and food. In equilibrium, the wage rate is equal to the value of labor's marginal product.

manufactures. Along the horizontal axis of Figure 3-4 we show the total labor supply L. Measuring from the left of the diagram, we show the value of the marginal product of labor in manufactures, which is simply the MPL_M curve from Figure 3-2 multiplied by P_M. This is the demand curve for labor in the manufacturing sector. Measuring from the right, we show the value of the marginal product of labor in food, which is the demand for labor in food. The equilibrium wage rate and allocation of labor between the two sectors is represented by point 1. At the wage rate w^1 the sum of labor demanded by manufactures (L_M^1) and food (L_F^1) just equals the total labor supply L.

There is a useful relationship between relative prices and output that emerges clearly from this analysis of labor allocation; this relationship applies to more general situations than that described by the specific factors model. Equations (3-4) and (3-5) imply that

$$MPL_M \times P_M = MPL_F \times P_F = w$$

or, rearranging, that

$$-MPL_F/MPL_M = -P_M/P_F. \tag{3-7}$$

The left side of equation (3-7) is the slope of the production possibility frontier at the actual production point; the right side is minus the relative price of manufactures. This result tells us that *at the production point the production possibility frontier must be tangent to a line whose slope is minus the price of manufactures divided by that of food.* The result is illustrated in Figure 3-5: if the relative price of manufactures is $(P_M/P_F)^1$ the economy produces at point 1.

What happens to the allocation of labor and the distribution of income when the prices of food and manufactures change? Notice that any price change can be broken into two parts: an equal proportional change in both P_M and P_F, and a change in only one price. For example, suppose that the price of manufactures rises 17 percent and the price of food rises 10 percent. We can analyze the effects of this by first asking what

FIGURE 3-5
Production in the specific factors model.
The economy produces at the point on its production possibility frontier where the slope of that frontier equals minus the relative price of manufactures.

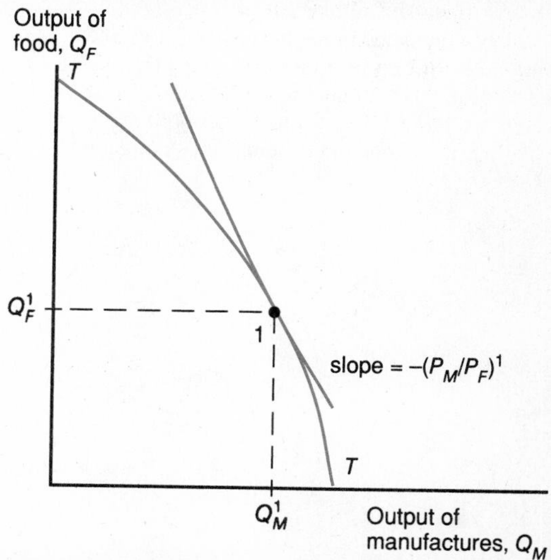

happens if manufactures and food prices both rise by 10 percent, then by finding out what happens if manufactures prices rise by 7 percent. This allows us to separate the effect of changes in the overall price level from the effect of changes in relative prices.

An Equal Proportional Change in Prices. Figure 3-6 shows the effect of an equal proportional increase in P_M and P_F. P_M rises from P_M^1 to P_M^2; P_F rises from P_F^1 to P_F^2. If both goods prices increase by 10 percent, the labor demand curves will both shift up by 10 percent as well. As you can see from the diagram, these shifts lead to a 10 percent increase in the wage rate from w^1 (point 1) to w^2 (point 2). The allocation of labor between the sectors and the outputs of the two goods do not change.

In fact, when P_M and P_F change in the same proportion, no real changes occur. The wage rate rises in the same proportion as the prices, so *real* wage rates, the ratios of the wage rate to the prices of goods, are unaffected. With the same amount of labor employed in each sector, receiving the same real wage rate, the real incomes of capital owners and landowners also remain the same. So everyone is in exactly the same position as before. This illustrates a general principle: changes in the overall price level have no real effects, that is, do not change any physical quantities in the economy. Only changes in relative prices—which in this case means the price of manufactures relative to food, P_M/P_F—affect welfare or the allocation of resources.

A Change in Relative Prices. Consider the effect of a price change that *does* affect relative prices. Figure 3-7 shows the effect of a change in the price of only one good, in this case a rise in P_M from P_M^1 and P_M^2. The effect of the increase in P_M is to shift up the manufacturing labor demand curve in the same proportion as the price increase. This shifts the equilibrium from point 1 to point 2. Notice two important facts about the results of this shift. First, although the wage rate rises, it does by *less* than the

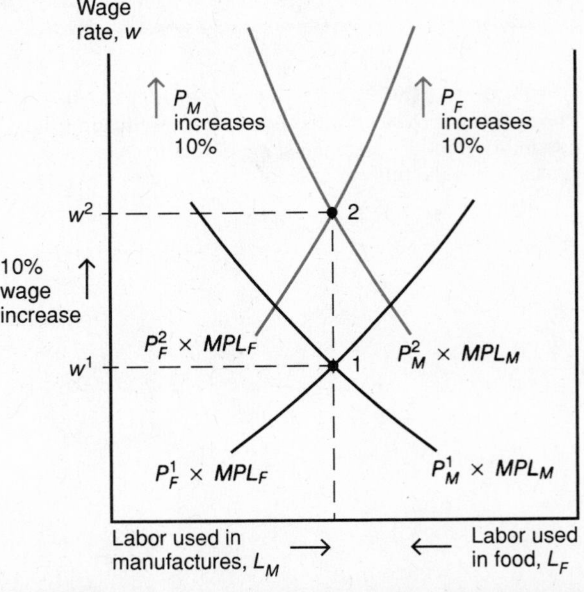

FIGURE 3-6
An equal proportional increase in the prices of manufactures and food.
The labor demand curves in manufactures and food both shift up in proportion to the rise in P_M from P_M^1 to P_M^2 and the rise in P_F from P_F^1 to P_F^2. The wage rate rises in the same proportion, from w^1 to w^2, the allocation of labor does not change.

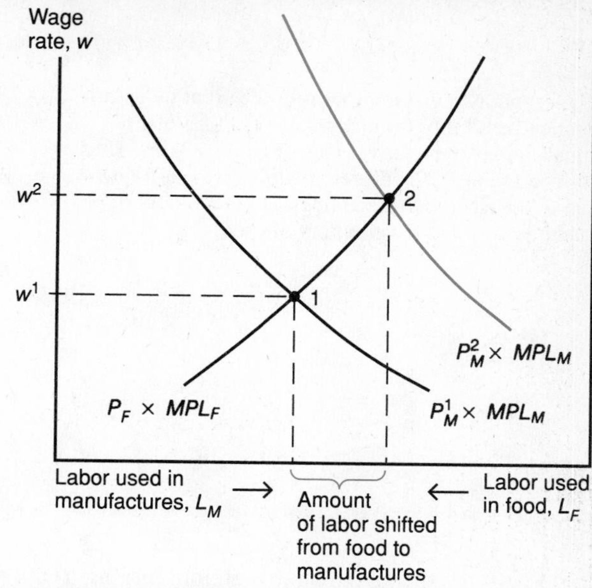

FIGURE 3-7
A rise in the price of manufactures.
The manufacturing labor demand curve rises in proportion to the increase in P_M, but the wage rate rises less than proportionately. Output of manufactures rises; output of food falls.

increase in the price of manufactures. This can be seen by comparing Figures 3-6 and 3-7. In Figure 3-6, which represents the results of a 10 percent increase in both P_M and P_F, we saw that w increased by 10 percent as well. If only P_M increases, w clearly rises by less—say 5 percent.

Second, when only P_M rises, in contrast to the case of a simultaneous rise in P_M and P_F, labor shifts from the food sector to the manufacturing sector and the output of manufactures rises while that of food falls.

The effect of a rise in the relative price of manufactures can also be seen directly by looking at the production possibility curve. In Figure 3-8, we show the effects of the same rise in the price of manufactures, which raises the *relative* price of manufactures from $(P_M/P_F)^1$ to $(P_M/P_F)^2$. The production point, which is always located where the slope of *TT* equals minus the relative price, shifts from 1 to 2. Food output falls and manufactures output rises as a result of the rise in the relative price of manufactures.

Since higher relative prices of manufactures lead to higher output of manufactures relative to that of food, we can draw a relative supply curve showing Q_M/Q_F as a function of P_M/P_F. This relative supply curve is shown as *RS* in Figure 3-9. As we showed in Chapter 2, we can also draw a relative demand curve, which is illustrated by the downward-sloping line *RD*. The equilibrium relative price $(P_M/P_F)^1$ and output $(Q_M/Q_F)^1$ are determined by the intersection of *RS* and *RD*.

RELATIVE PRICES AND THE DISTRIBUTION OF INCOME

So far we have examined the following aspects of the specific factors model: (1) the determination of production possibilities given an economy's resources and technology and (2) the determination of resource allocation, production, and relative prices in a

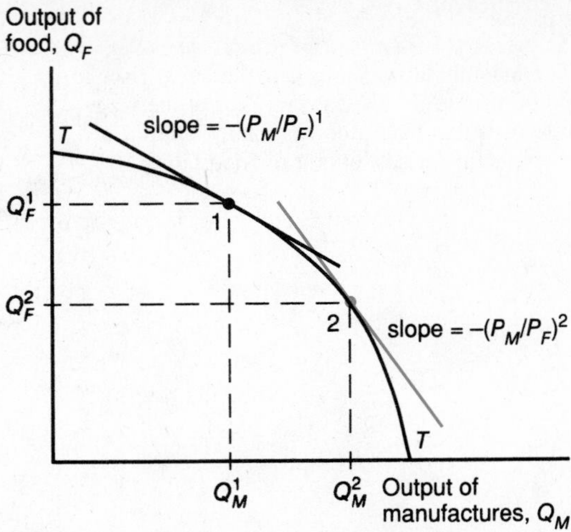

FIGURE 3-8
The response of output to a change in the relative price of manufactures.
The economy always produces at the point on its production possibility frontier where the slope of *TT* equals minus the relative price of manufactures. Thus an increase in P_M/P_F causes production to shift down and to the right, corresponding to higher output of manufactures and lower output of food.

market economy. Before turning to the effects of international trade we must consider the effect of changes in relative prices on the distribution of income.

Look again at Figure 3-7, which shows the effect of a rise in the price of manufactures. We have already noted that the demand curve for labor in the manufacturing sector will shift upward in proportion to the rise in P_M, so that if P_M rises by 10 percent, the curve defined by $P_M \times MPL_M$ also rises by 10 percent. We have also seen that unless the price of food also rises by at least 10 percent, w will rise by *less* than P_M. Thus if manufacturing prices rise by 10 percent, we would expect the wage rate to rise by only, say, 5 percent.

Let's look at what this outcome implies for the incomes of three groups: workers,

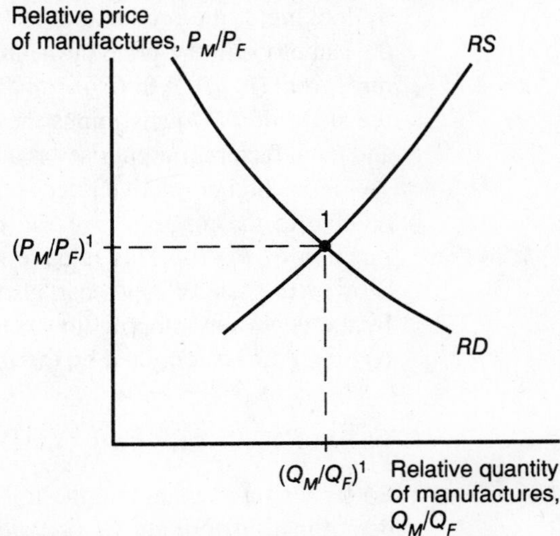

FIGURE 3-9
Determination of relative prices.
In the specific factors model a higher relative price of manufactures will lead to an increase in the output of manufactures relative to that of food. Thus the relative supply curve *RS* is upward-sloping. Equilibrium relative quantities and prices are determined by the intersection of *RS* with the relative demand curve *RD*.

owners of capital, and owners of land. Workers find that their wage rate has risen, but less than in proportion to the rise in P_M. Thus their real wage in terms of manufactures, w/P_M, falls, while their real wage in terms of food, w/P_F, rises. Given this information, we cannot say whether workers are better or worse off; this depends on the relative importance of manufactures and food in workers' consumption, a question that we will not pursue further.

Owners of capital, however, are definitely better off. The real wage rate in terms of manufactures has fallen, so that the profits of capital owners in terms of what they produce rises. That is, the income of capital owners will rise more than proportionately with the rise in P_M. Since P_M in turn has risen relative to P_F, the income of capitalists has clearly gone up in terms of both goods.

Conversely, landowners are definitely worse off. They lose for two reasons: the real wage in terms of food rises, squeezing their income, and the rise in manufactures prices reduces the purchasing power of any given income.

International Trade in the Specific Factors Model

Now that we know how the specific factors model works for a single economy, we can turn to an analysis of international trade. Imagine that two countries, Japan and America, trade with each other; let's examine the effects of this trade on their welfare.

For trade to take place, the two countries must differ in the relative price of manufactures that would prevail in the absence of trade. In Figure 3-9 we saw how P_M/P_F is determined in a single economy in the absence of trade. Japan and America could have different relative prices of manufactures either because they differ in their relative demand or because they differ in their relative supply. We will assume away demand differences: that is, we assume that at any given P_M/P_F, relative demand is the same in the two countries. If both countries face the same relative price of manufactures, they will consume food and manufactures in the same proportions. Thus both countries will have the same relative demand curve. We will therefore focus on differences in relative supply as the source of international trade.

Why might relative supply differ? The countries could have different technologies, as in the Ricardian model. Now that our model has more than one factor of production, however, the countries could also differ in their resources. It is worth examining how differences in resources can affect relative supply.

RESOURCES AND RELATIVE SUPPLY

The basic relationship between resources and relative supply is straightforward: a country with a lot of capital and not much land will tend to produce a high ratio of manufactures to food at any given prices, while a country with a lot of land and not much capital will do the reverse. Consider what would happen if one of the countries experienced an increase in the supply of some resource. Suppose, for example, that Japan were to increase its capital stock. The effects of such an increase are shown in Figure 3-10.

Other things equal, an increase in the quantity of capital would raise the marginal productivity of labor in the manufacturing sector. Thus the demand curve for labor in

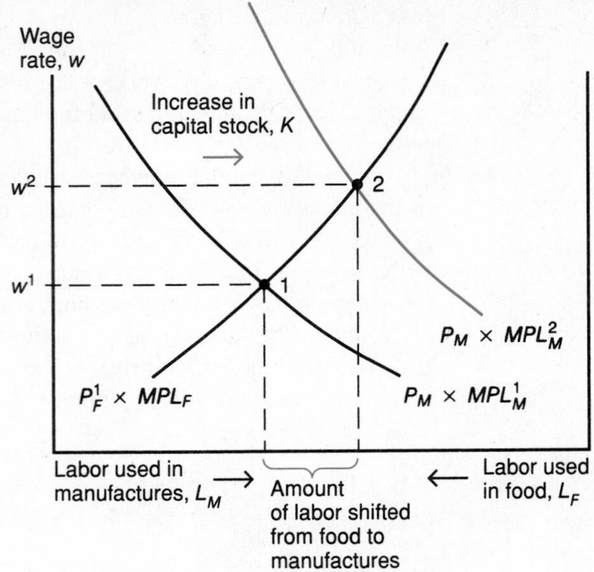

FIGURE 3-10
Changing the capital stock.
An increase in the capital stock raises the marginal product of labor in manufactures for any given level of employment. This raises the demand for labor in the manufacturing sector, which drives up the overall wage rate. Labor is pulled out of the food sector. Thus output of manufactures rises, while output of food falls.

manufacturing would shift to the right, from $P_M \times MPL_M^1$ to $P_M \times MPL_M^2$. At any given prices of manufactures and food, this increase in demand for manufacturing labor would shift the equilibrium from point 1 to point 2: more workers would be drawn into the manufacturing sector out of the food sector. Manufacturing output would rise, for two reasons: there would be more workers in the sector and they would have more capital to work with. Food output would fall because of reduced labor input. So at any given relative price of manufactures, the relative output of manufactures would rise. We therefore conclude that an increase in the supply of capital would shift the relative supply curve to the right.

Correspondingly, an increase in the supply of land would increase food output and reduce manufacturing output; the relative supply curve would shift left.

What about the effect of an increase in the labor force? This is a less clear-cut case. To induce employers to hire the additional workers, the wage rate must fall. This will lead to increased employment and output of *both* manufactures and food; the effect on relative output is ambiguous.

Suppose, however, that America and Japan have the same labor force, but that Japan has a larger supply of capital than America, while America has a larger supply of land than Japan. Then the situation will look like that in Figure 3-11. Japan's relative supply curve RS_J lies to the right of America's curve RS_A, because Japan's abundance of capital and scarcity of land leads it to produce a large quantity of manufactures and relatively little food at any given relative price of manufactures, whereas the reverse is true for America.

TRADE AND RELATIVE PRICES

In this model, as always, international trade leads to a convergence of relative prices, illustrated in Figure 3-11. Since relative demand is the same in Japan and America,

FIGURE 3-11
Trade and relative prices.
In the figure, Japan is assumed to have more capital per worker than America, while America has more land per worker than Japan. As a result, Japan's relative supply curve lies to the right of America's. When the two economies trade, the *world* relative supply curve RS_{WORLD} lies between the two national curves, and the equilibrium world relative price of manufactures—determined by the intersection of RS_{WORLD} with the relative demand curve RD_{WORLD}—lies between the levels of P_M/P_F that would have prevailed in the two countries in the absence of trade.

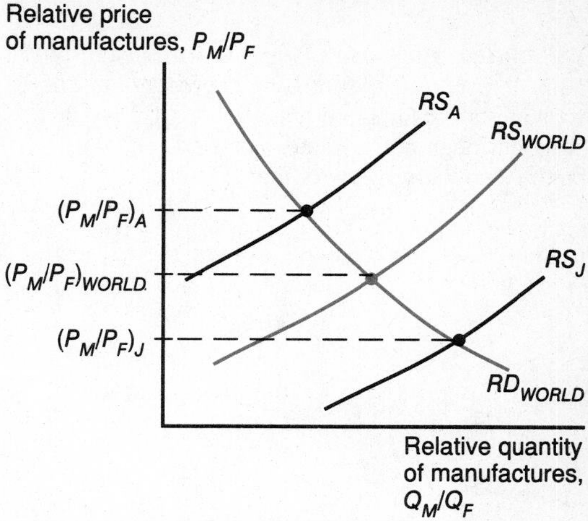

RD_{WORLD} is both each country's relative demand curve and the world relative demand curve when the two countries trade. RS_J and RS_A represent the relative supply curves of Japan and America, respectively. Japan is assumed to be relatively well-endowed with capital and poorly endowed with land, while America is the reverse, so RS_J lies to the right of RS_A. The pretrade relative price of manufactures in Japan, $(P_M/P_F)_J$, is lower than the pretrade relative price in America, $(P_M/P_F)_A$.

When the two countries open trade, they create an integrated world economy whose production of manufactures and food is the sum of the national outputs of the two goods. The world relative supply of manufactures (RS_{WORLD}) lies between the relative supplies in the two countries. The world relative price of manufactures, $(P_M/P_F)_{WORLD}$, therefore lies between the national pretrade prices. Trade has increased the relative price of manufactures in Japan and has lowered it in America.

THE PATTERN OF TRADE

If trade occurs initially because of differences in relative prices of manufactures, how does the convergence of P_M/P_F translate into a pattern of international trade? To answer this question, we need to state some basic relationships among prices, production, and consumption.

In a country that cannot trade, the output of a good must equal its consumption. If D_M is consumption of manufactures and D_F consumption of food, then in a closed economy $D_M = Q_M$ and $D_F = Q_F$. International trade makes it possible for the mix of manufactures and food consumed to differ from the mix produced. While the amounts of each good that a country consumes and produces may differ, however, a country cannot spend more than it earns: the *value* of consumption must be equal to the value of production. That is,

$$P_M \times D_M + P_F \times D_F = P_M \times Q_M + P_F \times Q_F. \quad \textbf{(3-8)}$$

Equation (3-8) can be rearranged to yield the following:

$$D_F - Q_F = (P_M/P_F) \times (Q_M - D_M). \quad \textbf{(3-9)}$$

FIGURE 3-12
The budget constraint for a trading economy. Point 1 represents the economy's production. The economy's consumption must lie along a line that passes through point 1 and has a slope equal to minus the relative price of manufactures.

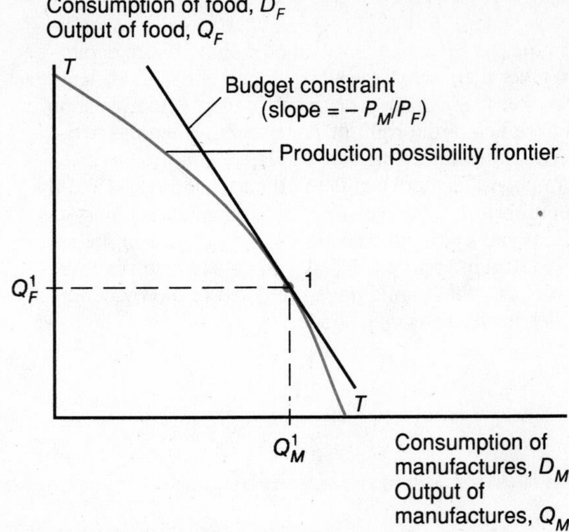

$D_F - Q_F$ is the economy's food *imports,* the amount by which its consumption of food exceeds its production. The right-hand side of the equation is the product of the relative price of manufactures and the amount by which production of manufactures exceeds consumption, that is, the economy's *exports* of manufactures. The equation, then, states that imports of food equal exports of manufactures times the relative price of manufactures. While it does not tell us how much the economy will import or export, the equation does show that the amount the economy can afford to import is limited, or constrained, by the amount it exports. Equation (3-9) is therefore known as a **budget constraint.**[2]

Figure 3-12 illustrates two important features of the budget constraint for a trading economy. First, the slope of the budget constraint is minus P_M/P_F, the relative price of manufactures. The reason is that consuming one less unit of manufactures saves the economy P_M; this is enough to purchase P_M/P_F extra units of food. Second, the budget constraint is tangent to the production possibility frontier at the point that represents the economy's choice of production given that relative price of manufactures, shown in the figure as point 1. That is, the economy can always afford to consume what it produces.

We can now use the budget constraints of Japan and America to construct a picture of the trading equilibrium. In Figure 3-13, we show the outputs, budget constraints, and consumption choices of Japan and America at equilibrium prices. In Japan, the rise in the relative price of manufactures leads to a rise in the consumption of food relative to manufactures and a fall in the relative output of food. Japan produces Q_F^J of food but consumes D_F^J; it therefore becomes a manufactures exporter and a food importer.

[2] The constraint that the value of consumption equals that of production (or, equivalently, that imports equal exports in value) may not hold when countries can borrow from other countries or lend to them. For now we assume that these possibilities are not available and that the budget constraint [equation (3-9)] therefore holds. International borrowing and lending are examined in Chapter 7, which shows that an economy's consumption *over time* is still constrained by the necessity of paying its debts to foreign lenders.

FIGURE 3-13
Trading equilibrium.
Japan's imports of food are exactly equal to America's exports, and America's imports of manufactures are exactly equal to Japan's exports.

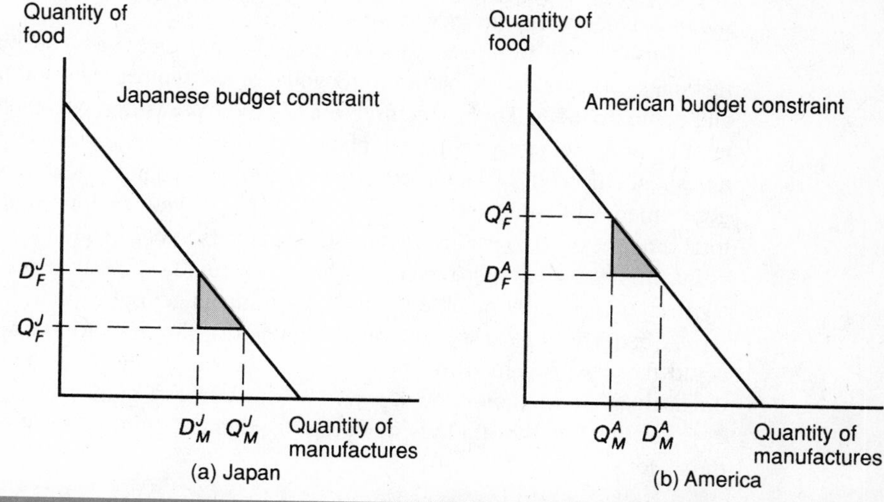

In America, the posttrade fall in the relative price of manufactures leads to a rise in the consumption of manufactures relative to food and a fall in the relative output of manufactures; America therefore becomes a manufactures importer and a food exporter. In equilibrium Japan's exports of manufactures must exactly equal America's imports and Japan's imports of food exactly equal America's exports. These equalities are shown by the equality of the two colored triangles in Figure 3-13.

Income Distribution and the Gains from Trade

We have seen how production possibilities are determined by resources and technology; how the choice of what to produce is determined by the relative price of manufactures; how changes in the relative price of manufactures affect the real incomes of different factors of production; and how trade affects both relative prices and the economy's budget constraint. Now we can ask the crucial question: who gains and who loses from international trade? We begin by asking how the welfare of particular groups is affected, and then how trade affects the welfare of the country as a whole.

To assess the effects of trade on particular groups, the key point is that international trade shifts the relative price of manufactures and food. Consider first what happens in Japan. We are assuming that in the absence of trade Japan would have had a lower relative price of manufactures than the rest of the world. Then trade, which leads to a convergence of relative prices, will mean a rise in P_M/P_F. In Japan, then (as we saw in the previous section), the result of a rise in P_M/P_F is that owners of capital are better off, workers experience an ambiguous shift in their position, and landowners are worse off.

In America, the effect of trade on relative prices is just the reverse: the relative price of manufactures falls. So in America landowners are better off and capital owners worse off, and the effect on workers is once again ambiguous.

The general outcome, then, is simple: *Trade benefits the factor that is specific to the export sector of each country but hurts the factor specific to the import-competing sectors, with ambiguous effects on mobile factors.*

Do the gains from trade outweigh the losses? One way you might try to answer this question would be to sum up the gains of the winners and the losses of the losers and compare them. The problem with this procedure is that we are comparing welfare, an inherently subjective thing. Suppose that capitalists are dull people who get hardly any satisfaction out of increased consumption, while landowners are bons vivants who get immense pleasure out of it. Then one might well imagine that trade reduces the total amount of pleasure in Japan. But the reverse could equally be true. More to the point, it is outside the province of what we normally think of as economic analysis to try to figure out how much enjoyment individuals get out of their lives.

A better way to assess the overall gains from trade is to ask a different question: could those who gain from trade compensate those who lose, and still be better off themselves? If so, then trade is *potentially* a source of gain to everyone.

To illustrate that trade is a source of potential gain for everyone, we proceed in three steps.

1. First, we notice that in the absence of trade the economy would have to produce what it consumed, and vice versa. Thus the *consumption* of the economy in the absence of trade would have to be a point on the *production* possibility frontier. In Figure 3-14, a typical pretrade consumption point is shown as point 2.

2. Next, we notice that it is possible for a trading economy to consume more of *both* goods than it would have in the absence of trade. The budget constraint in Figure

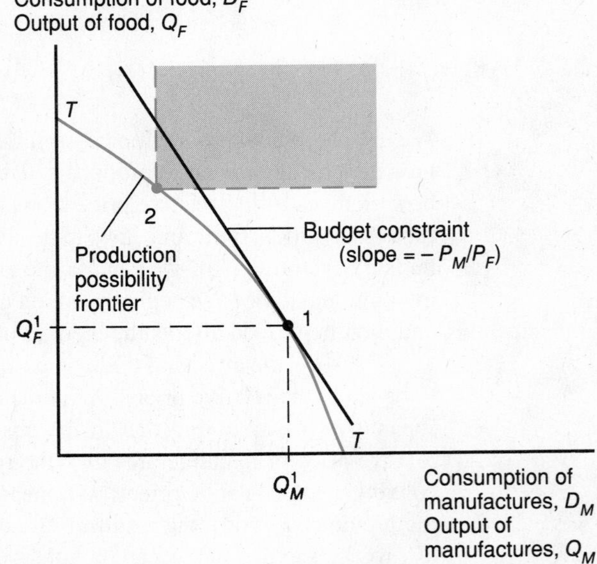

FIGURE 3-14
Trade expands the economy's consumption possibilities.
Before trade, the economy's production and consumption were at point 2. After trade, the economy can consume at any point on its budget constraint. The portion of the budget constraint in the colored region consists of feasible post-trade consumption choices with consumption of both goods higher than at the pretrade point 2.

3-14 represents all the possible combinations of food and manufactures that the c could consume given the world relative price of manufactures. Part of that budg constraint—the part in the colored region—represents situations in which the economy consumes more of both manufactures and food than it could in the absence of trade. Notice that this result does not depend on the assumption that pretrade production and consumption was at point 2; unless pretrade production was at point 1, so that trade has no effect on production at all, there is always a part of the budget constraint that allows consumption of more of both goods.

3. Finally, observe that if the economy as a whole consumes more of both goods, then it is possible in principle to give each *individual* more of both goods. This would make everyone better off. This shows, then, that it is possible to ensure that everyone is better off as a result of trade. Of course, everyone might be still better off if they had less of one good and more of the other, but this only reinforces the conclusion that everyone can potentially gain from trade.

The fundamental reason why trade potentially benefits a country is that it *expands the economy's choices.* This expansion of choice means that it is always possible to redistribute income in such a way that everyone gains from trade.[3]

That everyone *could* gain from trade unfortunately does not mean that everyone actually does. In the real world, the presence of losers as well as winners from trade is one of the most important reasons why trade is not free.

The Political Economy of Trade: A Preliminary View

Trade often produces losers as well as winners. This insight is crucial to understanding the considerations that actually determine trade policy in the modern world economy. Trade policy is examined in detail in Chapters 9 through 12; it is possible, however, to take a preliminary view at this point.

There are two ways to look at trade policy (or any government policy): (1) Given its objectives, what *should* the government do? What is its *optimal* trade policy? (2) What are governments likely to do in practice? The income distribution effects of trade are important to the first way of looking at the issue and are crucial to the second.

OPTIMAL TRADE POLICY

Suppose a government wants to maximize the welfare of its population. If everyone were exactly alike in tastes and in income there would be a straightforward solution: the government would choose policies that make the representative individual as well off as possible. In this homogeneous economy, free international trade would clearly serve the government's objectives.

When people are not exactly alike, however, the government's problem is less well-defined. The government must somehow weigh one person's gain against another

[3] The argument that trade is beneficial because it enlarges an economy's choices is much more general than this picture. For a thorough discussion see Paul Samuelson, "The Gains from International Trade Once Again," *Economic Journal* 72 (1962), pp. 820–829.

person's loss. If, for example, the Japanese government is relatively more concerned about hurting landowners than about helping capitalists, then international trade, which in our analysis benefited capital owners and hurt landowners in Japan, might be a bad thing from the Japanese government's point of view.

There are many reasons why one group might matter more than another, but one of the most compelling reasons is that some groups need special treatment because they are already relatively poor. There is widespread sympathy in the United States for restrictions on imports of garments and shoes, even though the restrictions raise consumer prices, because workers in these industries are already poorly paid. The gains that affluent consumers would realize if more imports were allowed do not matter as much to the U.S. public as the losses low-paid shoe and garment workers would suffer.

Does this mean that trade should be allowed only if it doesn't hurt lower-income people? Few international economists would agree. In spite of the real importance of income distribution, most economists remain strongly in favor of more or less free

Specific Factors and the Beginnings of Trade Theory

The modern theory of international trade began with the demonstration by David Ricardo, writing in 1817, that trade is mutually beneficial to countries. We studied Ricardo's model in Chapter 2. Ricardo used his model to argue for free trade, in particular for an end to the tariffs that restricted England's imports of food. Yet almost surely the British economy of 1817 was better described by a specific factors model than by the one-factor model Ricardo presented.

To understand the situation, recall that from the beginning of the French Revolution in 1789 until the defeat of Napoleon at Waterloo in 1815, Britain was almost continuously at war with France. This war interfered with Britain's trade: privateers (pirates licensed by foreign governments) raided shipping and the French attempted to impose a blockade on British goods. Since Britain was an exporter of manufactures and an importer of agricultural products, this limitation of trade raised the relative price of food in Britain. The profits of manufacturers suffered, but landowners actually prospered during the long war.

After the war, food prices in Britain fell. To avoid the consequences, the politically influential landowners were able to get legislation, the so-called Corn Laws, that imposed fees to discourage importation of grain. It was against these Corn Laws that Ricardo was arguing.

Ricardo knew that repeal of the Corn Laws would make capitalists better off but landowners worse off. From his point of view this was all to the good; a London businessman himself, he preferred hardworking capitalists to idle landed aristocrats. But he chose to present his argument in the form of a model that assumed away issues of internal income distribution.

Why did he do this? Almost surely the answer is political: while Ricardo was in reality to some extent representing the interest of a single group, he emphasized the gains to the nation as a whole. This was a clever and thoroughly modern strategy, one that pioneered the use of economic theory as a political instrument. Then as now, politics and intellectual progress are not incompatible: the Corn Laws were repealed nearly a century and a half ago, yet Ricardo's model of trade remains one of the great insights in economics.

trade. There are three main reasons why economists do *not* generally stress the income distribution effects of trade.

1. Income distribution effects are not specific to international trade. Every change in a nation's economy, including technological progress, shifting consumer preferences, exhaustion of old resources and discovery of new ones, and so on, affects income distribution. If every change in the economy were allowed only after it had been examined for its distributional effects, economic progress could easily end up snarled in red tape.
2. It is always better to allow trade and compensate those who are hurt by it than to prohibit the trade. (This applies to other forms of economic change as well.) All modern industrial countries provide some sort of "safety net" of income support programs (such as unemployment benefits and subsidized retraining and relocation programs) that can cushion the losses of groups hurt by trade. Economists would argue that if this cushion is felt to be inadequate, more support rather than less trade is the right answer.
3. Those who stand to lose from increased trade are typically better organized than those who stand to gain. This imbalance creates a bias in the political process that requires a counterweight. It is the traditional role of economists to strongly support free trade, pointing to the overall gains; those who are hurt usually have little trouble making their complaints heard.

Most economists, then, while acknowledging the effects of international trade on income distribution, believe that it is more important to stress the potential gains from trade than the possible losses to some groups in a country. Economists do not, however, often have the deciding voice in economic policy, especially when conflicting interests are at stake. Any realistic understanding of how trade policy is determined must look at the actual motivations of policy.

INCOME DISTRIBUTION AND TRADE POLITICS

It is easy to see why groups that lose from trade lobby their governments to restrict trade and protect their incomes. You might expect that those who gain from trade would lobby as strongly as those who lose from it, but this is rarely the case. In the United States and in most countries, those who want trade limited are more effective politically than those who want it extended. Typically, those who gain from trade in any particular product are a much less concentrated, informed, and organized group than those who lose.

A good example of this contrast between the two sides is the U.S. sugar industry. The United States has limited imports of sugar for many years; at the time of writing the price of sugar in the U.S. market was about twice its price in the world market. Most estimates put the cost to U.S. consumers of this import limitation at about $2 billion a year—that is, about $8 a year for every man, woman, and child. The gains to producers are much smaller, probably less than half as large.

If producers and consumers were equally able to get their interests represented, this policy would never have been enacted. In absolute terms, however, each consumer suffers very little. Eight dollars a year is not much; furthermore, most of the cost is hidden, because most sugar is consumed as an ingredient in other foods rather than purchased directly. Thus most consumers are unaware that the import quota even exists, let alone that it reduces their standard of living. Even if they were aware, $8 is not a large enough sum to provoke people into organizing protests and writing letters to their congressional representatives.

The sugar producers' situation is quite different. The average sugar producer gains thousands of dollars a year from the import quota. Furthermore, sugar producers are organized into trade associations and cooperatives that actively pursue their members' political interests. So the complaints of sugar producers about the effects of imports are loudly and effectively expressed.

As we will see in Chapters 9 through 12, the politics of import restriction in the sugar industry are an extreme example of a kind of political process that is common in international trade. That world trade in general became steadily freer from 1945 to 1980 depended, as we will see in Chapter 10, on a special set of circumstances that controlled what is probably an inherent political bias against international trade.

Summary

1. International trade often has strong effects on the distribution of income within countries, so that it often produces losers as well as winners. Income distribution effects arise for two reasons: factors of production cannot move instantaneously and costlessly from one industry to another, and changes in an economy's output mix have differential effects on the demand for different factors of production.

2. A useful model of income distribution effects is the *specific factors model,* which allows for a distinction between general-purpose factors that can move between sectors and factors that are specific to particular uses. In this model, differences in resources can cause countries to have different relative supply curves, and thus cause international trade.

3. In the specific factors model, factors specific to export sectors in each country gain from trade, while factors specific to import-competing sectors lose. Mobile factors that can work in either sector may either gain or lose.

4. Trade nonetheless produces overall gains in the limited sense that those who gain could in principle compensate those who lose while still remaining better off than before.

5. Most economists do not regard the effects of international trade on income distribution as a good reason to limit this trade. In its distributional effects, trade is no different from many other forms of economic change, which are not normally regulated. Furthermore, economists would prefer to address the problem of income distribution directly, rather than by interfering with trade flows.

6. Nonetheless, in the actual politics of trade policy income distribution is of crucial importance. This is true in particular because those who lose from trade are usually a much more informed, cohesive, and organized group than those who gain.

Key Terms

specific factors model
mobile factor
specific factor
production function
marginal product of labor
diminishing returns
budget constraint

Problems

1. In 1986, the price of oil on world markets dropped sharply. Since the United States is an oil-importing country, this was widely regarded as good for the U.S. economy. Yet in Texas and Louisiana 1986 was a year of economic decline. Why?
2. An economy can produce good 1 using labor and capital and good 2 using labor and land. The total supply of labor is 100 units. Given the supply of capital, the outputs of the two goods depends on labor input as follows:

Labor input to good 1	*Output of good 1*	*Labor input to good 2*	*Output of good 2*
0	0.0	0	0.0
10	25.1	10	39.8
20	38.1	20	52.5
30	48.6	30	61.8
40	57.7	40	69.3
50	66.0	50	75.8
60	73.6	60	81.5
70	80.7	70	86.7
80	87.4	80	91.4
90	93.9	90	95.9
100	100	100	100

   a. Graph the production functions for good 1 and good 2.

   b. Graph the production possibility frontier. Why is it curved?

3. The marginal product of labor curves corresponding to the production functions in problem 2 are as follows:

Workers employed	*MPL in sector 1*	*MPL in sector 2*
10	1.51	1.59
20	1.14	1.05
30	0.97	0.82
40	0.87	0.69
50	0.79	0.61
60	0.74	0.54
70	0.69	0.50
80	0.66	0.46
90	0.63	0.43
100	0.60	0.40

   a. Suppose that the price of good 2 relative to that of good 1 is 2. Determine graphically the wage rate and the allocation of labor between the two sectors.

b. Using the graph drawn for problem 2, determine the output of each sector. Then confirm graphically that the slope of the production possibility frontier at that point equals the relative price.

c. Suppose that the relative price of good 2 falls to 1. Repeat (a) and (b).

d. Calculate the effects of the price change on the income of the specific factors in sectors 1 and 2.

4. In the text we examined the impacts of increases in the supply of capital and land. But what if the mobile factor, labor, increases in supply?

a. Analyze the qualitative effects of an increase in the supply of labor in the specific factors model, holding the prices of both goods constant.

b. Graph the effect on the equilibrium for the numerical example in problems 2 and 3, given a relative price of 1, when the labor force expands from 100 to 140.

Further Reading

Avinash Dixit and Victor Norman. *Theory of International Trade.* Cambridge: Cambridge University Press, 1980. The problem of establishing gains from trade when some people may be made worse off has been the subject of a long debate. Dixit and Norman show it is always possible in principle for a country's government to use taxes and subsidies to redistribute income in such a way that everyone is better off with free trade than with no trade.

Michael Mussa. "Tariffs and the Distribution of Income: The Importance of Factor Specificity, Substitutability, and Intensity in the Short and Long Run." *Journal of Political Economy* 82 (1974), pp. 1191–1204. An extension of the specific factors model that relates it to the factor-proportions model of Chapter 4.

J. Peter Neary. "Short-Run Capital Specificity and the Pure Theory of International Trade." *Economic Journal* 88 (1978), pp. 488–510. A further treatment of the specific factors model that stresses how differing assumptions about mobility of factors between sectors affect the model's conclusions.

Mancur Olson. *The Logic of Collective Action.* Cambridge: Harvard University Press, 1965. A highly influential book that argues the proposition that in practice government policies favor small, concentrated groups over large ones.

David Ricardo. *The Principles of Political Economy and Taxation.* Homewood, IL: Irwin, 1963. While Ricardo's *Principles* emphasizes the national gains from trade at one point, elsewhere in his book the conflict of interest between landowners and capitalists is a central issue.

Appendix to Chapter 3 ●
Further Details on Specific Factors

The specific factors model developed in this chapter is such a convenient tool of analysis that we take the time here to spell out some of its details more fully. We give a fuller treatment of two related issues: (1) the relationship between marginal and total product within each sector; (2) the income distribution effects of relative price changes.

MARGINAL AND TOTAL PRODUCT

In the text we illustrated the production function in manufacturing two different ways. In Figure 3-1 we showed total output as a function of labor input, holding capital constant. We then observed that the slope of that curve is the marginal product of labor and illustrated that marginal product in Figure 3-2. We now want to demonstrate that the total output is measured by the area under the marginal product curve. (Students who are familiar with calculus will find this obvious: marginal product is the derivative of total, so total is the integral of marginal. Even for these students, however, an intuitive approach can be helpful.)

In Figure 3A-1 we show once again the marginal product curve in manufacturing. Suppose that we employ L_M person-hours. How can we show the total output of manufactures? Let's approximate this using the marginal product curve. First, let's ask what would happen if we used slightly fewer person-hours, say dL_M fewer. Then output would be less. The fall in output would be approximately

$$dL_M \times MPL_M,$$

FIGURE 3A-1
Showing that output is equal to the area under the marginal product curve.
By approximating the marginal product curve with a series of thin rectangles, one can show that the total output of manufactures is equal to the area under the curve.

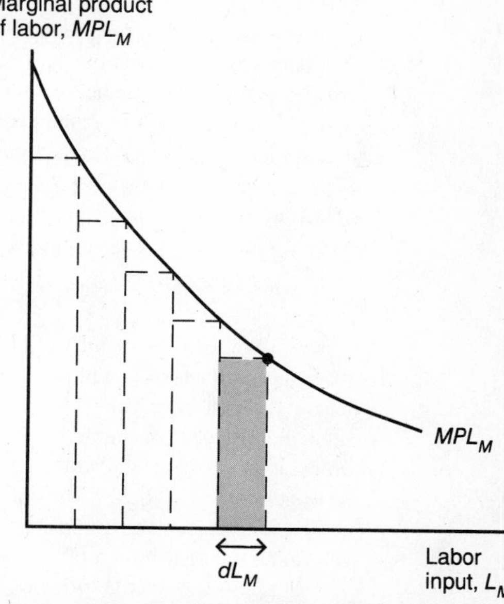

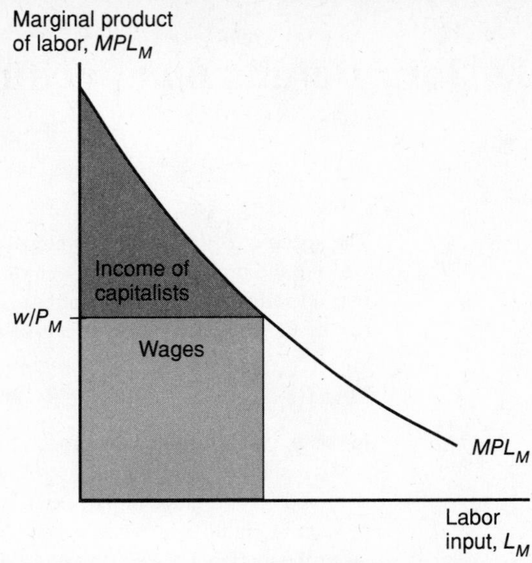

FIGURE 3A-2
The distribution of income within the manufacturing sector.
Labor income is equal to the real wage times employment. The rest of output accrues as income to the owners of capital.

that is, the reduction in the work force times the marginal product of labor at the initial level of employment. This reduction in output is represented by the area of the colored rectangle in Figure 3A-1. Now subtract another few person-hours; the output loss will be another rectangle. This time the rectangle will be taller, because the marginal product of labor rises as the quantity of labor falls. If we continue this process until all the labor is gone, our approximation of the total output loss will be the sum of all the rectangles shown in the figure. When no labor is employed, however, output will fall to zero. So we can approximate the total output of the manufacturing sector by the sum of the areas of all the rectangles under the marginal product curve.

This is, however, only an approximation, because we used the marginal product of only the first person-hour in each batch of labor removed. We can get a better approximation if we take smaller groups—the smaller the better. As the groups of labor removed get infinitesimally small, however, the rectangles get thinner and thinner, and we approximate ever more closely the total area under the marginal product curve. In the end, then, we find that the total output of manufactures produced with labor L_M is equal to the area under the marginal product of labor curve MPL_M up to L_M.

RELATIVE PRICES AND THE DISTRIBUTION OF INCOME

Figure 3A-2 uses the result we just found to show the distribution of income within the manufacturing sector for a given real wage. We know that employers will hire labor up to the point where the real wage in terms of manufactures, w/P_M, equals the marginal product. We can immediately read off the graph the total output of manufactures as the area under the marginal product curve. We can also read off the graph the part of manufacturing output that is paid out as wages, which is equal to the real wage times employment, and thus to the area of the rectangle shown. The part of the output that is kept by owners of capital, then, is the remainder. We can determine the distribution of food production between labor and landowners in the same way.

Suppose the relative price of manufactures now rises. We saw in Figure 3-7 that a rise in P_M/P_F lowers the real wage in terms of manufactures while raising it in terms of food. The effects

FIGURE 3A-3
A rise in P_M benefits the owners of capital.
The real wage in terms of manufactures falls, leading to a rise in the income of capital owners.

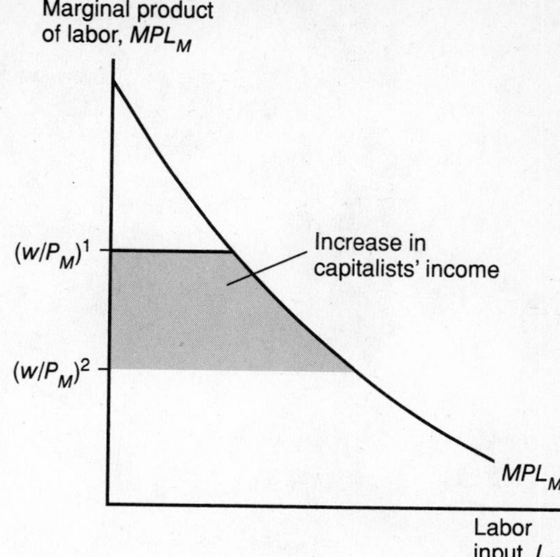

of this on the income of capitalists and landowners can be seen in Figures 3A-3 and 3A-4. In the manufactures sector, the real wage is shown as falling from $(w/P_M)^1$ to $(w/P_M)^2$; as a result capitalists receive increased income. In the food sector, the real wage rises from $(w/P_F)^1$ to $(w/P_F)^2$, and landowners receive less income.

This effect on incomes is reinforced by the change in P_M/P_F itself. Owners of capital receive more income *in terms of manufactures;* their purchasing power is further increased by the rise in the price of manufactures relative to food. Landowners receive less income *in terms of food;* they are made still worse off because of the rise in the relative price of manufactures.

FIGURE 3A-4
A rise in P_M hurts landowners.
The real wage in terms of food rises, reducing the income of land.

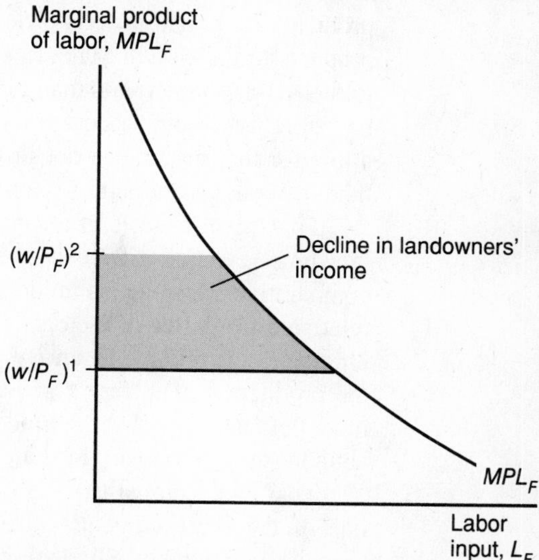

Resources and Trade: The Heckscher-Ohlin Model

Chapter 4

If labor were the only factor of production, as the Ricardian model assumes, comparative advantage could arise only because of international differences in labor productivity. In the real world, however, while trade is partly explained by differences in labor productivity, it also reflects differences in countries' *resources.* Canada exports forest products to the United States not because its lumberjacks are more productive relative to their U.S. counterparts than other Canadians but because sparsely populated Canada has more forested land per capita than the United States. A realistic view of trade must allow for the importance not just of labor, but of other factors of production such as land, capital, and mineral resources.

To explain the role of resource differences in trade, this chapter examines a model in which resource differences are the *only* source of trade. This model shows that comparative advantage is influenced by the interaction between nations' resources (the relative **abundance** of factors of production) and the technology of production (which influences the relative **intensity** with which different factors of production are used in the production of different goods). The same idea was present in the specific factors model of Chapter 3, but the model we study in this chapter puts the interaction between abundance and intensity in sharper relief.

That international trade is largely driven by differences in countries' resources is one of the most influential theories in international economics. Developed by two Swedish economists, Eli Heckscher and Bertil Ohlin (Ohlin received the Nobel Prize in economics in 1977), the theory is often referred to as the **Heckscher-Ohlin theory.** Because the theory emphasizes the interplay between the proportions in which different factors of production are available in different countries and the proportions in which they are used in producing different goods, it is also referred to as the **factor-proportions theory.**

To develop the factor-proportions theory we begin by describing an economy that does not trade, then ask what happens when two such economies trade with each other. Since the factor-proportions theory is both an important theory and a controversial one, the chapter concludes with a discussion of the empirical evidence for and against the theory.

A Model of a Two-Factor Economy

The simplest factor-proportions model is in many ways very similar to the specific factors model developed in Chapter 3. As in that model, it is assumed that each economy is able to produce two goods and that production of each good requires the use of two factors of production. In this case, however, we no longer assume that one of the factors used in each industry is specific to that industry. Instead, the *same* two factors are used in both sectors. This leads to a somewhat more difficult model, but also to some important new insights.

ASSUMPTIONS OF THE MODEL

The economy we are analyzing can produce two goods: cloth (measured in yards) and food (measured in calories). Production of these goods requires two inputs that are in limited supply: labor, which we measure in hours, and land, which we measure in acres. Initially we assume that the technology of production is one of **fixed coefficients;** that is, there is only one way to produce each good. A yard of cloth can be produced only using a certain fixed number of hours of labor and acres of land; we cannot use less land and more labor, or vice versa. The same is true for producing a calorie of food.

In general we would not expect the production of food and of cloth to require land and labor in the same proportions. Let's assume that cloth production is *labor-intensive,* that is, it requires a higher ratio of labor to land than food production. Food production is correspondingly more *land-intensive* than cloth production. Notice that the definition of labor or land intensity depends on the ratio of land to labor used in production, not the ratio of land or labor to output. Thus a good cannot be both land- and labor-intensive.

Let's define the following expressions:

$$\begin{aligned}
a_{TC} &= \text{acres of land required per yard of cloth,}\\
a_{LC} &= \text{hours of labor required per yard of cloth,}\\
a_{TF} &= \text{acres of land required per calorie of food,}\\
a_{LF} &= \text{hours of labor required per calorie of food,}\\
L &= \text{economy's supply of labor,}\\
T &= \text{economy's supply of land.}
\end{aligned}$$

The assumption that cloth production is labor-intensive and food production land-intensive can be stated in two equivalent ways:

$$a_{LC}/a_{TC} > a_{LF}/a_{TF}$$

or

$$a_{LC}/a_{LF} > a_{TC}/a_{TF}.$$

PRODUCTION POSSIBILITIES

The principle that underlies the derivation of a production possibility frontier in this model is the same as in earlier ones: the economy cannot use more of either input than it has available. If the country produces Q_C yards of cloth and Q_F calories of food, it must use $a_{LC}Q_C + a_{LF}Q_F$ hours of labor to produce these goods, and this amount must not exceed the total labor force L. The economy will also use $a_{TC}Q_C + a_{TF}Q_F$ acres of land, and this must not exceed the total supply of land T. Together, these two constraints define the economy's production possibilities. First, total use of labor cannot exceed the available supply:

$$a_{LC}Q_C + a_{LF}Q_F \leq L. \tag{4-1}$$

Second, total use of land must not exceed the available supply:

$$a_{TC}Q_C + a_{TF}Q_F \leq T. \tag{4-2}$$

The limited supplies of labor and land limit what the economy can produce.

By rearranging the labor constraint, we can write the expression

$$Q_F \leq L/a_{LF} - (a_{LC}/a_{LF})Q_C. \tag{4-3}$$

The logic behind this expression should be clear. If all labor (L) were used to produce food, there would be enough to produce at most L/a_{LF} calories, that is, the total labor force divided by the number of hours it takes to produce each calorie. If some cloth is also produced, each unit of cloth requires that a_{LC} units of labor be diverted from food production and thus reduces the maximum food output by a_{LC}/a_{LF} calories.

Similarly, by rearranging the land constraint we get

$$Q_F \leq T/a_{TF} - (a_{TC}/a_{TF})Q_C. \tag{4-4}$$

The labor and land constraints are illustrated in Figure 4-1. Because cloth is more labor-intensive than food— $a_{LC}/a_{LF} > a_{TC}/a_{TF}$ —the labor constraint is a steeper line than the land constraint.

The two-tone lines in Figure 4-1 show how the two constraints together determine the economy's production possibilities. If the economy is producing a high ratio of food to cloth, as at point 1, the binding constraint, that is, the constraint that actually limits production, is the land constraint. If, on the other hand, the economy is producing a low ratio of food to cloth, as at point 2, the labor constraint is the one that binds. The fact that which constraint is binding depends on the mix of goods the economy produces suggests that changes in the economy's resources will have uneven effects on its ability to produce different goods. Specifically, an increase in the economy's supply of land will expand production possibilities more in the direction of food than in that of cloth, while an increase in the supply of labor will expand production possibilities more in the direction of cloth than in that of food.

FIGURE 4-1
The production possibility frontier in the factor proportions model.
The limited supplies of labor and land constrain the economy's production. Because cloth is more labor-intensive than food, the labor constraint is steeper than the land constraint.

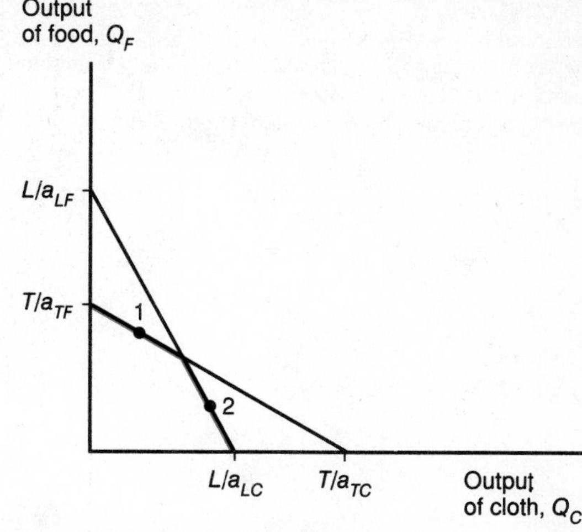

Figure 4-2 shows explicitly how an increase in the supply of land changes production possibilities. When the supply of land is increased from T^1 to T^2, the land constraint on the economy's production possibilities is relaxed, so that the production possibility frontier is shifted outward. What is immediately clear from the diagram, however, is that this is a **biased expansion of production possibilities**—that is, the expansion is greater, the higher the ratio of food to cloth in production. In fact, if the economy tries to produce a high ratio of cloth to food, the expansion of land supply does not permit any increase in production at all.

The biased effect of increases in resources on production possibilities is the key to understanding how differences in resources give rise to international trade.[1] An increase in the supply of land expands production possibilities disproportionately in the direction of food production, while an increase in the supply of labor expands them disproportionately in the direction of cloth production. Thus an economy with a high ratio of land to labor will be relatively better at producing food than an economy with a low ratio of land to labor. *More generally, an economy will tend to be relatively effective at producing goods that are intensive in the factors with which the country is relatively well endowed.*

GOODS PRICES AND FACTOR PRICES

In Chapter 3 the assumption that some factors of production were specific to particular sectors was shown to imply that changes in relative prices produce strong effects on income distribution. Since international trade leads to a convergence of relative prices, these effects on income distribution will sharply qualify the conclusion that trade produces gains for everyone. In the Heckscher-Ohlin model each factor of production

[1] The biased effect of resource changes on production was pointed out in a paper by the Polish economist T. M. Rybczynski, "Factor Endowments and Relative Commodity Prices," *Economica* 22 (1955), pp. 336–341. It is therefore known as the Rybczynski effect.

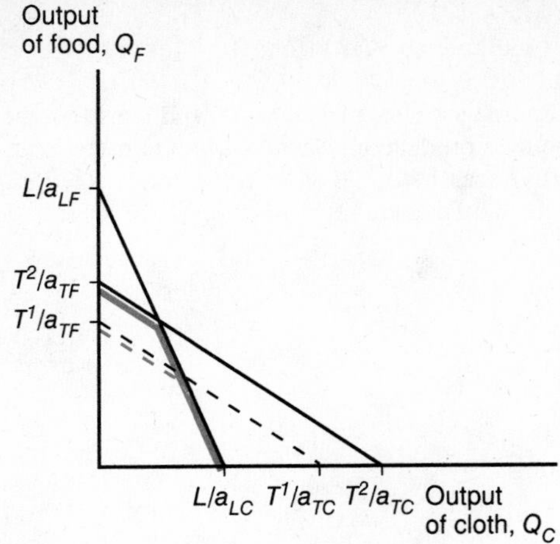

FIGURE 4-2
Increasing the supply of land.
When land supply is increased from T^1 to T^2, the land constaint is relaxed. This expands production possibilities in a direction biased toward food production.

can be used in both sectors, but because there are two factors income distribution may still be an issue. An analysis of the effects of changes in the prices of cloth and food on the earnings of land and labor involves the following:

P_C = price of 1 yard of cloth,
P_F = price of 1 calorie of food,
w = wage rate for 1 hour of labor,
r = rent that must be paid for the use of 1 acre of land.

To analyze the relationship between prices and earnings, we assume there is perfect competition in the production of cloth and food. This means that any monopoly profits are competed away, so that the price of each good is exactly equal to the cost of producing it. This cost, in turn, is the sum of the cost of land and labor used in production:

$$P_C = a_{LC}w + a_{TC}r, \quad \textbf{(4-5)}$$

$$P_F = a_{LF}w + a_{TF}r. \quad \textbf{(4-6)}$$

Equations (4-5) and (4-6) define combinations of w and r for which the cost of production equals the price for cloth and food, respectively. These two relationships are shown in Figure 4-3. Remember that we have assumed that cloth production is more labor-intensive than food production—that is,

$$a_{LC}/a_{TC} > a_{LF}/a_{TF}.$$

This implies that the cloth line must be steeper than the food line, as drawn.

The economy will produce both goods only if price equals cost in both sectors. This equality holds for both goods at the point in the diagram where the two lines cross, point 1, where $w = w^1$ and $r = r^1$. The diagram thus shows that we can determine factor prices given goods prices. Notice that we did *not* need to ask about the relative supplies of land and labor to do this: as long as both goods are produced, there is a one-to-one relationship between goods prices and factor prices.

FIGURE 4-3
Determination of factor prices.
The wage rate and the rental rate on land are determined by the requirement that price equal cost of production in both cloth and food.

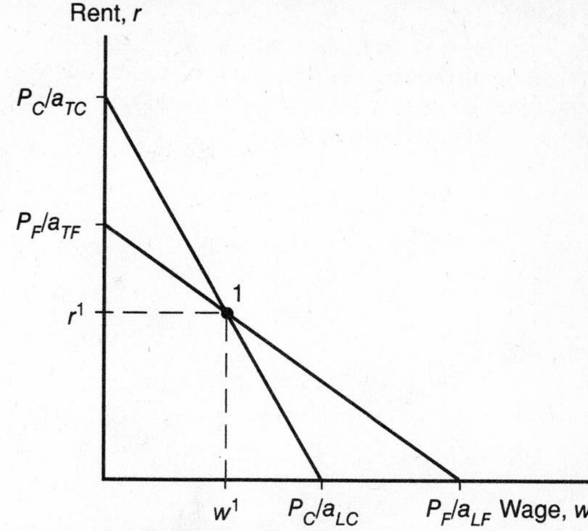

When goods prices change, factor prices will also change. You might not be surprised to find that when the price of cloth is increased, the price of labor rises more than that of land. In fact, however, the effect on the relative price of land and labor is so strong that the price of land actually *falls.*

In Figure 4-4, we show what happens when the price of cloth is increased from P^1_C to P^2_C. The increase in the price of cloth shifts the cloth line out. The equilibrium factor price point therefore shifts from point 1 to point 2. This movement involves a rise in the wage rate, from w^1 to w^2, and a fall in the rental rate on land, from r^1 to r^2. Similarly, a rise in the price of food would raise the rental rate on land and lower the wage rate.

When the price of cloth increases, the wage rate rises more than proportionately—that is, if the price of cloth increases by 10 percent, the wage rate will rise by more than 10 percent. This must be so because the rental on land actually falls. Consider the following numerical example. A yard of cloth takes 1 hour of labor and 1 acre of land to produce. Initially the labor and the land each cost \$5, and the price of cloth is \$10. Now suppose that the price of cloth rises by 10 percent, to \$11. When the price of cloth rises, we know that the rental on land actually falls, say to \$4.50. Correspondingly, the wage rate must therefore have risen to \$6.50—a 30 percent rise, three times as large as the increase in the price of cloth.

In a two-factor economy, then, changes in relative goods prices have very strong effects on income distribution. There is a **magnified effect of goods prices on factor prices.**[2] Because an increase in the price of cloth leads to a fall in the rent on land, someone who derives all her income from land rent will find her purchasing power reduced in terms of *both* goods. At the same time, the wage rate rises more than proportionately to the increase in the price of cloth; so someone who derives his income

[2] The effect of changes in relative goods prices on factor prices was first analyzed by Wolfgang Stolper and Paul Samuelson, ''Protection and Real Wages,'' *Review of Economic Studies* 9 (1941), pp. 58–73, and is thus known as the **Stolper-Samuelson effect.**

FIGURE 4-4
An increase in the price of cloth.
When the price of cloth rises from P_C^1 to P_C^2, the wage rate rises from w^1 to w^2, while the rental rate on land actually declines from r^1 to r^2.

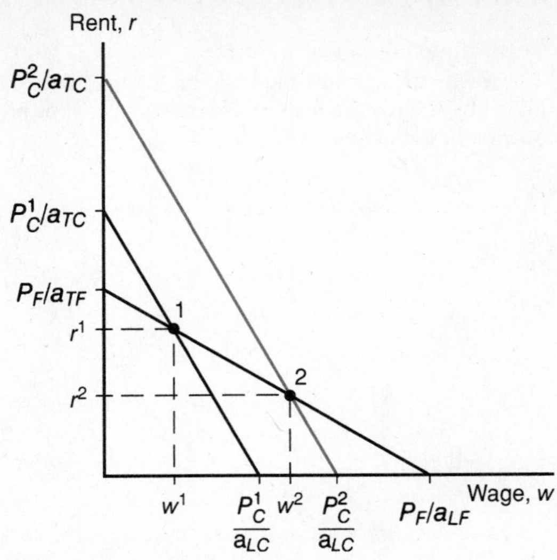

entirely from wages will find that his purchasing power has *increased* in terms of both goods.

ALLOWING SUBSTITUTION BETWEEN INPUTS

Up to now, we have examined an economy with fixed coefficients, where it takes a certain number of hours of labor and acres of land to make a yard of cloth and there is no way to trade off more land for less labor. The results must be modified slightly for an economy in which the ratio of land to labor in production can vary. (The two-factor model with **variable coefficients** is discussed in more detail in the appendix to this chapter.)

One difference is that there is no longer a simple, physical definition of which goods are land-intensive and which are labor-intensive: the ratio of land to labor used in production depends on the relative price of land and labor. In the United States, where land is abundant, cattle raising is land-intensive compared with wheat growing. Yet in Japan, where land is very scarce, cows may be raised with a lower land-labor ratio than the United States uses in growing wheat. When comparing factor intensities, we must therefore be careful always to compare the land-labor ratio that would have been used given the same incentives. Specifically, we describe cloth production as more labor-intensive than food production as long as the cloth sector will use a higher labor-land ratio than the food sector *when the two sectors face the same factor prices.*

Another difference that arises when factor substitution is allowed is that we can no longer say that only one resource constrains production at each point in time. In the fixed-coefficients model, production possibilities are defined by two constraints. If the economy tries to produce a high ratio of food to cloth, only the land constraint matters; if it tries to produce a high ratio of cloth to food, only the labor constraint matters. Once we allow trade-offs between use of the two factors, however, this sharp-edged result gets a little fuzzy. Even if the economy is producing mostly food and very little cloth, an increase in the labor supply will allow it to produce more of *either* good by substituting labor for land.

Because of the additional flexibility allowed by land-labor substitution, the production possibility frontier loses the ''kinked'' shape that it has in the case of fixed coefficients. Instead, it becomes more of a smooth curve, as illustrated by *TT* in Figure 4-5.

Although the shape of the production possibility frontier is softened by allowing land-labor substitution, the basic result of our fixed-coefficient analysis remains valid: increases in factor supplies shift production possibilities in a biased way (Figure 4-6). An increase in the labor supply shifts the production possibility curve outward from T^1T^1 to T^2T^2, but it shifts production possibilities out more in the direction of the labor-intensive product (cloth) than in the direction of the land-intensive product (food). Similarly, an increase in the supply of land would shift production possibilities out more in the direction of food than in the direction of cloth.

One conclusion that is *not* softened by allowing factor substitution is the relationship between goods prices and factor prices: a rise in the price of cloth leads to a more than proportional increase in the wage rate and to an actual fall in the price of land.

Effects of International Trade between Two-Factor Economies

Having outlined the production structure of a two-factor economy, we can now look at what happens when two such economies, Home and Foreign, trade. As always, Home and Foreign are similar along many dimensions. They have the same tastes and therefore have identical relative demands for food and cloth when faced with the same relative price of the two goods. They also have the same technology: a given amount of land and labor yields the same output of either cloth or food in the two countries. The only

FIGURE 4-5
Production possibilities with land-labor substitution.
The possibility of substitution removes the ''kink'' in the production possibility frontier, causing it instead to be a smooth curve.

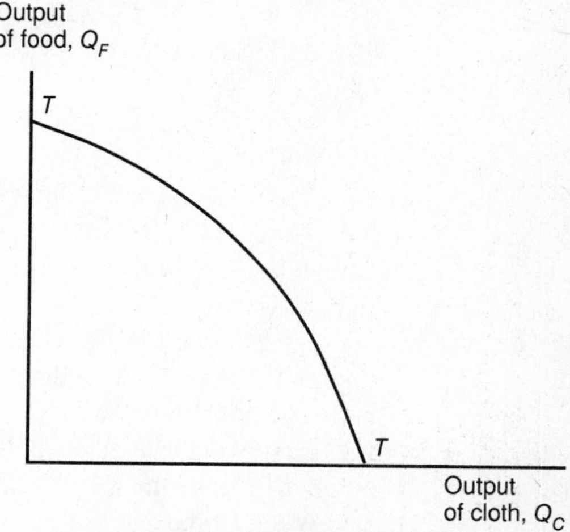

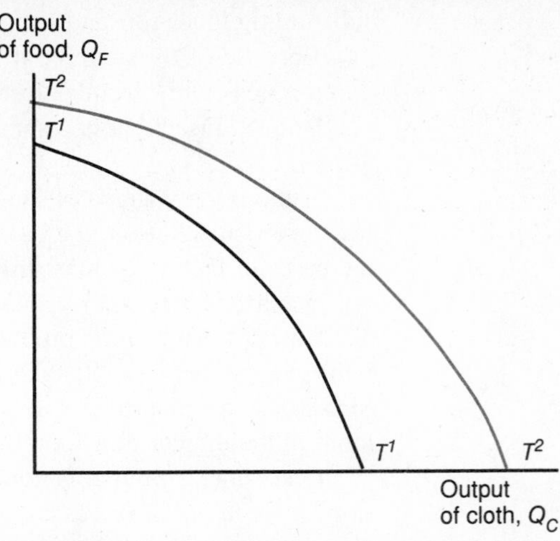

FIGURE 4-6
Biased expansion in production possibilities.
An increase in the labor supply, which shifts the production possibility frontier out from T^1T^1 to T^2T^2, shifts it out more in the direction of cloth than of food.

difference between the countries is in their resources: Home has a higher ratio of labor to land than Foreign does.

RELATIVE PRICES AND THE PATTERN OF TRADE

Since Home has a higher ratio of labor to land than Foreign, Home is *labor-abundant* and Foreign is *land-abundant.* Note that abundance is defined in terms of a ratio and not in absolute quantities. If America has 80 million workers and 200 million acres, while Britain has 20 million workers and 20 million acres, we consider Britain to be labor-abundant even though it has less total labor than America. ''Abundance'' is always defined in relative terms, by comparing the ratio of labor to land in the two countries, so that no country is abundant in everything.

Since cloth is the labor-intensive good, Home's production possibility frontier relative to Foreign's is shifted out more in the direction of cloth than in the direction of food. Thus, other things equal, Home tends to produce a higher ratio of cloth to food.

Because trade leads to a convergence of relative prices, one of the other things that will be equal is the price of cloth relative to food. Because the countries differ in their factor abundances, however, for any given ratio of the price of cloth to that of food Home will produce a higher ratio of cloth to food than Foreign will: Home will have a larger *relative supply* of cloth. Home's relative supply curve, then, lies to the right of Foreign's.

The relative supply schedules of Home (*RS*) and Foreign (*RS**) are illustrated in Figure 4-7. The relative demand curve, which we have assumed to be the same for both countries, is shown as *RD.* If there were no international trade, the equilibrium for Home would be at point 1, the equilibrium for Foreign at point 3. That is, in the absence of trade the relative price of cloth would be lower in Home than in Foreign.

When Home and Foreign trade with each other, their relative prices converge. The relative price of cloth rises in Home and declines in Foreign, and a new world relative

FIGURE 4-7
Trade leads to a convergence of relative prices. In the absence of trade, Home's equilibrium would be at point 1, where domestic relative supply *RS* intersects the relative demand curve *RD*. Similarly, Foreign's equilibrium would be at point 3. Trade leads to a world relative price that lies between the pretrade prices, e.g., at point 2.

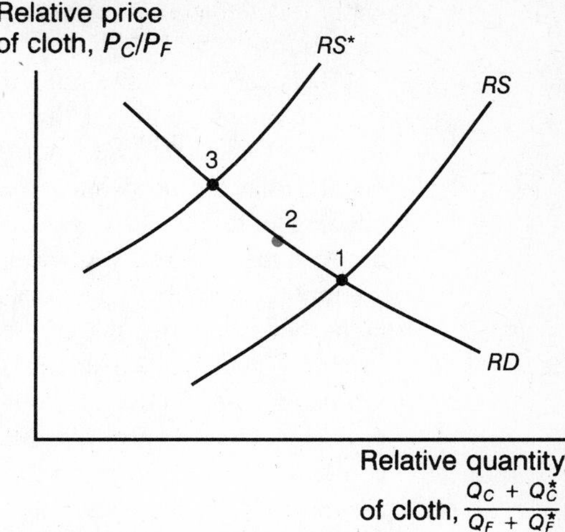

price of cloth is established at a point somewhere between the pretrade relative prices, say at point 2. In Home, the rise in the relative price of cloth leads to a rise in the production of cloth and a decline in relative consumption, so Home becomes an exporter of cloth and an importer of food. Conversely, the decline in the relative price of cloth in Foreign leads it to become an importer of cloth and an exporter of food.

To sum up what we have learned about the pattern of trade: Home has a higher ratio of labor to land than Foreign; that is, Home is abundant in labor and Foreign is abundant in land. Cloth production uses a higher ratio of labor to land in its production than food; that is, cloth is labor-intensive and food is land-intensive. Home, the labor-abundant country, exports cloth, the labor-intensive good; Foreign, the land-abundant country, exports food, the land-intensive good. The general statement of the result is: *Countries tend to export goods whose production is intensive in factors with which they are abundantly endowed.*

TRADE AND THE DISTRIBUTION OF INCOME

Trade produces a convergence of relative prices. Changes in relative prices, in turn, have strong effects on the relative earnings of labor and land. A rise in the price of cloth raises the purchasing power of labor in terms of both goods while lowering the purchasing power of land in terms of both goods. A rise in the price of food has the reverse effect. Thus international trade has a powerful effect on income distribution. In Home, where the relative price of cloth rises, people who get their income from labor gain from trade but those who derive their income from land are made worse off. In Foreign, where the relative price of cloth falls, the opposite happens: laborers are made worse off and landowners are made better off.

The resource of which a country has a relatively large supply (labor in Home, land in Foreign) is the **abundant factor** in that country, and the resource of which it has a relatively small supply (land in Home, labor in Foreign) is the **scarce factor.** The general conclusion about the income distribution effects of international trade is: *Owners of a country's abundant factors gain from trade, but owners of a country's scarce factors lose.*

This conclusion is similar to the one reached in our analysis of the case of specific factors. There we found that factors of production that are ''stuck'' in an import-competing industry lose from the opening of trade. Here we find that factors of production that are used intensively by the import-competing industry are hurt by the opening of trade. As a practical matter, however, there is an important difference between these two views. The specificity of factors to particular industries is often only a temporary problem: garment makers cannot become computer manufacturers overnight, but given time the U.S. economy can shift its manufacturing employment from declining sectors to expanding ones. Thus income distribution effects that arise because labor and other factors of production are immobile represent a temporary, transitional problem (which is not to say that such effects are not painful to those who lose). In contrast, effects of trade on the distribution of income among land, labor, and capital are more or less permanent.

We will see shortly that the trade pattern of the United States suggests that compared with the rest of the world the United States is abundantly endowed with highly skilled labor and that low-skilled labor is correspondingly scarce. This means that international trade tends to make low-skilled workers in the United States worse off—not just temporarily, but on a sustained basis. The negative effect of trade on low-skilled workers poses a persistent political problem. Industries that use low-skilled labor intensively, such as apparel and shoes, consistently demand protection from foreign competition, and their demands attract considerable sympathy because low-skilled workers are relatively badly off to begin with.

The distinction between income distribution effects due to immobility and those due to differences in factor intensity also reveals that there is frequently a conflict between short-term and long-term interests in trade. Consider a highly skilled U.S. worker who is employed in an industry that is intensive in low-skilled labor. Her short-term interest is to restrict international trade, because she cannot instantly shift jobs. Over the longer term, however, she would be better off with free trade, which will raise the income of skilled workers generally.

FACTOR PRICE EQUALIZATION

In the absence of trade, labor would earn less in Home than in Foreign, and land would earn more. Without trade, labor-abundant Home would have a lower relative price of cloth than land-abundant Foreign, and the difference in relative prices of *goods* implies an even larger difference in the relative prices of *factors.*

When Home and Foreign trade, the relative prices of goods converge. This convergence, in turn, causes convergence of the relative prices of land and labor. Thus there is clearly a tendency toward **equalization of factor prices.** How far does this tendency go?

The surprising answer is that in the model the tendency goes all the way. International trade leads to complete equalization of factor prices. Although Home has a higher ratio of labor to land than Foreign, once they trade with each other the wage rate and the rent on land are the same in both countries. To see this, refer back to

Figure 4-3, which shows that given the prices of cloth and food we can determine the wage rate and the rental rate without reference to the supplies of land and labor. If Home and Foreign face the same relative prices of cloth and food, they will also have the same factor prices.

To understand how this equalization occurs, we have to realize that when Home and Foreign trade with each other more is happening than a simple exchange of goods. In an indirect way the two countries are in effect trading factors of production. Home lets Foreign have the use of some of its abundant labor, not by selling the labor directly but by trading goods produced with a high ratio of labor to land for goods produced with a low labor-land ratio. The goods that Home sells require more labor to produce than the goods it receives in return; that is, more labor is *embodied* in Home's exports than in its imports. Thus Home exports its labor, embodied in its labor-intensive exports. Conversely, Foreign's exports embody more land than its imports, thus Foreign is indirectly exporting its land. When viewed this way, it is not surprising that trade leads to equalization of the two countries' factor prices.

Case Study

POLLUTION RIGHTS AS A RESOURCE

Environmental economists have long suggested using the market to help limit pollution efficiently. For example, the government might establish an overall limit on how much of some pollutant can be released per year, then auction off the rights to pollute. Such a program would give those firms that can cheaply reduce pollution an incentive to do so, while allowing firms for whom pollution control is prohibitively costly to buy pollution rights instead. The United States has already moved somewhat in this direction by allowing some firms who produce less than the legal amount of air pollution to sell their excess pollution allowance to other firms.

Widespread adoption of such a market-based environmental policy would in effect turn pollution rights into a scarce resource allocated by the market. And like other scarce resources, pollution rights would become a factor determining international trade. Countries that were "pollution rights-abundant"—that is, were willing to tolerate an unusually high quantity of pollution relative to their supplies of other factors—would tend to export "pollution-intensive" goods.

Who would be the pollution rights-abundant countries? One might expect that poorer countries would be more willing to trade off pollution for income than richer ones.

All this sounds economically very rational but it may sound equally highly immoral as a proposal that rich countries should "export their pollution" to the third world.

The collision between apparent economic good sense and morality became unpleasantly apparent in 1992 to Lawrence Summers, chief economist of the World Bank. An internal World Bank memo signed by Summers endorsed the idea that it might be economically rational for developing countries to impose somewhat weaker environmental standards than richer nations and noted that this might give them a de facto comparative advantage in some polluting industries. The text of the memo was leaked to the press, generating a firestorm of bad publicity (*People* magazine listed Summers as one of the leading "enemies of the environment"). In December of that year, it appeared that the controversy over the memo had blocked Summers from an expected appointment as chief economic adviser to President-Elect Bill Clinton.

Although this view of trade is clearly simple and appealing, there is a major problem: in the real world factor prices are not equalized. For example, there is an extremely wide range of wage rates across countries (Table 4-1). While some of these differences may reflect differences in the quality of labor, they are too wide to be explained away on this basis alone.

To understand why the model doesn't give us an accurate prediction, we need to look at its assumptions. Three assumptions crucial to the prediction of factor price equalization are in reality certainly untrue. These are the assumptions that (1) both countries produce both goods; (2) technologies are the same; and (3) trade actually equalizes the prices of goods in the two countries.

1. To derive the wage and rental rates from the prices of cloth and food in Figure 4-3, we assumed that the country produced both goods. This need not, however, be the case. A country with a very high ratio of labor to land might produce only cloth, while a country with a very high ratio of land to labor might produce only food. This implies that factor price equalization occurs only if the countries involved are sufficiently similar in their relative factor endowments. (A more thorough discussion of this point is given in the appendix to this chapter.) Thus, factor prices need not be equalized between countries with radically different ratios of capital to labor or of skilled to unskilled labor.

2. The proposition that trade equalizes factor prices will not hold if countries have different technologies of production. For example, a country with superior technology might have both a higher wage rate and a higher rental rate than a country with an inferior technology.

3. Finally, the proposition of complete factor price equalization depends on com-

TABLE 4-1 Comparative international wage rates

Country	*Hourly wage rate in 1988 (dollars)*
United States	13.90
Germany	18.07
Japan	13.14
Spain	8.75
Greece	4.61
Hong Kong	2.43
Taiwan	2.71
Korea	2.46

Source: U.S. Department of Labor, *Handbook of Labor Statistics,* 1989.

plete convergence of the prices of goods. In the real world, prices of goods are not fully equalized by international trade. This lack of convergence is due to both natural barriers (such as transportation costs) and barriers to trade such as tariffs, import quotas, and other restrictions.

Empirical Evidence on the Heckscher-Ohlin Model

Since the factor-proportions theory of trade is one of the most influential ideas in international economics, it has been the subject of extensive empirical testing. The results of this testing have not been favorable: countries do not in fact export the goods the theory predicts. The question then is what to make of this—does the factor-proportions theory still have any relevance for thinking about international trade?

TESTING THE HECKSCHER-OHLIN MODEL

Tests on U.S. Data. Until recently, and to some extent even now, the United States has been a special case among countries. The United States was until a few years ago much wealthier than other countries, and U.S. workers visibly worked with more capital per person than their counterparts in other countries. Even now, although some Western European countries and Japan have largely caught up, the United States continues to be high on the scale of countries as ranked by capital-labor ratios.

One would expect, then, that the United States would be an exporter of capital-intensive goods and an importer of labor-intensive goods. Surprisingly, however, this was not the case in the twenty-five years after World War II. In a famous study published in 1953, the economist Wassily Leontief (winner of the Nobel Prize in 1973) found that U.S. exports were less capital-intensive than U.S. imports.[3] This result is known as the **Leontief paradox.** It is the single biggest piece of evidence against the factor-proportions theory.

Table 4-2 illustrates the Leontief paradox as well as other information about U.S. trade patterns. We compare the factors of production used to produce $1 million worth of 1962 U.S. exports with those used to produce the same value of 1962 U.S. imports. As the first two lines in the table show, Leontief's paradox was still present in that year: U.S. exports were produced with a lower ratio of capital to labor than U.S. imports. As the rest of the table shows, however, other comparisons of imports and exports are more in line with what one might expect. The U.S. exported products that were more skilled labor-intensive than its imports. We also tended to export products that were "technology-intensive," requiring more scientists and engineers per unit of sales. These observations are consistent with the position of the United States as a high-skill country, with a comparative advantage in sophisticated products.

Why, then, do we observe the Leontief paradox? No one is quite sure. A plausible explanation, however, might be the following: The United States has a special advantage in producing new products or goods made with innovative technologies. Such products may well be *less* capital-intensive than products whose technology has had time to

[3] See Leontief, "Domestic Production and Foreign Trade: The American Capital Position Re-examined," *Proceedings of the American Philosophical Society* 97 (1953), pp. 331–349.

TABLE 4-2 Factor content of U.S. exports and imports for 1962

	Imports	*Exports*
Capital	$2,132,000	$1,876,000
Labor (person-years)	119	131
Average years of education	9.9	10.1
Proportion of engineers and scientists	.0189	.0255

Source: Robert Baldwin, ''Determinants of the Commodity Structure of U.S. Trade,'' *American Economic Review* 61 (March 1971), pp. 126–145.

mature and become suitable for mass production techniques. Thus the United States may be exporting goods that heavily use skilled labor and innovative entrepreneurship, while importing heavy manufactures that use large amounts of capital.[4]

Tests on Global Data. More recently, economists have attempted to test the Heckscher-Ohlin model using data for a large number of countries. An important study by Harry P. Bowen, Edward E. Leamer, and Leo Sveikauskas[5] is based on the idea, described earlier, that trading goods is actually an indirect way of trading factors of production. Thus if we were to calculate the factors of production embodied in a country's exports and imports, we should find that a country is a net exporter of the factors of production with which it is relatively abundantly endowed, a net importer of those with which it is relatively poorly endowed.

Table 4-3 shows one of Bowen et al.'s key tests. For a sample of twenty-seven countries and twelve factors of production, the authors calculated the ratio of each country's endowment of each factor to the world supply. They then compared these ratios with each country's share of world income. If the factor-proportions theory were right, a country would always export factors for which the factor share exceeded the income share, import factors for which it was less. In fact, for two-thirds of the factors of production, trade ran in the predicted direction less than 70 percent of the time. This result confirms the Leontief paradox on a broader level: trade just does not run in the direction that the Heckscher-Ohlin theory predicts.

IMPLICATIONS OF THE TESTS

The negative results of tests of the factor-proportions theory place international economists in a difficult position. We saw in Chapter 2 that empirical evidence broadly supports the Ricardian model's prediction that countries will export goods in which their labor is especially productive. Most international economists, however, regard the Ricardian model as too limited to serve as their basic model of international trade. By contrast, the Heckscher-Ohlin model has long occupied a central place in trade theory,

[4] Recent studies point to the disappearance of the Leontief paradox by the early 1970s. For example, see Robert M. Stern and Keith E. Maskus, ''Determinants of the Structure of U.S. Foreign Trade, 1958–76,'' *Journal of International Economics* 11 (May 1981), pp. 207–224. These studies show, however, the continuing importance of *human* capital in explaining U.S. exports.

[5] See Bowen, Leamer, and Sveikauskas, ''Multicountry, Multifactor Tests of the Factor Abundance Theory,'' *American Economic Review* 77 (December 1987), pp. 791–809.

TABLE 4-3 **Testing the Heckscher-Ohlin model**

Factor of production	*Predictive success**
Capital	.52
Labor	.67
Professional workers	.78
Managerial workers	.22
Clerical workers	.59
Sales workers	.67
Service workers	.67
Agricultural workers	.63
Production workers	.70
Arable land	.70
Pasture land	.52
Forest	.70

* Fraction of countries for which net exports of factor runs in predicted direction.
Source: Harry P. Bowen, Edward E. Leamer, and Leo Sveikauskas, ''Multicountry, Multifactor Tests of the Factor Abundance Theory,'' *American Economic Review* 77 (December 1987), pp. 791–809.

because it allows a simultaneous treatment of issues of income distribution and the pattern of trade. So the model that predicts trade best is too limiting for other purposes, while there is by now strong evidence against the pure Heckscher-Ohlin model.

The best answer at this point seems to be to return to the Ricardian idea that the trade pattern is largely driven by international differences in technology rather than resources. For example, the United States exports computers and aircraft not because its resources are specially suited to these activities, but because it is simply relatively more efficient at producing these goods than it is at automobile or steel production. This still leaves the reasons for technology differences unexplained. Understanding the sources of technological differences between countries is now a key topic of research.

While we return to the Ricardian explanation of trade, however, we do not return to the view that trade has no effects on the distribution of income. As long as more than one factor is used in production, trade will have important effects on income distribution. Thus it is still important to ask what factors are embodied in a country's exports and imports. The United States exports skilled labor-intensive products and imports unskilled labor-intensive products. Therefore, trade tends to benefit skilled U.S. workers at the expense of unskilled, even though U.S. factor endowments do not help much in predicting the pattern of trade. The Heckscher-Ohlin model thus retains a more limited use, as a way of predicting the income distribution effects of trade and trade policy.

Summary

1. To understand the role of resources in trade we begin by examining the effect of resources on a country's production possibilities. Increases in an economy's supply of a factor of production such as land shift the production possibility frontier out in a

biased way: an increase in the land supply shifts the frontier out more in the direction of land-intensive goods than in the direction of labor-intensive goods. As a result, countries are relatively effective at producing goods whose production is *intensive* in resources of which they have a relatively abundant supply.

2. Changes in relative prices of goods have very strong effects on the relative incomes earned by different resources. An increase in the price of the land-intensive good will raise the rent earned on land more than in proportion, while actually reducing the wage rate.

3. A country that has a large supply of one resource relative to its supply of other resources is *abundant* in that resource. A country will tend to produce relatively more of goods that use its abundant resources intensively. The result is the basic *Heckscher-Ohlin theory* of trade: *Countries tend to export goods that are intensive in the factors with which they are abundantly supplied.*

4. Because changes in relative prices of goods have very strong effects on the relative earnings of resources, and because trade changes relative prices, international trade has strong income distribution effects. The owners of a country's abundant factors gain from trade, but the owners of scarce factors lose.

5. In an idealized model international trade would actually lead to equalization of the prices of factors such as labor and capital between countries. In reality, complete *factor price equalization* is not observed because of wide differences in resources, barriers to trade, and international differences in technology.

6. Empirical evidence is generally negative on the idea that differences in resources are the main determinant of trade patterns. Instead, differences in technology probably play the key role, as we suggested in the Ricardian model. Nonetheless, the Heckscher-Ohlin model remains useful as a way to predict the income distribution effects of trade.

Key Terms

factor abundance
factor intensity
Heckscher-Ohlin theory (or factor-proportions theory)
fixed coefficients
biased expansion of production possibilities
magnified effect of goods prices on factor prices (or Stolper-Samuelson effect)
variable coefficients
abundant factor
scarce factor
equalization of factor prices
Leontief paradox

Problems

1. To produce a ton of steel requires 10 units of labor and 5 units of land. To produce a ton of wheat requires 2 units of labor and 4 units of land. The economy has a supply of 100 units of labor and 100 units of land.

a. Graph the labor and land constraints on the economy's production.

b. Find the production possibility frontier.

c. Suppose that the labor supply were increased to 110. Show how this would affect production possibilities.

2. Maintaining the assumptions of problem 1, suppose that the price of steel is 3 and the price of wheat is 1.

a. Graph the lines along which the price and production cost are equal for steel and wheat.

b. Determine the equilibrium wage rate and rental rate on land.

c. Suppose that the price of steel were to rise to 3.5. Graph the effect of this change, and find the effects on the wage and rental rates.

3. "The world's poorest countries cannot find anything to export. There is no resource that is abundant—certainly not capital nor land, and in small poor nations not even labor is abundant." Discuss.

4. The U.S. labor movement—which mostly represents blue-collar workers rather than professionals and highly educated workers—has traditionally favored limits on imports from less affluent countries. Is this a shortsighted policy or a rational one in view of the interests of union members? How does the answer depend on the model of trade?

5. There is substantial inequality of wage levels between regions within the United States. For example, wages of manufacturing workers in equivalent jobs are about 20 percent lower in the southeast than they are in the far west. Which of the explanations of failure of factor price equalization might account for this? How is this case different from the divergence of wages between the United States and Mexico (which is geographically closer to both the southeast and the far west than either is to the other)?

6. Explain why the Leontief paradox and the more recent Bowen, Leamer, and Sveikauskas results reported in the text contradict the factor-proportions theory.

7. Using the diagrammatic technique illustrated in Figures 4A-5 and 4A-6 in the appendix, examine the impact of a reduction in the supply of labor (for example, due to emigration). Show that the production of cloth falls but that production of food actually rises.

Further Reading

Alan Deardorff. "Testing Trade Theories and Predicting Trade Flows," in Ronald W. Jones and Peter B. Kenen, eds. *Handbook of International Economics.* Vol. 1. Amsterdam: North-Holland, 1984. A survey of empirical evidence on trade theories, especially the factor-proportions theory.

Ronald W. Jones. "Factor Proportions and the Heckscher-Ohlin Theorem." *Review of Economic Studies* 24 (1956), pp. 1–10. Extends Samuelson's 1948–1949 analysis (cited below), which focuses primarily on the relationship between trade and income distribution, into an overall model of international trade.

Ronald W. Jones. "The Structure of Simple General Equilibrium Models." *Journal of Political Economy* 73 (1965), pp. 557–572. A restatement of the Heckscher-Ohlin-Samuelson model in terms of elegant algebra.

Ronald W. Jones and J. Peter Neary. "The Positive Theory of International Trade," in Ronald W. Jones and Peter B. Kenen, eds. *Handbook of International Economics.* Vol. 1. Amsterdam: North-Holland, 1984. An up-to-date survey of many trade theories, including the factor-proportions theory.

Bertil Ohlin. *Interregional and International Trade.* Cambridge: Harvard University Press, 1933. The original Ohlin book presenting the factor-proportions view of trade remains interesting—its complex and rich view of trade contrasts with the more rigorous and simplified mathematical models that followed.

Robert Reich. *The Work of Nations.* New York: Basic Books, 1991. An influential tract that argues that the increasing integration of the United States in the world economy is widening the gap between skilled and unskilled workers.

Paul Samuelson. "International Trade and the Equalisation of Factor Prices." *Economic Journal* 58 (1948), pp. 163–184, and "International Factor Price Equalisation Once Again." *Economic Journal* 59 (1949), pp. 181–196. The most influential formalizer of Ohlin's ideas is Paul Samuelson (again!), whose two *Economic Journal* papers on the subject are classics.

Appendix to Chapter 4 • The Heckscher-Ohlin Model with Variable Coefficients

In the main body of this chapter we examined a two-factor model with *fixed coefficients.* That is, the ratio of land to labor used in the production of each good was assumed to be wholly determined by technology. This is a useful simplification, but in the real world the possibility of substitution between factors is important. For example, firms in a country with cheap labor may choose to use less capital-intensive and more labor-intensive techniques of production than they would in a country with expensive labor. We want to be sure the basic insights of our chapter are not lost when we allow for such substitution. This appendix briefly shows how a two-factor model of an economy works when coefficients are variable.

CHOICE OF TECHNIQUE

The key new element we need to introduce is that firms have a choice about the land- or labor-intensity of production of each good. They can choose to use less land per unit of output if they are willing to use more labor. Figure 4A-1 illustrates this trade-off for cloth. Curve *II,* which shows different bundles of labor and land that can produce 1 unit of cloth, is referred to as the *unit isoquant* for cloth.

Firms will choose the ratio of land to labor that minimizes the cost of producing cloth. The details of this choice are discussed in microeconomics texts. The basic result is not surprising:

FIGURE 4A-1
The unit isoquant for cloth.
The more labor that is used in producing a unit of cloth, the less land is needed.

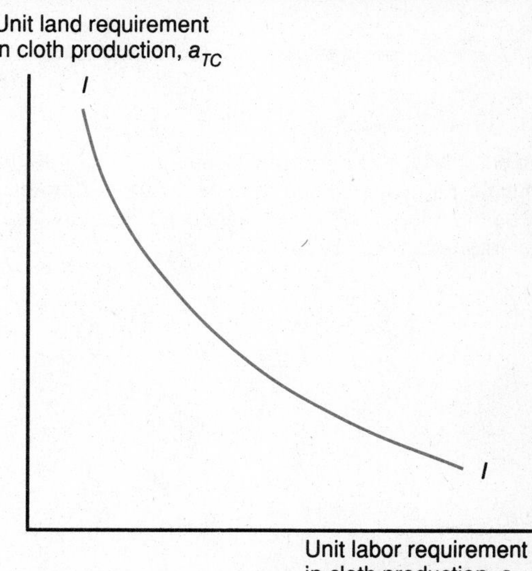

FIGURE 4A-2
Factor prices such that price equals cost.
The curve CC shows all combinations of w and r such that the cost of producing a unit of cloth equals its price. The higher w is, the lower r must be to leave the production cost the same.

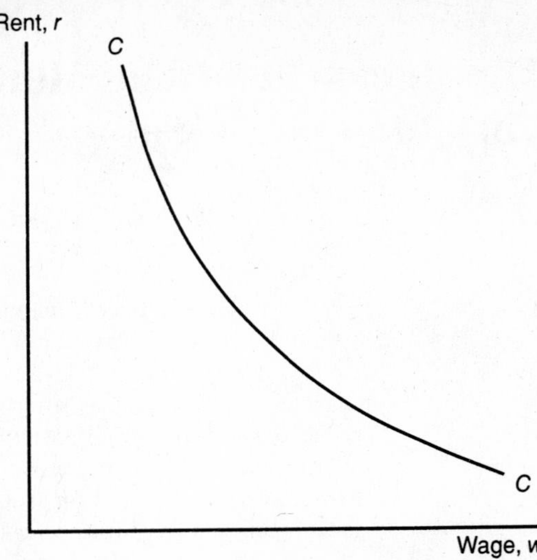

the cost-minimizing land-labor ratio a_{TC}/a_{LC} is inversely related to the ratio of the price of land to that of labor, r/w.

GOODS PRICES AND FACTOR PRICES

The price of each good must equal its cost of production. For any given price of a good, this requirement defines a set of possible factor prices. For example, given the price of cloth, the higher the wage rate w the lower must be the rental rate r (Figure 4A-2). The economy's factor prices must be such that the cost of production equals the price in both cloth and food (Figure 4A-3). Curve CC represents all combinations of w and r for which price equals cost in cloth,

FIGURE 4A-3
Determination of w and r.
In equilibrium, the cost of producing a unit of cloth must equal its price, and so must the cost of producing a unit of food. Thus w and r are determined by the intersection of CC and FF.

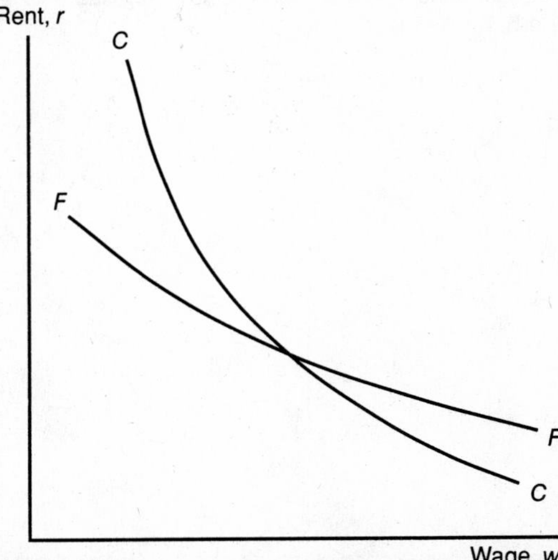

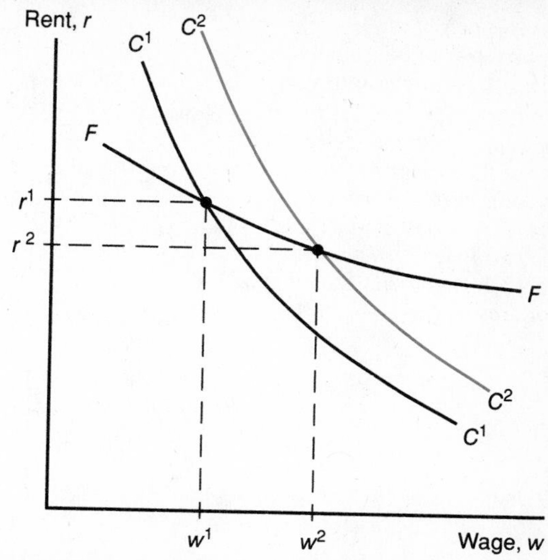

FIGURE 4A-4
A rise in the price of cloth.
An increase in the price of cloth shifts CC out from C^1C^1 to C^2C^2. This raises the wage rate from w^1 to w^2, while lowering the rental rate from r^1 to r^2.

while FF represents all combinations for which price and cost are equal in food. Since cloth is more labor-intensive and less land-intensive than food, the wage rate has relatively more effect on the cost of cloth production, and the rental on land less effect. As a result, to offset the effect of higher w on cloth production cost, r must fall more than is true for food; thus CC is steeper than FF.

If the price of cloth rises, the cloth industry is able to pay a higher wage, a higher rent on land, or both: CC shifts out from C^1C^1 to C^2C^2 (Figure 4A-4). This raises the wage rate from w^1 to w^2, while lowering r from r^1 to r^2. The rise in w must be more than proportional to the increase in P_C. Thus in the variable-coefficients model, as in the fixed-coefficients model, changes in relative prices have strong effects on the distribution of income.

ALLOCATION OF RESOURCES

To determine how the economy allocates resources between cloth and food production, given goods prices, we follow three steps: (1) Use goods prices to determine factor prices. (2) Use factor prices to determine the land-labor ratio in each sector. (3) Use the assumption that land and labor are both fully employed to determine resource allocation.

Figure 4A-5 shows how step 3 works. The economy's resources are represented by the sides of a box. The width of the box represents the economy's supply of labor, while its height represents the supply of land. We measure resources used to produce cloth from the lower left corner of the box (O_C) and resources used to produce food from the upper right corner (O_F). The ratio of land to labor in cloth production is shown by the slope of the line O_CC, while the land-labor ratio in food is the slope of O_FF.

The allocation of land and labor that allows both to be fully employed is at point 1, where O_CC and O_FF cross. The economy allocates O_CL_C units of labor and O_CT_C units of land to cloth production, O_FL_F labor and O_FT_F land to food production.

Now we ask what happens if the economy's supply of land increases (Figure 4A-6). The box expands, so that after the land supply increase the resources used in food are measured from O_F^2 instead of O_F^1. The key point is to look at resources used in cloth production. As the equilibrium allocation shifts from point 1 to point 2, both land and labor used in cloth production *fall*, from $O_CT_C^1$ to $O_CT_C^2$ and from $O_CL_C^1$ to $O_CL_C^2$, respectively. As a result, cloth production

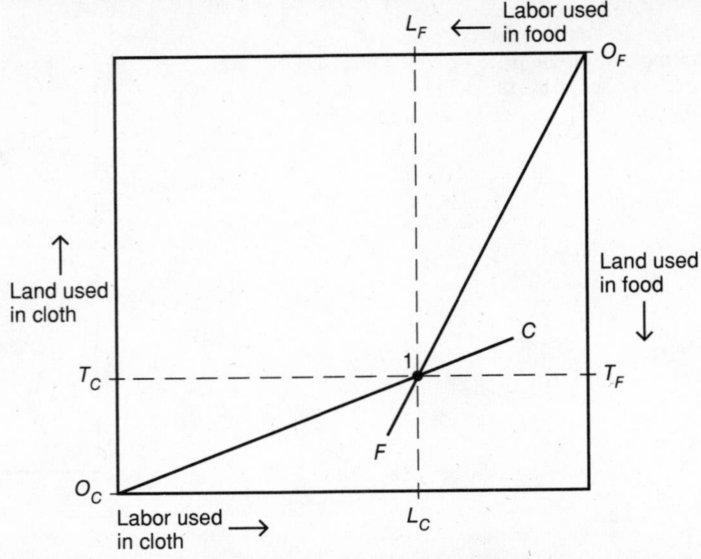

FIGURE 4A-5
Allocation of resources in the variable-coefficients case.
Inputs to cloth production are measured from the lower left corner of the box, inputs to food production from the upper right corner. Given the land-labor ratios in the two industries, point 1 is the only allocation that fully employs both resources.

declines. Correspondingly, land and labor employed to produce food, and thus food production, must rise.

The result that an increase in land supply actually leads to a fall in the production of the labor-intensive good confirms our result from the fixed-coefficients model: increases in factor supplies have strongly *biased* effects on production.

Finally, it is clear from Figure 4A-6 that if we were to keep increasing the economy's land supply, still holding goods prices fixed, eventually no resources at all would be used to produce cloth: the economy would specialize in food production. The general point is that a trading economy whose land-labor ratio is either very high or very low will specialize in producing only one good.

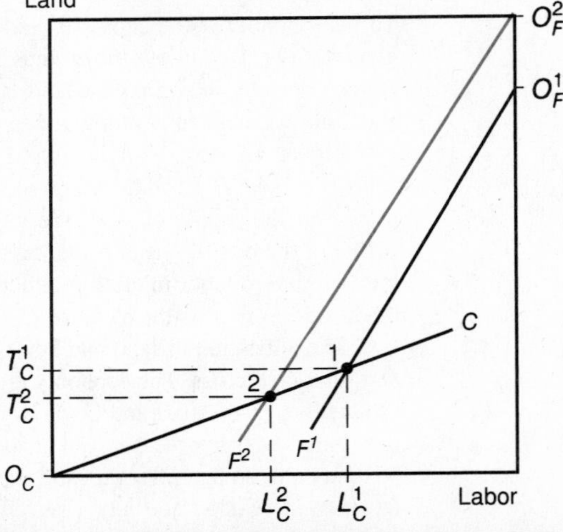

FIGURE 4A-6
An increase in the supply of land.
An increase in the supply of land expands the box and shifts the allocation of resources from point 1 to point 2. Production of food rises, but production of cloth actually falls.

The Standard Trade Model

Chapter 5

Previous chapters developed a number of different models, each of which illuminates a particular aspect of the supply side in international trade. To bring out important points, each model leaves out aspects of reality that the others stress. When we analyze real problems, we want to base our insights on a mixture of the models. For example, in the 1980s one of the central changes in world trade was the rapid growth in exports from Japan, Korea, and Taiwan. These countries experienced rapid productivity growth, with Japan overtaking the United States in many areas; to discuss the implications of this productivity growth we may want to apply the Ricardian model of Chapter 2. The changing pattern of trade has differential effects on different groups in the United States; to understand the effects of increased Pacific trade for U.S. income distribution, we may want to apply the specific factors model of Chapter 3. Finally, over time the resources of the East Asian nations have changed, as they accumulate capital and their labor grows more educated, while unskilled labor becomes scarcer. To understand the implications of this shift, we may wish to turn to the Heckscher-Ohlin model of Chapter 4.

In spite of the differences in their details, our models share a number of features.

1. The productive capacity of an economy can be summarized by its production possibility frontier, and differences in these frontiers give rise to trade.
2. Production possibilities determine a country's relative supply schedule.
3. World equilibrium is determined by world relative demand and a *world* relative supply schedule that lies between the national relative supply schedules.

Because of these common features, the models we have studied may be viewed as special cases of a more general model of a trading world economy. There are many important issues in international economics whose analysis can be conducted in terms of this general model, with only the details depending on which special model you choose. These include the effects of shifts in world supply resulting from economic growth; shifts in world demand resulting from foreign aid, war reparations, and other international transfers of income; and simultaneous shifts in supply and demand resulting from tariffs and export subsidies.

This chapter stresses those insights from international trade theory that are not strongly dependent on the details of the economy's supply side. We develop a standard model of a trading world economy of which the models of Chapters 2, 3, and 4 can be regarded as special cases and use this model to ask how a variety of changes in underlying parameters affect the world economy.

A Standard Model of a Trading Economy

The **standard trade model** is built on four key relationships: (1) the relationship between the production possibility frontier and the relative supply curve; (2) the relationship between relative prices and demand; (3) the determination of world equilibrium by world relative supply and world relative demand; and (4) the effect of the **terms of trade**—the price of a country's exports divided by the price of its imports—on a nation's welfare.

PRODUCTION POSSIBILITIES AND RELATIVE SUPPLY

For the purposes of our standard model we assume that each country produces two goods, food (F) and cloth (C), and that each country's production possibility frontier is a smooth curve like that illustrated by TT in Figure 5-1.[1]

The point on its production possibility frontier at which an economy actually produces depends on the price of cloth relative to food, P_C/P_F. It is a basic proposition of microeconomics that a market economy that is not distorted by monopoly or other market failures is efficient in production—that is, maximizes the value of output at given market prices, $P_C Q_C + P_F Q_F$.

We can indicate the market value of output by drawing a number of **isovalue lines**—that is, lines along which the value of output is constant. Each of these lines is defined by an equation of the form $P_C Q_C + P_F Q_F = V$, or by rearranging, $Q_F = V/P_F - (P_C/P_F)Q_C$, where V is the value of output. The higher V is, the farther out an isovalue line lies; thus isovalue lines farther from the origin correspond to higher values of output. The slope of an isovalue line is simply minus the relative price of cloth.

[1] We have seen that when there is only one factor of production, as in Chapter 2, the production possibility frontier is a straight line. For most models, however, it will be a smooth curve, and the Ricardian result can be viewed as an extreme case.

FIGURE 5-1
Relative prices determine the economy's output. An economy whose production possibility frontier is *TT* will produce at *Q*, which is on the highest possible isovalue line.

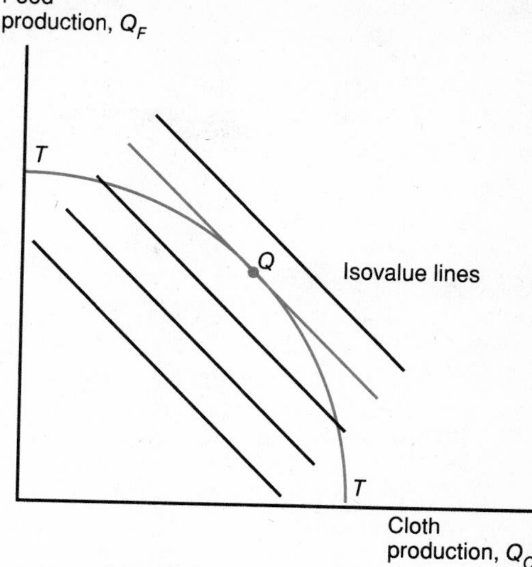

The economy will produce the highest value of output it can, which can be achieved by producing at point *Q*, where *TT* is just tangent to an isovalue line.[2]

Now suppose that P_C/P_F were to rise. Then the isovalue lines would be steeper than before. In Figure 5-2 the highest isovalue line the economy could reach before the change in P_C/P_F is shown as V^1V^1; the highest line after the price change is V^2V^2, the point at which the economy produces shifts from Q^1 to Q^2. Thus, as we might expect, a rise in the relative price of cloth leads the economy to produce more cloth and less food. The relative supply of cloth will therefore rise when the relative price of cloth rises.

RELATIVE PRICES AND DEMAND

Figure 5-3 shows the relationship among production, consumption, and trade in the standard model. As we pointed out in Chapter 3, the value of an economy's consumption equals the value of its production. Letting D_C and D_F be consumption of cloth and food, respectively, we must have

$$P_C D_C + P_F D_F = P_C Q_C + P_F Q_F = V.$$

The equation above says that production and consumption must lie on the same isovalue line.

The economy's choice of a point on the isovalue line depends on tastes. For our standard model, we make a useful simplifying assumption, namely that the economy's

[2] In our analysis of the specific factors model in Chapter 3 we showed explicitly that the economy always produces at a point on its production possibility curve where the slope of that curve equals the ratio of the two goods prices—that is, where the price line is tangent to the production possibility curve. Students may want to refer back to Chapter 3 to refresh their intuition.

FIGURE 5-2
How an increase in the relative price of cloth affects relative supply.
The isovalue lines become steeper, as shown by the shift from V^1V^1 to V^2V^2. As a result, equilibrium output shifts from Q^1 to Q^2.

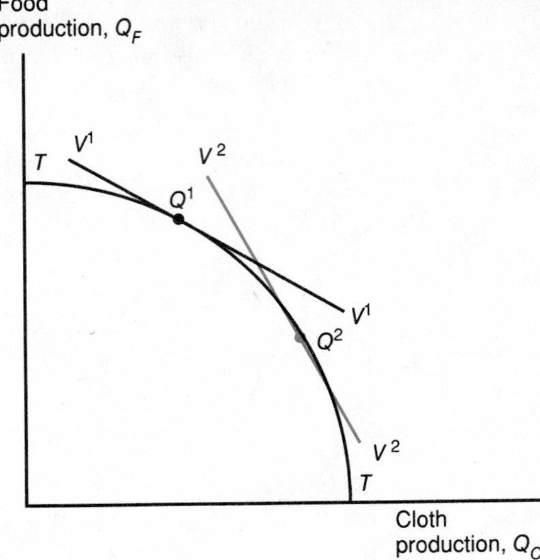

consumption decisions may be represented as if they were based on the tastes of a single representative individual.[3]

The tastes of an individual can be represented graphically by a series of **indifference curves.** An indifference curve traces a set of combinations of C and F consumption that leave the individual equally well off. Indifference curves have three properties:

1. They are downward-sloping: if an individual is offered less F, then to be made equally well off she must be given more C.
2. The farther up and to the right an indifference curve lies, the higher the level of welfare to which it corresponds: an individual will prefer more of both goods to less.
3. Each indifference curve gets flatter as we move to the right: the more C and the less F an individual consumes, the more valuable a unit of F is at the margin compared with a unit of C, so more C will have to be provided to compensate for any further reduction in F.

In Figure 5-3 we show a set of indifference curves for the economy that have these three properties. The economy will choose the point on the isovalue line that yields the highest possible welfare. This point is where the isovalue line is tangent to the highest reachable indifference curve, at D. Notice that at this point the economy is an exporter of C and an importer of F. (If this is not obvious, refer back to our discussion of the pattern of trade in Chapter 3.)

Now consider what happens when P_C/P_F is increased. In Figure 5-4 we show the

[3] There are several sets of circumstances that can justify this assumption. One is that all individuals have the same tastes and the same share of all resources. Another is that the government redistributes income so as to maximize its view of overall social welfare. Essentially, the assumption requires that effects of changing income distribution on demand not be too important.

FIGURE 5-3
Production, consumption, and trade in the standard model.
The economy produces at point Q and consumes at point D, which is the point where the isovalue line is tangent to the highest possible indifference curve.

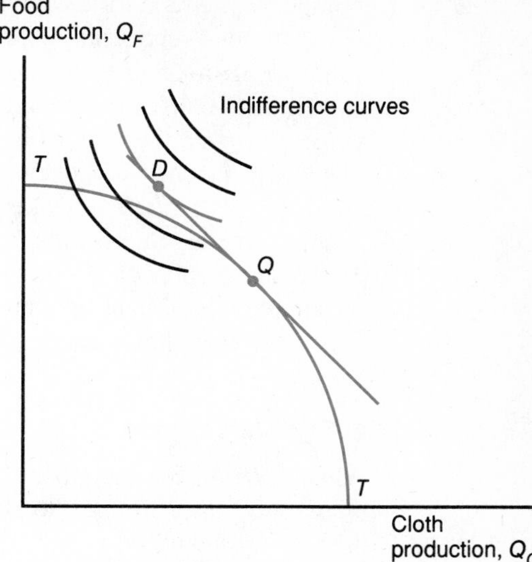

effects. First, the economy produces more C and less F, shifting production from Q^1 to Q^2. This shifts the isovalue line on which consumption must lie, from V^1V^1 to V^2V^2. The economy's consumption choice therefore also shifts, from D^1 to D^2.

The move from D^1 to D^2 reflects two effects of the rise in P_C/P_F. First, the economy has moved to a higher indifference curve: it is better off. The reason is that this economy

FIGURE 5-4
Effects of a rise in the relative price of cloth.
The isovalue line rotates from V^1V^1 to V^2V^2. Production shifts from Q^1 to Q^2, while consumption shifts from D^1 to D^2.

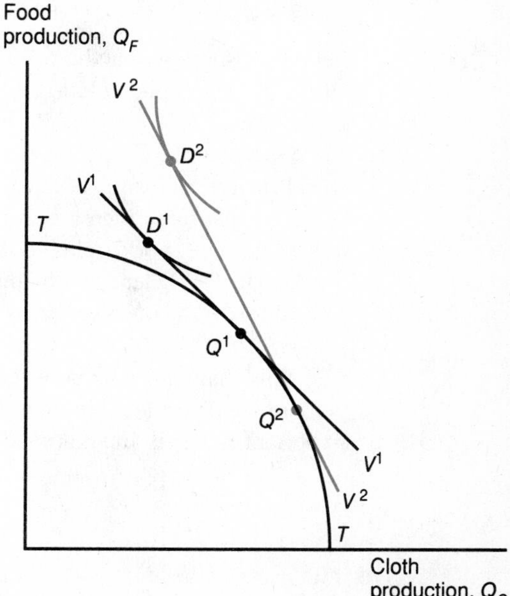

is an exporter of cloth. When the relative price of cloth rises, the economy can afford to import more food for any given volume of exports. Thus the higher relative price of its export good represents an advantage. Second, the change in relative prices leads to a shift along the indifference curve, toward food and away from cloth.

These two effects are familiar from basic economic theory. The rise in welfare is an *income effect;* the shift in consumption at any given level of welfare is a *substitution effect.* The income effect tends to increase consumption of both goods, while the substitution effect acts to make the economy consume less C and more F.

It is possible in principle that the income effect will be so strong that when P_C/P_F rises, consumption of both goods actually rises. Normally, however, the ratio of C consumption to F consumption will fall, that is, *relative* demand for C will decline. This is the case shown in the figure.

THE WELFARE EFFECT OF CHANGES IN THE TERMS OF TRADE

When P_C/P_F increases, a country that initially exports C is made better off, as illustrated by the movement from D^1 to D^2 in Figure 5-4. Conversely, if P_C/P_F were to decline, the country would be made worse off—for example, consumption might move back from D^2 to D^1.

If the country were initially an exporter of food instead of cloth, the direction of this effect would of course be reversed. An increase in P_C/P_F would mean a fall in P_F/P_C, and the country would be worse off; a fall in P_C/P_F would make it better off.

We cover all cases by defining the terms of trade as the price of the good a country initially exports divided by the price of the good it initially imports. The general statement, then, is that *a rise in the terms of trade increases a country's welfare, while a decline in the terms of trade reduces its welfare.*

DETERMINING RELATIVE PRICES

Let's now suppose that the world economy consists of two countries, once again named Home (which exports cloth) and Foreign (which exports food). Home's terms of trade are measured by P_C/P_F, while Foreign's are measured by P_F/P_C.

To determine P_C/P_F we find the intersection of world relative supply of cloth and world relative demand. The world relative supply curve (*RS* in Figure 5-5) is upward-sloping because an increase in P_C/P_F leads both countries to produce more cloth and less food. The world relative demand curve (*RD*) is downward-sloping because an increase in P_C/P_F leads both countries to shift their consumption mix away from cloth toward food. The intersection of the curves (point 1) determines the equilibrium relative price $(P_C/P_F)^1$.

Now that we know how relative supply, relative demand, the terms of trade, and welfare are determined in the standard model, we can use it to understand a number of important issues in international economics.

Economic Growth: A Shift of the *RS* Curve

The effects of economic growth in a trading world economy are a perennial source of concern and controversy. The debate revolves around two questions. First, is economic

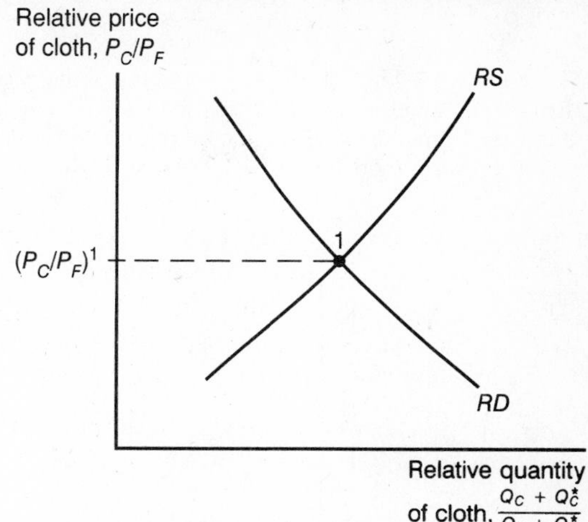

FIGURE 5-5
World relative supply and demand.
The higher P_C/P_F is, the larger the world supply of cloth relative to food (*RS*) and the lower the world demand for cloth relative to food (*RD*).

growth in other countries good or bad for our nation? Second, is growth in a country more or less valuable when that nation is part of a closely integrated world economy?

In assessing the effects of growth in other countries, common-sense arguments can be made on either side. On one side, economic growth in the rest of the world may be good for our economy because it means larger markets for our exports. On the other side, growth in other countries may mean increased competition for our exporters.

Similar ambiguities seem present when we look at the effects of growth at home. On one hand, growth in an economy's production capacity should be more valuable when that country can sell some of its increased production to the world market. On the other hand, the benefits of growth may be passed on to foreigners in the form of lower prices for the country's exports rather than retained at home.

The standard model of trade developed in the last section provides a framework than can cut through these seeming contradictions and clarify the effects of economic growth in a trading world.

GROWTH AND THE PRODUCTION POSSIBILITY FRONTIER

Economic growth means an outward shift of a country's production possibility frontier. This growth can result either from increases in a country's resources or from improvements in the efficiency with which these resources are used.

The international trade effects of growth result from the fact that such growth typically has a bias. Biased growth takes place when the production possibility frontier shifts out more in one direction than in the other. Figure 5-6a illustrates growth biased toward cloth, and Figure 5-6b shows growth biased toward food. In each case the production possibility frontier shifts from T^1T^1 to T^2T^2.

As you may recall, growth may be biased for two main reasons:

1. The Ricardian model of Chapter 2 shows that technological progress in o. sector of the economy will expand the economy's production possibilities more in th direction of that sector's output than in the direction of the other sector's output.

FIGURE 5-6
Biased growth.
Growth is biased if it shifts production possibilities out more toward one good than toward another. In both cases shown the production possibility frontier shifts out from T^1T^1 to T^2T^2. In case (a) this shift is biased toward cloth, in case (b) toward food.

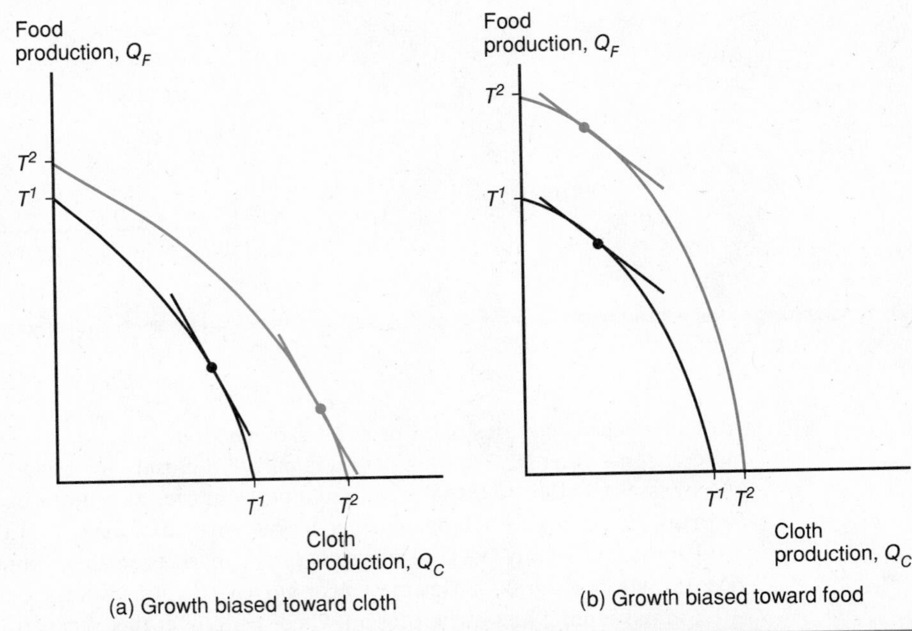

2. The specific factors model of Chapter 3 and the factor proportions model of Chapter 4 both showed that an increase in a country's supply of a factor of production—say, an increase in the capital stock resulting from saving and investment—will produce biased expansion of production possibilities. The bias will be in the direction of either the good to which the factor is specific or the good whose production is intensive in the factor whose supply has increased. Thus the same considerations that give rise to international trade will also lead to biased growth in a trading economy.

The biases of growth in Figure 5-6a and 5-6b are strong. In each case the economy is able to produce more of both goods, but at an unchanged relative price of cloth the output of food actually falls in Figure 5-6a, while the output of cloth actually falls in Figure 5-6b. Although growth is not always as strongly biased as it is in these examples, even growth that is more mildly biased toward cloth will lead, for any given relative price of cloth, to a rise in the output of cloth *relative* to that of food. The reverse is true for growth biased toward food.

RELATIVE SUPPLY AND THE TERMS OF TRADE

Suppose now that Home experiences growth strongly biased toward cloth, so that its output of cloth rises at any given relative price of cloth, while its output of food declines. Then for the world as a whole the output of cloth relative to food will rise at any given price and the world relative supply curve will shift to the right from RS^1 to RS^2 (Figure 5-7a). This shift results in a decrease in the relative price of cloth from $(P_C/P_F)^1$ to $(P_C/P_F)^2$, which represents a worsening of Home's terms of trade and an improvement in Foreign's terms of trade.

Notice that the important consideration here is not which economy grows but the bias of the growth. If Foreign had experienced growth biased toward cloth, the effect on the relative supply curve and thus on the terms of trade would have been the same. On the other hand, either Home or Foreign growth biased toward food (Figure 5-7b) leads to a *leftward* shift of the *RS* curve (RS^1 to RS^2) and thus to a rise in the relative price of cloth from $(P_C/P_F)^1$ to $(P_C/P_F)^2$. This increase is an improvement in Home's terms of trade, a worsening of Foreign's.

Growth that disproportionately expands a country's production possibilities in the direction of the good it exports (cloth in Home, food in Foreign) is **export-biased growth.** Similarly, growth biased toward the good a country imports is **import-biased growth.** Our analysis leads to the following general principle: *Export-biased growth tends to worsen a growing country's terms of trade, to the benefit of the rest of the world; import-biased growth tends to improve a growing country's terms of trade at the rest of the world's expense.*

INTERNATIONAL EFFECTS OF GROWTH

Using this principle, we are now in a position to resolve our questions about the international effects of growth. Is growth in the rest of the world good or bad for our country? Does the fact that our country is part of a trading world economy increase or decrease the benefits of growth? In each case the answer depends on the *bias* of the growth. Export-biased growth in the rest of the world is good for us, improving our terms of trade, while import-biased growth abroad worsens our terms of trade. Export-biased growth in our own country worsens our terms of trade, reducing the direct benefits of growth, while import-biased growth leads to an improvement of our terms of trade, a secondary benefit.

During the 1950s, many economists from poorer countries believed that their nations, which primarily exported raw materials, were likely to experience steadily declining terms of trade over time. They believed that growth in the industrial world would be marked by an increasing development of synthetic substitutes for raw materials, while growth in the poorer nations would take the form of a further extension of their capacity to produce what they were already exporting rather than a move toward industrialization. That is, the growth in the industrial world would be import-biased, while that in the less-developed world would be export-biased.

Some analysts suggested that growth in the poorer nations would actually be self-defeating. They argued that export-biased growth by poor nations would worsen their terms of trade so much that they would be worse off than if they had not grown at all. This situation is known to economists as the case of **immiserizing growth.**

In a famous paper published in 1958, the economist Jagdish Bhagwati of Columbia University showed that such perverse effects of growth can in fact arise within a rigorously specified economic model.[4] The conditions under which immiserizing

[4] "Immiserizing Growth: A Geometrical Note," *Review of Economic Studies* 25 (June 1958), pp. 201–205.

FIGURE 5-7
Growth and relative supply.
Growth biased toward cloth shifts the *RS* curve to the right (a), while growth biased toward food shifts it to the left (b).

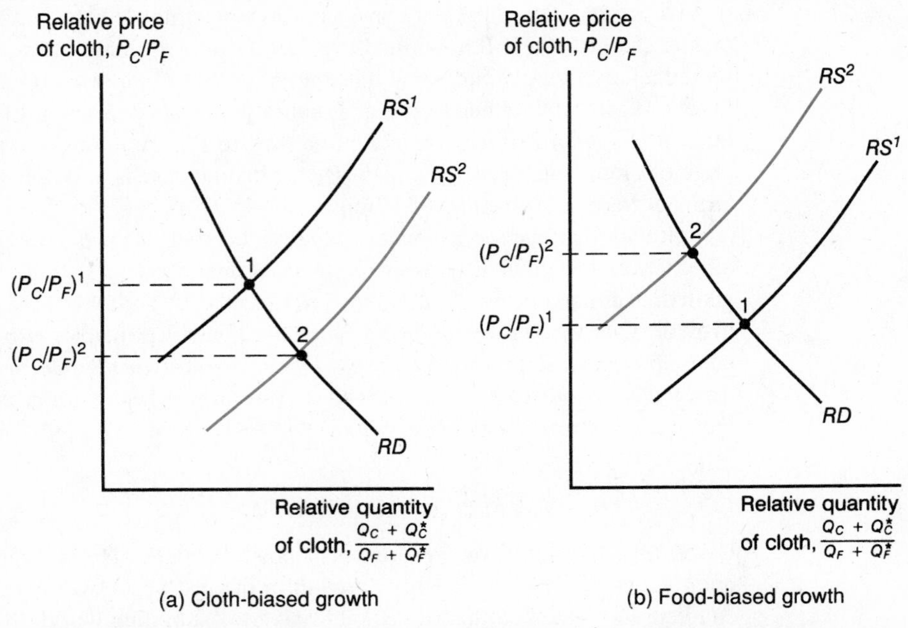

growth can occur are, however, extreme: strongly export-biased growth must be combined with very steep *RS* and *RD* curves, so that the change in the terms of trade is large enough to offset the initial favorable effects of an increase in a country's productive capacity. Most economists now regard the concept of immiserizing growth as more a theoretical point than a real-world issue.

While growth at home normally raises our own welfare even in a trading world, however, this is by no means true of growth abroad. Import-biased growth is not an unlikely possibility, and whenever the rest of the world experiences such growth, it worsens our terms of trade. Indeed, as we point out below, it is possible that the United States has suffered some loss of real income because of foreign growth over the postwar period.

Case Study

FOREIGN GROWTH AND THE U.S. TERMS OF TRADE

At the end of World War II the United States was the dominant world economy by any measure: it accounted for about half of the GNP of market economies, and its productivity and per capita income were far above those of any other major country. Since

1945, the rest of the world has closed some of this gap. By 1990, the United States accounted for less than a third of market economy GNP, and a number of industrial countries were approaching and in some cases surpassing U.S. levels of productivity. Has this catching-up process been good or bad for the United States?

In strictly economic terms, a good case can be made that the United States was hurt by growth in the rest of the world. Consider Figure 5-8, which shows an index of the U.S. terms of trade, excluding oil and agricultural products, from 1967 to 1991. From 1967 to 1980 there was a fairly consistent downward trend in the terms of trade, at a rate of about 1 percent per year. Most analysts would agree that the reversal of this trend during the 1980s was a temporary phenomenon associated with large inflows of foreign capital (see p. 102), and indeed the terms of trade worsened again after 1985.

Our standard model of trade suggests an explanation of the decline in the U.S. terms of trade. In 1967, the United States led the world in technology, the skill of its labor force, and capital per worker. As the rest of the world began to catch up, other countries became *more like the United States.* This meant that their growth was naturally biased toward those sectors in which the U.S. advantage was initially greatest. For example, in the early 1950s Japan's comparative advantage lay in labor-intensive industries like textiles; over time, it came to challenge the United States in capital-intensive industries like automobiles and steel. Growth in the rest of the world was import-biased, worsening the U.S. terms of trade.

One should not conclude that the United States made a mistake in helping Western Europe and Japan to recover from World War II! First, the United States had humanitarian and political reasons for restoring prosperity to its allies. Second, the costs of the terms of trade loss, while not negligible, were not overwhelming. We show in the Mathematical Postscript to this chapter that the real income costs of terms of trade loss is approxi-

FIGURE 5-8
The U.S. terms of trade.
Since the late 1960s the U.S. terms of trade (excluding oil and agricultural goods) have shown a persistent downward trend.
Source: *Survey of Current Business and National Trademark Databank.*

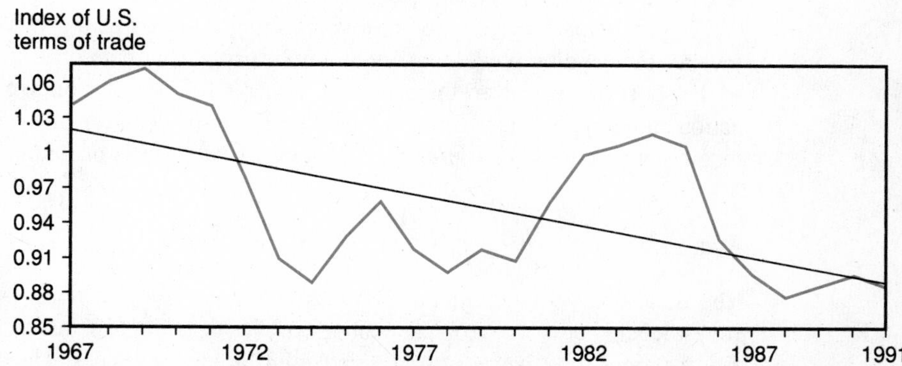

mately equal to the percentage loss multiplied by the share of imports in GNP. Since imports were less than 10 percent of GNP throughout the 1967–1980 period, a one percent per year terms of trade loss reduced the rate of growth of U.S. real income by at most 0.1 percent per year (over the period 1960–1991, U.S. growth averaged 3 percent annually). Finally, when the gains from economies of scale are taken into account (Chapter 6), growth in foreign markets may benefit a country even if its terms of trade worsen.

In any case, the decline in the U.S. terms of trade seems to have flattened out. The U.S. terms of trade in 1991 were only slightly worse than in 1980; the downward trend over the whole period from 1967 to 1991, shown in the figure, was only 0.7 percent. A decline at that rate reduces U.S. growth by only about 0.07 percent annually.

International Transfers of Income: Shifting the *RD* Curve

We now turn from terms of trade changes originating on the supply side of the world economy to changes that originate on the demand side.

Relative world demand for goods may shift for many reasons. Tastes may change: with rising concern over cholesterol, demand for fish has risen relative to the demand for red meat. Technology may also change demand: whale oil fueled lamps at one time but was supplanted by kerosene, later by gas, and finally by electricity. In international economics, however, perhaps the most important and controversial issue is the shift in world relative demand that can result from international **transfers of income.**

In the past, transfers of income between nations often occurred in the aftermath of wars. Germany demanded a payment from France after the latter's defeat in the Franco-Prussian war of 1871; after World War I the victorious Allies demanded large reparations payments from Germany (mostly never paid). After World War II, the United States provided aid to defeated Japan and Germany as well as to its wartime allies to help them rebuild. Since the 1950s, advanced countries have provided aid to poorer nations, although the sums have made a major contribution to the income of only a few of the very poorest countries.

International loans are not strictly speaking transfers of income, since the current transfer of spending power that a loan implies comes with an obligation to repay later. In the short run, however, the economic effects of a sum of money given outright to a nation and the same sum lent to that nation are similar. Thus an analysis of international income transfers is also useful in understanding the effects of international loans.

THE TRANSFER PROBLEM

The issue of how international transfers affect the terms of trade was raised in a famous debate between two great economists, Bertil Ohlin (one of the originators of the factor-proportions theory of trade) and John Maynard Keynes. The subject of the debate was the reparations payments demanded of Germany after World War I, and the question was how much of a burden these payments represented to the German economy.[5]

Keynes, who made a forceful case that the vengeful terms of the Allies (the "Carthaginian peace") were too harsh, argued that the monetary sums being demanded were an understatement of the true burden on Germany. He pointed out that to pay money to other countries Germany would have to export more and import less. To do this, he argued, Germany would have to make its exports cheaper relative to its imports. The resulting worsening of Germany's terms of trade would add an excess burden to the direct burden of the payment.

Ohlin questioned whether Keynes was right in assuming that Germany's terms of trade would worsen. He counterargued that when Germany raised taxes to finance its reparations, its demand for foreign goods would automatically decrease. At the same time, the reparation payment would be distributed in other countries in the form of reduced taxes or increased government spending, and some of the resulting increased foreign demand would be for German exports. Thus Germany might be able to reduce imports and increase exports without having its terms of trade worsen.

In the particular case in dispute the debate turned out to be beside the point: in the end, Germany paid very little of its reparations. The issue of the terms of trade effects of a transfer, however, arises in a surprisingly wide variety of contexts in international economics.

EFFECTS OF A TRANSFER ON THE TERMS OF TRADE

If Home makes a transfer of some of its income to Foreign, Home's income is reduced, and it must reduce its expenditure. Correspondingly, Foreign increases its expenditure. This shift in the national division of world spending may lead to a shift in world relative demand, thus affecting the terms of trade.

The shift in the *RD* curve (if it occurs) is the only effect of a transfer of income. The *RS* curve does not shift. As long as only income is being transferred, and not physical resources like capital equipment, the production of cloth and food for any given relative price will not change in either country. Thus the transfer problem is a purely demand-side issue.

The *RD* curve does not necessarily shift when world income is redistributed (this was Ohlin's point). If Foreign allocates its extra income between cloth and food in the same proportions that Home reduces its spending, then *world* spending on cloth and food will not change. The *RD* curve does not shift, and there is no terms of trade effect.

If the two countries do not allocate their change in spending in the same proportions, however, there will be a terms of trade effect, whose direction will depend on the difference in Home and Foreign spending patterns. Suppose that Home allocates a higher proportion of a marginal shift in expenditure to cloth than Foreign does. That is, Home has a higher **marginal propensity to spend** on cloth than Foreign. (Correspondingly, Home in this case must have a lower marginal propensity to spend on food.) Then at any given relative price Home's transfer payment to Foreign reduces demand for cloth and increases demand for food. The *RD* curve shifts to the left, from RD^1 to RD^2 (Figure 5-9), and equilibrium shifts from point 1 to point 2. This shift

[5] See Keynes, "The German Transfer Problem" and Ohlin, "The German Transfer Problem: A Discussion," both in *Economic Journal* 39 (1929), pp. 1–7 and pp. 172–182, respectively.

lowers the relative price of cloth from $(P_C/P_F)^1$ to $(P_C/P_F)^2$, worsening Home's terms of trade (because it exports cloth) while improving Foreign's. This is the case that Keynes described: the indirect effect of an international transfer on terms of trade reinforces its original effect on the incomes of the two countries.

There is, however, another possibility. If Home has a *lower* marginal propensity to spend on cloth, a transfer by Home to Foreign shifts the *RD* curve right, and improves Home's terms of trade at Foreign's expense. This effect offsets both the negative effect on Home's income and the positive effect on Foreign's income.

In general, then, *a transfer worsens the donor's terms of trade if the donor has a higher marginal propensity to spend on its export good than the recipient.* If the donor has a *lower* marginal propensity to spend on its export, its terms of trade will actually improve.

A paradoxical possibility is implied by this analysis. A transfer payment—say foreign aid—could conceivably improve the donor's terms of trade so much that it leaves the donor better off and the recipient worse off. In this case it is definitely better to give than to receive! Recent theoretical work has shown that this paradox, like the case of immiserizing growth, is possible in a rigorously specified model. The conditions are, however, even more stringent than those for immiserizing growth, and this possibility is almost surely purely theoretical.[6]

This analysis shows that the terms of trade effects of reparations and foreign aid can go either way. Thus Ohlin was right about the general principle. Many would still argue, however, that Keynes was right in suggesting that there is a presumption that transfers cause terms of trade effects that reinforce their effects on the incomes of donors and recipients.

PRESUMPTIONS ABOUT THE TERMS OF TRADE EFFECTS OF TRANSFERS

A transfer will worsen the donor's terms of trade if the donor has a higher marginal propensity to spend on its export good than the recipient. If differences in marginal propensities to spend were simply a matter of differences in taste, there would be no presumption either way: which good a country exports depends for the most part on differences in technology or resources, which need have nothing to do with tastes. When we look at actual spending patterns, however, each country seems to have a relative preference for its own goods. The United States, for example, produces only about 25 percent of the value of output of the world's market economies, so that total sales of U.S. goods are 25 percent of world sales. If spending patterns were the same everywhere, the United States would spend only 25 percent of its income on U.S. products. In fact, imports are only 11 percent of national income—that is, the United States spends 89 percent of its income domestically. On the other hand, the rest of the world spends less than 3 percent of its income on U.S. products. This certainly suggests that if the United States were to transfer some of its income to foreigners, the relative

[6] For examples of how an immiserizing transfer might occur, see Graciela Chichilnisky, "Basic Goods, the Effects of Commodity Transfers and the International Economic Order," *Journal of Development Economics* 7 (1980), pp. 505–519; and Jagdish Bhagwati, Richard Brecher, and Tatsuo Hatta, "The Generalized Theory of Transfers and Welfare," *American Economic Review* 73 (1983), pp. 606–618.

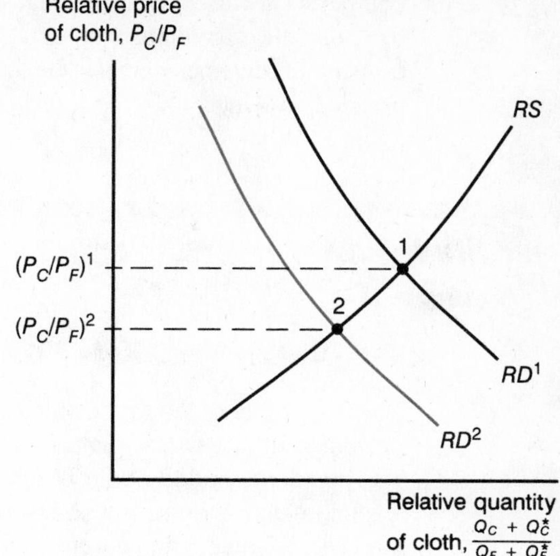

FIGURE 5-9
Effects of a transfer on the terms of trade.
If Home has a higher marginal propensity to spend on cloth than Foreign, a transfer of income by Home to Foreign shifts the *RD* curve left from RD^1 to RD^2, reducing the equilibrium relative price of cloth.

demand for U.S. goods would fall and the U.S. terms of trade would decline, just as Keynes argued.

The United States spends so much of its income at home because of barriers to trade, both natural and artificial. Transportation costs, tariffs, and import quotas cause residents of each country to buy a variety of goods and services at home rather than abroad. As we noted in Chapter 2, the effect of such barriers to trade is to create a set of nontraded goods. Even if every country divides its income among different goods in the same proportions, local purchase of nontraded goods will ensure that spending has a national bias.

Consider the following example. Suppose that there are not two but *three* goods: cloth, food, and haircuts. Only Home produces cloth, only Foreign produces food. Haircuts, however, are a nontraded good that each country produces for itself. Each country spends one-third of its income on each good. Even though these countries have the same tastes, each of them spends two-thirds of its income domestically and only one-third on imports.

Nontraded goods can give rise to what looks like a national preference for all goods produced domestically. But to analyze the effects of a transfer we need to know what happens to the supply and demand for *exports.* Here the crucial point is that nontraded goods compete with exports for resources. A transfer of income from the United States to the rest of the world lowers the demand for nontraded goods in the United States, releasing resources that can be used to produce U.S. exports. As a result, the supply of U.S. exports rises. At the same time, the rest of the world increases its demand for nontraded goods, drawing resources away from exports and reducing the supply of foreign exports (which are U.S. imports). The result is that a transfer by the United States to other countries may lower the price of U.S. exports relative to foreign, worsening U.S. terms of trade.

Demand shifts also cause resources to move between the nontraded and import-competing sectors. As a practical matter, however, most international economists believe that the effect of barriers to trade *is* to validate the presumption that an international transfer of income worsens the donor's terms of trade. Thus, Keynes was right in practice.

Case Study

THE TRANSFER PROBLEM FOR THE UNITED STATES

The magnitude of the terms of trade impacts from a transfer can be seen by looking at estimates for the United States. Based on estimates from past history, it appears that U.S. residents spend about 80 cents of a dollar of additional income on U.S. goods, while foreign residents will spend only 10 cents of that same dollar on goods made in the United States. Thus a transfer to the United States will raise the relative demand for U.S. goods and hence improve U.S. terms of trade.

During the period after 1982 the United States began receiving large inflows of loans from abroad: measured as a share of national income, these inflows peaked at 3.5 percent in 1987, and had declined to less than 1 percent at the time of writing. These were not true transfer payments, because they must eventually be repaid. For the time being, however, they not only allow the United States to spend more than its current income, they also raise the purchasing power of that income substantially. The transfer effect was a major contributor to the large temporary improvement in the U.S. terms of trade after 1980 (see Figure 5-8), which ran counter to the long-term downward trend we saw in our discussion of growth and trade earlier.

Tariffs and Export Subsidies: Simultaneous Shifts in *RS* and *RD*

Import tariffs and **export subsidies** are not usually put in place to affect a country's terms of trade. Government intervention in trade usually takes place for income distribution reasons, to promote industries thought to be crucial to the economy, or for balance of payments reasons (these motivations are examined in Chapters 10, 11, and 12). Whatever the motive for tariffs and subsidies, however, they do have terms of trade effects that can be understood using the standard trade model.

The distinctive feature of tariffs and export subsidies is that they create a difference between the prices at which goods are traded on the world market and their prices inside a country. The direct effect of a tariff (a tax levied on imports) is to make imported goods more expensive inside a country than they are outside. An export subsidy is a payment given to domestic producers who sell a good abroad; by giving an incentive to export, such subsidies raise the price of exported goods inside a country.

The price changes caused by tariffs and subsidies change both relative supply and relative demand. The result is a shift in the terms of trade of the country imposing the policy change and in the terms of trade of the rest of the world.

RELATIVE DEMAND AND SUPPLY EFFECTS OF A TARIFF

Tariffs and subsidies drive a wedge between the prices at which goods are traded internationally **(external prices)** and the prices at which they are traded within a country **(internal prices).** This means that we have to be careful in defining the terms of trade. The terms of trade are intended to measure the ratio at which countries exchange goods—for example, how many units of food can Home import for each unit of cloth that it exports? The terms of trade therefore correspond to external, not internal, prices. Thus we want to know how a tariff or export subsidy affects relative supply and demand *as a function of external prices.*

If Home imposes a 20 percent tariff on the value of food imports, the price of food relative to cloth faced by Home producers and consumers will be 20 percent higher than the relative price of food on the world market. Equivalently, the relative price of cloth on which Home residents base their decisions will be lower than that on the external market.

At any given world relative price of cloth, then, Home producers will face a lower relative cloth price and therefore will produce less cloth and more food. At the same time, Home consumers will shift their consumption toward cloth and away from food. From the point of view of the world as a whole, the relative supply of cloth will fall (from RS^1 to RS^2 in Figure 5-10) while the relative demand for cloth will rise (from RD^1 to RD^2). Clearly, the world relative price of cloth rises from $(P_C/P_F)^1$ to $(P_C/P_F)^2$, and thus Home's terms of trade improve at Foreign's expense.

The extent of this terms of trade effect depends on how large the country imposing

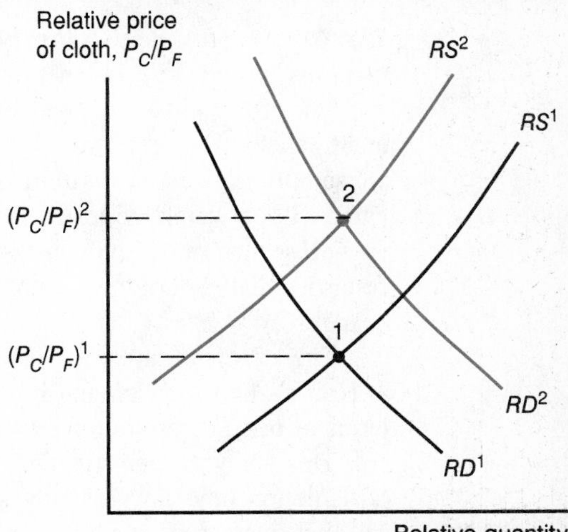

FIGURE 5-10
Effects of a tariff.
An import tariff imposed by Home both reduces the relative supply of cloth (from RS^1 to RS^2) and increases the relative demand (from RD^1 to RD^2). As a result, the relative price of cloth must rise.

the tariff is relative to the rest of the world—if the country is only a small part of the world, it cannot have much effect on world relative supply and demand and therefore cannot have much effect on relative prices. If the United States, a very large country, were to impose a 20 percent tariff, some estimates suggest that the U.S. terms of trade might rise by 15 percent. That is, the price of U.S. imports relative to exports might fall by 15 percent on the world market, while the relative price of imports would rise only 5 percent inside the United States. On the other hand, if Luxembourg or Paraguay were to impose a 20 percent tariff, the terms of trade effect would probably be too small to measure.

EFFECTS OF AN EXPORT SUBSIDY

Tariffs and export subsidies are often treated as similar policies, since they both seem to support domestic producers, but they have opposite effects on the terms of trade. Suppose that Home offers a 20 percent subsidy on the value of any cloth exported. For any given world prices this subsidy will raise Home's internal price of cloth relative to food by 20 percent. The rise in the relative price of cloth will lead Home producers to produce more cloth and less food, while leading Home consumers to substitute food for cloth. As illustrated in Figure 5-11, the subsidy will increase the world relative supply of cloth (from RS^1 to RS^2) and decrease the world relative demand for cloth (from RD^1 to RD^2), shifting equilibrium from point 1 to point 2. A Home export subsidy worsens Home's terms of trade and improves Foreign's.

IMPLICATIONS OF TERMS OF TRADE EFFECTS: WHO GAINS AND WHO LOSES?

The question of who gains and who loses from tariffs and export subsidies has two dimensions. First is the issue of the *international* distribution of income; second is the issue of the distribution of income *within* each of the countries.

The International Distribution of Income. If Home imposes a tariff, it improves its terms of trade at Foreign's expense. Thus tariffs hurt the rest of the world.

The effect on Home's welfare is not quite as clear-cut. The terms of trade improvement benefits Home; however, a tariff also imposes costs by distorting production and consumption incentives within Home's economy (see Chapter 9). The terms of trade gains will outweigh the losses from distortion only as long as the tariff is not too large: we will see later how to define an optimum tariff that maximizes net benefit. (For small countries that cannot have much impact on their terms of trade, the optimum tariff is near zero.)

The effects of an export subsidy are quite clear. Foreign's terms of trade improve at Home's expense, leaving it clearly better off. At the same time, Home loses from terms of trade deterioration *and* from the distorting effects of its policy.

This analysis seems to show that export subsidies never make sense. In fact, it is difficult to come up with any situation in which export subsidies would serve the national interest. The use of export subsidies as a policy tool usually has more to do with the peculiarities of trade politics than with economic logic.

Are foreign tariffs always bad for a country and foreign export subsidies always beneficial? Not necessarily. Our model is of a two-country world, where the other

FIGURE 5-11
Effects of a subsidy.
An export subsidy's effects are the reverse of those of a tariff. Relative supply of cloth rises, while relative demand falls. Home's terms of trade decline.

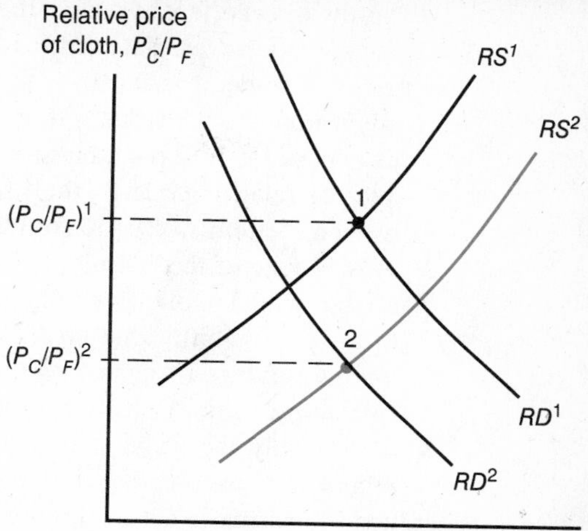

country exports the good we import and vice versa. In the real world of many countries, a foreign government may subsidize the export of a good that competes with U.S. exports; this foreign subsidy will obviously hurt the U.S. terms of trade. A good example of this effect is European subsidies to agricultural exports (see Chapter 9). Alternatively, a country may impose a tariff on something the United States also imports, lowering its price and benefiting the United States. We thus need to qualify our conclusions from a two-country analysis: subsidies to exports of things *the United States imports* help us, while tariffs *against U.S. exports* hurt us.

The view that subsidized foreign sales to the United States are good for us is not a popular one. When foreign governments are charged with subsidizing sales in the United States, the popular and political reaction is that this is unfair competition. Thus when a Commerce Department study determined that European governments were subsidizing exports of steel to the United States, our government demanded that they raise their prices. The standard model tells us that when foreign governments subsidize exports to the United States, the appropriate response from a national point of view should be to send them a note of thanks!

Of course this never happens, largely because of the effects of foreign subsidies on income distribution within the United States. If Europe subsidizes exports of steel to the United States, most U.S. residents gain from cheaper steel, but steelworkers, the owners of steel company stock, and industrial workers in general may not be so cheerful.

The Distribution of Income within Countries. Foreign tariffs or subsidies change the relative prices of goods. Such changes have strong effects on income distribution because of factor immobility and differences in the factor intensity of different industries.

At first glance, the direction of the effect of tariffs and export subsidies on relative prices, and therefore on income distribution, may seem obvious. A tariff has the direct effect of raising the internal relative price of the imported good, while an export subsidy has the direct effect of raising the internal relative price of the exported good. We have just seen, however, that tariffs and export subsidies have an indirect effect on a country's terms of trade. The terms of trade effect suggests a paradoxical possibility. A tariff might improve a country's terms of trade so much—that is, raise the relative price of its export good so much on world markets—that even after the tariff rate is added, the internal relative price of the import good *falls.* Similarly, an export subsidy might worsen the terms of trade so much that the internal relative price of the export good falls in spite of the subsidy. If these paradoxical results occur, the income distribution effects of trade policies will be just the opposite of what is expected.

The possibility that tariffs and export subsidies might have perverse effects on internal prices in a country was pointed out and demonstrated by the University of Chicago economist Lloyd Metzler and is known as the **Metzler paradox.**[7] This paradox has roughly the same status as immiserizing growth and a transfer that makes the recipient worse off: that is, it is possible in theory but will happen only under extreme conditions and is not likely in practice.

Leaving aside the possibility of a Metzler paradox, then, a tariff will help the import-competing sector at home while hurting the exporting sector; an export subsidy will do the reverse. These shifts in the distribution of income *within* countries are often more obvious and more important to the formation of policy than the shifts in the distribution of income *between* countries that result from changes in the terms of trade.

Summary

1. The *standard trade model* derives a world relative supply curve from production possibilities and a world relative demand curve from preferences. The price of exports relative to imports, a country's *terms of trade,* is determined by the intersection of the world relative supply and demand curves. Other things equal, a rise in a country's terms of trade increases its welfare. Conversely, a decline in a country's terms of trade will leave the country worse off.

2. Economic growth means an outward shift in a country's production possibility frontier. Such growth is usually *biased*—that is, the production possibility frontier shifts out more in the direction of some goods than in the direction of others. The immediate effect of biased growth is to lead, other things equal, to an increase in the world relative supply of the goods toward which the growth is biased. This shift in the world relative supply curve in turn leads to a change in the growing country's terms of trade, which can go in either direction. If the growing country's terms of trade improve, this improvement reinforces the initial growth at home but hurts the rest of the world. If the growing country's terms of trade worsen, this decline offsets some of the favorable effects of growth at home but benefits the rest of the world.

3. The direction of the terms of trade effects depends on the nature of the growth.

[7] See Metzler, "Tariffs, the Terms of Trade, and the Distribution of National Income," *Journal of Political Economy* 57 (February 1949), pp. 1–29.

Growth that is *export-biased* (growth that expands the ability of an economy to produce the goods it was initially exporting more than it expands the ability to produce goods that compete with imports) worsens the terms of trade. Conversely, growth that is *import-biased,* disproportionately increasing the ability to produce import-competing goods, improves a country's terms of trade. It is possible for import-biased growth abroad to hurt a country, a situation that may actually have happened to a mild degree to the United States in the postwar period.

4. International *transfers of income,* such as war reparations and foreign aid, may affect a country's terms of trade by shifting the world relative demand curve. If the country receiving a transfer spends a higher proportion of an increase in income on its export good than the giver, a transfer raises world relative demand for the recipient's export good and thus improves its terms of trade. This improvement reinforces the initial transfer and provides an indirect benefit in addition to the direct income transfer. On the other hand, if the recipient has a lower *propensity to spend* on its export at the margin than the donor, a transfer worsens the recipient's terms of trade, offsetting at least part of the transfer's effect.

5. In practice, most countries spend a much higher share of their income on domestically produced goods than foreigners do. This is not necessarily due to differences in taste but rather to barriers to trade, natural and artificial, which cause many goods to be nontraded. If nontraded goods compete with exports for resources, transfers will usually raise the recipient's terms of trade. The evidence suggests that this is, in fact, the case.

6. *Import tariffs* and *export subsidies* affect both relative supply and demand. A tariff raises relative supply of a country's import good while lowering relative demand. A tariff unambiguously improves the country's terms of trade at the rest of the world's expense. An export subsidy has the reverse effect, increasing the relative supply and reducing the relative demand for the country's *export* good, and thus worsening the terms of trade.

7. The terms of trade effects of an export subsidy hurt the subsidizing country and benefit the rest of the world, while those of a tariff do the reverse. This suggests that export subsidies do not make sense from a national point of view and that foreign export subsidies should be welcomed rather than countered. Both tariffs and subsidies, however, have strong effects on the distribution of income *within* countries, and these effects often weigh more heavily on policy than the terms of trade concerns.

Key Terms

standard trade model
terms of trade
isovalue lines
indifference curves
export-biased growth
import-biased growth
immiserizing growth
transfers of income
marginal propensity to spend
import tariff
export subsidy
external price
internal price
Metzler paradox

Problems

1. In some economies relative supply may be unresponsive to changes in prices. For example, if factors of production were completely immobile between sectors, the production possibility frontier would be right-angled, and output of the two goods would not depend on their relative prices. Is it still true in this case that a rise in the terms of trade increases welfare? Analyze graphically.
2. The counterpart to immobile factors on the supply side would be lack of substitution on the demand side. Imagine an economy where consumers always buy goods in rigid proportions—for example, one yard of cloth for every pound of food—regardless of the prices of the two goods. Show that an improvement in the terms of trade benefits this economy, as well.
3. Japan primarily exports manufactured goods, while importing raw materials such as food and oil. Analyze the impact on Japan's terms of trade of the following events:
   a. A war in the Middle East disrupts oil supply.
   b. Korea develops the ability to produce automobiles that it can sell in Canada and the United States.
   c. U.S. engineers develop a fusion reactor that replaces fossil fuel electricity plants.
   d. A harvest failure in Russia.
   e. A reduction in Japan's tariffs on imported beef and citrus fruit.
4. Countries *A* and *B* have two factors of production, capital and labor, with which they produce two goods, *X* and *Y*. Technology is the same in the two countries. *X* is capital-intensive; *A* is capital-abundant.
   Analyze the effects on the terms of trade and the welfare of the two countries of the following:
   a. An increase in *A*'s capital stock.
   b. An increase in *A*'s labor supply.
   c. An increase in *B*'s capital stock.
   d. An increase in *B*'s labor supply.
5. It is just as likely that economic growth will worsen a country's terms of trade as that it will improve them. Why, then, do most economists regard immiserizing growth, where growth actually hurts the growing country, as unlikely in practice?
6. In practice much foreign aid is "tied"; that is, it comes with restrictions that require that the recipient spend the aid on goods from the donor country. For example, France might provide money for an irrigation project in Africa, on the condition that the pumps, pipelines, and construction equipment be purchased from France rather than from Japan. How does such tying of aid affect the transfer problem analysis? Does tying of aid make sense from the donor's point of view? Can you think of a scenario in which tied aid actually makes the recipient worse off?
7. During 1989 a wave of political change swept over Eastern Europe, raising prospects not only of democracy but also of a shift from centrally planned to market economies. One consequence might be a shift in how *Western* Europe uses its

money: nations, especially Germany, that during the 1980s were lending heavily to the United States might start to lend to nearby Eastern European nations instead.

Using the analysis of the transfer problem, how do you think this should affect the prices of Western European goods relative to those from the United States and Japan? (Hint: how would the likely use of a dollar of financial resources differ in, say East Germany, from its use in the United States?)

8. Suppose that one country subsidizes its exports and the other country imposes a "countervailing" tariff that offsets its effect, so that in the end relative prices in the second country are unchanged. What happens to the terms of trade? What about welfare in the two countries?

Suppose, on the other hand, that the second country retaliates with an export subsidy of its own. Contrast the result.

Further Reading

Rudiger Dornbusch, Stanley Fischer, and Paul Samuelson. "Comparative Advantage, Trade, and Payments in a Ricardian Model with a Continuum of Goods." *American Economic Review,* 1977. This paper, cited in Chapter 2, also gives a clear exposition of the role of nontraded goods in establishing the presumption that a transfer improves the recipient's terms of trade.

J. R. Hicks. "The Long Run Dollar Problem." *Oxford Economic Papers* 2 (1953), pp. 117–135. The modern analysis of growth and trade has its origins in the fears of Europeans, in the early years after World War II, that the United States had an economic lead that could not be overtaken (this sounds dated today, but many of the same arguments have now resurfaced about Japan). The paper by Hicks is the most famous exposition.

Harry G. Johnson. "Economic Expansion and International Trade." *Manchester School of Social and Economic Studies* 23 (1955), pp. 95–112. The paper that laid out the crucial distinction between export- and import-biased growth.

Paul Samuelson. "The Transfer Problem and Transport Costs." *Economic Journal* 62 (1952), pp. 278–304 (Part I) and 64 (1954), pp. 264–289 (Part II). The transfer problem, like so many issues in international economics, was given its basic formal analysis by Paul Samuelson.

John Whalley. *Trade Liberalization among Major World Trading Areas.* Cambridge: MIT Press, 1985. The impact of tariffs on the international economy has been the subject of extensive study. Most impressive are the huge "computable general equilibrium" models, numerical models based on actual data that allow computation of the effects of changes in tariffs and other trade policies. Whalley's book presents one of the most carefully constructed of these.

Appendix to Chapter 5

Representing International Equilibrium with Offer Curves

For most purposes, analyzing international equilibrium in terms of relative supply and demand is the simplest and most useful technique. In some circumstances, however, it is useful to analyze trade in a diagram that shows directly what each country ships to the other. A diagram that does this is the *offer curve* diagram.

DERIVING A COUNTRY'S OFFER CURVE

In Figure 5-3 we showed how to determine a country's production and consumption given the relative price P_C/P_F. Trade is the difference between production and consumption. In an offer curve diagram we show directly the trade flows that correspond to any given relative price. On one axis of Figure 5A-1 we show the country's exports $(Q_C - D_C)$, on the other its imports $(D_F - Q_F)$. Point T in Figure 5A-1 corresponds to the situation shown in Figure 5-3 (production at Q, consumption at D). Since

$$(D_F - Q_F) = (Q_C - D_C) \times (P_C/P_F), \tag{5A-1}$$

the slope of the line from the origin of Figure 5A-1 to T is equal to P_C/P_F. T is Home's offer at the assumed relative price: at that price, Home residents are willing to trade $(Q_C - D_C)$ units of cloth for $(D_F - Q_F)$ units of food.

By calculating Home's offer at different relative prices, we trace out Home's *offer curve* (Figure 5A-2). We saw in Figure 5-4 that as P_C/P_F rises, Q_C rises, Q_F falls, D_F rises, and D_C may rise or fall. Desired $(Q_C - D_C)$ and $(D_F - Q_F)$, however, both normally rise if income effects are not too strong. In Figure 5A-2, T^1 is the offer corresponding to Q^1, D^1 in Figure 5-4; T^2 the offer corresponding to Q^2, D^2. By finding Home's offer at many prices, we trace out the Home offer curve OC.

FIGURE 5A-1
Home's desired trade at a given relative price.
At the relative price corresponding to the slope of the line from the origin, Home makes the offer to trade $Q_C - D_C$ units of cloth for $D_F - Q_F$ units of food.

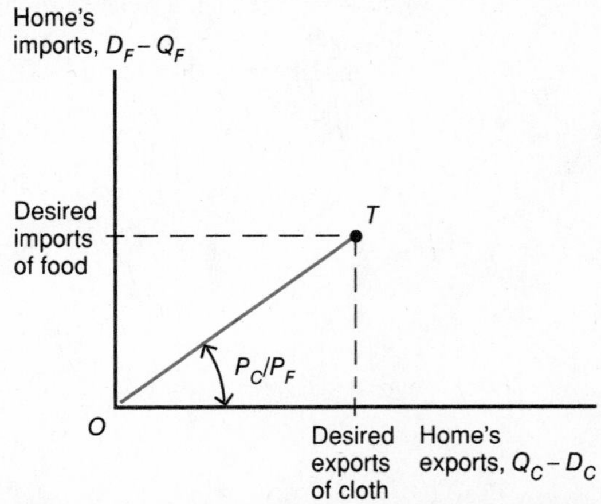

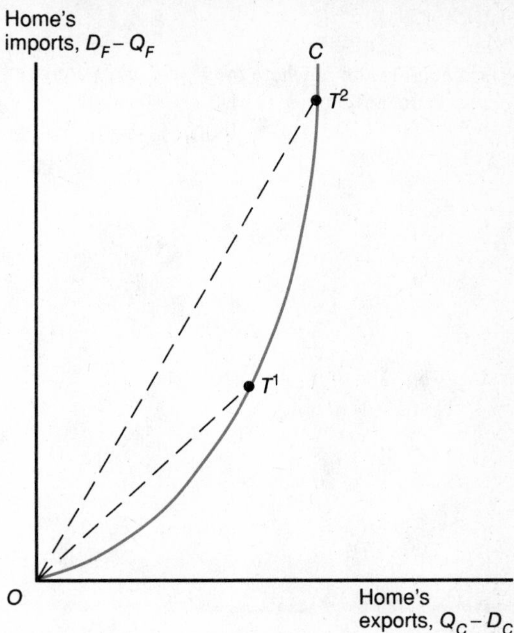

FIGURE 5A-2
Home's offer curve.
The offer curve is generated by tracing out how Home's offer varies as the relative price of cloth is changed.

Foreign's offer curve *OF* may be traced out in the same way (Figure 5A-3). On the vertical axis we plot ($Q^*_F - D^*_F$), Foreign's desired exports of food, while on the horizontal axis we plot ($D^*_C - Q^*_C$), desired imports of cloth. The lower P_C/P_F is, the more food Foreign will want to export and the more cloth it will want to import.

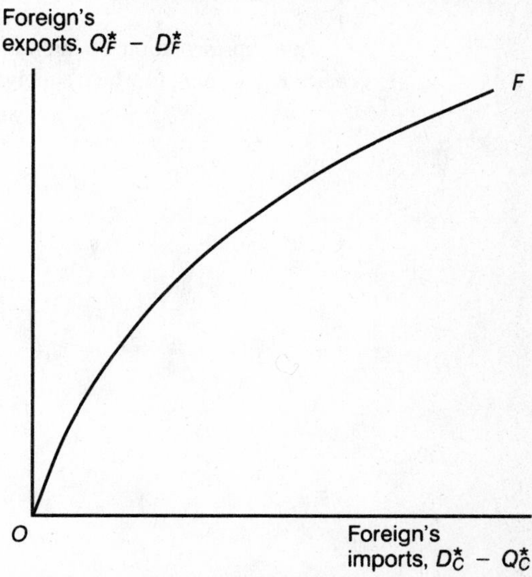

FIGURE 5A-3
Foreign's offer curve.
Foreign's offer curve shows how that country's desired imports of cloth and exports of food vary with the relative price.

FIGURE 5A-4
Offer curve equilibrium.
World equilibrium is where the Home and Foreign offer curves intersect.

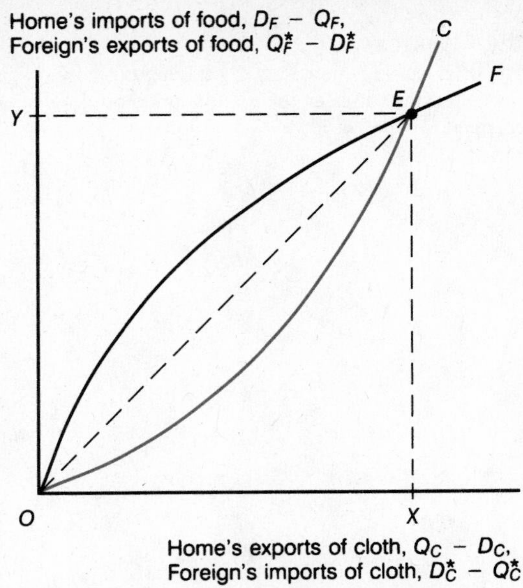

INTERNATIONAL EQUILIBRIUM

In equilibrium it must be true that $(Q_C - D_C) = (D_C^* - Q_C^*)$, and also that $(D_F - Q_F) = (Q_F^* - D_F^*)$. That is, world supply and demand must be equal for both cloth and food. Given these equivalences, we can plot the Home and Foreign offer curves on the same diagram (Figure 5A-4). Equilibrium is at the point where the Home and Foreign offer curves cross. At the equilibrium point *E* the relative price of cloth is equal to the slope of *OE*. Home's exports of cloth, which equal Foreign's imports, are *OX*. Foreign's exports of food, which equal Home's imports, are *OY*.

This representation of international equilibrium helps us see that equilibrium is in fact *general* equlibrium, in which supply and demand are equalized in both markets at the same time.

Economies of Scale, Imperfect Competition, and International Trade

Chapter 6

In Chapter 2 we pointed out that there are two reasons why countries specialize and trade. First, countries differ either in their resources or in technology and specialize in the things they do relatively well; second, economies of scale (or increasing returns) make it advantageous for each country to specialize in the production of only a limited range of goods and services. The past four chapters considered models in which all trade is based on comparative advantage—that is, differences between countries are the only reason for trade. This chapter introduces the role of economies of scale.

The analysis of trade based on economies of scale presents certain problems that we have so far avoided. Up to now we have assumed that markets are perfectly competitive, so that all monopoly profits are always competed away. When there are increasing returns, however, large firms usually have an advantage over small, so that markets tend to be dominated by one firm (monopoly) or, more often, by a few firms (oligopoly). When increasing returns enter the trade picture, then, markets usually become imperfectly competitive.

This chapter begins with an overview of the concept of economies of scale and the economics of imperfect competition. We then turn to two models of international trade in which economies of scale and imperfect competition play a crucial role: the monopolistic competition model and the dumping model. The rest of the chapter addresses the role of a different kind of increasing returns, external economies, in determining trade patterns.

Economies of Scale and International Trade: An Overview

The models of comparative advantage already presented were based on the assumption of constant returns to scale. That is, we assumed that if inputs to an industry were doubled, industry output would double as well. In practice, however, many industries are characterized by economies of scale (also referred to as increasing returns), so that production is more efficient the larger the scale at which it takes place. Where there are economies of scale, doubling the inputs to an industry will more than double the industry's production.

A simple example can help convey the significance of economies of scale for international trade. Table 6-1 shows the relationship between inputs and output of a hypothetical industry. Widgets are produced using only one input, labor; the table shows how the amount of labor required depends on the number of widgets produced. To produce 10 widgets, for example, requires 15 hours of labor, while to produce 25 widgets requires 30 hours. The presence of economies of scale may be seen from the fact that doubling the input of labor from 15 to 30 more than doubles the industry's output—in fact, output increases by a factor of 2.5. Equivalently, the existence of economies of scale may be seen by looking at the average amount of labor used to produce each unit of output: if output is only 5 widgets the average labor input per widget is 2 hours, while if output is 25 units the average labor input falls to 1.2 hours.

We can use this example to see why economies of scale provide an incentive for international trade. Imagine a world consisting of two countries, America and Britain, both of whom have the same technology for producing widgets, and suppose that initially each country produces 10 widgets. According to the table this requires 15 hours of labor in each country, so in the world as a whole 30 hours of labor produce 20 widgets. But now suppose that we concentrate world production of widgets in one country, say America, and let America employ 30 hours of labor in the widget industry. In a single country these 30 hours of labor can produce 25 widgets. So by concentrating production of widgets in America, the world economy can use the same amount of labor to produce 25 percent more widgets.

But where does America find the extra labor to produce widgets, and what happens to the labor that was employed in the British widget industry? To get the labor to expand its production of some goods, America must contract or abandon the production of others; these goods will then be produced in Britain instead, using the labor formerly

TABLE 6-1 Relationship of input to output for a hypothetical industry

Output	*Total labor input*	*Average labor input*
5	10	2
10	15	1.5
15	20	1.333333
20	25	1.25
25	30	1.2
30	35	1.166667

employed in the industries whose production has expanded in America. Imagine that there are many goods subject to economies of scale in production, and give them numbers: 1, 2, 3, ... To take advantage of economies of scale, each of the countries must concentrate on producing only a limited number of goods. Thus, for example, America might produce goods 1, 3, 5, and so on while Britain produces 2, 4, 6, and so on. If each country produces only some of the goods, then each good can be produced at a larger scale than would be the case if each country tried to produce everything, and the world economy can therefore produce more of each good.

How does international trade enter the story? Consumers in each country will still want to consume a variety of goods. Suppose that industry 1 ends up in America and industry 2 in Britain; then American consumers of good 2 will have to buy goods imported from Britain, while British consumers of good 1 will have to import it from America. International trade plays a crucial role: it makes it possible for each country to produce a restricted range of goods and to take advantage of economies of scale without sacrificing variety in consumption. Indeed, as we will see below, international trade typically leads to an increase in the variety of goods available.

Our example, then, suggests how mutually beneficial trade can arise as a result of economies of scale. Each country specializes in producing a limited range of products, which enables it to produce these goods more efficiently than if it tried to produce everything for itself; these specialized economies then trade with each other to be able to consume the full range of goods.

Unfortunately, to go from this suggestive story to an explicit model of trade based on economies of scale is not that simple. The reason is that economies of scale typically lead to a market structure other than that of perfect competition, and it is necessary to be careful about analyzing this market structure.

Economies of Scale and Market Structure

In the example in Table 6-1, we represented economies of scale by assuming that the labor input per unit of production is smaller the more units produced. We did not say how this production increase was achieved—whether existing firms simply produced more, or whether there was instead an increase in the number of firms. To analyze the effects of economies of scale on market structure, however, one must be clear about what kind of production increase is necessary to reduce average cost. **External econmies of scale** occur when the cost per unit depends on the size of the industry but not necessarily on the size of any one firm. **Internal economies of scale** occur when the cost per unit depends on the size of an individual firm but not necessarily on that of the industry.

The distinction between external and internal economies can be illustrated with a hypothetical example. Imagine an industry that initially consists of ten firms, each producing 100 widgets. Now consider two cases. First, suppose the industry were to double in size, so that it now consists of twenty firms, each one still producing 100 widgets. Will the efficiency of production rise? If so, this is a case of external economies of scale. That is, the efficiency of firms is increased by having a larger industry, even though each firm is the same size as before.

On the other hand, suppose the industry's output were held constant, but the number of firms cut in half, so that each firm produces 200 widgets. If the efficiency of production rises in this case, then there are internal economies of scale: a firm is more efficient if its output is larger.

External and internal economies of scale have different implications for the structure of industries. An industry where economies of scale are purely external (that is, where there are no advantages to large firms) will typically consist of many small firms and be perfectly competitive. Internal economies of scale, by contrast, give large firms a cost advantage over small and lead to an imperfectly competitive market structure.

Both external and internal economies of scale are important causes of international trade. Most recent research on the role of economies of scale in trade, has, however, focused on internal economies, for two reasons. First, internal economies of scale are easier to identify in practice than are external. Engineers can provide pretty good estimates of the gains from large-scale production in petrochemicals, aircraft, autos, and so on, whereas the size of external economies is more elusive. For example, there is clearly an advantage to firms in the computer industry from being close to each other—otherwise there would not be so many firms clustered around Boston's Route 128—but the dollar value of that clustering is very hard to pin down.

The second reason for research being focused on internal economies is that the story of international trade that emerges from recently developed models of trade under internal economies of scale is simpler than the story that emerges from external-economy models. The reasons for this difference are discussed later in this chapter when we turn to external-economy models.

We begin with a model of trade based on internal economies of scale. As we have just argued, however, internal economies of scale lead to a breakdown of perfect competition. This forces us to take time out to review the economics of imperfect competition before we can turn to the analysis of international trade.

The Theory of Imperfect Competition

In a perfectly competitive market, firms are *price takers.* That is, sellers of products believe that they can sell as much as they like at the current price and cannot influence the price they receive for their product. For example, a wheat farmer can sell as much wheat as she likes without worrying that if she tries to sell more she will depress the market price. The reason, of course, is that any individual wheat grower represents a tiny fraction of the global wheat market.

When only a few firms produce a good, however, matters are different. To take perhaps the most dramatic example, the aircraft manufacturing giant Boeing faces only two competitors in the production of large jet aircraft, Airbus and McDonnell-Douglas, and even these competitors do not offer close substitutes for many of Boeing's products (such as the 747). Boeing therefore knows that if it wants to sell more airplanes, it can do so only by significantly reducing its price. In **imperfect competition,** then, firms are aware that they can influence the prices of their products and that they can sell more only by reducing their price.

When firms are not price takers, it is necessary to develop additional tools to describe how they behave. The simplest market structure to examine is that of a **pure**

FIGURE 6-1
Monopolistic behavior.
A monopolistic firm chooses an output such that marginal revenue, the increase in revenue from selling an additional unit, equals marginal cost, the cost of producing an additional unit. This profit-maximizing output is shown as Q_M; the price at which this output is demanded is P_M. The marginal revenue curve *MR* lies below the demand curve *D*, because marginal revenue is always less than the price.

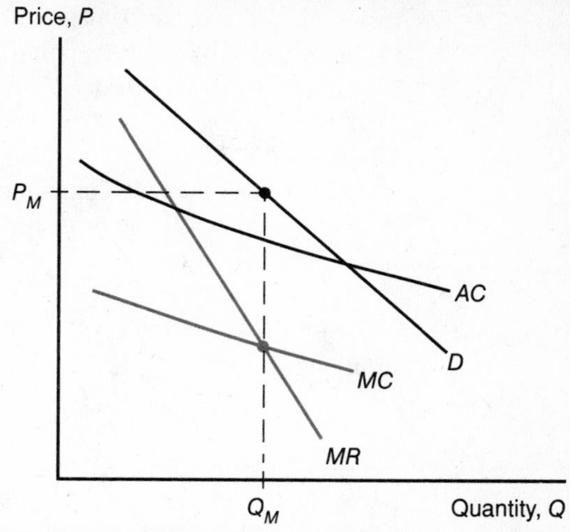

monopoly, where a firm faces no competition; the tools we develop can then be used to examine more complex market structures.

MONOPOLY: A BRIEF REVIEW

Figure 6-1 shows the position of a single, monopolistic firm. The firm faces a downward-sloping demand curve, shown in the figure as *D*. The downward slope of *D* indicates that the firm can sell more units of output only if the price of the output falls. As you may recall from basic microeconomics, corresponding to the demand curve is a **marginal revenue** curve. Marginal revenue is the extra or marginal revenue the firm gains from selling an additional unit. Marginal revenue for a monopolist is always less than the price because to sell an additional unit the firm must lower the price of *all* units (not just the marginal one). Thus for a monopolist the marginal revenue curve, *MR,* always lies below the demand curve.

Marginal Revenue and Price. For our analysis of the monopolistic competition model later in this section it is important to determine the relationship between the price the monopolist receives per unit and marginal revenue. Marginal revenue is always less than the price—but how much less? The relationship between marginal revenue and price depends on two things. First, it depends on how much output the firm is already selling: a firm that is not selling very many units will not lose much by cutting the price it receives on those units. Second, the gap between price and marginal revenue depends on the slope of the demand curve, which tells us how much the monopolist has to cut his price to sell one more unit of output. If the curve is very flat, then the monopolist can sell an additional unit with only a small price cut and will therefore not have to lower the price on units he would have sold otherwise by very much, so marginal revenue will be close to the price per unit. On the other hand, if the demand curve is very steep, selling an additional unit will require a large price cut, implying marginal revenue much less than price.

We can be more specific about the relationship between price and marginal revenue if we assume that the demand curve the firm faces is a straight line. When this is so, the dependence of the monopolist's total sales on the price it charges can be represented by an equation of the form

$$X = A - B \times P, \tag{6-1}$$

where X is the number of units the firm sells, P the price it charges per unit, and A and B are constants. We show in the appendix to this chapter that in this case marginal revenue is

$$\text{Marginal revenue} = MR = P - X/B, \tag{6-2}$$

implying

$$P - MR = X/B.$$

Equation (6-2) reveals that the gap between price and marginal revenue depends on the initial sales X of the firm and the slope parameter B of its demand curve. If sales X are larger, marginal revenue is lower, because cutting the price costs the firm more. The greater is B, that is, the more sales fall for any given increase in price, the closer is marginal revenue to the price of the good. Equation (6-2) is crucial for our analysis of the monopolistic competition model of trade (pp. 124–133).

Average and Marginal Costs. Returning to Figure 6-1, AC represents the firm's **average cost** of production, that is, its total cost divided by its output. Its downward slope reflects our assumption that there are economies of scale, so that the larger the firm's output is the lower are its costs per unit. MC represents the firm's **marginal cost** (the amount it costs the firm to produce one extra unit). We know from basic economics that when average costs are a decreasing function of output, marginal cost is always less than average cost. Thus MC lies below AC.

Equation (6-2) related price and marginal revenue. There is a corresponding formula relating average and marginal cost. Suppose the costs of a firm take the form

$$C = F + c \times X, \tag{6-3}$$

where F is a fixed cost that is independent of the firm's output, c is the firm's marginal cost, and X is once again the firm's output. (This is called a linear cost function.) *The fixed cost in a linear cost function gives rise to economies of scale, because the larger the firm's output, the less is the fixed cost per unit.* Specifically, the firm's average cost (total cost divided by output) is

$$\text{Average cost} = AC = C/X = F/X + c. \tag{6-4}$$

This average cost declines as X increases because the fixed cost is spread over a larger output.

If, for example, $F = 5$ and $c = 1$ the average cost of producing 10 units is $5/10 + 1 = 1.5$ and the average cost of producing 25 units is $5/25 + 1 = 1.2$. These numbers may look familiar, because they were used to construct Table 6-1. The relationship between output, average costs, and marginal costs given in Table 6-1 is shown graphically in Figure 6-2. Average cost approaches infinity at zero output and approaches marginal cost at very large output.

The profit-maximizing output of a monopolist is where marginal revenue (the revenue gained from selling an extra unit) equals marginal cost (the cost of producing

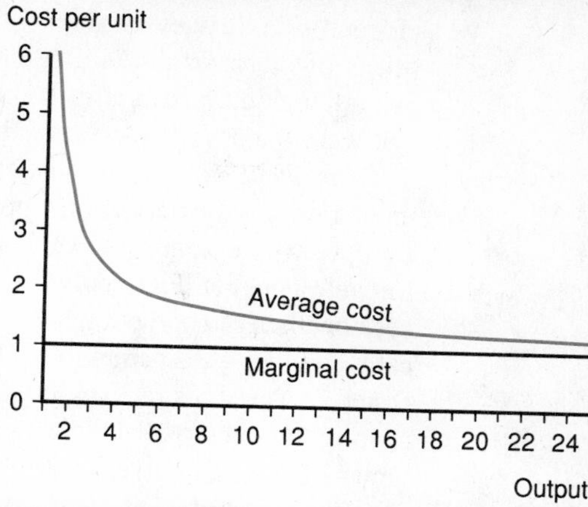

FIGURE 6-2
Average vs. marginal cost.
This figure illustrates the average and marginal costs corresponding to the total cost function $C = 5 + x$. Marginal cost is always 1; average cost declines as output rises.

an extra unit), that is, at the intersection of the *MC* and *MR* curves. In Figure 6-1 we can see that the price at which the profit-maximizing output Q_M is demanded is P_M, which is greater than average cost. When $P > AC$, the monopolist is earning some monopoly profits.[1]

MONOPOLISTIC COMPETITION

Monopoly profits rarely go uncontested. A firm making high profits normally attracts competitors. Thus situations of pure monopoly are rare in practice. Instead, the usual market structure in industries characterized by internal economies of scale is one of **oligopoly:** several firms, each of them large enough to affect prices, but none with an uncontested monopoly.

The general analysis of oligopoly is a complex and controversial subject, because in oligopolies the pricing policies of firms are *interdependent.* Each firm in an oligopoly will, in setting its price, consider not only the responses of consumers but also the expected responses of competitors. These responses, however, depend in turn on the competitors' expectations about the firm's behavior—and we are therefore in a complex game in which firms are trying to second-guess each others' strategies. We will briefly discuss the general problems of modeling oligopoly below. However, there is a special case of oligopoly, known as monopolistic competition, which is relatively easy to analyze. In recent years monopolistic competition models have been widely applied to international trade.

In **monopolistic competition** models two key assumptions are made to get around the problem of interdependence. First, each firm is assumed to be able to *differentiate its product* from that of its rivals. That is, its customers will not rush to buy other firms' products because of a slight price difference. Product differentiation assures that each firm has a monopoly in its particular product within an industry and is therefore

[1] The economic definition of profits is not the same as that used in conventional accounting, where any revenue over and above labor and material costs is called a profit. A firm that earns a rate of return on its capital less than what that capital could have earned in other industries is not making profits; from an economic point of view the normal rate of return on capital represents part of the firm's costs, and only returns over and above that normal rate of return represent profits.

somewhat insulated from competition. Second, each firm is assumed to take the prices charged by its rivals as given—that is, it ignores the impact of its own price on the prices of other firms. As a result, the monopolistic competition model assumes that even though each firm is in reality facing competition from other firms, it behaves as if it were a monopolist—hence the model's name.

Are there any monopolistically competitive industries in the real world? Some industries may be reasonable approximations. For example, the automobile industry in Europe, where a number of major producers (Ford, General Motors, Volkswagon, Renault, Peugeot, Fiat, Volvo—and more recently Nissan) offer substantially different yet nonetheless competing automobiles, may be fairly well described by monopolistically competitive assumptions. The main appeal of the monopolistic competition model is not, however, its realism, but is simplicity. As we will see in the next section of this chapter, the monopolistic competition model gives us a very clear view of how economies of scale can give rise to mutually beneficial trade.

Before we can examine trade, however, we need to develop a basic model of monopolistic competition. Let us therefore imagine an industry consisting of a number of firms. These firms produce differentiated products—that is, goods that are not exactly the same but that are substitutes for one another. Each firm is therefore a monopolist in the sense that it is the only firm producing its particular good, but the demand for its good depends on the number of other similar products available and on the prices of other firms in the industry.

Assumptions of the Model. We begin by describing the demand facing a typical monopolistically competitive firm. In general, we would expect a firm to sell more the larger the total demand for its industry's product and the higher the prices charged by its rivals. On the other hand, we expect the firm to sell less the greater the number of firms in the industry and the higher its own price. A particular equation for the demand facing a firm that has these properties is[2]

$$X = S \times [1/n - b \times (P - \overline{P})], \qquad \textbf{(6-5)}$$

where X is the firm's sales, S is the total sales of the industry, n the number of firms in the industry, P the price charged by the firm itself, and $\overline{P}$ the average price charged by its competitors. Equation (6-5) may be given the following intuitive justification: if all firms charge the same price, each will have a market share $1/n$. A firm charging more than the average of other firms will have a smaller market share, a firm charging less a larger share.[3]

It is helpful to assume that total industry sales S are unaffected by the average price $\overline{P}$ charged by firms in the industry. That is, we assume that firms can gain customers only at each others' expense. This is an unrealistic assumption, but it simplifies the analysis and helps focus on the competition among firms. In particular, it means that S is a measure of the size of the market and that if all firms charge the same price, each sells S/n units.

[2] Equation (6-5) can be derived from a model in which consumers have different preferences and firms produce varieties tailored to particular segments of the market. See Stephen Salop, "Monopolistic Competition with Outside Goods," *Bell Journal of Economics* 10 (1979), pp. 141–156 for a development of this approach.

[3] Equation (6-5) may be rewritten as $X = S/n - S \times b \times (P - \overline{P})$. If $P = \overline{P}$, this reduces to $X = S/n$. If $P > \overline{P}$, $X < S/n$, while if $P < \overline{P}$, $X > S/n$.

Next we turn to the costs of a typical firm. Here we simply assume that total and average costs of a typical firm are described by (6-3) and (6-4).

Market Equilibrium. To model the behavior of this monopolistically competitive industry, we will assume that all firms in this industry are *symmetric*—that is, the demand function and cost function are identical for all firms (even though they are producing and selling somewhat differentiated products). When the individual firms are symmetric, the state of the industry can be described without enumerating the features of all firms in detail: all we really need to know to describe the industry is how many firms there are and what price the typical firm charges. To analyze the industry, for example to assess the effects of international trade, we need to determine the number of firms n and the average price they charge $\overline{P}$. Once we have a method for determining n and $\overline{P}$, we can ask how they are affected by international trade.

Our method for determining n and $\overline{P}$ involves three steps. (1) First, we derive a relationship between the number of firms and the *average cost* of a typical firm. We show that this relationship is upward-sloping; that is, the more firms there are, the lower the output of each firm, and thus the higher its cost per unit of output. (2) We next show the relationship between the number of firms and the price each firm charges, which must equal $\overline{P}$ in equilibrium. We show that this relationship is downward-sloping: the more firms there are, the more intense is competition among firms, and as a result the lower the prices they charge. (3) Finally, we argue that when the price exceeds average cost additional firms will enter the industry, while when the price is less than average cost firms will exit. So in the long run the number of firms is determined by the intersection of the curve that relates average cost to n and the curve that relates price to n.

1. *The number of firms and average cost.* As a first step toward determining n and $\overline{P}$, we ask how the average cost of a typical firm depends on the number of firms in the industry. Since all firms are symmetric in this model, in equilibrium they will all charge the same price. But when all firms charge the same price, so that $P = \overline{P}$, equation (6-5) tells us that $X = S/n$—that is, each firm's output is a share $1/n$ of the total industry sales. But we saw in equation (6-4) that average cost depends inversely on a firm's output. We therefore conclude that average cost depends on the size of the market and the number of firms in the industry:

$$AC = F/X + c = n \times F/S + c. \qquad \textbf{(6-6)}$$

Equation (6-6) tells us that other things equal, *the more firms there are in the industry the higher is average cost.* The reason is that the more firms there are, the less each firm produces. For example, imagine an industry with total sales of 1 million widgets annually. If there are five firms in the industry, each will sell 200,000 annually. If there are ten firms, each will sell only 100,000, and therefore each firm will have higher average cost. The upward-sloping relationship between n and average cost is shown as CC in Figure 6-3.

2. *The number of firms and the price.* Meanwhile, the price the typical firm charges also depends on the number of firms in the industry. In general, we would expect that the more firms there are, the more intense will be the competition among them, and hence the lower the price. This turns out to be true in this model, but proving it takes a moment. The basic trick is to show that each firm faces a straight-line demand

FIGURE 6-3
Equilibrium in a monopolistically competitive market.
The number of firms in a monopolistically competitive market, and the prices they charge, are determined by two relationships. On one side, the more firms there are, the more intensely they compete, and hence the lower is the industry price. This relationship is represented by *PP*. On the other side, the more firms there are, the less each firm sells and therefore the higher is its average cost. This relationship is represented by *CC*. If price exceeds average cost, the industry will be making profits and additional firms will enter the industry; if price is less than average cost, the industry will be incurring losses and firms will leave the industry. The equilibrium price and number of firms occurs when price equals average cost, at the intersection of *PP* and *CC*.

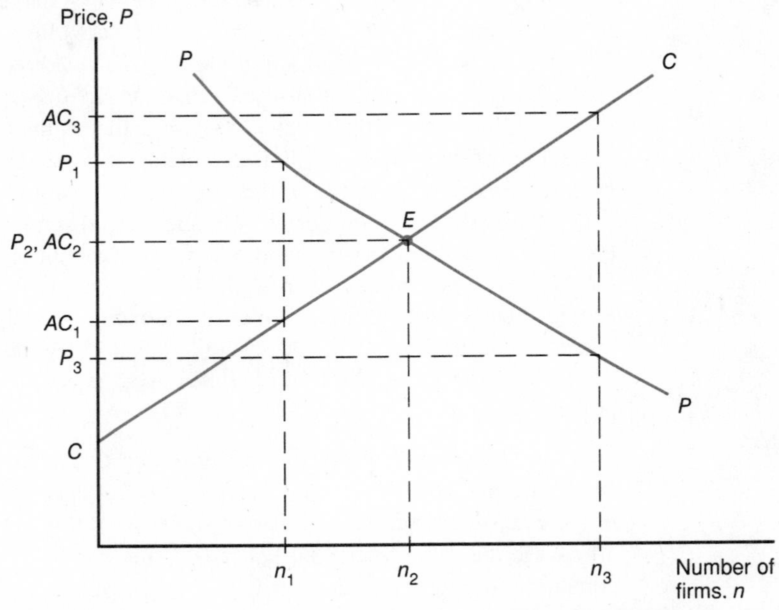

curve of the form we showed in equation (6-1), and then to use equation (6-2) to determine prices.

First recall that in the monopolistic competition model firms are assumed to take each others' prices as given—that is, each firm ignores the possibility that if it changes its price other firms will also change theirs. If each firm treats $\overline{P}$ as given, we can rewrite the demand curve (6-5) in the form

$$X = (S/n + S \times b \times \overline{P}) - S \times b \times P, \qquad \textbf{(6-7)}$$

where b is the parameter in equation (6-5) that measured the sensitivity of each firm's market share to the price it charges. Now this is in the same form as (6-1), with $S/n + S \times b \times \overline{P}$ in place of the constant term A and $S \times b$ in place of the slope coefficient B. So we can plug these values back into the formula for marginal revenue (6-2), which gives us a marginal revenue for a typical firm of

$$MR = P - X/(S \times b). \qquad \textbf{(6-8)}$$

Profit-maximizing firms will set marginal revenue equal to their marginal cost c, so that

$$MR = P - X/(S \times b) = c,$$

which can be rearranged to give the following equation for the price charged by a typical firm:

$$P = c + X/(S \times b). \qquad \textbf{(6-9)}$$

We have already noted, however, that if all firms charge the same price, each will sell an amount $X = S/n$. Plugging this back into (6-9) gives us a relationship between the number of firms and the price each firm charges:

$$P = c + 1/(b \times n). \qquad \textbf{(6-10)}$$

Equation (6-10) says algebraically that *the more firms there are in the industry, the lower the price each firm will charge.* Equation (6-10) is shown in Figure 6-3 as the downward-sloping curve *PP*.

3. *The equilibrium number of firms.* Let us now ask what Figure 6-3 means. We have summarized an industry by two curves. The downward-sloping curve *PP* shows that the more firms there are in the industry, the lower the price each firm will charge. This makes sense: the more firms there are, the more competition each firm faces. The upward-sloping curve *CC* tells us that the more firms there are in the industry, the higher the average cost of each firm. This also makes sense: if the number of firms increases, each firm will sell less, so firms will not be able to move as far down their average cost curve.

The two schedules intersect at point E, corresponding to the number of firms n_2. The significance of n_2 is that it is the *zero-profit* number of firms in the industry. When there are n_2 firms in the industry, their profit-maximizing price is P_2, which is exactly equal to their average cost AC_2.

What we will now argue is that in the long run the number of firms in the industry tends to move toward n_2, so that point E describes the industry's long-run equilibrium.

To see why, suppose that n were less than n_2, say n_1. Then the price charged by firms would be P_1, while their average cost would be only AC_1. Thus firms would be making monopoly profits. Conversely, suppose that n were greater than n_2, say n_3. Then firms would charge only the price P_3, while their average cost would be AC_3, firms would be suffering losses.

Over time, firms will enter an industry that is profitable, exit one in which they lose money. The number of firms will rise over time if it is less than n_2, fall if it is greater. This means that n_2 is the equilibrium number of firms in the industry and P_2 the equilibrium price.[4]

We have now developed a model of a monopolistically competitive industry in which we can determine the equilibrium number of firms and the average price that firms charge. We can use this model to derive some important conclusions about the role of economies of scale in international trade. But before we do, we should take a moment to note some limitations of the monopolistic competition model.

[4] This analysis slips past a slight problem: the number of firms in an industry must, of course, be a whole number like 5 or 8. What if n_2 turns out to equal 6.37? The answer is that there will be 6 firms in the industry, all making small monopoly profits, but not challenged by new entrants because everyone knows that a seven-firm industry would lose money. In most examples of monopolistic competition, this whole-number or ''integer constraint'' problem turns out not to be very important, and we ignore it here.

LIMITATIONS OF THE MONOPOLISTIC COMPETITION MODEL

The monopolistic competition model captures certain key elements of markets where there are economies of scale and thus imperfect competition. However, few industries are well described by monopolistic competition. Instead, the most common market structure is one of small-group oligopoly, where only a few firms are actively engaged in competition. In this situation the key assumption of the monopolistic competition model, which is that each firm will behave as if it were a true monopolist, is likely to break down. Instead, firms will be aware that their actions influence the actions of other firms and will take this interdependence into account.

Two kinds of behavior arise in the general oligopoly setting but are excluded by assumption from the monopolistic competition model. The first is *collusive* behavior. Each firm may keep its price higher than the apparent profit-maximizing level as part of an understanding that other firms will do the same; since each firm's profits are higher if its competitors charge high prices, such an understanding can raise the profits of all the firms (at the expense of consumers). Collusive price-setting behavior may be managed through explicit agreements (illegal in the United States) or through tacit coordination strategies, such as allowing one firm to act as a price leader for the industry.

Firms may also engage in *strategic* behavior; that is, they may do things that seem to lower profits, but that affect the behavior of competitors in a desirable way. For example a firm may build extra capacity not to use it but to deter potential rivals from entering its industry.

These possibilities for both collusive and strategic behavior make the analysis of oligopoly a complex matter. There is no one generally accepted model of oligopoly behavior, which makes modeling trade in oligopolistic industries problematic.

The monopolistic competition approach to trade is attractive because it avoids these complexities. Even though it may leave out some features of the real world, the monopolistic competition model is widely accepted as a way to provide at least a first cut at the role of economies of scale in international trade.

Monopolistic Competition and Trade

Underlying the application of the monopolistic competition model to trade is the idea that trade increases market size. In industries where there are economies of scale, both the variety of goods that a country can produce and the scale of its production are constrained by the size of the market. By trading with each other, and therefore forming an integrated world market that is bigger than any individual national market, nations are able to loosen these constraints. Each country can specialize in producing a narrower range of products than it would in the absence of trade; yet by buying goods that it does not make from other countries, each nation can simultaneously increase the variety of goods available to its consumers. As a result, trade offers an opportunity for mutual gain even when countries do not differ in their resources or technology.

Suppose, for example, that there are two countries, each with an annual market for 1 million automobiles. By trading with each other, these countries can create a combined market of 2 million autos. In this combined market, more varieties of automobiles can be produced, at lower average costs, than in either market alone.

The monopolistic competition model can be used to show how trade improves the trade-off between scale and variety that individual nations face. We will begin by showing how a larger market leads, in the monopolistic competition model, to both a lower average price and the availability of a greater variety of goods. Applying this result to international trade, we observe that trade creates a world market larger than any of the national markets that comprise it. Integrating markets through international trade therefore has the same effects as growth of a market within a single country.

THE EFFECTS OF INCREASED MARKET SIZE

The number of firms in a monopolistically competitive industry and the prices they charge are affected by the size of the market. In larger markets there usually will be both more firms and more sales per firm; consumers in a large market will be offered both lower prices and a greater variety of products than consumers in small markets.

To see this in the context of our model, look again at the *CC* curve in Figure 6-3, which showed that average costs per firm are higher the more firms there are in the industry. The definition of the *CC* curve is given by equation (6-6):

$$AC = F/X + c = n \times F/S + c.$$

Examining this equation, we see that an increase in total sales *S* will reduce average costs for any given number of firms *n*. The reason is that if the market grows while the number of firms is held constant, sales per firm will increase and the average cost of each firm will therefore decline. Thus if we compare two markets, one with higher *S* than the other, the *CC* curve in the larger market will be below that in the smaller one.

Meanwhile, the *PP* curve in Figure 6-3, which relates the price charged by firms to the number of firms, does not shift. The definition of that curve is given in equation (6-10):

$$P = c + 1/(b \times n).$$

The size of the market does not enter into this equation, so an increase in *S* does not shift the *PP* curve.

Figure 6-4 uses this information to show the effect of an increase in the size of the market on long-run equilibrium. Initially, equilibrium is at point 1, with a price P_1 and a number of firms n_1. An increase in the size of the market, measured by industry sales *S*, shifts the *CC* curve down from C_1C_1 to C_2C_2, while it has no effect on the *PP* curve. The new equilibrium is at point 2: the number of firms increases from n_1 to n_2, while the price falls from P_1 to P_2.

Clearly, consumers would prefer to be part of a large market rather than a small one. At point 2, a greater variety of products is available at a lower price than at point 1.

GAINS FROM AN INTEGRATED MARKET: A NUMERICAL EXAMPLE

International trade can create a larger market. We can illustrate the effects of trade on prices, scale, and the variety of goods available with a specific numerical example.

Imagine that automobiles are produced by a monopolistically competitive industry. The demand curve facing any given producer of automobiles is described by equation

FIGURE 6-4
Effects of a larger market.
An increase in the size of the market allows each firm, other things equal, to produce more and thus have lower average cost. This is represented by a downward shift in *CC*. The result is a simultaneous increase in the number of firms (and hence in the variety of goods available) and fall in the price of each good.

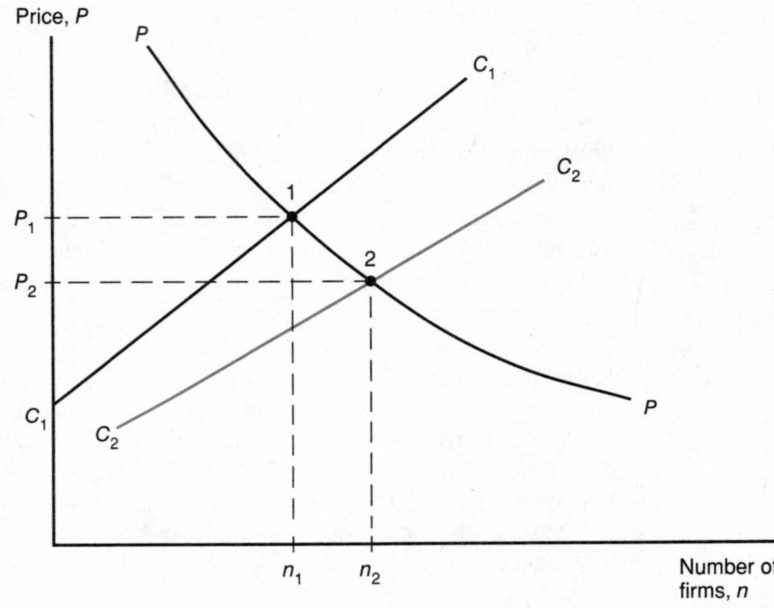

(6-5), with $b = 1/30{,}000$ (this value has no particular significance; it was chosen to make the example come out neatly). Thus the demand facing any one producer is given by

$$X = S \times [1/n - (1/30{,}000) \times (P - \overline{P})],$$

where X is the number of automobiles sold per firm, S the total sales of the industry, n the number of firms, P the price that a firm charges, and $\overline{P}$ the average price of other firms. We also assume that the cost function for producing automobiles is described by equation (6-3), with a fixed cost $F = \$750{,}000{,}000$ and a marginal cost $c = \$5000$ per automobile (again these values are chosen to give nice results). The total cost is

$$C = 750{,}000{,}000 + (5000 \times X).$$

The average cost curve is therefore

$$AC = (750{,}000{,}000/X) + 5000.$$

Now suppose there are two countries, Home and Foreign. Home has annual sales of 900,000 automobiles; Foreign has annual sales of 1.6 million. The two countries are assumed, for the moment, to have the same costs of production.

FIGURE 6-5
Equilibrium in the Home automobile market.
This figure shows the *PP* and *CC* curves corresponding to the example in the text, with a market size of 900,000 automobiles. Equilibrium, determined by the intersection of the *PP* and *CC* curves, occurs with six firms and an industry price of $10,000 per auto.

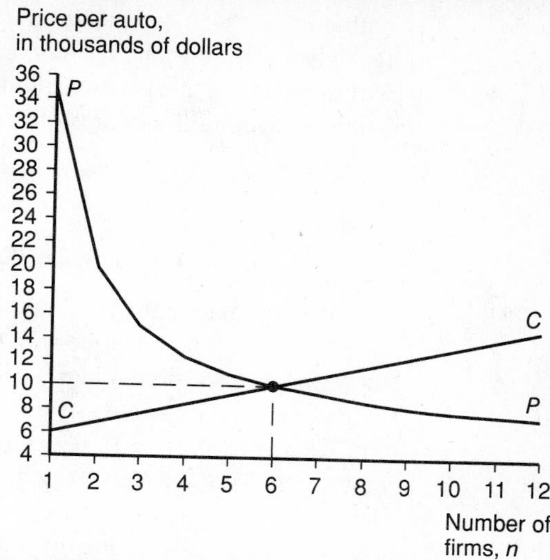

Figure 6-5 shows the *PP* and *CC* curves for the Home auto industry. We find that in the absence of trade, Home would have six automobile firms, selling at a price of $10,000 each. (It is also possible to solve for n and P algebraically, as shown in the Mathematical Postscript to this chapter). To confirm that this is the long-run equilibrium, we need to show both that the pricing equation (6-10) is satisfied and that the price equals average cost.

Substituting the actual values of the marginal cost c, the demand parameter b, and the number of Home firms n into equation (6-10), we find

$$P = \$10{,}000 = c + 1/(b \times n) = \$5000 + 1/[(1/30{,}000) \times 6] = \$5000 + \$5000,$$

so the condition for profit maximization—that marginal revenue equal marginal cost—is satisfied. Each firm sells 900,000 units/6 firms = 150,000 units/firm. Its average cost is therefore

$$AC = (\$750{,}000{,}000/150{,}000) + \$5000 = \$10{,}000.$$

Since the average cost of $10,000 per unit is the same as the price, all monopoly profits have been competed away. Thus 6 firms, selling at a price of $10,000, with each firm producing 150,000 cars, is the long-run equilibrium in the Home market.

What about Foreign? By drawing the *PP* and *CC* curves we find that when the market is for 1.6 million automobiles, the curves intersect at $n = 8$, $P = 8750$. That is, in the absence of trade Foreign's market would support eight firms, each producing 200,000 automobiles, and selling them at a price of $8750. We can again confirm that this solution satisfies the equilibrium conditions:

$$P = \$8750 = c + 1/(b \times n) = \$5000 + 1/[(1/30{,}000) \times 8] = \$5000 + \$3750,$$

and

$$AC = (\$750{,}000{,}000/200{,}000) + \$5000 = \$8750.$$

Now suppose it is possible for Home and Foreign to trade automobiles costlessly with one another. This creates a new, integrated market with total sales of 2.5 million. By drawing the *PP* and *CC* curves one more time, we find that this integrated market will support ten firms, each producing 250,000 cars and selling them at a price of \$8000. The conditions for profit maximization and zero profits are again satisfied:

$$P = \$8000 = c + 1/(b \times n) = \$5000 + 1/[(1/30{,}000) \times 10] = \$5000 + \$3000$$

and

$$AC = (\$750{,}000{,}000/250{,}000) + \$5000 = \$8000.$$

We summarize the results of creating an integrated market in Table 6-2. The table compares each market alone with the integrated market. The integrated market supports more firms, each producing at a larger scale and selling at a lower price, than either national market did on its own.

Clearly everyone is better off as a result of integration. In the larger market, consumers have a wider range of choice, yet each firm produces more and is therefore able to offer its product at a lower price.

To realize these gains from integration, the countries must engage in international trade. To achieve economies of scale, each firm must concentrate its production in one country—either Home or Foreign. Yet it must sell its output to customers in both markets. So each product will be produced in only one country and exported to the other.

ECONOMIES OF SCALE AND COMPARATIVE ADVANTAGE

Our example of a monopolistically competitive industry says little about the pattern of trade that results from economies of scale. The model assumes that the cost of production is the same in both countries and that trade is costless. These assumptions mean that although we know that the integrated market will support ten firms, we cannot say where they will be located. For example, four firms might be in Home and six in Foreign—but it is equally possible, as far as this example goes, that all ten will be in Foreign (or in Home).

To say more than that the market will support ten firms, it is necessary to go behind the partial equilibrium framework that we have considered so far and think about how economies of scale interact with comparative advantage to determine the pattern of international trade.

TABLE 6-2 Hypothetical example of gains from market integration

	Home market, before trade	*Foreign market, before trade*	*Integrated market, after trade*
Total sales of autos	900,000	1,600,000	2,500,000
Number of firms	6	8	10
Sales per firm	150,000	200,000	250,000
Average cost	10.00	8.75	8.00
Price	10.00	8.75	8.00

Let us therefore now imagine a world economy consisting, as usual, of our two countries Home and Foreign. Each of these countries has two factors of production, capital and labor. We assume that Home has a higher overall capital-labor ratio than Foreign, that is, that Home is the capital-abundant country. Let's also imagine that there are two industries, manufactures and food, with manufactures the more capital-intensive industry.

The difference between this model and the factor proportions model of Chapter 4 is that we now suppose that manufactures is not a perfectly competitive industry producing a homogeneous product. Instead, it is a monopolistically competitive industry in which a number of firms all produce differentiated products. *Because of economies of scale, neither country is able to produce the full range of manufactured products by itself; thus, although both countries may produce some manufactures, they will be producing different things.* The monopolistically competitive nature of the manufactures industry makes an important difference to the trade pattern, a difference that can best be seen by looking at what would happen if manufactures were *not* a monopolistically competitive sector.

If manufactures were *not* a differentiated product sector, we know from Chapter 4 what the trade pattern would look like. Because Home is capital-abundant and manufactures capital-intensive, Home would have a larger relative supply of manufactures and would therefore export manufactures and import food. Schematically, we can represent this trade pattern with a diagram like Figure 6-6. The length of the arrows indicates the value of trade in each direction; the figure shows that Home would export manufactures equal in value to the food it imports.

If we assume that manufactures is a monopolistically competitive sector (each firm's products are differentiated from other firms'), Home will still be a *net* exporter of manufactures and an importer of food. However, Foreign firms in the manufactures sector will produce products different from those that Home firms produce. Because some Home consumers will prefer Foreign varieties, Home, although running a trade surplus in manufactures, will import as well as export within the industry. With manufactures monopolistically competitive, then, the pattern of trade will look like Figure 6-7.

We can think of world trade in a monopolistic competition model as consisting of two parts. There will be two-way trade *within* the manufacturing sector. This exchange of manufactures for manufactures is called **intraindustry trade.** The remainder of trade is an exchange of manufactures for food called **interindustry trade.**

Notice these four points about this pattern of trade:

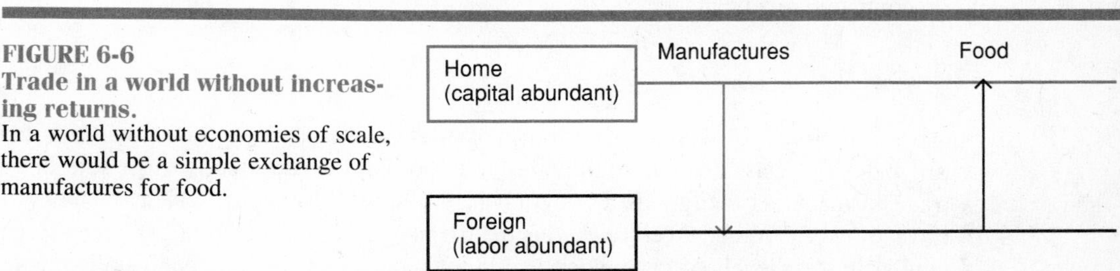

FIGURE 6-6
Trade in a world without increasing returns.
In a world without economies of scale, there would be a simple exchange of manufactures for food.

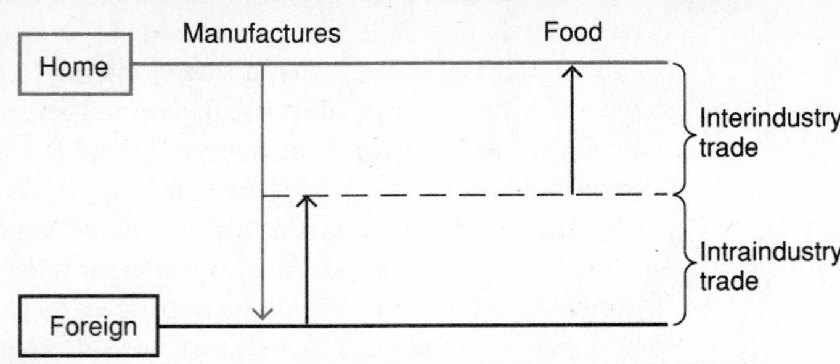

FIGURE 6-7
Trade with increasing returns and monopolistic competition.
If manufactures is a monopolistically competitive industry, Home and Foreign will produce differentiated products. As a result, even if Home is a net exporter of manufactured goods, it will import as well as export manufactures, giving rise to intraindustry trade.

1. *Interindustry* trade reflects comparative advantage. The pattern of interindustry trade is that Home, the capital-abundant country, is a net exporter of capital-intensive manufactures and a net importer of labor-intensive food. So comparative advantage continues to be a major part of the trade story.

2. *Intraindustry* trade does *not* reflect comparative advantage. Even if the countries had the same overall capital-labor ratio, their firms would continue to produce differentiated products and the demand of consumers for products made abroad would continue to generate intraindustry trade. It is economies of scale that keep each country from producing the full range of products for itself; thus economies of scale can be an independent source of international trade.

3. The pattern of intraindustry trade itself is unpredictable. We have not said anything about which country produces which goods within the manufactures sector because there is nothing in the model to tell us. All we know is that the countries will produce different products. Since history and accident determine the details of the trade pattern, an unpredictable component of the trade pattern is an inevitable feature of a world where economies of scale are important. Notice, however, that the unpredictability is not total. While the precise pattern of intraindustry trade within the manufactures sector is arbitrary, the pattern of interindustry trade between manufactures and food is determined by underlying differences between countries.

4. The relative importance of intraindustry and interindustry trade depends on how similar countries are. If Home and Foreign are similar in their capital-labor ratios, then there will be little interindustry trade, and intraindustry trade, based ultimately on economies of scale, will be dominant. On the other hand, if the capital-labor ratios are very different, so that, for example, Foreign specializes completely in food production, there will be no intraindustry trade based on economies of scale. All trade will be based on comparative advantage.

THE SIGNIFICANCE OF INTRAINDUSTRY TRADE

About one-fourth of world trade consists of two-way exchanges of goods within standard industrial classifications. Intraindustry trade plays a particularly large role in the trade in manufactured goods among advanced industrial nations, which accounts for most of world trade. Over time, the industrial countries have become increasingly similar in their levels of technology and in the availability of capital and skilled labor.

Since the major trading nations have become similar in technology and resources, there is often no clear comparative advantage within an industry, and much of international trade therefore takes the form of two-way exchanges within industries—probably driven in large part by economies of scale—rather than interindustry specialization driven by comparative advantage.

Table 6-3 shows measures of the importance of intraindustry trade for a number of U.S. manufacturing industries in 1989. The measure shown is intraindustry trade/total trade. The measure ranges from 0.99 for power-generating equipment—an industry in which U.S. exports and imports are nearly equal—to 0.00 for footwear, an industry in which the U.S. has large imports but virtually no exports. The measure would be zero for an industry in which the United States was only an exporter or only an importer, not both; it would be one in an industry for which U.S. exports exactly equaled U.S. imports.

Table 6-3 shows that in many industries a large part of trade is intraindustry rather than interindustry. The industries are ranked by the relative importance of intraindustry trade, those with higher intraindustry trade first. Industries with high levels of intraindustry trade tend to be sophisticated manufactured goods, such as chemicals, pharmaceuticals, and power-generating equipment. These goods are exported principally by advanced nations and are probably subject to important economies of scale in production. At the other end of the scale, the industries with very little intraindustry trade are typically labor-intensive products, such as footwear and apparel. These are goods that the U.S. imports primarily from less-developed countries, where comparative advantage is clear-cut and is the primary determinant of U.S. trade with these countries.

WHY INTRAINDUSTRY TRADE MATTERS

Table 6-3 shows that a sizeable part of international trade is intraindustry trade rather than the interindustry trade we studied in Chapters 2 through 5. But does the importance of intraindustry trade change any of our conclusions?

First, intraindustry trade produces extra gains from international trade, over and above those from comparative advantage, because intraindustry trade allows countries

TABLE 6-3 Indexes of intraindustry trade for U.S. industries, 1989

Industry	Index
Power-generating equipment	0.99
Office machines	0.98
Electric machinery	0.89
Inorganic chemicals	0.88
Organic chemicals	0.81
Medicines and pharmaceutical products	0.73
Telecommunications equipment	0.53
Road vehicles	0.53
Iron and steel	0.48
Clothing and accessories	0.15
Footwear	0.00

to benefit from larger markets. As we have seen, by engaging in intraindustry trade a country can simultaneously reduce the number of products it produces *and* increase the variety of goods available to domestic consumers. By producing fewer varieties, a country can produce each at larger scale, with higher productivity and lower costs. At the same time, consumers benefit from the increased range of choice. In our numerical example of the gains from integrating a market, Home consumers found that intraindustry trade expanded their range of choice from six automobile models to ten even as it reduced the price of autos from $10,000 to $8000. As the case study of the North American auto industry indicates (p. 133), the advantages of creating an integrated industry in two countries can be substantial in reality as well.

In our earlier analysis of the distribution of gains from trade (Chapters 3 and 4), we were pessimistic about the prospects that everyone will benefit from trade, even though international trade could potentially raise everyone's income. In the models discussed earlier, trade had all its effects through changes in relative prices, which in turn have very strong effects on the distribution of income.

Suppose, however, that intraindustry trade is the dominant source of gains from trade. This will happen (1) when countries are similar in their relative factor supplies, so that there is not much interindustry trade, and (2) when scale economies and product differentiation are important, so that the gains from larger scale and increased choice are large. In these circumstances the income distribution effects of trade will be small and there will be substantial extra gains from intraindustry trade. The result may well be that despite the effects of trade on income distribution, everyone gains from trade.

When will this be most likely to happen? Intraindustry trade tends to be prevalent between countries that are similar in their capital-labor ratios, skill levels, and so on. Thus, intraindustry trade will be dominant between countries at a similar level of economic development. Gains from this trade will be large when economies of scale are strong and products are highly differentiated. This is more characteristic of sophisticated manufactured goods than of raw materials or more traditional sectors (such as textiles or footwear). Trade without serious income distribution effects, then, is most likely to happen in manufactures trade between advanced industrial countries.

This conclusion is borne out by postwar experience, particularly in Western Europe. In 1957 the major countries of continental Europe established a free trade area in manufactured goods, the Common Market, or European Economic Community (EEC). (The United Kingdom entered the EEC later, in 1973.) The result was a rapid growth of trade: trade within the EEC grew twice as fast as world trade as a whole during the 1960s. One might have expected this rapid growth in trade to produce substantial dislocations and political problems. The growth in trade, however, was almost entirely intraindustry rather than interindustry; drastic economic dislocation did not occur. Instead of, say, workers in France's electrical machinery industry being hurt while those in Germany's gained, workers in both sectors gained from the increased efficiency of the integrated European industry. The result was that the growth in trade within Europe presented far fewer social and political problems than anyone anticipated.

There is both a good and a bad side to this favorable view of intraindustry trade. The good side is that under some circumstances trade is relatively easy to live with and therefore relatively easy to support politically. The bad side is that trade between very different countries or where scale economies and product differentiation are not important remains politically problematic. In fact, the progressive liberalization of trade that characterized the thirty-year period from 1950 to 1980 was primarily concentrated on trade in manufactures among the advanced nations, as we will see in Chapter 10. If progress on other kinds of trade is important, the past record does not give us much encouragement.

Case Study

INTRAINDUSTRY TRADE IN ACTION: THE NORTH AMERICAN AUTO PACT

An unusually clear-cut example of the role of economies of scale in generating beneficial international trade is provided by the growth in automotive trade between the United States and Canada during the second half of the 1960s. While the case does not fit our model exactly, it does show that the basic concepts we have developed are useful in the real world.

Before 1965, tariff protection by Canada and the United States produced a Canadian auto industry that was largely self-sufficient, neither importing nor exporting much. The Canadian industry was controlled by the same firms as the U.S. industry—a departure from our model, since we have not yet examined the role of multinational firms—but these firms found it cheaper to have largely separate production systems than to pay the tariffs. Thus the Canadian industry was in effect a miniature version of the U.S. industry, at about one-tenth the scale.

The Canadian subsidiaries of U.S. firms found that small scale was a substantial disadvantage. This was partly because Canadian plants had to be smaller than their U.S. counterparts. Perhaps more important, U.S. plants could often be "dedicated"—that is, devoted to producing a single model or component—while Canadian plants had to produce several different things, requiring the plants to shut down periodically to change over from producing one item to producing another, to hold larger inventories, to use less specialized machinery, and so on. The Canadian auto industry had a labor productivity about 30 percent lower than that of the United States.

In an effort to remove these problems, the United States and Canada agreed in 1964 to establish a free trade area in automobiles (subject to certain restrictions). This allowed the auto companies to reorganize their production. Canadian subsidiaries of the auto firms sharply cut the number of products made in Canada. For example, General Motors cut in half the number of models assembled in Canada. The overall level of Canadian production and employment was, however, maintained. This was achieved by importing from the United States products no longer made in Canada and exporting the products Canada continued to make. In 1962, Canada exported $16 million worth of automotive products to the United States while importing $519 million worth. By 1968 the numbers were $2.4 and $2.9 billion, respectively. In other words, both exports and imports increased sharply: intraindustry trade in action.

The gains seem to have been substantial. By the early 1970s the Canadian industry was comparable to the U.S. industry in productivity.

Dumping

The monopolistic competition model helps us understand how increasing returns promote international trade. As we noted earlier, however, this model assumes away many of the issues that can arise when firms are imperfectly competitive. Although it recognizes that imperfect competition is a necessary consequence of economies of scale, the monopolistic competition analysis does not focus on the possible consequences of imperfect competition itself for international trade.

In reality, imperfect competition has some important consequences for international trade. The most striking of these is that firms do not necessarily charge the same price for goods that are exported and those that are sold to domestic buyers.

THE ECONOMICS OF DUMPING

In imperfectly competitive markets, firms sometimes charge one price for a good when that good is exported and a different price for the same good when it is sold domestically. In general, the practice of charging different customers different prices is called **price discrimination.** The most common form of price discrimination in international trade is **dumping,** a pricing practice in which a firm charges a lower price for exported goods than it does for the same goods sold domestically. Dumping is a controversial issue in trade policy, where it is widely regarded as an ''unfair'' practice and is subject to special rules and penalties. We will discuss the policy dispute surrounding dumping in Chapter 10. For now, we present some basic economic analysis of the dumping phenomenon.

Dumping can occur only if two conditions are met. First, the industry must be imperfectly competitive, so that firms set prices rather than taking market prices as given. Second, markets must be *segmented,* so that domestic residents cannot easily purchase goods intended for export. Given these conditions, a monopolistic firm may find that it is profitable to engage in dumping.

An example may help to show how dumping can be a profit-maximizing strategy. Imagine a firm that currently sells 1000 units of a good at home and 100 units abroad. Currently selling the good at $20 per unit domestically, it gets only $15 per unit on export sales. One might imagine that the firm would conclude that additional domestic sales are much more profitable than additional exports.

Suppose, however, that to expand sales by one unit, in either market, would require reducing the price by $.01. Reducing the domestic price by a penny, then, would increase sales by one unit—directly adding $19.99 in revenue, but reducing the receipts on the 1000 units that would have sold at the $20 price by $10. So the marginal revenue from the extra unit sold is only $9.99. On the other hand, reducing the price charged to foreign customers and thereby expanding exports by one unit would directly increase revenue by only $14.99. The indirect cost of reduced receipts on the 100 units that would have been sold at the original price, however, would be only $1, so that marginal revenue on export sales would be $13.99. It would therefore be more profitable in this case to expand exports rather than domestic sales, even though the price received on exports is lower.

This example could be reversed, with the incentive being to charge less on domestic than foreign sales. However, price discrimination in favor of exports is more common.

Since international markets are imperfectly integrated due to both transportation costs and protectionist trade barriers, domestic firms usually have a larger share of home markets than they do of foreign markets. This in turn usually means that their foreign sales are more affected by their pricing than their domestic sales. A firm with a 20 percent market share need not cut its price as much to double its sales as a firm with an 80 percent share. So firms typically see themselves as having less monopoly power, and a greater incentive to keep their prices low, on exports than on domestic sales.

Figure 6-8 offers a diagrammatic example of dumping. It shows an industry in which there is a single monopolistic domestic firm. The firm sells in two markets: a domestic market, where it faces the demand curve D_{DOM}, and an export market. In the export market we take the assumption that sales are highly responsive to the price the firm charges to an extreme, assuming the firm can sell as much as it wants at the price P_{FOR}. The horizontal line P_{FOR} is thus the demand curve for sales in the foreign market.

FIGURE 6-8
Dumping.
The figure shows a monopolist that faces a demand curve D_{DOM} for domestic sales, but which can also sell as much as it likes at the export price P_{FOR}. Since an additional unit can always be sold at P_{FOR}, the firm increases output until the marginal cost equals P_{FOR}; this profit-maximizing output is shown as $Q_{MONOPOLY}$. Since the firm's marginal cost is P_{FOR}, it sells output on the domestic market up to the point where marginal revenue equals P_{FOR}; this profit-maximizing level of domestic sales is shown as Q_{DOM}. The rest of its output, $Q_{MONOPOLY} - Q_{DOM}$, is exported.

The price at which domestic consumers demand Q_{DOM} is P_{DOM}. Since $P_{DOM} > P_{FOR}$, the firm sells exports at a lower price than it charges domestic consumers.

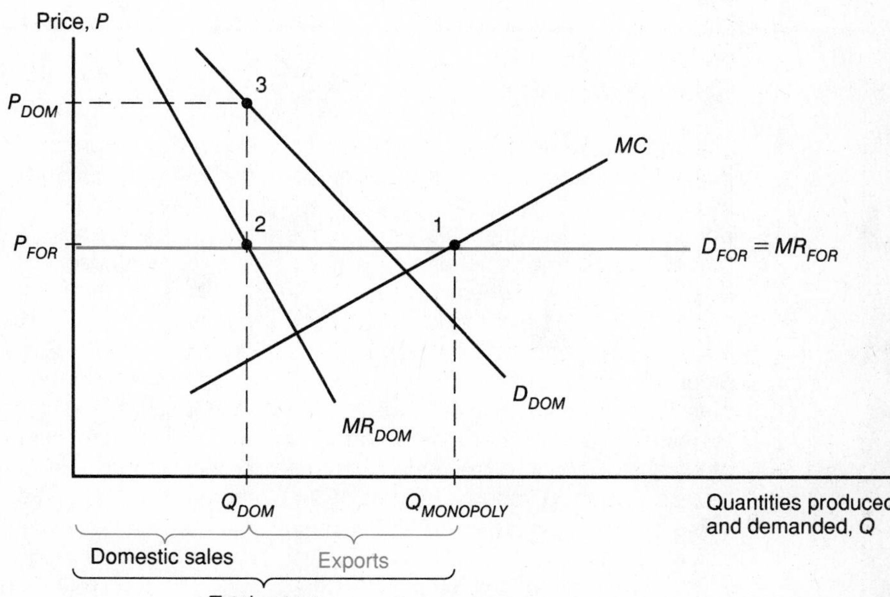

We assume the markets are segmented, so that the firm can charge a higher price for domestically sold goods than it does for exports. *MC* is the marginal cost curve for total output, which can be sold on either market.

To maximize profits, the firm must set marginal revenue equal to marginal cost in *each* market. Marginal revenue on domestic sales is defined by the curve MR_{DOM}, which lies below D_{DOM}. Export sales take place at a constant price P_{FOR}, so the marginal revenue for an additional unit exported is just P_{FOR}. To set marginal cost equal to marginal revenue in both markets it is necessary to produce the quantity $Q_{MONOPOLY}$, to sell Q_{DOM} on the domestic market, and to export $Q_{MONOPOLY} - Q_{DOM}$. The cost of producing an additional unit in this case is equal to P_{FOR}, the marginal revenue from exports, which in turn is equal to the marginal revenue for domestic sales.

The quantity Q_{DOM} will be demanded domestically at a price of P_{DOM}, which is above the export price P_{FOR}. Thus the firm is indeed dumping, selling more cheaply abroad than at home.

In both our numerical example and Figure 6-8, the reason the firm chooses to dump is the difference in the responsiveness of sales to price in the export and domestic markets. In Figure 6-8 we assume the firm can increase exports without cutting its price, so marginal revenue and price coincide on the export market. Domestically, by contrast, increased sales do lower the price. This is an extreme example of the general condition for price discrimination presented in microeconomics courses: firms will price-discriminate when sales are more price-responsive in one market than in another.[5] (In this case we have assumed export demand is infinitely price-responsive.)

[5] The formal condition for price discrimination is that firms will charge lower prices in markets in which they face a higher *elasticity* of demand, where the elasticity is the percentage decrease in sales that results from a 1 percent increase in price. Firms will dump if they perceive a higher elasticity on export sales than on domestic sales.

Reverse Dumping

Our analysis of international price discrimination focuses on the case of dumping, where firms charge a lower price on exports than on domestic sales. This focus reflects several considerations: in practice, this is the usual direction of price discrimination; dumping tends to increase trade, while price discrimination in the other direction tends to reduce it; and accusations of dumping are frequent in international trade disputes, while charges of excessive export prices are not. Nonetheless, there are important cases of "reverse dumping": charging a higher price to foreign customers than domestic.

A notable example of reverse dumping occurred for European luxury automobiles in 1984 and 1985. When the dollar rose sharply against European currencies, European manufacturers such as Volvo and Mercedes chose not to cut their U.S. prices, even though the equivalent dollar prices of their cars in Europe had dropped greatly. Thus a Mercedes could be bought in Germany for as much as 40 percent less than it cost in the United States. The gap was so large that many U.S. buyers started purchasing cars in Europe and shipping them home. The situation probably could not have gone on forever, but it was eventually resolved through a decline in the dollar rather than a change in pricing policy.

Dumping is widely regarded as an unfair practice in international trade. There is no good economic justification for regarding dumping as particularly harmful, but U.S. trade law prohibits foreign firms from dumping in our market and automatically imposes tariffs when such dumping is discovered.

The situation shown in Figure 6-8 is simply an extreme version of a wider class of situations in which firms have an incentive to sell exports for a lower price than the price they charge domestic customers.

Case Study

ANTIDUMPING AS PROTECTIONISM

In the United States and a number of other countries, dumping is regarded as an unfair competitive practice. Firms that claim to have been injured by foreign firms who dump their products in the domestic market at low prices can appeal, through a quasi-judicial procedure, to the Commerce Department for relief. If their complaint is ruled valid—and from 1980 to 1989 54 percent of foreign companies accused of dumping were deemed guilty—an "antidumping duty" is imposed, equal to the calculated difference between the actual and "fair" price of imports.

Economists have never been very happy with the idea of singling dumping out as a prohibited practice. For one thing, price discrimination between markets may be a perfectly legitimate business strategy—like the discounts that airlines offer to students, senior citizens, and travelers who are willing to stay over a weekend. Also, the legal definition of dumping deviates substantially from the economic definition. Since it is often difficult to prove that foreign firms charge higher prices to domestic than export customers, the United States and other nations instead often try to calculate a supposed fair price based on estimates of foreign production costs. This "fair price" rule can interfere with perfectly normal business practices: a firm may well be willing to sell a product for a loss while it is lowering its costs through experience or breaking into a new market.

In spite of almost universal negative assessments from economists, however, formal complaints about dumping have been filed with growing frequency since about 1970. Is this just cynical abuse of the law, or does it reflect a real increase in the importance of dumping? The answer may be a little of both.

Why may dumping have increased? Because of the uneven pace at which countries have opened up their markets. Since 1970 trade liberalization and deregulation have opened up international competition in a number of previously sheltered industries. For example, it used to be taken for granted that telephone companies would buy their equipment from domestic manufacturers. With the breakup of AT&T in the United States and the privatization of phone companies in other countries, this is no longer the case everywhere. But in Japan and several European countries the old rules still apply. It is not surprising that the manufacturers of telephone equipment in these countries would continue to charge high prices at home while offering lower prices to customers in the United States—or at least that they would be accused of doing so.

At the time of writing, the United States had imposed antidumping duties on European steel exports, threatening to undermine trade negotiations already in progress. And Japan, usually the party accused of dumping, had turned accuser, imposing duties on allegedly dumped steel from China.

RECIPROCAL DUMPING

The analysis of dumping suggests that price discrimination can actually give rise to international trade. Suppose there are two monopolies, each producing the same good, one in Home and one in Foreign. To simplify the analysis, assume that these two firms have the same marginal cost. Suppose also that there are some costs of transportation between the two markets, so that if the firms charge the same price there will be no trade. In the absence of trade, each firm's monopoly would be uncontested.

If we introduce the possibility of dumping, however, trade may emerge. Each firm will limit the quantity it sells in its home market, recognizing that if it tries to sell more it will drive down the price on its existing domestic sales. If a firm can sell a little bit in the other market, however, it will add to its profits even if the price is lower than in the domestic market, because the negative effect on the price of existing sales will fall on the other firm, not on itself. So each firm has an incentive to ''raid'' the other

A Concrete Example of Dumping

A particularly clear-cut example of dumping in practice, and of the conflict between political and economic analysis, involves U.S. imports of cement.

The cement industry has traditionally been marked by strong collusion among producers that keeps prices well above marginal production cost. This is true in the United States as well as other countries. In the United States, however, the combination of strong antitrust enforcement and a large national market has made the cement industry more competitive than elsewhere. Thus cement is generally cheaper in the United States than in other countries.

Nonetheless, foreign producers find it profitable to sell cement in the U.S. market. Japanese firms sell cement in California; Venezuelan and Mexican firms sell it in Florida.

During 1990 and 1991 the U.S. cement industry filed antidumping suits against firms from all three nations and won its cases easily: there was no question that foreign firms were selling cement at lower prices than they charged at home, and that the imports were hurting U.S. producers.

But was the decision in the interests of the United States as a whole? Why should the United States refuse to accept an offer of cheap imports, that is, of more favorable terms of trade, regardless of the motive? In Chapter 10 we will consider some reasons why protecting certain industries can raise welfare, but it is safe to say that cement production fits none of the criteria. In fact, the motivation for the antidumping charges may even have been slightly sinister: large firms that own both cement and concrete plants may have been trying to squeeze out smaller competitors who use imported cement to make concrete.

market, selling a few units at a price that (net of transportation costs) is lower than the home market price but still above marginal cost.

If both firms do this, however, the result will be the emergence of trade even though there was (by assumption) no initial difference in the price of the good in the two markets, and even though there are some transportation costs. Even more peculiarly, there will be two-way trade in the same product. For example, a cement plant in country A might be shipping cement to country B while a cement plant in B is doing the reverse. The situation in which dumping leads to two-way trade in the same product is known as **reciprocal dumping.**[6]

This may seem like a strange case, and it is admittedly probably rare in international trade for exactly identical goods to be shipped in both directions at once. However, the reciprocal dumping effect probably tends to increase the volume of trade in goods that are not quite identical.

Is such peculiar and seemingly pointless trade socially desirable? The answer is ambiguous. It is obviously wasteful to ship the same good, or close substitutes, back and forth when transportation is costly. However, notice that the emergence of reciprocal dumping in our story eliminates what were initially pure monopolies, leading to some competition. The increased competition represents a benefit that may offset the waste of resources in transportation. The net effect of such peculiar trade on a nation's economic welfare is therefore uncertain.

External Economies and International Trade

In the monopolistic competition model of trade it is presumed that the economies of scale that give rise to international trade occur at the level of the individual firm. That is, the larger any particular firm's output of a product, the lower its average cost. The inevitable result of such economies of scale at the level of the firm is imperfect competition, which in turn allows such practices as dumping.

As we pointed out early in this chapter, however, not all scale economies apply at the level of the individual firm. For a variety of reasons, it is often the case that concentrating production of an industry in one or a few locations reduces the industry's costs, even if the individual firms in the industry remain small. For example, a geographically concentrated industry may provide a local market for a greater variety of specialized services that support the industry's operations or for a larger and more flexible market in specialized kinds of labor. The advantages of having a local concentration of firms play an obvious role in determining the location of many kinds of economic activity within the United States. Among the better known examples are the concentration of semiconductor manufacturers in California's "Silicon Valley," the similar concentration of computer firms around Route 128 in Massachusetts, and—much bigger than either—the concentration of financial and banking firms in New York. It is probable that similar factors explain persistent national advantages in industries for which there is no obvious advantage in resources—for example, Swiss exports of watches.

[6] The possibility of reciprocal dumping was first noted by James Brander, "Intraindustry Trade in Identical Commodities," *Journal of International Economics* 11 (1981), pp. 1–14.

Examples of External Economies

It is often difficult to disentangle the roles of external economies and comparative advantage in leading countries to become exporters in particular industries. For example, Italy has a strong world market position in fashionable clothing and accessories, based on Milan's role as a fashion center. Some of that role is clearly self-reinforcing: the cluster of designers supports specialized services like dressmaking and modeling, and the reputation of Milan as a fashion center is itself an asset that leads ambitious designers to settle there. Yet one might argue that Italy's national character and interests would have guaranteed a strong fashion position even without the historical accidents that created the Milan scene. There are, however, a number of well-documented cases of external economies at work. Here we briefly describe three examples.

Our first example is not strictly about international trade; it concerns the strong localization of the production of carpets in the United States. (It is relevant, however, since the United States covers such a large area that there is not much difference between interregional trade in the United States and international trade within Europe.) Most carpet manufacture in the United States takes place in the vicinity of the small Georgia city of Dalton. Economies of scale at the level of the firm are not large: the Dalton area supports several dozen manufacturers. Nor is there any obvious advantage in resources or costs that would make Dalton stand out over many other possible sites. Why, then, has Dalton become the carpet capital?

It turns out that Dalton has a long tradition in handicraft production of "tufted" sweaters, shawls, bed linens, and so on that began when a teenager named Catherine Evans made a tufted bedspread as a wedding gift in 1895. Before World War II most carpets in the United States were woven, for the most part in the Northeast. After the war, however, a new process for making carpets was developed; this "tufting" method involved running loops of yarn through a woven backing, then cutting the loops. Dalton's base of people experienced in tufting gave it a head start over possible rival sites in this superior new technology, a head start that proved self-reinforcing as the town developed a network of firms that specialized in supplying the backings, dying the yarn, and so on.

Another concentration of a large number of small firms, but this time selling to the international market, may be found in

When economies of scale apply at the level of the industry rather than the firm, they are called *external economies.* External economies, like economies of scale that are internal to firms, may play an important role in international trade, but they are quite different in their effects. For one thing, external economies need not lead to imperfect competition, since it is possible that individual firms may remain small in spite of important advantages to large scale at the industry level. More important for the assessment of trade is the possibility that trade in the presence of external economies may not be beneficial to all countries.

EXTERNAL ECONOMIES AND THE PATTERN OF TRADE

When there are external economies of scale, a country that has large production in some industry will tend, other things equal, to have low costs of producing that good.

the Northern Italian town of Sassuolo. In this case, the product is ceramic tile. Italy is the leading exporter of ceramic tile, accounting for about 60 percent of world exports in the industry; virtually all of these exported tiles come from Sassuolo and vicinity. The ceramic tile industry does not exhibit strong economies of scale at the level of the individual firm. Instead, more than 100 small firms are clustered together in Sassuolo. While there is no Catherine Evans in the history of Sassuolo, in general the story of its origins resembles that of Dalton: a traditional local handicraft industry provided the base of skills that gave the town a head start in developing a modern industry.

If Dalton and Sassuolo sound like relatively small examples (although in each case the industry employs thousands of people), consider London's role as a financial center. London is the main center for international financial transactions within Europe and between Europe and the rest of the world. This is big business: some estimates suggest that Britain may earn $10 billion each year from London's role as an international financial center.

Why is London a great financial center? It is not a cheap or easy place to operate, given high rents and traffic congestion. Nor is it the center of an especially dominant national economy: although Britain was once Europe's industrial leader, its gross domestic product in 1990 was only 66 percent that of Germany and was less than that of either France or Italy. The answer seems to be that financial deals, such as large corporate bond issues, mergers, takeovers, and so on, still require face-to-face contact among the investment bankers and lawyers who put these deals together—which means that financial institutions and the law firms that cater to their needs need to be near each other, and thus that a financial center, once established, tends to be self-perpetuating.

London became a great financial center when Britain was the world's greatest manufacturer and investor—when British investors financed the digging of the Suez Canal, the building of the railroads that opened up Canada's prairies and Argentina's pampas, and the gold rushes in Australia and South Africa. Even though those days are long gone, London is still the best place for European investment bankers to meet each other and their clients, and so its business has expanded along with international capital flows.

This gives rise to an obvious circularity, since a country that can produce a good cheaply will also therefore tend to produce a lot of that good. Strong external economies tend to confirm existing patterns of interindustry trade, whatever their original sources: countries that start out as large producers in certain industries, for whatever reason, tend to remain large producers. They may do so even if some other country could potentially produce the goods more cheaply.

Figure 6-9 illustrates this point. We show the cost of producing a watch as a function of the number of watches produced annually. Two countries are shown: "Switzerland" and "Thailand." The Swiss cost of producing a watch is shown as AC_{SWISS}; the Thai cost as AC_{THAI}. D represents the world demand for watches, which we assume can be satisfied either by Switzerland or by Thailand.

Suppose that the economies of scale in watch production are entirely external to firms, and that since there are no economies of scale at the level of the firm the watch

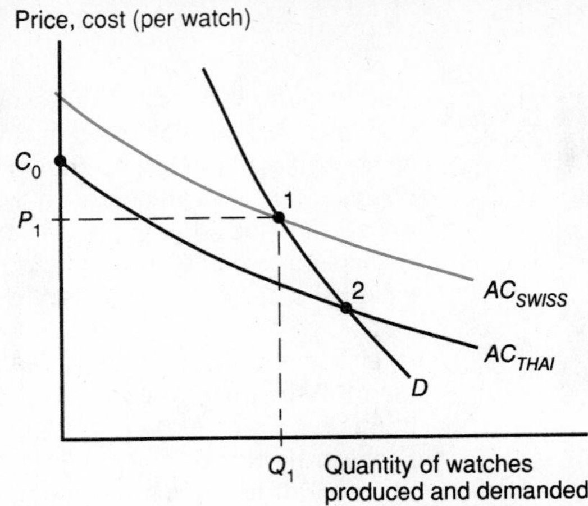

FIGURE 6-9
External economies and specialization.
The average cost curve for Thailand, AC_{THAI}, lies below the average cost curve for Switzerland, AC_{SWISS}. Thus Thailand could potentially supply the world market more cheaply than Switzerland. If the Swiss industry gets established first, however, it may be able to sell watches at the price P_1, which is below the cost C_0 that an individual Thai firm would face if it began production on its own. So a pattern of specialization established by historical accident may persist even when new producers could potentially have lower costs.

industry in each country consists of many small perfectly competitive firms. Competition therefore drives the price of watches down to its average cost.

We assume that the Thai cost curve lies below the Swiss curve, say because Thai wages are lower than Swiss. This means that at any given level of production, Thailand could manufacture watches more cheaply than Switzerland. One might hope that this would always imply that Thailand will in fact supply the world market. Unfortunately, this need not be the case. Suppose that Switzerland, for historical reasons, establishes its watch industry first. Then initially world watch equilibrium will be established at point 1 in Figure 6-9, with Swiss production of Q_1 units per year and a price of P_1. Now introduce the possibility of Thai production. If Thailand could take over the world market, the equilibrium would move to point 2. However, if there is no initial Thai production ($Q = 0$), any individual Thai firm considering manufacture of watches will face a cost of production of C_0. As we have drawn it, this cost is above the price at which the established Swiss industry can produce watches. So although the Thai industry could potentially make watches more cheaply than Switzerland, Switzerland's head start enables it to hold onto the industry.

As this example shows, external economies potentially give a strong role to historical accident in determining who produces what, and may allow established patterns of specialization to persist even when they run counter to comparative advantage.

TRADE AND WELFARE WITH EXTERNAL ECONOMIES

Trade based on external economies has more ambiguous effects on national welfare than either trade based on comparative advantage or trade based on economies of scale at the level of the firm. There may be gains to the world economy from concentrating production in particular industries to realize external economies. On the other hand, there is no guarantee that the right country will produce a good subject to external economies, and it is possible that trade based on external economies may actually leave a country worse off than it would have been in the absence of trade.

An example of how a country can actually be worse off with trade than without is shown in Figure 6-10. In this example, as before, we imagine that Thailand and Switzerland could both manufacture watches, that Thailand could make them more cheaply, but that Switzerland has gotten there first. D_{WORLD} is the world demand for watches, and, given that Switzerland produces the watches, the equilibrium is at point 1. However, we now add to the figure the Thai demand for watches, D_{THAI}. If no trade in watches were allowed and Thailand were forced to be self-sufficient, then the Thai equilibrium would be at point 2. Because of its lower average cost curve, the price of Thai-made watches at point 2, P_2, is actually lower than the price of Swiss-made watches at point 1, P_1.

We have shown a situation in which the price of a good that Thailand imports would actually be lower if there were no trade and the country were forced to produce the good for itself. Clearly in this situation trade leaves the country worse off than it would be in the absence of trade.

There is an incentive in this case for Thailand to protect its potential watch industry from foreign competition. Before concluding that this justifies protectionism, however, we should note that in practice identifying cases like that in Figure 6-10 is far from easy. Indeed, as we will emphasize in Chapters 11 and 12, the difficulty of identifying external economies in practice is one of the main arguments against activist government policies toward trade.

DYNAMIC INCREASING RETURNS

Some of the most important external economies probably arise from the accumulation of knowledge. When an individual firm improves its products or production techniques through experience, other firms are likely to imitate the firm and benefit from its

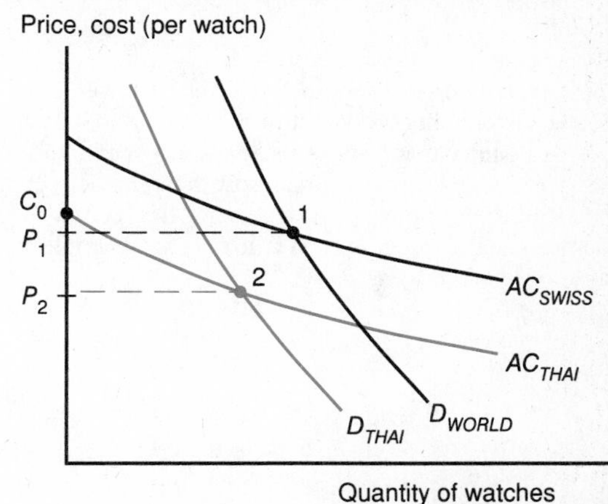

FIGURE 6-10
External economies and losses from trade.
When there are external economies, trade can potentially leave a country worse off than it would be in the absence of trade. In this example, Thailand imports watches from Switzerland, which is able to supply the world market (D_{WORLD}) at a price (P_1) low enough to block entry by Thai producers. Yet if Thailand were to block all trade in watches, it would be able to supply its domestic market (D_{THAI}) at the lower price P_2.

knowledge. This spillover of knowledge gives rise to a situation in which the production costs of individual firms fall as the industry as a whole accumulates experience.

Notice that external economies arising from the accumulation of knowledge differ somewhat from the external economies considered so far, in which industry costs depend on current output. In this alternative situation industry costs depend on experience, usually measured by the cumulative output of the industry to date. For example, the cost of producing a ton of steel might depend negatively on the total number of tons of steel produced by a country since the industry began. This kind of relationship is often summarized by a **learning curve** that relates unit cost to cumulative output. Such learning curves are illustrated in Figure 6-11. They are downward-sloping because of the effect of the experience gained through production on costs. When costs fall with cumulative production over time, rather than with the current rate of production, this is referred to as a case of **dynamic increasing returns.**

Like ordinary external economies, dynamic external economies can lock in an initial advantage or head start in an industry. In Figure 6-11, the learning curve L is that of a country that pioneered an industry, while L^* is that of another country that has lower input costs—say, lower wages—but less production experience. Provided that the first country has a sufficiently large head start, the potentially lower costs of the second country may not allow it to enter the market. For example, suppose the first country has a cumulative output of Q_L units, giving it a unit cost of C_1, while the second country has never produced the good. Then the second country will have an initial start-up cost C_0^* that is higher than the current unit cost, C_1, of the established industry.

Dynamic scale economies, like external economies at a point in time, potentially justify protectionism. Suppose that a country could have low enough costs to produce a good for export if it had more production experience, but that given the current lack of experience the good cannot be produced competitively. Such a country might increase its long-term welfare either by encouraging the production of the good by a subsidy or by protecting it from foreign competition until the industry could stand on

FIGURE 6-11
The learning curve.
The learning curve shows that unit cost is lower, the greater the cumulative output of a country's industry to date. A country that has extensive experience in an industry (L) may have lower unit cost than another country with little or no experience, even if the second country's learning curve (L^*) is lower, for example because of lower wages.

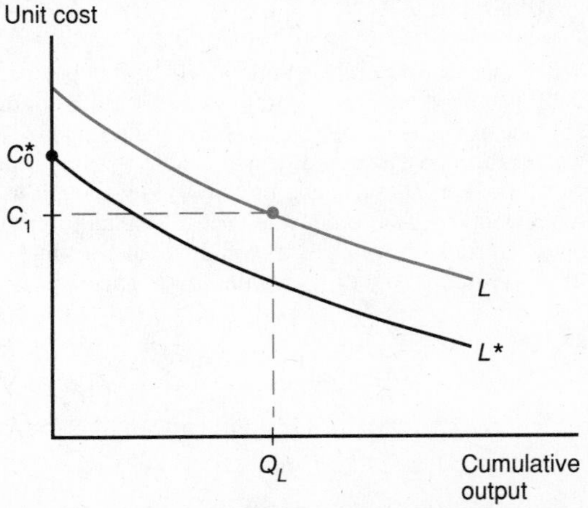

its own feet. The argument for temporary protection of industries to enable them to gain experience is known as the **infant industry argument** and has played an important role in debates over the role of trade policy in economic development. We will discuss the infant industry argument at greater length in Chapter 11, but for now we simply note that situations like that illustrated in Figure 6-11 are just as hard to identify in practice in those involving nondynamic increasing returns.

Summary

1. Trade need not be the result of comparative advantage. Instead, it can result from *increasing returns* or *economies of scale*—that is, from a tendency of unit costs to be lower with larger output. Economies of scale give countries an incentive to specialize and trade even in the absence of differences between countries in their resources or technology.
2. Economies of scale normally lead to a breakdown of perfect competition, so that trade in the presence of economies of scale must be analyzed using models of *imperfect competition.* Two important models of this kind are the *monopolistic competition* model and the *dumping* model. A third model, that of *external economies,* is consistent with perfect competition.
3. In monopolistic competition, an industry contains a number of firms producing *differentiated products.* These firms act as individual monopolists, but additional firms enter a profitable industry until monopoly profits are competed away. Equilibrium is affected by the size of the market: a large market will support a larger number of firms, each producing at larger scale and thus lower average cost, than a small market.
4. International trade allows creation of an integrated market that is larger than any one country's market, and thus makes it possible simultaneously to offer consumers a greater variety of products and lower prices.
5. In the monopolistic competition model, trade may be divided into two kinds. Two-way trade in differentiated products within an industry is called *intraindustry trade;* trade that exchanges the products of one industry for the products of another is called *interindustry trade.* Intraindustry trade reflects economies of scale, interindustry trade reflects comparative advantage. Intraindustry trade does not generate the same strong effects on income distribution as interindustry trade.
6. *Dumping* occurs when a monopolistic firm charges a lower price on exports than it charges domestically. It is a profit-maximizing strategy when export sales are more price-responsive than domestic sales, and when firms can effectively segment markets, that is, prevent domestic customers from buying goods intended for export markets. *Reciprocal dumping* occurs when two monopolistic firms dump into each others' home markets; such reciprocal dumping can be a cause of international trade.
7. *External economies* are economies of scale that occur at the level of the industry instead of the firm. They give an important role to history and accident in determining the pattern of international trade. When external economies are important, a country starting with a large industry may retain that advantage even if another country could potentially produce the same goods more cheaply. When external economies are important, countries can conceivably lose from trade.

Key Terms

external economies of scale
internal economies of scale
imperfect competition
pure monopoly
marginal revenue
average cost
marginal cost
oligopoly
monopolistic competition
intraindustry trade
interindustry trade
price discrimination
dumping
reciprocal dumping
learning curve
dynamic increasing returns
infant industry argument

Problems

1. For each of the following examples, explain whether this is a case of external or internal economies of scale:
   a. Most musical wind instruments in the United States are produced by more than a dozen factories in Elkhart, Indiana.
   b. All Hondas sold in the United States are either imported or produced in Marysville, Ohio.
   c. All airframes for Airbus, Europe's only producer of large aircraft, are assembled in Toulouse, France.
   d. Hartford, Connecticut is the insurance capital of the northeastern United States.
2. In perfect competition, firms set price equal to marginal cost. Why isn't this possible when there are internal economies of scale?
3. It is often argued that the existence of increasing returns is a source of conflict between countries, since each country is better off if it can increase its production in those industries characterized by economies of scale. Evaluate this view in terms of both the monopolistic competition and the external economy models.
4. Suppose the two countries we considered in the numerical example on pages 125–128 were to integrate their automobile market with a third country with an annual market for 3.75 million automobiles. Find the number of firms, the output per firm, and the price per automobile in the new integrated market after trade.
5. Evaluate the relative importance of economies of scale and comparative advantage in causing the following:
   a. Most of the world's aluminum is smelted in Norway or Canada.
   b. Half of the world's large jet aircraft are assembled in Seattle.
   c. Most semiconductors are manufactured in either the United States or Japan.
   d. Most Scotch whiskey comes from Scotland.
   e. Much of the world's best wine comes from France.
6. The United States and Canada recently established a free trade area; on the other hand, despite large potential gains, free trade between the United States and Mexico

is considered politically more difficult to achieve. Explain why in terms of the theory of intraindustry trade.

7. There are some shops in Japan that sell *Japanese* goods imported back from the United States at a discount over the prices charged by regular shops. How is this possible?

Further Reading

Frank Graham. ''Some Aspects of Protection Further Considered'' *Quarterly Journal of Economics* 37 (1923), pp. 199–227. An early warning that international trade may be harmful in the presence of external economies of scale.

Elhanan Helpman and Paul Krugman. *Market Structure and Foreign Trade.* Cambridge: MIT Press, 1985. A technical presentation of monopolistic competition and other models of trade with economies of scale.

Henryk Kierzkowski, ed. *Monopolistic Competition in International Trade.* Oxford: Clarendon Press, 1984. A collection of papers representing many of the leading researchers in imperfect competition and international trade.

Staffan Burenstam Linder. *An Essay on Trade and Transformation.* New York: John Wiley and Sons, 1961. An early and influential statement of the view that trade in manufactures among advanced countries mainly reflects forces other than comparative advantage.

Michael Porter. *The Competitive Advantage of Nations.* New York: Free Press, 1990. A best-selling book that explains national export success as the result of self-reinforcing industrial clusters, that is, external economies.

Appendix to Chapter 6 ● Determining Marginal Revenue

In our exposition of monopoly and monopolistic competition, we found it useful to have an algebraic statement of the marginal revenue faced by a firm given the demand curve it faced. Specifically, we asserted that if a firm faces the demand curve

$$X = A - B \times P, \qquad \textbf{(6A-1)}$$

its marginal revenue is

$$MR = P - (1/B) \times X. \qquad \textbf{(6A-2)}$$

In this appendix we demonstrate why this is true.

Notice first that the demand curve can be rearranged to state the price as a function of the firm's sales rather than the other way around. By rearranging (6A-1) we get

$$P = (A/B) - (1/B) \times X. \qquad \textbf{(6A-3)}$$

The revenue of a firm is simply the price it receives per unit multiplied by the number of units it sells. Letting R denote the firm's revenue, we have

$$R = P \times X = [(A/B) - (1/B) \times X] \times X. \qquad \textbf{(6A-4)}$$

Let us next ask how the revenue of a firm changes if it changes its sales. Suppose that the firm decides to increase its sales by a small amount dX, so that the new level of sales is $X' = X + dX$. Then the firm's revenue after the increase in sales, R', will be

$$\begin{aligned} R' &= P' \times X' = [(A/B) - (1/B) \times (X + dX)] \times (X + dX) \qquad \textbf{(6A-5)} \\ &= [(A/B) - (1/B) \times X] \times X + [(A/B) - (1/B) \times X] \times dX \\ &\quad - (1/B) \times X \times dX - (1/B) \times (dX)^2. \end{aligned}$$

Equation (6A-5) can be simplified by substitution in from (6A-1) and (6A-4) to get

$$R' = R + P \times dX - (1/B) \times X \times dX - (1/B) \times (dX)^2. \qquad \textbf{(6A-6)}$$

When the change in sales dX is small, however, its square $(dX)^2$ is very small (e.g., the square of 1 is 1, but the square of 1/10 is 1/100). So for a small change in X, the last term in (6A-6) can be ignored. This gives us the result that the *change* in revenue from a small change in sales is

$$R' - R = [P - (1/B) \times X] \times dX. \qquad \textbf{(6A-7)}$$

So the increase in revenue *per unit of additional sales*—which is the definition of marginal revenue—is

$$MR = (R' - R)/dX = P - (1/B) \times X,$$

which is just what we asserted in equation (6A-2).

International Factor Movements

Chapter 7

Up to this point we have concerned ourselves entirely with international *trade*. That is, we have focused on the causes and effects of international exchanges of goods and services. Movement of goods and services is not, however, the only form of international integration. This chapter is concerned with another form of integration, international movements of factors of production, or **factor movements.** Factor movements include labor migration, the transfer of capital via international borrowing and lending, and the subtle international linkages involved in the formation of multinational corporations.

The principles of international factor movement do not differ in their essentials from those underlying international trade in goods. Both international borrowing and lending and international labor migration can be thought of as analogous in their causes and effects to the movement of goods analyzed in Chapters 2 through 5. The role of the multinational corporation may be understood by extending some of the concepts developed in Chapter 6. So when we turn from trade in goods and services to factor movements we do not make a radical shift in emphasis.

Although there is a fundamental economic similarity between trade and factor movements, however, there are major differences in the political context. A labor-abundant country may under some circumstances import capital-intensive goods; under other circumstances it may acquire capital by borrowing abroad. A capital-abundant country may import labor-intensive goods or begin employing migrant workers. A country that is too small to support firms of efficient size may import goods where large firms have an advantage or allow those goods to be produced locally by subsidiaries of foreign firms. In each case the alternative strategies may be similar in their purely economic consequences but radically different in their political acceptability.

On the whole, international factor movement tends to raise even more political difficulties than international trade. Thus factor movements are subject to more restriction than trade in goods. Immigration restrictions are nearly universal. Until recently several European countries, such as France, maintained controls on capital movements even though they had virtually free trade in goods with their neighbors. Investment by foreign-based multinational corporations is regarded with suspicion and tightly regulated through much of the world. The result is that factor movements are probably less important in practice than trade in goods, which is why we took an analysis of trade in the absence of factor movements as our starting point. Nonetheless, factor movements are very important, and it is valuable to spend a chapter on their analysis.

This chapter is in three parts. We begin with a simple model of international labor mobility. We then proceed to an analysis of international borrowing and lending, in which we show that this lending can be interpreted as trade *over time:* the lending country gives up resources now to receive repayment in the future, while the borrower does the reverse. Finally, the last section of the chapter analyzes multinational corporations.

International Labor Mobility

We begin our discussion with an analysis of the effects of labor mobility. In the modern world, restrictions on the flow of labor are legion—just about every country imposes restrictions on immigration. Thus labor mobility is less prevalent in practice than capital mobility. It remains important, however; it is also simpler in some ways to analyze than capital movement, for reasons that will become apparent later in the chapter.

A ONE-GOOD MODEL WITHOUT FACTOR MOBILITY

As in the analysis of trade, the best way to understand factor mobility is to begin with a world that is not economically integrated, then examine what happens when international transactions are allowed. Let's assume that we have, as usual, a two-country world consisting of Home and Foreign, each with two factors of production, land and labor. We assume for the moment, however, that this world is even simpler than the one we examined in Chapter 4, in that the two countries produce only *one* good, which we will simply refer to as "output." Thus there is no scope for ordinary trade, the exchange of different goods, in this world. The only way for these economies to become integrated with each other is via movement of either land or labor. Land almost by definition cannot move, so this is a model of integration via international labor mobility.

Before we introduce factor movements, however, let us analyze the determinants of the level of output in each country. Land (T) and labor (L) are the only scarce resources. Thus the output of each country will depend, other things equal, on the quantity of these factors available. The relationship between the supplies of factors on one side and the output of the economy on the other is referred to as the economy's production function, which we denote by $Q(T, L)$.

We have already encountered the idea of a production function in Chapter 3. As we noted there, a useful way to look at the production function is to ask how output depends on the supply of one factor of production, holding the quantity of the other factor fixed. This is done in Figure 7-1, which shows how a country's output varies as its employment of labor is varied, holding fixed the supply of land; the figure is the same as Figure 3-1. The slope of the production function measures the increase in output that would be gained by using a little more labor and is thus referred to as the *marginal product of labor.* As the curve is drawn in Figure 7-1, the marginal product of labor is assumed to fall as the ratio of labor to land rises. This is the normal case: as a country seeks to employ more labor on a given amount of land, it must move to increasingly labor-intensive techniques of production, and this will normally become increasingly difficult the further the substitution of labor for land goes.

Figure 7-2, corresponding to Figure 3-2, contains the same information as Figure 7-1 but plots it in a different way. We now show directly how the marginal product of labor depends on the quantity of labor employed. We also indicate that the real wage earned by each unit of labor is equal to labor's marginal product. This will be true as long as the economy is perfectly competitive, which we assume to be the case.

What about the income earned by land? As we showed in the appendix to Chapter 3, the total output of the economy can be measured by the area under the marginal product curve. Of that total output, wages earned by workers equal the real wage rate times the employment of labor, and hence equal the indicated area on the figure. The remainder, also shown, equals rents earned by landowners.

Assume that Home and Foreign have the same technology but different overall land-labor ratios. If Home is the labor-abundant country, workers in Home will earn less than those in Foreign, while land in Home earns more than in Foreign. This obviously creates an incentive for factors of production to move. Home workers would like to move to Foreign; Foreign landowners would also like to move their land to Home, but we are supposing that this is impossible. Our next step is to allow workers to move and see what happens.

FIGURE 7-1
An economy's production function.
The larger the supply of labor, the larger is output; however, the marginal product of labor declines as more workers are employed.

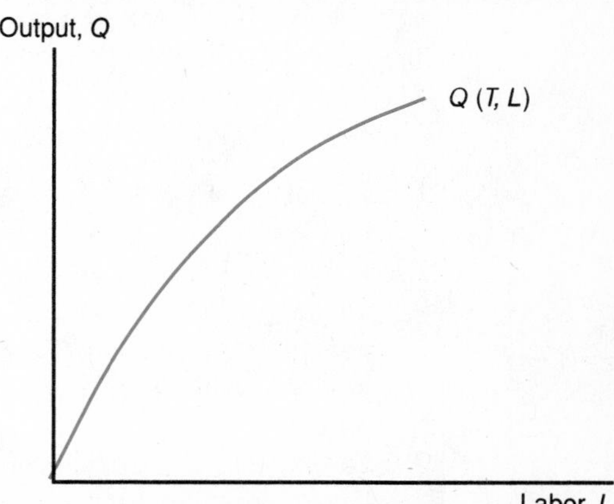

FIGURE 7-2
The marginal product of labor.
The marginal product of labor declines with employment. The area under the marginal product curve equals total output.

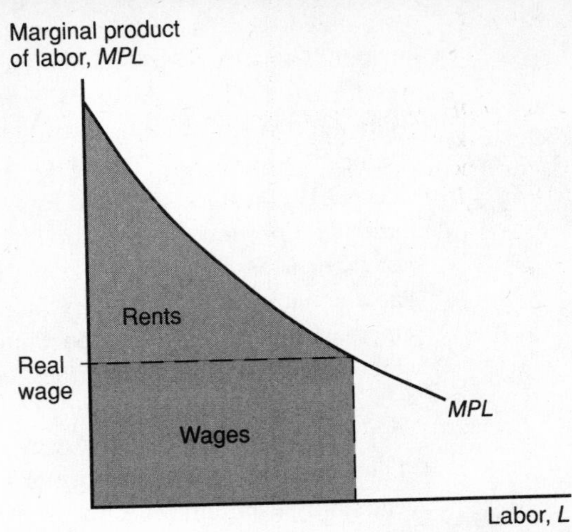

INTERNATIONAL LABOR MOVEMENT

Now suppose that workers are able to move between our two countries. Workers will move from Home to Foreign. This movement will reduce the Home labor force and thus raise the real wage in Home, while increasing the labor force and reducing the real wage in Foreign. If there are no obstacles to labor movement, this process will continue until the marginal product of labor is the same in the two countries.

Figure 7-3 illustrates the causes and effects of international labor mobility. The horizontal axis represents the total world labor force. The workers employed in Home are measured from the left, the workers employed in Foreign from the right. On the vertical axis is shown the marginal product of labor in each country. Initially we assume that there are OL^1 workers in Home, L^1O^* workers in Foreign. Given this allocation, the real wage rate would be lower in Home (point *C*) than in Foreign (point *B*). If workers can move freely to whichever country offers the higher real wage, they will move from Home to Foreign until the real wage rates are equalized. The eventual distribution of the world's labor force will be one with OL^2 workers in Home, L^2O^* workers in Foreign (point *A*).

Three points should be noted about this redistribution of the world's labor force.

1. It leads to a convergence of real wage rates. Real wages rise in Home, fall in Foreign.
2. It increases the world's output as a whole. Foreign's output rises by the area under its marginal product curve from L^1 to L^2, while Home's falls by the corresponding area under its marginal product curve. We see from the figure that Foreign's gain is larger than Home's loss, by an amount equal to the colored area *ABC* in the figure.
3. Despite this gain, some people are hurt by the change. Those who would originally have worked in Home receive higher real wages, but those who would originally have worked in Foreign receive lower real wages. Landowners in Foreign benefit

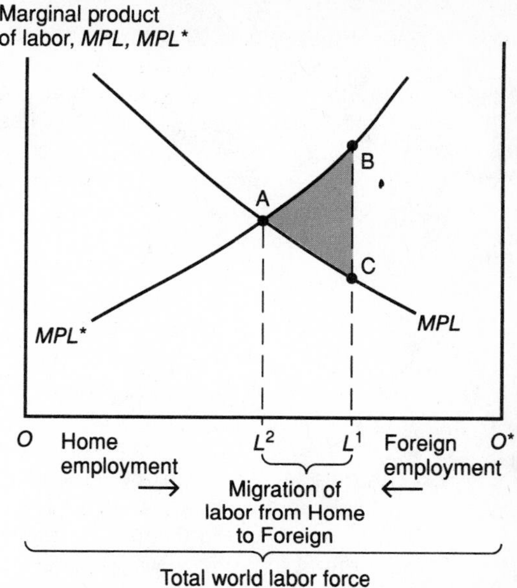

FIGURE 7-3
Causes and effects of international labor mobility.
Initially OL^1 workers are employed in Home, while L^1O^* workers are employed in Foreign. Labor migrates from Home to Foreign until OL^2 workers are employed in Home, L^2O^* in Foreign, and wages are equalized.

from the larger labor supply, but landowners in Home are made worse off. As in the case of the gains from international trade, then, international labor mobility, while allowing everyone to be made better off in principle, leaves some groups worse off in practice.

EXTENDING THE ANALYSIS

We have just seen that a very simple model tells us quite a lot about both why international factor movements occur and what effects they have. Labor mobility in our simple model, like trade in the model of Chapter 4, is driven by international differences in resources; also like trade, it is beneficial in the sense that it increases world production yet is associated with strong income distribution effects that make those gains problematic.

Let us consider briefly how the analysis is modified when we add some of the complications we have assumed away.

We need to remove the assumption that the two countries produce only one good. Suppose, then, that the countries produce two goods, one more labor-intensive than the other. We already know from our discussion of the factor-proportions model in Chapter 4 that in this case trade offers an alternative to factor mobility. Home can in a sense export labor and import land by exporting the labor-intensive good and importing the land-intensive good. It is possible in principle for such trade to lead to a complete equalization of factor prices without any need for factor mobility. If this happened, it would of course remove any incentive for labor to move from Home to Foreign.

In practice, while trade is indeed a substitute for international factor movement, it is not a perfect substitute. The reasons are those already summarized in Chapter 4.

International Labor Mobility in Practice: "Guest Workers" in Europe

The great age of international labor mobility was the late nineteenth and early twentieth centuries, when tens of millions of workers moved from Europe to North and South America and millions of Indians and Chinese emigrated to Africa, the West Indies, and Southeast Asia. Since 1920, great movements of population have been limited by immigration restrictions, and most large population shifts have been political consequences of war and civil strife. A major example of economically based migration, however, has been the mobility of labor within Europe. From the 1950s to the early 1970s the affluent countries of Western Europe attracted millions of workers from the less prosperous areas to the south and southeast: Portugal, Spain, southern Italy, Yugoslavia, Greece, Turkey, and North Africa. These so-called guest workers often stayed only temporarily and left their families behind in their home countries.

The guest worker phenomenon illustrates both the potential benefits and the problems raised by international labor mobility. By migrating, workers were able to earn much more—sometimes ten times more—than they could have earned at home. During the 1960s and early 1970s, with the richer Western European economies at near-full employment, the availability of migrant workers helped to keep growth from being constrained by labor supply. Although a simple model suggests that workers in the more prosperous countries would have been better off without competition from immigrants, by and large immigrants ended up in low-skill jobs that domestic workers were not anxious to take.

Even during the period of rapid growth, however, migration raised serious social and political issues. Guest workers inevitably came to constitute a sort of second-class citizenry in their host countries, especially in Switzerland, where by the early 1970s they were one-third of the labor force. Inevitably, the position of migrants as hewers of wood and drawers of water for wealthier societies produced feelings of bitterness and inferiority. The Swiss author Max Frisch wrote, "We asked for workers, but human beings came."

The northward migration of workers within Europe came to a sudden halt with the slowdown in Western European growth that followed the rise in oil prices in 1973. In an environment of rising unemployment, guest workers typically found themselves in the position of "last hired, first fired," so that the attractiveness of migration faded. While some workers continued to head north, many others returned home. From 1960 to 1969, net emigration from Greece, Italy, Portugal, and Spain was 2.2 million; from 1970 to 1979, it was only 75,000.

Complete factor price equalization is not observed in the real world because countries are sometimes too different in their resources to remain unspecialized; there are barriers to trade, both natural and artificial; and there are differences in technology as well as resources between countries.

We might wonder on the other side whether factor movements do not remove the incentive for international trade. Again the answer is that while in a simple model movement of factors of production can make international trade in goods unnecessary, in practice there are substantial barriers to free movement of labor, capital, and other potentially mobile resources. And some resources cannot be brought together—Canadian forests and Caribbean sunshine cannot migrate.

Extending the simple model of factor mobility, then, does not change its fundamental message. The main point is that trade in factors is in purely economic terms very much like trade in goods, occurring for much the same reasons and producing similar results.

International Borrowing and Lending

International movements of capital are a prominent feature of the international economic landscape. It is tempting to analyze these movements in a way parallel to our analysis of labor mobility, and this is sometimes a useful exercise. There are some important differences, however. When we speak of international labor mobility, it is clear that workers are physically moving from one country to another. International capital movements are not so simple. When we speak of capital flows from the United States to Mexico, we do not mean that U.S. machines are literally being unbolted and shipped south. We are instead talking of a *financial* transaction. A U.S. bank lends to a Mexican firm, or U.S. residents buy stock in Mexico, or a U.S. firm invests through its Mexican subsidiary. We focus for now on the first type of transaction, in which U.S. residents make loans to Mexicans—that is, the U.S. residents grant Mexicans the right to spend more than they earn today in return for a promise to repay in the future.

The analysis of financial aspects of the international economy is the subject of the second half of this book. It is important to realize, however, that financial transactions do not exist simply on paper. They have real consequences. International borrowing and lending, in particular, can be interpreted as a kind of international trade. The trade is not of one good for another at a point in time but of goods today for goods in the future. This kind of trade is known as **intertemporal trade;** we will have much more to say about it later in this text, but for present purposes a simple model will be sufficient to make our point.[1]

INTERTEMPORAL PRODUCTION POSSIBILITIES AND TRADE

Even in the absence of international capital movements, any economy faces a trade-off between consumption now and consumption in the future. Economies usually do not consume all of their current output; some of their output takes the form of investment in machines, buildings, and other forms of productive capital. The more investment an economy undertakes now, the more it will be able to produce and consume in the future. To invest more, however, an economy must release resources by consuming less (unless there are unemployed resources, a possibility we temporarily disregard). Thus there is a trade-off between current and future consumption.

Let's imagine an economy that consumes only one good and will exist for only two periods, which we will call present and future. Then there will be a trade-off between present and future production of the consumption good, which we can summarize by drawing an **intertemporal production possibility frontier.** Such a frontier

[1] The appendix to this chapter contains a more detailed examination of the model developed in this section.

is illustrated in Figure 7-4. It looks just like the production possibility frontiers we have been drawing between two goods at a point in time.

The shape of the intertemporal production possibility frontier will differ among countries. Some countries will have production possibilities that are biased toward present output, while others are biased toward future output. We will ask what real differences these biases correspond to in a moment, but first let's simply suppose that there are two countries, Home and Foreign, with different intertemporal production possibilities. Home's possibilities are biased toward current consumption, while Foreign's are biased toward future consumption.

Reasoning by analogy, we already know what to expect. In the absence of international borrowing and lending, we would expect the relative price of future consumption to be higher in Home than in Foreign, and thus if we open the possibility of trade over time, we would expect Home to export present consumption and import future consumption.

This may, however, seem a little puzzling. What is the relative price of future consumption, and how does one trade over time?

THE REAL INTEREST RATE

The answer to the second question is that a country, like an individual, can trade over time by borrowing or lending. Consider what happens when an individual borrows: she is initially able to spend more than her income or, in other words, to consume more than her production. Later, however, she must repay the loan with interest, and therefore in the future she consumes *less* than she produces. By borrowing, then, she has in effect traded future consumption for current consumption. The same is true of a borrowing country.

Clearly the price of future consumption in terms of present consumption has

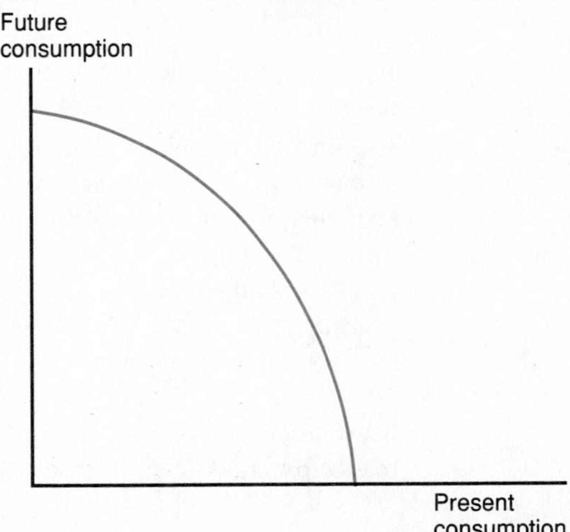

FIGURE 7-4
The intertemporal production possibility frontier.
A country can trade off current for future consumption in the same way that it can produce more of one good by producing less of another.

something to do with the interest rate. As we will see in the second half of this book, in the real world the interpretation of interest rates is complicated by the possibility of changes in the overall price level. Let us bypass that problem for now by supposing that loan contracts are specified in ''real'' terms: when a country borrows, it gets the right to purchase some quantity of consumption in present in return for repayment of some larger quantity in future. Specifically, the quantity of repayment in future will be $(1 + r)$ times the quantity borrowed in present. Then r is the **real interest rate** on borrowing. And it is clear also that, since the trade-off is one unit of consumption in present for $(1 + r)$ units in future, the relative price of future consumption is $1/(1 + r)$.

The parallel with our standard trade model is now complete. If borrowing and lending are allowed, the relative price of future consumption, and thus the world real interest rate, will be determined by the world relative supply and demand for future consumption. Home, whose intertemporal production possibilities are biased toward present consumption, will export present consumption and import future consumption. That is, Home will lend to foreign in the first period and receive repayment in the second.

INTERTEMPORAL COMPARATIVE ADVANTAGE

We have assumed that Home's intertemporal production possibilities are biased toward present production. But what does this mean? The sources of intertemporal comparative advantage are somewhat different from those that give rise to ordinary trade.

A country that has a comparative advantage in future production of consumption goods is one that in the absence of international borrowing and lending would have a low relative price of future consumption, that is, a high real interest rate. This high real interest rate corresponds to a high return on investment—that is, a high return to diverting resources from current production of consumption goods to production of capital goods, construction, and other activities that enhance the economy's future ability to produce. So countries that borrow in the international market will be those where highly productive investment opportunities are available relative to current productive capacity, while countries that lend will be those where such opportunities are not available domestically.

The pattern of international borrowing and lending in the 1970s illustrates the point. Table 23-2 (p. 686) compares the international lending of three groups of countries: industrial countries, non-oil developing countries, and major oil exporters. From 1973 to 1981, the oil exporters lent $384 billion, the less-developed countries borrowed $409 billion, and the industrial countries borrowed a much smaller amount, $64 billion. In the light of our model, this is not surprising. During the 1970s, as a result of a spectacular increase in oil prices, oil exporters like Saudi Arabia found themselves with very high current income. They did not, however, find any comparable increase in their domestic investment opportunities. With small populations, limited resources other than oil, and little expertise in industrial or other production, their natural reaction was to invest much of their increased earnings abroad. By contrast, rapidly developing countries such as Brazil and Korea expected to have much higher incomes in the future and saw highly productive investment opportunities in their growing industrial sectors.

Changes in the Pattern of Capital Movements in the 1980s

The 1980s brought some surprising changes in the pattern of international trade in capital. Borrowing by developing countries was sharply curtailed, while the United States, traditionally a capital exporter, suddenly emerged as the world's largest capital importer.

Figure 7-5 shows the net capital exports of the United States and of a group of capital-importing developing countries from 1980 to 1991.

The reasons for the decline in developing country borrowing are no mystery: a collapse of confidence in these countries' ability to repay their debts, the so-called "debt crisis," choked off virtually all private financial flows to many countries after 1982. We will discuss the debt crisis and its implications at considerable length in Chapter 23.

The causes of the sudden shift of the United States to capital importer are a source of dispute. Optimists attribute the surge of capital imports to the emergence of new investment opportunities; in terms of our model, this would be an outward shift in intertemporal production possibilities biased toward the future. Pessimists instead argue that the United States simply shifted its consumption toward the present at the expense of the future. We will show in Chapter 13 that most indicators support the pessimistic interpretation, although the dispute has by no means ended.

Nor were the trends of the 1980s necessarily permanent. In the early 1990s there was a surprise revival of willingness by investors to put money into at least some developing countries. A few countries, notably Mexico, found themselves receiving capital inflows at rates as high as or higher than before the debt crisis. Also, for the first time, investors in advanced countries began to look with favor on the stock markets of a number of developing countries, sending stock prices soaring.

FIGURE 7-5
Changing patterns of international trade in capital.
During the 1980s, the capital imports of developing countries tapered off under the impact of the debt crisis, while the United States emerged as the world's largest importer of capital.

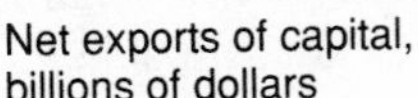

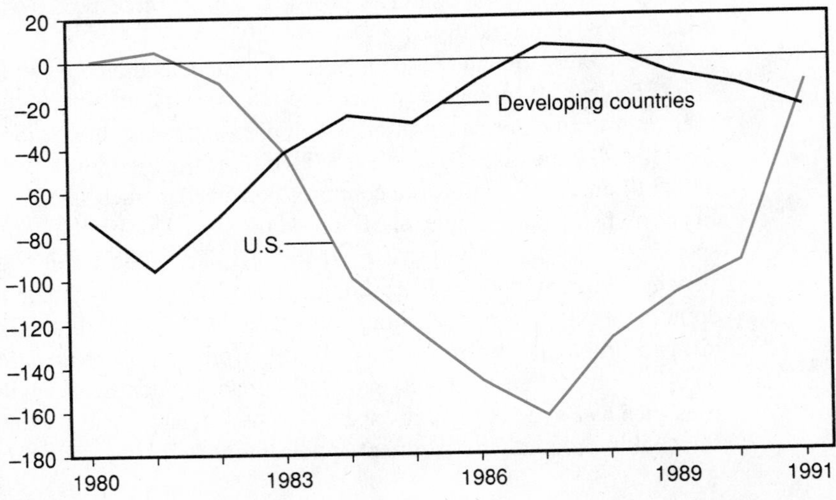

Direct Foreign Investment and Multinational Firms

In the last section we focused on international borrowing and lending. This is a relatively simple transaction, in that the borrower makes no demands on the lender other than that of repayment. An important part of international capital movement, however, takes a different form, that of **direct foreign investment.** By direct foreign investment we mean international capital flows in which a firm in one country creates or expands a subsidiary in another. The distinctive feature of direct foreign investment is that it involves not only a transfer of resources but also the acquisition of *control.* That is, the subsidiary does not simply have a financial obligation to the parent company; it is part of the same organizational structure.

Multinational firms are often a vehicle for international borrowing and lending. Parent companies often provide their foreign subsidiaries with capital, in the expectation of eventual repayment. To the extent that multinational firms provide financing to their foreign subsidiaries, direct foreign investment is an alternative way of accomplishing the same things as international lending. This still leaves open the question, however, of why direct investment rather than some other way of transferring funds is chosen. In any case, the existence of multinational firms does not necessarily reflect a net capital flow from one country to another. Multinationals sometimes raise money for the expansion of their subsidiaries in the country where the subsidiary operates rather than in their home country. Furthermore, there is a good deal of two-way foreign direct investment among industrial countries, U.S. firms expanding their European subsidiaries at the same time that European firms expand their U.S. subsidiaries, for example.

The point is that while multinational firms sometimes act as a vehicle for international capital flows, it is probably a mistake to view direct foreign investment as primarily an alternative way for countries to borrow and lend. Instead, the main point of direct foreign investment is to allow the formation of multinational organizations. That is, it is the extension of control that is the essential purpose.

But why do firms seek to extend control? Economists do not have as fully developed a theory of multinational enterprise as they do of many other issues in international economics. There is some theory on the subject, however, which we now review.

THE THEORY OF MULTINATIONAL ENTERPRISE

The basic necessary elements of a theory of multinational firms can best be seen by looking at an example. Consider the Mexican auto industry. In terms of production Mexico is largely self-sufficient in automobiles, assembling nearly all the cars sold there and producing most of the components for those cars as well. The firms that produce the autos, however, are subsidiaries of major U.S. automakers. This arrangement is familiar, but we should realize that there are two obvious alternatives. On one side, instead of producing in Mexico the U.S. firms could produce in the United States and export to Mexico. On the other side, firms owned and controlled by residents of Mexico could produce automobiles. Why, then, do we have this particular arrangement, in which the *same* firms produce in *different* countries?

The modern theory of multinational enterprise starts by distinguishing between the two questions of which this larger question is composed. First, why is a good produced in two (or more) different countries rather than one? This is known as the question of **location.** Second, why is production in different locations done by the same firm rather than by separate firms? This is known, for reasons that will become apparent in a moment, as the question of **internalization.** We need a theory of location to explain why Mexico does not import its automobiles from the United States; we need a theory of internalization to explain why Mexico's auto industry is not independently controlled.

The theory of location is not a difficult one in principle. It is, in fact, just the theory of trade that we developed in Chapters 2 through 6. The location of production is often determined by resources. Aluminum mining must be located where the bauxite is, aluminum smelting near cheap electricity. Minicomputer manufacturers locate their skill-intensive design facilities in Massachusetts or northern California, their labor-intensive assembly plants in Ireland or Singapore. Alternatively, transport costs and other barriers to trade may determine location. The Mexican auto industry exists in large part because of import quotas and other protective measures that limit imports. The point is that the factors that determine a multinational corporation's decisions about where to produce are probably not much different from those that determine the pattern of trade in general.

The theory of internalization is another matter. Why not have independent auto companies in Mexico? We may note first that there are always important transactions between a multinational's operations in different countries. The output of one subsidiary is often an input into the production of another. Or technology developed in one country may be used in others. Or management may usefully coordinate the activities of plants in several countries. These transactions are what tie the multinational firm together, and the firm presumably exists so as to facilitate these transactions. But international transactions need not be carried out inside a firm. Components can be sold in an open market, and technology can be licensed to other firms. Multinationals exist because it turns out to be more profitable to carry out these transactions within a firm rather than between firms. This is why the motive for multinationals is referred to as "internalization."

We have defined a concept, but we have not yet explained what gives rise to internalization. Why are some transactions more profitably conducted within a firm rather than between firms? Here there are a variety of theories, none as well-grounded either in theory or in evidence as our theories of location. We may note two influential views, however, about why activities in different countries may usefully be integrated in a single firm.

The first view stresses the advantages of internalization for **technology transfer.** Technology, broadly defined as any kind of economically useful knowledge, can sometimes be sold or licensed. There are important difficulties in doing this, however. Often the technology involved in, say, running a factory has never been written down; it is embodied in the knowledge of a group of individuals and cannot be packaged and sold. Also, it is difficult for a prospective buyer to know how much knowledge is worth—if the buyer knew as much as the seller, there would be no need to buy! Finally, property rights in knowledge are often hard to establish. If a European firm licenses technology to a U.S. firm, other U.S. firms may legally imitate that technology. All these problems may be reduced if a firm, instead of selling technology, sets about capturing the returns in other countries by setting up foreign subsidiaries.

The second view stresses the advantages of internalization for **vertical integration.**

If one firm (the "upstream" firm) produces a good that is used as an input for another firm (the "downstream" firm), a number of problems can result. For one thing, if each has a monopoly position, they may get into a conflict as the downstream firm tries to hold the price down while the upstream firm tries to raise it. There may be problems of coordination if demand or supply is uncertain. Finally, a fluctuating price may impose excessive risk on one or the other party. If the upstream and downstream firms are combined into a single "vertically integrated" firm, these problems may be avoided or at least reduced.

It should be clear that these views are by no means as rigorously worked out as the analysis of trade carried out elsewhere in this book. The economic theory of organizations—which is what we are talking about when we try to develop a theory of multinational corporations—is still in its infancy. This is particularly unfortunate because in practice multinationals are a subject of heated controversy.

MULTINATIONAL FIRMS IN PRACTICE

Multinational firms play an important part in world trade and investment. For example, about half of U.S. imports are transactions between "related parties." By this we mean that the buyer and the seller are to a significant extent owned and presumably controlled by the same firm. Thus half of U.S. imports can be regarded as transactions between branches of multinational firms. At the same time, 24 percent of U.S. assets abroad consists of the value of foreign subsidiaries of U.S. firms. So U.S. trade and investment, while not dominated by multinational firms, are to an important extent conducted by such firms.

Multinational firms may, of course, be either domestic or foreign-owned. Foreign-owned multinational firms play an important role in most economies and an increasingly important role in the United States. Table 7-1 compares the role of foreign-owned firms in the five largest market economies. The table reveals several interesting points. First is the large role of foreign firms in European countries—a role that has, however, not changed much over the past decade. Second is the rapidly increasing importance of foreign firms in the United States. As late as 1977 the United States had relatively few foreign- as opposed to domestically owned multinationals operating on its territory. Third is the still small degree of foreign ownership in Japan.

The important question, however, is what difference multinationals make. With only a limited understanding of why multinationals exist, this is a hard question to answer. Nonetheless, the existing theory suggests some preliminary answers.

Notice first that much of what multinationals do could be done without multinationals, although perhaps not as easily. Two examples are the shift of labor-intensive production from industrial countries to labor-abundant nations and capital flows from capital-abundant countries to capital-scarce countries. Multinational firms are sometimes the agents of these changes and are therefore either praised or condemned for their actions (depending on the commentator's point of view). But these shifts reflect the "location" aspect of our theory of multinationals, which is really no different from ordinary trade theory. If multinationals were not there, the same things would still happen, though perhaps not to the same extent. This observation leads international economists to attribute less significance to multinational enterprise than most lay observers.

TABLE 7-1 Comparison of roles of foreign-owned firms in five largest market economies

		1977	*1986*
United States			
	(a)	5	10
	(b)	3	7
	(c)	5	9
Japan			
	(a)	2	1
	(b)	2	1
	(c)	2	1
France			
	(a)	24	27
	(b)	18	21
	(c)	NA	NA
Germany			
	(a)	17	18
	(b)	14	13
	(c)	17	17
United Kingdom			
	(a)	2	20
	(b)	15	14
	(c)	NA	14

(a) Share of foreign-owned firms in sales
(b) Share of foreign-owned firms in manufacturing employment
(c) Share of foreign-owned firms in assets
Source: D. Julius and S. Thomsen, ''Foreign-owned Firms, Trade, and Economic Integration,'' *Tokyo Club Papers* 2, Royal Institute of Economic Affairs, 1988.

Notice, too, that in a broad sense what multinational corporations do by creating organizations that extend across national boundaries is similar to the effects of trade and simple factor mobility; that is, it is a form of international economic integration. By analogy with the other forms of international integration we have studied, we would expect multinational enterprise to produce overall gains but to produce income distribution effects that leave some people worse off. These income distribution effects are probably mostly effects *within* rather than *between* countries.

To sum up, multinational corporations probably are not as important a factor in the world economy as their visibility would suggest; their role is neither more nor less likely to be beneficial than other international linkages. This does not, however, prevent them from being cast in the role of villains or (more rarely) heroes, as we will see in our discussion of trade and development in Chapter 11.

Case Study

FOREIGN DIRECT INVESTMENT IN THE UNITED STATES

Until recently, the United States was almost always thought of as a "home" country for multinational enterprises rather than a "host" country for foreign-based multinationals. Indeed, in 1968 the French author Jean-Jacques Servan-Schreiber titled his best-selling warning against the growth of multinationals *The American Challenge*. Correspondingly, the U.S. government has traditionally defended multinational firms against critics like Servan-Schreiber and third world advocates of a new international economic order. During the 1980s, however, the shoe shifted to the other foot, as the United States became a target of unprecedented direct foreign investment from other advanced nations.

Figure 7-6 shows the flow of foreign direct investment in the United States since 1973, measured as a share of national income.[2] There have been two waves of direct investment since the late 1970s: a first wave from 1978 to 1981 and a second, larger wave from 1986 to 1990. By 1990, about 4 percent of U.S. workers were employed by

[2] The measure shown in Figure 7-6 is derived from the balance of payments, described in Chapter 13. It measures expenditures by foreign corporations either to establish control over U.S. enterprises or to expand their investments in enterprises they already control. For technical reasons this is an incomplete measure of the rate at which foreign firms actually are expanding their U.S. holdings, but it is nonetheless a useful indicator of changes in the foreign investment flow.

FIGURE 7-6
Foreign direct investment in the United States.
Foreign direct investment flows into the United States surged in 1978–1981 and again after 1986, rapidly raising the share of U.S. production controlled by foreign firms.

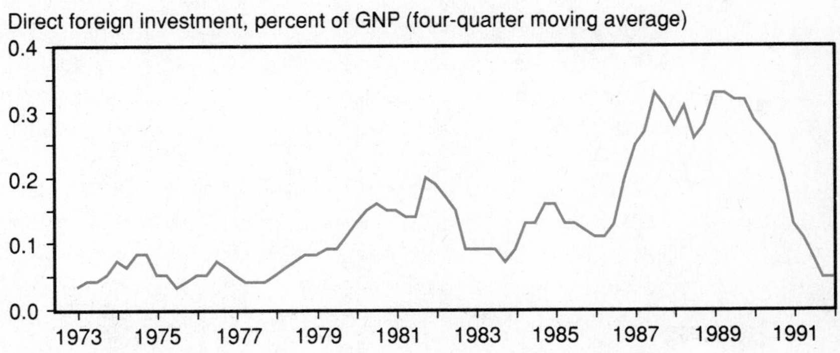

Source: *Survey of Current Business*, various issues.

foreign-owned firms. Foreign ownership was concentrated in finance and manufacturing; by 1990 more than 12 percent of U.S. manufacturing assets, and more than 20 percent of banking assets, were foreign-owned.

Foreign investment in the United States has come from a variety of sources and taken a variety of forms. The most publicized investments have been Japan's establishment of manufacturing plants in the United States, especially in the auto industry. Five Japanese auto firms have built assembly plants in America, plants that produced 11 percent of U.S.-manufactured cars in 1991. Many other investments, however, took the form of acquisition of existing U.S. firms, often by European or Canadian rather than Japanese corporations. Examples include the acquisition of Tropicana by Seagram's, the Canadian distiller, and of Sohio by British Petroleum (BP).

Why did foreign firms come to the United States? As we have stressed, we need to understand both why goods are produced in the United States and why foreign firms rather than U.S. firms produce them. Explaining the location decision seems complicated. One explanation is a shift in relative costs: U.S. wages, which used to be the highest in the world, are no longer so high—the fall of the dollar from 1985 to 1987 brought U.S. wages to a level lower than German wages and not much higher than Japanese wages. Another explanation is fear of protectionism: foreign firms, especially Japanese firms, were setting up production in the United States either in anticipation of import quotas or to buy off protectionist sentiment by providing jobs in the United States. As for why foreign rather than U.S. firms were doing the producing, foreign firms apparently believe they have superior technology or management technique that allows them to produce more efficiently than local U.S. competitors.

Notice that the flow of *direct* investment to the United States, shown in Figure 7-6, has not been closely correlated with overall U.S. capital imports, shown in Figure 7-5. The first wave of direct investment came before the emergence of large-scale capital imports; the second wave did not commence as soon as large capital imports began, but actually emerged as U.S. imports of capital were beginning to decline. This lack of correlation underscores the point that direct foreign investment is not primarily a way of transferring capital.

Predictably, the political reaction to growing foreign direct investment in the United States has echoed the reaction of other countries to U.S. investment in the past: alarm, coupled with demands for restriction. The Omnibus Trade and Competitiveness Act of 1988, reflecting this reaction, contains provisions allowing the president to block foreign acquisitions of U.S. firms on national security grounds—with the definition of national security deliberately left vague. At the time of writing this power was being exercised with circumspection: only three acquisitions had been blocked, all of them in industries with clear military applications. Nonetheless, many experts felt that the U.S. government could, if it so chose, use its authority to screen foreign investments on economic as well as military grounds.

For a while, however, the issue seems likely to lie fairly dormant. Many foreign investors seem to have concluded after several years of aggressive buying in the United States that they had not been getting very good returns on their money; Japanese investors in particular also found their financial resources reduced by a massive decline in the Japanese stock market beginning in 1990. For these reasons, among others, the rate of foreign direct investment into the United States fell sharply in 1990, and the political temperature fell with it.

Japan in the Entertainment Business

During 1990 and 1991 there was a strong public backlash in the United States against the sale of U.S. corporations to foreigners. This backlash was fueled by the publicity given to several huge actual or proposed Japanese acquisitions. Ironically, however, the deals that attracted the most attention were almost certainly very good deals for the United States and, at least in retrospect, bad deals for Japan.

Two of the highly publicized deals involved entertainment companies. First, the Japanese consumer electronics firm Sony bought the entertainment firm Columbia Pictures. The idea behind the deal was that there would be a profitable synergy between Columbia's movie, television, and music business and the Sony VCRs, CD players, and so on that would play them. Not to be left in the cold, Sony's rival Matsushita similarly acquired the American firm MCA.

The furor over these acquisitions led to the abandonment of a third proposed Japanese acquisition, in which Mitsubishi Estates, a real estate investment firm, had planned to purchase New York's famous Rockefeller Center, home of Radio City Music Hall.

While the public reacted negatively to these deals, however, it was hard to see what the United States had to lose. There has been some legitimate concern about Japanese acquisition of U.S. high-technology companies; some observers fear that the owners will in effect strip them of their knowledge, or move the research activities overseas. It is unlikely, however, that Sony will want to make films for the American market in Japan, or that MCA will start showing a preference for Japanese rock stars. The prospects for harm from foreign ownership of Rockefeller Center are even more remote—Japanese Rockettes?

Moreover, it seems clear with the benefit of hindsight that both Sony and Matsushita overpaid heavily for their acquisitions—in Sony's case, probably at least twice what Columbia was really worth. Had Rockefeller Center been sold, the Japanese purchaser would surely have taken a heavy loss, as the New York real estate market plunged soon afterward.

Summary

1. International *factor movements* can sometimes substitute for trade, so it is not surprising that international migration of labor is similar in its causes and effects to international trade based on differences in resources. Labor moves from countries where it is abundant to countries where it is scarce. This movement raises total world output, but it also generates strong income distribution effects, so that some groups are hurt.

2. International borrowing and lending can be viewed as a kind of international trade, but one that involves trade of present consumption for future consumption rather than trade of one good for another. The relative price at which this *intertemporal trade* takes place is one plus the *real rate of interest.*

3. Multinational firms, while they often serve as vehicles for international borrowing and lending, primarily exist as ways of extending control over activities taking place in two or more different countries. The theory of multinational firms is not as well-developed as other parts of international economics. A basic framework can be presented that stresses two crucial elements that explain the existence of a multinational:

a *location* motive that leads the activities of the firm to be in different countries, and an *internalization* motive that leads these activities to be integrated in a single firm.

4. The location motives of multinationals are the same as those behind all international trade. The internalization motives are less well understood; current theory points to two main motives: the need for a way to *transfer technology* and the advantages in some cases of *vertical integration.*

Key Terms

factor movements
intertemporal trade
intertemporal production possibility frontier
real interest rate
direct foreign investment
location and internalization motives of multinationals
technology transfer
vertical integration

Problems

1. In Home and Foreign there are two factors of production, land and labor, used to produce only one good. The land supply in each country and the technology of production are exactly the same. The marginal product of labor in each country depends on employment as follows:

Number of workers employed	*Marginal product of last worker*
1	20
2	19
3	18
4	17
5	16
6	15
7	14
8	13
9	12
10	11
11	10

Initially, there are 11 workers employed in Home, but only 3 workers in Foreign.

Find the effect of free movement of labor from Home to Foreign on employment, production, real wages, and the income of landowners in each country.

2. Suppose that a labor-abundant country and a land-abundant country both produce labor- and land-intensive goods with the same technology. Drawing on the analysis in Chapter 4, first analyze the conditions under which trade between the two countries eliminates the incentive for labor to migrate. Then, using the analysis in Chapter 5, show that a tariff by one country will create an incentive for labor migration.

3. Explain the analogy between international borrowing and lending and ordinary international trade.
4. Which of the following countries would you expect to have intertemporal production possibilities biased toward current consumption goods, and which biased toward future consumption goods?
   - **a.** A country, like Argentina or Canada in the last century, that has only recently been opened for large-scale settlement and is receiving large inflows of immigrants.
   - **b.** A country, like the United Kingdom in the late nineteenth century or the United States today, that leads the world technologically but is seeing that lead eroded as other countries catch up.
   - **c.** A country that has discovered large oil reserves that can be exploited with little new investment (like Saudi Arabia).
   - **d.** A country that has discovered large oil reserves that can be exploited only with massive investment (like Norway, whose oil lies under the North Sea).
   - **e.** A country like South Korea that has discovered the knack of producing industrial goods and is rapidly gaining on advanced countries.
5. Which of the following is a direct foreign investment, and which is not?
   - **a.** A Saudi businessman buys $10 million of IBM stock.
   - **b.** The same businessman buys a New York apartment building.
   - **c.** A French company merges with an American company; stockholders in the U.S. company exchange their stock for shares in the French firm.
   - **d.** An Italian firm builds a plant in Russia and manages the plant as a contractor to the Russian government.
6. The Karma Computer Company has decided to open a Brazilian subsidiary. Brazilian import restrictions have prevented the firm from selling into that market, while the firm has been unwilling to sell or lease its patents to Brazilian firms because it fears this will eventually hurt its technological advantage in the U.S. market. Analyze Karma's decision in terms of the theory of multinational enterprise.

Further Reading

Richard A. Brecher and Robert C. Feenstra. "International Trade and Capital Mobility Between Diversified Economies." *Journal of International Economics* 14 (May 1983), pp. 321–339. A synthesis of the theories of trade and international factor movements.

Richard E. Caves. *Multinational Enterprises and Economic Analysis.* Cambridge: Harvard University Press, 1982. A view of multinational firms' activities.

Wilfred J. Ethier. "The Multinational Firm." *Quarterly Journal of Economics* 101 (November 1986), pp. 805–833. Models the internalization motive of multinationals.

Irving Fisher. *The Theory of Interest.* New York: Macmillan, 1930. The ''intertemporal'' approach described in this chapter owes its origin to Fisher.

Edward M. Graham and Paul R. Krugman. *Foreign Direct Investment in the United States.* Washington, D.C.: Institute for International Economics, 1989. A survey of the surge of foreign investment in the United States, with an emphasis on policy issues.

Charles P. Kindleberger. *American Business Abroad.* New Haven: Yale University Press, 1969. A good discussion of the nature and effects of multinational firms, written at a time when such firms were primarily United States-based.

Charles P. Kindleberger. *Europe's Postwar Growth: The Role of Labor Supply.* Cambridge: Harvard University Press, 1967. A good account of the role of labor migration during its height in Europe.

G. D. A. MacDougall. ''The Benefits and Costs of Private Investment from Abroad: A Theoretical Approach.'' *Economic Record* 36 (1960), pp. 13–35. A clear analysis of the costs and benefits of factor movement.

Robert A. Mundell. ''International Trade and Factor Mobility.'' *American Economic Review* 47 (1957), pp. 321–335. The paper that first laid out the argument that trade and factor movement can substitute for each other.

Jeffrey Sachs. ''The Current Account and Macroeconomic Adjustment in the 1970s.'' *Brookings Papers on Economic Activity,* 1981. A study of international capital flows that takes the approach of viewing such flows as intertemporal trade.

Appendix to Chapter 7
More on Intertemporal Trade

This appendix contains a more detailed examination of the two-period intertemporal trade model described in the chapter. The concepts used are the same as those used in Chapter 5 to analyze international exchanges of different consumption goods at a *single* point in time. In the present setting, however, the trade model explains international patterns of investment and borrowing and the determination of the *intertemporal* terms of trade (that is, the real interest rate).

First consider Home, whose intertemporal production possibility frontier is shown in Figure 7A-1. Recall that the quantities of present and future consumption goods produced at Home depend on the amount of present consumption goods invested to produce future goods. As currently available resources are diverted from present consumption to investment, production of present consumption, Q_P, falls and production of future consumption, Q_F, rises. Increased investment therefore shifts the economy up and to the left along the intertemporal production possibility frontier.

The chapter showed that the price of future consumption in terms of present consumption is $1/(1 + r)$, where r is the real interest rate. Measured in terms of present consumption, the value of the economy's total production over the two periods of its existence is therefore

$$V = Q_P + Q_F/(1 + r).$$

Figure 7A-1 shows the isovalue lines corresponding to the relative price $1/(1 + r)$ for different values of V. These are straight lines with slope $-(1 + r)$ (because future consumption is on the vertical axis). As in the standard trade model, firms' decisions lead to a production pattern that maximizes the value of production at market prices, $Q_P + Q_F/(1 + r)$. Production therefore occurs at point Q. The economy invests the amount shown, leaving Q_P^1 available for present

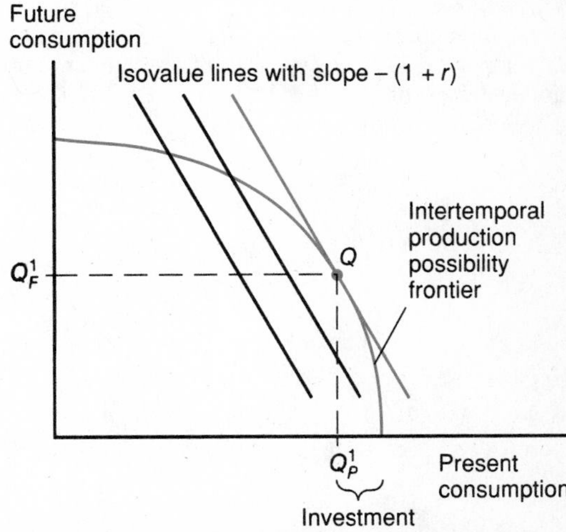

FIGURE 7A-1
Determining Home's intertemporal production pattern.
At a world real interest rate of r, Home's investment level maximizes the value of production over the two periods that the economy exists.

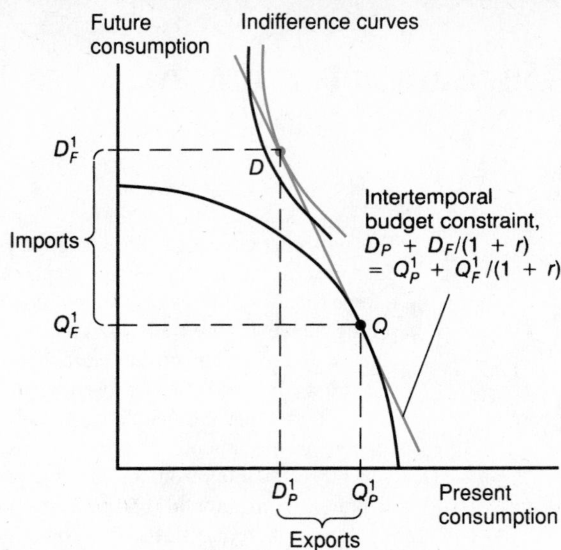

FIGURE 7A-2
Determining Home's intertemporal consumption pattern.
Home's consumption places it on the highest indifference curve touching its intertemporal budget constraint. The economy exports $Q_P^1 - D_P^1$ units of present consumption and imports $D_F^1 - Q_F^1 = (1 + r) \times (Q_P^1 - D_P^1)$ units of future consumption.

consumption and producing an amount Q_F^1 of future consumption when the first-period investment pays off.

Notice that at point Q, the extra future consumption that would result from investing an additional unit of present consumption just equals $(1 + r)$. It would be inefficient to push investment beyond point Q because the economy could do better by lending additional present consumption to foreigners instead. Figure 7A-1 implies that a rise in the world real interest rate r, which steepens the isovalue lines, causes investment to fall.

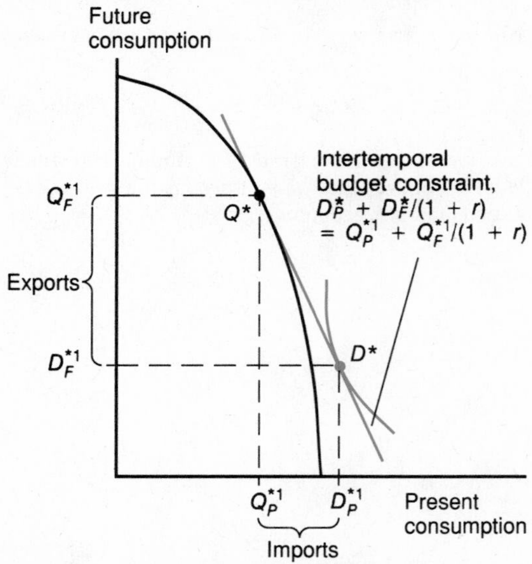

FIGURE 7A-3
Determining Foreign's intertemporal production and consumption patterns.
Foreign produces at point Q^* and consumes at point D^*, importing $D_P^{*1} - Q_P^{*1}$ units of present consumption and exporting $Q_F^{*1} - D_F^{*1} = (1 + r) \times (D_P^{*1} - Q_P^{*1})$ units of future consumption.

FIGURE 7A-4
International intertemporal equilibrium in terms of offer curves.
Equilibrium is at point E (with interest rate r^1) because desired Home exports of present consumption equal desired Foreign imports and desired Foreign exports of future consumption equal desired Home imports.

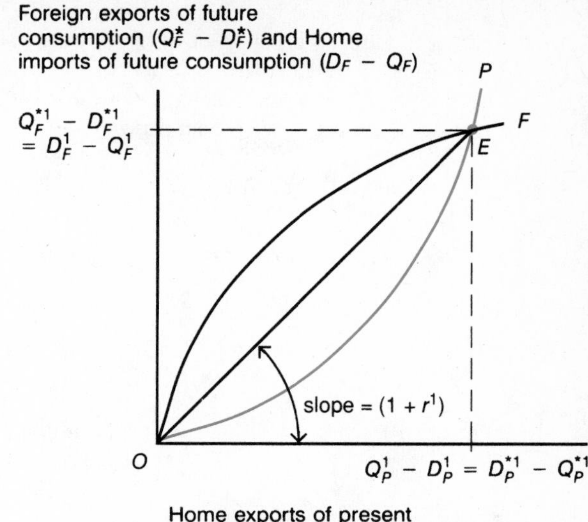

Figure 7A-2 shows how Home's consumption pattern is determined for a given world interest rate. Let D_P and D_F represent the demands for present and future consumption goods, respectively. Since production is at point Q, the economy's consumption possibilities over the two periods are limited by the *intertemporal budget constraint:*

$$D_P + D_F/(1 + r) = Q_P^1 + Q_F^1/(1 + r).$$

This constraint states that the value of Home's consumption over the two periods (measured in terms of present consumption) equals the value of consumption goods produced in the two periods (also measured in present consumption units). Put another way, production and consumption must lie on the same isovalue line.

Point D, where Home's budget constraint touches the highest attainable indifference curve, shows the present and future consumption levels chosen by the economy. Home's demand for present consumption, D_P^1, is smaller than its production of present consumption, Q_P^1, so it exports (that is, lends) $Q_P^1 - D_P^1$ units of present consumption to Foreigners. Correspondingly, Home imports $D_F^1 - Q_F^1$ units of future consumption from abroad when its first-period loans are repaid to it with interest. The intertemporal budget constraint implies that $D_F^1 - Q_F^1 = (1 + r) \times (Q_P^1 - D_P^1)$, so that trade is *intertemporally* balanced.

Figure 7A-3 shows how investment and consumption are determined in Foreign. Foreign is assumed to have a comparative advantage in producing *future* consumption goods. The diagram shows that at a real interest rate of r, Foreign borrows consumption goods in the first period and repays this loan using consumption goods produced in the second period. Because of its relatively rich domestic investment opportunities and its relative preference for present consumption, Foreign is an importer of present consumption and an exporter of future consumption.

As in Chapter 5 (appendix), international equilibrium can be portrayed by an offer curve diagram. Recall that a country's offer curve is the result of plotting its desired exports against its desired imports. Now, however, the exchanges plotted involve present and future consumption.

Figure 7A-4 shows that the equilibrium real interest rate is determined by the intersection of the Home and Foreign offer curves *OP* and *OF* at point *E*. The ray *OE* has slope $(1 + r^1)$, where r^1 is the equilibrium world interest rate. At point *E*, Home's desired export of present consumption equals Foreign's desired import of present consumption. Put another way, at point *E*, Home's desired first-period lending equals Foreign's desired first-period borrowing. Supply and demand are therefore equal in both periods.

Regional Economic Issues
Chapter 8

In 1992 several publishers of maps introduced a new kind of globe. A standard globe is, of course, a sphere representing the earth on which the territories of different nations are painted in a variety of colors. On the new globes, however, countries are no longer painted on. Instead, they consist of snap-on plastic sections that can be removed and replaced.

Why did the map makers introduce these new globes? So that customers could be sent ''update'' kits: sets of replacement snap-on parts that would allow them to keep up with changes in political boundaries without buying new globes! In the 1990s nations, once stable entities, began to divide and recombine with dizzying speed. East Germany, recently a sovereign state, no longer exists since being absorbed into what was once West Germany. The Soviet Union has dissolved into its constituent republics, giving the world a whole new set of unfamiliar countries like Belarus and Tadjikistan. Czechoslovakia has split into the Czech and Slovak republics. And even peaceful, generally prosperous Canada is torn by political divisions that could break it into two or more separate states.

These spectacular political upheavals have suddenly changed the definition of important parts of world trade. We normally draw a firm distinction between **interregional trade,** the flows of goods that take place *inside* countries, and the international trade that is the subject of this book. Yet in today's world of shifting boundaries definitions may suddenly change. Flows of goods between East and West Germany used to be considered international trade; now they are simply interregional trade within a reunified country. Conversely, shipments from Ukraine to Belarus used to be simply interregional trade; now they are part of international trade.

There are also less spectacular but still important changes in the world economy that seem to blur the distinction between regions and nations. Most notably, the nations of the European Community (EC) have embarked on a series of measures designed to unify their economies. The Single European Act, passed in 1986 and scheduled to take effect in 1992,[1] is intended to remove all barriers to the free flow of goods, services, capital, and even labor between EC nations. If it succeeds, the economies of, say, France and Germany will eventually be as unified as those of the East Coast and the Midwest in the United States. This unity will be further reinforced if Europe succeeds in establishing a common currency. (We discuss Europe's efforts to unify its currency, including some of the problems it has recently encountered, in Chapter 21.) If Europe succeeds in establishing a truly unified market, what is now international economics within Europe will become indistinguishable from regional economics within the United States.[2]

The new instability in what used to be unchangeable national boundaries has led recently to a resurgence of interest in the field of **regional economics.** By looking at the ways that regions interact within countries, economists hope to find clues about the effects of changes in political boundaries on national economies. If Quebec separates from the rest of Canada, what will happen to the former Canadian economy? We can get some idea by comparing the trade among Canadian provinces with the trade between Canadian provinces and the United States. If Europe forms a truly integrated market, how will relations among its nations change? We can get some idea by comparing trade and factor movements between European countries with those between U.S. states.

In this chapter we discuss how our understanding of internatinal economics can be increased by studying regional economies. We begin by asking a fundamental question: What defines a nation as an economic unit? Then we turn to some comparisons between the economics of regions within a country and the economics of separate nations. Finally, we turn to some of the characteristic problems of regional economics and ask to what extent they may begin to manifest themselves in the international economy as well.

● What Is a Country?

There is a widely available map entitled "The Earth at Night." It was not drawn by a cartographer—it is a collage of nighttime photographs taken by satellites. It shows the parts of the earth's surface that are illuminated by human activity—for the most part oil fields (where unused natural gas is flared) and cities.

The most striking aspect of the map is what it does *not* show. There is no sign of

[1] The changes taking place under this act are popularly referred to as "1992." In practice, many of the provisions of the Single European Act will not take effect on schedule.

[2] The blurring of the lines between international and regional economics is more pronounced in Europe than anywhere else, largely because geography and economic development make it a far more cohesive economic unit than other continents. It is useful to compare Europe and South America in this regard: Europe has only 30 percent of South America's land mass, yet it has a population that is 60 percent larger and a purchasng power at least five times as large. Because South American nations are quite far apart and relatively poor, they do not sell very much to each other: more than 80 percent of their exports go to other continents. By contrast, the compact and wealthy European market generates intensive trade, with more than 70 percent of exports of European countries going to other European countries.

the political boundaries between countries. There are clearly defined regions where cities cluster together, but they do not correspond to national units. On one side, the United States has several distinct urban clusters: the Boston-Washington corridor, the industrial heartland along the Great Lakes, the urban sprawls of Southern and Northern California. On the other, Europe has a dense belt of cities that runs roughly from Liverpool to Prague, crossing the boundaries of at least nine countries (a region known to European geographers as the ''hot banana''). An alien spaceship arriving at night would never guess that the United States is one country, or the European Community twelve.

The view from space reminds us that the political boundaries between countries are artificial and may have little to do with the natural lines of commerce. Instead, political boundaries have been set by historical processes driven by war and diplomacy, which often produce geographical units that are peculiar when viewed in economic terms.

The boundary between Canada and the United States is a good example. At the time the United States became a separate country while Canada remained a British colony, the parts of Canada that had been colonized by Europeans formed a reasonably compact unit around the St. Lawrence River. As Canada extended itself westward, however, it became, in economic terms, a very long, narrow country indeed. Figure 8-1 shows an ''economic'' map of the United States and Canada. Each Canadian province is represented by a solid circle, each of the thirty most populous U.S. states by an open circle, with the area of each circle proportional to income. The map conveys clearly the impression that if the United States and Canada were a single nation, each Canadian province would find the bulk of its market in what is now the United States, rather than in other parts of Canada. One might say that Canada is, in effect, closer to the United States than it is to itself.

Yet it is also clear that in reality national boundaries *do* matter. In fact, Canada is much more of an economic unit than it seems to be when viewed from space. This is not an accident: nations may not be natural economic units, but government policies often turn them into economic units all the same.

HOW GOVERNMENTS CREATE NATIONAL ECONOMIES

New York is about the same distance from Los Angeles that it is from London: it takes about 6 hours to fly, a few seconds to send a fax. Nonetheless, New York's economy remains much more closely linked to that of Los Angeles than to that of London because national boundaries impose significant barriers to doing business.

One reason is that governments impose explicit **barriers to trade.** The protectionist policies we study in Chapters 9–12—tariffs, import quotas, and their variations—have traditionally separated national economies. Tariff barriers among advanced industrial countries have been steadily reduced since their peak in the 1930s, and in some cases major countries have formed free trade zones that are free from all such restrictions. But explicit trade restrictions remain a significant barrier to international trade.

Even where deliberate restrictions on trade are small, the mere fact that countries collect any tariffs imposes significant ''red tape'' costs on international trade. For example, trade among the member countries of the European Community is free from all tariffs and import quotas. Nonetheless, until 1992, goods crossing national boundaries within the European Community had to pass through customs checks. This process

FIGURE 8-1
An economic map of North America.
The dark circles represent Canadian provinces, the open circles U.S. states. In each case the area of the circle represents the political unit's income. The map suggests that if there were no political boundary, Canadian provinces would trade mostly with the U.S. rather than with each other.
Source: *Statistical Abstract of the United States,* 1992 and Statistics Canada, *Canada,* 1992.

was often a serious and costly nuisance: at busy times the lines of trucks waiting to be cleared could extend for miles and require drivers to wait, their engines idling, for several hours. The same is true for movement of people: it takes a good deal more time to fly from London to Paris than to fly from New York to Washington, even though the time spent in the air is the same, because of the time spent clearing emigration and immigration procedures.

Differences in national currencies impose another set of nuisance costs on international trade. Some of these costs involve the expense of changing one currency into another. One well-known calculation is that if you were to visit all twelve nations of the European Community in succession, changing your money into local currency at each point but never buying anything, you would return to your starting point with only 40 percent of your original sum. (Remember, however, that firms engaged in international trade, who change money on a large scale, get much better exchange rates than tourists who stop at airport foreign exchange windows.) Fluctuating exchange rates also create risk in international transactions; this risk can usually be hedged (see Chapter 14), but, again, only at a cost.

Yet another reason why international trade is less than trade between regions of a country is that regulations and standards may differ in ways that make selling products difficult. France and Great Britain have completely free trade with each other. In Britain, however, cars drive on the left, in France on the right; British electrical outlets are designed to accommodate three-pronged plugs with flat pins, while French outlets take two-pronged plugs with round pins. These arbitrary differences mean that a British resident cannot shop for a car in France, because it will have the steering wheel on the wrong side, and that a French resident cannot buy a toaster in England, because its plug will not fit his or her wall socket. These obvious barriers to trade are matched by thousands of more subtle ones. A product that meets French health and safety regulations may fail to meet those in Germany, not because the German regulations are stricter, but simply because they are different.

Hidden barriers to trade in services are even greater than those to trade in goods. Many service industries, such as banking and insurance, are subject to extensive government regulation designed to protect both consumers and taxpayers (who will have to bail out these institutions if they fail). When the rules are different across countries, it becomes difficult for businesses to operate across borders, since a multinational firm that meets one country's guidelines may fail to meet another's.

Finally, one important limitation on the integration of international markets is the fact that *people* do not move freely across borders. All modern countries maintain immigration restrictions that make it difficult for foreigners to enter a country or to take jobs once there. Such barriers to the movement of people can, to an important degree, limit trade in goods and services as well. As anyone in business knows, people are most likely to become aware of business opportunities—including export opportunities—through personal contacts. In the United States, such personal contacts are geographically far-flung: many residents of the East Coast have friends or family members in California and vice versa. The informal information networks provided by personal connections are much thinner across national borders, simply because there is so much less international migration.

The overall result of these various obstacles to international trade is that national markets are far more integrated than international markets. A recent study[3] of the trade of Canadian provinces makes this point clearly. As we saw in Figure 8-1, Canada seems to make very little sense as a geographical unit. In that figure, we indicate the Canadian province of Ontario, centered on Toronto; the western Canadian province of British Columbia; and the U.S. state of California. Notice that California is a bigger economy than the whole of Canada, and its market is about 10 times as large as that of British Columbia. And Vancouver, the major city of British Columbia, is nearly as far from Toronto as Los Angeles. One might therefore expect California to be a much more important market for Ontario than British Columbia. In fact, however, in 1988 Ontario exported only $1.4 billion to California, versus $5.0 billion to British Columbia.

In today's world, then, there remains a basic difference between international and interregional trade. But will this difference persist? A recent best-selling book by the

[3] John McCallum. ''International Borders and Trade Patterns: The Case of Canada and the United States,'' mimeo: McGill University, November 1992.

management consultant Kenichi Ohmae was entitled *The Borderless World;* its thesis was that companies will soon be competing in a truly global market. To what extent is the division between international and regional economics in the process of dissolving?

FROM INTERNATIONAL TO INTERREGIONAL TRADE

In at least two major parts of the world economy there are moves underway to make international markets as well integrated as national markets. In North America, the United States and Canada signed a free trade pact in 1989 and at the time of writing they appeared likely to join Mexico in the North American Free Trade Agreement (NAFTA). Trade has been free from tariffs in the European Community since its founding in 1957, but there has been a major push to remove many of the remaining obstacles to unified markets.

The European effort is an impressive exercise. The main focus of ''1992'' has been on setting common regulations for business, so that a German firm can sell a good or service in France as easily as a New York firm sells its wares in Illinois. This has involved negotiating standards in some 300 areas, a process that has sometimes caused considerable conflict (see box). There is little question that by eliminating differences

Food Fights in Europe

Most modern nations impose health and quality standards on food. These standards are intended to assure consumers that when, for example, they buy ground beef it will neither be bulked up with fat and gristle nor handled in a way that might lead to contamination. Such standards differ between countries, however, and the need to package exported food to meet foreign standards is a significant cost of international trade. Part of the job of the European bureaucrats engaged in "1992" was to set common European standards for food.

Unfortunately, this harmonization of standards has led to conflicts because of differences in national tastes and attitudes—and there is no area in which those differences are greater than food.

First to become angry were the British. Part of the traditional English breakfast is the traditional English breakfast sausage, the "banger." These sausages are made with relatively little meat and are bulked up with cereal filler. As a result of their high cereal content, traditional bangers would not have met the original EC guidelines that set a minimum meat content for any product labelled "sausage"! British opponents of European unity were quick to use the case as an example of how bureaucrats in Brussels would undermine their national identity.

Soon afterward came the French. For health reasons, the European Community proposed new guidelines on manufacture of cheese. To the horror of French gourmets, these guidelines would have banned some traditional French cheeses, including Camembert.

The European Community backed down in both cases, but there are doubtless other conflicts to come. Indeed, in the fall of 1992 a new dispute arose, this time over the British custom of hanging slaughtered turkeys for a day to improve their flavor. At the time of writing, this dispute was still unresolved.

in regulations and the nuisance costs of border checks, the European Community will achieve a significant integration of markets.

Exactly how far this integration will finally go remains uncertain, however. European nations, in spite of the short distances that separate them, have significant cultural differences. At the most basic level, there is the difference in language: France and Britain will soon be linked by a tunnel underneath the English Channel, but they will be divided for the next few centuries by their native tongues. Beyond this, European countries continue to have surprisingly different preferences—there are hardly any English-style pubs in France or Germany, for example—which may in effect segment their markets for many consumer goods. Some observers predict that the results of "1992" will be disappointing and that it will be a very long time before the European market begins to look as unified as that in the United States.

In North America, nothing like the European effort at integration is planned. U.S., Canadian, and Mexican regulations and standards will continue to be set independently after NAFTA. Yet in one important respect NAFTA will be more than a free trade agreement. A major part of the negotiations has involved foreign direct investment, setting ground rules that will ensure the free operation of multinational firms across the borders of the three nations. There is some evidence that this aspect of NAFTA may be very important. Notably, the U.S. and Canadian automobile industries—which involve the same companies in both countries—show a trade pattern that seems pretty much to ignore the border. This pattern suggests that with completely free direct investment, other markets may also become truly continental.

Despite the moves toward integration in Europe and North America it seems unlikely that we will see a "borderless world," or for that matter even borderless continents, anytime soon. That is, regions will continue to be different from nations for some years to come. Nonetheless, it is useful to compare regional economics with international economics to get some clues about future trends in the international economy.

Comparing Regions and Nations

The differences between regions and nations are quantitative, not qualitative. That is, the same forces are at work in interregional and international trade, but their relative importance is different. In particular, regions within a country tend to be much more specialized than countries and experience much greater factor mobility.

SPECIALIZATION AND TRADE

Regions within a country tend to be more specialized and engage in more trade than countries, even when the regions are themselves as large as countries.

Consider, for example, the geography of automobile production in the United States and in Europe. In the United States, automobile production grew up serving a unified national market, free of tariffs and other barriers to trade. This made it possible to develop a single dominant auto-producing center. In the industry's formative years several producers in the Detroit area took the lead in the market, and Detroit's initial advantage proved self-reinforcing. That is, the concentration of automobile manufacturing around Detroit supported a network of specialized suppliers and skilled labor that further enhanced the attractiveness of Detroit as a place to build cars—in the terminology of Chapter 6, *external economies* led to the emergence of Detroit as America's "Motor City."

The geographic concentration of U.S. auto manufacturing peaked around 1940, when 75 percent of U.S. auto manufacturing took place within 150 miles of Detroit. Since then changes in the industry have caused a gradual drift away from the original center. Still, as Table 8-1 shows, even now most of the U.S. auto industry remains concentrated in the Midwest.

In Europe, by contrast, motor vehicle industries emerged for the most part between the world wars and served protected domestic markets. Thus the United Kingdom, France, Germany, and Italy all had their own auto industries. After World War II trade became gradually freer, and today there is free trade among all four countries. Nonetheless, as Table 8-1 shows, auto production remains far more evenly spread among the four large European nations than among U.S. regions with comparable population.

What does this difference in locational patterns mean for specialization and trade? The traditional U.S. auto manufacturing area surrounding Detroit has almost as large a population as Belgium or the Netherlands; yet in 1940, and even now, Detroit concentrated to a far greater degree than either of those countries on producing one kind of product. In other words, the regional economy was more specialized than national economies of the same size. And because in 1940 nearly all the cars bought in the United States were made in or near Detroit, long-distance shipments of automobiles within the United States were much larger than in Europe.

The automobile example is by no means unique. We saw in Chapter 6 how the United States has come to have most of its carpet production concentrated near Dalton, Georgia and has come to have high technology concentrations in Silicon Valley in California and Route 128 in Massachusetts. There are similar concentrations in Europe, but they are much smaller, because until recently they were not free to serve the whole European market. Even more striking is the concentration of banking and financial services: financial activity in the United States is concentrated in New York and Chicago to an extent that is far greater than anything one sees in Europe.

Because each industry in the United States has been free to concentrate geographically, each region in the United States tends to specialize in a few key industries and to sell the great bulk of the output of these industries to faraway markets rather than local consumers. Countries, by contrast, even in Europe, are usually less export-oriented and correspondingly do considerably less trade.

TABLE 8-1 Distribution of auto production, 1985 (percent)

	U.S.		*European Community*
Midwest	66.3	Germany	38.5
South	25.4	France	31.1
West	5.1	Italy	17.6
Northeast	3.2	U.K.	12.9

Source: Automotive Industry Association, *Automotive Facts and Figures,* 1989.

If international markets become more integrated, we can expect to see the geography of production gradually come to resemble that of the United States. For example, in a truly integrated European market there would probably be a dominant financial center playing a role similar to that of New York. The interesting political question is whether, say, France would meekly accept a downgrading of Paris to financial satellite of London. Similarly, one might expect aircraft production to concentrate somewhere; would the British cheerfully concede that Toulouse will be the European equivalent of Seattle, where Boeing makes most large U.S. commercial jets?

If the world economy as a whole becomes increasingly integrated, the process may go even further. Perhaps in the long run there will be only one great financial center. Will it be London, Tokyo, or New York? Will Europe, the United States, or Japan be willing to accept the outcome if their center doesn't win? Merely posing these questions helps show why it is difficult to integrate markets among nations as well as markets within nations.

FACTOR MOBILITY

If there is one overwhelming difference between the way markets function within countries and between countries, it is the mobility of labor. Movement of labor between advanced countries is too small to make much economic difference. There is some migration from poor countries to rich, not all of it legal, but overall international labor mobility is quite small.

By contrast, labor mobility within countries can be very large. The United States, despite the distances that relocating workers must move, provides the most impressive example. Over the fifty-year period from 1940 to 1990, the overall U.S. population grew by 89 percent. In the Northeast, however, the population grew only 41 percent, thanks to a steady outward flow of workers and their families, while California's population grew 331 percent. In effect, the population of the Northeast was 25 percent less and that of California 128 percent more than they would have been in the absence of migration.

It also appears that labor mobility in the United States is highly responsive to changes in economic conditions and provides an important safety valve for troubled regions. One recent study[4] found that when a local slump—like the downturn in the Texas oil industry in the 1980s or the 1990s slide in defense jobs in California—hits a U.S. state, it leads to only a temporary rise in that state's unemployment rate. The reason is not that the state regains the jobs it lost, but that workers leave for other states. Normally, within six years the state is back to the national average unemployment rate.

There is very little prospect that international labor mobility will rise to levels approximating those within countries anytime in the foreseeable future. Within the European Community, "1992" now guarantees citizens of any member country the legal right to live and work in any other. Language and cultural barriers remain high enough, however, that it is hard to imagine that large-scale migration will take place. On a global basis, there are tens of millions of people in poor countries who would be eager to migrate to richer countries in search of higher wages, but there is vehement political opposition to allowing this kind of large-scale migration.

[4] Olivier Blanchard and Lawrence Katz. "Regional Evolutions," *Brookings Papers on Economic Activity* 2:1992.

While there is thus little prospect of a large increase in labor mobility among countries, however, there has been increasing mobility of other factors. As pointed out in Chapter 22, there has been considerable liberalization of capital movements in the last few years. And foreign direct investment surged in the 1980s. Among the most significant aspects both of ''1992'' in Europe and of the free trade agreements in North America has been increased freedom for multinational firms to operate across borders. In the United States, we are accustomed to the way local markets are linked by the continent-wide reach of large firms, and rarely even stop to think about where they are headquartered—how may people know or care where McDonald's or Wal-Mart was founded? By the year 2005, European consumers may no more think of, say, Volkswagen as a specifically German firm than Americans think of Dupont as a specifically Delaware firm.

Problems of Regional Economics

We have seen that even Europe is far from becoming as integrated an economy as the United States, and that we are very far indeed from becoming a ''borderless world.'' Yet both goods and capital markets *are* becoming more integrated, and international economic issues are becoming a little more like regional issues.

The main difference between regional and international economic issues is in the mobility of factors of production: highly mobile between regions, less mobile between nations. This difference has two consequences. First, because regions must compete to hold on to mobile factors, the long-run ability of a region to export a good depends on *absolute* rather than *comparative* advantage. Second, movements of capital and especially labor often give rise to cumulative processes of *uneven development.*

ABSOLUTE VERSUS COMPARATIVE ADVANTAGE

In our first model of international trade, the Ricardian model of Chapter 2, we developed the crucial concept that trade depends on *comparative* advantage, not *absolute* advantage. That is, you cannot predict whether a country will export a good simply by asking whether it produces that good more efficiently than other countries do; you have to ask how the country's relative productivity in that industry compares with its relative productivity in other industries.

We saw this principle demonstrated in a particular example (Table 2-1) in which one country is more productive than another in all sectors. Nonetheless, the less productive country (Foreign) is still able to export the good (wine) in which it has a smaller productivity disadvantage. In the example, labor in the less productive economy ends up with a wage only one-third as high as that in the more productive nation; nonetheless, trade is beneficial to both countries.

But what if Home and Foreign were not two separate countries, but two regions of a single country, with high mobility of labor between them? Then one would expect workers to move from the low-wage Foreign region to the high-wage Home region. If all workers were mobile in the long run, the low-productivity Foreign regional economy would simply disappear.

Suppose that instead of being less productive in all sectors, Foreign were actually more efficient than Home in producing wine, although less productive in cheese. What would happen? The answer is that labor would move toward whichever region offered higher wages. In the long run, then, wages would have to be the same in the two regions. Given equal wages, Home would produce cheese, in which it is more efficient, while Foreign would produce wine.

In general, in an economy in which labor moves freely between regions, one would expect a long-run tendency toward equal wages. And if all regions must pay more or less the same wages, regions will only be able to export goods in which they have an **absolute advantage**—that is, goods they can produce with lower unit labor requirements than any other region.

In Chapter 2 we ridiculed the ''expert'' who asserted that ''many small countries have no comparative advantage in anything.'' Every country has a comparative advantage in something. It is, however, certainly true that many regions have *absolute* advantage in at best a few goods and services. As a result, such regions are unable to attract or hold a large population. Within the United States, there are large tracts of mountain and desert land that are very thinly populated—indeed, the nighttime satellite map we referred to earlier in this chapter shows nearly half the country virtually blank.

Changes in tastes or technology can change the pattern of absolute advantage. Sometimes such changes can open up regions for development. Irrigation, for example, turned areas of California that had previously been virtually uninhabited desert into valuable farmland. In other cases, however, a region may lose its previous advantages. The subsequent process of depopulation can be dramatic. For example, the population of the western part of the U.S. Great Plains—an arid area traditionally dependent on ranching and limited farming—has seen its population thin out to the point that many small towns have simply ceased to exist. Population and land value have declined to the point that there is a serious proposal to return an area about 1.5 times the size of California to wilderness status. Another region with shrinking population is Central Appalachia, where the decline of the coal industry has led to massive outmigration (see box).

Anatomy of a Declining Region

Countries always have a comparative advantage in something, but regions may have no absolute advantage in anything and may therefore be largely depopulated by shifts in tastes or technology.

The classic example in the United States is Central Appalachia, consisting of Eastern Kentucky plus parts of several neighboring states. This region is heavily dependent on coal mining. After World War II, however, the industry went into a deep slump: in the nation as a whole, many customers shifted from coal to oil and gas for home heating fuel. Furthermore, the deep-coal mining of the Appalachian area faced competition from the less labor-intensive strip mining of shallower deposits elsewhere.

The region has not managed to find an alternative industrial base and has experienced a sharp decline in population. Between 1945 and 1990, the population of the United States increased 80 percent; the population of the central Appalachian area fell by more than one-third.

Is there anything wrong with regional decline? We saw in Chapter 7 that international factor movements are normally a source of efficiency gains, for the same reasons that trade in goods and services is normally beneficial. The same is true for movements of labor between regions of the same country. In particular, migrants normally raise their own real income substantially by moving. If coal miners from Appalachia can double their real income by moving to Chicago and taking jobs in the service sector, why should anyone object?

In practice, however, governments frequently try to discourage out-migration from declining regions and try to establish new industries to take the place of declining sectors. There are several reasons for this policy concern.

One reason is more cultural than economic: many countries seem to feel it is important to preserve regional traditions as part of their cultural mix and therefore try to maintain existing populations rather than adopt a laissez-faire attitude toward economic changes that threaten to depopulate regions. Such cultural concerns are part of the motivation behind the European attempts to support farmers, which we discuss in Chapter 9.

A second, more narrowly economic problem with regional decline is that not all people are equally mobile, and the out-migration of part of a region's population can further impoverish those who stay behind. For example, it is often true that skilled and educated workers are the first to leave, and that their departure reduces job opportunities for the less skilled workers who remain. It may be difficult to hold on to providers of key services, like doctors and schoolteachers. The departure of workers can also deplete the tax base of regions that must still provide services to older residents. In principle the gains from those who leave should be sufficient to allow them to compensate those left behind and still be better off. In practice, such compensation is rare, and regions with declining population often find that those who remain experience a fall in income.

Finally, policy makers have often been concerned about the possibility that regional decline will become a self-reinforcing process—that a region that loses some industries will become increasingly unattractive to other industries, leading to a cumulative process of decline. The argument that success and failure of regions tend to be self-reinforcing is generally referred to as the concept of *uneven development.*

AGGLOMERATION ECONOMIES AND UNEVEN DEVELOPMENT

In relatively poor countries there are often large differences in the level of income between regions *within* the country. In Brazil, for example, the urbanized, industrialized southeast of the nation has a per capita income three times that of the less-developed northeast. In Mexico the Federal District around Mexico City and the manufacturing regions along the U.S. border have per capita incomes almost four times as high as those in the south of the country.

In advanced nations, where labor is usually more mobile, income differences are not usually as large. What we see, instead, are highly uneven geographical distributions of population. In the United States, a huge nation whose natural resources are widely dispersed, most of the population is concentrated in a few urban belts—indeed, 25 percent lies in the almost continuous chain of cities from Boston to Washington.

Why are wealth and population so highly concentrated geographically? It is hard to argue that the concentration of population in the Boston-Washington corridor or in the Valley of Mexico is due to inherent advantages of the site. Instead, geographers point to a variety of ways in which initial advantages of particular sites, which may represent nothing more than historical accident, tend to be reinforced over time. Such self-reinforcing processes are often referred to as examples of **cumulative causation.**

The clearest example of cumulative causation involves the interaction of economies of scale (which we studied in Chapter 6), transportation costs, and labor mobility. This process can perhaps best be seen by considering a simple example.

In this example, we make the following assumptions:

1. There are two regions, East and West.
2. There are a number of firms, each producing a different good.
3. Each firm sells a total of 10 million units of its good.
4. It costs $1 to ship a unit of a good from East to West or vice versa.
5. Economies of scale are strong enough that in spite of transport costs each firm builds only one plant to serve both regions.
6. Of the 10 million units each firm sells, 60 percent (6 million units) are sold to consumers who are immobile and evenly divided between regions. The other 40 percent (4 million units), however, are sold either to other firms or to people working for those firms. The location of these sales depends on where firms choose to locate. Thus if *all* firms choose to produce in East, a typical firm will sell 7 million units there: 3 million to the immobile consumers in East and 4 million to firms and their workers located in East. Only 3 million units will be sold to immobile consumers in West.
7. Firms try to choose a location that minimizes the costs of shipping their goods to consumers.

Given assumption 6, the best location for a firm depends on what other firms decide to do. If all other firms choose to locate in East, a firm will sell most of its output in East—and East will therefore be the firm's own preferred location. If, on the other hand, all other firms choose to locate in West, West will be the preferred location. Table 8-2 shows how the shipping costs of a typical firm depend not only on its own location but on the location choices made by other firms. Because a firm minimizes shipping costs by locating close to the majority of its customers, the typical firm will want to locate in the same place other firms are located. Clearly, then, a concentration of firms in *either* location, once established, will be self-sustaining.

TABLE 8-2 Hypothetical shipping costs (in millions of dollars)

	Shipping costs of a firm when its factory is located in: *East*	*West*
And all other plants are located in:		
East	3 (for goods shipped from East to West)	7 (for goods shipped from West to East)
West	7 (for goods shipped from East to West)	3 (for goods shipped from West to East)

Let's back up and consider the intuition for what is happening in this example. We have considered an economy in which firms face economies of scale that are large enough to make them want to produce in only one location and transport costs that make them prefer locations close to their largest market. But the market will be largest precisely where large numbers of other firms have chosen to locate. Suppose that for whatever reason one region starts with a larger industrial base than the other. The region with the most firms and hence the larger market would attract firms from the other region, further reinforcing its market size advantage, and so on. This circular process of cumulative causation would eventually lead to concentration of industry in only one region.

There is a similarity between our story of cumulative causation and our discussion of external economies as a source of specialization in Chapter 6. Indeed, the market size effects discussed above are, in effect, a kind of external economy which may be reinforced by other external economies such as knowledge spillovers, advantages of large labor markets, and so on. External economies associated with the concentration of resources or industry in a particular location play a crucial role in all of regional and urban economics, and have a special name: **agglomeration economies.**

In Chapter 6 we saw that when external economies play a large role in trade, who produces what may be determined largely by historical accidents. Uneven regional development may similarly be determined by historical contingency. For example, the massive population concentration in America's Northeast Corridor is evidently due not to the region's natural resources, but to the historical fact that 17th and 18th century European immigrants settled the East coast first and that the original urban and industrial settlements were therefore along that coast. Within that urban belt, New York remains the largest city—in large part because in 1820 the Hudson River (which reached the sea at New York) was linked to the Great Lakes by the Erie Canal.

Why does the possibility of uneven development pose a problem for economic policy? We have just seen that when shifts in absolute advantage lead some regions to suffer losses in employment, this shrinkage can cause social and economic difficulties. It is inevitable that regions will sometimes have bad luck, as Appalachia did when its coal industry shrank. But the theory of uneven development suggests that regional decline will not be simply the result of bad luck: there may be a systematic process in which some regions gain at the expense of others.

The problems that uneven development can cause are illustrated by the situation in Italy. The unification of Italy in 1860 was followed by growing economic inequality between the industrial, increasingly modern north of the country and the backward southern part, known as the Mezzogiorno. Since World War II, the Mezzogiorno has received massive aid from the north, yet has remained poor; its poverty has bred crime and corruption. In recent years, as Europe as a whole has experienced considerable economic difficulties, growing numbers of northern Italians have come to feel hostile toward the south, seeing it as a drain on their income and a bad influence on their politics. Indeed, the Lombard League, a political party that wants the affluent north to secede from the poorer south, has won significant numbers of votes in recent elections.

The Italian example is very much on the minds of German policy makers today, as a result of German reunification (see Chapter 20). They fear that the former East Germany will become Germany's Mezzogiorno: that industry will prefer to remain in the already prosperous West and that the most motivated and skilled workers from the East will move out, leaving behind a permanently backward region.

The experience of the United States suggests, however, that the forces that work toward uneven development may not be as powerful as they once were. In the early twentieth century, the U.S. economy was marked by great regional inequality. The great bulk of U.S. manufacturing was concentrated in the so-called "Manufacturing Belt" in the Northeast and along the Great Lakes. Meanwhile, the South remained predominantly agricultural and poor. Since World War II, however, there has been both a decentralization of manufacturing, as industry has moved to the Sunbelt states of the South and West, and a substantial narrowing of interstate differences in per capita income.

Why did manufacturing in the United States spread out? Geographers suggest two reasons: the growth of the U.S. market made it possible for manufacturers to have a large number of efficient scale plants, and the emergence of new technologies like automobiles and airplanes together with an improved road network reduced per-mile transportation costs of manufactured goods. Recall the assumptions underlying the example in Table 8-2. We assumed for that example that economies of scale were sufficient to induce each firm to build only one plant. In the late nineteenth century, many firms did have only a few plants serving the whole U.S. market. But as the market grew and it became possible to have a number of efficient scale plants in different parts of the country, firms spread out to improve their access to markets. For example, automobile manufacturers began to establish assembly plants in each major region of the country instead of assembling all cars in the Detroit area—and tire manufacturers, who ship much of their output directly to the factories where they are put onto new cars, followed suit.

The fall in transportation costs also reduced the incentive for firms to concentrate together. Industries such as textiles had long tended to cluster near their original homes in the Northeast and the industrial Midwest, near their traditional customers and suppliers. With lower transport costs, some of them became willing to trade off greater distance for locations, such as the southern United States, that offered cheaper labor and land.

In Europe, economists agonize over the contrasting models of Italy, where political and economic unification did little if anything to produce convergence between regions, and the United States, in which regional inequality has diminished to the point that it is no longer a major issue. The European Community contains a number of "peripheral" regions—Ireland, Portugal, much of Spain, Southern Italy, and Greece—whose average per capita income is less than half that of the rest of the Community. What will happen to these regions, which are relatively distant from markets? These regions already receive aid from the community, known as "cohesion funds," that subsidize the construction of roads, telephone networks, schools, and other public investments that it is hoped will promote development. Some European leaders have called for a large increase in these funds. At the time of writing, however, the richer nations appeared very reluctant to support any large increase in aid.

Summary

1. Economists normally draw a sharp distinction between international trade, which takes place between countries, and the *interregional trade* that takes place within

a country. Recent political turmoil has, however, blurred that distinction, leading to a renewal of interest in *regional economics.*

2. Countries are not "natural" economic units: the regions that make up countries would not necessarily be each others' main trading partners in the absence of political boundaries. In practice, however, trade between regions of a single country is usually greater than international trade. The reasons include deliberate *barriers to trade* set up by countries, the costs imposed by moving between different national currencies, differences in national regulations and standards, and immigration restrictions that limit international labor mobility.

3. The Single European Act, generally referred to as "1992," is intended to remove many of the obstacles that still limit trade within the European Community. The North American Free Trade Agreement, in a more limited way, aims to do the same for Canada, the United States, and Mexico. To the extent that these moves succeed, international economics and regional economics will become more similar on both continents.

4. The same forces drive trade between regions as those that drive trade between nations. However, there are quantitative differences. Regions tend to be more specialized and engage in more trade, especially because integrated markets allow greater specialization due to external economies. There is also much greater mobility of factors of production, especially labor, between regions than between nations.

5. The high mobility of factors means that in the long run a region's exports, unlike a country's, are not determined by comparative advantage. Since wages tend to be equalized across regions, long-run patterns of regional specialization reflect *absolute advantage* instead.

6. Regional economies are often characterized by *uneven development,* a process of *cumulative causation* in which regions with an initial advantage due to accidents of history attract increasing amounts of industry and employment away from less lucky regions. The external economies associated with large concentrations of population and industry are known as *agglomeration economies.* While uneven development has often occurred, however, the U.S. experience since World War II suggests that the forces of uneven development may have become weaker over time.

Key Terms

interregional trade
regional economics
barriers to trade
absolute advantage
uneven development
cumulative causation
agglomeration economies

Problems

1. There is some possibility that the French-speaking Canadian province of Quebec could at some point become an independent nation. How might independence for Quebec affect the flows of goods and services between Quebec and other Canadian provinces?

2. In 1993 many people in France were outraged when the Hoover vacuum cleaner company decided to close its plant in the city of Dijon, and concentrate its operations at its other European plant (in Glasgow, Scotland). Explain why "1992" may have encouraged Hoover to do this, and why other such controversies may become increasingly common in Europe.

3. Imagine an economy consisting of two regions: California and Montana. These regions can produce two goods, wine and cattle. Labor is the only factor of production. In California it takes two workers to produce a cow, but only one to produce a gallon of wine. In Montana, it takes only one worker to produce a cow, but five to produce a gallon of wine.

We assume that the relative demand for cattle is

$$\frac{\textit{cows}}{\textit{gallons of wine}} = \frac{1}{10} \times \frac{\textit{price per gallon}}{\textit{price per cow}}$$

a. Assume initially that Montana and California each have 1 million workers, and that workers are not mobile between regions. Determine prices, production, and the pattern of trade.

b. Now suppose that workers can move between the two regions, and that they move to whichever region offers the higher wage rate. (We assume that all workers are the same, that it is climate that makes their productivity different in California and Montana.) Determine prices, production, and regional work forces in this case. (Hint: start from the point that wages must be equal in the two regions, and use this fact to determine which goods are produced where.)

c. Compare your answers under (a) and (b), and explain how this relates to the discussion in the text of the difference between *absolute* and *comparative* advantage.

4. "The growing integration of the European economy will be devastating for Europe's less productive regions. In a highly integrated economy, regions must have absolute rather than merely comparative advantage to export. This problem will be compounded by the immobility of labor: in Europe, unlike the United States, workers will not leave the less productive regions in search of jobs elsewhere." What's wrong with this plausible-sounding quote?

5. We showed in the text how cumulative causation can lead to the concentration of population in one region. But will the population always end up in the right place? Here's an example that suggests that it may not.

Imagine a country with two regions, East and West. As in the text, we suppose that there are a number of firms, each producing a different good. Economies of scale are sufficiently strong that each firm will produce its goods in only one location, which it will choose to minimize shipping costs. Each firm sells 10 million units of its good in total. Of this, 60 percent of the sales are to geographically immobile farmers, while 40 percent are to workers who work for the firms themselves.

In the text we assumed that farmers were equally divided between the two regions. Now, however, we assume that three-fourths of the farmers, accounting for 45 percent of the demand, are located in West, while only one-fourth are in East.

a. Discuss the location choice of a firm given that (i) all other firms choose to locate in East (ii) all other firms choose to locate in West. Show that in each case concentration of all firms in the region is in fact self-sustaining.

b. Try to make an argument that one of these outcomes is better than the other. (Hint: think about transportation costs.)

6. Maintain the assumptions of problem 5, but now return to the assumption that farmers are evenly split between East and West. We now suppose, however, that firms have the option of maintaining *two* plants, one in each region, and thereby avoiding any shipping costs. Suppose that it costs $1 to ship each unit between East and West, and that it costs $4 million to open a second plant. Each producer chooses the number and location of plants to minimize the sum of these plant costs and transportation costs. For example, if a producer has only one plant in East, and sells 3 million units in West, she incurs $3 million in shipping costs; she can eliminate these costs by opening a second plant in West, but this costs $4 million and is therefore not a good idea.

a. Assume that all other producers have only one plant in East. How many plants should our firm have, and where?

b. Now assume that all other producers have two plants, one in each region. As a result, 50 percent of our firm's sales take place in each region. What is our optimal plant location strategy now?

c. Many governments have tried to promote decentralization of population, to avoid the concentration in a few regions so characteristic of modern economies. In the light of this example, is there any prospect for success?

Further Reading

Michael Chisholm. *Regions in Recession and Resurgence.* London: Unwin Hyman, 1990. A survey of major trends in thinking about regional economic development and how well they match actual experience.

Peter Dicken and Peter E. Lloyd. *Location in Space: Theoretical Perspectives in Economic Geography.* New York: HarperCollins, 1990. An excellent textbook in "location theory," the field that tries to explain the spatial pattern of economic activity.

European Commission. *One Market, One Money.* Brussels: European Commission, 1990. The European Commission's study of the likely effects of economic and monetary union within Europe contains an extensive discussion of possible impacts on the relatively poor "peripheral" regions of the country.

Riccardo Faini. "Increasing Returns, Nontraded Inputs, and Regional Development." *Economic Journal* 94 (1984), pp. 308–323. A theoretical model of cumulative causation and uneven development, inspired by the problem of Italy's Mezzogiorno.

Walter Isard. *Location and Space-Economy.* Cambridge, MA: MIT Press, 1956. A classic work by the founder of the field of regional science.

Paul Krugman. *Geography and Trade.* Cambridge: MIT Press, 1991. Three lectures on the relationship between international and regional economics.

David Myers. "Emergence of the American Manufacturing Belt: An Interpretation." *Journal of Historical Geography* 9 (1983), pp. 145–174. An insightful discussion of the reasons why the nineteenth century saw a differentiation of the United States into an industrialized East and an agricultural West and South.

Michael Porter. *The Competitive Advantage of Nations.* New York: Free Press, 1990. A best-selling book by a leading management consultant who concludes, surprisingly, that the relevant units for global competition are often regions rather than whole nations.

Allan Pred. *The Spatial Dynamics of U.S. Urban-Industrial Growth, 1800–1914.* Cambridge: MIT Press, 1966. An influential study of cumulative causation in the emergence of major United States cities.

Part Two International Trade Policy

The Instruments of Trade Policy

Chapter 9

Previous chapters have answered the question, ''Why do nations trade?'' by *describing* the causes and effects of international trade and the functioning of a trading world economy. While this question is interesting in itself, its answer is much more interesting if it helps answer the question, ''What should a nation's trade policy be?'' Should the United States use a tariff or an import quota to protect its automobile industry against competition from Japan and Korea? Who will benefit and who will lose from an import quota? Will the benefits outweigh the costs?

This chapter examines the policies that governments adopt toward international trade, policies that involve a number of different actions. These actions include taxes on some international transactions, subsidies for other transactions, legal limits on the value or volume of particular imports, and many other measures. The chapter provides a framework for understanding the effects of the most important instruments of trade policy.

Basic Tariff Analysis

A tariff, the simplest of trade policies, is a tax levied when a good is imported. **Specific tariffs** are levied as a fixed charge for each unit of goods imported (for example, $3 per barrel of oil). **Ad valorem tariffs** are taxes that are levied as a fraction of the value of the imported goods (for example, the 25 percent U.S. tariff on imported trucks). In either case the effect of the tariff is to raise the cost of shipping goods to a country.

Tariffs are the oldest form of trade policy and have traditionally been used as a source of government income. Until the introduction of the income tax, for instance, the U.S. government raised most of its revenue from tariffs. Their true purpose, however, has usually been not only to provide revenue but to protect particular domestic sectors. In the early nineteenth century the United Kingdom used tariffs (the famous Corn Laws) to protect its agriculture from import competition. In the late nineteenth century both Germany and the United States protected their new industrial sectors by imposing tariffs on imports of manufactured goods. The importance of tariffs has declined in modern times, because modern governments usually prefer to protect domestic industries through a variety of **nontariff barriers.** Nonetheless, an understanding of the effects of a tariff remains a vital basis for understanding other trade policies.

In developing the theory of trade in Chapters 2 through 7 we adopted a *general equilibrium* perspective. That is, we were keenly aware that events in one part of the economy have repercussions elsewhere. However, in many (though not all) cases trade policies toward one sector can be reasonably well understood without going into detail about the repercussions of that policy in the rest of the economy. For the most part, then, trade policy can be examined in a *partial equilibrium* framework. The rest of the economy is always there in the background, however. When the effects on the economy as a whole become crucial, we will refer back to general equilibrium analysis.

SUPPLY, DEMAND, AND TRADE IN A SINGLE INDUSTRY

Let's suppose there are two countries, Home and Foreign, both of which consume and produce wheat, which can be costlessly transported between the countries. In each country wheat is a simple competitive industry in which the supply and demand curves are functions of the market price. Normally Home supply and demand will depend on the price in terms of Home currency, and Foreign supply and demand will depend on the price in terms of Foreign currency, but we assume that the exchange rate between the currencies is not affected by whatever trade policy is undertaken in this market. Thus, we quote prices in both markets in terms of Home currency.

Trade will arise in such a market if prices are different in the absence of trade. Suppose that in the absence of trade the price of wheat is higher in Home than it is in Foreign. Now allow foreign trade. Since the price of wheat in Home exceeds the price in Foreign, shippers begin to move wheat from Foreign to Home. The export of wheat raises its price in Foreign and lowers its price in Home until the difference in prices has been eliminated.

To determine the world price and the quantity traded, it is helpful to define two new curves: the Home **import demand curve** and the Foreign **export supply curve,** which are derived from the underlying domestic supply and demand curves. Home import demand is the excess of what Home consumers demand over what Home producers supply; Foreign export supply is the excess of what Foreign producers supply over what Foreign consumers demand.

Figure 9-1 shows how the Home import demand curve is derived. At the price P^1 Home consumers demand D^1, while Home producers supply only S^1, so Home import demand is $D^1 - S^1$. If we raise the price to P^2, Home consumers demand only D^2, while Home producers raise their supply to S^2, so import demand falls to $D^2 - S^2$. Thus the import demand curve MD is downward-sloping. At P_A, Home supply and

FIGURE 9-1
Deriving Home's import demand curve.
As the price of the good increases, Home consumers demand less, while Home producers supply more, so that the demand for imports declines.

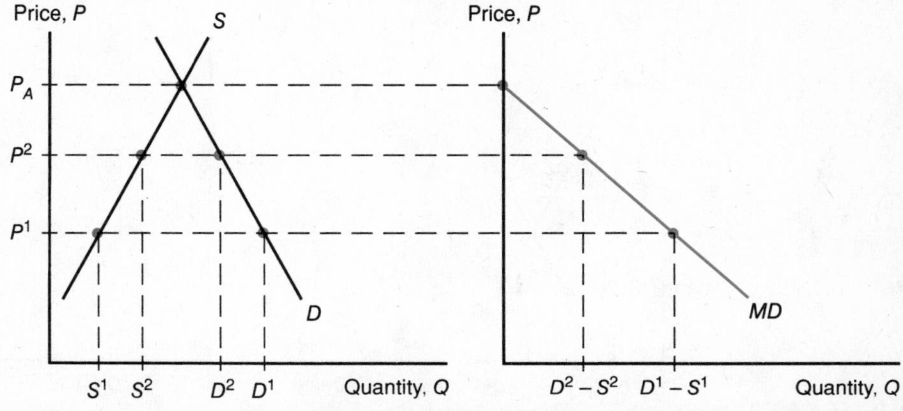

demand are equal in the absence of trade, so the Home import demand curve crosses zero.

Figure 9-2 shows how the Foreign export supply curve *XS* is derived. At P^1 Foreign producers supply S^{*1}, while Foreign consumers demand only D^{*1}, so the supply available for export is $S^{*1} - D^{*1}$. At P^2 Foreign producers raise their supply to S^{*2} and Foreign consumers lower their demand to D^{*2}, so export supply rises to $S^{*2} - D^{*2}$. Thus the Foreign export supply curve is upward-sloping. If the price were as low as P^*_A, supply and demand would be equal in the absence of trade, so the Foreign export supply curve crosses zero at P^*_A.

World equilibrium occurs when Home import demand equals Foreign export supply (Figure 9-3). At the price P_W, where the two curves cross, world supply equals world demand. At the equilibrium point 1 in Figure 9-3,

$$\text{Home demand} - \text{Home supply} = \text{Foreign supply} - \text{Foreign demand}.$$

By adding and subtracting from both sides, this can be rearranged to say that

$$\text{Home demand} + \text{Foreign demand} = \text{Home supply} + \text{Foreign supply}$$

or, in other words,

$$\text{World demand} = \text{world supply}.$$

EFFECTS OF A TARIFF

From the point of view of someone shipping goods, a tariff is just like a cost of transportation. If Home imposes a tax of $2 on every bushel of wheat imported, shippers will be unwilling to move the wheat unless the price difference between the two markets is at least $2.

FIGURE 9-2
Deriving Foreign's export supply curve.
As the price of the good rises, Foreign producers supply more while Foreign consumers demand less, so that the supply available for export rises.

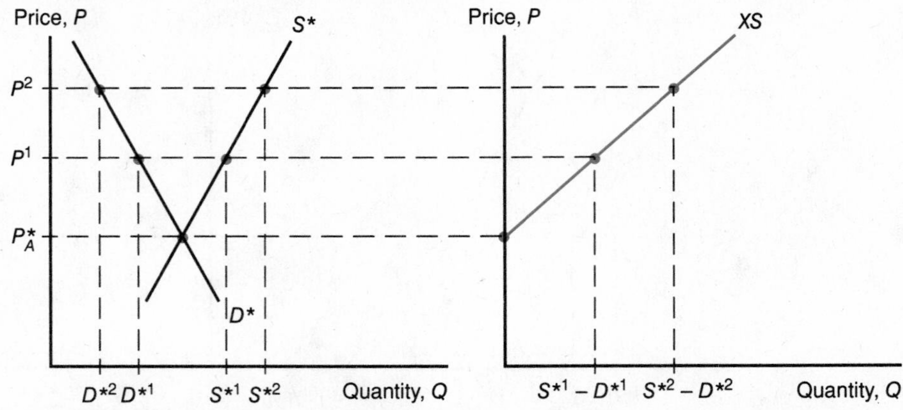

Figure 9-4 illustrates the effects of a specific tariff of $t per unit of wheat. In the absence of a tariff, the price of wheat would be equalized at P_W in both Home and Foreign. With the tariff in place, however, shippers are not willing to move wheat from Foreign to Home unless the Home price exceeds the Foreign price by at least $t. Thus the price in Home rises and the price in Foreign falls, until the price difference is $t. Introducing a tariff drives a wedge between the prices in the two markets. The tariff raises the price in Home to P_T and lowers the price in Foreign to $P^*_T = P_T - t$. In

FIGURE 9-3
World equilibrium.
The equilibrium world price is where Home import demand equals Foreign export supply.

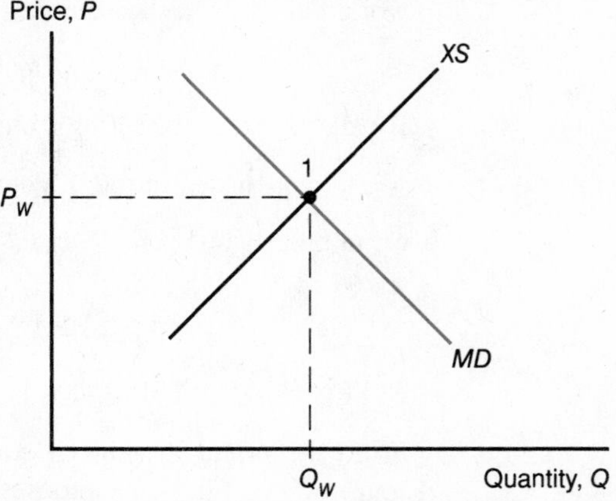

FIGURE 9-4
Effects of a tariff.
A tariff raises the price in Home while lowering the price in Foreign. The volume traded declines.

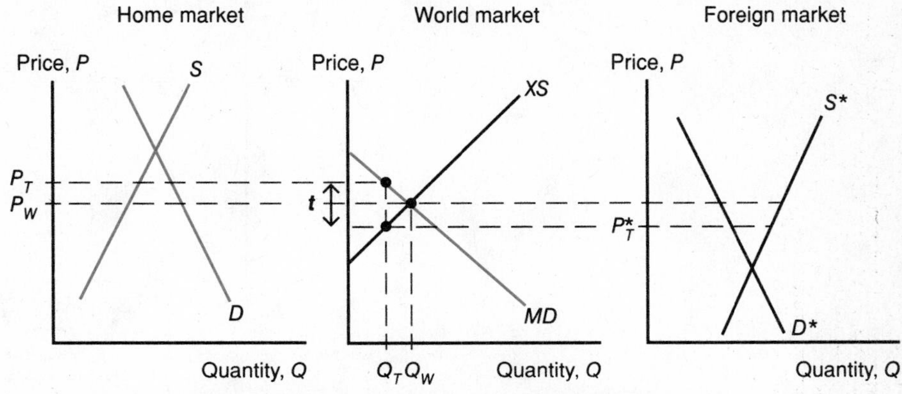

Home producers supply more at the higher price, while consumers demand less, so that fewer imports are demanded. In Foreign the lower price leads to reduced supply and increased demand, and thus a smaller export supply. Thus the volume of wheat traded declines from Q_W, the free-trade volume, to Q_T, the volume with a tariff. At the trade volume Q_T, Home import demand equals Foreign export supply when $P_T - P_T^* = t$.

The increase in the price in Home, from P_W to P_T, is less than the amount of the tariff, because part of the tariff is reflected in a decline in Foreign's export price and thus is not passed on to Home consumers. This is the normal result of a tariff and of any trade policy that limits imports. The size of this effect, however, is often in practice very small. When a small country imposes a tariff, its share of the world market for the goods it imports is usually minor to begin with, so that its import reduction has very little effect on the world price. For all practical purposes, the foreign export price of imported goods can be taken as given in many cases.

The effects of a tariff in the "small country" case where a country cannot affect foreign export prices are illustrated in Figure 9-5. In this case a tariff raises the price of the imported good by the full amount of the tariff, from P_W to $P_W + t$. Production rises from S^1 to S^2, while consumption falls from D^1 to D^2.

MEASURING THE AMOUNT OF PROTECTION

A tariff on an imported good raises the price received by domestic producers of that good. This effect is often the tariff's principal objective—to *protect* domestic producers from the low prices that would result from import competition. In analyzing trade policy in practice, it is important to ask how much protection a tariff or other trade

FIGURE 9-5
A tariff in a small country.
When a country is small, a tariff cannot lower the foreign price of the good it imports.

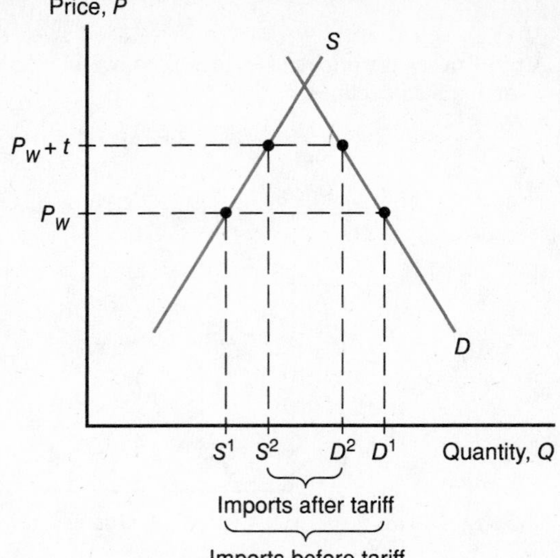

policy actually provides. The answer is usually expressed as a percentage of the price that would prevail under free trade. An import quota on sugar could, for example, raise the price received by U.S. sugar producers by 45 percent.

Measuring protection would seem to be straightforward in the case of a tariff: if the tariff is an ad valorem tax proportional to the value of the imports, the tariff rate itself should measure the amount of protection; if the tariff is specific, dividing the tariff by the price net of the tariff gives us the ad valorem equivalent.

There are two problems in trying to calculate the rate of protection this simply. First, if the small country assumption is not a good approximation, part of the effect of a tariff will be to lower foreign export prices rather than to raise domestic prices, and the effect of trade policies on foreign export prices is sometimes significant. In theory (through rarely in practice) a tariff could actually lower the price received by domestic producers (the Metzler paradox discussed in Chapter 5).

The second problem is that tariffs may have very different effects on different stages of production of a good. A simple example illustrates this point.

Suppose that an automobile sells on the world market for $8000 and that the parts out of which that automobile is made sell for $6000. Let's compare two countries: one that wants to develop an auto assembly industry and one that already has an assembly industry and wants to develop a parts industry.

To encourage a domestic auto industry, the first country places a 25 percent tariff on imported autos, allowing domestic assemblers to charge $10,000 instead of $8000. In this case it would be wrong to say that the assemblers receive only 25 percent protection. Before the tariff, domestic assembly would take place only if it could be done for $2000 (the difference between the $8000 price of a completed automobile and the $6000 cost of parts) or less; now it will take place even if it costs as much as $4000 (the difference between the $10,000 price and the cost of parts). That is, the 25 percent tariff rate provides assemblers with an **effective rate of protection** of 100 percent.

Now suppose the second country, to encourage domestic production of parts, imposes a 10 percent tariff on imported parts, raising the cost of parts to domestic assemblers from \$6000 to \$6600. Even though there is no change in the tariff on assembled automobiles, this policy makes it less advantageous to assemble domestically. Before the tariff it would have been worth assembling a car locally if it could be done for \$2000 (\$8000 − \$6000); after the tariff local assembly takes place only if it can be done for \$1400 (\$8000 − \$6600). The tariff on parts, then, while providing positive protection to parts manufacturers, provides negative effective protection to assembly at the rate of −30 percent (−600/2000).

Reasoning similar to that seen in this example has led economists to make elaborate calculations to measure the degree of effective protection actually provided to particular industries by tariffs and other trade policies. Trade policies aimed at promoting economic development, for example (Chapter 11), often lead to rates of effective protection much higher than the tariff rates themselves.[1]

Costs and Benefits of a Tariff

A tariff raises the price of a good in the importing country and lowers it in the exporting country. As a result of these price changes, consumers lose in the importing country and gain in the exporting country. Producers gain in the importing country and lose in the exporting country. In addition, the government imposing the tariff gains revenue. To compare these costs and benefits, it is necessary to quantify them. The method for measuring costs and benefits of a tariff depends on two concepts common to much microeconomic analysis: consumer and producer surplus.

CONSUMER AND PRODUCER SURPLUS

Consumer surplus measures the amount a consumer gains from a purchase by the difference between the price he actually pays and the price he would have been willing to pay. If, for example, a consumer would have been willing to pay \$8 for a bushel of wheat but the price is only \$3, the consumer surplus gained by the purchase is \$5.

Consumer surplus can be derived from the market demand curve (Figure 9-6). For example, suppose the maximum price at which consumers will buy 10 units of a good is \$10. Then the tenth unit of the good purchased must be worth \$10 to consumers. If it were worth less, they would not purchase it; if it were worth more, they would have been willing to purchase it even if the price were higher. Now suppose that to get consumers to buy 11 units the price must be cut to \$9. Then the eleventh unit must be worth only \$9 to consumers.

[1] The effective rate of protection for a sector is formally defined as $(V_T - V_W)/V_W$, where V_W is value added in the sector at world prices and V_T value added in the presence of trade policies. In terms of our example, let P_A be the world price of an assembled automobile, P_C the world price of its components, t_A the ad valorem tariff rate on imported autos, and t_C the ad valorem tariff rate on components. You can check that if the tariffs don't affect world prices, they provide assemblers with an effective protection rate of

$$\frac{V_T - V_W}{V_W} = t_A + P_C\left(\frac{t_A - t_C}{P_A - P_C}\right).$$

FIGURE 9-6
Deriving consumer surplus from the demand curve.
Consumer surplus on each unit sold is the difference between the actual price and what consumers would have been willing to pay.

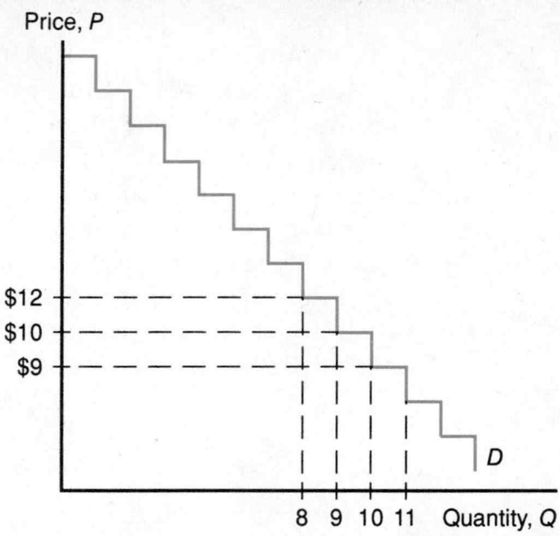

Suppose that the price is $9. Then consumers are just willing to purchase the eleventh unit of the good and thus receive no consumer surplus from their purchase of that unit. They would have been willing to pay $10 for the tenth unit, however, and thus receive $1 in consumer surplus from that unit. They might have been willing to pay $12 for the ninth unit; if so, they receive $3 of consumer surplus on that unit, and so on.

Generalizing from this example, if P is the price of a good and Q the quantity demanded at that price, then consumer surplus is calculated by subtracting P times Q from the area under the demand curve up to Q (Figure 9-7). If the price is P^1, the quantity demanded is Q^1 and the consumer surplus is measured by the area labeled *a*. If the price falls to P^2, the quantity demanded rises to Q^2 and consumer surplus rises to equal *a* plus the additional area *b*.

Producer surplus is an analogous concept. A producer willing to sell a good for $2 but receiving a price of $5 gains a producer surplus of $3. The same procedure used to derive consumer surplus from the demand curve can be used to derive producer surplus from the supply curve. If P is the price and Q the quantity supplied at that price, then producer surplus is P times Q minus the area under the supply curve up to Q (Figure 9-8). If the price is P^1, the quantity supplied will be Q^1, and producer surplus is measured by the area *c*. If the price rises to P^2, the quantity supplied rises to Q^2, and producer surplus rises to equal *c* plus the additional area *d*.

Some of the difficulties related to the concepts of consumer and producer surplus are technical issues of calculation that we can safely disregard. More important is the question of whether the direct gains to producers and consumers in a given market accurately measure the *social* gains. Additional benefits and costs not captured by consumer and producer surplus are at the core of the case for trade policy activism discussed in Chapter 10. For now, however, we will focus on costs and benefits as measured by consumer and producer surplus.

FIGURE 9-7
Geometry of consumer surplus.
Consumer surplus is equal to the area under the demand curve and above the price.

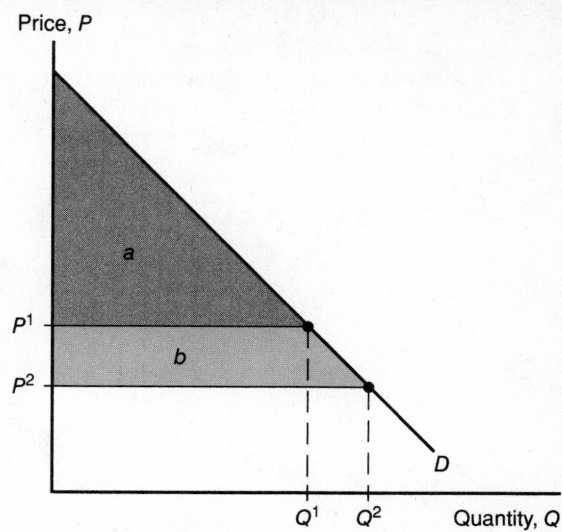

MEASURING THE COSTS AND BENEFITS

Figure 9-9 illustrates the costs and benefits of a tariff for the importing country.

The tariff raises the domestic price from P_W to P_T but lowers the foreign export price from P_W to P_T^* (refer back to Figure 9-4). Domestic production rises from S^1 to S^2, while domestic consumption falls from D^1 to D^2. The costs and benefits to different groups can be expressed as sums of the areas of five regions, labeled *a, b, c, d, e*.

Consider first the gain to domestic producers. They receive a higher price and therefore have higher producer surplus. Referring back to Figure 9-8, their gain may

FIGURE 9-8
Geometry of producer surplus.
Producer surplus is equal to the area above the supply curve and below the price.

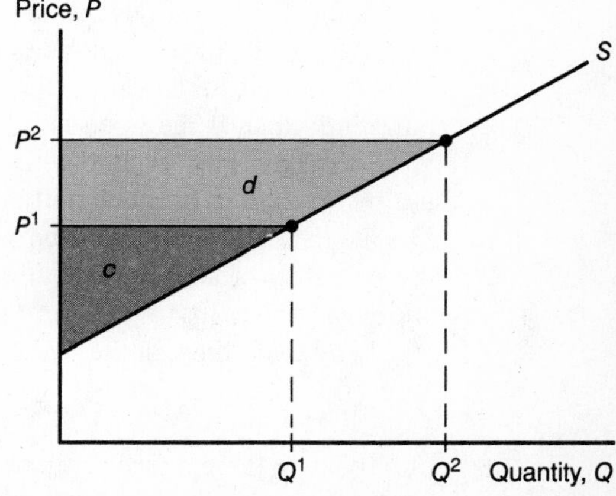

FIGURE 9-9
Costs and benefits of a tariff.
The costs and benefits to different groups can be represented as sums of the five areas *a, b, c, d,* and *e*.

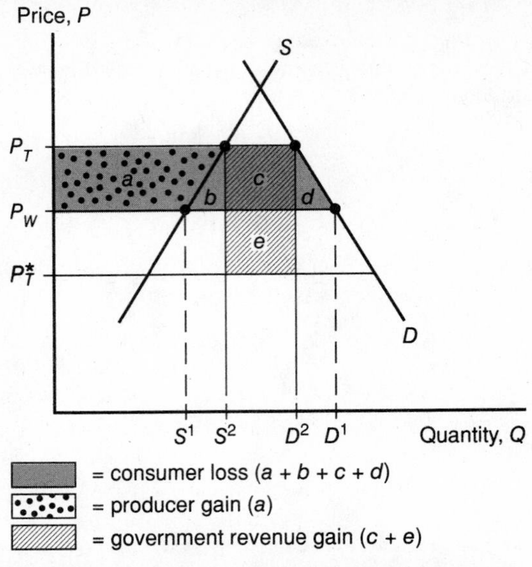

be measured by *a*, the increase in the difference between $P \times Q$ and the area under the supply curve.

Domestic consumers also face a higher price and are therefore worse off. Referring to Figure 9-7, the loss to domestic consumers is equal to the sum $a + b + c + d$, the reduction in the difference between the area under the demand curve and $P \times Q$.

There is a third player here as well: the government. The government gains by collecting tariff revenue. This is equal to the tariff rate *t* times the volume of imports $Q_T = D^2 - S^2$. Since $t = P_T - P^*_T$, the government's revenue is equal to the sum of the two areas *c* and *e*.

Since these gains and losses accrue to different people, the overall cost-benefit evaluation of a tariff depends on how much we value a dollar's worth of benefit to each group. If, for example, the producer gain accrues mostly to wealthy owners of resources, while the consumers are poorer than average, the tariff will be viewed differently than if the good is a luxury bought by the affluent but produced by low-wage workers. Further ambiguity is introduced by the role of the government: will it use its revenue to finance vitally needed public services or waste it on cost overruns? Despite these problems, it is common for analysts of trade policy to attempt to compute the net effect of a tariff on national welfare by assuming that at the margin a dollar's worth of gain or loss to each group is of the same social worth.

Let's look, then, at the net effect of a tariff on welfare. The net cost of a tariff is

$$\text{Consumer loss} - \text{producer gain} - \text{government revenue} \tag{9-1}$$

or, replacing these concepts by the areas in Figure 9-9,

$$(a + b + c + d) - a - (c + e) = b + d - e. \tag{9-2}$$

That is, there are two "triangles" whose area measures loss and a "rectangle" whose area measures an offsetting gain. A useful way to interpret these gains and losses is the following: the loss triangles represent the **efficiency loss** that arises because a tariff distorts incentives, while the rectangle represents the **terms of trade gain** that arise because a tariff lowers foreign export prices.

The gain depends on the ability of the tariff-imposing country to drive down foreign export prices. If the country cannot affect world prices (the "small country" case illustrated in Figure 9-5), region *e,* which represents the terms of trade gain, disappears, and it is clear that the tariff reduces welfare. It distorts the incentives of both producers and consumers by inducing them to act as if imports were more expensive than they actually are. The cost of an additional unit of consumption to the economy is the price of an additional unit of imports, yet because the tariff raises the domestic price above the world price, consumers reduce their consumption to the point where that marginal unit yields them welfare equal to the tariff-inclusive domestic price. The value of an additional unit of production to the economy is the price of the unit of imports it saves, yet domestic producers expand production to the point where the marginal cost is equal to the tariff-inclusive price. Thus the economy produces at home additional units of the good that it could purchase more cheaply abroad.

The net welfare effects of a tariff, then, are summarized in Figure 9-10. The negative effects consist of the two triangles *b* and *d.* The first triangle is a **production distortion loss,** resulting from the fact that the tariff leads domestic producers to produce too much of this good. The second triangle is a domestic **consumption distortion loss,** resulting from the fact that a tariff leads consumers to consume too little of the good. Against these losses must be set the terms of trade gain measured by the rectangle *e,* which results from the decline in the foreign export price caused by a tariff.

FIGURE 9-10
Net welfare effects of a tariff.
The colored triangles represent efficiency losses, while the rectangle represents a terms of trade gain.

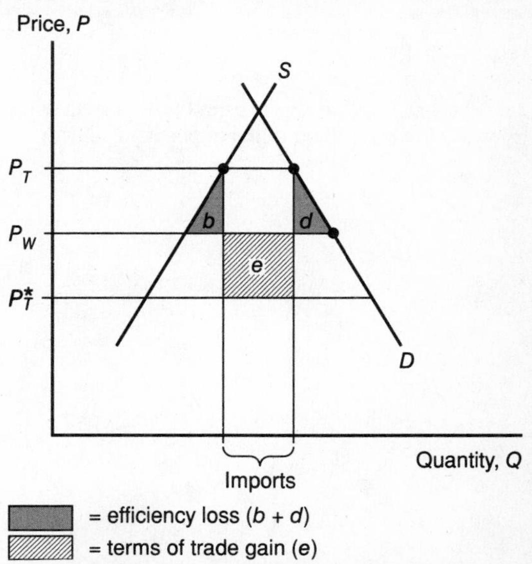

In the important case of a small country that cannot significantly affect foreign prices, this last effect drops out, so that the costs of a tariff unambiguously exceed its benefits.

Other Instruments of Trade Policy

Tariffs are the simplest trade policies, but in the modern world most government intervention in international trade takes other forms, such as export subsidies, import quotas, voluntary export restraints, and local content requirements. Fortunately, once we understand tariffs it is not too difficult to understand these other trade instruments.

EXPORT SUBSIDIES: THEORY

An **export subsidy** is a payment to a firm or individual that ships a good abroad. Like a tariff, an export subsidy can be either specific (a fixed sum per unit) or ad valorem (a proportion of the value exported). When the government offers an export subsidy, shippers will export the good up to the point where the domestic price exceeds the foreign price by the amount of the subsidy.

The effects of an export subsidy on prices are exactly the reverse of those of a tariff (Figure 9-11). The price in the exporting country rises from P_W to P_S, but because the price in the importing country falls from P_W to P_S^*, the price rise is less than the subsidy. In the exporting country, consumers are hurt, producers gain, and the government loses because it must expend money on the subsidy. The consumer loss is the area $a + b$; the producer gain is the area $a + b + c$; the government subsidy is the area $b + c + d + e + f + g$. The net welfare loss is therefore the sum of the areas $b + d + e + f + g$. Of these, b and d represent consumption and production distortion

FIGURE 9-11
Effects of an export subsidy.
An export subsidy raises prices in the exporting country while lowering them in the importing country.

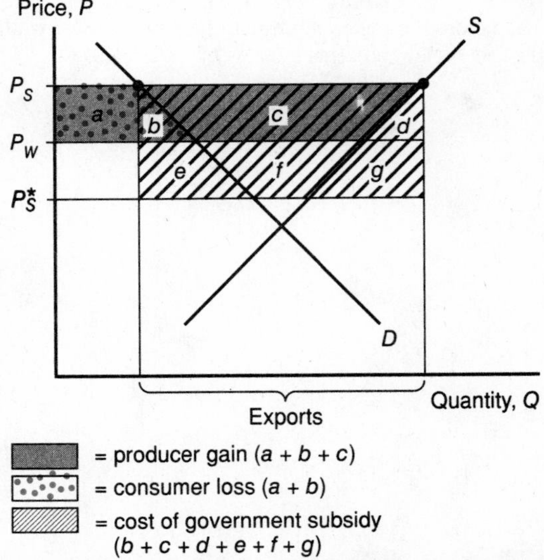

losses of the same kind that a tariff produces. In addition, and in contrast to a tariff, the export subsidy *worsens* the terms of trade by lowering the price of the export in the foreign market from P_W to P_S^*. This leads to the additional terms of trade loss $e + f + g$, equal to $P_W - P_S^*$ times the quantity exported with the subsidy. So an export subsidy unambiguously leads to costs that exceed its benefits.

Case Study

EUROPE'S COMMON AGRICULTURAL POLICY

Since 1957, six Western European nations—Germany, France, Italy, Belgium, the Netherlands, and Luxembourg—have been members of the European Economic Community; they were later joined by the United Kingdom, Ireland, Denmark, Greece, and, most recently, Spain and Portugal. Now called the European Community (EC) its two biggest effects are on trade policy. First, the members of the European Community have removed all tariffs with respect to each other, creating a customs union (discussed in the next chapter). Second, the agricultural policy of the European Community has developed into a massive export subsidy program.

The European Community's Common Agricultural Policy (CAP) began not as an export subsidy, but as an effort to guarantee high prices to European farmers by having the European Community buy agricultural products whenever the prices fell below specified support levels. To prevent this policy from drawing in large quantities of imports, it was initially backed by tariffs that offset the difference between European and world agricultural prices.

Since the 1970s, however, the support prices set by the European Community have turned out to be so high that Europe, which would under free trade be an importer of most agricultural products, was producing more than consumers were willing to buy. The result was that the European Community found itself obliged to buy and store huge quantities of food. At the end of 1985, European nations had stored 780,000 tons of beef, 1.2 million tons of butter, and 12 million tons of wheat. To avoid unlimited growth in these stockpiles, the European Community turned to a policy of subsidizing exports to dispose of surplus production.

Figure 9-12 shows how the CAP works. It is, of course, exactly like the export subsidy shown in Figure 9-11, except that Europe would actually be an importer under free trade. The support price is set not only above the world price that would prevail in its absence but also above the price that would equate demand and supply even without imports. To export the resulting surplus, an export subsidy is paid that offsets the difference between European and world prices. The subsidized exports themselves tend to depress the world price, increasing the required subsidy. Cost-benefit analysis would clearly show that the combined costs to European consumers and taxpayers exceed the benefits to producers.

At the time of writing the CAP was under substantial political pressure. This concern did not primarily reflect cost-benefit analysis, however. Instead, the problems were the budgetary strain from the subsidies—approximately 15 billion dollars annually—and conflict with the United States. The United States made a sharp reduction in Europe's agricultural subsidies one of its key demands in the Uruguay round of trade talks described in Chapter 10. At the time of writing, those talks were still stalled, largely because of the insistence of France in particular on maintaining high agricultural subsidies.

IMPORT QUOTAS: THEORY

An **import quota** is a direct restriction on the quantity of some good that may be imported. The restriction is usually enforced by issuing licenses to some group of individuals or firms. For example, the United States has a quota on imports of foreign cheese. The only firms allowed to import cheese are certain trading companies, each of which is allocated the right to import a maximum number of pounds of cheese each year; the size of each firm's quota is based on the amount of cheese it imported in the past. In some important cases, notably sugar and apparel, the right to sell in the United States is given directly to the governments of exporting countries.

It is important to avoid the misconception that import quotas somehow limit imports without raising domestic prices. *An import quota always raises the domestic price of the imported good.* When imports are limited, the immediate result is that at the initial price the demand for the good exceeds domestic supply plus imports. This causes the price to be bid up until the market clears. In the end, an import quota will raise domestic prices by the same amount as a tariff that limits imports to the same level (except in the case of domestic monopoly, when the quota raises prices more than this; see the second appendix to this chapter).

The difference between a quota and a tariff is that with a quota the government receives no revenue. When a quota instead of a tariff is used to restrict imports, the sum of money that would have appeared as government revenue with a tariff is collected by whomever receives the import licenses. License holders are able to buy imports and

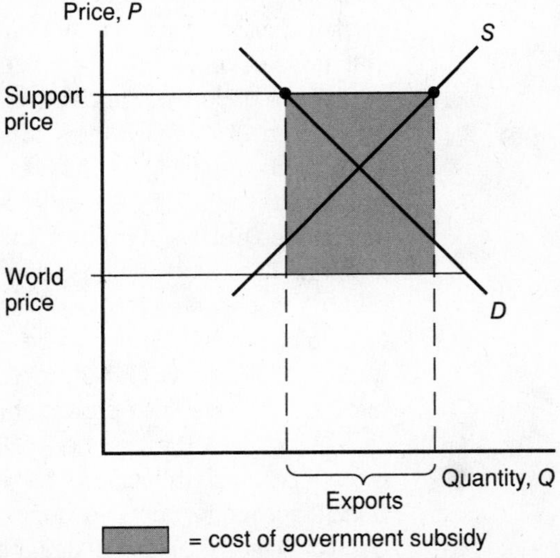

FIGURE 9-12
Europe's common agricultural program.
Agricultural prices are fixed above world market levels, and an export subsidy is used to dispose of the resulting surplus.

resell them at a higher price in the domestic market. The profits received by the holders of import licenses are known as **quota rents.** In assessing the costs and benefits of an import quota, it is crucial to determine who gets the rents. When the rights to sell in the domestic market are assigned to governments of exporting countries, as is often the case, the transfer of rents abroad makes the costs of a quota substantially higher than the equivalent tariff.

Case Study

AN IMPORT QUOTA IN PRACTICE: U.S. SUGAR

The U.S. sugar problem is similar in its origins to the European agricultural problem: a domestic price guarantee by the federal government has led to U.S. prices above world market levels. Unlike the European Community, however, the domestic supply in the United States does not exceed domestic demand. Thus the United States has been able to keep domestic prices at the target level with an import quota on sugar.

As it happens, the Federal Trade Commission (FTC), has quantified the likely costs and benefits of the sugar quota, allowing us to place numbers into our framework.[2] Before we proceed to these numbers, however, it is important to note two special features of U.S. sugar policy that affect the results.

First is that the import quota is combined with a tariff. The effect of this is to make the rents associated with the quota smaller than they would otherwise have been or, to put it another way, to allow the U.S. government to capture part of those rents. The second special feature is that the rights to sell in the United States—the import licenses—are allocated to twenty-four foreign governments, who then allocate these to their own residents. Thus whatever rents are not captured by the tariff accrue to foreigners.

Figure 9-13 shows the effects of the sugar quota, as estimated by the FTC. Notice that the United States is assumed to be a "small" country in terms of the world sugar market; this reflects a judgment that, given time, world sugar supply is highly elastic. The FTC estimates the normal world sugar price at 15 cents a pound, requiring a quota to raise the U.S. price to its support level of 21.8 cents. The difference between U.S. and world prices is thus 6.8 cents. Since the tariff rate is only 2.8 cents, the right to sell in the United States is worth 6.8 − 2.8 = 4.0 cents per pound. Under free trade, imports would be 13.04 billion pounds, but under the quota they are restricted to 5.96 billion pounds.

The welfare effects of the sugar quota are indicated by the five areas *f, g, h, i, j*. Because the quota raises the price, U.S. consumers lose the consumer surplus $f + g + h + i + j$. The value of this lost surplus is $1.266 billion. U.S. producers gain from the higher price, with the area *f* measuring their gain; the value of this gain is $616 million. The U.S. government also collects tariff revenue, in the amount measured by the area *i*; this is simply the volume of imports times the tariff rate, equaling $167 million.

The net effect to the United States is a loss: $f + g + h + i + j - f - i = g + j + h =$ \$483 million. Of this net loss, the areas *g* and *j* represent the production distortion and consumption distortion losses. Area *h* consists of rents collected by foreigners; it

[2] David G. Tarr and Morris E. Morkre, *Aggregate Costs to the United States of Tariffs and Quotas on Imports* (Washington, D.C.: Federal Trade Commission, 1984).

equals $238 million. This sum, which represents a pure transfer to foreigners, is thus just as important a part of the U.S. loss as efficiency costs.

A final postscript: during 1985 there was a sharp fall in the world price of sugar, to levels well below the FTC's estimates. The difference between U.S. and world sugar prices became so large as to make extreme efforts to evade the quota profitable. For example, some firms began importing Canadian pancake mix, which contains a high proportion of sugar but is not subject to the quota, and processing it to extract the sugar. These events provoked a crisis in the administration of the sugar import quota. Fortunately or unfortunately, the crisis abated in the later 1980s, as rising world sugar prices removed some of the pressure.

VOLUNTARY EXPORT RESTRAINTS

A variant on the import quota is the **voluntary export restraint (VER),** also known as a voluntary restraint agreement (VRA). (Welcome to the bureaucratic world of trade policy, where everything has a three-letter symbol.) A VER is a quota on trade imposed from the exporting country's side instead of the importer's. The most famous example is the limitation on auto exports to the United States enforced by Japan since 1981.

Voluntary export restraints are generally imposed at the request of the importer and are agreed to by the exporter to forestall other trade restrictions. As we will see in Chapter 10, certain political and legal advantages have made VERs preferred instruments of trade policy in recent years. From an economic point of view, however, a voluntary export restraint is exactly like an import quota where the licenses are assigned to foreign governments and is therefore very costly to the importing country.

FIGURE 9-13
The U.S. import quota on sugar.
The quantitative limit on imports raises domestic prices and generates rents for the recipients of the right to sell in the United States.

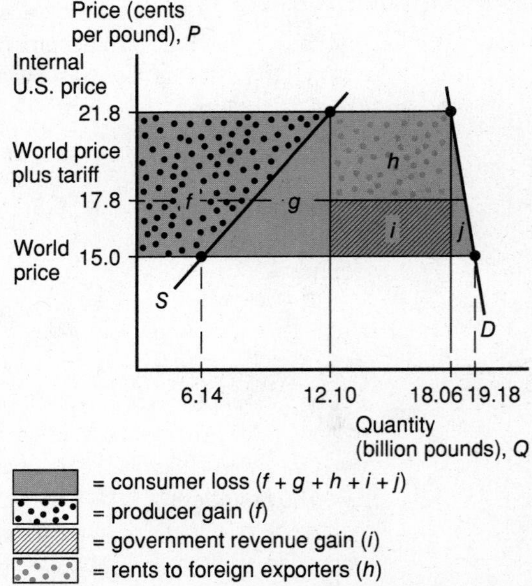

A VER is always more costly to the importing country than a tariff that limits imports by the same amount. The difference is that what would have been revenue under a tariff becomes rents earned by foreigners under the VER, so that the VER clearly produces a loss.

A recent study of the effects of the three major U.S. voluntary export restraints—in textiles and apparel, steel, and automobiles—found that about two-thirds of the cost to consumers of these restraints is accounted for by the rents earned by foreigners.[3] In other words, the bulk of the cost represents a transfer of income rather than a loss of efficiency. This calculation also emphasizes the point that from a national point of view, VERs are much more costly than tariffs. Given this, the widespread preference of governments for VERs over other trade policy measures requires some careful analysis.

Some voluntary export agreements cover more than one country. The most famous multilateral agreement is the Multifiber Arrangement, an agreement that limits textile exports from twenty-two countries. Such multilateral voluntary restraint agreements are known by yet another three-letter abbreviation as OMAs, for orderly marketing agreements.

[3] See the study by David G. Tarr in this chapter's Further Reading.

The Case of the Forbidden Phone Booths

Anyone who has visited Britain remembers the distinctive red steel telephone booths found throughout the country. Although the British phone booth has long been popular, in 1985 the British phone service began replacing them with more open, accessible, and vandal-proof models. Peculiarly, this led to a trade dispute with the United States.

The problem began when the British, rather than simply melting down the old phone booths, decided to try to sell them. They soon discovered they had a market in the United States. Many Americans were interested in buying a traditional British phone booth, whether to decorate shopping malls, to place in the gardens of Beverly Hills homes, or for other purposes. There seemed to be a perfect match between America's idea of the old Britain and Britain's march toward the future.

When the phone booths began to arrive in the United States, however, they were impounded by U.S. Customs because of an orderly marketing agreement in iron and steel products between the United States and Europe, including Britain. This agreement sets a limit on the quantity of iron and steel products that Britain may export to the United States. Since old phone booths are mostly iron and steel, the United States refused to allow them in unless Britain reduced its exports of some other product. (Specifically, the United States contended that the phone booths fell under a category defined in the OMA as "other other.") The British denounced this action, claiming that phone booths should be classified not as iron and steel, but as antiques—a category for which there is so far no U.S. import restriction.

As a result of high-level negotiations, the British eventually agreed to the U.S. demands, and the phone booths became available to U.S. buyers in limited quantities and at premium prices. At the time of writing, mail order catalogues were offering British phone booths at $3500.

Case Study

A VOLUNTARY EXPORT RESTRAINT IN PRACTICE: JAPANESE AUTOS

For much of the 1960s and 1970s the U.S. auto industry was largely insulated from import competition by the difference in the kinds of cars bought by U.S. and foreign consumers. U.S. buyers, living in a large country with low gasoline taxes, preferred much larger cars than Europeans and Japanese, and, by and large, foreign firms have chosen not to challenge the United States in the large-car market.

In 1979, however, sharp oil price increases and temporary gasoline shortages caused the U.S. market to shift abruptly toward smaller cars. Japanese producers, whose costs had been falling relative to their U.S. competitors in any case, moved in to fill the new demand. As the Japanese market share soared and U.S. output fell, strong political forces in the United States demanded protection for the U.S. industry. Rather than act unilaterally and risk creating a trade war, the U.S. government asked the Japanese government to limits its exports. The Japanese, fearing unilateral U.S. protectionist measures if they did not do so, agreed to limit their sales. The first agreement, in 1981, limited Japanese exports to the United States to 1.68 million automobiles. A revision raised that total to 1.85 million in 1984–1985. In 1985, the agreement was allowed to lapse, but the Japanese government indicated its intention to continue to restrict its exports.

The effects of this voluntary export restraint are complicated by several factors. First, Japanese and U.S. cars are clearly not perfect substitutes. Second, the Japanese industry to some extent responded to the quota by upgrading its quality, selling larger autos with more features. Third, the auto industry is clearly not perfectly competitive. Nonetheless, the basic results were what the discussion of voluntary export restraints earlier would have predicted: the price of Japanese cars in the United States rose, with the rent captured by Japanese firms. The U.S. government estimates the total costs to the United States at $3.2 billion in 1984, primarily in transfers to Japan rather than efficiency losses.

LOCAL CONTENT REQUIREMENTS

A **local content requirement** is a regulation that requires that some specified fraction of a final good be produced domestically. In some cases this fraction is specified in physical units, like the U.S. oil import quota in the 1960s (see below). In other cases the requirement is stated in value terms, by requiring that some minimum share of the price of a good represent domestic value added. Local content laws have been widely used by developing countries trying to shift their manufacturing base from assembly back into intermediate goods. In the United States, a local content bill for automobiles was proposed in 1982 but was never acted on.

From the point of view of the domestic producers of parts, a local content regulation provides protection in the same way an import quota does. From the point of view of

What's a Domestic Car?

For the most part, domestic content requirements have been imposed by developing countries trying to encourage industrialization. But the worldwide expansion of the Japanese auto industry, partly in response to barriers to direct exports from Japan, has brought the domestic content issue to the United States and Europe.

The key point is that when Japanese auto manufacturers expand abroad, they begin by building assembly plants. These plants produce finished cars, but many of the parts continue to be imported from Japan. As a result, Japanese cars made in the United States have a much smaller share of domestic value added than a car made by the Big Three (domestic cars still have about 90 percent domestic value added; cars made by Japanese "transplants" typically had only about 30 percent U.S. content at first, although the number has risen to around 60 percent as they have begun to purchase more of the parts in the United States).

The relatively low domestic content of Japanese-made cars created a major trade dispute in Europe and threatens to provoke a serious dispute in the United States.

In Europe, the problem arose over Nissan cars made in Britain. Britain, with its relatively low wages and free-market government, has been a favorite site for Japanese investors. (The use of English, which Japanese managers are more likely to speak than any other Western language, is also a factor.) And the United Kingdom is part of the European Community, which guarantees British-made goods free access to any other European nation.

Or does it? In 1990 France declared that the Nissan Bluebird, a Japanese car made in Britain, was a Japanese product—and hence would be included under France's VER with Japan, which limits Japanese cars to about 3 percent of the French market. The French declared that the Bluebird did not contain enough European value added to be considered a European good to which free trade must apply. The British were, unsurprisingly, furious. In the end the dispute was papered over, thanks in part to assurances from Nissan that the local content of its cars would soon be rising sharply.

In the United States, 1992 was marked by huge losses and huge layoffs at once-mighty General Motors. Auto imports from Japan were not a major factor in these losses: imports had remained consistently below the peak levels of the voluntary export restraints of the 1980s. Competition from Japanese cars produced in the United States was, however, cutting into GM's market share (as was competition from Ford, which had been much more successful than GM at matching Japanese productivity levels). The result was growing pressure to extend voluntary export restraints to Japanese cars produced in the United States. At time of writing, rumors were flying that the new Clinton administration had already agreed to such a deal—but it was unclear whether the rumors were true, especially since it was hard to see how such a deal could be legal.

the firms that must buy locally, however, the effects are somewhat different. Local content does not place a strict limit on imports. It allows firms to import more, provided that they also buy more domestically. This means that the effective price of inputs to the firm is an average of the price of imported and domestically produced inputs.

Consider, for example, the earlier automobile example in which the cost of imported parts is \$6000. Suppose that to purchase the same parts domestically would cost \$10,000 but that assembly firms are required to use 50 percent domestic parts. Then they will face an average cost of parts of \$8000 ($0.5 \times \$6000 + 0.5 \times \$10,000$), which will be reflected in the final price of the car.

The important point is that a local content requirement does not produce either government revenue or quota rents. Instead, the difference between the prices of imports and domestic goods in effect gets averaged in the final price and is passed on to consumers.

An interesting innovation in local content regulations has been to allow firms to satisfy their local content requirement by exporting instead of using parts domestically. This has become important in several cases: for example, U.S. auto firms operating in Mexico have chosen to export some components from Mexico to the United States, even though those components could be produced in the United States more cheaply, because this allows them to use less Mexican content in producing cars in Mexico for Mexico's market.

Case Study

A LOCAL CONTENT SCHEME: THE OIL IMPORT QUOTA IN THE 1960S

Local content regulations are widely used as part of the industrialization strategies of less-developed countries. In most cases, however, the details of the schemes are too complex to be easily summarized. To illustrate a fairly simple local content scheme in practice, we go back to the 1960s and early 1970s to describe the working of the U.S. oil import quota.

As its name suggests, the oil import quota was intended to set a quantitative limit on U.S. oil imports. Unlike many import limitations, however, this legislation did not allocate rights to import on a fixed basis to foreign governments or domestic firms. Instead, it allowed domestic firms to compete for quota rights in a way that turned it effectively into a local content requirement.

Imported oil is not sold directly to final consumers. It must first be processed into refined products such as gasoline and heating oil. The oil import quota based the amount of imported oil a refiner was allowed to purchase on the total amount of oil it refined. That is, by refining, say, eight barrels of domestic crude oil the refiner would be allowed to purchase one barrel of cheaper imported oil. (In fact the proportions depended on the size of the refiner; small refiners were allowed to purchase a higher proportion of imported oil than large.)

What was particularly interesting about the scheme was that refiners were not required to use or even actually take delivery of the imported oil. They could instead sell their import rights (known as "tickets") to other refiners. In general, inland refiners sold their rights to coastal ones, generating a substantial market in which the right to import sold at a well-defined price.

The results were straightforward. Domestic oil sold at a higher price than imported: about \$3.25 per barrel versus \$2. Correspondingly, the price of an import "ticket" was about \$1.25. Consumer prices of refined products appeared to reflect the average price of oil, which lay between the import and domestic prices.

Estimates of the effects of the oil import quota suggest that it cost consumers about \$5 billion per year. Most of this, however, was a redistribution to oil producers rather than a net cost to the economy as a whole; the net cost may have been on the order of \$1 to \$2 billion.

OTHER TRADE POLICY INSTRUMENTS

There are many other ways in which governments influence trade. We list some of them briefly.

1. *Export credit subsidies.* This is like an export subsidy except that it takes the form of a subsidized loan to the buyer. The United States, like most countries, has a government institution, the Export-Import Bank, that is devoted to providing at least slightly subsidized loans to aid exports.
2. *National procurement.* Purchases by the government or strongly regulated firms can be directed toward domestically produced goods even when these goods are more expensive than imports. The classic example is the European telecommunications industry. The nations of the European Community in principle have free trade with each other. The main purchasers of telecommunications equipment, however, are phone companies—and in Europe these companies have until recently all been government-owned. These government-owned telephone companies buy from domestic suppliers even when the suppliers charge higher prices than suppliers in other countries. The result is that there is very little trade in telecommunications equipment within Europe.
3. *Red tape barriers.* Sometimes a government wants to restrict imports without doing so formally. Fortunately or unfortunately, it is easy to twist normal health, safety, and customs procedures so as to place substantial obstacles in the way of trade. The classic example is the French decree in 1982 that all Japanese videocassette recorders must pass through the tiny customs house at Poitiers—effectively limiting the actual imports to a handful.

Summary

1. In contrast to our earlier analysis, which stressed the general equilibrium interaction of markets, for analysis of trade policy it is usually sufficient to use a *partial equilibrium* approach.
2. A tariff drives a wedge between foreign and domestic prices, raising the domestic price but by less than the tariff rate. An important and relevant special case, however, is that of a "small" country that cannot have any substantial influence on foreign prices. In the small country case a tariff is fully reflected in domestic prices.
3. The costs and benefits of a tariff or other trade policy may be measured using the concepts of *consumer surplus* and *producer surplus.* Using these concepts, we can show that the domestic producers of a good gain, because a tariff raises the price they receive; the domestic consumers lose, for the same reason. There is also a gain in government revenue.

4. If we add together the gains and losses from a tariff, we find that the net effect on national welfare can be separated into two parts. There is an *efficiency loss,* which results from the distortion in the incentives facing domestic producers and consumers. On the other hand, there is a *terms of trade gain,* reflecting the tendency of a tariff to drive down foreign export prices. In the case of a small country that cannot affect foreign prices, the second effect is zero, so that there is an unambiguous loss.

5. The analysis of a tariff can be readily adapted to other trade policy measures, such as *export subsidies, import quotas,* and *voluntary export restraints.* An export subsidy causes efficiency losses similar to a tariff but compounds these losses by causing a deterioration of the terms of trade. Import quotas and voluntary export restraints differ from tariffs in that the government gets no revenue. Instead, what would have been government revenue accrues as *rents* to the recipients of import licenses in the case of a quota and to foreigners in the case of a voluntary export restraint.

Key Terms

specific tariff
ad valorem tariff
nontariff barriers
import demand curve
export supply curve
effective rate of protection
consumer surplus
producer surplus
efficiency loss
terms of trade gain
production distortion loss
consumption distortion loss
export subsidy
import quota
quota rent
voluntary export restraint (VER)
local content requirement

Problems

1. Home's demand curve for wheat is

$$D = 100 - 20P.$$

Its supply curve is

$$S = 20 + 20P.$$

Derive and graph Home's *import* demand schedule. What would the price of wheat be in the absence of trade?

2. Now add Foreign, which has a demand curve

$$D^* = 80 - 20P$$

and a supply curve

$$S^* = 40 + 20P.$$

a. Derive and graph Foreign's *export* supply curve and find the price of wheat that would prevail in Foreign in the absence of trade.

b. Now allow Foreign and Home to trade with each other, at zero transportation cost. Find and graph the equilibrium under free trade. What is the world price? What is the volume of trade?

3. Home imposes a specific tariff of 0.5 on wheat imports.

a. Determine and graph the effects of the tariff on the following: (1) the price of wheat in each country; (2) the quantity of wheat supplied and demanded in each country; (3) the volume of trade.

b. Determine the effect of the tariff on the welfare of each of the following groups: (1) Home import-competing producers; (2) Home consumers; (3) the Home government.

c. Show graphically and calculate the terms of trade gain, the efficiency loss, and the total effect on welfare of the tariff.

4. Suppose that Foreign had been a much larger country, with domestic demand

$$D^* = 800 - 200P, \; S^* = 400 + 200P.$$

(Notice that this implies that the Foreign price of wheat in the absence of trade would have been the same as in problem 2.)

Recalculate the free trade equilibrium and the effects of a 0.5 specific tariff by Home. Relate the difference in results to the discussion of the "small country" case in the text.

5. The aircraft industry in Europe receives aid from several governments, according to some estimates equal to 20 percent of the purchase price of each aircraft. For example, an airplane that sells for $50 million may have cost $60 million to produce, with the difference made up by European governments. At the same time, approximately half the purchase price of a "European" aircraft represents the cost of components purchased from other countries (including the United States). If these estimates are correct, what is the *effective* rate of protection received by European aircraft producers?

6. Return to the example of problem 2. Starting from free trade, assume that Foreign offers exporters a subsidy of 0.5 per unit. Calculate the effects on the price in each country and on welfare, both of individual groups and of the economy as a whole, in both countries.

7. The nation of Acirema is "small," unable to affect world prices. It imports peanuts at the price of $10 per bag. The demand curve is

$$D = 400 - 10P.$$

The supply curve is

$$S = 50 + 5P.$$

Determine the free trade equilibrium. Then calculate and graph the following effects of an import quota that limits imports to 50 bags.

a. The increase in the domestic price

b. The quota rents

c. The consumption distortion loss

d. The production distortion loss

Further Reading

Jagdish Bhagwati. "On the Equivalence of Tariffs and Quotas," in Robert E. Baldwin et al., eds. *Trade, Growth, and the Balance of Payments.* Chicago: Rand McNally, 1965. The classic comparison of tariffs and quotas under monopoly.

W. M. Corden. *The Theory of Protection.* Oxford: Clarendon Press, 1971. A general survey of the effects of tariffs, quotas, and other trade policies.

Robert W. Crandall. *Regulating the Automobile.* Washington, D.C.: Brookings Institution, 1986. Contains an analysis of the most famous of all voluntary export restraints.

Kala Krishna. "Trade Restrictions as Facilitating Practices." *Journal of International Economics* 26 (May 1989), pp. 251–270. A pioneering analysis of the effects of import quotas when both foreign and domestic producers have monopoly power, showing that the usual result is an increase in the profits of both groups—at consumers' expense.

D. Rousslang and A. Suomela. "Calculating the Consumer and Net Welfare Costs of Import Relief." U.S. International Trade Commission Staff Research Study 15. Washington, D.C.: International Trade Commission, 1985. An exposition of the framework used in this chapter, with a description of how the framework is applied in practice to real industries.

David G. Tarr. *A General Equilibrium Analysis of the Welfare and Employment Effects of U.S. Quotas in Textiles, Autos, and Steel.* Washington, D.C.: Federal Trade Commission, 1989. An up-to-date assessment of the impacts of the three most important U.S. protectionist policies.

Appendix I to Chapter 9 ●
Tariff Analysis in General Equilibrium

The text of this chapter takes a partial equilibrium approach to the analysis of trade policy. That is, it focuses on the effects of tariffs, quotas, and other policies in a single market without explicitly considering the consequences for other markets. This partial equilibrium approach usually is adequate, and it is much simpler than a full general equilibrium treatment that takes cross-market effects into account. Nonetheless, it is sometimes important to do the general equilibrium analysis. In Chapter 5 we presented a brief discussion of the effects of tariffs in general equilibrium. This appendix presents a more detailed analysis.

The analysis proceeds in two stages. First, we analyze the effects of a tariff in a small country, one that cannot affect its terms of trade; then we analyze the case of a large country.

A TARIFF IN A SMALL COUNTRY

Imagine a country that produces and consumes two goods, manufactures and food. The country is small, unable to affect its terms of trade; we will assume that it exports manufactures and imports food. Thus the country sells its manufactures to the world market at a given world price P^*_M and buys food at a given world price P^*_F.

Figure 9AI-1 illustrates the position of this country in the absence of a tariff. The economy produces at the point on its production possibility frontier that is tangent to a line with slope $-P^*_M/P^*_F$, indicated by Q^1. This line also defines the economy's budget constraint, that is, all the consumption points it can afford. The economy chooses the point on the budget constraint that is tangent to the highest possible indifference curve; this point is shown as D^1.

Now suppose the government imposes an ad valorem tariff at a rate t. Then the price of

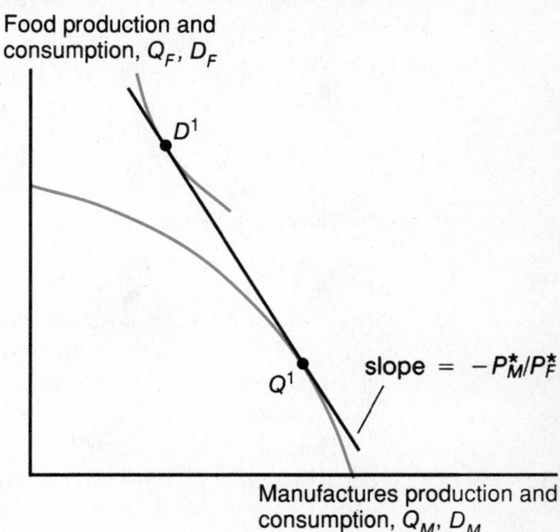

FIGURE 9AI-1
Free trade equilibrium for a small country.
The country produces at the point on its production frontier that is tangent to a line whose slope equals relative prices, and consumes at the point on the budget line tangent to the highest possible indifference curve.

FIGURE 9AI-2
A tariff in a small country.
The country produces less of its export good and more of its imported good. Consumption is also distorted. The result is a reduction in both welfare and the volume of the country's trade.

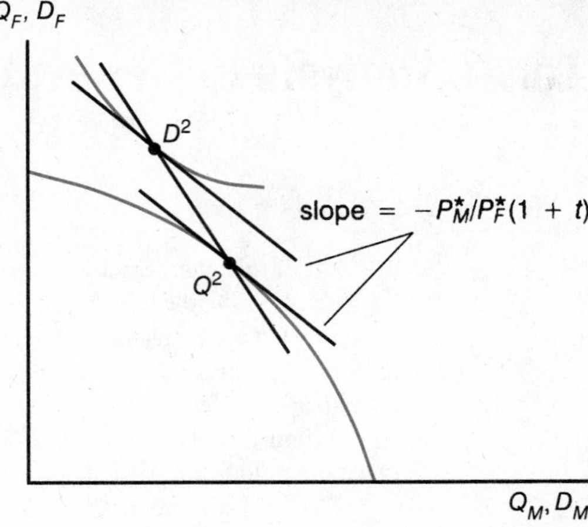

food facing both consumers and domestic producers rises to $P^*_F(1 + t)$, and the relative price line therefore gets flatter, with a slope $-P^*_M/P^*_F(1 + t)$.

The effect of this fall in the relative price of manufactures on production is straightforward: output of manufactures falls, while output of food rises. In Figure 9AI-2, this shift in production is shown by the movement of the production point from Q^1, shown in Figure 9AI-1, to Q^2.

The effect on consumption is more complicated; the tariff generates revenue, which must be spent somehow. In general, the precise effect of a tariff depends on exactly how the government spends the tariff revenue. Consider the case in which the government returns any tariff revenue to consumers. In this case the budget constraint of consumers is *not* the line with slope $-P^*_M/P^*_F(1 + t)$ that passes through the production point Q^2; consumers can spend more than this, because in addition to the income they generate by producing goods they receive the tariff revenue collected by the government.

How do we find the true budget constraint? Notice that trade must still be balanced at world prices. That is,

$$P^*_M \times (Q_M - D_M) = P^*_F \times (D_F - Q_F)$$

where Q refers to output and D to consumption of manufactures and food respectively. The left-hand side of this expression therefore represents the value of exports at world prices, while the right-hand side represents the value of imports. This expression may be rearranged to show that the value of consumption equals the value of production at world prices:

$$P^*_M \times Q_M + P^*_F \times Q_F = P^*_M \times D_M + P^*_F \times D_F.$$

This defines a budget constraint that passes through the production point Q^2, with a slope of $-P^*_M/P^*_F$. The consumption point must lie on this new budget constraint.

Consumers will not, however, choose the point on the new budget constraint at which this constraint is tangent to an indifference curve. Instead, the tariff causes them to consume less food and more manufactures. In Figure 9AI-2 the consumption point after the tariff is shown as D^2: it lies on the new budget constraint, but on an indifference curve that is tangent to a line with slope $-P^*_M/P^*_F(1 + t)$. This line lies above the line with the same slope that passes through the production point Q^2; the difference is the tariff revenue redistributed to consumers.

By examining Figure 9AI-2 and comparing it with Figure 9AI-1, we can see three important points:

1. Welfare is less with a tariff than under free trade. That is, D^2 lies on a lower indifference curve than D^1.
2. The reduction in welfare comes from two effects. (a) The economy no longer produces at a point that maximizes the value of income at world prices. The budget constraint that passes through Q^2 lies inside the constraint passing through Q^1. (b) Consumers do not choose the welfare-maximizing point on the budget constraint; they do not move up to an indifference curve that is tangent to the economy's true budget constraint. Both (a) and (b) result from the fact that domestic consumers and producers face prices that are different from world prices. The loss in welfare due to inefficient production (a) is the general equilibrium counterpart of the production distortion loss we described in the partial equilibrium approach in this chapter, and the loss in welfare due to inefficient consumption (b) is the counterpart of the consumption distortion loss.
3. Trade is reduced by the tariff. Exports and imports are both less after the tariff is imposed than before.

These are the effects of a tariff imposed by a small country. We next turn to the effects of a tariff imposed by a large country.

A TARIFF IN A LARGE COUNTRY

To address the large country case, we use the offer curve technique developed in the appendix to Chapter 5. We consider two countries: Home, which exports manufactures and imports food, and its trading partner Foreign. In Figure 9AI-3, Foreign's offer curve is represented by *OF*. Home's offer curve in the absence of a tariff is represented by OM^1. The free trade equilibrium is determined by the intersection of *OF* and OM^1, at point 1, with a relative price of manufactures on the world market $(P^*_M/P^*_F)^1$.

Now suppose that Home imposes a tariff. We first ask, how would its trade change if there were no change in its terms of trade? We already know the answer from the small country analysis: for a given world price, a tariff reduces both exports and imports. Thus if the world relative price of manufactures remained at $(P^*_M/P^*_F)^1$, Home's offer would shift in from point 1

FIGURE 9AI-3
Effect of a tariff on the terms of trade.
The tariff causes the country to trade less at any *given* terms of trade; thus its offer curve shifts in. This implies, however, that the terms of trade must improve. The gain from improved terms of trade may offset the losses from the distortion of production and consumption, which reduce welfare at any given terms of trade.

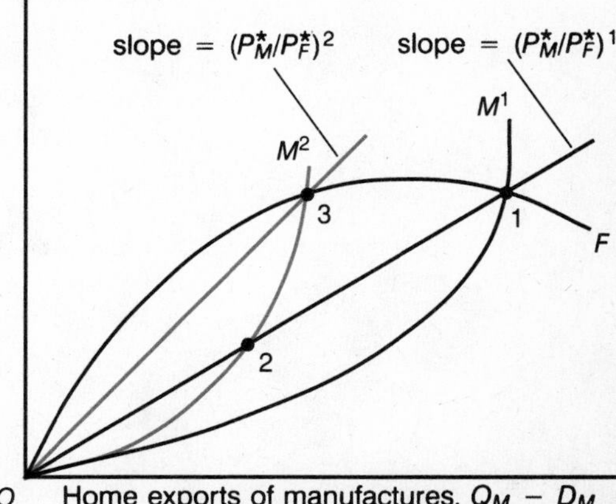

to point 2. More generally, if Home imposes a tariff its overall offer curve will shrink in to a curve like OM^2, passing through point 2.

But this shift in Home's offer curve will change the equilibrium terms of trade. In Figure 9AI-3, the new equilibrium is at point 3, with a relative price of manufactures $(P^*_M/P^*_F)^2 > (P^*_M/P^*_F)^1$. That is, the tariff improves Home's terms of trade.

The effects of the tariff on Home's welfare are ambiguous. On one side, if the terms of trade did not improve, we have just seen from the small country analysis that the tariff would reduce welfare. On the other side, the improvement in Home's terms of trade tends to increase welfare. So the welfare effect can go either way, just as in the partial equilibrium analysis.

Appendix II to Chapter 9 ●
Tariffs and Import Quotas in the Presence of Monopoly

The trade policy analysis in this chapter assumed that markets are perfectly competitive, so that all firms take prices as given. As we argued in Chapter 6, however, many markets for internationally traded goods are imperfectly competitive. The effects of international trade policies can be affected by the nature of the competition in a market.

When we analyze the effects of trade policy in imperfectly competitive markets, a new consideration appears: international trade limits monopoly power, and policies that limit trade may therefore increase monopoly power. Even if a firm is the only producer of a good in a country, it will have little ability to raise prices if there are many foreign suppliers and free trade. If imports are limited by a quota, however, the same firm will be free to raise prices without fear of competition.

The link between trade policy and monopoly power may be understood by examining a model in which a country imports a good and its import-competing production is controlled by only *one* firm. The country is small on world markets, so that the price of the import is unaffected by its trade policy. For this model, we examine and compare the effects of free trade, a tariff, and an import quota.

THE MODEL WITH FREE TRADE

Figure 9AII-1 shows free trade in a market where a domestic monopolist faces competition from imports. D is the domestic demand curve: demand for the product by domestic residents. P_W is the world price of the good; imports are available in unlimited quantities at that price. The domestic industry is assumed to consist of only a single firm, whose marginal cost curve is MC.

If there were no trade in this market, the domestic firm would behave as an ordinary profit-

FIGURE 9AII-1
A monopolist under free trade.
The threat of import competition forces the monopolist to behave like a perfectly competitive industry.

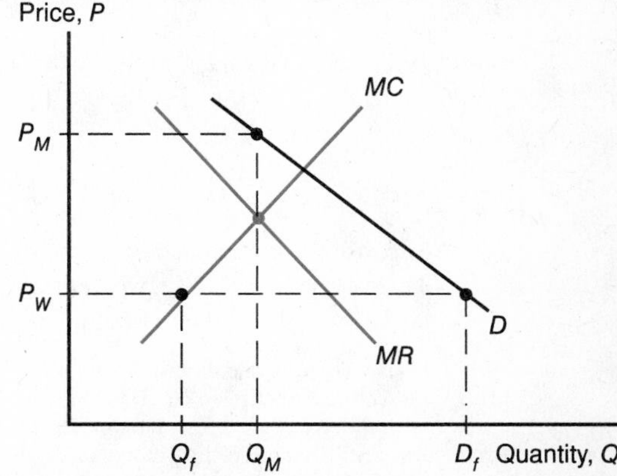

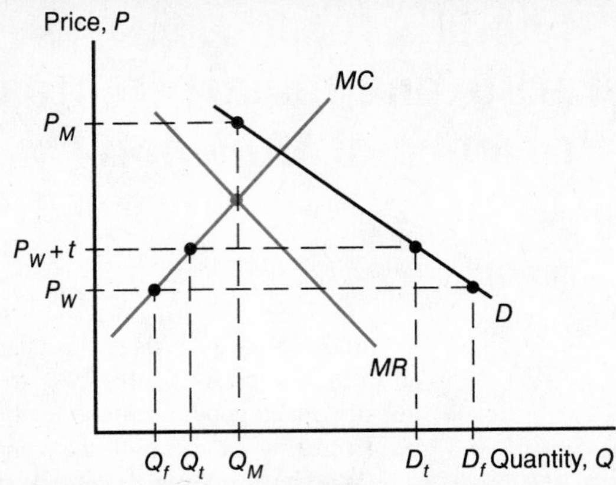

FIGURE 9AII-2
A monopolist protected by a tariff.
The tariff allows the monopolist to raise its price, but the price is still limited by the threat of imports.

maximizing monopolist. Corresponding to D is a marginal revenue curve MR, and the firm would choose the monopoly profit-maximizing level of output Q_M and price P_M.

With free trade, however, this monopoly behavior is not possible. If the firm tried to charge P_M, or indeed any price above P_W, nobody would buy its product, because cheaper imports would be available. Thus international trade puts a lid on the monopolist's price at P_W.

Given this limit on its price, the best the monopolist can do is produce up to the point where marginal cost is equal to the world price, at Q_f. At the price P_W, domestic consumers will demand D_f units of the good, so imports will be $D_f - Q_f$. This outcome, however, is exactly what would have happened if the domestic industry had been perfectly competitive. With free trade, then, the fact that the domestic industry is a monopoly does not make any difference to the outcome.

THE MODEL WITH A TARIFF

The effect of a tariff is to raise the maximum price the domestic industry can charge. If a specific tariff t is charged on imports, the domestic industry can now charge $P_W + t$ (Figure 9AII-2). The industry still is not free to raise its price all the way to the monopoly price, however, because consumers will still turn to imports if the price rises above the world price plus the tariff. Thus the best the monopolist can do is to set price equal to marginal cost, at Q_t. The tariff raises the domestic price as well as the output of the domestic industry, while demand falls to D_t and thus imports fall. However, the domestic industry still produces the same quantity as if it were perfectly competitive.[1]

THE MODEL WITH AN IMPORT QUOTA

Suppose the government imposes a limit on imports, restricting their quantity to a fixed level $\bar{Q}$. Then the monopolist knows that when it charges a price above P_W, it will not lose all its sales.

[1] There is one case in which a tariff will have different effects on a monopolistic industry than on a perfectly competitive one. This is the case where a tariff is so high that imports are completely eliminated (a prohibitive tariff). For a competitive industry, once imports have been eliminated, any further increase in the tariff has no effect. A monopolist, however, will be forced to limit its price by the *threat* of imports even if actual imports are zero. Thus an increase in a prohibitive tariff will allow a monopolist to raise its price closer to the profit-maximizing price P_M.

FIGURE 9AII-3
A monopolist protected by an import quota.
The monopolist is now free to raise prices, knowing that the domestic price of imports will rise too.

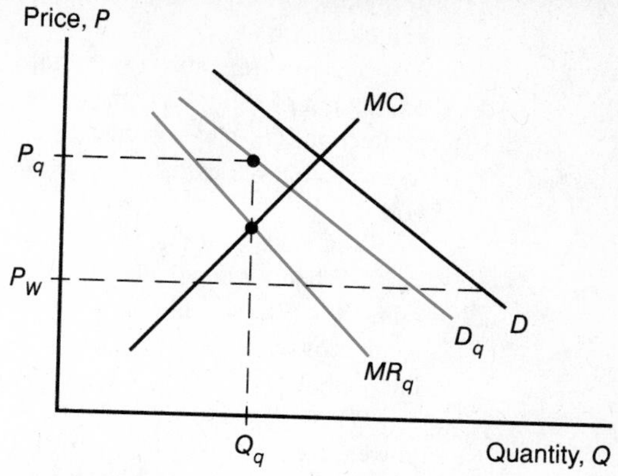

Instead, it will sell whatever domestic demand is at that price, minus the allowed imports $\bar{Q}$. Thus the demand facing the monopolist will be domestic demand less allowed imports. We define the postquota demand curve as D_q; it is parallel to the domestic demand curve D but shifted $\bar{Q}$ units to the left (Figure 9AII-3).

Corresponding to D_q is a new marginal revenue curve MR_q. The firm protected by an import quota maximizes profit by setting marginal cost equal to this new marginal revenue, producing Q_q and charging the price P_q. (The license to import one unit of the good will therefore yield a rent of $P_q - P_W$.)

COMPARING A TARIFF AND A QUOTA

We now ask how the effects of a tariff and a quota compare. To do this, we compare a tariff and a quota that lead to *the same level of imports* (Figure 9AII-4). The tariff level t leads to a level

FIGURE 9AII-4
Comparing a tariff and a quota.
A quota leads to lower domestic output and a higher price than a tariff that yields the same level of imports.

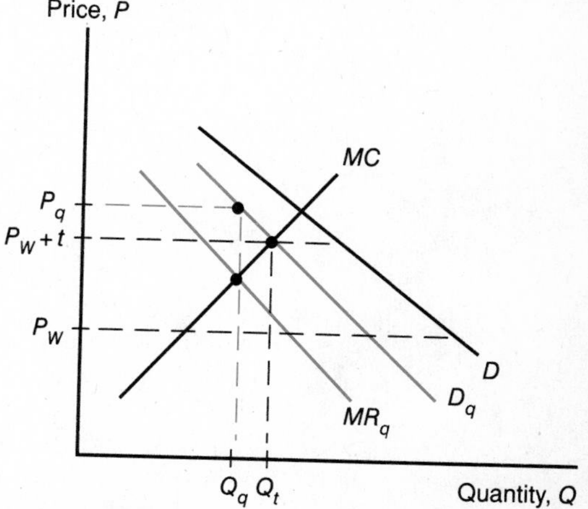

of imports $\bar{Q}$; we therefore ask what would happen if instead of a tariff the government simply limited imports to $\bar{Q}$.

We see from the figure that the results are not the same. The tariff leads to domestic production of Q_t and a domestic price of $P_W + t$. The quota leads to a lower level of domestic production, Q_q, and a higher price, P_q. When protected by a tariff the monopolistic domestic industry behaves as if it were perfectly competitive; when protected by a quota it clearly does not.

The reason for this difference is that an import quota creates more monopoly power than a tariff. When monopolistic industries are protected by tariffs, domestic firms know that if they raise their prices too high they will still be undercut by imports. An import quota, on the other hand, provides absolute protection: no matter how high the domestic price, imports cannot exceed the quota level.

This comparison seems to say that if governments are concerned about domestic monopoly power, they should prefer tariffs to quotas as instruments of trade policy. In fact, however, protection has increasingly drifted away from tariffs toward nontariff barriers, including import quotas. To explain this, we need to look at considerations other than economic efficiency that motivate governments.

The Political Economy of Trade Policy

Chapter 10

In 1981, the United States asked Japan to limit its exports of autos to the United States. This raised the prices of imported cars and forced U.S. consumers to buy domestic autos they clearly did not like as much. While Japan was willing to accommodate the U.S. government on this point, it was unwilling to do so on another—a request that Japan eliminate import quotas on beef and citrus products—quotas that forced Japanese consumers to buy incredibly expensive domestic products instead of cheap imports from the United States. The governments of both countries were thus determined to pursue policies that, according to the cost-benefit analysis developed in Chapter 9, produced more costs than benefits. Clearly, government policies reflect objectives that go beyond simple measures of cost and benefit.

In this chapter we examine some of the reasons governments either should not or, at any rate, do not base their policy on economists' cost-benefit calculations. The examination of the forces motivating trade policy in practice continues in Chapters 11 and 12, which discuss the characteristic trade policy issues facing developing and advanced countries, respectively.

The first step toward understanding actual trade policies is to ask what reasons there are for governments *not* to interfere with trade—that is, what is the case for free trade? With this question answered, arguments for intervention can be examined as challenges to the assumptions underlying the case for free trade.

The Case for Free Trade

Few countries have anything approaching completely free trade. The city-state of Hong Kong may be the only modern nation with no tariffs or import quotas. Nonetheless, since the time of Adam Smith economists have advocated free trade as an ideal toward which trade policy should strive. The reasons for this advocacy are not quite as simple as the idea itself. At one level, theoretical models suggest that free trade will avoid the efficiency losses associated with protection. Many economists believe that free trade produces additional gains beyond the elimination of production and consumption distortions. Finally, even among economists who believe free trade is a less than perfect policy, many believe free trade is usually better than any other policy a government is likely to follow.

FREE TRADE AND EFFICIENCY

The **efficiency case for free trade** is simply the reverse of the cost-benefit analysis of a tariff. Figure 10-1 shows the basic point once again for the case of a small country that cannot influence foreign export prices. A tariff causes a net loss to the economy measured by the area of the two triangles; it does so by distorting the economic incentives of both producers and consumers. Conversely, a move to free trade eliminates these distortions and increases national welfare.

A number of efforts have been made to add the total costs of distortions due to tariffs and import quotas in particular economies. Table 10-1 presents some representative estimates. It is noteworthy that the costs of protection to the United States are measured as quite small relative to national income. This situation reflects two facts: (1) the United States is relatively less dependent on trade than other countries, and (2) with some major exceptions, U.S. trade is fairly free. By contrast, some smaller countries that impose very restrictive tariffs and quotas are estimated to lose as much as 10 percent of their potential national income to distortions caused by their trade policies.

FIGURE 10-1
The efficiency case for free trade.
A trade restriction, such as a tariff, leads to production and consumption distortions.

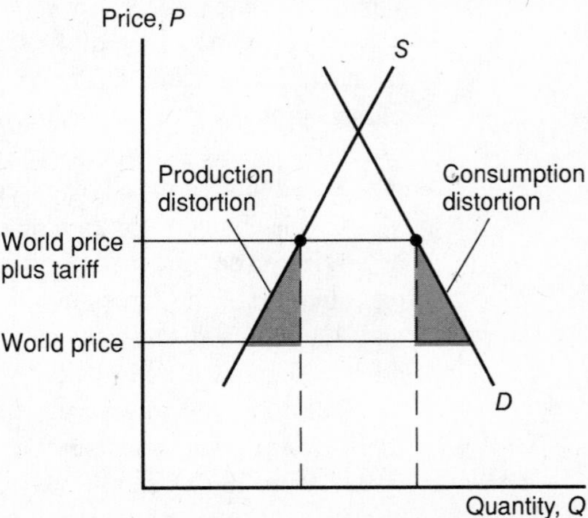

TABLE 10-1 Estimated cost of protection, as a percentage of national income

Brazil (1966)	9.5
Pakistan (1963)	6.2
Mexico (1960)	2.5
United States (1983)	0.26

Source: Bela Balassa. *The Structure of Protection in Developing Countries.* Baltimore: The Johns Hopkins Press, 1971; and David G. Tarr and Morris E. Morkre. *Aggregate Costs to the United States of Tariffs and Quotas on Imports.* Washington, D.C.: Federal Trade Commission, 1984.

ADDITIONAL GAINS FROM FREE TRADE[1]

There is a widespread belief among economists that calculations of the kind reported in Table 10-1, even though they report substantial gains from free trade in some cases, do not represent the whole story. In small countries in general and developing countries in particular, many economists would argue that there are important gains from free trade not accounted for in conventional cost-benefit analysis.

One kind of additional gain involves economies of scale. Protected markets not only fragment production internationally, but by reducing competition and raising profits, they also lead too many firms to enter the protected industry. With a proliferation of firms in narrow domestic markets, the scale of production of each firm becomes inefficient. A good example of how protection leads to inefficient scale is the case of the Argentine automobile industry, which emerged because of import restrictions. An efficient scale assembly plant should make from 80 thousand to 200 thousand automobiles per year, yet in 1964 the Argentine industry, which produced only 166 thousand cars, had no less than thirteen firms! Some economists argue that the need to deter excessive entry and the resulting inefficient scale of production is a reason for free trade that goes beyond the standard cost-benefit calculations.

Another argument for free trade is that by providing entrepreneurs with an incentive to seek new ways to export or compete with imports, free trade offers more opportunities for learning and innovation than are provided by a system of "managed" trade, where the government largely dictates the pattern of imports and exports. Chapter 11 discusses the experiences of less-developed countries that discovered unexpected export opportunities when they shifted from systems of import quotas and tariffs to more open trade policies.

These additional arguments for free trade are for the most part not quantified. Recently, however, the Canadian economists Richard Harris and David Cox attempted to quantify the gains for Canada of free trade with the United States, taking into account the gains from a more efficient scale of production within Canada. They estimate that Canada's real income would rise by 8.6 percent—an increase about three times as large as the one typically estimated by economists who do not take into account the gains from economies of scale.[2]

[1] The additional gains from free trade that are discussed here are sometimes referred to as "dynamic" gains, because increased competition and innovation may need more time to take effect than the elimination of production and consumption distortions.

[2] See Harris and Cox, *Trade, Industrial Policy, and Canadian Manufacturing* (Toronto: Ontario Economic Council, 1984); and, by the same authors, "Trade Liberalization and Industrial Organization: Some Estimates for Canada," *Journal of Political Economy* 93 (February 1985), pp. 115–145.

If the additional gains from free trade are as large as some economists believe, the costs of distorting trade with tariffs, quotas, export subsidies, and so on are correspondingly larger than the conventional cost-benefit analysis measures.

POLITICAL ARGUMENT FOR FREE TRADE

A **political argument for free trade** reflects the fact that a political commitment to free trade may be a good idea in practice even though there may be better policies in principle. Economists often argue that trade policies in practice are dominated by special-interest politics rather than consideration of national costs and benefits. Economists can sometimes show that in theory a selective set of tariffs and export subsidies could increase national welfare, but in reality any government agency attempting to pursue a sophisticated program of intervention in trade would probably be captured by interest groups and converted into a device for redistributing income to politically influential sectors. If this argument is correct, it may be better to advocate free trade without exceptions, even though on purely economic grounds free trade may not always be the best conceivable policy.

The three arguments outlined in the previous section probably represent the standard view of most international economists, at least in the United States.

1. The conventionally measured costs of deviating from free trade are large.
2. There are other benefits from free trade that add to the costs of protectionist policies.
3. Any attempt to pursue sophisticated deviations from free trade will be subverted by the political process.

Nonetheless, there are intellectually respectable arguments for deviating from free trade, and these arguments deserve a fair hearing.

National Welfare Arguments against Free Trade

Most tariffs, import quotas, and other trade policy measures are undertaken primarily to protect the income of particular interest groups. Politicians often claim, however, that the policies are being undertaken in the interest of the nation as a whole, and sometimes they are even telling the truth. Although economists often argue that deviations from free trade reduce national welfare, there are, in fact, some theoretical grounds for believing that activist trade policies can sometimes increase the welfare of the nation as a whole.

Case Study

THE GAINS FROM 1992

The Single European Act, which was supposed to eliminate all obstacles to trade within Europe by the end of 1992, is running a little behind schedule. Nonetheless, an impressive set of market-opening measures began taking effect in 1992. These measures have been hailed by economists and businesses alike. But how big will the gains be?

Enthusiasts point out that in spite of free trade, Europe remains divided into a number of local markets. Italian homes are typically equipped with Italian appliances, German homes with German appliances. They claim that 1992 will dissolve the barriers that separate these local markets, creating more competition and allowing production at more efficient scale.

Skeptics are not so sure: they suggest that the segmentation of European markets has more to do with enduring cultural differences than with laws.

Consider the case of washing machines. The washing machines in U.S. homes are pretty much the same wherever you go. Not so in Europe. Italian machines are typically small, slow, and very gentle; German machines are larger, faster, and rough on clothes. And so each country in effect has its own washing machine industry. Is this wasteful duplication?

Not necessarily. Italian middle-class families tend to have fewer clothes than their German counterparts, because they prefer to buy a small, stylish, and relatively expensive wardrobe rather than a lot of cheaper, less stylish clothing. Thus, Italians naturally prefer gentler washing machines that conserve their clothing investment. The Germans, like the Americans, want their clothes done quickly and don't worry too much about style.

The point is, of course, that differences in fashion sense, like many other cultural differences between European nations, may be deeply resistant to mere changes in trade regulations. In general, it seems likely that it will be a long time before Europe becomes a market as unified as the United States. And in the end, why should it? As some (but only some!) of the Europeans say, *vive la difference!*

THE TERMS OF TRADE ARGUMENT FOR A TARIFF

One argument for deviating from free trade comes directly out of cost-benefit analysis: for a large country that is able to affect the prices of foreign exporters, a tariff lowers the price of imports and thus generates a terms of trade benefit. This benefit must be set against the costs of the tariff, which arise because the tariff distorts production and consumption incentives. It is possible, however, that in some cases the terms of trade benefits of a tariff outweigh its costs, so there is a **terms of trade argument for a tariff.**

The appendix to this chapter shows that for a sufficiently small tariff the terms of trade benefits must outweigh the costs. Thus at small tariff rates a large country's welfare is higher than with free trade (Figure 10-2). As the tariff rate is increased, however, the costs eventually begin to grow more rapidly than the benefits and the curve relating national welfare to the tariff rate turns down. A tariff rate that completely prohibits trade (t_P in Figure 10-2) leaves the country worse off than with free trade; further increases in the tariff rate beyond t_P have no effect, so the curve flattens out.

At point 1 on the curve in Figure 10-2, corresponding to the tariff rate t_O, national welfare is maximized. The tariff rate t_O that maximizes national welfare is the **optimum tariff.** (By convention the phrase optimum tariff is usually used to refer to the tariff justified by a terms of trade argument rather than to the best tariff given all possible considerations.) The optimum tariff rate is always positive but less than the prohibitive rate (t_P) that would eliminate all imports.

FIGURE 10-2
The optimum tariff.
For a large country, there is an optimum tariff t_O at which the marginal gain from improved terms of trade just equals the marginal efficiency loss from production and consumption distortion.

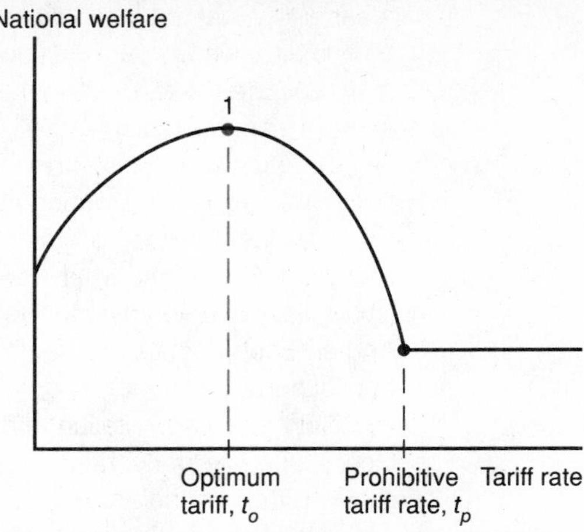

What policy would the terms of trade argument dictate for *export* sectors? Since an export subsidy *worsens* the terms of trade, and therefore unambiguously reduces national welfare, the optimal policy in export sectors must be a negative subsidy—that is, a *tax* on exports that raises the price of exports to foreigners. Like the optimum tariff, the optimum export tax is always positive but less than the prohibitive tax that would eliminate exports completely.

The policy of Saudi Arabia and other oil exporters has been to tax their exports of oil, raising the price to the rest of the world. Although oil prices fell in the mid-1980s, it is hard to argue that Saudi Arabia would have been better off under free trade.

The terms of trade argument against free trade has some important limitations, however. Most small countries have very little ability to affect the world prices of either their imports or other exports, so that the terms of trade argument is of little practical importance. For big countries like the United States, the problem is that the terms of trade argument amounts to an argument for using national monopoly power to extract gains at other countries' expense. The United States could surely do this to some extent, but such a predatory policy would probably bring retaliation from other large countries. A cycle of retaliatory trade moves would, in turn, undermine the attempts at international trade policy coordination described later in this chapter.

The terms of trade argument against free trade, then, is intellectually impeccable but of doubtful usefulness. In practice, it is emphasized more by economists as a theoretical proposition than it is used by governments as a justification for trade policy.

THE DOMESTIC MARKET FAILURE ARGUMENT AGAINST FREE TRADE

Leaving aside the issue of the terms of trade, the basic theoretical case for free trade rested on cost-benefit analysis using the concepts of consumer and producer surplus. Many economists have made a case against free trade based on the counterargument that these concepts, producer surplus in particular, do not properly measure costs and benefits.

Why might producer surplus not properly measure the benefits of producing a good? We consider a variety of reasons in the next two chapters: these include the possibility that the labor used in a sector would otherwise be unemployed or underemployed, the existence of defects in the capital or labor markets that prevent resources from being transferred as rapidly as they should be to sectors that yield high returns, and the possibility of technological spillovers from industries that are new or particularly innovative. These can all be classified under the general heading of **domestic market failures.** That is, each of these examples is one in which some market in the country is not doing its job right—the labor market is not clearing, the capital market is not allocating resources efficiently, and so on.

Suppose, for example, that the production of some good yields experience that will improve the technology of the economy as a whole but that the firms in the sector cannot appropriate this benefit and therefore do not take it into account in deciding how much to produce. Then there is a **marginal social benefit** to additional production that is not captured by the producer surplus measure. This marginal social benefit can serve as a justification for tariffs or other trade policies.

Figure 10-3 illustrates the domestic market failure argument against free trade. Figure 10-3a shows the conventional cost-benefit analysis of a tariff for a small country (which rules out terms of trade effects). Figure 10-3b shows the marginal benefit from production that is not taken account of by the producer surplus measure. The figure shows the effects of a tariff that raises the domestic price from P_W to $P_W + t$. Production rises from S^1 to S^2, with a resulting production distortion indicated by the area labeled

FIGURE 10-3
The domestic market failure argument for a tariff.
If production of a good yields extra social benefits not captured as producer surplus, a tariff can increase welfare.

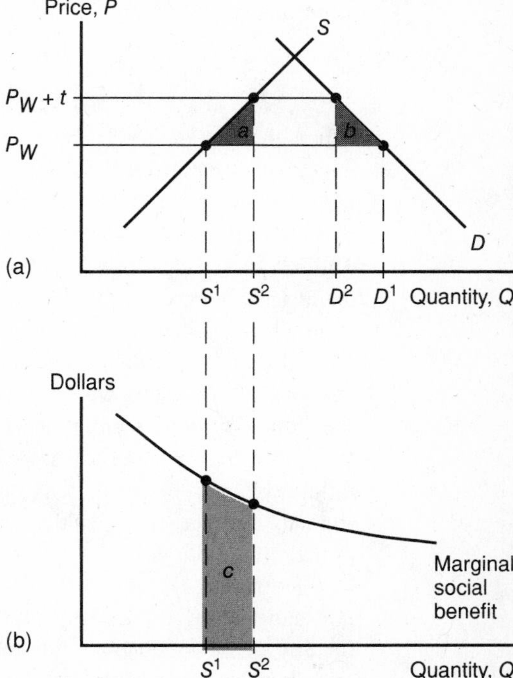

a. Consumption falls from D^1 to D^2, with a resulting consumption distortion indicated by the area *b*. If we considered only consumer and producer surplus, we would find that the costs of the tariff exceed its benefits. Figure 10-3b shows, however, that this calculation overlooks an additional benefit that may make the tariff preferable to free trade. The increase in production yields a social benefit that may be measured by the area under the marginal social benefit curve from S^1 to S^2, indicated by *c*. In fact, by an argument similar to that in the terms of trade case, we can show that if the tariff is small enough the area *c* must always exceed the area $a + b$ and that there is some welfare-maximizing tariff that yields a level of social welfare higher than that of free trade.

The domestic market failure argument against free trade is a particular case of a more general concept known in economics as the **theory of the second best.** This theory states that a hands-off policy is desirable in any one market only if all other markets are working properly. If they are not, a government intervention that appears to distort incentives in one market may actually increase welfare by offsetting the consequences of market failures elsewhere. For example, if the labor market is malfunctioning and fails to deliver full employment, a policy of subsidizing labor-intensive industries, which would be undesirable in a full-employment economy, might turn out to be a good idea. It would be better to fix the labor market, for example, by making wages more flexible, but if for some reason this cannot be done, intervening in other markets may be a ''second-best'' way of alleviating the problem.

When economists apply the theory of the second best to trade policy, they argue that imperfections in the *internal* functioning of an economy may justify interfering in its external economic relations. This argument accepts that international trade is not the source of the problem but suggests nonetheless that trade policy can provide at least a partial solution.

HOW CONVINCING IS THE MARKET FAILURE ARGUMENT?

When they were first proposed, market failure arguments for protection seemed to undermine much of the case for free trade. After all, who would want to argue that the real economies we live in are free from market failures? In poorer nations, in particular, market imperfections seem to be legion. For example, unemployment and massive differences between rural and urban wage rates are present in many less-developed countries (Chapter 11). The evidence that markets work badly is less glaring in advanced countries, but it is easy to develop hypotheses suggesting major market failures there as well—for example, the inability of innovative firms to reap the full rewards of their innovations. How can we defend free trade given the likelihood that there are interventions that could raise national welfare?

There are two lines of defense for free trade: the first argues that domestic market failures should be corrected by domestic policies aimed directly at the problems' sources; the second argues that economists cannot diagnose market failure well enough to prescribe policy.

The point that domestic market failure calls for domestic policy changes, not international trade policies, can be made by cost-benefit analysis, modified to account for any unmeasured marginal social benefits. Figure 10-3 showed that a tariff might raise welfare, despite the production and consumption distortion it causes, because it leads to additional production that yields social benefits. If the same production increase were achieved via a production subsidy rather than a tariff, however, the price to consumers would not increase and the consumption loss *b* would be avoided. In other words, by targeting directly the particular activity we want to encourage, a production subsidy would avoid some of the side costs associated with a tariff.

This example illustrates a general principle when dealing with market failures: it is always preferable to deal with market failures as directly as possible, because indirect policy responses lead to unintended distortions of incentives elsewhere in the economy. Thus, trade policies justified by domestic market failure are never the most efficient response; they are always ''second-best'' rather than ''first-best'' policies.

This insight has important implications for trade policymakers: any proposed trade policy should always be compared with a purely domestic policy aimed at correcting the same problem. If the domestic policy appears too costly or has undesirable side effects, the trade policy is almost surely even less desirable—even though the costs are less apparent.

In the United States, for example, an import quota on automobiles has been supported on the grounds that it is necessary to save the jobs of autoworkers. The advocates of an import quota argue that U.S. labor markets are too inflexible for autoworkers to remain employed either by cutting their wages or by finding jobs in other sectors. Now consider a purely domestic policy aimed at the same problem: a subsidy to firms that employ autoworkers. Such a policy would encounter massive political opposition. For one thing, to preserve current levels of employment without protection would require large subsidy payments, which would either increase the federal government budget deficit or require a tax increase. Furthermore, autoworkers are among the highest-paid workers in the manufacturing sector; the general public would surely object to subsidizing them. It is hard to believe an employment subsidy for autoworkers could pass Congress. Yet an import quota *would be even more expensive,* because while bringing about the same increase in employment, it would also distort consumer choice. The only difference is that the costs would be less visible, taking the form of higher automobile prices rather than direct government outlays.

Critics of the domestic market failure justification for protection argue that this case is typical: most deviations from free trade are adopted not because their benefits exceed their costs but because the public fails to understand their true costs. Comparing the costs of trade policy with alternative domestic policies is a useful way to focus attention on how large these costs are.

The second defense of free trade is that because market failures are typically hard to identify precisely, it is difficult to be sure about the appropriate policy response. For example, suppose there is urban unemployment in a less-developed country; what is the appropriate policy? One hypothesis (examined more closely in Chapter 11) says that a tariff to protect urban industrial sectors will draw the unemployed into productive work and thus generate social benefits that more than compensate for its costs. Another hypothesis says, however, that this policy will encourage so much migration to urban areas that unemployment will, in fact, increase. It is difficult to say which of these hypotheses is right. While economic theory says much about the working of markets that function properly, it provides much less guidance on those that don't; there are many ways in which markets can malfunction, and the choice of a second-best policy depends on the details of the market failure.

The difficulty of ascertaining the right second-best trade policy to follow reinforces the political argument for free trade mentioned earlier. If trade policy experts are highly uncertain about how policy should deviate from free trade and disagree among themselves, it is all too easy for trade policy to ignore national welfare altogether and become dominated by special-interest politics. If the market failures are not too bad to start with, a commitment to free trade might in the end be a better policy than opening the Pandora's box of a more flexible approach.

This is, however, a judgment about politics rather than economics. We need to realize that economic theory does *not* provide a dogmatic defense of free trade, something that it is often accused of doing.

Income Distribution and Trade Policy

The discussion so far has focused on national welfare arguments for and against tariff policy. It is appropriate to start there, both because a distinction between national welfare and the welfare of particular groups helps to clarify the issues and because the advocates of trade policies usually claim they will benefit the nation as a whole. When looking at the actual politics of trade policy, however, it becomes necessary to deal with the reality that there is no such thing as national welfare; there are only the desires of individuals, which get more or less imperfectly reflected in the objectives of government.

The previous discussion showed that a tariff or other trade policy usually has opposite effects on the welfare of domestic producers and consumers. While no single theory explains how governments decide on their trade policy, several influential hypotheses have been offered.

WEIGHTED SOCIAL WELFARE

According to one view of trade policy, the government (at least implicitly) goes through calculations like the cost-benefit analysis in Chapter 9, but with a difference: a dollar of gain to different groups is not weighted equally. Instead, some groups are counted more heavily than others, with the result that deviations from free trade serve the purpose of redistributing income to the favored groups. This is referred to as **weighted social welfare.**

In the United States, government policy often seems to favor low-wage workers. In many less-developed countries, and in resource-rich industrial countries such as Australia, the government seems consistently to favor urban workers over agricultural interests.

This view is appealing because it incorporates the politics of trade policy into our basic analysis with only a small modification (weighted dollars of gain). In itself, however, it is not enough to explain many features of actual trade policy.

CONSERVATIVE SOCIAL WELFARE

A useful way to look at fairly short-run changes in trade policy is the **conservative social welfare** view that governments are reluctant to allow large changes in income distribution regardless of who gains and who loses. If import competition threatens to make producers in an industry much worse off, the producers are liable to get protection regardless of whether they are a group normally favored by public policy. Thus the U.S. government was unwilling to let its auto industry suffer at foreign hands after 1979, even though the Reagan administration was in principle strongly committed to free trade.

An intriguing aspect of the conservative social welfare view is that it helps explain how temporary trade policies can become permanent. Consider the case of Latin American industrialization. During the 1930s, many Latin American countries imposed import quotas and tariffs as an emergency response to the balance-of-payments problems brought on by worldwide depression. These barriers led to the emergence of domestic industries, which produced substitutes for imports. Because of World War II, imports continued to be restricted through the mid-1940s. By the time a return to freer trade was possible, so much capital was invested and so many workers were employed in the import-substituting industries that removal of import restrictions had become politically unthinkable. Such restrictions remain in much of Latin America to this day.

The irreversibility of protection that results from conservative social welfare is often used as another argument for free trade. Even where a temporary tariff could be desirable, it may be better to avoid risking the creation of a vested interest in permanent protection.

COLLECTIVE ACTION

Many trade policies seem to involve heavy costs to the general public compared with the benefits they provide. How can such apparently irrational policies exist? A frequent answer draws on the famous insight by the economist Mancur Olson that political action, or **collective action,** while it may be in the interest of a *group,* is not usually in the interest of any individual member of that group.[3] Only if interest groups are small and/or well organized will they make themselves felt politically.

The sugar quota discussed in Chapter 9, for example, cost consumers $1.266 billion, while benefiting sugar producers and the government by only $783 million—not a very good bargain. The consumer loss, however, comes to less than $8 per capita: something few people would notice, especially since most sugar is purchased as an ingredient in other foods rather than directly. In fact, only a tiny fraction of the American voting public is aware that there is a sugar quota or that it raises their cost of living. And, since an individual's protest will not by itself change the policy, it is not in the interests of individual consumers to be any better informed.

The sugar producers, by contrast, are well aware that the quota can easily be worth tens or even hundreds of thousands of dollars to an individual sugar producer. Furthermore, sugar producers are organized to act collectively to lobby Congress and make political contributions. It is therefore not surprising that a policy that produces far more costs than benefits is also almost unchallengeable politically.

Theories that emphasize the problem of collective political action conclude that trade policy generally favors small, well-organized groups, even when cost-benefit calculations do not support protection or when the beneficiaries are not the groups one expects the political system to favor in general.

[3] See Olson, *The Logic of Collective Action* (Cambridge: Harvard University Press, 1965).

WHO GETS PROTECTED?

We have now discussed three possible views of the way concerns over income distribution affect trade policy. To conclude this section, we consider briefly who actually gets protected in the world economy.

At a broad level, two generalizations stand out. In countries with strong comparative advantage in manufacturing, farmers get protected, while in countries with a comparative advantage in agricultural or natural resource production, the industrial sector gets protected. Thus Europe and Japan, densely populated areas with highly productive industry, provide price supports, import restrictions, and (in the case of Europe) export subsidies that provide their farmers with prices as much as ten times as high as world levels. At the same time, resource-rich countries like Australia and less-developed economies like India offer their industrial sectors rates of effective protection that sometimes run to hundreds of percent.

In the case of the United States, we can describe specifically who gets protected. Although a number of small industries—ranging from color televisions to motorcycles to pasta—have received trade protection over the years, most U.S. protection is concentrated on just four industries: autos, steel, sugar, and textiles and clothing.

Notice how disparate these industries are. Autos and steel are capital-intensive industries whose workers receive wages much higher than the U.S. average. Textiles and especially clothing is a labor-intensive industry whose workers are among the most poorly paid in the manufacturing sector. Sugar is an agricultural sector, unique primarily in that sugar is one of the few agricultural products in which the United States has both domestic production (unlike, say, coffee) and a comparative disadvantage (unlike wheat). This means that generalizations about the politics of trade policy should be taken cautiously. In the United States, at least, there is no ''typical'' protected industry.

International Negotiations and Trade Policy

Our discussion of the politics of trade policy has not been very encouraging. We have argued that it is difficult to devise trade policies that raise national welfare and that trade policy is often dominated by interest group politics. ''Horror stories'' of trade policies that produce costs that greatly exceed any conceivable benefits abound; it is easy to be highly cynical about the practical side of trade theory.

Yet, in fact, from the mid-1930s until about 1980 the United States and other advanced countries gradually removed tariffs and some other barriers to trade, and by so doing aided a rapid increase in international integration. Figure 10-4 shows the average U.S. tariff rate on dutiable imports from 1920 to 1991; after rising sharply in the early 1930s, the rate has steadily declined.[4] Most economists believe this progressive

[4] Measures of changes in the average rate of protection can be problematic, because the composition of imports changes—partly because of tariff rates themselves. Imagine, for example, a country that imposes a tariff on some goods that is so high that it shuts off all imports of these goods. Then the average tariff rate on goods actually imported will be zero! To try to correct for this, the measure we use in Figure 10-4 shows the rate only on ''dutiable'' imports; that is, it excludes imports that for some reason were exempt from tariff. At their peak, U.S. tariff rates were so high that goods subject to tariffs accounted for only one-third of imports; by 1975 that share had risen to two-thirds. As a result, the average tariff rate on all goods fell much less than the rate on dutiable goods. The numbers shown in Figure 10-4, however, give a more accurate picture of the major liberalization of trade actually experienced by the United States.

FIGURE 10-4
The U.S. tariff rate.
After rising sharply at the beginning of the 1930s, the average tariff rate of the United States has steadily declined.

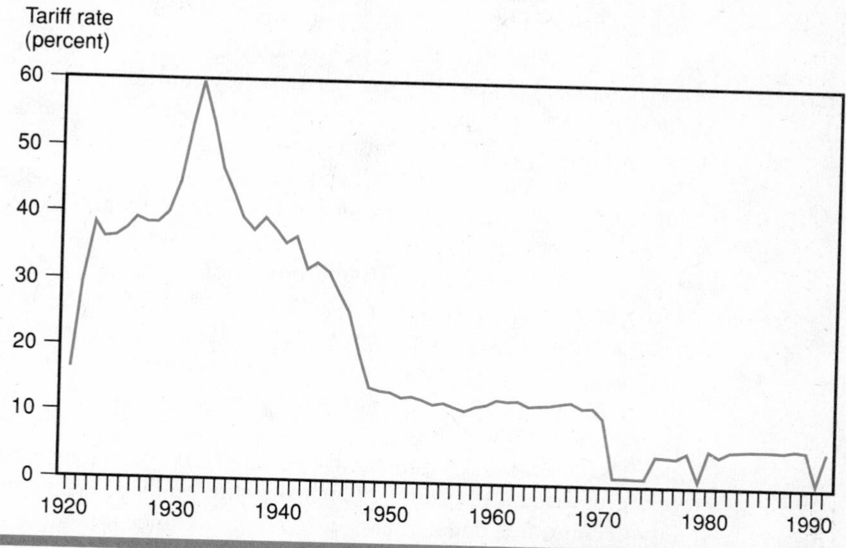

trade liberalization was highly beneficial. Given what we have said about the politics of trade policy, however, how was this removal of tariffs politically possible?

At least part of the answer is that the great postwar liberalization of trade was achieved through **international negotiation.** That is, governments agreed to engage in mutual tariff reduction. These agreements linked reduced protection for each country's import-competing industries to reduced protection by other countries against that country's export industries. Such a linkage, as we will now argue, helps to offset some of the political difficulties that would otherwise prevent countries from adopting good trade policies.

THE ADVANTAGES OF NEGOTIATION

There are at least two reasons why it is easier to lower tariffs as part of a mutual agreement to do so than as a unilateral policy. First, a mutual agreement helps mobilize support for freer trade. Second, negotiated agreements on trade can help governments avoid getting caught in destructive trade wars.

The effect of international negotiations on support for freer trade is straightforward. We have noted that import-competing producers are usually better informed and organized than consumers. International negotiations can bring in domestic exporters as a counterweight. The United States and Japan, for example, could reach an agreement in which the United States refrains from imposing import quotas to protect some of its manufacturers from Japanese competition in return for removal of Japanese barriers to U.S. exports of agricultural or high-technology products to Japan. U.S. consumers might not be effective politically in opposing such import quotas on foreign goods, even though these quotas may be costly to them, but exporters who want access to foreign markets may, through their lobbying for mutual elimination of import quotas, protect consumer interests.

International negotiation can also help to avoid a **trade war.** The concept of a trade war can best be illustrated with a stylized example.

Imagine that there are only two countries in the world, the United States and Japan, and that these countries have only two policy choices, free trade or protection. Suppose that these are unusually clear-headed governments that can assign definite numerical values to their satisfaction with any particular policy outcome (Table 10-2).

The particular values of the payoffs given in the table represent two assumptions. First we assume that each country's government would choose protection if it could take the other country's policy as given. That is, whichever policy Japan chooses, the U.S. government is better off with protection. This assumption is by no means necessarily true; many economists would argue that free trade is the best policy for the nation, regardless of what other governments do. Governments, however, must act not only in the public interest but in their own political interest. For the reasons discussed in the previous section, governments often find it politically difficult to avoid giving protection to some industries.

The second assumption built into Table 10-2 is that even though each government acting individually would be better off with protection, they would both be better off if both chose free trade. That is, the U.S. government has more to gain from an opening of Japanese markets than it has to lose from opening its own markets, and the same is true for Japan. We can justify this assumption simply by appealing to the gains from trade.

To those who have studied game theory, this situation is known as a **Prisoner's dilemma.** Each government, making the best decision for itself, will choose to protect. These choices lead to the outcome in the lower right box of the table. Yet both governments are better off if neither protects: the upper left box of the table yields a payoff that is higher for both countries. By acting unilaterally in what appear to be their best interests, the governments fail to achieve the best outcome possible. If the countries act unilaterally to protect, there is a trade war that leaves both worse off. Trade wars are not as serious as shooting wars, but avoiding them is similar to the problem of avoiding armed conflict or arms races.

Obviously, Japan and the United States need to establish an agreement (such as a treaty) to refrain from protection. Each government will be better off if it limits its own

TABLE 10-2 The problem of trade warfare

U.S. \ Japan	*Free trade*	*Protection*
Free trade	U.S. 10, Japan 10	U.S. −10, Japan 20
Protection	U.S. 20, Japan −10	U.S. −5, Japan −5

freedom of action, provided the other country limits its freedom of action as well. A treaty can make everyone better off.

This is a highly simplified example. In the real world there are both many countries and many gradations of trade policy between free trade and complete protection against imports. Nonetheless, the example suggests both that there is a need to coordinate trade policies through international agreements and that such agreements can actually make a difference. Indeed, the current system of international trade is built around a series of international agreements.

INTERNATIONAL TRADE AGREEMENTS: A BRIEF HISTORY

Internationally coordinated tariff reduction as a trade policy dates back to the 1930s. In 1930, the United States passed a remarkably irresponsible tariff law, the Smoot-Hawley Act. Under this act, tariff rates rose steeply and U.S. trade fell sharply; some economists argue that the Smoot-Hawley Act helped deepen the Great Depression. Within a few years after the act's passage, the U.S. administration concluded that tariffs needed to be reduced, but this posed serious problems of political coalition building. Any tariff reduction would be opposed by those members of Congress whose districts contained firms producing competing goods, while the benefits would be so widely diffused that few in Congress could be mobilized on the other side. To reduce tariff rates, tariff reduction needed to be linked to some concrete benefits for exporters. The initial solution to this political problem was bilateral tariff negotiations. The United States would approach some country that was a major exporter of some good—say, a sugar exporter—and offer to lower tariffs on sugar if that country would lower its tariffs on some U.S. exports. The attractiveness of the deal to U.S. exporters would help counter the political weight of the sugar interest. In the foreign country, the attractiveness of the deal to foreign sugar exporters would balance the political influence of import-competing interests. Such bilateral negotiations helped reduce the average duty on U.S. imports from 59 percent in 1932 to 25 percent shortly after World War II.

Bilateral negotiations, however, do not take full advantage of international coordination. For one thing, benefits from a bilateral negotiation may "spill over" to countries that have not made any concessions. For example, if the United States reduces tariffs on coffee as a result of a deal with Brazil, Colombia will also gain from a higher world coffee price. Furthermore, some advantageous deals may inherently involve more than two countries: the United States sells more to Europe, Europe sells more to Saudi Arabia, Saudi Arabia sells more to Japan, and Japan sells more to the United States. Thus the next step in international trade liberalization was to proceed to multilateral negotiations involving a number of countries.

Since 1945, there have been seven major multilateral trade agreements. The first five of these took the form of "parallel" bilateral negotiations, where each country negotiates pairwise with a number of countries at once. For example, if Germany were to offer a tariff reduction that would benefit both France and Italy, it could ask both of them for reciprocal concessions. The ability to make more extensive deals, together with the worldwide economic recovery from the war, helped to permit substantial tariff reductions.

The sixth multilateral trade agreement, known as the Kennedy Round, was com-

Environmentalism or Protectionism?

As we mentioned in Chapter 9, "red tape"—bureaucratic measures applied at the border—can limit international trade even when tariffs are low. But when are red tape barriers allowed under international law?

There are some cases in which countries have a clear right to limit the international flow of goods for health and safety reasons. For example, the United States requires fumigation of imported produce to ensure that destructive pests are not introduced to U.S. farms. This procedure does not constitute unwarranted interference with trade, since there is a clear economic justification. The United States even allows individual states such as California to impose similar requirements on shipments of fruits and vegetables from other states, even though the Constitution prohibits restrictions of interstate trade.

Conversely, there are other red tape barriers that are clearly spurious—such as the Japanese refusal in the early 1980s to permit importation of U.S. aluminum baseball bats on the grounds that they were unsuited to Japanese conditions.

There is, however, an extensive gray area, involving regulations that serve laudable goals through questionable means.

In 1990 the United States tested this gray area when, in response to environmentalist concerns, it banned the import of tuna caught by methods that kill large numbers of dolphins. (In some areas of the Pacific, herds of these intelligent marine mammals on the surface are a sign of schools of tuna below. Encircling the dolphins with large nets is an effective way to catch tuna cheaply, but it kills many dolphins too.) Mexico, which exports tuna to the United States, appealed to the GATT. An international tribunal ruled in Mexico's favor: the United States has no right to use trade policy to impose its environmental standards on other countries.

The legal reasoning behind this decision was clear, yet it left U.S. environmentalists understandably upset. (We might note that the moral and even economic case for the U.S. action on tuna seems, even in retrospect, a lot better than the case for antidumping duties, yet such duties are an accepted part of international trade law.) It seems likely that there will be future trade policy challenges over a variety of environmental issues, some of them even more compelling—for example, can we refuse to import goods whose production endangers the ozone layer? Many experts expect that so-called "trade and environment" issues will be at the top of the agenda in any future world trade negotiations.

pleted in 1967. This agreement involved an across-the-board 50 percent reduction in tariffs by the major industrial countries, except for specified industries whose tariffs were left unchanged. The negotiations were over which industries to exempt rather than over the size of the cut for industries not given special treatment. Overall, the Kennedy Round reduced average tariffs by about 35 percent.

Finally, the so-called Tokyo Round of trade negotiations (completed in 1979) reduced tariffs by a formula more complex than that of the Kennedy Round. In addition, new codes were established in an effort to control the proliferation of nontariff barriers, such as voluntary export restraints and orderly marketing agreements. At the time of writing, an eighth round of multilateral trade negotiations—the Uruguay Round—was still being negotiated. (The Uruguay Round was supposed to have been concluded in

1990. A dispute between the United States and Europe over agriculture delayed its completion, and as of early 1993 there was still a risk that the talks might fail.)

The multilateral tariff reductions since World War II have taken place under the umbrella framework of the **General Agreement on Tariffs and Trade (GATT),** established in 1947. The GATT embodies a set of rules of conduct for international trade policy that are monitored by a bureaucracy headquartered in Geneva. As with any law, the provisions of the GATT are complex in detail, but the main constraints it places on trade policy are:

1. Export subsidies: Signatories to the GATT may not use export subsidies, except for agricultural products (an exception originally insisted on by the United States but now primarily exploited by the European Community).
2. Import quotas: Signatories to the GATT may not impose unilateral quotas on imports, except when imports threaten ''market disruption'' (an undefined phrase usually interpreted to mean surges of imports that threaten to put a domestic sector suddenly out of business).
3. Tariffs: Any new tariff or increase in a tariff must be offset by reductions in other tariffs to compensate the affected exporting countries.

Not all countries are members of the GATT. In particular, developing countries are by and large outside these rules. Nearly all advanced countries are members, however, and the trade policies they adopt are to some extent conditioned by the need to remain ''GATT-legal.''

STRESSES ON THE TRADING SYSTEM

As we noted, the GATT framework helped promote a fairly steady liberalization of trade among industrial countries from the end of World War II until about 1980. Unfortunately, since that time progress in some areas of international trade has been offset by increased barriers to trade in other areas. There is a widespread perception among policy makers that the GATT is in trouble; that even though an agreement is expected in the current Uruguay Round, this agreement will not be enough either to control growing barriers to trade or to counter growing political pressure for protectionism.

The stresses on the GATT arise from a variety of sources. One important source is that protectionists have simply become more skillful at evading the rules of the GATT. Increasingly, protection by industrial countries takes the form of voluntary export restraints administered by the exporters at the importer's request. The exporters agree to do this rather than face the possibility that the importer will impose a unilateral tariff or import quota. For example, when the United States wanted to reduce automobile imports in 1981, it did not impose an import quota. Instead, it asked Japan to limit its exports. Implicit in this request was the threat that if Japan did not agree, the United States would act on its own. We saw in Chapter 9 that a VER transfers rents to the foreign exporters, while a tariff or quota administered by the importer will not. So the Japanese preferred to go along with the U.S. request rather than take the chance of facing a worse outcome.

Why does this kind of deal undermine the GATT? Because while restrictions on *imports* are policed by the GATT, restrictions (as opposed to subsidies) on *exports* are not.[5] So in terms of the working of the system, what happened in 1981 was an action—Japanese restriction of exports—against which the GATT has no effective sanctions.

Another important source of stress on the GATT arises from the huge trade imbalances that, as we saw in Chapter 1, emerged in the 1980s. In the United States, in particular, low exports and high imports have fueled a surge of protectionist pressure.

Furthermore, GATT members disagree over how (if at all) the organization's rules should be extended to cover areas such as international trade in services, foreign direct investment, agricultural policy, and intellectual property rights.

The stresses on the GATT, however, go beyond both legal difficulties and the current trade imbalances. The structure of the world economy has changed in ways that make the existing system look increasingly inadequate. Many analysts have stressed two changes in particular:

1. The relative decline of the United States. At the inception of the GATT, the United States was overwhelmingly the world's dominant economy, producing about half the output of the world's market economies and with a national income eight times that of its nearest rival. Although the U.S. economy continued to grow over the next forty years, other economies grew faster, so that the U.S. output share was down to about 25 percent by 1990. Many economists expect that by the year 2000 the United States will be only one among equals: the increasingly unified nations of Western Europe will have an economy larger than that of the United States, while Japan's economy will be a close rival.

This matters because the relative decline of the United States deprives the world trading system of a natural leader. During the years of rapid trade liberalization the United States took the lead in pressing for increased trade, often offering somewhat more in concessions than it received. (This was not sheer altruism. U.S. officials regarded increased trade as an aid to other foreign policy objectives, notably maintenance of a common front against the Soviet Union.) In today's world, the United States is neither able nor willing to continue in that role.

2. The rise of Japan. Japan was a country in ruins when the GATT was created. By the 1990s it had become the world's second largest economy and largest exporter. Japan's economic institutions remain, however, very different from those of both the United States and Western Europe. Many foreign businessmen claim that in spite of low tariff rates, Japan's markets are effectively closed by informal barriers to many imports (a claim the Japanese deny). We will discuss the Japan issue at greater length in Chapter 12. Whatever the truth, there is a widespread belief that trade negotiations do little or nothing to give foreign firms access to Japan's markets.

This belief undermines the political basis of international negotiation, in which the interests of exporters serve as a counterweight to the interests of import-competing sectors. If exporters regard the concessions of one of the most important players as irrelevant, the counterweight is largely lost.

During the 1980s a gradual increase in trade restrictions that evaded the GATT largely offset the effects of the Tokyo Round in liberalizing trade; in the view of many analysts the net movement was away from free trade, not toward it. And there was

[5] Strictly speaking, export restraints are prohibited by the same part of the GATT that prohibits import restraints. Under the GATT, however, a case must be brought by a complaining party—normally the exporter. Since a "voluntary" restraint has already enlisted the complicity of the exporting nation, there is usually nobody left to complain.

widespread concern at the end of the decade that a crisis of trade policy might be looming. Nevertheless, the late 1980s were marked by major moves toward freer trade, not for the world as a whole, but at a regional level. Both in Europe and between the United States and Canada there were new agreements to remove remaining trade barriers. Such special arrangements among limited groups of countries are known as **preferential trading agreements.** They have always been a part of the international system, but they have assumed even greater importance recently.

PREFERENTIAL TRADING AGREEMENTS

The international trade agreements that we have described so far all involved a ''nondiscriminatory'' reduction in tariff rates. For example, when the United States agrees with Germany to lower its tariff on imported machinery, the new tariff rate applies to machinery from any nation rather than just imports from Germany. Such nondiscrimination is normal in most tariffs. Indeed, the United States grants many countries a status known formally as that of ''most favored nation'' (MFN), a guarantee that their exporters will pay tariffs no higher than that of the nation that pays the lowest. All countries granted MFN status pay the same rates. Tariff reductions under GATT always are made on an MFN basis.

There are some important cases, however, in which nations establish preferential trading agreements under which the tariffs they apply to each others' products are lower than the rates on the same goods coming from other countries. The simplest case is one in which two or more countries eliminate all tariffs on trade with each other while continuing to maintain tariff barriers against the rest of the world. Such agreements are known variously as **customs unions, common markets,** and **free trade areas.** The most important customs union in the modern world is the European Community, which unites twelve European nations in a zone without any tariffs or explicit quotas (although a variety of administrative obstacles to trade still persist). Since more than a third of world trade takes place within this European free trade area, preferential trading arrangements are an important real-world issue. Furthermore, a number of other customs unions exist, albeit on a smaller scale, and, as noted above, the United States and Canada have recently agreed to establish mutual free trade.

Subject to the qualifications mentioned earlier in this chapter, tariff reduction is a good thing that raises economic efficiency. At first it might seem that preferential tariff reductions are also good, if not as good as reducing tariffs all around. After all, isn't half a loaf better than none?

Perhaps surprisingly, this conclusion is too optimistic. It is possible for a country to make itself worse off by joining a customs union. The reason may be illustrated by a hypothetical example, using Britain, France, and the United States. The United States is a low-cost producer of wheat ($4 per bushel), France a medium-cost producer ($6 per bushel), and Britain a high-cost producer ($8 per bushel). Both Britain and France maintain tariffs against all wheat imports. If Britain forms a customs union with France, the tariff against French, but not U.S., wheat will be abolished. Is this good or bad for Britain? To answer this, consider two cases.

First, suppose that Britain's initial tariff was high enough to exclude wheat imports from either France or the United States. For example, with a tariff of $5 per bushel it would cost $9 to import U.S. wheat and $11 to import French wheat, so British consumers would buy $8 British wheat instead. When the tariff on French wheat is

Do Trade Preferences Have Appeal?

In early 1993 the members of the European Community slipped into a bunch of trouble over the question of trade preferences for bananas.

Most of the world's banana exports come from several small Central American nations—the original "banana republics." Several European nations have, however, traditionally bought their bananas instead from their past or present West Indian colonies in the Caribbean. To protect the island producers, France and the United Kingdom impose import quotas against the "dollar bananas" of Central America, which are typically about 40 percent cheaper than the West Indian product. Germany, however, which has never had West Indian colonies, allows free entry to dollar bananas.

With the integration of European markets after 1992, the existing banana regime will become impossible to maintain, because it will be easy to import the cheaper dollar bananas into Germany and then ship them elsewhere in Europe. As a result, the European Commission announced plans to impose a new common European import quota against dollar bananas. Germany angrily protested the move and even denied its legality: the Germans pointed out that the Treaty of Rome, which established the European Community, contains an explicit guarantee (the "banana protocol") that Germany would be able to import bananas freely.

Why are the Germans so exercised about bananas? During the years of Communist rule in East Germany, bananas were a rare luxury. The sudden availability of inexpensive bananas after the fall of the Berlin Wall made them a symbol of freedom. So the German government is very unwilling to introduce a policy that will sharply increase banana prices.

At the time of writing, efforts to negotiate a resolution to Europe's banana split had proved fruitless.

eliminated, imports from France will replace British production. From Britain's point of view this is a gain, because it costs \$8 to produce a bushel of wheat domestically, while Britain needs to produce only \$6 worth of export goods to pay for a bushel of French wheat.

On the other hand, suppose the tariff was lower, for example, \$3 per bushel, so that before joining the customs union Britain bought its wheat from the United States (at a cost to consumers of \$7 per bushel) rather than producing its own wheat. When the customs union is formed, consumers will buy French wheat at \$6 rather than U.S. wheat at \$7. So imports of wheat from the United States will cease. However, U.S. wheat is really cheaper than French wheat; the \$3 tax that British consumers must pay on U.S. wheat returns to Britain in the form of government revenue and is therefore not a net cost to the British economy. Britain will have to devote more resources to exports to pay for its wheat imports and will be worse off rather than better off.

This possibility of a loss is another example of the theory of the second best. Think of Britain as initially having two policies that distort incentives: a tariff against U.S. wheat and a tariff against French wheat. Although the tariff against French wheat may seem to distort incentives, it may help to offset the distortion of incentives resulting from the tariff against the United States, by encouraging consumption of the cheaper U.S. wheat. Thus, removing the tariff on French wheat can actually reduce welfare.

Returning to our two cases, notice that Britain gains if the formation of a customs

The Oilseed Dispute

During the fall of 1992, as negotiators tried desperately to reach an agreement that would end the Uruguay Round of trade talks, a trade war between the United States and Europe almost erupted over an issue so obscure that only a few specialists had previously been aware of it.

The problem was oilseeds—the various crops (e.g., sunflowers) whose seeds may be pressed to yield edible oils. The point of dispute was the claim by the United States that European nations, primarily France, had in effect failed to honor an earlier agreement to open their markets to American oilseeds. They had in fact reduced their tariffs, but had compensated by offering production subsidies to their farmers, leaving little scope for increased imports. Over a six-year period the United States had twice brought the oilseed issue before GATT arbitration panels, and in each case the panels had ruled in America's favor and ordered France to eliminate its subsidies, but France had refused.

Faced with this refusal, the United States announced in November 1992 that it would retaliate with new tariffs on $300 million of European products, notably French white wines. For a few weeks it seemed as if a full-scale trade war might be about to break out. In the end, however, France backed down under pressure from other members of the European Community.

The whole episode was an object lesson in the realities of trade policy. One might naively suppose that great global negotiations must involve conflicts over great national interests. European oilseed production is only about 10 million metric tons annually, and the price per ton is typically less than $100—in other words, the European oilseed industry amounts to only about $1 billion in sales, in a $5 trillion European economy. Yet France was willing to endanger the Uruguay Round to defend its policy of protecting the crop, a policy that was almost certainly against national interest in the first place.

union leads to new trade—French wheat replacing domestic production—while it loses if the trade within the customs union simply replaces trade with countries outside the union. In the analysis of preferential trading arrangements, the first case is referred to as **trade creation,** while the second is **trade diversion.** Whether a customs union is desirable or undesirable depends on whether it largely leads to trade creation or trade diversion.

Case Study

RECENT REGIONAL TRADING AGREEMENTS

While many were growing pessimistic about the prospects for the GATT, the late 1980s and early 1990s saw several dramatic moves toward closer trade ties among neighboring countries.

The most ambitious of these moves was the attempt to create a unified market in Europe, generally referred to as "1992." We have already described this effort in this chapter and in Chapter 8. It is unusual in that the countries involved already constituted a customs union, with no tariffs or quotas on internal trade. What Europe was aiming for was something deeper—in effect, to eliminate completely the distinction among its different national economies. It remains to be seen how successful the attempt will be in economic terms, but there is no question that "1992" was a remarkable political achievement.

Moves toward free trade in North America were in their way equally remarkable. Both Canada and Mexico have historically feared that their national identities would be swallowed up by the far larger economy of the United States and have thus traditionally pursued protectionist policies against U.S. goods. Since the 1960s Canada and the United States have moved steadily toward freer trade (recall our discussion of the auto pact in Chapter 6), and by the late 1980s Canadian tariffs on U.S. goods averaged only 2 percent. Still, it was a political milestone in 1989 when Canada and the United States agreed to eliminate virtually all trade barriers over the next ten years.

Even more dramatic was the tentative 1992 agreement by Canada, the United States, and Mexico to form a North American Free Trade Area (generally known as NAFTA). Here again much of the move to free trade had already taken place: beginning in 1987, Mexico sharply reduced its tariff rates and dismantled many of its import restrictions. By 1992, the average Mexican tariff on U.S. goods was only 10 percent, while the U.S. tariff on Mexican goods was only 4 percent. Nonetheless, the decision to go all the way to free trade and to lock in previous liberalization by treaty was a powerful political symbol. Indeed, NAFTA aroused significant opposition from labor groups in the United States, who feared that competition from Mexican labor would hurt some U.S. workers. At the time of writing it was still possible that this opposition would block congressional ratification of NAFTA.

Finally, in 1991 the South American nations of Brazil, Uruguay, and Argentina formed a customs union, generally known as Mercosur. Few observers gave the union much chance of success, given past failures in the region and the political and economic turmoil in Brazil. In its first year of operation, however, Mercosur astonished the skeptics as trade among its members surged by 50 percent.

There are two obvious questions about these moves toward free trade at a regional level. First, why have they succeeded when global trade negotiations appear stalled? Second, is the apparent trend toward regional trading agreements a good thing?

There are several answers to the first question. Close neighbors often find it easier to trust each other than less similar nations. France and Germany, or Canada and the United States, do not have the problems of radical differences in economic institutions that bedevil U.S. trade relations with Japan. Special political factors also play a role. For the United States, NAFTA is a way to strengthen a reformist, pro-United States Mexican government. For the members of Mercosur, the trade alliance is a bit of mutual support for freely elected governments in a region where democracy has historically been a sometime thing.

Are the agreements a good thing? Most analysts believe the direct effects of NAFTA and "1992" will be clearly positive (there has been little careful study of Mercosur). That is, the gains from trade creation will outweigh any losses from trade diversion. The concern is instead that the large economic blocs being formed may turn protectionist against the outside world—for example, that 1992 will pave the way for "Fortress Europe." All of the policymakers involved deny that this will happen; it remains to be seen if they are right.

Summary

1. Although few countries practice free trade, most economists continue to hold up free trade as a desirable policy. This advocacy rests on three lines of argument. First is a formal case for the efficiency gains from free trade that is simply the cost-benefit analysis of trade policy read in reverse. Second, many economists believe that free trade produces additional gains that go beyond this formal analysis. Finally, given the difficulty of translating complex economic analysis into real policies, even those who do not see free trade as the best imaginable policy see it as a useful rule of thumb.

2. There is an intellectually respectable case for deviating from free trade. One argument that is clearly valid in principle is that countries can improve their *terms of trade* through optimal tariffs and export taxes. This argument is not too important in practice, however. Small countries cannot have much influence on their import or export prices, so they cannot use tariffs or other policies to raise their terms of trade. Large countries, on the other hand, *can* influence their terms of trade, but in imposing tariffs they run the risk of disrupting trade agreements and provoking retaliation.

3. The other argument for deviating from free trade rests on *domestic market failures.* If some domestic market, such as the labor market, fails to function properly, deviating from free trade can sometimes help reduce the consequences of this malfunctioning. The *theory of the second best* states that if one market fails to work properly it is no longer optimal for the government to abstain from intervention in other markets. A tariff may raise welfare if there is a *marginal social benefit* to production of a good that is not captured by producer surplus measures.

4. Although market failures are probably common, the domestic market failure argument should not be applied too freely. First, it is an argument for domestic policies rather than trade policies; tariffs are always an inferior, "second-best" way to offset domestic market failure, which is always best treated at its source. Furthermore, market failure is difficult to analyze well enough to be sure of the appropriate policy recommendation.

5. In practice, trade policy is dominated by considerations of income distribution. No single way of modeling the politics of trade policy exists, but several useful ideas have been proposed. First is the concept of *weighted social welfare.* In this view, governments weight an additional dollar of gain or loss differently depending on who is affected, so that trade policy attempts to benefit favored groups. Second is the idea of *conservative social welfare.* In this view, governments are reluctant to allow any group to suffer large losses. Third is the problem of *collective action.* In this view, trade policy is determined by the differential ability of groups to organize to act politically in their collective interest, even though it may be in the interest of individuals to abstain.

6. If trade policy were made on a purely domestic basis, progress toward freer trade would be very difficult to achieve. In fact, however, industrial countries have achieved substantial reductions in tariffs through a process of *international negotiation.* International negotiation helps the cause of tariff reduction in two ways: it helps broaden the constituency for freer trade by giving exporters a direct stake, and it helps governments avoid the mutually disadvantageous *trade wars* that internationally uncoordinated policies could bring.

7. Although some progress was made in the 1930s toward trade liberalization via bilateral agreements, since World War II international coordination has taken place primarily via multilateral agreements under the auspices of the *General Agreement on*

Tariffs and Trade. The GATT, which comprises both a bureaucracy and a set of rules of conduct, is the central institution of the international trading system. Although it was a huge success for three decades, the GATT now faces serious problems.

8. In addition to the overall reductions in tariffs that have taken place through multilateral negotiation, some groups of countries have negotiated *preferential trading agreements* under which they lower tariffs with respect to each other but not the rest of the world. The simplest examples are those of *customs unions.* The economic value of joining a customs union is ambiguous. If joining leads to replacement of high-cost domestic production by imports from within the customs union—the case of *trade creation*—the country gains. If, on the other hand, joining leads to replacement of cheap imports from outside the union by more expensive imports from inside—the case of *trade diversion*—the country loses.

Key Terms

efficiency case for free trade
political argument for free trade
terms of trade argument for a tariff
optimum tariff
domestic market failure
marginal social benefit
theory of the second best
weighted social welfare
conservative social welfare
collective action
international negotiation
trade war
Prisoner's dilemma
General Agreement on Tariffs and Trade (GATT)
preferential trading agreements
customs union
common market
free trade area
trade creation
trade diversion

Problems

1. "For a small country like the Philippines, a move to free trade would have huge advantages. It would let consumers and producers make their choices based on the real costs of goods, not artificial prices determined by government policy; it would allow escape from the confines of a narrow domestic market; it would open new horizons for entrepreneurship; and, most important, it would help to clean up domestic politics." Separate out and identify the arguments for free trade in this statement.

2. Which of the following are potentially valid arguments for tariffs or export subsidies, and which are not (explain your answers)?

a. "The more oil the United States imports, the higher the price of oil will go in the next world shortage."

b. "The growing exports of off-season fruit from Chile, which now accounts for 80 percent of the U.S. supply of such produce as winter grapes, are contributing to sharply falling prices of these former luxury goods."

c. ''U.S. farm exports don't just mean higher incomes for farmers—they mean higher income for everyone who sells goods and services to the U.S. farm sector.''

d. ''Semiconductors are the crude oil to technology; if we don't produce our own chips, the flow of information that is crucial to every industry that uses microelectronics will be impaired.''

e. ''The real price of timber has fallen 40 percent, and thousands of timber workers have been forced to look for other jobs.''

3. A small country can import a good at a world price of 10 per unit. The domestic supply curve of the good is

$$S = 50 + 5P.$$

The demand curve is

$$D = 400 - 10P.$$

In addition, each unit of production yields a marginal social benefit of 10.

a. Calculate the total effect on welfare of a tariff of 5 per unit levied on imports.

b. Calculate the total effect of a production subsidy of 5 per unit.

c. Why does the production subsidy produce a greater gain in welfare than the tariff?

d. What would the *optimal* production subsidy be?

4. Suppose that demand and supply are exactly as described in problem 3 but there is no marginal social benefit to production. However, for political reasons the government counts a dollar's worth of gain to producers as being worth \$2 of either consumer gain or government revenue. Calculate the effects *on the government's objective* of a tariff of 5 per unit.

5. ''There is no point in the United States complaining about trade policies in Japan and Europe. Each country has a right to do whatever is in its own best interest. Instead of complaining about foreign trade policies, the United States should let other countries go their own way, and give up our own prejudices about free trade and follow suit.'' Discuss both the economics and the political economy of this viewpoint.

6. Which of the following actions would be legal under GATT, and which would not?

a. A U.S. tariff of 20 percent against any country that exports more than twice as much to the United States as it imports in return.

b. A subsidy to U.S. wheat exports, aimed at recapturing some of the markets lost to the European Community.

c. A U.S. tariff on Canadian lumber exports, not matched by equivalent reductions on other tariffs.

d. A Canadian tax on lumber *exports,* agreed to at the demand of the United States to placate U.S. lumber producers.

e. A program of subsidized research and development in areas related to high-technology goods such as electronics and semiconductors.

f. Special government assistance for workers who lose their jobs because of import competition.

7. As a result of political and economic liberalization in Eastern Europe, there has been widespread speculation that Eastern European nations such as Poland and Hungary may join the European Community. Discuss the potential economic *costs* of such an expansion of the European Community, from the point of view of (1) Western Europe; (2) Eastern Europe; and (3) other nations.

Further Reading

Robert E. Baldwin. *The Political Economy of U.S. Import Policy.* Cambridge: MIT Press, 1985. A basic reference on how and why trade policies are made in the United States.

Robert E. Baldwin, ed. *Recent Issues and Initiatives in U.S. Trade Policy.* Cambridge: National Bureau of Economic Research, 1984. Essays on some of the issues that are relevant to current policy debate.

Robert E. Baldwin. ''Trade Policies in Developed Countries,'' in Ronald W. Jones and Peter B. Kenen, eds. *Handbook of International Economics.* Vol. 1. Amsterdam: North-Holland, 1984. A comprehensive survey of theory and evidence on a broad range of trade-related policies.

Jagdish Bhagwati, ed. *Import Competition and Response.* Chicago: University of Chicago Press, 1982. Analytical papers on the economic and political issues raised when imports compete with domestic production.

Jagdish Bhagwati. *Protectionism.* Cambridge: MIT Press, 1988. A cogent summary of the arguments for and against protectionism, ending with a set of proposals for strengthening free trade.

Congressional Budget Office. *The GATT Negotiations and U.S. Trade Policy.* Washington, D.C.: U.S. Government Printing Office, 1987. A useful survey of key issues in the Uruguay Round of negotiations.

W. Max Corden. *Trade Policy and Economic Welfare.* Oxford: Clarendon Press, 1974. A careful survey of economic arguments for and against protection.

Harry Flam. ''Product Markets and 1992: Full Integration, Large Gains?'' *The Journal of Economic Perspectives,* Fall 1992, pp. 7–30. A careful review of the possible economic effects of ''1992,'' the effort to integrate European markets. Notable for the way it tries to test the common belief that there will be large ''dynamic'' gains from removing trade barriers, even though the measured costs of those barriers appear small.

John H. Jackson. *The World Trading System.* Cambridge: MIT Press, 1989. A comprehensive view of the legal framework of international trade, with emphasis on the role of the GATT.

Dominick Salvatore, ed. *The New Protectionist Threat to World Welfare.* Amsterdam: North-Holland, 1987. A collection of essays on the causes and consequences of increasing protectionist pressure in the 1980s.

Robert M. Stern, ed. *U.S. Trade Policies in a Changing World Economy.* Cambridge: MIT Press, 1987. More essays on current trade policy issues.

Appendix to Chapter 10 ●
Proving that the Optimum Tariff Is Positive

A tariff always improves the terms of trade of a large country but at the same time distorts production and consumption. This appendix shows that for a sufficiently small tariff the terms of trade gain is always larger than the distortion loss. Thus there is always an optimal tariff that is positive.

To make the point, we focus on the case where all demand and supply curves are *linear,* that is, are straight lines.

DEMAND AND SUPPLY

We assume that Home, the importing country, has a demand curve whose equation is

$$D = a - b\tilde{P}, \qquad \textbf{(10A-1)}$$

where $\tilde{P}$ is the internal price of the good, and a supply curve whose equation is

$$Q = e + f\tilde{P}. \qquad \textbf{(10A-2)}$$

Home's import demand is equal to the difference between domestic demand and supply,

$$D - Q = (a - e) - (b + f)\tilde{P}. \qquad \textbf{(10A-3)}$$

Foreign's export supply is also a straight line,

$$(Q^* - D^*) = g + hP_W, \qquad \textbf{(10A-4)}$$

where P_W is the world price. The internal price in Home will exceed the world price by the tariff,

$$\tilde{P} = P_W + t. \qquad \textbf{(10A-5)}$$

THE TARIFF AND PRICES

A tariff drives a wedge between internal and world prices, driving the internal Home price up and the world price down (Figure 10A-1).

In world equilibrium, Home import demand equals Foreign export supply:

$$(a - e) - (b + f) \times (P_W + t) = g + hP_W. \qquad \textbf{(10A-6)}$$

Let P_F be the world price that would prevail if there were no tariff. Then a tariff t will raise the internal price to

$$\tilde{P} = P_F + th/(b + f + h), \qquad \textbf{(10A-7)}$$

while lowering the world price to

$$P_W = P_F - t(b + f)/(b + f + h). \qquad \textbf{(10A-8)}$$

(For a small country, foreign supply is highly elastic, that is, h is very large. So for a small country a tariff will have little effect on the world price while raising the domestic price almost one-for-one.)

FIGURE 10A-1
Effects of a tariff on prices.
In a linear model we can calculate the exact effect of a

Price, P

Foreign export

Trade Policy in Developing Countries

Chapter 11

So far we have analyzed the instruments of trade policy and its objectives without specifying the context—that is, without saying much about the country undertaking these policies. Each country has its own distinctive history and issues, but in discussing economic policy one broad distinction is between two groups of countries. On one side are the developed or advanced countries: North America, Western Europe, Japan, and a few others. These countries, whatever their economic problems, are by the standards of the rest of the world highly successful economies. With only about 15 percent of the world's population, the advanced countries account for about 70 percent of the world's production and international trade. Given how well these economies perform, it is reasonable to suppose that their economic systems are fairly efficient, so neither the demands on trade policy nor the expectations placed on it are usually very large.

Most of the world's population, however, lives in **developing countries** that lag far behind these advanced nations.[1] Developing countries span the range from rapidly growing nations such as South Korea (which may soon be ''graduated'' into the category of advanced countries) to nations such as Ethiopia that live on the edge of subsistence. Despite the huge differences among developing countries, however, their shared relative backwardness creates some common themes in their trade policies. First, many developing nations have tried to use trade policy to favor manufacturing as

[1] *Developing country* is a term used by international organizations that has now become standard, even though some ''developing'' countries have had declining living standards for a decade or more. A more descriptive but less polite term is *less-developed countries* (LDCs).

opposed to traditional sectors such as agriculture and mining in the hope that this would help them catch up with wealthier countries. Second, many poorer countries have tried to use trade policy to cure the problem of uneven development or dualism *within* the country. Finally, developing countries sometimes argue that their relative poverty is not their own fault but is instead due to an unfair international economic system, and they have at times tried to use international negotiation to bring about changes in that system.

In this chapter we examine the special issues of trade policy raised by each of these considerations. In the next chapter we turn to the different concerns of the advanced countries.

Trade Policy to Promote Manufacturing

Perhaps the most distinctive difference between trade policy in advanced countries and in poor countries is that in developing countries policy is more consistently preoccupied with the encouragement of manufacturing as opposed to other sectors of the economy. This preoccupation is, to some extent, a result of the symbolic importance of manufacturing as a sign of national development. Most advanced nations are mainly exporters of manufactured goods, while poor nations are usually exporters of "primary" products such as agricultural produce and minerals. Thus, countries seeking to demonstrate their strength and independence often want conspicuous domestic industries such as steel or petrochemicals. Beyond the symbolism of manufacturing development, however, governments in many nations have been strongly influenced by theoretical arguments for trade policy to promote manufacturing. The most important of these arguments is the *infant industry argument* for temporary protection of the manufacturing sector against import competition, which we mentioned in Chapter 6.

WHY MANUFACTURING IS FAVORED: THE INFANT INDUSTRY ARGUMENT

According to the infant industry argument, developing countries have a *potential* comparative advantage in manufacturing, but new manufacturing industries in developing countries cannot initially compete with well-established manufacturing in developed countries. To allow manufacturing to get a toehold, governments should temporarily support new industries, until they have grown strong enough to meet international competition. Thus it makes sense, according to this argument, to use tariffs or import quotas as temporary measures to get industrialization started. It is a historical fact that the world's three largest market economies all began their industrialization behind trade barriers: the United States and Germany had high tariff rates on manufacturing in the nineteenth century, while Japan had extensive import controls until the 1970s.

Problems with the Infant Industry Argument. The infant industry argument seems highly plausible, and in fact it has been persuasive to many governments. Yet economists have pointed out many pitfalls in the argument, suggesting that it must be used cautiously.

First, it is not always good to try to move today into the industries that will have a comparative advantage in the future. Suppose that a country that is currently labor-abundant is in the process of accumulating capital: when it accumulates enough capital, it will have a comparative advantage in capital-intensive industries. That does not mean it should try to develop these industries immediately. In the 1980s, for example, Korea became an exporter of automobiles; it would probably not have been a good idea for Korea to have tried to develop its auto industry in the 1960s, when capital and skilled labor were still very scarce.

Second, protecting manufacturing does no good unless the protection itself helps make industry competitive. Pakistan and India have protected their manufacturing sectors for decades and have recently begun to develop significant exports of manufactured goods. The goods they export, however, are light manufactures like textiles, not the heavy manufactures that they protected; a good case can be made that they would have developed their manufactured exports even if they had never protected manufacturing. Some economists have warned of the case of the "pseudo infant industry," where industry is initially protected, then becomes competitive for reasons that have nothing to do with the protection. In this case infant industry protection ends up looking like a success but may actually have been a net cost to the economy.

More generally, the fact that it is costly and time-consuming to build up an industry is not an argument for government intervention unless there is some domestic market failure. If an industry is supposed to be able to earn high enough returns to capital, labor, and other factors of production to be worth developing, then why don't private investors develop the industry without government help? Sometimes it is argued that private investors take into account only the current returns in an industry and fail to take account of the future prospects, but this is not consistent with market behavior. In advanced countries at least, investors often back projects whose returns are uncertain and lie far in the future. (Consider, for example, the U.S. biotechnology industry, which attracted hundreds of millions of dollars of capital years before it made even a single commercial sale.)

Market Failure Justifications for Infant Industry Protection. To justify the infant industry argument, it is necessary to go beyond the plausible but questionable view that industries always need to be sheltered when they are new. Whether infant industry protection is justified depends on an analysis of the kind we discussed in Chapter 10. That is, the argument for protecting an industry in its early growth must be related to some particular set of market failures that prevent private markets from developing the industry as rapidly as they should. Sophisticated proponents of the infant industry argument have identified two market failures as reasons why infant industry protection may be a good idea: **imperfect capital markets** and the problem of **appropriability.**

The *imperfect capital markets justification* for infant industry protection is as follows. If a developing country does not have a set of financial institutions (such as efficient stock markets and banks) that would allow savings from traditional sectors (such as agriculture) to be used to finance investment in new sectors (such as manufacturing), then growth of new industries will be restricted by the ability of firms in these industries to earn current profits. Thus low initial profits will be an obstacle to investment even if the long-term returns on this investment are high. The first-best policy is to create a better capital market, but protection of new industries, which would raise profits and thus allow more rapid growth, can be justified as a second-best policy option.

The *appropriability argument* for infant industry protection can take many forms, but all have in common the idea that firms in a new industry generate social benefits for which they are not compensated. For example, the firms that first enter an industry may have to incur ''start-up'' costs of adapting technology to local circumstances or of opening new markets. If other firms are able to follow their lead without incurring these start-up costs, the pioneers will be prevented from reaping any returns from these outlays. Thus, pioneering firms may, in addition to producing physical output, create intangible benefits (such as knowledge or new markets) in which they are unable to establish property rights. In some cases the social benefits from creation of a new industry will exceed its costs, yet because of the problem of appropriability no private entrepreneurs will be willing to enter. The first-best answer is to compensate firms for their intangible contributions. When this is not possible, however, there is a second-best case for encouraging entry into a new industry by using tariffs or other trade policies.

Both the imperfect capital markets argument and the appropriability case for infant industry protection are clearly special cases of the *market failures* justification for interfering with free trade (Chapter 10). The difference is that in this case the arguments apply specifically to new industries rather than to any industry. The general problems with the market failure approach remain, however. In practice it is difficult to evaluate which industries really warrant special treatment, and there are risks that a policy intended to promote development will end up being captured by special interests. There are many stories of infant industries that have never grown up and remain dependent on protection.

HOW MANUFACTURING IS FAVORED: IMPORT-SUBSTITUTING INDUSTRIALIZATION

Although there are doubts about the infant industry argument, many developing countries have seen this argument as a compelling reason to provide special support for the development of manufacturing industries. In principle such support could be provided in a variety of ways. For example, countries could provide subsidies to manufacturing production in general, or they could focus their efforts on subsidies for the export of some manufactured goods in which they believe they can develop a comparative advantage. In most developing countries, however, the basic strategy for industrialization has been to develop industries oriented toward the domestic market by using trade restrictions such as tariffs and quotas to encourage the replacement of imported manufactures by domestic products. The strategy of encouraging domestic industry by limiting imports of manufactured goods is known as the strategy of **import-substituting industrialization.**

One might ask why a choice needs to be made. Why not encourage both import substitution and exports? The answer goes back to the general equilibrium analysis of tariffs in Chapter 5: a tariff that reduces imports also necessarily reduces exports. By protecting import-substituting industries, countries draw resources away from actual or potential export sectors. So a country's choice to seek to substitute for imports is also a choice to discourage export growth.

The reasons why import substitution rather than export growth has usually been chosen as an industrialization strategy are a mixture of economics and politics. First, until the 1970s many developing countries were skeptical about the possibility of exporting manufactured goods (although this skepticism also calls into question the infant industry argument for manufacturing protection). They believed that industrialization was necessarily based on a substitution of domestic industry for imports rather than on a growth of manufactured exports. Second, in many cases import-substituting industrialization policies dovetailed naturally with existing political biases. We have already noted the case of Latin American nations that were compelled to develop substitutes for imports during the 1930s because of the Great Depression and during the first half of the 1940s because of the wartime disruption of trade (Chapter 10). In these countries import substitution directly benefited powerful, established interest groups, while export promotion had no natural constituency.

The 1950s and 1960s saw the high tide of import-substituting industrialization. Developing countries typically began by protecting final stages of industry, such as food processing and automobile assembly. In the larger developing countries, domestic products almost completely replaced imported consumer goods (although the manufacturing was often carried out by foreign multinational firms). Once the possibilities for replacing consumer goods imports had been exhausted, these countries turned to protection of intermediate goods, such as automobile bodies, steel, and petrochemicals.

In most developing economies, the import-substitution drive stopped short of its logical limit: sophisticated manufactured goods such as computers, precision machine tools, and so on continued to be imported. Nonetheless, the larger countries pursuing import-substituting industrialization reduced their imports to remarkably low levels. Usually, the smaller a country's economic size (as measured, for example, by the value of its total output) the larger will be the share of imports and exports in national income. Yet as Table 11-1 shows, India, with a domestic market less than 5 percent that of the United States, exported a smaller fraction of its output than the United States did in 1990. Brazil is the most extreme case: in 1990, exports were only 7 percent of output, a share less than that of the United States and far less than that of large industrial countries such as Germany.

As a strategy for encouraging growth of manufacturing, import-substituting industrialization has clearly worked. Latin American economies now generate almost as large a share of their output from manufacturing as advanced nations. (India generates less, but only because its poorer population continues to spend a high proportion of its income on food.) For these countries, however, the encouragement of manufacturing was not a goal in itself; it was a means to the end goal of economic development. Has import-substituting industrialization promoted economic development? Here serious

TABLE 11-1 Exports as a percentage of national income, 1990

Brazil	7
India	8
United States	10
Japan	11
West Germany	32
South Korea	32
Hong Kong	137
Singapore	190

Source: World Bank. *World Development Report.* Washington, D.C.: World Bank, 1992.

doubts have appeared. Although many economists approved of import-substitution measures in the 1950s and early 1960s, since the 1960s import-substituting industrialization has come under increasingly harsh criticism. Indeed, much of the focus of economic analysts and of policy makers has shifted from trying to encourage import substitution to trying to correct the damage done by bad import-substitution policies.

RESULTS OF FAVORING MANUFACTURING: PROBLEMS OF IMPORT-SUBSTITUTING INDUSTRIALIZATION

The attack on import-substituting industrialization starts from the fact that many countries that have pursued import substitution have not shown any signs of catching up with the advanced countries. In some cases, the development of a domestic manufacturing base seems to have led to a stagnation of per capita income instead of an economic takeoff. This is true of India, which, after 20 years of ambitious economic plans between the early 1950s and the early 1970s, found itself with per capita income only a few percent higher than before. It is also true of Argentina, once considered a wealthy country, whose economy has grown at a snail's pace for decades. Other countries, such as Mexico, have achieved economic growth but have not narrowed the gap between themselves and advanced countries. Only a few developing countries really seem to have moved dramatically upward on the income scale—and these countries either have never pursued import substitution or have moved sharply away from it.

Why didn't import-substituting industrialization work the way it was supposed to? The most important reason seems to be that the infant industry argument was not as universally valid as many people assumed. A period of protection will not create a competitive manufacturing sector if there are fundamental reasons why a country lacks a comparative advantage in manufacturing. Experience has shown that the reasons for failure to develop often run deeper than a simple lack of experience with manufacturing. Poor countries lack skilled labor, entrepreneurs, and managerial competence and have problems of social organization that make it difficult to maintain reliable supplies of everything from spare parts to electricity. These problems may not be beyond the reach of economic policy, but they cannot be solved by *trade* policy: an import quota can allow an inefficient manufacturing sector to survive, but it cannot directly make that sector more efficient. The infant industry argument is that, given the temporary shelter of tariffs or quotas, the manufacturing industries of less-developed nations will learn to be efficient. In practice, this is not always, or even usually, true.

With import substitution failing to deliver the promised benefits, attention has turned to the costs of the policies used to promote industry. On this issue, a growing body of evidence shows that the protectionist policies of many less-developed countries have badly distorted incentives. Part of the problem has been that many countries have used excessively complex methods to promote their infant industries. That is, they have used elaborate and often overlapping import quotas, exchange controls, and domestic content rules instead of simple tariffs. It is often difficult to determine how much protection an administrative regulation is actually providing, and studies show that the degree of protection is often both higher and more variable across industries than the government intended. As Table 11-2 shows, some industries in Latin America and South Asia have been protected by regulations that are the equivalent of tariff rates of 200 percent or more. These high rates of effective protection have allowed industries to exist even when their cost of production is three or four times the price of the imports

TABLE 11-2 Effective protection of manufacturing in some developing countries (percent)

Mexico (1960)	26
Philippines (1965)	61
Brazil (1966)	113
Chile (1961)	182
Pakistan (1963)	271

Source: Bela Balassa. *The Structure of Protection in Developing Countries.* Baltimore: Johns Hopkins Press, 1971.

they replace. Even the most enthusiastic advocates of market failure arguments for protection find rates of effective protection that high difficult to defend.

A further cost that has received considerable attention is the tendency of import restrictions to promote production at inefficiently small scale. The domestic markets of even the largest developing countries are only a small fraction of the size of that of the United States or the European Community. Often, the whole domestic market is not large enough to allow an efficient-scale production facility. Yet when this small market is protected, say, by an import quota, if only a single firm were to enter the market it could earn monopoly profits. The competition for these profits typically leads several firms to enter a market that does not really even have room enough for one, and production is carried out at highly inefficient scale. The answer for small countries to the problem of scale is, as noted in Chapter 6, to specialize in the production and export of a limited range of products and to import other goods. Import-substituting industrialization eliminates this option by focusing industrial production on the domestic market.

Those who criticize import-substituting industrialization also argue that it has aggravated other problems, such as income inequality and unemployment (discussed later in this chapter under Problems of the Dual Economy).

Despite the criticism of import-substituting industrialization by economists, few countries that followed policies of import substitution have dismantled their trade barriers. The reason for this reluctance to change policy is only partly that they continue to believe in import substitution as a development strategy. An equally important factor is that at this point a lot of capital has been invested in industries that could not survive without protection, and many workers in protected industries would be hurt if that protection were removed. Thus there is now a vested interest in the continuation of import-substitution policies.

ANOTHER WAY TO FAVOR MANUFACTURING: INDUSTRIALIZATION THROUGH EXPORTS

Although the attempt to promote industrialization through import substitution has now fallen into disfavor among economists, not all industrialization among less-developed countries has been a failure. Since the mid-1960s, a small group of initially poor countries has combined rapid growth of output and living standards with industrialization oriented primarily toward export rather than domestic markets. These countries

Trade Liberalization and Economic Growth: The Case of China

For much of the 1980s, the world's most populous nation seemed to be well on the road to becoming the biggest NIC of them all. After moderates drove radical Maoists from power in 1976, they instituted a series of economic reforms that allowed much greater play for market forces generally, and that opened up the Chinese economy to international trade in particular.

The result of the opening of China to trade was a dramatic increase in both imports and exports. In 1976 exports were only 5.6 percent of China's national income, and imports only 5.3 percent. By 1987 exports were up to 15.8 percent, while imports had risen to 17.3 percent. Most of the new Chinese exports were manufactures rather than raw materials: very low Chinese wages allowed China to become a competitive exporter of labor-intensive manufactured goods, and inexpensive Chinese products began appearing in increasing numbers on world markets. Meanwhile, many of the imports were capital goods, used to aid a rapid expansion of manufacturing capacity. China's industrial production grew at a remarkable 12 percent annual rate between 1977 and 1988.

This manufacturing expansion did not come at the expense of agriculture. On the contrary, agricultural production also expanded rapidly, at more than a 6 percent annual rate. Compared with the previous decade, during which political turmoil had crippled the economy, this amounted to a virtual economic miracle—and a classic demonstration of the potential of export-oriented industrialization.

China remains a poor nation in per capita terms. But because its population is huge, the rapid growth of production has turned it into a major economic force. International comparisons of output are difficult (we discuss some of the issues involved in Chapter 16), but by 1992 some analysts were suggesting that China might already be the world's second-largest economy, pulling ahead of Japan.

are often referred to as **newly industrializing countries,** or **NICs.** The most spectacular performers among the NICs have been the four Asian countries of South Korea, Hong Kong, Taiwan, and Singapore, sometimes referred to facetiously as the "Gang of Four" (after the allegedly villainous clique ousted by the current Chinese government).

Aside from their rapid growth, the most remarkable thing about the Gang of Four is their openness to international trade. Table 11-1 shows some comparative figures for the shares of exports in national income. The contrast between the NICs and the import-substituting industrializers is clear.[2]

For the most part, the NICs have not followed policies of strict free trade (except for Hong Kong, which is the least regulated economy in the world). Compared with the import-substituting nations, however, all of the highly successful countries seem to have rates of protection that are both lower and less variable across sectors.

[2] It may seem puzzling that Singapore's export share exceeds 100 percent. However, no paradox is involved. National income, as explained in Chapter 13, measures the value *added* by the economy, not the total value of the goods it produces. Singapore often buys partly finished manufactures from abroad, processes them further, then exports them. For example, fabric woven in the United States may be sewn by Singapore workers into garments, which are then exported. The value added—the difference between what the imported fabric cost and the price of the finished clothing—can easily be less than the cost of the fabric. When this is the typical pattern, imports and exports will end up larger than national income.

The big question about the NICs is whether their success can be emulated by other developing countries. Does Korea do so well because of its relatively low rate of protection or because of other factors? If, say, Mexico were to abandon its strategy of import substitution, would its growth rate sharply accelerate? Obviously countries differ, and it might be that the successful NICs do well because of social factors such as a national commitment to education or work ethic. On the other hand, thirty years ago, few people would have said that Korea had a society well suited to economic growth. It was only after trade policy changed that Korea began to look like a winner. Was this success just a coincidence?

Whatever the final verdict on the causes of success in the NICs, the remarkable achievements of export-oriented development have shattered the old belief that industrialization must be aimed at the domestic market.

Problems of the Dual Economy

While the trade policy of less-developed countries is partly a response to their relative backwardness as compared with advanced nations, it is also a response to uneven development *within* the country. Often a relatively modern, capital-intensive, high-wage industrial sector exists in the same country as a very poor traditional agricultural sector. The division of a single economy into two sectors that appear to be at very different levels of development is referred to as **economic dualism,** and an economy that looks like this is referred to as a **dual economy.**

Why does dualism have anything to do with trade policy? One answer is that dualism is probably a sign of markets working poorly: in an efficient economy, for example, workers would not earn hugely different wages in different sectors. Whenever markets are working badly, there may be a market failure case for deviating from free trade. The presence of economic dualism is often used to justify tariffs that protect the apparently more efficient manufacturing sector.

A second reason for linking dualism to trade policy is that trade policy may itself have a great deal to do with dualism. As import-substituting industrialization has come under attack, some economists have argued that import-substitution policies have actually helped to create the dual economy or at least aggravate some of its symptoms.

THE SYMPTOMS OF DUALISM

There is no precise definition of a dual economy, but in general a dual economy is one in which there is a ''modern'' sector (typically producing manufactured goods that are protected from import competition) that contrasts sharply with the rest of the economy in a number of ways:

1. The value of output per worker is much higher in the modern sector than in the rest of the economy. In most developing countries, the goods produced by a worker in the manufacturing sector carry a price several times that of the goods produced by an agricultural worker. Sometimes this difference runs as high as fifteen to one.

2. Accompanying the high value of output per worker is a higher wage rate. Industrial workers may earn ten times what agricultural laborers make (although their wages still seem low in comparison with North America, Western Europe, or Japan).

3. Although wages are high in the manufacturing sector, however, returns on capital are not necessarily higher. In fact, it often seems to be the case that capital earns *lower* returns in the industrial sector.

4. The high value of output per worker in the modern sector is at least partly due to a higher capital intensity of production. Manufacturing in less-developed countries typically has much higher capital intensity than agriculture (this is *not* true of advanced countries, where agriculture is quite capital-intensive). In the developing world, agricultural workers often work with primitive tools, while industrial facilities are not much different from those in advanced nations.

5. Many less-developed countries have a persistent unemployment problem. Especially in urban areas, there are large numbers of people either without jobs or with only occasional, extremely low-wage employment. These urban unemployed coexist with the relatively well-paid urban industrial workers.

Case Study

ECONOMIC DUALISM IN INDIA

The economy of India presents a classic case of economic dualism. In a country of over 700 million people, only 6 million are employed in the manufacturing sector. These manufacturing workers, however, produce 15 percent of the gross national product and receive wages more than six times as high as agricultural wages. Manufacturing is far more capital-intensive than agriculture; indeed, for the past thirty years investment on capital equipment for the tiny manufacturing labor force has consistently been larger than total investment in agriculture.

This sharp distinction between manufacturing and agriculture has actually grown over time. Since 1960, for example, the real wages of manufacturing workers have risen by about 80 percent, while those of farm workers have risen only about 5 percent.

Why is the gap between sectors so large? It seems likely that government policies play a key role. In India, government subsidies and protectionist policies have encouraged investment in manufacturing, and in the most capital-intensive sectors in particular. At the same time, labor laws designed to protect workers' interests have probably helped the bargaining position of unions, enabling organized workers to win large wage increases even though there are millions of workers who would be willing to take their jobs at lower wages.

In the heady early days of independence, India's economic planners hoped that the manufacturing sector would eventually grow and absorb the traditional economy. But from 1960 to 1980, manufacturing employment in India grew at an annual rate of only 3 percent, not much faster than the nation's population.

In the early 1990s India began limited moves toward economic reform, removing some barriers to trade and foreign investment. It was unclear, however, whether there was a political consensus for a radical change of policy.

DUAL LABOR MARKETS AND TRADE POLICY

The symptoms of dualism are present in many countries and are clear signs of an economy that is not working well, especially in its labor markets. The trade policy implications of these symptoms have been a subject of great dispute among students of economic development.

In the 1950s, many economists argued that wage differences between manufacturing and agriculture provided another justification, beyond the infant industry argument, for encouraging manufacturing at agriculture's expense. This argument, known as the **wage differentials argument,** can be stated in market failure terms. Suppose that, for some reason, an equivalent worker would receive a higher wage in manufacturing than he would in agriculture. Whenever a manufacturing firm decides to hire an additional worker, then, it generates a marginal social benefit for which it receives no reward, because a worker gains a wage increase when he moves from agriculture to manufacturing. This is in contrast to what would happen without a wage difference, where the marginal worker would be indifferent between manufacturing and agricultural employment and there would be no marginal social benefit of hiring a worker other than the profits earned by the hiring firm.

The effects of a wage differential on the economy's allocation of labor can be illustrated using the *specific factors model* presented in Chapter 3. Assume that an economy produces only two goods, manufactures and food. Manufactures are produced using labor and capital; food is produced using labor and land. Then the allocation of resources can be represented with a diagram like Figure 11-1. The vertical axis represents wage rates and marginal products; the horizontal axis represents employment. Employment in manufactures is measured from the left origin O_M, while employment in food is measured from the right origin O_F. MPL_M is the marginal product of labor in manufactures, MPL_F the marginal product in food; P_M is the price of manufactures, P_F the price of food. Thus the two curves in the figure represent the *value* of the marginal product of an additional worker in each sector.

When there is a wage differential, workers in manufactures must be paid a higher wage than workers in food; in the figure the manufactures wage is assumed to be w_M, the food wage w_F. Employers in each sector will hire workers up to the point where the value of a worker's marginal product equals his wage; thus employment in manufactures is $O_M L^1$ (point *B*), employment in food is $L^1 O_F$ (point *C*).

Suppose the economy were now able to shift one worker from food to manufactures. Manufactures output would rise; food output would fall. The value of the additional manufactures output, however, would be the wage rate in manufactures, w_M, while the value of the reduction in food output would be the lower wage rate in food, w_F. The total value of the economy's output, then, would rise by $w_M - w_F$. The fact that the value of output can be increased by shifting labor from food to manufactures shows that the economy is allocating too little labor to manufactures. An efficient economy would set the marginal product of labor equal in both sectors, which would be achieved if $O_M L^2$ workers were employed in manufactures, $L^2 O_F$ in food (point *A*). (The increase in output achieved by moving to this efficient allocation of labor would be equal to the colored area *ABC* in the figure.)

If there is a wage differential, then, markets will misallocate labor; firms in the industrial sector will hire too few workers. A government policy that induces them to hire more can raise national welfare.

As usual, trade policy is not the first-best policy to expand manufacturing employ-

FIGURE 11-1
The effects of a wage differential.
If manufactures must pay a higher wage than food, the economy will employ too few workers in manufactures and too many in food.

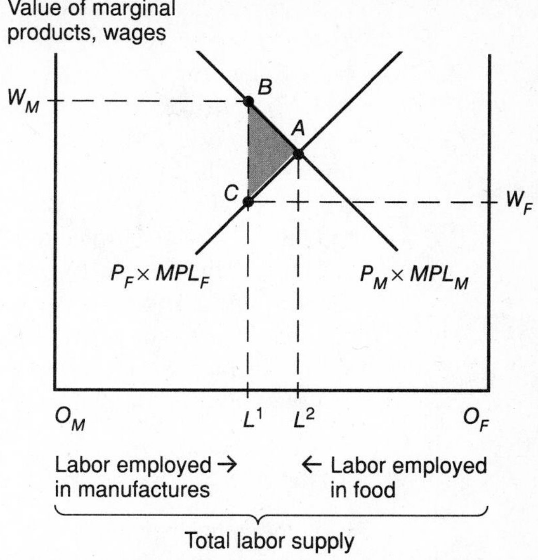

ment. Ideally, government policy should target employment directly, either by eliminating the wage differential or by subsidizing firms to hire more workers. A subsidy to manufacturing production is not as good, because it encourages capital as well as labor to move into manufacturing[3]—and capital does not receive an especially high return in manufacturing. A tariff or import quota is still worse, because it also distorts demand. Nonetheless, as a second-best alternative (or more strictly third-best), a tariff on manufactures could be justified by the wage differentials argument.

In the 1950s and 1960s this seemed to be a fairly convincing argument. In a famous paper published in 1970, however, the economists John Harris and Michael Todaro offered a devastating reinterpretation of the labor markets of less-developed countries.[4] They pointed out a link between rural-urban migration and unemployment that undermines the case for favoring manufacturing employment, even though manufacturing does offer higher wages.

Harris and Todaro began from the observation that countries with highly dualistic economies also seem to have a great deal of urban unemployment. Although one might suppose that this unemployment strengthens the case for creating more urban jobs in manufacturing, Harris and Todaro pointed out that despite this unemployment, migration from rural to urban areas continues. They concluded that rural workers were willing to come to the cities and take the risk of being unemployed in return for the chance of

[3] This cannot be seen in the specific factors model, because that model assumes that capital cannot be used in the agricultural sector. In the factor-proportions model, however, the superiority of a wage subsidy to a production subsidy can be demonstrated. See Harry G. Johnson, ''Optimal Trade Intervention in the Presence of Domestic Distortions,'' in Robert E. Baldwin et al., *Trade, Growth, and the Balance of Payments* (Chicago: Rand McNally, 1965), pp. 3–34.

[4] John R. Harris and Michael P. Todaro, ''Migration, Unemployment, and Development: A Two-Sector Analysis,'' *American Economic Review* 60 (1970), pp. 126–142.

getting high-paying industrial jobs. The chance of getting a job depends, of course, on how many jobs are available.

According to the Harris-Todaro model, an increase in the number of manufacturing jobs will lead to a rural-urban migration so large that urban unemployment actually rises. When an additional worker is hired by the manufacturing sector, two or three more workers may leave agriculture to swell the ranks of the urban unemployed. Although the lucky worker gains, his wage gain will be largely (maybe even completely) offset by the wage losses of the newly unemployed. The supposed social benefit of additional manufacturing employment is therefore lost.

Like the infant industry argument, the wage differentials argument for protection is now in disfavor with economists. This is partly because of arguments like that of Harris and Todaro and partly because of the general backlash against import-substitution policies. In fact, trade policies adopted as a response to economic dualism are now often accused of actually making that dualism worse.

TRADE POLICY AS A CAUSE OF ECONOMIC DUALISM

Trade policy has been accused both of widening the wage differential between manufacturing and agriculture and of fostering excessive capital intensity.

The reasons for huge wage differentials between agriculture and industry are not well understood. Some economists believe these differentials are a natural market response. Firms, so the argument goes, offer high wages to ensure low turnover and high work effort in countries not used to the discipline of industrial work. Other economists argue, however, that the wage differentials also reflect the monopoly power of unions whose industries are sheltered by import quotas from foreign competition. With freer trade, they argue, industrial wages would be lower and agricultural wages higher. If so, dualism—and unemployment—may be worsened by import restrictions, especially those undertaken in the name of import substitution.

The excessive capital intensity of manufacturing is partly due to relatively high wages, which give firms an incentive to substitute capital for labor. To the extent that trade restrictions are responsible for these high wages, they are to blame. Also, in some countries a controlled banking system in effect provides subsidized credit to industrial firms, making capital-labor substitution cheap. The most direct channel, however, has been through selective import control. In many cases, imports of capital goods enter without tariff or other restriction, and sometimes with de facto import subsidies. This policy further encourages the use of capital-intensive techniques.

Negotiations between Developing and Advanced Countries: The North-South Debate

So far we have focused on how individual developing countries have tried to use their own trade policies to help themselves grow. Since World War II, however, developing countries have also tried to get the advanced countries to change their policies. The result has been a set of running arguments often called the **North-South debate** because (with the exception of Australia and New Zealand) all the advanced countries are in the temperate zones of the Northern Hemisphere, while most developing countries lie in the tropics.

Three questions have been at the heart of the North-South debate:

1. Have poor nations been exploited? Is the affluence of the advanced nations achieved to some degree at the expense of developing countries?
2. What is the role of foreign capital in development? Is investment by advanced nations in developing countries good or bad for them?
3. Should the prices of developing country exports be higher? Should cartels be organized to raise the prices of raw materials?

ARE POOR NATIONS EXPLOITED?

Poor nations and their advocates in the advanced countries have often claimed that the wealth of the rich nations is based on exploitation. This position was easier to argue when much of the less-developed world was under direct political domination from Europe. (Actually, at the height of imperialism, few colonies paid enough tribute to repay the cost of administering them. But there were some examples of brutal, exploitation, especially in Africa.) In the modern world, the case for exploitation must rest on something about the transactions between North and South that works to the South's disadvantage.

It is clear that trade between advanced countries and developing countries is marked by "unequal exchange." Developing nations use much more labor to produce the goods they export to advanced nations than these nations use to produce the goods they supply in return. The Ricardian model presented in Chapter 2 showed, however, that this is not a useful way to look at international exchange. Given the low productivity of developing countries in both manufacturing and agriculture, unequal exchange is inevitable: it is not an indication that the poor countries are losing from their trade.

A more sophisticated view of exploitation comes from the same line of thought as the infant industry argument. Suppose developing countries could potentially develop efficient manufacturing industries but they cannot get started in the face of competition from established industries in the advanced nations. Then it might be that the division of the world into rich manufacturing nations and poor agricultural countries is a historical accident—the rich countries just got there first, and their industrial development precluded development by the rest of the world. This view is sometimes called the doctrine of **uneven development.** Unlike the concept of unequal exchange, which the model in Chapter 2 showed to be misconceived, but like the infant industry argument, uneven development makes sense. The question is whether it is true.

The answer is that uneven development is hard to justify given the experience of the last few decades. On one side, the doctrine depends on the correctness of the infant industry argument. Yet the history of import-substitution policies shows that even with decades of protection from foreign competition, many developing countries have not been able to develop efficient manufacturing sectors. On the other side, some developing countries have done very well at selling manufactures in world markets without infant industry protection. Both the failure of protected industries to achieve efficiency and the success of unprotected industries indicate that competition from established industries in advanced countries is not the main factor inhibiting growth in developing countries.

Many people—not all of them from developing countries—would like to believe the poverty of most of the world is caused by the wealth of the lucky advanced nations. The sheer awfulness of world poverty makes us want to find villains. In fact, however, it is hard to find evidence that the wealth of the advanced countries has been achieved at the expense of developing nations.

THE ROLE OF FOREIGN CAPITAL AND MULTINATIONAL FIRMS IN DEVELOPMENT

The doctrine of uneven development concerns the effects of foreign *trade* on development. Many less-developed countries have been equally concerned about the effects of foreign *investment,* especially when it comes as direct investment by multinational firms. Does an important role by foreign multinationals hurt the economy of a less-developed country?

At one level the opposition to foreign multinationals is based on concern over national sovereignty. In the past, some countries have felt that foreign firms dominate their economies and have too much influence over their politics. The caricature of the ''banana republic'' that is virtually owned by the United Fruit Company has sometimes had a basis in reality. Even in a country as large as Mexico, foreign companies dominated the economy and had powerful political influence in the early years of the twentieth century; it was partly a nationalistic reaction to this foreign control that set off the Mexican revolution of 1910–1920. As is the case for international investment generally, foreign ownership declined during the period between the wars and has never regained the relative importance it had in the years before World War I. Despite some scare talk, national sovereignty has not been much threatened in the postwar period. A rise in multinational operations during the 1950s and 1960s did, however, raise some legitimate economic concerns.

Essentially, recent concern over multinationals has focused on technology: the kind that multinationals use (the issue of **appropriate technology**) and the way in which it is made available to others (the issue of **technology transfer**).

Appropriate Technology. Those who raise the appropriate technology issue argue that multinational firms bring with them a technology that is suited to the capital-abundant, labor-scarce economies in which they are based but not to the poor economies to which they come. The slogan ''small is beautiful,'' coined by the development theorist E. F. Schumacher, has popularized the view that less-developed countries need small-scale, labor-intensive methods rather than the large-scale, capital-intensive methods that allegedly characterize the operations of multinationals.

Defenders of multinationals reply that multinationals are no more inclined to use inappropriate technology than domestically owned firms and that when they do it is because they are given inappropriate incentives. When multinationals produce manufactures in dualistic economies, for example, they face relatively high wages and government policies that encourage them to import expensive machinery. Given these incentives the multinationals adopt capital-intensive techniques similar to the ones they use at home. Given different incentives, they would behave differently.

There is some evidence to support this view. Consider Mexico, which until the 1980s pursued a policy of import-substituting industrialization and which has the characteristic problems of dualism: a capital-intensive manufacturing sector that offers too few jobs to employ the growing population of urban unemployed. Since 1966, U.S. firms have been allowed to establish plants in northern Mexico that export to the United States and receive special exemption from both U.S. and Mexican restrictions on trade:

raw materials can be imported from the United States without tariff or import restrictions, and the United States has agreed to charge tariffs only on the value added, not the total value of goods exported from Mexico. Because powerful unions are absent, wages in these export-oriented manufacturing plants—known as *maquiladoras*—are lower than wages in the older import-substituting industries. Also, no special incentives have been offered to these new plants to import expensive capital goods. The results are dramatic: the *maquiladoras* of northern Mexico are only about one-tenth as capital-intensive as the traditional manufacturing sector. Despite having only modest investment, the offshore manufacturing now employs some 25 percent of Mexican industrial workers. The Mexican experience suggests that when multinationals are given an incentive to use appropriate technology, they are as likely to use it as domestic firms.

Technology Transfer. The technology transfer issue is a cousin to the infant industry issue of appropriability. Recall that infant industries are supposed to yield extra benefits in the form of experience and knowledge that diffuse to other sectors of the economy. Critics of multinationals argue that when an infant industry consists of foreign firms the technology is developed elsewhere and is not *transferred* to the rest of the domestic economy. Thse critics would prefer to see domestically owned firms that either license technology from abroad or develop it themselves. They believe that even though these firms might initially have higher costs than a multinational, the indirect benefits would be larger.

While there is no hard evidence on how technology transfer by multinationals compares with that by domestic firms, it might be informative to ask whether the NICs, which seem to have been successful at adopting advanced technology, have relied on multinationals. The answer is that they vary enormously. On one side, Korea and Hong Kong have relied primarily on local entrepreneurs to develop their industry. On the other side, Taiwan and Singapore rely heavily on multinationals—so much so in the case of Singapore that some observers have characterized it as a ''contract labor'' economy that hires itself out to foreign firms. All four economies have done spectacularly well at improving their living standards.

RAISING THE EXPORT PRICES OF DEVELOPING COUNTRIES: COMMODITY EXPORT CARTELS

Despite their efforts at industrialization, most developing countries remain exporters of agricultural products and minerals—often called ''commodities''—and importers of manufactures. Thus, the terms of trade of developing countries as a group are related to the prices of commodities relative to those of manufactured goods. Governments of poor nations have therefore always been interested in ways to raise commodity prices. The most promising route to increased commodity prices has often seemed to be the formation of **commodity export cartels,** in which a group of countries exporting the same commodity agree to restrict supply and drive up the price.

We saw in Chapter 10 that a country that is a large exporter of some good can raise its welfare at other countries' expense by imposing an export tax. If there are several exporting nations, however, each individual country will be restrained from imposing a large export tax, because some of the benefit of the higher prices that result will accrue to other exporters rather than the taxing country. The basic idea of an export cartel is that several exporters acting together take into account the benefits that each gains from the export taxes of the others and they will therefore succeed in raising prices (and their welfare) more than if they acted independently.

For example, suppose Brazil and Colombia were the world's only coffee exporters. If Brazil were to impose a tax on its coffee exports to raise world prices, some consumers would shift to Colombian coffee; this shift would limit how high an export tax Brazil could profitably impose. Colombia would feel similarly constrained. If Brazil and Colombia agreed to raise coffee prices together, however, they would both feel free to raise prices higher, to their mutual gain (and the rest of the world's loss).

Gains from forming a cartel are greatest when the cartel controls much of world production, when there is little ability on the part of consumers to switch away from the product, and when alternative sources of supply are difficult to develop. Over the years there have been many attempts to form export cartels, in commodities ranging from coffee to oil to tin. For the most part, however, these cartels either broke apart or were less successful in raising prices than their founders hoped. The reasons have partly to do with the limits on cartel power: most cartels have controlled too little of world production and have faced both substitution by consumers and competition from alternative sources. Equally important, cartels have trouble imposing discipline on their own members. Each country has an incentive to cheat, undercutting the rest of the cartel so as to sell more. If too many members cheat, the "honest" members will find that it is not worth trying to support the price.

Case Study

OPEC

Most commodity export cartels have been unimpressive in their results, but there has been one spectacular exception. The Organization of Petroleum Exporting Countries (OPEC), founded in 1961, was able during the 1970s to engineer a huge rise in the price of oil. For a time, it seemed as though OPEC could serve as a model for other commodity exporters. In fact, however, OPEC's success has remained unique, and OPEC itself fell on hard times in the mid-1980s.

What was special about OPEC? Part of the answer is that political disturbances helped disrupt the supply of oil and drive up the price: the Arab-Israeli war of 1973 led to an Arab embargo, while the fall of the Shah in Iran (1979) and the Iran-Iraq war (begun in 1980) reduced deliveries from the Persian Gulf. Also, OPEC accounted for more than half of world oil production outside the U.S.S.R. in the early 1970s, and both the supply and demand for oil are inelastic in the short run.

Cheating by cartel members was less of a problem for OPEC than other cartels, at least at first, because of the dominant role of Saudi Arabia. In effect, the Saudis had a large enough market share that they were willing to support the price by reducing output even when other members of OPEC produced more than they were supposed to.

These special circumstances explain why oil could be more effectively cartelized than other commodities. And even OPEC eventually ran into problems: by 1986, long-run shifts in demand and increasing supply from non-OPEC sources had forced price reductions to levels that, in real terms, were the lowest since 1973.

Despite the failure of attempts to raise prices through export cartels, developing countries continue to argue that something should be done to improve their terms of trade, which fell during the mid-1980s to the lowest levels since the Great Depression. At times they have proposed that advanced countries fund price-support programs, in which international organizations would buy up commodities whenever their prices fell to some minimum level; such programs would be extremely expensive, however, and there is no sentiment in the industrial countries for providing the necessary resources.

Summary

1. Trade policy in less-developed countries can be analyzed using the same analytical tools used to discuss advanced countries. The particular issues characteristic of *developing countries* are, however, different. In particular, trade policy in developing countries is concerned with three objectives: promoting industrialization, coping with the uneven development of the domestic economy, and attempting to undo what is perceived as unfair or exploitative economic relations with advanced countries.

2. Government policy to promote industrialization has often been justified by the infant industry argument, which says that new industries need a temporary period of protection from competition from established competitors in other countries. The infant industry argument is valid only if it can be cast as a market failure argument for intervention. Two usual justifications are the existence of *imperfect capital markets* and the problem of *appropriability* of knowledge generated by pioneering firms.

3. Using the infant industry argument as justification, many less-developed countries have pursued policies of *import-substituting industrialization* in which domestic industries are created under the protection of tariffs or import quotas. Although these policies have succeeded in promoting manufacturing, by and large they have not delivered the expected gains in economic growth and living standards. Many economists are now harshly critical of the results of import substitution, arguing that it has fostered high-cost, inefficient production.

4. A small group of developing countries has managed to industrialize not through import substitution but through development of manufactured exports. These *newly industrializing countries* (NICs) have achieved rapid growth in output and living standards. A major question is whether other countries, by moving away from import-substitution policies, can achieve similar success.

5. Most developing countries are characterized by economic *dualism:* a high-wage, capital-intensive industrial sector coexists with a low-wage traditional sector. Dual economies also often have a serious problem of urban unemployment.

6. The difference in wages between the modern and traditional sectors has sometimes been used as a case for tariff protection of the industrial sector. This is the *wage differentials* case for protection. This view no longer receives much credence among economists, however. More recent analyses suggest that protection will lead to more rural-urban migration, which worsens the urban unemployment problem and may worsen the symptoms of dualism.

7. Governments of developing countries and their supporters have argued that the current international economic system is unfair and that the poverty of the developing world is related to advanced countries' wealth. The most coherent view of this kind is the doctrine of *uneven development,* which is related to the infant industry

argument. According to this doctrine, advanced countries were just lucky in getting established in the industrial sector first, forestalling industrial development by later competitors. A review of the evidence, however, finds little support for the view that advanced nations grew wealthy at the expense of others.

8. On a less global level, multinational enterprises have been accused of failing to provide benefits to their host countries, either because they use *inappropriate technology* or because they fail to make a *technology transfer* that improves the technological level of the rest of the economy. Defenders of multinationals argue that multinationals use inappropriate technology because they are faced with distorted incentives. On the technology transfer issue, some countries have done well with extensive foreign investment and others have done well without it, so that it is hard to reach any definite answer.

9. Most developing countries export commodities, and they have always tried to find ways to raise commodity prices. In the 1970s the success of OPEC led to hopes that *commodity export cartels* could improve the terms of trade of many developing countries. It seems, however, that OPEC benefited from uniquely favorable conditions (and OPEC itself has come on hard times).

Key Terms

developing countries
imperfect capital markets
appropriability
import-substituting industrialization
newly industrializing countries (NICs)
economic dualism
dual economy
wage differentials argument
North-South debate
uneven development
appropriate technology
technology transfer
commodity export cartels

Problems

1. ''Japan's experience makes the infant industry case for protection better than any theory. In the early 1950s Japan was a poor nation that survived by exporting textiles and toys. The Japanese government protected what at first were inefficient, high-cost steel and automobile industries, and those industries came to dominate world markets.'' Discuss critically.

2. A country currently imports automobiles at $8000 each. Its government believes domestic producers could manufacture autos for only $6000 given time but that there would be an initial shakedown period during which autos would cost $10,000 to produce domestically.

a. Suppose that each firm that tries to produce autos must go through the shakedown period of high costs on its own. Under what circumstances would the existence of the initial high costs justify infant industry protection?

b. Now suppose, on the contrary, that once one firm has borne the costs of learning to produce autos at $6000 each, other firms can imitate it and do the same. Explain how this can prevent development of a domestic industry, and how infant industry protection can help.

3. Why might import substituting industrialization be more successful in large developing countries such as Brazil than in smaller nations such as Ghana?

4. The very small economy of Cantabrigia has a total labor force of twenty workers. These workers can produce two goods, manufactures and food. In production of manufactures, the *marginal* product of labor depends on employment as follows:

Number of workers	*Marginal product of last worker*
1	20
2	18
3	16
4	14
5	12
6	11
7	10
8	9
9	8
10	7

In the food sector the marginal product of labor is independent of employment, and is 9. The world price of a unit of manufactures is $10, so is the world price of a unit of food.

a. Suppose there were no distortion in the labor market; find the wage rate, the allocation of labor between manufactures and food, and the output of each good.

b. Now suppose that for some reason the minimum wage in the manufactures sector is $150. Full employment, however, is maintained. Find the output of the economy in this case. How large is the cost of the distortion?

c. Finally, suppose that workers migrate from the country to the city until the wage of city workers multiplied by the probability of being employed equals the rural wage. Find the level of output and unemployment.

5. Suppose a country has the Harris-Todaro problem—that is, for some reason urban wages are much higher than rural, leading to inefficiently low manufacturing production, but at the same time there is high urban unemployment because rural workers migrate to the cities in search of high-wage jobs. What policy or combination of policies would you advocate to solve this problem?

6. "Import quotas on capital-intensive industrial goods and subsidies for the import of capital equipment were meant to create manufacturing jobs in many developing countries. Unfortunately, they have probably helped create the urban unemployment problem." Explain this remark.

7. Explain the distinction between the doctrines of unequal exchange and uneven development. Why is there a natural relationship between the uneven development doctrine and the case for import-substituting industrialization?

8. Suppose that foreign firms, other things equal, tend to use more capital-intensive techniques than domestic firms. Suppose also that your economy is dualistic for other reasons. Does this offer a possible argument against foreign investment?

9. Suppose two countries produce bauxite for the world market. In each country the cost of producing bauxite is \$10 per ton. The world demand curve for bauxite may be written

$$P = 40 - 0.1Q,$$

where Q is the total production by both countries combined. Note that this demand curve is written showing price as a function of quantity; it could equally well be written the other way, in which case the curve would be

$$Q = 400 - 10P.$$

It is possible to show that if the two countries choose independent profit-maximizing levels of bauxite output, each will produce 100 tons; if they agree to maximize their profits jointly, each will produce only 75 tons.

a. Compare the profits of the two countries when they each produce 100 tons with profits when they organize a cartel and each produces 75 tons.

b. What happens if one of the countries honors its agreement to produce only 75 tons but the other cheats and produces 100 tons?

Further Reading

Jagdish N. Bhagwati, ed. *The New International Economic Order.* Cambridge: MIT Press, 1977. The North-South debate reached its height in the late 1970s, with widespread demands for a "new international economic order" that would redistribute income from rich to poor nations. This volume gives a good overview of the debate.

Jagdish N. Bhagwati and T. N. Srinivasan, "Trade Policy and Development," in Rudiger Dornbusch and Jacob A. Frenkel, eds. *International Economic Policy: Theory and Evidence.* Baltimore: Johns Hopkins University Press, 1979, pp. 1–35. Reviews research findings on the links between trade policy and economic development.

W. Max Corden. *Trade Policy and Economic Welfare.* Oxford: Clarendon Press, 1974. A clear analytical discussion of the role of trade policy in economic development.

Anne O. Krueger. "Trade Policies in Developing Countries," in Ronald W. Jones and Peter B. Kenen, eds. *Handbook of International Economics,* Vol. 1. Amsterdam: North-Holland, 1984. An analytical survey of developing country trade issues.

W. Arthur Lewis. *The Theory of Economic Development.* Homewood, IL: Irwin, 1955. A good example of the upbeat view taken of trade policies for economic development during the import-substitution high tide of the 1950s and 1960s.

I. M. D. Little. *Economic Development.* New York: Basic Books, 1982. An entertaining discussion of the not always scientific process by which ideas about trade policy for developing countries have come into and out of vogue.

I. M. D. Little, Tibor Scitovsky, and Maurice Scott. *Industry and Trade in Some Developing Countries.* New York: Oxford University Press, 1970. A key work in the emergence of a more downbeat view of import substitution in the 1970s and 1980s.

Dani Rodrik. "Imperfect Competition, Scale Economies and Trade Policy in Developing Countries," in Robert E. Baldwin, ed. *Trade Policy Issues and Empirical Analysis.* Chicago: University of Chicago Press, 1988. Looks at commercial policy in developing countries from the perspective of trade models with imperfect competition.

World Bank. *World Development Report 1991: The Challenge of Development.* Washington, D.C.: World Bank, 1991. A comprehensive survey of evidence on development policy.

Industrial Policy in Advanced Countries
Chapter 12

Most of the world's income is generated by a handful of advanced industrial countries: the nations of Western Europe and North America, plus Japan, Australia, and New Zealand. These are lucky countries, whose prosperity is the envy of the rest of the world. Even wealthy countries, however, want to add to their wealth through economic growth. Throughout the industrial world, economic growth was much slower in the 1970s and 1980s than it was in the 1950s and 1960s. In Western Europe, this slower growth was accompanied by rising unemployment. In the United States, employment has grown steadily but productivity growth has been sluggish, and important segments of the population are worse off economically than they were in 1970. In Japan, growth continues to outpace that in the rest of the industrial world, but there too its pace slowed after 1970.

How can a country accelerate the pace of its economic growth? One possible answer is to adopt an **industrial policy,** in which the government attempts to channel resources into sectors that it views as important for future economic growth. This chapter reviews the debate over the usefulness and appropriate form of industrial policy for an advanced nation like the United States. The first part of the chapter considers some popular arguments for industrial policy that are *not* based on careful economic analysis, and criticizes their weaknesses. The second part reviews some sophisticated arguments that do make good economic sense, and asks how they might be applied in practice. The third part turns to a brief survey of experience with industrial policy in Japan and elsewhere.

Popular Arguments for Industrial Policy

Industrial policy is an attempt by a government to encourage resources to move into particular sectors that the government views as important to future economic growth. Since this means moving resources out of other sectors, industrial policy always promotes some parts of the domestic economy at the expense of others. The case for such a policy therefore stands or falls on the issue of **criteria for selection:** how do we choose which sectors should be encouraged at the expense of the rest?

It is important not to confuse the question of which sectors the government should encourage with the question of which sectors should grow. In a market economy some sectors will be growing and other shrinking as a result of natural market forces. To devise a useful industrial policy, a government must do more than decide which are the industries of the future; it must answer the much more difficult question: Which sectors should be growing or shrinking *more rapidly than they would if left to the market?* For example, we may be able to say that U.S. comparative advantage is shifting from traditional "smokestack" industries like steel and automobiles to new high-technology areas like computers and biotechnology. But this observation does not necessarily imply that the U.S. government should actively encourage workers and investment to move into the new sectors, since these resources are shifting to the new industries in any case as a result of market incentives. To justify an active government program that encourages the shift of resources, it would be necessary to show that for some reason the shift is taking place too slowly—that there is a market failure justification for government intervention.

Currently popular arguments for industrial policy are not usually cast in market failure form. Instead, they suggest plausible criteria for identifying desirable industries that the government should encourage. In particular, proponents of a U.S. industrial policy have argued that the U.S. government should encourage the growth of (1) industries with high value added per worker, (2) industries that have a "linkage" role with regard to other industries, (3) industries that have future growth potential, and (4) industries that have been targeted by foreign governments. While on the surface these criteria seem reasonable, a close analysis reveals that each is badly flawed.

ENCOURAGING INDUSTRIES WITH HIGH VALUE ADDED PER WORKER

The value added by an industry is the difference between the value of its output and the value of the inputs it buys from other industries. The sum of value added in all industries is a country's national income. Value added per worker varies considerably across industries. This has led many commentators to argue that a country can raise its national income by shifting its industrial mix toward those industries with **high value added per worker.**

The problem with this argument is that it fails to ask *why* some sectors have higher value added per worker than others. Commentators often presume that high-value-added sectors must pay higher wage rates or earn higher rates of profit than low-value-added sectors. But if that were the case, labor and capital would have a market incentive to move into high-value-added industries, without need for special government encouragement. In fact, however, high value added per worker usually reflects high inputs per worker. High-value-added sectors are often capital-intensive, like petrochemicals. In such industries the high value added per worker is compensated for by extremely high capital costs, so that neither wages nor profit rates are particularly out of line. In other cases, high value added reflects human capital: high levels of training or skill.

Suppose that high-value-added sectors are those that have large inputs of capital per worker. Could we then argue that a country can raise its national income by expanding these sectors at the expense of others? As we saw in Chapter 4, if a country accumulates capital, it will indeed both grow richer and shift its industrial mix toward capital-intensive sectors and away from labor-intensive sectors. This shift does not, however, need a special government policy, because it will happen as a natural consequence of market forces. The government might encourage saving and investment, which will lead to capital accumulation and eventually automatically lead to a shift in industrial structure toward capital goods. Encouraging saving, however, is not industrial policy. An industrial policy would involve deliberately subsidizing or otherwise encouraging growth of the capital-intensive industries for a *given* supply of capital.

Will such an industrial policy raise national welfare? Not unless it helps correct some market failure. If there is no market failure, the initial allocation of resources will already be optimal, and the government-sponsored reallocation cannot improve on it. If there *is* a market failure, there is still no reason to assume the market failure leads to insufficient allocation of resources to capital-intensive sectors, rather than excessive allocation to these sectors.

What would happen if a country did subsidize its capital-intensive industries? Other things equal, a given amount of capital will employ fewer workers in capital- than in labor-intensive sectors. So a shift of capital toward the capital-intensive part of the economy will initially tend to reduce employment. Although the unemployment may eventually be eliminated by a fall in real wages that encourages all sectors to substitute labor for capital, the initial increase in unemployment is hardly the result one looks for from an industrial policy.

ENCOURAGING LINKAGE INDUSTRIES

A recurrent view in discussions of industrial policy has been that governments should offer special encouragement to sectors that supply inputs to the rest of the economy. The idea is that expansion of industries producing intermediate goods has multiplied effects through the encouragement of industries that use what they produce. For example, some observers argue that Japanese subsidies to investment in steel, by leading to cheaper steel, encouraged growth of all those industries that use steel, such as shipbuilding and autos.

The popularity of the **linkage argument** stems from the feeling that producing intermediate goods that can be used in a variety of sectors is a more fundamental economic activity than producing consumer goods that simply provide satisfaction to households. It is hard to escape the feeling that the makers of steel or semiconductors are doing something more serious than the makers of toys or toothpaste.

Again, however, if there is no market failure, there is no reason to expect markets to devote too few resources to the production of intermediate goods. A basic proposition of economics is that with competitive markets the earnings of any input are equal to the value of its marginal product. Thus at the margin a dollar's worth of capital services will add one dollar to the value of production of the sector in which it is employed, whether it be steel, autos, shipbuilding, or any other. It is also true that a dollar's worth of steel will similarly be worth one dollar in any alternative use.

The linkage argument is that the government should direct more investment into steel as opposed to autos or shipbuilding than the private market would have. Will this raise national income? In the absence of a market failure, it will not. A dollar of capital services reallocated from autos to steel lowers the value of auto output by one dollar and raises the value of steel output by one dollar. The extra steel output can now be used to raise auto output back to its original level, *but not higher;* this only confirms that the original allocation was optimal in that it could not be improved on.

PROMOTING INDUSTRIES WITH FUTURE GROWTH POTENTIAL

Another common argument is that industrial policy should seek to channel resources into industries with high potential for future growth. There is no question that technological change, shifting patterns of demand, and shifting comparative advantage lead to very different growth rates of industries within an economy. Sometimes, though not always, it is possible to predict which industries will grow fastest. Should the government try to ''pick winners'' and encourage labor and capital to move into the industries with the highest growth prospects?

Again the answer is that properly functioning markets will make such a government role unnecessary. Firms making investment choices and workers making career choices are already trying to pick the winning industries. Only if the government can do a better job of picking the winners than these private market participants can it improve on the market outcome. To put it another way, if everyone knows an industry will grow rapidly, capital and labor will move into that industry even without special government encouragement. Unless there is some market failure, adding additional incentives to move into the sector will actually overdo it. It *is* possible to invest too much in a high-growth industry, as the later discussion of experience with steel and aircraft will make clear.

The argument that the government should always promote growth sectors amounts to saying that private markets systematically undervalue future growth prospects. This argument is close to the infant industry argument (Chapter 11) and has been strongly criticized on the grounds that there is no clear evidence for the kinds of market failures that would make it valid. The same criticism applies with even more force in the case of advanced industrial countries, where markets presumably work more efficiently. In the United States, private investors often support ventures, such as the Alaskan oil pipeline and the development of biotechnology, that involve large initial expenditures in return for uncertain profits that will occur only after a long delay. Looking at these examples, both of which have attracted huge amounts of private investment, it is hard to argue that private markets are systematically shortsighted.

COUNTERING THE EFFECTS OF OTHER COUNTRIES' INDUSTRIAL POLICIES

A final criterion for industrial policy that is particularly popular in U.S. discussion is the idea of industrial policy as a defensive measure. Suppose other countries provide support to an industry, leading to a contraction of that industry in the United States.

Shouldn't the United States respond by supporting the industry? If it does not, the argument runs, the United States will, in effect, be allowing its industrial structure to be determined by other countries' industrial policies.

To see what is wrong with this argument, let's first imagine a different scenario. Suppose other countries get more efficient at producing some good, say textiles, and that as a result textile prices on world markets fall. What is the appropriate U.S. response? Because this is a shift in comparative advantage, the United States should accommodate it by moving resources out of textiles and into other sectors. Furthermore, markets will tend to make this adjustment automatically, because the reduced relative price of textiles will provide the incentive. Unless there is some market failure in the U.S. economy, there is no need for a special government policy either to stop or to accelerate the pace of adjustment.

Now return to the issue of industrial targeting, and suppose the price of textiles falls, not because of a shift in comparative advantage but because other countries subsidize textile production. Should the United States respond differently? It should not. *From the point of view of the United States,* it makes no difference whether the price of textiles falls because of changes in foreign technology or because of foreign subsidies. In either case, the response that maximizes U.S. welfare is to shift resources out of textiles. A farmer deciding whether to grow wheat or corn needs to know their relative price, but the right decision does not depend on whether this price is the result of natural market forces or of government price supports. The same is true of a country setting its industrial mix. The French economist Frédéric Bastiat once wrote that the fact that other countries have rocks in their harbors is no reason to throw rocks in our own—that is, the fact that other countries distort their production with protection and subsidies is no reason for us to distort our own.

The usual counterargument is that if the United States does not respond to foreign industrial targeting, other countries will drive us out of key industries. This presumes, however, that the sectors other countries are targeting are especially important for economic growth. Certainly the fact that another country chooses to target a sector is not in and of itself evidence of a market failure requiring government intervention. The defensive argument for industrial policy in effect commits us to accepting other countries' judgments about which sectors should be encouraged—and as we will see, the record on judgment either by the United States or by other governments is not especially good.

So far we have examined a series of criteria for industrial policy that have influenced popular discussion. These criteria seem appealing but do not stand up to thoughtful economic analysis. Should the government dismiss the case for activist industrial policy? If its advocates cannot present better arguments, why should thoughtful observers take industrial policy seriously? There are two answers to this. The first is a practical one: although these ideas may not convince economists, they do influence actual policy. Thus it is important to ask how industrial policy has worked in practice (the evidence on this issue is covered later in this chapter).

The second answer to dismissing the idea of industrial policy is that to restrict the discussion to popular criteria is not to give the idea of industrial policy a fair hearing. Although popular critera for industrial policy may not hold up well, there are more carefully conceived arguments that we should examine carefully. These arguments do not carry the political appeal of the simplistic arguments above, but they do have more intellectual substance.

Sophisticated Arguments for Industrial Policy

Nothing in the analytical framework developed in Chapters 9 and 10 rules out the desirability of industrial policy. That framework *does* show that activist government policy needs a specific kind of justification—namely, it must offset some preexisting domestic market failure. The problem with the popular arguments for industrial policy is precisely that they do not link the case for government intervention to any particular failure of the assumptions on which the case for laissez-faire rests.

The problem with market failure arguments for intervention is how to know a market failure when you see one. Economists studying industrial countries have identified two kinds of market failure that seem to be present and relevant to the industrial policies of advanced countries. One of these is the inability of firms in high-technology industries to capture the benefits of that part of their contribution to knowledge that spills over to other firms. The other is the presence of monopoly profits in highly concentrated oligopolistic industries.

TECHNOLOGY AND EXTERNALITIES

The discussion of the infant industry argument in Chapter 11 noted that there is a potential market failure arising from difficulties of appropriating knowledge. If firms in an industry generate knowledge that other firms can also use without paying for it, the industry is in effect producing some extra output—the marginal social benefit of the knowledge—that is not reflected in the incentives of firms. Where such **externalities** (benefits that accrue to parties external to the firms) can be shown to be important, there is a good case for subsidizing the industry.

At an abstract level this argument is the same for the infant industries of less-developed countries as it is for the established industries of the advanced countries. In advanced countries, however, the argument has a special edge because in those countries there are some industries in which the generation of knowledge is in many ways the central aspect of the enterprise. These industries, called **high-technology industries,** include computers, electronics, and aerospace. In high-technology industries, firms devote a great deal of their resources to improving technology, either by explicit spending on research and development or by being willing to take initial losses on new products and processes to gain experience. Such activities take place in nearly all industries, of course, so that there is no sharp line between high-tech and the rest of the economy. There are clear differences in degree, however, and it makes sense to talk of a high-technology sector in which investment in knowledge is the key part of the business.

The point for industrial policy is that while firms can appropriate some of the benefits of their own investment in knowledge (otherwise they would not be investing!), they usually cannot appropriate them fully. Some of the benefits accrue to other firms that can imitate the ideas and techniques of the leaders. In electronics, for example, it is not uncommon for firms to ''reverse engineer'' their rivals' designs, taking their products apart to figure out how they work and how they were made. Because patent laws provide only weak protection for innovators, there is a reasonable presumption that under laissez-faire high-technology firms do not receive as strong an incentive to innovate as they should.

The Case for Government Support of High-Technology Industries. Should the U.S. government subsidize high-technology industries? While there is a pretty good case for such a subsidy, we need to exercise some caution. Two questions in particular arise: first, the ability of government policy to target the right thing; second, the quantitative importance of the argument.

Although high-technology industries probably produce extra social benefits because of the knowledge they generate, much of what goes on even in a high-technology industry has nothing to do with generating knowledge. There is no reason to subsidize the employment of capital or nontechnical workers in high-technology industries; on the other hand, innovation and technological spillovers happen to some extent even in industries that are mostly not at all high-tech. A general principle is that trade and industrial policy should be targeted specifically on the activity in which the market failure occurs. Thus policy should seek to subsidize the generation of knowledge that firms cannot appropriate. A general subsidy for a set of industries in which this kind of knowledge generation is believed to go on is a pretty blunt instrument for the purpose.

Perhaps, instead, government should subsidize research and development wherever it occurs. The problem here is one of definition. How do we know when a firm is engaged in creating knowledge? A loose definition could lend itself to abuse: who is to say whether paper clips and company cars were really supporting the development of knowledge or were placed in the research department's budget to inflate the subsidy? A strict definition, on the other hand, would risk favoring large, bureaucratic forms of research where the allocation of funds can be strictly documented over the smaller, informal organizations that are widely believed to be the key to the most original thinking.

The United States *does* in effect subsidize research and development (R&D), at least as compared with other kinds of investment. Research and development can be claimed by firms as a current expense and thus counts as an immediate deduction against the corporate profit tax. By constrast, investment in plant and equipment cannot be claimed as an immediate expense and can be written off only through gradual depreciation. This effective favorable treatment for knowledge is an accident of tax history rather than an explicit policy, but we should note it before concluding that the United States spends too little on R&D or that the high-technology sector needs further encouragement. To reach such a conclusion we would need to know how much subsidy is justified.

How Important Are Externalities? The question of the appropriate level of subsidy for high technology depends on the answer to a difficult empirical problem: How important, quantitatively, is the technological spillover argument for targeting high-technology industries? Is the optimal subsidy 10, 20, or 100 percent? The honest answer is that no one has a good idea. It is in the nature of externalities, benefits that do not carry a market price, that they are hard to measure.

Further, even if the externalities generated by high-technology industries could be shown to be large, there may be only a limited incentive for any one country to support these industries. The reason is that many of the benefits of knowledge created in one country may in fact accrue to firms in other countries. Thus if, say, a Belgian firm develops a new technique for making steel, most of the firms that can imitate this technique will be in other European countries, the United States, and Japan rather than in Belgium. A world government might find it worthwhile to subsidize this innovation; the Belgian government might not. Such problems of appropriability at the level of the *nation* (as opposed to the firm) are less severe but still important even for a nation as large as the United States.

Despite the criticism, the technological spillover argument is probably the best case one can make intellectually for an active industrial policy. In contrast to the simplistic criteria for choosing industries, which can be strongly rejected, the case for or against targeting ''knowledge-intensive'' industries is a judgment call.

IMPERFECT COMPETITION AND STRATEGIC TRADE POLICY

During the 1980s a new argument for industrial targeting received substantial theoretical attention. Originally proposed by the economists Barbara Spencer and James Brander of the University of British Columbia, this argument locates the market failure that justifies government intervention in the lack of perfect competition. In some industries, they point out, there are only a few firms in effective competition. Because of the small number of firms, the assumptions of perfect competition do not apply. In particular, there will typically be **excess returns;** that is, firms will make profits above what equally risky investments elsewhere in the economy can earn. There will be an international competition over who gets these profits.

Spencer and Brander noticed that, in this case, it is possible in principle for a government to alter the rules of the game to shift these excess returns from foreign to domestic firms. In the simplest case, a subsidy to domestic firms, by deterring investment and production by foreign competitors, can raise the profits of domestic firms by more than the amount of the subsidy. Setting aside the effects on consumers—for example, when the firms are selling only in foreign markets—this capture of profits from foreign competitors would mean the subsidy raises national income at other countries' expense.

The Brander-Spencer Analysis: An Example. The **Brander-Spencer analysis** can be illustrated with a simple example in which there are only two firms competing, each from a different country. Bearing in mind that any resemblance to actual events may be coincidental, let's call the firms Boeing and Airbus, and the countries the United States and Europe. Suppose there is a new product, 150-seat aircraft, that both firms are capable of making. For simplicity, assume each firm can make only a yes/no decision: either to produce 150-seat aircraft or not.

Table 12-1 illustrates how the profits earned by the two firms might depend on their decisions. (The setup is similar to the one we used to examine the interaction of different countries' trade policies in Chapter 10.) Each row corresponds to a particular decision by Boeing, each column to a decision by Airbus. In each box are two entries: the entry on the lower left represents the profits of Boeing, while that on the upper right represents the profits of Airbus.

As set up, the table reflects the following assumption: either firm alone could earn profits making 150-seat aircraft, but if both firms try to produce them, both will make losses. Which firm will actually get the profits? This depends on who gets there first. Suppose Boeing is able to get a small head start and commits itself to produce 150-

TABLE 12-1 Two-firm competition

Boeing \ *Airbus*	*Produce*	*Don't produce*
Produce	−5, −5	100, 0
Don't produce	0, 100	0, 0

seat aircraft before Airbus can get going. Airbus will find that it has no incentive to enter. The outcome will be in the upper right of the table, with Boeing earning profits.

Now comes the Brander-Spencer point: the European government can reverse this situation. Suppose the European government commits itself to pay its firm a subsidy of 25 if it enters. The result will be to change the table of payoffs to that represented in Table 12-2. It is now profitable for Airbus to produce 150-seat aircraft whatever Boeing does.

Let's work through the implications of this shift. Boeing now knows that whatever it does, it will have to compete with Airbus and will therefore lose money if it chooses to produce. So now it is Boeing that will be deterred from entering. In effect, the government subsidy has removed the advantage of a head start that we assumed was Boeing's and has conferred it on Airbus instead.

The end result is that the equilibrium shifts from the upper right of Table 12-1 to the lower left of Table 12-2. Airbus ends up with profits of 125 instead of 0, profits that arise because of a government subsidy of only 25. That is, the subsidy raises profits by more than the amount of the subsidy itself, because of its deterrent effect on foreign competition. The subsidy has this effect because it creates an advantage for Airbus comparable with the *strategic* advantage it would have had if it, not Boeing, had had a head start in the industry. For this reason the argument for industrial policy based on imperfect competition is often referred to as the **strategic trade policy** argument.

Problems with the Brander-Spencer Analysis. This hypothetical example might seem to indicate that the strategic trade policy argument provides a compelling case for government activism. A subsidy by the European government sharply raises profits of a European firm at the expense of its foreign rivals. Leaving aside the interest of

TABLE 12-2 Effects of a subsidy to Airbus

Boeing \ *Airbus*	*Produce*	*Don't produce*
Produce	−5, 20	100, 0
Don't produce	0, 125	0, 0

TABLE 12-3 Two-firm competition: An alternative case

Boeing \ Airbus	Produce	Don't produce
Produce	Boeing −5, Airbus −20	Boeing 125, Airbus 0
Don't produce	Boeing 0, Airbus 100	Boeing 0, Airbus 0

consumers, this seems clearly to raise European welfare (and reduce U.S. welfare). Shouldn't the U.S. government put this argument into practice?

In fact, the strategic justification for trade policy, while it has attracted much interest, has also received much criticism. Critics argue that to make practical use of the theory would require more information than is likely to be available, that such policies would risk foreign retaliation, and that in any case the domestic politics of trade and industrial policy would prevent use of such subtle analytical tools.

The problem of insufficient information has two aspects. The first is that even when looking at an industry in isolation, it may be difficult to fill in the entries in a table like Table 12-1 with any confidence. And if the government gets it wrong, a subsidy policy may turn out to be a costly misjudgment. To see this, suppose that instead of Table 12-1 the reality is represented by the seemingly similar payoffs in Table 12-3. The numbers are not much different, but the difference in crucial. In Table 12-3, Boeing is assumed to have some underlying advantage—maybe a better technology—so that even if Airbus enters, Boeing will still find it profitable to produce. Airbus, however, cannot produce profitably if Boeing enters.

In the absence of a subsidy, the outcome in Table 12-3 will be in the upper right corner; Boeing produces and Airbus does not. Now suppose that, as in the previous case, the European government provides a subsidy of 25, which is sufficient to induce Airbus to produce. The new table of payoffs is illustrated as Table 12-4. The result is that both firms produce: the outcome is in the upper left. In this case Airbus, which receives a subsidy of 25, earns profits of only 5. That is, we have reversed the result above, in which a subsidy raised profits by more than the amount of the subsidy. The

TABLE 12-4 Effects of a subsidy to Airbus

Boeing \ Airbus	Produce	Don't produce
Produce	Boeing 5, Airbus 5	Boeing 125, Airbus 0
Don't produce	Boeing 0, Airbus 125	Boeing 0, Airbus 0

reason for the difference in outcome is that this time the subsidy has failed to act as a deterrent to Boeing.

Initially the two cases look very similar, yet in one case a subsidy looks like a good idea, while in the other it looks like a terrible idea. It seems the desirability of strategic trade policies depends on an exact reading of the situation. This leads some economists to ask whether we are ever likely to have enough information to use the theory effectively.

The information requirement is complicated by the fact that we cannot consider industries in isolation. If one industry is subsidized, it will draw resources from other industries and lead to increases in their costs. Thus, even a policy that succeeds in giving U.S. firms a strategic advantage in one industry will tend to cause strategic disadvantage elsewhere. To ask whether the policy is justified, the U.S. government needs to weigh these offsetting effects. Even if the government has a precise understanding of one industry, this is not enough; it needs an equally precise understanding of those industries with which that industry competes for resources.

If a proposed strategic trade policy can overcome these criticisms, it still faces the problem of foreign retaliation, essentially the same problem faced when considering the use of a tariff to improve the terms of trade (Chapter 10). Strategic policies are **beggar-thy-neighbor policies** that increase our welfare at other countries' expense. These policies therefore risk a trade war that leaves everyone worse off. Few economists would advocate that the United States be the initiator of such policies. Instead, the most that is usually argued for is that the United States itself be prepared to retaliate when other countries appear to be using strategic policies aggressively.

Finally, can theories like this ever be used in a political context? We discussed this issue in Chapter 10, where the reasons for skepticism were placed in the context of a political skeptic's case for free trade.

Industrial Policy in Practice

The theory of industrial policy is a special case of the domestic market failure analysis laid out in Chapter 10. The principles are therefore fairly simple, even though the details may be complex. No such underlying simplicity ties together the *practice* of industrial policy, however. There is a great deal of controversy even over what the industrial policies of major countries have tried to accomplish, let alone how successful they were. What follows is a brief review of some salient facts about industrial policy, followed by a discussion of some famous cases.

THE INDUSTRIAL POLICY OF JAPAN

Japan is the spectacular success story of the advanced industrial world, having emerged from postwar devastation and economic weakness into decades of spectacular growth. Japan also has had the most visible industrial policy of the industrial countries. But what was the content of that policy?

Experts on Japan point out that it is necessary to distinguish two phases in Japan's industrial policy.[1] From 1950 until the early 1970s, the Japanese economy was run in such a way that government agencies had a great deal of direct control over the allocation of resources. Since the mid-1970s, the government's role has been more subtle and ambiguous. It is a mistake to discuss the current role of the Japanese government in electronics and computers in the same context as its earlier role in steel, shipbuilding, and other heavy industries.

Early Japanese Industrial Policy. From the end of World War II until the 1970s, Japan was run as a "shortage" economy. Both the price of foreign currency and the interest rate were kept below the levels at which supply would have equaled demand, so that foreign exchange and credit were rationed. The allocation of these scarce resources was essentially controlled by the government, especially by the Ministry of Finance and the famous Ministry of International Trade and Industry (MITI). Their control over vital resources gave these ministries great power over the direction of the economy's growth. This power was further reinforced by the use of tariffs and import restrictions to protect selected industries.

During the 1950s and 1960s, the ministries used this power to follow a growth strategy similar to what the advocates of the "popular" criteria we discussed earlier might have suggested. The government channeled funds into heavy industries with high value added per worker and away from traditional labor-intensive industries such as textiles. They tried to encourage those industries that they believed reflected Japan's future comparative advantage rather than its current trade pattern. Intermediate goods industries such as steel were special favorites.

The result is history: Japan's economy grew extremely rapidly. Indeed, it is Japan's success that helps lend plausibility to the popular arguments we discussed.

The crucial question is whether Japan's industrial policy was really the key to the rapid growth. Might the economy have grown just as rapidly without the policy? There are at least two reasons to be cautious about attributing success primarily to the industrial policy.

First, we are not sure whether the activities of Japan's government were actually pushing Japan into heavy industry faster than they would have gone under laissez-faire. Japan's industrial policy was not applied to an otherwise unregulated economy. Instead, the government first disconnected the normal channels of allocation, by rationing foreign exchange and credit, then made up for the lack of a market by allocating these resources directly. Some economists have argued that in the end Japan arrived at the same outcome as if the government had stayed out of the picture. To put it another way, the government may have been making sensible investment decisions, but the market might have made similar decisions if left to itself. There is some evidence supporting this view in Japan's pattern of trade in the 1970s, which was not very different from what would have been predicted from its resources and level of economic development, even without its industrial policy.

Second, there is the possibility that the dynamism of Japanese industry had its roots in factors other than industrial policy and that Japan would have done well in any case. Reasons for Japan's success are many: Japan had the highest savings rate in the

[1] For a clear summary of Japan's industrial policy, see Kozo Yamamura, "Caveat Emptor: The Industrial Policy of Japan," in Paul R. Krugman, ed., *Strategic Trade Policy and the New International Economics* (Cambridge: MIT Press, 1986).

world, an effective educational system, good labor-management relations, and a business-oriented culture in which the most ambitious and talented channeled their energy into corporate management. It is possible that industrial policy may have been a minor positive factor or even a drag on economic growth. Some of Japan's most successful industries, notably automobiles and consumer electronics, were not among those that received high priority.

The Japanese industrial policy of the 1950s and 1960s remains the picture of Japan that many retain. The country is seen as "Japan, Inc.," a society in which the allocation of resources is under the central control of MITI. Such a picture has become increasingly out of date, however. Since 1970, the traditional levers of Japanese industrial policy have lost much of their force. Foreign exchange and credit are no longer scarce and rationed, while the use of trade restrictions has become constrained by the demand of other countries that Japan open its markets. Industrial policy since 1975 or so has taken a different and more subtle form.

Current Japanese Industrial Policy. Japan's industrial policy since the mid-1970s has aimed at encouraging a new set of industries, the "knowledge-intensive," or high-technology, industries. The tools of industrial policy have been a combination of modest subsidies for research and development and encouragement of joint government-industry research projects aimed at developing promising new technologies. The whole enterprise has been on a much smaller scale relative to the total economy than the old industrial policy.

The justification for targeting high technology is not especially clear. The Japanese themselves do not seem to be clear whether they are targeting high technology because it is the growth sector of the future or because it is a generator of technological spillovers. The new Japanese industrial policy is, however, easier to justify in terms of a market failure argument than the old one.

How much effect do the new policies have? The industries targeted since 1975 remain a small part of Japan's economy. Neither automobiles nor consumer electronics (televisions, stereos, VCRs, and so on) are part of the high-technology area that has been the focus of research joint ventures. So the Japanese consumer products that have made Japan's export success so visible do not reflect the new industrial policy. Japan has, however, become a significant producer of some products in which recent industrial policy has played a key role. Most famous and most important of these is semiconductor chips, a case we will examine shortly.

This brief history gives some perspective on the reality of Japan's policy. Japan is often seen as an almost militarily organized society, centrally commanded to achieve economic objectives. This view exaggerated the role of the Japanese government even during its period of greatest influence and exaggerates it still more today.

INDUSTRIAL POLICY IN OTHER COUNTRIES

Other countries have pursued industrial policies to some degree in the postwar period, though none with the degree of government control, or success, that Japan did. France has pursued industrial policies with varying degrees of vigor. Also, the United States, though without an explicit industrial strategy, does have policies—notably its support of agriculture and military procurement—that look to some observers like industrial policies.

The HDTV Debate

In 1988 and 1989 concerns over lagging U.S. technology came to focus on one issue in particular: the apparent decision on the part of U.S. electronics firms not to compete in the emerging market for high-definition television (HDTV).

High-definition television will represent in effect a cross between a television and a computer. It will receive a digitized signal, process it, and produce a picture with about twice the resolution and substantially higher quality than current television screens. Enthusiasts argue that the new technology will transform both consumer electronics and business applications. For example, while HDTV would have only a modest effect on the viewability of current-sized television sets, it would make a large difference on bigger sets; if new technologies for large, flat-screen televisions become economically practical, they would both require and encourage use of HDTV technology. Similarly, HDTV could be important for business workstations and other computer applications where image quality is crucial.

As of 1989, while both Japanese and European firms were investing substantial sums in the development of HDTV, no U.S. firms were doing so. This led to widespread concern that the U.S. was once again about to lose a technological race and to calls for a government-subsidized program to keep the U.S. competitive in HDTV.

The HDTV case illustrates quite clearly, however, the difficulty of making industrial policy. At first sight HDTV has all the characteristics of an industry suitable for targeting. It is undeniably a high-technology industry, which might be expected to generate externalities both through the technology it develops and by providing a domestic market for other high-technology products, such as semiconductors. It is also likely to be a fairly concentrated industry, so that a strategic trade policy argument can also be made on HDTV's behalf. To many members of Congress the case for subsidizing the development of a U.S. HDTV industry seemed overwhelming.

Yet there were serious doubts. Skeptics—notably the Congressional Budget Office—pointed out that there was considerable uncertainty about the size of the eventual market for HDTV, suggesting that hype about its prospects could easily lead to worldwide overcapacity. Moreover, they argued that even if the HDTV market turned out to be as large as, say, the market for ordinary television sets, it will still represent only a small part of the market for the high-technology items, mainly sem-

French Industrial Policy. The aspect of French industrial policy that has attracted the most attention has been the efforts of the government to bolster French firms in technological competition with foreign firms. Since the 1960s, the French government has worried that world technology will become dominated by large U.S. or, more recently, Japanese companies. To prevent this domination, the government has attempted to ensure that there are French firms, called national champions, that can compete on world markets. To create national champions, the French government has encouraged mergers of smaller firms into large units. It has also used its influence over demand to provide privileged markets, for example, by requiring the state-run phone company to buy its telecommunications and computer equipment from French firms. And in a few cases, notably aircraft, extensive government subsidies have been used to promote industries that are regarded as key.

How has France's industrial policy worked? The French economy performed quite

iconductors, for which its development was allegedly crucial. Advocates of an HDTV program countered that HDTV would be much more important for certain specialized applications, which they alleged would then generate important externalities to more broadly defined technologies.

One peculiar aspect of the debate was the question of what constitutes an American product. In the absence of a U.S. government program to support HDTV, it seemed likely that Japanese and European firms would dominate the industry. However, it also seemed likely that much of the *production* of these firms would take place in the United States. Although most of the color televisions sold in the United States are manufactured by foreign firms, most of them are made in this country—with the major exception being the sets made by the U.S. firm Zenith, which are made in Mexico. Both advocates and opponents of an HDTV program agreed that most HDTV manufacturing for the U.S. market would take place in the United States, whoever won the technology race. Thus the HDTV debate was really as much a debate about foreign direct investment as about industrial policy.

The great irony of the HDTV debate, however, is that it turned out to be beside the point, because surprise technological developments made the HDTV systems that Japanese and European firms were working on obsolete before they were introduced. New techniques for compressing data appear to have completely changed the nature of the game. Suppose a network is transmitting a television show in which the actors spend several minutes in front of a background that includes a large area of blue sky. The old technique would send several thousand instructions each fraction of a second, repeatedly telling the television to color each "pixel" (small area of the screen) blue. The new methods would, in effect, inform the "intelligent" television that "the whole top left part of the screen should be colored blue until further notice." It turns out that data compression will allow HDTV to be introduced much more cheaply and with much less change in current methods of broadcasting than the techniques previously contemplated.

To cap the irony, at the time of writing it appears that U.S. firms are ahead in developing these new techniques, suggesting they may win the competition after all.

well until the late 1970s, achieving rates of growth slightly higher than Germany's and much higher than Britain's. Since then France has had severe unemployment, but this is a problem shared by almost all of Europe. Notable about France, however, is that while the economy as a whole has done well, the sectors most coveted by the government have not. France's computer industry remains dependent on protected markets, and efforts to develop an aircraft industry have achieved technological success only at the cost of heavy monetary losses. For this reason few would regard France's industrial policy as the key to its economic growth.

U.S. Industrial Policy. The United States has a commitment to free market ideology that would preclude any explicit government direction of the economy such as that of Japan during the early phase. There are some areas, however, in which the U.S. government has had a major role in promoting industries.

The most notable of these areas is agriculture. Here the U.S. government has come closest to the kind of industrial policy that we might recommend on the basis of the sophisticated criteria discussed earlier. Recall that the problem of appropriating knowledge can be a reason for intervening in an industry. In agriculture, which remains mostly a matter of family farms, this problem is especially acute: a farmer who makes a major innovation can be imitated by thousands of others, who derive the benefits without sharing the risks. To alleviate this problem, the U.S. government has long engaged both in research into agricultural techniques and in the dissemination of improved techniques through the Agricultural Extension Service. Also, the government has taken a leading role in large-scale projects, such as irrigation facilities, that require collective action. These interventions fit nicely into a market failure framework and are commended even by economists who are skeptical about most industrial policy.

Another major role for the U.S. government is in defense. Both because it has a larger national income than other industrial countries and because it spends relatively more on defense, the U.S. government is far and away the world's largest market for military hardware. Not surprisingly, the United States dominates the production of military goods such as fighter aircraft that involve large economies of scale. In some cases it is likely that U.S. spending on military goods has helped give U.S. firms an advantage in civilian markets as well. For example, one of the most successful civilian aircraft produced by Boeing, the Boeing 707 (introduced in 1960), owed a great deal to a previously developed military plane (the B-52 bomber). The military market surely sometimes helps U.S. firms gain economies of scale that help them in civilian markets—the Boeing 707 continues to be manufactured, long after its civilian sales are over, as the AWACS reconnaissance plane. Military research and development sometimes gives U.S. firms knowledge that they can apply elsewhere. As usual in industrial policy issues, however, the quantitative importance of these effects is a matter of dispute. European commentators, who sometimes feel they are losing a race with the United States and Japan, have suggested that in practice the United States has as effective an industrial policy as Japan.

Case Studies of Industrial Policy

How effective is industrial policy? Industrial policy has been applied in a wide variety of industries. To see the difficulties involved in evaluation, we examine three examples: Japan's targeting of steel in the 1960s and early 1970s, European support of aircraft production, and Japan's targeting of semiconductors in the late 1970s and early 1980s.

Case Study

JAPANESE TARGETING OF STEEL (1960–EARLY 1970s)

Beginning in the 1950s the Japanese government designated steel as a sector that should receive priority in growth. Japanese steel production tripled from 1963 to 1970, not only meeting the rapidly growing demands of the domestic economy but also making Japan the world's largest exporter. This development was especially remarkable given that virtually all the raw materials for steel making have to be imported into resource-poor Japan from other countries. When a world steel glut developed after the energy crisis in 1973, Japan's industry had the most modern plants with the lowest operating costs and was thus able to continue to operate in an environment in which the steel industries of other industrial countries were either contracting sharply (as in the United States) or being supported by government subsidy (as in Europe).

This experience raises two major questions. Was government policy the cause of steel's rapid growth? Was this policy good for Japan's economy?

Given the previous description of Japan's industrial policy, we must ask whether the government's targeting of steel only moved the economy in the same direction market forces would have moved it anyway. Japan would probably have developed a comparative advantage in steel even with laissez-faire. On one side, Japan's high savings rate gave it a growing comparative advantage in capital-intensive industries like steel. On the other side, falling transport costs and the emergence of new sources of iron ore and coal made it less necessary for steel industries in general to locate near coal fields or iron deposits. Thus Japan might well have had a growing steel industry even without government intervention. Nonetheless, it is a good guess that the Japanese government encouraged steel to grow even faster than it would have in a free market economy. This is supported by the observation that Japan's steel industry grew rapidly despite a profit rate substantially *below* the average for Japanese manufacturing.

The more important question, however, is whether the policy accelerated Japanese economic growth. In answering this question, it is important to be careful. The policy was successful in making the steel industry grow—but that is not the question. The question is whether it made the Japanese economy *as a whole* grow faster. This amounts to asking whether the resources used in steel yielded a higher payoff to society than they would have elsewhere.

As noted above, the return directly earned by the resources used in steel was actually not as high as the return the same resources were earning elsewhere. Capital invested in steel earned a rate of return only a little more than half the average rate of return in Japanese manufacturing even during the prosperous 1960s and earned an even lower return during the 1970s.[2] Japan's promotion of steel can be justified only if there were marginal social benefits not included in the market return.

Economists who have studied the issue have not identified important marginal social benefits. Steel is not a "high-technology" industry that could be expected to yield important technological externalities. Nor are there high returns to be snatched from foreign rivals by strategic trade policy. Creation of jobs did not represent an extra benefit in Japan, because the economy was already running at full employment. Unless a plausible source of marginal social benefits can be identified, we must conclude that the targeting of steel—despite the industry's growth—was a mistake. It diverted resources to areas where their return was lower than elsewhere and thus acted as a drag on Japan's growth.

The case of Japanese steel is instructive. It is a reminder that the economic success of an industrial policy cannot be measured simply by looking at the growth or market share of the targeted industry.

[2] See Paul R. Krugman, "Targeted Industrial Policies: Theory and Evidence," in Dominick Salvatore, ed., *The New Protectionist Threat to World Welfare* (Amsterdam: North-Holland, 1987).

Case Study

EUROPEAN SUPPORT OF AIRCRAFT IN THE 1970s AND 1980s

The continued U.S. dominance in the manufacture of aircraft is a potent symbol of U.S. technological prowess. It is a symbol especially visible to policy makers, who spend much of their time flying between meetings. It is not surprising, then, that there is a long history of attempts by European governments to develop aircraft industries that can compete with the U.S. firms. In the 1950s and 1960s, these efforts were undertaken at a national level, with little success. Since the late 1960s, however, there have been two major cooperative efforts at government-sponsored aircraft development in Europe.

One of these was the joint development by Britain and France of a supersonic aircraft, the Concorde. Construction of a supersonic passenger plane became technologically feasible in the late 1960s, but private airplane manufactures were unconvinced that it would be profitable to develop. A political campaign to have the U.S. government finance development of such a plane failed. In Europe, however, France and Britain agreed to foot the bill for development. The logic behind this agreement was complex. To some extent there was hope of large technological spillovers. More important, however, was the prestige appeal of the project and the usefulness of the Concorde as a symbol of European cooperation.

In commercial terms the results have been disastrous. Concordes are extremely expensive to run, and the saving of a few hours in travel time has not been enough to counteract this difference in expense. Only a few Concordes have been sold, and those were bought by the state-owned airlines of Britain and France. The best that can be said of the Concorde is that the experience of its development may have yielded technological spillovers to the next European attempt at aircraft production, the Airbus.

Airbus is a consortium of European governments that produces large passenger airplanes that compete directly with the main U.S. strength. The costs of capital and some of the other costs have been subsidized by the member governments. Unlike the Concorde project, Airbus has succeeded in producing planes that are commercially viable: the A300 family of wide-bodied, medium-range passenger jets is comparable in performance and operating costs with U.S. planes and has achieved significant sales. Unfortunately, after years of subsidy Airbus continues to have production costs substantially higher than Boeing, its chief U.S. competitor. Airbus has taken a sizable market share, but only at the cost of continuing subsidy.

The Airbus experience is particularly interesting because it fits well into our discussion of strategic trade policy. The economies of scale in large passenger aircraft production are so huge that there is probably room for only one or two profitable producers in the whole world market. The European subsidy to Airbus could be viewed as an attempt to overcome Boeing's head start and snatch some of that profitable market for Europe. Unfortunately, the outcome looks more like Tables 12-3 and 12-4 than like Tables 12-1 and 12-2. Boeing has *not* been driven out, and Airbus is absorbing a lot of government money.

Case Study

JAPANESE TARGETING OF SEMICONDUCTORS (MID-1970s TO DATE)

As we noted earlier, since the mid-1970s Japanese industrial policy has shifted to a focus on high-technology industries. The best-known and most controversial case has been semiconductors. Semiconductor chips, complex electronic circuits etched at microscopic scale onto chips of silicon, are key components of many new products. Until the mid-1970s, the technology for making such chips was largely a U.S. monopoly. Japan made a deliberate effort to break into this industry, with the government sponsoring joint research projects and at least initially providing a protected domestic market. In the late 1970s and early 1980s Japanese producers shocked their U.S. competitors by taking a dominant share of the market for one kind of chip, random access memories.

That Japan targeted semiconductors, and that the industry achieved a large market share, is fact. What is hotly disputed is how much support the Japanese industry actually received, how decisive that support was, and whether the policy helped Japan and/or hurt the United States.

We know that not much government money was provided; the subsidy component of the targeting was actually quite small. We also know that explicit home market protection, by tariffs and quotas, was mostly removed after the mid-1970s. Some would argue that, in fact, the Japanese semiconductor industry succeeded with little government help.

Others argue that more subtle government help was crucial. The proponents of this view argue that the joint research projects, which would have been blocked in the United States by antitrust laws, were a highly effective way of improving the technology. They also argue that the Japanese market was effectively closed through a tacit "buy Japanese" policy discreetly encouraged by the government. As evidence they note that U.S. firms had a much smaller market share in Japan than in the United States or Europe.

Economists do not know which of these views is correct. (It may be that the Japanese don't know either.) If we assume for the sake of argument that government policy was, in fact, crucial, was it a good idea?

As in the case of steel, the direct returns on Japan's investment in semiconductors have been quite low. Exact figures are not available, but it is generally believed that Japanese firms have earned a low rate of return on semiconductors since the late 1970s. So any gains from the encouragement of chips must be located in the technological externalities.

Now comes the great uncertainty. Unlike steel, semiconductor production—a highly dynamic industry where knowledge is the main source of competitive advantage—is exactly the kind of sector where the external economy argument should apply. But were the externalities large enough to justify the cost? Nobody knows.

This brief survey of three industrial policies in practice is not comprehensive. Each example does, however, illustrate an important point: an industrial policy cannot be judged by asking whether the targeted industries grew. All three cases are of industries that did eventually grow and achieve substantial market share, but this does not mean that policies accelerated economic growth, because an industrial policy will not accelerate overall growth unless it corrects a market failure. In the case of steel, it is hard to identify a market failure, so the Japanese government's promotion of steel probably retarded economic growth by channeling resources into an area of low return. In the case of aircraft, European subsidies may in principle have helped Airbus gain a strategic advantage, but it is doubtful whether any advantage was gained in fact. In the case of semiconductors, the justification for the Japanese targeting rests on presumed external economies that have not been measured.

Some extravagant claims have been made about the effectiveness of industrial policy. We cannot show that such policies never work, but we can show that they have not always worked and that assessing them requires a more careful analysis of data than most observers have carried out.

Summary

1. *Industrial policy* is an attempt by a government to shift the allocation of resources to promote economic growth. Industrial policy has been extensively practiced in Japan, is important in France, and exists to some extent in many countries, including the United States.

2. Advocates of industrial policy often base their case for intervention on criteria that do not have their basis in economic theory. The most often cited criteria are the alleged need to target industries with *high value added per worker,* linkage industries, industries with high growth prospects, and industries that have been targeted by foreign governments. A careful examination of these criteria shows that they are badly flawed and likely to lead to undesirable results if used as the basis for government policy.

3. More sophisticated criteria for industrial policy are based on the existence of domestic market failures. Two arguments for industrial policy in particular have attracted the attention of international economists. One is the argument that governments should promote industries that yield *technological externalities.* The other is the *strategic trade policy* argument that governments can help domestic firms seize monopoly profits from foreign competitors. These criteria are valid in terms of economic theory; however, many economists worry that they are too subtle and require too much information to be useful in practice.

4. Industrial policy in practice is much more varied and uncertain in effect than popular descriptions might indicate. Japan's industrial policy has shifted from extensive government control over the economy in the 1950s and 1960s to a much lighter government hand today. Other countries have had less consistent policies; even the United States has, in effect, had a widely approved industrial policy in agriculture, and some foreigners allege that the U.S. defense budget acts like an industrial policy for the high-technology industries.

5. Assessing the effect of industrial policies is not easy. Looking at market shares or the growth of the industry is not enough. Instead, one must do a cost-benefit analysis.

An examination of some major examples of industrial policy is not very encouraging about the track record of governments in their targeting.

Key Terms

industrial policy
criteria for selection
high value added per worker
linkage argument
externalities
high-technology industries
excess returns
Brander-Spencer analysis
strategic trade policy
beggar-thy-neighbor policies

Problems

1. Suppose the U.S. government were able to determine which industries will grow most rapidly over the next twenty years. Why doesn't this automatically mean that the nation should have a policy of supporting these industries' growth?
2. The U.S. Commerce Department has urged that the United States provide special support for its high-technology industries. It argues that these industries have the prospect of rapid future growth, provide inputs to many other industries, and generate technology that benefits the whole economy. Furthermore, some U.S. high-technology industries such as aircraft and microelectronics face challenges by government-supported foreign competitors. Which of these arguments might be valid reasons for the United States to have an industrial policy targeting these industries?
3. If the United States had its way, it would demand that Japan spend more money on basic research in science and less on applied research into industrial applications. Explain why in terms of the analysis of appropriability.
4. Tables 12-1 and 12-2 presented a situation in which European governments were able to use a subsidy to achieve a strategic advantage, while Tables 12-3 and 12-4 presented a situation in which it could not. What is the crucial distinction between these two cases? That is, what is the general rule for determining when a subsidy can work?
5. "The new strategic trade policy argument demonstrates the wisdom of policies like that of Korea, which subsidizes its exports across the board. The subsidy gives each industry the strategic advantage it needs to establish itself in world competition." Discuss.
6. Does the U.S. military budget help or hurt the strategic position of U.S. high-technology industries? Make the case for either point of view.
7. It appears that Japan earned a low market rate of return on both its investment in steel in the late 1960s and early 1970s and its investment in semiconductors in the late 1970s and 1980s. What possible justification for these investments can be given? Why is the text more sympathetic to the possibility that semiconductor targeting was a good policy than it is to the case for steel targeting?

8. France, in addition to its occasional stabs at industrial policy, pursues an active nationalist *cultural* policy, promoting French art, music, fashion, cuisine, and so on. This may be primarily a matter of attempting to preserve a national identity in an increasingly homogeneous world, but some French officials also defend this policy on economic grounds. In what sense could some features of such a policy be defended as a kind of industrial policy?

Further Reading

James A. Brander and Barbara J. Spencer. ''Export Subsidies and International Market Share Rivalry.'' *Journal of International Economics* 16 (1985), pp. 83–100. A basic reference on the potential role of subsidies as a tool of strategic trade policy.

James A. Brander and Barbara J. Spencer. ''International R&D Rivalry and Industrial Strategy.'' *Review of Economic Studies* 50 (1983), pp. 707–722. The first exposition of the case for ''strategic'' industrial policy.

Avinash K. Dixit and A. S. Kyle. ''The Use of Protection and Subsidies for Entry Promotion and Deterrence.'' *American Economic Review* 75 (1985), pp. 139–152. An extension of the Brander-Spencer analysis that looks at the broader game between governments as well as the competition between firms.

Elhanan Helpman and Paul Krugman. *Trade Policy and Market Structure.* Cambridge: MIT Press, 1989. A survey and synthesis of the literature on strategic trade policy and related topics.

Paul R. Krugman, ed. *Strategic Trade Policy and the New International Economics.* Cambridge: MIT Press, 1986. A collection of papers by leading exponents and critics of the idea of strategic trade policy.

Ira Magaziner and Robert Reich. *Minding America's Business.* New York: Random House, 1982. An eloquent and clearly written tract in favor of a national industrial policy for the United States.

Bruce Scott and George C. Lodge, eds. *U.S. Competitiveness in the World Economy.* Cambridge: Harvard University Press, 1987. A collection of papers arguing the case for a U.S. industrial policy.

Part Three
Exchange Rates and Open-Economy Macroeconomics

National Income Accounting and the Balance of Payments

Chapter 13

As the United States prepared for the Persian Gulf War in the summer of 1990, its economy slipped into a long-lasting economic slowdown that soon spread to Europe and Japan. The percentage of unemployed workers in America's labor force rose from 5.3 percent in 1989 to nearly 8 percent in 1992; other industrial countries faced similar increases in jobless rates. Coming after nearly eight years of relative prosperity, the recession of the early 1990s inflicted immense financial and personal hardships on many people throughout the world. Presidents and prime ministers fell from power as a result. Was this worldwide slump an inexplicable accident? Or can economic analysis shed light on its causes and suggest ways to avoid similar contractions in the future?

Previous chapters have been concerned primarily with the problem of making the best use of the world's scarce productive resources at a single point in time. The branch of economics called **microeconomics** studies this problem from the perspective of individual firms and consumers. Microeconomics works "from the bottom up" to show how individual economic actors, by pursuing their own interests, collectively determine how resources are used. In our study of international microeconomics we have learned how individual production and consumption decisions produce patterns of international trade and specialization. We have seen that while free trade usually encourages efficient resource use, government intervention or market failures can cause waste even when all factors of production are fully employed.

With this chapter we shift our focus and ask: How can economic policy ensure that factors of production *are* fully employed? And what determines how an economy's capacity to produce goods and services changes over time? To answer these questions we must understand **macroeconomics,** the branch of economics that studies how economies' overall levels of employment, production, and growth are determined. Like microeconomics, macroeconomics is concerned with the effective use of scarce resources. But while microeconomics focuses on the economic decisions of individuals, macroeconomics analyzes the behavior of the economy as a whole. In our study of international macroeconomics, we will learn how the interactions of national economies influence the worldwide pattern of macroeconomic activity.

Macroeconomic analysis emphasizes four aspects of economic life that we have usually kept in the background until now to simplify our discussion of international economics:

1. *Unemployment.* We know that in the real world workers may be unemployed and factories may be idle. Macroeconomics studies the factors that cause unemployment and the steps governments can take to prevent it. A main concern of international macroeconomics is the problem of ensuring full employment in economies open to international trade.
2. *Saving.* In earlier chapters we usually assumed that every country consumes an amount exactly equal to its income—no more and no less. In reality, though, households can put aside part of their income to provide for the future, or they can borrow temporarily to spend more than they earn. A country's saving or borrowing behavior affects domestic employment and future levels of national wealth. From the standpoint of the international economy as a whole, the world saving rate determines how quickly the world stock of productive capital can grow.
3. *Trade imbalances.* As we saw in earlier chapters, the value of a country's imports equals the value of its exports when spending equals income. This state of balanced trade is seldom attained by actual economies, however. Trade imbalances play a large role in the following chapters because they redistribute wealth among countries and are a main channel through which one country's macroeconomic policies affect its trading partners. It should be no surprise, therefore, that trade imbalances, particularly when they are large and persistent, quickly can become a source of international discord.
4. *Money and the price level.* The trade theory you have studied so far is a barter theory, one in which goods are exchanged directly for other goods on the basis of their relative prices. In practice it is more convenient to use money, a widely acceptable medium of exchange, in transactions, and to quote prices in terms of money. Because money changes hands in virtually every transaction that takes place in a modern economy, fluctuations in the supply of money or the demand for it can affect both output and employment. International macroeconomics takes into account that every country uses a currency and that a monetary change in one country (for example, a change in money supply) can have effects that spill across its borders to other countries. Stability in money price levels is an important goal of international macroeconomic policy.

This chapter takes the first step in our study of international macroeconomics by explaining the accounting concepts economists use to describe a country's level of production and its international transactions. To get a complete picture of the macroeconomic linkages among economies that engage in international trade, we have to master two related and essential tools. The first of these tools, **national income accounting,** records all the expenditures that contribute to a country's income and output.

The second tool, **balance of payments accounting,** helps us keep track of both changes in a country's indebtedness to foreigners and the fortunes of its export- and import-competing industries. The balance of payments accounts also show the connection between foreign transactions and national money supplies.

The National Income Accounts

Of central concern to macroeconomic analysis is a country's **gross national product (GNP),** the value of all final goods and services produced by its factors of production and sold on the market in a given time period. GNP, which is the basic measure of a country's output studied by macroeconomists, is calculated by adding up the market value of all expenditures on final output. GNP therefore includes the value of goods like bread sold in a supermarket and textbooks sold in a bookstore, as well as the value of services provided by supermarket checkers and baggers and by university professors. Because output cannot be produced without the aid of factor inputs, the expenditures that make up GNP are closely linked to the employment of labor, capital, and other factors of production.

To distinguish among the different types of expenditure that make up a country's GNP, government economists and statisticians who compile national income accounts divide GNP among the four possible uses for which a country's output is purchased: *consumption* (the amount consumed by private domestic residents), *investment* (the amount put aside by private firms to build new plant and equipment for future production), *government purchases* (the amount used by the government), and the *current account balance* (the amount of net exports of goods and services to foreigners). The term *national income accounts,* rather than *national output accounts,* is used to describe this fourfold classification because a country's income in fact equals its output. Thus, the national income accounts can be thought of as classifying each transaction that contributes to national income according to the type of expenditure that gives rise to it. Figure 13-1 shows how U.S. GNP was divided among its four components in 1991.[1]

Why is it useful to divide GNP into consumption, investment, government purchases, and the current account? One major reason is that we cannot hope to understand the cause of a particular recession or boom without knowing how the main categories of spending have changed. And without such an understanding, we cannot recommend a sound policy response. In addition, the national income accounts provide information essential for studying why some countries are rich—that is, have a high level of GNP relative to population size—while some are poor.

NATIONAL PRODUCT AND NATIONAL INCOME

Our first task in understanding how economists analyze GNP is to explain in greater detail why the GNP a country generates over some time period must equal its **national income,** the income earned in that period by its factors of production.

[1] Our definition of the current account is not strictly accurate when a country is a net donor or recipient of foreign gifts. This possibility, along with some others, also complicates our identification of GNP with national income. We describe later in this chapter how the definitions of national income and the current account must be changed in such cases.

FIGURE 13-1
U.S. GNP and its components, 1991.
America's $5.7 trillion 1991 gross national product can be broken down into the four components shown.
Source: U.S. Department of Commerce, *Survey of Current Business,* June 1992.

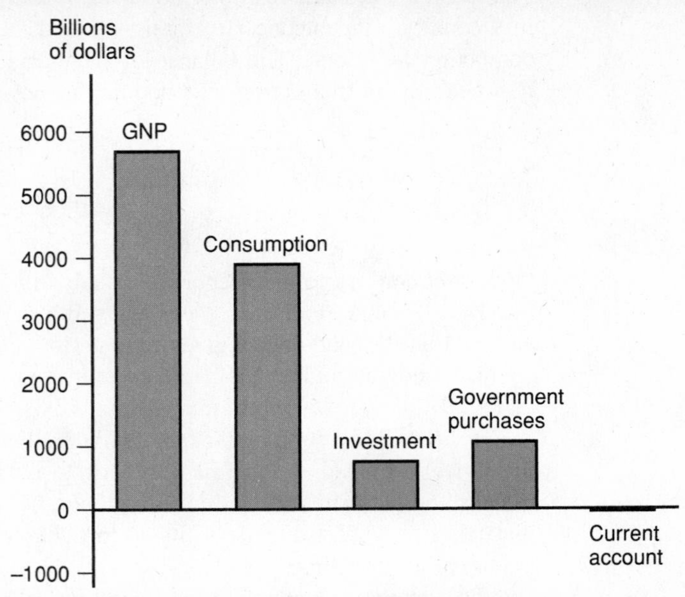

The reason for this equality is that every dollar used to purchase goods or services automatically ends up in somebody's pocket. A visit to the doctor provides a simple example of how an increase in national output raises national income by the same amount. The $75 you pay the doctor represents the market value of the services he or she provides for you, so your visit raises GNP by $75. But the $75 you pay the doctor also raises his or her income. So national income rises by $75.

The principle that output and income are the same also applies to goods, even goods that are produced with the help of many factors of production. Consider the example of an economics textbook. When you purchase a new book from the publisher, the value of your purchase enters GNP. But your payment enters the income of the productive factors that have cooperated in producing the book, because the publisher must pay for their services with the proceeds of sales. First, there are the authors, editors, artists, and typesetters who provide the labor inputs necessary for the book's production. Second, there are the publishing company's shareholders, who receive dividends for having financed acquisition of the capital used in production. Finally, there are the suppliers of paper and ink, who provide the intermediate materials used in producing the book.

The paper and ink purchased by the publishing house to produce the book are *not* counted separately in GNP because their contribution to the value of national output is already included in the book's price. It is to avoid such double counting that we allow only the sale of *final* goods and services to enter into the definition of GNP: sales of intermediate goods, such as paper and ink purchased by a publisher, are not counted. Notice also that the sale of a used textbook does not enter GNP. Our definition counts only final goods and services that are *produced,* and a used textbook does not qualify: it was counted in GNP at the time it was first sold. Equivalently, the sale of a used textbook does not generate income for any factor of production.

CAPITAL DEPRECIATION, INTERNATIONAL TRANSFERS, AND INDIRECT BUSINESS TAXES

Because we have defined GNP and national income so that they are necessarily equal, their equality is really an identity. Some adjustments to the definition of GNP must be made, however, before the identification of GNP and national income is entirely correct in practice.

1. GNP does not take into account the economic loss due to the tendency of machinery and structures to wear out as they are used. This loss, called *depreciation,* reduces the income of capital owners. To calculate national income over a given period, we must therefore subtract from GNP the depreciation of capital over the period. GNP less depreciation is called *net national product (NNP).*
2. A country's income may include gifts from residents of foreign countries, called *unilateral transfers.* Examples of unilateral transfers are pension payments to retired citizens living abroad, reparation payments, and foreign aid such as relief funds donated to drought-stricken nations. For the United States in 1991, the balance of such payments amounted to around $8 billion, representing a 0.14 percent of GNP net transfer from foreigners. Net unilateral transfers are part of a country's income but are not part of its product, and they must be added to NNP in calculations of national income.
3. National income depends on the prices producers *receive* for their goods, GNP on the prices purchasers *pay.* These two sets of prices need not, however, be identical. For example, sales taxes make buyers pay more than sellers receive, leading GNP to overestimate national income. The amount of this tax wedge, called *indirect business taxes,* must therefore be subtracted from GNP in calculating true national income.

National income equals GNP *less* depreciation, *plus* net unilateral transfers, *less* indirect business taxes. The difference between GNP and national income is by no means an insignificant amount, but macroeconomics has little to say about it, and it is of little importance for macroeconomic analysis. Therefore, for the purposes of this text we usually use the terms *GNP* and *national income* interchangeably, emphasizing the distinction between the two only when it is essential.

GROSS DOMESTIC PRODUCT

Most countries other than the United States have long reported **gross domestic product (GDP)** rather than GNP as their primary measure of national economic activity. In 1991, the United States began to follow this practice as well. GDP is supposed to measure the volume of production within a country's borders. GNP equals GDP *plus* net receipts of factor income from the rest of the world. These net receipts are the income domestic residents earn on wealth they hold in other countries less the payments domestic residents make to foreign owners of wealth located at home.

GDP does not correct, as GNP does, for the portion of countries' production carried out using services provided by foreign-owned capital. Consider an example. The earnings of a Spanish factory with British owners are counted in Spain's GDP but are part of Britain's GNP. The services British capital provides in Spain are a service export from Britain, therefore they are added to British GDP in calculating British GNP. At the same time, to figure Spain's GNP we must subtract from its GDP the corresponding service import from Britain.

As a practical matter, movements in GDP and GNP usually do not differ greatly. We will focus on GNP in this book, however, because GNP tracks national income more closely than GDP and national welfare depends more directly on national income than on domestic product.

National Income Accounting in a Closed Economy

Before discussing the national income accounts for an open economy, that is, one that trades with other economies, we discuss the hypothetical case of a closed economy that does not trade with the outside world. Because a closed economy's residents cannot purchase foreign output or sell their own output to foreigners, there are only three types of expenditure that generate national income in an economy closed to international trade: consumption, investment, and government purchases. Put another way, the fourth component of spending on an *open* economy's output, the current account, makes no contribution to national income in a *closed* economy because exports and imports both must equal zero.

While no economy is truly closed to international trade, a hypothetical closed economy is a good starting point for our discussion of national income accounting because the relations among the components of expenditure on GNP are simpler there than in an open economy. In addition, a preliminary exploration of the closed-economy case will serve to highlight the central role of trade in the macroeconomics of open economies.

CONSUMPTION

The portion of GNP purchased by the private sector to fulfill current wants is called **consumption.** Purchases of movie tickets, food, dental work, and washing machines all fall into this category. Consumption expenditure is the largest component of GNP in most economies. In the United States, for example, the fraction of GNP devoted to consumption has fluctuated in a range of about 62 to 66 percent since the Korean War.

INVESTMENT

The part of output used by private firms to produce future output is called **investment.** Investment spending may be viewed as the portion of GNP used to increase the nation's stock of capital. Steel and bricks used to build a factory are part of investment spending, as are services provided by a technician who helps build business computers. Firms' purchases of inventories are also counted in investment spending because carrying inventories is just another way for firms to transfer output from current use to future use. Investment is usually more variable than consumption. In the United States, (gross) investment has fluctuated between 12 and 19 percent of GNP in recent years. While we often use the word *investment* to describe individual households' purchases of stocks, bonds, or real estate, you should be careful not to confuse this everyday meaning of the word with the economic definition of investment as a component of GNP. When you buy a share of Genentech stock, you are buying neither a good nor a service, so your purchase does not show up in GNP.

The criteria used by national income accountants to distinguish investment from consumption sometimes may seem arbitrary. This is because they adopt the convention that investment activity can be carried out only by firms. An individual's purchase of a book from its publisher is considered consumption, but when a bookstore buys the same book the transaction is counted in inventory investment.

A related practice in national income accounting is the treatment as consumption of household spending on consumer durables, goods that are not consumed at once (as are milk and fresh fruit) but are used continuously over many years. The purchase of a washing machine, which yields services over a long period, seems like a form of investment, but, according to the definitions used to construct GNP accounts, it is not. Because of its importance to the economy, one type of consumer-durable spending, spending on newly built private homes, is counted in investment. For the sake of consistency, GNP accounts treat a homeowner as a firm selling housing services to herself. Correspondingly, estimated rental payments reflecting the value of these housing services are included in GNP as part of consumption.

Finally, if we think of investment as any spending aimed at raising future productivity, research or educational expenditures might logically be classified as investment. National income accountants do not follow this reasoning in measuring investment.

GOVERNMENT PURCHASES

Any goods and services purchased by federal, state, or local governments are classified as **government purchases** in the national income accounts. Included in government purchases are federal military spending, government support of cancer research, and government funds spent on highway repair and education. Government transfer payments are certainly a part of the government's total expenditure, but transfer payments do not require the recipient to give the government any goods or services in return. Thus, transfer payments like social security, unemployment, and welfare benefits are not included in government purchases.

Government purchases currently take up about 20 percent of U.S. GNP, and this share has not risen much since the late 1950s. (The corresponding figure for 1959, for example, was also around 20 percent.) In 1929, however, government purchases accounted for only 8.5 percent of U.S. GNP.

The National Income Identity for a Closed Economy

For a closed economy, the division of GNP into consumption, investment, and government purchases is exhaustive. Any final good or service that is not purchased by households or the government must be used by firms to produce new plant, equipment, and inventories. What happens to consumption goods that cannot be sold immediately to consumers or the government? Firms (perhaps reluctantly) add such goods to their existing inventories, thus increasing investment.

Our reasoning leads to a fundamental identity for closed economies. Let Y stand for GNP, C for consumption, I for investment, and G for government purchases. Since all of a closed economy's output must be consumed, invested, or bought by the government, we can write

$$Y = C + I + G.$$

The relationship above is an identity because C, I, and G are defined to ensure that it always holds.[2] You should be careful not to confuse identities, which hold by definition, with equilibrium conditions, which describe the equality of market supply and demand. Equilibrium conditions hold true only when price and quantity are at their equilibrium levels.

AN IMAGINARY CLOSED ECONOMY

Table 13-1 shows the national income accounts for an imaginary closed economy, Agraria, whose only output is wheat. Each citizen of Agraria is a consumer of wheat, but each is also a farmer and therefore can be viewed as a firm. Farmers invest by putting aside a portion of each year's crop as seed for the following year's planting. There is also a government that appropriates part of the crop to feed the Agrarian army. Of Agraria's total annual crop of 100 bushels of wheat, 65 bushels are consumed by civilians in the current year, 25 are stored away to be used in the future as seed, and 10 go to feed the army in the current year.

IMPLICATIONS FOR NATIONAL SAVING

Simple as it is, the GNP identity has many illuminating implications. To explain the most important of these implications, we define the concept of **national saving,** that is, the portion of output, Y, that is not devoted to household consumption, C, or government purchases, G.[3] *In a closed economy, national saving always equals investment.* This tells us that the economy as a whole can increase its wealth only by accumulating new capital.

Let S stand for national saving. Our definition of S tells us that

$$S = Y - C - G.$$

Since the GNP identity, $Y = C + I + G$, may also be written as $I = Y - C - G$, then

$$S = I,$$

and national saving must equal investment in a closed economy.

If you return to Table 13-1, you will see that saving and investment are indeed equal in the imaginary economy of Agraria. Current use of wheat by the private sector and government is $65 + 10 = 75$ bushels. The 25 bushels invested by farmers are the same 25 bushels the economy saves.

The finding that saving equals investment may be surprising because households can save but, according to the rules of GNP accounting, cannot invest (except in owner-occupied housing). The key to understanding why saving must equal investment is that S is the sum of *all* the saving decisions of every household, firm, and government

[2] If Y is thought of as NNP rather than GNP, the identity holds if investment is defined as *net investment,* that is, investment less depreciation.

[3] The U.S. national income accounts assume that government purchases are not used to enlarge the nation's capital stock. We follow this convention here by subtracting *all* government purchases from output to calculate national saving. Most other countries' national accounts distinguish between government consumption and government investment (for example, investment by publicly owned enterprises) and include the latter as part of national saving. Often, however, government investment figures include purchases of military equipment.

TABLE 13-1 National income accounts for Agraria, a closed economy (bushels of wheat)

GNP (total output)	=	*consumption*	+	*investment*	+	*government purchases*
100	=	65	+	25	+	10

agency in the economy. Suppose a household lowers its consumption by $100 to buy a bond from the U.S. government. The government then uses the $100 to buy white paint to touch up the columns of the White House. In this case, neither investment nor *national* saving is affected: the $100 increase in household saving is exactly offset by an additional $100 government purchase (a $100 decrease in *government* saving). Suppose, however, that the same household uses its savings to purchase a newly issued $100 corporate bond from IBM, and that IBM in turn uses the money to buy bricks for a new office building. Then national saving and investment both rise by $100. The $100 in resources that the household makes available to IBM is used by the firm to increase the stock of plant and equipment that can be used to produce output in the future.

What happens to national saving, S, when a household saves by buying a piece of land in the country? Doesn't national saving rise without any corresponding increase in investment? The answer to this question is ''not necessarily'': when one household raises its saving to acquire land, the household that sells the land may be lowering its saving, by an equal amount, through the action of selling some of its wealth so that it can consume more. Overall saving, S, would not change in this case. In a closed economy, saving can take place *in the aggregate* only through enlarging the stock of capital.

National Income Accounting for an Open Economy

In this section we extend the national income accounting framework to open economies. In an open economy, the national income identity must be modified because some domestic output is exported to foreigners while some domestic income is spent on imported foreign products.

The main lesson of this section concerns the relation among national saving, investment, and trade imbalances. We will see that in open economies, saving and investment are not necessarily equal as they are in a closed economy. This is because countries can save by exporting more than they import, and they can dissave—that is, reduce their wealth—by exporting less than they import.

THE NATIONAL INCOME IDENTITY FOR AN OPEN ECONOMY

We derived the national income identity for a closed economy by assuming that all output was consumed or invested by the country's citizens or purchased by its government. When foreign trade is possible, however, some output is purchased by foreigners while some domestic spending goes to purchase goods and services produced abroad. The GNP identity for open economies shows how the national income a country earns by selling its goods and services is divided between sales to domestic residents and sales to foreign residents.

Since residents of an open economy may spend some of their income on imports, that is, goods and services purchased from abroad, only the portion of their spending that is not devoted to imports is part of domestic GNP. The value of imports, denoted by *IM,* must be substracted from total domestic spending, $C + I + G$, to find the portion of domestic spending that generates domestic national income. Imports from abroad add to foreign countries' GNPs but do not add directly to domestic GNP.

Similarly, the goods and services sold to foreigners make up a country's exports. Exports, denoted by *EX,* are the amount foreign residents' purchases add to the national income of the domestic economy.

The national income of an open economy is therefore the sum of domestic and foreign expenditure on the goods and services produced by domestic factors of production. Thus, the national income identity for an open economy is

$$Y = C + I + G + EX - IM. \quad \textbf{(13-1)}$$

To make this identity concrete, let's suppose that the imaginary country Agraria can import milk from the rest of the world in exchange for exports of wheat. We cannot draw up the Agrarian national income accounts without knowing the price of milk in terms of wheat because all the components in the GNP identity (13-1) must be measured in the same units. If we assume the price of milk is 0.5 bushel of wheat per gallon, and that at this price Agrarians want to consume 40 gallons of milk, then Agraria's imports are equal in value to 20 bushels of wheat.

In Table 13-2, we see that, as before, Agraria's total output is 100 bushels of wheat. Consumption is now divided between wheat and milk, however, with 55 bushels of wheat and 40 gallons of milk (equal in value to 20 bushels of wheat) consumed over the year. The value of consumption in terms of wheat is $55 + (0.5 \times 40) = 55 + 20 = 75$.

The 100 bushels of wheat produced by Agraria are used as follows: 55 are consumed by domestic residents, 25 are invested, 10 are purchased by the government, and 10 are exported abroad. National income ($Y = 100$) equals domestic spending ($C + I + G = 110$) plus exports ($EX = 10$) less imports ($IM = 20$).

TABLE 13-2 National income accounts for Agraria, an open economy (bushels of wheat)

GNP (total output)	=	*consumption*	+	*investment*	+	*government purchases*	+	*exports*	−	*imports*
100	=	75[a]	+	25	+	10	+	10	−	20[b]

[a] 55 bushels of wheat plus (0.5 bushel per gallon) × (40 gallons of milk).
[b] 0.5 bushel per gallon × 40 gallons of milk.

THE CURRENT ACCOUNT AND FOREIGN INDEBTEDNESS

In reality a country's foreign trade is exactly balanced only rarely. The difference between exports of goods and services and imports of goods and services is known as the **current account balance** (or current account). If we denote the current account by *CA,* we can express this definition in symbols as

$$CA = EX - IM.$$

When a country's imports exceed its exports, we say the country has a *current account deficit.* A country has a *current account surplus* when its exports exceed its imports.[4]

The GNP identity, equation (13-1), shows one reason why the current account is important in international macroeconomics. Since the right-hand side of (13-1) is total expenditure on domestic output, changes in the current account can be associated with changes in output and, thus, employment.

The current account is also important because it measures the size and direction of international borrowing. When a country imports more than it exports, it is buying more from foreigners than it sells to them and must somehow finance this current account deficit. How does it pay for additional imports once it has spent its export earnings? Since the country as a whole can import more than it exports only if it can borrow the difference from foreigners, a country with a current account deficit must be increasing its net foreign debts by the amount of the deficit.[5]

Similarly, a country with a current account surplus is earning more from its exports that it spends on imports. This country finances the current account deficit of its trading partners by lending to them. The foreign wealth of a surplus country rises because foreigners pay for any imports not covered by their exports by issuing IOUs that they will eventually have to redeem. The preceding reasoning shows that *a country's current account balance equals the change in its net foreign wealth.*

We have defined the current account as the difference between exports and imports. Equation (13-1) says that the current account is also equal to the difference between national income Y and domestic residents' spending $C + I + G$:

$$Y - (C + I + G) = CA.$$

It is only by borrowing abroad that a country can have a current account deficit and use more output than it is currently producing. If it uses less than its output, it has a current account surplus and is lending the surplus to foreigners.[6] International borrowing and lending were identified with *intertemporal trade* in Chapter 7. A country with a current account deficit is importing present consumption and exporting future consumption. A country with a current account surplus is exporting present consumption and importing future consumption.

[4] In addition to net exports of goods and services, the current account balance includes net unilateral transfers, which we discussed briefly above. Following our earlier assumption, we continue to ignore transfers for now to simplify the discussion. We will see how transfers enter the current account later in this chapter when we analyze the U.S. balance of payments in detail.

[5] Alternatively, a country could finance a current account deficit by using previously accumulated foreign wealth to pay for imports. This country would be running down its net foreign wealth, which is the same as running up its net foreign debts.

[6] The sum $C + I + G$ is often called domestic *absorption* in the literature on international macroeconomics. Using this terminology, we can describe the current account surplus as the difference between income and absorption.

As an example, consider again the imaginary economy of Agraria described in Table 13-2. The total value of its consumption, investment, and government purchases, at 110 bushels of wheat, is greater than its output of 100 bushels. This inequality would be impossible in a closed economy; it *is* possible in this open economy because Agraria now imports 40 gallons of milk, worth 20 bushels of wheat, but exports only 10 bushels of wheat. The current account deficit of 10 bushels is the value of Agraria's borrowing from foreigners, which the country will have to repay in the future.

Figure 13-2 gives a vivid illustration of how a string of current account deficits can add up to a large foreign debt. The figure plots the United States' current account balance since the late 1970s along with a measure of the nation's stock of net foreign wealth. As you can see, the United States had accumulated substantial foreign wealth by the early 1980s, when a sustained current account deficit of proportions unprecedented in the twentieth century opened up. In 1987 the country became a net debtor to foreigners for the first time since World War I.

As the Case Study on p. 325 shows, it is surprisingly hard to measure accurately by the early 1980s, when a sustained current account deficit on proportions unprece-Figure 13-2 and disagree over when the United States became a debtor country and how large its foreign debt really is. But there is no question that a large decrease in U.S. foreign assets did occur over the 1980s.

SAVING AND THE CURRENT ACCOUNT

In a closed economy, saving and investment must always be equal. In an open economy, however, saving and investment can differ. Remembering that national saving, S, equals $Y - C - G$ and that $CA = EX - IM$, we can rewrite the GNP identity (13-1) as

$$S = I + CA.$$

The equation highlights an important difference between open and closed economies: *An open economy can save either by building up its capital stock or by acquiring foreign wealth, but a closed economy can save only by building up its capital stock.*

Unlike a closed economy, an open economy with profitable investment opportunities does not have to increase its saving in order to exploit them. The preceding expression shows that it is possible simultaneously to raise investment and foreign borrowing without changing saving. For example, if New Zealand decides to build a new hydroelectric plant, it can import the materials it needs from the United States and borrow American funds to pay for them. This transaction raises New Zealand's domestic investment because the imported materials contribute to expanding the country's capital stock. The transaction also raises New Zealand's current account deficit by an amount equal to the increase in investment. New Zealand's saving does not have to change, even though investment rises. For this to be possible, however, U.S. residents must be willing to save more so that the resources needed to build the plant are freed for New Zealand's use. The result is another example of intertemporal trade, in which New Zealand imports present consumption (when it borrows from the United States) and exports future consumption (when it pays off the loan).

Because one country's savings can be borrowed by a second country to increase the second country's stock of capital, a country's current account surplus is often referred to as its *net foreign investment.* Of course, when one country lends to another to finance investment, part of the income generated by the investment in future years

FIGURE 13-2
The U.S. current account and net foreign wealth position, 1977–1991.
A string of current account deficits in the 1980s reduced America's net foreign wealth until, by the decade's end, the country had accumulated a substantial net foreign debt.
Source: U.S. Department of Commerce, *Survey of Current Business,* June 1992, p. 49.

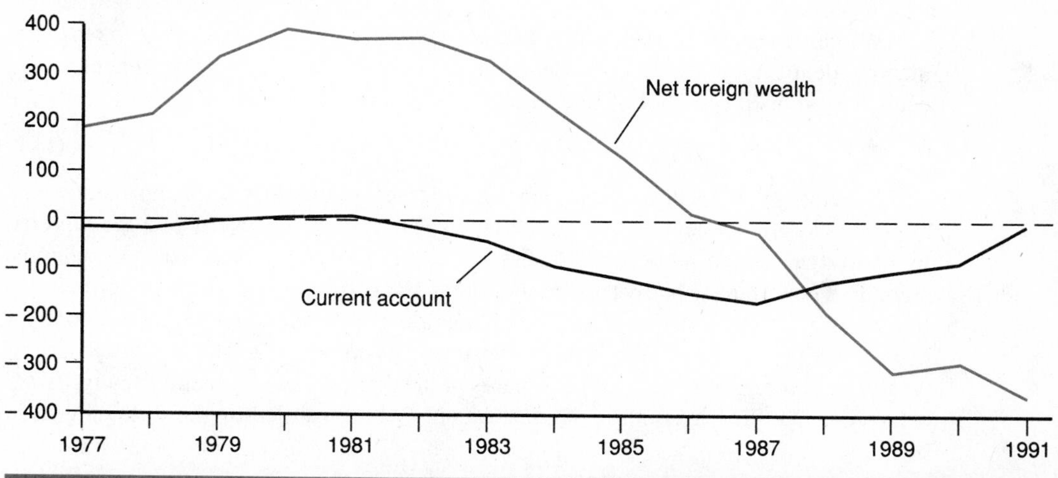

must be used to pay back the lender. Domestic investment and foreign investment are two different ways in which a country can use current savings to increase its future income.

PRIVATE AND GOVERNMENT SAVING

So far, our discussion of saving has not stressed the distinction between saving decisions made by the private sector and saving decisions made by the government. Unlike private saving decisions, however, government saving decisions are often made with an eye toward their effect on output and employment. The national income identity can help us to analyze the channels through which government saving decisions influence macroeconomic conditions. To use the national income identity in this way, we first have to divide national saving into its private and government components.

Private saving is defined as the part of disposable income that is saved rather than consumed. Disposable income is national income, Y, less the net taxes collected from households and firms by the government, T.[7] Private saving, denoted S^p, can therefore be expressed as

$$S^p = Y - T - C.$$

[7] Net taxes are taxes less government transfer payments. The term *government* refers to the federal, state, and local governments considered as a single unit.

Government saving is defined similarly to private saving. The government's "income" is its net tax revenue, T, while its "consumption" is government purchases, G. If we let S^g stand for government saving, then

$$S^g = T - G.$$

The two types of saving we have defined, private and government, add up to national saving. To see why, recall the definition of national saving, S, as $Y - C - G$. Then

$$S = Y - C - G = (Y - T - C) + (T - G) = S^p + S^g.$$

We can use the definitions of private and government saving to rewrite the national income identity in a form that is useful for analyzing the effects of government saving decisions on open economies. Because $S = S^p + S^g = I + CA$,

$$S^p = I + CA - S^g = I + CA - (T - G) = I + CA + (G - T). \qquad \textbf{(13-2)}$$

Equation (13-2) relates private saving to domestic investment, the current account surplus, and government saving. To interpret equation (13-2), we define the **government budget deficit** as $G - T$, that is, as government saving preceded by a minus sign. The government budget deficit measures the extent to which the government is borrowing to finance its expenditures. Equation (13-2) then states that a country's private saving can take three forms: investment in domestic capital (I), purchases of wealth from foreigners (CA), and purchases of the domestic government's newly-issued debt ($G - T$).[8] The usefulness of equation (13-2) is illustrated by the following Case Study.

Case Study

DO GOVERNMENT BUDGET DEFICITS WORSEN THE CURRENT ACCOUNT?

Unusually large imbalances in the current accounts of the United States and Japan developed in the 1980s, with America's current account moving to a record deficit and Japan's to a record surplus. The huge U.S. current account deficit led many Americans to favor protection for industries whose sales were hurt by a flood of foreign imports. Because much of Japan's export surplus went to the United States, Japan became a leading target for many of the proposed measures. Also fueling U.S. resentment of the Japanese current account surplus were Japan's very visible acquisitions in the United States, for example the purchase of property in New York's Rockefeller Center late in 1989.

Some international policy makers blamed the current account imbalances on growing government budget deficits in the United States and shrinking government deficits in Japan. The administration of President Ronald Reagan, which had engineered the

[8] In a closed economy the current account is always zero, so equation (13-2) is simply $S^p = I + (G - T)$.

American government deficits by cutting taxes and increasing government purchases, tried at first to deflect blame for the worsening of the U.S. current account. Administration officials pointed to buoyant domestic investment as the cause, citing investment incentives that had accompanied the tax-cut legislation.

Identity (13-2), which can be written as

$$CA = S^p - I - (G - T),$$

provides a framework for analyzing the current accounts of the United States and Japan in the 1980s. Because private saving, investment, the current account, and the government deficit are jointly determined variables, we cannot fully determine the cause of a current account change by using the identity above alone. Nonetheless, the identity can give us some useful clues.

The table below presents data on the four variables linked by identity (13-2) for the United States. (The variables are expressed as percentages of GNP so that their values in different years can be compared more easily; they don't add up exactly as required by (13-2) because of errors in data collection.) We examine gross saving and investment rates, rather than net, because the depreciation data used to calculate the net flows are very unreliable.

United States (percentage of GNP)

Year	CA	S^p	I	G − T
1981	0.2	19.1	18.2	1.0
1982	−0.4	19.4	15.8	3.4
1983	−1.2	18.7	15.9	4.1
1984	−2.6	19.5	18.9	2.9
1985	−3.0	18.2	17.6	3.1
1986	−3.4	16.9	16.8	3.4
1987	−3.6	16.1	16.5	2.5
1988	−2.6	16.4	16.2	2.0
1989	−1.9	15.8	16.0	1.5
1990	−1.6	15.4	14.5	2.5
1991	−0.1	15.6	12.8	3.0

Source: *Economic Report of the President, 1992,* and U.S. Department of Commerce, *Survey of Current Business,* June 1992.

Identity (13-2) tells us that, other things equal, a rise in private saving must increase the current account surplus; a rise in investment or the government budget deficit must lower it. The U.S. data above show that between 1981 and 1983, the current account moved from a small surplus of 0.2 percent of GNP to a deficit of 1.2 percent of GNP as the government budget deficit rose sharply from 1 to 4.1 percent of GNP. A large fall in investment (from 18.2 to 15.8 percent of GNP) accompanied the U.S. economy's slide into a severe recession in 1981–1982.

The American economy grew quickly in 1984 and investment recovered sharply in that year, rising to 18.9 percent of GNP. Private saving rose compared with 1983, and with government tax revenues increasing automatically as the economy grew the government deficit declined from 4.1 to 2.9 percent of GNP. But the investment surge of 1984 was so large that the current account deficit (measured as a fraction of GNP) widened to 2.6 percent of GNP, a level unmatched since the nineteenth century.

The events of 1984 do not, however, prove the Reagan administration's case that high investment caused the U.S. current account deficit to widen. If we compare 1985–1986, when the recovery from recession had leveled off, with 1981, we see that the gap between private saving and investment is a bit smaller in the later years but that both of the "twin deficits" are much higher. Higher government budget deficits would have resulted in much higher current account deficits in 1982 and 1983 had investment not plummeted in the recession. This fall in investment temporarily masked the effect on the current account of the higher government deficits, but that effect was apparent by 1985, once investment had returned closer to normal levels.

Between 1987 and 1989 public-sector belt-tightening reduced the government's deficit; at the same time the current account deficit finally fell below 2 percent of GNP. As the United States slipped into a new recession in 1990, tax revenues fell and the government deficit again ballooned. Despite an accompanying fall in private saving, however, the external deficit continued to drop, with the United States reaching approximate current account balance in 1991. The reason: a dizzying fall in investment to a level not seen even during the 1981–1982 recession.

Let's look next at comparable figures for Japan so that we can analyze its current account surplus:

Japan (percentage of GNP)

Year	CA	S^p	I	G − T
1981	0.4	34.9	30.7	3.8
1982	0.6	33.7	29.5	3.6
1983	1.8	33.3	28.0	3.6
1984	2.8	32.5	27.7	2.1
1985	3.6	31.8	27.4	0.8
1986	4.3	32.4	27.2	0.9
1987	3.6	31.4	28.3	−0.5
1988	2.7	31.0	29.7	−1.5
1989	2.0	30.2	30.7	−2.5
1990	1.2	30.6	32.3	−2.9

Source: Current account and general government deficit ratios from International Monetary Fund, *World Economic Outlook,* May 1992. Investment ratio calculated from GNP and investment data reported in OECD Economic Survey of Japan, 1990–1991. Private saving ratio calculated as a residual.

Japan's current account surplus swelled after 1981 despite a declining private saving rate. (Japan's gross private saving rate remained, however, nearly twice that of the United States!) The growing current account surplus reflected both a declining investment rate and a shrinking government budget deficit. Unlike the U.S. national income accounts, the Japanese accounts classify investment spending by the government as part of *I* rather than of *G*. Part of the fall in investment after 1981 resulted from the Japanese government's attempt to reduce its borrowing by cutting the growth of its investment spending.

Only after 1986 did Japan's current account surplus appear to decline as a share of GNP, a steadily rising government surplus notwithstanding. Accompanying this change were a fall in private saving and a substantial rise in investment, part of which was due to higher public investment.

As in the U.S. case, we see that changes in the Japanese government budget deficit have been an important factor behind the country's current account performance. The data confirm a tendency for increases in the government budget deficit to lower the current account surplus while decreases in the government budget deficit raise it. But the data also show that this relationship is not a simple one.

The Balance of Payments Accounts

In the previous section, we examined the components of the national income accounts: consumption, investment, government purchases, and the current account (the measure of a country's net foreign investment or, equivalently, of the difference between its exports and imports). In addition to national income accounts, government economists and statisticians also keep balance of payments accounts, a detailed record of the composition of the current account balance and of the many transactions that finance it. Balance of payments figures are of great interest to the general public, as indicated by the attention that various news media pay to them. But press reports sometimes confuse different measures of international payments flows. Should we be alarmed or cheered by a *Wall Street Journal* headline proclaiming "U.S. Chalks Up Record Balance of Payments Deficit"? A thorough understanding of balance of payments accounting will help us evaluate the implications of a country's international transactions.

A country's balance of payments accounts keep track of both its payments to and its receipts from foreigners. Any transaction resulting in a payment to foreigners is entered in the balance of payments accounts as a *debit* and is given a negative ($-$) sign. Any transaction resulting in a receipt from foreigners is entered as a *credit* and is given a positive ($+$) sign.

Two types of international transaction are recorded in the balance of payments:

1. Transactions that involve the export or import of goods or services and therefore enter directly into the current account. When a French consumer imports American blue jeans, for example, the transaction enters the U.S. balance of payments accounts as a credit on current account.

2. Transactions that involve the purchase or sale of assets. An **asset** is any one of the forms in which wealth can be held, such as money, stocks, factories, government debt, land, or rare postage stamps. The **capital account** of the balance of payments records all international purchases or sales of assets. When an American buys a French château, the transaction enters the U.S. balance of payments as a debit on capital account. It may seem strange to give a negative sign to a purchase of assets and a

positive sign to a sale of assets. It will seem less so if you think in terms of the U.S. "importing" (purchasing) assets and the U.S. "exporting" (selling) assets and give the transaction the same sign you would give to an import (−) or export (+) transaction recorded in the current account. The difference between a country's exports and imports of assets is called its capital account balance, or capital account for short.

You will find the complexities of the balance of payments accounts less confusing if you keep in mind the following simple rule of double-entry bookkeeping: *Every international transaction automatically enters the balance of payments twice, once as a credit and once as a debit.* This principle of balance of payments accounting holds true because every transaction has two sides: if you buy something from a foreigner you must pay him in some way, and the foreigner must then somehow spend or store your payment. An example will clarify how the principle operates in practice.

Imagine that you buy a typewriter from the Italian firm Olivetti and pay for your purchase with a $1000 check. Since your purchase represents a payment to a foreigner, it enters the current account of the U.S. balance of payments as a $1000 debit. On the other side of the transaction, Olivetti now has your check and must do something with it. If it deposits the check in an American bank, Olivetti has purchased a U.S. asset—a bank deposit worth $1000—and the transaction shows up as a $1000 credit in the U.S. balance of payments capital account. But suppose Olivetti deposits the check at its Italian bank. Now the Italian bank must do something with the check, and any action it takes will ultimately result in a credit item in the U.S. balance of payments. If, for example, the Italian bank lends the $1000 to an Italian firm that uses it to import personal computers from the United States, $1000 must be credited to the U.S. current account. We can never be sure where the flip side of a given transaction will show up, but we can be sure that it will show up somewhere.

Because any international transaction automatically gives rise to two offsetting entries in the balance of payments, the current account balance and the capital account balance automatically add up to zero:

$$\text{Current account} + \text{capital account} = 0. \qquad \textbf{(13-3)}$$

This identity can also be understood by recalling the relation linking the current account to international lending and borrowing. Because the current account is the change in a country's net foreign assets, the current account necessarily equals the difference between a country's purchases of assets from foreigners and its sales of assets to them, that is, the capital account balance preceded by a minus sign.

We now turn to a more detailed description of the balance of payments accounts, using as an example the U.S. accounts for 1991. Table 13-3 reproduces the record of America's international transactions in that year.

THE CURRENT ACCOUNT, ONCE AGAIN

As you have learned, the current account balance measures a country's net exports of goods and services. Table 13-3 shows that U.S. exports were $704.9 billion in 1991 while U.S. imports were $716.6 billion. Because imports give rise to payments to foreigners, they enter the accounts with a negative sign, as shown.

The balance of payments accounts divide exports and imports into three finer categories. The first is *merchandise* trade, that is, exports or imports of goods. The

TABLE 13-3 U.S. balance of payments accounts for 1991 (billions of dollars)

	Credits	*Debits*
Current account		
(1) Exports	+704.9	
Of which:		
Merchandise	+416.0	
Investment income received	+125.3	
Other services	+163.6	
(2) Imports		−716.6
Of which:		
Merchandise		−489.4
Investment income paid		−108.9
Other services		−118.3
(3) Net unilateral transfers	+8.0	
Balance on current account [(1) + (2) + (3)]		−3.7
Capital account		
(4) U.S. assets held abroad (increase −)		−62.2
Of which:		
Official reserve assets	+5.8	
Other assets		−68.0
(5) Foreign assets held in U.S. (increase +)	+67.0	
Of which:		
Official reserve assets	+18.4	
Other assets	+48.6	
Balance on capital account [(4) + (5)]	+4.8	
Statistical discrepancy [sum of (1) through (5) with sign reversed]		−1.1

Source: U.S. Department of Commerce, *Survey of Current Business,* June 1992, p. 79.

second category, *investment income,* is made up of international interest and dividend payments and the repatriated earnings of domestically owned firms operating abroad. If you own a share of a German firm's stock and receive a dividend payment of $5, that payment shows up in the accounts as a U.S. investment income receipt of $5. The final category, *other services,* includes items such as payments for legal assistance, tourists' expenditures, and shipping fees.

We include income on foreign investments in the current account because that income is compensation for the *services* provided by foreign investments. This idea, as we saw earlier, is behind the distinction between GNP and GDP. When a U.S. corporation builds a plant in Canada, for instance, the productive services the plant generates are viewed as a service export from the United States to Canada equal in value to the profits the plant yields for its American owner. To be consistent, we must be sure to include these profits in American GNP and not in Canadian GNP. Remember, the definition of GNP refers to goods and services generated by a country's factors of production, but it does *not* specify that those factors must work within the borders of the country that owns them.

Before calculating the current account, we must include one additional type of international transaction that we have largely ignored until now. In discussing the relation between GNP and national income, we defined unilateral transfers between countries as international gifts, that is, payments that do not correspond to the purchase of any good, service, or asset. Net unilateral transfers are considered part of the current account as well as part of national income, and the identity $Y = C + I + G + CA$ holds exactly if Y is interpreted as GNP *plus* net transfers. In 1991, the U.S. balance of unilateral transfers was \$8.0 billion.[9]

The table shows a 1991 current account balance of \$704.9 billion − \$716.6 billion + \$8.0 billion = −\$3.7 billion, a deficit. The negative sign means that current payments exceeded current receipts and that U.S. residents used more output than they produced. Since these current account transactions were paid for in some way, we know that this negative \$3.7 billion entry must be offset by a positive \$3.7 billion entry in the other part of the balance of payments, the capital account.

THE CAPITAL ACCOUNT

Just as the current account is the difference between sales of goods and services to foreigners and purchases of goods and services from them, the capital account measures the difference between sales of assets to foreigners and purchases of assets located abroad. When the United States borrows \$1 from foreigners, it is selling them an asset—a promise that they will be repaid \$1, with interest, in the future. Such a transaction enters the capital account with a positive sign because the loan is itself a payment to the United States, or a **capital inflow.** When the United States lends abroad, however, a payment is made to foreigners and the capital account is debited. This transaction involves the purchase of an asset from foreigners and is called a **capital outflow.**

To cover its 1991 current account deficit of \$3.7 billion, the United States required a net capital inflow of \$3.7 billion. In other words, its net borrowing or sales of assets to foreigners should have amounted to \$3.7 billion. We can look again at Table 13-3 to see exactly how this net capital inflow came about.

The table records separately increases in U.S. holdings of assets located abroad (which are capital outflows and enter with a negative sign) and increases in foreign holdings of assets located in the United States (which are capital inflows and enter with a positive sign).

According to Table 13-3, U.S. assets held abroad increased by \$62.2 billion in 1991, contributing a −\$62.2 billion entry to the U.S. balance of payments. Foreign assets held in the United States rose by \$67.0 billion in the year, and these purchases are shown with a positive sign. We calculate the balance on capital account as \$67.0 billion − \$62.2 billion = \$4.8 billion, a surplus.

[9] This item also includes workers' remittances—wages workers earn abroad and send home to their dependents. These remittances could be classified more appropriately as a payment made to the home country for the export of labor services, and therefore as part of GNP; in practice, however, they are not.

THE STATISTICAL DISCREPANCY

We come out with a capital account surplus of \$4.8 billion rather than the smaller \$3.7 billion capital account surplus we expected. If every balance of payments credit automatically generates an equal counterpart debit, and vice versa, how is this difference possible? The reason is that information about the offsetting debit and credit items associated with a given transaction may be collected from different sources. For example, the import debit that a shipment of VCRs from Japan generates may come from a U.S. customs inspector's report and the corresponding capital account credit from a report by the U.S. bank in which the check paying for the VCRs is deposited. Because data from different sources may differ in coverage, accuracy, and timing, the balance of payments accounts seldom balance in practice as they must in theory. Account keepers force the two sides to balance by adding to the accounts a statistical discrepancy. For 1991, unrecorded (or misrecorded) international transactions generated a balancing debit of −\$1.1 billion.

We have no way of knowing exactly how to allocate this discrepancy between the current and capital accounts. (If we did, it wouldn't be a discrepancy!) The capital account is the most likely culprit, since it is notoriously difficult to keep track of the complicated financial trades between residents of different countries. But we cannot conclude that net capital outflows were \$1.1 billion higher than recorded, because the current account is also suspect. Balance of payments accountants consider merchandise trade data relatively reliable, but data on services are not. Such service transactions as sales of financial advice and computer programming assistance may escape detection. Accurate measurement of international interest and dividend receipts is particularly difficult. (See the box on page 322.)

OFFICIAL RESERVE TRANSACTIONS

Although there are many types of capital account transaction, one type is important enough to merit separate discussion. This type of transaction involves the purchase or sale of official reserve assets by central banks.

An economy's **central bank** is the institution responsible for managing the supply of money. In the United States, the central bank is the Federal Reserve System. **Official international reserves** are foreign assets held by central banks as a cushion against national economic misfortune. At one time official reserves consisted largely of gold, but today central banks' reserves include substantial foreign financial assets, particularly U.S. dollar assets such as Treasury bills. The Federal Reserve itself holds only a small level of official reserve assets other than gold; its own holdings of dollar assets are not considered international reserves.

Central banks often buy or sell international reserves in private asset markets to affect macroeconomic conditions in their economies. Official transactions of this type are called **official foreign exchange intervention.** One reason why foreign exchange intervention can alter macroeconomic conditions is that it is a way for the central bank to inject money into the economy or withdraw it from circulation. We will have much more to say later about the causes and consequences of foreign exchange intervention.

Government agencies other than central banks may hold foreign reserves and intervene officially in exchange markes. The U.S. Treasury, for example, operates an Exchange Stabilization Fund that sometimes plays an active role in market trading. Because the operations of such agencies usually have no noticeable impact on the

The Mystery of the Missing Surplus

Because the world as a whole is a closed economy, world saving must equal world investment and world spending must equal world output. Individual countries can run current account surpluses or deficits to invest or borrow abroad. Because one country's lending is another country's borrowing, however, the sum of all these individual current account imbalances necessarily equals zero.

Or does it? National current account data show that the world as a whole is running a substantial current account *deficit* that increased shaprly in the early 1980s and has remained high. Below are figures for the sum total of all countries' current account balances since 1979.

The global discrepancies in the table are far greater in magnitude than most reported national current accounts. Since positive and negative errors cancel out in the summation leading to the global figures, discrepancies of this size raise the worrisome possibility that the national current account statistics on which policy makers base decisions are seriously inaccurate.

What explains the theoretically impossible deficit shown by total world current account numbers? Your first reaction may be to blame the problem on the statistical discrepancies that bedevil the national income and balance of payments accounts of individual countries. An additional complication is introduced by timing factors. Goods that leave one country's ports near the end of an accounting year, for example, may not reach their destination in time to be recorded in the recipient's import statistics for the same year.

A general appeal to accounting anomalies such as these does not explain, however, why the world as a whole should appear to be persistently in deficit (rather than in surplus) or why that deficit should have tripled in the early 1980s. A more plausible hypothesis links the missing surplus to one specific cause of accounting discrepancies at the national level, the systematic misreporting of international interest income flows. Interest payments earned abroad are often not reported to government authorities in the recipient's home country. In many cases such interest payments are credited directly to a foreign bank account and do not even cross

money supply, however, we will simplify our discussion by speaking (when this is not too misleading) as if the central bank alone holds foreign reserves and intervenes.

When a central bank purchases or sells a foreign asset, the transaction appears in its country's capital account just as if the same transaction had been carried out by a private citizen. A transaction in which the central bank of Germany (called the Bundesbank) acquires dollar assets might occur as follows. A U.S. auto dealer imports a Volkswagen from Germany and pays the auto company with a check for $15,000. Volkswagen does not want to invest the money in dollar assets, but it so happens that the Bundesbank is willing to give Volkswagen German money in exchange for the $15,000 check. The Bundesbank's international reserves rise by $15,000 as a result of the deal. Because the Bundesbank's dollar reserves are part of total German assets held in the United States, the latter rise by $15,000. This transaction therefore results in a positive $15,000 entry in the U.S. capital account, the other side of the −$15,000 entry in the U.S. current account due to the purchase of the car.[10]

[10] To test your understanding, see if you can explain why the same sequence of actions causes a $15,000 improvement in Germany's current account but a $15,000 worsening of its capital account.

Measured world current account balance, 1979–1991 (billions of U.S. dollars)

1979	1980	1981	1982	1983	1984	1985	1986	1987	1988	1989	1990	1991
−24.9	−38.5	−68.3	−100.2	−61.2	−73.4	−80.8	−63.7	−44.2	−67.5	−104.4	−127.8	−121.9

Source: International Monetary Fund, *World Economic Outlook,* 1986–1992, Table A30.

national borders. There is thus a consistent tendency to observe a negative global balance of international interest flows.

World interest rates rose sharply after 1980, and the size of the world interest payment discrepancy increased with them. The interest payment hypothesis therefore offers a potential explanation for the increase in the global deficit. The downturn in world interest rates after the mid-1980s provides partial confirmation of the hypothesis, since the world current account deficit did drop as interest rates fell. The large increase in the discrepancy between 1988 and 1989 is puzzling, though: interest rates in most of the main industrial countries did rise after 1987, but the rise seems too small to have more than doubled the world payments gap.

Other measurement problems are probably at work, as an International Monetary Fund (IMF) study of the current account discrepancy concluded (see Further Reading). The IMF found that while interest payments explain a good part of the discrepancy, several additional factors are involved. For example, much of the world's merchant shipping fleet is registered in countries that do not report maritime freight earnings to the IMF. These unrecorded earnings make up a significant portion of the missing world surplus.

Table 13-3 shows the size and direction of official reserve transactions involving the United States. United States official reserve assets—that is, international reserves held by the Federal Reserve—*fell* by \$5.8 billion (recall that a positive sign here means a decline in U.S. assets held abroad, that is, an "export" of assets to foreigners). Foreign central banks purchased \$18.4 billion to add to their reserves. The net increase in foreign official reserve claims on the U.S. *less* the net increase in U.S. official reserves is the *balance of official reserve transactions,* which stood at \$18.4 billion − (−\$5.8 billion) = \$24.2 billion in 1991.

You can think of this \$24.2 billion balance as measuring the degree to which monetary authorities in the U.S. and abroad joined with other lenders to cover the U.S. current account deficit. In the example above, the Bundesbank, by acquiring a \$15,000 U.S. bank deposit, indirectly finances an American import of a \$15,000 German car. The bookkeeping offset to the balance of official reserve transactions is called the **official settlements balance** or (in less formal usage) the **balance of payments.** This balance is the sum of the current account balance, the nonreserve portion of the capital account balance, and the statistical discrepancy, and it indicates the payments gap that official reserve transactions need to cover. Thus the U.S. balance of payments in 1991

TABLE 13-4 Calculating the U.S. official settlements balance for 1991 (billions of dollars)

	Credits	*Debits*
Current account		
(1) Exports	+704.9	
(2) Imports		−716.6
(3) Net unilateral transfers	+8.0	
(4) Balance on current account [(1) + (2) + (3)]		−3.7
Nonreserve capital account		
(5) U.S. assets held abroad (excluding U.S. official reserves) (increase −)		−68.0
(6) Foreign assets held in U.S. (excluding foreign official reserves) (increase +)	+48.6	
(7) Balance on nonreserve capital account [(5) + (6)]		−19.4
(8) Statistical discrepancy		−1.1
(9) Official settlements balance [(4) + (7) + (8)]		−24.2
Official reserve transactions		
(10) U.S. official reserve assets held abroad (increase −)	+5.8	
Of which:		
Gold	—	
Special Drawing Rights		−0.2
Reserve position in the International Monetary Fund		−0.4
Foreign currencies	+6.3	
(11) Foreign official reserve assets held in U.S. (increase +)	+18.4	
Of which:		
U.S. government securities	+17.1	
Other U.S. government liabilities	+1.6	
Liabilities reported by U.S. banks, not included elsewhere		−1.7
Other	+1.4	
(12) Balance of official reserve transactions [(10) + (11)]	+24.2	

Source: U.S. Department of Commerce, *Survey of Current Business,* June 1992, p. 79. Totals may differ from sums because of rounding.

was -24.2 billion, that is, the balance of official reserve transactions with its sign reversed.

Table 13-4 reorganizes the major categories in Table 13-3 to emphasize the role of official reserve transactions in bridging the gap between the current account deficit and the *nonreserve* portion of the capital account surplus. The balance of payments played an important historical role as a measure of disequilibrium in international payments, and for many countries it still plays this role. A negative balance of payments (a deficit) may signal a crisis, for it means that a country is running down its international reserve assets or incurring debts to foreign monetary authorities.

Like any summary measure, however, the balance of payments must be interpreted with caution. To return to our running example, the German Bundesbank's decision to expand its U.S. bank deposit holdings by $15,000 swells the measured U.S. balance of payments deficit by the same amount. Suppose the Bundesbank instead places its $15,000 with Barclays Bank in London, which in turn deposits the money with Bankers Trust in New York. Nonreserve U.S. capital inflows rise by $15,000 in this case, and the U.S. balance of payments deficit does not rise. But this ''improvement'' in the balance of payments is of little economic importance: it makes no difference to the United States whether it borrows the Bundesbank's money directly or through a London bank.

Case Study

IS THE UNITED STATES THE WORLD'S BIGGEST DEBTOR?

The Bureau of Economic Analysis (BEA) of the U.S. Department of Commerce oversees the vast data collection operation behind the U.S. national income and product accounts and balance of payments statistics. In addition, the BEA reports annual estimates of the "international investment position of the United States"—the country's net foreign wealth. These estimates showed that at the end of 1991 the United States had a *negative* net foreign wealth position far greater than that of any other single country.

We saw earlier that the current account balance measures the flow of new net claims on foreign wealth that a country acquires by exporting more goods and services than it imports. This flow is not, however, the only factor that causes a country's net foreign wealth to change. In addition, changes in the market price of wealth previously acquired can alter a country's net foreign wealth. When Japan's stock market lost more than half of its value between 1990 and 1992, for example, American and European owners of Japanese shares saw the value of their claims on Japan plummet, and Japan's net *foreign* wealth increased as a result. The BEA must adjust the value of existing claims for such capital gains and losses before arriving at its estimate of U.S. net foreign wealth.

The BEA now reports two estimates of U.S. net foreign wealth that differ in their treatment of foreign direct investments (see Chapter 7). Until 1991 foreign direct investments were valued at their historical, that is, original, purchase prices. This practice understated the value of U.S. net foreign wealth, because most foreign direct investments in the United States were acquired more recently than U.S. direct investments

TABLE 13-5 International investment position of the United States at year end, 1990 and 1991 (millions of dollars)

Line	Type of investment	Position 1990[r]	Changes in position in 1991 (decrease (−))					Position 1991[r]
			Attributable to:				Total	
			Capital flows	Valuation adjustments				
				Price changes	Exchange rate changes[1]	Other changes[2]		
			(a)	(b)	(c)	(d)	(a+b+c+d)	
	Net international investment position of the United States:							
1	**With direct investment positions at current cost (line 3 less line 24)**	**−294,836**	**−4,760**	**−58,627**	**−5,592**	**2,313**	**−66,667**	**−361,503**
2	**With direct investment positions at market value (line 4 less line 25)**	**−272,027**	**−4,760**	**−107,976**	**1,232**	**1,697**	**−109,808**	**−381,835**
	U.S. assets abroad:							
3	**With direct investment positions at current cost (lines 5+10+15)**	**1,884,199**	**62,220**	**19,796**	**−7,060**	**1,147**	**76,102**	**1,960,301**
4	**With direct investment positions at market value (lines 5+10+16)**	**1,977,053**	**62,220**	**64,674**	**−236**	**3,331**	**129,988**	**2,107,041**
5	U.S. official reserve assets	174,664	−5,763	−9,848	167	3	−15,441	159,223
6	Gold	102,406	....	[3] −9,848	....	[4] 3	−9,845	92,561
7	Special drawing rights	10,989	177	....	74	....	251	11,240
8	Reserve position in the International Monetary Fund	9,076	367	....	45	....	412	9,488
9	Foreign currencies	52,193	−6,307	....	48	....	−6,259	45,934
10	U.S. Government assets, other than official reserve assets	82,230	−3,397	....	−103	−1	−3,501	78,729
11	U.S. credits and other long-term assets[5]	81,787	−4,399	....	−32	−1	−4,432	77,355
12	Repayable in dollars	80,462	−4,284	....	....	−49	−4,333	76,129
13	Other[6]	1,325	−115	....	−32	48	−99	1,226
14	U.S. foreign currency holdings and U.S. short-term assets	443	1,002	....	−71	....	931	1,374
	U.S. private assets:							
15	With direct investment at current cost (lines 17+19+22+23)	1,627,305	71,379	29,644	−7,124	1,145	95,044	1,722,349
16	With direct investment at market value (lines 18+19+22+23)	1,720,159	71,379	74,522	−300	3,329	148,930	1,869,089
	Direct investment abroad:							
17	At current cost	623,587	27,135	9,850	−6,551	1,239	31,673	655,260
18	At market value	716,441	27,135	54,728	273	3,423	85,559	802,000
19	Foreign securities	241,748	45,017	19,794	−673	....	64,138	305,886
20	Bonds	131,715	14,861	2,892	−1,856	....	15,897	147,612
21	Corporate stocks	110,033	30,156	16,902	1,183	....	48,241	158,274
22	U.S. claims on unaffiliated foreigners reported by U.S. nonbanking concerns.	109,821	−5,526	....	100	52	−5,374	104,447
23	U.S. claims reported by U.S. banks, not included elsewhere	652,149	4,753	....	....	−146	4,607	656,756
	Foreign assets in the United States:							
24	**With direct investment at current cost (lines 26+33)**	**2,179,035**	**66,980**	**78,423**	**−1,468**	**−1,166**	**142,769**	**2,321,804**
25	**With direct investment at market value (lines 26+34)**	**2,249,080**	**66,980**	**172,650**	**−1,468**	**1,634**	**239,796**	**2,488,876**
26	Foreign official assets in the United States	371,101	18,407	7,937	....	−838	25,506	396,607
27	U.S. Government securities	296,971	17,116	4,918	....	−987	21,047	318,018
28	U.S. Treasury securities	286,702	15,815	4,358	....	−987	19,186	305,888
29	Other	10,269	1,301	560	....	....	1,861	12,130
30	Other U.S. Government liabilities[7]	17,212	1,600	....	....	....	1,600	18,812
31	U.S. liabilities reported by U.S. banks, not included elsewhere	39,880	−1,668	....	....	149	−1,519	38,361
32	Other foreign official assets	17,038	1,359	3,019	....	....	4,378	21,416
	Other foreign assets:							
33	With direct investment at current cost (lines 35+37+38+41+42)	1,807,934	48,573	70,486	−1,468	−328	117,263	1,925,197
34	With direct investment at market value (lines 36+37+38+41+42)	1,877,979	48,573	164,713	−1,468	2,472	214,290	2,092,269
	Direct investment in the United States:							
35	At current cost	466,515	11,497	9,534	....	−524	20,507	487,022
36	At market value	536,560	11,497	103,761	....	2,276	117,534	654,094
37	U.S. Treasury securities	130,716	16,241	6,635	....	1,073	23,949	154,665
38	U.S. securities other than U.S. Treasury securities	471,888	34,918	54,317	−1,468	....	87,767	559,655
39	Corporate and other bonds	240,713	25,743	12,025	−1,468	....	36,300	277,013
40	Corporate stocks	231,175	9,175	42,292	....	....	51,467	282,642
41	U.S. liabilities to unaffiliated foreigners reported by U.S. nonbanking concerns.	45,379	−405	....	....	−1,213	−1,618	43,761
42	U.S. liabilities reported by U.S. banks, not included elsewhere	693,436	−13,678	....	....	336	−13,342	680,094

[r] Revised.
[p] Preliminary.
1. Represents gains or losses on foreign currency-denominated assets due to their revaluation at current exchange rates.
2. Includes changes in coverage, statistical discrepancies, and other adjustments to the value of assets.
3. Reflects changes in the value of the official gold stock due to fluctuations in the market price of gold.
4. Reflects changes in gold stock from U.S. Treasury sales of gold medallions and commemorative and bullion coins; also reflects replenishment through open market purchases. These demonetizations/monetizations are not included in international transactions capital flows.
5. Also includes paid-in capital subscriptions to international financial institutions and outstanding amounts of miscellaneous claims that have been settled through international agreements to be payable to the U.S. Government over periods in excess of 1 year. Excludes World War I debts that are not being serviced.
6. Includes indebtedness that the borrower may contractually, or at its option, repay with its currency, with a third country's currency, or by delivery of materials or transfer of services.
7. Primarily U.S. Government liabilities associated with military sales contracts and other transactions arranged with or through foreign official agencies.

Source: U.S. Department of Commerce, Bureau of Economic Analysis, *Survey of Current Business,* June 1992, p. 47.

abroad, and the values of these investments have tended to rise over time. Now the BEA uses two different methods to place current values on foreign direct investments: the *current cost* method, which values direct investments at the cost of buying them today, and the *market value* method, which is meant to measure the price at which the investments could be sold. These methods can lead to different valuations, because the cost of replacing a particular direct investment and the price it would command if sold on the market may be hard to measure. (The net foreign wealth data graphed in FIgure 13-2 are current cost estimates.)

Table 13-5 reproduces the BEA's account of how it made its valuation adjustments to find the U.S. net foreign position at the end of 1991. Starting with its estimate of 1990 net foreign wealth (−$294.8 billion at current cost or −$272.0 billion at market value), the BEA (column a) subtracted the amount of the 1991 U.S. net capital inflow of $4.8 billion—the sum of lines 4 and 5 in Table 13-3. (Do you remember why a capital *inflow* to the United States results in a *reduction* in U.S. net foreign assets?) Then the BEA adjusted the values of previously held assets for various changes in their dollar prices (columns b, c, and d). As you can see from column b, the value of foreign assets in the United States rose more than that of U.S. assets abroad, mainly because the U.S. stock and bond markets were more buoyant than those in other countries in 1991. Thus, U.S. net foreign wealth *fell* by far more than the $4.8 billion in new net capital inflows from abroad. Based on the current cost method for valuing direct investments, the BEA's 1991 estimate of U.S. net foreign wealth was −$361.5 billion. On a market value basis, the BEA places 1991 net foreign wealth even lower, at −$381.8 billion.

This debt is almost as large as the total foreign debt owed by all the Western Hemisphere's developing countries, which totaled $433.4 billion in 1991. To put these figures in perspective, however, it is important to realize that the U.S. net foreign debt (at current cost) amounted to only 6.4 percent of its GNP, while that of Argentina, Brazil, Mexico, Venezuela, and the other Western Hemisphere debtors was more than 40 percent of their collective GNP! Thus, the U.S. external debt represents a much lower income drain than that of its southern neighbors.

The United States certainly is the world's biggest debtor. There is no reason to be alarmed, however, because the U.S. GNP is also the world's largest and the U.S. is not in danger of being unable to repay its foreign debts. Remember also that foreign borrowing may not always be a bad idea: a country that borrows abroad to undertake profitable domestic investments can pay back its creditors and still have money left over (Chapter 7). Unfortunately for the United States, most of its foreign borrowing over the 1980s financed government budget deficits rather than investment, as we saw in the last Case Study. Future generations of U.S. citizens therefore will face a real burden in repaying the resulting foreign debt.

Summary

1. International *macroeconomics* is concerned with the full employment of scarce economic resources and price level stability throughout the world economy. Because they reflect national expenditure patterns and their international repercussions, the

national income accounts and the *balance of payments accounts* are essential tools for studying the macroeconomics of open, interdependent economies.

2. A country's *gross national product (GNP)* is equal to the income received by its factors of production. The national income accounts divide national income according to the types of spending that generate it: *consumption, investment, government purchases,* and the *current account balance.*

3. In an economy closed to international trade, GNP must be consumed, invested, or purchased by the government. By using current output to build plant, equipment, and inventories, investment transforms present output into future output. For a closed economy, investment is the only way to save in the aggregate, so the sum of the saving carried out by the private and public sectors, *national saving,* must equal investment.

4. In an open economy, GNP equals the sum of consumption, investment, government purchases, and net exports of goods and services. Trade does not have to be balanced if the economy can borrow from and lend to the rest of the world. The difference between the economy's exports and imports, the current account balance, equals the difference between the economy's output and its total use of goods and services.

5. The current account also equals the country's net lending to foreigners. Unlike a closed economy, an open economy can save by domestic *and* foreign investment. National saving therefore equals domestic investment plus the current account balance.

6. Balance of payments accounts provide a detailed picture of the composition and financing of the current account. All transactions between a country and the rest of the world are recorded in its balance of payments accounts. The accounts are based on the convention that any transaction resulting in a payment to foreigners is entered with a minus sign while any transaction resulting in a receipt from foreigners is entered with a plus sign.

7. Transactions involving goods and services appear in the current account of the balance of payments, while international sales or purchases of *assets* appear in the *capital account.* Any current account deficit must be matched by an equal capital account surplus, and any current account surplus by a capital account deficit. This feature of the accounts reflects the fact that discrepancies between export earnings and import expenditures must be matched by a promise to repay the difference, usually with interest, in the future.

8. International asset transactions carried out by *central banks* are included in the capital account. Any central bank transaction in private markets for foreign-currency assets is called *official foreign exchange intervention.* One reason intervention is important is that central banks use it as a way of altering the amount of money in circulation. A country has a deficit in its *balance of payments* when it is running down its *official international reserves* or borrowing from foreign central banks; it has a surplus in the opposite case.

Key Terms

microeconomics
macroeconomics
national income accounting
balance of payments accounting
gross national product (GNP)
national income

private saving
government budget deficit
asset
gross domestic product (GDP)
consumption
investment
government purchases
national saving
current account balance
capital account
capital inflow
capital outflow
central bank
official international reserves
official foreign exchange intervention
official settlements balance (or balance of payments)

Problems

1. We stated above that GNP accounts avoid double counting by including only the value of *final* goods and services sold on the market. Should the measure of imports used in the GNP accounts therefore be defined to include only imports of final goods and services from abroad? What about exports?
2. Equation (13-2) tells us that to reduce a current account deficit, a country must increase its private saving, reduce domestic investment, or cut its government budget deficit. Yet, as we saw in the Case Study of the American and Japanese current accounts in the 1980s, many people recommended restrictions on imports from Japan and other countries to reduce the American current account deficit. How would higher U.S. barriers to imports affect its private saving, domestic investment, and government deficit? Do you agree that import restrictions would necessarily reduce a U.S. current account deficit?
3. Explain how each of the following transactions generates two entries—a credit and a debit—in the American balance of payments accounts, and describe how each entry would be classified:
   a. An American buys a share of German stock, paying by writing a check on an account with a Swiss bank.
   b. An American buys a share of German stock, paying the seller with a check on an American bank.
   c. The French government carries out an official foreign exchange intervention in which it uses dollars held in an American bank to buy French currency from its citizens.
   d. A tourist from Detroit buys a meal at an expensive restaurant in Lyons, France, paying with a VISA credit card.
   e. A California winegrower contributes a case of cabernet sauvignon for a London wine tasting.
   f. A U.S.-owned factory in Britain uses local earnings to buy additional machinery.
4. A New Yorker travels to New Jersey to buy a $100 telephone answering machine. The New Jersey company that sells the machine then deposits the $100 check in its account at a New York bank. How would these transactions show up in the balance of payments accounts of New York and New Jersey? What if the New Yorker pays cash for the machine?

5. The nation of Pecunia had a current account deficit of $1 billion and a nonreserve capital account surplus of $500 million in 1994.
   a. What was the balance of payments of Pecunia in that year? What happened to the country's net foreign assets?
   b. Assume that foreign central banks neither buy nor sell Pecunian assets. How did the Pecunian central bank's foreign reserves change in 1994? How would this official intervention show up in the balance of payments accounts of Pecunia?
   c. How would your answer to (b) change if you learned that foreign central banks had purchased $600 million of Pecunian assets in 1994? How would these official purchases enter foreign balance of payments accounts?
   d. Draw up the Pecunian balance of payments accounts for 1994 under the assumption that the event described in (c) occurred in that year.
6. Can you think of reasons why a government might be concerned about a large current account deficit or surplus? Why might a government be concerned about its official settlements balance (that is, its balance of payments)?
7. Do data on the U.S. official settlements balance give an accurate picture of the extent to which foreign central banks buy and sell dollars in currency markets?
8. Is it possible for a country to have a current account deficit at the same time it has a surplus in its balance of payments? Explain your answer, using hypothetical figures for the current and nonreserve capital accounts. Be sure to discuss the possible implications for official international reserve flows.

Further Reading

Peter Hooper and J. David Richardson, eds. *International Economic Transactions.* Chicago: University of Chicago Press, 1991. Useful papers on international economic measurement.

David H. Howard. "Implications of the U.S. Current Account Deficit." *Journal of Economic Perspectives* 3 (Fall 1989), pp. 153–165. Examines how recent U.S. current account deficits may affect American welfare and net foreign wealth.

International Monetary Fund. *Final Report of the Working Party on the Statistical Discrepancy in World Current Account Balances.* Washington, D.C.: International Monetary Fund, September 1987. Discusses the statistical discrepancy in the world current account balance, its implications for policy analysis, and recommendations for more accurate measurement.

Robert E. Lipsey. "Changing Patterns of International Investment in and by the United States," in Martin S. Feldstein, ed. *The United States in the World Economy.* Chicago: University of Chicago Press, 1988, pp. 475–545. Historical perspective on capital flows to and from the United States.

Rita M. Maldonado. "Recording and Classifying Transactions in the Balance of Payments." *International Journal of Accounting* 15 (Fall 1979), pp. 105–133. Provides detailed examples of how various international transactions enter the balance of payments accounts.

James E. Meade. *The Balance of Payments,* Chapters 1–3. London: Oxford University Press, 1952. A classic analytical discussion of balance of payments concepts.

Lois Stekler. "Adequacy of International Transactions and Position Data for Policy Coordination," in William H. Branson, Jacob A. Frenkel, and Morris Goldstein, eds. *International Policy Coordination and Exchange Rate Fluctuations.* Chicago: University of Chicago

Press, 1990, pp. 347–371. A critical look at the interpretation of official data on current accounts and external indebtedness.

Robert M. Stern, Charles F. Schwartz, Robert Triffin, Edward M. Bernstein, and Walther Lederer. *The Presentation of the Balance of Payments: A Symposium,* Princeton Esays in International Finance 123. International Finance Section, Department of Economics, Princeton University, August 1977. A discussion of changes in the presentation of the U.S. balance of payments accounts.

U.S. Bureau of the Budget, Review Committee for Balance of Payments Statistics. *The Balance of Payments Statistics of the United States: A Review and Appraisal.* Washington, D.C.: Government Printing Office, 1965. A major official reappraisal of U.S. balance of payments accounting procedures. Chapter 9 focuses on conceptual difficulties in defining surpluses and deficits in the balance of payments.

Exchange Rates and the Foreign Exchange Market: An Asset Approach

Chapter 14

In 1985 American students flocked to Europe in record numbers to enjoy the castles of the Loire valley, the cuisine of Tuscany, and the London theater. By the 1990s, however, their younger brothers and sisters were finding that a summer vacation in Europe had become an expensive luxury. What economic forces had raised the price of foreign travel? One major factor was a sharp rise in the dollar prices of foreign currencies, a development that made foreign food, lodging, and transport more expensive for Americans.

The price of one currency in terms of another is called an **exchange rate.** At 3 P.M. New York time on December 4, 1992, you would have needed 62.76 cents to buy one unit of the German currency, the Deutschemark (DM), so the dollar's exchange rate against the DM was $0.6276 per DM. Because of their strong influence on the current account and other macroeconomic variables, exchange rates are among the most important prices in an open economy.

Because an exchange rate, as the price of one country's money in terms of another's, is also an asset price, the principles governing the behavior of other asset prices also govern the behavior of exchange rates. As you will recall from Chapter 13, the defining characteristic of an asset is that it is a form of wealth, a way of transferring purchasing power from the present into the future. The price that an asset commands today is therefore directly related to the goods and services buyers expect it to yield in the future. Similarly, *today's* dollar/DM exchange rate is closely tied to people's expectations about the *future* level of that rate. Just as the price of Microsoft stock rises immediately on favorable news about Microsoft's future prospects, so do exchange rates respond immediately to any news concerning future currency values.

Our general goals in this chapter are to understand the role of exchange rates in international trade and how exchange rates are determined. To begin, we first learn how exchange rates allow us to compare the prices of different countries' goods and services. Next we describe the international asset market in which currencies are traded and show how equilibrium exchange rates are determined in that market. A final section underlines our asset market approach by showing how today's exchange rate responds to changes in the expected future values of exchange rates.

Exchange Rates and International Transactions

Each country has a currency in which the prices of goods and services are quoted—the dollar in the United States, the DM in Germany, the pound sterling in Britain, the yen in Japan, and the peso in Mexico, to name just a few. Exchange rates play a central role in international trade because they allow us to compare the prices of goods and services produced in different countries. A consumer deciding which of two American cars to buy must compare their dollar prices, for example, $32,000 (for a Lincoln Continental) or $18,000 (for a Ford Taurus). But how is the same consumer to compare either of these prices with the 1,800,000 yen (¥1,800,000) it costs to import a Subaru from Japan? To make this comparison, he must know the relative price of dollars and yen.

The relative prices of currencies are reported daily in newspapers' financial sections. Table 14-1 shows the dollar exchange rates for currencies traded in New York at 3 P.M. on December 4, 1992, as reported in the *Wall Street Journal.* Notice that an exchange rate can be quoted in two ways; as the price of the foreign currency in terms of dollars (for example, $0.008003 per yen) or as the price of dollars in terms of the foreign currency (for example, ¥124.95 per dollar). The first of these exchange rate quotations (dollars per foreign currency unit) is said to be in *direct* (or "American") terms, the second (foreign currency units per dollar) in *indirect* (or "European") terms.

Households and firms use exchange rates to translate foreign prices into domestic currency terms. Once the money prices of domestic goods and imports have been expressed in terms of the same currency, households and firms can compute the *relative* prices that affect international trade flows.

DOMESTIC AND FOREIGN PRICES

If we know the exchange rate between two countries' currencies, we can compute the price of one country's exports in terms of the other country's money. For example, how many dollars would it cost to buy an Edinburgh Woolen Mill sweater costing 50 British pounds (£50)? The answer is found by multiplying the price of the sweater in pounds, 50, by the price of a pound in terms of dollars—the dollar's exchange rate against the pound. At an exchange rate of $1.50 per pound (expressed in American terms), the dollar price of the sweater is

$$(1.50\ \$/£) \times (£50) = \$75.$$

TABLE 14-1 Exchange rate quotations

CURRENCY TRADING

EXCHANGE RATES

Friday, December 4, 1992

The New York foreign exchange selling rates below apply to trading among banks in amounts of $1 million and more, as quoted at 3 p.m. Eastern time by Bankers Trust Co., Telerate and other sources. Retail transactions provide fewer units of foreign currency per dollar.

	U.S. $ equiv.		Currency per U.S. $	
Country	Fri.	Thurs.	Fri.	Thurs.
Argentina (Peso)	1.01	1.01	.99	.99
Australia (Dollar)	.6930	.6955	1.4430	1.4378
Austria (Schilling)	.08929	.08975	11.20	11.14
Bahrain (Dinar)	2.6522	2.6522	.3771	.3771
Belgium (Franc)	.03053	.03067	32.76	32.60
Brazil (Cruzeiro)	.0001007	.0001016	9934.00	9839.00
Britain (Pound)	1.5595	1.5645	.6412	.6392
30-Day Forward	1.5553	1.5604	.6430	.6409
90-Day Forward	1.5469	1.5521	.6465	.6443
180-Day Forward	1.5367	1.5422	.6507	.6484
Canada (Dollar)	.7827	.7848	1.2777	1.2742
30-Day Forward	.7796	.7817	1.2827	1.2792
90-Day Forward	.7746	.7771	1.2910	1.2868
180-Day Forward	.7682	.7673	1.3017	1.3032
Czechoslovakia (Koruna)				
Commercial rate	.0357398	.0357398	27.9800	27.9800
Chile (Peso)	.002707	.002703	369.41	369.90
China (Renminbi)	.181028	.181028	5.5240	5.5240
Colombia (Peso)	.001730	.001636	578.00	611.15
Denmark (Krone)	.1621	.1626	6.1700	6.1483
Ecuador (Sucre)				
Floating rate	.000529	.000529	1892.00	1892.00
Finland (Markka)	.19417	.19560	5.1500	5.1124
France (Franc)	.18493	.18553	5.4075	5.3900
30-Day Forward	.18391	.18442	5.4375	5.4225
90-Day Forward	.18185	.18232	5.4990	5.4850
180-Day Forward	.17945	.17986	5.5725	5.5600
Germany (Mark)	.6276	.6313	1.5933	1.5840
30-Day Forward	.6249	.6286	1.6003	1.5909
90-Day Forward	.6197	.6234	1.6138	1.6040
180-Day Forward	.6136	.6172	1.6298	1.6202
Greece (Drachma)	.004779	.004808	209.25	208.00
Hong Kong (Dollar)	.12914	.12916	7.7435	7.7425
Hungary (Forint)	.0122714	.0122684	81.4900	81.5100
India (Rupee)	.03549	.03549	28.18	28.18
Indonesia (Rupiah)	.0004854	.0004854	2060.00	2060.00
Ireland (Punt)	1.6573	1.6635	.6034	.6011
Israel (Shekel)	.3802	.3803	2.6305	2.6295
Italy (Lira)	.0007157	.0007109	1397.25	1406.59
Japan (Yen)	.008003	.008019	124.95	124.70
30-Day Forward	.008005	.008017	124.92	124.74
90-Day Forward	.008006	.008022	124.90	124.65
180-Day Forward	.008015	.008030	124.77	124.54
Jordan (Dinar)	1.4789	1.4789	.6762	.6762
Kuwait (Dinar)	3.3328	3.3328	.3001	.3001
Lebanon (Pound)	.000534	.000534	1871.00	1871.00
Malaysia (Ringgit)	.3937	.3942	2.5400	2.5365
Malta (Lira)	2.7174	2.7174	.3680	.3680
Mexico (Peso)				
Floating rate	.0003213	.0003213	3112.00	3112.00
Netherland (Guilder) ..	.5583	.5616	1.7910	1.7807
New Zealand (Dollar) .	.5170	.5182	1.9342	1.9298
Norway (Krone)	.1511	.1542	6.6200	6.4865
Pakistan (Rupee)	.0393	.0393	25.44	25.44
Peru (New Sol)	.6351	.6430	1.57	1.56
Philippines (Peso)	.04032	.04032	24.80	24.80
Poland (Zloty)	.00006820	.00006786	14662.00	14736.00
Portugal (Escudo)	.007050	.007050	141.85	141.85
Saudi Arabia (Riyal) ..	.26702	.26702	3.7450	3.7450
Singapore (Dollar)	.6090	.6098	1.6421	1.6400
South Africa (Rand)				
Commercial rate	.3327	.3336	3.0053	2.9978
Financial rate	.2128	.2083	4.7000	4.8000
South Korea (Won)	.0012723	.0012723	786.00	786.00
Spain (Peseta)	.008726	.008754	114.60	114.24
Sweden (Krona)	.1470	.1474	6.8030	6.7859
Switzerland (Franc) ...	.7004	.7072	1.4277	1.4140
30-Day Forward	.6989	.7058	1.4308	1.4168
90-Day Forward	.6959	.7027	1.4369	1.4230
180-Day Forward	.6928	.6998	1.4434	1.4290
Taiwan (Dollar)	.039683	.039698	25.20	25.19
Thailand (Baht)	.03920	.03920	25.51	25.51
Turkey (Lira)	.0001220	.0001221	8195.00	8189.00
United Arab (Dirham)	.2723	.2723	3.6725	3.6725
Uruguay (New Peso)				
Financial	.000283	.000283	3531.00	3531.00
Venezuela (Bolivar)				
Floating rate	.01290	.01291	77.52	77.47
SDR	1.39109	1.38909	.71886	.71990
ECU	1.23490	1.23960	....	....

Special Drawing Rights (SDR) are based on exchange rates for the U.S., German, British, French and Japanese currencies. Source: International Monetary Fund.

European Currency Unit (ECU) is based on a basket of community currencies.

OPTIONS

PHILADELPHIA EXCHANGE

Option & Underlying	Strike Price	Calls—Last			Puts—Last		
		Dec	Jan	Mar	Dec	Jan	Mar
50,000 Australian Dollars-cents per unit.							
ADollr.....	67	r	r	r	r	r	0.59
69.46	68	1.34	r	r	r	r	r
69.46	69	r	r	r	0.19	r	1.24
69.46	70	0.08	r	r	0.80	r	1.85
69.46	71	r	r	0.60	r	r	r
31,250 British Pound-German Mark cross.							
BPd-GMk	238	r	r	r	0.08	r	r
247.81 ..	250	1.00	r	r	r	r	r
247.81 ..	252	0.50	r	r	r	r	r
247.81 ..	254	r	1.76	r	r	r	r
31,250 British Pounds-European Style.							
BPound ..	157½	1.22	2.30	r	r	r	r
31,250 British Pounds-cents per unit.							
BPound .	145	r	r	r	0.10	r	1.35
156.45 ..	147½	r	8.95	r	0.05	r	r
156.45 ..	150	r	7.50	r	r	1.15	2.80
156.45 ..	152½	4.68	6.40	6.11	0.20	2.00	r
156.45 ..	155	1.80	3.65	6.10	0.85	2.90	4.20
156.45 ..	157½	1.70	r	r	2.30	3.90	r
156.45 ..	160	0.60	1.52	2.75	r	5.07	r
156.45 ..	162½	r	1.16	2.15	r	r	r
156.45 ..	165	0.10	1.00	r	9.30	r	11.90
156.45 ..	167½	r	r	1.31	r	r	r
156.45 ..	180	r	r	r	r	r	24.72
50,000 Canadian Dollars-European Style.							
CDollar....	78½	r	r	r	r	r	1.69
78.48	79½	r	r	r	1.18	r	r
50,000 Canadian Dollars-cents per unit.							
CDollr.....	77	r	r	r	r	0.46	r

TABLE 14-1 continued

78.48	78	r	r	r	0.23	r	r
78.48	78½	r	0.50	0.76	r	r	r
78.48	79	r	r	r	0.85	r	r
78.48	80	r	0.18	r	r	r	r
250,000 French Francs-10ths of a cent per unit.							
FFranc....	16½	r	s	r	r	s	0.94
185.55 ...	17½	r	r	r	0.14	r	r
185.55 ...	18¼	r	r	r	r	r	6.32
185.55 ...	18½	r	r	r	r	r	7.40
185.55 ...	18¾	0.48	r	4.10	r	r	9.00
185.55 ...	20	r	r	r	15.00	r	r
62,500 German Mark-Japanese Yen cross.							
GMk-YJn .	77	r	r	r	0.20	1.01	r
78.66	78	r	r	r	r	r	2.20
62,500 German Marks-European Style.							
DMark	60	2.75	r	r	r	0.37	r
63.13	61½	r	r	s	r	0.77	s
63.13	62½	r	r	s	0.33	r	s
63.13	64	0.31	r	r	r	r	r
63.13	66	r	0.25	r	r	r	r
62,500 German Marks-cents per unit.							
DMark	55	r	r	r	r	r	0.19
63.13	58	r	r	r	r	0.18	0.58
63.13	59	r	r	r	r	0.29	0.85
63.13	59½	r	r	s	0.02	r	s
63.13	60	r	r	r	0.03	0.44	1.07
63.13	60½	r	r	s	0.05	0.47	s
63.13	61	r	r	r	r	0.59	1.53
63.13	61½	r	r	s	0.12	0.97	s
63.13	62	0.86	1.68	2.29	0.26	1.08	2.05
63.13	62½	0.67	1.27	s	0.40	1.36	s
63.13	63	0.36	1.11	1.50	0.68	1.62	2.56
63.13	63½	0.24	1.15	s	r	r	s
63.13	64	0.17	0.71	1.13	r	2.26	3.12
63.13	64½	0.08	r	s	1.45	r	s
63.13	65	r	r	r	r	r	3.88
63.13	65½	r	r	s	2.30	r	s
63.13	66	0.06	0.28	r	3.25	3.42	r
63.13	67	r	r	0.39	4.19	r	r
63.13	70	r	r	r	r	r	7.62
6,250,000 Japanese Yen-100ths of a cent per unit.							
JYen......	74	r	r	r	r	r	0.11
80.27	76	r	r	r	r	r	0.26
80.27	78	r	r	r	r	r	0.64
80.27	78½	r	r	s	0.02	r	s
80.27	79	r	r	r	0.06	0.43	r
80.27	79½	r	r	s	0.10	r	s
80.27	80	r	r	r	0.25	0.80	1.30
80.27	80½	0.20	0.70	s	0.55	0.96	s
80.27	81	0.10	r	1.13	r	r	r
80.27	81½	0.04	r	s	r	r	s
80.27	82	r	r	r	1.85	r	r
80.27	83	r	r	r	r	r	3.28
80.27	85	r	r	0.22	r	r	r
6,250,000 Japanese Yen-European Style.							
JYen......	80½	0.23	r	s	r	r	s
80.27	81½	0.04	r	s	r	r	s
62,500 Swiss Francs-European Style.							
SFranc....	68½	r	r	s	0.27	1.10	s
62,500 Swiss Francs-cents per unit.							
SFranc....	66	r	r	r	r	r	1.05
70.69	67	r	r	r	r	r	1.32
70.69	68	r	r	r	0.17	0.92	1.68
70.69	68½	r	r	s	0.28	r	s
70.69	69	1.36	r	3.19	0.33	1.17	2.07
70.69	69½	r	r	s	0.55	r	s
70.69	70	0.74	r	r	0.75	1.70	r
70.69	70½	0.42	r	s	0.80	r	s
70.69	71	0.35	1.15	r	1.36	2.30	3.28
70.69	71½	0.31	r	s	1.46	r	s
70.69	72	0.32	0.76	1.34	2.40	r	r
70.69	72½	0.24	0.63	s	r	r	s
70.69	74	r	r	0.98	r	r	r
70.69	75	r	0.26	r	r	r	r
70.69	76	r	r	r	6.09	r	r
62,500 German Marks EOM-cents per unit.							
DMark ...	64½	0.19	r	s	r	r	s
6,250,000 Japanese Yen EOM-100ths of a cent per unit.							
JYen	78	r	r	s	r	0.31	s
80.27	80	r	r	s	0.36	r	s
80.27	82½	r	0.31	s	r	r	s

Total Call Vol 22,913 Call Open Int 680,935
Total Put Vol 18,027 Put Open Int 668,357

FUTURES PRICES

CURRENCY

	Open	High	Low	Settle	Change	Lifetime High	Lifetime Low	Open Interest
JAPAN YEN (IMM)–12.5 million yen; $ per yen (.00)								
Dec	.8018	.8033	.8000	.8003	– .0018	.8419	.7410	37,490
Mr93	.8035	.8036	.8002	.8007	– .0019	.8372	.7445	10,153
June	.8050	.8050	.8022	.8016	– .0020	.8340	.7745	402
Sept	....	....	....	.8036	– .0020	.8070	.8070	869
Dec	....	....	....	.8061	– .0020	.8085	.8081	1,423
Est vol 16,982; vol Thur 8,136; open int 50,337, +536.								
DEUTSCHEMARK (IMM)–125,000 marks; $ per mark								
Dec	.6315	.6334	.6250	.6269	– .0035	.7117	.5645	104,589
Mr93	.6249	.6256	.6171	.6189	– .0036	.7025	.5724	17,933
June	.6170	.6180	.6120	.6127	– .0036	.6920	.6070	2,008
Sept	....	....	....	.6084	– .0035	.6720	.6320	302
Est vol 79,482; vol Thur 39,304; open int 124,845, –789.								
CANADIAN DOLLAR (IMM)–100,000 dlrs.; $ per Can $								
Dec	.7834	.7839	.7804	.7812	– .0021	.8740	.7685	23,516
Mr93	.7749	.7766	.7733	.7736	– .0025	.8712	.7610	3,876
June	.7703	.7704	.7681	.7678	– .0025	.8360	.7532	2,142
Sept	.7648	.7648	.7648	.7632	– .0025	.8335	.7515	771
Dec	.7600	.7600	.7600	.7592	– .0019	.8310	.7470	412
Est vol 6,376; vol Thur 5,415; open int 30,718, –849.								
BRITISH POUND (IMM)–62,500 pds.; $ per pound								
Dec	1.5624	1.5836	1.5546	1.5592	– .0032	1.9746	1.5012	25,932
Mr93	1.5502	1.5700	1.5424	1.5470	– .0034	1.9400	1.4900	5,186
June	1.5500	1.5500	1.5330	1.5368	– .0038	1.9100	1.4810	296
Est vol 18,143; vol Thur 16,378; open int 31,414, –475.								
SWISS FRANC (IMM)–125,000 francs; $ per franc								
Dec	.7070	.7096	.6965	.6998	– .0066	.8209	.6280	38,908
Mr93	.7030	.7049	.6920	.6949	– .0072	.8140	.6785	7,322
June	.6915	.7010	.6880	.6917	– .0074	.8070	.6750	661
Est vol 32,384; vol Thur 22,783; open int 46,897, –642.								
AUSTRALIAN DOLLAR (IMM)–100,000 dlrs.; $ per A.$								
Dec	.6945	.6945	.6920	.6924	– .0026	.7462	.6808	4,769
Mr93	.6900	.6903	.6886	.6889	– .0026	.7450	.6775	314
Est vol 513; vol Thur 1,104; open int 5,083, –185.								
U.S. DOLLAR INDEX (FINEX)–1,000 times USDX								
Dec	90.35	90.93	90.01	90.80	+ .32	94.93	79.85	6,133
Mr93	91.80	92.40	91.52	92.30	+ .32	93.28	81.45	1,058
Est vol 3,680; vol Thur 2,031; open int 7,196, +926.								
The Index: High 90.77; Low 89.77; Close 90.61 +.39								

From *Wall Street Journal* December 7, 1992.

A change in the dollar/pound exchange rate would alter the sweater's dollar price. At an exchange rate of \$1.25 per pound, the sweater would cost only

$$(1.25\ \$/£) \times (£50) = \$62.50,$$

assuming its price in terms of pounds remained the same. At an exchange rate of \$1.75 per pound, the sweater's dollar price would be higher, equal to

$$(1.75\ \$/£) \times (£50) = \$87.50.$$

Changes in exchange rates are described as depreciations or appreciations. A **depreciation** of the pound against the dollar is a fall in the dollar price of pounds, for example, a change in the exchange rate from \$1.50 per pound to \$1.25 per pound. The preceding example shows that *all else equal, a depreciation of a country's currency makes its goods cheaper for foreigners.* A rise in the pound's price in terms of dollars—for example, from \$1.50 per pound to \$1.75 per pound—is an **appreciation** of the pound against the dollar. *All else equal, an appreciation of a country's currency makes its goods more expensive for foreigners.*

The exchange rate changes discussed in the example simultaneously alter the prices Britons pay for American goods. At an exchange rate of \$1.50 per pound, the pound price of a pair of American designer jeans costing \$45 is (\$45)/(1.50 \$/£) = £30. A change in the exchange rate from \$1.50 per pound to \$1.25 per pound, while a depreciation of the pound against the dollar, is also a rise in the pound price of dollars, an *appreciation* of the dollar against the pound. This appreciation of the dollar makes the American jeans more expensive for Britons by raising their pound price to

$$(\$45)/(1.25\ \$/£) = £36.$$

The change in the exchange rate from \$1.50 per pound to \$1.75 per pound—an appreciation of the pound against the dollar but a depreciation of the dollar against the pound—lowers the pound price of the jeans to

$$(\$45)/(1.75\ \$/£) = £25.71.$$

As you can see, descriptions of exchange rate changes as depreciations or appreciations can be bewildering, because when one currency depreciates against another, the second currency must simultaneously appreciate against the first. To avoid confusion in discussing exchange rates, we must always keep track of which of the two currencies we are examining has depreciated or appreciated against the other.

If we remember that a depreciation of the dollar against the pound is at the same time an appreciation of the pound against the dollar, we reach the following conclusion: *When a country's currency depreciates, foreigners find that its exports are cheaper and domestic residents find that imports from abroad are more expensive. An appreciation has opposite effects: foreigners pay more for the country's products and domestic consumers pay less for foreign products.*

EXCHANGE RATES AND RELATIVE PRICES

Import and export demands, like the demands for all goods and services, are influenced by *relative* prices, such as the price of sweaters in terms of designer jeans. We have just seen how exchange rates allow individuals to compare domestic and foreign money prices by expressing them in a common currency unit. Carrying this analysis one step further, we can see that exchange rates also allow individuals to compute the relative prices of goods and services whose money prices are quoted in different currencies.

An American trying to decide how much to spend on American jeans and how much to spend on British sweaters must translate their prices into a common currency to compute the price of sweaters in terms of jeans. As we have seen, an exchange rate of $1.50 per pound means that an American pays $75 for a sweater priced at £50 in Britain. Because the price of a pair of American jeans is $45, the price of sweaters in terms of jeans is ($75 per sweater)/($45 per pair of jeans) = 1.67 pairs of jeans per sweater. Naturally, a Briton faces the same relative price of (£50 per sweater)/(£30 per pair of jeans) = 1.67 pairs of jeans per sweater.

Table 14-2 shows the relative prices implied by exchange rates of $1.25 per pound, $1.50 per pound, and $1.75 per pound, on the assumption that the dollar price of jeans and the pound price of sweaters are unaffected by the exchange rate changes. To test your understanding, try to calculate these relative prices for yourself and confirm that the outcome of the calculation is the same for a Briton and for an American.

The table shows that if the goods' money prices do not change, an appreciation of the dollar against the pound makes sweaters cheaper in terms of jeans (each pair of jeans buys more sweaters) while a depreciation of the dollar against the pound makes sweaters more expensive in terms of jeans (each pair of jeans buys fewer sweaters). The computations illustrate a general principle: *All else equal, an appreciation of a country's currency raises the relative price of its exports and lowers the relative price of its imports. Conversely, a depreciation lowers the relative price of a country's exports and raises the relative price of its imports.*

The Foreign Exchange Market

Just as other prices in the economy are determined by the interaction of buyers and sellers, exchange rates are determined by the interaction of the households, firms, and financial institutions that buy and sell foreign currencies to make international payments. The market in which international currency trades take place is called the **foreign exchange market.**

THE ACTORS

The major participants in the foreign exchange market are commercial banks, corporations that engage in international trade, nonbank financial institutions such as asset-

TABLE 14-2 $/£ exchange rates and the relative price of American designer jeans and British sweaters

Exchange rate ($/£)	1.25	1.50	1.75
Relative price (pairs of jeans/sweater)	1.39	1.67	1.94

Note: The above calculations assume unchanged money prices of $45 per pair of jeans and £50 per sweater.

Making the Most of a Cheap Dollar

In 1992 the dollar depreciated against foreign currencies, reaching new lows against both the Deutschemark and the Japanese yen. As a result, American goods and services became unusually cheap relative to those available in Europe and Japan. Not only were United States exporters able to sell more abroad, but millions of foreign tourists flocked to the U.S. to enjoy cheap vacations and stuff their suitcases with clothing, jewelry, antiques, and appliances that would have been much more costly to buy at home.

Reporting on the trend, Sylvia Nasar of the *New York Times* gave this description of the situation: "To the Swiss businessman just off the Concorde, the $120 tab for a room at the Plaza looks like the lunch check back home. To the teenager from Paris, the $9 sticker on the tape at Tower Records or the $30 tag on a pair of Levi 501's reads like the big signs that say buy one, get one free."* She noted that at current exchange rates a businessman traveling to Chicago, for example, would find the cost of an overnight hotel stay to be only one-half to one-third the cost of comparable accommodations in major European cities.

Some American companies set up toll-free telephone lines to allow convenient mail-order purchases by European buyers. One Briton who shopped by phone had a California company ship him a personal computer that was twice as expensive in the United Kingdom as in the United States. Despite substantial British taxes on imports, he saved roughly $1100—and the computer arrived after only four days.**

The cheap dollar had lowered American prices to the point where foreigners could actually profit by flying to the United States to shop: even after subtracting the cost of air tickets and hotel rooms, they were saving money! Swissair, the Swiss airline, planned a winter travel package to bring Europeans into Chicago for a weekend of shopping at suburban Gurnee Mall. British Airways offered a pre-Christmas package including round-trip airfare to New York and two nights in a hotel, all for $580.† Transoceanic shopping expeditions were not, however, an entirely new phenomenon. As recently as 1985, when the dollar was riding high, Americans had flown to Europe in search of bargains.

* "Weak Dollar Makes U.S. World's Bargain Bazaar," *New York Times*, September 28, 1992, p. A1.

** See "Shoppers Fly to Buy with Fistfuls of Dollars," *The Independent on Sunday*, September 6, 1992, p. 8.

† See "London Journal: Dollar's Pounding Shocks Tourists," *New York Times*, August 31, 1992, p. A4.

management firms and insurance companies, and central banks. Individuals may also participate in the foreign exchange market—for example, the tourist who buys foreign currency at a hotel's front desk—but such cash transactions are an insignificant fraction of total foreign exchange trading.

We now describe the major actors in the market and their roles.

1. *Commercial banks.* Commercial banks are at the center of the foreign exchange market because almost every sizable international transaction involves the debiting and crediting of accounts at commercial banks in various financial centers. Thus, the vast majority of foreign exchange transactions involve the exchange of *bank deposits* denominated in different currencies.

Let's look at an example. Suppose Exxon Corporation wishes to pay DM 160,000 to a German supplier. First, Exxon gets an exchange rate quotation from its own commercial bank, the Third National Bank. Then it instructs Third National to debit Exxon's dollar account and pay DM 160,000 into the supplier's account at a German bank. If the exchange rate quoted to Exxon by Third National is $0.35 per DM, $56,000 (= $0.35 per DM × DM 160,000) is debited from Exxon's account. The final result of the transaction is the exchange of a $56,000 deposit at Third National Bank (now owned by the German bank that supplied the DM) for the DM 160,000 deposit used by Third National to pay Exxon's German supplier.

As the example shows, banks routinely enter the foreign exchange market to meet the needs of their customers—primarily corporations. A bank may also transact in foreign currencies to alter the currency composition of its own assets and liabilities. In addition, it is normal practice in the foreign exchange market for a bank to quote to other banks exchange rates at which it is willing to buy currencies from them and sell currencies to them. Banks may work through specialized foreign exchange brokers when they wish to trade anonymously and keep potential competitors in the dark.

Foreign currency trading among banks—called **interbank trading**—accounts for most of the activity in the foreign exchange market. In fact, the exchange rates listed in Table 14-1 are interbank rates, the rates banks charge to each other. No amount less than $1 million is traded at those rates. The rates available to corporate customers, called ''retail'' rates, are usually less favorable than the ''wholesale'' interbank rates. The differential between the retail and wholesale rates is the bank's compensation for doing the business.

Because their international operations are so extensive, large commercial banks are well-suited to bring buyers and sellers of currencies together. A multinational corporation wishing to convert $100,000 into Swedish kronor might find it difficult and costly to locate other corporations wishing to sell the right amount of kronor. By serving many customers simultaneously through a single large purchase of kronor, a bank can economize on these search costs.

2. *Corporations.* Corporations with operations in several countries frequently make or receive payments in currencies other than that of the country in which they are headquartered. To pay workers at a plant in Mexico, for example, IBM may need Mexican pesos. If IBM has only dollars earned by selling computers in the United States, it can acquire the pesos it needs by buying them with its dollars in the foreign exchange market.

3. *Nonbank financial institutions.* In recent years, deregulation of financial markets in the United States, Japan, and other countries has encouraged nonbank financial institutions to offer their customers a broader range of services, many of them indistinguishable from those offered by banks. Among these have been services involving foreign exchange transactions. Institutional investors, such as pension funds, often trade foreign currencies.

4. *Central banks.* In the previous chapter we learned that central banks sometimes intervene in foreign exchange markets. While the volume of central bank transactions is typically not large, the impact of these transactions may be great. The reason for this impact is that participants in the foreign exchange market watch central bank actions closely for clues about future macroeconomic policies that may affect exchange rates. Government agencies other than central banks may also trade in the foreign exchange market, but central banks are the most regular official participants.

CHARACTERISTICS OF THE MARKET

Foreign exchange trading takes place in many financial centers, with the largest volume of trade occurring in such major cities as London (the largest market), New York, Tokyo, Frankfurt, and Singapore. The worldwide volume of foreign exchange trading is enormous, and it has ballooned in recent years. In April 1989, the average total value of global foreign exchange trading was over $500 billion *per day,* of which $187 billion was traded daily in London, $129 billion in the United States, and $115 billion in Tokyo. Only three years later, in April 1992, the daily global value of foreign exchange trading had nearly doubled to $1 trillion, of which $303 billion was traded daily in London, $192 billion in New York, and $128 billion in Tokyo.[1]

Direct telephone, fax, and computer links among the major foreign exchange trading centers make each a part of a single world market on which the sun never sets. Economic news released at any time of the day is immediately transmitted around the world and may set off a flurry of activity by market participants. Even after trading in New York has finished, New York-based banks and corporations with affiliates in other time zones can remain active in the market. Foreign exchange traders may deal from their homes when a late-night communication alerts them to important developments in a financial center on another continent. Devices like the Reuter Pocketwatch, a palm-sized portable monitor, allow traders in Hong Kong, Toronto, London, and other cities to keep an uninterrupted watch over key currency rates.

The integration of financial centers implies that there can be no significant difference between the dollar/DM exchange rate quoted in New York at 9 A.M. and the dollar/DM exchange rate quoted in London at the same time (which corresponds to 3 P.M. London time). If the DM were selling for $0.30 in New York and $0.35 in London, profits could be made through **arbitrage,** the process of buying a currency cheap and selling it dear. At the prices listed above, a trader could, for instance, purchase the DM 1 million in New York for $300,000 and immediately sell the DM in London for $350,000, making a pure profit of $50,000. If all traders tried to cash in on the opportunity, however, their demand for DM in New York would drive up the dollar price of DM there, and their supply of DM in London would drive down the dollar price of DM there. Very quickly, the difference between the New York and London exchange rates would disappear. Since foreign exchange traders carefully watch their computer screens for arbitrage opportunities, the few that arise are small and very short-lived.

While a foreign exchange transaction can involve any two currencies, most transactions between banks involve exchanges of foreign currencies for U.S. dollars. This is true even when a bank's goal is to sell one nondollar currency and buy another! A bank wishing to sell Dutch guilders and buy Austrian schillings, for example, will usually sell its guilders for dollars and then use the dollars to buy schillings. While this procedure may appear roundabout, it is actually cheaper for the bank than the alternative of trying to find a holder of schillings who wishes to buy guilders. The advantage of

[1] April 1989 figures come from surveys carried out simultaneously by the Federal Reserve Bank of New York, the Bank of England, the Bank of Japan, the Bank of Canada, and monetary authorities from France, Italy, the Netherlands, Singapore, Hong Kong, and Australia. (Germany declined to participate because of reservations about the survey method's accuracy.) See "Japanese Influence Grows in Global Currency Market," *Wall Street Journal,* September 14, 1989, p. C1. For April 1992 survey results see "Currency Markets Resisting Powers of Central Banks," *New York Times,* September 25, 1992, p. A1. Daily U.S. foreign currency trading in 1980 averaged only around $18 billion.

trading through the dollar is a result of the United States' importance in the world economy. Because the volume of international transactions involving dollars is so great, it is not hard to find parties willing to trade dollars against guilders or schillings. In contrast, relatively few transactions require direct exchanges of guilders for schillings.[2]

Because of its pivotal role in so many foreign exchange deals, the dollar is sometimes called a **vehicle currency.** A vehicle currency is one that is widely used to denominate international contracts made by parties who do not reside in the country that issues the vehicle currency.[3] Dollars changed hands in 70 percent of the foreign exchange trades carried out in April 1992.

After the dollar, the DM and the yen play the most important roles in the foreign exchange market. In April 1992, 38 percent of all foreign exchange transactions involved DM. The pound sterling, once second only to the dollar as a key international currency, has declined in importance. In April 1992 its share in world foreign exchange trading was just 14 percent.

SPOT RATES AND FORWARD RATES

The foreign exchange transactions we have been discussing take place on the spot: two parties agree to an exchange of bank deposits and execute the deal immediately. Exchange rates governing such "on-the-spot" trading are called **spot exchange rates,** and the deal is called a spot transaction.

The term *spot* is a bit misleading because even spot exchanges usually become effective only two days after a deal is struck. The delay occurs because in most cases it takes two days for payment instructions (such as checks) to be cleared through the banking system.[4] Suppose Apple Computer has pounds in an account at the National Westminster Bank in London but sells them to the Bank of America in San Francisco, which has offered Apple a more favorable spot exchange rate for pounds than the bank where it has its dollar account, Wells Fargo. On Monday, June 20, Apple pays the pounds to Bank of America with a pound check drawn on National Westminster, while Bank of America, to pay Apple, wires dollars into Apple's account at Wells Fargo. Normally, Apple cannot use the dollars it has bought, nor can Bank of America use its pounds, until Wednesday, June 22, two business days later. In the jargon of the foreign exchange market, the *value date* for a spot transaction—the date on which the parties actually receive the funds they have purchased—occurs two business days after the deal is made.

Foreign exchange deals sometimes specify a value date further away than two days—30 days, 90 days, 180 days, or even several years. The exchange rates quoted in such transactions are called **forward exchange rates.** In a thirty-day forward transaction, for example, two parties may agree on April 1 to a spot exchange of £100,000

[2] The guilder/schilling exchange rate can be calculated from the dollar/guilder and dollar/schilling rates as the dollar/schilling rate divided by the dollar/guilder rate. If the dollar/guilder rate is $0.30 per guilder and the dollar/schilling rate is $0.06 per schilling, then the guilder/schilling exchange rate is (0.06 $/schilling)/(0.30 $/guilder) = 0.20 guilders/schilling. Exchange rates between nondollar currencies are called "cross rates" by foreign exchange traders.

[3] For a more detailed discussion of vehicle currencies, see Stephen P. Magee and Ramesh K. S. Rao, "Vehicle and Nonvehicle Currencies in International Trade," *American Economic Review* 70 (May 1980), pp. 368–373.

[4] A major exception involves trades of U.S. dollars for Canadian dollars in New York. These are executed with a one-day lag. Trades of dollars for Mexican pesos also have a one-day lag.

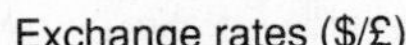

FIGURE 14-1
Dollar/pound spot and forward exchange rates, 1974–1992.
Spot and forward exchange rates tend to move in a highly correlated fashion.
Source: OECD, *Main Economic Indicators.* Rates shown are ninety-day forward exchange rates and spot exchange rates, at end of month.

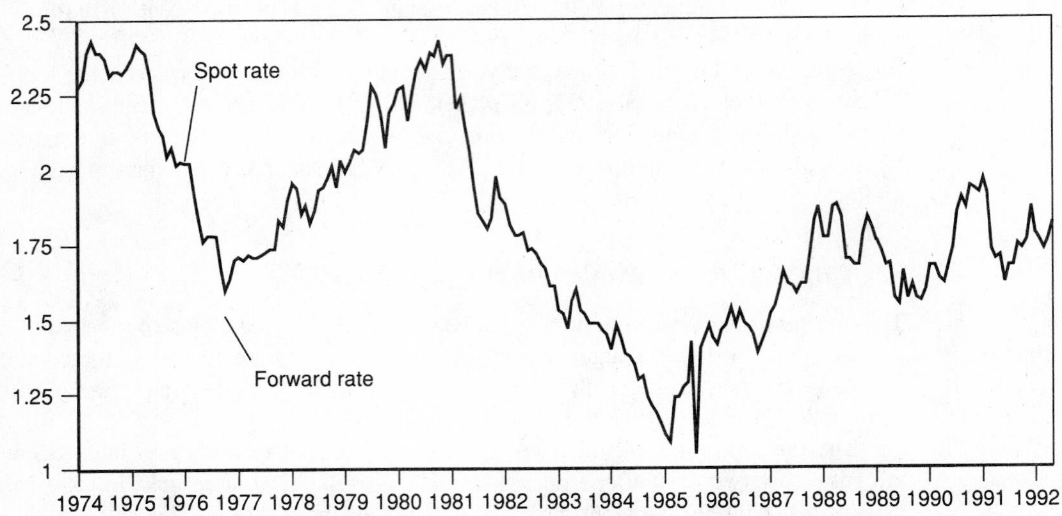

for $136,000 on May 1. The thirty-day forward exchange rate is therefore $1.36 per pound, and it is generally different from the spot rate and from the forward rates applied to different value dates. When you agree to sell pounds for dollars on a future date at a forward rate agreed on today, you have "sold pounds forward" and "bought dollars forward."

Table 14-1 reports forward exchange rates for the most heavily traded foreign currencies. (The forward quotations, when available, are listed below the corresponding spot quotations.) Forward and spot exchange rates, while not necessarily equal, do move closely together, as illustrated for dollar/pound rates in Figure 14-1. The appendix to this chapter, which discusses how forward exchange rates are determined, explains this close relationship between movements in spot and forward rates.

An example shows why parties may wish to engage in forward exchange transactions. Suppose an American who imports radios from Japan knows that in thirty days he must pay yen to a Japanese supplier for a shipment arriving then. The importer can sell each radio for $100 and must pay his supplier ¥25,000 per radio; so his profit depends on the dollar/yen exchange rate. At the current spot exchange rate of $0.0038 per yen, the importer would pay ($0.0038 per yen) × (¥25,000 per radio) = $95 per radio and would therefore make $5 on each radio imported. But the importer will not have the funds to pay the supplier until the radios arrive and are sold. If over the next thirty days the dollar unexpectedly depreciates to $0.0041 per yen, the importer will have to pay ($0.0041 per yen) × (¥25,000 per radio) = $102.50 per radio and so will take a $2.50 *loss* on each.

To avoid this risk, the importer can make a thirty-day forward exchange deal with his bank. If the bank agrees to sell yen to the importer in thirty days at a rate of $0.0039, the importer is assured of paying no more than ($0.0039 per yen) × (¥25,000 per radio) = $97.50 per radio to the supplier. By buying yen and selling dollars forward, the importer is guaranteed a profit of $2.50 per radio and is insured against the possibility that a sudden exchange rate change will turn a profitable importing deal into a loss.

From now on, when we mention an exchange rate without specifying whether it is a spot rate or a forward rate, we will always be referring to the spot rate.

FOREIGN EXCHANGE SWAPS

A foreign exchange *swap* is a spot sale of a currency combined with a forward repurchase of the currency. For example, a multinational company has just received $1 million from sales and knows it will have to pay those dollars to a California supplier in three months. The company's asset-management department would meanwhile like to invest the $1 million in Swiss francs. A three-month swap of dollars into Swiss francs may result in lower brokers' fees than the two separate transactions of selling dollars for spot Swiss francs and selling the Swiss francs for dollars on the forward market. Swaps make up a significant proportion of all foreign exchange trading.

FUTURES AND OPTIONS

Table 14-1 lists price data for several other financial instruments traded in the foreign exchange market. Like forward contracts, these instruments involve future exchanges of currencies. The timing and terms of the exchanges can differ, however, from those specified in forward contracts, giving traders additional flexibility in avoiding foreign exchange risk. Only fifteen years ago, some of these instruments were not traded on organized exchanges.

When you buy a *futures contract,* you buy a promise that a specified amount of foreign currency will be delivered on a specified date in the future. A forward contract between you and some other private party is an alternative way to ensure that you receive the same amount of foreign currency on the date in question. But while you have no choice about fulfilling your end of a forward deal, you can sell your futures contract on an organized futures exchange, realizing a profit or loss right away. Such a sale might appear advantageous, for example, if your views about the future spot exchange rate were to change.

A *foreign exchange option* gives its owner the right to buy or sell a specified amount of foreign currency at a specified price at any time up to a specified expiration date. The other party to the deal, the option's seller, is required to sell or buy the foreign currency at the discretion of the option's owner, who is under no obligation to exercise his right.

Imagine that you are uncertain about when in the next month a foreign currency payment will arrive. To avoid the risk of a loss, you may wish to buy a *put option* giving you the right to sell the foreign currency at a known exchange rate at any time during the month. If instead you expect to make a payment abroad sometime in the month, a *call option,* which gives you the right to buy foreign currency at a known

How Multinationals Manage Their Foreign Exchange Risks

Corporations with multinational operations are among the most important players in the foreign exchange market. Because both revenues and expenses are denominated in many different currencies, an unexpected exchange rate shift can potentially result in huge profit gains—or losses. Multinationals eliminate some of the risk of unexpected currency fluctuations through forward trading, swaps, or more complex financial transactions. For example, an American-based company expecting a payment in yen can buy a yen put option, which fully protects it from a dollar loss in case the yen suddenly depreciates but allows it to keep any dollar gains from a surprise yen appreciation. As the foreign exchange market has grown in complexity and size, the financial officers of most large corporations have become increasingly sophisticated in its ways.

Eastman Kodak, headquartered in Rochester, New York, is a leader in this respect. The company set up its own foreign exchange trading room in the late 1980s, hoping to turn a profit by managing Kodak's "exposure"—that is, its net asset position—in foreign currencies. Similarly, Mobil Corporation is setting up a trading room in London. The oil Mobil sells is priced in dollars, but the company's costs are paid in other currencies as well as in dollars. Mobil therefore cannot afford to be caught off guard by a sudden dollar depreciation.*

Profitable as such ventures can be, they do not eliminate all of a company's currency-related risks. Forward contracts and options with a horizon longer than a couple of years are still relatively costly to arrange, so various exchange market activities, while effective in countering short-term risks, are less effective in countering long-term risks. Moreover, the more limited nature of most short-term risks makes them inherently easier to guard against than long-term risks.

Long-term risks, however, can be substantial. For example, a steep appreciation of the dollar against foreign currencies over the first half of the 1980s made Kodak's photography products more expensive compared with foreign brands. As a result, Kodak had to give up a greater

price, might be attractive. Options can be written on many underlying assets (including foreign exchange futures), and, like futures, they are freely bought and sold.

The Demand for Foreign Currency Assets

We have now seen how banks, corporations, and other institutions trade foreign currency bank deposits in a worldwide foreign exchange market that operates twenty-four hours a day. To understand how exchange rates are determined by the foreign exchange market, we first must ask how the major actors' demands for different types of foreign currency deposits are determined.

The demand for a foreign currency bank deposit is influenced by the same considerations that influence the demand for any other asset. Chief among these considerations is our view of what the deposit will be worth in the future. A foreign currency deposit's

share of its world market to foreign competitors like Fuji Photo Film of Japan. When the dollar began falling in 1985, Kodak (like many other American companies) looked for ways to avoid the effects of such punishing exchange rate swings in the future.

Kodak is now more wary of making long-term commitments that might become uncomfortable after an adverse exchange rate movement. When it signs long-term supply contracts, Kodak may insist on linking the amount purchased, or the price, to current exchange rates. The company takes exchange rate prospects into account before making decisions to open production facilities in foreign countries.

Notice that the decision to open a foreign plant is itself a way of guarding against exchange risk. If Kodak could open a plant in Japan, its ability to take advantage of Japanese production costs would partially offset the loss of competitiveness it would suffer if a sudden appreciation of the dollar were to raise American costs relative to Japanese. This was one consideration that led Japanese auto manufacturers like Honda to open U.S. plants in the mid-1980s, when the yen was relatively weak against the dollar.**

Kodak gets nearly half of its revenues from foreign sales, so its potential gain from reducing exchange rate risk is large. The company's precautions have not made it entirely immune to exchange rate risks, however. In 1989, the photo giant was forced to fire 3 percent of its U.S. workers when the dollar, rather than depreciating against foreign currencies as the company had guessed when it projected future costs, strengthened instead. As in the early 1980s, this unexpected currency movement hurt Kodak by making its photographic products more expensive relative to those sold by its foreign competitors.

* See "Companies Learn to Live With Dollar's Volatility," *New York Times,* August 31, 1992, p. C1.

** A second consideration was the threat of stricter U.S. restrictions on imports from Japan.

future value depends in turn on two factors: the interest rate it offers and the expected change in the currency's exchange rate against other currencies.

ASSETS AND ASSET RETURNS

As you will recall, people can hold wealth in many forms—stocks, bonds, cash, real estate, rare wines, diamonds, and so on. The object of acquiring wealth—of saving—is to transfer purchasing power into the future. We may do this to provide for our retirement years, for our heirs, or simply because we earn more than we need to spend in a particular year and prefer to save the balance for a rainy day.

Defining Asset Returns. Because the object of saving is to provide for future consumption, we judge the desirability of an asset largely on the basis of its **rate of return,** that is, the percentage increase in value it offers over some time period. For example, suppose that at the beginning of 1996 you pay $100 for a share of stock issued by Financial Soothsayers, Inc. If the stock pays you a dividend of $1 at the beginning of 1997, and if the stock's price rises from $100 to $109 per share over the year, then you have earned a rate of return of 10 percent on the stock over 1996—that is, your initial $100 investment has grown in value to $110, the sum of the $1 dividend and the $109 you could get by selling your share. Had Financial Soothsayers stock still paid out its $1 dividend but dropped in price to $89 per share, your $100 investment would be worth only $90 by year's end, giving a rate of return of *negative* 10 percent.

You often cannot know with certainty the return that an asset will actually pay after you buy it. Both the dividend paid by a share of stock and the share's resale price, for example, may be hard to predict. Your decision therefore must be based on an *expected* rate of return. To calculate an expected rate of return over some time period, you make your best forecast of the asset's total value at the period's end. The percentage difference between that expected future value and the price you pay for the asset today equals the asset's expected rate of return over the time period.

When we measure an asset's rate of return, we compare how an investment in the asset changes in total value between two dates. In the previous example, we compared how the value of an investment in Financial Soothsayers stock changed between 1996 ($100) and 1997 ($110) to conclude that the rate of return on the stock was 10 percent per year. We call this a *dollar* rate of return because the two values we compare are expressed in terms of dollars. It is also possible, however, to compute different rates of return by expressing the two values in terms of a foreign currency or a commodity such as gold.

The Real Rate of Return. The expected rate of return that savers consider in deciding which assets to hold is the expected **real rate of return,** that is, the rate of return computed by measuring asset values in terms of some broad representative basket of products that savers regularly purchase. It is the expected real return that matters because the ultimate goal of saving is future consumption, and only the *real* return measures the goods and services a saver can buy in the future in return for giving up some consumption (that is, saving) today.

To continue our example, suppose the dollar value of an investment in Financial Soothsayers stock increases by 10 percent between 1996 and 1997 but that the dollar prices of all goods and services *also* increase by 10 percent. Then in terms of output—that is, in *real* terms—the investment would be worth no more in 1996 than in 1997. With a real rate of return of zero, Financial Soothsayers stock would not be a very desirable asset.

Although savers care about expected real rates of return, rates of return expressed in terms of a currency can still be used to *compare* real returns on *different* assets. Even if all dollar prices rise by 10 percent between 1996 and 1997, a rare bottle of wine whose dollar price rises by 25 percent is still a better investment than a bond whose dollar value rises by 20 percent. The real rate of return offered by the wine is 15 percent (= 25 percent − 10 percent) while that offered by the bond is only 10 percent (= 20 percent − 10 percent). Notice that the difference between the dollar returns of the two assets (25 percent − 20 percent) must equal the difference between their real returns (15 percent − 10 percent). The reason for this equality is that, given the two assets' dollar returns, a change in the rate at which the dollar prices of goods are rising changes both assets' real returns by the same amount.

The distinction between real rates of return and dollar rates of return illustrates an important concept in studying how savers evaluate different assets: the returns on two assets cannot be compared unless they are measured in the *same* units. For example, it makes no sense to compare directly the real return on the bottle of wine (15 percent in our example) with the dollar return on the bond (20 percent) or to compare the dollar return on old paintings with the DM return on gold. Only after the returns are expressed in terms of a common unit of measure—for example, all in terms of dollars—can we tell which asset offers the highest expected real rate of return.

RISK AND LIQUIDITY

All else equal, individuals prefer to hold those assets offering the highest expected real rate of return. Our later discussions of particular assets will show, however, that ''all else'' often is not equal. Some assets may be valued by savers for attributes other than the expected real rate of return they offer. Savers care about two main characteristics of an asset other than its return: its **risk,** that is, the variability it contributes to savers' wealth, and its **liquidity,** that is, the ease with which the asset can be sold or exchanged for goods.

1. *Risk.* An asset's real return is usually unpredictable and may turn out to be quite different from what savers expect when they purchase the asset. In our last example, savers found the expected real rate of return on an investment in bonds (10 percent) by subtracting from the expected rate of increase in the investment's dollar value (20 percent) the expected rate of increase in dollar prices (10 percent). But if expectations are wrong and the bonds' dollar value stays constant instead of rising by 20 percent, the saver ends up with a real return of *negative* 10 percent (= 0 percent − 10 percent). Savers dislike uncertainty and are reluctant to hold assets that make their wealth highly variable. An asset with a high expected rate of return may appear undesirable to savers if its realized rate of return fluctuates widely.
2. *Liquidity.* Assets also differ according to the cost and speed at which savers can dispose of them. A house, for example, is not very liquid because its sale usually requires time and the services of brokers, inspectors, and lawyers. In contrast, cash is the most liquid of assets: it is always acceptable at face value as payment for goods or other assets. Savers prefer to hold some liquid assets as a precaution against unexpected expenses that might force them to sell less liquid assets at a loss. They will therefore consider an asset's liquidity as well as its expected return and risk in deciding how much of it to hold.

INTEREST RATES

As in other asset markets, participants in the foreign exchange market base their demands for deposits of different currencies on a comparison of these assets' expected rates of return. To compare returns on different deposits, market participants need two pieces of information. First, they need to know how the money values of the deposits will change. Second, they need to know how exchange rates will change so that they can translate rates of return measured in different currencies into comparable terms.

The first piece of information needed to compute the rate of return on a deposit of a particular currency is the currency's **interest rate,** the amount of that currency an individual can earn by lending a unit of the currency for a year. At a dollar interest rate of 0.10 (quoted as 10 percent per year), the lender of $1 receives $1.10 at the end of the year, $1 of which is principal and 10 cents of which is interest. Looked at from the other side of the transaction, the interest rate on dollars is also the amount that must be paid to borrow $1 for a year. When you buy a U.S. Treasury bill, you earn the interest rate on dollars because you are lending dollars to the U.S. government.

Interest rates play an important role in the foreign exchange market because the large deposits traded there pay interest, each at a rate reflecting its currency of denomination. For example, when the interest rate on dollars is 10 percent per year, a $100,000 deposit is worth $110,000 after a year; when the interest rate on DM is 5 percent per year, a DM 100,000 deposit is worth DM 105,000 after a year. Deposits pay interest because they are really loans from the depositor to the bank. When a corporation or a financial institution deposits a currency in a bank, it is lending that currency to the bank rather than using it for some current expenditure. In other words, the depositor is acquiring an asset denominated in the currency it deposits.

The dollar interest rate is simply the dollar rate of return on dollar deposits. You "buy" the deposit by lending a bank $100,000, and when you are paid back with 10 percent interest at the end of the year your asset is worth $110,000. This gives a rate of return of (110,000 − 100,000)/100,000 = 0.10, or 10 percent per year. Similarly, a foreign currency's interest rate measures the foreign currency return on deposits of that currency. Figure 14-2 shows the behavior of monthly interest rates on dollars and DM since mid-1973. These interest rates are not measured in comparable terms, so there is no reason for them to be close to each other or to move in similar ways over time.[5]

EXCHANGE RATES AND ASSET RETURNS

The interest rates offered by a dollar and a DM deposit tell us how their dollar and DM values will change over a year. The other piece of information we need to compare the rates of return offered by dollar and DM deposits is the expected change in the dollar/DM exchange rate over the year.

An example will show how exchange rates are used together with interest rates to calculate comparable rates of return. Suppose the dollar interest rate is 10 percent per year while the DM interest rate is 5 percent per year. This means a deposit of $1 pays $1.10 after a year while a deposit of DM 1 pays DM 1.05 after a year. Suppose also that today's exchange rate (quoted in American terms) is $0.350 per DM, but that you expect the rate to be $0.380 per DM in a year (perhaps because you expect unfavorable developments in the U.S. economy). To see which of these deposits, DM or dollar, offers a higher expected rate of return, you must ask the question: If I use dollars to buy a DM deposit, how many dollars will I get back after a year? When you answer this question, you are calculating the dollar rate of return on a DM deposit because you are comparing its dollar price today with its dollar value a year from today.

The answer can be found in three steps. First, use today's dollar/DM exchange rate to figure out the dollar price of a DM deposit of, say, DM 1. Second, use the DM interest rate to find the amount of DM you will have a year from now if you purchase a DM 1 deposit today. Third, use the exchange rate you expect to prevail a year from today to calculate the dollar value of those DM.

[5] Chapter 7 discussed *real* interest rates, which are simply real rates of return on loans, that is, interest rates expressed in terms of a consumption basket. Interest rates expressed in terms of currencies are called *nominal* interest rates. The connection between real and nominal interest rates is discussed in detail in Chapter 16.

FIGURE 14-2
Interest rates on dollar and Deutschemark deposits, 1973–1991.
Since dollar and DM interest rates are not measured in comparable terms, they can move quite differently over time.
Source: Morgan Guaranty Trust Company of New York, *World Financial Markets.* Rates shown are one-month Euro-deposit rates, at end of month.

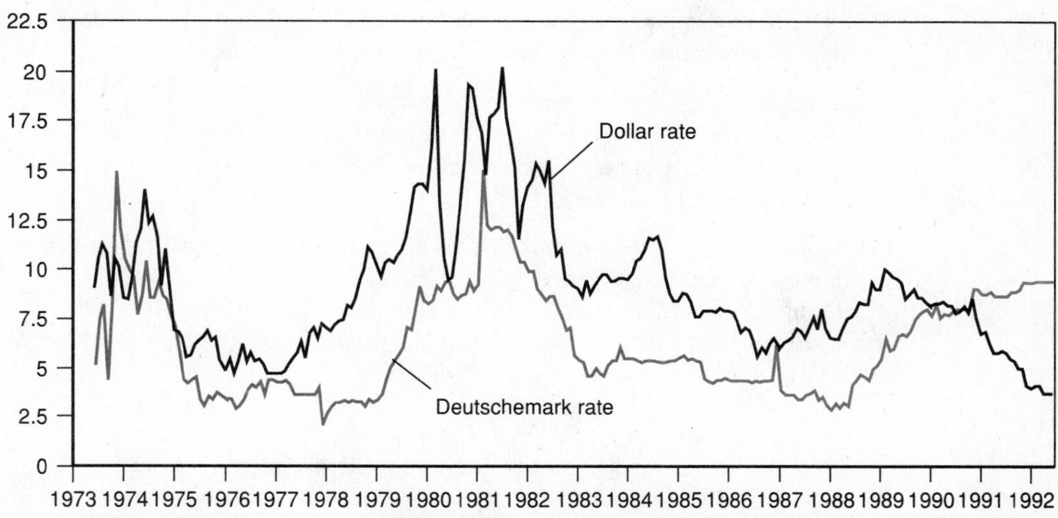

Step 1 is easy. If the exchange rate today is \$0.350 per DM, the dollar price of a DM 1 deposit is just \$0.350. Step 2 is also easy. You know that the interest rate on DM deposits is 5 percent per year. So at the end of a year your DM 1 deposit is worth DM 1.05. Step 3 is a bit harder because you do not actually know what the exchange rate will be a year from now. If you expect the dollar to depreciate against the DM over the coming year so that the exchange rate twelve months from today is \$0.380 per DM, then you'd expect the dollar value of your DM deposit to be (\$0.380 per DM) × (DM 1.05) = \$0.399 after a year.

Now that you know the dollar price of a DM 1 deposit today (\$0.350) and can forecast its value in a year (\$0.399), you can calculate the expected *dollar* rate of return on a DM deposit as (0.399 − 0.350)/0.350 = 0.14, or 14 percent per year. Since the dollar rate of return on dollar deposits is only 10 percent per year, you would expect to do better by holding your wealth in the form of DM deposits. Despite the fact that the dollar interest rate exceeds the DM interest rate by 5 percent per year, the DM's expected appreciation against the dollar gives DM holders a prospective capital gain that is large enough to make DM deposits the higher-yield asset.

A SIMPLE RULE

There is a simple rule that shortens this calculation. First, define the **rate of depreciation** of the dollar against the DM as the percentage increase in the dollar/DM exchange rate over a year. In the last example, the dollar's expected depreciation rate is (0.380

− 0.350)/0.350 = 0.086, or roughly 9 percent per year. Once you have calculated the rate of depreciation of the dollar against the DM, our rule is this: *The dollar rate of return on DM deposits is approximately the DM interest rate plus the rate of depreciation of the dollar against the DM.* In other words, to translate the DM return on DM deposits into dollar terms, you need to add the rate at which the DM's dollar price rises over a year to the DM interest rate.

In our example, the sum of the DM interest rate (5 percent) and the expected depreciation rate of the dollar (roughly 9 percent) is about 14 percent, which is what we found to be the expected dollar return on DM deposits in our first calculation.

We summarize our discussion by introducing some notation:

R_{DM} = today's interest rate on one-year DM deposits,
$E_{\$/DM}$ = today's price of DM in terms of dollars (number of dollars per DM),
$E^e_{\$/DM}$ = dollar/DM exchange rate (number of dollars per DM) expected to prevail a year from today.

(The superscript ^{e} attached to this last exchange rate indicates that it is a forecast of the future exchange rate based on what people know today.)

Using these symbols, we write the expected rate of return on a DM deposit, measured in terms of dollars, as the sum of (1) the DM interest rate and (2) the expected rate of dollar depreciation against the DM,

$$R_{DM} + (E^e_{\$/DM} - E_{\$/DM})/E_{\$/DM}.$$

This expected return is what must be compared with the interest rate on one-year dollar deposits, $R_\$$, in deciding whether dollar or DM deposits offer the higher expected rate of return.[6] The expected rate of return difference between dollar and DM deposits is therefore equal to $R_\$$ less the above expression,

$$R_\$ - [R_{DM} + (E^e_{\$/DM} - E_{\$/DM})/E_{\$/DM}] = R_\$ - R_{DM} - (E^e_{\$/DM} - E_{\$/DM})/E_{\$/DM}. \qquad \textbf{(14-1)}$$

When the difference above is positive, dollar deposits yield the higher expected rate of return; when it is negative, DM deposits yield the higher expected rate of return.

Table 14-3 carries out some illustrative comparisons. In case 1, the interest difference in favor of dollar deposits is 4 percent per year ($R_\$ - R_{DM} = 0.10 - 0.06 = 0.04$), and no change in the exchange rate is expected [$(E^e_{\$/DM} - E_{\$/DM})/E_{\$/DM} = 0.00$]. This means that the expected annual real rate of return on dollar deposits is 4 percent higher than that on DM, so that, other things equal, you would prefer to hold your wealth as dollar rather than DM deposits. In case 2 the interest difference is the same (4 percent), but it is just offset by an expected depreciation rate of the dollar of 4 percent. The two assets therefore have the same expected rate of return.

Case 3 is similar to the one discussed earlier: a 4 percent interest difference in favor of dollar deposits is more than offset by an 8 percent expected depreciation of

[6] If you compute the expected dollar return on DM deposits using the exact three-step method we described before introducing the simple rule, you'll find that it actually equals

$$(1 + R_{DM})(E^e_{\$/DM}/E_{\$/DM}) - 1.$$

This exact formula can be rewritten, however, as

$$R_{DM} + (E^e_{\$/DM} - E_{\$/DM})/E_{\$/DM} + R_{DM} \times (E^e_{\$/DM} - E_{\$/DM})/E_{\$/DM}.$$

The expression above is very close to the formula derived from the simple rule when, as is usually the case, the product $R_{DM} \times (E^e_{\$/DM} - E_{\$/DM})/E_{\$/DM}$ is a small number.

TABLE 14-3 Comparing dollar rates of return on dollar and DM deposits

Case	Dollar interest rate $R_\$$	DM interest rate R_{DM}	Expected rate of dollar depreciation against DM $\frac{E^e_{\$/DM} - E_{\$/DM}}{E_{\$/DM}}$	Rate of return difference between dollar and DM deposits $R_\$ - R_{DM} - \frac{(E^e_{\$/DM} - E_{\$/DM})}{E_{\$/DM}}$
1	0.10	0.06	0.00	0.04
2	0.10	0.06	0.04	0.00
3	0.10	0.06	0.08	−0.04
4	0.10	0.12	−0.04	0.02

the dollar, so DM deposits are preferred by market participants. In case 4, there is a 2 percent interest difference in favor of DM deposits, but the dollar is expected to *appreciate* against the DM by 4 percent over the year. The expected rate of return on dollar deposits is therefore 2 percent per year higher than that on DM.

So far we have been translating all returns into dollar terms. But the rate of return differentials we calculated would have been the same had we chosen to express returns in terms of DM or in terms of some third currency. Suppose, for example, we wanted to measure the return on dollar deposits in terms of DM. Following our simple rule, we would add to the dollar interest rate $R_\$$ the expected rate of depreciation of the DM against the dollar. But the expected rate of depreciation of the DM against the dollar is approximately the expected **rate of appreciation** of the dollar against the DM, that is, the expected rate of depreciation of the dollar against the DM with a minus sign in front of it. This means that in terms of DM, the return on a dollar deposit is

$$R_\$ - (E^e_{\$/DM} - E_{\$/DM})/E_{\$/DM}.$$

The difference between the expression above and R_{DM} is identical to equation (14-1). Thus, it makes no difference to our comparison whether we measure returns in terms of dollars or DM, as long as we measure in terms of a single currency.

RETURN, RISK, AND LIQUIDITY IN THE FOREIGN EXCHANGE MARKET

We observed earlier that a saver deciding which assets to hold may care about assets' riskiness and liquidity in addition to their expected real rates of return. Similarly, the demand for foreign currency assets depends not only on returns but on risk and liquidity. Even if the expected dollar return on DM deposits is higher than that on dollar deposits, for example, people may be reluctant to hold DM deposits if the payoff to holding them varies erratically.

There is no consensus among economists about the importance of risk in the foreign exchange market. Even the definition of "foreign exchange risk" is a topic of debate. For now we will avoid the complex questions involved by assuming that the real returns on all deposits have equal riskiness, regardless of the currency of denomination. In other words, we are assuming that risk differences do not influence the demand for foreign currency assets. We discuss the role of foreign exchange risk in greater detail, however, in Chapters 18 and 22.[7]

Some market participants may be influenced by liquidity factors in deciding which currencies to hold. Most of these participants are firms and individuals involved in international trade. An American importer of French goods, for example, may find it convenient to hold French francs for routine payments even if the expected rate of return on francs is lower than that on dollars. Because payments connected with international trade make up a very small fraction of total foreign exchange transactions, we ignore the liquidity motive for holding foreign currencies.

We are therefore assuming for now that participants in the foreign exchange market base their demands for foreign currency assets exclusively on a comparison of those assets' expected rates of return. The main reason for making this assumption is that it simplifies our analysis of how exchange rates are determined in the foreign exchange market. In addition, the risk and liquidity motives for holding foreign currencies appear to be of secondary importance for many of the international macroeconomic issues discussed in the next few chapters.

Equilibrium in the Foreign Exchange Market

We now use what we have learned about the demand for foreign currency assets to describe how exchange rates are determined. We will show that the exchange rate at which the market settles is the one that makes market participants content to hold existing supplies of deposits of all currencies. When market participants willingly hold the existing supplies of deposits of all currencies, we say that the foreign exchange market is in equilibrium.

The description of exchange rate determination given in this section is only a first step: a full explanation of the exchange rate's current level can be given only after we examine how participants in the foreign exchange market form their expectations about exchange rates they expect to prevail in the future. The next two chapters look at the factors that influence expectations of future exchange rates. For now, however, we will take expected future exchange rates as given.

INTEREST PARITY: THE BASIC EQUILIBRIUM CONDITION

The foreign exchange market is in equilibrium when deposits of all currencies offer the same expected rate of return. The condition that the expected returns on deposits of any two currencies are equal when measured in the same currency is called the **interest parity condition.** It implies that potential holders of foreign currency deposits view them all as equally desirable assets.

[7] In discussing spot and forward foreign exchange transactions, some textbooks make a distinction between foreign exchange "speculators"—market participants who allegedly care only about expected returns—and "hedgers"—market participants whose concern is to avoid risk. We depart from this textbook tradition because it can mislead the unwary: while the speculative and hedging motives are both potentially important in exchange rate determination, the same person can be both a speculator and a hedger if she cares about both return and risk. Our assumption that risk is unimportant in determining the demand for foreign currency assets means, in terms of the traditional language, that the speculative motive for holding foreign currencies is far more important than the hedging motive.

Let's see why the foreign exchange market is in equilibrium only when the interest parity condition holds. Suppose the dollar interest rate is 10 percent and the DM interest rate is 6 percent, but that the dollar is expected to depreciate against the DM at an 8 percent rate over a year. (This is case 3 in Table 14-3.) In the circumstances described, the rate of return on DM deposits would be 4 percent per year higher than that on dollar deposits. We assumed at the end of the last section that individuals always prefer to hold deposits of currencies offering the highest expected return. This means that if the expected return on DM deposits is 4 percent greater than that on dollar deposits, no one will be willing to continue holding dollar deposits, and holders of dollar deposits will be trying to sell them for DM deposits. There will therefore be an excess supply of dollar deposits and an excess demand for DM deposits in the foreign exchange market.

As a contrasting example, suppose that dollar deposits again offer a 10 percent interest rate but DM deposits offer a 12 percent rate and the dollar is expected to *appreciate* against the DM by 4 percent over the coming year. (This is case 4 in Table 14-3.) Now the return on dollar deposits is 2 percent higher. In this case no one would demand DM deposits, so they would be in excess supply and dollar deposits would be in excess demand.

When, however, the dollar interest rate is 10 percent, the DM interest rate is 6 percent, and the dollar's expected depreciation rate against the DM is 4 percent, dollar and DM deposits offer the same rate of return and participants in the foreign exchange market are willing to hold either. (This is case 2 in Table 14-3.)

Only when all expected rates of return are equal—that is, when the interest parity condition holds—is there no excess supply of some type of deposit and no excess demand for another. The foreign exchange market is in equilibrium when no type of deposit is in excess demand or excess supply. We can therefore say that the foreign exchange market is in equilibrium when the interest parity condition holds.

To express interest parity between dollar and DM deposits symbolically, we can use expression (14-1), which shows the difference between the two assets' expected rates of return measured in dollars. The expected rates of return are equal when

$$R_{\$} = R_{DM} + (E^{e}_{\$/DM} - E_{\$/DM})/E_{\$/DM}. \qquad \textbf{(14-2)}$$

You probably suspect that when dollar deposits offer a higher return than DM deposits, the dollar will appreciate against the DM as investors all try to shift their funds into dollars. Conversely, the dollar should depreciate against the DM when it is DM deposits that initially offer the higher return. This intuition is exactly correct. To understand the mechanism at work, however, we must take a careful look at how exchange rate changes like these help to maintain equilibrium in the foreign exchange market.

HOW CHANGES IN THE CURRENT EXCHANGE RATE AFFECT EXPECTED RETURNS

As a first step in understanding how the foreign exchange market finds its equilibrium, we examine how changes in today's exchange rate affect the expected return on a foreign currency deposit when interest rates and expectations about the future exchange rate do not change.

It is easiest to begin with an example. We ask how a change in today's dollar/DM exchange rate, all else held constant, changes the expected return, measured in terms of dollars, on DM deposits. Suppose that today's dollar/DM rate is \$0.365 per DM and the exchange rate you expect for this day next year is \$0.383 per DM. Then the expected rate of dollar depreciation against the DM is (0.383 − 0.365)/0.365 = 0.05, or 5 percent per year. This means that when you buy a DM deposit, you not only earn the interest R_{DM} but also get a 5 percent "bonus" in terms of dollars. Now suppose that today's exchange rate suddenly jumps up to \$0.370 per DM (a depreciation of the dollar and an appreciation of the DM) but the expected future rate is *still* \$0.383 per DM. What has happened to the "bonus" you expected to get from the DM's increase in value in terms of dollars? The expected rate of dollar depreciation is now only (0.383 − 0.370)/0.370 = 0.035, or 3.5 percent instead of 5 percent. Since R_{DM} has not changed, the dollar return on DM deposits, which is the sum of R_{DM} and the expected rate of dollar depreciation, has *fallen* by 1.5 percent per year (5 percent − 3.5 percent).

In Table 14-4 we work out the dollar return on DM deposits for various levels of today's dollar/DM exchange rate $E_{\$/DM}$, always assuming the expected *future* exchange rate remains fixed at \$0.383 per DM and the DM interest rate is 5 percent per year. As you can see, a rise in today's dollar/DM exchange rate (a depreciation of the dollar against the DM) always *lowers* the expected dollar return on DM deposits (as in our example), while a fall in today's dollar/DM rate (an appreciation of the dollar against the DM) always *raises* this return.

It may run counter to your intuition that a depreciation of the dollar against the DM makes DM deposits less attractive relative to dollar deposits (by lowering the expected dollar return on DM deposits) while an appreciation of the dollar makes DM deposits more attractive. This result will seem less surprising if you remember we have assumed that the expected future dollar/DM rate and interest rates do not change. A dollar depreciation today, for example, means the dollar now needs to depreciate by a *smaller* amount to reach any given expected future level. If the expected future dollar/DM exchange rate does not change when the dollar depreciates today, the dollar's expected future depreciation against the DM therefore falls, or, alternatively, the dollar's expected future appreciation rises. Since interest rates also are unchanged, today's

TABLE 14-4 Today's dollar/DM exchange rate and the expected dollar return on DM deposits when $E^e_{\$/DM}$ = \$0.383 per DM

Today's dollar/DM exchange rate $E_{\$/DM}$	*Interest rate on DM deposits* R_{DM}	*Expected dollar depreciation rate against DM* $\frac{0.383 - E_{\$/DM}}{E_{\$/DM}}$	*Dollar return on DM deposits* $R_{DM} + \frac{0.383 - E_{\$/DM}}{E_{\$/DM}}$
0.395	0.05	−0.03	0.02
0.383	0.05	0.00	0.05
0.375	0.05	0.02	0.07
0.370	0.05	0.035	0.085
0.365	0.05	0.05	0.10

dollar depreciation thus makes DM deposits less attractive compared with dollar deposits.

Put another way, a current dollar depreciation that affects neither exchange rate expectations nor interest rates leaves the expected future dollar payoff of a DM deposit the same but raises the deposit's current dollar cost. This change naturally makes DM deposits less attractive relative to dollars.

It may also run counter to your intuition that *today's* exchange rate can change while the exchange rate expected for the *future* does not. We will indeed study cases later in this book when both of these rates do change at once. We nonetheless hold the expected future exchange rate constant in the present discussion because that is the clearest way to illustrate the effect of today's exchange rate on expected returns. If it helps, you can imagine we are looking at the impact of a *temporary* change so brief that it has no effect on the exchange rate expected for next year.

Figure 14-3 shows the calculations in Table 14-4 in a graphic form that will be helpful in our analysis of exchange rate determination. The vertical axis in the figure measures today's dollar/DM exchange rate and the horizontal axis measures the expected dollar return on DM deposits. For fixed values of the expected future dollar/DM exchange rate and the DM interest rate, the relation beween today's dollar/DM exchange rate and the expected dollar return on DM deposits defines a downward-sloping schedule.

FIGURE 14-3
How changes in the dollar/DM exchange rate affect the dollar return on DM deposits, given $E^e_{\$/DM} =$ 0.383 and $R_{DM} = .05$.
An appreciation of the dollar against the DM raises the expected return on DM deposits, measured in terms of dollars.

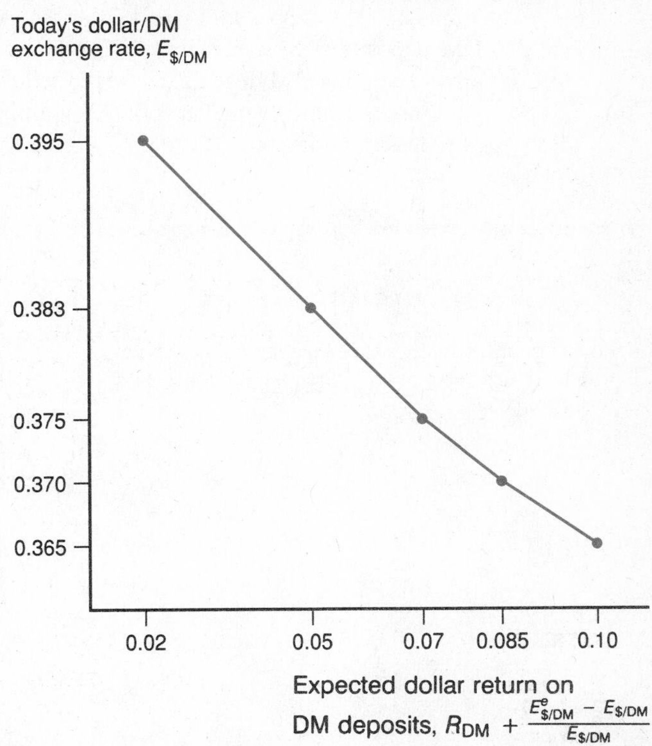

THE EQUILIBRIUM EXCHANGE RATE

Now that we understand why the interest parity condition must hold if the foreign exchange market is in equilibrium and how today's exchange rate affects the expected return on foreign currency deposits, we can see how equilibrium exchange rates are determined. Our main conclusion will be that exchange rates always adjust to maintain interest parity. We continue to assume that the dollar interest rate $R_{\$}$, the DM interest rate R_{DM}, and the expected future dollar/DM exchange rate $E^e_{\$/DM}$, are all *given.*

Figure 14-4 illustrates how the equilibrium dollar/DM exchange rate is determined under this assumption. The vertical schedule in the graph indicates the given level of $R_{\$}$, the return on dollar deposits measured in terms of dollars. The downward-sloping schedule shows how the expected return on DM deposits measured in terms of dollars depends on the current dollar/DM exchange rate. This second schedule is derived in the same way as the one shown in Figure 14-3.

The equilibrium dollar/DM rate is the one indicated by the intersection of the two schedules at point 1, $E^1_{\$/DM}$. At this exchange rate, the returns on dollar and DM assets are equal, so that the interest parity condition (14-2),

$$R_{\$} = R_{DM} + (E^e_{\$/DM} - E^1_{\$/DM})/E^1_{\$/DM},$$

is satisfied.

Let's see why the exchange rate will tend to settle at point 1 in Figure 14-4 if it is initially at a point such as 2 or 3. Suppose first that we are at point 2, with the exchange rate equal to $E^2_{\$/DM}$. The downward-sloping schedule measuring the expected dollar return on DM deposits tells us that at the exchange rate $E^2_{\$/DM}$, the rate of return on DM deposits is less than the rate of return on dollar deposits, $R_{\$}$. In this situation anyone holding DM deposits wishes to sell them for the more lucrative dollar deposits: the foreign exchange market is out of equilibrium because participants are *unwilling* to hold DM deposits.

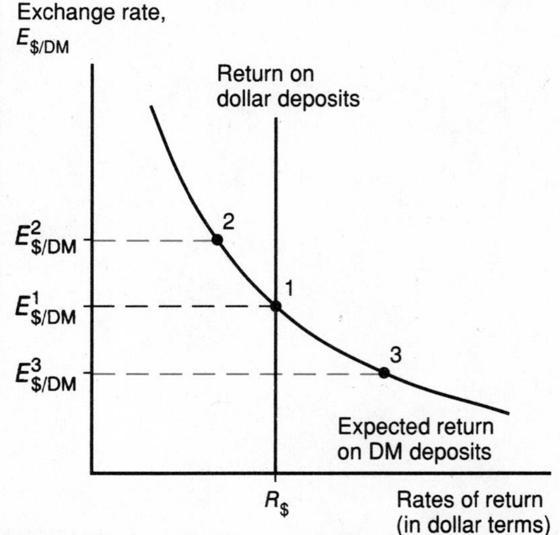

FIGURE 14-4
Determination of the equilibrium dollar/DM exchange rate.
Equilibrium in the foreign exchange market is at point 1, where the expected dollar returns on dollar and DM deposits are equal.

How does the exchange rate adjust? The unhappy owners of DM deposits attempt to sell them for dollar deposits, but because the return on dollar deposits is higher than that on DM deposits at the exchange rate $E^2_{\$/DM}$, no holder of a dollar deposit is willing to sell it for DM at that rate. As DM holders try to entice dollar holders to trade by offering them a better price for dollars, the dollar/DM exchange rate falls toward $E^1_{\$/DM}$; that is, DM become cheaper in terms of dollars. Once the exchange rate reaches $E^1_{\$/DM}$, DM and dollar deposits offer equal returns and holders of DM deposits no longer have an incentive to try to sell them for dollars. The foreign exchange market is therefore in equilibrium. In falling from $E^2_{\$/DM}$ to $E^1_{\$/DM}$, the exchange rate equalizes the expected returns on the two types of deposit by increasing the rate at which the dollar is expected to depreciate in the future, thereby making DM deposits more attractive.

The same process works in reverse if we are initially at point 3 with an exchange rate of $E^3_{\$/DM}$. At point 3, the return on DM deposits exceeds that on dollar deposits, so there is now an excess supply of the latter. As unwilling holders of dollar deposits bid for the more attractive DM deposits, the price of DM in terms of dollars tends to rise; that is, the dollar tends to depreciate against the DM. When the exchange rate has moved to $E^1_{\$/DM}$, rates of return are equalized across currencies and the market is in equilibrium. The depreciation of the dollar from $E^3_{\$/DM}$ to $E^1_{\$/DM}$ makes DM deposits less attractive relative to dollar deposits by reducing the rate at which the dollar is expected to depreciate in the future.[8]

Interest Rates, Expectations, and Equilibrium

Having seen how exchange rates are determined, we now take a look at how current exchange rates are affected by changes in interest rates and in expectations about the future. In our discussion we will see that the exchange rate (which is the relative price of two assets) responds to factors that alter the expected rates of return on those two assets.

THE EFFECT OF CHANGING INTEREST RATES ON THE CURRENT EXCHANGE RATE

We often read in the newspaper that the dollar is strong because U.S. interest rates are high or that it is falling because U.S. interest rates are falling. Can these statements be explained using our analysis of the foreign exchange market?

To answer this question we again turn to a diagram. Figure 14-5 shows a rise in the interest rate on dollars, from $R^1_\$$ to $R^2_\$$, as a rightward shift of the vertical schedule. At the initial exchange rate $E^1_{\$/DM}$, the expected return on dollar deposits is now higher than that on DM deposits by an amount equal to the distance between points 1 and 1′. As we have seen, this difference causes the dollar to appreciate to $E^2_{\$/DM}$ (point 2).

[8] We could have developed our diagram from the perspective of Germany, with the DM/dollar exchange rate $E_{DM/\$}$ ($= 1/E_{\$/DM}$) on the vertical axis, a schedule vertical at R_{DM} to indicate the DM return on DM deposits, and a downward-sloping schedule showing how the DM return on dollar deposits varies with $E_{DM/\$}$. An exercise at the end of the chapter asks you to show that this alternative way of looking at equilibrium in the foreign exchange market gives the same answers as the method used in the text.

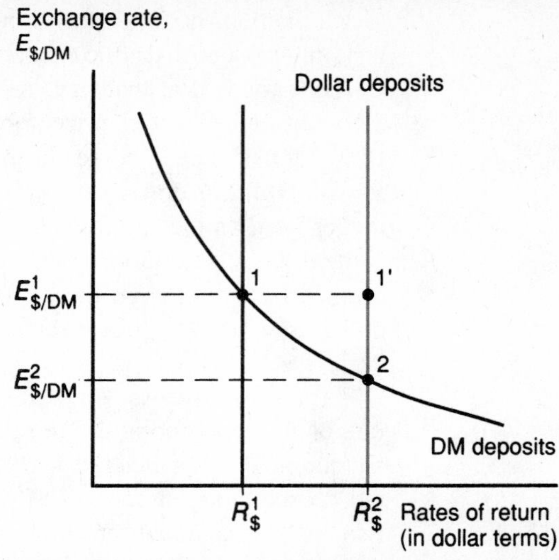

FIGURE 14-5
Effect of a rise in the dollar interest rate.
A rise in the interest rate offered by dollar deposits causes the dollar to appreciate from $E^1_{\$/DM}$ (point 1) to $E^2_{\$/DM}$ (point 2).

Because there has been no change in the DM interest rate or in the expected future exchange rate, the dollar's appreciation today raises the expected dollar return on DM deposits by increasing the rate at which the dollar is expected to depreciate in the future.

Figure 14-6 shows the effect of a rise in the DM interest rate R_{DM}. This change causes the downward-sloping schedule (which measures the expected dollar return on DM deposits) to shift rightward. (To see why, ask yourself how a rise in the DM interest rate alters the dollar return on DM deposits, given the current exchange rate and the expected future rate.)

At the initial exchange rate $E^1_{\$/DM}$ the expected depreciation rate of the dollar is the same as before the rise in R_{DM}, so the expected return on DM deposits now exceeds that on dollar deposits. The dollar/DM exchange rate rises (from $E^1_{\$/DM}$ to $E^2_{\$/DM}$) to eliminate the excess supply of dollar assets at point 1. As before, the dollar's depreciation against the DM eliminates the excess supply of dollar assets by lowering the expected dollar rate of return on DM deposits. A rise in German interest rates therefore leads to a depreciation of the dollar against the DM or, looked at from the German perspective, an appreciation of the DM against the dollar.

Our discussion shows that, all else equal, *an increase in the interest paid on deposits of a currency causes that currency to appreciate against foreign currencies.*

Before we conclude that the newspaper account of the effect of interest rates on exchange rates is correct, we must remember that our assumption of a *constant* expected future exchange rate often is unrealistic. In many cases a change in interest rates will be accompanied by a change in the expected future exchange rate. This change in the expected future exchange rate will depend, in turn, on the economic causes of the interest rate change. We compare different possible relationships between interest rates and expected future exchange rates in Chapter 16. Keep in mind for now that in the real world, we cannot predict how a given interest rate change will alter exchange rates unless we know *why* the interest rate is changing.

FIGURE 14-6
Effect of a rise in the DM interest rate.
A rise in the interest rate paid by DM deposits causes the dollar to depreciate from $E^1_{\$/DM}$ (point 1) to $E^2_{\$/DM}$ (point 2). (This figure also describes the effect of a rise in the expected future \$/DM exchange rate.)

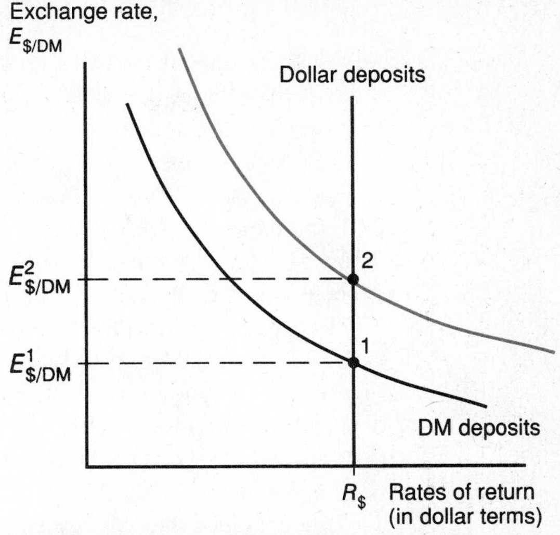

The Perils of Forecasting Exchange Rates

If exchange rates are asset prices that respond immediately to changes in expectations and interest rates, they should have properties similar to those of other asset prices, for example, stock prices. Like stock prices, exchange rates should respond strongly to "news," that is, unexpected economic and political events; and, like stock prices, they therefore should be very hard to forecast.

Despite the notorious difficulty of forecasting stock prices, there is no shortage of newsletters and television programs devoted to stock market prediction. Similarly, numerous firms sell exchange rate forecasts to individual investors, international corporations, and others with financial interests in the foreign exchange market. In a well-known study, Richard M. Levich of New York University surveyed the track record of a dozen exchange rate forecasting companies through 1982.*

The results were depressing for would-be exchange rate oracles but encouraging for the asset approach to exchange rates. Levich found little evidence over his sample period that professional forecasters do systematically better than an individual who, for example, uses the three-month forward exchange rate as a forecast of the spot rate that will materialize in three months.** This finding does not mean that forward rates are accurate predictors; on the contrary, the evidence suggests that forward rates usually contain little information useful in predicting future spot rates (as we shall see in Chapter 22). What Levich's results do show is that inherently unpredictable "news" plays such a dominant role in determining exchange rates that exchange rate movements, like movements in stock prices, are almost completely impossible to forecast.

* See "Evaluating the Performance of the Forecasters," in Donald R. Lessard, ed., *International Financial Management: Theory and Application,* 2nd edition (New York: John Wiley and Sons, 1985), pp. 218–233.

** This chapter's appendix suggests one reason for thinking that forward exchange rates might be closely related to expected future spot rates.

THE EFFECT OF CHANGING EXPECTATIONS ON THE CURRENT EXCHANGE RATE

Figure 14-6 may also be used to study the effect on today's exchange rate of a rise in the expected future dollar/DM exchange rate, $E^e_{\$/DM}$.

Given today's exchange rate, a rise in the expected future price of DM in terms of dollars raises the dollar's expected depreciation rate. For example, if today's exchange rate is \$0.365 per DM and the rate expected to prevail in a year is \$0.383 per DM, the expected depreciation rate of the dollar against the DM is (0.383 − 0.365)/0.365 = 0.05; if the expected future exchange rate now rises to \$0.387 per DM, the expected depreciation rate also rises, to (0.387 − 0.365)/0.365 = 0.06.

Because a rise in the expected depreciation rate of the dollar raises the expected dollar return on DM deposits, the downward-sloping schedule shifts to the right, as in Figure 14-6. At the initial exchange rate $E^1_{\$/DM}$ there is now an excess supply of dollar deposits: DM deposits offer a higher expected rate of return (measured in dollar terms) than do dollar deposits. The dollar therefore depreciates against the DM until equilibrium is reached at point 2.

We conclude that, all else equal, *a rise in the expected future exchange rate causes a rise in the current exchange rate. Similarly, a fall in the expected future exchange rate causes a fall in the current exchange rate.*

Summary

1. An *exchange rate* is the price of one country's currency in terms of another country's currency. Exchange rates play a role in spending decisions because they enable us to translate different countries' prices into comparable terms. All else equal, a *depreciation* of a country's currency against foreign currencies (a rise in the home currency prices of foreign currencies) makes its exports cheaper and its imports more expensive. An *appreciation* of its currency (a fall in the home currency prices of foreign currencies) makes its exports more expensive and its imports cheaper.

2. Exchange rates are determined in the *foreign exchange market.* The major participants in that market are commercial banks, international corporations, nonbank financial institutions, and national central banks. Commercial banks play a pivotal role in the market because they facilitate the exchanges of interest-bearing bank deposits that make up the bulk of foreign exchange trading. Even though foreign exchange trading takes place in many financial centers around the world, modern telecommunication technology links those centers together into a single market that is open twenty-four hours a day. An important category of foreign exchange trading is *forward* trading, in which parties agree to exchange currencies on some future date at a prenegotiated exchange rate. In contrast, *spot* trades are (for practical purposes) settled immediately.

3. Because the exchange rate is the relative price of two assets, it is most appropriately thought of as being an asset price itself. The basic principle of asset pricing is that an asset's current value depends on its expected future purchasing power. In evaluating an asset, savers look at the expected *rate of return* it offers, that is, the rate at which the value of an investment in the asset is expected to rise over time. It is possible to measure an asset's expected rate of return in different ways, each depending

on the units in which the asset's value is measured. Savers care about an asset's expected *real rate of return,* the rate at which its value expressed in terms of a representative output basket is expected to rise.

4. When relative asset returns are relevant, as in the foreign exchange market, it is appropriate to compare expected changes in assets' currency values, provided those values are expressed in the same currency. If *risk* and *liquidity* factors do not strongly influence the demands for foreign currency assets, participants in the foreign exchange market always prefer to hold those assets yielding the highest expected rate of return.

5. The returns on deposits traded in the foreign exchange market depend on *interest rates* and expected exchange rate changes. To compare the expected rates of return offered by dollar and DM deposits, for example, the return on DM deposits must be expressed in dollar terms by adding to the DM interest rate the expected *rate of depreciation* of the dollar against the DM (or *rate of appreciation* of the DM against the dollar) over the deposit's holding period.

6. Equilibrium in the foreign exchange market requires *interest parity;* that is, deposits of all currencies must offer the same expected rate of return when returns are measured in comparable terms.

7. For given interest rates and a given expectation of the future exchange rate, the interest parity condition tells us the current equilibrium exchange rate. When the expected return on DM deposits exceeds that on dollar deposits, for example, the dollar immediately depreciates against the DM. Other things equal, a dollar depreciation today reduces the expected dollar return on DM deposits by reducing the depreciation rate of the dollar against the DM expected for the future. Similarly, when the expected return on DM deposits is below that on dollar deposits, the dollar must immediately appreciate against the DM. Other things equal, a current appreciation of the dollar makes DM deposits more attractive by increasing the dollar's expected future depreciation against the German currency.

8. All else equal, a rise in dollar interest rates causes the dollar to appreciate against the DM while a rise in DM interest rates causes the dollar to depreciate against the DM. Today's exchange rate is also altered by changes in its expected future level. If there is a rise in the expected future level of the dollar/DM rate, for example, then at unchanged interest rates today's dollar/DM rate will also rise.

Key Terms

exchange rate
depreciation
appreciation
foreign exchange market
interbank trading
arbitrage
vehicle currency
spot exchange rate
forward exchange rate
rate of return
real rate of return
risk
liquidity
interest rate
rate of depreciation
rate of appreciation
interest parity condition

Problems

1. In Munich a bratwurst costs 2 DM; a hot dog costs \$1 at Boston's Fenway Park. At an exchange rate of \$0.5 per DM, what is the price of a bratwurst in terms of hot dogs? All else equal, how does this relative price change if the dollar appreciates to \$0.4 per DM? Compared with the initial situation, has a hot dog become more or less expensive relative to a bratwurst?
2. A U.S. dollar costs 8 French francs, but the same dollar can be purchased for 2 Swiss francs. What is the French franc/Swiss franc exchange rate?
3. Calculate the dollar rates of return on the following assets:
   a. A painting whose price rises from \$200,000 to \$250,000 in a year.
   b. A bottle of a rare Burgundy, Domaine de la Romanée-Conti 1978, whose price rises from \$180 to \$216 between 1993 and 1994.
   c. A £10,000 deposit in a London bank in a year when the interest rate on pounds is 10 percent and the \$/£ exchange rate moves from \$1.50 per pound to \$1.38 per pound.
4. What would be the real rates of return on the assets in the preceding question if the price changes described were accompanied by a simultaneous 10 percent increase in all dollar prices?
5. Suppose the dollar interest rate and the pound sterling interest rate are the same, 5 percent per year. What is the relation between the current equilibrium \$/£ exchange rate and its expected future level? Suppose the expected future \$/£ exchange rate, \$1.52 per pound, remains constant as Britain's interest rate rises to 10 percent per year. If the U.S. interest rate also remains constant, what is the new equilibrium \$/£ exchange rate?
6. Traders in asset markets suddenly learn that the interest rate on dollars will decline in the near future. Use the diagrammatic analysis of the chapter to determine the effect on the *current* dollar/DM exchange rate, assuming current interest rates on dollar and DM deposits do not change.
7. We noted that we could have developed our diagrammatic analysis of foreign exchange market equilibrium from the perspective of Germany, with the DM/dollar exchange rate $E_{DM/\$}$ ($= 1/E_{\$/DM}$) on the vertical axis, a schedule vertical at R_{DM} to indicate the DM return on DM deposits, and a downward-sloping schedule showing how the DM return on dollar deposits varies with $E_{DM/\$}$. Derive this alternative picture of equilibrium and use it to examine the effect of changes in interest rates and the expected future exchange rate. Do your answers agree with those we found earlier?
8. The following report appeared in the *New York Times* on August 7, 1989 ("Dollar's Strength a Surprise," p. D1):

   > But now the sentiment is that the economy is heading for a "soft landing," with the economy slowing significantly and inflation subsiding, but without a recession.
   >
   > This outlook is good for the dollar for two reasons. A soft landing is not as disruptive as a recession, so the foreign investments that support the dollar are more likely to continue.

Also, a soft landing would not force the Federal Reserve to push interest rates sharply lower to stimulate growth. Falling interest rates can put downward pressure on the dollar because they make investments in dollar-denominated securities less attractive to foreigners, prompting the selling of dollars. In addition, the optimism sparked by the expectation of a soft landing can even offset some of the pressure on the dollar from lower interest rates.

a. Show how you would interpret the third paragraph of this report using this chapter's model of exchange rate determination.

b. What additional factors in exchange rate determination might help you explain the second paragraph?

9. Suppose the dollar exchange rates of the DM and the pound sterling are equally variable. The DM, however, tends to depreciate unexpectedly against the dollar when the return on the rest of your wealth is unexpectedly high, while the pound tends to appreciate unexpectedly in the same circumstances. As a U.S. resident, which currency, the DM or the pound, would you consider riskier?

10. Does any of the discussion in this chapter lead you to believe that dollar deposits may have liquidity characteristics different from those of other currency deposits? If so, how would the differences affect the interest differential between, say, dollar and French franc deposits? Do you have any guesses about how the liquidity of DM, pound sterling, and yen deposits may be changing over time?

11. In October 1979, the U.S. central bank (the Federal Reserve System) announced it would play a less active role in limiting fluctuations in dollar interest rates. After this new policy was put into effect, the dollar's exchange rates against foreign currencies became more volatile. Does our analysis of the foreign exchange market suggest any connection between these two events?

12. Imagine that everyone in the world pays a tax of τ percent on interest earnings and on any capital gains due to exchange rate changes. How would such a tax alter the analysis of the interest parity condition? How does the answer change if the tax applies to interest earnings but *not* to capital gains, which are untaxed?

13. Suppose the one-year forward $/DM exchange rate is $0.38 per DM and the spot exchange rate is $0.362 per DM. What is the forward premium on DM (the forward discount on dollars)? What is the difference between the interest rate on one-year dollar deposits and that on one-year DM deposits (assuming no political risk)?

Further Reading

J. Orlin Grabbe. *International Financial Markets,* 2nd edition. New York: Elsevier Science Publishing Co., 1991. Chapters 3–6, 7, 10, and 11 are especially pertinent to topics discussed in this chapter.

Peter B. Kenen. *The Role of the Dollar as an International Currency.* Occasional Paper 13. New York: Group of Thirty, 1983. Evidence on the U.S. dollar's use in international trade and financial transactions.

John Maynard Keynes. *A Tract on Monetary Reform,* Chapter 3. London: Macmillan, 1923. Classic analysis of the forward exchange market and covered interest parity.

Paul R. Krugman. "The International Role of the Dollar: Theory and Prospect," in John F. O. Bilson and Richard C. Marston, eds. *Exchange Rate Theory and Practice.* Chicago: University of Chicago Press, 1984, pp. 261–278. Theoretical and empirical analysis of the dollar's position as an "international money."

Roger M. Kubarych. *Foreign Exchange Markets in the United States,* revised edition. New York: Federal Reserve Bank of New York, 1983. A detailed description of the structure and functions of the foreign exchange market.

Ronald I. McKinnon. *Money in International Exchange: The Convertible Currency System.* New York: Oxford University Press, 1979. Theoretical and institutional analysis of the place of the foreign exchange market in international monetary relations.

Michael Mussa. "Empirical Regularities in the Behavior of Exchange Rates and Theories of the Foreign Exchange Market," in Karl Brunner and Allan H. Meltzer, eds. *Policies for Employment, Prices and Exchange Rates,* Carnegie-Rochester Conference Series on Public Policy 11. Amsterdam: North-Holland, 1979, pp. 9–57. Examines the empirical basis of the asset price approach to exchange rate determination.

Julian Walmsley. *The Foreign Exchange Handbook: A User's Guide.* New York: John Wiley and Sons, 1983. A basic text on the terminology and institutions of the foreign exchange market.

Appendix to Chapter 14

Forward Exchange Rates and Covered Interest Parity

This appendix explains how forward exchange rates are determined. Under the assumption that the interest parity condition always holds, a forward exchange rate equals the spot exchange rate expected to prevail on the forward contract's value date.

As the first step in the discussion, we point out the close connection among the forward exchange rate between two currencies, their spot exchange rate, and the interest rates on deposits denominated in those currencies. The connection is described by the *covered interest parity* condition, which is similar to the (noncovered) interest parity condition defining foreign exchange market equilibrium but involves the forward exchange rate rather than the expected future spot exchange rate.

To be concrete, we again consider dollar and DM deposits. Suppose you want to buy a DM deposit with dollars but would like to be *certain* about the number of dollars it will be worth at the end of a year. You can avoid exchange rate risk by buying a DM deposit and, at the same time, selling the proceeds of your investment forward. When you buy a DM deposit with dollars and at the same time sell the principal and interest forward for dollars, we say you have "covered" yourself, that is, avoided the possibility of an unexpected depreciation of the DM.

The covered interest parity condition states that the rates of return on dollar deposits and "covered" foreign deposits must be the same. An example will clarify the meaning of the condition and illustrate why it must always hold. Let $F_{\$/DM}$ stand for the one-year forward price of DM in terms of dollars, and suppose $F_{\$/DM} = \$0.387$ per DM. Assume that at the same time, the spot exchange rate $E_{\$/DM} = \$0.365$ per DM, $R_{\$} = 0.10$, and $R_{DM} = 0.05$. The (dollar) rate of return on a dollar deposit is clearly 0.10, or 10 percent per year. What is the rate of return on a covered DM deposit?

We answer this question as in the chapter. A DM 1 deposit costs \$0.365 today, and it is worth DM 1.05 after a year. If you sell DM 1.05 forward today at the forward exchange rate of \$0.387 per DM, the dollar value of your investment at the end of a year is (\$0.387 per DM) × DM 1.05 = \$0.406. The rate of return on a covered purchase of a DM deposit is therefore (0.406 − 0.365)/0.365 = 0.11. This 11 percent per year rate of return exceeds the 10 percent offered by dollar deposits, so covered interest parity does not hold. In this situation, no one would be willing to hold dollar deposits; everyone would prefer covered DM deposits.

More formally, we can express the covered return on a DM deposit as

$$\frac{F_{\$/DM}(1 + R_{DM}) - E_{\$/DM}}{E_{\$/DM}},$$

which is approximately equal to

$$R_{DM} + \frac{F_{\$/DM} - E_{\$/DM}}{E_{\$/DM}}$$

when the product $R_{DM} \times (F_{\$/DM} - E_{\$/DM})/E_{\$/DM}$ is a small number. The covered interest parity condition can therefore be written

$$R_{\$} = R_{DM} + (F_{\$/DM} - E_{\$/DM})/E_{\$/DM}.$$

The quantity

$$(F_{\$/DM} - E_{\$/DM})/E_{\$/DM}$$

is called the *forward premium* on DM against dollars. (It is also called the *forward discount* on dollars against DM.) Using this terminology, we can state the covered interest parity condition as follows: *The interest rate on dollar deposits equals the interest rate on DM deposits plus the forward premium on DM against dollars (the forward discount on dollars against DM).*

There is strong empirical evidence that the covered interest parity condition holds for different foreign currency deposits issued within a single financial center. Indeed, currency traders often set the forward exchange rates they quote by looking at current interest rates and spot exchange rates and using the covered interest parity formula.[1] Deviations from covered interest parity can occur, however, if the deposits being compared are located in different countries. These deviations occur when asset holders fear that governments may impose regulations which prevent the free movement of foreign funds across national borders. Our derivation of the covered interest parity condition implicitly assumed there was no political risk of this kind.[2]

By comparing the (noncovered) interest parity condition,

$$R_{\$} = R_{DM} + (E^e_{\$/DM} - E_{\$/DM})/E_{\$/DM},$$

with the *covered* interest parity condition, you will find that both conditions can be true at the same time only if the one-year forward \$/DM rate quoted today equals the spot exchange rate people expect to materialize a year from today:

$$F_{\$/DM} = E^e_{\$/DM}.$$

This makes intuitive sense. When two parties agree to trade foreign exchange on a date in the future, the exchange rate they agree on is the spot rate they expect to prevail on that date. The important difference between covered and noncovered transactions should be kept in mind, however. Covered transactions do not involve exchange rate risk, noncovered transactions do.[3]

The theory of covered interest parity helps explain the close correlation between movements in spot and forward exchange rates shown in Figure 14-1, a correlation typical of all major currencies. The unexpected economic events that affect expected asset returns often have a relatively small effect on international interest rate differences between deposits with short maturities (for example, three months). To maintain covered interest parity, therefore, spot and forward rates for the corresponding maturities must change roughly in proportion to each other.

We conclude this appendix with one further application of the covered interest parity condition. To illustrate the role of forward exchange rates, the chapter used the example of an American importer of Japanese radios anxious about the \$/¥ exchange rate he would face in 30 days when the time came to pay his supplier. In the example, the importer solved his problem by selling forward for yen enough dollars to cover the cost of the radios. But he could have solved his problem in a different, more complicated way. He could have (1) borrowed dollars from his bank; (2) sold those dollars immediately for yen at the spot exchange rate and placed

[1] Empirical evidence supporting the covered interest parity condition is provided by Frank McCormick in "Covered Interest Arbitrage: Unexploited Profits? Comment," *Journal of Political Economy* 87 (April 1979), pp. 411–417, and by Kevin Clinton in "Transactions Costs and Covered Interest Arbitrage: Theory and Evidence," *Journal of Political Economy* 96 (April 1988), pp. 358–370.

[2] For a more detailed discussion of the role of political risk in the forward exchange market, see Robert Z. Aliber, "The Interest Parity Theorem: A Reinterpretation," *Journal of Political Economy* 81 (November/December 1973), pp. 1451–1459. Of course, actual restrictions on cross-border money movements can also cause covered interest parity deviations.

[3] We indicated in the text that the (noncovered) interest parity condition, while a useful simplification, may not always hold exactly if the riskiness of currencies influences demands in the foreign exchange market. Therefore, the forward rate may differ from the expected future spot rate by a risk factor even if *covered* interest parity holds true. As noted earlier, the role of risk in exchange rate determination is discussed more fully in Chapters 18 and 22.

the yen in a 30-day yen bank deposit; (3) then, after 30 days, used the proceeds of the maturing yen deposit to pay his Japanese supplier; and (4) used the realized proceeds of his U.S. radio sales, less his profits, to repay his original dollar loan.

Which course of action—the forward purchase of yen or the sequence of four transactions described in the preceding paragraph—is more profitable for the importer? We leave it to you, as an exercise, to show that the two strategies yield the same profit when the covered interest parity condition holds.

Money, Interest Rates, and Exchange Rates
Chapter 15

Chapter 14 showed how the exchange rate between currencies depends on two factors, the interest that can be earned on deposits of those currencies and the expected future exchange rate. To understand fully the determination of exchange rates, however, we have to learn how interest rates themselves are determined and how expectations of future exchange rates are formed. In the next three chapters we examine these topics by building an economic model that links exchange rates, interest rates, and other important macroeconomic variables such as the inflation rate and output.

The first step in building the model is to explain the effects of a country's money supply and of the demand for its money on its interest rate and exchange rate. Because exchange rates are the relative prices of national monies, factors that affect a country's money supply or demand are among the most powerful determinants of its currency's exchange rate against foreign currencies. It is therefore natural to begin a deeper study of exchange rate determination with a discussion of money supply and money demand.

Monetary developments influence the exchange rate *both* by changing interest rates *and* by changing people's expectations about future exchange rates. Expectations about future exchange rates are closely connected with expectations about the future money prices of countries' products; these price movements, in turn, depend on changes in money supply and demand. In examining monetary influences on the exchange rate, we therefore look at how monetary factors influence output prices along with interest rates. Expectations of future exchange rates depend on many factors other than money, however, and these nonmonetary factors are taken up in the next chapter.

Once the theories and determinants of money supply and demand are laid out, we use them to examine how equilibrium interest rates are determined by the equality of money supply and money demand. Then we combine our model of interest rate determination with the interest parity condition to study the effects of monetary shifts on the exchange rate, given the prices of goods and services, the level of output, and market expectations about the future. Finally, we take a first look at the long-term effects of monetary changes on output prices and expected future exchange rates.

Money Defined: A Brief Review

We are so accustomed to using money that we seldom notice the roles it plays in almost all of our everyday transactions. As with many other modern conveniences, we take money for granted until something goes wrong with it! In fact, the easiest way to appreciate the importance of money is to imagine what economic life would be like without it.

In this section we do just that. Our purpose in carrying out this "thought experiment" is to distinguish money from other assets and to describe the characteristics of money that lead people to hold it. These characteristics are central to an analysis of the demand for money.

MONEY AS A MEDIUM OF EXCHANGE

The most important function of money is to serve as a *medium of exchange,* a generally accepted means of payment. To see why a medium of exchange is necessary, imagine how time-consuming it would be for people to purchase goods and services in a world where the only type of trade possible was barter trade—the trade of goods or services for other goods or services.

Money eliminates the enormous search costs connected with a barter system because it is universally acceptable. It eliminates these search costs by enabling an individual to sell the goods and services she produces to people other than the producers of the goods and services she wishes to consume. A complex modern economy would cease functioning without some standardized and convenient means of payment.

MONEY AS A UNIT OF ACCOUNT

Money's second important role is as a *unit of account,* that is, as a widely recognized measure of value. It is in this role that we encountered money in Chapter 14: prices of goods, services, and assets are typically expressed in terms of money. Exchange rates allow us to translate different countries' money prices into comparable terms.

The convention of quoting prices in money terms simplifies economic calculations by making it easy to compare the prices of different commodities. The international price comparisons in Chapter 14, which used exchange rates to compare the prices of different countries' outputs, are similar to the calculations you would have to do many times each day if different commodities' prices were not expressed in terms of a standardized unit of account. If the calculations in Chapter 14 gave you a headache, imagine what it would be like to have to calculate the relative prices of each good and service you consume in terms of several other goods and services. This thought experiment should give you a keener appreciation of using money as a unit of account.

MONEY AS A STORE OF VALUE

Because money can be used to transfer purchasing power from the present into the future, it is also an asset, or a *store of value.* This attribute is essential for any medium of exchange because no one would be willing to accept it in payment if its value in terms of goods and services evaporated immediately.

Money's usefulness as a medium of exchange, however, automatically makes it the most *liquid* of all assets. As you will recall from the last chapter, an asset is said to be liquid when it can be transformed into goods and services rapidly and without high transaction costs, such as brokers' fees. Since money is readily acceptable as a means of payment, money sets the standard against which the liquidity of other assets is judged.

WHAT IS MONEY?

Currency and bank deposits on which checks may be written certainly qualify as money. These are widely accepted means of payment that can be transferred between owners at low cost. Households and firms hold currency and checking deposits as a convenient way of financing routine transactions as they arise. Assets such as real estate do not qualify as money because, unlike currency and checking deposits, they lack the essential property of liquidity.

When we speak of the **money supply** in this book, we are referring to the monetary aggregate the Federal Reserve calls M1, that is, the total amount of currency and checking deposits held by households and firms. In the United States at the end of 1991, the total money supply amounted to $898.1 billion, equal to 15.8 percent of that year's GNP.[1]

The large deposits traded by participants in the foreign exchange market are not considered part of the money supply. These deposits are less liquid than money and are not used to finance routine transactions.

HOW THE MONEY SUPPLY IS DETERMINED

An economy's money supply is controlled by its central bank. The central bank directly regulates the amount of currency in existence and also has indirect control over the amount of checking deposits issued by private banks. The procedures through which the central bank controls the money supply are complex, and we assume for now that

[1] A broader Federal Reserve measure of money supply, M2, includes time deposits, but these are less liquid than the assets included in M1 because the funds in them typically cannot be withdrawn early without penalty. An even broader measure, known as M3, is also tracked by the Fed. A decision on where to draw the line between money and near-money must be somewhat arbitrary and therefore controversial. For further discussion of this question, see Frederic S. Mishkin, *The Economics of Money, Banking and Financial Markets,* 3rd ed., Chapter 2 (New York: HarperCollins Publishers, 1992).

the central bank simply sets the size of the money supply at the level it desires. We go into the money supply process in more detail, however, in Chapters 18 and 22.

The Demand for Money by Individuals

Having discussed the functions of money and the definition of the money supply, we now examine the factors that determine the amount of money an individual desires to hold. The determinants of individual money demand can be derived from the theory of asset demand discussed in the last chapter.

We saw in the last chapter that individuals base their demand for an asset on three characteristics:

1. The expected return the asset offers compared with the returns offered by other assets.
2. The riskiness of the asset's expected return.
3. The asset's liquidity.

While liquidity plays no important role in determining the relative demands for assets traded in the foreign exchange market, households and firms hold money *only* because of its liquidity. To understand how the economy's households and firms decide the amount of money they wish to hold, we must look more closely at how the three considerations listed above influence money demand.

EXPECTED RETURN

Currency pays no interest. Checking deposits often do pay some interest, but they offer a rate of return that usually fails to keep pace with the higher return offered by less liquid forms of wealth. When you hold money, you therefore sacrifice the higher interest rate you could earn by holding your wealth in a government bond, a large time deposit, or some other relatively illiquid asset. It is this last rate of interest we have in mind when we refer to ''the'' interest rate. Since the interest paid on currency is zero while that paid on ''checkable'' deposits tends to be relatively constant, the difference in rates of return between money in general and less liquid alternative assets is reflected by the market interest rate: the higher the interest rate, the more you sacrifice by holding wealth in the form of money.[2]

Suppose, for example, that the interest rate you could earn from a U.S. Treasury bill is 10 percent per year. If you use $10,000 of your wealth to buy a Treasury bill, you will be paid $11,000 by Uncle Sam at the end of a year, but if you choose instead to keep the $10,000 as cash in a safe-deposit box, you give up the $1000 interest you

[2] Many of the illiquid assets that individuals can choose from do not pay their returns in the form of interest. Stocks, for example, pay returns in the form of dividends and capital gains. The family summer house on Cape Cod pays a return in the form of capital gains and the pleasure of vacations at the beach. The assumption behind our analysis of money demand is that once allowance is made for risk, all assets other than money offer an expected rate of return (measured in terms of money) equal to the interest rate. This assumption allows us to use the interest rate to summarize the return an individual forgoes by holding money rather than an illiquid asset.

could have earned by buying the Treasury bill. You thus sacrifice a 10 percent rate of return by holding your $10,000 as money.

The theory of asset demand developed in the last chapter shows how changes in the rate of interest affect the demand for money. The theory states that, other things equal, people prefer assets offering higher expected returns. Because an increase in the interest rate is a rise in the rate of return on less liquid assets relative to the rate of return on money, individuals will want to hold more of their wealth in nonmoney assets that pay the market interest rate and less of their wealth in the form of money if the interest rate rises. We conclude that *all else equal, a rise in the interest rate causes the demand for money to fall.*

We can also describe the influence of the interest rate on money demand in terms of the economic concept of *opportunity cost*—the amount you sacrifice by taking one course of action rather than another. The interest rate measures the opportunity cost of holding money rather than interest-bearing bonds. A rise in the interest rate therefore raises the cost of holding money and causes money demand to fall.

RISK

Risk is not an important factor in money demand. It is risky to hold money because an unexpected increase in the prices of goods and services could reduce the value of your money in terms of the commodities you consume. Since interest-paying assets such as government bonds have face values fixed in terms of money, however, the same unexpected increase in prices would reduce the real value of those assets by the same percentage. Because any change in the riskiness of money causes an equal change in the riskiness of bonds, changes in the risk of holding money need not cause individuals to reduce their demand for money and increase their demand for interest-paying assets.

LIQUIDITY

The main benefit of holding money comes from its liquidity. Households and firms hold money because it is the easiest way of financing their everyday purchases. Some large purchases can be financed through the sale of a substantial illiquid asset. An art collector, for example, could sell one of her Picassos to buy a house. To finance a continuing stream of smaller expenditures at various times and for various amounts, however, households and firms have to hold some money.

An individual's need for liquidity rises when the average daily value of his transactions rises. A student who takes the bus every day, for example, does not need to hold as much cash as a business executive who takes taxis during rush hour. We conclude that *a rise in the average value of transactions carried out by a household or firm causes its demand for money to rise.*

Aggregate Money Demand

Our discussion of how individual households and firms determine their demands for money can now be applied to derive the determinants of **aggregate money demand,** the total demand for money by all households and firms in the economy. Aggregate money demand is just the sum of all the economy's individual money demands.

Three main factors determine aggregate money demand:

1. *The interest rate.* A rise in the interest rate causes each individual in the economy to reduce her demand for money. All else equal, aggregate money demand therefore falls when the interest rate rises.
2. *The price level.* The economy's **price level** is the price of a broad reference basket of goods and services in terms of currency. If the price level rises, individual households and firms must spend more money than before to purchase their usual weekly baskets of goods and services. To maintain the same level of liquidity as before the price level increase, they will therefore have to hold more money.
3. *Real national income.* When real national income (GNP) rises, more goods and services are being sold in the economy. This increase in the real value of transactions raises the demand for money, given the price level.

If P is the price level, R is the interest rate, and Y is real GNP, the aggregate demand for money, M^d, can be expressed as

$$M^d = P \times L(R,Y), \tag{15-1}$$

where the value of $L(R,Y)$ falls when R rises, and rises when Y rises.[3] To see why we have specified that aggregate money demand is *proportional* to the price level, imagine that all prices doubled but the interest rate and everyone's *real* incomes remained unchanged. The money value of each individual's average daily transactions would then simply double, as would the amount of money each wished to hold.

We usually write the aggregate money demand relation (15-1) in the equivalent form

$$M^d/P = L(R,Y), \tag{15-2}$$

and call $L(R,Y)$ aggregate *real* money demand. This way of expressing money demand shows that the aggregate demand for liquidity, $L(R,Y)$, is not a demand for a certain number of currency units but is instead a demand to hold a certain amount of purchasing power in liquid form. The ratio M^d/P—that is, desired money holdings measured in terms of a typical reference basket of commodities—equals the amount of purchasing power people would like to hold in liquid form. For example, if people wished to hold \$1000 in cash at a price level of \$100 per commodity basket, their real money holdings would be equivalent to \$1000/(\$100 per basket) = 10 baskets. If the price level doubled (to \$200 per basket), the purchasing power of their \$1000 in cash would be halved, since it would now be worth only 5 baskets.

Figure 15-1 shows how aggregate real money demand is affected by the interest rate for a fixed level of real income, Y. The aggregate real money demand schedule $L(R,Y)$ slopes downward because a fall in the interest rate raises the desired real money holdings of each household and firm in the economy.

For a given level of real GNP, changes in interest rates cause movements *along* the $L(R,Y)$ schedule. Changes in real GNP, however, cause the schedule itself to shift.

[3] Naturally, $L(R,Y)$ rises when R falls, and falls when Y falls.

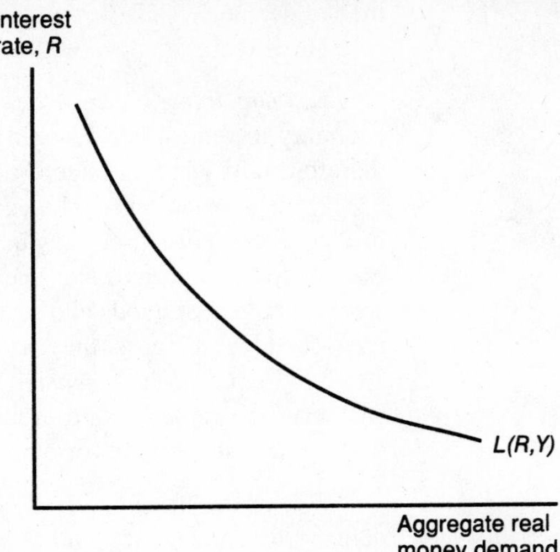

FIGURE 15-1
How aggregate real money demand depends on the interest rate for a given real income level, *Y*.
The graph shows that for a given income level, real money demand rises as the interest rate falls.

Figure 15-2 shows how a rise in real GNP from Y^1 to Y^2 affects aggregate real money demand. Because a rise in real GNP raises aggregate real money demand for a given interest rate, the schedule $L(R,Y^2)$ lies to the right of $L(R,Y^1)$ when Y^2 is greater than Y^1.

The Equilibrium Interest Rate: The Interaction of Money Supply and Demand

As you might expect from other economics courses you've taken, the money market is in equilibrium when the money supply set by the central bank equals aggregate money demand. In this section we see how the interest rate is determined by money market equilibrium, given the price level and output, both of which are temporarily assumed to be unaffected by monetary changes.

EQUILIBRIUM IN THE MONEY MARKET

If M^s is the money supply, the condition for equilibrium in the money market is

$$M^s = M^d. \qquad \textbf{(15-3)}$$

After dividing both sides of this equality by the price level, we can express the money market equilibrium condition in terms of aggregate real money demand as

$$M^s/P = L(R,Y). \qquad \textbf{(15-4)}$$

Given the price level and output, the equilibrium interest rate is the one at which aggregate real money demand equals the real money supply.

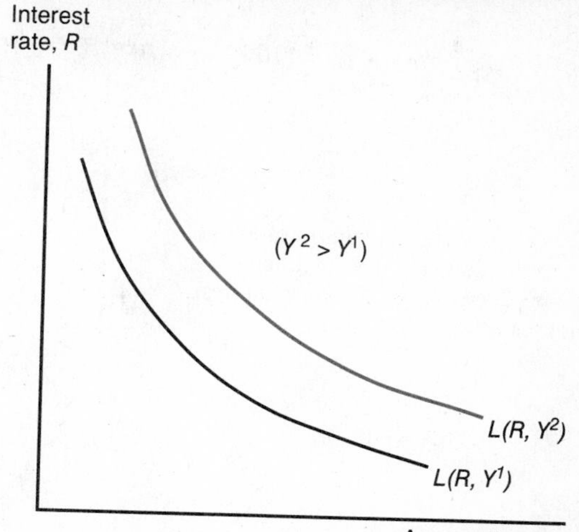

FIGURE 15-2
Effect on the aggregate real money demand schedule of a rise in real income from Y^1 to Y^2. An increase in real income causes the demand for real money balances to rise at every level of the interest rate.

In Figure 15-3, the aggregate real money demand schedule intersects the real money supply schedule at point 1 to give an equilibrium interest rate of R^1. The money supply schedule is vertical at M^s/P because M^s is set by the central bank while P is taken as given.

Let's see why the interest rate tends to settle at its equilibrium level by considering what happens if the market is initially at point 2, with an interest rate, R^2, that is above R^1.

At point 2 the demand for real money holdings falls short of the supply by $Q^1 - Q^2$, so there is an excess supply of money. If individuals are holding more money than they desire given the interest rate of R^2, they will attempt to reduce their liquidity by using some money to purchase interest-bearing assets. In other words, individuals will attempt to get rid of their excess money by lending it to others. Since there is an aggregate excess supply of money at R^2, however, not everyone can succeed in doing this: there are more people who would like to lend money to reduce their liquidity than there are people who would like to borrow it to increase theirs. Those who cannot unload their extra money try to tempt potential borrowers by lowering the interest rate they charge for loans below R^2. The downward pressure on the interest rate continues until the rate reaches R^1. At this interest rate, anyone wishing to lend money can do so because the aggregate excess supply of money has disappeared; that is, supply once again equals demand. Once the market reaches point 1, there is therefore no further tendency for the interest rate to drop.[4]

Similarly, if the interest rate is initially at a level R^3 below R^1, it will tend to rise.

[4] Another way to view this process is as follows: We saw in the last chapter that an asset's rate of return falls when its current price rises relative to its future value. When there is an excess supply of money, the current money prices of illiquid assets that pay interest will be bid up as individuals attempt to reduce their money holdings. This rise in current asset prices lowers the rate of return on nonmoney assets, and since this rate of return is equal to the interest rate (after adjustment for risk), the interest rate also must fall.

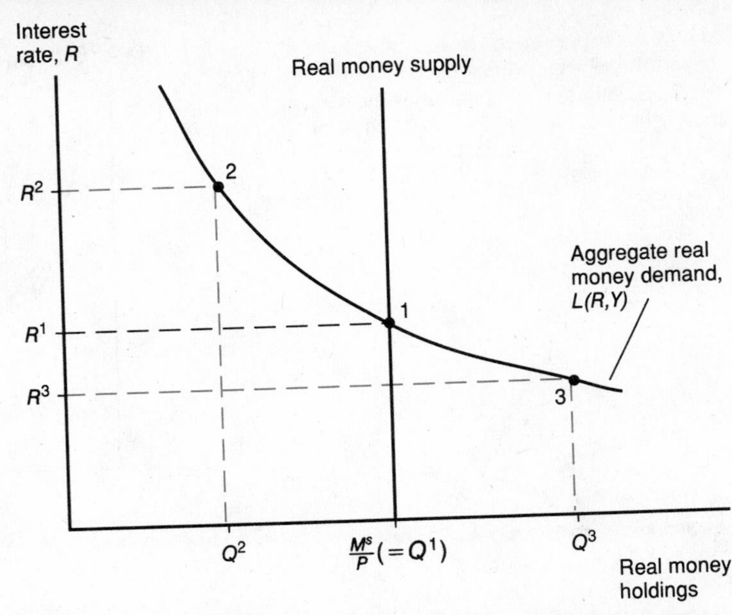

FIGURE 15-3
Determination of the equilibrium interest rate by the equality of aggregate real money demand and the real money supply (with *P* and *Y* given).
With a real money supply of M^s/P, money-market equilibrium is at point 1 and the equilibrium interest rate is R^1.

As Figure 15-3 shows, there is excess demand for money equal to $Q^3 - Q^1$ at point 3. Individuals therefore attempt to sell interest-bearing assets such as bonds to increase their money holdings (that is, they sell bonds for cash). At point 3, however, not everyone can succeed in selling enough interest-bearing assets to satisfy his or her demand for money. Thus, people bid for money by offering to borrow at progressively higher interest rates and push the interest rate upward toward R^1. Only when the market has reached point 1 and the excess demand for money has been eliminated does the interest rate stop rising.

We can summarize our findings as follows: *The market always moves toward an interest rate at which the real money supply equals aggregate real money demand. If there is initially an excess supply of money, the interest rate falls, and if there is initially an excess demand, it rises.*

INTEREST RATES AND THE MONEY SUPPLY

The effect of increasing the money supply at a given price level is illustrated in Figure 15-4. Initially the money market is in equilibrium at point 1, with a money supply M^1 and an interest rate R^1. Since we are holding P constant, a rise in the money supply to M^2 increases the real money supply from M^1/P to M^2/P. With a real money supply of M^2/P, point 2 is the new equilibrium and R^2 is the new, lower interest rate that induces people to hold the increased available real money supply.

The process through which the interest rate falls is by now familiar. After M^s is increased by the central bank, there is initially an excess real supply of money at the old equilibrium interest rate, R^1, which previously balanced the market. Since people

FIGURE 15-4
Effect of an increase in the money supply on the interest rate for a given price level, *P*, and real income level, *Y*.
An increase in the money supply from M^1 to M^2 reduces the interest rate from R^1 (point 1) to R^2 (point 2).

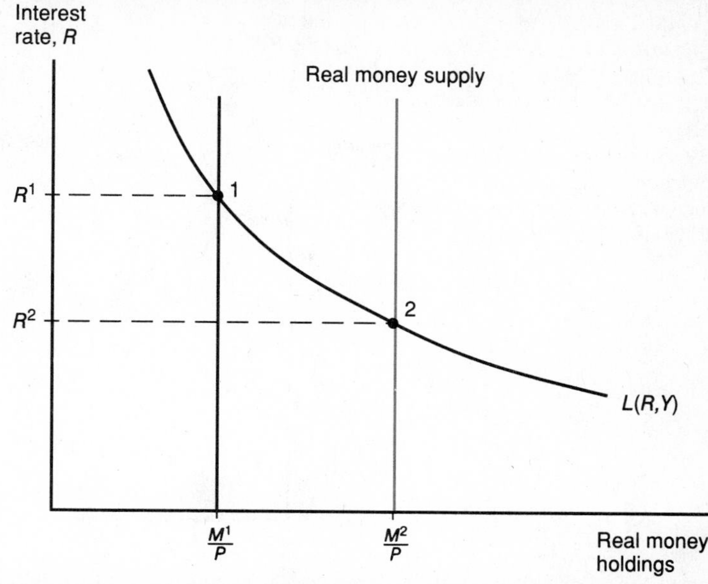

are holding more money than they desire, they use their surplus funds to bid for assets that pay interest. The economy as a whole cannot reduce its money holdings, so interest rates are driven down as unwilling money holders compete to lend their excess cash balances. At point 2 in Figure 15-4, the interest rate has fallen sufficiently to induce an increase in real money demand equal to the increase in the real money supply.

By running the above policy experiment in reverse, we can see how a reduction of the money supply forces interest rates upward. A fall in M^s causes an excess demand for money at the interest rate that previously balanced supply and demand. People attempt to sell interest-bearing assets—that is, to borrow—to rebuild their depleted real money holdings. Since they cannot all be successful when there is excess money demand, the interest rate is pushed upward until everyone is content to hold the smaller real money stock.

We conclude that *an increase in the money supply lowers the interest rate, while a fall in the money supply raises the interest rate, given the price level and output.*

OUTPUT AND THE INTEREST RATE

Figure 15-5 shows the effect on the interest rate of a rise in the level of output from Y^1 to Y^2, given the money supply and the price level. As we saw earlier, an increase in output causes the entire aggregate real money demand schedule to shift to the right, moving the equilibrium away from point 1. At the old equilibrium interest rate, R^1, there is an excess demand for money equal to $Q^2 - Q^1$ (point 1′). Since the real money supply is given, the interest rate is bid up until it reaches the higher new equilibrium level R^2 (point 2). A fall in output has opposite effects, causing the aggregate real money demand schedule to shift to the left and therefore causing the equilibrium interest rate to fall.

FIGURE 15-5
Effect on the interest rate of a rise in real income from Y^1 to Y^2, given the real money supply.
By shifting the real money demand function to the right, a rise in real income raises the interest rate from R^1 (point 1) to R^2 (point 2).

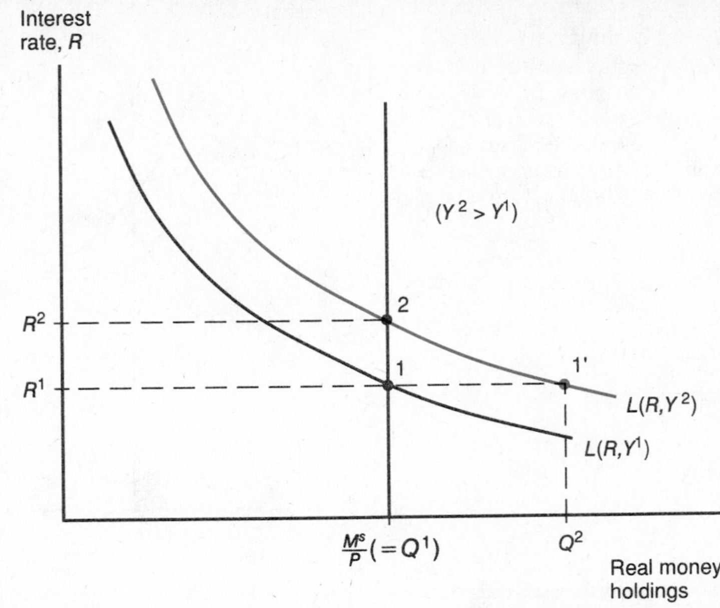

We conclude that *an increase in real output raises the interest rate, while a fall in real output lowers the interest rate, given the price level and the money supply.*

The Money Supply and the Exchange Rate in the Short Run

In Chapter 14 we learned about the interest parity condition, which predicts how interest rate movements influence the exchange rate, given expectations about the exchange rate's future level. Now that we know how shifts in a country's money supply affect the interest rate on nonmoney assets denominated in its currency, we can see how monetary changes affect the exchange rate. We will discover that an increase in a country's money supply causes its currency to depreciate in the foreign exchange market, while a reduction in the money supply causes its currency to appreciate.

In this section we continue to take the price level (along with real output) as given, and for that reason we label the analysis of this section **short run.** The **long-run** analysis of an economic event allows for the complete adjustment of the price level (which may take a long time) and for full employment of all factors of production. Later in this chapter we examine the long-run effects of money supply changes on the price level, the exchange rate, and other macroeconomic variables. Our long-run analysis will show how the money supply influences exchange rate expectations, which we also continue to take as given for now.

LINKING MONEY, THE INTEREST RATE, AND THE EXCHANGE RATE

To analyze the relation between money and the exchange rate in the short run, we combine two diagrams that we have already studied separately. The first of these (introduced as Figure 14-4) shows how the equilibrium exchange rate is determined in the foreign exchange market, given interest rates and expectations about future exchange rates. The second diagram, introduced as Figure 15-3, shows how a country's equilibrium interest rate is determined in its money market. Let's assume once again that we are studying the dollar/DM exchange rate, that is, the price of DM in terms of dollars.

Figure 15-6 combines the diagrams we used earlier to show equilibrium in the foreign exchange and U.S. money markets. The lower part of Figure 15-6 reproduces

FIGURE 15-6
Simultaneous equilibrium in the U.S. money market and the foreign-exchange market.
Both asset markets are in equilibrium at the interest rate $R^1_\$$ and exchange rate $E^1_{\$/DM}$ such that money supply equals money demand (point 1) and the interest parity condition holds (point 1′).

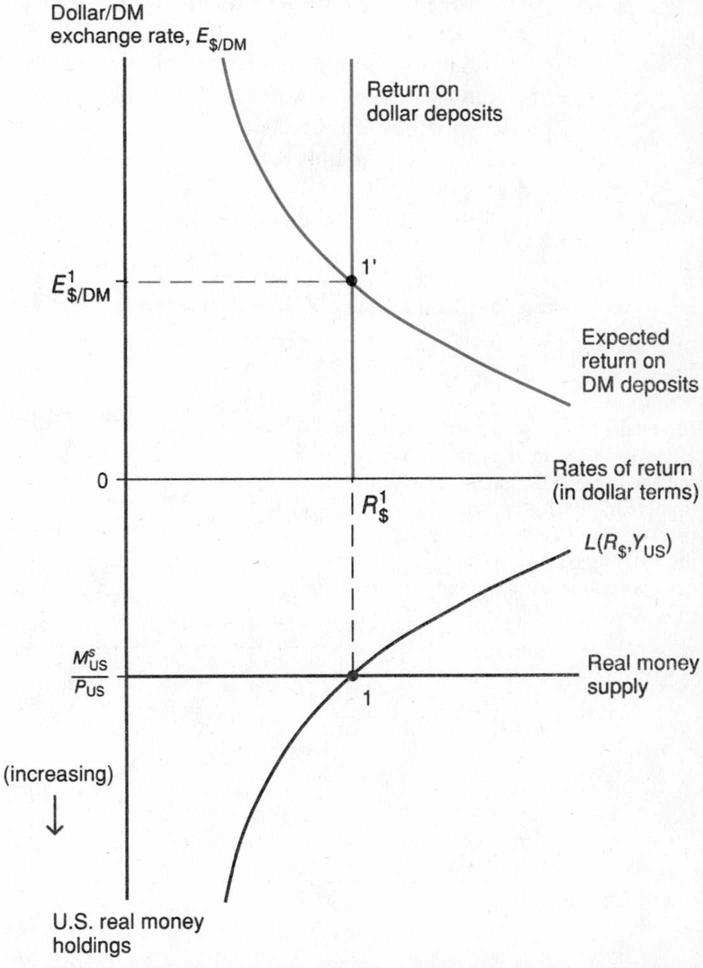

the picture of money market equilibrium developed in the previous section. For convenience, however, that picture has here been rotated clockwise by 90 degrees: we now measure dollar interest rates on the horizontal axis starting at point 0, and the U.S. real money supply is measured from 0 on the descending vertical axis. Money market equilibrium is shown at point 1, where the dollar interest rate $R^1_\$$ induces people to demand real balances equal to the U.S. real money supply, M^s_{US}/P_{US}.

The upper part of Figure 15-6 shows equilibrium in the foreign exchange market. As you will remember from Chapter 14, the downward-sloping schedule shows the expected return on DM deposits, measured in terms of dollars. The schedule slopes downward because of the effect of current exchange rate changes on expectations of future depreciation: a strengthening of the dollar today (a fall in $E_{\$/DM}$) relative to its *given* expected future level makes DM deposits more attractive by leading people to anticipate a sharper dollar depreciation in the future. The dollar interest rate determined in the money market, $R^1_\$$, defines the vertical schedule in the figure's upper portion. At the intersection of the two schedules (point 1′), the expected rates of return on dollar and DM deposits are equal, and therefore interest parity holds. $E^1_{\$/DM}$ is the equilibrium exchange rate.

Figure 15-6 emphasizes the link between the U.S. money market (bottom) and the foreign exchange market (top)—the U.S. money market determines the dollar interest rate, which in turn affects the exchange rate that maintains interest parity. (Of course, there is a similar link between the German money market and the foreign exchange market that operates through changes in the DM interest rate.)

Figure 15-7 illustrates these linkages. The U.S. and German central banks, the

FIGURE 15-7
Money-market/exchange rate linkages.
Monetary policy actions by the Fed affect the U.S. interest rate, changing the dollar/DM exchange rate that clears the foreign exchange market. The Bundesbank can affect the exchange rate by changing the German money supply and interest rate.

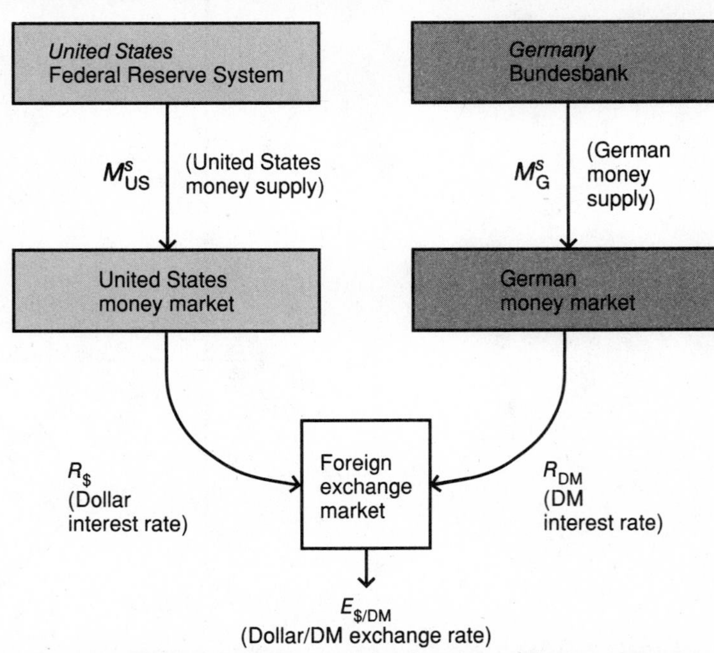

Federal Reserve and the Bundesbank, determine the U.S. and German money supplies, M^s_{US} and M^s_G. Given the price levels and national incomes of the two countries, equilibrium in national money markets leads to the dollar and DM interest rates $R_\$$ and R_{DM}. These interest rates feed into the foreign exchange market where, given expectations about the future dollar/DM exchange rate, the current rate $E_{\$/DM}$ is determined by the interest parity condition.

U.S. MONEY SUPPLY AND THE DOLLAR/DM EXCHANGE RATE

We now use our model of asset market linkages to ask how the dollar/DM exchange rate changes when the Federal Reserve changes the U.S. money supply M^s_{US}. The effects of this change are summarized in Figure 15-8.

FIGURE 15-8
Effect on the dollar/DM exchange rate and dollar interest rate of an increase in the U.S. money supply (given P_{US} and Y_{US}).
When the money supply rises from M^1_{US} to M^2_{US}, the dollar interest rate declines (as money-market equilibrium is reestablished at point 2) and the dollar depreciates against the DM (as foreign exchange market equilibrium is reestablished at point 2′).

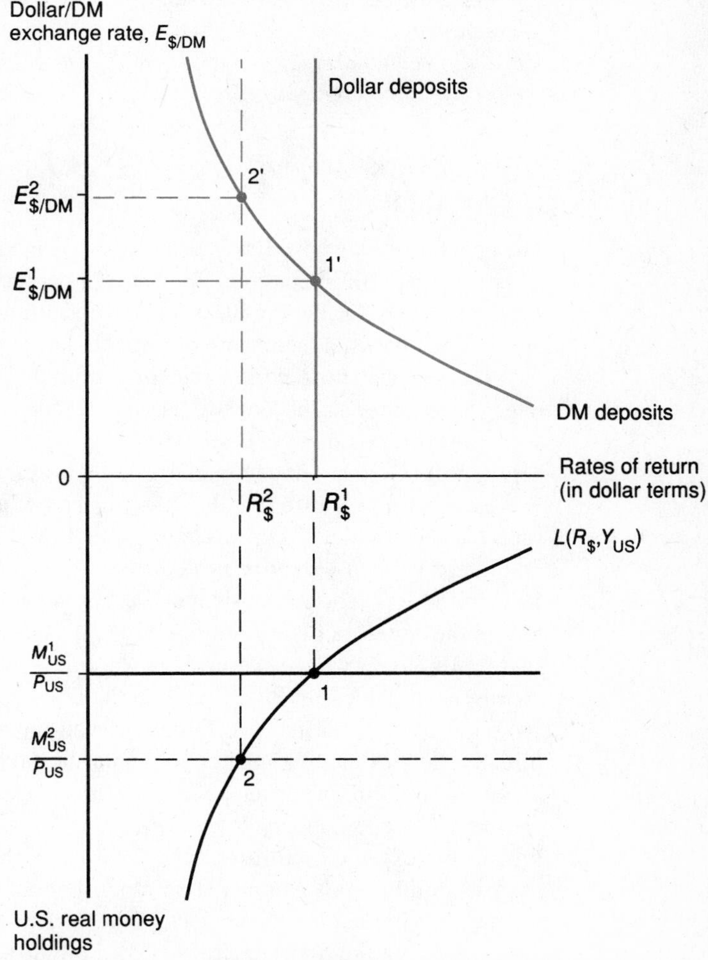

At the initial money supply M^1_{US}, the money market is in equilibrium at point 1 with an interest rate $R^1_\$$. Given the DM interest rate and the expected future exchange rate, a dollar interest rate of $R^1_\$$ implies that foreign exchange market equilibrium occurs at point 1′, with an exchange rate equal to $E^1_{\$/DM}$.

What happens when the Federal Reserve raises the U.S. money supply from M^1_{US} to M^2_{US}? This increase sets in train the following sequence of events: (1) At the initial interest rate $R^1_\$$ there is an excess supply of money in the U.S. money market, so the dollar interest rate falls to $R^2_\$$ as the money market reaches its new equilibrium position (point 2). (2) Given the initial exchange rate $E^1_{\$/DM}$ and the new, lower interest rate on dollars, $R^2_\$$, the expected return on DM deposits is greater then that on dollar deposits. Holders of dollar deposits therefore try to sell them for DM deposits, which are momentarily more attractive. (3) The dollar depreciates to $E^2_{\$/DM}$ as holders of dollar deposits bid for DM deposits. The foreign exchange market is once again in equilibrium at point 2′ because the exchange rate's move to $E^2_{\$/DM}$ causes a fall in the dollar's expected future depreciation rate sufficient to offset the fall in the dollar interest rate.

We conclude that *an increase in a country's money supply causes its currency to depreciate in the foreign exchange market.* By running Figure 15-8 in reverse, you can see that *a reduction in a country's money supply causes its currency to appreciate in the foreign exchange market.*

GERMAN MONEY SUPPLY AND THE DOLLAR/DM EXCHANGE RATE

The conclusions we have reached also apply when the Bundesbank changes Germany's money supply. An increase in M^s_G causes a depreciation of the DM (that is, an appreciation of the dollar, or a fall in $E_{\$/DM}$), while a reduction in M^s_G causes an appreciation of the DM (that is, a depreciation of the dollar, or a rise in $E_{\$/DM}$).

The mechanism at work, which runs from the German interest rate to the exchange rate, is the same as the one we just analyzed. It is a good exercise to verify these assertions by drawing figures similar to Figures 15-6 and 15-8 that illustrate the linkage between the German money market and the foreign exchange market.

Here we use a different approach to show how changes in the German money supply affect the dollar/DM exchange rate. In Chapter 14 we learned that a fall in the DM interest rate, R_{DM}, shifts the downward-sloping schedule in the upper part of Figure 15-6 to the left. The reason is that for any level of the exchange rate, a fall in R_{DM} lowers the expected rate of return on DM deposits. Since a rise in the German money supply M^s_G lowers R_{DM}, we can see the effect on the exchange rate by shifting the appropriate schedule in Figure 15-6 to the left.

The result of an increase in the German money supply is shown in Figure 15-9. Initially the U.S. money market is in equilibrium at point 1 and the foreign exchange market is in equilibrium at point 1′, with an exchange rate $E^1_{\$/DM}$. An increase in Germany's money supply lowers R_{DM} and therefore shifts to the left the schedule linking the expected return on DM deposits to the exchange rate. Foreign exchange market equilibrium is restored at point 2′, with an exchange rate of $E^2_{\$/DM}$. We see that the increase in German money causes the DM to depreciate against the dollar (that is, causes a fall in the dollar price of DM). Similarly, a fall in Germany's money supply would cause the DM to appreciate against the dollar ($E_{\$/DM}$ would rise). The change in

FIGURE 15-9
Effect of an increase in the German money supply on the dollar/DM exchange rate.
By lowering the dollar return on DM deposits, an increase in Germany's money supply causes the dollar to appreciate against the DM. Equilibrium in the foreign exchange market shifts from point 1′ to point 2′, but equilibrium in the U.S. money market remains at point 1.

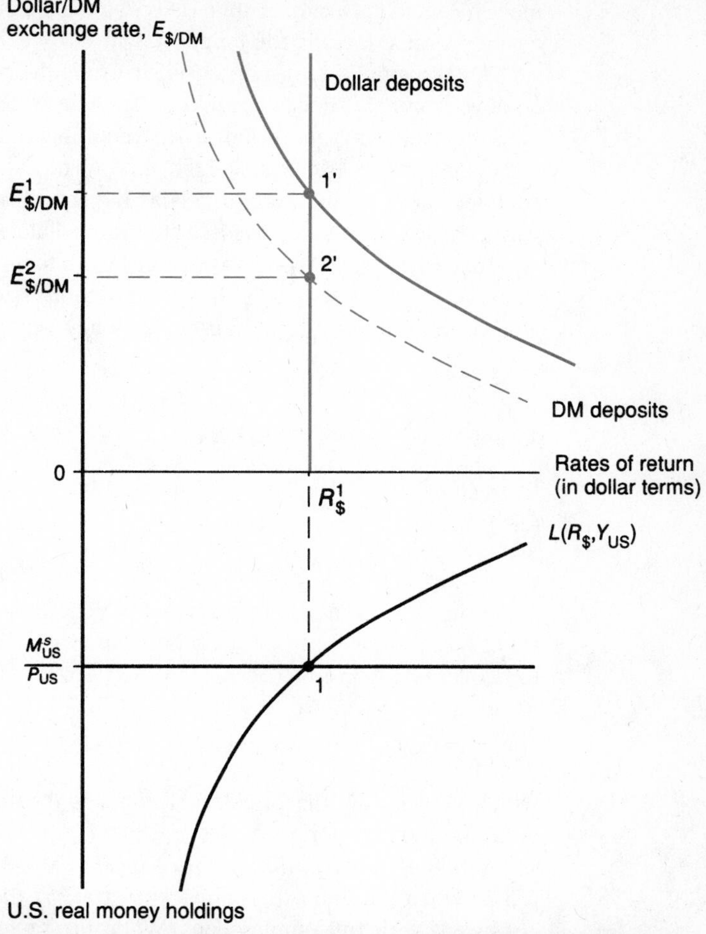

the German money supply does not disturb the U.S. money market equilibrium, which remains at point 1.[5]

Money, the Price Level, and the Exchange Rate in the Long Run

Our short-run analysis of the link between countries' money markets and the foreign exchange market rested on the simplifying assumption that price levels and exchange

[5] The U.S. money market equilibrium remains at point 1 because the price adjustments that equilibrate the German money market and the foreign exchange market after the increase in Germany's money supply do not change either the money supply or money demand in the United States, given Y_{US} and P_{US}.

rate expectations were given. To extend our understanding of how money supply and money demand affect exchange rates, we must examine how monetary factors affect a country's price level in the long run.

An economy's **long-run equilibrium** is the position it would eventually reach if no new economic shocks occurred during the adjustment to full employment. You can think of long-run equilibrium as the equilibrium that would be maintained after all wages and prices had had enough time to adjust to their market-clearing levels. An equivalent way of thinking of it is as the equilibrium that would occur if prices were perfectly flexible and always adjusted immediately to preserve full employment.

In studying how monetary changes work themselves out over the long run, we will examine how such changes shift the economy's long-run equilibrium. Our main tool is once again the theory of aggregate money demand.

MONEY AND MONEY PRICES

If the price level and output are fixed in the short run, the condition (15-4) of money market equilibrium,

$$M^s/P = L(R,Y),$$

determines the domestic interest rate, R. The money market always moves to equilibrium, however, even if we drop our "short-run" assumption and think of periods of time over which P and Y, as well as R, can vary. The above equilibrium condition can therefore be rearranged to give

$$P = M^s/L(R,Y), \qquad \textbf{(15-5)}$$

which shows how the price level depends on the interest rate, real output, and the domestic money supply.

The *long-run equilibrium price level* is just the value of P that satisfies condition (15-5) when the interest rate and output are at their long-run levels, that is, at levels consistent with full employment. When the money market is in equilibrium and all factors of production are fully employed, the price level will remain steady if the money supply, the aggregate money demand function, and the long-run values of R and Y remain steady.

One of the most important predictions of the above equation for P concerns the relationship between a country's price level and its money supply, M^s: *All else equal, an increase in a country's money supply causes a proportional increase in its price level.* If, for example, the money supply doubles (to $2M^s$) but output and the interest rate do not change, the price level must also double (to $2P$) to maintain equilibrium in the money market.

The economic reasoning behind this very precise prediction follows from our observation above that the demand for money is a demand for *real* money holdings: Real money demand is not altered by an increased in M^s that leaves R and Y (and thus aggregate real money demand $L(R,Y)$) unchanged. If aggregate real money demand does not change, however, the money market will remain in equilibrium only if the real money supply also stays the same. To keep the real money supply M^s/P constant, P must rise in proportion to M^s.

THE LONG-RUN EFFECTS OF MONEY SUPPLY CHANGES

Our theory of how the money supply affects the price level *given* the interest rate and output is not yet a theory of how money supply changes affect the price level in the long run. To develop such a theory, we still have to determine the long-run effects of a money supply change on the interest rate and output. This is easier than you might think. As we now argue, *a change in the supply of money has no effect on the long-run values of the interest rate or real output.*[6]

The best way to understand the long-run effects of money supply on the interest rate and output is to think first about a *currency reform,* in which a country's government redefines the national currency unit. For example, the government of France reformed its currency on January 1, 1960, simply by issuing ''new'' French francs, each equal to 100 ''old'' French francs. The effect of this reform was to lower the number of currency units in circulation, and all franc prices, to $\frac{1}{100}$ of their old franc values. But the redefinition of the monetary unit had no effect on real output, the interest rate, or the relative prices of goods: all that occurred was a one-shot change in all values measured in francs. A decision to measure distance in half-miles rather than miles would have as little effect on real economic variables as the French government's decision to chop two zeros off the end of every magnitude measured in terms of money.

An increase in the supply of a country's currency has the same effect in the long run as a currency reform. A doubling of the money supply, for example, has the same long-run effect as a currency reform in which each unit of currency is replaced by two units of ''new'' currency. If the economy is initially fully employed, every money price in the economy eventually doubles, but real GNP, the interest rate, and all relative prices return to their long-run or full-employment levels.

Why is a money supply change just like a currency reform in its effects on the economy's long-run equilibrium? The full-employment output level is determined by the economy's endowments of labor and capital, so in the long run real output does not depend on the money supply. Similarly, the interest rate is independent of the money supply in the long run. If the money supply and all prices double permanently, there is no reason why people previously willing to exchange \$1 today for \$1.10 a year from now should not be willing afterward to exchange \$2 today for \$2.20 a year from now, so the interest rate will remain at 10 percent per annum. Relative prices also remain the same if all money prices double, since relative prices are just ratios of money prices. Thus, money supply changes do not change the long-run allocation of resources. Only the absolute level of money prices changes.[7]

[6] The preceding statement refers only to changes in the *level* of the nominal money supply and not, for example, to changes in the *rate* at which the money supply is growing over time. The proposition that a one-time change in the level of the money supply has no effects on the long-run values of real economic variables is often called the *long-run neutrality of money.* In contrast, changes in the money supply growth rate need not be neutral in the long run. At the very least, a sustained change in the monetary growth rate will eventually affect equilibrium real money balances by raising the money interest rate (as discussed in the next chapter).

[7] To understand more fully why a one-time change in the money supply does not change the long-run level of the interest rate, it may be useful to think of interest rates measured in terms of money as defining relative prices of currency units available on different dates. If the dollar interest rate is R percent per annum, giving up \$1 today buys you $\$(1 + R)$ next year. Thus, $1/(1 + R)$ is the relative price of future dollars in terms of current dollars, and this relative price would not change if the real value of the monetary unit were scaled up or down by the same factor on all dates.

When studying the effect of an increase in the money supply over long time periods, we are therefore justified in assuming that the long-run values of R and Y will not be changed by a change in the supply of money. Thus, we can draw the following conclusion from equation (15-5): *A permanent increase in the money supply causes a proportional increase in the price level's long-run value. In particular, if the economy is initially at full employment, a permanent increase in the money supply eventually will be followed by a proportional increase in the price level.*

EMPIRICAL EVIDENCE ON MONEY SUPPLIES AND PRICE LEVELS

In looking at actual data on money and prices, we should not expect to see an exact proportional relationship over long periods, partly because output, the interest rate, and the aggregate real money demand function can shift for reasons that have nothing to do with the supply of money. Output changes as a result of capital accumulation and technological advance, for example, and money demand behavior may change as a result of demographic trends or financial innovations such as electronic cash-transfer facilities. In addition, actual economies are rarely in positions of long-run equilibrium. Nonetheless, we should expect the data to show a clear-cut positive association between money supplies and price levels. If real-world data did not provide strong evidence that

FIGURE 15-10
Monetary growth and price-level change in the seven main industrial countries, 1973–1991.
In a cross-section of countries, long-term changes in money supplies and price levels show a clear positive correlation.
Source: OECD, *Main Economic Indicators,* and IMF, *International Financial Statistics* (for the United Kingdom).

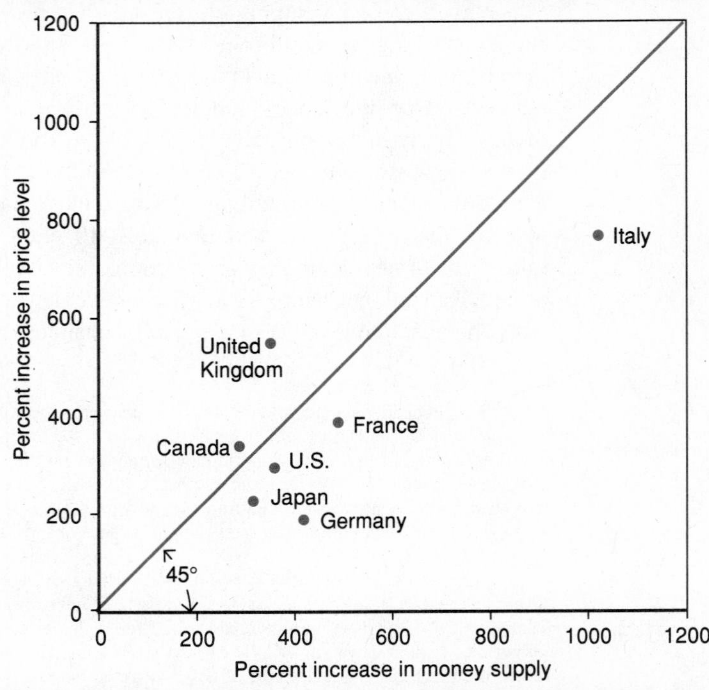

Money as a Weapon of War

Iraq lost the Persian Gulf War of 1990–1991 but the country's strongman, Saddam Hussein, remained in power. During 1992 Saddam's victorious but frustrated enemies deployed a subtle financial weapon in their drive to encourage his overthrow. They attacked Iraq's currency, the dinar, by smuggling millions of fake dinar notes into the country. Their plan was based on a prediction of our monetary model: a series of massive injections of carefully forged currency should cause a series of proportionally massive jumps in the price level, destabilizing economic activity throughout Iraq by reducing the usefulness of money.*

Counterfeiting is a nagging problem in many countries. To see why Iraq was especially vulnerable to currency sabotage, however, it helps to understand how various governments actually produce their currencies. The largest industrial countries issue high-quality banknotes that are very difficult to imitate. Only Germany and Canada among the large industrial countries allow specialized private printing firms to produce significant amounts of national currency; the others print most money in state-owned facilities. Governments in the developing world are, however, more likely to rely on banknotes printed in the West. With the breakup of the former Soviet bloc into a multitude of independent states, each desiring its own currency, the best-established Western banknote suppliers are enjoying an exceptional boom in business.**

Prior to the Gulf War, Iraq's currency was printed in Britain. Once Iraq's relations with Britain and other Western countries broke down, however, the country was forced to print its own notes on lower-quality paper. The fall in the quality of genuine notes made them easier to copy; soon, a group of nations said to include Saudi Arabia, Israel, Iran, and the United States was bombarding Iraq with bogus dinars difficult to tell apart from the real thing. In an unusual example of life imitating economic theory, U.S. helicopters allegedly dropped dinars onto villages in Iraq's southern marshlands.

Iraq took stern measures to stem the inflow: it withdrew all 100-dinar notes from circulation and imposed a penalty of life imprisonment for circulating fake dinars. Those caught smuggling counterfeit money into the country became eligible for a death sentence. The rise in the price level continued, however, in part because Iraq's government itself was issuing currency at a rapid clip to pay for urgent public services.

* "Fake-Money Flood Is Aimed at Crippling Iraq's Economy," *New York Times,* May 27, 1992, p. A1.

** Ironically, many of the would-be customers lack the hard currency needed to pay for their money. See "Scramble for a License to Print Money," *Financial Times,* September 9, 1992, p. 19.

money supplies and price levels move together in the long run, the usefulness of the theory of money demand we have developed would be in severe doubt.

Evidence on the money supply/price level linkage for the world's seven largest industrial countries is shown in Figure 15-10. The horizontal axis measures percentage increases in money supplies between 1973 and 1991, the vertical axis percentage increases in price levels. As you can see, there is a strong positive relation between money supply and price level for this group of countries. In countries plotted close to the 45-degree line, money supplies and price levels increased more or less in proportion over 1973–1991. In Canada, for example, both the money supply and the price level rose by a factor of about 4. In some cases, however, the observations stray from the 45-degree line along which increases in money and prices are proportional. Germany's price level, for example, rose by a much smaller percentage than its money supply, as indicated by that country's position far below the 45-degree line.

As we observed above, we should expect these discrepancies because the theory of money demand predicts exactly proportional increases in money and price levels only when no other factors affecting the money market (such as real income per capita) change at the same time. These other factors, however, have not remained constant in the countries shown. Countries close to the 45-degree line in Figure 15-10 are those in which the effects on money market equilibrium of factors other than money supply roughly offset each other. The main lesson to be drawn from Figure 15-10 is that the data confirm the strong long-run link between national money supplies and national price levels predicted by economic theory.

MONEY AND THE EXCHANGE RATE IN THE LONG RUN

The domestic currency price of foreign currency is one of the many prices in the economy that rise in the long run after a permanent increase in the money supply. If you think again about the effects of a currency reform, you will see how the exchange rate moves in the long run. Suppose, for example, that the U.S. government replaced every pair of ''old'' dollars with one ''new'' dollar. Then if the dollar/DM exchange rate had been 0.30 *old* dollars per DM before the reform, it would change to 0.15 *new* dollars per DM immediately after the reform. In much the same way, a halving of the U.S. money supply would eventually lead the dollar to appreciate from an exchange rate of 0.30 dollars/DM to one of 0.15 dollars/DM. Since the dollar prices of all U.S. goods and services would also decrease by half, this 50 percent appreciation of the dollar leaves the *relative* prices of all U.S. and foreign goods and services unchanged.

We conclude that, all else equal, *a permanent increase in a country's money supply causes a proportional long-run depreciation of its currency against foreign currencies. Similarly, a permanent decrease in a country's money supply causes a proportional long-run appreciation of its currency against foreign currencies.*

Inflation and Exchange Rate Dynamics

In this section we tie together our short-run and long-run findings about the effects of monetary changes by examining the process through which the price level adjusts to its long-run position. An economy experiences **inflation** when its price level is rising and **deflation** when its price level is falling. Our examination of inflation will give us a deeper understanding of how the exchange rate adjusts to monetary disturbances in the economy.

SHORT-RUN PRICE RIGIDITY VERSUS LONG-RUN PRICE FLEXIBILITY

Our analysis of the short-run effects of monetary changes assumed that a country's price level, unlike its exchange rate, does not jump immediately. This assumption cannot be exactly correct, because many commodities, such as agricultural products, are traded in markets where prices adjust sharply every day as supply or demand conditions shift. In addition, exchange rate changes themselves may affect the prices of some tradable goods and services that enter into the commodity basket defining the price level.

Many prices in the economy, however, are written into long-term contracts and cannot be changed immediately when changes in the money supply occur. The most important prices of this type are workers' wages, which are negotiated only periodically in many industries. Wages do not enter indices of the price level directly, but they make up a large fraction of the cost of producing goods and services. Since output prices depend heavily on production costs, the behavior of the overall price level is influenced by the sluggishness of wage movements. The short-run "stickiness" of price levels is illustrated by Figure 15-11, which compares data on month-to-month per-

FIGURE 15-11
Variability of the dollar/DM exchange rate and of the U.S./German price-level ratio.
The much greater month-to-month variability of the exchange rate suggests that price levels are relatively sticky in the short run.
Source: OECD, *Main Economic Indicators.*

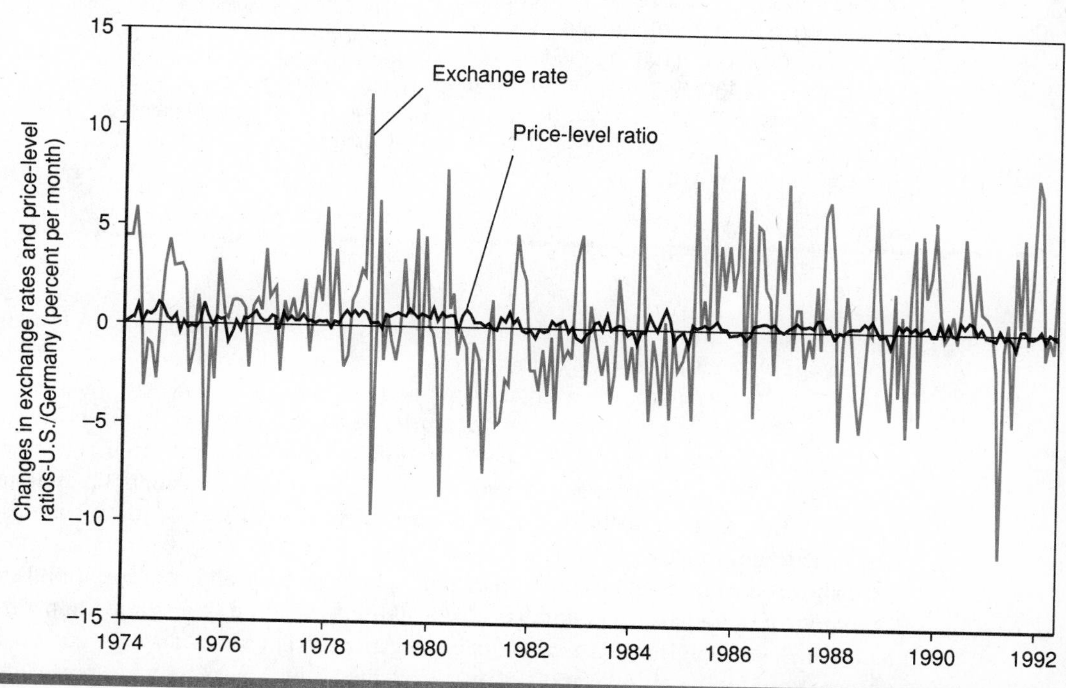

Money Supply Growth and Hyperinflation in Bolivia

In 1984 and 1985, the small Latin American country of Bolivia experienced *hyperinflation*—an explosive and seemingly uncontrollable inflation in which money loses value rapidly and may even go out of use.* During hyperinflations the magnitudes of monetary changes are so enormous that the "long-run" effects of money on the price level can occur very quickly. These episodes therefore provide laboratory conditions well-suited for testing long-run theories about the effects of money supplies on prices.

Below we show data on Bolivia's money supply and price level during the hyperinflation. An official exchange rate between the Bolivian peso and the U.S. dollar was controlled by the Bolivian government during this period, so we list instead values for an exchange rate that better reflected market forces, the price of dollars in terms of pesos on the La Paz black market.

The data show a clear tendency for the money supply, price level, and exchange rate to move in step, as the theory in the text would predict. Moreover, the trends in the price level and exchange rate are of the same order of magnitude: the price level rose by 22,908 percent between April 1984 and July 1985 and the peso price of dollars rose by 24,662 percent over the same period. These percentage changes actually are greater than the corresponding percentage increase in the money supply (which is "only" 17,433 percent), but the difference is to be expected. Exploding inflation causes real money demand to fall over time, and this additional monetary change makes money prices rise even more quickly than the money supply itself rises.

We chose July 1985 as the endpoint for the comparison because the Bolivian government introduced a dramatic stabilization plan near the end of August 1985. You can see in the data how the money supply and, more dramatically, the price level and exchange rate all began to level out in the two months after August. Chapter 23 will say more about how Bolivia escaped from the grip of its hyperinflation.

* In a classic paper, Columbia University economist Phillip Cagan drew the line between inflation and hyperinflation at an inflation rate of 50 percent per month (which, through the power of compounding, comes out to 12,875 percent per year). See "The Monetary Dynamics of Hyperinflation," in Milton Friedman, ed., *Studies in the Quantity Theory of Money* (Chicago: University of Chicago Press, 1956), pp. 25–117.

centage changes in the dollar/DM exchange rate, $E_{\$/DM}$, with data on month-to-month percentage changes in the ratio of money price levels in the United States and Germany, P_{US}/P_G. As you can see, the exchange rate is much more variable than relative price levels, a fact consistent with the view that price levels are relatively rigid in the short run. The pattern shown in the figure applies to all of the main industrial countries in recent years. In light of this and other evidence, we will therefore continue to assume that the price level is given in the short run and does not take significant jumps in response to policy changes.

This assumption would not be reasonable, however, for all countries at all times. In extremely inflationary conditions, such as those seen recently in some Latin American countries, long-term contracts specifying money payments may go out of use. Automatic price level indexation of wage payments may also be widespread under highly inflationary conditions. Such developments make the price level much less rigid

Macroeconomic data for Bolivia, April 1984–October 1985

Month	Money supply (billions of pesos)	Price level (relative to 1982 average = 1)	Exchange rate (pesos per dollar)
1984			
April	270	21.1	3,576
May	330	31.1	3,512
June	440	32.3	3,342
July	599	34.0	3,570
August	718	39.1	7,038
September	889	53.7	13,685
October	1,194	85.5	15,205
November	1,495	112.4	18,469
December	3,296	180.9	24,515
1985			
January	4,630	305.3	73,016
February	6,455	863.3	141,101
March	9,089	1,078.6	128,137
April	12,885	1,205.7	167,428
May	21,309	1,635.7	272,375
June	27,778	2,919.1	481,756
July	47,341	4,854.6	885,476
August	74,306	8,081.0	1,182,300
September	103,272	12,647.6	1,087,440
October	132,550	12,411.8	1,120,210

Source: Juan-Antonio Morales, "Inflation Stabilization in Bolivia," in Michael Bruno et al., eds., *Inflation Stabilization: The Experience of Israel, Argentina, Brazil, Bolivia, and Mexico* (Cambridge: MIT Press, 1988), Table 7A-1. Money supply is M1.

than it would be under moderate inflation, and large price level jumps become possible. (See the box on Bolivia on page 390.)

Our analysis assuming short-run price rigidity is therefore most applicable to countries with histories of relative price level stability, such as the United States. Even in the cases of low-inflation countries, there is a lively academic debate over the possibility that seemingly sticky wages and prices are in reality quite flexible.[8]

Although the price levels appear to display short-run stickiness in many countries,

[8] For a discussion of this debate, and empirical evidence that U.S. aggregate prices and wages show significant rigidity, see the book by Hall and Taylor listed in Further Reading. A study by Dennis W. Carlton of individual U.S. industries also finds evidence of price rigidity. See Carlton, "The Rigidity of Prices," *American Economic Review* 76 (September 1986), pp. 637–658. For evidence on Germany, see Alberto Giovannini and Julio J. Rotemberg, "Exchange-Rate Dynamics with Sticky Prices: The Deutsche Mark, 1974–1982," *Journal of Business & Economic Statistics* 7 (April 1989), pp. 169–178.

a change in the money supply creates immediate demand and cost pressures that eventually lead to *future* increases in the price level. These pressures come from three main sources:

1. *Excess demand for output and labor.* An increase in the money supply has an expansionary effect on the economy, raising the total demand for final goods and services. To meet this demand, producers of goods and services must employ workers overtime and make new hires. Even if wages are given in the short run, the additional demand for labor allows workers to ask for higher wages in the next round of wage negotiations. Producers are willing to pay these higher wages, for they know that in a booming economy it will not be hard to pass higher wage costs on to consumers through higher product prices.

2. *Inflationary expectations.* If everyone expects the price level to rise in the future, their expectation will increase the pace of inflation today. Workers bargaining over wage contracts will insist on higher money wages to counteract the effect on their *real* wages of the anticipated general increase in prices. Producers, once again, will give in to these wage demands if they expect product prices to rise and cover the additional wage costs.

3. *Raw materials prices.* Many raw materials used in the production of final goods, for example, petroleum products and metals, are sold in markets where prices adjust sharply even in the short run. By causing the prices of such materials to jump upward, a money supply increase raises production costs in materials-using industries. Eventually, producers in those industries will raise product prices to cover their higher costs.

PERMANENT MONEY SUPPLY CHANGES AND THE EXCHANGE RATE

We now apply our analysis of inflation to study the adjustment of the dollar/DM exchange rate following a *permanent* increase in the U.S. money supply. Figure 15-12 shows both the short-run (Figure 15-12a) and long-run (Figure 15-12b) effects of this disturbance. We assume the economy starts with all variables at their long-run levels and that output remains constant as the economy adjusts to the money supply change.

Figure 15-12a assumes the U.S. price level is initially given at P^1_{US}. An increase in the nominal money supply from M^1_{US} to M^2_{US} therefore raises the real money supply from M^1_{US}/P^1_{US} to M^2_{US}/P^1_{US} in the short run, lowering the interest rate from $R^1_\$$ (point 1) to $R^2_\$$ (point 2). So far our analysis follows exactly as it did earlier in this chapter.

The first change in our analysis comes when we ask how the American money supply change affects the foreign exchange market. As before, the fall in the U.S. interest rate is shown as a leftward shift in the vertical schedule giving the dollar return on dollar deposits. This is no longer the whole story, however, for the money supply increase now affects *exchange rate expectations.* Because the U.S. money supply change is permanent, people expect a long-run increase in all dollar prices, including the exchange rate, which is the dollar price of DM. As you will recall from Chapter 14, a rise in the expected future dollar/DM exchange rate (a future dollar depreciation) raises the expected dollar return on DM deposits; it thus shifts the downward-sloping schedule in the top part of Figure 15-12a to the right. The dollar depreciates against the DM, moving from an exchange rate of $E^1_{\$/DM}$ (point 1′) to $E^2_{\$/DM}$ (point 2′). Notice

FIGURE 15-12
Short-run and long-run effects of an increase in the U.S. money supply (given real output, *Y*).
(a) Short-run adjustment of the asset markets. (b) How the interest rate, price level, and exchange rate move over time as the economy approaches its long-run equilibrium.

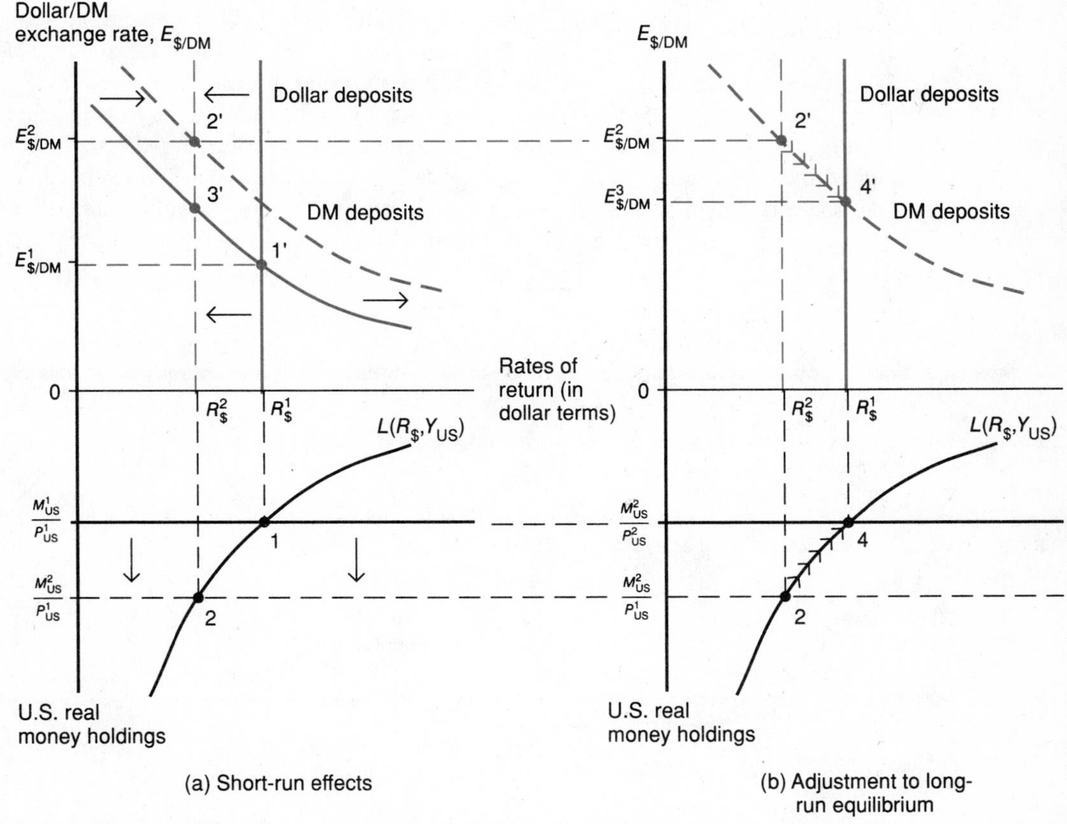

that the dollar depreciation is *greater* than it would be if the expected future dollar/DM exchange rate stayed fixed (as it might if the money supply increase were temporary rather than permanent). If the expectation $E^e_{\$/DM}$ did not change, the new short-run equilibrium would be at point 3′ rather than at point 2′.

Figure 15-12b shows how the interest rate and exchange rate behave as the price level rises during the economy's adjustment to its long-run equilibrium. The price level begins to rise from the initially given level P^1_{US}, eventually reaching P^2_{US}. Because the long-run increase in the price level must be proportional to the increase in the money supply, the final *real* money supply, M^2_{US}/P^2_{US}, is shown equal to the initial real money supply, M^1_{US}/P^1_{US}. Since output is given and the real money supply has returned to its original level, the equilibrium interest rate must again equal $R^1_\$$ in the long run (point

4). The interest rate therefore rises from $R^2_\$$ (point 2) to $R^1_\$$ (point 4) as the price level rises from P^1_{US} to P^2_{US}.

The rising U.S. interest rate has exchange rate effects that can also be seen in Figure 15-12b: the dollar *appreciates* against the DM in the process of adjustment. If exchange rate expectations do not change further during the adjustment process, the foreign exchange market moves to its long-run position along the downward-sloping schedule defining the dollar return on DM deposits. The market's path is just the path traced out by the vertical dollar interest rate schedule as it moves rightward because of the price level's gradual rise. In the long run (point 4′) the equilibrium exchange rate, $E^3_{\$/DM}$, is higher than at the original equilibrium, point 1′. Like the price level, the dollar/DM exchange rate has risen in proportion to the increase in the money supply.

Figure 15-13 shows time paths like the ones just described for the U.S. money supply, the dollar interest rate, the U.S. price level, and the dollar/DM exchange rate. The figure is drawn so that the long-run increases in the price level (Figure 15-13c) and exchange rate (Figure 15-13d) are proportional to the increase in the money supply (Figure 15-13a).

FIGURE 15-13
Time paths of U.S. economic variables after a permanent increase in the U.S. money supply.
After the money supply increases at time t_0 in panel (a), the interest rate (in panel [b]), price level (in panel [c]), and exchange rate (in panel [d]) move as shown toward their long-run levels. The exchange rate overshoots in the short run.

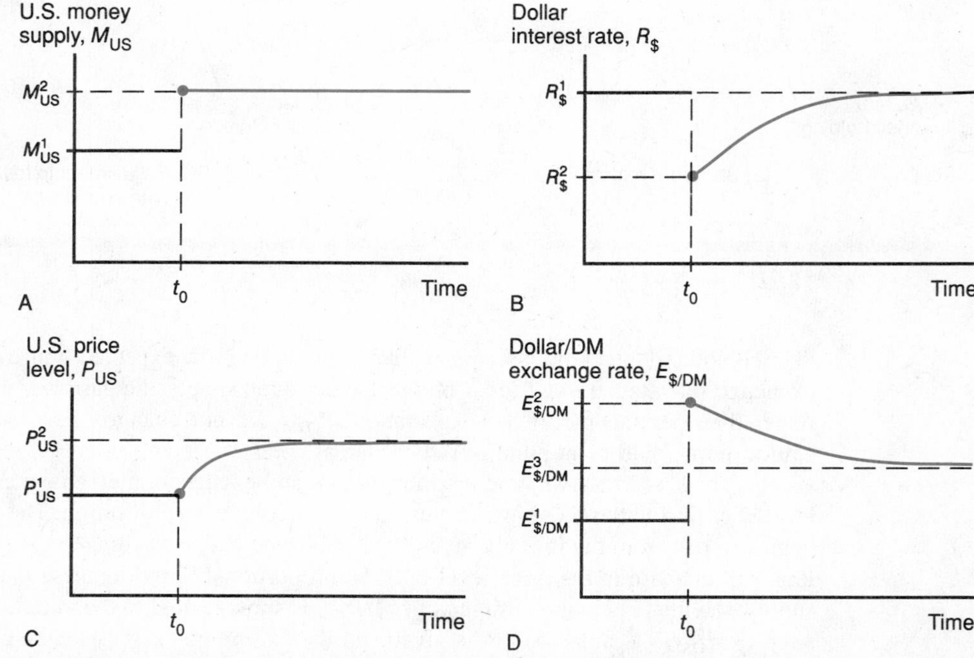

EXCHANGE RATE OVERSHOOTING

In its initial depreciation after a money supply rise, the exchange rate jumps from $E^1_{\$/DM}$ up to $E^2_{\$/DM}$, a depreciation greater than its *long-run* depreciation from $E^1_{\$/DM}$ to $E^3_{\$/DM}$ (see Figure 15-13d). The exchange rate is said to overshoot when its immediate response to a disturbance is greater than its long-run response. **Exchange rate overshooting** is an important phenomenon because it helps explain why exchange rates move so sharply from day to day.

The economic explanation of overshooting comes from the interest parity condition. The explanation is easiest to grasp if we assume that before the money supply increase first occurs, no change in the dollar/DM exchange rate is expected, so that $R^1_{\$}$ equals R_{DM}, the given interest rate on DM deposits. A permanent increase in the U.S. money supply doesn't affect R_{DM}, so it causes $R^1_{\$}$ to fall below R_{DM} and remain below that interest rate (Figure 15-13b) until the U.S. price level has completed the long-run adjustment to P^2_{US} shown in Figure 15-13c. For the foreign exchange market to be in equilibrium during this adjustment process, however, the interest difference in favor of DM deposits must be offset by an expected *appreciation* of the dollar against the DM, that is, by an expected fall in $E_{\$/DM}$. Only if the dollar/DM exchange rate overshoots $E^3_{\$/DM}$ initially will market participants expect a subsequent appreciation of the dollar against the DM.

Overshooting is a direct consequence of the short-run rigidity of the price level. In a hypothetical world where the price level could adjust immediately to its new long-run level after a money supply increase, the dollar interest rate would not fall because prices *would* adjust immediately and prevent the real money supply from rising. Thus, there would be no need for overshooting to maintain equilibrium in the foreign exchange market. The exchange rate would maintain equilibrium simply by jumping to its new long-run level right away.

Summary

1. Money is held because of its liquidity. When considered in real terms, *aggregate money demand* is not a demand for a certain number of currency units but is instead a demand for a certain amount of purchasing power. Aggregate real money demand depends negatively on the opportunity cost of holding money (measured by the domestic interest rate) and positively on the volume of transactions in the economy (measured by real GNP).

2. The money market is in equilibrium when the real *money supply* equals aggregate real money demand. With the *price level* and real output given, a rise in the money supply lowers the interest rate and a fall in the money supply raises the interest rate. A rise in real output raises the interest rate, given the price level, while a fall in real output has the opposite effect.

3. By lowering the domestic interest rate, an increase in the money supply causes the domestic currency to depreciate in the foreign exchange market (even when expectations of future exchange rates do not change). Similarly, a fall in the domestic money supply causes the domestic currency to appreciate against foreign currencies.

4. The assumption that the price level is given in the *short run* is a good approx-

imation to reality in countries with moderate inflation, but it is a misleading assumption over the *long run.* Permanent changes in the money supply push the *long-run equilibrium* price level proportionally in the same direction but do not influence the long-run values of output, the interest rate, or any relative prices. One important money price whose long-run equilibrium level rises in proportion to a permanent money supply increase is the exchange rate, the domestic currency price of foreign currency.

5. An increase in the money supply can cause the exchange rate to overshoot its long-run level in the short run. If output is given, a permanent money supply increase, for example, causes a more-than-proportional short-run depreciation of the currency, followed by an appreciation of the currency to its long-run exchange rate. *Exchange rate overshooting,* which heightens the volatility of exchange rates, is a direct result of sluggish short-run price level adjustment and the interest parity condition.

Key Terms

money supply
aggregate money demand
price level
short run
long run
long-run equilibrium
inflation
deflation
exchange rate overshooting

Problems

1. Suppose there is a reduction in aggregate real money demand, that is, a negative shift in the aggregate real money demand function. Trace the short-run and long-run effects on the exchange rate, interest rate and price level.

2. How would you expect a fall in a country's population to alter its aggregate money demand function? Would it matter if the fall in population were due to a fall in the number of households or to a fall in the average size of a household?

3. The *velocity* of money, V, is defined as the ratio of real GNP to real money holdings, $V = Y/(M/P)$ in this chapter's notation. Use equation (15-4) to derive an expression for velocity and explain how velocity varies with changes in R and in Y. (Hint: The effect of output changes on V depends on the elasticity of aggregate money demand with respect to real output, which economists believe to be less than unity.) What is the relationship between velocity and the exchange rate?

4. What is the short-run effect on the exchange rate of an increase in domestic real GNP, given expectations about future exchange rates?

5. Does our discussion of money's usefulness as a medium of exchange and unit of account suggest reasons why some currencies become vehicle currencies for foreign exchange transactions? (The concept of a vehicle currency was discussed in Chapter 14.)

6. If a currency reform has no effects on the economy's real variables, why do governments typically institute currency reforms in connection with broader programs aimed at halting runaway inflation? (There are many instances other than

the French case mentioned in the text. Recent examples include Israel's switch from the pound to the shekel, Argentina's switches from the peso to the austral and back to the peso, and Brazil's switches from the cruzeiro to the cruzado, from the cruzado to the cruzeiro, and from the cruzeiro to the cruzeiro real.)

7. Imagine that the central bank of an economy with unemployment doubles its money supply. In the long run, full employment is restored and output returns to its full employment level. On the assumption that the interest rate before the money supply increase equals the long-run interest rate, is the long-run increase in the price level more than proportional or less than proportional to the money supply change? What if the interest rate was initially below its long-run level?

8. Between 1984 and 1985, the money supply in the United States increased to $641.0 billion from $570.3 billion, while that of Brazil increased to 106.1 billion cruzados from 24.4 billion. Over the same period, the U.S. consumer price index rose to 100 from a level of 96.6, while the corresponding index for Brazil rose to 100 from a level of only 31. Calculate the 1984–1985 rates of money supply growth and inflation for the U.S. and Brazil, respectively. Assuming that other factors affecting the money markets did not change too dramatically, how do these numbers match up with the predictions of this chapter's model? How would you explain the apparently different responses of U.S. compared with Brazilian prices?

9. Continuing with the preceding question, note that the monetary value of output in 1985 was $4,010 billion in the U.S., 1,418 billion cruzados in Brazil. Refer back to question 3 and calculate velocity for the two countries in 1985. Why do you think velocity was so much higher in Brazil?

10. In our discussion of short-run exchange rate overshooting, we assumed that real output was given. Assume instead that an increase in the money supply raises real output in the short run (an assumption that will be justified in Chapter 17). How does this affect the extent to which the exchange rate overshoots when the money supply first increases? Is it likely that the exchange rate *under*shoots? (Hint: In Figure 15-12a, allow the aggregate real money demand schedule to shift in response to the increase in output.)

Further Reading

Rudiger Dornbusch. ''Expectations and Exchange Rate Dynamics,'' *Journal of Political Economy* 84 (December 1976), pp. 1161–1176. A theoretical analysis of exchange rate overshooting.

Jacob A. Frenkel and Michael L. Mussa. ''The Efficiency of Foreign Exchange Markets and Measures of Turbulence,'' *American Economic Review* 70 (May 1980), pp. 374–381. Contrasts the behavior of national price levels with that of exchange rates and other asset prices.

Benjamin M. Friedman. ''Lessons on Monetary Policy from the 1980s.'' *Journal of Economic Perspectives* 2 (Summer 1988), pp. 51–72. A clear account of U.S. monetary and price level experience in the 1980s.

Robert E. Hall and John B. Taylor. *Macroeconomics: Theory, Performance, and Policy,* 3rd edition. New York: Norton, 1991. Chapters 16 and 17 contain a detailed discussion of short-run price rigidity and longer-run price adjustment in closed economies.

Richard M. Levich. *''Overshooting'' in the Foreign Exchange Market.* Occasional Paper 5. New York: Group of Thirty, 1981. An examination of the theory and evidence on exchange rate overshooting.

Price Levels and the Exchange Rate in the Long Run

Chapter 16

At the end of 1970 you could have bought 358 Japanese yen with a single American dollar; by Christmas 1980 a dollar was worth only 203 yen. Despite a temporary comeback during the 1980s, the dollar's price in yen had slumped almost to 100 by the summer of 1993. Many investors found these price changes difficult to predict, and as a result fortunes were lost—and made—in the foreign exchange market. What economic forces lie behind such dramatic long-term movements in exchange rates?

We have seen that exchange rates are determined by interest rates and expectations about the future, which are, in turn, influenced by conditions in national money markets. To understand fully long-term exchange rate movements, however, we have to extend our model in two directions. First, we must complete our account of the linkages among monetary policies, inflation, interest rates, and exchange rates. Second, we must examine factors other than money supplies and demands—for example, demand shifts in markets for goods and services—that also can have sustained effects on exchange rates.

The model of long-run exchange rate behavior that we develop in this chapter provides the framework that actors in asset markets use to forecast future exchange rates. Because the expectations of these agents influence exchange rates immediately, however, predictions about *long-run* movements in exchange rates are important *even in the short run.* We therefore will draw heavily on this chapter's conclusions when we begin our study of *short-run* interactions between exchange rates and output in Chapter 17.

In the long run, national price levels play a key role in determining both interest rates and the relative prices at which countries' products are traded. A theory of how national price levels interact with exchange rates is thus central to understanding why exchange rates can change dramatically over periods of several years. We begin our analysis by discussing the theory of **purchasing power parity (PPP),** which explains movements in the exchange rate between two countries' currencies by changes in the countries' price levels. Next, we examine reasons PPP may fail to give accurate long-run predictions and show how the theory must sometimes be modified to account for supply or demand shifts in countries' output markets. Finally, we look at what our extended PPP theory predicts about how changes in money and output markets affect exchange and interest rates.

The Law of One Price

To understand the market forces that might give rise to the results predicted by the purchasing power parity theory, we discuss first a related but distinct proposition known as the **law of one price.** The law of one price states that in competitive markets free of transportation costs and official barriers to trade (such as tariffs), identical goods sold in different countries must sell for the same price when their prices are expressed in terms of the same currency. For example, if the dollar/pound exchange rate is \$1.50 per pound, a sweater that sells for \$45 in New York must sell for £30 in London. The dollar price of the sweater when sold in London is then (\$1.50 per pound) × (£30 per sweater) = \$45 per sweater, the same as its price in New York.

Let's continue with this example to see why the law of one price must hold when trade is free and there are no transport costs or other trade barriers. If the dollar/pound exchange rate were \$1.45 per pound, you could buy a sweater in London by converting \$43.50 (= \$1.45 per pound × £30) into £30 in the foreign exchange market. Thus, the dollar price of a sweater in London would be only \$43.50. If the same sweater were selling for \$45 in New York, U.S. importers and British exporters would have an incentive to buy sweaters in London and ship them to New York, pushing the London price up and the New York price down until prices were equal in the two locations. Similarly, at an exchange rate of \$1.55 per pound, the dollar price of sweaters in London would be \$46.50 (= \$1.55 per pound × £30), \$1.50 more than in New York. Sweaters would be shipped from west to east until a single price prevailed in the two markets.

The law of one price is a restatement, in terms of currencies, of a principle that was important in the trade theory portion of this book: When trade is open and costless, identical goods must trade at the same relative prices regardless of where they are sold. We remind you of that principle here because it provides one link between the domestic prices of goods and exchange rates. We can state the law of one price formally as follows: Let P^i_{US} be the dollar price of good i when sold in the U.S., P^i_G the corresponding DM price in Germany. Then the law of one price implies that the dollar price of good i is the same wherever it is sold,

$$P^i_{US} = (E_{\$/DM}) \times (P^i_G).$$

Equivalently, the dollar/DM exchange rate is the ratio of good i's U.S. and German money prices,

$$E_{\$/DM} = P^i_{US}/P^i_G.$$

indexes they publish using an internationally standardized basket of commodities. Absolute PPP makes no sense, however, unless the two baskets whose prices are compared in equation (16-1) are the same. (There is no reason to expect *different* commodity baskets to sell for the same price!) The notion of relative PPP therefore comes in handy when we have to rely on government price level statistics to evaluate PPP. It makes logical sense to compare percentage exchange rate changes to inflation differences, as above, even when countries base their price *level* estimates on product baskets that differ in coverage and composition.

Relative PPP is important also because it may be valid even when absolute PPP is not. Provided the factors causing deviations from absolute PPP are more or less stable over time, percentage *changes* in relative price levels can still approximate percentage *changes* in exchange rates.

A Long-Run Exchange Rate Model Based on PPP

When combined with the framework of money demand and supply we developed in Chapter 15, the theory of PPP leads to a useful theory of how exchange rates and monetary factors interact in the long run. Because factors that do not influence money supply or money demand play no explicit role in this theory, it is known as the **monetary approach to the exchange rate.** The monetary approach is this chapter's first step in developing a general long-run theory of exchange rates.

We think of the monetary approach as a *long-run* and not a short-run theory because it does not allow for the price rigidities that seem important in explaining short-run macroeconomic developments, in particular departures from full employment. Instead, the monetary approach proceeds as if prices could adjust right away to maintain full employment as well as PPP. Here, as in the previous chapter, when we refer to a variable's ''long-run'' value we mean the variable's equilibrium value in a hypothetical world of perfectly flexible output and factor market prices.

There is actually considerable controversy among macroeconomists about the sources of apparent price level stickiness, with some maintaining that prices and wages only appear rigid and in reality adjust immediately to clear markets. To an economist of the aforementioned school, this chapter's models would describe the short-run behavior of an economy in which the speed of price level adjustment is so high that no significant unemployment ever occurs.

THE FUNDAMENTAL EQUATION OF THE MONETARY APPROACH

To develop the monetary approach's predictions for the dollar/DM exchange rate, we will assume that in the long run the foreign exchange market sets that rate so that PPP holds (see equation (16-1)):

$$E_{\$/DM} = P_{US}/P_{G}.$$

In other words, we assume the above equation would hold in a world where there were no market rigidities to prevent the exchange rate and other prices from adjusting immediately to levels consistent with full employment.

In the previous chapter, equation (15-5) showed how we can explain domestic price levels in terms of domestic money demands and supplies. In the United States,

$$P_{US} = M^s_{US}/L(R_{\$}, Y_{US}), \tag{16-3}$$

while in Germany,

$$P_G = M^s_G/L(R_{DM}, Y_G), \tag{16-4}$$

As before, we have used the symbol M^s to stand for a country's money supply and $L(R,Y)$ to stand for its aggregate real money demand, which is a decreasing function of the interest rate and an increasing function of real output.[2]

Equations (16-3) and (16-4) show how the monetary approach to the exchange rate comes by its name. According to the statement of PPP in equation (16-1), the dollar price of a DM is simply the dollar price of U.S. output divided by the DM price of German output. These two price levels, in turn, are determined completely by the supply and demand for each country's money: the United States price level is the U.S. money supply divided by U.S. real money demand, as shown in (16-3), and Germany's price level similarly is the German money supply divided by German real money demand, as shown in (16-4). The monetary approach therefore makes the general prediction that *the exchange rate, which is the relative price of American and German money, is fully determined in the long run by the relative supplies of those monies and the relative real demands for them.* Shifts in interest rates and output levels affect the exchange rate only through their influences on money demand.

In addition, the monetary approach makes a number of specific predictions about the long-run effects on the exchange rate of changes in money supplies, interest rates, and output levels:

1. *Money supplies.* Other things equal, a permanent rise in the U.S. money supply M^s_{US} causes a proportional increase in the long-run U.S. price level P_{US}, as equation (16-3) shows. Because under PPP, $E_{\$/DM} = P_{US}/P_G$, however, $E_{\$/DM}$ also rises in the long run in proportion to the increase in the U.S. money supply. (For example, if M^s_{US} rises by 10 percent, P_{US} and $E_{\$/DM}$ both eventually rise by 10 percent as well.) Thus, an increase in the U.S. money supply causes a proportional long-run *depreciation* of the dollar against the DM. Conversely, equation (16-4) shows that a permanent increase in the German money supply causes a proportional increase in the long-run German price level. Under PPP, this price level rise implies a proportional long-run *appreciation* of the dollar against the DM (which is the same as a proportional depreciation of the DM against the dollar).
2. *Interest rates.* A rise in the interest rate $R_{\$}$ on dollar-denominated assets lowers real U.S. money demand $L(R_{\$}, Y_{US})$. By (16-3) the long-run U.S. price level rises, and under PPP the dollar must depreciate against the DM in proportion to this U.S. price level increase. A rise in the interest rate R_{DM} on DM-denominated assets has the reverse long-run exchange rate effect. Because real German money demand $L(R_{DM}, Y_G)$ falls, Germany's price level rises, by (16-4). Under PPP, the dollar must appreciate against the DM in proportion to Germany's price level increase.

[2] To simplify the notation, we assume identical money demand functions for the United States and Germany.

3. *Output levels.* A rise in U.S. output raises real U.S. money demand $L(R_\$,Y_{US})$, leading by (16-3) to a fall in the long-run U.S. price level. According to PPP, there is an appreciation of the dollar against the DM. Symmetrically, a rise in German output raises $L(R_{DM},Y_G)$ and, by (16-4), causes a fall in Germany's long-run price level. PPP predicts that this development will make the dollar depreciate against the DM.

To understand these predictions, remember that the monetary approach, like any long-run theory, essentially assumes that price levels adjust as quickly as exchange rates do—that is, right away. For example, a rise in real U.S. output raises the transactions demand for real U.S. money balances. According to the monetary approach, the U.S. price level drops *immediately* to bring about a market-clearing increase in the supply of real balances. PPP implies that this instantaneous American price deflation is accompanied by an instantaneous dollar appreciation on the foreign exchanges.

The monetary approach leads to a result familiar from Chapter 15, that the long-run foreign exchange value of a country's currency moves in proportion to its money supply (prediction 1 above). The theory also raises what seems to be a paradox (prediction 2). In our previous examples, we always found that a currency *appreciates* when the interest rate it offers rises relative to foreign interest rates. How is it that we have now arrived at precisely the opposite conclusion—that a rise in a country's interest rate *depreciates* its currency by lowering the real demand for its money?

At the end of Chapter 14 we warned that no account of how a change in interest rates affects the exchange rate is complete until we specify *exactly why interest rates have changed.* This point explains the apparent contradiction in our findings about interest and exchange rates. To resolve the puzzle, however, we must first examine more closely how monetary policies and interest rates are connected in the long run.

ONGOING INFLATION, INTEREST PARITY, AND PPP

In the last chapter we saw that a permanent increase in the *level* of a country's money supply ultimately results in a proportional rise in its price level but has no effect on the long-run values of the interest rate or real output. The conceptual experiment of a one-time, stepwise money supply change is useful for thinking about the long-run effects of money, but it is not too realistic as a description of actual monetary policies. More often, the monetary authorities choose a *growth rate* for the money supply, say, 5 or 10 or 50 percent per year, and then allow money to grow gradually, through small but frequent increases. What are the long-run effects of a policy that allows the money supply to grow smoothly forever at a positive rate?

The reasoning in Chapter 15 suggests that continuing money supply growth will require a continuing rise in the price level—a situation of *ongoing* inflation. As firms and workers catch on to the fact that the money supply is growing steadily at, say, a 10 percent annual rate, they will adjust by raising prices and wages by the same 10 percent every year, thus keeping their real incomes constant. Full-employment output depends on supplies of productive factors, but it is safe to assume that factor supplies, and thus output, are unaffected over the long run by different choices of a constant growth rate for the money supply. *Other things equal, money supply growth at a constant rate eventually results in ongoing price level inflation at the same rate, but changes in this long-run inflation rate do not affect the full-employment output level or the long-run relative prices of goods and services.*

The interest rate, however, is definitely not independent of the money supply growth rate in the long run. While the long-run interest rate does not depend on the absolute level of the money supply, continuing growth in the money supply eventually will affect the interest rate. The easiest way to see how a permanent increase in inflation affects the long-run interest rate is by combining PPP with the interest rate parity condition on which our previous analysis of exchange rate determination was built.

As in the preceding two chapters, the condition of interest parity between dollar and DM assets is

$$R_{\$} = R_{DM} + (E^e_{\$/DM} - E_{\$/DM})/E_{\$/DM}$$

(recall equation (14-2), page 353). Now let's ask how this parity condition, which must hold in the long run as well as in the short run, fits with the other parity condition we are assuming in our long-run model, purchasing power parity. According to relative PPP, the percentage change in the dollar/DM exchange rate over the next year, say, will equal the difference between the inflation rates of the United States and Germany over that year (see equation (16-2)). Since people understand this relationship, however, it must also be true that they *expect* the percentage exchange rate change to equal the U.S.-German inflation difference. The interest parity condition written above now tells us the following: *If people expect relative PPP to hold, the difference between the interest rates offered by dollar and DM deposits will equal the difference between the inflation rates expected, over the relevant horizon, in the United States and in Germany.*

Some additional notation is helpful in deriving this result more formally. If P^e is the price level expected in a country for a year from today, the expected inflation rate in that country, π^e, is the expected percentage increase in the price level over the coming year,

$$\pi^e = (P^e - P)/P.$$

If relative PPP holds, however, market participants will also expect it to hold, which means that we can replace the actual depreciation and inflation rates in equation (16-2) with the values the market expects to materialize:

$$(E^e_{\$/DM} - E_{\$/DM})/E_{\$/DM} = \pi^e_{US} - \pi^e_{G}.$$

By combining this ''expected'' version of relative PPP with the interest parity condition

$$R_{\$} = R_{DM} + (E^e_{\$/DM} - E_{\$/DM})/E_{\$/DM}$$

and rearranging, we arrive at a formula that expresses the international interest rate difference as the difference between expected national inflation rates:

$$R_{\$} - R_{DM} = \pi^e_{US} - \pi^e_{G}. \quad \textbf{(16-5)}$$

If, as PPP predicts, currency depreciation is expected to offset the international inflation difference (so that the expected dollar depreciation rate is $\pi^e_{US} - \pi^e_{G}$), the interest rate difference must equal the expected inflation difference.

THE FISHER EFFECT

Equation (16-5) gives us the long-run relationship between ongoing inflation and interest rates that we need to explain the monetary approach's predictions about how interest rates affect exchange rates. The equation tells us that *all else equal, a rise in a country's expected inflation rate will eventually cause an equal rise in the interest rate that deposits of its currency offer. Similarly, a fall in the expected inflation rate will eventually cause a fall in the interest rate.*

This long-run relationship between inflation and interest rates is called the **Fisher effect.** The Fisher effect implies, for example, that if U.S. inflation were to rise permanently from a constant level of 5 percent per year to a constant level of 10 percent per year, dollar interest rates would eventually catch up with the higher inflation, rising by 5 percentage points per year from their initial level. These changes would leave the *real rate of return* on dollar assets, measured in terms of U.S. goods and services, unchanged. The Fisher effect is therefore another example of the general idea that in the long run, purely monetary developments should have no effect on an economy's relative prices.[3]

The Fisher effect is behind the seemingly paradoxical monetary approach prediction that a currency depreciates in the foreign exchange market when its interest rate rises relative to foreign currency interest rates. In the long-run equilibrium assumed by the monetary approach, a rise in the difference between home and foreign interest rates occurs only when expected home inflation rises relative to expected foreign inflation. This is certainly not the case in the short run, when the domestic price level is sticky. In the short run, as we saw in Chapter 15, the interest can rise when the domestic money supply *falls* because the sticky domestic price level leads to an excess demand for real money balances at the initial interest rate. Under the flexible-price monetary approach, however, the price level would fall right away and thus make the interest rate change unnecessary.

We can better understand how interest rates and exchange rates interact under the monetary approach by thinking through an example. Our example illustrates why the monetary approach associates sustained interest rate hikes with current as well as future currency depreciation, sustained interest rate slumps with appreciation.

Imagine that at time t_0 the Federal Reserve unexpectedly increases the growth rate of the U.S. money supply from π to the higher level $\pi + \Delta\pi$. Figure 16-1 illustrates how this change affects the dollar/DM exchange rate $E_{\$/DM}$, as well as other U.S. variables, under the assumptions of the monetary approach. To simplify the graphs we assume that in Germany the inflation rate remains constant at zero.

Figure 16-1a shows the sudden acceleration of U.S. money supply growth at time t_0. (We have scaled the horizontal axes of the graphs so that constant slopes represent constant proportional growth rates of variables.) The policy change generates expectations of more rapid currency depreciation in the future: under PPP the dollar will now depreciate at rate $\pi + \Delta\pi$ rather than at the lower rate π. Interest parity therefore requires the dollar interest rate to rise, as shown in Figure 16-1b, from its initial level $R^1_\$$ to a new level that reflects the extra expected dollar depreciation, $R^2_\$ = R^1_\$ + \Delta\pi$ (see equation (16-5)). Notice that this adjustment leaves the DM interest rate unchanged; but since Germany's money supply and output haven't changed, the original DM interest rate will still maintain equilibrium in Germany's money market.

You can see from Figure 16-1a that the *level* of the money supply does not actually

[3] The effect is named after Irving Fisher, one of the great American economists of the early twentieth century. The effect is discussed at length in his book, *The Theory of Interest* (New York: Macmillan, 1930). Fisher, incidentally, gave an early account of the interest parity condition on which our theory of foreign exchange market equilibrium is based.

FIGURE 16-1
Long-run time paths of U.S. economic variables after a permanent increase in the growth rate of the U.S. money supply.
After the money-supply growth rate increases at time t_0 in panel (a), the interest rate (in panel [b]), price level (in panel [c]), and exchange rate (in panel [d]) move to new long-run equilibrium paths. (The money supply, price level, and exchange rate are all measured on a *natural logarithmic* scale, which makes variables that change at constant proportional rates appear as straight lines when they are graphed against time. The slope of the line equals the variable's proportional growth rate.)

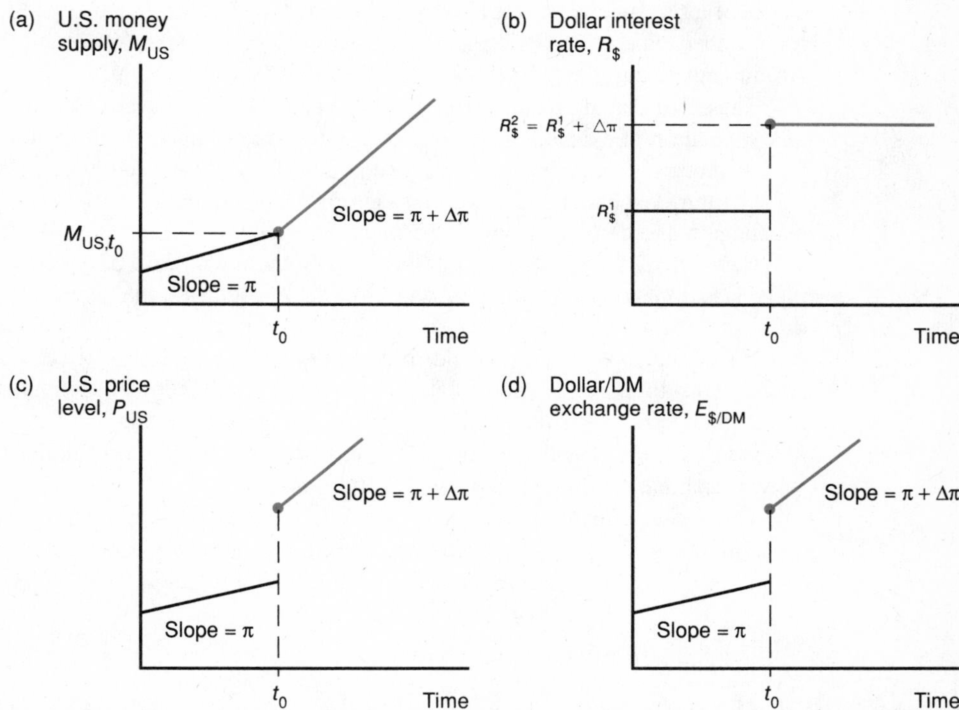

jump upward at t_0—only the *future growth rate* changes. Since there is no immediate increase in the money supply, but there is an interest rate rise that reduces money demand, there would be an excess supply of real U.S. money balances at the price level prevailing just prior to t_0. In the face of this potential excess supply the U.S. price level does jump at t_0 (see Figure 16-1c), reducing the real money supply so that it again equals real money demand (see equation (16-3)). Along with the upward jump in P_{US} at t_0, Figure 16-1d shows the simultaneous proportional upward jump in $E_{\$/DM}$ implied by PPP.

How can we visualize the reaction of the foreign exchange market at time t_0? The dollar interest rate rises in our example not because of a change in current levels of money supply or demand, but solely because people expect more rapid future money supply growth and dollar depreciation. As investors respond by moving into foreign deposits offering higher expected returns, the dollar depreciates sharply in the foreign exchange market, moving to a new trend line along which depreciation is more rapid than it was up to time t_0.[4]

Notice how different assumptions about the speed of price level adjustment lead to contrasting predictions about how exchange and interest rates interact. In the example of a fall in the money supply under sticky prices, an interest rate rise is needed to preserve money market equilibrium, given that the price level cannot do so by dropping immediately in response to the money supply reduction. In that sticky price case, an interest rate rise is associated with lower expected inflation and a long-run currency appreciation, so the currency appreciates immediately. In our monetary-approach example of a rise in money supply growth, however, an interest rate increase is associated with higher expected inflation and a currency that will be weaker on all future dates. An immediate currency *depreciation* is the result.[5]

These contrasting results of interest rate changes underlie our earlier warning that an explanation of exchange rates based on interest rates must carefully account for the factors that cause interest rates to move. These factors can simultaneously affect expected future exchange rates and can therefore have a decisive impact on the foreign exchange market's response to the interest rate change.

Figure 16-2 bears out the main long-run prediction of the Fisher effect. The figure plots inflation rates and interest rates for three countries that have had somewhat different inflationary experiences since 1970: Switzerland, the United States, and Italy. In each country interest rates tend to rise after inflation rises as prices adjust and as people learn to expect higher inflation in the future; reductions in inflation eventually lower interest rates for the same reason. Moreover, the average level of interest rates is lowest in Switzerland, which has the lowest average inflation rate, and highest in Italy, which has the highest average inflation rate.

The Fisher effect can be broadly correct even when PPP is not, so we can't take the evidence in Figure 16-2 as confirmation of the monetary approach. We now look at evidence bearing more directly on the validity of PPP itself.

Empirical Evidence on PPP and the Law of One Price

How well does the PPP theory explain actual data on exchange rates and national price levels? A brief answer is that all versions of the PPP theory do badly in explaining the facts. In particular, changes in national price levels often tell us little or nothing about exchange rate movements.

Do not conclude from this evidence, however, that the effort you've put into

[4] In the general case in which Germany's inflation rate π_G is not zero, the dollar, rather than depreciating against the DM at rate π before t_0 and at rate $\pi + \Delta\pi$ afterward, depreciates at rate $\pi - \pi_G$ until t_0 and at rate $\pi + \Delta\pi - \pi_G$ thereafter.

[5] National money supplies typically trend upward over time, as in Figure 16-1a. Such trends lead to corresponding upward trends in price levels; if two countries' price level trends differ, PPP implies a trend in their exchange rate as well. From now on, when we refer to a change in the money supply, price level, or exchange rate, we will mean by this a change in the variable *relative to its previously expected trend rate of increase*. When instead we want to consider changes in trends themselves, we will say so explicitly.

FIGURE 16-2
Inflation and interest rates in Switzerland, the United States, and Italy, 1970–1991.

Inflation and interest rates show a long-run tendency to move together, as the Fisher effect suggests.

Source: OECD, *Main Economic Indicators.* Inflation rates are year-to-year percentage changes in consumer price indexes. Interest rates: Switzerland, yield of confederation bonds; United States, 3-month Treasury bill rate; Italy, bond yields of credit institutions; all measured at end of second quarter.

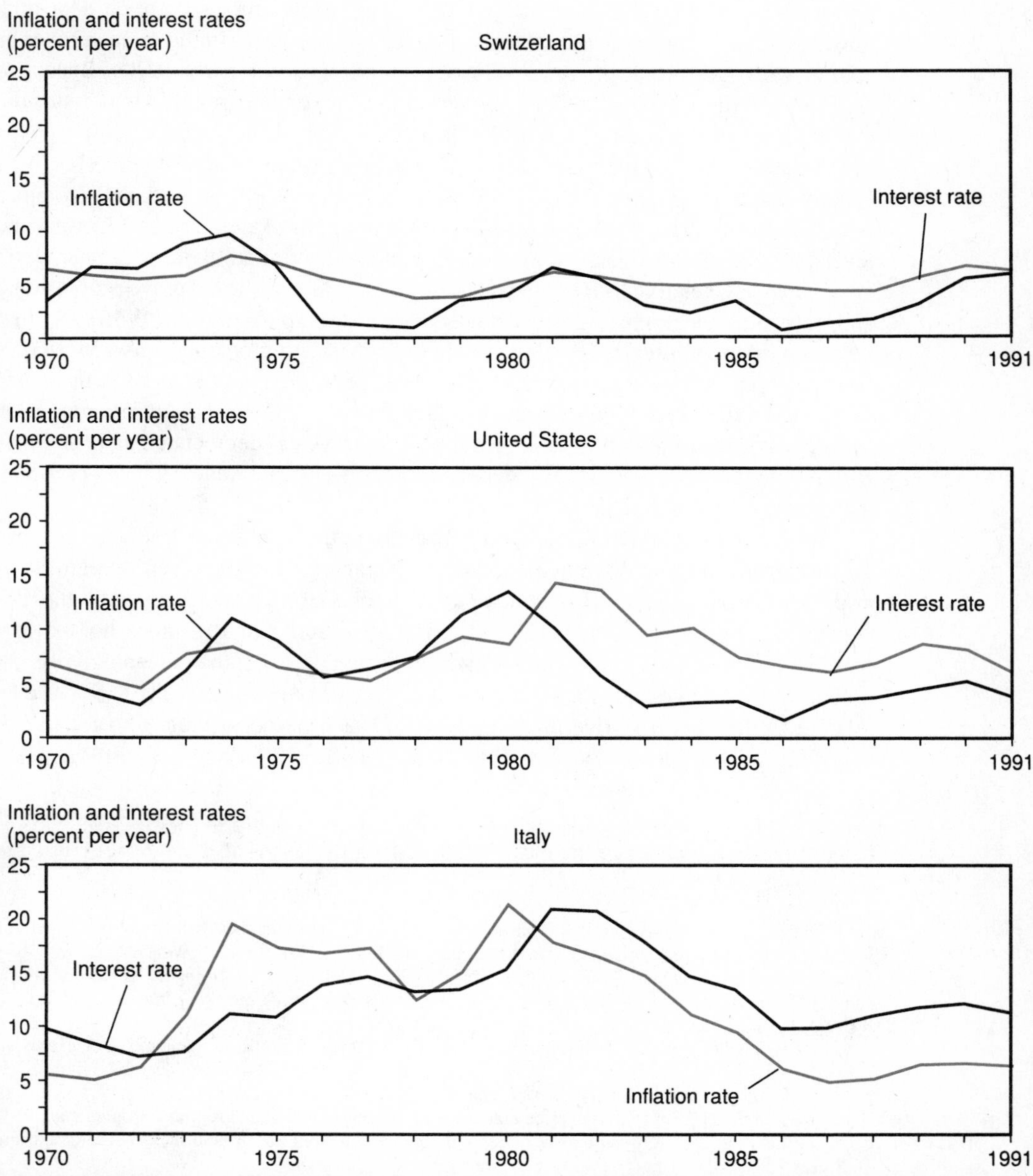

learning about PPP has been wasted. As we'll see later in this chapter, PPP is a key building-block of exchange rate models more realistic than the monetary approach. Indeed, the empirical failures of PPP give us important clues about how more realistic models should be set up.

To test *absolute* PPP, economic researchers compare the international prices of a broad reference basket of commodities, making careful adjustments for intercountry quality differences among supposedly identical goods. These comparisons typically conclude that absolute PPP is way off the mark: the prices of identical commodity baskets, when converted to a single currency, differ substantially across countries. Even the law of one price does not fare well in some recent studies of price data broken down by commodity type. Manufactured goods that are very similar to each other have sold at widely different prices in various markets since the early 1970s. Because the argument leading to absolute PPP builds on the law of one price, it is not surprising that PPP does not stand up well to the data.[6]

Relative PPP is sometimes a reasonable approximation to the data, but it, too, usually performs poorly. Figure 16-3 illustrates relative PPP's weakness by plotting both the dollar/DM exchange rate, $E_{\$/DM}$, and the ratio of the U.S. and German price levels, P_{US}/P_G. Price levels are measured by indexes reported by the U.S. and German governments.[7] Relative PPP predicts that $E_{\$/DM}$ and P_{US}/P_G should move proportionally, and, as you can see in the figure, this was more or less so through 1970. But PPP broke down completely after 1970, with the dollar depreciating sharply between 1970 and 1973 even though U.S. prices *fell* slightly relative to German prices over those years. From 1973 through 1979, PPP is somewhat more successful: as U.S. prices rose relative to German prices, the dollar (in all but one of these years) depreciated against the DM. But the magnitude of the dollar's depreciation between 1973 and 1979 was far greater than relative PPP would predict.

A dramatic violation of relative PPP occurs in the years after 1979. In those years the dollar first sustained a massive appreciation against the DM even though the U.S. price level continued to rise relative to that of Germany; subsequently the dollar depreciated by far more than PPP would predict. Relative PPP does hold over the period 1964–1983 taken as a whole: over those two decades, the percentage rise in the dollar/DM exchange rate is very close to the percentage increase in the U.S. price level relative to the German price level. In view of the wide departures from relative PPP over long subperiods of the 1964–1983 span and after 1983, however, PPP appears to be of limited use even as a long-run explanation of exchange rate movements.

Studies of other currencies largely confirm the results in Figure 16-3. Relative PPP has not held up well since the early 1970s, but in the 1960s it is a more reliable guide

[6] Some of the negative evidence on absolute PPP is discussed in the Case Study presented below. Regarding the law of one price, see, for example, Peter Isard, "How Far Can We Push the Law of One Price?" *American Economic Review* 67 (December 1977), pp. 942–948; and Irving B. Kravis and Robert E. Lipsey, "Price Behavior in the Light of Balance of Payments Theories," *Journal of International Economics* 8 (May 1978), pp. 193–246.

[7] The price level measures in Figure 16-3 are index numbers, not dollar amounts. For example, the U.S. consumer price index (CPI) was 100 in the base year 1967 and 298.4 in 1983, so the dollar price of a reference commodity basket of typical U.S. consumption purchases nearly tripled between 1967 and 1983. Base years for the U.S. and German price indexes were chosen so that their 1964 ratio would equal the 1964 exchange rate, but this imposed equality does *not* mean that absolute PPP held in 1964. Although Figure 16-3 uses CPIs, other price indexes lead to similar pictures.

FIGURE 16-3
The dollar/DM exchange rate and relative U.S./German price levels, 1964–1991.
The graph shows that relative PPP does not explain the dollar/DM exchange rate after 1970.
Source: OECD, *Main Economic Indicators*. Exchange rates and price levels are end-of-year data.

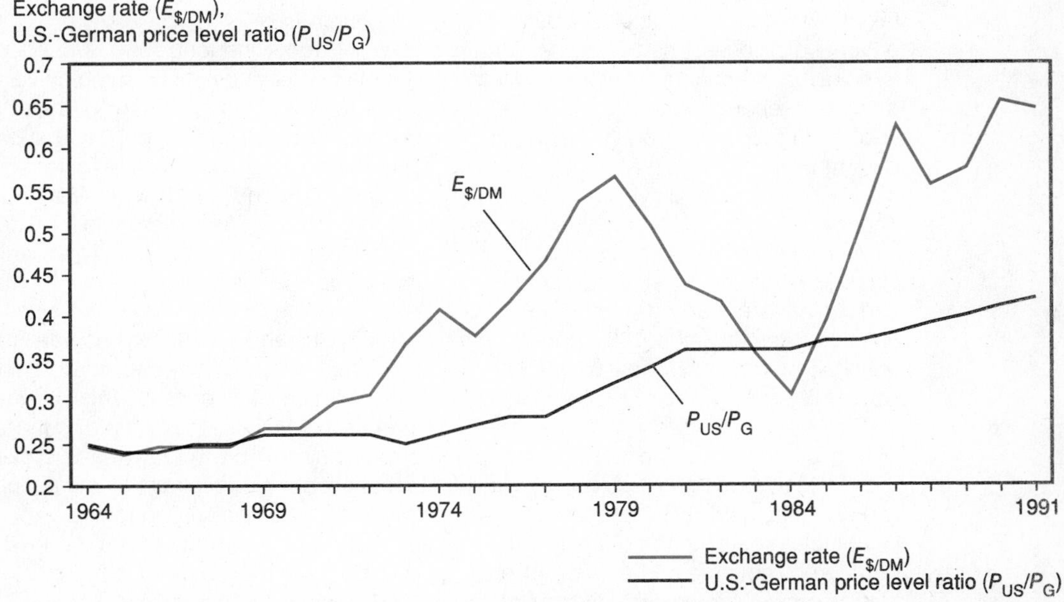

to the relationship among exchange rates and national price levels.[8] As you will learn later in this book, between the end of World War II in 1945 and the early 1970s exchange rates were fixed within narrow internationally agreed margins through the intervention of central banks in the foreign exchange market. During the first half of the 1920s, when many exchange rates were market-determined as in the 1970s, 1980s, and 1990s, important deviations from relative PPP also occurred.[9]

[8] See, for example, Hans Genberg, "Purchasing Power Parity under Fixed and Flexible Exchange Rates," *Journal of International Economics* 8 (May 1978), pp. 247–276; Jacob A. Frenkel, "The Collapse of Purchasing Power Parities during the 1970s," *European Economic Review* 16 (1981), pp. 145–165; and Robert E. Cumby and Maurice Obstfeld, "International Interest Rate and Price Level Linkages under Flexible Exchange Rates: A Review of Recent Evidence," in John F. O. Bilson and Richard C. Marston, eds., *Exchange Rate Theory and Practice* (Chicago: University of Chicago Press, 1984), pp. 121–151.

[9] See Paul R. Krugman, "Purchasing Power Parity and Exchange Rates: Another Look at the Evidence," *Journal of International Economics* 8 (August 1978), pp. 397–407; and Paul De Grauwe, Marc Janssens, and Hilde Leliaert, *Real-Exchange-Rate Variability from 1920 to 1926 and 1973 to 1982,* Princeton Studies in International Finance 56 (International Finance Section, Department of Economics, Princeton University, September 1985).

Some Meaty Evidence on the Law of One Price

In the summer of 1986, the *Economist* magazine conducted an extensive survey on the prices of Big Mac hamburgers at McDonald's restaurants throughout the world. This apparently whimsical undertaking was not the result of an outbreak of editorial giddiness. The magazine wanted to poke fun at economists who confidently declare exchange rates to be "overvalued" or "undervalued" on the basis of PPP comparisons. Since Big Macs are "sold in 41 countries, with only the most trivial changes of recipe," the magazine argued, a comparison of hamburger prices should serve as a "medium-rare guide to whether currencies are trading at the right exchange rates."* Since 1986, the *Economist* has periodically updated its calculations.

One way of interpreting the *Economist* survey is as a test of the law of one price. Viewed in this way, the results of the initial test are quite startling. The dollar prices of Big Macs turned out to be wildly different in different countries. The price of a Big Mac in New York was 50 percent higher than in Australia and 64 percent higher than in Hong Kong. In contrast, a Parisian Big Mac cost 54 percent more than its New York counterpart; a Tokyo Big Mac cost 50 percent more. Only in Britain and Ireland were the dollar prices of the burgers close to New York levels.

How can this dramatic violation of the law of one price be explained? As the *Economist* noted, transport costs and government regulations are part of the explanation. Product differentiation is probably an important additional factor. Because relatively few close substitutes for Big Macs are available in some countries, product differentiation may give McDonald's some power to tailor prices to the local market. Finally, remember that the price of a Big Mac must cover not only the cost of ground meat and buns, but also the wages of serving people, rent, electricity, and so on. The prices of these nonfood inputs can differ sharply in different countries.

What about the long run? Subsequent Big Mac surveys have shown no universal tendency toward a narrowing of the 1986 price differentials. The April 1989 survey showed the Big Mac selling for only 12 percent more in Paris than in Manhattan but selling for 153 percent more in Manhattan than in Hong Kong.** Significantly, the magazine also reported price differences among the four American cities of Atlanta, Chicago, New York, and San Francisco that were in many cases larger than the international disparities! This suggests that of the possible factors causing the law of one price to break down in this case, direct government restraint of international trade is not the most important.

We have reproduced the table that summarized the *Economist*'s April 18, 1992 survey report. Column 1 reports local-currency prices for Big Macs. Column 2 is the local price of a Big Mac divided by its average dollar price in the four U.S. cities mentioned above. This "implied PPP" is the exchange rate—quoted in indirect terms, as foreign currency units per dollar—that would prevail if the law of one price governed hamburger prices.

The last column gives the percentage by which the actual price of a dollar in column 3 exceeds or falls short of the hamburger-PPP rate in column 2. (It is often said that a currency is "overvalued" when its exchange rate makes domestic goods look expensive relative to similar goods sold abroad and "undervalued" in the opposite case.) Thus, the reported 33 percent undervaluation of the dollar relative to

The hamburger standard

Big Mac prices

Country	Prices* in local currency	Implied PPP** of the dollar	Actual exchange rate 10/4/92	% over(+) or under(-) valuation of dollar
Argentina	Peso3.30	1.51	0.99	-34
Australia	A$2.54	1.16	1.31	+13
Belgium	BFr108	49.32	33.55	-32
Brazil	Cr3,800	1,735	2,153	+24
Britain	£1.74	0.79	0.57	-28
Canada	C$2.76	1.26	1.19	-6
China	Yuan6.30	2.88	5.44	+89
Denmark	DKr27.25	12.44	6.32	-49
France	FFr18.10	8.26	5.55	-33
Germany	DM 4.50	2.05	1.64	-20
Holland	Fl 5.35	2.44	1.84	-24
Hong Kong	HK$8.90	4.06	7.73	+91
Hungary	Forint133	60.73	79.70	+31
Ireland	I£1.45	0.66	0.61	-8
Italy	Lire4,100	1872	1,233	-34
Japan	¥380	174	133	-24
Russia	Rouble58	26.48	98.95†	+273
Singapore	S$4.75	2.17	1.65	-24
S.Korea	Won2,300	1,050	778	-26
Spain	Ptas315	144	102	-29
Sweden	SKr25.50	11.64	5.93	-49
United States††	$2.19	—	—	—
Venezuela	Bs 170	77.63	60.63	-22

Source: McDonald's * prices may vary locally, ** Purchasing-power parity: local price divided by dollar price, † Market rate, †† New York, Chicago, San Francisco and Atlanta

the French franc means that the price of a Big Mac in the United States was only two-thirds the dollar price of a Parisian Big Mac. Similarly, the U.S. price was nearly 91 percent higher than the Hong Kong price.

Notice that the world's cheapest Big Macs, by far, are sold in Russia. It is doubtful McDonald's is making much money in that market, despite the low wages Russian workers earn. The operation has generated much favorable publicity for the company, however, and McDonald's Moscow beachhead gives it a strategic position that may prove profitable in the future as Russian living standards rise.

* "On the Hamburger Standard," *Economist,* September 6–12, 1986.

** "The Hamburger Standard," *Economist,* April 15, 1989.

Explaining the Problems with PPP

What explains the negative empirical results described in the previous section? There are several immediate problems with our rationale for the PPP theory of exchange rates, which was based on the law of one price:

1. Contrary to the assumption of the law of one price, transport costs and restrictions on trade certainly do exist. These trade barriers may be high enough to prevent some goods and services from being traded between countries.
2. Monopolistic or oligopolistic practices in goods markets may interact with transport costs and other trade barriers to weaken further the link between the prices of similar goods sold in different countries.
3. Because the inflation data reported in different countries are based on different commodity baskets, there is no reason for exchange rate changes to offset official measures of inflation differences, even when there are no barriers to trade and all products are tradable.

TRADE BARRIERS AND NONTRADABLES

Transport costs and trade restrictions make it expensive to move goods between markets located in different countries and therefore weaken the law of one price mechanism underlying PPP. Suppose once again that the same sweater sells for $45 in New York and for £30 in London, but that it costs $2 to ship a sweater between the two cities. At an exchange rate of $1.45 per pound, the dollar price of a London sweater is ($1.45 per pound) × (£30) = $43.50, but an American importer would have to pay $43.50 + $2 = $45.50 to purchase the sweater in London and get it to New York. At an exchange rate of $1.45 per pound, it therefore would not pay to ship sweaters from London to New York, even though their dollar price would be higher in the latter location. Similarly, at an exchange rate of $1.55 per pound, an American exporter would lose money by shipping sweaters from New York to London even though the New York price of $45 would then be below the dollar price of the sweater in London, $46.50.

The lesson of this example is that transport costs sever the close link between exchange rates and goods prices implied by the law of one price. The greater the transport costs, the greater the range over which the exchange rate can move, given goods prices in different countries. Official trade restrictions such as tariffs have a similar effect, because a fee paid to the customs inspector affects the importer's profit in the same way as an equivalent shipping fee. Either type of trade impediment weakens the basis of PPP by allowing the purchasing power of a given currency to differ more widely from country to country. For example, in the presence of trade impediments, a dollar need not go as far in Tokyo as in Chicago—and it doesn't, as anyone who has been to Tokyo has found out.

As you will recall from Chapter 2, transport costs may be so large relative to the cost of producing some goods and services that they can never be traded internationally at a profit. Such goods and services are called *nontradables.* The time-honored classroom example of a nontradable is the haircut. A Frenchman desiring an American haircut would have to transport himself to the United States or transport an American barber to France; in either case, the cost of transport is so large relative to the price of the service being purchased that (tourists excepted) French haircuts are consumed only by residents of France while American haircuts are consumed only by residents of the United States.

The existence in all countries of nontraded goods and services whose prices are not linked internationally allows systematic deviations even from relative PPP. Because the price of a nontradable is determined entirely by its *domestic* supply and demand curves, shifts in those curves may cause the domestic price of a broad commodity basket to change relative to the foreign price of the same basket. Other things equal, a rise in the price of a country's nontradables will raise its price level relative to foreign price levels (measuring all countries' price levels in terms of a single currency). Looked at another way, the purchasing power of any given currency will fall in countries where the prices of nontradables rise.

Each country's price level includes a wide variety of nontradables, including (along with haircuts) routine medical treatment, aerobic dance instruction, and housing, among others. Broadly speaking, we can identify traded goods with manufactured products, raw materials, and agricultural products. Nontradables are primarily services and the output of the construction industry. There are naturally exceptions to this rule. For example, financial services provided by banks and brokerage houses often can be traded internationally. In addition, trade restrictions, if sufficiently severe, can cause goods that would normally be traded to become nontraded. Thus, in most countries some manufactures are nontraded.

We can get a very rough idea of the importance of nontradables in the American economy by looking at the contribution of the service and construction industries to U.S. GNP. In 1991, the output of these industries accounted for about 60 percent of U.S. GNP.

Numbers like these are likely to understate the importance of nontradables in determining national price levels. Even the prices of tradable products usually include costs of nontraded distribution and marketing services that bring goods from producers to consumers. (See ''Some Meaty Evidence on the Law of One Price,'' page 412.) Nontradables help explain the wide departures from relative PPP illustrated by Figure 16-3.

DEPARTURES FROM FREE COMPETITION

When trade barriers and imperfectly competitive market structures occur together, linkages between national price levels are weakened further. An extreme case occurs when a single firm sells a commodity for different prices in different markets. (Recall the analysis of dumping in Chapter 6.) In the early 1990s, for example, a Nissan automobile built at the Japanese company's Sunderland plant in northeast England could be bought from a dealer near the plant for £16,215. The same model sold in Japan for only £13,375—despite the cost to Nissan of shipping the car 10,600 miles from Sunderland to Tokyo.[10]

Such discriminatory pricing would be difficult to enforce if it were not costly for drivers to buy autos in Japan and ship them to England. Similarly, if consumers viewed Volkswagens and Fiats as good substitutes for the Nissan, competition among producers

[10] ''Why Buyers in Tokyo Spend $5,000 Less for UK-Built Nissan,'' *Financial Times,* October 5, 1992, p. 16.

would keep the U.K. price of the Japanese cars from getting wildly out of line with production costs. The combination of product differentiation and segmented markets, however, leads to large violations of the law of one price and absolute PPP. Shifts in market structure and demand over time can invalidate relative PPP.

INTERNATIONAL DIFFERENCES IN PRICE LEVEL MEASUREMENT

Government measures of the price level differ from country to country. One reason for these differences is that people living in different countries spend their income in different ways. The average Italian consumes more olive oil than her American counterpart, the average Japanese more sushi, and the average Frenchwoman more croissants. In constructing a reference commodity basket to measure purchasing power, it is therefore likely that the Italian government will put a relatively high weight on olive oil, the Japanese government a high weight on sushi, and the French government a high weight on croissants.

Because relative PPP makes predictions about price *changes* rather than price *levels,* it is a sensible concept regardless of the baskets used to define price levels in the countries being compared. If all U.S. prices increase by 10 percent and the dollar depreciates against foreign currencies by 10 percent, relative PPP will be satisfied (assuming there are no changes abroad) for any domestic and foreign choices of price level indexes.

Change in the relative prices of basket components, however, can cause relative PPP to fail tests that are based on official price indexes. For example, a rise in the relative price of fish would raise the dollar price of a Japanese government reference commodity basket relative to that of a U.S. government basket, simply because fish takes up a larger share of the Japanese basket. Relative price changes could lead to PPP violations like those shown in Figure 16-3 even if trade were free and costless.

PPP IN THE SHORT RUN AND IN THE LONG RUN

The factors we have examined so far in explaining the PPP theory's poor empirical performance can cause national price levels to diverge even in the long run, after all prices have had time to adjust to their market-clearing levels. As we discussed in Chapter 15, however, many prices in the economy are sticky and take time to adjust fully. Departures from PPP may therefore be even greater in the short run than in the long run.

An abrupt depreciation of the dollar against foreign currencies, for example, makes farm equipment in the United States cheaper relative to similar equipment produced abroad. As farmers throughout the world shift their demand for tractors and reapers to U.S. producers, the price of American farm equipment tends to rise to reduce the divergence from the law of one price caused by the dollar's depreciation. It takes time for this process of price increase to be complete, however, and prices for U.S. and foreign farm equipment may differ considerably while markets adjust to the exchange rate change.

You might suspect that short-run price stickiness and exchange rate volatility help explain a phenomenon we noted in discussing Figure 16-3, that violations of relative PPP have been much more flagrant over periods when exchange rates have floated.

Recent empirical research supports this interpretation of the data. In a careful study covering many countries and historical episodes, Michael Mussa of the University of Chicago compared the extent of short-run deviations from PPP under fixed and floating exchange rates. He found that floating exchange rates systematically lead to much larger and more frequent short-run deviations from relative PPP.[11]

Case Study

WHY PRICE LEVELS ARE LOWER IN POORER COUNTRIES

Research on international price level differences has uncovered a striking empirical regularity: when expressed in terms of a single currency, countries' price levels are positively related to the level of real income per capita. In other words, a dollar, when converted to local currency at the market exchange rate, generally goes much further in a poor country than in a rich one.

The previous section's discussion of the role of nontraded goods in the determination of national price levels suggests that international variations in the prices of nontradables may contribute to price level discrepancies between rich and poor nations. Figure 16-4 shows that when nontradables are defined as services and construction, the relative price of nontradables (in terms of tradables) does rise systematically with per capita real output. Higher prices for nontradables in richer countries therefore contribute to those countries' higher overall price levels.[12]

One reason for the lower relative price of nontradables in poor countries was suggested by Bela Balassa and by Paul Samuelson.[13] The Balassa-Samuelson theory assumes that the labor forces of poor countries are less productive than those of rich countries in the tradables sector but that international productivity differences in nontradables are negligible. If the prices of traded goods are roughly equal in all countries, however, lower labor productivity in the tradables industries of poor countries implies lower wages than abroad, lower production costs in nontradables, and therefore a lower price of nontradables. Rich countries with higher labor productivity in the tradables sector will tend to have higher nontradables prices and higher price levels. Productivity statistics give some empirical support to the Balassa-Samuelson differential productivity postulate. And it is plausible that international productivity differences are sharper in traded than in nontraded goods. Whether a country is rich or poor, a barber can give

[11] See Mussa, ''Nominal Exchange Rate Regimes and the Behavior of Real Exchange Rates: Evidence and Implications,'' in Karl Brunner and Allan H. Meltzer, eds., *Real Business Cycles, Real Exchange Rates and Actual Policies,* Carnegie-Rochester Conference Series on Public Policy 25 (Amsterdam: North-Holland, 1986), pp. 117–214.

[12] The price indexes for tradable goods underlying Figure 16-4 actually show that tradables as well as nontradables tend to be cheaper in poorer countries.

[13] See Balassa, ''The Purchasing Power Parity Doctrine: A Reappraisal,'' *Journal of Political Economy* 72 (December 1964), pp. 584–596, and Samuelson, ''Theoretical Notes on Trade Problems,'' *Review of Economics and Statistics* 46 (May 1964), pp. 145–154. The Balassa-Samuelson theory was foreshadowed by some observations of Ricardo. See Jacob Viner, *Studies in the Theory of International Trade* (New York: Harper & Brothers, 1937), p. 315.

FIGURE 16-4
Ratio of price indexes for nontradable and tradable goods and services, 1975.
The relative price of a country's nontradables tends to rise as its real per capita income rises.
Horizontal axis measures average per capita levels of national output for the following six income groups:
1. Malawi, Kenya, India, Pakistan, Sri Lanka, Zambia, Thailand, Philippines
2. Korea, Malaysia, Colombia, Jamaica, Syria, Brazil
3. Romania, Mexico, Yugoslavia, Iran, Uruguay, Ireland
4. Hungary, Poland, Italy, Spain
5. U.K., Japan, Austria, Netherlands, Belgium, Luxembourg, France, Denmark, Germany
6. U.S.

Source: Irving B. Kravis and Robert E. Lipsey, *Toward an Explanation of National Price Levels* (Princeton Studies in International Finance 52, November 1983), Table 2.

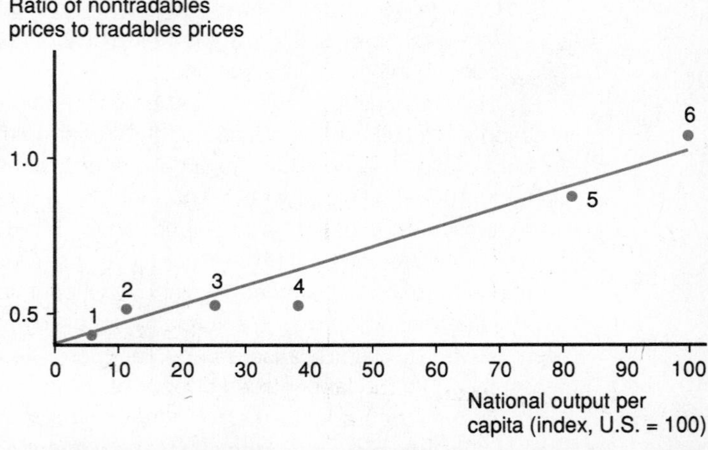

only so many haircuts in a week, but there may be significant scope for productivity differences across countries in the manufacture of traded goods like personal computers.

An alternative theory that attempts to explain the lower price levels of poor countries was put forth by Jagdish Bhagwati and by Irving Kravis of the University of Pennsylvania and Robert Lipsey of the City University of New York.[14] The Bhagwati-Kravis-Lipsey view relies on differences in endowments of capital and labor rather than productivity differences, but it also predicts that the relative price of nontradables increases as real per capita income increases. Rich countries have high capital-labor ratios, while poor countries have more labor relative to capital. Because rich countries have higher capital-labor ratios, the marginal productivity of labor is greater in rich countries than in poor countries, and the former will therefore have a higher wage level than the latter.[15]

[14] See Kravis and Lipsey, *Toward an Explanation of National Price Levels,* Princeton Studies in International Finance 52 (International Finance Section, Department of Economics, Princeton University, November 1983); and Bhagwati, "Why Are Services Cheaper in the Poor Countries?" *Economic Journal* 94 (June 1984), pp. 279–286.

[15] This argument assumes that factor endowment differences between rich and poor countries are sufficiently great that factor-price equalization cannot hold.

Nontradables, which consist largely of services, are naturally labor-intensive relative to tradables. Because labor is cheaper in poor countries and is used intensively in producing nontradables, nontradables also will be cheaper there than in the rich, high-wage countries. Once again, this international difference in the relative price of nontradables suggests that overall price levels, when measured in a single currency, should be higher in rich countries than in poor.

Beyond Purchasing Power Parity: A General Model of Long-Run Exchange Rates

Why devote so much discussion to the purchasing power parity theory when it is fraught with exceptions and apparently contradicted by the data? We examined the implications of PPP so closely because its basic idea of relating long-run exchange rates to long-run national price levels is a useful starting point. The monetary approach presented above, which assumed PPP, is too simple to give accurate predictions about the real world, but we can generalize it by taking account of some of the reasons why PPP predicts badly in practice. In this section we develop a generalized model of long-run exchange rate determination that, while more complicated than the monetary approach, is better at explaining how exchange rates really behave.

Our generalized model provides another reason why PPP is a useful concept, for the model shows that in those important situations where monetary changes are the dominant cause of economic fluctuations, the predictions of the simple monetary approach *are* accurate over the long run.

The long-run analysis below continues to ignore short-run complications caused by sticky prices. An understanding of how exchange rates behave in the long run is, as mentioned earlier, a prerequisite for the more complicated short-run analysis that we undertake in the next chapter.

THE REAL EXCHANGE RATE

As the first step in extending the PPP theory, we define the concept of a **real exchange rate.** The real exchange rate between two countries' currencies is a broad summary measure of the prices of one country's goods and services relative to the other's. It is natural to introduce the real exchange rate concept at this point because the major prediction of PPP is that real exchange rates never change, at least not permanently. To extend our model so that it describes the world more accurately, we need to examine systematically the forces that can cause dramatic and permanent changes in real exchange rates.

As we shall see, real exchange rates are important not only for quantifying deviations from PPP; they also are a basis for analyzing macroeconomic demand and supply conditions in open economies. When we wish to differentiate a real exchange rate, which is the relative price of two output baskets, from a relative price of two currencies, we will refer to the latter as a **nominal exchange rate.** But when there is no risk of confusion we will continue to use the shorter term *exchange rate* to cover nominal exchange rates.

Real exchange rates are defined, however, in terms of nominal exchange rates and price levels. So before we can give a more precise definition of real exchange rates, we need to clarify the price level measure we will be using. Let P_{US}, as usual, be the price level in the United States, and P_G the price level in Germany. Since we will not be assuming absolute PPP (as we did in our discussion of the monetary approach), we no longer assume the price level can be measured by the same basket of commodities in the U.S. as in Germany. Because we will soon want to link our analysis to monetary factors, we require instead that each country's price index give a good representation of the purchases that motivate its residents to demand its money supply.

No measure of the price level does this perfectly, but we must settle on some measure before the real exchange rate can be defined formally. To be concrete, you can think of P_{US} as the dollar price of an unchanging basket containing the typical weekly purchases of U.S. households and firms; P_G, similarly, is based on an unchanging basket reflecting the typical weekly purchases of German households and firms. The point to remember is that *the United States price level will place a relatively heavy weight on commodities produced and consumed in America, the German price level a relatively heavy weight on commodities produced and consumed in Germany.*[16]

Having described the reference commodity baskets used to measure price levels, we can now formally define the *real dollar/DM exchange rate,* denoted $q_{\$/DM}$, as the dollar price of the German basket relative to that of the American. We can express the real exchange rate as the dollar value of Germany's price level divided by the U.S. price level or, in symbols, as

$$q_{\$/DM} = (E_{\$/DM} \times P_G)/P_{US}. \qquad \textbf{(16-6)}$$

A numerical example will clarify the concept of the real exchange rate. Imagine that the German reference commodity basket costs DM 100 (so that P_G = DM 100 per German basket), that the U.S. basket costs \$50 (so that P_{US} = \$50 per U.S. basket), and that the nominal exchange rate is $E_{\$/DM}$ = \$0.50 per DM. The real dollar/DM exchange rate would then be

$$\begin{aligned} q_{\$/DM} &= \frac{(\$0.50 \text{ per DM}) \times (\text{DM } 100 \text{ per German basket})}{(\$50 \text{ per U.S. basket})} \\ &= (\$50 \text{ per German basket})/(\$50 \text{ per U.S. basket}) \\ &= 1 \text{ U.S. basket per German basket.} \end{aligned}$$

A rise in the real dollar/DM exchange rate $q_{\$/DM}$ (which we call a **real depreciation** of the dollar against the DM) can be thought of in several equivalent ways. Most obviously, (16-6) shows this change to be a fall in the purchasing power of a dollar within Germany's borders relative to its purchasing power within the United States. This change in relative purchasing power occurs because the dollar prices of German goods ($E_{\$/DM} \times P_G$) rise relative to those of U.S. goods (P_{US}).

In terms of our numerical example, a 10 percent nominal dollar depreciation, to $E_{\$/DM}$ = \$0.55 per DM, causes $q_{\$/DM}$ to rise to 1.1 U.S. baskets per German basket, a *real* dollar depreciation of 10 percent against the DM. (The same change in $q_{\$/DM}$ could result from a 10 percent rise in P_G or a 10 percent fall in P_{US}.) The real depreciation

[16] A similar presumption was made in our discussion of the transfer problem in Chapter 5. As we observed in that chapter, nontradables are one important factor behind the relative preference for home products.

means that the dollar's purchasing power over German goods and services falls by 10 percent relative to its purchasing power over U.S. goods and services.

Alternatively, even though many of the items entering national price levels are nontraded, it is useful to think of the real exchange rate $q_{\$/DM}$ as the relative price of German products in general in terms of American products, that is, the price at which hypothetical trades of American for German commodity baskets would occur if trades at domestic prices were possible. The dollar is considered to *depreciate* in real terms against the mark when $q_{\$/DM}$ rises because the hypothetical purchasing power of America's products in general over Germany's declines. America's goods and services become cheaper relative to Germany's.

A **real appreciation** of the dollar against the DM is a fall in $q_{\$/DM}$. This fall indicates a decrease in the relative price of products purchased in Germany, or a rise in the dollar's German purchasing power compared with that in the United States.[17]

Our convention for describing real depreciations and appreciations of the dollar against the DM is the same one we use for nominal exchange rates (that is, $E_{\$/DM}$ up is a dollar depreciation, $E_{\$/DM}$ down an appreciation). Equation (16-6) shows that at *unchanged* output prices, nominal depreciation (appreciation) implies real depreciation (appreciation), and vice versa. Our discussion of real exchange rate changes thus includes, as a special case, an observation we made in Chapter 14: with the domestic money prices of goods held constant, a nominal dollar depreciation makes U.S. goods cheaper compared with foreign goods, while a nominal dollar appreciation makes them more expensive.

Equation (16-6) makes it easy to see why the real exchange rate can never change when relative PPP holds. Under relative PPP, a 10 percent rise in $E_{\$/DM}$, for instance, would always be exactly offset by a 10 percent fall in the price level ratio P_G/P_{US}, leaving $q_{\$/DM}$ unchanged.

DEMAND, SUPPLY, AND THE LONG-RUN REAL EXCHANGE RATE

It should come as no surprise that in a world where PPP does not hold, the long-run values of real exchange rates, just like other relative prices that clear markets, depend on demand and supply conditions. Since a real exchange rate tracks changes in the relative price of two countries' expenditure baskets, however, conditions in *both* countries matter. Changes in countries' output markets can be complex, and we do not want to digress into an exhaustive (and exhausting) catalogue of the possibilities. We focus instead on two specific cases that are both easy to grasp and important in practice for explaining why the long-run values of real exchange rates can change.

1. *A change in world relative demand for American products.* Imagine that total world spending on American goods and services rises relative to total world spending on German goods and services. Such a change could rise from several sources, for example, a shift in private U.S. demand away from German goods and toward American goods; a similar shift in private foreign demand toward American goods; or an increase in U.S. government demand falling primarily on U.S. output. Any increase in relative

[17] Since $E_{DM/\$} = 1/E_{\$/DM}$, so that $q_{\$/DM} = P_G/(E_{DM/\$} \times P_{US}) = 1/q_{DM/\$}$, a real depreciation of the dollar against the DM is the same as a real appreciation of the DM against the dollar (that is, a rise in the purchasing power of the DM within the United States relative to its purchasing power within Germany, or a fall in the relative price of American products in terms of German).

Productivity Growth and the Real Dollar/Yen Exchange Rate

If tradables' prices are not too sensitive to purely domestic conditions, a productivity increase in tradables will cause a real domestic currency appreciation—a comparative rise in the domestic price level. The reasoning follows the Balassa-Samuelson argument that price levels should rise with per capita income (see the Case Study on

FIGURE 16-5
The real dollar/yen exchange rate, 1970–1992.
The U.S. dollar has steadily depreciated in real terms against the Japanese yen. A main reason for this strong trend is the relatively rapid productivity growth in the industries that produce Japan's tradable goods.
Source: Quarterly nominal exchange rate and CPI data from OECD, *Main Economic Indicators.*

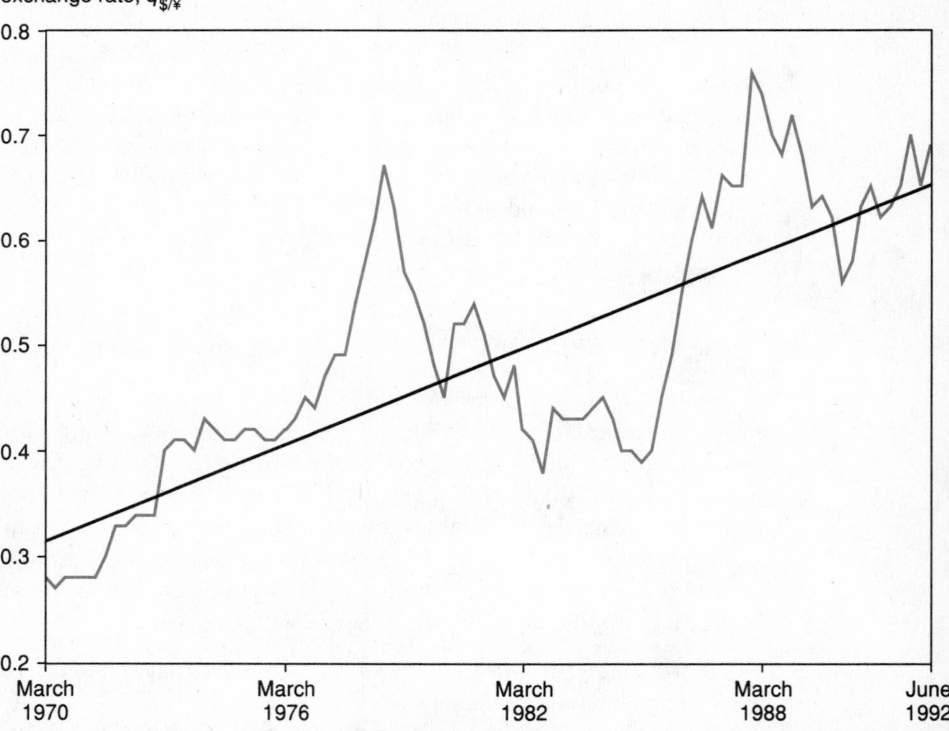

p. 417). Higher factor productivity in tradables induces labor and capital to migrate out of the nontradable sector, reducing the supply of nontradables and thus raising their relative price. If the greater supply of domestic tradables does not cause too large a fall in the terms of trade, however, the domestic-to-foreign price level ratio also will rise.

Results in agreement with this theory come from a recent study of the dollar/yen real exchange rate by University of Pennsylvania economist Richard Marston.* Marston used industry-level data for the United States and Japan to calculate the growth of labor productivity in tradables and nontradables over the years 1973–1983. He found that in the United States, productivity increased by 13.2 percent more in tradables than in nontradables. In Japan, however, productivity growth in tradables outstripped that in nontradables by a massive 73.2 percent.

Our earlier reasoning implies that the price of nontradables in terms of tradables should have risen in both countries but the increase should have been greater in Japan. If relative tradables prices do not vary greatly in the long run, we'd expect this pattern of relative price changes within the two countries to cause a real appreciation of the yen against the dollar.

This reasoning fits the facts quite well. Marston found that the relative price of nontradables rose by 12.3 percent in the United States; the corresponding number for Japan was 56.9 percent. While the price of Japanese tradables did fall sharply relative to that of American tradables, the end result was still a 9 percent real appreciation of the yen against the dollar.

Figure 16-5 shows quarterly data on the real dollar/yen exchange rate, $q_{\$/¥}$, since 1970. (Remember in looking at the figure that a rise in $q_{\$/¥}$ is a real depreciation of the dollar against the yen and a real appreciation of the yen against the dollar.) The trend discussed by Marston—that Japan's price level, measured in dollars, has risen steadily relative to the U.S. price level—actually has characterized the entire post-World War II era, and in particular has continued beyond the end of Marston's sample in 1983.

Between 1970 and 1992, the dollar depreciated against the yen in real terms at an average annual rate of about 3.9 percent. Japan and America have not, however, had radically different inflation experiences over the post-1970 period as a whole. The *real* exchange rate trend shown in Figure 16-5 has therefore caused much of the long-term *nominal* depreciation of the dollar against the yen mentioned in this chapter's first paragraph.

* Richard C. Marston, "Real Exchange Rates and Productivity Growth in the United States and Japan," in Sven W. Arndt and J. David Richardson, eds., *Real-Financial Linkages among Open Economies* (Cambridge, MA: MIT Press, 1987), pp. 71–96.

world demand for U.S. products causes an excess demand for them at the previous real exchange rate. To restore equilibrium, the relative price of American output in terms of German will therefore have to rise: the relative prices of U.S. nontradables will rise and the prices of tradables produced in the United States, and consumed intensively there, will rise relative to the prices of tradables made in Germany. These changes all work to reduce $q_{\$/DM}$, the relative price of Germany's reference expenditure basket in terms of the United States'. We conclude that *an increase in world relative demand for U.S. output causes a long-run real appreciation of the dollar against the DM (a fall in* $q_{\$/DM}$*). Similarly, a fall in world relative demand for U.S. output causes a long-run real depreciation of the dollar against the DM (a rise in* $q_{\$/DM}$*).*

2. *A change in relative output supply.* Suppose that the productive efficiency of U.S. labor and capital rises. Since Americans spend part of their increased income on foreign goods, the supplies of all types of U.S. goods and services increase relative to the demand for them, the result being an excess relative supply of American output at the previous real exchange rate. A fall in the relative price of American products—both nontradables and tradables—shifts demand toward them and eliminates the excess supply. This price change is a real depreciation of the dollar against the DM, that is, an increase in $q_{\$/DM}$. *A relative expansion of U.S. output causes a long-run real depreciation of the dollar against the DM (*$q_{\$/DM}$ *rises). A relative expansion of German output causes a long-run real appreciation of the dollar against the DM (*$q_{\$/DM}$ *falls).*

NOMINAL AND REAL EXCHANGE RATES IN LONG-RUN EQUILIBRIUM

We now pull together what we have learned in this chapter and the last one to show how long-run nominal exchange rates are determined. One central conclusion is that changes in national money supplies and demands give rise to the proportional long-run movements in nominal exchange rates and international price level ratios predicted by the relative purchasing power parity theory. Demand and supply shifts in national output markets, however, cause nominal exchange rate movements that do not conform to PPP.

Recall our definition of the real dollar/DM exchange rate as

$$q_{\$/DM} = (E_{\$/DM} \times P_G)/P_{US}.$$

(See equation (16-6).) If we now solve this equation for the nominal exchange rate, we get an equation that gives us the nominal dollar/DM exchange rate as the real dollar/DM exchange rate times the U.S.-German price level ratio:

$$E_{\$/DM} = q_{\$/DM} \times (P_{US}/P_G). \tag{16-7}$$

Formally speaking, the only difference between (16-7) and equation (16-1), on which we based our exposition of the monetary approach to the exchange rate, is that (16-7) accounts for possible deviations from PPP by adding the *real* exchange rate as an additional determinant of the nominal exchange rate. *The equation implies that for a given real dollar/DM exchange rate, changes in money demand or supply in Germany or the United States affect the long-run nominal dollar/DM exchange rate as in the monetary approach. Changes in the long-run real exchange rate, however, also affect the long-run nominal exchange rate.* The long-run theory of exchange rate determination implied by equation (16-7) thus includes the valid elements of the monetary approach, but in addition it corrects the monetary approach by allowing for nonmonetary factors that can cause sustained deviations from purchasing power parity.

Assuming that all variables start out at their long-run levels, we can now understand the most important determinants of long-run swings in nominal exchange rates:

1. *A shift in relative money supply levels.* Consider an increase in the level of the U.S. money supply. As you will remember from Chapter 15, a permanent one-time increase in a country's money supply has no effect on the long-run levels of output, the interest rate, or any relative price (including the real exchange rate). Thus, (16-3) implies once again that P_{US} rises in proportion to M_{US}, while (16-7) shows that the U.S. price level is the sole variable changing in the long run along with the nominal exchange rate $E_{\$/DM}$. Because the real exchange rate $q_{\$/DM}$ does not change, the nominal exchange rate change is consistent with relative PPP: the only long-run effect of the U.S. money supply increase is to raise all dollar prices, including the dollar price of the DM, in proportion to the increase in the money supply. It should be no surprise that this result is the same as the one we found using the monetary approach, since that approach is designed to account for the long-run effects of monetary changes.

2. *A shift in relative money supply growth rates.* A permanent increase in the *growth rate* of the U.S. money supply raises the long-run U.S. inflation rate and, through the Fisher effect, raises the dollar interest rate relative to the DM interest rate. Because relative U.S. real money demand therefore declines, equation (16-3) implies that P_{US} rises (as shown in Figure 16-1). Because the change bringing this outcome about is purely monetary, however, it is neutral in its long-run effects; specifically, it does not alter the long-run *real* dollar-DM exchange rate. According to (16-7), then, $E_{\$/DM}$ rises in proportion to the increase in P_{US} (a depreciation of the dollar against the DM). Once again, a purely monetary change brings about a long-run nominal exchange rate shift in line with relative PPP, just as the monetary approach predicted.

3. *A change in relative output demand.* This type of change is *not* covered by the monetary approach, so now the more general perspective we've developed, in which the real exchange rate can change, is essential. Since a change in relative output demand does not affect long-run national price levels—these depend solely on the factors appearing in equations (16-3) and (16-4)—the long-run nominal exchange rate in (16-7) will change only insofar as the real exchange rate changes. Consider an increase in world relative demand for U.S. products. Earlier in this section we saw that a rise in demand for U.S. products causes a long-run real appreciation of the dollar against the DM (a fall in $q_{\$/DM}$); this change is simply a rise in the relative price of U.S. output. Given that long-run national price levels are unchanged, however, (16-7) tells us that a long-run *nominal* appreciation of the dollar against the DM (a fall in $E_{\$/DM}$) must also occur. This prediction highlights the important fact that even though exchange rates are nominal prices, they respond to nonmonetary as well as monetary events, even over long horizons.

4. *A change in relative output supply.* As we saw earlier in this section, an increase in relative U.S. output supply causes the dollar to depreciate in real terms against the DM, lowering the relative price of U.S. output. This rise in $q_{\$/DM}$ is not, however, the only change in equation (16-7) implied by a relative rise in U.S. output. In addition, the U.S. output increase raises the transactions demand for real U.S. money balances, raising aggregate U.S. real money demand and, by (16-3), pushing the long-run U.S. price level down. Referring back to equation (16-7), you will see that since

TABLE 16-1 Effects of money market and output market changes on the long-run nominal dollar/DM exchange rate, $E_{\$/DM}$.

Change	*Effect on the long-run nominal dollar/DM exchange rate,* $E_{\$/DM}$
Money market	
1. Increase in U.S. money supply level	Proportional increase (nominal depreciation of $)
2. Increase in German money supply level	Proportional decrease (nominal depreciation of DM)
3. Increase in U.S. money supply growth rate	Increase (nominal depreciation of $)
4. Increase in German money supply growth rate	Decrease (nominal depreciation of DM)
Output market	
1. Increase in demand for U.S. output	Decrease (nominal appreciation of $)
2. Increase in demand for German output	Increase (nominal appreciation of DM)
3. Output supply increase in the United States	Ambiguous
4. Output supply increase in Germany	Ambiguous

$q_{\$/DM}$ rises while P_{US} falls, the output and money market effects of a change in output supply work in opposite directions, so that the net effect on $E_{\$/DM}$ is *ambiguous.* Our analysis of an output-supply change illustrates that even when a disturbance originates in a single market (in this case, the output market), its influence on exchange rates may depend on repercussion effects that are channeled through other markets.

We conclude that *when all disturbances are monetary in nature, exchange rates obey relative PPP in the long run. In the long run, a monetary disturbance affects only the general purchasing power of a currency, and this change in purchasing power changes equally the currency's value in terms of domestic and foreign goods. When disturbances occur in output markets, the exchange rate is unlikely to obey relative PPP, even in the long run.*[18]

Table 16-1 summarizes these conclusions regarding the effects of monetary and output market changes on long-run nominal exchange rates.

In the chapters that follow, we will appeal to this section's general long-run exchange rate model even when we are discussing *short-run* macroeconomic events.

[18] These conclusions help explain why empirical applications of the monetary approach have been more successful in data where the most prominent changes are monetary in nature. For an econometric application of the monetary approach to the German hyperinflation of the 1920s, see Jacob A. Frenkel, "A Monetary Approach to the Exchange Rate: Doctrinal Aspects and Empirical Evidence," in Jan Herin, Assar Lindbeck, and Johan Myhrman, eds., *Flexible Exchange Rates and Stabilization Policy* (Boulder, CO: Westview Press, 1977), pp. 68–92. The approach's failure to explain data from the 1970s is documented in Rudiger Dornbusch, "Exchange Rate Economics: Where Do We Stand?" *Brookings Papers on Economic Activity* 1:1980, pp. 143–185.

Long-run factors are important for the short run because of the central role expectations about the future play in the day-to-day determination of exchange rates. The long-run exchange rate model of this section will provide the anchor for market expectations, that is, the framework market participants use to forecast future exchange rates on the basis of information at hand today.

International Interest Rate Differences and the Real Exchange Rate

Earlier in this chapter we saw that relative PPP, when combined with interest parity, implies that international interest rate differences equal differences in countries' expected inflation rates. Because relative PPP does not hold true in general, however, the relation between international interest rate differences and national inflation rates is likely to be more complex in practice than that simple formula suggests. Despite this complexity, economic policy makers who hope to influence exchange rates, as well as private individuals who wish to forecast them, cannot succeed without understanding the factors that cause countries' interest rates to differ.

In this section we therefore extend our earlier discussion of the Fisher effect to include real exchange rate movements. We do this by showing that in general, interest rate differences between countries depend not only on differences in expected inflation, as the monetary approach asserts, but also on expected changes in the real exchange rate.

We begin by recalling that the change in $q_{\$/DM}$, the real dollar/DM exchange rate, is the *deviation* from relative PPP; that is, the change in $q_{\$/DM}$ is the percentage change in the nominal dollar/DM exchange rate less the international difference in inflation rates between the United States and Germany. We thus arrive at the corresponding relationship between the *expected* change in the real exchange rate, the *expected* change in the nominal rate, and *expected* inflation,

$$(q^e_{\$/DM} - q_{\$/DM})/q_{\$/DM} = [(E^e_{\$/DM} - E_{\$/DM})/E_{\$/DM}] - (\pi^e_{US} - \pi^e_{G}), \qquad \textbf{(16-8)}$$

where $q^e_{\$/DM}$ (as per our usual notation) is the real exchange rate expected for a year from today.

Now return to the interest parity condition between dollar and DM deposits,

$$R_{\$} - R_{DM} = (E^e_{\$/DM} - E_{\$/DM})/E_{\$/DM}.$$

An easy rearrangement of (16-8) shows that the expected rate of change in the *nominal* dollar/DM exchange rate is just the expected rate of change in the *real* dollar/DM exchange rate *plus* the U.S.-German expected inflation difference. Combining (16-8) with the above interest parity condition, we thus are led to the following breakdown of the international interest gap:

$$R_{\$} - R_{DM} = [(q^e_{\$/DM} - q_{\$/DM})/q_{\$/DM}] + (\pi^e_{US} - \pi^e_{G}). \qquad \textbf{(16-9)}$$

Notice that when the market expects relative PPP to prevail, $q^e_{\$/DM} = q_{\$/DM}$ and the first term on the right side of this equation drops out. In this special case, (16-9) reduces to the simpler (16-5), which we derived by assuming relative PPP.

In general, however, the dollar-DM interest difference is the sum of *two* components: (1) the expected rate of real dollar depreciation against the DM and (2) the expected inflation difference between the United States and Germany. For example, if U.S. inflation will be 5 percent per year forever and German inflation zero, the long-run interest difference between dollar and DM deposits need not be the 5 percent that PPP (and interest parity) would suggest. If, in addition, everyone knows that output demand and supply trends will make the dollar decline against the DM in real terms at a rate of 1 percent per year, the international interest spread will actually be 6 percent.

Real Interest Parity

Economics makes an important distinction between **nominal interest rates,** which are rates of return measured in monetary terms, and **real interest rates,** which are rates of return measured in *real* terms, that is, in terms of a country's output. Because real rates of return often are uncertain, we usually will refer to *expected* real interest rates. The interest rates we discussed in connection with the interest parity condition and the determinants of money demand were nominal rates, for example, the dollar return on dollar deposits. But for many other purposes, economists need to analyze behavior in terms of real rates of return. No one who is thinking of investing money, for example, could make a decision knowing only that the nominal interest rate is 15 percent. The investment would be quite attractive at zero inflation, but disastrously unattractive if inflation were bounding along at 100 percent per year![19]

We conclude this chapter by showing that when the nominal interest parity condition equates nominal interest rate differences between currencies to expected changes in *nominal* exchange rates, a *real* interest parity condition equates expected real interest rate differences to expected changes in *real* exchange rates. Only when relative PPP is expected to hold (meaning no real exchange rate change is anticipated) are expected real interest rates in all countries identical.

The expected real interest rate, denoted r^e, is defined as the nominal interest rate, R, less the expected inflation rate, π^e:

$$r^e = R - \pi^e.$$

In other words, the expected real interest rate in a country is just the real rate of return a domestic resident expects to earn on a loan of its currency. The definition of the expected real interest rate clarifies the generality of the forces behind the Fisher effect: any increase in the expected inflation rate that does not alter the expected real interest rate must be reflected, one for one, in the nominal interest rate.

A useful consequence of the preceding definition is a formula for the difference in expected real interest rates between two countries such as the United States and Germany:

$$r^e_{US} - r^e_G = (R_\$ - \pi^e_{US}) - (R_{DM} - \pi^e_G).$$

[19] We could get away with examining nominal return *differences* in the foreign exchange market because (as Chapter 14 showed) nominal return differences equal real return differences for any given investor. In the context of the money market, the *nominal* interest rate is the *real* rate of return you sacrifice by holding interest-barren currency.

If we rearrange equation (16-9) and combine it with the equation above, we get the desired *real interest parity condition:*

$$r^e_{US} - r^e_G = (q^e_{\$/DM} - q_{\$/DM})/q_{\$/DM}. \qquad \textbf{(16-10)}$$

Equation (16-10) looks much like the nominal interest parity condition from which it is derived, but it explains differences in expected *real* interest rates between the United States and Germany by expected movements in the dollar/DM *real* exchange rate.

Expected real interest rates are the same in different countries when relative PPP is expected to hold (in which case (16-10) implies that $r^e_{US} = r^e_G$). More generally, however, expected real interest rates in different countries need not be equal, even in the long run, if continuing change in output markets is expected.[20] Suppose, for example, that productivity in the Korean tradables sector is expected to rise during the next two decades while productivity stagnates in Korean nontradables and in all U.S. industries. If the Balassa-Samuelson hypothesis is valid, people should expect the U.S. dollar to depreciate in real terms against Korea's currency, the won, as the prices of Korea's nontradables trend upward. Equation (16-10) thus implies that the expected real interest rate should be higher in the United States than in Korea.

Do such real interest differences imply unnoticed profit opportunities for international investors? Not necessarily. A cross-border real interest difference does imply that residents of two countries perceive different real rates of return on wealth. Nominal interest parity tells us, however, that any *given* investor expects the same real return on domestic and foreign currency assets. Two investors residing in different countries need not calculate this single real rate of return in the same way if relative PPP does not link the prices of their consumption baskets, but there is no way either can profit from their disagreement by shifting funds between currencies.

Summary

1. The *purchasing power parity* theory, in its absolute form, asserts that the exchange rate between countries' currencies equals the ratio of their price levels, as measured by the money prices of a reference commodity basket. An equivalent statement of PPP is that the purchasing power of any currency is the same in any country. Absolute PPP implies a second version of the PPP theory, *relative PPP,* which predicts that percentage changes in exchange rates equal differences in national inflation rates.

2. A building block of the PPP theory is the *law of one price,* which states that under free competition and in the absence of trade impediments, a good must sell for a single price regardless of where in the world it is sold. Proponents of the PPP theory often argue, however, that its validity does not require the law of one price to hold for every commodity.

3. The *monetary approach to the exchange rate* uses PPP to explain long-term

[20] The two-period analysis of international borrowing and lending in Chapter 7 assumed that all countries face a single worldwide real interest rate. Relative PPP must hold in that analysis, however, because there is only one consumption good in each period.

exchange rate behavior exclusively in terms of money supply and demand. In that theory long-run international interest differentials result from different national rates of ongoing inflation, as the *Fisher effect* predicts. Sustained international differences in monetary growth rates are, in turn, behind different long-term rates of continuing inflation. The monetary approach thus finds that a rise in a country's interest rate will be associated with a depreciation of its currency. Relative PPP implies that international interest differences, which equal the expected percentage change in the exchange rate, also equal the international expected inflation gap.

4. The empirical support for PPP and the law of one price is weak in recent data. The failure of these propositions in the real world is related to trade barriers and departures from free competition. In addition, different definitions of price levels in different countries bedevil attempts to test PPP using the price indexes governments publish. For some products, including many services, international transport costs are so steep that these products become nontradable.

5. Deviations from relative PPP can be viewed as changes in a country's *real exchange rate,* the price of a typical foreign expenditure basket in terms of the typical domestic expenditure basket. All else equal, a country's currency undergoes a long-run *real appreciation* against foreign currencies when the world relative demand for its output rises. In this case the country's real exchange rate, as just defined, falls. The home currency undergoes a long-run *real depreciation* against foreign currencies when home output expands relative to foreign output. In this case the real exchange rate rises.

6. The long-run determination of *nominal exchange rates* can be analyzed by combining two theories: the theory of the long-run *real* exchange rate and the theory of how domestic monetary factors determine long-run price levels. A stepwise increase in a country's money stock ultimately leads to a proportional increase in its price level and a proportional fall in its currency's foreign exchange value, just as relative PPP predicts. Changes in monetary growth rates also have long-run effects consistent with PPP. Supply or demand changes in output markets, however, cause exchange rate movements that do not conform to PPP.

7. The interest parity condition equates international differences in *nominal interest rates* to the expected percentage change in the nominal exchange rate. If interest parity holds in this sense, a real interest parity condition equates international differences in expected *real interest rates* to the expected change in the real exchange rate. Real interest parity also implies that international differences in nominal interest rates equal the difference in expected inflation *plus* the expected percentage change in the real exchange rate.

Key Terms

purchasing power parity (PPP)
law of one price
relative PPP
monetary approach to the exchange rate
Fisher effect
real exchange rate
nominal exchange rate
real depreciation
real appreciation
nominal interest rate
real interest rate

Problems

1. Suppose Brazil's inflation rate is 100 percent over one year but the inflation rate in Holland is only 5 percent. According to relative PPP, what should happen over the year to the Dutch guilder's exchange rate against the Brazilian cruzeiro?
2. Discuss why it is often asserted that exporters suffer when their home currencies appreciate in real terms against foreign currencies and prosper when their home currencies depreciate in real terms.
3. Other things equal, how would you expect the following shifts to affect a currency's real exchange rate against foreign currencies?
   a. The overall level of spending doesn't change, but domestic residents decide to spend more of their income on nontraded products and less on tradables.
   b. Foreign residents shift their demand away from their own goods and toward the home country's exports.
4. Large-scale wars typically bring a suspension of international trading and financial activities. Exchange rates lose much of their relevance under these conditions, but once the war is over governments wishing to fix exchange rates face the problem of deciding what the new rates should be. The PPP theory has often been applied to this problem of postwar exchange rate realignment. Imagine that you are a British Chancellor of the Exchequer and World War I has just ended. Explain how you would figure out the dollar/pound exchange rate implied by PPP. When might it be a bad idea to use the PPP theory in this way?
5. In the late 1970s Britain seemed to have struck it rich. Having developed its North Sea oil-producing fields in earlier years, Britain suddenly found its real income higher as a result of a dramatic increase in world oil prices in 1979–1980. In the early 1980s, however, oil prices receded as the world economy slid into a deep recession and world oil demand faltered.

   Below, we show index numbers for the average real exchange rate of the pound against several foreign currencies. (Such average index numbers are called real *effective* exchange rates.) A rise in one of these numbers indicates a real *appreciation* of the pound, that is, an increase in Britain's price level relative to the average price level abroad measured in pounds. A fall is a real depreciation.

Real effective exchange rate of the pound sterling, 1976–1984 (1980 = 100)

1976	*1977*	*1978*	*1979*	*1980*	*1981*	*1982*	*1983*	*1984*
68.3	66.5	72.2	81.4	100.0	102.8	100.0	92.5	89.8

Source: International Monetary Fund, *International Financial Statistics.* The real exchange rate measures are based on indexes of net output prices called value-added deflators.

   Use the clues we have given about the British economy to explain the rise and fall of the pound's real effective exchange rate between 1978 and 1984. Pay particular attention to the role of nontradables.

6. Every week the Federal Reserve announces how quickly the money supply grew in the week ending ten days previously. (There is a ten-day delay because it takes that long to assemble data on bank deposits.) Economists have noticed that when the announced increase in the money supply is greater than expected, nominal interest rates *rise* just after the announcement; they *fall* when the market learns the money supply grew more slowly than expected. Two competing explanations of this phenomenon are (1) unexpectedly high money growth raises expected inflation and thus raises nominal interest rates through the Fisher effect; and (2) unexpectedly high money growth leads the market to expect future Fed action to reduce the money supply, causing a decrease in the amount of deposits supplied to the public by banks but no increase in expected inflation. How would you use data from the foreign exchange market to decide between these two hypotheses? (For an answer, see the paper by Engel and Frankel in Further Reading.)
7. Explain how permanent shifts in national real money-demand functions affect real and nominal exchange rates in the long run.
8. In Chaper 5 we discussed the effect of transfers between countries, such as the indemnity imposed on Germany after World War I. Use the theory developed in this chapter to discuss the mechanisms through which a permanent transfer from Germany to France would affect the real French franc/DM exchange rate in the long run.
9. Continuing with the preceding problem, discuss how the transfer would affect the long-run *nominal* exchange rate between the two currencies.
10. A country imposes a tariff on imports from abroad. How does its action change the long-run real exchange rate between home and foreign currency? How is the long-run nominal exchange rate affected?
11. Imagine that two identical countries have restricted imports to identical levels, but one has done so using tariffs while the other has done so using quotas. After these policies are in place, both countries experience identical, balanced expansions of domestic spending. Where should the demand expansion cause a greater real currency appreciation, in the tariff-using country or in the quota-using country?
12. Explain how the nominal dollar/DM exchange rate would be affected (all else equal) by permanent changes in the expected rate of real depreciation of the dollar against the DM.
13. Can you suggest an event that would cause a country's nominal interest rate to rise and its currency to appreciate simultaneously, in a world of perfectly flexible prices?
14. Suppose that the expected real interest rate in the United States is 9 percent per year while that in Germany is 3 percent per year. What do you expect to happen to the real dollar/DM exchange rate over the next year?
15. In the short run of a model with sticky prices, a reduction in the money supply raises the nominal interest rate and appreciates the currency (see Chapter 15). What happens to the expected real interest rate? Explain why the subsequent path of the real exchange rate satisfies the real interest parity condition.
16. Discuss the following statement: ''When a change in a country's nominal interest rate is caused by a rise in the expected real interest rate, the domestic currency

appreciates. When the change is caused by a rise in expected inflation, the currency depreciates.''

17. The difference between the nominal interest rate and the actual inflation rate is often called the ex post real interest rate (as opposed to the ex ante, or expected real interest rate). Figure 16-2 shows that between 1976 and 1980, the ex post real interest rate in Switzerland was usually positive while that in the United States was usually negative. Assume that people were able to forecast inflation accurately in both countries during these years. What would you guess about the dollar's strength against the Swiss franc in the foreign exchange market between 1976 and 1980? What do you think happened to the dollar/Swiss franc exchange rate in 1981–1982? Check your answer by looking up the history of the exchange rate. (See, for example, the International Monetary Fund's publication, *International Financial Statistics.*)

Further Reading

Gustav Cassel. *Post-war Monetary Stabilization.* New York: Columbia University Press, 1928. Applies the purchasing power parity theory of exchange rates in analyzing the monetary problems that followed World War I.

Robert E. Cumby and Frederic S. Mishkin. ''The International Linkage of Real Interest Rates: The U.S.-European Connection.'' *Journal of International Money and Finance* 5 (March 1986), pp. 5–23. An econometric study of the relationship between real interest rates in the United States and Europe.

Rudiger Dornbusch. ''Purchasing Power Parity,'' in *The New Palgrave: A Dictionary of Economics.* Vol. 3. New York: Stockton Press, 1987, pp. 1075–1085. Examines the role of the purchasing power parity theory in international macroeconomics.

Rudiger Dornbusch. ''The Theory of Flexible Exchange Rate Regimes and Macroeconomic Policy,'' in Jan Herin, Assar Lindbeck, and Johan Myhrman, eds. *Flexible Exchange Rates and Stabilization Policy.* Boulder, CO: Westview Press, 1977, pp. 123–143. Develops a long-run model of exchange rates incorporating traded and nontraded goods and services.

Charles Engel and Jeffrey Frankel. ''Why Money Announcements Move Interest Rates: An Answer from the Foreign Exchange Market,'' in *Sixth West Coast Academic/Federal Reserve Economic Research Seminar* (Economic Review Conference Supplement). San Francisco: Federal Reserve Bank of San Francisco, 1983, pp. 1–26. Studies the link between Fed money announcements, interest rates, and the exchange rate.

Irving B. Kravis. ''Comparative Studies of National Incomes and Prices.'' *Journal of Economic Literature* 22 (March 1984), pp. 1–39. An account of the findings of a United Nations-sponsored research project that compared the real incomes and price levels of more than 100 countries.

Robin Marris. ''Comparing the Incomes of Nations: A Critique of the International Comparison Project.'' *Journal of Economic Literature* 22 (March 1984), pp. 40–57. A critical appraisal of the research described in the previous reading by Kravis.

Lloyd A. Metzler. ''Exchange Rates and the International Monetary Fund,'' in *International Monetary Policies.* Postwar Economic Studies 7. Washington, D.C.: Board of Governors of the Federal Reserve System, 1947, pp. 1–45. The author applies purchasing power parity with skill and skepticism to evaluate the fixed exchange rates established by the International Monetary Fund after World War II.

Frederic S. Mishkin. *The Economics of Money, Banking and Financial Markets,* 3rd edition. New York: HarperCollins Publishers, 1992. Chapter 6 discusses inflation and the Fisher effect.

Lawrence Officer. *Purchasing Power Parity and Exchange Rates: Theory, Evidence and Relevance.* Greenwich, CT: JAI Press Inc., 1982. A comprehensive review of the history and validity of the purchasing power parity doctrine.

Alan C. Stockman. ''The Equilibrium Approach to Exchange Rates.'' *Federal Reserve Bank of Richmond Economic Review* 73 (March/April 1987), pp. 12–30. Theory and evidence on an equilibrium exchange rate model similar to the long-run model of this chapter.

Output and the Exchange Rate in the Short Run

Chapter 17

When the real gross national product of the United States fell by 2.5 percent in 1982, many observers blamed the slump on the sharp appreciation of the dollar that had occurred since 1980. In 1984, however, U.S. real GNP *rose* by a whopping 6.8 percent despite another sizable appreciation of the dollar. This chapter will help us understand the complicated factors that cause output and exchange rate changes by completing the macroeconomic model built in the last two chapters.

Chapters 15 and 16 explained the connections among exchange rates, interest rates, and price levels but always assumed that output levels were given. Those chapters give us only a partial picture of how macroeconomic changes affect an open economy because events that change exchange rates, interest rates, and price levels may also affect output. Now we complete the picture by examining how output and the exchange rate are determined in the short run.

Our discussion combines what we have learned about asset markets and the long-run behavior of exchange rates with a new element, a theory of how the output market adjusts to demand changes when product prices in the economy are themselves slow to adjust. As we learned in Chapter 15, institutional factors like long-term nominal contracts can give rise to "sticky" or slowly adjusting output market prices. By putting a short-run model of the output market together with our models of the foreign exchange and money markets (the asset markets), we build a model that explains all the important macroeconomic variables in an open economy. The long-run exchange rate model of the preceding chapter provides the framework that participants in the asset markets use to form their expectations about future exchange rates.

Output changes may push the economy away from full employment; they may also be coupled with swings in the merchandise trade balance and the current account. The links among output and other macroeconomic variables are therefore of great concern to economic policy makers. We will use this chapter's model to examine how macroeconomic policy tools affect the economy and how those tools can be used to maintain full employment.

Determinants of Aggregate Demand in an Open Economy

To analyze how output is determined in the short run when product prices are sticky, we introduce the concept of **aggregate demand** for a country's output. Aggregate demand is the amount of a country's goods and services demanded by households and firms throughout the world. Just as the output of an individual good or service depends in part on the demand for it, a country's overall short-run output level depends on the aggregate demand for its products. The economy is at full employment in the long run (by definition), so in the long run, a country's output depends only on the available domestic supplies of factors of production such as labor and capital. As we will see, however, these productive factors can be over- or underemployed in the short run as a result of shifts in aggregate demand that have not yet had their full long-run effects on prices.

In Chapter 13 we learned that an economy's output can be divided among the four different types of expenditure that generate national income: consumption, investment, government purchases, and the current account. Correspondingly, aggregate demand for an open economy's output is the sum of consumption demand (C), investment demand (I), government demand (G), and net export demand, that is, the current account (CA). Each of these components of aggregate demand depends on various factors. In this section we examine the factors that determine consumption demand and the current account. Government demand will be discussed later in this chapter when we examine the effects of fiscal policy; for now we assume that G is given. To avoid complicating our model, we also assume that investment demand is given. The determinants of investment demand are incorporated into the model in Appendix I to this chapter.

DETERMINANTS OF CONSUMPTION DEMAND

In this chapter we view the amount a country's residents wish to consume as depending on disposable income, Y^d (that is, national income less taxes, $Y - T$).[1] (C, Y, and T, are all measured in terms of domestic output units.) With this assumption, a country's desired consumption level can be written as a function of disposable income:

$$C = C(Y^d).$$

[1] A more complete model would allow other factors, such as real wealth and the real interest rate, to affect consumption plans. This chapter's Appendix I takes account of the real interest rate's effect on consumption demand.

Because each consumer naturally demands more goods and services as his or her real income rises, we expect consumption to increase as disposable income increases at the aggregate level, too. Thus, consumption demand and disposable income are positively related. When disposable income rises, however, consumption demand generally rises by *less* because part of the income increase is saved.

DETERMINANTS OF THE CURRENT ACCOUNT

The current account balance, viewed as the demand for a country's exports less that country's own demand for imports, is determined by two main factors: the domestic currency's real exchange rate against foreign currency (that is, the price of a typical foreign expenditure basket in terms of domestic expenditure baskets) and domestic disposble income. (In reality, a country's current account depends on many other factors, such as the level of foreign expenditure, but for now we regard these other factors as being held constant.[2])

We express a country's current account balance as a function of its currency's real exchange rate, $q = EP^*/P$, and of domestic disposable income, Y^d:

$$CA = CA(EP^*/P, Y^d).$$

As a reminder of the last chapter's discussion, note that the domestic currency prices of representative foreign and domestic expenditure baskets are, respectively, EP^* and P, where E (the nominal exchange rate) is the price of foreign currency in terms of domestic, P^* is the foreign price level, and P is the home price level. The *real* exchange rate q, defined as the price of the foreign basket in terms of the domestic one, is therefore EP^*/P. If, for example, the representative basket of German goods and services costs DM 100 (P^*), the representative U.S. basket costs \$50 (P), and the dollar/DM exchange rate is \$0.40 per DM (E), then the price of the German basket in terms of U.S. baskets is

$$\begin{aligned} EP^*/P &= \frac{(0.40\ \$/\text{DM}) \times (100\ \text{DM/German basket})}{(50\ \$/\text{U.S. basket})} \\ &= 0.8\ \text{U.S. basket/German basket.} \end{aligned}$$

Real exchange rate changes affect the current account because they reflect changes in the prices of domestic goods and services relative to foreign. Disposable income affects the current account through its effect on total spending by domestic consumers. To understand how these real exchange rate and disposable income effects work, it is helpful to look separately at the demand for a country's exports, EX, and the demand for imports by the country's residents, IM. As we saw in Chapter 13, the current account is related to exports and imports by the identity

$$CA = EX - IM$$

when CA, EX, and IM all are measured in terms of domestic output.

[2] In Chapter 20 we study a two-country framework that takes account of how events in the domestic economy affect foreign output and how these changes in foreign output, in turn, feed back to the domestic economy. As the previous footnote observed, we are ignoring a number of factors (such as wealth and interest rates) that affect consumption along with disposable income. Since some part of any consumption change goes into imports, these omitted determinants of consumption also help to determine the current account. Following the convention of Chapter 13, we are also ignoring unilateral transfers in analyzing the current account balance.

HOW REAL EXCHANGE RATE CHANGES AFFECT THE CURRENT ACCOUNT

You will recall that a representative domestic expenditure basket includes some imported products but places a relatively heavier weight on goods and services produced domestically. At the same time, the representative foreign basket is skewed toward goods and services produced in the foreign country. Thus a rise in the price of the foreign basket in terms of domestic baskets, say, will be associated with a rise in the relative price of foreign output in general relative to domestic.[3]

To determine how such a change in the relative price of national outputs affects the current account, other things equal, we must ask how it affects both EX and IM. If EP^*/P rises, for example, foreign products have become more expensive relative to domestic products: each unit of domestic output now purchases fewer units of foreign output. Foreign consumers will respond to this price shift by demanding more of our exports. This response by foreigners will therefore raise EX and will tend to improve the domestic country's current account.

The effect of the same real exchange rate increase on IM is more complicated. Domestic consumers respond to the price shift by purchasing fewer units of the more expensive foreign products. Their response does not imply, however, that IM must fall. IM denotes the value of imports *measured in terms of domestic output,* and not the volume of foreign products imported: because a rise in EP^*/P tends to raise the value of each unit of imports in terms of domestic output units, imports measured in domestic output units may rise as a result of a rise in EP^*/P even if imports decline when measured in foreign output units. IM can therefore rise or fall when EP^*/P rises, so the effect of a real exchange rate change on the current account CA is ambiguous.

Whether the current account improves or worsens depends on which effect of a real exchange rate change is dominant, the *volume effect* of consumer spending shifts on export and import quantities or the *value effect,* which changes the domestic output worth of a given volume of foreign imports. We assume for now that the volume effect of a real exchange rate change always outweighs the value effect, so that, other things equal, a real depreciation of the currency improves the current account and a real appreciation of the currency worsens the current account.[4]

HOW DISPOSABLE INCOME CHANGES AFFECT THE CURRENT ACCOUNT

The second factor influencing the current account is domestic disposable income. Since a rise in Y^d causes domestic consumers to increase their spending on *all* goods, including imports from abroad, an increase in disposable income worsens the current account, other things equal. (An increase in Y^d has no effect on export demand because we are holding foreign income constant and not allowing Y^d to affect it.)

[3] The real exchange rate is being used here essentially as a convenient summary measure of the relative prices of domestic against foreign products. A more exact (but much more complicated) analysis would work explicitly with separate demand and supply functions for each country's nontradables and tradables but would lead to conclusions very much like those we reach below.

[4] This assumption requires that import and export demands be relatively *elastic* with respect to the real exchange rate. Appendix II to this chapter describes a precise condition, called the Marshall-Lerner condition, under which the assumption in the text will be valid. The appendix also examines empirical evidence on the time horizon over which the Marshall-Lerner condition holds.

The table below summarizes our discussion of how real exchange rate and disposable income changes influence the domestic current account.

Change	*Effect on current account, CA*
Real exchange rate, EP^*/P ↑	CA ↑
Real exchange rate, EP^*/P ↓	CA ↓
Disposable income, Y^d ↑	CA ↓
Disposable income, Y^d ↓	CA ↑

The Equation of Aggregate Demand

We now combine the four components of aggregate demand to get an expression for total aggregate demand, denoted D:

$$D = C(Y - T) + I + G + CA(EP^*/P, Y - T),$$

where we have written disposable income Y^d as output Y less taxes T. This equation shows that aggregate demand for home output can be written as a function of the real exchange rate, disposable income, investment demand, and government spending:

$$D = D(EP^*/P, Y - T, I, G).$$

We now want to see how aggregate demand depends on the real exchange rate and domestic GNP given the level of taxes, T, investment demand, I, and government purchases, G.

THE REAL EXCHANGE RATE AND AGGREGATE DEMAND

A rise in EP^*/P makes domestic goods and services cheaper relative to foreign goods and services and shifts both domestic and foreign spending from foreign goods to domestic goods. As a result, CA rises (as assumed in the previous section) and aggregate demand D therefore goes up. *A real depreciation of the home currency raises aggregate demand for home output, other things equal; a real appreciation lowers aggregate demand for home output.*

REAL INCOME AND AGGREGATE DEMAND

The effect of domestic real income on aggregate demand is slightly more complicated. If taxes are fixed at a given level, a rise in Y represents an equal rise in disposable income Y^d. While this rise in Y^d raises consumption, it worsens the current account by raising home spending on foreign imports. The first of these effects raises aggregate demand, but the second lowers it. Since the increase in consumption is divided between higher spending on home products and higher spending on foreign imports, however, the first effect (the effect of disposable income on total consumption) is greater than the second (the effect of disposable income on import spending alone). Therefore, *a rise in domestic real income raises aggregate demand for home output, other things equal, and a fall in domestic real income lowers aggregate demand for home output.*

Figure 17-1 shows the relation between aggregate demand and real income Y for fixed values of the real exchange rate, taxes, investment demand, and government spending. As Y rises, consumption rises by a fraction of the increase in income. Part of this increase in consumption, moreover, goes into import spending. The effect of an increase in Y on the aggregate demand for home output is therefore smaller than the accompanying rise in consumption demand, which is smaller, in turn, than the increase in Y. We show this in Figure 17-1 by drawing the aggregate demand schedule with a slope less than 1.

How Output Is Determined in the Short Run

Having discussed the factors that influence the demand for an open economy's output, we now study how output is determined in the short run. We show in this section that the output market is in equilibrium when real output Y equals the aggregate demand for domestic output:

$$Y = D(EP^*/P, Y - T, I, G). \tag{17-1}$$

The equality of aggregate supply and demand therefore determines the short-run equilibrium output level.[5]

Our analysis of real output determination applies to the short run because we assume that the money prices of goods and services are *temporarily fixed.* As we will see later in the chapter, the short-run real output changes allowed by temporarily fixed prices eventually cause price level changes that move the economy to its long-run equilibrium. In long-run equilibrium, factors of production are fully employed, the level of real output is completely determined by factor supplies, and the real exchange rate has adjusted to equate the long-run real output level to aggregate demand.[6]

The determination of national output in the short run is illustrated in Figure 17-2, where we again graph aggregate demand as a function of output for fixed levels of the real exchange rate, taxes, investment demand, and government spending. The intersection (at point 1) of the aggregate demand schedule and a 45-degree line drawn from the origin (the equation $D = Y$) gives us the unique output level Y^1 at which aggregate demand equals output.

Let's use Figure 17-2 to see why output tends to settle at Y^1 in the short run. At an output level of Y^2, aggregate demand (point 2) is higher than output. Firms therefore

[5] Superficially, equation (17-1), which may be written as $Y = C(Y^d) + I + G + CA(EP^*/P, Y^d)$, looks like the GNP identity we discussed in Chapter 13, $Y = C + I + G + CA$. How do the two equations differ? They differ in that (17-1) is an equilibrium condition, not an identity. As you will recall from Chapter 13, the investment quantity I appearing in the GNP identity includes *undesired* or involuntary inventory accumulation by firms, so that the GNP identity always holds as a matter of definition. The investment demand appearing in equation (17-1), however, is *desired* or planned investment. Thus, the GNP identity always holds but equation (17-1) holds only if firms are not unwillingly building up or drawing down inventories of goods.

[6] Thus, equation (17-1) also holds in long-run equilibrium, but the equation determines the long-run real exchange rate when Y is at its long-run value.

FIGURE 17-1
Aggregate demand as a function of output.
Other things equal, a rise in output raises aggregate demand, but by a smaller amount.

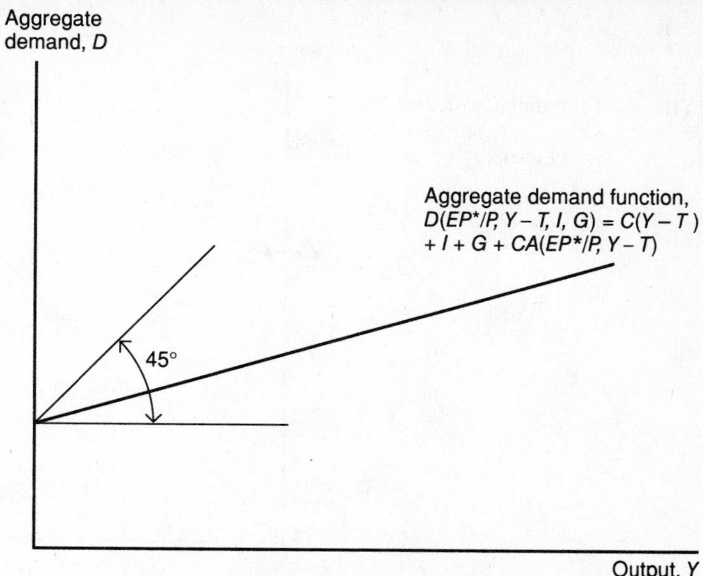

increase their production to meet this excess demand. (If they did not, they would have to meet the excess demand out of inventories, reducing investment below the desired level *I*.) Thus, output expands until national income reaches Y^1.

At point 3 there is an excess supply of domestic output and firms find themselves involuntarily accumulating inventories (involuntarily raising their investment spending above its desired level). As inventories start to build up, firms cut back on production; only when output has fallen to Y^1 will firms be content with their level of production. Once again, output settles at point 1, the point at which output exactly equals aggregate demand. In this short-run equilibrium, consumers, firms, the government, and foreign buyers of domestic products are all able to realize their desired expenditures with no output left over.

Output Market Equilibrium in the Short Run: The *DD* Schedule

Now that we understand how output is determined for a given real exchange rate EP^*/P, let's look at how the exchange rate and output are simultaneously determined in the short run. To understand this process, we need two elements. The first element, developed in this section, is the relationship between output and the exchange rate (the *DD* schedule) that must hold when the output market is in equilibrium. The second element, developed in the next section, is the relationship between output and the exchange rate that must hold when the home money market and the foreign exchange market (the asset markets) are in equilibrium. As we will see, both elements are

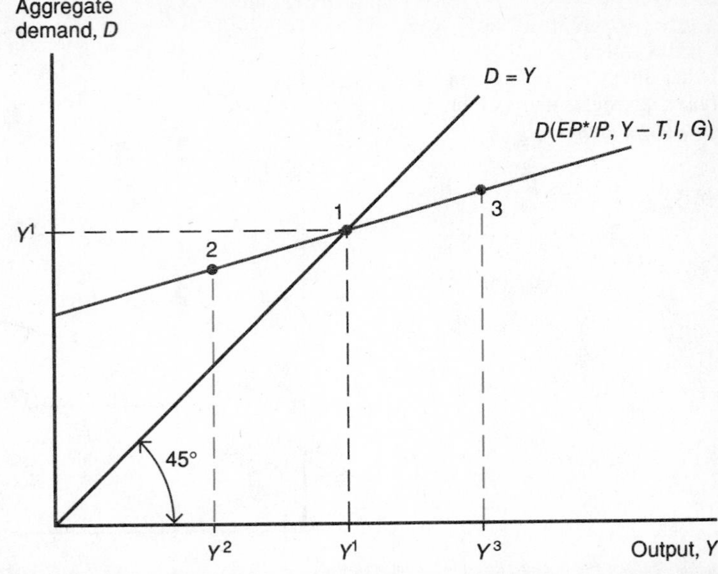

FIGURE 17-2
The determination of output in the short run.
In the short run output settles at Y^1 (point 1), where aggregate demand equals aggregate supply.

necessary because the economy as a whole is in equilibrium only when both the output market and the asset markets are in equilibrium.

OUTPUT, THE EXCHANGE RATE, AND OUTPUT MARKET EQUILIBRIUM

Figure 17-3 illustrates the first relationship between the exchange rate and output, the one implied by output market equilibrium. Specifically, the figure illustrates the effect of a depreciation of the domestic currency against foreign currency (that is, a rise in E from E^1 to E^2) for fixed values of the domestic price level P and the foreign price level P^*. With fixed price levels at home and abroad, the rise in the nominal exchange rate makes foreign goods and services more expensive relative to domestic goods and services. This relative price change shifts the aggregate demand schedule upward.

The fall in the relative price of domestic output shifts the aggregate demand schedule upward because at each level of domestic output, the demand for domestic products is now higher. Output expands from Y^1 to Y^2 as firms find themselves faced with excess demand at initial production levels.

Although we have considered the effect of a change in E with P and P^* held fixed, it is straightforward to analyze the effects of changes in P or P^* on output. *Any rise in the real exchange rate* EP*/P *(whether due to a rise in* E, *a rise in* P*, *or a fall in* P) *will cause an upward shift in the aggregate demand function and an expansion of output, all else equal.* (A rise in P^*, for example, has effects qualitatively identical to those of a rise in E.) *Similarly, any fall in* EP*/P, *regardless of its cause (a fall in* E, *a fall in* P*, *or a rise in* P), *will cause output to contract, all else equal.* (A rise in P, with E and P^* held fixed, for example, makes domestic products more expensive

FIGURE 17-3
Output effect of a currency depreciation with fixed output prices.
A rise in the exchange rate from E^1 to E^2 raises aggregate demand and output, all else equal.

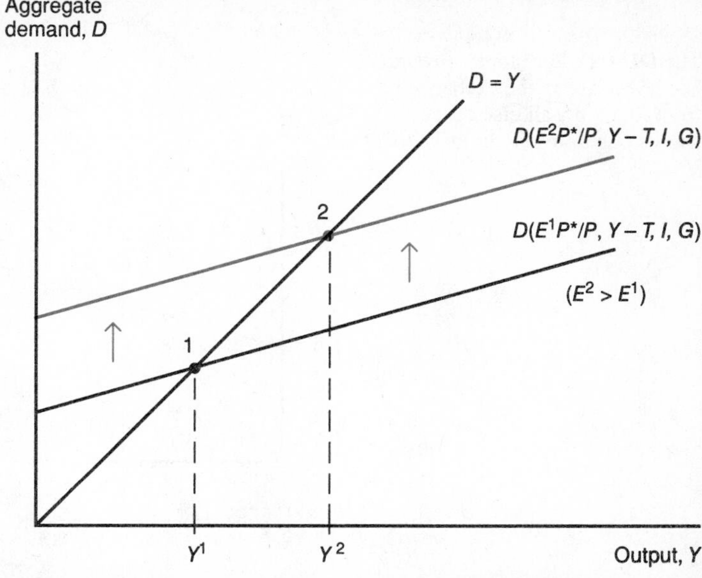

relative to foreign products, reduces aggregate demand for domestic output, and causes output to fall.)

DERIVING THE *DD* SCHEDULE

If we assume P and P^* are fixed in the short run, a depreciation of the domestic currency (a rise in E) is associated with a rise in domestic output, Y, while an appreciation (a fall in E) is associated with a fall in Y. This association provides us with one of the two relationships between E and Y needed to describe the short-run macroeconomic behavior of an open economy. We summarize this relationship by the *DD* schedule, which shows all combinations of output and the exchange rate such that the output market is in short-run equilibrium with aggregate demand equal to aggregate supply.

Figure 17-4 shows how to derive the *DD* schedule, which relates E and Y when P and P^* are fixed. The upper part of the figure reproduces the result of Figure 17-3 (a depreciation of the domestic currency shifts the aggregate demand function upward, causing output to rise). The *DD* schedule in the lower part shows the resulting relationship between the exchange rate and output (given that P and P^* are held constant). Point 1 on the *DD* schedule gives the output level Y^1 at which aggregate demand equals aggregate supply when the exchange rate is E^1. A depreciation of the currency to E^2 leads to the higher output level Y^2 according to the figure's upper part, and this information allows us to locate point 2 on *DD*.

FACTORS THAT SHIFT THE *DD* SCHEDULE

A number of factors affect the position of the *DD* schedule: the levels of government demand, taxes, and investment: the domestic and foreign price levels; variations in

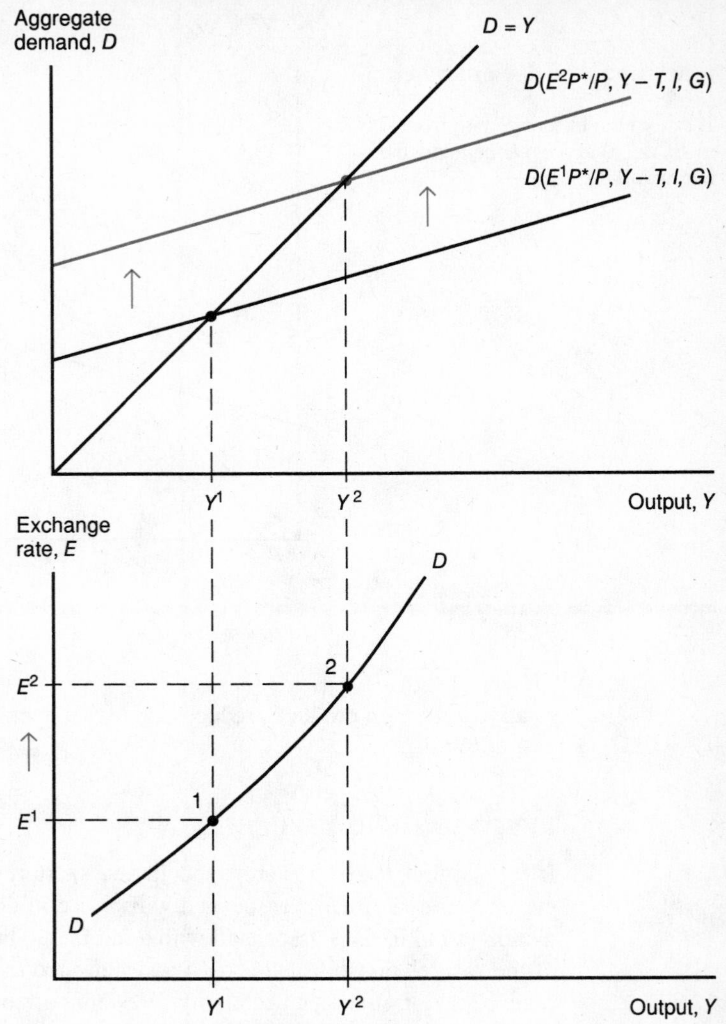

FIGURE 17-4
Deriving the *DD* schedule.
The *DD* schedule slopes upward because a rise in the exchange rate from E^1 to E^2, all else equal, causes output to rise from Y^1 to Y^2.

domestic consumption behavior; and the foreign demand for home output. To understand the effects of shifts in these factors, we must study how the *DD* schedule shifts when they change.

1. *A change in* G. Figure 17-5 shows the effect on *DD* of a rise in government purchases, *G*. Before the increase in *G*, the relevant *DD* curve is D^1D^1 in the lower part of the figure. As shown in the upper part, the exchange rate E^0 leads to an equilibrium output level Y^1 at the initial level of government demand; so point 1 is one point on D^1D^1.

An increase in *G* causes the aggregate demand schedule in the upper part of the figure to shift upward. Everything else remaining unchanged, output increases. Point 2

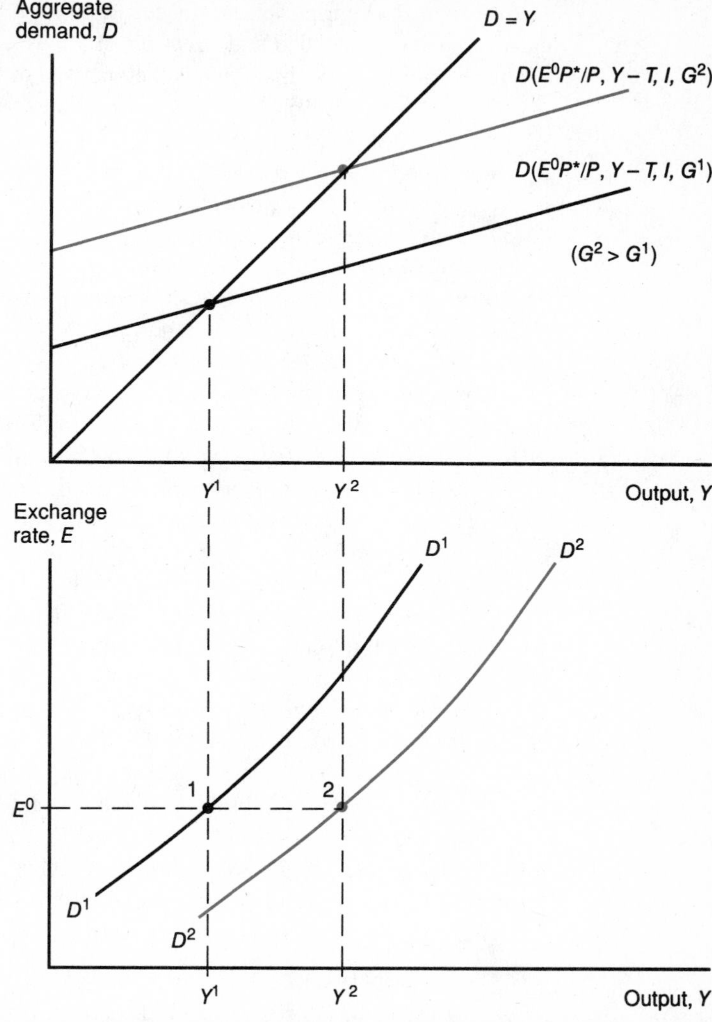

FIGURE 17-5
Government demand and the position of the *DD* schedule.
A rise in government demand from G^1 to G^2 raises output at every level of the exchange rate. The change therefore shifts *DD* to the right.

in the bottom part shows the higher level of output Y^2 at which aggregate demand and supply are now equal, given an unchanged exchange rate of E^0. Point 2 is on the new *DD* curve, D^2D^2.

For any level of the exchange rate, the level of output equating aggregate demand and supply is higher after the increase in *G*. This implies that *an increase in* G *causes* DD *to shift to the right, as shown in Figure 17-5. Similarly, a decrease in* G *causes* DD *to shift to the left.*

The method and reasoning we have just used to study how an increase in *G* shifts the *DD* curve can be applied to all the cases that follow. So we give only a brief summary of the results, leaving it to you to provide a more detailed analysis using diagrams similar to Figure 17-5.

2. *A change in* T. Taxes, T, affect aggregate demand by changing disposable income, and thus consumption, for any level of Y. It follows that an increase in taxes causes the aggregate demand function of Figure 17-1 to shift *downward* given the exchange rate E. Since this effect is the opposite of that of an increase in G, an increase in T must cause the DD schedule to shift leftward. Similarly, a fall in T causes a rightward shift of DD.

3. *A change in* I. An increase in investment demand has the same effect as an increase in G: the aggregate demand schedule shifts upward and DD shifts to the right. A fall in investment demand shifts DD to the left.

4. *A change in* P. Given E and P^*, an increase in P makes domestic output more expensive relative to foreign output and lowers net export demand. The DD schedule shifts to the left as aggregate demand falls. A fall in P makes domestic goods cheaper and causes a rightward shift of DD.

5. *A change in* P*. Given E and P, a rise in P^* makes foreign goods and services relatively more expensive. Aggregate demand for domestic output therefore rises and DD shifts to the right. Similarly, a fall in P^* causes DD to shift to the left.

6. *A change in the consumption function.* Suppose residents of the home economy suddenly decide they want to consume more and save less at each level of disposable income. If the increase in consumption spending is not devoted entirely to imports from abroad, aggregate demand for domestic output rises and the aggregate demand schedule shifts upward for any given exchange rate E. This implies a shift to the right of the DD schedule. An autonomous fall in consumption (if it is not entirely due to a fall in import demand) shifts DD to the left.

7. *A demand shift between foreign and domestic goods.* Suppose there is no change in the domestic consumption function but domestic and foreign residents suddenly decide to devote more of their spending to goods and services produced in the home country. If home disposable income and the real exchange rate remain the same, this shift in demand *improves* the current account by raising exports and lowering imports. The aggregate demand schedule shifts upward and DD therefore shifts to the right. The same reasoning shows that a shift in world demand away from domestic products and toward foreign products causes DD to shift to the left.

You may have noticed that a simple rule allows you to predict the effect on DD of any of the disturbances we have discussed: *Any disturbance that raises aggregate demand for domestic output shifts the* DD *schedule to the right; any disturbance that lowers aggregate demand for domestic output shifts the* DD *schedule to the left.*

Asset Market Equilibrium in the Short Run: The *AA* Schedule

We have now derived the first element in our account of short-run exchange rate and income determination, the relation between the exchange rate and output consistent with the equality of aggregate demand and supply. That relation is summarized by the DD schedule, which shows all exchange rate and output levels that lead to short-run equilibrium in the output market. As we noted at the beginning of the preceding section, however, equilibrium in the economy as a whole requires equilibrium in the asset markets as well as in the output market, and there is no reason in general why points on the *DD* schedule should lead to asset market equilibrium.

To complete the story of short-run equilibrium, we therefore introduce a second element to ensure that the exchange rate and output level consistent with output market equilibrium are also consistent with asset market equilibrium. The schedule of exchange rates and output levels consistent with equilibrium in the domestic money market and the foreign exchange market is called the *AA* schedule.

OUTPUT, THE EXCHANGE RATE, AND ASSET MARKET EQUILIBRIUM

In Chapter 14 we studied the interest parity condition, which states that the foreign exchange market is in equilibrium only when the expected rates of return on domestic and foreign currency deposits are equal. In Chapter 15 we learned how the interest rates that enter the interest parity relationship are determined by the equality of real money supply and real money demand in national money markets. Now we combine these asset market equilibrium conditions to see how the exchange rate and output must be related when all asset markets simultaneously clear. Because the focus for now is on the domestic economy, the foreign interest rate is taken as given.

For a given expected future exchange rate E^e, the interest parity condition describing foreign exchange market equilibrium is

$$R = R^* + (E^e - E)/E,$$

where R is the interest rate on domestic currency deposits and R^* is the interest rate on foreign currency deposits. In Chapter 15 we saw that the domestic interest rate satisfying the interest parity condition must also equate the real domestic money supply (M^s/P) to aggregate real money demand:

$$M^s/P = L(R,Y).$$

You will recall that aggregate real money demand $L(R,Y)$ rises when the interest rate falls because a fall in R makes interest-bearing nonmoney assets less attractive to hold. (Conversely, a rise in the interest rate lowers real money demand.) A rise in real output increases real money demand by raising the volume of monetary transactions people must carry out (and a fall in real output reduces real money demand by reducing transactions needs).

We now use the diagrammatic tools developed in Chapter 15 to study the changes in the exchange rate that must accompany output changes so that asset markets remain in equilibrium. Figure 17-6 shows the equilibrium domestic interest rate and exchange rate associated with the output level Y^1 for a given nominal money supply, M^s, a given domestic price level, P, a given foreign interest rate, R^*, and a given value of the expected future exchange rate, E^e. In the lower part of the figure, we see that with real output at Y^1 and the real money supply at M^s/P, the interest rate R^1 clears the home money market (point 1) while the exchange rate E^1 clears the foreign exchange market (point 1′). The exchange rate E^1 clears the foreign exchange market because it equates the expected rate of return on foreign deposits, measured in terms of domestic currency, to R^1.

A rise in output from Y^1 to Y^2 raises aggregate real money demand from $L(R,Y^1)$ to $L(R,Y^2)$, shifting out the entire money demand schedule in Figure 17-6. This shift, in turn, raises the equilibrium domestic interest rate to R^2 (point 2). With E^e and R^*

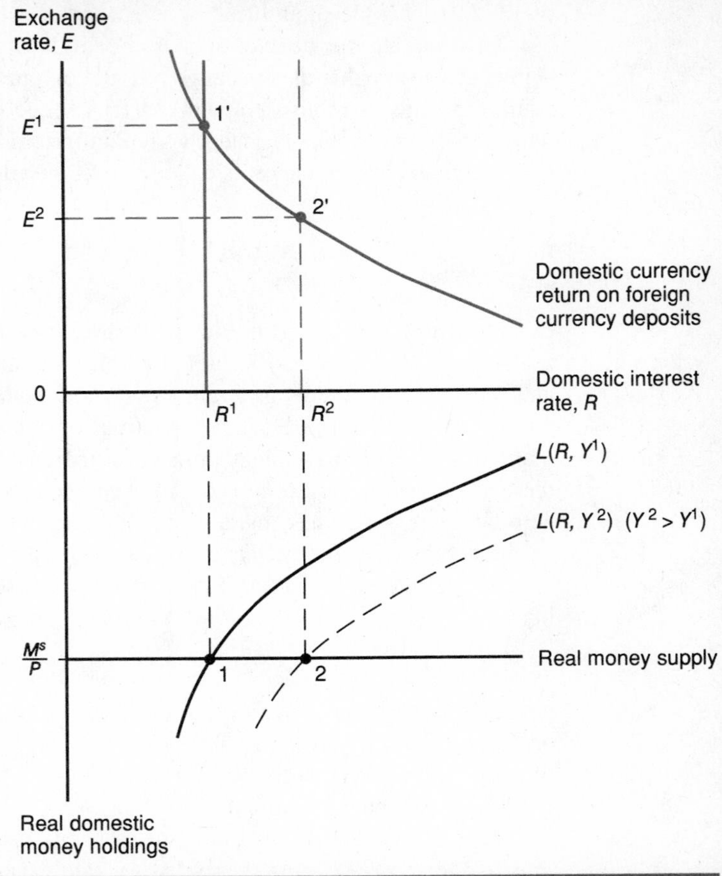

FIGURE 17-6
Output and the exchange rate in asset market equilibrium.
For the asset markets to remain in equilibrium, a rise in output must be accompanied by an appreciation of the currency, all else equal.

fixed, the domestic currency must appreciate from E^1 to E^2 to bring the foreign exchange market back into equilibrium at point 2′. The domestic currency appreciates by just enough that the increase in the rate at which it is expected to *depreciate* in the future offsets the increased interest rate advantage of home currency deposits. *For asset markets to remain in equilibrium, a rise in domestic output must be accompanied by an appreciation of the domestic currency, all else equal, and a fall in domestic output must be accompanied by a depreciation.*

DERIVING THE *AA* SCHEDULE

While the *DD* schedule plots exchange rates and output levels at which the output market is in equilibrium, the *AA* schedule relates exchange rates and output levels that keep the money and foreign exchange markets in equilibrium. Figure 17-7 shows the *AA* schedule. From Figure 17-6 we see that for any output level Y^1, there is a unique exchange rate E^1 satisfying the interest parity condition (given the real money supply, the foreign interest rate, and the expected future exchange rate). Our previous reasoning tells us that other things equal, a rise in Y^1 to Y^2 will produce an appreciation of the domestic currency, that is, a fall in the exchange rate from E^1 to E^2. The *AA* schedule therefore has a negative slope, as shown.

FIGURE 17-7
The *AA* schedule.
The asset market equilibrium schedule *AA* slopes downward because a rise in output, all else equal, causes a rise in the home interest rate and a domestic currency appreciation.

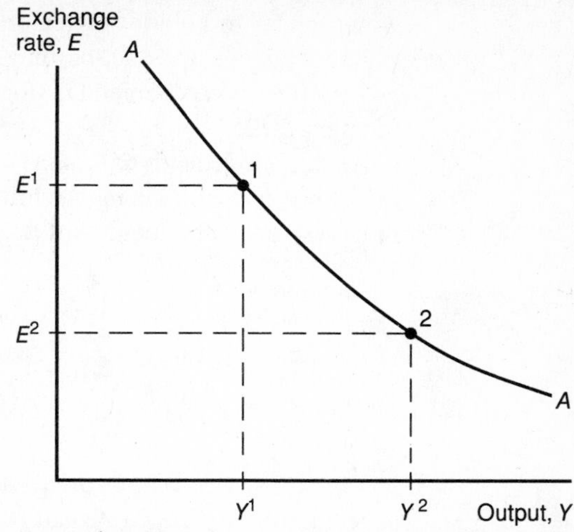

FACTORS THAT SHIFT THE *AA* SCHEDULE

Five factors cause the *AA* schedule to shift: changes in the domestic money supply, M^s; changes in the domestic price level, *P;* changes in the expected future exchange rate, E^e; changes in the foreign interest rate, R^*; and shifts in the aggregate real money demand schedule.

1. *A change in* M^s. For a fixed level of output, an increase in M^s causes the domestic currency to depreciate in the foreign exchange market, all else equal (that is, *E* rises). Since for each level of output the exchange rate *E* is higher after the rise in M^s, the rise in M^s causes *AA* to shift *upward.* Similiarly, a fall in M^s causes *AA* to shift *downward.*

2. *A change in* P. An increase in *P* reduces the *real* money supply and drives the interest rate upward. Other things (including *Y*) equal, this rise in the interest rate causes *E* to fall. The effect of a rise in *P* is therefore a downward shift of *AA*. A fall in *P* results in an upward shift of *AA*.

3. *A change in* E^e. Suppose participants in the foreign exchange market suddenly revise their expectations about the exchange rate's future value so that E^e rises. Such a change shifts the curve in the top part of Figure 17-6 (which measures the expected domestic currency return on foreign currency deposits) to the right. The rise in E^e therefore causes the domestic currency to depreciate, other things equal. Because the exchange rate producing equilibrium in the foreign exchange market is higher after a rise in E^e, given output, *AA* shifts upward when a rise in the expected future exchange rate occurs. It shifts downward when the expected future exchange rate falls.

4. *A change in* R^*. A rise in R^* raises the expected return on foreign currency deposits and therefore shifts the downward-sloping schedule at the top of Figure 17-6 to the right. Given output, the domestic currency must depreciate to restore interest parity. A rise in R^* therefore has the same effect on *AA* as a rise in E^e: it causes an upward shift. A fall in R^* results in a downward shift of *AA*.

5. *A change in real money demand.* Suppose domestic residents decide they would prefer to hold lower real money balances at each output level and interest rate. (Such a change in asset-holding preferences is a *reduction in money demand.*) A reduction in money demand implies an inward shift of the aggregate real money demand function $L(R,Y)$ for any fixed level of Y, and it thus results in a lower interest rate and a rise in E. A reduction in money demand therefore has the same effect as an increase in the money supply, in that it shifts AA upward. The opposite disturbance of an increase in money demand would shift AA downward.

Short-Run Equilibrium for an Open Economy: Putting the *DD* and *AA* Schedules Together

By assuming that output prices are temporarily fixed, we have derived two separate schedules of exchange rate and output levels: the DD schedule, along which the output market is in equilibrium, and the AA schedule, along which the asset markets are in equilibrium. A short-run equilibrium for the economy as a whole must lie on *both* schedules because such a point must bring about equilibrium simultaneously in the output and asset markets. We can therefore find the economy's short-run equilibrium by finding the intersection of the DD and AA schedules. Once again, it is the assumption that output prices are temporarily fixed that makes this intersection a *short-run* equilibrium. The analysis in this section continues to assume that the foreign interest rate R^* and the expected future exchange rate E^e also are fixed.

Figure 17-8 combines the DD and AA schedules to locate short-run equilibrium. The intersection of DD and AA at point 1 is the only combination of exchange rate and output consistent with both the equality of aggregate demand and aggregate supply *and* asset market equilibrium. The short-run equilibrium levels of the exchange rate and output are therefore E^1 and Y^1.

To convince yourself that the economy will indeed settle at point 1, imagine that

FIGURE 17-8
Short-run equilibrium: The intersection of *DD* and *AA*.
The short-run equilibrium of the economy occurs at point 1, where the output and asset markets simultaneously clear.

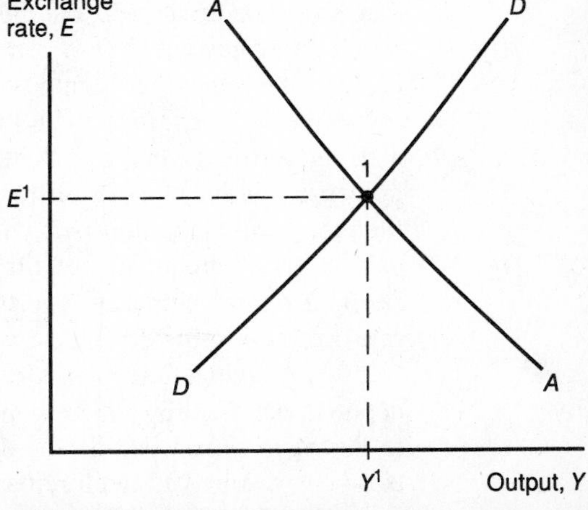

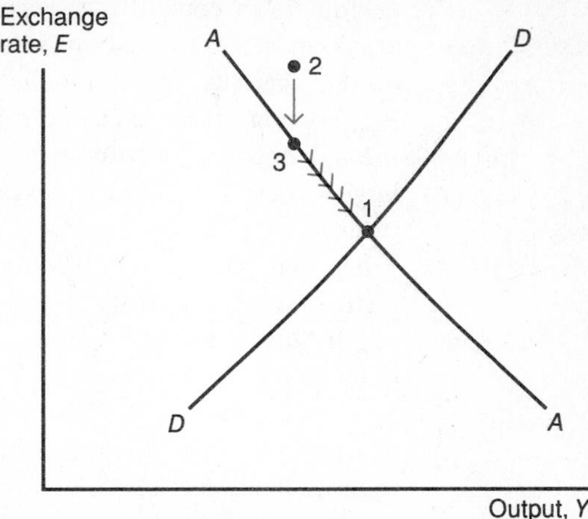

FIGURE 17-9
How the economy reaches its short-run equilibrium.
Because asset markets adjust very quickly, the exchange rate jumps immediately from point 2 to point 3 on *AA*. The economy then moves to point 1 along *AA* as output rises to meet aggregate demand.

the economy is instead at a position like point 2 in Figure 17-9. At point 2, which lies above *AA* and *DD*, both the output and asset markets are out of equilibrium. Because *E* is so high relative to *AA*, the rate at which *E* is expected to fall in the future is also high relative to the rate that would maintain interest parity. The high expected future appreciation rate of the domestic currency implies that the expected domestic currency return on foreign deposits is below that on domestic deposits, so there is an excess demand for the domestic currency in the foreign exchange market. The high level of *E* at point 2 also makes domestic goods cheap for foreign buyers (given the goods' domestic-currency prices), causing an excess demand for output at that point.

The excess demand for domestic currency leads to an immediate fall in the exchange rate. This appreciation equalizes the expected returns on domestic and foreign deposits and places the economy at point 3 on the asset market equilibrium curve *AA*. But since point 3 is above the *DD* schedule, there is still excess demand for domestic output. As firms raise production to avoid depleting their inventories, the economy travels along *AA* to point 1, where aggregate demand and supply are equal. Because asset prices can jump immediately while changes in production plans take some time, the asset markets remain in continual equilibrium even while output is changing.

The exchange rate falls as the economy approaches point 1 along *AA* because rising national output causes money demand to rise, pushing the interest rate steadily upward. (The currency must appreciate steadily to lower the expected rate of future domestic currency appreciation and maintain interest parity.) Once the economy has reached point 1 on *DD*, aggregate demand equals output and producers no longer face involuntary inventory depletion. The economy therefore settles at point 1, the only point at which the output *and* asset markets clear.

Temporary Changes in Monetary and Fiscal Policy

Now that we have seen how the economy's short-run equilibrium is determined, we can study how shifts in government macroeconomic policies affect output and the exchange rate. Our interest in the effects of macroeconomic policies stems from their usefulness in counteracting economic disturbances that cause fluctuations in output, employment, and inflation. In this section we learn how government policies can be used to maintain full employment in open economies.

We concentrate on two types of government policy, **monetary policy,** which works through changes in the money supply, and **fiscal policy,** which works through changes in government spending or taxes.[7] To avoid the complications that would be introduced by ongoing inflation, however, we do not look at situations in which the money supply grows over time. Thus, the only type of monetary policies we will study explicitly are stepwise increases or decreases in money supplies.[8]

In this section we examine *temporary* policy shifts, shifts that the public expects to be reversed in the near future. The expected future exchange rate E^e is now assumed to equal the long-run exchange rate discussed in Chapter 16, that is, the exchange rate that prevails once full employment is reached and domestic prices have adjusted fully to past disturbances in the output and asset markets. In line with this interpretation, a temporary policy change does *not* affect the long-run expected exchange rate E^e.

We assume throughout that events in the economy we are studying do not influence the foreign interest rate R^* or price level P^*, and that the domestic price level P is fixed in the short run.

MONETARY POLICY

The short-run effect of a temporary increase in the domestic money supply is shown in Figure 17-10. An increased money supply shifts A^1A^1 upward to A^2A^2 but does not

[7] Other policies, such as commercial policies, have macroeconomic side effects. Such policies, however, are not used routinely for purposes of macroeconomic stabilization, so we do not discuss them in this chapter. (A problem at the end of this chapter does ask you to think about the macroeconomic effects of a tariff.)

[8] You can extend the results below to a setting with ongoing inflation by thinking of the exchange rate and price level changes we describe as departures from time paths along which E and P trend upward at constant rates.

FIGURE 17-10
Effects of a temporary increase in the money supply.
By shifting A^1A^1 upward, a temporary increase in the money supply causes a currency depreciation and a rise in output.

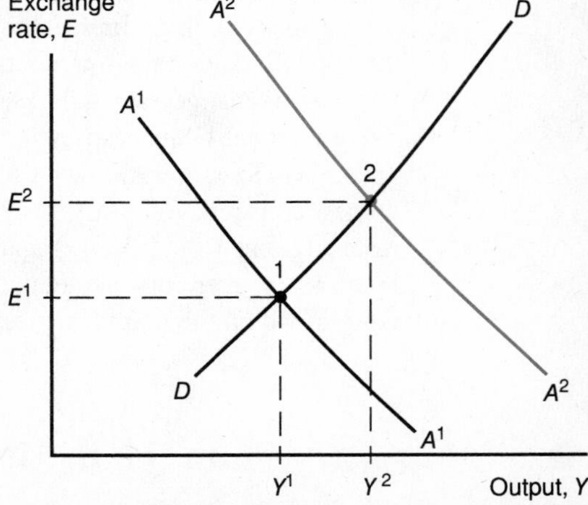

affect the position of *DD*. The upward shift of the asset market equilibrium schedule moves the economy from point 1, with exchange rate E^1 and output Y^1, to point 2, with exchange rate E^2 and output Y^2. An increase in the money supply causes a depreciation of the domestic currency, an expansion of output, and therefore an increase in employment.

We can understand the economic forces causing these results by recalling our earlier discussions of asset market equilibrium and output determination. At the initial output level Y^1 and given the fixed price level, an increase in money supply must push down the home interest rate *R*. We have been assuming the monetary change is temporary and does not affect the expected future exchange rate E^e, so to preserve interest parity in the face of a decline in *R* (given that R^* does not change), the exchange rate must depreciate immediately to create the expectation that the home currency will appreciate in the future at a faster rate than was expected before *R* fell. The immediate depreciation of the domestic currency, however, makes home products cheaper relative to foreign products. There is therefore an increase in aggregate demand, which must be matched by an increase in output.

FISCAL POLICY

As we saw earlier, expansionary fiscal policy can take the form of an increase in government demand, a cut in taxes, or some combination of the two that raises aggregate demand. A temporary fiscal expansion (which does not affect the expected future exchange rate) therefore shifts the *DD* schedule to the right but does not move *AA*.

Figure 17-11 shows how expansionary fiscal policy affects the economy in the short run. Initially the economy is at point 1, with an exchange rate E^1 and output Y^1. Suppose the government decides to spend $5 billion to develop a new space shuttle. This one-time increase in government purchases moves the economy to point 2, causing the currency to appreciate to E^2 and output to expand to Y^2. The economy would respond in a similar way to a temporary cut in taxes.

What economic forces produce the movement from point 1 to point 2? The increase

FIGURE 17-11
Effects of a temporary fiscal expansion.
By shifting D^1D^1 to the right, a temporary fiscal expansion causes a currency appreciation and a rise in output.

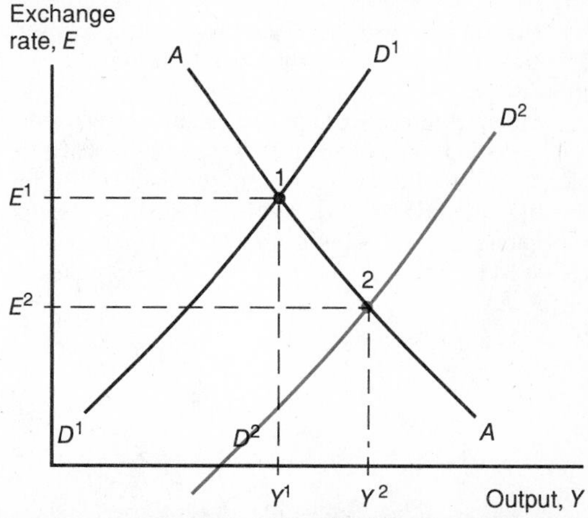

in output caused by the increase in government spending raises the transactions demand for real money holdings. Given the fixed price level, this increase in money demand pushes the interest rate R upward. Because the expected future exchange rate E^e and the foreign interest rate R^* have not changed, the domestic currency must appreciate to create the expectation of a subsequent depreciation just large enough to offset the higher international interest rate difference in favor of domestic currency deposits.

POLICIES TO MAINTAIN FULL EMPLOYMENT

The analysis of this section can be applied to the problem of maintaining full employment in open economies. Because temporary monetary expansion and temporary fiscal expansion both raise output and employment, they can be used to counteract the effects of temporary disturbances that lead to recession. Similarly, disturbances that lead to overemployment can be offset through contractionary macroeconomic policies.

Figure 17-12 illustrates this use of macroeconomic policy. Suppose the economy's initial equilibrium is at point 1, where output equals its full-employment level, denoted Y^f. Suddenly there is a temporary shift in consumer tastes away from domestic products. As we saw earlier in this chapter, such a shift is a decrease in aggregate demand for domestic goods, and it causes the curve D^1D^1 to shift leftward, to D^2D^2. At point 2, the new short-run equilibrium, the currency has depreciated to E^2 and output, at Y^2, is below its full-employment level. Because the shift in preferences is assumed to be temporary, it does not affect E^e, so there is no change in the position of A^1A^1.

To restore full employment, the government may use monetary or fiscal policy, or both. A temporary fiscal expansion shifts D^2D^2 back to its original position, restoring full employment and returning the exchange rate to E^1. A temporary money supply increase shifts the asset market equilibrium curve to A^2A^2 and places the economy at point 3, a move that restores full employment but causes the home currency to depreciate even further.

Another possible cause of recession is a temporary increase in the demand for

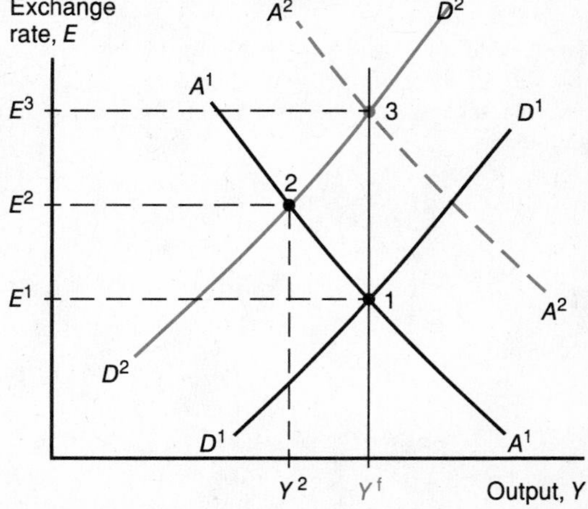

FIGURE 17-12
Policies to maintain full employment after a temporary fall in world demand for domestic products.
A temporary fall in world demand shifts D^1D^1 to the left, reducing output (point 2). Temporary fiscal expansion can restore full employment (point 1) by shifting the DD schedule back to its original position. Temporary monetary expansion restores full employment (point 3) by shifting A^1A^1 to A^2A^2. The two policies differ in their exchange-rate effects.

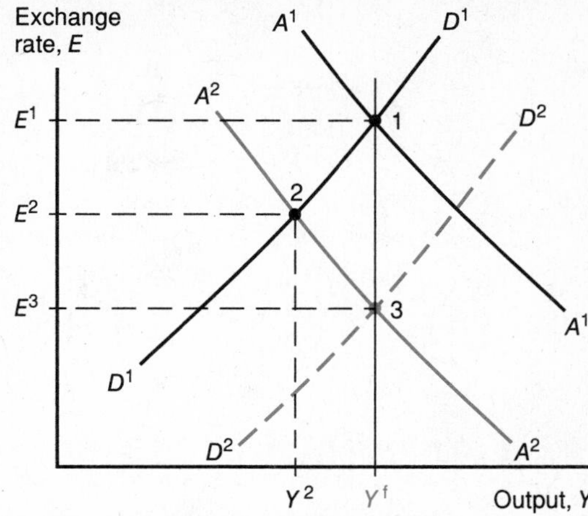

FIGURE 17-13
Policies to maintain full employment after a money-demand increase.
After a temporary money-demand increase, either an increase in the money supply or temporary fiscal ease can be used to maintain full employment. The two policies have different exchange-rate effects.

money, illustrated in Figure 17-13. An increase in money demand pushes up the domestic interest rate and appreciates the currency, thereby making domestic goods more expensive and causing output to contract. Figure 17-13 shows this asset market disturbance as the downward shift of A^1A^1 to A^2A^2, which moves the economy from its initial full-employment equilibrium at point 1 to point 2.

Expansionary macroeconomic policies can again restore full employment. A temporary money supply increase moves the economy back to its initial position at point 1, completely offsetting the increase in money demand by giving domestic residents the additional money they desire to hold. Temporary fiscal expansion shifts D^1D^1 to D^2D^2 and restores full employment at point 3. But the move to point 3 involves an even greater appreciation of the currency.

SOME PROBLEMS OF POLICY FORMULATION

The apparent ease with which full employment is maintained in our model is misleading, and you should not come away from our discussion of policy with the idea that it is easy to keep the macroeconomy on a steady course. Here are just a few of the many problems that can arise:

1. In practice it is sometimes hard to be sure whether a disturbance to the economy originates in the output or asset markets. Yet a government concerned about the exchange rate effect of its policy response needs to know this before it can choose between monetary and fiscal policy.

2. Real-world policy choices are frequently determined by political necessities rather than by detailed consideration of whether shocks to the economy are real or monetary. Shifts in fiscal policy often can be made only after lengthy legislative deliberation, while monetary policy, in contrast, is usually exercised by the central bank. To avoid procedural delays, governments are likely to respond to disturbances by changing monetary policy even when a shift in fiscal policy would be more appropriate.

3. Another problem with fiscal policy is its impact on the government budget. A tax cut or spending increase may lead to a government budget deficit that must sooner or later be closed by a fiscal reversal. Unfortunately, there is no guarantee that the government will have the political will to synchronize these actions with the state of the business cycle. The state of the electoral cycle may be more important.

4. Policies that appear to act swiftly in our simple model operate in reality with lags of varying length. At the same time, the difficulty of evaluating the size and persistence of a given shock makes it hard to know precisely how much monetary or fiscal medicine to administer. These uncertainties force policy makers to base their actions on forecasts and hunches that may turn out to be quite wide of the mark.

Permanent Shifts in Monetary and Fiscal Policy

A permanent policy shift affects not only the current value of the government's policy instrument (the money supply, government spending, or taxes) but also the *long-run* exchange rate. This in turn affects expectations about future exchange rates. Because these changes in expectations have a major influence on the exchange rate prevailing in the short run, the effects of permanent policy shifts differ from those of temporary shifts. In this section we look at the effects of permanent changes in monetary and fiscal policy, in both the short and long run.[9]

To make it easier to grasp the long-run effects of policies, we assume that the economy is initially at a long-run equilibrium position and that the policy changes we examine are the only economic changes that occur (our usual "other things equal" clause). These assumptions mean that the economy starts out at full employment with the exchange rate at its long-run level and with no change in the exchange rate expected. In particular, we know that the domestic interest rate must initially equal the foreign rate, R^*.

A PERMANENT INCREASE IN THE MONEY SUPPLY

Figure 17-14 shows the short-run effects of a permanent increase in the money supply on an economy initially at its full-employment output level Y^f (point 1). As we saw earlier, even a temporary increase in M^s causes the asset market equilibrium schedule A^1A^1 to shift upward. Because the increase in M^s is now permanent, however, it also affects the exchange rate expected for the future, E^e. Chapter 15 showed how a permanent increase in the money supply affects the long-run exchange rate: a permanent increase in M^s must ultimately lead to a proportional rise in E. Therefore, the rise in M^s causes E^e, the expected future exchange rate, to rise proportionally.

Because a rise in E^e accompanies a *permanent* increase in the money supply, the upward shift of A^1A^1 to A^2A^2 is greater than that caused by an equal, but transitory, increase. At point 2, the economy's new short-run equilibrium, Y and E are both higher than they would be were the change in the money supply temporary. (Point 3 shows the equilibrium that might result from a temporary increase in M^s.)

[9] You may be wondering whether a permanent change in fiscal policy is always possible. For example, if a government starts with a balanced budget, doesn't a fiscal expansion lead to a deficit, and thus require an eventual fiscal contraction? Problem 3 at the end of this chapter suggests an answer.

FIGURE 17-14
Short-run effects of a permanent increase in the money supply.
A permanent increase in the money supply, which moves the economy from point 1 to point 2, has stronger effects on the exchange rate and output than an equal temporary increase, which moves the economy only to point 3.

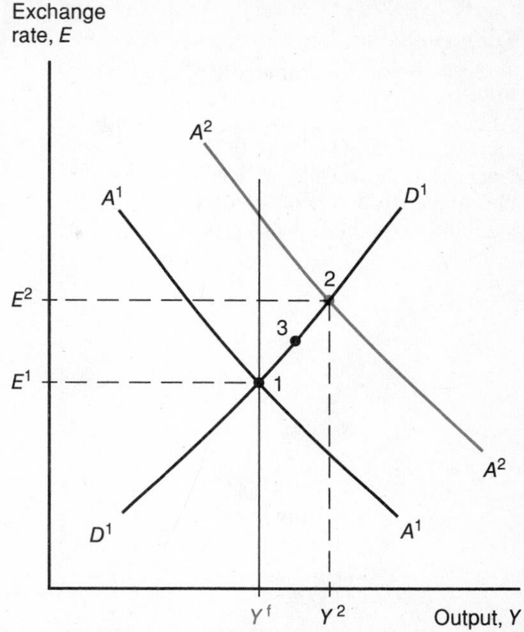

ADJUSTMENT TO A PERMANENT INCREASE IN THE MONEY SUPPLY

The increase in the money supply shown in Figure 17-14 is not reversed by the central bank, so it is natural to ask how the economy is affected *over time.* At the short-run equilibrium, shown as point 2 in Figure 17-14, output is above its full-employment level and labor and machines are working overtime. Upward pressure on the price level develops as workers demand higher wages and producers raise prices to cover their increasing production costs. Chapter 15 showed that while an increase in the money supply must eventually cause all money prices to rise in proportion, it has no lasting effect on output, relative prices, or interst rates. Over time, the inflationary pressure that follows a permanent money supply expansion pushes the price level to its new long-run value and returns the economy to full employment.

Figure 17-15 will help you visualize the adjustment back to full employment. Whenever output is greater than its full-employment level Y^f and productive factors are working overtime, the price level P is rising to keep up with rising production costs. Although the DD and AA schedules are drawn for a constant price level P, we have seen how increases in P cause them to shift. A rise in P makes domestic goods more expensive relative to foreign goods, discouraging exports and encouraging imports. A rising domestic price level therefore causes D^1D^1 to shift to the left over time. Because a rising price level steadily reduces the real money supply over time, A^2A^2 also travels to the left as prices rise.

The DD and AA schedules stop shifting only when they intersect at the full-employment output level Y^f; as long as output differs from Y^f, the price level will change and the two schedules will continue to shift. The schedules' final positions are shown in Figure 17-15 as D^2D^2 and A^3A^3. At point 3, their intersection, the exchange

FIGURE 17-15
Long-run adjustment to a permanent increase in the money supply.
After a permanent money-supply increase, a steadily increasing price level shifts the *DD* and *AA* schedules to the left until a new long-run equilibrium (point 3) is reached.

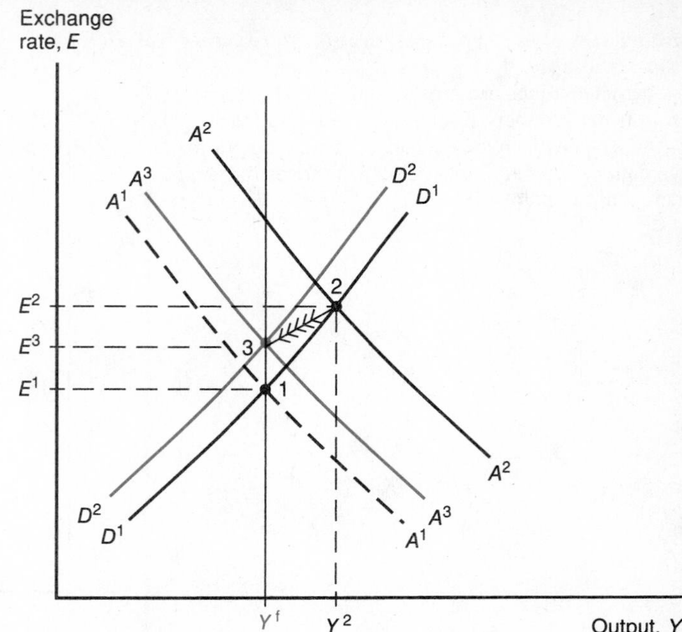

rate, *E*, and the price level, *P*, have risen in proportion to the increase in the money supply, as required by the long-run neutrality of money. (A^2A^2 does not shift all the way back to its original position because E^e is permanently higher after a permanent increase in the money supply: it too has risen by the same percentage as M^s.)

Notice that along the adjustment path between the initial short-run equilibrium (point 2) and the long-run equilibrium (point 3), the domestic currency actually appreciates (from E^2 to E^3) following its initial sharp depreciation (from $E^1$to E^2). This exchange rate behavior is an example of the *overshooting* phenomenon discussed in Chapter 15, in which the exchange rate's initial response to some change is greater than its long-run response.[10]

We can draw on our conclusions to describe the proper policy response to a permanent monetary disturbance. A permanent increase in money demand, for example, can be offset with a permanent increase in the money supply of equal magnitude. Such a policy maintains full employment, but because the price level would fall in the absence of the policy, the policy will not have inflationary consequences. Instead, monetary expansion can move the economy straight to its long-run, full-employment position. Keep in mind, however, that it may be hard in practice to diagnose the origin or persistence of a particular shock to the economy.

A PERMANENT FISCAL EXPANSION

A permanent fiscal expansion not only has an immediate impact in the output market but also affects the asset markets through its impact on long-run exchange rate expec-

[10] While the exchange rate initially overshoots in the case shown in Figure 17-15, overshooting does not have to occur in all circumstances.

FIGURE 17-16
Effects of a permanent fiscal expansion.
Because a permanent fiscal expansion changes exchange-rate expectations, it shifts A^1A^1 leftward as it shifts D^1D^1 to the right. The effect on output (point 2) is nil if the economy starts in long-run equilibrium. A comparable *temporary* fiscal expansion, in contrast, would leave the economy at point 3.

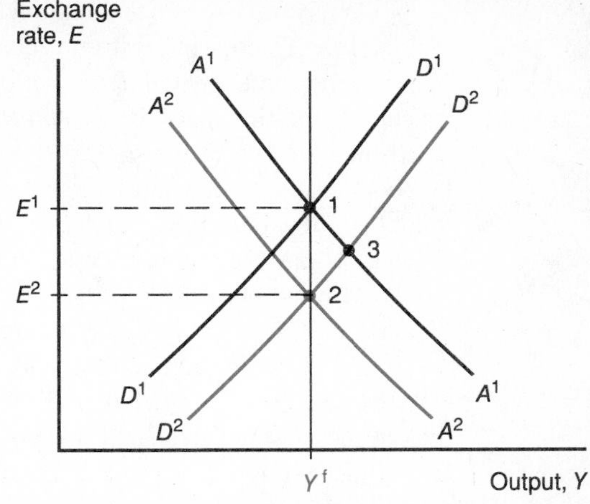

tations. Figure 17-16 shows the short-run effects of a government decision to spend an extra $5 billion a year on its space travel program forever. As before, the direct effect of this rise in G on aggregate demand causes D^1D^1 to shift right to D^2D^2. But because the increase in government demand for domestic goods and services is permanent in this case, it causes a long-run appreciation of the currency, as we saw in Chapter 16. The resulting fall in E^e pushes the asset market equilibrium schedule A^1A^1 downward to A^2A^2. Point 2, where the new schedules D^2D^2 and A^2A^2 intersect, is the economy's short-run equilibrium, and at that point the currency has appreciated from its initial level while output is unchanged.

The important result illustrated in Figure 17-16 is that when a fiscal expansion is permanent, the additional currency appreciation caused by the shift in exchange rate expectations reduces the policy's expansionary effect on output. Without this additional expectations effect due to the permanence of the fiscal change, equilibrium would initially be at point 3, with higher output and a smaller appreciation. The greater the downward shift of the asset market equilibrium schedule, the greater the appreciation of the currency. This appreciation ''crowds out'' aggregate demand for domestic products by making them more expensive relative to foreign products.

Figure 17-16 is drawn to show a case in which fiscal expansion, contrary to what you might have guessed, has no net effect on output. This case is not, however, a special one; in fact, it is inevitable under the assumptions we have made. The argument that establishes this point requires five steps; by taking the time to understand it you will solidify your understanding of the ground we have covered so far:

1. As a first step, convince yourself (perhaps by reviewing Chapter 15) that because the fiscal expansion does not affect the money supply, M^s, or the long-run values of the domestic interest rate and output, which equal R^* and Y^f, it can have no impact on the long-run price level.
2. Next, recall our assumption that the economy starts out in long-run equilibrium with the domestic interest rate R just equal to the foreign rate R^* and output equal to Y^f. Observe also that the fiscal expansion leaves the real money supply M^s/P unchanged in the short run (neither the numerator nor the denominator changes).
3. Now imagine, contrary to what Figure 17-16 shows, that output *did* rise above

Y^f. Because M^s/P doesn't change in the short run (step 2), the domestic interest rate R would have to rise above its initial level of R^* to keep the money market in equilibrium. Since the foreign interest rate remains at R^*, however, a rise in Y to any level above Y^f implies an expected *depreciation* of the domestic currency (by interest parity).

4. Notice that there is something wrong with this conclusion: we already know (from step 1) that the long-run price level is not affected by the fiscal expansion, so people can expect a nominal domestic currency depreciation just after the policy change only if the currency depreciates in *real* terms as the economy returns to long-run equilibrium. Such a real depreciation, by making domestic products relatively cheap, would only worsen the initial situation of overemployment that we have imagined to exist, and thus would prevent output from ever actually returning to Y^f.

5. Finally, conclude that the apparent contradiction is resolved only if output does *not* rise at all after the fiscal policy move. The only logical possibility is that the currency appreciates right away to its new long-run value. This appreciation crowds out just enough net export demand to leave output at the full-employment level despite the higher level of G.

Notice that this exchange rate change, which allows the output market to clear at full employment, leaves the asset markets in equilibrium as well. Since the exchange rate has jumped to its new long-run value, R remains at R^*. With output also at Y^f, however, the long-run money market equilibrium condition $M^s/P = L(R^*, Y^f)$ still holds, as it did before the fiscal action. So our story hangs together: the currency appreciation that a permanent fiscal expansion provokes immediately brings the asset makets as well as the output market to positions of long-run equilibrium.

We conclude that *if the economy starts at long-run equilibrium, a permanent change in fiscal policy has no net effect on output. Instead, it causes an immediate and permanent exchange rate jump that offsets exactly the fiscal policy's direct effect on aggregate demand.*

Macroeconomic Policies and the Current Account

Policy makers are often concerned about the level of the current account. As we will discuss more fully in Chapter 19, an excessive imbalance in the current account—either a surplus or a deficit—may have undesirable long-run effects on national welfare. Large external imbalances may also generate political pressures for government restrictions on trade. It is therefore important to know how monetary and fiscal policies aimed at domestic objectives affect the current account.

Figure 17-17 shows how the *DD-AA* model can be extended to illustrate the effects of macroeconomic policies on the current account. In addition to the *DD* and *AA* curves, the figure contains a new curve, labled *XX,* which shows combinations of the exchange rate and output at which the current account balance is equal to some desired level, say $CA(EP^*/P, Y - T) = X$. The curve slopes upward because, other things equal, a rise in output encourages spending on imports and thus worsens the current account if it is not accompanied by a currency depreciation.

The central feature of Figure 17-17 is that *XX* is *flatter* than *DD*. The reason is

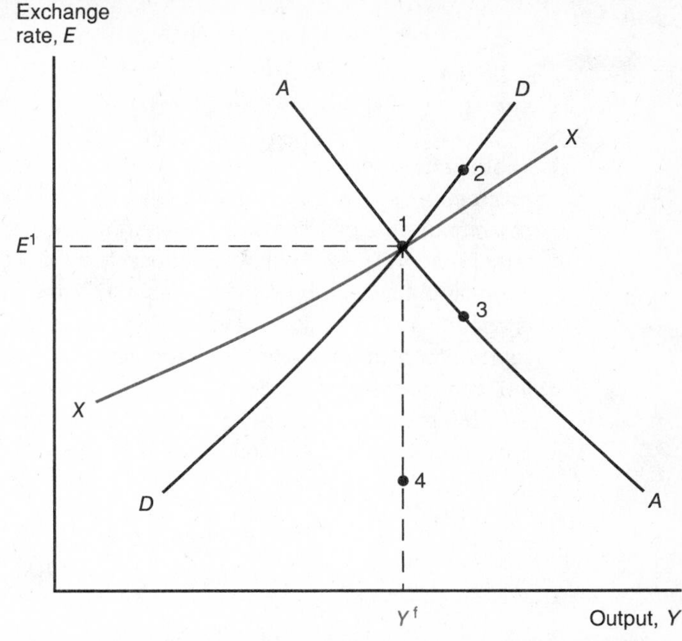

FIGURE 17-17
How macroeconomic policies affect the current account.
Along the curve *XX*, the current account is constant at the level $CA = X$. Monetary expansion moves the economy to point 2 and thus raises the current account balance. Temporary fiscal expansion moves the economy to point 3 while permanent fiscal expansion moves it to point 4; in either case the current account balance falls.

seen by asking how the current account changes as we move up along the *DD* curve from point 1, where all three curves intersect (so that, initially, $CA = X$). As we increase *Y* in moving up along *DD*, the *domestic* demand for domestic output rises by less than the rise in output itself (since some income is saved and some spending falls on imports). Along *DD*, however, *total aggregate demand has to equal supply.* To prevent an excess supply of home output, *E* therefore must rise sharply enough along *DD* to make export demand rise faster than imports. In other words, net foreign demand—the current account—must rise sufficiently along *DD* as output rises to take up the slack left by domestic saving. Thus to the right of point 1, *DD* is in the region above *XX*, where $CA > X$; similar reasoning shows that *DD* lies below *XX* (where $CA < X$) to the left of point 1.

The current account effects of macroeconomic policies can now be examined. As shown earlier, an increase in the money supply, for example, shifts the economy to a position like point 2, expanding output and depreciating the currency. Since point 2 lies above *XX*, the current account has improved as a result of the policy action. *Monetary expansion causes the current account balance to increase in the short run.*

Consider next a temporary fiscal expansion. This action shifts *DD* to the right and moves the economy to point 3 in the figure. Because the currency appreciates and income rises, there is a deterioration in the current account. A permanent fiscal expansion has the additional effect of shifting *AA* leftward, producing an equilibrium at point 4. Like point 3, point 4 is below *XX*, so once again the current account worsens. *Expansionary fiscal policy reduces the current account balance.*

Case Study

U.S. MONETARY AND FISCAL POLICY IN ACTION, 1979–1983

The effects of monetary and fiscal policy we have just studied are illustrated by U.S. macroeconomic policy in the tumultuous period between 1979 and 1983. Table 17-1 summarizes the courses of monetary policy, measured by the growth rate of the money supply, and of fiscal policy. Because fiscal policy may operate through a change in government spending or taxes, Table 17-1 measures the extent to which fiscal policy is contractionary by the size of the government budget surplus, $T - G$. The higher the budget surplus, the more contractionary is fiscal policy. A negative value of $T - G$ indicates a government deficit.

The two major U.S. policy initiatives taken in the years 1979–1983 were a contractionary shift in monetary policy late in 1979 and a drastic cut in taxes legislated in 1981. These policy actions preceded the sharpest U.S. (and, indeed, worldwide) recession since the Great Depression of the 1930s. The recession reached its low point in the

TABLE 17-1 U.S. macroeconomic data, 1979–1983

	1979	*1980*	*1981*	*1982*	*1983*
Annualized growth rate of nominal money supply (M1) (percent per year)	7.0	6.6	6.5	8.8	9.4
Annualized growth rate of real money supply (M1) (percent per year)	−4.3	−6.9	−3.9	2.7	6.2
Government surplus (as a percent of GNP)	0.5	−1.3	−1.0	−3.5	−3.8
Annualized growth rate of real GNP (percent per year)	2.5	−0.2	1.9	−2.5	3.6
Dollar interest rate (percent per year, year average)	12.1	14.3	16.6	13.3	9.9
Dollar/DM exchange rate (dollars per DM, year average)	0.5452	0.5502	0.4419	0.4119	0.3916

Note: Data on nominal money growth come from Tables 20-2 and 20-5. Real money supply growth rate is calculated as nominal money supply growth less inflation, with inflation data taken from Tables 20-1 and 20-4. Government surplus is from Table 20-6. GNP growth rate is from International Monetary Fund, *World Economic Outlook*, April 1987. Interest rate is six-month London interbank offered rate, from World Bank, *World Development Report 1986*. Exchange rate is from *Economic Report of the President, 1988*.

United States in 1982. Together with a phased buildup of military spending, the 1981 tax cut (which took effect in stages starting in 1982) led to a sharply increased government budget deficit. Between 1981 and 1983 the deficit rose from 1.0 to 3.8 percent of GNP. (The relation of the government deficit to the large U.S. current account deficit that also emerged in the early 1980s was discussed in the Case Study in Chapter 13.)

Table 17-1 also shows the slowdown in monetary growth after 1979, which appears as a string of negative growth rates for the *real* money supply. The analysis of the previous section suggests that monetary contraction should result in a rise in the dollar interest rate, a fall in output, and a currency appreciation. The interest rate did, in fact, rise from 12.1 to 14.3 percent per year, while the growth rate of real GNP became negative (−0.2 percent per year in 1980).[11]

The table shows little change in the average dollar/DM exchange rate between 1979 and 1980. In fact, the large appreciation of the dollar against foreign currencies between 1980 and 1981 began at the end of 1980 as monetary growth became particularly restrictive and participants in the foreign exchange market became convinced that slow monetary growth would continue into the future.

Although the data show a relatively small change in the government surplus as a fraction of GNP between 1979 and 1981, the tax cuts legislated in 1981 affected expectations about future government deficits and exchange rates and therefore moved the exchange rate immediately. The dollar appreciated in 1981, as our model would predict. As already noted, tight monetary policy also pushed the dollar in this direction.

The dollar's appreciation, which came before the legislated fiscal expansion had come fully into force, reduced aggregate demand for U.S. output and helped contribute to a sharp decline in GNP in 1982 (when output fell by 2.5 percent). The other factor contributing to this fall in output was the continuing restrictive stance of monetary policy in the first half of the year. For 1982, we must be careful about interpreting the sharp increase in the government deficit ratio as indicating expansionary fiscal policy only. The high ratio of the deficit to GNP also reflects the fall in GNP as well as the fall in government tax receipts that always occurs in recessions when national income falls. In fact, the expansionary impact of fiscal policy really became strong only late in 1982 and in 1983.[12]

Responding to the deep slump, the Federal Reserve adopted a more expansionary

[11] The growth rate of output in 1980 was so low in part because of a series of oil price increases sparked by the Iranian revolution. These events are discussed more fully in Chapter 20.

[12] To measure the stance of fiscal policy in a way that does not depend on the condition of the economy, economists often calculate a *full-employment government budget surplus*. It is defined as the budget surplus that would have been observed, given tax rates and spending policies, had the economy been at full employment. For 1979–1983, the full-employment *federal* budget surplus (measured as a percentage of full-employment GNP) was as follows:

1979	*1980*	*1981*	*1982*	*1983*
−1.0	−1.6	−0.9	−1.8	−2.7

Notice that these numbers, unlike those in the third row of Table 17-1, do not take account of the budget surpluses of U.S. state and local governments. They do, however, tell the same basic story about the direction of U.S. fiscal policy. The source for the full-employment surplus estimates is Robert J. Gordon, *Macroeconomics*, 4th ed. (Boston: Little, Brown, 1987), pp. 583–587.

monetary policy in the second half of 1982 and in 1983. As our theory would predict, the interest rate fell sharply (from 13.3 to 9.9 percent) and output expanded (at a 3.6 percent rate) in 1983. Continuing fiscal expansion strengthened the dollar further, but because monetary growth was so rapid, the dollar appreciated by an amount smaller than in the previous two years.[13]

Gradual Trade Flow Adjustment and Current Account Dynamics

An important assumption underlying the *DD-AA* model is that other things equal, a real depreciation of the home currency immediately improves the current account while a real appreciation causes the current account immediately to worsen. In reality, however, the behavior underlying trade flows may be far more complex than we have so far suggested, involving dynamic elements—on the supply as well as the demand side—that lead the current account to adjust only gradually to exchange rate changes. In this section we discuss some dynamic factors that seem important in explaining actual patterns of current account adjustment and indicate how their presence might modify the predictions of our model.

THE J-CURVE

It is often observed that a country's current account *worsens* immediately after a real currency depreciation and begins to improve only some months later, contrary to the assumption we made in deriving the *DD* curve. If the current account initially worsens after a depreciation, its time path, shown in Figure 17-18, has an initial segment reminiscent of a *J* and therefore called the **J-curve.**

The current account, measured in domestic output, can deteriorate sharply right after a real currency depreciation (the move from point 1 to point 2 in the figure) because most import and export orders are placed several months in advance. In the first few months after the depreciation, export and import volumes therefore may reflect buying decisions that were made on the basis of the old real exchange rate: the primary effect of the depreciation is to raise the value of the precontracted level of imports in terms of domestic products. Because exports measured in domestic output do not change while imports measured in domestic output rise, there is an initial fall in the current account, as shown.

Even after the old export and import contracts have been fulfilled, it still takes time for new shipments to adjust fully to the relative price change. On the production side, producers of exports may have to install additional plant and equipment and hire new workers. To the extent that imports consist of intermediate materials used in

[13] The expansion of 1983 helped set off a 1984 boom in investment demand. The resulting increase in aggregate demand helps explain a fact mentioned in this chapter's introduction—the rapid rise in U.S. GNP that accompanied the dollar's further 1984 appreciation. A slump accompanied the dollar's 1980–1982 appreciation because the appreciation was caused by different factors than the appreciation of 1984—tight money and expected *future* fiscal expansion.

FIGURE 17-18
The J-curve.
The J-curve describes the time lag with which a real currency depreciation improves the current account.

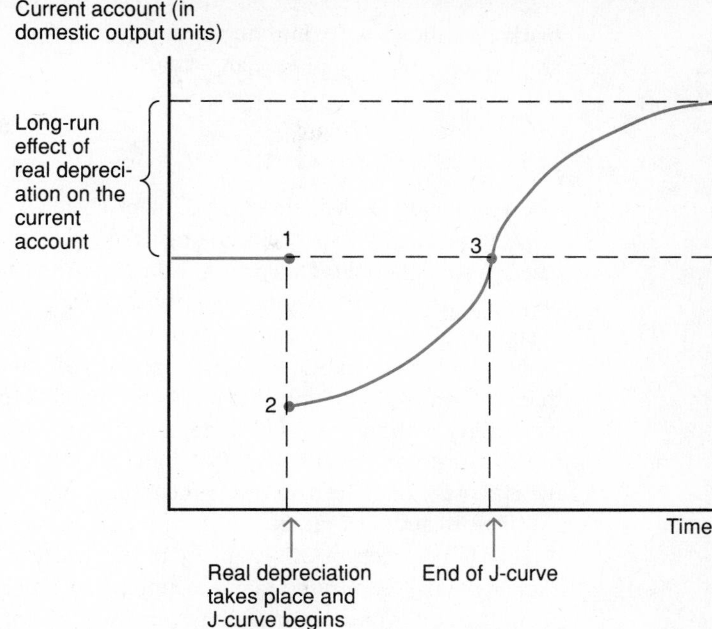

domestic manufacturing, import adjustment will also occur gradually as importers switch to new production techniques that economize on intermediate inputs. There are lags on the consumption side as well. To expand significantly foreign consumption of domestic exports, for example, it may be necessary to build new retailing outlets abroad, a time-consuming process.

The result of these lags in adjustment is the gradually improving current account shown in Figure 17-18 as the move from point 2 to point 3. Only after point 3 does the current account exceed its predepreciation level. Eventually, the increase in the current account tapers off as the adjustment to the real depreciation is completed.

Empirical evidence indicates for most industrial countries a J-curve lasting more than six months but less than a year. Thus, point 3 in the figure is typically reached within a year of the real depreciation and the current account continues to improve afterward.[14]

The existence of a significant J-curve effect forces us to modify some of our earlier conclusions, at least for the short run of a year or less. Monetary expansion, for example, can depress output initially by depreciating the home currency. In this case, it may take some time before an increase in the money supply results in an improved current account and therefore in higher aggregate demand.

If expansionary monetary policy actually depresses output in the short run, the domestic interest rate will need to fall further than it normally would to clear the home

[14] See the discussion of Table 17AII-1 in Appendix II.

money market. Correspondingly, the exchange rate will overshoot more sharply to create the larger expected domestic currency appreciation required for foreign exchange market equilibrium. By introducing an additional source of overshooting, J-curve effects amplify the volatility of exchange rates.

THE BEACHHEAD EFFECT

The picture of gradual trade adjustment sketched above is one in which firms can always marginally expand or contract their production and marketing facilities dedicated to foreign trade. This picture is inaccurate as a general rule because firms starting an export or import venture often must incur considerable *sunk costs*—one-time investments that must be made before even a small volume of overseas transactions can be undertaken profitably. A French exporter of mineral water, for example, may need to conduct a large, one-time advertising campaign to establish a beachhead in the U.S. market. By withdrawing even temporarily from that market, however, the exporter loses his investment as Americans forget about his product. A subsequent decision to re-enter the U.S. will force the exporter to incur the sunk cost of a ''media blitz'' all over again.

This **beachhead effect,** the tendency for sunk costs to deter firms from abandoning established markets or entering new ones, clearly slows the response of trade flows to exchange rates. Returning to our example, the French exporter may have established a position in the American sparkling water market when the dollar was strong and French products could be sold in the United States at high franc prices. Having incurred a sunk cost in the past, however, the exporter may find it profitable to continue selling in the United States even after a big depreciation of the dollar against the franc; and he will be reluctant to leave the American market and thus lose the sunk investment until he is quite sure he will not want to re-enter in the near future. The dollar will have to depreciate far beyond the point at which exporters first entered, and remain there for some time, before the supply of French mineral water to the U.S. dries up.

Beachhead effects due to sunk costs result in a lower responsiveness of trade flows to exchange rate changes than would be implied by less extreme forms of adjustment cost. Indeed, beachhead effects may even lead to exchange rate ranges within which the decisions of trading firms do not respond at all to exchange rates.[15]

EXCHANGE RATE PASS-THROUGH AND INFLATION

Our discussion of how the current account is determined in the *DD-AA* model has assumed that nominal exchange rate changes cause proportional changes in real exchange rates in the short run. Because the *DD-AA* model assumes that the nominal output prices P and P^* cannot suddenly jump, movements in the real exchange rate, $q = EP^*/P$, correspond perfectly in the short run to movements in the nominal rate, E. In reality, however, even the short-run correspondence between nominal and real exchange rate movements, while quite close, is less than perfect. To understand fully how *nominal* exchange rate movements affect the current account in the short run, we

[15] A general implication of adjustment costs is that *permanent* real exchange rate changes are likely to have stronger current account effects than *temporary* changes. A more sophisticated model than the one we have analyzed would, at the very least, add the expected long-run real exchange rate to the list of determinants of the current account.

need to examine more closely the linkage between the nominal exchange rate and the prices of exports and imports.

The domestic currency price of foreign output is the product of the exchange rate and the foreign currency price, or EP^*. We have assumed until now that when E rises, for example, P^* remains fixed so that the domestic currency price of goods imported from abroad rises in proportion. The percentage by which import prices rise when the home currency depreciates by one percent is known as the degree of **pass-through** from the exchange rate to import prices. In the version of the *DD-AA* model we studied above, the degree of pass-through is 1; any exchange rate change is passed through completely to import prices.

Contrary to this assumption, however, exchange rate pass-through can be incomplete. One possible reason for incomplete pass-through is international market segmentation, which allows imperfectly competitive firms to charge different prices for the same product in different countries. A large foreign firm supplying automobiles to the United States may be so worried about losing market share that it does not immediately raise its U.S. prices by 10 percent when the dollar depreciates by 10 percent, despite the fact that its revenue from American sales, measured in its own currency, will decline. Similarly, the firm may hesitate to lower its U.S. prices by 10 percent after a dollar appreciation of that size because it can thereby earn higher profits without investing resources immediately in expanding its shipments to the U.S. In either case the firm may wait to find out if the currency movement reflects a definite trend before making price and production commitments that are costly to undo.

We thus see that while a permanent nominal exchange rate change may be fully reflected in import prices in the long run, the degree of pass-through may be far less than 1 in the short run. Incomplete pass-through will have complicated effects, however, on the timing of current account adjustment. On the one hand, the short-run J-curve effect of a nominal currency change will be dampened by a low responsiveness of import prices to the exchange rate. On the other hand, incomplete pass-through implies that currency movements have less-than-proportional effects on the relative prices determining trade volumes. The failure of relative prices to adjust quickly will in turn be accompanied by a slow adjustment of trade volumes.

Notice also how the link between nominal and real exchange rates may be further weakened by *domestic* price responses. In highly inflationary economies, for example, it is difficult to alter the real exchange rate EP^*/P simply by changing the nominal rate E, because the resulting increase in aggregate demand quickly sparks domestic inflation, which in turn raises P. To the extent that a country's export prices rise when its currency depreciates, any favorable effect on its competitive position in world markets will be dissipated. Such price increases, however, like partial pass-through, may weaken the J-curve.

Summary

1. The *aggregate demand* for an open economy's output consists of four components, corresponding to the four components of GNP: consumption demand, investment demand, government demand, and the current account (net export demand). An

important determinant of the current account is the real exchange rate, the ratio of the foreign price level (measured in domestic currency) to the domestic price level.

2. Output is determined in the short run by the equality of aggregate demand and aggregate supply. When aggregate demand is greater than output, firms increase production to avoid unintended inventory depletion. When aggregate demand is less than output, firms cut back production to avoid unintended accumulation of inventories.

3. The economy's short-run equilibrium occurs at the exchange rate and output level where—given the price level, the expected future exchange rate, and foreign economic conditions—aggregate demand equals aggregate supply and the asset markets are in equilibrium. In a diagram with the exchange rate and real output on its axes, the short-run equilibrium can be visualized as the intersection of an upward-sloping *DD* schedule, along which the output market clears, and a downward-sloping *AA* schedule, along which the asset markets clear.

4. A temporary increase in the money supply, which does not alter the long-run expected exchange rate, causes a depreciation of the currency and a rise in output. Temporary fiscal expansion also results in a rise in output, but it causes the currency to appreciate. *Monetary policy* and *fiscal policy* can be used by the government to offset the effects of disturbances to output and employment.

5. Permanent shifts in the money supply, which do alter the long-run expected exchange rate, cause sharper exchange rate movements and therefore have stronger short-run effects on output than transitory shifts. If the economy is at full employment, a permanent increase in the money supply leads to a rising price level that ultimately reverses the effect on the real exchange rate of the nominal exchange rate's initial depreciation. In the long run, output returns to its initial level and all money prices rise in proportion to the increase in the money supply.

6. Because permanent fiscal expansion changes the long-run expected exchange rate, it causes a sharper currency appreciation than an equal temporary expansion. If the economy starts out in long-run equilibrium, the additional appreciation makes domestic goods and services so expensive that the resulting ''crowding out'' of net export demand nullifies the policy's effect on output and employment. In this case, a permanent fiscal expansion has no expansionary effect at all.

7. If exports and imports adjust gradually to real exchange rate changes, the current account may follow a *J-curve* pattern after a real currency depreciation, first worsening and then improving. If such a J-curve exists, currency depreciation may have a contractionary initial effect on output, and exchange rate overshooting will be amplified. *Beachhead effects* accentuate the J-curve by slowing firms' responses to exchange rate changes. Limited exchange rate *pass-through,* along with domestic price increases, may reduce the effect of a nominal exchange rate change on the real exchange rate.

Key Terms

aggregate demand
monetary policy
fiscal policy
J-curve
beachhead effect
pass-through

Problems

1. How does the *DD* schedule shift if there is a decline in investment demand?
2. Suppose the government imposes a tariff on all imports. Use the *DD-AA* model to analyze the effects this measure would have on the economy. Analyze both temporary and permanent tariffs.
3. Imagine that Congress passes a constitutional amendment requiring the U.S. government to maintain a balanced budget at all times. Thus, if the government wishes to change government spending, it must change taxes by the same amount, that is, $\Delta G = \Delta T$ always. Does the constitutional amendment imply that the government can no longer use fiscal policy to affect employment and output? (Hint: Analyze a ''balanced-budget'' increase in government spending, one that is accompanied by an equal tax hike.)
4. Suppose there is a permanent fall in private aggregate demand for a country's output (a downward shift of the entire aggregate demand schedule). What is the effect on output? What government policy response would you recommend?
5. How does a permanent cut in taxes affect the current account? What about a permanent increase in government spending? Reread the first Case Study in Chapter 13 and see if your answer accurately reflects the U.S. experience in the early 1980s.
6. If a government initially has a balanced budget but then cuts taxes, it is running a deficit that it must somehow finance. Suppose people think the government will finance its deficit by printing the extra money it now needs to cover its expenditures. Would you still expect the tax cut to cause a currency appreciation?
7. You observe that a country's currency depreciates but its current account worsens at the same time. What data might you look at to decide whether you are witnessing a J-curve effect? What other macroeconomic change might bring about a currency depreciation coupled with a deterioration of the current account, even if there is no J-curve?
8. A new government is elected and announces that once it is inaugurated, it will increase the money supply. Use the *DD-AA* model to study the economy's response to this announcement.
9. Many economists put part of the blame for the persistent U.S. current account deficit of the late 1980s on the apparently small size of the relative price change between U.S. imports and exports. The first Case Study in Chapter 13, however, linked the slow current account adjustment to private and government saving behavior. Try to give a unified account of the current account data, reconciling both price and expenditure effects.
10. How would you draw the *DD-AA* diagram when the current account's response to exchange rate changes follows a J-curve? Use this modified diagram to examine the effects of temporary and permanent changes in monetary and fiscal policy.
11. What does the Marshall-Lerner condition look like if the country whose real exchange rate changes does *not* start out with a current account of zero? (The Marshall-Lerner condition is derived in Appendix II under the ''standard'' assumption of an initially balanced current account.)

12. Our model takes the price level P as given in the short run, but in reality the currency appreciation caused by a permanent fiscal expansion might cause P to fall a bit by lowering some import prices. If P can fall slightly as a result of a permanent fiscal expansion, is it still true that there are no output effects? (As above, assume an initial long-run equilibrium.)
13. Suppose that interest parity does not hold exactly, but that the true relationship is $R = R^* + (E^e - E)/E + \rho$ where ρ is a term measuring the differential riskiness of domestic versus foreign deposits. Suppose a permanent rise in domestic government spending, by creating the prospect of future government deficits, also raises ρ, that is, makes domestic currency deposits more risky. Evaluate the policy's output effects in this situation.
14. If an economy does *not* start out at full employment, is it still true that a permanent change in fiscal policy has no current effect on output?
15. See if you can retrace the steps in the five-step argument on p. 459 to show that a permanent fiscal expansion cannot cause output to *fall.*

Further Reading

Victor Argy and Michael G. Porter. "The Forward Exchange Market and the Effects of Domestic and External Disturbances under Alternative Exchange Rate Systems." *International Monetary Fund Staff Papers* 19 (November 1972), pp. 503–532. Advanced analysis of a macroeconomic model similar to the one in this chapter.

Victor Argy and Joanne K. Salop. "Price and Output Effects of Monetary and Fiscal Policies under Flexible Exchange Rates." *International Monetary Fund Staff Papers* 26 (June 1979), pp. 224–256. The effects of macroeconomic policies under alternative institutional assumptions about wage indexation and the wage-price adjustment process in general.

Richard E. Baldwin. "Hysteresis in Import Prices: The Beachhead Effect." *American Economic Review* 78 (September 1988), pp. 773–785. Theoretical and empirical investigation of beachhead effects in recent U.S. trade balance adjustment.

Ralph C. Bryant et al., eds. *Empirical Macroeconomics for Interdependent Economies.* Washington, D.C.: Brookings Institution, 1988. This study compares what twelve leading econometric models predict about the domestic and foreign effects of individual countries' macroeconomic policies.

Rudiger Dornbusch. "Exchange Rate Expectations and Monetary Policy." *Journal of International Economics* 6 (August 1976), pp. 231–244. A formal examination of monetary policy and the exchange rate in a model with a J-curve.

Rudiger Dornbusch and Paul Krugman. "Flexible Exchange Rates in the Short Run." *Brookings Papers on Economic Activity* 3:1976, pp. 537–575. Theory and evidence on short-run macroeconomic adjustment under floating exchange rates.

Jacob A. Frenkel and Assaf Razin. "The Mundell-Fleming Model a Quarter Century Later: A Unified Exposition." *International Monetary Fund Staff Papers* 34 (December 1987), pp. 567–620. Further variations and background on models like the ones this chapter studies.

Morris Goldstein and Mohsin S. Khan. "Income and Price Effects in International Trade," in Ronald W. Jones and Peter B. Kenen, eds. *Handbook of International Economics,* Vol. 2. Amsterdam: North-Holland Publishing Company, 1985. Surveys empirical work on the macroeconomic determinants of trade balances.

Paul R. Krugman. "Pricing to Market When the Exchange Rate Changes," in Sven W. Arndt and J. David Richardson, eds. *Real-Financial Linkages among Open Economies.* Cambridge: MIT Press, 1987, pp. 49–70. Theoretical discussion of interactions between exchange rates and import prices.

Robert Z. Lawrence. ''U.S. Current Account Adjustment: An Appraisal.'' *Brookings Papers on Economic Activity* 2:1990, pp. 343–392. Thorough statistical analysis of U.S. current account behavior in the late 1980s.

Rachel McCulloch. ''Macroeconomic Policy and Trade Performance: International Implications of U.S. Budget Deficits,'' in Robert E. Baldwin, Carl B. Hamilton, and André Sapir, eds. *Issues in US-EC Trade Relations.* Chicago: University of Chicago Press, 1988, pp. 349–368. An account of macroeconomic influences on U.S. competitiveness and trade.

Ellen E. Meade. ''Exchange Rates, Adjustment, and the J-Curve.'' *Federal Reserve Bulletin* 74 (October 1988), pp. 633–644. Analyzes J-curve effects in the U.S. current account response to the dollar's depreciation between early 1985 and 1988.

Robert A. Mundell. *International Economics,* Chapter 17. New York: Macmillan, 1968. A classic account of macroeconomic policy effects under floating exchange rates.

Appendix I to Chapter 17 ●
The *IS-LM* Model and the *DD-AA* Model

In this appendix we examine the relationship between the *DD-AA* model of the chapter and another model frequently used to answer questions in international macroeconomics, the *IS-LM* model. The *IS-LM* model generalizes the *DD-AA* model by allowing the real domestic interest rate to affect aggregate demand.

The diagram usually used to analyze the *IS-LM* model has the nominal interest rate and output, rather than the nominal exchange rate and output, on its axes. Like the *DD-AA* diagram, the *IS-LM* diagram determines the short-run equilibrium of the economy as the intersection of two individual market equilibrium curves, called *IS* and *LM*. The *IS* curve is the schedule of nominal interest rates and output levels at which the output and foreign exchange markets are in equilibrium, while the *LM* curve shows points at which the money market is in equilibrium.[1]

The *IS-LM* model assumes that investment, and some forms of consumer purchases (such as purchases of autos and other durable goods), are negatively related to the expected real interest rate. When the expected real interest rate is low, firms find it profitable to borrow and undertake investment plans. (The appendix to Chapter 7 presented a model of this link between investment and the real interest rate.) A low expected real interest rate also makes it more profitable to carry inventories rather than alternative assets. For both these reasons, we would expect investment to rise when the expected real interest rate falls. Similarly, because consumers find borrowing cheap and saving unattractive when the real interest rate is low, interest-responsive consumer purchases also rise when the real interest rate falls.

In the *IS-LM* model, aggregate demand is therefore written as a function of the real exchange rate, disposable income, *and* the real interest rate,

$$D(EP^*/P, Y - T, R - \pi^e)$$
$$= C(Y - T, R - \pi^e) + I(R - \pi^e) + G + CA(EP^*/P, Y - T, R - \pi^e),$$

where π^e is the expected inflation rate and $R - \pi^e$ therefore the expected real interest rate. The model assumes that P, P^*, G, T, R^*, and E^e are all given. (To simplify the notation, we've left G out of the aggregate demand function D.)

To find the *IS* curve of R and Y combinations such that aggregate demand equals output,

$$Y = D(EP^*/P, Y - T, R - \pi^e),$$

we must first write this output market equilibrium condition so that it does not depend on E.

We solve for E using the interest parity condition, $R = R^* + (E^e - E)/E$. If we solve this equation for E, the result is

$$E = E^e/(1 + R - R^*).$$

Substitution of this expression into the aggregate demand function shows that we can express the condition for output market equilibrium as

$$Y = D[E^eP^*/P(1 + R - R^*), Y - T, R - \pi^e].$$

[1] In a closed-economy context, the original exposition of the *IS-LM* model is in J. R. Hicks, "Mr. Keynes and the 'Classics': A Suggested Interpretation," *Econometrica* 5 (April 1937), pp. 147–159. Hicks's article still makes enjoyable and instructive reading today. The name *IS* comes from the fact that in a closed economy (but not necessarily in an open economy!) the output market is in equilibrium when investment (I) and saving (S) are equal. Along the *LM* schedule, real money demand (L) equals the real money supply (M^s/P in our notation).

To get a complete picture of how output changes affect goods market equilibrium, we must remember that the inflation rate in the economy depends positively on the gap between actual output, Y, and full employment output, Y^f. We therefore write π^e as an increasing function of that gap:

$$\pi^e = \pi^e(Y - Y^f).$$

Under this assumption on expectations, the goods market is in equilibrium when

$$Y = D[E^eP^*/P(1 + R - R^*), Y - T, R - \pi^e(Y - Y^f)].$$

This condition shows that a fall in the nominal interest rate R raises aggregate demand through two channels: (1) Given the expected future exchange rate, a fall in R causes a domestic currency depreciation that improves the current account. (2) Given expected inflation, a fall in R directly encourages consumption and investment spending that falls only partly on imports. Only the second of these channels—the effect of the interest rate on spending—would be present in a closed-economy *IS-LM* model.

The *IS* curve is found by asking how output must respond to such a fall in the interest rate to maintain output market equilibrium. Since a fall in R raises aggregate demand, the output market will remain in equilibrium after R falls only if Y rises. The *IS* curve therefore slopes downward, as shown in Figure 17AI-1. Even though the *IS* and *DD* curves both reflect output market equilibrium, *IS* slopes downward while *DD* slopes upward. The reason for this difference is that the interest rate and the exchange rate are inversely related by the interest parity condition, given the expected future exchange rate.[2]

The slope of the *LM* (or money market equilibrium) curve is much easier to derive. Money market equilibrium holds when $M^s/P = L(R, Y)$. Because a rise in the interest rate reduces money demand, it results in an excess supply of money for a given output level. To maintain equilibrium in the money market after R rises, Y must therefore rise also (because a rise in output stimulates

[2] In concluding that *IS* has a negative slope, we have argued that a rise in output reduces the excess demand for output caused by a fall in R. This reduction in excess demand occurs because while consumption demand rises with a rise in output, it rises by less. Notice, however, that a rise in output also raises expected inflation and thus stimulates demand. So it is conceivable that a fall in output, not a rise, eliminates excess demand in the output market. We assume this perverse possibility (which would give an upward-sloping *IS* curve) does not arise.

FIGURE 17AI-1
Short-run equilibrium in the *IS-LM* model.
Equilibrium is at point 1, where the output and asset markets simultaneously clear.

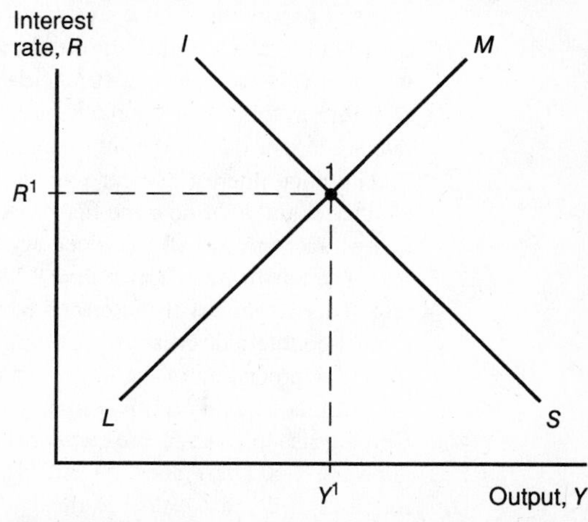

FIGURE 17AI-2
Effects of permanent and temporary increases in the money supply in the *IS-LM* model.
A temporary increase in the money supply shifts the *LM* curve alone to the right, but a permanent increase shifts both the *IS* and *LM* curves in that direction.

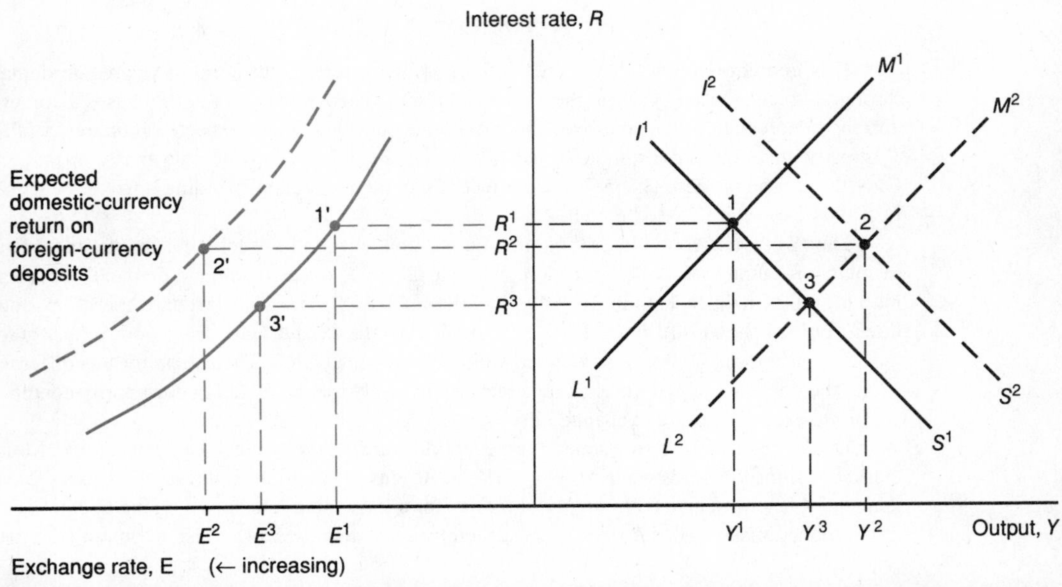

the transactions demand for money). The *LM* curve thus has a positive slope, as shown in Figure 17AI-1. The intersection of the *IS* and *LM* curves at point 1 determines the short-run equilibrium values of output, Y^1, and the nominal interest rate, R^1. The equilibrium interest rate, in turn, determines a short-run equilibrium exchange rate through the interest parity condition.

The *IS-LM* model can be used to analyze the effects of monetary and fiscal policies. A temporary increase in the money supply, for example, shifts *LM* to the right, lowering the interest rate and expanding output. A *permanent* increase in the money supply, however, shifts *LM* to the right but also shifts *IS* to the right, since in an open economy that schedule depends on E^e, which now rises. The right-hand side of Figure 17AI-2 shows these shifts. At the new short-run equilibrium following a permanent increase in the money supply (point 2), output and the interest rate are higher than at the short-run equilibrium (point 3) following an equal temporary increase. The nominal interest rate can even be higher at point 2 than at point 1. This possibility provides another example of how the Fisher expected inflation effect of Chapter 16 can push the nominal interest rate upward after a monetary expansion.

The left-hand side of Figure 17AI-2 shows how the monetary changes affect the exchange rate. This is our usual picture of equilibrium in the foreign exchange market, but it has been rotated counterclockwise so that a movement to the left along the horizontal axis is an increase in *E* (a depreciation of the home currency). The interest rate R^2 following a permanent increase in the money supply implies foreign exchange market equilibrium at point 2′, since the accompanying rise in E^e shifts the curve that measures the expected domestic currency return on foreign deposits. That curve does not shift if the money supply increase is temporary, so the equilibrium interest rate R^3 that results in this case leads to foreign exchange equilibrium at point 3′.

FIGURE 17AI-3
Effects of permanent and temporary fiscal expansions in the *IS-LM* model.
Temporary fiscal expansion has a positive effect on output while permanent fiscal expansion has none.

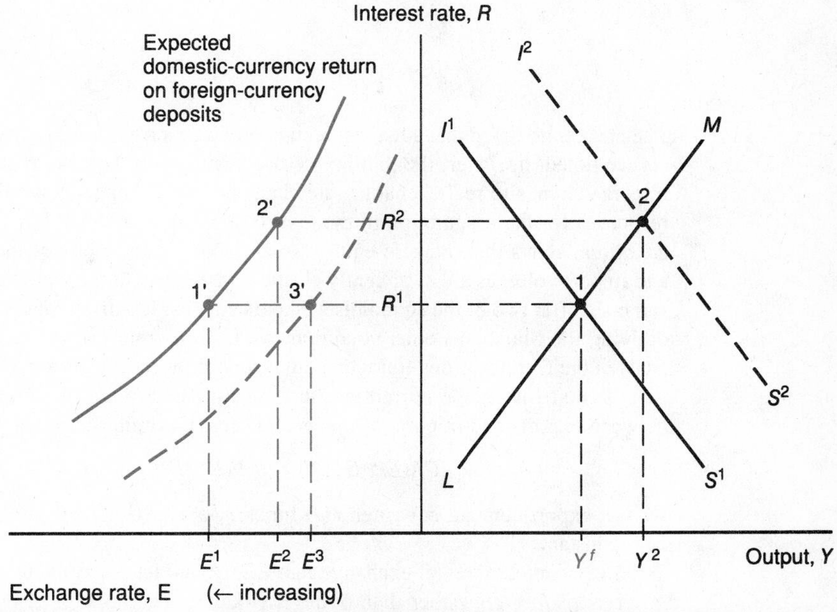

Fiscal policy is analyzed in Figure 17AI-3, which assumes a long-run equilibrium starting point. A temporary increase in government spending, for example, shifts I^1S^1 to the right but has no effect on *LM*. The new short-run equilibrium at point 2 shows a rise in output and a rise in the nominal interest rate, while the foreign exchange market equilibrium at point 2′ indicates a temporary currency appreciation. A permanent increase in government spending causes a fall in the long-run equilibrium exchange rate and thus a fall in E^e. The *IS* curve therefore does not shift out as much as in the case of a temporary policy. In fact, it does not shift at all: as in the *DD-AA* model, *a permanent fiscal expansion has no effect on output or the home interest rate.* The reason why permanent fiscal policy moves are weaker than transitory can be seen in the figure's left-hand side (point 3′). The accompanying change in exchange rate expectations generates a sharper currency appreciation and thus, through the response of net exports, a complete ''crowding out'' effect on aggregate demand.[3]

[3] One way the *IS-LM* model differs from the *DD-AA* model is that in the former, monetary expansion can cause a deterioration of the current account (even when there are no J-curve effects) by lowering the real interest rate and thus encouraging domestic spending. We leave it to the interested student to derive the *IS-LM* version of this chapter's *XX* curve.

Appendix II to Chapter 17 ●
The Marshall-Lerner Condition and Empirical Estimates of Trade Elasticities

The chapter assumed that a real depreciation of a country's currency improves its current account. As we noted, however, the validity of this assumption depends on the response of export and import volumes to real exchange rate changes. In this appendix we derive a condition on those responses for the assumption in the text to be valid. The condition, called the *Marshall-Lerner condition,* states that, all else equal, a real depreciation improves the current account if export and import volumes are sufficiently elastic with respect to the real exchange rate. (The condition is named after two of the economists who discovered it, Alfred Marshall and Abba Lerner.) After deriving the Marshall-Lerner condition, we look at empirical estimates of trade elasticities and analyze their implications for actual current account responses to real exchange rate changes.

To start, write the current account, measured in domestic output units, as the difference between exports and imports of goods and services similarly measured:

$$CA(EP^*/P, Y^d) = EX(EP^*/P) - IM(EP^*/P, Y^d).$$

Above, export demand is written as a function of EP^*/P alone because foreign income is being held constant.

Let q denote the real exchange rate EP^*/P and let EX^* denote domestic imports measured in terms of *foreign,* rather than domestic, output. The notation EX^* is used because domestic imports from abroad, measured in foreign output, equal the volume of foreign exports to the home country. If we identify q with the price of foreign products in terms of domestic products, then IM and EX^* are related by

$$IM = q \times EX^*,$$

that is, imports measured in domestic output = (domestic output units/foreign output unit) × (imports measured in foreign output units).[1]

The current account can therefore be expressed as

$$CA(q, Y^d) = EX(q) - q \times EX^*(q, Y^d).$$

Now let EX_q stand for the effect of a rise in q (a real depreciation) on export demand and let EX^*_q stand for the effect of a rise in q on import volume. Thus,

$$EX_q = \Delta EX/\Delta q, \quad EX^*_q = \Delta EX^*/\Delta q.$$

As we saw in the chapter, EX_q is positive (a real depreciation makes home products relatively cheaper and stimulates exports) while EX^*_q is negative (a relative cheapening of home products

[1] As we warned earlier in the chapter, the identification of the real exchange rate with relative output prices is not quite exact since, as we defined it, the real exchange rate is the relative price of expenditure baskets. For most practical purposes, however, the discrepancy is not qualitatively important. A more serious problem with our analysis is that national outputs consist in part of nontradables, and the real exchange rate covers their prices as well as those of tradables. To avoid the additional complexity that would result from a more detailed treatment of the composition of national outputs, we assume in deriving the Marshall-Lerner condition that the real exchange rate can be approximately identified with the relative price of imports in terms of exports.

reduces domestic import demand). Using these definitions, we can now ask how a rise in q affects the current account, all else equal.

If superscript ^{1} indicates the initial value of a variable while superscript ^{2} indicates its value after q has changed by $\Delta q = q^2 - q^1$, then the change in the current account caused by a real exchange rate change Δq is

$$\begin{aligned}\Delta CA &= CA^2 - CA^1 = (EX^2 - q^2 \times EX^{*2}) - (EX^1 - q^1 \times EX^{*1}) \\ &= \Delta EX - (q^2 \times \Delta EX^*) - (\Delta q \times EX^{*1}).\end{aligned}$$

Dividing through by Δq gives the current account's response to a change in q,

$$\Delta CA/\Delta q = EX_q - (q^2 \times EX^*_q) - EX^{*1}.$$

This equation summarizes the two current account effects of a real depreciation discussed in the text, the *volume* effect and the *value* effect. The terms involving EX_q and EX^*_q represent the volume effect, the effect of the change in q on the number of output units exported and imported. These terms are always positive because $EX_q > 0$ and $EX^*_q < 0$. The last term above, EX^{*1}, represents the value effect, and it is preceded by a minus sign. This last term tells us that a rise in q worsens the current account to the extent that it raises the domestic output value of the initial volume of imports.

We are interested in knowing when the right-hand side of the equation above is positive, so that a real depreciation causes the current account balance to increase. To answer this question, we first define the *elasticity of export demand* with respect to q,

$$\eta = (q^1/EX^1)EX_q,$$

and the *elasticity of import demand* with respect to q,

$$\eta^* = -(q^1/EX^{*1})EX^*_q.$$

(The definition of η^* involves a minus sign because $EX^*_q < 0$ and we are defining trade elasticities as positive numbers.) Returning to our equation for $\Delta CA/\Delta q$, we multiply its right-hand side by (q^1/EX^1) to express it in terms of trade elasticities. Then if the current account is initially zero (that is, $EX^1 = q^1 \times EX^{*1}$), this last step shows that $\Delta CA/\Delta q$ is positive when

$$\eta + (q^2/q^1)\eta^* - 1 > 0.$$

If the change in q is assumed to be small, so that $q^2 \approx q^1$, the condition for an increase in q to improve the current account is

$$\eta + \eta^* > 1.$$

This is the Marshall-Lerner condition. The condition states that if the current account is initially zero, a real currency depreciation causes a current account surplus if the sum of the relative price elasticities of export and import demand exceeds 1. (If the current account is not zero initially, the condition becomes substantially more complex.) In applying the Marshall-Lerner condition, remember that its derivation assumes that disposable income is held constant when q changes.

Now that we have the Marshall-Lerner condition, we can ask whether empirical estimates of trade equations imply price elasticities consistent with this chapter's assumption that a real exchange rate depreciation improves the current account. Table 17AII-1 presents International Monetary Fund elasticity estimates for trade in manufactured goods. The table reports export and import price elasticities measured over three successively longer time horizons, and thus allows for the possibility that export and import demands adjust gradually to relative price changes, as in our discussion of the J-curve and beachhead effects. "Impact" elasticities measure the response of trade flows to relative price changes in the first six months after the change; "short-run" elasticities apply to a one-year adjustment period; and "long-run" elasticities measure the response of trade flows to the price changes over a hypothetical infinite adjustment period.

TABLE 17AII-1 Estimated price elasticities for international trade in manufactured goods

	η			η^*		
Country	*Impact*	*Short-run*	*Long-run*	*Impact*	*Short-run*	*Long-run*
Austria	0.39	0.71	1.37	0.03	0.36	0.80
Belgium	0.18	0.59	1.55	—	—	0.70
Britain	—	—	0.31	0.60	0.75	0.75
Canada	0.08	0.40	0.71	0.72	0.72	0.72
Denmark	0.82	1.13	1.13	0.55	0.93	1.14
France	0.20	0.48	1.25	—	0.49	0.60
Germany	—	—	1.41	0.57	0.77	0.77
Italy	—	0.56	0.64	0.94	0.94	0.94
Japan	0.59	1.01	1.61	0.16	0.72	0.97
Netherlands	0.24	0.49	0.89	0.71	1.22	1.22
Norway	0.40	0.74	1.49	—	0.01	0.71
Sweden	0.27	0.73	1.59	—	—	0.94
Switzerland	0.28	0.42	0.73	0.25	0.25	0.25
United States	0.18	0.48	1.67	—	1.06	1.06

Note: Estimates are taken from Jacques R. Artus and Malcolm D. Knight, *Issues in the Assessment of the Exchange Rates of Industrial Countries,* Occasional Paper 29. Washington, D.C.: International Monetary Fund, July 1984, Table 4. Unavailable estimates are indicated by dashes.

For most countries, the impact elasticities are so small that the sum of the impact export and import elasticities is less than 1. Since the impact elasticities usually fail to satisfy the Marshall-Lerner condition, the estimates support the existence of an initial J-curve effect that causes the real current account to deteriorate immediately following a real depreciation.

It is also true, however, that most countries represented in the table satisfy the Marshall-Lerner condition in the short run and that virtually all do so in the long run. The evidence is therefore consistent with the assumption made in the chapter: except over short time periods, a real depreciation is likely to improve the current account while a real appreciation is likely to worsen it.

Fixed Exchange Rates and Foreign Exchange Intervention

Chapter 18

In the past several chapters we have developed a model that helps us understand how a country's exchange rate and national income are determined by the interaction of asset and output markets. Using that model, we saw how monetary and fiscal policies can be used to maintain full employment and a stable price level.

To keep our discussion simple, we assumed that exchange rates are *completely* flexible, that is, that national monetary authorities themselves do not trade in the foreign exchange market to influence exchange rates. In reality, however, the assumption of complete exchange rate flexibility is rarely accurate. As we mentioned earlier, the world economy operated under a system of *fixed* dollar exchange rates between the end of World War II and 1973, with central banks routinely trading foreign exchange to hold their exchange rates at internationally agreed levels. Industrialized countries now operate under a hybrid system of **managed floating exchange rates**—a system in which governments may attempt to moderate exchange rate movements without keeping exchange rates rigidly fixed. Most developing countries have retained some form of government exchange rate fixing, for reasons that we discuss in Chapter 23.

In this chapter we study how central banks intervene in the foreign exchange market to fix exchange rates and how macroeconomic policies work when exchange rates are fixed. The chapter will help us understand the role of central bank foreign exchange intervention in the determination of exchange rates under a system of managed floating.

Why Study Fixed Exchange Rates?

A discussion of fixed exchange rates may seem outdated in an era when newspaper headlines regularly highlight sharp changes in the exchange rates of the major industrial country currencies. Our interest in fixed exchange rates, however, is not the result of nostalgia, antiquarianism, or an unhealthy obsession with hypothetical worlds. There are four reasons why we must understand fixed exchange rates before analyzing contemporary macroeconomic policy problems:

1. *Managed floating.* As noted above, central banks often intervene in currency markets to influence exchange rates. So while the dollar exchange rates of the industrial countries' currencies are not currently fixed by governments, they are not left to fluctuate freely either. The system of floating dollar exchange rates is often referred to as a *dirty float,* to distinguish it from a *clean float* in which governments make no direct attempts to influence foreign currency values. (The model of the exchange rate developed in earlier chapters assumed a cleanly floating, or completely flexible, exchange rate.[1]) Because the present monetary system is a hybrid of the ''pure'' fixed and floating rate systems, an understanding of fixed exchange rates gives us insight into the effects of foreign exchange intervention when it occurs under floating rates.

2. *Regional currency arrangements.* Some countries belong to *exchange rate unions,* organizations whose members agree to fix their mutual exchange rates while allowing their currencies to fluctuate in value against the currencies of nonmember countries. The most important exchange rate union is the **European Monetary System (EMS),** which began operating in 1979 and whose members include France and Germany. Until August 1993, the DM and the French franc, for example, had a fixed relative price, but the prices of both of those currencies in terms of dollars could change from day to day. As this book is written, the EMS remains in a transitional managed float, but its core members hope to return to fixed exchange rates.

3. *Developing countries.* While industrial countries generally allow their currencies to float against the dollar, these economies account for less than a sixth of the world's countries. Almost all developing countries try to peg the values of their currencies, often in terms of the dollar, but sometimes in terms of a nondollar currency or some ''basket'' of currencies chosen by the authorities. Thailand pegs its currency to a basket, for example, while Argentina pegs to the U.S. dollar and Senegal pegs to the French franc. No examination of the problems of developing countries would get very far without taking into account the implications of fixed exchange rates.

4. *Lessons of the past for the future.* Fixed exchange rates were the norm in many periods, such as the decades before World War I, between the mid-1920s and 1931, and again between 1945 and 1973. Today, many economists and policy makers dissatisfied with floating exchange rates are proposing new international agreements that would resurrect some form of fixed-rate system. Would this plan benefit the world economy? Who would gain or lose from such a system? To compare the merits of fixed and floating exchange rates (the topic of Chapter 20), the functioning of fixed rates must be understood.

[1] It is questionable whether a truly clean float has ever existed in reality. Most government policies affect the exchange rate, and governments rarely undertake policies without considering their exchange rate implications.

Central Bank Intervention and the Money Supply

In Chapter 15 we defined an economy's money supply as the total amount of currency and checking deposits held by its households and firms and assumed that the central bank determined the amount of money in circulation. To understand the effects of central bank intervention in the foreign exchange market, we need to look first at how central bank financial transactions affect the money supply.[2]

THE CENTRAL BANK BALANCE SHEET

The main tool we will use in studying central bank transactions in asset markets is the **central bank balance sheet,** which records both the assets held by the central bank and its liabilities. Like any other balance sheet, the central bank balance sheet is organized according to the principles of double-entry bookkeeping. Any acquisition of an asset by the central bank results in a positive change on the assets side of the balance sheet, while any increase in the bank's liabilities results in a positive change on the balance sheet's liabilities side.

A balance sheet for the central bank of the imaginary country of Pecunia is shown below.

Central bank balance sheet

Assets		*Liabilities*	
Foreign assets	$1000	Deposits held by private banks	$500
Domestic assets	$1500	Currency in circulation	$2000

The assets side of the Bank of Pecunia's balance sheet lists two types of assets, *foreign assets* and *domestic assets.* Foreign assets consist mainly of foreign currency bonds owned by the central bank. These foreign assets make up the central bank's official international reserves, and their level changes when the central bank intervenes in the foreign exchange market by buying or selling foreign exchange. For historical reasons discussed later in this chapter, a central bank's international reserves also include any gold that it owns. The defining characteristic of international reserves is that they be either claims on foreigners or a universally acceptable means of making international payments (for example, gold). In the present example, the central bank's holdings of foreign assets are worth $1000.

Domestic assets are central bank holdings of claims to future payments by its own citizens and domestic institutions. These claims usually take the form of domestic government bonds and loans to domestic private banks. The Bank of Pecunia owns

[2] As we pointed out in Chapter 13, government agencies other than central banks may intervene in the foreign exchange market, but their intervention operations, unlike those of central banks, have no significant effect on national money supplies. (In the terminology introduced below, interventions by agencies other than central banks are automatically *sterilized.*) To simplify our discussion, we continue to assume, when the assumption is not misleading, that central banks alone carry out foreign exchange intervention.

$1500 in domestic assets. Its total assets therefore equal $2500, the sum of foreign and domestic asset holdings.

The liabilities side of the balance sheet lists as liabilities the deposits of private banks and currency in circulation, both notes and coin. (Nonbank firms and households generally cannot deposit money at the central bank, while banks are generally required by law to hold central bank deposits as partial backing for their own liabilities.) Private bank deposits are liabilities of the central bank because the money may be withdrawn whenever private banks need it. Currency in circulation is considered a central bank liability mainly for historical reasons: at one time, central banks were obliged to give a certain amount of gold or silver to anyone wishing to exchange domestic currency for one of those precious metals. The balance sheet above shows that Pecunia's private banks have deposited $500 at the central bank. Currency in circulation equals $2000, so the central bank's total liabilities amount to $2500.

The central bank's total assets equal its total liabilities plus its net worth, which we have assumed in the present example to be zero. Because changes in central bank net worth are not important to our analysis we will also ignore those.[3]

The additional assumption that net worth is constant means that the changes in central bank assets we will consider *automatically* cause equal changes in central bank liabilities. When the central bank purchases an asset, for example, it can pay for it in one of two ways. A cash payment raises the supply of currency in circulation by the amount of the bank's asset purchase. A payment by check promises the check's owner a central bank deposit equal in value to the asset's price. When the recipient of the check deposits it in her account at a private bank, the private bank's claims on the central bank (and thus the central bank's liabilities to private banks) rise by the same amount. In either case, the central bank's purchase of assets automatically causes an equal increase in its liabilities. Similarly, asset sales by the central bank involve either the withdrawal of currency from circulation or the reduction of private banks' claims on the central bank, and thus a fall in central bank liabilities to the private sector.

THE CENTRAL BANK BALANCE SHEET AND THE MONEY SUPPLY

The central bank balance sheet is so important because changes in the central bank's assets cause the domestic money supply to move in the same direction. Our discussion of the equality between changes in central bank assets and liabilities illustrates the mechanism at work.

When the central bank buys an asset from the public, for example, its payment—whether cash or check—directly enters the money supply. The increase in central bank liabilities associated with the asset purchase thus causes the money supply to expand. The money supply shrinks when the central bank sells an asset to the public because the cash or check the central bank receives in payment goes out of circulation, reducing the central bank's liabilities to the public. Changes in the level of central bank asset holdings cause the money supply to change in the same direction because they require equal changes in the central bank's liabilities.

[3] There are several ways in which a central bank's net worth could change. For example, the government might allow its central bank to keep a fraction of the interest earnings on its assets, and this interest flow would raise the bank's net worth if reinvested. Such changes in net worth tend to be small enough empirically that they can usually be ignored for purposes of macroeconomic analysis.

The process we have described may be familiar to you from studying central bank open-market operations in earlier courses. By definition, open-market operations involve the purchase or sale of domestic assets, but official transactions in foreign assets have the same direct effect on the money supply. You will also recall that when the central bank buys assets, for example, the accompanying increase in the money supply is generally *larger* than the initial asset purchase because of multiple deposit creation within the private banking system. This *money multiplier* effect, which magnifies the impact of central bank transactions on the money supply, reinforces our main conclusion: *Any central bank purchase of assets automatically results in an increase in the domestic money supply, while any central bank sale of assets automatically causes the money supply to decline.*[4]

FOREIGN EXCHANGE INTERVENTION AND THE MONEY SUPPLY

To see in greater detail how foreign exchange intervention affects the money supply, let's look at an example. Suppose the Bank of Pecunia goes to the foreign exchange market and sells $100 worth of foreign bonds for Pecunian money. The sale reduces official holdings of foreign assets from $1000 to $900, causing the assets side of the central bank balance sheet to shrink from $2500 to $2400.

The payment the Bank of Pecunia receives for these foreign assets automatically reduces its liabilities by $100 as well. If the Bank of Pecunia is paid with domestic currency, the currency goes into its vault and out of circulation. Currency in circulation therefore falls by $100. As a result of the foreign asset sale, the central bank's balance sheet changes as follows:

Central bank balance sheet after $100 foreign asset sale (buyer pays with currency)

Assets		*Liabilities*	
Foreign assets	$900	Deposits held by private banks	$500
Domestic assets	$1500	Currency in circulation	$1900

After the sale, assets still equal liabilities, but both have declined by $100, equal to the amount of currency the Bank of Pecunia has taken out of circulation through its intervention in the foreign exchange market. The change in the central bank's balance sheet implies a decline in the Pecunian money supply.

What happens if the buyer of the foreign assets pays the Bank of Pecunia with a $100 check drawn on an account at Pecuniacorp, a private domestic bank? The Bank of Pecunia debits $100 from Pecuniacorp's central bank account and Pecuniacorp debits

[4] For a detailed description of multiple deposit creation and the money multiplier, see Frederic S. Mishkin, *The Economics of Money, Banking and Financial Markets,* 3rd ed., Chapter 15 (New York: HarperCollins Publishers, 1992).

$100 from the buyer's checking account. Private bank deposits with the central bank fall by $100, and the Bank of Pecunia's balance sheet becomes as shown below.

Central bank balance sheet after $100 foreign asset sale (buyer pays with a check)

Assets		*Liabilities*	
Foreign assets	$900	Deposits held by private banks	$400
Domestic assets	$1500	Currency in circulation	$2000

Once again, the Bank of Pecunia's liabilities fall by $100 and the Pecunian money supply shrinks.

A $100 *purchase* of foreign assets by the Bank of Pecunia would cause its liabilities to increase by $100. If the central bank paid for its purchase in cash, currency in circulation would rise by $100. If it paid by writing a check on itself, private bank deposits at the Bank of Pecunia would ultimately rise by $100. In either case, there would be a rise in the domestic money supply.

STERILIZATION

Central banks sometimes carry out equal foreign and domestic asset transactions in opposite directions to nullify the impact of their foreign exchange operations on the domestic money supply. This type of policy is called **sterilized foreign exchange intervention.** We can understand how sterilized foreign exchange intervention works by considering the following example.

Suppose once again that the Bank of Pecunia sells $100 of its foreign assets and receives as payment a $100 check on the private bank Pecuniacorp. This transaction causes the central bank's foreign assets and its liabilities to decline simultaneously by $100, and there is therefore a fall in the domestic money supply. If the central bank wishes to negate the effect of its foreign asset sale on the money supply, it can *buy* $100 of domestic assets, such as government bonds. This second action increases the Bank of Pecunia's domestic assets *and* its liabilities by $100 and so completely offsets the money supply effect of the $100 sale of foreign assets. If the central bank buys the government bonds with a check, for example, the two transactions (a $100 sale of foreign assets and a $100 purchase of domestic assets) have the following net effect on its balance sheet.

Central bank balance sheet before sterilized $100 foreign asset sale

Assets		*Liabilities*	
Foreign assets	$1000	Deposits held by private banks	$500
Domestic assets	$1500	Currency in circulation	$2000

Central bank balance sheet after sterilized $100 foreign asset sale

Assets		Liabilities	
Foreign assets	$900	Deposits held by private banks	$500
Domestic assets	$1600	Currency in circulation	$2000

The $100 decrease in the central bank's foreign assets is matched with a $100 increase in domestic assets, and the liabilities side of the balance sheet does not change. The sterilized foreign exchange sale therefore has no effect on the money supply.

THE BALANCE OF PAYMENTS AND THE MONEY SUPPLY

In our discussion of balance of payments accounting in Chapter 13, we defined a country's balance of payments (or official settlements balance) as net purchases of foreign assets by the home central bank less net purchases of domestic assets by foreign central banks. Looked at differently, the balance of payments is the sum of the current account and the nonreserve component of the capital account, that is, the international payments gap that central banks must finance through their reserve transactions. A home balance of payments deficit, for example, means the country's net foreign reserve liabilities are increasing: some combination of reserve sales by the home central bank and reserve purchases by foreign central banks is covering a home current account deficit not fully matched by net nonreserve capital inflows, or a home current account surplus that falls short of net nonreserve capital outflows.

What we have learned in this section illustrates the important connection between the balance of payments and the growth of money supplies at home and abroad. *If central banks are not sterilizing and the home country has a balance of payments surplus, for example, any associated increase in the home central bank's foreign assets implies an increased home money supply. Similarly, any associated decrease in a foreign central bank's claims on the home country implies a decreased foreign money supply.*

The extent to which a measured balance of payments disparity will affect home and foreign money supplies is, however, quite uncertain in practice. For one thing, we have to know how the burden of balance of payments adjustment is divided among central banks, that is, how much financing of the payments gap is done through home official intervention and how much through foreign. This division depends on various factors, such as the macroeconomic goals of the central banks and institutional arrangements governing intervention (discussed later in this chapter). Second, central banks may be sterilizing to counter the monetary effects of reserve changes. Finally, as we noted in Chapter 13 (p. 325), some central bank transactions indirectly help to finance a foreign country's balance of payments deficit, but they do not show up in the latter's published balance of payments figures. Such transactions may nonetheless affect the monetary liabilities of the bank that undertakes them.

How the Central Bank Fixes the Exchange Rate

Having seen how central bank foreign exchange transactions affect the money supply, we can now look at how a central bank fixes the domestic currency's exchange rate through foreign exchange intervention.

To hold the exchange rate constant, a central bank must always be willing to trade currencies at the fixed exchange rate with the private actors in the foreign exchange market. For example, to fix the DM/dollar rate at DM 2.00 per dollar, the German Bundesbank must be willing to buy DM with its dollar reserves, and in any amount the market desires, at a rate of DM 2.00 per dollar. The bank must also be willing to buy any amount of dollar assets the market wants to sell for DM at that exchange rate. If the Bundesbank did not remove such excess supplies or demands for DM by intervening in the market, the exchange rate would have to change to restore equilibrium.

The central bank can succeed in holding the exchange rate fixed only if its financial transactions ensure that asset markets remain in equilibrium when the exchange rate is at its fixed level. The process through which asset market equilibrium is maintained is illustrated by the model of simultaneous foreign exchange and money market equilibrium used in previous chapters.

FOREIGN EXCHANGE MARKET EQUILIBRIUM UNDER A FIXED EXCHANGE RATE

To begin, we consider how equilibrium in the foreign exchange market can be maintained when the central bank fixes the exchange rate permanently at the level E^0. The foreign exchange market is in equilibrium when the interest parity condition holds, that is, when the domestic interest rate, R, equals the foreign interest rate, R^*, plus $(E^e - E)/E$, the expected rate of depreciation of the domestic currency against foreign currency. When the exchange rate is fixed at E^0, however, and market participants expect it to remain fixed, the expected rate of domestic currency depreciation is zero. The interest parity condition therefore implies that E^0 is today's equilibrium exchange rate only if

$$R = R^*.$$

Because no exchange rate change is expected by participants in the foreign exchange market, they are content to hold the available supplies of domestic and foreign currency deposits only if these offer the same interest rate.[5]

To ensure equilibrium in the foreign exchange market when the exchange rate is fixed permanently at E^0, the central bank must therefore hold R equal to R^*. Because the domestic interest rate is determined by the interaction of real money demand and the real money supply, we must look at the money market to complete our analysis of exchange rate fixing.

[5] Even when an exchange rate is currently fixed at some level, market participants may expect the central bank to change it. In such situations the home interest rate must equal the foreign interest rate plus the expected depreciation rate of the domestic currency (as usual) for the foreign exchange market to be in equilibrium. We examine this type of situation later in this chapter, but for now we assume that no one expects the central bank to alter the exchange rate.

MONEY MARKET EQUILIBRIUM UNDER A FIXED EXCHANGE RATE

To hold the domestic interest rate at R^*, the central bank's foreign exchange intervention must adjust the money supply so that R^* equates aggregate real domestic money demand and the real money supply:

$$M^s/P = L(R^*, Y).$$

Given P and Y, the above equilibrium condition tells what the money supply must be if a permanently fixed exchange rate is consistent with asset market equilibrium at a foreign interest rate of R^*.

When the central bank intervenes to hold the exchange rate fixed, it must *automatically* adjust the domestic money supply so that money market equilibrium is maintained with $R = R^*$. Let's look at an example to see how this process works. Suppose the central bank has been fixing E at E^0 and that asset markets initially are in equilibrium. Suddenly output rises. A necessary condition for holding the exchange rate permanently fixed at E^0 is that the central bank restore current asset market equilibrium at that rate, *given* that people expect E^0 to prevail in the future. So we frame our question as: What monetary measures keep the current exchange rate constant given unchanged expectations about the future rate?

A rise in output raises the demand for domestic money, and this increase in money demand normally would push the domestic interest rate upward. To prevent the appreciation of the home currency that would occur (given that people expect an exchange rate of E^0 in the future), the central bank must intervene in the foreign exchange market by buying foreign assets. This foreign asset purchase eliminates the excess demand for domestic money because the central bank issues money to pay for the foreign assets it buys. The bank automatically increases the money supply in this way until asset markets again clear with $E = E^0$ and $R = R^*$.

If the central bank does *not* purchase foreign assets when output increases but instead holds the money stock constant, can it still keep the exchange rate fixed at E^0? The answer is no. If the central bank did not satisfy the excess demand for money caused by a rise in output, the domestic interest rate would begin to rise above the foreign rate R^* to balance the home money market. Traders in the foreign exchange market, perceiving that domestic currency deposits were offering a higher rate of return (given expectations), would begin to bid up the price of domestic currency in terms of foreign currency. In the absence of central bank intervention, the exchange rate thus would fall below E^0. To prevent this appreciation, the bank must sell domestic currency and buy foreign assets, thereby increasing the money supply and preventing any excess money demand from pushing the home interest rate above R^*.

A DIAGRAMMATIC ANALYSIS

The preceding mechanism of exchange rate fixing can be pictured using a diagrammatic tool developed earlier. Figure 18-1 shows the simultaneous equilibrium of the foreign exchange and domestic money markets when the exchange rate is fixed at E^0 and is expected to remain fixed at E^0 in the future.

Money market equilibrium is initially at point 1 in the lower part of the figure.

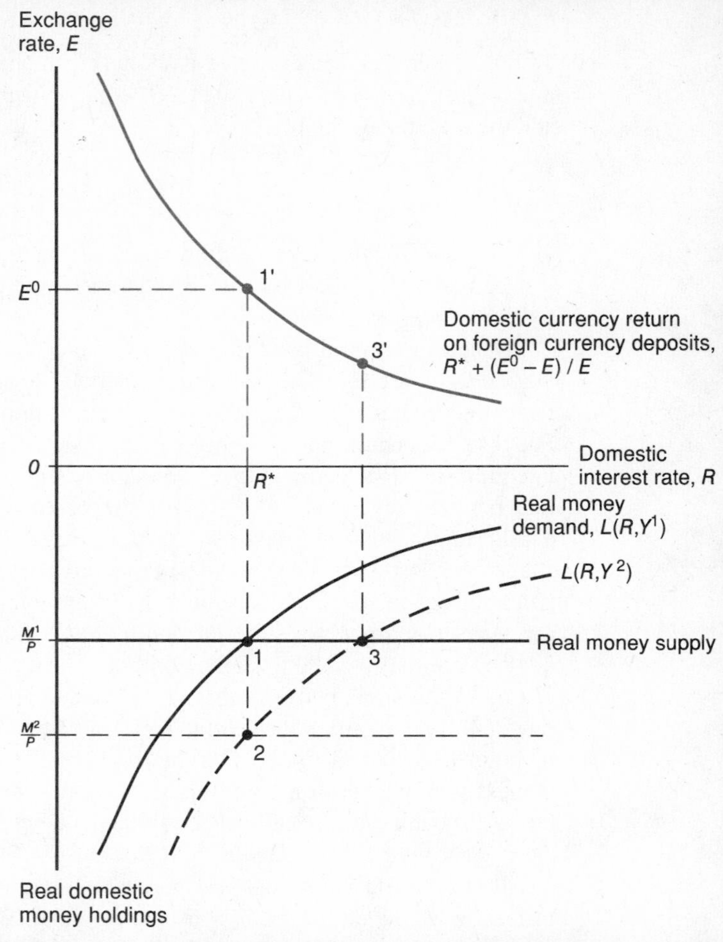

FIGURE 18-1
Asset market equilibrium with a fixed exchange rate, E^0.
To hold the exchange rate fixed at E^0 when output rises from Y^1 to Y^2, the central bank must purchase foreign assets and thereby raise the money supply from M^1 to M^2.

The diagram shows that for a given price level P and a given national income level Y^1, the money supply must equal M^1 when the domestic interest rate equals the foreign rate R^*. The upper part of the figure shows the equilibrium of the foreign exchange market at point 1′. If the expected future exchange rate is E^0, the interest parity condition holds when $R = R^*$ only if today's exchange rate also equals E^0.

To see how the central bank must react to macroeconomic changes to hold the exchange rate permanently at E^0, let's look again at the example of an increase in income. A rise in income (from Y^1 to Y^2) raises the demand for real money holdings at every interest rate, thereby shifting the aggregate money demand function in Figure 18-1 downward. As noted above, a necessary condition for maintaining the fixed rate is to restore *current* asset market equilibrium given that E^0 is still the expected future exchange rate. So we can assume that the downward-sloping curve in the figure's top panel doesn't move.

If the central bank were to take no action, the new money market equilibrium would be at point 3. Because the domestic interest rate is above R^* at point 3, the currency would have to appreciate to bring the foreign exchange market to equilibrium at point 3′.

The central bank cannot allow this appreciation of the domestic currency to occur if it is fixing the exchange rate, so it will buy foreign exchange. As we have seen, the increase in the central bank's foreign assets is accompanied by an expansion of the domestic money supply. The central bank will continue to purchase foreign assets until the domestic money supply has expanded to M^2. At the resulting money market equilibrium (point 2 in the figure), the domestic interest rate again equals R^*. Given this domestic interest rate, the foreign exchange market equilibrium remains at point 1′ with the equilibrium exchange rate still equal to E^0.

Stabilization Policies with a Fixed Exchange Rate

Having seen how the central bank uses foreign exchange intervention to fix the exchange rate, we can now analyze the effects of various macroeconomic policies. In this section we consider three possible policies, monetary policy, fiscal policy, and an abrupt change in the exchange rate's fixed level, E^0.

The stabilization policies we studied in the last chapter have surprisingly different effects when the central bank fixes the exchange rate rather than allowing the foreign exchange market to determine it. By fixing the exchange rate, the central bank gives up its ability to influence the economy through monetary policy. Fiscal policy, however, becomes a more potent tool for affecting output and employment.

As in the last chapter, we use the *DD-AA* model to describe the economy's short-run equilibrium. You will recall that the *DD* schedule shows combinations of the exchange rate and output for which the output market is in equilibrium, the *AA* schedule shows combinations of the exchange rate and output for which the asset markets are in equilibrium, and the short-run equilibrium of the economy as a whole is at the intersection of *DD* and *AA*. To apply the model to the case of a permanently fixed exchange rate, we add the assumption that the expected future exchange rate, E^e, equals the rate E^0 at which the central bank is pegging.

MONETARY POLICY

Figure 18-2 shows the economy's short-run equilibrium as point 1 when the central bank fixes the exchange rate at the level E^0. Output equals Y^1 at point 1, and, as in the last section, the money supply is at the level where a domestic interest rate equal to the foreign rate (R^*) clears the domestic money market. Suppose now that to increase output, the central bank decides to increase the money supply through a purchase of domestic assets.

Figure 18-3 shows the effect of such a policy action. Under a floating exchange rate, the increase in the central bank's domestic assets would push the original asset market equilibrium curve A^1A^1 rightward to A^2A^2 and would therefore result in a new equilibrium at point 2 and a currency depreciation. To prevent this depreciation and hold the rate at E^0, the central bank sells foreign assets for domestic money in the foreign exchange market. The money the bank receives goes out of circulation, and the asset market equilibrium curve shifts back toward its initial position as the home money

FIGURE 18-2
Short-run equilibrium in the *DD-AA* model with a fixed exchange rate, E^0.
Equilibrium is shown at point 1, where the output and asset markets simultaneously clear at an exchange rate of E^0 and output level of Y^1.

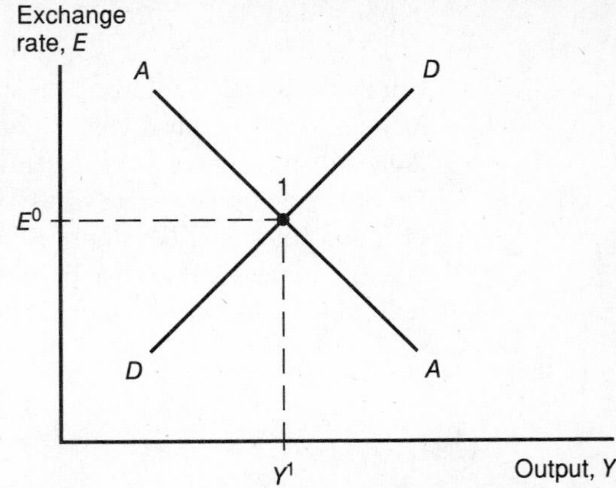

supply falls. Only when the money supply has returned to its original level, so that the asset market schedule is again A^1A^1, is the exchange rate no longer under pressure. The attempt to increase the money supply under a fixed exchange rate thus leaves the economy at its initial equilibrium (point 1). *Under a fixed exchange rate, central bank monetary policy tools are powerless to affect the economy's money supply or its output.*

This result is very different from our finding in Chapter 17 that a central bank can use monetary policy to raise the money supply and output when the exchange rate floats, so it is instructive to ask why the difference arises. By purchasing domestic assets under a floating rate, the central bank causes an initial excess supply of domestic money that simultaneously pushes the domestic interest rate downward and weakens the currency. Under a fixed exchange rate, however, the central bank will resist any tendency for the currency to depreciate by selling foreign assets for domestic money and so removing the initial excess supply of money its policy move has caused. Because any increase in the domestic money supply, no matter how small, will cause the domestic currency to depreciate, the central bank must continue selling foreign assets

FIGURE 18-3
Monetary expansion is ineffective under a fixed exchange rate.
The initial shift of A^1A^1 to A^2A^2 is reversed immediately, and the economy's equilibrium remains at point 1.

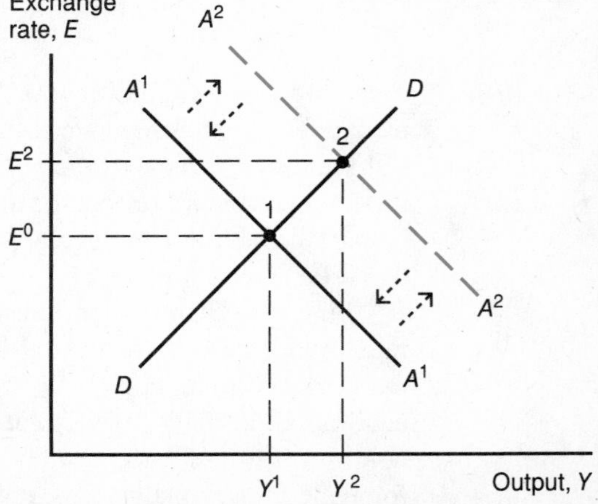

until the money supply has returned to its original level. In the end, the increase in the central bank's domestic assets is exactly offset by an equal *decrease* in the bank's official international reserves. Similarly, an attempt to decrease the money supply through a sale of domestic assets would cause an equal *increase* in reserves that would keep the money supply from changing in the end. Under fixed rates, monetary policy can affect international reserves but nothing else.

By fixing the exchange rate, then, the central bank loses its ability to use monetary policy for the purpose of macroeconomic stabilization. However, the government's second key stabilization tool, fiscal policy, is more effective under a fixed rate than under a floating rate.

FISCAL POLICY

Figure 18-4 illustrates the effects of expansionary fiscal policy when the economy's initial equilibrium is at point 1. As we saw in Chapter 17, fiscal expansion shifts the output market equilibrium schedule to the right. D^1D^1 therefore shifts to D^2D^2 in the figure. If the central bank refrained from intervening in the foreign exchange market, output would rise to Y^2 and the exchange rate would fall to E^2 (a currency appreciation) as a result of a rise in the home interest rate.

How does the central bank intervention hold the exchange rate fixed after the fiscal expansion? The process is the one we illustrated in Figure 18-1. Initially, there is an excess demand for money because the rise in output raises money demand. To prevent the excess money demand from pushing up the home interest rate and appreciating the currency, the central bank must buy foreign assets with money, thereby increasing the money supply. In terms of Figure 18-4, intervention holds the exchange rate at E^0 by shifting A^1A^1 rightward to A^2A^2. At the new equilibrium (point 3), output is higher than

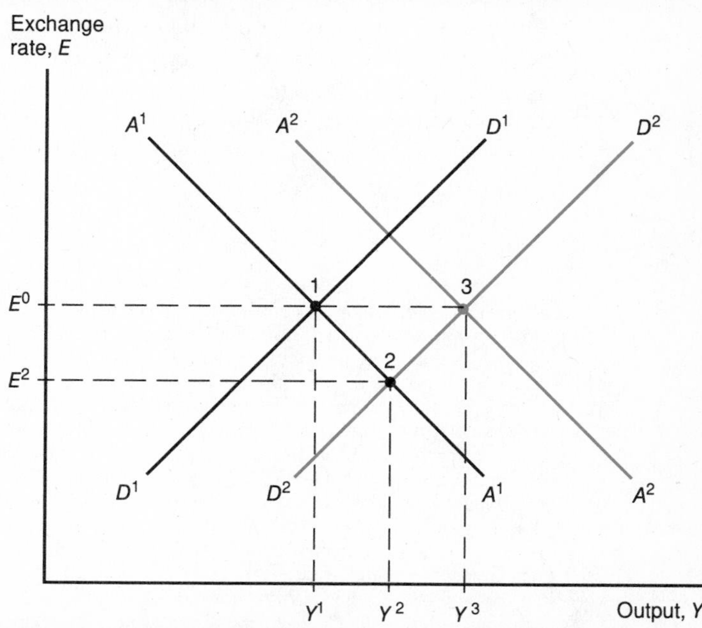

FIGURE 18-4
Fiscal expansion under a fixed exchange rate.
Fiscal expansion and the intervention that accompanies it move the economy from point 1 to point 3 by causing both the *DD* and *AA* schedules to shift.

originally, the exchange rate is unchanged, and official international reserves (and the money supply) are higher.

Unlike monetary policy, fiscal policy can be used to affect output under a fixed exchange rate. Indeed, it is even more effective than under a floating rate! Under a floating rate, fiscal expansion is accompanied by an appreciation of the domestic currency that makes domestic goods and services more expensive and so tends to counteract the policy's positive direct effect on aggregate demand. To prevent this appreciation, a central bank that is fixing the exchange rate is forced to expand the money supply through foreign exchange purchases. The additional expansionary effect of this involuntary increase in the money supply explains why fiscal policy is more potent than under a floating rate.

CHANGES IN THE EXCHANGE RATE

A country that is fixing its exchange rate sometimes decides on a sudden change in the foreign currency value of the domestic currency. A **devaluation** occurs when the central bank raises the domestic currency price of foreign currency, E, and a **revaluation** occurs when the central bank lowers E. All the central bank has to do to devalue or revalue is announce its willingness to trade domestic against foreign currency, in unlimited amounts, at the new exchange rate.[6]

Figure 18-5 shows how a devaluation affects the economy. A rise in the level of the fixed exchange rate, from E^0 to E^1, makes domestic goods and services cheaper relative to foreign goods and services (given that P and P^* are fixed in the short run). Output therefore moves to the higher level Y^2 shown by point 2 on the DD schedule. Point 2, however, does not lie on the initial asset market equilibrium schedule A^1A^1: at point 2, there is initially an excess demand for money due to the rise in transactions accompanying the output increase. This excess money demand would push the home interest rate above the world interest rate if the central bank did not intervene in the foreign exchange market. To maintain the exchange rate at its new fixed level E^1, the central bank must therefore buy foreign assets and expand the money supply until the asset market curve reaches A^2A^2 and passes through point 2. Devaluation therefore causes a rise in output, a rise in official reserves, and an expansion of the money supply. A private capital inflow matches the central bank's reserve gain (an official outflow) in the balance of payments accounts.[7]

[6] We observe a subtle distinction between the terms *devaluation* and *depreciation* (and between *revaluation* and *appreciation*). Depreciation (appreciation) is a rise in E (a fall in E) when the exchange rate floats, while devaluation (revaluation) is a rise in E (a fall in E) when the exchange rate is pegged. Depreciation (appreciation) thus involves the active voice (as in "the currency appreciated"), while devaluation (revaluation) involves the passive voice (as in "the currency was devalued"). Put another way, devaluation (revaluation) reflects a deliberate government decision while depreciation (appreciation) is an outcome of government actions and market forces acting together.

[7] After the home currency is devalued, market participants expect that the new higher exchange rate, rather than the old rate, will prevail in the future. The change in expectations alone shifts A^1A^1 to the right, but without central bank intervention this by itself is insufficient to move A^1A^1 all the way to A^2A^2. At point 2, as at point 1, $R = R^*$ if the foreign exchange market clears. Because output is higher at point 2 than at point 1, however, real money demand is also higher at the former point. With P fixed, an expansion of the money supply is therefore necessary to make point 2 a position of money market equilibrium, that is, a point on the new AA schedule. Central bank purchases of foreign assets are therefore a necessary part of the economy's shift to its new fixed exchange rate equilibrium.

FIGURE 18-5
Effect of a currency devaluation from E^0 to E^1.
The economy's equilibrium moves from point 1 to point 2 as both output and the money supply expand.

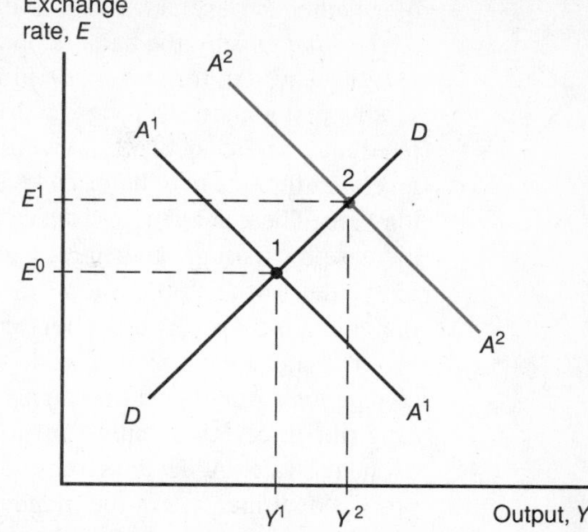

The effects of devaluation illustrate the three main reasons why governments sometimes choose to devalue their currencies. First, devaluation allows the government to fight domestic unemployment despite the lack of effective monetary policy. If government spending and budget deficits are politically unpopular, for example, or if the legislative process is slow, a government may opt for devaluation as the most convenient way of boosting aggregate demand. A second reason for devaluing is the resulting improvement in the current account, a development the government may believe to be desirable. The third motive behind devaluations is their effect on the central bank's foreign reserves. If the central bank is running low on reserves, a sudden, one-time devaluation can be used to draw in more.[8]

ADJUSTMENT TO FISCAL POLICY AND EXCHANGE RATE CHANGES

If fiscal and exchange rate changes occur when there is full employment and the policy changes are maintained indefinitely, they will ultimately cause the domestic price level to move in such a way that full employment is restored. To understand this dynamic process, we discuss the economy's adjustment to fiscal expansion and devaluation in turn.

If the economy is initially at full employment, fiscal expansion raises output, and this rise in output above its full-employment level causes the domestic price level, *P*, to begin rising. As *P* rises home output becomes more expensive, so aggregate demand gradually falls, returning output to the initial, full-employment level. Once this point is reached, the upward pressure on the price level comes to an end. There is no real

[8] Because an unexpected devaluation lowers the foreign currency value of the government's domestic currency liabilities to the private sector, the initial reserve gain by the central bank is financed essentially by a surprise tax on holders of government bonds and money.

appreciation in the short run, as there is with a floating exchange rate, but regardless of whether the exchange rate is floating or fixed, the real exchange rate appreciates *in the long run* by the same amount.[9] In the present case real appreciation (a fall in EP^*/P) takes the form of a rise in P rather than a fall in E.

At first glance, the long-run price level increase caused by a fiscal expansion under fixed rates seems inconsistent with the conclusion of Chapter 15 that for a given output level and interest rate the price level and the money supply move proportionally in the long run. There is no inconsistency because fiscal expansion *does* cause a money supply increase by forcing the central bank to intervene in the foreign exchange market. To fix the rate throughout the adjustment process, the central bank ultimately must increase the money supply through intervention in proportion to the long-run increase in P.

The adjustment to a devaluation is similar. In fact, since a devaluation does not change long-run demand or supply conditions in the output market, the increase in the long-run price level caused by a devaluation is proportional to the increase in the exchange rate. A devaluation under a fixed rate has the same long-run effect as a proportional increase in the money supply under a floating rate. Like the latter policy, devaluation is neutral in the long run, in the sense that its only effect on the economy's long-run equilibrium is a proportional rise in all nominal prices and in the domestic money supply.

Balance of Payments Crises and Capital Flight

Until now we have assumed that participants in the foreign exchange market believe that a fixed exchange rate will be maintained at its current level forever. In many practical situations, however, the central bank may find it undesirable or infeasible to maintain the current fixed exchange rate. The central bank may be running short on foreign reserves, for example, or it may face high domestic unemployment. Because market participants know the central bank may respond to such situations by devaluing the currency, it would be unreasonable for them to expect the current exchange rate to be maintained forever.

The market's belief in an impending change in the exchange rate gives rise to a **balance of payments crisis,** a sharp change in official foreign reserves sparked by a change in expectations about the future exchange rate. In this section we use our model of asset market equilibrium to examine how balance of payments crises can occur under fixed exchange rates.

Figure 18-6 shows the asset markets in equilibrium at points 1 (the money market) and 1′ (the foreign exchange market) with the exchange rate fixed at E^0 and expected to remain there indefinitely. M^1 is the money supply consistent with this initial equilibrium. Suppose a sudden deterioration in the current account, for example, leads the foreign exchange market to expect the government to devalue in the future and adopt

[9] To see this, observe that the long-run equilibrium real exchange rate, EP^*/P, must in either case satisfy the same equation, $Y^f = D(EP^*/P, Y^f - T, I, G)$, where Y^f, as in Chapter 17, is the full-employment output level.

FIGURE 18-6
Capital flight, the money supply, and the interest rate.
To hold the exchange rate fixed at E^0 after the market decides it will be devalued to E^1, the central bank must use its reserves to finance a private capital outflow that shrinks the money supply and raises the home interest rate.

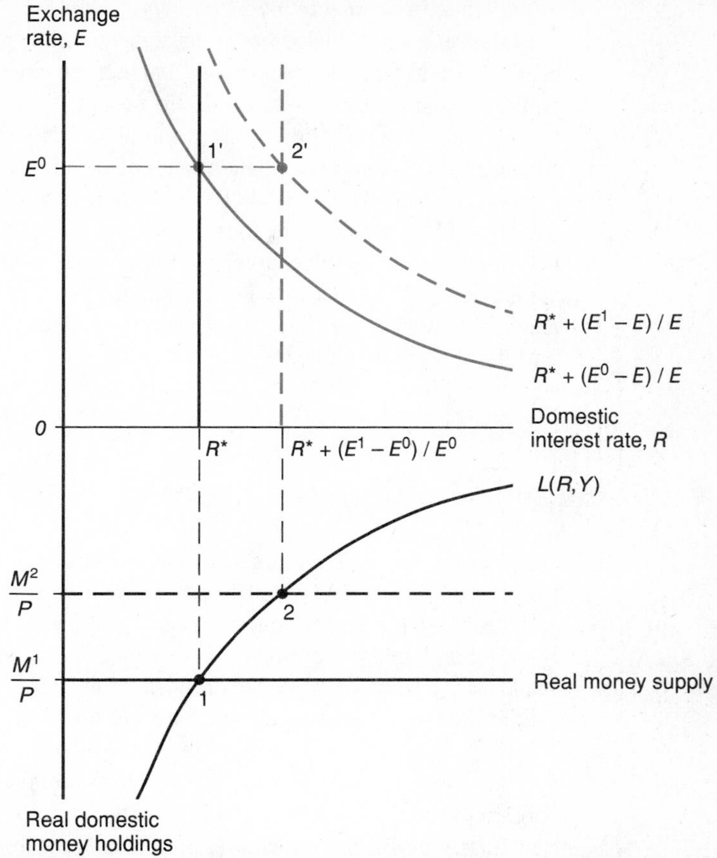

a new fixed exchange rate, E^1, that is higher than the current rate, E^0. The figure's upper part shows this change in expectations as a rightward shift in the downward-sloping curve that measures the expected domestic currency return on foreign currency deposits. Since the current exchange rate still is E^0, equilibrium in the foreign exchange market (point 2′) requires a rise in the domestic interest rate to $R^* + (E^1 - E^0)/E^0$, which now equals the expected domestic currency return on foreign currency assets.

Initially, however, the domestic interest rate remains at R^*, which is below the new expected return on foreign assets. This differential causes an excess demand for foreign currency assets in the foreign exchange market; to continue holding the exchange rate at E^0 the central bank must sell foreign reserves and thus shrink the domestic money supply. The bank's intervention comes to an end once the money supply has fallen to M^2, so that the money market is in equilibrium at the interest rate $R^* + (E^1 - E^0)/E^0$ that clears the foreign exchange market (point 2). *The expectation of a future devaluation causes a balance of payments crisis marked by a sharp fall in reserves and a rise in the home interest rate above the world interest rate. Similarly,* *an expected revaluation causes an abrupt rise in foreign reserves together with a fall in the home interest rate below the world rate.*

The reserve loss accompanying a devaluation scare is often labeled **capital flight** because the associated debit in the balance of payments accounts is a private capital outflow. Residents flee the domestic currency by selling it to the central bank for foreign exchange; they then invest the proceeds abroad. Capital flight is of particular concern to the government when fears of devaluation arise because the central bank's reserves are low to begin with. By pushing reserves even lower, capital flight may force the central bank to devalue sooner and by a larger amount than planned.[10]

For the rest of this chapter we continue to assume that no exchange rate changes are expected by the market when exchange rates are fixed. But we draw on the preceding analysis repeatedly in later chapters when we discuss various countries' experiences with fixed exchange rates.

Managed Floating and Sterilized Intervention

In previous sections we argued that a central bank gives up its ability to influence output through monetary policy when it maintains a fixed exchange rate. Under managed floating, however, monetary policy is influenced by exchange rate changes without being completely subordinate to the requirements of a fixed rate. Instead, the central bank faces a trade-off between domestic objectives such as employment or the inflation rate and exchange rate stability. Suppose the central bank tries to expand the money supply to fight domestic unemployment, for example, but at the same time carries out foreign asset sales to restrain the resulting depreciation of the home currency. The foreign exchange intervention will tend to *reduce* the money supply, hindering but not necessarily nullifying the central bank's attempt to reduce unemployment.

Discussions of foreign exchange intervention in policy forums and newspapers often appear to ignore the intimate link between intervention and the money supply that we explored in detail above. In reality, however, these discussions often assume that foreign exchange intervention is being *sterilized,* so that opposite domestic asset transactions prevent it from affecting the money supply. Empirical studies of central bank behavior confirm this assumption and consistently show central banks to have practiced sterilized intervention throughout the twentieth century and earlier.[11]

[10] If aggregate demand depends on the real interest rate (as in the *IS-LM* model), capital flight reduces output by shrinking the money supply and raising the real interest rate. This possibly contractionary effect of capital flight is another reason why policy makers hope to avoid it.

[11] Three empirical studies of recent experiences are Leroy O. Laney and Thomas D. Willett, ''The International Liquidity Explosion and Worldwide Inflation: The Evidence from Sterilization Coefficient Estimates,'' *Journal of International Money and Finance* 1 (August 1982), pp. 141–152; Robert E. Cumby and Maurice Obstfeld, ''Capital Mobility and the Scope for Sterilization: Mexico in the 1970s,'' in Pedro Aspe Armella, Rudiger Dornbusch, and Maurice Obstfeld, eds., *Financial Policies and the World Capital Market: The Problem of Latin American Countries* (Chicago: University of Chicago Press, 1983), pp. 245–269; and Cristina Mastropasqua, Stefano Micossi, and Roberto Rinaldi, ''Interventions, Sterilization, and Monetary Policy in European Monetary System Countries, 1979–87,'' in Francesco Giavazzi, Stefano Micossi, and Marcus Miller, eds., *The European Monetary System* (Cambridge, Eng.: Cambridge University Press, 1988), pp. 252–287.

In spite of widespread sterilized intervention, there is considerable disagreement among economists about its effects. In this section we study the role of sterilized intervention in exchange rate management.

PERFECT ASSET SUBSTITUTABILITY AND THE INEFFECTIVENESS OF STERILIZED INTERVENTION

When a central bank carries out a sterilized foreign exchange intervention, its transactions leave the domestic money supply unchanged. A rationale for such a policy is difficult to find using the model of exchange rate determination developed above, for the model predicts that without an accompanying change in the money supply, the central bank's intervention will not affect the domestic interest rate and therefore will not affect the exchange rate.

Our model also predicts that sterilization will be fruitless under a fixed exchange rate. The example of a fiscal expansion illustrates why a central bank might wish to sterilize under a fixed rate and why our model says the policy will fail. Recall that to hold the exchange rate constant when fiscal policy becomes more expansive, the central bank must buy foreign assets and expand the home money supply. The policy raises output but also causes inflation, which the central bank may try to avoid by sterilizing the increase in the money supply that its fiscal policy has induced. But as quickly as the central bank sells domestic assets to reduce the money supply, it will have to *buy* more foreign assets to keep the exchange rate fixed. The ineffectiveness of monetary policy under a fixed exchange rate implies that sterilization is a self-defeating policy.

The key feature of our model that leads to these results is the assumption that the foreign exchange market is in equilibrium only when the expected returns on domestic and foreign currency bonds are the same.[12] This assumption is often called **perfect asset substitutability.** Two assets are perfect substitutes when, as our model assumed, investors don't care how their portfolios are divided between them provided both yield the same expected rate of return. With perfect asset substitutability in the foreign exchange market, the exchange rate is therefore determined so that the interest parity condition holds. When this is the case there is nothing a central bank can do through foreign exchange intervention that it could not do as well through purely domestic open-market operations.

In contrast to perfect asset substitutability, **imperfect asset substitutability** exists when it is possible for assets' expected returns to differ in equilibrium. As we saw in Chapter 14, the main factor that may lead to imperfect asset substitutability in the foreign exchange market is *risk.* If bonds denominated in different currencies have different degrees of risk, investors may be willing to earn lower expected returns on bonds that are less risky. Correspondingly, they will hold a very risky asset only if the expected return it offers is relatively high.

In a world of perfect asset substitutability, participants in the foreign exchange market care only about expected rates of return; since these rates are determined by

[12] We are assuming that all interest-bearing (nonmoney) assets denominated in *the same* currency, whether illiquid time deposits or government bonds, are perfect substitutes in portfolios. The single term *bonds* will generally be used to refer to all these assets.

monetary policy, actions such as sterilized intervention that do not affect the money supply also do not affect the exchange rate. Under imperfect asset substitutability both risk *and* return matter, so central bank actions that alter the riskiness of domestic currency assets can move the exchange rate even when the money supply does not change. To understand how sterilized intervention can alter the riskiness of domestic currency assets, however, we must modify our model of equilibrium in the foreign exchange market.

FOREIGN EXCHANGE MARKET EQUILIBRIUM UNDER IMPERFECT ASSET SUBSTITUTABILITY

When domestic and foreign currency bonds are perfect substitutes, the foreign exchange market is in equilibrium only if the interest parity condition holds:

$$R = R^* + (E^e - E)/E. \tag{18-1}$$

When domestic and foreign currency bonds are *imperfect* substitutes, the condition above does not hold in general. Instead, equilibrium in the foreign exchange market requires that the domestic interest rate equal the expected domestic currency return on foreign bonds *plus* a **risk premium,** ρ, that reflects the difference between the riskiness of domestic and foreign bonds:

$$R = R^* + (E^e - E)/E + \rho. \tag{18-2}$$

Appendix I to this chapter develops a detailed model of foreign exchange market equilibrium with imperfect asset substitutability. The main conclusion of that model is that the risk premium on domestic assets rises when the stock of domestic government bonds available to be held by the public rises and falls when the central bank's domestic assets rise. It is not hard to grasp the economic reasoning behind this result. Private investors become more vulnerable to unexpected changes in the home currency's exchange rate as the stock of domestic government bonds they hold rises. Investors will be unwilling to assume the increased risk of holding more domestic government debt, however, unless they are compensated by a higher expected rate of return on domestic currency assets. An increased stock of domestic government debt will therefore raise the difference between the expected returns on domestic and foreign currency bonds. Similarly, when the central bank buys domestic assets, the market need no longer hold them; private vulnerability to home currency exchange rate risk is thus lower, and the risk premium on home currency assets falls.

This alternative model of foreign market equilibrium implies that the risk premium depends positively on the stock of domestic government debt, denoted by B, less the domestic assets of the central bank, denoted by A:

$$\rho = \rho(B - A). \tag{18-3}$$

The risk premium on domestic bonds therefore rises when $B - A$ rises. This relation between the risk premium and the central bank's domestic asset holdings allows the bank to affect the exchange rate through sterilized foreign exchange intervention. It also implies that official operations in domestic and foreign assets may differ in their asset market impacts.[13]

[13] The stock of central bank domestic assets is often called domestic *credit.*

THE EFFECTS OF STERILIZED INTERVENTION WITH IMPERFECT ASSET SUBSTITUTABILITY

Figure 18-7 modifies our earlier picture of asset market equilibrium by adding imperfect asset substitutability to illustrate how sterilized intervention can affect the exchange rate. The lower part of the figure, which shows the money market in equilibrium at point 1, does not change. The upper part of the figure is also much the same as before, except that the downward-sloping schedule now shows how the *sum* of the expected domestic currency return on foreign assets *and* the risk premium depends on the exchange rate. The curve continues to slope downward because the risk premium itself is assumed not to depend on the exchange rate. Equilibrium in the foreign exchange market is at point 1′, which corresponds to a domestic government debt of B and central bank domestic asset holdings of A^1. At that point, the domestic interest rate equals the risk-adjusted domestic currency return on foreign deposits [as in equation (18-2)].

Let's use the diagram to examine the effects of a sterilized purchase of foreign assets by the central bank. By matching its purchase of foreign assets with a sale of

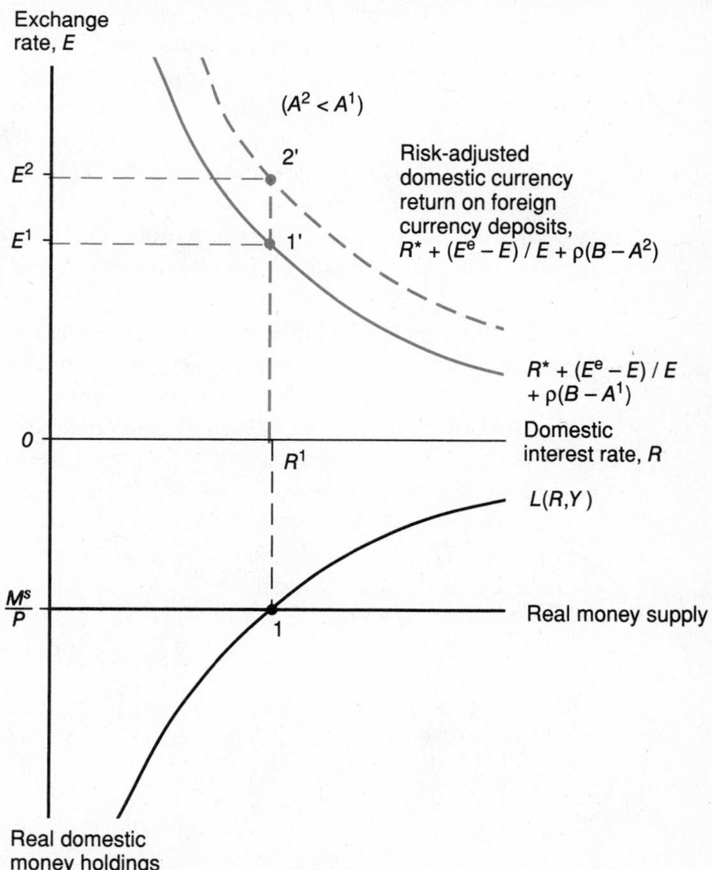

FIGURE 18-7
Effect of a sterilized central bank purchase of foreign assets under imperfect asset substitutability.
A sterilized purchase of foreign assets leaves the money supply unchanged but raises the risk-adjusted return that domestic currency deposits must offer in equilibrium. Other things equal, this depreciates the domestic currency.

domestic assets, the central bank holds the money supply constant at M^s and avoids any change in the lower part of Figure 18-7. As a result of the domestic asset sale, however, the central bank's domestic assets are lower (they fall to A^2) and the stock of domestic assets that the market must hold, $B - A^2$, is therefore higher than the initial stock $B - A^1$. This increase pushes the risk premium ρ upward and shifts to the right the negatively sloped schedule in the upper part of the figure. The foreign exchange market now settles at point 2′, and the domestic currency depreciates.

With imperfect asset substitutability, even sterilized purchases of foreign exchange cause the home currency to depreciate. Similarly, sterilized sales of foreign exchange cause the home currency to appreciate. A slight modification of our analysis shows that the central bank can also use sterilized intervention to hold the exchange rate fixed as it varies the money supply to achieve domestic objectives such as full employment. In effect, the exchange rate and monetary policy can be managed independently of each other in the short run when sterilized intervention is effective.

EVIDENCE ON THE EFFECTS OF STERILIZED INTERVENTION

In the early 1980s, European countries called on the United States to intervene systematically in the foreign exchange market and resist sharp movements in the dollar's exchange rate against other currencies. Leaders of the seven largest industrial economies discussed intervention at an economic summit meeting held at Versailles in June 1982.[14] As a result of the discussion, government economists in the summit countries were asked to prepare a study of the effects of alternative intervention practices.

The conclusions of the study were published in 1983 as the "Report of the Working Group on Exchange Market Intervention." The report asked in particular if sterilized intervention might allow central banks to manage exchange rates without corresponding adjustments in domestic monetary policies. Little evidence was found to support the idea that sterilized intervention had been a major independent factor influencing exchange rates.

This conclusion agrees with the one reached by most academic studies of sterilized intervention.[15] As we discuss at length in Chapter 22, however, there is also considerable evidence against the view that bonds denominated in different currencies are perfect substitutes. Some economists conclude from these conflicting results that while risk premiums are important, they do not depend on central bank asset transactions in the simple way our model assumes.[16] Others contend that the tests that have been used to detect the effects of sterilized intervention are flawed.[17] Given the meager evidence that sterilized intervention has a reliable effect on exchange rates, however, a skeptical attitude is probably in order.

[14] The countries represented were Britain, Canada, France, Germany, Italy, Japan, and the United States.

[15] An article by Kenneth Rogoff analyzes Canadian data and surveys results for other countries. See Rogoff, "On the Effects of Sterilized Intervention: An Analysis of Weekly Data," *Journal of Monetary Economics* 14 (September 1984), pp. 133–150. The findings of the Federal Reserve participants in the Versailles project are summarized in the piece by Henderson and Sampson in Further Reading.

[16] For this view, see Robert J. Hodrick and Sanjay Srivastava, "An Investigation of Risk and Return in Forward Foreign Exchange," *Journal of International Money and Finance* 3 (April 1984), pp. 5–29.

[17] See, for example, Richard N. Cooper, "Comment," *Brookings Papers on Economic Activity* 2:1985, pp. 451–456.

THE SIGNALING EFFECT OF INTERVENTION

A phenomenon sometimes referred to as the **signaling effect of foreign exchange intervention** is an important complicating factor in econometric efforts to study the effects of sterilization. Our discussion of sterilized intervention has assumed that it does not change the market's exchange rate expectations. If market participants are unsure about the future direction of macroeconomic policies, however, sterilized intervention may given an indication of where the central bank expects (or desires) the exchange rate to move. This signal, in turn, can alter the market's view of the future and cause an immediate exchange rate change even when bonds denominated in different currencies are perfect substitutes.

The signaling effect is most important when the government is unhappy with the exchange rate's level and declares in public that it will alter monetary or fiscal policies to bring about a change. By simultaneously intervening on a sterilized basis, the central bank sometimes lends credibility to this announcement. A sterilized purchase of foreign assets, for example, may convince the market that the central bank intends to bring about a home currency depreciation because the bank will lose money if an appreciation occurs instead. Even central banks must watch their budgets!

A government may be tempted to exploit the signaling effect for temporary benefits, however, even when it has no intention of changing monetary or fiscal policy to bring about a different long-run exchange rate. The result of crying ''Wolf!'' too often is the same in the foreign exchange market as elsewhere. If governments do not follow up on their exchange market signals with concrete policy moves, the signals soon become ineffective. Thus, intervention signaling cannot be viewed as a policy weapon to be wielded independently of monetary and fiscal policy. The box on page 503 gives examples of how the signaling effect can work—or backfire.[18]

Reserve Currencies in the World Monetary System

Until now, we have studied a single country that fixes its exchange rate in terms of a hypothetical single foreign currency by trading domestic for foreign assets when necessary. In the real world there are many currencies, and it is possible for a country to fix the exchange rates of its domestic currency against some foreign currencies while allowing them to float against others. This has been the case in the European Monetary System, whose members have held their mutual exchange rates fixed while allowing their currencies' dollar prices to fluctuate.

[18] For discussion of the role played by the signaling effect in more recent exchange rate experience, see Owen F. Humpage, ''Intervention and the Dollar's Decline,'' *Federal Reserve Bank of Cleveland Economic Review* 24 (Quarter 2, 1988), pp. 2–16; Maurice Obstfeld, ''The Effectiveness of Foreign-Exchange Intervention: Recent Experience, 1985–1988'' in William H. Branson, Jacob A. Frenkel, and Morris Goldstein, eds., *International Policy Coordination and Exchange Rate Fluctuations* (Chicago: University of Chicago Press, 1990), pp. 197–237; and Kathryn M. Dominguez and Jeffrey A. Frankel, *Does Foreign Exchange Intervention Work?* (Washington, D.C.: Institute for International Economics, 1993).

This section and the next adopt a global perspective and study the macroeconomic behavior of the world economy under two possible systems for fixing the exchange rates of *all* currencies against each other.

The first such fixed-rate system is very much like the one we have been studying. In it, one currency is singled out as a **reserve currency,** the currency central banks hold in their international reserves, and each nation's central bank fixes its currency's exchange rate against the reserve currency by standing ready to trade domestic money for reserve assets at that rate. Between the end of World War II and 1973, the U.S. dollar was the main reserve currency and almost every country pegged the dollar exchange rate of its currency.

The second fixed-rate system (studied in the next section) is a **gold standard.** Under a gold standard, central banks peg the prices of their currencies in terms of gold, and hold gold as official international reserves. The heyday of the international gold standard was between 1870 and 1914, although many countries attempted unsuccessfully to restore a permanent gold standard after the end of World War I in 1918.

Both reserve currency standards and the gold standard result in fixed exchange rates between *all* pairs of currencies in the world. But the two systems have very different implications about how countries share the burden of balance of payments financing and about the growth and control of national money supplies.

THE MECHANICS OF A RESERVE CURRENCY STANDARD

The workings of a reserve currency system are illustrated by the system based on the U.S. dollar set up at the end of World War II. Under that system, every central bank fixed the dollar exchange rate of its currency through foreign exchange market trades of domestic currency for dollar assets. The frequent need to intervene meant that each central bank had to have on hand sufficient dollar reserves to meet any excess supply of its currency that might arise. Central banks therefore held a large portion of their international reserves in the form of U.S. Treasury bills and short-term dollar deposits, which pay interest and can be turned into cash at relatively low cost.

Because each currency's dollar price was fixed by its central bank, the exchange rate between any two currencies was automatically fixed as well through arbitrage in the foreign exchange market. How did this process work? Let's suppose the French franc price of dollars was fixed at FFr 5 per dolar while the DM price of dollars was fixed at DM 4 per dollar. The exchange rate between the franc and the DM had to remain constant at DM 0.80 per franc = (DM 4 per dollar) ÷ (FFr 5 per dollar), even though no central bank was directly trading francs for DM to hold the relative price of those two currencies fixed. At a DM/FFr rate of DM 0.85 per franc, for example, you could have made a sure profit of $6.25 by selling $100 to the French central bank, the Bank of France, for ($100) × (FFr 5 per dollar) = FFr 500, selling your FFr 500 in the foreign exchange market for (FFr 500) × (DM 0.85 per franc) = DM 425, and then selling the DM to the German Bundesbank for (DM 425) ÷ (DM 4 per dollar) = $106.25. With everyone trying to exploit this profit opportunity by selling francs for DM in the foreign exchange market, however, the DM would have appreciated against the franc until the DM/FFr rate reached DM 0.80 per franc. Similarly, at a rate of DM 0.75 per franc, pressure in the foreign exchange market would have forced the DM to depreciate against the franc until the rate of DM 0.80 per franc was reached.

Even though each central bank tied its currency's exchange rate only to the dollar,

Games Governments Play

Faced with accelerating inflation and a sharply depreciating dollar, U.S. President Jimmy Carter announced on November 1, 1978, that the dollar's foreign exchange value was too low and that the U.S. Treasury and Federal Reserve were taking actions to strengthen the currency. A week earlier the president had announced another anti-inflation program to halt the dollar's slide but had mentioned no specifics about monetary policy. As a result of this vagueness, the dollar had plummeted against the yen and DM, despite massive sterilized dollar purchases by the Bank of Japan and the Bundesbank.

Having previously disappointed the market, President Carter was more specific on November 1. Two main policy shifts were announced. First, the United States would borrow Swiss francs, marks, and yen (in the market and from central banks) and use the proceeds to buy dollars in the foreign exchange market. Whether these dollar purchases would be sterilized or allowed to reduce the U.S. money supply was not stated. Second, the Federal Reserve would take contractionary monetary measures—an increase in the discount rate at which it lends money to U.S. banks and a rise in required reserves on some bank deposits.

The foreign exchange market's initial reaction to this second announcement was favorable, and the dollar soon appreciated by 7.5 percent against the Swiss franc, 7 percent against the DM, and 5 percent against the yen. By the summer of 1979, however, the U.S. money supply was ballooning and the dollar once again took a nosedive. Substantial sterilized intervention by the Fed and foreign central banks made little apparent difference: the markets no longer believed the United States seriously intended to slow down monetary growth.

The dollar firmed only in October 1979, when a new Federal Reserve chairman known for his monetary conservatism, Paul A. Volcker, announced a credible program of money supply control.

market forces automatically held all other exchange rates—called cross rates—constant at the values implied by the dollar rates. Thus, the post-World War II exchange rate system was one in which exchange rates between any two currencies were fixed.[19]

THE ASYMMETRIC POSITION OF THE RESERVE CENTER

In a reserve currency system the country whose currency is held as reserves occupies a special position because it never has to intervene in the foreign exchange market. The reason is that if there are N countries with N currencies in the world, there are only $N - 1$ exchange rates against the reserve currency. If the $N - 1$ nonreserve currency countries fix their exchange rates against the reserve currency, there is no exchange rate left for the reserve center to fix. Thus the center country need never intervene and bears none of the burden of financing its balance of payments.

This set of arrangements puts the reserve-issuing country in a privileged position because it can use its monetary policy for macroeconomic stabilization even though it

[19] The rules of the postwar system actually allowed currencies' dollar values to move as much as 1 percent above or below the ''official'' values. This meant cross rates could fluctuate by as much as 4 percent.

has fixed exchange rates. We saw earlier in this chapter that when a country must intervene to hold its exchange rate constant, an attempt to expand its money supply is bound to be frustrated by losses of international reserves. But because the reserve center is the one country in the system that can enjoy fixed exchange rates without the need to intervene, it is still able to use monetary policy for stabilization purposes.

What would be the effect of a purchase of domestic assets by the central bank of the reserve currency country? The resulting expansion in its money supply would momentarily push its interest rate below those prevailing abroad, and thereby cause an excess demand for foreign currencies in the foreign exchange market. To prevent their currencies from appreciating against the reserve currency, all other central banks in the system would be forced to buy reserve assets with their own currencies, expanding their money supplies and pushing their interest rates down to the level established by the reserve center. Output throughout the world, as well as at home, would expand after a purchase of domestic assets by the reserve country.

Our account of monetary policy under a reserve currency system points to a basic asymmetry. The reserve country has the power to affect its own economy, as well as foreign economies, by using monetary policy. Other central banks are forced to relinquish monetary policy as a stabilization tool, and instead must passively "import" the monetary policy of the reserve center because of their commitment to peg their currencies to the reserve currency.

This inherent asymmetry of a reserve system places immense economic power in the hands of the reserve country and is therefore likely to lead eventually to policy disputes within the system. Such problems helped cause the breakdown of the postwar "dollar standard" in 1973, a topic we discuss in detail in Chapter 19.

The Gold Standard

An international gold standard avoids the asymmetry inherent in a reserve currency standard by avoiding the "*N*th currency" problem. Under a gold standard, each country fixes the price of its currency in terms of gold by standing ready to trade domestic currency for gold whenever necessary to defend the official price. Because there are *N* currencies and *N* prices of gold in terms of those currencies, no single country occupies a privileged position within the system: each is responsible for pegging its currency's price in terms of the official international reserve asset, gold.

THE MECHANICS OF A GOLD STANDARD

Because countries tie their currencies to gold under a gold standard, official international reserves take the form of gold. Gold standard rules also require each country to allow unhindered imports and exports of gold across its borders. Under these arrangements, a gold standard, like a reserve currency system, results in fixed exchange rates between all currencies. For example, if the dollar price of gold is pegged at $35 per ounce by the Federal Reserve while the pound price of gold is pegged at £14.58 per ounce by Britain's central bank, the Bank of England, the dollar/pound exchange rate must be constant at ($35 per ounce) ÷ (£14.58 per ounce) = $2.40 per pound. The same arbitrage process that holds cross exchange rates fixed under a reserve currency system keeps exchange rates fixed under a gold standard as well.[20]

SYMMETRIC MONETARY ADJUSTMENT UNDER A GOLD STANDARD

Because of the inherent symmetry of a gold standard, no country in the system occupies a privileged position by being relieved of the commitment to intervene. By considering the international effects of a purchase of domestic assets by one central bank, we can see in more detail how monetary policy works under a gold standard.

Suppose the Bank of England decides to increase its money supply through a purchase of domestic assets. The initial increase in Britain's money supply will put downward pressure on British interest rates and make foreign currency assets more attractive than British assets. Holders of pound deposits will attempt to sell them for foreign deposits, but no *private* buyers will come forward. Under floating exchange rates, the pound would depreciate against foreign currencies until interest parity had been re-established. This depreciation cannot occur when all currencies are tied to gold, however. What happens? Because central banks are obliged to trade their currencies for gold at fixed rates, unhappy holders of pounds can sell these to the Bank of England for gold, sell the gold to other central banks for their currencies, and use these currencies to purchase deposits that offer interest rates higher than the interest rate on pounds. Britain therefore experiences a private capital outflow and foreign countries experience an inflow.

This process re-establishes equilibrium in the foreign exchange market. The Bank of England loses foreign reserves since it is forced to buy pounds and sell gold to keep the pound price of gold fixed. Foreign central banks gain reserves as they *buy* gold with their currencies. Countries share equally in the burden of balance of payments adjustment. Because official foreign reserves are declining in Britain and increasing abroad, the British money supply is falling, pushing the British interest rate back up, and foreign money supplies are rising, pushing foreign interest rates down. Once interest rates have again become equal across countries, asset markets are in equilibrium and there is no further tendency for the Bank of England to lose gold or for foreign central banks to gain it.

Our example illustates the symmetric nature of international monetary adjustment under a gold standard. Whenever a country is losing reserves and seeing its money supply shrink as a consequence, foreign countries are gaining reserves and seeing their money supplies expand. In contrast, monetary adjustment under a reserve currency standard is highly asymmetric. Countries can gain or lose reserves without inducing any change in the money supply of the reserve currency country, and only the latter country has the ability to influence domestic and world monetary conditions.[21]

[20] In practice, the costs of shipping gold and insuring it in transit determined narrow ''gold points'' within which currency exchange rates could fluctuate.

[21] Originally, gold coins were a substantial part of the currency supply in gold standard countries. A country's gold losses to foreigners therefore did not have to take the form of a fall in central bank gold holdings: private citizens could melt gold coins into ingots and ship them abroad, where they were either reminted as foreign gold coins or sold to the foreign central bank for paper currency. In terms of our earlier analysis of the central bank balance sheet, circulating gold coins are considered to make up a component of the monetary base that is not a central bank liability. Either form of gold export would thus result in a fall in the domestic money supply and an increase in foreign money supplies.

Intervention Arrangements in the European Monetary System

In March 1979, eight members of the European Community—France, Germany, Italy, Belgium, Denmark, Ireland, Luxembourg, and the Netherlands—agreed to fix their mutual exchange rates and float jointly against the U.S. dollar within a European Monetary System (EMS). Spain joined the EMS exchange rate mechanism in June 1989, Britain in October 1990, and Portugal in April 1992. Britain dropped out after only twenty-three months, when a speculative crisis shattered several EMS parities in September 1992. At the same time Italy set the lira afloat. The EC governments had hoped the EMS would evolve into a unified monetary area with a single central bank and a single EC currency. As a result of the currency crisis and the factors behind it, however, the EMS now faces an uncertain future. We will discuss the EMS experience in detail in Chapter 21.

Bilateral exchange rates within the EMS are not literally fixed; rather, they are allowed to fluctuate within specified limits called *margins*. Each participating currency is also assigned a "central" exchange rate against the European Currency Unit (ECU), a basket containing specified amounts of EC currencies. (Not coincidentally, *écu* is the name of an ancient French silver coin.) When a currency's market exchange rate against the ECU diverges sufficiently from its central rate, the central bank that issues the currency is expected to intervene and possibly take other actions to correct the situation.

In return for contributing 20 percent of their gold and dollar holdings to a European Monetary Cooperation Fund, central banks in the EMS receive equivalent holdings of ECUs. ECUs can be used, along with other types of international reserves, to purchase domestic currency from member central banks that acquire it in intervention operations but do not wish to hold it.

Intervention burdens may be shared symmetrically within the EMS, but they need not be. If the French franc depreciates to its lower limit against the DM, for example, the French central bank must rectify the situation by selling DM reserves; at the same time, the German central bank must lend the necessary DM to the Bank of France. EMS rules thus call for a symmetric intervention procedure when an exchange rate reaches the limit of its range, one in which the weak-currency country loses reserves and the other gains them.

Much intervention takes place *within* the EMS exchange rate margins, however, and such intervention does not oblige other central banks to take action. If the Bank of France buys DM assets and adds them to its reserves, for example, the Bundesbank is not required to intervene as long as the franc stays within its margins.

In addition, the symmetry of intervention at the margins is no guarantee that the resulting adjustments in national money supplies are symmetric. There is little at present to prevent a central bank from trying to shift the burden of monetary adjustment onto its EMS partners by sterilizing its foreign exchange intervention.

BENEFITS AND DRAWBACKS OF THE GOLD STANDARD

Advocates of the gold standard argue that it has another desirable property besides symmetry. Because central banks throughout the world are obliged to fix the money price of gold, they cannot allow their money supplies to grow more rapidly than real money demand, since such rapid monetary growth eventually raises the money prices of all goods and services, including gold. A gold standard therefore places automatic limits on the extent to which central banks can cause increases in national price levels through expansionary monetary policies. These limits make the real values of national monies more stable and predictable, thereby enhancing the transactions economies arising from the use of money (see Chapter 15). No such limits to money creation exist under a reserve currency system; the reserve currency country faces no automatic barrier to unlimited money creation.

Offsetting this benefit of a gold standard are some drawbacks:

1. The gold standard places undesirable constraints on the use of monetary policy to fight unemployment. In a worldwide recession, it might be desirable for all countries to expand their money supplies jointly even if this were to raise the price of gold in terms of national currencies.

2. Tying currency values to gold ensures a stable overall price level only if the *relative* price of gold and other goods and services is stable. For example, suppose the dollar price of gold is $35 per ounce while the price of gold in terms of a typical output basket is $\frac{1}{3}$ basket per ounce. This implies a price level of $105 per output basket. Now suppose that there is a major gold discovery in South America and the relative price of gold in terms of output falls to $\frac{1}{4}$ basket per ounce. With the dollar price of gold unchanged at $35 per ounce, the price level would have to rise from $105 to $140 per basket. In fact, studies of the gold standard era do reveal surprisingly large price level fluctuations arising from such changes in gold's relative price.[22]

3. An international payments system based on gold is problematic because central banks cannot increase their holdings of international reserves as their economies grow unless there are continual new gold discoveries. Every central bank would need to hold some gold reserves to fix its currency's gold price and as a buffer against unforeseen economic mishaps, so central banks might bring about world unemployment as they attempted to compete for reserves by selling domestic assets and thus shrinking their money supplies.

4. The gold standard could give countries with potentially large gold production, such as Russia and South Africa, considerable ability to influence macroeconomic conditions throughout the world through market sales of gold.

Because of these drawbacks, few economists favor a return to the gold standard today. As early as 1923, the British economist John Maynard Keynes characterized gold as a "barbarous relic" of an earlier international monetary system.[23] After coming to office in 1981, President Reagan set up a special commission under the direction of monetary scholar Anna Jacobson Schwartz to study whether the United States should return to the gold standard. The commission recommended against a return to gold. While most central banks continue to hold gold as part of their international reserves, the price of gold now plays no special role in influencing countries' monetary policies.

[22] See, for example, Richard N. Cooper, "The Gold Standard: Historical Facts and Future Prospects," *Brookings Papers on Economic Activity* 1:1982, pp. 1–45.

[23] See Keynes, "Alternative Aims in Monetary Policy," reprinted in his *Essays in Persuation* (New York: W. W. Norton & Company, 1963). For a recent dissenting view on the gold standard, see Robert A. Mundell, "International Monetary Reform: The Optimal Mix in Big Countries," in James Tobin, ed., *Macroeconomics, Prices and Quantities* (Washington, D.C.: Brookings Institution, 1983), pp. 285–293.

THE GOLD EXCHANGE STANDARD

Halfway between the gold standard and a pure reserve currency standard is the **gold exchange standard.** Under a gold exchange standard central banks' reserves consist of gold *and* currencies whose prices in terms of gold are fixed, and each central bank fixes its exchange rate to a currency with a fixed gold price. A gold exchange standard can operate like a gold standard in restraining excessive monetary growth throughout the world, but it allows more flexibility in the growth of international reserves, which can consist of assets besides gold. A gold exchange standard is, however, subject to the other limitations of a gold standard listed above.

The post-World War II reserve currency system centered on the dollar was, in fact, originally set up as a gold exchange standard. While foreign central banks did the job of pegging exchange rates, the U.S. Federal Reserve was responsible for holding the dollar price of gold at $35 an ounce. By the mid-1960s, the system operated in practice more like a pure reserve currency system than a gold standard. For reasons examined in the next chapter, President Nixon unilaterally severed the dollar's link to gold in August 1971, shortly before the system of fixed dollar exchange rates was abandoned.

Summary

1. There is a direct link between central bank intervention in the foreign exchange market and the domestic money supply. When a country's central bank purchases foreign assets, the country's money supply automatically increases. Similarly, a central bank sale of foreign assets automatically lowers the money supply. The *central bank balance sheet* shows how foreign exchange intervention affects the money supply because the central bank's liabilities, which rise or fall when its assets rise or fall, are the base of the domestic money supply process. The central bank can negate the money supply effect of intervention through *sterilization.* Absent sterilization, there is a link between the balance of payments and national money supplies that depends on how central banks share the burden of financing payments gaps.

2. A central bank can fix the exchange rate of its currency against foreign currency if it is willing to trade unlimited amounts of domestic money against foreign assets at that rate. To fix the exchange rate, the central bank must intervene in the foreign exchange market whenever this is necessary to prevent the emergence of an excess demand or supply of domestic currency assets. In effect, the central bank adjusts its foreign assets—and so, the domestic money supply—to ensure that asset markets are always in equilibrium under the fixed exchange rate.

3. A commitment to fix the exchange rate forces the central bank to sacrifice its ability to use monetary policy for stabilization. A purchase of domestic assets by the central bank causes an equal fall in its official international reserves, leaving the money supply and output unchanged. Similarly, a sale of domestic assets by the bank causes foreign reserves to rise by the same amount but has no other effects.

4. Fiscal policy, unlike monetary policy, has a more powerful effect on output under fixed exchange rates than under floating rates. Under a fixed exchange rate, fiscal

expansion does not, in the short run, cause a real appreciation that "crowds out" aggregate demand. Instead, it forces central bank purchases of foreign assets and an expansion of the money supply. *Devaluation* also raises aggregate demand and the money supply in the short run. (*Revaluation* has opposite effects.) In the long run, fiscal expansion causes a real appreciation, an increase in the money supply, and a rise in the home price level, while devaluation causes the long-run levels of the money supply and prices to rise in proportion to the exchange rate change.

5. *Balance of payments crises* occur when market participants expect the central bank to change the exchange rate from its current level. If the market decides a devaluation is coming, for example, the domestic interest rate rises above the world interest rate and foreign reserves drop sharply as private capital flows abroad.

6. A system of *managed floating* allows the central bank to retain some ability to control the domestic money supply, but at the cost of greater exchange rate instability. If domestic and foreign bonds are *imperfect substitutes,* however, the central bank may be able to control both the money supply and the exchange rate through sterilized foreign exchange intervention. Empirical evidence provides little support for the idea that sterilized intervention has a significant direct effect on exchange rates. Even when domestic and foreign bonds are *perfect substitutes,* so that there is no *risk premium,* sterilized intervention may operate indirectly through a *signaling effect* that changes market views of future policies.

7. A world system of fixed exchange rates in which countries peg the prices of their currencies in terms of a *reserve currency* involves a striking asymmetry. The reserve currency country, which does not have to fix any exchange rate, can influence economic activity both at home and abroad through its monetary policy. In contrast, all other countries are unable to influence their output or foreign output through monetary policy. This policy asymmetry reflects the fact that the reserve center bears none of the burden of financing its balance of payments.

8. A *gold standard,* in which all countries fix their currencies' prices in terms of gold, avoids the asymmetry inherent in a reserve currency standard and also places constraints on the growth of countries' money supplies. But the gold standard has serious drawbacks that make it impractical as a way of organizing today's international monetary system. Even the dollar-based *gold exchange standard* set up after World War II ultimately proved unworkable.

Key Terms

managed floating exchange rates
European Monetary System (EMS)
central bank balance sheet
sterilized foreign exchange intervention
devaluation
revaluation
balance of payments crisis
capital flight
perfect asset substitutability
imperfect asset substitutability
risk premium
signaling effect of foreign exchange intervention
reserve currency
gold standard
gold exchange standard

Problems

1. Show how an expansion in the central bank's domestic assets ultimately affects its balance sheet under a fixed exchange rate. How are the central bank's transactions in the foreign exchange market reflected in the balance of payments accounts?
2. Do the exercises in the previous question for an increase in government spending.
3. Describe the effects of an unexpected devaluation on the central bank's balance sheet and on the balance of payments accounts.
4. Explain why a devaluation improves the current account in this chapter's model. (Hint: Consider the *XX* curve developed in the last chapter.)
5. The following paragraphs appeared in the *New York Times* on September 22, 1986 (see ''Europeans May Prop the Dollar,'' p. D1):

   To keep the dollar from falling against the West German mark, the European central banks would have to sell marks and buy dollars, a procedure known as intervention. But the pool of currencies in the marketplace is vastly larger than all the governments' holdings.

   Billions of dollars worth of currencies are traded each day. Without support from the United States and Japan, it is unlikely that market intervention from even the two most economically influential members of the European Community—Britain and West Germany—would have much impact on the markets. However, just the stated intention of the Community's central banks to intervene could disrupt the market with its psychological effect.

   Economists say that intervention works only when markets turn unusually erratic, as they have done upon reports of the assassination of a President, or when intervention is used to push the markets along in a direction where they are already headed anyway.

   a. Do you agree with the statement in the article that Germany has little ability to influence the exchange rate of the DM?

   b. Do you agree with the last paragraph's evaluation of the efficacy of intervention?

   c. Describe how ''just the stated intention'' to intervene could have a ''psychological effect'' on the foreign exchange market.

   d. Try your hand at rewriting the above paragraphs in more precise language so that they reflect what you learned in this chapter.
6. Can you think of reasons why a government might willingly sacrifice some of its ability to use monetary policy so that it can have more stable exchange rates?
7. How does fiscal expansion affect a country's current account under a fixed exchange rate?
8. Explain why temporary and permanent fiscal expansions do not have different effects under fixed exchange rates, as they do under floating.
9. Devaluation is often used by countries to improve their current accounts. Since the current account equals national saving less domestic investment, however (see Chapter 13), this improvement can occur only if investment falls, saving rises, or both. How might devaluation affect national saving and domestic investment?

10. Using the *DD-AA* model, analyze the output and balance of payments effects of an import tariff under fixed exchange rates. What would happen if all countries in the world simultaneously tried to improve employment and the balance of payments by imposing tariffs?

11. When a central bank devalues after a balance of payments crisis, it usually gains foreign reserves. Can this capital inflow be explained using our model? What would happen if the market believed *another* devaluation was to occur in the near future?

12. Suppose that under the postwar "dollar standard" system foreign central banks had held dollar reserves in the form of green dollar bills hidden in their vaults rather than U.S. Treasury bills. Would the international monetary adjustment mechanism have been symmetric or asymmetric? (Hint: Think about what happens to the U.S. and German money supplies, for example, when the German Bundesbank sells DM for dollar bills that it then keeps.)

13. To avoid deflation due to insufficient gold supplies, countries have sometimes adopted a "bimetallic" monetary standard in which the currency has fixed prices in terms of both gold *and* silver. (The United States was technically on a bimetallic standard until 1873.) Can you see any special problems that a bimetallic standard might cause?

14. "When domestic and foreign bonds are perfect substitutes, a central bank should be indifferent about using domestic or foreign assets to implement monetary policy." Discuss.

15. United States foreign exchange intervention is sometimes done by an Exchange Stabilization Fund or ESF (a branch of the Treasury Department) that manages a portfolio of U.S. government and foreign currency bonds. An ESF intervention to support the yen, for example, would take the form of a portfolio shift out of dollar and into yen assets. Show that ESF interventions are automatically sterilized and thus do not alter money supplies. How do ESF operations affect the foreign exchange risk premium?

16. Use a diagram like Figure 18-7 to explain how a central bank can alter the domestic interest rate, while holding the exchange rate fixed, under imperfect asset substitutability.

Further Reading

Anatol Balbach. "The Mechanics of Intervention in Exchange Markets." *Federal Reserve Bank of St. Louis Review* 60 (February 1978), pp. 2–7. A detailed account of central bank intervention procedures.

William H. Branson. "Causes of Appreciation and Volatility of the Dollar," in *The U.S. Dollar—Recent Developments, Outlook, and Policy Options.* Kansas City: Federal Reserve Bank of Kansas City, 1985, pp. 33–52. Develops and applies a model of exchange rate determination with imperfect asset substitutability.

Dale W. Henderson and Stephanie Sampson. "Intervention in Foreign Exchange Markets: A Summary of Ten Staff Studies," *Federal Reserve Bulletin* 69 (November 1983), pp. 830–

836. Presents the major findings of the Federal Reserve intervention study that followed the June 1982 Versailles economic summit meeting.

Ronald I. McKinnon. *A New Tripartite Monetary Agreement or a Limping Dollar Standard?* Princeton Essays in International Finance 106. International Finance Section, Department of Econmics, Princeton University, October 1974. Critical analysis of intervention arrangements under the post-World War II fixed exchange rate system.

Robert A. Mundell. ''Capital Mobility and Stabilization Policy under Fixed and Flexible Exchange Rates.'' *Canadian Journal of Economics and Political Science* 29 (November 1963), pp. 475–485. Reprinted as Chapter 18 in Mundell's *International Economics.* New York: Macmillan, 1968. Classic account of the effects of monetary and fiscal policies under alternative exchange rate regimes.

Michael Mussa. ''The Exchange Rate, the Balance of Payments and Monetary and Fiscal Policy under a Regime of Controlled Floating,'' in Jan Herin, Assar Lindbeck, and Johan Myhrman, eds. *Flexible Exchange Rates and Stabilization Policy.* Boulder, CO: Westview Press, 1977, pp. 97–116. An exposition of the monetary approaches to the balance of payments and the exchange rate.

Michael Mussa. *The Role of Official Intervention.* Occasional Paper 6. New York: Group of Thirty, 1981. Discusses the theory and practice of central bank foreign exchange intervention under a dirty float.

Maurice Obstfeld. ''Can We Sterilize? Theory and Evidence.'' *American Economic Review* 72 (May 1982), pp. 45–50. A review of research on sterilized foreign exchange intervention under fixed and floating exchange rates.

Anna J. Schwartz. *Money in Historical Perspective.* Chicago: University of Chicago Press, 1987. Chapters 13–16 cover the gold standard and alternative exchange rate systems.

Warren E. Weber. ''Do Sterilized Interventions Affect Exchange Rates?'' *Federal Reserve Bank of Minneapolis Quarterly Review* 10 (Summer 1986), pp. 14–23. More evidence on whether sterilized intervention influences exchange rates.

Appendix I to Chapter 18 ●
Equilibrium in the Foreign Exchange Market with Imperfect Asset Substitutability

This appendix develops a model of the foreign exchange market in which risk factors may make domestic currency and foreign currency assets imperfect substitutes. The model gives rise to a risk premium that can separate the expected rates of return on domestic and foreign assets.[1]

DEMAND

Because individuals dislike risky situations in which their wealth may vary greatly from day to day, they decide how to allocate wealth among different assets by looking at the riskiness of the resulting portfolio as well as at the expected return it offers. Someone who puts her wealth entirely into British pounds, for example, may expect a high return but can be wiped out if the pound unexpectedly depreciates. A more sensible strategy is to invest in several currencies, even if some have lower expected returns than the pound, and thus reduce the impact on wealth of bad luck with any one currency. By spreading risk in this way among several currencies, an individual can reduce the variability of her wealth.

Considerations of risk make it reasonable to assume that an individual's demand for interest-bearing domestic currency assets increases when the interest they offer (R) rises relative to the domestic currency return on foreign currency assets $[R^* + (E^e - E)/E]$. Put another way, an individual will be willing to increase the riskiness of her portfolio by investing more heavily in domestic currency assets only if she is compensated by an increase in the relative expected return on those assets.

We summarize this assumption by writing individual i's demand for domestic currency bonds, B_i^d, as an increasing function of the rate-of-return difference between domestic and foreign bonds,

$$B_i^d = B_i^d[R - R^* - (E^e - E)/E].$$

Of course, B_i^d also depends on other factors specific to individual i, such as her wealth and income. The demand for domestic currency bonds can be negative or positive, and in the former case individual i is a net borrower in the home currency, that is, a *supplier* of domestic currency bonds.

To find the *aggregate* private demand for domestic currency bonds, we need only add up individual demands B_i^d for all individuals i in the world. This summation gives the aggregate demand for domestic currency bonds, B^d, which is also an increasing function of the expected rate of return difference in favor of domestic currency assets. Therefore,

$$\begin{aligned}\text{Demand} &= B^d[R - R^* - (E^e - E)/E] \\ &= \text{sum (for all } i\text{) of } B_i^d[R - R^* - (E^e - E)/E].\end{aligned}$$

Since some private individuals may be borrowing, and therefore supplying bonds, B^d should be interpreted as the private sector's *net* demand for domestic currency bonds.

[1] The Mathematical Postscript to Chapter 22 develops a microeconomic model of individual demand for risky assets.

Appendix II to Chapter 18 ● The Monetary Approach to the Balance of Payments

The close link discussed above between a country's balance of payments and its money supply suggests that fluctuations in central bank reserves can be thought of as the result of changes in the money market. This method of analyzing the balance of payments is called the *monetary approach to the balance of payments*. The monetary approach was developed in the 1950s and 1960s by the International Monetary Fund's research department under Jacques J. Polak, and by Harry G. Johnson, Robert A. Mundell, and their students at the University of Chicago.[1]

The monetary approach can be illustrated through a simple model linking the balance of payments to developments in the money market. To begin, recall that the money market is in equilibrium when the real money supply equals real money demand, that is, when

$$M^s/P = L(R,Y). \qquad \textbf{(18AII-1)}$$

Now let F^* denote the central bank's foreign assets (measured in domestic currency) and A its domestic assets (domestic credit). If μ is the *money multiplier* that defines the relation between total central bank assets ($F^* + A$) and the money supply, then

$$M^s = \mu(F^* + A). \qquad \textbf{(18AII-2)}$$

The change in central bank foreign assets over any time period, ΔF^*, equals the balance of payments (for a nonreserve currency country). By combining (18AII-1) and (18AII-2), we can express the central bank's foreign assets as

$$F^* = (1/\mu)PL(R,Y) - A.$$

If we assume that μ is a constant, the balance of payments surplus is

$$\Delta F^* = (1/\mu)\Delta[PL(R,Y)] - \Delta A. \qquad \textbf{(18AII-3)}$$

The last equation summarizes the monetary approach. The first term on its right-hand side reflects changes in nominal money demand and tells us that, all else equal, an increase in money demand will bring about a balance of payments surplus and an accompanying increase in the money supply that maintains money market equilibrium. The second term in the balance of payments equation reflects supply factors in the money market. An increase in domestic credit raises money supply relative to money demand, all else equal; so the balance of payments must go into deficit to reduce the money supply and restore money market equilibrium.

Because the balance of payments equals the sum of the current and (nonreserve) capital account surpluses (see Chapter 13), much of the economics literature that appeared before the monetary approach was developed explained balance of payments movements as the result of current or capital account changes. An important contribution of the monetary approach was to stress that in many situations, balance of payments problems result directly from imbalances in

[1] Many original articles using the monetary approach are collected in Jacob A. Frenkel and Harry G. Johnson, eds., *The Monetary Approach to the Balance of Payments* (London: George Allen and Unwin, 1976), and International Monetary Fund, *The Monetary Approach to the Balance of Payments* (Washington, D.C.: International Monetary Fund, 1977).

the money market and a policy solution that relies on monetary policy is therefore most appropriate. A large balance of payments deficit may be the result of excessive domestic credit creation, for example. Even though this balance of payments deficit will generally involve deficits in both the current and private capital accounts, it would be misleading to view it as fundamentally due to an exogenous fall in relative world demand for domestic goods or assets.

There are many realistic cases, however, in which a balance of payments analysis based on the monetary approach is roundabout and possibly misleading as a guide to policy. Suppose, for example, that a temporary fall in foreign demand for domestic products does occur. This change will cause a fall in the current account and in the balance of payments, but these effects can be counteracted (when rigid capital account restrictions are not in place) by a temporarily expansionary fiscal policy.

Because output and thus money demand fall, the monetary approach also predicts that a balance of payments deficit will result from a fall in export demand. It would be wrong, however, for policy makers to conclude that because the balance of payments deficit is associated with a fall in money demand, a contraction of domestic credit is the best response. If the central bank were to restrict domestic credit to improve the balance of payments, unemployment would remain high and might even rise.

While the monetary approach is an extremely useful analytical tool, it must be applied with caution in seeking solutions to macroeconomic problems. It is most useful for formulating solutions to policy problems that are a direct result of shifts in domestic money demand or supply.

Appendix III to Chapter 18 ● The Timing of Balance of Payments Crises

In the text we modeled a balance of payments crisis as a sudden loss of confidence in the central bank's promise to hold the exchange rate fixed in the future. Our analysis said nothing, however, about the factors that determine when (if ever) such a loss of confidence will occur. Perhaps surprisingly, a currency crisis often is not the result of arbitrary shifts in market sentiment, as exasperated policy makers embroiled in crises sometimes contend. Instead, simple economic theory may allow us to predict the date of a crisis through a careful analysis of government policies and the market's rational response to them.[1]

It is easiest to make the main points using the assumptions and notation of the monetary approach to the balance of payments (as developed in Appendix II to this chapter) and the monetary approach to the exchange rate (Chapter 16). To simplify we will assume that output prices are perfectly flexible and output is constant at its full-employment level. We will also assume that market participants have perfect foresight concerning the future, an assumption that rules out arbitrary shifts in expectation.

The precise timing of a payments crisis cannot be determined independently of government policies. In particular, we have to describe not only how the government is behaving today, but also how it plans to react to future events in the economy. Two assumptions about official behavior are made: (1) The central bank is allowing the stock of domestic credit, A, to expand steadily, and will do so forever. (2) The central bank is currently fixing the exchange rate at the level E^0, but it will allow the exchange rate to float freely forever if its foreign reserves, F^*, ever fall to zero. Furthermore, the authorities will defend E^0 to the bitter end by selling foreign reserves at that price as long as they have any to sell.

These assumptions are not very realistic, but other more complicated stories would lead to similar conclusions. You can think of assumption 1 as reflecting the government's need to finance its budget deficit by borrowing money *directly* from the central bank. Such a policy course would increase A over time by increasing the central bank's claims on government—which do count as domestic assets. You can think of assumption 2 as reflecting a limit on the central bank's ability to borrow foreign reserves to defend its currency from speculative attack. Once the central bank has used up its reserves and foreign currency credit lines, it has no choice but to give up the game and withdraw from the foreign exchange market.

The problem with the central bank's policies is that they are inconsistent with maintaining a fixed exchange rate indefinitely. The monetary approach suggests that foreign reserves will fall steadily as domestic assets continually rise. Eventually, therefore, reserves will have to run out and the fixed exchange rate E^0 will have to be abandoned. In fact, speculators will force the issue by mounting a speculative attack and buying all of the central bank's reserves while reserves are still at a positive level.

We can describe the timing of this crisis with the help of a definition and a diagram. The *shadow* floating exchange rate at time t, denoted E_t^s, is the exchange rate that would prevail at

[1] Models of balance of payments crisis are developed in Paul Krugman, ''A Model of Balance-of-Payments Crises,'' *Journal of Money, Credit and Banking* 11 (August 1979), pp. 311–325; Robert P. Flood and Peter M. Garber, ''Collapsing Exchange Rate Regimes: Some Linear Examples,'' *Journal of International Economics* 17 (August 1984), pp. 1–14; and Maurice Obstfeld, ''Rational and Self-fulfilling Balance-of-Payments Crises,'' *American Economic Review* 76 (March 1986), pp. 72–81.

time t if the central bank held no foreign reserves, allowed the currency to float, but continued to allow domestic credit to grow over time. We know from the monetary approach to the exchange rate that the result would be a situation of *ongoing inflation* in which E^s_t trended upward over time in proportion to the domestic credit growth rate. The upper panel of Figure 18AIII-1 shows this upward trend in the shadow floating rate, together with the level E^0 at which the exchange rate is initially pegged. The time T indicated on the horizontal axis is defined as the date on which the shadow exchange rate reaches E^0.

The lower panel of the figure shows how reserves behave over time when domestic credit is steadily growing. (An increase in reserves is a move down from the origin along the vertical axis.) We have shown the path of reserves as a kinked curve that falls gradually until time T, at which time reserves drop in a single stroke to zero. This precipitous reserve loss (of size F^*_T) is the speculative attack that forces the end of the fixed exchange rate, and we now argue that such an attack must occur precisely at time T if assets markets are to clear at each moment.

We are assuming that output Y is fixed, so equation (18AII-3) tells us that reserves will fall over time at the same rate that domestic credit grows as long as the domestic interest rate R doesn't change. What do we know about the behavior of the interest rate? We know that while the exchange rate is convincingly fixed, R will equal the foreign interest rate R^* because no

FIGURE 18AIII-1
How the timing of a balance of payments crisis is determined.
The market stages a speculative attack and buys the remaining foreign reserve stock F^*_T at time T, when the shadow floating exchange rate E^s_T just equals the precollapse fixed exchange rate E^0.

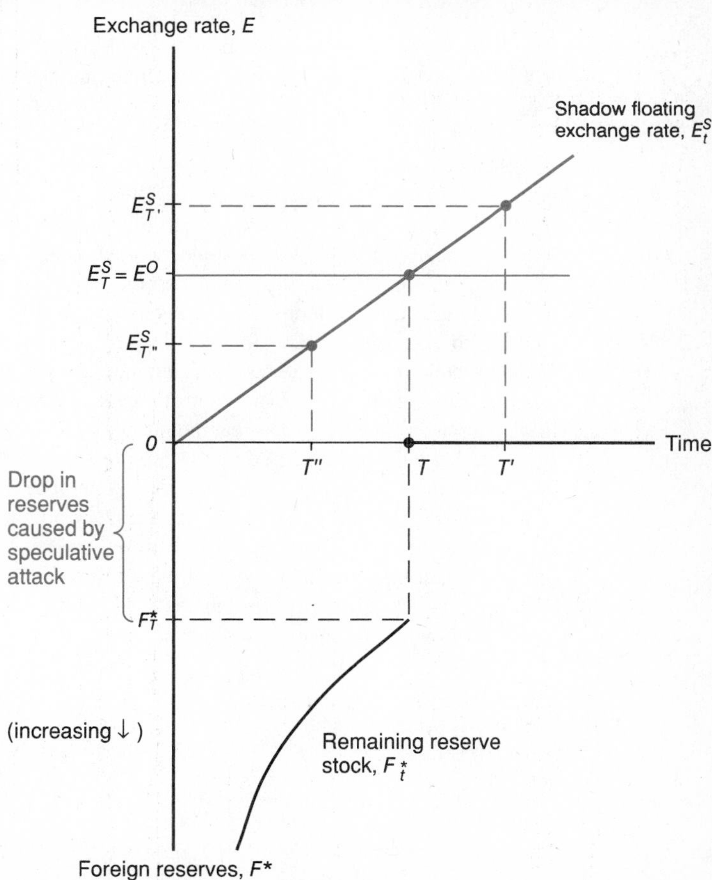

depreciation is expected. Thus, reserves fall gradually over time, as shown in Figure 18AIII-1, as long as the exchange rate remains fixed at E^0.

Imagine now that reserves first hit zero at a time like T', which is *later* than time T. Our shadow exchange rate E^s is defined as the equilibrium floating rate that prevails when foreign reserves are zero, so if reserves first hit zero at time T', the authorities abandon E^0 forever and the exchange rate jumps immediately to the higher level $E^s_{T'}$. There is something wrong with this "equilibrium," however: each market participant knows that the home currency will depreciate very sharply at time T' and will try to profit by buying foreign reserves from the central bank, at the lower price E^0, just an instant *before* T'. Thus the central bank will lose all of its reserves before T', contrary to our assumption that reserves first hit zero *at* T'. So we have not really been looking at an equilibrium after all.

Do we get to an equilibrium by assuming instead that speculators buy out the official reserve stock at a time like T'' that is *earlier* than time T? Again the answer is no, as you can see by considering the choices facing an individual asset holder. He knows that if central bank reserves reach zero at time T'', the currency will appreciate from E^0 to $E^{es}_{T''}$ as the central bank leaves the foreign exchange market. It therefore will behoove him not to join any speculative attack that pushes reserves to zero at time T''; in fact, he would prefer to *sell* as much foreign currency as possible to the central bank just before time T'' and then buy it back at the lower market-determined price that would prevail after a crisis. Since every market participant would find it in his or her interest to act in this way, however, a speculative attack simply can't occur before time T. No speculator would want to buy central bank reserves at the price E^0, knowing that an immediate discrete capital loss was at hand.

Only if foreign reserves hit zero precisely at time T are asset markets continually in equilibrium. As noted above, time T is defined by the condition

$$E^s_T = E^0,$$

which states that if reserves suddenly drop to zero at time T, the exchange rate remains initially at its pegged level, and only subsequently floats upward.

The absence of any foreseen initial jump in the exchange rate, either upward or downward, removes the opportunities for arbitrage (described above) that prevent speculative attacks at times like T' or T''. In addition, the money market remains in equilibrium at time T, even though the exchange rate doesn't jump, because two factors offset each other exactly. As reserves drop sharply to zero, the money supply falls [see equation (18AII-2)]. We also know that at the moment the fixed exchange rate is abandoned, people will expect the currency to begin depreciating over time. The domestic interest rate R will therefore move upward to maintain interest parity, and this change reduces real money demand in line with the fall in the real money supply.

We have therefore tied down the exact date on which a balance of payments crisis forces the authorities off the fixed exchange rate. Note once again that in our example, a crisis must occur at *some* point because profligate monetary policies make one inevitable. The fact that a crisis occurs while the central bank's foreign reserves are still positive might suggest to superficial observers that ill-founded market sentiment is leading to a premature panic. This is not the case. The speculative attack we have analyzed is the only outcome that does not confront market participants with arbitrage opportunities.[2]

[2] Our finding that reserves fall to zero in a single attack comes from our assumptions that the market can foresee perfectly the future course of events and that trading takes place continuously. If we were to allow instead some discrete uncertainty—for example, about the rate of domestic credit growth—the domestic interest rate would rise as a collapse became more probable, causing a series of "speculative" money-demand reductions prior to the final depletion of foreign reserves. Each of these preliminary attacks would be similar to the type of crisis described in the chapter.

Part Four
International Macroeconomic Policy

The International Monetary System, 1870–1973

Chapter 19

In the previous two chapters we saw how a single country can use monetary, fiscal, and exchange rate policy to change the levels of employment and production within its borders. Although the analysis usually assumed that macroeconomic conditions in the rest of the world were not affected by the actions of the country we were studying, this assumption is not, in general, a valid one: any change in the home country's real exchange rate automatically implies an opposite change in foreign real exchange rates, and any shift in overall domestic spending is likely to change domestic demand for foreign goods. Unless the home country is insignificantly small, developments within its borders affect macroeconomic conditions abroad and therefore complicate the task of foreign policy makers.

The inherent interdependence of open national economies has sometimes made it more difficult for governments to achieve such policy goals as full employment and price level stability. The channels of interdependence depend, in turn, on the monetary and exchange rate arrangements that countries adopt—a set of institutions called the *international monetary system.* This chapter examines how the international monetary system influenced macroeconomic policy making and performance during three periods: the gold standard era (1870–1914), the interwar period (1918–1939), and the post-World War II years during which exchange rates were fixed under the Bretton Woods agreement (1945–1973).

In an open economy, macroeconomic policy has two basic goals, internal balance (full employment with price stability) and external balance (avoiding excessive imbalances in international payments). Because a country cannot alter its international payments position without automatically causing an opposite change of equal magnitude in the payments position of the rest of the world, one country's pursuit of its macroeconomic goals inevitably influences how well other countries attain their goals. The goal of external balance therefore offers a clear illustration of how policy actions taken abroad may change an economy's position relative to the position its government prefers.

Throughout the period 1870–1973, with its various international currency arrangements, how did countries try to attain internal and external balance, and how successful were they? Did policy makers worry about the foreign repercussions of their actions, or did each adopt nationalistic measures that were self-defeating for the world economy as a whole? The answers to these questions depend on the international monetary system in effect at the time.

Macroeconomic Policy Goals in an Open Economy

In open economies, policy makers are motivated by the goals of internal and external balance. Simply defined, **internal balance** requires the full employment of a country's resources and domestic price level stability. **External balance** is attained when a country's current account is neither so deeply in deficit that the country may be unable to repay its foreign debts in the future nor so strongly in surplus that foreigners are put in that position.

In practice, neither of these definitions captures the full range of potential policy concerns. Along with full employment and stability of the overall price level, for example, policy makers may have a particular domestic distribution of income as an additional internal target. Depending on exchange rate arrangements, policy makers may worry about swings in balance of payments accounts other than the current account. To make matters even more complicated, the line between external and internal goals can be a fuzzy one. How should one classify an employment target for export industries, for example, when export growth influences the economy's ability to repay its foreign debts?

The simple definitions of internal and external balance given above, however, capture the goals that most policy makers share regardless of the particular economic environment. We therefore organize our analysis around these definitions and discuss possible additional aspects of internal or external balance when they are relevant.

INTERNAL BALANCE: FULL EMPLOYMENT AND PRICE LEVEL STABILITY

When a country's productive resources are fully employed and its price level is stable, the country is in internal balance. The waste and hardship that occur when resources are underemployed is clear. If a country's economy is "overheated" and resources are *over*employed, however, waste of a different (though probably less hamful) kind occurs. For example, workers on overtime might prefer to be working less and enjoying leisure, but their contracts require them to put in longer hours during periods of high demand.

Machines that are being worked more intensely than usual will tend to suffer more frequent breakdowns and to depreciate more quickly.

Under- and overemployment also lead to general price level movements that reduce the economy's efficiency by making the real value of the monetary unit less certain and thus a less useful guide for economic decisions. Since domestic wages and prices rise when the demands for labor and output exceed full-employment levels, and fall in the opposite case, the government must prevent substantial movements in aggregate demand relative to its full-employment level to maintain a stable, predictable price level.

Inflation or deflation can occur even under conditions of full employment, of course, if the expectations of workers and firms about future monetary policy lead to an upward or downward wage-price spiral. Such a spiral can continue, however, only if the central bank fulfills expectations through continuing injections or withdrawals of money (Chapter 15).

One particularly disruptive effect of an unstable price level is its effect on the real value of loan contracts. Because loans tend to be denominated in the monetary unit, unexpected price level changes cause income to be redistributed between creditors and debtors. A sudden increase in the U.S. price level, for example, makes those with dollar debts better off, since the money they owe to lenders is now worth less in terms of goods and services. At the same time, the price level increase makes creditors worse off. Because such accidental income redistribution can cause considerable distress to those who are hurt, governments have another reason to maintain price level stability.[1]

Theoretically, a perfectly predictable trend of rising or falling prices would not be too costly, since everyone would be able to calculate easily the real value of money at any point in the future. But in the real world, there appears to be no such thing as a predictable inflation rate. Indeed, experience shows that the unpredictability of the general price level is magnified tremendously in periods of rapid price level change. The costs of inflation have been most apparent recently in countries like Argentina and Brazil, where astronomical price level increases caused the domestic currencies practically to stop functioning as units of account. (Both countries had currency reforms as a result of the public's flight from domestic money.)

To avoid price level instability, therefore, the government must prevent large fluctuations in output, which are also undesirable in themselves. In addition, it must avoid ongoing inflation and deflation by ensuring that the domestic money supply does not grow too quickly or too slowly.

EXTERNAL BALANCE: THE OPTIMAL LEVEL OF THE CURRENT ACCOUNT

The notion of external balance is more difficult to define than internal balance because there are no natural benchmarks like "full employment" or "stable prices" to apply

[1] The situation is somewhat different when the government itself is a major debtor in domestic currency. In such cases, a surprise inflation that reduces the real value of government debt may be a convenient way of taxing the public. This method of taxation has been quite common in developing countries (see Chapter 23), but elsewhere it has generally been applied with reluctance and in extreme situations (for example, during wars). A policy of trying to surprise the public with inflation undermines the government's credibility and, through the Fisher effect, worsens the terms on which the government can borrow in the future.

to an economy's external transactions. Whether an economy's trade with the outside world poses macroeconomic problems depends on several factors, including the economy's particular circumstances, conditions in the outside world, and the institutional arrangements governing its economic relations with foreign countries. A country that is committed to fix its exchange rate against a foreign currency, for example, may well adopt a different definition of external balance than one whose currency floats.

International economics textbooks often identify external balance with balance in a country's current account. While this definition is appropriate in some circumstances, it is not helpful as a general rule. Recall from Chapter 13 that a country with a current account deficit is borrowing resources from the rest of the world that it will have to pay back in the future. This situation is not necessarily undesirable. For example, the country's opportunities for investing the borrowed resources may be attractive relative to the opportunities available in the rest of the world. In this case, paying back loans from foreigners poses no problem because a profitable investment will generate a return high enough to cover the interest and principal on those loans. Similarly, a current account surplus may pose no problem if domestic savings are being invested more profitably abroad than they would be at home.

More generally, we may think of current account imbalances as providing another example of how countries gain from trade. The trade involved is what we have called *intertemporal trade,* that is, the trade of consumption over time (Chapter 7). Just as countries with differing abilities to produce goods at a single point in time gain from concentrating their production on what they do best and trading, countries can gain from concentrating the world's investment in those economies best able to turn current output into future output. Countries with weak investment opportunities should invest little at home and channel their savings into more productive investment activity abroad. Put another way, countries where investment is relatively unproductive should be net exporters of currently available output (and thus have current account surpluses), while countries where investment is relatively productive should be net importers of current output (and have current account deficits). To pay off their foreign debts when the investments mature, the latter countries export output to the former countries and thereby complete the exchange of present output for future output.

Other considerations may also justify an unbalanced current account. A country where output drops temporarily (for example, because of an unusually bad crop failure) may wish to borrow from foreigners to avoid the sharp temporary fall in its consumption that would otherwise occur. In the absence of this borrowing, the price of present output in terms of future output would be higher in the low-output country than abroad, so the intertemporal trade that eliminates this price difference leads to mutual gains.

Insisting that all countries be in current account equilibrium makes no allowance for these important gains from trade over time. Thus, no realistic policy maker would want to adopt a balanced current account as a policy target appropriate in all circumstances.

At a given point, however, policy makers generally adopt *some* current account target as an objective, and this target defines their external balance goal. While the target level of the current account is generally not zero, governments usually try to avoid extremely large external surpluses or deficits unless they have clear evidence that large imbalances are justified by potential intertemporal trade gains. (After the sharp rise in oil prices in the early 1970s, for example, Norway's government allowed extensive foreign borrowing to fund the development of the country's North Sea oil reserves.) Governments are cautious because the exact current account balance that maximizes the gains from intertemporal trade is difficult if not impossible to figure out. In addition, this optimal current account balance can change unpredictably over time as conditions in the economy change. Current account balances that are very wide of the mark can, however, cause serious problems.

Problems with Excessive Current Account Deficits. Why do governments prefer to avoid current account deficits that are too large? As noted, a current account deficit (which means that the economy is borrowing from abroad) may pose no problem if the borrowed funds are channeled into productive domestic investment projects that pay for themselves with the revenue they generate in the future. Sometimes, however, large current account deficits represent temporarily high consumption resulting from misguided government policies or some other malfunction in the economy. At other times, the investment projects that draw on foreign funds may be badly planned and based on overoptimistic expectations about future profitability. In such cases, the government might wish to reduce the current account deficit immediately rather than face problems in repaying debts to foreigners later. In particular, a large current account deficit caused by an expansionary fiscal policy that does not simultaneously make domestic investment opportunities more profitable may signal a need for the government to restore external balance by changing its economic course.

At times the external target is imposed from abroad rather than chosen by the domestic government. When countries begin to have trouble meeting their payments on past foreign loans, foreign creditors become reluctant to lend them new funds and may even demand immediate repayment of the earlier loans. Since 1982, many developing economies (particularly those in Latin America) have faced this problem of a limited ability to borrow abroad. In such cases, the home government may have to take severe action to reduce the country's desired borrowing from foreigners to feasible levels.

Problems with Excessive Current Account Surpluses. An excessive current account surplus poses problems that are different from those posed by deficits. A surplus in the current account implies that a country is accumulating assets located abroad. Why are growing domestic claims to foreign wealth ever a problem? One potential reason stems from the fact that, for a given level of national saving, an increased current account surplus implies lower investment in domestic plant and equipment. (This follows from the national income indentity, $S = CA + I$, which says that total domestic saving, S, is divided between foreign asset accumulation, CA, and domestic investment, I.) Several factors might lead policy makers to prefer that domestic savings be devoted to higher levels of domestic investment and lower levels of foreign investment. First, the returns on domestic capital may be easier to tax than those on assets abroad. Second, an addition to the home capital stock may reduce domestic unemployment and therefore lead to higher national income than an equal addition to foreign assets. Finally, domestic investment by one firm may have beneficial technological spillover effects on other domestic producers that the investing firm does not capture. In this case also, the nation gains more at the margin from investing at home rather than abroad.

If a large home current account surplus reflects excessive external borrowing by foreigners, the home country may in the future find itself unable to collect the money it is owed. Put another way, the home country may lose part of its foreign wealth if foreigners find they have borrowed more than they can repay. In contrast, nonrepayment of a loan between domestic residents leads to a redistribution of national wealth within the home country but causes no change in the level of national wealth.

Excessive current account surpluses may also be inconvenient for political reasons. Countries with large surpluses can become targets for discriminatory protectionist measures by trading partners with external deficits. To avoid such damaging restrictions, surplus countries may try to keep their surpluses from becoming too large.

Although high surpluses, like deficits, can pose problems, governments whose economies are in deficit usually face much more intense pressures to restore external balance. This difference reflects a basic asymmetry. A borrowing country is dependent on its creditors, who may withdraw their credit at any time. In contrast, a lending country faces no such market-imposed limit on its surplus. Its government often can postpone external adjustment, if it chooses, for an indefinite period, even though the surplus may be detrimental to national welfare.

To summarize, the goal of external balance is a level of the current account that allows the most important gains from trade over time to be realized without risking the problems discussed above. Because governments do not know this current account level exactly, they usually try to avoid large deficits or surpluses unless there is clear evidence of large gains from intertemporal trade.

International Macroeconomic Policy under the Gold Standard, 1870–1914

The gold standard period between 1870 and 1914 was based on ideas about international macroeconomic policy very different from those that have formed the basis of international monetary arrangements in the second half of the twentieth century. Nevertheless, the period warrants attention because subsequent attempts to reform the international monetary system on the basis of fixed exchange rates can be viewed as attempts to build on the strengths of the gold standard while avoiding its weaknesses. (Some of these strengths and weaknesses were discussed in Chapter 18.) This section looks at how the gold standard functioned in practice before World War I and examines how well it enabled countries to attain goals of internal and external balance.

ORIGINS OF THE GOLD STANDARD

The gold standard had its origin in the use of gold coins as a medium of exchange, unit of account, and store of value. While gold has been used in this way since ancient times, the gold standard as a legal institution dates from 1819, when the British Parliament passed the Resumption Act. This law derived its name from its requirement that the Bank of England *resume* its practice—discontinued four years after the outbreak of the Napoleonic Wars (1793–1815)—of exchanging currency notes for gold on demand at a fixed rate. The Resumption Act marks the first adoption of a true gold standard because it simultaneously repealed long-standing restrictions on the export of gold coins and bullion from Britain.

Later in the nineteenth century, Germany, Japan, and other countries also adopted the gold standard. At the time, Britain was the world's leading economic power, and other nations hoped to achieve similar economic success by imitating British institutions. The United States effectively joined the gold standard in 1879 when it pegged to gold the paper ''greenbacks'' issued during the Civil War. The U.S. Gold Standard Act of 1900 institutionalized the dollar-gold link. Given Britain's preeminence in international trade and the advanced development of its financial institutions, London naturally became the center of the international monetary system built on the gold standard.

EXTERNAL BALANCE UNDER THE GOLD STANDARD

Under the gold standard, the primary responsibility of a central bank was to preserve the official parity between its currency and gold; to maintain this price, the central bank needed an adequate stock of gold reserves. Policy makers therefore viewed external balance not in terms of a current account target but as a situation in which the central bank was neither gaining gold from abroad nor (more important) losing gold to foreigners at too rapid a rate.

In the modern terminology of Chapter 13, central banks tried to avoid sharp fluctuations in the *balance of payments* (or official settlements balance), the sum of the current account balance and the nonreserve component of the capital account balance. Because international reserves took the form of gold during this period, the surplus or deficit in the balance of payments had to be financed by gold shipments between central banks.[2] To avoid large gold movements, central banks adopted policies that pushed the nonserve component of the capital account surplus (or deficit) into line with the current account deficit (or surplus). A country is said to be in **balance of payments equilibrium** when the sum of its current and its nonreserve capital account equals zero, so that the current account balance is financed entirely by international lending without reserve movements.

Many governments took a laissez-faire attitude toward the current account. Britain's current account surplus between 1870 and World War I averaged 5.2 percent of its GNP, a figure that is remarkably high by post-1945 standards. (Today, a current account/GNP ratio half that size would be considered sizable.) Several borrowing countries, however, did experience difficulty at one time or another in paying their foreign debts. Perhaps because Britain was the world's leading exporter of international economic theory as well as of capital during these years, the economic writing of the gold standard era places little emphasis on problems of current account adjustment.[3]

THE PRICE-SPECIE-FLOW MECHANISM

The gold standard contains some powerful automatic mechanisms that contribute to the simultaneous achievement of balance of payments equilibrium by all countries. The

[2] In reality, central banks had begun to hold foreign currencies in their reserves even before 1914. (The pound sterling was the leading reserve currency.) It is still true, however, that the balance of payments was financed mainly by gold shipments during this period.

[3] While the economic consequences of the current account were often ignored (at least by surplus countries), governments sometimes restricted international lending by their residents to put political pressure on foreign governments. The political dimensions of international capital flows before World War I are examined in a famous study by Herbert Feis, *Europe, the World's Banker* (New Haven: Yale University Press, 1930).

most important of these, the **price-specie-flow mechanism,** was recognized by the eighteenth century (when precious metals were referred to as ''specie''). David Hume, the Scottish philosopher, in 1752 described the price-specie-flow mechanism as follows:

> Suppose four-fifths of all the money in Great Britain to be annihilated in one night, and the nation reduced to the same condition, with regard to specie, as in the reigns of the Harrys and the Edwards, what would be the consequence? Must not the price of all labour and commodities sink in proportion, and everything be sold as cheap as they were in those ages? What nation could then dispute with us in any foreign market, or pretend to navigate or to sell manufactures at the same price, which to us would afford sufficient profit? In how little time, therefore, must this bring back the money which we had lost, and raise us to the level of all the neighbouring nations? Where, after we have arrived, we immediately lose the advantage of the cheapness of labour and commodities; and the farther flowing in of money is stopped by our fulness and repletion.
>
> Again, suppose that all the money in Great Britain were multiplied fivefold in a night, must not the contrary effect follow? Must not all labour and commodities rise to such an exorbitant height, that no neighbouring nations could afford to buy from us; while their commodities, on the other hand, became comparatively so cheap, that, in spite of all the laws which could be formed, they would run in upon us, and our money flow out; till we fall to a level with foreigners, and lose that great superiority of riches which had laid us under such disadvantages?[4]

It is easy to translate Hume's description of the price-specie-flow mechanism into more modern terms. Suppose that Britain's current account surplus is greater than its nonreserve capital account deficit. Because foreigners' net imports from Britain are not being financed entirely by British loans, the balance must be matched by flows of international reserves—that is, of gold—into Britain. These gold flows automatically reduce foreign money supplies and swell Britain's money supply, pushing foreign prices downward and British prices upward. (Notice that Hume fully understood the lesson of Chapter 15 that price levels and money supplies move proportionally in the long run.[5])

The simultaneous rise in British prices and fall in foreign prices—a real appreciation of the pound, given the fixed exchange rate—reduces foreign demand for British goods and services and at the same time increases British demand for foreign goods and services. These demand shifts work in the direction of reducing Britain's current account surplus and reducing the foreign current account deficit. Eventually, therefore, reserve movements stop and both countries reach balance of payments equilibrium. The same process also works in reverse, eliminating an initial situation of foreign surplus and British deficit.

[4] Hume, ''Of the Balance of Trade,'' reprinted (in abridged form) in Barry Eichengreen, ed., *The Gold Standard in Theory and History* (London: Methuen, 1985), pp. 39–48.

[5] As mentioned in the footnote on p. 505, there are several ways in which the reduction in foreign money supplies, and the corresponding increase in Britain's money supply, might have occurred in Hume's day. Foreign residents could have melted gold coins into bars and used them to pay for imports. The British recipients of the gold bars could have then sold them to the Bank of England for British coins or paper currency. Alternatively, the foreign residents could have sold paper money to their central banks in return for gold and shipped this gold to Britain. Since gold coins were then part of the money supply, both transactions would have affected money supplies in the same way.

THE GOLD STANDARD "RULES OF THE GAME": MYTH AND REALITY

The price-specie-flow mechanism could operate automatically under the gold standard to bring countries' current and capital accounts into line and eliminate international gold movements. But the reactions of central banks to gold flows across their borders furnished another potential mechanism to help restore balance of payments equilibrium. Central banks that were persistently losing gold faced the risk of becoming unable to meet their obligation to redeem currency notes. They were therefore motivated to contract their domestic asset holdings when gold was being lost, pushing domestic interest rates upward and attracting inflows of capital from abroad. Central banks gaining gold had much weaker incentives to eliminate their own imports of the metal. The main incentive was the greater profitability of interest-bearing domestic assets compared with "barren" gold. A central bank that was accumulating gold might be tempted to purchase domestic assets, thereby increasing capital outflows and driving gold abroad.

These domestic credit measures, if undertaken by central banks, reinforced the price-specie-flow mechanism in pushing all countries toward balance of payments equilibrium. After World War I, the practices of selling domestic assets in the face of a deficit and buying domestic assets in the face of a surplus came to be known as the gold standard "rules of the game"—a phrase apparently coined by Keynes. Because such measures speeded the movement of all countries toward their external balance goals, they increased the efficiency of the automatic adjustment processes inherent in the gold standard.

Later research has shown that the supposed "rules of the game" of the gold standard were frequently violated before 1914. As noted, the incentives to obey the rules applied with greater force to deficit than to surplus countries, so in practice it was the deficit countries that bore the burden of bringing the payments balances of *all* countries into equilibrium. By hoarding gold, the surplus countries worsened a problem of international policy coordination inherent in the system: deficit countries competing for a limited supply of gold reserves might adopt overcontractionary monetary policies that harmed employment while doing little to improve their reserve positions.

In fact, countries often reversed the rules and *sterilized* gold flows, that is, sold domestic assets when foreign reserves were rising and bought domestic assets as foreign reserves fell. Government interference with private gold exports also undermined the system. The picture of smooth and automatic balance of payments adjustment before World War I therefore did not always match reality. Governments sometimes ignored both the "rules of the game" and the effects of their actions on other countries.[6]

INTERNAL BALANCE UNDER THE GOLD STANDARD

By fixing the prices of currencies in terms of gold, the gold standard aimed to limit monetary growth in the world economy and thus to ensure stability in world price levels. While price levels within gold standard countries did not rise as much between

[6] An influential modern study of central bank practices under the gold standard is Arthur I. Bloomfield, *Monetary Policy under the International Gold Standard: 1880–1914* (New York: Federal Reserve Bank of New York, 1959).

Hume versus the Mercantilists

David Hume's forceful account of the price-specie-flow mechanism is another example of the skillful use of economic theory to mold economic policy. An influential school of economic thinkers called *mercantilists* held that without severe restrictions on international trade and payments, Britain might find itself impoverished and without an adequate supply of circulating monetary gold as a result of balance of payments deficits. Hume refuted their arguments by demonstrating that the balance of payments would automatically regulate itself to ensure an adequate supply of money in every country.

Mercantilism, which originated in the seventeenth century, held that silver and gold were the mainstays of national wealth and essential to vigorous commerce. Mercantilists therefore viewed specie outflows with alarm and had as a main policy goal a continuing surplus in the balance of payments (that is, a continuing inflow of precious metals). As the mercantilist writer Thomas Mun put it around 1630: "The ordinary means therefore to increase our wealth and treasure is by foreign trade, wherein we must ever observe this rule: to sell more to strangers yearly than we consume of theirs in value."

Hume's reasoning showed that a perpetual surplus is impossible: since specie inflows drive up domestic prices and restore equilibrium in the balance of payments, any surplus eventually eliminates itself. Similarly, a shortage of currency leads to low domestic prices and a foreign payments surplus that eventually brings into the country as much money as needed. Government interference with international transactions, Hume argued, would harm the economy without bringing about the ongoing increase in "wealth and treasure" that the mercantilists favored.

Hume pointed out that the mercantilists overemphasized a single and relatively minor component of national wealth, precious metals, while ignoring the nation's main source of wealth, its productive capacity. In making this observation Hume was putting forward a very modern view. Well into the twentieth century, however, policy makers concerned with external balance often focused on international gold flows at the expense of broader indicators of changes in national wealth. Since the mercantilists were discredited by the attacks of Hume and like-minded thinkers, this relative neglect of the current account and its relation to domestic investment and productivity is puzzling. Perhaps mercantilistic instincts survived in the hearts of central bankers.

1870 and 1914 as over the period after World War II, national price levels moved unpredictably over shorter horizons as periods of inflation and deflation followed each other. The gold standard's mixed record on price stability reflected a problem discussed in the last chapter, change in the relative prices of gold and other commodities.

In addition, the gold standard does not seem to have done much to ensure full employment. The U.S. unemployment rate, for example, averaged 6.8 percent between 1890 and 1913, but it averaged under 5.7 percent between 1946 and 1992.[7]

[7] Data on price levels are given by Cooper (cited on p. 507 in Chapter 18) and data for U.S. unemployment are adapted from the same source. Caution should be used in comparing gold standard and post-World War II unemployment data because the methods used to assemble the earlier data were much cruder. A critical study of pre-1930 U.S. unemployment data is Christina Romer, "Spurious Volatility in Historical Unemployment Data," *Journal of Political Economy* 94 (February 1986), pp. 1–37.

A fundamental cause of short-term internal instability under the pre-1914 gold standard was the subordination of economic policy to external objectives. Before World War I, governments had not assumed responsibility for maintaining internal balance as fully as they did after World War II. The importance of internal policy objectives increased after World War I as a result of the worldwide economic instability of the interwar years, 1918–1939. And the unpalatable internal consequences of attempts to restore the gold standard after 1918 helped mold the thinking of the architects of the fixed exchange rate system adopted after 1945. To understand how the post-World War II international monetary system tried to reconcile the goals of internal and external balance, we therefore must examine the economic events of the period between the two world wars.

The Interwar Years, 1918–1939

Governments abandoned the gold standard during World War I and financed part of their massive military expenditures by printing money. Further, labor forces and productive capacity had been reduced sharply through war losses. As a result, price levels were higher everywhere at the war's conclusion in 1918.

Several countries experienced runaway inflation as their governments attempted to aid the reconstruction process through public expenditures. These governments financed their purchases simply by printing the money they needed, as they sometimes had during the war. The result was a sharp rise in money supplies and price levels.

THE GERMAN HYPERINFLATION

The most celebrated episode of interwar inflation is the German hyperinflation, during which Germany's price index rose from a level of 262 in January 1919 to a level of 126,160,000,000,000 in December 1923—a factor of 481.5 billion!

The Versailles Treaty ending World War I saddled Germany with a huge burden of reparations payments to the Allies. Rather than raising taxes to meet these payments, the German government ran its printing presses. The inflation accelerated most dramatically in January 1923 when France, citing lagging German compliance with the Versailles terms, sent its troops into Germany's industrial heartland, the Ruhr. German workers went on strike to protest the French occupation, and the German government supported their action by issuing even more money to pay them. Within the year, the price level rose by a factor of 452,998,200. Under these conditions, people were unwilling to hold the German currency, which became all but useless.

The hyperinflation was ended toward the end of 1923 as Germany instituted a currency reform, obtained some relief from its reparations burdens, and moved toward a balanced government budget.

THE FLEETING RETURN TO GOLD

The United States returned to gold in 1919. By the early 1920s, other countries yearned increasingly for the comparative financial stability of the gold standard era. In 1922, at a conference in Genoa, Italy, a group of countries including Britain, France, Italy, and

Japan agreed on a program calling for a general return to the gold standard and cooperation among central banks in attaining external and internal objectives. Realizing that gold supplies might be inadequate to meet central banks' demands for international reserves (a problem of the gold standard noted in Chapter 18), the Genoa Conference sanctioned a partial gold *exchange* standard in which smaller countries could hold as reserves the currencies of several large countries whose own international reserves would consist entirely of gold.

In 1925, Britain returned to the gold standard by pegging the pound to gold at the prewar price. Chancellor of the Exchequer Winston Churchill, a champion of the return to the old parity, argued that any deviation from the prewar price would undermine world confidence in the stability of Britain's financial institutions, which had played the leading role in international finance during the gold standard era. Though Britain's price level had been falling since the war, in 1925 it was still higher than in the days of the prewar gold standard. To return the pound price of gold to its prewar level, the Bank of England was therefore forced to follow contractionary monetary policies that contributed to severe unemployment.

The depression in Britain that accompanied the return to gold had been predicted by Keynes and others, but it was not unprecedented. More than a century earlier, Britain's return to the gold standard at the parity prevailing before the Napoleonic Wars had also set off a sustained and deep depression. In both cases, the return to an exchange rate made obsolete by wartime price level increases amounted to a *revaluation* of the pound against foreign currencies, a move that shifted world demand away from British products.

British stagnation in the 1920s accelerated London's decline as the world's leading financial center. Britain's economic weakening proved problematic for the stability of the restored gold standard. In line with the recommendations of the Genoa Conference, many countries held international reserves in the form of pound deposits in London. Britain's gold reserves were limited, however, and the country's persistent stagnation did little to inspire confidence in its ability to meet its foreign obligations. The onset of the Great Depression after 1929 was accompanied by bank failures throughout the world. Britain was forced off gold in 1931 when foreign holders of pounds (including several central banks) lost confidence in Britain's commitment to maintain its currency's value and began converting their pound holdings to gold.

INTERNATIONAL ECONOMIC DISINTEGRATION

As the Depression continued, many countries renounced their gold standard obligations and allowed their currencies to float in the foreign exchange market. The United States left the gold standard in 1933 but returned to it in 1934, having raised the dollar price of gold from $20.67 to $35 per ounce. Several other countries also returned to some form of gold standard after devaluation. These "competitive depreciations" were undertaken by each country in the hope of conserving gold and shifting world demand toward its output. They largely offset each other, however, and thus helped countries overcome unemployment only to the extent that worldwide monetary expansion was encouraged by higher money prices of gold.

Major economic harm was done by restrictions on international trade and payments, which proliferated as countries attempted to discourage imports and keep aggregate demand bottled up at home. The Smoot-Hawley tariff imposed by the United States in 1930 had a damaging effect on employment abroad. The foreign response involved retaliatory trade restrictions and preferential trading agreements among groups of countries.

Uncertainty about government policies led to sharp reserve movements for countries with pegged exchange rates and sharp exchange rate movements for those with floating rates. Prohibitions on private capital account transactions were used by many countries to limit these effects of foreign exchange market developments. Some governments also used administrative methods or multiple exchange rates to allocate scarce foreign exchange reserves among competing uses. Trade barriers and deflation in the industrial economies of America and Europe led to widespread repudiations of international debts, particularly by Latin American countries, whose export markets were disappearing. In short, the world economy disintegrated into increasingly autarkic national units in the early 1930s.

Currency depreciation, like tariff policy, is called a *beggar-thy-neighbor policy* when it benefits the home country only because it worsens economic conditions abroad (Chapter 12). During the worldwide depression, beggar-thy-neighbor policies inevitably provoked foreign retaliation and often left all countries worse off in the end.

Considerable turbulence in world markets continued until the beginning of World War II in 1939, in spite of limited moves toward international economic cooperation in the late 1930s. In the face of the Great Depression, many countries had resolved the choice between external and internal balance by curtailing their trading links with the rest of the world and eliminating, by government decree, the possibility of any significant external imbalance. But this path, by reducing the gains from trade, imposed high costs on the world economy and contributed to the slow recovery from depression, which in many countries was still incomplete in 1939. All countries would have been better off in a world with freer international trade, provided international cooperation had helped each country preserve its external balance and financial stability without sacrificing internal policy goals. It was this realization that inspired the blueprint for the postwar international monetary system, the **Bretton Woods agreement.**

The Bretton Woods System and the International Monetary Fund

In July 1944, representatives of forty-four countries meeting in Bretton Woods, New Hampshire, drafted and signed the Articles of Agreement of the **International Monetary Fund (IMF).** Even as the war continued, statesmen in the Allied countries were looking ahead to the economic needs of the postwar world. Remembering the disastrous economic events of the interwar period, they hoped to design an international monetary system that would foster full employment and price stability while allowing individual countries to attain external balance without imposing restrictions on international trade.[8]

The system set up by the Bretton Woods agreement called for fixed exchange rates

[8] The same conference set up a second institution, the World Bank, whose goals were to help the belligerents rebuild their shattered economies and to help the former colonial territories develop and modernize theirs. Only in 1947 was the General Agreement on Tariffs and Trade (GATT) inaugurated as a forum for the multilateral reduction of trade barriers. The GATT was meant as a prelude to the creation of an International Trade Organization (ITO) whose goals in the trade area would parallel those of the IMF in the financial area. Unfortunately, the ITO was doomed by the failures of Congress and Parliament to ratify its charter.

against the U.S. dollar and an unvarying dollar price of gold—$35 an ounce. Member countries held their official international reserves largely in the form of gold or dollar assets and had the right to sell dollars to the Federal Reserve for gold at the official price. The system was thus a gold exchange standard, with the dollar as its principal reserve currency. In the terminology of Chapter 18, the dollar was the ''*N*th currency'' in terms of which the $N - 1$ exchange rates of the system were defined. The United States itself intervened only rarely in the foreign exchange market. Usually, the $N - 1$ foreign central banks intervened when necessary to fix the system's $N - 1$ exchange rates, while the United States was responsible in theory for fixing the dollar price of gold.

GOALS AND STRUCTURE OF THE IMF

The IMF Articles of Agreement were heavily influenced by the interwar experience of financial and price level instability, unemployment, and international economic disintegration. The articles tried to avoid a repetition of those events through a mixture of discipline and flexibility.

The major discipline on monetary management was the requirement that exchange rates be fixed to the dollar, which, in turn, was tied to gold. If a central bank other than the Federal Reserve pursued excessive monetary expansion, it would lose international reserves and eventually become unable to maintain the fixed dollar exchange rate of its currency. Since high U.S. monetary growth would lead to dollar accumulation by foreign central banks, the Fed itself was constrained in its monetary policies by its obligation to redeem those dollars for gold. The official gold price of $35 an ounce served as a further brake on American monetary policy, since that price would be pushed upward if too many dollars were created. Fixed exchange rates were viewed as more than a device for imposing monetary discipline on the system, however. Rightly or wrongly, the interwar experience had convinced the Fund's architects that floating exchange rates were a cause of speculative instability and were harmful to international trade.

The interwar experience had shown also that national governments would not be willing to maintain both free trade and fixed exchange rates at the price of long-term domestic unemployment. After the experience of the Great Depression, governments were widely viewed as responsible for maintaining full employment. The IMF agreement therefore tried to incorporate sufficient flexibility to allow countries to attain external balance in an orderly fashion without sacrificing internal objectives or fixed exchange rates.

Two major features of the IMF Articles of Agreement helped promote this flexibility in external adjustment:

1. *IMF lending facilities.* The IMF stood ready to lend foreign currencies to members to tide them over periods during which their current accounts were in deficit but a tightening of monetary or fiscal policy would have an adverse effect on domestic employment. A pool of gold and currencies contributed by members provided the IMF with the resources to be used in these lending operations.

How did IMF lending work? On joining the Fund, a new member was assigned a *quota,* which determined both its contribution to the reserve pool and its right to draw on IMF resources. Each member contributed to the Fund an amount of gold equal in value to one-fourth of its quota. The remaining three-fourths of its quota took the form of a contribution of its own national currency. A member was entitled to use its own currency to purchase temporarily from the Fund gold or foreign currencies equal in value to its gold subscription. Further gold or foreign currencies (up to a limit) could be borrowed from the Fund, but only under increasingly stringent Fund supervision of the borrower's macroeconomic policies. **IMF conditionality** is the name for this surveillance over the policies of member countries who are heavy borrowers of Fund resources.

2. *Adjustable parities.* Although each country's exchange rate was fixed, it could be changed—devalued or revalued against the dollar—if the IMF agreed that the country's balance of payments was in a situation of "fundamental disequilibrium." The term *fundamental disequilibrium* was not defined in the Articles of Agreement, but the clause was meant to cover countries that suffered permanent adverse international shifts in the demand for their products. Without a devaluation, such a country would experience higher unemployment and a higher current account deficit until the domestic price level fell enough to restore internal and external balance. A devaluation, on the other hand, could simultaneously improve employment and the current account, thus sidestepping a long and painful adjustment process during which international reserves might in any case run out. Remembering Britain's experience with an overvalued currency after 1925, the IMF's founders built in the flexibility of (hopefully infrequent) exchange rate changes. This flexibility was not available, however, to the "*N*th currency" of the Bretton Woods system, the U.S. dollar.

CONVERTIBILITY

Just as the general acceptability of national currency eliminates the costs of barter within a single economy, the use of national currencies in international trade makes the world economy function more efficiently. To promote efficient multilateral trade, the IMF Articles of Agreement urged members to make their national currencies convertible as soon as possible. A **convertible currency** is one that may be freely exchanged for foreign currencies. The U.S. and Canadian dollars became convertible in 1945. This meant, for example, that a Canadian resident who acquired U.S. dollars could use them to make purchases in the United States, could sell them in the foreign exchange market for Canadian dollars, or could sell them to the Bank of Canada, which then had the right to sell them to the Federal Reserve (at the fixed dollar/gold exchange rate) in return for gold. General *in*convertibility would make international trade extremely difficult. A French citizen might be unwilling to sell goods to a German in return for inconvertible DM because these DM would then be usable only subject to restrictions imposed by the German government. With no market in inconvertible francs, the German would be unable to obtain French currency to pay for the French goods. The only way of trading would therefore be through barter, the direct exchange of goods for goods.

The IMF articles called for convertibility on *current* account transactions only: countries were explicitly allowed to restrict capital account transactions provided they permitted the free use of their currencies for transactions entering the current account. The experience of 1918–1939 had led policy makers to view private capital movements as a factor leading to economic instability, and they feared that speculative movements of "hot money" across national borders might sabotage their goal of tree trade based

participants wished to hold. This loss of foreign reserves, if large enough, might force a devaluation by leaving the Bank of England without enough reserves to prop up the exchange rate.

Similarly, countries with large current account surpluses might be viewed by the market as candidates for revaluation. In this case their central banks would find themselves swamped with official reserves, the result of selling the home currency in the foreign exchange market to keep it from appreciating. A country in this position would face the problem of having its money supply grow uncontrollably, a development that could push the price level up and upset internal balance.

Balance of payments crises became increasingly frequent and violent throughout the 1960s and early 1970s. A record British trade balance deficit in early 1964 led to a period of intermittent speculation against the pound that complicated British policy making until November 1967, when the pound was finally devalued. France devalued its franc and Germany revalued its DM in 1969 after similar speculative attacks. These crises became so massive by the early 1970s that they eventually brought down the Bretton Woods structure of fixed exchange rates. The events leading up to the system's collapse are covered later in this chapter.

The possibility of a balance of payments crisis therefore lent increased importance to the external goal of a current account target. Even current account imbalances justified by differing international investment opportunities or caused by purely temporary factors might fuel market suspicions of an impending parity change. In this environment, policy makers had additional incentives to avoid sharp current account changes.

Analyzing Policy Options under the Bretton Woods System

To describe the problem an individual country (other than the United States) faced in pursuing internal and external balance under the Bretton Woods system of fixed exchange rates, let's return to the framework used in Chapter 18. Assume that domestic and foreign interest rates are always equal,

$$R = R^*,$$

where R is the domestic interest rate and R^* the foreign interest rate. As noted above, this equality does not fit the Bretton Woods facts exactly (particularly just after 1958), but it leads to a fairly accurate picture of the external constraints policy makers then faced in using their macroeconomic tools. The framework will show how a country's position with respect to its internal and external goals depends on the level of its fixed exchange rate, E, and its fiscal policy. Throughout, E is the domestic currency price of the dollar. The analysis applies to the short run because the home and foreign price levels (P and P^*, respectively) are assumed to be fixed.[10]

[10] By assumption there is no ongoing balance of payments crisis, that is, no expectation of a future exchange rate change. The point of this assumption is to highlight the difficult choices policy makers faced, even under favorable conditions.

MAINTAINING INTERNAL BALANCE

First consider internal balance. If both P^* and E are permanently fixed, domestic inflation depends primarily on the amount of aggregate demand pressure in the economy, not on expectations of future inflation. Internal balance therefore requires only full employment, that is, that aggregate demand equal the full-employment level of output, Y^f.[11]

Recall that aggregate demand for domestic output is the sum of consumption, C, investment I, government purchases, G, and the current account, CA. Consumption is an increasing function of disposable income, $Y - T$, where T denotes net taxes. The current account surplus is a decreasing function of disposable income and an increasing function of the real exchange rate, EP^*/P (Chapter 17). Finally, investment is assumed constant. The condition of internal balance is therefore

$$Y^f = C(Y^f - T) + I + G + CA(EP^*/P, Y^f - T). \qquad \textbf{(19-1)}$$

Equation (19-1) shows the policy tools that affect aggregate demand and therefore affect output in the short run. Fiscal expansion (a rise in G or a fall in T) stimulates aggregate demand and causes output to rise. Similarly, a devaluation of the currency (a rise in E) makes domestic goods and services cheaper relative to those sold abroad and also increases demand and output. The policy maker can hold output steady at its full employment level, Y^f, through fiscal policy or exchange rate changes.

Notice that monetary policy is not a policy tool under fixed exchange rates. This is because, as shown in Chapter 18, an attempt by the central bank to alter the money supply by buying or selling domestic assets will cause an offsetting change in foreign reserves, leaving the domestic money supply unchanged. Domestic asset transactions by the central bank can be used to alter the level of foreign reserves but not to affect the state of employment and output.

The *II* schedule in Figure 19-1 shows combinations of exchange rates and fiscal policy that hold output constant at Y^f and thus maintain internal balance. The schedule is downward-sloping because currency devaluation (a rise in E) and fiscal expansion (a rise in G or a fall in T) both tend to raise output. To hold output constant, a revaluation of the currency (which reduces aggregate demand) must therefore be matched by fiscal expansion (which increases aggregate demand). Schedule *II* shows precisely how the fiscal stance must change as E changes to maintain full employment. To the right of *II* fiscal policy is more expansionary than needed for full employment, so the economy's productive factors are overemployed. To the left of *II* fiscal policy is too restrictive, and there is unemployment.

MAINTAINING EXTERNAL BALANCE

We have seen how fiscal policy or exchange rate changes can be used to influence output and thus help the government achieve its internal goal of full employment. How do these policy tools affect the economy's external balance? To answer this question, assume the government has a target value, X, for the current account surplus. The goal

[11] If P^* is unstable because of foreign inflation, for example, full employment alone will not guarantee price stability under a fixed exchange rate. This complex problem is considered below when worldwide inflation under fixed exchange rates is examined.

of external balance requires the government to manage fiscal policy and the exchange rate so that the equation

$$CA(EP^*/P, Y - T) = X \qquad \textbf{(19-2)}$$

is satisfied.

Given P and P^*, a rise in E makes domestic goods cheaper and improves the current account. Fiscal expansion, however, has the opposite effect on the current account. A fall in T raises output, Y; the resulting increase in disposable income raises home spending on foreign goods and worsens the current account. Similarly, a rise in G causes CA to fall by increasing Y.

To maintain its current account at X as it devalues the currency (that is, as it raises E), the government must expand its purchases or lower taxes. Figure 19-1 therefore shows that the XX schedule, along which external balance holds, is positively sloped. The XX schedule shows how much fiscal expansion is needed to hold the current account surplus at X as the currency is devalued by a given amount.[12] Since a rise in E raises net exports, the current account is in surplus, relative to its target level X, above XX. Similarly, below XX the current account is in deficit relative to its target level.[13]

EXPENDITURE-CHANGING AND EXPENDITURE-SWITCHING POLICIES

The II and XX schedules divide the diagram into four regions, sometimes called the "four zones of economic discomfort." Each of these zones represents the effects of different policy settings. In zone 1 the level of employment is too high and the current account surplus too great; in zone 2 the level of employment is too high but the current account deficit is too great; in zone 3 there is underemployment and an excessive deficit; and in zone 4 underemployment is coupled with a current account surplus greater than the target level. Used together, fiscal and exchange rate policy can place the economy at the intersection of II and XX (point 1), the point at which both internal and external balance hold. Point 1 shows the policy setting that places the economy in the position that the policy maker would prefer.

If the economy is initially away from point 1, appropriate adjustments in fiscal policy and the exchange rate are needed to bring about internal and external balance. The change in fiscal policy that moves the economy to point 1 is called an **expenditure-**

[12] Can you see how to derive the XX schedule in Figure 19-1 from the different (but related) XX schedule shown in Figure 17-17 on p. 461? Hint: Use the latter diagram to analyze the effects of fiscal expansion.

[13] Since the central bank does not affect the economy when it raises its foreign reserves by an open-market sale of domestic assets, no separate reserve constraint is shown in Figure 19-1. In effect, the bank can borrow reserves freely from abroad by selling domestic assets to the public. (During a devaluation scare this tactic would not work because no one would want to sell the bank foreign assets for domestic money.) Our analysis, however, assumes perfect asset substitutability between domestic and foreign bonds (see Chapter 18). Under imperfect asset substitutability, central bank domestic asset sales to attract foreign reserves would drive up the domestic interest rate relative to the foreign rate. Thus, while imperfect asset substitutability would give the central bank an additional policy tool (monetary policy), it would also make the bank responsible for an additional policy target (the domestic interest rate). If the government is concerned about the domestic interest rate because it affects investment, for example, the additional policy tool would not necessarily increase the set of attractive policy options. Imperfect substitutability was exploited by central banks under Bretton Woods, but it did not get countries out of the policy dilemmas illustrated in the text.

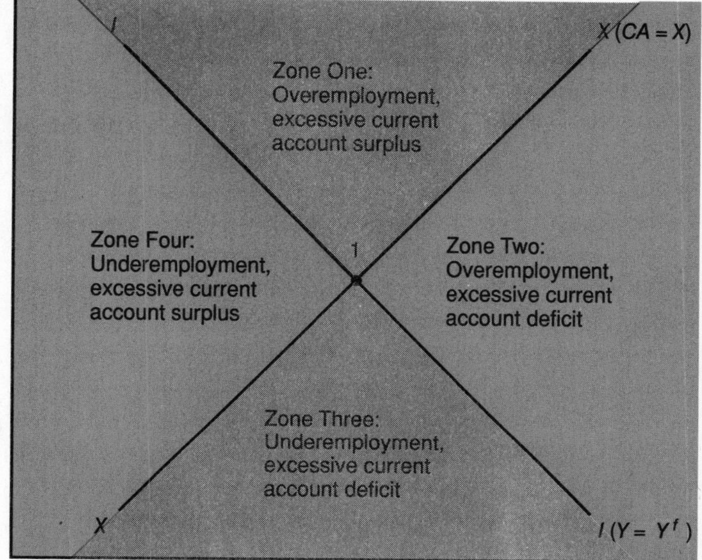

FIGURE 19-1
Internal balance (*II*), external balance (*XX*), and the "four zones of economic discomfort."
The diagram shows what different levels of the exchange rate and fiscal ease imply for employment and the current account. Along *II,* output is at its full-employment level, Y^f. Along *XX,* the current account is at its target level, *X.*

changing policy because it alters the *level* of the economy's total demand for goods and services. The accompanying exchange rate adjustment is called an **expenditure-switching policy** because it changes the *direction* of demand, shifting it between domestic output and imports. In general, both expenditure changing and expenditure switching are needed to reach internal and external balance.

Under the Bretton Woods rules, exchange rate changes (expenditure-switching policy) were supposed to be infrequent. This left fiscal policy as the main tool for moving the economy toward internal and external balance. But as Figure 19-1 shows, one instrument, fiscal policy, is generally insufficient to attain the two goals of internal and external balance. Only if the economy had been displaced horizontally from point 1 would fiscal policy be able to do the job alone. In addition, fiscal policy is an unwieldy tool, since it often cannot be implemented without legislative approval. Another drawback is that a fiscal expansion, for example, might have to be reversed after some time if it leads to chronic government budget deficits.

As a result of the exchange rate's inflexibility, policy makers sometimes found themselves in dilemma situations. With the fiscal policy and exchange rate indicated by point 2 in Figure 19-2, there is underemployment and an excessive current account deficit. Only the combination of devaluation and fiscal expansion indicated in the figure moves the economy to internal and external balance (point 1). Expansionary fiscal policy, acting alone, can eliminate the unemployment by moving the economy to point 3, but the cost of reduced unemployment is a larger external deficit. While contractionary fiscal policy alone can bring about external balance (point 4), output falls as a result

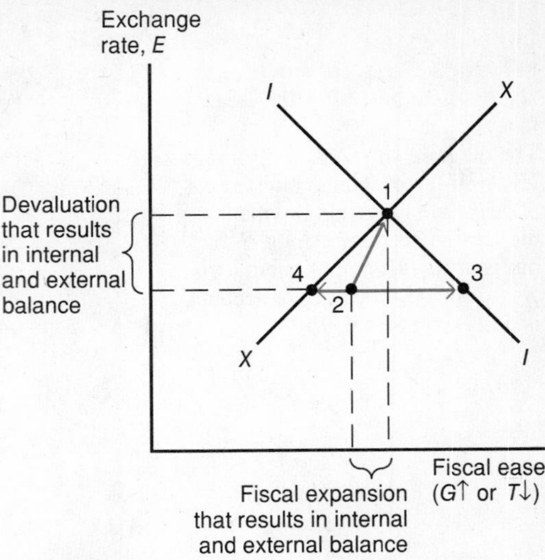

FIGURE 19-2
Policies to bring about internal and external balance.
Unless the currency is devalued and the degree of fiscal ease increased, internal and external balance (point 1) cannot be reached. Acting alone, fiscal policy can attain *either* internal balance (point 3) or external balance (point 4), but only at the cost of increasing the economy's distance from the goal that is sacrificed.

and the economy moves further from internal balance. It is no wonder that policy dilemmas such as the one at point 2 gave rise to suspicions that the currency was about to be devalued. Devaluation improves the current account and aggregate demand by raising the real exchange rate EP^*/P in one stroke; the alternative is a long and politically unpalatable period of unemployment to bring about an equal rise in the real exchange rate through a fall in P.[14]

In practice, countries did sometimes use changes in their exchange rates to move closer to internal and external balance, although the changes were typically accompanied by balance of payments crises. Many countries also tightened controls on capital account transactions to sever the links between domestic and foreign interest rates and make monetary policy more effective. In this they were only partly successful, as the events leading to the breakdown of the system were to prove.

The External Balance Problem of the United States

The external balance problem of the United States was different from the one faced by other countries in the Bretton Woods system. As the issuer of the *N*th currency, the United States was not responsible for pegging dollar exchange rates. Its main responsibility was to hold the dollar price of gold at $35 an ounce and, in particular, to

[14]As an exercise to test understanding, show that a fall in *P*, all else equal, lowers both *II* and *XX*, moving point 1 vertically downward.

guarantee that foreign central banks could convert their dollar holdings into gold at that price. For this purpose it had to hold sufficient gold reserves.

Because the United States was required to trade gold for dollars with foreign central banks, the possibility that other countries might convert their dollar reserves into gold was a potential external constraint on U.S. macroeconomic policy. In practice, however, foreign central banks were willing to hold on to the dollars they accumulated, since these paid interest and represented an international money *par excellence.* And the logic of the gold exchange standard dictated that foreign central banks should continue to accumulate dollars. World gold supplies were not growing quickly enough to keep up with world economic growth, so the only way central banks could maintain adequate international reserve levels (barring deflation) was by accumulating dollar assets. Official gold conversions did occur on occasion, and these depleted the American gold stock and caused concern. But as long as most central banks were willing to add dollars to their reserves and forgo the right of redeeming those dollars for American gold, the U.S. external constraint appeared looser than that faced by other countries in the system.[15]

In an influential book that appeared in 1960, the economist Robert Triffin of Yale University called attention to a fundamental long-run problem of the Bretton Woods system, the **confidence problem.**[16] At the time Triffin wrote, the U.S. gold stock exceeded its dollar liabilities to foreign central banks. But Triffin realized that as central banks' international reserve needs grew over time, their holdings of dollars would necessarily grow until they exceeded the U.S. gold stock. Since the United States had promised to redeem these dollars at $35 an ounce, it would no longer have the ability to meet its obligations should all dollar holders simultaneously try to convert their dollars into gold. This would lead to a confidence problem: central banks, knowing that their dollars were no longer "as good as gold," might become unwilling to accumulate more dollars and might even bring down the system by attempting to cash in the dollars they already held. There was a historical precedent for Triffin's prediction. Recall that in 1931, official holders of pounds, aware how meager Britain's gold holdings were, helped bring down the gold standard system by suddenly attempting to redeem their pounds for gold.

One possible solution suggested at the time was an increase in the official price of gold in terms of the dollar and all other currencies. But such an increase would have been inflationary and would have had the politically unattractive consequence of enriching the main gold-producing countries. Further, an increase in gold's price would have caused central banks to expect further decreases in the gold value of their dollar reserve holdings in the future, thus possibly worsening the confidence problem rather than solving it!

Triffin himself proposed a plan in which the IMF issued its own currency, which central banks would hold as international reserves in place of dollars. According to this

[15] France, in particular, was *not* willing to continue accumulating dollars. President Charles de Gaulle, criticizing the Bretton Woods system for the "exorbitant privilege" it allowed the United States to enjoy, converted a large portion of France's dollar holdings into gold in 1965. But de Gaulle's aggressive action, part of his broader campaign against the alleged "Anglo-Saxon" dominance of the Western alliance, was atypical of the behavior of most countries.

[16] See Triffin, *Gold and the Dollar Crisis* (New Haven: Yale University Press, 1960).

plan, the IMF would ensure adequate growth of the supply of international reserves in much the same way a central bank ensures adequate growth of the domestic money supply. In effect, Triffin's plan would have transformed the IMF into a world central bank.[17]

In 1967, IMF members agreed to the creation of the **Special Drawing Right (SDR),** an artificial reserve asset similar to the IMF currency Triffin had envisioned. SDRs are used in transactions between central banks, but their creation had relatively little impact on the functioning of the international monetary system. Their impact was limited partly because by the late 1960s, the system of fixed exchange rates was beginning to show strains that would soon lead to its collapse. These strains were closely related to the special position of the United States.

Case Study

THE DECLINE AND FALL OF THE BRETTON WOODS SYSTEM

The system of fixed parities made it difficult for countries to attain simultaneous internal and external balance without discrete exchange rate adjustments. As it became easier to transfer funds across borders, however, the very possibility that exchange rates *might* be changed set off speculative capital movements that made the task facing policy makers even harder. The story of the Bretton Woods system's breakdown is the story of countries' unsuccessful attempts to reconcile internal and external balance under its rules.

The Calm before the Storm: 1958–1965

In 1958, the same year currency convertibility was restored in Europe, the U.S. current account surplus fell sharply. In 1959, it moved into deficit. Although the current account improved in 1960 as the U.S. economy entered a recession, foreign central banks converted nearly $2 billion of their dollar holdings into gold in that year, after having converted around $3 billion in 1958 and 1959. The year 1960 marked the end of the period of "dollar shortage" and the beginning of a period dominated by fears that the United States might devalue the dollar relative to gold. The price of gold in the London market, where most trading then took place, reflected these worries about the dollar's future. Late in the year, the price of gold rose from its official price of $35 an ounce. Only after central bank intervention in the gold market and a statement from presidential candidate John F. Kennedy ruling out a devaluation did gold's price return to the official level.

On the whole, the period from 1961 to 1965 was a calm one for the United States, although some other countries, most notably Britain, faced external problems. The U.S. current account surplus widened and the threat of large-scale conversions of dollars into gold by foreign central banks receded. Continuing private capital outflows from the United States, which augmented the dollar component of foreign official reserves, were, however, a source of concern to the Kennedy and Johnson administrations. In 1963,

[17] Triffin's plan was similar to one Keynes had advanced while the IMF was first being designed in the early 1940s. Keynes's blueprint was not adopted, however.

therefore, the United States moved to discourage capital outflows by imposing a tax on purchases of foreign assets by Americans. In 1965, further measures to discourage capital outflows were taken.

Early in this period, Germany faced a dilemma between internal and external balance that was to recur more dramatically toward the end of the decade. In 1960, Germany experienced an employment boom coupled with large inflows of international reserves. In terms of Figure 19-1, the German authorities found themselves in zone 1. Attempts to restrain the boom through contractionary monetary policy only succeeded in increasing the Bundesbank's international reserves more quickly as the central bank was forced to sell DM for dollars to keep the DM from appreciating. A small revaluation of the DM (by 5 percent) in March 1961 moved the economy closer to internal and external balance as output growth slowed and the current account surplus declined. Although the system successfully avoided a major crisis in this case, this was in part due to the foreign exchange market's perception that the DM revaluation reflected German macroeconomic problems rather than American problems. That perception was to change over the next decade.

The Vietnam Military Buildup and the Great Society: 1965–1968

Many economists view the U.S. macroeconomic policy package of 1965–1968 as a major blunder that helped unravel the system of fixed exchange rates. In 1965, government military purchases began rising as President Lyndon B. Johnson widened America's involvement in the Vietnam conflict. At the same time, other categories of government spending also rose dramatically as the president's "Great Society" programs (which included funds for public education and urban redevelopment) expanded. Figure 19-3a shows how the growth rate of nominal government purchases began to rise, slowly in 1965 and then quite sharply the next year. These increases in government expenditures were not matched by a prompt increase in taxes: 1966 was an election year, and President Johnson was reluctant to invite close congressional scrutiny of his spending by asking for a tax increase.

The result was a substantial fiscal expansion that helped set U.S. prices rising and caused a sharp fall in the U.S. current account surplus (Figures 19-3b and 19-3c). Although monetary policy (as measured by the growth rate of the money supply) initially turned contractionary as output expanded, the negative effect of the resulting high interest rates on the construction industry led the Federal Reserve to choose a much more expansionary monetary course in 1967 and 1968 (Figure 19-3d). As Figure 19-3b shows, this further push to the domestic price level left the United States with an inflation rate near 6 percent per year by the end of the decade. Only in June 1968 was a tax increase signed into law. But by then, considerable damage had been done to the U.S. economy and the international monetary system.

From the Gold Crisis to the Collapse: 1968–1973

Early signals of future problems came from the London gold market. In late 1967 and early 1968, private speculators began buying gold in anticipation of a rise in its dollar price. It was thought at the time that the speculation had been triggered by the British pound's devaluation in November 1967, but the sharp U.S. monetary expansion over 1967 and rising U.S. inflation probably influenced speculative sentiments as well. After massive gold sales by the Federal Reserve and European central banks, the Bank of

FIGURE 19-3
U.S. macroeconomic data, 1964–1972.
Source: *Economic Report of the President, 1985.* Money supply growth rate is the December to December percentage increase in M1. Inflation rate is the percentage increase in each year's average consumer price index over the average consumer price index for the previous year.

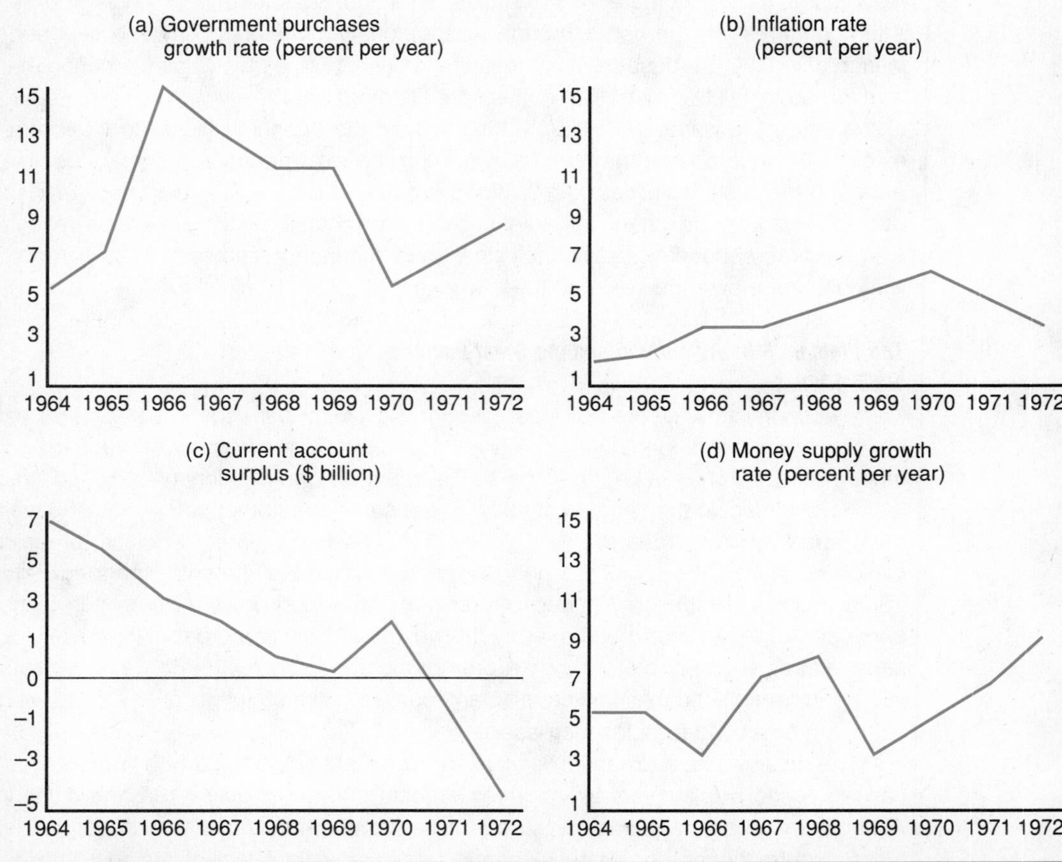

England closed the gold market on March 15, 1968. Two days later the central banks announced the creation of a *two-tier* gold market, with one tier private and the other official. Private gold traders would continue to trade on the London gold market, but the gold price set there would be allowed to fluctuate. In contrast, central banks would continue to transact with each other in the official tier at the official gold price of $35 an ounce.

The creation of the two-tier market was a turning point for the Bretton Woods system. A prime goal of the gold exchange standard created at Bretton Woods was to prevent inflation by tying down gold's dollar price. By severing the link between the supply of dollars and a fixed *market* price of gold, the central banks had jettisoned the system's built-in safeguard against inflation. The new arrangements did not eliminate the external constraint on the United States altogether, because foreign central banks retained the right to purchase gold for dollars from the Federal Reserve. But the *official* price of gold had been reduced to a fictitious device for squaring accounts among central banks; it no longer placed an automatic constraint on worldwide monetary growth.

The June 1968 tax increase helped push the U.S. economy into a recession by 1970, but, as Figure 19-3b shows, inflation rose in that year. By then, inflationary expectations had become entrenched in the economy and were affecting wage settlements even in the face of recession. Falling aggregate demand did, however, contribute to an improvement in the U.S. current account in 1970.

The improvement in the U.S. current account proved transitory. Adverse balance of payments figures released in early 1971 helped set off massive private purchases of DM in the foreign exchange market, motivated by expectations that the DM would be revalued against the dollar. On a single day, May 4, 1971, the Bundesbank had to buy $1 billion to hold its dollar exchange rate fixed in the face of the great demand for its currency. On the morning of May 5, the Bundesbank purchased $1 billion during the first hour of foreign exchange trading alone! At that point the Bundesbank gave up and allowed its currency to float. The alternative was to see the German money supply balloon even further as a result of Bundesbank dollar purchases.

As the weeks passed, the markets became increasingly convinced that the dollar would have to be devalued against all the major European currencies. U.S. unemployment was still high in 1971 and the U.S. price level had risen substantially over the previous years. To restore full employment and a balanced current account, the United States somehow had to bring about a real depreciation of the dollar.

That real depreciation could be brought about in two ways. The first option was a fall in the U.S. price level in response to domestic unemployment, coupled with a rise in foreign price levels in response to continuing purchases of dollars by foreign central banks. The second option was a fall in the dollar's nominal value in terms of foreign currencies. The first route—unemployment in the United States and inflation abroad—seemed a painful one for policy makers to follow. The markets rightly guessed that a change in the dollar's value was inevitable. Their realization led to renewed sales of dollars in the foreign exchange market that reached a climax in August 1971.

Devaluation was no easy matter for the United States, however. Any other country could change its exchange rates against all currencies simply by fixing its *dollar* rate at a new level. But as the *N*th currency, the dollar could be devalued only if foreign governments agreed to peg their currencies against the dollar at new rates. In effect, all countries had to agree simultaneously to *revalue* their currencies against the dollar. Dollar devaluation could therefore be accomplished only through extensive multilateral negotiations. And some foreign countries were not anxious to revalue because revaluation would make their goods more expensive relative to U.S. goods and would therefore hurt their export- and import-competing industries.

President Richard M. Nixon forced the issue on August 15, 1971. First, he ended U.S. gold losses by announcing the United States would no longer automatically sell gold to foreign central banks for dollars. This action effectively cut the remaining link between the dollar and gold. Second, the president announced a 10 percent tax on all imports into the United States, to remain effective until America's trading partners agreed to revalue their currencies against the dollar. A number of domestic stabilization measures were announced at the same time, including a freeze on wages and prices aimed at reducing U.S. inflation.

An international agreement on exchange rate realignment was reached in December 1971 at the Smithsonian Institution in Washington, D.C. On average, the dollar was devalued against foreign currencies by about 8 percent, and the 10 percent import surcharge that the United States had imposed to force the realignment was removed. The official gold price was raised to $38 an ounce, but the move had no economic significance because the United States did not agree to resume sales of gold to foreign central banks. The Smithsonian agreement made clear that the last remnant of the gold standard had been abandoned.

The Smithsonian realignment, although hailed at the time by President Nixon as "the most significant monetary agreement in the history of the world," was in shambles less than fifteen months later. A sharp deterioration of the U.S. current account in 1972, together with sharply higher U.S. monetary growth prior to that year's presidential election, convinced markets that the Smithsonian dollar devaluation had been insufficient. Throughout 1972 there were further speculative capital flows out of dollars and into other currencies, particularly the DM and the yen. Germany tightened controls on capital inflows to impede reserve movements that were bloating Germany's money supply.

Early in February 1973, another massive speculative attack on the dollar started and the foreign exchange maket was closed while the United States and its main trading partners negotiated on dollar support measures. A further 10 percent devaluation of the dollar was announced on February 12, but speculation against the dollar resumed as soon as governments allowed the foreign exchange market to reopen. After European central banks purchased $3.6 billion on March 1 to prevent their currencies from appreciating, the foreign exchange market was closed down once again.

When the foreign exchange market reopened on March 19, the currencies of Japan and most European countries were floating against the dollar.[18] The floating of the industrialized countries' dollar exchange rates was viewed at the time as a temporary response to unmanageable speculative capital movements. But the interim arrangements adopted in March 1973 turned out to be permanent and marked the end of fixed exchange rates and the beginning of a turbulent new period in international monetary relations.

Worldwide Inflation and the Transition to Floating Rates

The acceleration of American inflation in the late 1960s, shown in Figure 19-3b, was a worldwide phenomenon. Table 19-1 shows that by the end of the 1960s, inflation had also speeded up in European economies. The theory in Chapter 18 predicts that when the reserve currency country speeds up its monetary growth, as the United States did in the second half of the 1960s, one effect is an automatic increase in monetary growth rates and inflation abroad as foreign central banks purchase the reserve currency

[18] Many developing countries continued to peg to the dollar, and a number of European countries were continuing to peg their mutual exchange rates as part of an informal arrangement called the "snake." As we see in Chapter 21, the snake ultimately evolved into the European Monetary System.

TABLE 19-1 Inflation rates in European countries, 1966–1972 (percent per year)

Country	*1966*	*1967*	*1968*	*1969*	*1970*	*1971*	*1972*
Britain	3.6	2.6	4.6	5.2	6.5	9.7	6.9
France	2.8	2.8	4.4	6.5	5.3	5.5	6.2
Germany	3.4	1.4	2.9	1.9	3.4	5.3	5.5
Italy	2.1	2.1	1.2	2.8	5.1	5.2	5.3

Source: Organization for Economic Cooperation and Development. *Main Economic Indicators: Historical Statistics, 1964–1983.* Paris: OECD, 1984. Figures are percentage increases in each year's average consumer price index over that of the previous year.

to maintain their exchange rates and expand their money supplies in the process. One interpretation of the Bretton Woods system's collapse is that foreign countries were forced to *import* U.S. inflation through the mechanism described in Chapter 18: to stabilize their price levels and regain internal balance, they had to abandon fixed exchange rates and allow their currencies to float. How much blame for the system's breakdown can be placed on U.S. macroeconomic policies?

To understand how inflation can be imported from abroad unless exchange rates are adjusted, look again at the graphical picture of internal and external balance shown in Figure 19-1. Suppose the home country is faced with foreign inflation. Above, the foreign price level, P^*, was assumed to be given; now, however, P^* rises as a result of inflation abroad. Figure 19-4 shows the effect on the home economy.

You can see how the two schedules shift by asking what would happen if the nominal exchange rate were to fall in proportion to the rise in P^*. In this case, the real exchange rate EP^*/P would be unaffected (given P), and the economy would remain in internal balance or in external balance if either of these conditions originally held. Figure 19-4 therefore shows that for a given initial exchange rate, a rise in P^* shifts both I^1I^1 and X^1X^1 downward by the same distance (equal to the proportional increase in P^* times the initial exchange rate). The intersection of the new schedules I^2I^2 and X^2X^2 (point 2) lies directly below point 1.

If the economy is at point 1, a rise in P^*, *given* the fixed exchange rate and the domestic price level, therefore strands the economy in zone 1 with overemployment and an undesirably high surplus in its current account. The factor that causes this outcome is a real currency depreciation that shifts world demand toward the home country (EP^*/P rises because P^* rises).

If nothing is done by the government, overemployment puts upward pressure on the domestic price level, and this pressure gradually shifts the two schedules back to their original positions. The schedules stop shifting once P has risen in proportion to P^*. At this stage the real exchange rate, employment, and the current account are at their initial levels, so point 1 is once again a position of internal and external balance.

The way to avoid the imported inflation is to revalue the currency (that is, lower E) and move to point 2. A revaluation restores internal and external balance immediately, without domestic inflation, by using the nominal exchange rate to offset the effect

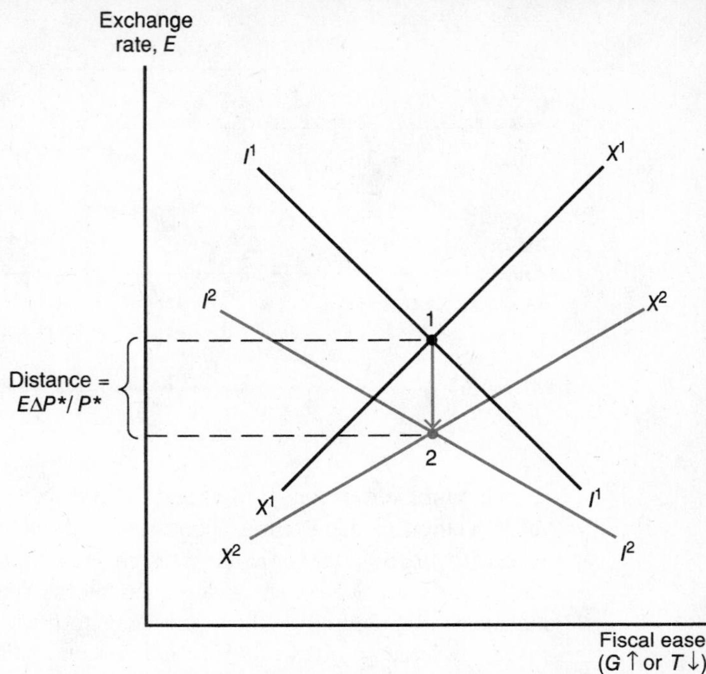

FIGURE 19-4
Effect on internal and external balance of a rise in the foreign price level, P^*.
After P^* rises, point 1 is in Zone One (overemployment and an excessive surplus). Revaluation (a fall in E) restores balance immediately by moving the policy setting to point 2.

of the rise in P^* on the real exchange rate. Only an expenditure-switching policy is needed to respond to a pure increase in foreign prices.

The rise in domestic prices that occurs when no revaluation takes place requires a rise in the domestic money supply, since prices and the money supply move proportionally in the long run. The mechanism that brings this rise about is foreign exchange intervention by the home central bank. As domestic output and prices rise after the rise in P^*, the real money supply shrinks and the demand for real money holdings increases. To prevent the resulting upward pressure on the home interest rate from appreciating the currency, the central bank must purchase international reserves and expand the home money supply. In this way, inflationary policies pursued by the reserve center spill over into foreign countries' money supplies.

The close association between U.S. and foreign inflation evident in Figure 19-3 and Table 19-1 suggests that some European inflation was imported from the United States. But the timing of the inflationary surges in different countries suggests that factors peculiar to individual economies also played a role. In Britain, for example, inflation speeds up markedly in 1968, the year following the pound's devaluation. Since (as seen in the last chapter) devaluation is neutral in the long run, it must raise the long-run domestic price level proportionally. The devaluation is probably part of the explanation for the rise in British inflation. Strikes in France in 1968 led to large wage increases, a French-German currency crisis, and a devaluation of the franc in 1969. These events partly explain the sharp increase in French inflation in 1968–1969. The role of imported inflation was greatest in Germany, where the painful earlier experience with hyperinflation had made policy makers determined to resist price level increases.

Evidence on money supplies confirms that European and Japanese monetary growth accelerated in the late 1960s, as our theory predicts. Table 19-2 shows the evolution of the international reserves and money supply of West Germany over the years 1968–1972. The table shows how monetary growth rose dramatically after 1969 as the Bundesbank's international reserves expanded.[19] This evidence is consistent with the view that American inflation was imported into Germany through the Bundesbank's purchases of dollars in the foreign exchange market.

The acceleration of German money growth probably cannot be explained entirely as a direct consequence of the acceleration in U.S. monetary growth, however. A comparison of Figure 19-3 and Table 19-2 shows that German monetary growth accelerated by much more than U.S. monetary growth after 1969. This difference suggests that much of the growth in Germany's international reserves reflected speculation on a possible dollar devaluation in the early 1970s and the resulting shift by market participants away from dollar assets and into DM assets.

U.S. monetary policy certainly contributed to inflation abroad by its direct effect on prices and money supplies. It helped wreck the fixed rate system by confronting foreign policy makers with a choice between fixed rates and imported inflation. But the U.S. fiscal policy that helped make a dollar devaluation necessary also contributed to foreign inflation by giving further encouragement to speculative capital flows out of dollars. U.S. fiscal policy in the later 1960s must be viewed as an additional cause of the Bretton Woods system's demise.

Thus, the collapse of the Bretton Woods system was due, in part, to the lopsided macroeconomic power of the United States. But it was also due to the fact that the key expenditure-switching tool needed for internal and external balance—discrete exchange rate adjustment—inspired speculative attacks that made both internal and external balance progressively more difficult to achieve. The architects of the Bretton Woods system had hoped its most powerful member would see beyond purely domestic goals and adopt policies geared to the welfare of the world economy as a whole. When the United States proved unwilling to shoulder this responsibility after the mid-1960s, the fixed exchange rate system came apart.

[19] The behavior of reserves in 1968 and 1969—a large increase followed by a large decrease—reflects speculation on a DM revaluation against the franc during the French-German currency crisis of those years.

TABLE 19-2 Changes in Germany's money supply and international reserves, 1968–1972 (percent per year)

Growth rate of	*1968*	*1969*	*1970*	*1971*	*1972*
Money supply	6.4	−6.3	8.9	12.3	14.7
Official international reserves	37.8	−43.6	215.7	36.1	35.8

Source: Organization for Economic Cooperation and Development. *Main Economic Indicators: Historical Statistics, 1964–1983.* Paris: OECD, 1984. Figures are percentage increases in each year's end-of-year money supply or international reserves over the level at the end of the previous year. Official reserves are measured net of gold holdings.

Summary

1. In an open economy, policy makers try to maintain *internal balance* (full employment and a stable price level) and *external balance* (a current account level that is neither so negative that the country may be unable to repay its foreign debts nor so positive that foreigners are put in that position). The definition of external balance depends on a number of factors, including the exchange rate regime and world economic conditions. Because each country's macroeconomic policies have repercussions abroad, a country's ability to reach internal and external balance depends on the policies other countries adopt.

2. The gold standard system contains a powerful automatic mechanism for assuring external balance, the *price-specie-flow mechanism.* The flows of gold accompanying deficits and surpluses cause price changes that reduce current account imbalances and therefore tend to return all countries to external balance. The system's performance in maintaining internal balance was mixed, however. With the eruption of World War I in 1914, the gold standard was suspended.

3. Attempts to return to the prewar gold standard after 1918 were unsuccessful. As the world economy moved into general depression after 1929, the restored gold standard fell apart and international economic integration weakened. In the turbulent economic conditions of the period, governments made internal balance their main concern and tried to avoid the external balance problem by partially shutting their economies off from the rest of the world. The result was a world economy in which all countries' situations could have been bettered through international cooperation.

4. The architects of the *International Monetary Fund* (IMF) hoped to design a fixed exchange rate system that would encourage growth in international trade while making the requirements of external balance sufficiently flexible that they could be met without sacrificing internal balance. To this end, the IMF charter provided financing facilities for deficit countries and allowed exchange rate adjustments in conditions of ''fundamental disequilibrium.'' All countries pegged their currencies to the dollar. The United States pegged to gold and agreed to exchange gold for dollars with foreign central banks at a price of $35 an ounce.

5. After *currency convertibility* was restored in Europe in 1958, countries' financial markets became more closely integrated, monetary policy became less effective (except for the United States), and movements in international reserves became more volatile. These changes revealed a key weakness in the system. To reach internal and external balance at the same time, *expenditure-switching* as well as *expenditure-changing* policies were needed. But the possibility of expenditure-switching policies (exchange rate changes) could give rise to speculative capital flows that undermined fixed exchange rates. As the main reserve currency country, the United States faced a unique external balance problem: the *confidence problem* that would arise as foreign official dollar holdings inevitably grew to exceed U.S. gold holdings.

6. U.S macroeconomic policies in the late 1960s helped cause the breakdown of the Bretton Woods system by early 1973. Overexpansionary U.S. fiscal policy contributed to the need for a devaluation of the dollar in the early 1970s, and fears that this would occur touched off speculative capital flows out of dollars that caused foreign money supplies to balloon. Higher U.S. money growth fueled inflation at home and abroad, making foreign government increasingly reluctant to continue importing U.S.

inflation through fixed exchange rates. A series of international crises beginning in the spring of 1971 led in stages to the abandonment of both the dollar's link to gold and fixed dollar exchange rates for the industrialized countries.

Key Terms

internal balance
external balance
balance of payments equilibrium
price-specie-flow mechanism
Bretton Woods agreement
International Monetary Fund (IMF)
IMF conditionality
convertible currency
expenditure-changing policy
expenditure-switching policy
confidence problem
Special Drawing Right (SDR)

Problems

1. If you were in charge of macroeconomic policies in a small open economy, what qualitative effect would each of the following events have on your target for external balance?

a. Large deposits of uranium are discovered in the interior of your country.

b. The world price of your main export good, copper, rises permanently.

c. The world price of copper rises temporarily.

d. There is a temporary rise in the world price of oil.

2. Under a gold standard of the kind analyzed by Hume, describe how balance of payments equilibrium between two countries, A and B, would be restored after a transfer of income from B to A.

3. In spite of the flaws of the pre-1914 gold standard, exchange rate changes were rare. In contrast, such changes became quite frequent in the interwar period. Can you think of reasons for this contrast?

4. Under a gold standard, countries may adopt excessively contractionary monetary policies as all scramble in vain for a larger share of the limited supply of world gold reserves. Can the same problem arise under a reserve currency standard when bonds denominated in different currencies are all perfect substitutes?

5. A central bank that adopts a fixed exchange rate may sacrifice its autonomy in setting domestic monetary policy. It is sometimes argued that when this is the case, the central bank also gives up the ability to use monetary policy to combat the wage-price spiral. The argument goes like this: ''Suppose workers demand higher wages and employers give in, but that the employers then raise output prices to cover their higher costs. Now the price level is higher and real balances are momentarily lower, so to prevent an interest rate rise that would appreciate the currency, the central bank must buy foreign exchange and expand the money supply. This action accommodates the initial wage demands with monetary growth and the economy moves permanently to a higher level of wages and prices. With a fixed exchange rate there is thus no way of keeping wages and prices down.'' What is wrong with this argument?

6. Economists have long debated whether the growth of dollar reserve holdings in the Bretton Woods years was ''demand-determined'' (that is, determined by central banks' desire to add to their international reserves) or ''supply-determined'' (that is, determined by the speed of U.S. monetary growth). What would your answer be? What are the consequences for analyzing the relationship between growth in the world stock of international reserves and worldwide inflation?

7. Suppose the central bank of a small country is faced by a rise in the world interest rate, R^*. What is the effect on its foreign reserve holdings? On its money supply? Can it offset either of these effects through domestic open-market operations?

8. How might restrictions on private capital account transactions alter the problem of attaining internal and external balance with a fixed exchange rate? What costs might such restrictions involve?

Further Reading

Michael D. Bordo and Barry Eichengreen, eds. *A Retrospective on the Bretton Woods System.* Chicago: University of Chicago Press, 1993. A collection of essays re-evaluating the Bretton Woods experience.

W. Max Corden. ''The Geometric Representation of Policies to Attain Internal and External Balance,'' in Richard N. Cooper, ed. *International Finance.* Harmondsworth, Eng.: Penguin Books, 1969, pp. 256–290. A classic diagrammatic analysis of expenditure-switching and expenditure-changing macroeconomic policies.

Leland Crabbe. ''The International Gold Standard and U.S. Monetary Policy from World War I to the New Deal.'' *Federal Reserve Bulletin* 75 (June 1989), pp. 423–440. An account of the evolving U.S. role in the international monetary system during the fifteen years after World War I.

Barry Eichengreen, ed. *The Gold Standard in Theory and History.* London: Methuen, 1985. A valuable collection of readings on the performance of the gold standard in different historical periods.

Barry Eichengreen. *Golden Fetters.* New York: Oxford University Press, 1992. Analyzes international macroeconomic interactions under the interwar gold standard.

Richard N. Gardner. *Sterling-Dollar Diplomacy in Current Perspective.* New York: Columbia University Press, 1980. Readable account of the negotiations that established the IMF, World Bank, and GATT.

Charles P. Kindleberger. *The World in Depression 1929–1939.* Revised edition. Berkeley and Los Angeles: University of California Press, 1986. A leading international economist examines the causes and effects of the Great Depression.

Lawrence B. Krause and Walter S. Salant, eds. *Worldwide Inflation: Theory and Recent Experience.* Washington, D.C.: Brookings Institution, 1977. A collection of analytical studies on global inflationary experience in the 1960s and early 1970s.

Robert A. Mundell. *Monetary Theory.* Pacific Palisades, CA: Goodyear, 1971. The book's second part discusses international monetary problems of the late Bretton Woods years.

Ragnar Nurkse. *International Currency Experience: Lessons of the Inter-war Period.* Geneva: League of Nations, 1944. Classic critique of the nationalistic macroeconomic policies many countries adopted between the world wars.

Maurice Obstfeld. "International Finance," in *The New Palgrave: A Dictionary of Economics.* Vol. 2. New York: Stockton Press, 1987, pp. 898–906. Discusses changing conceptions of internal and external balance.

Michael Parkin. "A 'Monetarist' Analysis of the Generation and Transmission of World Inflation: 1958–71." *American Economic Review* 67 (February 1977), pp. 164–171. Proposes a monetary explanation of world inflation under the Bretton Woods system.

Robert Solomon. *The International Monetary System, 1945–1981.* New York: Harper & Row, 1982. Chapters 1–14 chronicle international monetary relations between World War II and the early 1970s. The author was chief of the Federal Reserve's international finance division during the period leading up to the breakdown of fixed exchange rates.

Macroeconomic Policy and Coordination Under Floating Exchange Rates

Chapter 20

As the Bretton Woods system of fixed exchange rates began to show signs of strain in the late 1960s, many economists recommended that countries allow currency values to be determined freely in the foreign exchange market. When the governments of the industrialized countries adopted floating exchange rates early in 1973, they viewed their step as a temporary emergency measure and were not consciously following the advice of the economists then advocating a permanent floating-rate system. So far, however, it has proved impossible to put the fixed-rate system back together again: the dollar exchange rates of the industrialized countries have continued to float since 1973.

The advocates of floating saw it as a way out of the conflicts between internal and external balance that often arose under the rigid Bretton Woods exchange rates. By the mid-1980s, however, economists and policy makers had become more skeptical about the benefits of an international monetary system based on floating rates. Some critics describe the post-1973 currency arrangements as an international monetary ''nonsystem,'' a free-for-all in which national macroeconomic policies are frequently at odds. Many observers now feel that the current exchange rate system is badly in need of reform.

Why has the performance of floating rates been so disappointing, and what direction should reform of the current system take? In this chapter our models of fixed and floating exchange rates are applied to examine the recent performance of floating rates and to compare the macroeconomic policy problems of different exchange rate regimes.

The Case for Floating Exchange Rates

As international currency crises of increasing scope and frequency erupted in the late 1960s, most economists began advocating greater flexibility of exchange rates. Many argued that a system of floating exchange rates (one in which central banks did not intervene in the foreign exchange market to fix rates) would not only automatically ensure exchange rate flexibility but would also produce several other benefits for the world economy. The case for floating exchange rates rested on three major claims:

1. *Monetary policy autonomy.* If central banks were no longer obliged to intervene in currency markets to fix exchange rates, governments would be able to use monetary policy to reach internal and external balance. Further, no country would be forced to import inflation (or deflation) from abroad.
2. *Symmetry.* Under a system of floating rates the inherent asymmetries of Bretton Woods would disappear and the United States would no longer be able to set world monetary conditions all by itself. At the same time, the United States would have the same opportunity as other countries to influence its exchange rate against foreign currencies.
3. *Exchange rates as automatic stabilizers.* Even in the absence of an active monetary policy, the swift adjustment of market-determined exchange rates would help countries maintain internal and external balance in the face of changes in aggregate demand. The long and agonizing periods of speculation preceding exchange rate realignments under the Bretton Woods rules would not occur under floating.

MONETARY POLICY AUTONOMY

Under the Bretton Woods fixed-rate system, countries other than the United States had little scope to use monetary policy to attain internal and external balance. Monetary policy was weakened by the mechanism of offsetting capital flows (discussed in Chapter 18). A central bank purchase of domestic assets, for example, would put temporary downward pressure on the domestic interest rate and cause the domestic currency to weaken in the foreign exchange market. The exchange rate then had to be propped through central bank sales of official foreign reserves. Pressure on the interest and exchange rates disappeared, however, only when official reserve losses had driven the domestic money supply back down to its original level. Thus, in the closing years of fixed exchange rates, central banks imposed increasingly stringent restrictions on international payments to keep control over their money supplies. These restrictions were only partially successful in strengthening monetary policy, and they had the damaging side effect of distorting international trade.

Advocates of floating rates pointed out that removal of the obligation to peg currency values would restore monetary control to central banks. If, for example, the central bank faced unemployment and wished to expand its money supply in response, there would no longer be any legal barrier to the currency depreciation this would cause. As in the analysis of Chapter 17, the currency depreciation would reduce unemployment by lowering the relative price of domestic products and increasing world demand for them. Similarly, the central bank of an overheated economy could cool down activity by contracting the money supply without worrying that undesired reserve inflows would undermine its stabilization effort. Enhanced control over monetary policy would allow countries to dismantle their distorting barriers to international payments.

Advocates of floating also argued that floating rates would allow each country to choose its own desired long-run inflation rate rather than passively importing the inflation rate established abroad. We saw in the last chapter that a country faced with a rise in the foreign price level will be thrown out of balance and ultimately will import the foreign inflation if it holds its exchange rate fixed: by the end of the 1960s many countries felt that they were importing inflation from the United States. By revaluing its currency—that is, by lowering the domestic currency price of foreign currency—a country can insulate itself completely from an inflationary increase in foreign prices, and so remain in internal and external balance. One of the most telling arguments in favor of floating rates was their ability, in theory, to bring about automatically exchange rate changes that insulate economies from ongoing foreign inflation.

The mechanism behind this insulation is purchasing power parity (Chapter 16). Recall that when all changes in the world economy are monetary, PPP holds true in the long run: exchange rates eventually move to offset exactly national differences in inflation. If U.S. monetary growth leads to a long-run doubling of the U.S. price level, while Germany's price level remains constant, PPP predicts that the long-run DM price of the dollar will be halved. This nominal exchange rate change leaves the *real* exchange rate between the dollar and DM unchanged and thus maintains Germany's internal and external balance. In other words, the long-run exchange rate change predicted by PPP is exactly the change that insulates Germany from U.S. inflation.

A money-induced increase in U.S. prices also causes an *immediate* appreciation of foreign currencies against the dollar when the exchange rate floats. In the short run, the size of this appreciation can differ from what PPP predicts, but the foreign exchange speculators who might have mounted an attack on fixed dollar exchange rates speed the adjustment of floating rates. Since they know foreign currencies will appreciate according to PPP in the long run, they act on their expectations and push exchange rates in the direction of their long-run levels.

Countries operating under the Bretton Woods rules were forced to choose between matching U.S. inflation to hold their dollar exchange rates fixed or deliberately revaluing their currencies in proportion to the rise in U.S. prices. Under floating, however, the foreign exchange market automatically brings about the exchange rate changes that shield countries from U.S. inflation. Since this outcome does not require any government policy decisions, the revaluation crises that occurred under fixed exchange rates are avoided.[1]

SYMMETRY

The second argument put forward by the advocates of floating was that abandonment of the Bretton Woods system would remove the asymmetries that caused so much international disagreement in the 1960s and early 1970s. There were two main asymmetries, both the result of the dollar's central role in the international monetary system. First, because central banks pegged their currencies to the dollar and accumulated dollars as international reserves, the U.S. Federal Reserve played the leading role in

[1] Countries can also avoid importing undesired *deflation* by floating, since the analysis above goes through, in reverse, for a fall in the foreign price level.

determining the world money supply and central banks abroad had little scope to determine ther own domestic money supplies. Second, any foreign country could devalue its currency against the dollar in conditions of ''fundamental disequilibrium,'' but the system's rules did not give the United States the option of devaluing against foreign currencies. Thus, when the dollar was at last devalued in December 1971, it was only after a long and economically disruptive period of multilateral negotiation.

A system of floating exchange rates, its proponents argued, would do away with these asymmetries. Since countries would no longer peg dollar exchange rates or need to hold dollar reserves for this purpose, each would be in a position to guide monetary conditions at home. For the same reason, the United States would not face any special obstacle to altering its exchange rate through monetary or fiscal policies. All countries' exchange rates would be determined symmetrically by the foreign exchange market, not by government decisions.[2]

EXCHANGE RATES AS AUTOMATIC STABILIZERS

The third argument in favor of floating rates concerned their ability, theoretically, to promote swift and relatively painless adjustment to certain types of economic changes. One such change, discussed above, is foreign inflation. Figure 20-1, which uses the *DD-AA* model, examines another type of change by comparing the economy's response under a fixed and a floating exchange rate to a temporary fall in foreign demand for its exports.

A fall in demand for the home country's exports reduces aggregate demand for every level of the exchange rate, E, and so shifts the *DD* schedule leftward from D^1D^1 to D^2D^2. (Recall that the *DD* schedule shows exchange rate and output pairs for which aggregate demand equals aggregate output.) Figure 20-1a shows how this shift affects the economy's equilibrium when the exchange rate floats. Because the demand shift is assumed to be temporary, it does not change the long-run expected exchange rate and so does not move the asset market equilibrium schedule A^1A^1. (Recall that the *AA* schedule shows exchange rate and output pairs at which the foreign exchange market and the domestic money market are in equilibrium.) The economy's short-run equilibrium is therefore at point 2; compared with the initial equilibrium at point 1, the currency depreciates (E rises) and output falls. Why does the exchange rate rise from E^1 to E^2? As demand and output fall, reducing the transactions demand for money, the home interest rate must also decline to keep the money market in equilibrium. This fall in the home interest rate causes the domestic currency to depreciate in the foreign exchange market, and the exchange rate therefore rises from E^1 to E^2.

The effect of the same export demand disturbance under a fixed exchange rate is shown in Figure 20-1b. Since the central bank must prevent the currency depreciation that occurs under a floating rate, it buys domestic money with foreign currency, an action that contracts the money supply and shifts A^1A^1 left to A^2A^2. The new short-run equilibrium of the economy under a fixed exchange rate is at point 3, where output equals Y^3.

[2] The symmetry argument is not an argument against fixed-rate systems in general, but an argument against the specific type of fixed-exchange rate system that broke down in the early 1970s. As we saw in Chapter 18, a fixed-rate system based on a gold standard can be completely symmetric. The creation of an artificial reserve asset, the SDR, in the late 1960s was an attempt to attain the symmetry of a gold standard without the other drawbacks of that system.

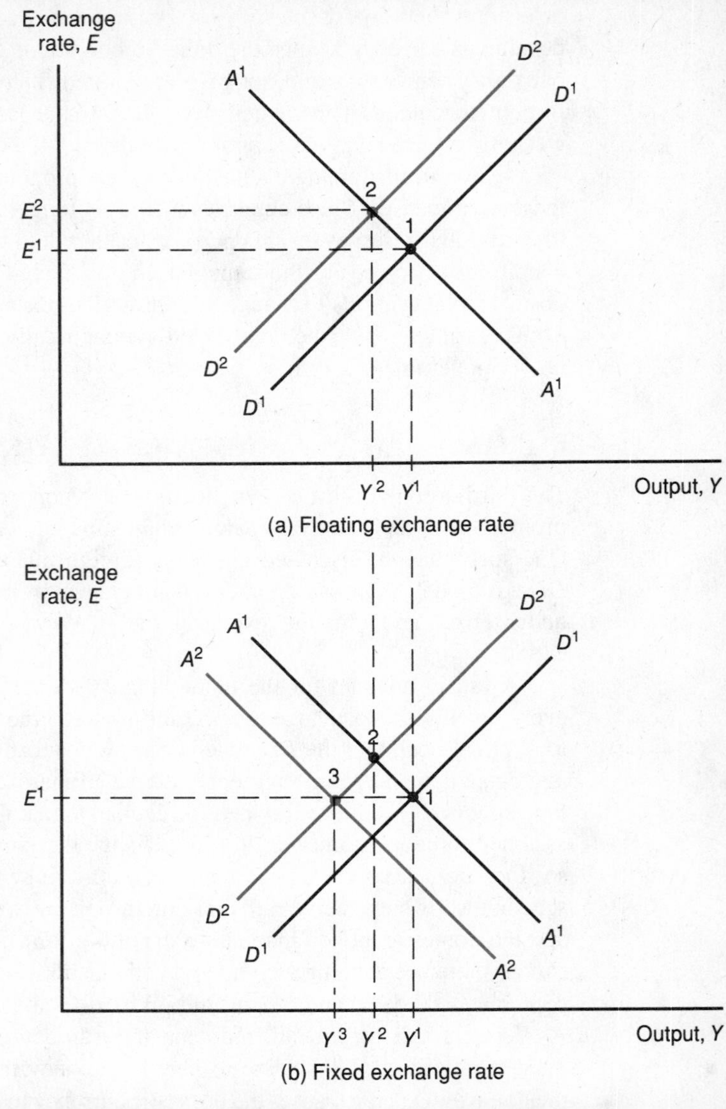

FIGURE 20-1
Effects of a fall in export demand under floating and fixed exchange rates.
With a floating rate (a), output falls only to Y^2 as the currency's depreciation shifts demand back toward domestic goods. With a fixed rate (b), output falls all the way to Y^3 as the central bank reduces the money supply.

Figure 20-1 shows that output actually falls more under a fixed rate than under a floating rate, dropping all the way to Y^3 rather than Y^2. In other words, the movement of the floating exchange rate stabilizes the economy by reducing the shock's effect on employment relative to its effect under a fixed rate. Currency depreciation in the floating rate case makes domestic goods and services cheaper when the demand for them falls, partially offsetting the initial reduction in demand. In addition to reducing the departure from internal balance caused by the fall in export demand, the depreciation reduces the current account deficit that occurs under fixed rates by making domestic products more competitive in international markets.

We have considered the case of a transitory fall in export demand, but even stronger conclusions can be drawn when there is a *permanent* fall in export demand. In this case, the expected exchange rate E^e also rises and AA shifts upward as a result. A permanent shock causes a greater depreciation than a temporary one, and the movement of the exchange rate therefore cushions domestic output more when the shock is permanent.

Under the Bretton Woods system, a fall in export demand such as the one shown in Figure 20-1b would, if permanent, have led to a situation of "fundamental disequilibrium" calling for a devaluation of the currency or a long period of domestic unemployment as export prices fell. Uncertainty about the government's intentions would have encouraged speculative capital outflows, further worsening the situation by depleting central bank reserves and contracting the domestic money supply at a time of unemployment. Advocates of floating rates pointed out that the foreign exchange market would automatically bring about the required *real* currency depreciation through a movement in the nominal exchange rate. This exchange rate change would reduce or eliminate the need to push the price level down through unemployment, and because it would occur immediately there would be no risk of speculative disruption, as there would be under a fixed rate.

The Case against Floating Exchange Rates

The experience with floating exchange rates between the world wars had left many doubts about how they would function in practice if the Bretton Woods rules were scrapped. Some economists were skeptical of the claims advanced by the advocates of floating and predicted instead that floating rates would have adverse consequences for the world economy. The case against floating rates rested on five main arguments:

1. *Discipline.* Central banks freed from the obligation to fix their exchange rates might embark on inflationary policies. In other words, the "discipline" imposed on individual countries by a fixed rate would be lost.
2. *Destabilizing speculation and money market disturbances.* Speculation on changes in exchange rates could lead to instability in foreign exchange markets, and this instability, in turn, might have negative effects on countries' internal and external balances. Further, disturbances to the home money market could be more disruptive under floating than under a fixed rate.
3. *Injury to international trade and investment.* Floating rates would make relative international prices more unpredictable and thus injure international trade and investment.
4. *Uncoordinated economic policies.* If the Bretton Woods rules on exchange rate adjustment were abandoned, the door would be opened to competitive currency practices harmful to the world economy. As happened during the interwar years, countries might adopt policies without considering their possible beggar-thy-neighbor aspects. All countries would suffer as a result.
5. *The illusion of greater autonomy.* Floating exchange rates would not really give countries more policy autonomy. Changes in exchange rates would have such pervasive macroeconomic effects that central banks would feel compelled to intervene

heavily in foreign exchange markets even without a formal commitment to peg. Thus, floating would increase the uncertainty in the economy without really giving macroeconomic policy greater freedom.

DISCIPLINE

Proponents of floating rates argue they give governments more freedom in the use of monetary policy. Some critics of floating rates believed that floating rates would lead to license rather than liberty: freed of the need to worry about losses of foreign reserves, governments might embark on overexpansionary fiscal or monetary policies. Factors ranging from political objectives (such as stimulating the economy in time to win an election) to simple incompetence might set off an inflationary spiral. In the minds of those who made the discipline argument, the German hyperinflation of the 1920s epitomized the kind of monetary instability that floating rates might allow.

The pro-floaters' response to the discipline criticism was that a floating exchange rate would bottle up inflationary disturbances within the country whose government was misbehaving; it would then be up to its voters, if they wished, to elect a government with better policies. The Bretton Woods arrangements ended up imposing relatively little discipline on the United States, which certainly contributed to the acceleration of worldwide inflation in the late 1960s. Unless a sacrosanct link between currencies and a commodity such as gold were at the center of a system of fixed rates, the system would remain susceptible to human tampering. As discussed in Chapter 18, however, commodity-based monetary standards suffer from difficulties that make them undesirable in practice.

DESTABILIZING SPECULATION AND MONEY MARKET DISTURBANCES

An additional concern arising out of the experience of the interwar period was the possibility that speculation in currency markets might fuel wide gyrations in exchange rates. If foreign exchange traders saw that a currency was depreciating, it was argued, they might sell the currency in the expectation of future depreciation regardless of the currency's longer-term prospects; and as more traders jumped on the bandwagon by selling the currency the expectations of depreciation would be realized. Such **destabilizing speculation** would tend to accentuate the fluctuations around the exchange rate's long-run value that would occur normally as a result of unexpected economic disturbances. Aside from interfering with international trade, destabilizing sales of a weak currency might encourage expectations of future inflation and set off a domestic wage-price spiral that would encourage further depreciation. Countries could be caught in a "vicious circle" of depreciation and inflation that might be difficult to escape.

Advocates of floating rates questioned whether destabilizing speculators could stay in business. Anyone who persisted in selling a currency after it had depreciated below its long-run value or in buying a currency after it had appreciated above its long-run value was bound to lose money over the long term. Destabilizing speculators would thus be driven from the market, the pro-floaters argued, and the field would be left to speculators who had avoided long-term losses by speeding the adjustment of exchange rates *toward* their long-run values.

Proponents of floating also pointed out that capital flows could behave in a destabilizing manner under fixed rates. An unexpected central bank reserve loss might set up expectations of a devaluation and spark a reserve hemorrhage as speculators dumped domestic currency assets. Such capital flight might actually force an unnecessary devaluation if government measures to restore confidence proved insufficient.

A more telling argument against floating rates is that they make the economy more vulnerable to shocks coming from the domestic money market. Figure 20-2 uses the *DD-AA* model to illustate this point. The figure shows the effect on the economy of a rise in real domestic money demand (that is, a rise in the real balances people desire to hold at each level of the interest rate and income) under a floating exchange rate. Because a lower level of income is now needed (given E) for people to be content to hold the available real money supply, A^1A^1 shifts leftward to A^2A^2: income falls from Y^1 to Y^2 as the currency appreciates from E^1 to E^2. The rise in money demand works exactly like a fall in the money supply, and if it is permanent it will lead eventually to a fall in the home price level. Under a fixed exchange rate, however, the change in money demand does not affect the economy at all. To prevent the home currency from appreciating, the central bank buys foreign reserves with domestic money until the real money supply rises by an amount equal to the rise in real money demand. This intervention has the effect of keeping A^1A^1 in its original position, preventing any change in output or the price level.

A fixed exchange rate therefore automatically prevents instability in the domestic money market from affecting the economy. This is a powerful argument in favor of fixed rates *if* most of the shocks that buffet the economy come from the home money market (that is, if they result from shifts in *AA*). But as we saw in the previous section, fixing the exchange rate will worsen macroeconomic performance on average if output market shocks (that is, shocks involving shifts in *DD*) predominate.

INJURY TO INTERNATIONAL TRADE AND INVESTMENT

Critics of floating also charged that the inherent variability of floating exchange rates would injure international trade and investment. Fluctuating currencies make importers more uncertain about the prices they will have to pay for goods in the future and make

FIGURE 20-2
A rise in money demand under a floating exchange rate.
A rise in money demand works exactly like a fall in the money supply, causing the currency to appreciate and output to fall. Under a fixed exchange rate the central bank would prevent A^1A^1 from shifting by purchasing foreign exchange and thus automatically expanding the money supply to meet the rise in money demand.

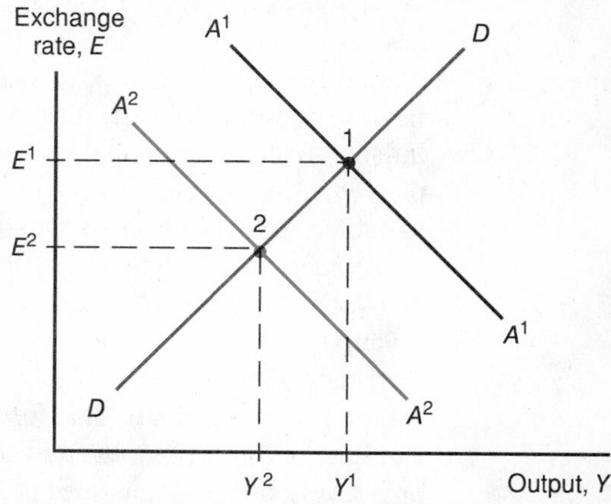

exporters more uncertain about the prices they will receive. This uncertainty, it was claimed, would make it costlier to engage in international trade, and as a result trade volumes—and with them the gains countries realize through trade—would shrink. Similarly, greater uncertainty about the payoffs on investments might interfere with productive international capital flows.

Supporters of floating countered that international traders could avoid exchange rate risk through transactions in the forward exchange market (see Chaper 14), which would grow in scope and efficiency in a floating-rate world. The skeptics replied that forward exchange markets would be expensive to use and that it was doubtful that forward transactions could be used to cover all risks. A long-term investment abroad yielding payoffs over a period of ten years, for example, could not be covered easily in the forward market, where the maturities of the contracts available are typically much shorter than ten years.

At a more general level, opponents of floating rates feared that the usefulness of each country's money as a guide to rational planning and calculation would be reduced. A currency becomes less useful as a unit of account if its purchasing power over imports becomes less predictable.

UNCOORDINATED ECONOMIC POLICIES

Some defenders of the Bretton Woods system felt that its rules had helped promote orderly international trade by outlawing the competitive currency depreciations that occurred during the Great Depression. With countries once again free to alter their exchange rates at will, they argued, history might repeat itself. Countries might again follow self-serving macroeconomic policies that hurt all countries and, in the end, helped none.

In rebuttal, the pro-floaters replied that the Bretton Woods rules for exchange rate adjustment were cumbersome. In addition, the rules were inequitable because, in practice, it was deficit countries that came under pressure to adopt restrictive macroeconomic policies or devalue. The fixed-rate system had "solved" the problem of international cooperation on monetary policy only by giving the United States a dominant position that it ultimately abused.

THE ILLUSION OF GREATER AUTONOMY

A final line of criticism held that the policy autonomy promised by the advocates of floating rates was, in part, illusory. True, a floating rate could in theory shut out foreign inflation over the long haul and allow central banks to set their money supplies as they pleased. But, it was argued, the exchange rate is such an important macroeconomic variable that policy makers would find themselves unable to take domestic monetary policy measures without considering their effects on the exchange rate.

Particularly important to this view was the role of the exchange rate in the domestic inflation process. A currency depreciation that raised import prices might induce workers to demand higher wages to maintain their customary standard of living. Higher wage settlements would then feed into final goods prices, fueling price level inflation and further wage hikes. In addition, currency depreciation would immediately raise the prices of imported goods used in the production of domestic output. Therefore, floating rates could be expected to quicken the pace at which the price level responded to increases in the money supply. While floating rates implied greater central bank control over the nominal money supply, M^s, they did not necessarily imply correspondingly greater control over the policy instrument that affects employment and other real economic variables, the *real* money supply, M^s/P. The response of domestic prices to exchange rate changes would be particularly rapid in economies where imports make up a large share of the domestic consumption basket: in such countries, currency changes have significant effects on the purchasing power of workers' wages.

The skeptics also maintained that the insulating properties of a floating rate are very limited. They conceded that the exchange rate would adjust *eventually* to offset foreign price inflation due to excessive monetary growth. In a world of sticky prices, however, countries are nonetheless buffeted by foreign monetary developments, which affect real interest rates and real exchange rates in the short run. Further, there is no reason, even in theory, why one country's fiscal policies cannot have repercussions abroad.

Critics of floating thus argued that its potential benefits had been oversold relative to its costs. Macroeconomic policy makers would continue to labor under the constraint of avoiding excessive exchange rate fluctuations. But by abandoning fixed rates, they would have forgone the benefits for world trade and investment of predictable currency values.

Case Study

EXCHANGE RATE EXPERIENCE BETWEEN THE OIL SHOCKS, 1973–1980

Which group was right, the advocates of floating rates or the critics? In this Case Study and the next we survey the experience with floating exchange rates since 1973 in an attempt to answer this question. To avoid future disappointment, however, it is best to state up front that, as is often the case in economics, the data do not lead to a clear verdict. Although a number of predictions made by the critics of floating were borne out by subsequent events, it is also unclear whether a regime of fixed exchange rates would have survived the series of economic storms that has shaken the world economy since 1973.

The First Oil Shock and Its Effects, 1973–1975

As the industrialized countries' exchange rates were allowed to float in March 1973, an official group representing all IMF members was preparing plans to restore world monetary order. Formed in the fall of 1972, this group, called the Committee of Twenty, had been assigned the job of designing a new system of fixed exchange rates free of the asymmetries of Bretton Woods. By the time the committee issued its final "Outline of Reform" in July 1974, however, an upheaval in the world petroleum market had made an early return to fixed exchange rates unthinkable.

Energy Prices and the 1974–1975 Recession. In October 1973, war broke out between Israel and the Arab countries. To protest support of Israel by the United States and the Netherlands, Arab members of the Organization of Petroleum Exporting Countries

(OPEC), an international cartel including most large oil producers, imposed an embargo on oil shipments to those two countries (Chapter 11). Fearing more general disruptions in oil shipments, buyers bid up market oil prices as they tried to build precautionary inventories. Encouraged by these developments in the oil market, OPEC countries began raising the price they charged to their main customers, the large oil companies. By March 1974, the oil price had quadrupled from its prewar price of $3 per barrel to $12 per barrel.

The massive increase in the price of oil raised the energy prices paid by consumers and the operating costs of energy-using firms and also fed into the prices of nonenergy petroleum products, such as plastics. To understand the impact of these price increases, think of them as a large tax on oil importers imposed by the oil producers of OPEC. The oil shock had the same macroeconomic effect as a simultaneous increase in consumer and business taxes: consumption and investment slowed down everywhere, and the world economy was thrown into recession.

Because the price increase raised the import bills of oil importers, it worsened the current account deficits of many countries. The overall current account balance of the industrialized countries, taken as a group, went from $20.3 billion in 1973 to −$10.8 billion in 1974, while the overall current account of the less-developed countries that were not major oil exporters moved from −$11.3 billion to −$37.0 billion. The increased current account deficits of these two groups corresponded to a greater current account surplus for the main oil exporters. The total current account surplus of those countries rose from $6.7 billion to $68.3 billion between 1973 and 1974. (Data on 1973–1986 current account balances for the three major groups of countries described here are given in Table 23-2, p. 686.[3])

The Acceleration of Inflation. The model we developed in Chapters 14 through 18 predicts that inflation tends to rise in booms and fall in recessions. As the world went into deep recession in 1974, however, inflation accelerated in most countries. Table 20-1 shows how inflation in the seven largest industrial countries spurted upward in that year. In a number of these countries inflation rates came close to doubling even though unemployment was rising.

What happened? An important contributing factor was the oil shock itself: by directly raising the prices of petroleum products and the costs of energy-using industries, the increase in the oil price caused price levels to jump upward. Further, the worldwide inflationary pressures that had built up since the end of the 1960s had become entrenched in the wage-setting process and were continuing to contribute to inflation in spite of the deteriorating employment picture. The same inflationary expectations that were driving new wage contracts were also putting additional upward pressure on commodity prices as speculators built up stocks of commodities whose prices they expected to rise.

Finally, the oil crisis, as luck would have it, was not the only supply shock troubling the world economy at the time. From 1972 on, a coincidence of adverse supply disturbances pushed farm prices upward and thus contributed to the general inflation. These

[3] The fall in the U.S. current account surplus, from $9.1 billion in 1973 to $7.6 billion in 1974, was relatively minor. This was because the United States, itself an oil producer, was less dependent on oil imports than were many other countries. In contrast, Japan, which is heavily dependent on energy imports, moved from a surplus of $0.1 billion to a deficit of $4.5 billion.

TABLE 20-1 Inflation rates in major industrialized countries, 1973–1980 (percent per year)

Country	*1973*	*1974*	*1975*	*1976*	*1977*	*1978*	*1979*	*1980*
United States	6.2	11.1	9.1	5.7	6.5	7.6	11.3	13.5
Britain	9.2	16.0	24.2	16.5	15.8	8.3	13.4	18.0
Canada	7.6	10.9	10.8	7.5	8.0	8.9	9.2	10.2
France	7.3	13.7	11.8	9.6	9.4	9.1	10.8	13.6
Germany	6.9	7.0	6.0	4.5	3.7	2.7	4.1	5.5
Italy	10.8	19.1	17.0	16.8	17.0	12.1	14.8	21.2
Japan	11.7	24.5	11.8	9.3	8.1	3.8	3.6	8.0

Source: Organization for Economic Cooperation and Development. *Economic Outlook: Historical Statistics, 1960–1986.* Paris: OECD, 1987. Figures are percentage increases in each year's average consumer price index over the average consumer price index for the previous year.

supply disturbances included poor harvests in the United States and the Soviet Union; shortages of sugar and cocoa; and the mysterious disappearance of the Peruvian anchovies from their customary feeding grounds. Although you may think anchovies are important only to consumers of pizza and Caesar salad, they are also important to farmers since they are used in the fish meal that is fed to livestock. The precipitous drop in the anchovy catch led to sharp increases in the prices of competing feed grains (mainly corn and soybeans).

Stagflation. To describe the unusual macroeconomic conditions of 1974–1975, economists coined a new word that has since become commonplace: **stagflation,** a combination of stagnating output and high inflation. Stagflation was the result of two factors:

1. Increases in commodity prices that directly raised inflation while at the same time depressing aggregate demand and supply.
2. Expectations of future inflation that fed into wages and other prices in spite of recession and rising unemployment.

Even before the oil shock hit, the move to floating rates had allowed the industrialized countries to adopt more restrictive monetary and fiscal policies aimed at restraining the accelerating inflation. The slowdown in money growth was most dramatic in Germany, whose Bundesbank used its new-found control over the money supply to reduce its annual monetary growth rate from 14.7 percent in 1972 to a mere 2.6 percent in 1973 (compare Tables 19-2, p. 553, and 20-2). A significant monetary slowdown also took place in the United States, where the Fed allowed the money supply to grow by only 5.6 percent in 1973 and 4.4 percent in 1974, as compared with 9.2 percent in 1972 (see Figure 19-3, p. 548, and Table 20-2). These initially restrictive policies helped deepen the 1974-1975 slump.

Regaining Internal and External Balance. The commodity shocks left most oil importers further from both internal and external balance than they were when floating began in 1973. Countries were in no position to give up the expenditure-switching advantages

TABLE 20-2 Money supply growth rates in major industrialized countries, 1973–1980 (percent per year)

Country	*1973*	*1974*	*1975*	*1976*	*1977*	*1978*	*1979*	*1980*
United States	5.6	4.4	4.8	6.6	8.0	8.3	7.0	6.6
Britain	5.1	10.8	18.0	11.2	21.7	16.3	9.1	4.0
Canada	11.1	5.8	23.1	1.9	11.7	8.3	3.7	10.5
France	9.7	11.6	16.6	7.3	11.7	11.1	12.8	6.9
Germany	2.6	10.9	13.5	3.9	11.4	14.3	4.2	3.8
Italy	24.2	11.0	12.2	19.7	21.4	25.8	24.4	13.5
Japan	16.8	8.6	11.2	13.0	7.1	10.8	7.9	−1.5

Source: Organization for Economic Cooperation and Development. *Economic Outlook: Historical Statistics, 1960–1986.* Paris: OECD, 1987. (France 1978 from OECD. *Main Economic Indicators: Historical Statistics, 1964–1983.* Paris OECD, 1984.) Figures are percentage increases in the end-of-year money stock M1 over the corresponding value for the previous year.

of exchange rate flexibility and burden monetary policy with the job of defending a fixed rate. No commitment to fixed rates would have been credible in a period when countries were experiencing such different inflation rates and suffering shocks that permanently altered production costs. The speculative attacks that had brought the fixed-rate system down would have quickly undermined any attempt to fix parities anew.

How did countries use their policy tools to regain internal and external balance? As the recession deepened over 1974 and early 1975, most governments shifted to expansionary fiscal and monetary policies. Table 20-2 shows that in the seven largest industrial countries, monetary growth rates rose between 1974 and 1975 as central banks reacted to rising unemployment. As a result of these policy actions, a strong output recovery was underway in most industrialized countries by the second half of 1975. At the same time inflation was falling (see Table 20-1). Unfortunately, however, the unemployment rates of industrialized countries failed to return to prerecession levels even as output recovered.

The 1974 current account deficit of the industrial countries, taken as a group, turned to a surplus in 1975 as spending fell, and was near zero in 1976. The OPEC countries, which could not raise spending quickly enough to match their increased income, were running a substantial current account surplus in 1975 and 1976, but this was matched by the deficit of the oil-importing developing countries. Because the non-oil-developing countries did not cut their spending as sharply as industrial countries, GNP growth in developing countries as a group did not become negative in 1975, as it did in many developed countries. The developing countries financed their oil deficits in part by borrowing funds that the OPEC countries had deposited in the industrial countries' financial centers. This "recycling" of the OPEC surplus, which took place over the years 1974–1977, is an important element in our examination of the developing country debt crisis and the growth of international capital markets (see Chapters 22 and 23).

Most economists and policy makers viewed the international adjustment to the first oil shock as a success for floating exchange rates. Freed of the need to defend a fixed exchange rate, each government had chosen the monetary and fiscal response that best suited its goals. The United States and Germany had even been able to relax the capital controls they had set up before 1974. This relaxation eased the adjustment problem of the developing countries, which were able to borrow more easily from developed country financial markets to maintain their own spending and economic growth. In turn, the relative strength of the developing world's demand for industrial country exports helped mitigate the severity of the 1974–1975 recession.

Rambouillet and Jamaica: Revising the IMF's Charter, 1975–1976

Because floating rates had seemed to function well in conditions of adversity, the governments of the industrialized countries acknowledged late in 1975 that they were prepared to live with floating exchange rates for the indefinite future. Meeting at the Château de Rambouillet, near Paris, in the first of a series of annual economic summit meetings, leaders of the main industrial countries called on the IMF to revise its Articles of Agreement to take account of the reality of floating exchange rates. The participating governments committed themselves to countering "erratic fluctuations" in exchange rates but made no provision for a return to fixed parities.

In response to the Rambouillet decisions, the IMF's directors met at Kingston, Jamaica, in January 1976 to approve a revision of the fourth IMF Article of Agreement, which covered exchange rate arrangements. The new Article IV implicitly endorsed floating rates by freeing each member country to choose any exchange rate system it preferred. Governments were urged to follow macroeconomic policies that would promote price stability and growth, and they were to avoid "manipulating exchange rates . . . to gain an unfair competitive advantage over other members," as had occurred during the interwar period when many countries engineered beggar-thy-neighbor currency depreciations. But more detailed restrictions were not placed on IMF members' policies.

The amended Article IV called on the IMF to monitor members' exchange rate policies to ensure compliance with the new guidelines. Although this "surveillance" of exchange rate policies went beyond IMF conditionality in that it applied even to countries not borrowing from the Fund, no mechanism was created to give the Fund clout in influencing nonborrowers' policies. In practice, therefore, the new article did no more than sanction what had already existed for nearly three years: a scheme of decentralized policy making in which each country pursued what it perceived as its own interest.

The Weak Dollar, 1976–1979

As the recovery from the 1974–1975 recession slowed in late 1976 and unemployment remained persistently high, the United States urged the two other industrial giants, Germany and Japan, to join it in adopting expansionary policies that would pull the world economy out of its doldrums. Only at the Bonn economic summit of July 1978 did Germany and Japan, less fearful of inflation than they had been two years earlier, agree to join the United States as "locomotives" of world economic growth. Until then, the United States had been attempting to go it alone, and its policies, while causing a sharp drop in the U.S. unemployment rate (to 6.0 percent in 1978 from a recession high of 8.3 percent in 1975), had reignited inflation and pushed the U.S. current acount into deficit. In contrast, inflation in Germany and Japan had reached relatively low levels by 1978 (see Table 20-1).

The result of this policy imbalance—vigorous expansion in the United States unmatched by expansion abroad—was a steep depreciation of the dollar starting in 1976. The depreciation of the dollar in these years is evident in Figure 20-3, which shows both **nominal and real effective exchange rate indexes** of the dollar. These indexes measure, respectively, the price of a dollar in terms of a basket of foreign currencies and the price of U.S. output in terms of a basket of foreign outputs. Thus, a rise in either index is a (nominal or real) dollar appreciation, while a fall is a depreciation.

The dollar's depreciation was an appreciation of the DM and yen, a development that put deflationary pressure on the German and Japanese economies by deflecting aggregate demand away from their exports and toward U.S. exports. To offset this negative stimulus to their economies, the Bundesbank and Bank of Japan intervened heavily in the foreign exchange market, buying dollars and issuing their own currencies in exchange. This foreign exchange intervention helps explain Germany's rapid money supply growth in 1977–1978 and Japan's in 1978 (see Table 20-2). In 1979, after the adoption of the expansionary measures promised at the Bonn summit, unemployment fell in both Japan and Germany.

FIGURE 20-3
Nominal and real effective dollar exchange rate indexes, 1975–1990.
The indexes are measures of the nominal and real value of the U.S. dollar in terms of a basket of fifteen industrial-country currencies. An increase is a dollar appreciation, a decrease a dollar depreciation. For both indexes, the 1985 value is 100.
Source: International Monetary Fund, *International Financial Statistics Yearbook,* 1991.

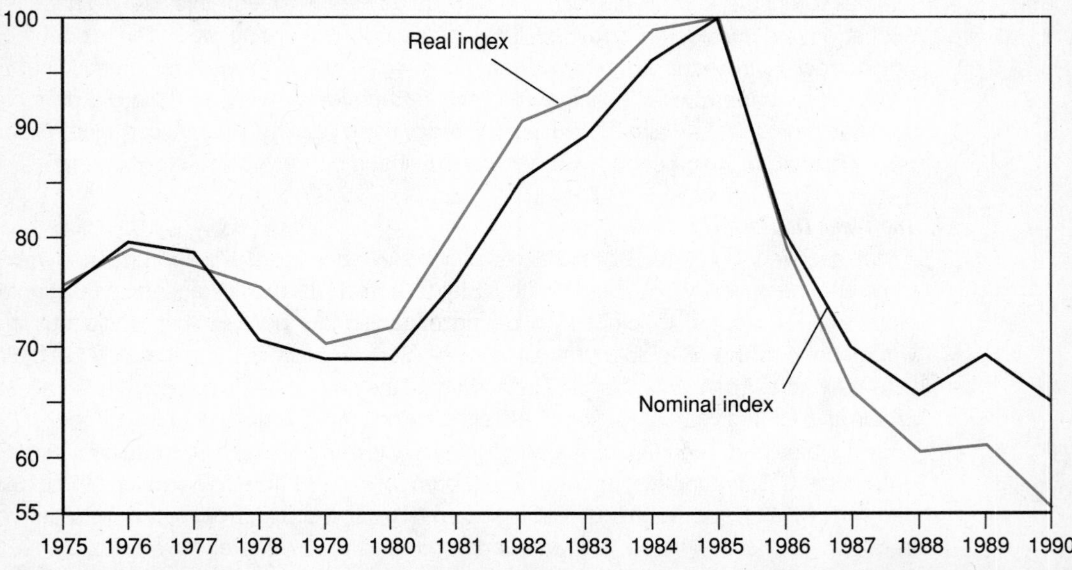

International investors had little confidence in the dollar's future value in view of the widening gap between U.S. and foreign inflation rates. In addition, the weakening dollar helped fuel U.S. inflation by raising import prices and the inflation expectations of wage setters. To restore confidence in the dollar, President Carter appointed a new Federal Reserve Board chairman with broad experience in international financial affairs, Paul A. Volcker. The dollar remained weak in the foreign exchange market until October 1979, when Volcker announced a tightening of U.S. monetary policy and the adoption by the Fed of more stringent procedures for controlling money supply growth.

The German and Japanese foreign exchange intervention of 1977–1978, along with the sharp U.S. monetary turnaround of 1979, illustrated the truth of one point made by the critics of floating exchange rates. Governments could not be indifferent to the behavior of exchange rates and inevitably surrendered some of their policy autonomy in other areas to prevent exchange rate movements they viewed as harmful to their economies.

The Second Oil Shock, 1979–1980

The fall of the Shah of Iran in 1979 sparked a second round of oil price increases by disrupting oil exports from that country. Oil prices rose from around $13 per barrel in 1978 to nearly $32 per barrel in 1980 as importers stockpiled oil to guard against possible supply cutoffs. As they had after the 1973–1974 episode, oil-importing economies faced stagflation. Table 20-1 shows that inflation accelerated sharply in all the industrialized economies between 1978 and 1980. Output growth generally slowed and unemployment generally rose, but the effects were neither as uniform nor as dramatic as those of the first oil shock. Oil-importing developing countries, like the developed countries, experienced higher inflation coupled with slower growth.

As in the earlier oil shock, the industrial countries as a group ran a current account deficit that then declined, while the non-oil-producing developing countries ran persistent high deficits rather than adjusting spending downward (see Table 23-2, p. 686). But in contrast to what happened after the first round of oil price hikes, the developing world's deficit caused serious problems for the world financial system later in the 1980s.

In 1975, macroeconomic policy makers in the industrial countries had responded to the first oil shock with expansionary monetary and fiscal policies. They responded very differently to the second oil shock. Over 1979 and 1980, monetary growth was actually *restricted* in most major industrial countries in an attempt to offset the rise in inflation accompanying the oil price increase. Several countries undertook contractionary fiscal measures at the same time. After struggling to reduce the higher inflation of the early 1970s, central banks were now worried that the 1978–1980 upswing in inflation might be hard to reverse later if it were allowed to be built into inflationary expectations and the wage-setting process. The sharp depreciation of the U.S. dollar after 1976 provided an additional motive for restrictive American monetary policy, as we have seen.

The fight against inflation had a high price in terms of employment and output. Unemployment appeared to take a ratchet step upward by 1981 (see Table 20-3), and restrictive macroeconomic policies blocked a decisive output recovery. In fact, the recovery from the oil shock barely had time to start up before the world economy, in 1981, plunged into the deepest recession since the Great Depression of the 1930s.

TABLE 20-3 Unemployment rates in major industrialized countries, 1979–1993 (percent of labor force)

Year	United States	Britain	Canada	France	Germany	Italy	Japan
1979	5.8	4.5	7.4	5.9	3.2	7.8	2.1
1980	7.2	6.1	7.5	6.3	3.2	7.7	2.0
1981	7.6	9.1	7.6	7.4	4.5	8.5	2.2
1982	9.7	10.4	11.0	8.1	6.4	9.2	2.3
1983	9.6	11.2	11.8	8.3	7.9	10.0	2.7
1984	7.5	11.4	11.2	9.7	7.9	10.1	2.7
1985	7.2	11.6	10.5	10.3	8.0	10.2	2.6
1986	7.0	11.8	9.5	10.4	7.7	11.2	2.8
1987	6.2	10.4	8.8	10.5	7.6	12.1	2.9
1988	5.5	8.2	7.8	10.0	7.6	12.2	2.5
1989	5.3	6.2	7.5	9.4	6.9	12.1	2.3
1990	5.5	5.9	8.1	8.9	6.2	11.1	2.1
1991	6.7	8.3	10.3	9.5	6.7	11.0	2.1
1992	7.4	10.1	11.3	10.2	7.7	10.7	2.2
1993	7.0	10.7	11.1	11.2	10.1	10.9	2.5

Source: Organization for Economic Cooperation and Development. *OECD Economic Outlook* 53 (June 1993), Tables 53 and R19. From 1991 on, data for Germany include the former East Germany.

A Two-Country Model of Macroeconomic Interdependence under a Floating Rate

Before discussing macroeconomic interactions between the United States and the rest of the world in the 1980s and 1990s, we will develop a model to analyze the transmission of policies between countries linked by a floating exchange rate. The model is applied to the short run in which output prices can be assumed to be fixed.

Imagine a world of two countries, Home and Foreign. In previous models the home country's current account balance has been written as a function of its real exchange rate and its income. In reality, however, the level of GNP abroad influences foreign demand for the home country's exports and therefore the home current account balance. The model of Chapters 17 and 18 implicitly assumed the home country was too small to influence foreign income, the level of which we took as fixed. The model cannot adequately illuminate the macroeconomic interdependence of national economies unless it is extended to apply to large countries like the United States.

As the first step in this extension, we now assume that Home's current account is a function of the real exchange rate, EP^*/P, its own disposable income, $Y - T$, *and* Foreign's disposable income, $Y^* - T^*$, where Y^* denotes Foreign's output and T^* Foreign's taxes. E is the Home currency price of Foreign's currency and EP^*/P is the real exchange rate, the price of Foreign output in terms of Home output. Home's current account is therefore

$$CA = CA(EP^*/P, Y - T, Y^* - T^*).$$

A real depreciation of Home's currency (a rise in EP^*/P) is assumed to cause an increase in its current account balance, while a rise in Home disposable income leads to a fall. Our previous model ignored the effect of Foreign disposable income on Home's current account, but in a model of two interacting economies we must ask how a rise in $Y^* - T^*$ affects CA. Because a rise in Foreign disposable income raises Foreign spending on Home products, it raises Home exports. A rise in Foreign disposable income therefore causes an increase in Home's current account balance.

Aggregate demand for Home output is, as always, the sum of Home's spending, $C + I + G$, and its current account, CA. Aggregate supply and demand are therefore equal in Home when

$$Y = C(Y - T) + I + G + CA(EP^*/P, Y - T, Y^* - T^*). \qquad \textbf{(20-1)}$$

Foreign's current account, CA^*, also depends on the relative price of Home and Foreign products, EP^*/P, and on disposable income in the two countries. In fact, in a world of two countries, Home's current account surplus must exactly equal Foreign's current account deficit when both balances are measured in terms of a common unit. Since Home exports are Foreign imports and Home imports are Foreign exports, any Home export surplus is necessarily matched by a corresponding Foreign import surplus. In terms of Foreign output, Foreign's current account is

$$CA^* = -CA(EP^*/P, Y - T, Y^* - T^*) \div (EP^*/P).$$

CA is divided by the real exchange rate EP^*/P, the price of Foreign output in terms of Home output, to convert it into the Foreign output units used to measure CA^*.

Clearly, a rise in Home income, by worsening Home's current account CA, improves CA^*; in the same way, a rise in Foreign income worsens CA^*. Although the effect of a change in EP^*/P on CA^* is more complicated, we assume that a rise in EP^*/P (a relative cheapening of Home output) causes CA^* to fall at the same time it causes CA to rise.[4] In the Foreign output market demand equals supply when

$$Y^* = C^*(Y^* - T^*) + I^* + G^* - (P/EP^*) \times CA(EP^*/P, Y - T, Y^* - T^*). \qquad \textbf{(20-2)}$$

Assuming temporarily that the real exchange rate EP^*/P is constant at a given level, Figure 20-4 shows how the Home and Foreign output levels are determined. The *HH* schedule shows the Home and Foreign output levels at which aggregate demand equals aggregate supply *in Home*. *HH* slopes upward because a rise in Y^* increases Home exports, raising aggregate demand and calling forth a higher level of Home

[4] The complication behind this assumption is related to the one behind the Marshall-Lerner condition (see Chapter 17, Appendix II). We have already assumed that a rise in EP^*/P causes CA to rise. But this is not always sufficient to imply that CA^* falls at the same time, because $CA^* = -CA \div (EP^*/P)$. For example, if Home has a current account surplus ($CA > 0$), a rise in EP^*/P pushes CA further away from zero. This tends to make CA^* more negative than it was, but at the same time it pushes CA^* closer to zero by increasing the denominator of $-CA \div (EP^*/P)$—that is, by making Foreign's exports more expensive relative to its imports from Home. These two effects work in opposite directions, but the second will be small if current accounts are initially near zero.

FIGURE 20-4
Output determination in a two-country world.
For a given real exchange rate, the intersection of *HH* (along which the Home output market clears) and *FF* (along which the Foreign output market clears) determines short-run equilibrium output levels in the two countries.

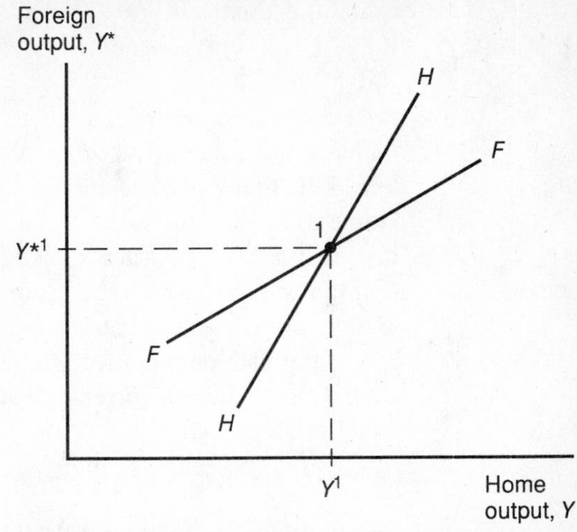

output, Y. The *FF* schedule shows the Home and Foreign output levels at which aggregate demand equals aggregate supply *in Foreign.* Like *HH, FF* has a positive slope, and for the same reason: a rise in Y raises demand for Foreign exports, and Foreign output, Y^*, must rise to meet this increase in aggregate demand. At the intersection of *HH* and *FF* (point 1), aggregate demand and supply are equal in *both* countries, given the real exchange rate.

Notice that *HH* is drawn to be steeper than *FF*. The slopes of the two schedules differ in this way because a rise in a country's output has a greater effect on its own output market than on the foreign one. Along *HH*, then, a large increase in Y^* is needed to remove the excess supply of Home output caused by a rise in Y. Likewise, along *FF*, a large increase in Y is needed to restore balance in the Foreign output market after a rise in Y^*.[5]

Changes in fiscal policy at home or abroad shift the schedules by altering government purchases, G and G^*, and net taxes, T and T^*. In addition, fiscal policies affect *HH* and *FF* by altering the exchange rate, E (Chapter 17). Home fiscal expansion causes E to fall (an appreciation of Home currency against Foreign currency), while Foreign fiscal expansion causes E to rise (a depreciation of Home currency against Foreign currency). Monetary policies can also move the two schedules by influencing the

[5] More formally, let s be the fraction of any increase in Home income that goes into saving and m the fraction that is spent on imports from Foreign. Let s^* and m^* denote the corresponding fractions for Foreign. Then an increase ΔY in Home output leads to an excess supply $(s + m)\Delta Y$ in Home's output market, which must be matched by an increase in Foreign demand equal to $(EP^*/P)m^*\Delta Y^*$ along *HH*. The slope of *HH* is therefore $\Delta Y^*/\Delta Y = (s + m)/[(EP^*/P)m^*]$. An identical argument shows that the slope of *FF* is $\Delta Y^*/\Delta Y = m/[(EP^*/P)(s^* + m^*)]$. From these equations, the slope of *HH* is greater than that of *FF* when $(s + m)/m^* > m/(s^* + m^*)$, that is, when $(s + m)(s^* + m^*) > mm^*$. This last inequality is always true, however, when none of the fractions that appear in it is a negative number.

The dependence of each country's equilibrium output on foreign output (for a given real exchange rate) is called the *export multiplier effect,* because changes in the demand for a country's exports can have an effect on its output several times as large. Using the formulas just given for the slopes of *HH* and *FF*, you can check that a unit increase in Foreign demand for Home exports raises Home output by $1/(s + m)$. Similarly, Foreign's export multiplier is $1/(s^* + m^*)$. Both numbers are likely to exceed 1.

exchange rate. Both monetary and fiscal policies are at the heart of recent exchange rate experience, and we now apply our two-country framework to these recent events.

Case Study

DISINFLATION, RECOVERY, AND GLOBAL SLUMP, 1980–1993

The years after 1980 brought a number of dramatic changes in the world economy. On the positive side, inflation rates throughout the industrialized world fell to their lowest levels since the Bretton Woods years (see Table 20-4). At long last, some measure of price stability seemed to have been restored. But the negative events of the period were so severe that they threatened the relatively open world trading and financial system that had been built up so laboriously after World War II. At times, the international community seemed on the verge of replaying the economic tragedy of the interwar years. Many economists and policy makers began to see floating exchange rates as a major cause of the world economy's problems and urged a return to more limited exchange rate flexibility.

Disinflation and the 1981–1983 Recession

In October 1979, Federal Reserve Chairman Volcker announced an abrupt change in U.S. monetary policy aimed at fighting domestic inflation and stemming the dollar's fall. Volcker's monetary slowdown convinced the foreign exchange market that the Fed chairman would make good his promise to wring inflation out of the American economy. With the November 1980 election of President Reagan, who had campaigned on an anti-inflation platform, the dollar's value soared. Between the end of 1979 and the end of 1981, the dollar appreciated against the DM by 23.2 percent. U.S. interest rates also rose sharply late in 1979; by 1981, short-term interest rates in the United States were nearly double their 1978 levels.

TABLE 20-4 Inflation rates in major industrialized countries, 1981–1991, and 1961–1971 average (percent per year)

Country	1981	1982	1983	1984	1985	1986	1987	1988	1989	1990	1991	1961–1971 average
United States	10.4	6.1	3.2	4.3	3.5	1.9	3.7	4.1	4.8	5.4	4.2	3.1
Britain	11.9	8.6	4.6	5.0	6.1	3.4	4.1	4.9	7.8	9.5	5.9	4.6
Canada	12.5	10.8	5.8	4.3	4.0	4.2	4.4	4.0	5.0	4.8	5.6	2.9
France	13.4	11.8	9.6	7.4	5.8	2.7	3.1	2.7	3.6	3.4	3.2	4.3
Germany	6.3	5.3	3.3	2.4	2.2	−0.1	0.2	1.3	2.8	2.7	3.5	3.0
Italy	19.5	16.5	13.1	10.6	8.6	6.1	4.6	5.0	6.6	6.1	6.4	4.2
Japan	4.9	2.7	1.9	2.2	2.0	0.6	0.1	0.7	2.3	3.1	3.3	5.9

Source: Organization for Economic Cooperation and Development. *Main Economic Indicators,* 1992. Figures are percentage increases in each year's average consumer price index over the average consumer price index for the previous year.

Figure 20-5, which shows the effect of a Home monetary slowdown in the two-country model, will help you understand the effects of the Volcker policy change both in the United States and abroad. By pushing up the U.S. interest rate and causing investors to expect a stronger dollar in the future, the U.S. action led to an immediate appreciation of the dollar. This appreciation made U.S. (Home) goods more expensive relative to Foreign goods, thereby raising the level of Foreign output, Y^*, needed to maintain the demand for Home output at any given level Y. Figure 20-5 shows this change as an upward shift of H^1H^1 to H^2H^2. The appreciation of the dollar (the Home currency) affects Foreign's output market as well; since Foreign output becomes relatively cheaper, F^1F^1 shifts leftward, to F^2F^2.

As a result of the two shifts, Home output falls, Foreign output rises, and the world economy moves from its initial equilibrium at point 1 to a new equilibrium at point 2. It may seem surprising at first that monetary contraction at Home raises output abroad, since the fall in Home output causes a direct reduction in Home's demand for imports. This last reduction in Home's import demand is, however, a secondary effect of the initial switch in world spending from Home to Foreign goods.[6]

[6] You may be wondering if it can ever happen that Home output *rises,* which is what would occur if the upward shift of H^1H^1 were less than that of F^1F^1. To prove that this outcome is impossible, let Z (a positive quantity measured in Home output units) equal the switch in aggregate demand from Home to Foreign products caused by the Home currency's appreciation and recall the notation introduced in the last footnote. If Foreign demand for Home goods rises by $Z = (EP^*/P)m^*\Delta Y^*$ (where EP^*/P is the new real exchange rate), Home output Y does not change. The upward shift of H^1H^1 is therefore $Z/[(EP^*/P)m^*]$. How must Y^* change to maintain goods market equilibrium in Foreign, given Y? Since world demand for Foreign products rises by $Z/(EP^*/P)$, a Foreign output increase given by

$$Z/(EP^*/P) + (1 - s^* - m^*)\Delta Y^* = \Delta Y^*$$

leaves aggregate demand and supply equal in Foreign for a given value of Y. The solution of this last equation is $\Delta Y^* = Z/[(EP^*/P)(s^* + m^*)]$, which equals the upward shift of F^1F^1. This number is smaller than the upward shift of H^1H^1. Thus, Home monetary contraction must cause a fall in Home's output.

A similar argument shows that the leftward shift of F^1F^1 always exceeds that of H^1H^1, so that Foreign output always rises. (See problem 6 at the end of this chapter.) The model's predictions would be somewhat more complicated if real interest rates influenced spending decisions (as in Chapter 17, Appendix I).

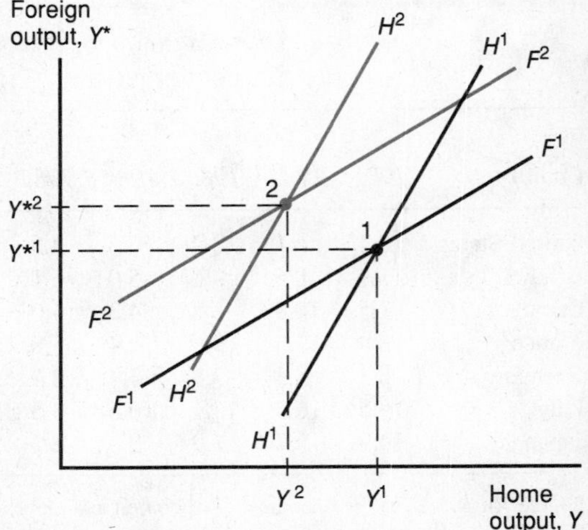

FIGURE 20-5
Monetary contraction in Home.
Monetary contraction in Home, by appreciating its currency relative to Foreign's, causes Home output to fall (from Y^1 to Y^2) and Foreign output to rise (from Y^{*1} to Y^{*2}).

As the model suggests, the Fed's monetary slowdown did have a negative effect on America's output and employment. The dollar's appreciation was not welcomed abroad, however, even though it may have lent foreign economies some positive stimulus in a period of slow growth. The reason was that a stronger dollar hindered foreign countries in their own fights against inflation, both by raising the import prices they faced and by encouraging higher wage demands by their workers. A stronger dollar had the opposite effect in the United States, hastening the decline of inflation there. The tight U.S. monetary policy therefore had a beggar-thy-neighbor effect on foreign economies, in that it lowered American inflation in part by exporting inflation to foreign economies.

Foreign central banks responded by intervening in the foreign exchange market to slow the dollar's rise. Through the process of selling dollar reserves and buying their own currencies, some central banks reduced their monetary growth rates for 1980 and 1981, driving interest rates upward (see Tables 20-2 and 20-5).[7]

Synchronized monetary contraction in the United States and abroad, following fast on the heels of the second oil shock, threw the world economy into a deep recession, the most severe since the Great Depression of the 1930s. Table 20-3 shows how unemployment moved in the major industrial countries. In 1982 and 1983, unemployment throughout the world rose to levels unprecedented in the post-World War II period. You can appreciate the severity of the unemployment rates shown in the table by comparing them with the average unemployment rate for the same seven countries over the years 1963–1972 (a mere 3.2 percent). As Table 20-4 shows, however, monetary contraction and the recession it brought quickly led to a dramatic drop in the inflation rates of industrialized countries.

Fiscal Policies, the Current Account, and the Resurgence of Protectionism

During his election campaign, President Reagan had promised to lower taxes and balance the federal budget. He made good on the first of these promises in 1981 when

[7] The extent to which such money growth reductions occurred is not always apparent in Tables 20-2 and 20-5, which show annual percentage changes in *year-end* money stocks. In Japan, for example, the change in the *year-average* money stock was only 3.3 percent between 1980 and 1981.

TABLE 20-5 Money supply growth rates in major industrialized countries, 1981–1987 (percent per year)

Country	*1981*	*1982*	*1983*	*1984*	*1985*	*1986*	*1987*
United States	6.5	8.7	9.8	5.8	12.2	16.9	3.5
Britain	2.6	3.1	6.9	5.6	3.7	6.2	3.3
Canada	0.9	2.8	8.2	0.3	9.2	5.6	8.8
France	12.4	9.6	13.0	11.1	6.7	6.0	4.4
Germany	−0.8	7.0	8.3	6.2	6.3	7.4	7.4
Italy	10.2	16.7	12.9	12.4	10.4	10.7	7.4
Japan	10.1	4.9	2.1	4.9	4.6	8.4	6.8

Source: Organization for Economic Cooperation and Development. *Main Economic Indicators.* Data defined as in Table 20-2 with the exception of Britain, where M0 is now used as the money supply measure.

Congress approved legislation lowering personal taxes and providing fiscal investment incentives to businesses. At the same time, the Reagan administration pushed for an acceleration of defense spending, accompanied by cuts in government spending on domestic programs. The net result of these and subsequent congressional actions was a ballooning U.S. government budget deficit and a sharp fiscal stimulus to the economy. Table 20-6 shows the U.S. government budget surplus as a percentage of GNP after 1979.

Figure 20-6 illustrates the effects of a Home fiscal expansion in the two-country model. Because fiscal expansion by Home causes its currency (the dollar) to appreciate, Foreign products become relatively cheap and world demand for them rises. Foreign output, Y^*, therefore must rise for every level of Home output, Y, as represented by the upward shift of F^1F^1 to F^2F^2. Since Home is a large country, the impact of its fiscal expansion on the aggregate demand for its output is positive, in spite of the domestic currency's appreciation, and so Y must rise for every value of Y^*. This rise in Home aggregate demand implies that H^1H^1 shifts rightward to H^2H^2. Output goes up both in Home and in Foreign as the world economy moves to point 2 from its initial position at point 1.

As we noted in Chapter 17 (pp. 462–464), an analysis of U.S. fiscal moves is complicated because the fiscal policy mandated in 1981 was a phased one that began only in 1982, and whose expansionary impact was probably not felt fully until 1983. The *anticipation* of future fiscal expansion in 1981 would simply have appreciated the dollar, shifting F^1F^1 up as shown in Figure 20-6 but shifting the other schedule left rather than right. These changes would have tended to deepen the early stages of the 1981–1983 recession in the United States, while giving less stimulus abroad than Figure 20-6, suggests. Only by late 1982 or 1983 is Figure 20-6 an accurate portrayal of the global effects of U.S. fiscal policy.

All along, however, the U.S. fiscal stance encouraged continuing dollar appreciation (see Figure 20-3), as did the contractionary fiscal policies pursued at the time by Germany and Japan. By February 1985, the dollar's cumulative appreciation against the DM since the end of 1979 was 47.9 percent. The recession reached its low point in the United States in December 1982, and output began to recover both there and abroad as the U.S. fiscal stimulus was transmitted to foreign countries through the dollar's steady appreciation. Also contributing to the recovery was a looser Federal Reserve monetary policy.

Foreign central banks remained fearful of encouraging inflation through expansionary policies of their own. As easier U.S. money brought dollar interest rates down in the second half of 1982, however, some foreign central banks began to feel they could ease their monetary policies without causing their currencies to depreciate too sharply

TABLE 20-6 U.S. government budget surplus as a percentage of GNP, 1979–1991 (percent)

1979	*1980*	*1981*	*1982*	*1983*	*1984*	*1985*	*1986*	*1987*	*1988*	*1989*	*1990*	*1991*
0.4	−1.3	−1.0	−3.4	−4.1	−2.9	−3.1	−3.4	−2.5	−2.0	−1.6	−2.5	−3.0

Source: *Economic Report of the President, 1992* and U.S. Department of Commerce, *Survey of Current Business,* June 1992.

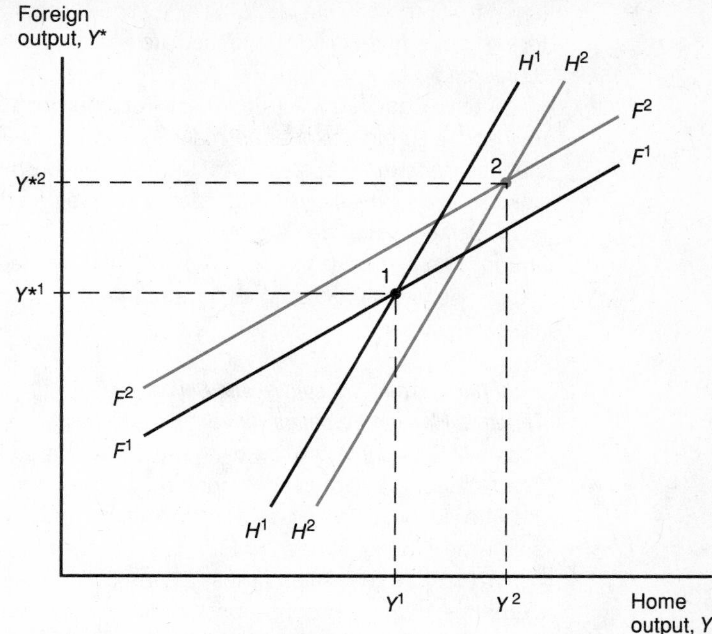

FIGURE 20-6
Fiscal expansion in Home.
A Home fiscal expansion raises output at home and abroad.

(see Table 20-5). By early 1984, U.S. unemployment had fallen and U.S. output was growing rapidly. Unemployment remained high in other industrialized countries, however, and the growth of output abroad was slow by historical standards.

While the U.S. fiscal expansion contributed to world recovery, growing federal budget deficits raised serious worries about the future stability of the world economy. Increasing government deficits were not met with offsetting increases in private saving or decreases in investment, so the American current account balance deteriorated sharply (recall Chapter 13's Case Study of the link between the government deficit and the current account, pp. 314–317). By 1987, the United States had become a net debtor to foreign countries and its current account deficit was at the postwar record level of 3.6 percent of GNP. Some analysts worried that foreign creditors would lose confidence in the future value of the dollar assets they were accumulating and sell them, causing a sudden, precipitous dollar depreciation.

Equally worrisome was the strong dollar's impact on the distribution of income within the United States. The dollar's appreciation had reduced U.S. inflation and allowed consumers to purchase imports more cheaply, but those hurt by the terms of trade change were better organized and more vocal than those who had benefited. Persistently poor economic performance in the 1980s had led to increased pressures on governments to protect declining industries in the exporting and import-competing sectors. As the U.S. recovery slowed late in 1984, protectionist pressures snowballed.

By making American exports more expensive for foreigners while cheapening foreign imports, the dollar's real appreciation had reduced demand in several sectors of the American economy, for example, agriculture, textiles, steel, and autos. In late 1984, these sectors stepped up their demands for protective legislation, resulting in an avalanche of protectionist trade bills. As the threat of American trade restrictions grew, foreign governments vowed to retaliate against any restrictive trade measures the United States might take.

The Reagan administration had, from the start, adopted a policy of "benign neglect" toward the foreign exchange market, refusing to intervene except in unusual circumstances (for example, after a would-be assassin shot President Reagan). Administration officials took the position that the market was best able to determine the appropriate level of the exchange rate, and the president himself appeared to view the dollar's strength as a market vote of confidence in his economic policies. By 1985, however, the link between the strong dollar and the gathering protectionist storm became impossible to ignore.

From the Plaza to the Louvre and Beyond: Trying to Manage Exchange Rates

Faster U.S. monetary growth in 1985 brought some dollar depreciation but failed to head off congressional sentiment in favor of import restrictions. Fearing a disaster for the international trading system, economic officials of the Group of Five (G-5) countries—the United States, Britain, France, Germany, and Japan—announced at New York's Plaza Hotel on September 22, 1985, that they would jointly intervene in the foreign exchange market to bring about a dollar depreciation. Th dollar dropped sharply the next day and continued to decline through 1986 and early 1987 as the United States maintained its loose monetary policy and pushed dollar interest rates down relative to foreign currency rates. (See Figure 20-3 and Table 20-5.)

The G-5 Plaza announcement represented a sharp change in the policy of the Reagan administration, a reversal of its opposition to foreign exchange intervention. After late 1985, when the collaborative intervention operations backing up the Plaza declaration ended, the United States stood aloof from the foreign exchange market for more than a year. Nonetheless, the Plaza communiqué indicated growing dissatisfaction in government circles with the performance of floating exchange rates and marked the start of a period in which countries including the United States readily intervened, sometimes massively and in a cooperative fashion, to influence exchange rates.

The dollar moved differently against different currencies during its 1986 depreciation, depreciating more sharply against the DM and yen than against the currencies of some other trading partners. The current account surpluses of Japan and Germany (when measured in dollars) continued to rise, however, and the external U.S. deficit rose substantially. Congress failed to make a dramatic dent in the federal budget deficit in 1985–1986, and without the necessary expenditure-changing policy of fiscal contraction, it is no surprise that the U.S. external balance problem didn't go away. The lags in trade balance response discussed in Chapter 17 were probably stretched out by the policy of relying so heavily on nominal exchange rate changes whose effects on real relative prices might be temporary. As a result, pressures for protection, although temporarily held off by the dollar's depreciation, remained threatening. Politically unable to change its own fiscal course quickly, the Reagan administration repeatedly urged Japan and Germany to adopt more expansionary macroeconomic policies in the hope that increased demand from those countries would help shrink the U.S. deficit and resolve the trade problem. These urgings accomplished little, despite several international accords to promote global trade adjustment through coordinated macroeconomic policies.

By the end of 1986, the dollar's exchange rate had become a focus of disagreement among governments. Faced with foreign reluctance to adopt expenditure-changing policies, American leaders continued their push to restore external balance through the expenditure-switching policy of further dollar depreciation. Leaders of other industrial countries, however, felt the appreciation of their currencies had gone far enough. Their own tradables industries were finding it difficult to meet foreign competition, and so the expenditure change of a U.S. fiscal and monetary contraction appeared preferable to them. This impasse led to more-or-less open competitive currency manipulation by the end of 1986, as the dollar plunged, Japan and Germany intervened in vain to stop it, and the United States stood aside. Only when the United States re-entered the foreign exchange market early in 1987 did the dollar stabilize.

A renewed effort to cooperate on exchange rates followed a meeting at the Louvre in Paris on February 22, 1987. Finance ministers and central bank governors from the G-5 countries plus Canada issued a statement pledging to stabilize nominal exchange rates around the levels then prevailing, which the officials viewed as "broadly consistent with underlying economic fundamentals," including the requirement of generalized external balance. The Louvre accord was far more, however, than a mere verbal pronouncement on exchange rates. In an unpublished agreement, governments set up target zones for exchange rates and agreed to defend them by intervening in the foreign exchange market. While these target zones were not made public, observers believe the Louvre accord called for bands of plus or minus 5 percent around the rates of DM 1.8250 per dollar and ¥ 153.50 per dollar. (In contrast, exchange rates in the weeks after the Plaza announcement were in the neighborhood of DM 2.750 per dollar and ¥ 250 per dollar.)

After adjusting the range for the yen/dollar rate in April 1987, the industrial countries succeeded in maintaining their new exchange rate bands for several months. The U.S. external deficit remained high, however, and the dollar stayed under heavy selling pressure; the bands thus could be maintained only with the help of slow U.S. money supply growth and a steadily rising interest difference favoring dollar assets. Market participants wondered whether the U.S. economy would be thrown into recession to enforce nominal exchange rate targets that seemed increasingly inconsistent with current account equilibrium, given output prices in the United States and abroad.

In October 1987 the brief period of exchange stability ended abruptly when the U.S. stock market dropped and then crashed following American criticism of a German interest rate hike. Major stock markets around the world followed Wall Street's dizzying plunge. In the United States, a more general economic crisis was turned aside by the new Federal Reserve chairman, Alan Greenspan, who announced the Fed's readiness to provide liquidity to a troubled financial system. Governors of foreign central banks acted similarly and interest rates throughout the world declined. In the process, however, U.S. authorities allowed the dollar to depreciate far beyond its Louvre limits.

New exchange rate zones were subsequently established, but these apparently have been changed on several occasions, never with on-the-record public acknowledgment. Figure 20-7 gives an overview of exchange rate movements after the Louvre accord. Skeptics argue that the implicit zones for exchange rates had no real force and that the authorities' reluctance to announce the zones, rather than keeping

FIGURE 20-7
Exchange rate changes since the Louvre accord.
The dollar prices of the DM and yen took wide swings after the February 1987 Louvre meeting despite an initial international agreement to keep those exchange rates within bands 10 percent wide.
Source: OECD, *Main Economic Indicators.*

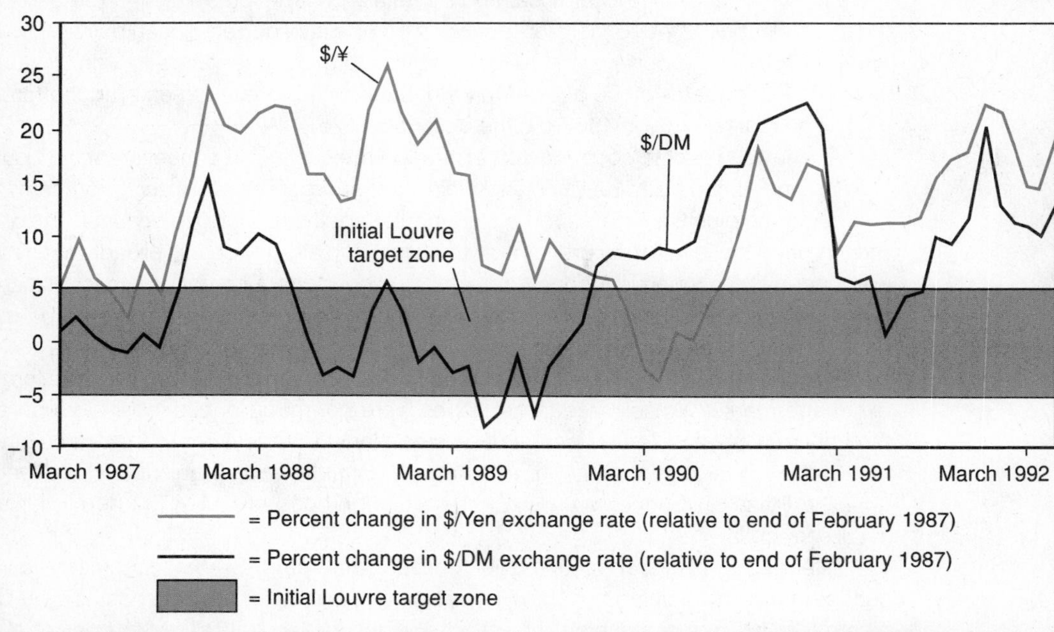

the market guessing, served mainly to cover repeated official failures to stand up to market pressures. Supporters argue that exchange rates would have moved even more than they did had zones not been adopted. What seems clear is that official attempts to influence exchange rates have been successful only when backed up by changes in monetary or fiscal policy rather than the milder expedient of sterilized intervention (which at times has been heavy). Authorities have thus faced genuine and sometimes painful trade-offs between internal balance and exchange stability, as the United States did in October 1987, and none of them has shown that in a crunch, exchange stability is the more important of these two goals.

Global Slump Once Again

Toward the end of the 1980s inflationary pressures reappeared in the main industrial countries (see Table 20-4). Inflation was the result of national developments rather than a global shock, and it emerged with different timing and force in each country.

In the United States, rapid monetary growth in 1985 and 1986 (Table 20-5) helped push inflation upward by 1987 and 1988. A period of exceptionally tight Federal Reserve monetary policy (Table 20-7) tilted the U.S. economy into a prolonged economic down-

TABLE 20-7 Money supply growth rates in major industrialized countries 1988–1992 (percent per year)

Country	*1988*	*1989*	*1990*	*1991*	*1992*
United States	5.0	0.9	4.0	8.7	14.1
Britain	8.5	5.4	2.5	3.0	2.3
Canada	6.8	2.6	−1.9	4.3	7.6
France	2.8	8.3	3.9	−4.6	0.0
Germany	10.9	5.5	29.7	3.4	10.9
Italy	11.0	12.8	6.9	11.4	1.2
Japan	10.3	−2.0	6.2	8.8	1.9

Source: Organization for Economic Cooperation and Development. *Main Economic Indicators.* Data defined as in Table 20-5. Starting at the end of 1990, German money supply data cover the unified eastern and western parts of the country.

turn by the summer of 1990. Economic stagnation in the United States was a major reason for President George Bush's defeat in his 1992 re-election attempt.

Loose monetary policy in Britain in 1988 similarly contributed to higher inflation there by 1989 (Table 20-4). Despite this inflation, Britain entered the European Monetary System exchange rate mechanism in October 1990, agreeing to peg the pound sterling to the European Currency Unit at an exchange rate that probably made British exports too expensive relative to foreign goods. This was the same mistake Britain had made in returning to the gold standard in 1925, and, as Table 20-3 shows, British unemployment quickly began to rise.

Japan's inflation picked up in 1989, possibly the result of a relatively loose monetary policy over 1986–1988. Two very visible symptoms of these pressures were skyrocketing prices for Japanese real estate and stocks. The Bank of Japan's strategy of puncturing these asset price bubbles through restrictive monetary policy and high interest rates succeeded well, and Tokyo's Nikkei stock price index lost more than half its value between 1990 and 1992. Unfortunately, the sharp fall in asset prices threw Japan's banking system into crisis and the economy into recession by early 1992.

The German economy faced a unique situation as the 1990s began. Starting in 1989 countries throughout Eastern Europe, including the eastern portion of Germany occupied by Soviet forces at the end of World War II, shook off Communist rule and began the painful task of moving from centrally planned to market economies. (See Chapter 24 for further discussion.) West and East Germany rushed to reunite, with economic unification coming on July 1, 1990, even before political unification. One element of the unification agreement required much of the East German money supply to be converted to DM at an exchange rate of DM 1 per East German mark, despite the latter currency's much lower black-market value and purchasing power. This move, which was approved by West Germany's government over the vigorous opposition of the German Bundesbank, led to a 29.7 percent growth in Germany's DM money supply over 1990 (Table 20-7).

Money supply growth was only one of several factors contributing to higher German inflation after 1990. The federal German government began a program of massive fiscal expansion to finance infrastructure investment and transfer payments (largely unemployment compensation) in the former East Germany. That area's residents, starved for the high-quality consumer goods denied them under Communism, spent heavily on imports from the West. Finally, Germany's labor unions, facing the unexpectedly high tax bill for reunification, mounted a wage offensive. The results were inflationary pressure, rising government debt, and a current account deficit. As we see in the next chapter, the Bundesbank's tight money response to the inflationary pressure caused grave difficulties for its EMS partners, with dramatic consequences for the stability of the system's fixed exchange rates.

In 1993 the major industrialized countries were all suffering from hesitant growth, if not actual recession. While the dollar's exchange rates against the yen and the EMS currencies were not a major focus of international disagreement, exchange rate relations within Europe were in flux. The plight of the industrialized countries provided a poor springboard for meeting the two critical economic challenges of the day: the strengthening of free-market reform initiatives in the debt-burdened developing world (Chapter 23) and the integration of the former Soviet bloc into the world economy (Chapter 24).

What Has Been Learned Since 1973?

The first two sections of this chapter outlined the main elements of the cases for and against floating exchange rates. Having examined the events of the recent floating-rate period, we now compare experience with the predictions made before 1973 by the proponents and opponents of floating and ask whether recent history supports a definitive judgment about reforming the current exchange rate system.

MONETARY POLICY AUTONOMY

There is no question that floating gave central banks the ability to control their money supplies and to choose their preferred rates of trend inflation. A comparison of Tables 20-1 and 20-4 (which show inflation rates over the floating-rate period) with Table 19-1 and Figure 19-3 (which apply to the fixed-rate period) shows that floating rates allowed a much larger international divergence in inflation rates. Did exchange depreciation offset inflation differentials between countries over the floating-rate period? Figure 20-8 compares domestic currency depreciation against the dollar with the difference between domestic and U.S. inflation for the six largest industrial market economies outside the United States. The PPP theory predicts that the points in the figure should lie along the 45-degree line, but this is not exactly the case. While Figure 20-8 therefore confirms the lesson of Chapter 16 that PP has not held closely, it does show that on balance, high-inflation countries have tended to have weaker currencies than their low-inflation neighbors.

While the inflation insulation part of the policy autonomy argument is broadly

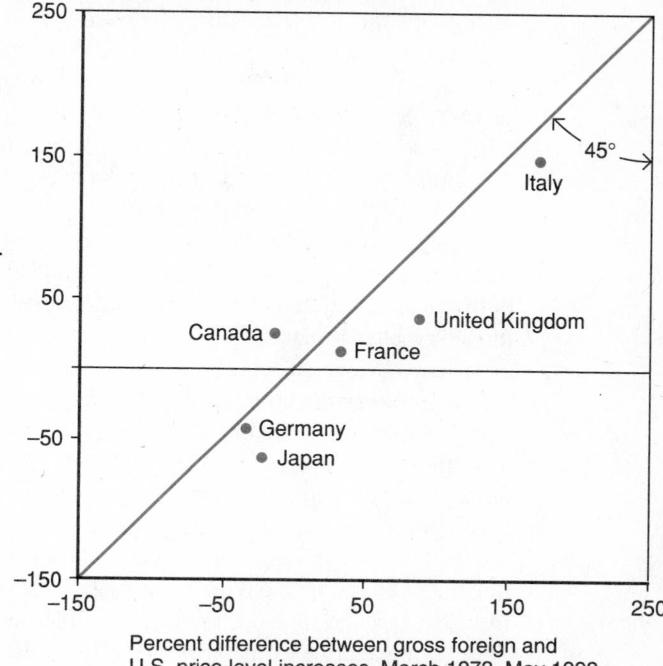

FIGURE 20-8
Exchange rate trends and inflation differentials, 1973–1993
Over the floating-rate period as a whole, higher inflation has been associated with greater currency depreciation. The exact relationship predicted by relative PPP, however, has not held for most countries. The inflation difference on the horizontal axis is calculated as $(\pi - \pi_{us}) \div (1 + \pi_{us}/100)$ using the exact relative PPP relation given in footnote 1 on p. 401.
Source: OECD, *Main Economic Indicators.*

supported as a *long-run* proposition, economic analysis and experience both show that in the short run, the effects of monetary as well as fiscal changes are transmitted across national borders under floating rates. The two-country macroeconomic model developed earlier, for example, shows that monetary policy affects output in the short run both at home and abroad as long as it alters the real exchange rate. The critics of floating were therefore right in claiming that floating rates would not insulate countries completely from foreign policy shocks.

Experience has also given dramatic support to the skeptics who argued that no central bank can be indifferent to its currency's value in the foreign exchange market. After 1973, central banks intervened repeatedly in the foreign exchange market to alter currency values, and even the Reagan administration's laissez-faire policy on exchange rates was abandoned when the G-5 Plaza initiative of September 1985 was launched. The post-1973 floating of exchange rates is often characterized as a ''dirty float'' rather than a ''clean float'' because central banks intervened on a discretionary basis and continued to hold foreign exchange reserves (Chapter 18). Advocates of floating had argued that central banks would not need to hold foreign reserves, but between 1972 and November 1991, the international reserves of the industrial countries rose in value from $113 billion to $429 billion (with a particularly large jump in 1987 due to the target zone arrangements set up at the Louvre).

Why did central banks continue to intervene even in the absence of any formal obligation to do so? As we saw in the example of a change in domestic money demand, intervention to fix the exchange rate can stabilize output and the price level when certain disturbances occur, and central banks sometimes felt that exchange rate movements were due to such factors. But even in the presence of output market disturbances, central banks wanted to slow exchange rate movements to prevent sharp changes in the international competitiveness of their tradable goods sectors. Such changes, if reversed later, might generate excessive sectoral employment fluctuations, and they might also lead to pressures for protection. Finally, central banks worried that even temporary exchange rate shifts might have medium-term inflationary effects that would be hard to wring out of the economy.

Those skeptical of the autonomy argument had also predicted that while floating would allow central banks to control nominal money supplies, their ability to affect output would still be limited by the price level's tendency to respond more quickly to monetary changes under a floating rate. This prediction was partially borne out by experience. Monetary changes clearly had a much greater short-run effect on the *real* exchange rate under a floating nominal exchange rate than under a fixed one, increasing the immediate influence of money on output in some countries. In many cases, however, this influence turned out to be short-lived. The quick response of the exchange rate to money supply changes affected import prices and wage settlements, shortening the time span over which money could alter real economic activity without changing nominal output prices. The link between exchange depreciation and inflation was illustrated by the U.S. experience of 1976–1979 and by the rapid inflation that resulted from attempts by Britain, France, and Italy, at various times, to spur output growth through monetary expansion. The U.S. disinflation after 1979 illustrated that a floating rate could also speed the translation of monetary contraction into lower inflation.

SYMMETRY

Because central banks continued to hold dollar reserves and intervene, the international monetary system did not become symmetric after 1973. The DM and the yen gained importance as international reseve currencies (and the British pound declined), but the dollar remained the primary component of most central banks' official reserves.

Economist Ronald McKinnon of Stanford University has argued that the current floating-rate system is similar in some ways to the asymmetric reserve currency system underlying the Bretton Woods arrangements.[8] When Germany and Japan intervened in 1977–1978 to prevent their currencies from appreciating in the face of rapid U.S. monetary growth, their own money supplies expanded with no offsetting reduction in U.S. money. McKinnon suggests that this increase in the world money supply, which would have been dampened under a more symmetric monetary adjustment mechanism, helped fuel the synchronized upswing in industrial country inflation rates at the end of the 1970s. Similarly, foreign intervention to slow the dollar's rise after 1979 led to monetary contraction abroad with no symmetric increase in the U.S. money supply. The resulting world monetary crunch was harsher because of this asymmetry, which therefore helped deepen the recession that followed.

[8] Ronald I. McKinnon, *An International Standard for Monetary Stabilization,* Policy Analyses in International Economics 8 (Washington, D.C.: Institute for International Economics, 1984).

THE EXCHANGE RATE AS AN AUTOMATIC STABILIZER

The world economy has undergone major structural changes since 1973. Because these shifts changed relative national output prices (Figure 20-8), it is doubtful that any pattern of fixed exchange rates would have been viable without some significant parity changes. The industrial economies certainly wouldn't have weathered the two oil shocks as well as they did while defending fixed exchange rates. In the absence of capital controls, speculative attacks similar to those that brought down the Bretton Woods system would have occurred periodically, as the recent experience of the European Monetary System has shown (Chapter 21). Under floating, however, many countries were able to relax the capital controls put in place earlier. The progressive loosening of controls spurred the rapid growth of a global financial industry and allowed countries to realize greater gains from intertemporal trade.

The effects of the U.S. fiscal expansion after 1981 illustrate the stabilizing properties of a floating exchange rate. As the dollar appreciated, U.S. inflation was slowed, American consumers enjoyed an improvement in their terms of trade, and economic recovery was spread abroad.

The dollar's appreciation after 1981 also illustrates a problem with the view that floating rates can cushion the economy from real disturbances such as shifts in aggregate demand. Even though *overall* output and the price level may be cushioned, some sectors of the economy may be hurt. For example, while the dollar's appreciation helped transmit U.S. fiscal expansion abroad in the 1980s, it worsened the plight of American agriculture, which did not benefit directly from the higher government demand. Real exchange rate changes can do damage by causing excessive adjustment problems in some sectors and by generating calls for increased protection.

Permanent changes in goods market conditions require eventual adjustment in real exchange rates that can be speeded by a floating-rate system. Foreign exchange intervention to peg nominal exchange rates cannot prevent this eventual adjustment because money is neutral in the long run and thus is powerless to alter relative prices permanently. The events of the 1980s show, however, that if it is costly for factors of production to move between sectors of the economy, there is a case for pegging rates in the face of temporary output market shocks. Unfortunately, this lesson leaves policy makers with the difficult task of determining which disturbances are temporary and which are permanent.

An indictment of floating exchange rates is sometimes based on the poor economic growth performance of industrial countries in the 1970s and 1980s compared with the 1950s and 1960s. As noted above, unemployment rates in industrial countries rose sharply after the 1960s; in addition, labor productivity and real GNP growth rates dropped. These adverse developments followed the adoption of floating dollar exchange rates, but this coincidence does not prove that floating rates were their cause. Although economists have not yet fully explained the growth slowdown or the rise in unemployment rates, the likely culprits are structural changes that had little to do with floating rates. Examples include the oil price shocks, restrictive labor market practices, and worker displacement caused by the emergence of several developing countries as major exporters of manufactured goods. Much of the international trade of the European Monetary System has taken place at fixed exchange rates, yet the record of EMS countries in generating jobs and keeping down unemployment has not been superior to that of the United States or Japan.

DISCIPLINE

Did countries abuse the autonomy afforded by floating rates? Inflation rates did accelerate after 1973 and remained high through the second oil shock. But the concerted disinflation in industrial countries after 1979 proved that central banks could control inflation under floating rates. On several occasions, voters in industrial countries showed that they viewed a weak currency as a sign of economic mismanagement. For this reason, currency depreciation sometimes brought sharp changes in monetary policies, as in the United States in 1979.

The system placed fewer obvious restraints on unbalanced fiscal policies, for example, the high U.S. government budget deficits of the 1980s. While some observers felt that fixed rates would have forced a more moderate American fiscal stance, their arguments were not compelling. In the late 1960s, fixed rates had failed to restrain the Johnson administration's fiscal expansion, a policy move that contributed to the collapse of the Bretton Woods system, nor did the EMS restrain Germany in the early 1990s.

DESTABILIZING SPECULATION

Floating exchange rates have exhibited much more day-to-day volatility than the early advocates of floating would have predicted, but as we saw in Chapter 14, exchange rates are asset prices, and so considerable volatility is to be expected. The asset price nature of exchange rates was not well understood by economists before the 1970s.

Even with the benefit of hindsight, however, short-term exchange rate movements can be quite difficult to relate to actual news about economic events that affect currency values. Part of the difficulty is that government officials often try to influence exchange rates by hinting at intended policy changes, thus making expectations about future macroeconomic policies volatile. The question of whether exchange rate volatility has been ''excessive'' relative to the theoretical determinants of exchange rates is a controversial one and provides an active research area for academic economists (Chapter 22).

Over the longer term, however, exchange rates have roughly reflected fundamental changes in monetary and fiscal policies, and their broad movements do not appear to be the result of destabilizing speculation. The decline of the dollar in the late 1970s (Figure 20-3) coincides with loose U.S. monetary policies, while its steep ascent between 1980 and 1985 occurred as the United States embarked on disinflation and a fiscal expansion of a size unprecedented in peacetime. While most economists agree that the direction of these exchange rate swings was appropriate, there is continuing debate about their magnitude. Some feel the foreign exchange market overreacted to government actions and that more systematic foreign exchange intervention would have been beneficial.

The experience with floating rates has not supported the idea that arbitrary exchange rate movements can lead to ''vicious circles'' of inflation and depreciation. Britain, Italy, and, to a lesser extent, France experienced inflationary spirals similar to those predicted by the vicious circle theory. But the currency depreciation that accompanied these spirals was not the arbitrary result of destabilizing exchange rate speculation. As Figure 15-10 (page 386) shows, industrial countries with poor inflation performances under floating exchange rates have also tended to have relatively rapid rates of monetary growth.

INTERNATIONAL TRADE AND INVESTMENT

Critics of floating had predicted that international trade and investment would suffer as a result of increased uncertainty. The prediction was certainly wrong with regard to investment, for international financial intermediation expanded strongly after 1973 as countries lowered barriers to capital movement (see Chapter 22).

There is controversy about the effects of floating rates on international trade. The use of forward markets expanded dramatically, just as advocates of floating had foreseen, and innovative financial instruments were developed to help traders avoid exchange rate risk. But some economists contend that the costs of avoiding exchange rate risk have had an effect similar to increased international transport costs in reducing the available gains from trade. They argue that as a result of these costs, international trade has grown more slowly than it would have under a hypothetical fixed exchange rate regime.

A very crude but direct measure of the extent of a country's international trade is the average of its imports and exports of goods and services, divided by its output. Figure 20-9 plots this number for six of the main industrial market economies over the period from the mid-1950s to the early 1990s. For most countries, the extent of trade shows a rising trend over the whole period, with no marked slowdown in trend after the move to floating. The figure probably exaggerates the growth of world trade in the decade after 1973 because a number of factors (notably the two OPEC shocks) caused the prices of tradable goods to rise relative to the prices of those that do not enter trade. Even after correcting for the resulting bias, however, it is difficult to make a strong case that the volume of world trade has grown more slowly over the entire period since the move to floating exchange rates. Further, to compare world trade growth before and after the early 1970s is to stack the deck against floating rates, because while the 1950s and 1960s were periods of dramatic trade liberalization, the 1970s and 1980s were marked by a surge in nontariff barriers to trade.[9]

Evaluation of the effects of floating rates on world trade is complicated further by the activities of multinational firms, many of which expanded their international production operations in the years after 1973. Facing a more turbulent economic environment, multinationals may have spread their activities over more countries in the hope of reducing their dependence on any individual government's economic policies. Because trade and capital movements can substitute for each other, however, the displacement of some trade by multinational firms' overseas production does not necessarily imply that welfare-improving trade gains have been lost.[10]

International trade has recently been threatened by the resurgence of protectionism, a symptom of slower economic growth and wide swings in real exchange rates. It is possible, however, that similar pressures to limit trade would have emerged under fixed exchange rates.

[9] There is a large econometric literature that studies how exchange rate volatility affects trade growth, and some authors reach conclusions different from those in the preceding paragraph. Unfortunately, various researchers differ in terms of their measures of trade volume, definitions of exchange rate volatility, and choices of estimation period, so it is difficult to draw unambiguous conclusions from this body of work. A recent study pointing to negative effects of exchange rate variability is Paul De Grauwe, "Exchange Rate Variability and the Slowdown in Growth of International Trade," *International Monetary Fund Staff Papers* 35 (March 1988), pp. 63–84.

[10] A recent study documenting the growth of U.S. multinationals' foreign exporting activities is Robert E. Lipsey and Irving B. Kravis, "The Competitiveness and Comparative Advantage of U.S. Multinationals, 1957–1984," *Banca Nazionale del Lavoro Quarterly Review* (June 1987), pp. 147–165.

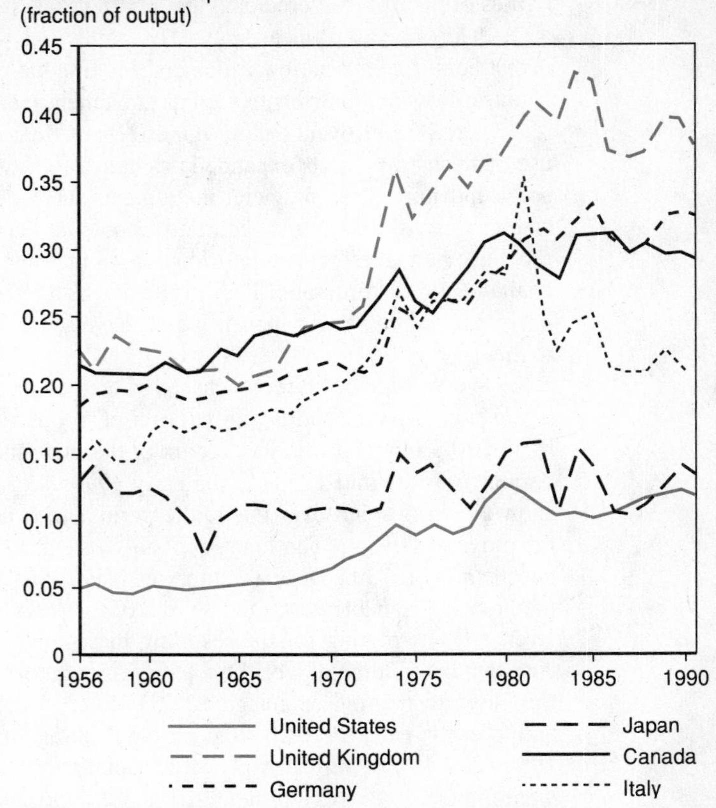

FIGURE 20-9
Trade in goods and services as a proportion of the output of major industrial countries, 1956–1991.
Floating exchange rates do not appear to have reduced the trend growth rate of world trade.
Source: IMF, *International Financial Statistics.*

POLICY COORDINATION

Floating exchange rates themselves have not promoted international policy coordination. On several occasions, for example, during the disinflation of the early 1980s, industrial countries as a group could have attained their macroeconomic goals more effectively by negotiating a joint approach to common objectives. The appendix to this chapter presents a formal model that illustrates how all countries can gain through international policy coordination.

While beggar-thy-neighbor policies sometimes have been a problem, critics of floating have not made a strong case that the problem would disappear under an alternative currency regime. Under fixed rates, for example, countries can always devalue their currencies unilaterally to attain nationalistic goals. The results of the informal target zone arrangements set up by the Louvre accord illustrate the wide gap between agreeing on exchange rates and true policy coordination.

Governments, like people, often are motivated by their own interest rather than that of the community. Legal penalties discourage antisocial actions by individuals, but it is a more difficult matter to design sanctions that bind sovereign governments. It seems doubtful that an exchange rate system alone can restrain a government from following its own perceived interest when it formulates macroeconomic policies.

Directions for Reform

The recent experience with floating exchange rates shows that neither side in the debate over floating was entirely right in its predictions. The floating-rate system has not been free of serious problems, but neither has it been the fiasco its opponents predicted it would be.

An important lesson of this chapter and the previous one is that no exchange rate system works well when countries "go it alone" and follow narrowly perceived self-interest. The Bretton Woods system functioned reasonably well until the United States unilaterally adopted overexpansionary policies under President Johnson. The EMS experience surveyed in the next chapter provides another example. Similarly, the worst problems of the floating-rate system occurred when countries failed to take coordinated action on common macroeconomic problems. Globally balanced and stable policies are a prerequisite for the successful performance of any international monetary system.

Current proposals to reform the international monetary system run the gamut from a more elaborate system of target zones for the dollar to the resurrection of fixed rates to the introduction of a single world currency. Because countries seem unwilling to give up the autonomy floating dollar rates have given them, it is unlikely that any of these changes is in the cards.[11] Since the Plaza announcement of September 1985, however, the United States has tended to show a greater awareness of its interdependence with other industrial economies. Although this development has not prevented serious international disagreement over policies, it certainly is a positive step toward improving the existing system.

With greater policy cooperation among the main players, there is no reason why floating exchange rates should not function tolerably well in the future. International policy cooperation is not unprecedented, as the GATT rounds of tariff reduction and the founding of the IMF indicate. Events of the last few years suggest, however, that cooperation should be sought as an end in itself and not as the indirect result of exchange rate rules that eventually are discredited through repeated amendment or violation.

Summary

1. The weaknesses of the Bretton Woods system led many economists to advocate floating exchange rates before 1973. They made three main arguments in favor of floating. First, they argued that floating rates would give national macroeconomic policy makers greater autonomy in managing their economies. Second, they predicted that floating rates would remove the asymmetries of the Bretton Woods arrangements. Third, they pointed out that floating exchange rates would quickly eliminate the "fundamental disequilibriums" that had led to parity changes and speculative attacks under fixed rates.

2. Critics of floating rates advanced several counterarguments. Some feared that

[11] An extended target zone proposal is outlined in John Williamson and Marcus H. Miller, *Targets and Indicators: A Blueprint for the International Coordination of Macroeconomic Policies,* Policy Analyses in International Economics 22 (Washington, D.C.: Institute for International Economics, 1987). McKinnon, op. cit., presents a program for re-establishing fixed rates for the dollar, yen, and DM. The case for a single world currency is made by Richard N. Cooper, "A Monetary System for the Future," *Foreign Affairs* 63 (1984), pp. 166–184.

floating would encourage monetary and fiscal excesses and beggar-thy-neighbor policies. Other lines of criticism asserted that floating rates would be subject to *destabilizing speculation* and that uncertainty over exchange rates would retard international trade and investment. Finally, a number of economists questioned whether countries would be willing in practice to disregard the exchange rate in formulating their monetary and fiscal policies. The exchange rate, they felt, was an important enough price that it would become a target of macroeconomic policy in its own right.

3. Between 1973 and 1980 floating rates seemed on the whole to function well. In particular, it is unlikely that the industrial countries could have maintained fixed exchange rates in the face of the *stagflation* caused by two oil shocks. The dollar suffered a sharp depreciation after 1976, however, as the United States adopted macroeconomic policies more expansionary than those of other industrial countries.

4. A sharp turn toward slower monetary growth in the United States, coupled with a rising U.S. government budget deficit, contributed to massive dollar appreciation between 1980 and early 1985. Other industrial economies pursued disinflation along with the United States, and the resulting worldwide monetary slowdown, coming soon after the second oil shock, led to the deepest recession since the 1930s. As the recovery from the recession slowed in late 1984 and the U.S. current account began to register record deficits, political pressure for wide-ranging trade restrictions gathered momentum in Washington. The drive for protection was slowed (but not defeated) by the September 1985 decision of the Group of Five countries to take concerted action to bring down the dollar. An experiment with vaguely defined exchange rate target zones, initiated by the Louvre accord of February 1987, had mixed success in promoting more stable currency values. Exchange rate stability was downplayed as a prime policy goal in the early 1990s. Instead, governments struggled to restrain domestic inflation while restoring economic growth.

5. The experience of floating does not fully support either the early advocates of that exchange rate system or its critics. One unambiguous lesson of experience, however, is that no exchange rate system functions well when international economic cooperation breaks down. Severe limits on exchange rate flexibility are unlikely to be reinstated in the near future. But increased consultation among policy makers in the industrial countries should improve the performance of floating rates.

Key Terms

destabilizing speculation

stagflation

nominal and real effective exchange rate indexes

Problems

1. Use the *DD-AA* model to examine the effects of a one-time rise in the foreign price level, P^*. If the expected future exchange rate E^e rises immediately in proportion to P^* (in line with PPP), show that the exchange rate will also appreciate immediately in proportion to the rise in P^*. If the economy is initially in internal and external balance, will its position be disturbed by such a rise in P^*?

2. Analyze a transitory increase in the foreign interest rate, R^*. Under which type of exchange rate is there a smaller effect on output—fixed or floating?

3. Suppose now that R^* rises permanently. What happens to the economy, and how does your answer depend on whether the change reflects a rise in the foreign real interest rate or in foreign inflation expectations (the Fisher effect)?

4. If the foreign *inflation rate* rises permanently, would you expect a floating exchange rate to insulate the domestic economy in the short run? What would happen in the long run? In answering the latter question, pay attention to the long-run relationship between domestic and foreign nominal interest rates.

5. Imagine that domestic and foreign currency bonds are imperfect substitutes and that investors suddenly shift their demand toward foreign currency bonds, raising the risk premium on domestic assets (Chapter 18). Which exchange rate regime minimizes the effect on output—fixed or floating?

6. In the two-country model of this chapter, show that Foreign output must rise as a result of monetary contraction in Home.

7. How would you analyze the use of monetary and fiscal policy to maintain internal and external balance under a floating exchange rate?

8. The chapter described how the United States tried after 1985 to reduce its current account deficit by accelerating monetary growth and depreciating the dollar. Assume that the United States was in internal balance but external balance called for an expenditure-reducing policy (a cut in the government budget deficit) as well as the expenditure switching caused by currency depreciation. How would you expect the use of monetary expansion alone to affect the U.S. economy in the short and long runs?

9. After 1985 the United States asked Germany and Japan to adopt fiscal and monetary expansion as ways of increasing foreign demand for U.S. output and reducing the American current account deficit. Would fiscal expansion by Germany and Japan have accomplished these goals? What about monetary expansion? Would your answer change if you thought different German and Japanese policies might facilitate different U.S. policies?

10. We mentioned in the text that a high volume of foreign exchange intervention occurred in 1987 in connection with the Louvre accord. What data might allow you to tell whether a large portion of this intervention was sterilized? Try to find the relevant data for Germany and Japan in back issues of the IMF's *International Financial Statistics.*

11. Suppose the U.S. and Japanese governments both want to depreciate their currencies to help their tradables industries but fear the resulting inflation. The two policy choices available to them are (1) expansionary monetary policy and (2) no change in monetary policy. Develop an analysis like the one in the appendix to show the consequences of different policy choices. Can Japan and the United States do better by cooperating than by acting individually?

Further Reading

Richard N. Cooper. ''Economic Interdependence and Coordination of Economic Policies,'' in Ronald W. Jones and Peter B. Kenen, eds. *Handbook of International Economics.* Vol. 2.

Amsterdam: North-Holland Publishing Company, pp. 1195–1234. Examines the interaction among national economic policies and the scope for international coordination.

Andrew Crockett and Morris Goldstein, *Strengthening the International Monetary System,* Occasional Paper 50. Washington, D.C.: International Monetary Fund, 1987. Reviews the performance of floating exchange rates, the IMF's role in the current international monetary system, and options for reform.

I. M. Destler and C. Randall Henning. *Dollar Politics: Exchange Rate Policymaking in the United States.* Washington, D.C.: Institute for International Economics, 1989. Describes how political pressures have influenced U.S. policy toward exchange rates.

Rudiger Dornbusch and Jeffrey A. Frankel. "The Flexible Exchange Rate System: Experience and Alternatives," in S. Borner, ed., *International Finance and Trade.* London: Macmillan, 1988. An overview of recent exchange rate experience and reform proposals.

Martin S. Feldstein. "Distinguished Lecture on Economics in Government: Thinking about International Economic Coordination." *Journal of Economic Perspectives* 2 (Spring 1988), pp. 3–13. The case *against* international macroeconomic policy coordination.

Milton Friedman. "The Case for Flexible Exchange Rates," in *Essays in Positive Economics.* Chicago: University of Chicago Press, 1953, pp. 157–203. A classic exposition of the merits of floating exchange rates.

Harry G. Johnson. "The Case for Flexible Exchange Rates, 1969." *Federal Reserve Bank of St. Louis Review* 51 (June 1969), pp. 12–24. An influential statement of the case for replacing the Bretton Woods system by floating rates.

Charles P. Kindleberger, "The Case for Fixed Exchange Rates, 1969," in *The International Adjustment Mechanism,* Conference Series 2. Boston: Federal Reserve Bank of Boston, 1970, pp. 93–108. Prescient analysis of problems with a floating-rate system.

Michael Mussa. "Macroeconomic Interdependence and the Exchange Rate Regime," in Rudiger Dornbusch and Jacob A. Frenkel, eds. *International Economic Policy.* Baltimore: Johns Hopkins University Press, 1979, pp. 160–204. Analyzes macroeconomic policy interactions under fixed and floating exchange rates.

Maurice Obstfeld. "Floating Exchange Rates: Experience and Prospects." *Brookings Papers on Economic Activity* 2:1985, pp. 369–450. Compares the merits of fixed and floating rates in light of the macroeconomic events of the previous decade.

Maurice Obstfeld. "The Effectiveness of Foreign-Exchange Intervention: Recent Experience, 1985–1988," in William H. Branson, Jacob A. Frenkel, and Morris Goldstein, eds., *International Policy Coordination and Exchange Rate Fluctuations.* Chicago: University of Chicago Press, 1990. Assesses the attempt by industrial countries to coordinate their exchange rate policies during the late 1980s.

Robert D. Putnam and Nicholas Bayne. *Hanging Together: Cooperation and Conflict in the Seven-Power Summits,* 2nd edition. Newbury Park, CA: Sage Publications, 1988. Describes the economic summit meetings of the Big Seven industrial countries.

Robert Solomon. *The International Monetary System, 1945–1981.* New York: Harper & Row, 1982. Chapters 15–19 cover the early years of floating exchange rates.

John Williamson. *The Exchange Rate System,* 2nd edition. Policy Analyses in International Economics 5. Washington, D.C.: Institute for International Economics, 1985. An indictment of floating exchange rates and a case for target zones.

Appendix to Chapter 20 ● International Policy Coordination Failures

This appendix illustrates the importance of macroeconomic policy coordination by showing how all countries can suffer as a result of self-centered policy decisions. The phenomenon is another example of the Prisoner's Dilemma of game theory (Chapter 10). Governments can achieve macroeconomic outcomes that are better for all if they choose policies cooperatively.

These points are made using an example based on the disinflation of the early 1980s. Recall that contractionary monetary policies in the industrial countries helped throw the world economy into a deep recession in 1981. Countries hoped to reduce inflation by slowing monetary growth, but the situation was complicated by the influence of exchange rates on the price level. A government that adopts a less restrictive monetary policy than its neighbors is likely to face a currency depreciation that partially frustrates its attempts to disinflate.

Many observers feel that in their individual attempts to resist currency depreciation, the industrial countries as a group adopted overly tight monetary policies that deepened the recession. All governments would have been happier if everyone had adopted looser monetary policies, but given the policies that other governments did adopt, it was not in the interest of any individual government to change course.

The argument above can be made more precise with a simple model. There are two countries, Home and Foreign, and each country has two policy options, a very restrictive monetary policy and a somewhat restrictive monetary policy. Figure 20A-1, which is similar to a diagram we used to analyze trade policies, shows the results in Home and Foreign of different policy choices by the two countries. Each row corresponds to a particular monetary policy decision by Home and each column to a decision by Foreign. The boxes contain entries giving changes in annual inflation rates ($\Delta\pi$ and $\Delta\pi^*$) and unemployment rates (ΔU and ΔU^*). Within each box, lower-left entries are Home outcomes and upper-right entries are Foreign outcomes.

The hypothetical entries in Figure 20A-1 can be understood in terms of this chapter's two-country model. Under somewhat restrictive policies, for example, inflation rates fall by 1 percent

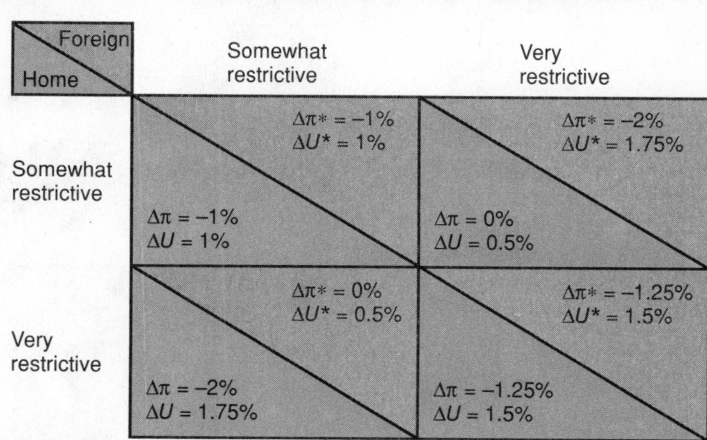

FIGURE 20A-1
Hypothetical effects of different monetary policy combinations on inflation and unemployment.
Monetary policy choices in one country affect the outcomes of monetary policy choices made abroad.

and unemployment rates rise by 1 percent in both countries. If Home suddenly shifts to a very restrictive policy while Foreign stands pat, Home's currency appreciates, its inflation drops further, and its unemployment rises. Home's additional monetary contraction, however, has two effects on Foreign. Foreign's unemployment rate falls, but because Home's currency appreciation is a currency *de*preciation for Foreign, Foreign inflation goes back up to its predisinflation level. In Foreign, the deflationary effects of higher unemployment are offset by the inflationary impact of a depreciating currency on import prices and wage demands. Home's sharper monetary crunch therefore has a beggar-thy-neighbor effect on Foreign, which is forced to "import" some inflation from Home.

To translate the outcomes in Figure 20A-1 into policy payoffs, we assume each government wishes to get the biggest reduction in inflation at the lowest cost in terms of unemployment. That is, each government wishes to maximize $-\Delta\pi/\Delta U$, the inflation reduction per point of increased unemployment. The numbers in Figure 20A-1 lead to the payoff matrix shown as Figure 20A-2.

How do Home and Foreign behave faced with the payoffs in this matrix? Assume each government "goes it alone" and picks the policy that maximizes its own payoff given the other player's policy choice. If Foreign adopts a somewhat restrictive policy, Home does better with a very restrictive policy (payoff $= \frac{8}{7}$) than with a somewhat restrictive one (payoff $= 1$). If Foreign is very restrictive, Home still does better by being very restrictive (payoff $= \frac{5}{6}$) than by being somewhat restrictive (payoff $= 0$). So no matter what Foreign does, Home's government will always choose a very restrictive monetary policy.

Foreign finds itself in a symmetric position. It, too, is better off with a very restrictive policy regardless of what Home does. The result is that both countries will choose very restrictive monetary policies, and each will get a payoff of $\frac{5}{6}$.

Notice, however, that *both* countries are actually better off if they simultaneously adopt the somewhat retrictive policies. The resulting payoff for each is 1, which is greater than $\frac{5}{6}$. Under this last policy configuration, inflation falls less in the two countries, but the rise in unemployment is far less than under very restrictive policies.

Since both countries are better off with somewhat restrictive policies, why aren't these adopted? The answer is at the root of the problem of policy coordination. Our analysis assumed that each country "goes it alone" by maximizing its own payoff. Under this assumption, a situation where both countries were somewhat restrictive would not be stable: each country

FIGURE 20A-2
Payoff matrix for different monetary policy moves.
Each entry equals the reduction in inflation per unit rise in the unemployment rate (calculated as $-\Delta\pi/\Delta U$). If each country "goes it alone," they both choose very restrictive policies. Somewhat restrictive policies, if adopted by both countries, lead to an outcome better for both.

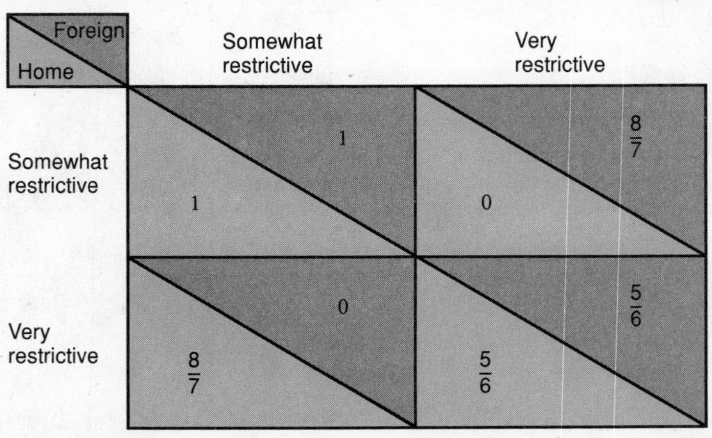

would want to reduce its monetary growth further and use its exchange rate to hasten disinflation at its neighbor's expense.

For the superior outcome in the upper-left corner of the matrix to occur, Home and Foreign must reach an explicit agreement, that is, they must *coordinate* their policy choices. Both countries must agree to forgo the beggar-thy-neighbor gains offered by very restrictive policies, and each country must abide by this agreement in spite of the incentive to cheat. If Home and Foreign can cooperate, both end up with a preferred mix of inflation and unemployment.

The reality of policy coordination is more complex than in this simple example because the choices and outcomes are more numerous and more uncertain. These added complexities make policy makers less willing to commit themselves to cooperative agreements and less certain that their counterparts abroad will live up to the agreed terms.

Optimum Currency Areas and the European Experience

Chapter 21

Between the first oil shock in 1973–1974 and the late 1980s, Europe's macroeconomic performance lagged behind that of other industrial regions. In the years 1979–1987, for example, the number of jobs available in European Community (EC) countries grew at an annual average rate of only 0.1 percent; Japan's pace of job creation for the same period was 9 times faster than that of the EC and the United States' pace was 16 times faster. Over the same period, output growth, another measure of economic success, averaged 2.4 percent per year in the United States and 3.9 percent per year in Japan, compared with only 1.8 percent per year in the EC.

Europe's lackluster record was widely blamed on "Eurosclerosis"—a pattern of social legislation and market rigidities that blocked the flow of labor and capital to their most productive uses. Hoping to revitalize their economies, the EC's leaders set out in the mid-1980s to remove the bewildering array of government regulations and trade restrictions that continued to harm economic efficiency despite the process of mutual trade liberalization the EC countries had begun in 1957. The initial success of this program and its apparent acceptance by the public encouraged EC heads of state to agree in December 1991 to a more radical step toward a unified European market: a timetable for replacing the individual national currencies in Europe by a single EC currency.

Only a year later, this bold plan appeared to be in disarray. Facing domestic recession and waning voter support for further European unification, EC members were trying desperately to stay on the road toward a single currency. Meanwhile, the European Monetary System (EMS) of fixed EC exchange rates was being battered by the most violent speculative attacks on industrial country currencies since the Bretton Woods system's final collapse twenty years earlier.

This chapter focuses on Europe's recent attempt at monetary union to illustrate the economic benefits and costs of fixed exchange rate agreements and more comprehensive currency unification schemes. As we see in Europe's experience, the effects of joining a fixed exchange rate agreement are complex and depend crucially on microeconomic *and* macroeconomic factors. Our discussion of Europe will throw light not only on the forces promoting greater unification of national economies but also on the forces that make a country think twice before giving up completely its control over domestic monetary policy.

Why Has Europe Favored Mutually Fixed Exchange Rates?

The Bretton Woods system that fell apart in 1973 fixed every member country's exchange rate against the U.S. dollar and as a result also fixed the exchange rate between every pair of nondollar currencies. Earlier chapters described the reasons for the Bretton Woods system's breakdown and how countries hoped to free their monetary policies by changing from fixed dollar exchange rates to floating rates. While allowing their currencies to float against the dollar, however, EC countries have tried progressively to narrow the extent to which they let their currencies fluctuate against each other. As a result, many EC currencies until recently took part in a concerted float against the dollar and therefore rose or fell against the U.S. currency by more or less equal percentages.

Even before 1973 EC members were examining ways to coordinate their monetary policies more closely and to reduce the limited intra-European exchange rate fluctuations allowed under Bretton Woods. These initiatives, which continued and gathered momentum after dollar exchange rates began to float in 1973, illustrate the economic and political forces behind the recent failed drive toward monetary unification in Europe.

EUROPEAN CURRENCY REFORM INITIATIVES, 1969–1978

European Community leaders meeting at The Hague in December 1969 initiated the drive toward European monetary unification. They appointed Pierre Werner, prime minister and finance minister of Luxembourg, to head a committee that would outline concrete steps for eliminating intra-European exchange rate movements, centralizing EC monetary policy decisions, and lowering remaining trade barriers within Europe. The Werner report, adopted by the EC in March 1971, proposed a three-phase program that, when completed, would result in locked EC exchange rates and the integration of the individual national central banks into a federated European system of banks.

What prompted the EC countries to seek closer coordination of monetary policies and greater exchange rate stability in the late 1960s? There were three main motives, one reflecting political changes in the world economy, one reflecting hopes for the evolution of the EC, and one reflecting the administrative problems that exchange rate changes caused for the EC:

1. *To enhance Europe's role in the world monetary system.* The currency crises of 1969 were accompanied by declining European confidence in the readiness of the United States to place its international monetary responsibilities ahead of its national interests (Chapter 19). By speaking with a single voice on monetary issues, EC countries hoped to defend more effectively their economic interests in the face of an increasingly self-absorbed United States.

2. *To turn the European Community into a truly unified market.* Even though the 1957 Treaty of Rome creating the EC had established a customs union, significant official barriers to the movements of goods and factors within Europe remained. A consistent goal of EC members has been to eliminate all such barriers and transform the EC into a huge unified market on the model of the United States. European officials believed, however, that exchange rate uncertainty, like official trade barriers, was a major factor reducing trade within Europe. In their view, a truly unified European market could never be achieved unless mutual European exchange rates were fixed.

3. *To avoid disrupting the Common Agricultural Policy.* Perhaps the most pressing motive of all was the tremendous difficulty of adjusting the EC's Common Agricultural Policy (CAP) to exchange rate changes (recall our discussion of the economic inefficiency of the CAP in Chapter 9).

The CAP guarantees EC farmers minimum support prices for their products. Wishing to treat all EC farmers symmetrically, the CAP specifies its support prices in terms of a basket of EC currencies that since 1979 has been called the *European Currency Unit* (ECU).

This mode of quoting agricultural support prices leads immediately, however, to a problem: when exchange rates within Europe are realigned, some countries' farmers find that the real value of their support prices has risen, while others are in the opposite position.

A simple example illustrates this effect. If the EC support price for wheat is 10 ECUs per bushel and an ECU is worth FFr 5, French wheat growers receive FFr 50 per bushel (= FFr 5 per ECU × 10 ECU/bushel). If, at the same time, an ECU is worth 3 DM, German farmers will get DM 30 per bushel of wheat (= DM 3 per ECU × 10 ECU/bushel).

Suppose now that there is a currency realignment, so that France devalues its currency to FFr 6 per ECU, while Germany revalues its currency to DM 2 per ECU.[1] What effect does this change have on the domestic currency prices received by French and German wheat growers? The price the French grower receives for wheat rises from FFr 50 to FFr 60 per bushel (= FFr 6 per ECU × 10 ECU/bushel), while the price the German grower receives *falls* from DM 30 to DM 20 per bushel (= DM 2 per ECU × 10 ECU per bushel). Clearly, the currency realignment increases the French farmer's income and reduces the German farmer's income.

Such redistributions have always provoked political outcry, and the European Community therefore was forced to adopt complex and costly administrative measures to offset them.[2] A desire to avoid the financial contortions needed to prevent sharp variations in farmers' incomes is one of the main factors behind EC policy makers'

[1] Remember that because the ECU is a *basket* of EC currencies, a depreciation of the franc against the ECU, other things equal, automatically results in an appreciation of the DM against the ECU.

[2] Specifically, the European Community required that the *domestic currency* prices of agricultural products be held constant during a transition period following realignments—in our example, at FFr 50 per bushel of wheat in France and at DM 30 per bushel of wheat in Germany. Notice, though, that at these old

TABLE 21-1 A brief glossary of Euronyms

CAP	Common Agricultural Policy
EC	European Community
ECU	European Currency Unit
EMS	European Monetary System
EMU	European Monetary Union
ERM	Exchange Rate Mechanism

dislike of variable exchange rates. (Of course the first-best policy, were it politically possible, would be to scrap the CAP.)

The considerations leading EC policy makers to favor mutual currency stability have changed little since the late 1960s. The Werner committee's vision was, however, ahead of its time. Faced with the economic turbulence surrounding the 1971–1973 dollar crises, most European leaders did not want to give up completely the ability to direct domestic monetary policy toward domestic goals. Instead, Germany, the Netherlands, Belgium, and Luxembourg—joined for periods by other European countries—participated in an informal joint float against the dollar known as the "snake." French, Italian, and British participation in the snake arrangements of the 1970s was brief and sporadic; nonetheless, the snake served as a prologue to the more comprehensive European Monetary System.

THE EUROPEAN MONETARY SYSTEM: FROM 1979 TO THE PRESENT

The eight original participants in the European Monetary System's exchange rate mechanism—France, Germany, Italy, Belgium, Denmark, Ireland, Luxembourg, and the Netherlands—began operating a formal network of mutually pegged exchange rates in March 1979. In Chapter 18 we described how EMS intervention arrangements work to restrict the exchange rates of participating currencies within specified fluctuation margins.[3]

When the EMS was founded on the initiative of France and Germany, skeptics predicted that the system would do no better than its predecessor the snake: speculative attacks would soon shatter its parities, forcing France, Italy, and some of the smaller countries out. The prospects for a successful fixed-rate area Europe seemed bleak indeed

---

domestic currency prices, but at the *new* exchange rates, wheat is priced at 8.33 ECU/bushel in France (= 1/6 ECU/franc × FFr 50 per bushel) and at 15 ECU/bushel (= 1/2 ECU/DM × DM 30 bushel) in Germany. How could the EC prevent people from buying wheat in France and selling it in Germany, thereby making arbitrage profits on the price difference? The EC prevented arbitrage by setting up a tax on French wheat exports and a subsidy on German wheat exports. These taxes and subsidies on agricultural trade within Europe, called Monetary Compensation Amounts (MCAs), were among the many trade regulations scheduled for removal by the EC 1992 project (see pp. 610–611). For a more detailed discussion of MCAs, see the book by Giavazzi and Giovannini listed in Further Reading.

[3] As a technical matter, all twelve EC members automatically are members of the EMS, but only those who enforce the fluctuation margins belong to the EMS exchange rate mechanism (ERM). Currently Greece is the only EMS country never to have joined the ERM. Nonetheless it participates in the European Monetary Cooperation Fund and its currency, the drachma, is part of the basket defining the ECU.

in early 1979, when recent yearly inflation rates ranged from Germany's 2.7 percent to Italy's 12.1 percent (see Table 20-1). Through a mixture of policy cooperation and realignment, however, the EMS fixed exchange rate club survived and even grew, adding Spain to its ranks in 1989, Britain in 1990, and Portugal early in 1992. Only in September 1992 did this growth suffer a sudden setback when Britain and Italy left the EMS exchange rate mechanism at the start of an ongoing European currency crisis that forced the remaining members within a year to retreat to very wide exchange rate margins. We discuss the causes and effects of this crisis later in this chapter.

The EMS's operation has been aided by several safety valves that initially helped reduce the frequency of such crises. Most exchange rates "fixed" by the EMS until August 1993 actually could fluctuate up or down by as much as 2.25 percent relative to an assigned par value. Spain's peseta and Portugal's escudo had bands of ± 6 percent, as did the British pound until its recent float against EMS currencies started in September 1992. The Italian lira likewise had a 6 percent band until January 1990, when Italy adopted the standard narrow band. Inflationary instability was common in Italy during the 1970s, and the country's special exchange rate band was meant to give it a greater latitude than other exchange rate mechanism members to choose monetary policies. Similarly, the recent new members, Spain, Portugal, and Britain, desired greater room for maneuver during their initiation periods and therefore also chose to start out with wide bands. In August 1993 all EMS bands (other than that between the DM and Dutch guilder) were widened to ± 15 percent under the pressure of speculative attacks.

As another crucial safety valve, the EMS developed generous provisions for the extension of credit from strong- to weak-currency members. If the French franc depreciates too far against the DM, for example, Germany's central bank, the Bundesbank, is expected to lend the Bank of France DM that can be sold for francs in the foreign exchange market.

Finally, during the system's initial years of operation several members (notably France and Italy) reduced the possibility of speculative attack by maintaining exchange controls that directly limited domestic residents' sales of home for foreign currencies. All French, Italian, Danish, and Belgian controls were dismantled in a series of stages completed in 1990. At the time of the crisis of September 1992, when several EMS members backtracked and tightened their exchange controls, the remaining restrictions on payments within the EC had been scheduled to be scrapped within a few years.

The EMS has always gone through periodic currency realignments. In all, eleven realignments occurred between the start of the EMS in March 1979 and January 1987. Exchange controls played the important role of shielding members' reserves from speculators during these adjustments.

Starting in 1987, the phased removal of exchange controls increased the possibility of speculative attacks and thus reduced governments' willingness to consider devaluing or revaluing. At the same time, the countries that dismantled their controls sharply reduced their power to reach national employment or inflation goals through domestic monetary policy (recall the monetary policy ineffectiveness result of Chapter 18). Freedom of payments and capital movements within the EC has always been a key element of EC countries' plan to turn Europe into a unified single market. By agreeing to remove exchange controls, EC governments were saying that it was less important to use monetary and exchange rate policy for domestic purposes than to speed up progress toward a single European market.

FIGURE 21-1
The EMS currency grid.
The grid shows the relative positions of EMS currencies within their permitted fluctuation bands. The first of the two grids shown above, panel (a), dates from shortly before the onset of the autumn 1992 currency crisis. In mid-September Britain and Italy withdrew their currencies from the EMS exchange rate mechanism; by mid-December (panel [b]) neither had reentered the system. In August 1993 most remaining ERM currencies moved to ±15 percent exchange rate bands.
Source: *Financial Times,* September 7, 1992, page 1, and December 14, 1992, page 1.

(a)

European Monetary System: The D-Mark remains at the top of the grid, following Friday's poor employment figures in the US which triggered heavy investment in the Germany currency. The D-Mark, the hardest currency in Europe, is normally at the center of the table, allowing the monetary policies and exchange rates of other currencies to be altered around it. Its strong position is putting pressure on other member currencies, with sterling still firmly at the bottom of the table. But the UK government's decision last week to buy pounds on the foreign exchanges by means of an Ecu10bn ($14.3bn) loan has eased the pound's differential against the strongest currencies in the system. **Currencies, Page 31**

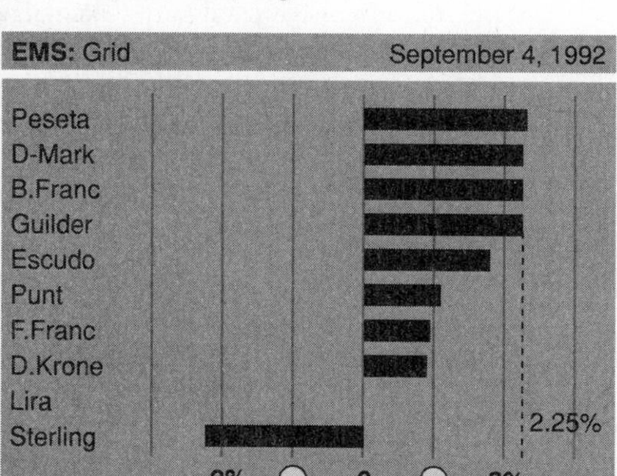

The chart shows the member currencies of the exchange rate mechanism measured against the weakest currency in the EMS's narrow 2.25 per cent fluctuation band. In practice, currencies in the EMS narrow band cannot rise more than 2.25 per cent from the weakest currency in that part of the system. Sterling, the Spanish peseta and the Portuguese escudo operate with 6 per cent fluctuation bands.

(b)

European monetary system: Tension within the exchange rate mechanism grew last week as the Bundesbank intervened to support the French franc. The Belgian and Dutch central banks helped to support the Danish krone while the Irish punt looked extremely vulnerable. The French franc has the strongest chance of withstanding any realignment, but even analysts who believe the French economy has the fundamental strength to avoid devaluation are concerned. More bearish economists are convinced that devaluation is imminent. **Currencies, Page 29; Lex, Page 19**

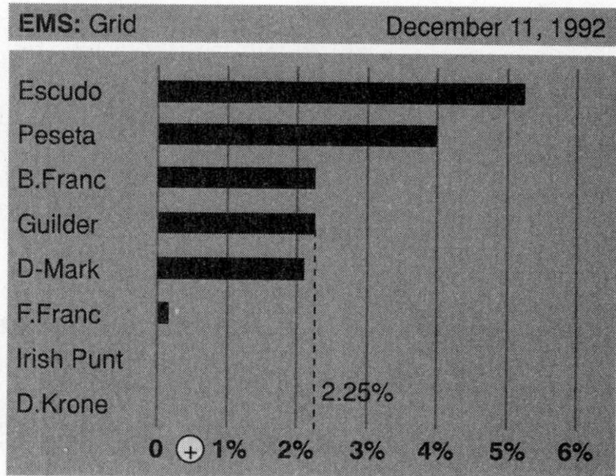

The chart shows the member currencies of the exchange rate mechanism measured against the weakest currency in the EMS's narrow 2.25 per cent fluctuation band. In practice, currencies in the narrow band cannot rise more than 2.25 per cent from the weakest currency in that part of the system. The Spanish peseta and the Portuguese escudo operate with 6 per cent fluctuation bands.

For a period of five and a half years after January 1987, no adverse economic event was able to shake the EC's commitment to its single-market plan, and the EMS thus was free of serious currency crises. As we see below, however, domestic macroeconomic problems became more urgent late in 1992; as a result, the system's fixed exchange rates gave way.

Figure 21-1 shows the London *Financial Times'* weekly capsule summary of currencies' positions within the EMS.[4] As we discuss in the box on p. 608, these graphs give a snapshot of currencies' relative positions within their EMS bilateral exchange rate bands. The two summaries we have selected—one from early September 1992 and one from December 1992—also illustrate the strains and setbacks that the system suffered during the autumn of 1992.

GERMAN MONETARY DOMINANCE AND THE CREDIBILITY THEORY OF THE EMS

Earlier, we identified three main reasons why the European Community sought to fix exchange rates through the EMS: a desire to defend Europe's economic interests more effectively on the world stage, the ambition to achieve greater internal economic unity, and the complexity of adjusting the Common Agricultural Policy to intra-European currency realignments.

Recent experience suggests an additional explanation for the EMS's existence. By fixing their exchange rates against the DM, the other EMS countries in effect imported the German Bundesbank's credibility as an inflation fighter and thus discouraged the development of inflationary pressures at home—pressures they might otherwise have been tempted to accommodate through monetary expansion. This view, the **credibility theory of the EMS,** is a variant of the "discipline" argument against floating exchange rates (Chapter 20): the political costs of violating an international exchange rate agreement can restrain governments from depreciating their currencies to gain the short-term advantage of an economic boom at the long-term cost of higher inflation.

To evaluate the credibility theory, we need first to understand how the German Bundesbank gained its low-inflation reputation. Germany's experiences with hyperinflation in the 1920s and again after World War II left its electorate with a deeply rooted fear of inflation. For this reason, the law establishing the Bundesbank singled out the defense of the DM's real value as the central bank's primary goal. Consistent with this goal, the bank's governing council has powers and membership rules that make it unusually independent of pressures from the politicians who run the rest of the German government.[5]

The way EMS intervention practices have evolved since the mid-1980s supports the view that Germany's EMS partners have sought to import its anti-inflation credibility. Increasingly, EMS countries other than Germany have come to hold DM in their reserves and to use these as an intervention medium when their exchange rates get too far from the official DM parity. (Germany also carries out some interventions in EMS currencies, especially during turbulent periods, but it instantly sterilizes any effects that these interventions might have on Germany's money supply.) The result is a system that functions very much in the asymmetric way the Bretton Woods system did under U.S. dominance. In practice, the EMS's *N*th currency problem (Chapter 18) has been

[4] Luxembourg is not shown separately because its franc is equivalent to Belgium's franc as the result of a currency union between the two countries.

[5] Two interesting studies show that central bank independence appears to result in lower inflation. See Vittorio Grilli, Donato Masciandaro, and Guido Tabellini, "Political and Monetary Institutions and Public Financial Policies in the Industrial Countries," *Economic Policy* 13 (October 1991), pp. 341–392; and Alberto Alesina and Lawrence H. Summers, "Central Bank Independence and Macroeconomic Performance," *Journal of Money, Credit and Banking* 25 (May 1993), pp. 151–162.

FIGURE 21-2
Inflation convergence within the EMS.
Shown are the differences between domestic inflation and German inflation for six of the original EMS members, Belgium, Denmark, France, Ireland, Italy, and the Netherlands. As of 1992 all national inflation rates except Italy's were below the German level; and Italy's rate was close to Germany's and much lower than at the system's birth.
Source: CPI inflation rates from OECD, *Main Economic Indicators.*

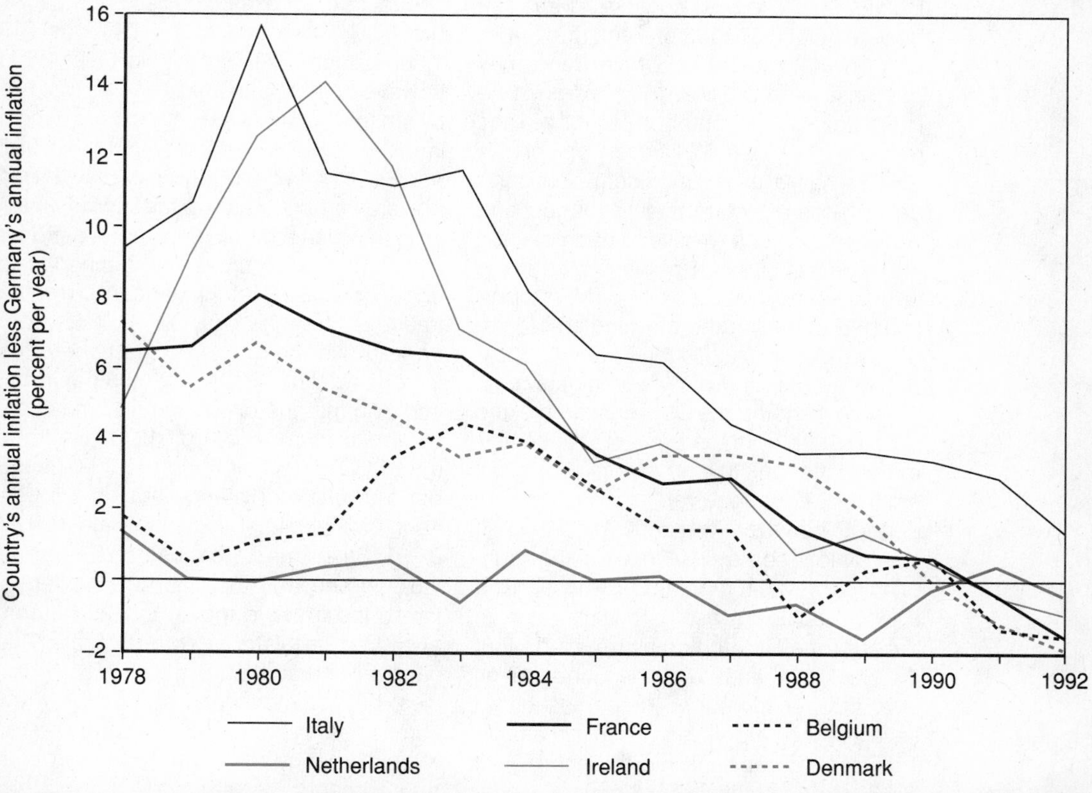

solved by having Germany set the system's monetary policy while the other countries peg their currencies' DM exchange rates.

Policy makers in inflation-prone EMS countries, such as Italy, clearly gained credibility by placing monetary policy decisions in the hands of the German central bank. Devaluation was still possible, but only subject to EMS restrictions. Because politicians also fear they will look incompetent to voters if they devalue, a government's decision to peg to the DM reduces both its willingness and ability to create domestic inflation.[6]

Added support for the credibility theory comes from the behavior of inflation rates

[6] The general theory that an inflation-prone country gains from vesting its monetary policy decisions with a "conservative" central bank is developed in an influential paper by Kenneth Rogoff. See "The Optimal Degree of Commitment to an Intermediate Monetary Target," *Quarterly Journal of Economics* 100 (November 1985), pp. 1169–1189. For application to the EMS, see Francesco Giavazzi and Marco Pagano, "The Advantage of Tying One's Hands: EMS Discipline and Central Bank Credibility," *European Economic Review* 32 (June 1988), pp. 1055–1082.

The EMS Currency Grid

An intricate EMS "currency grid" defines margins within which the exchange rate between any two members' currencies may fluctuate. At the end of 1992 the exchange rate between the French franc and DM, for example, was confined to a range between DM 0.30494 per franc (the upper limit on the number of DM a franc may purchase) and DM 0.29153 per franc (the lower limit on the number of DM a franc may purchase). Similarly, every pair of currencies has a permitted fluctuation band defining the two currencies' strongest and weakest positions relative to each other.

The exact position of these margins is of critical importance for the EMS's operation. One reason the margins are so important is their place in the EMS rule book. When the French franc depreciates to its lower limit against the DM, for example, the rules require both the Bank of France and the Bundesbank to intervene in support of the franc. Exchange rate margins are important, however, for another reason. If speculators see a DM/FFr exchange rate of only DM 0.29153 per franc, meaning the franc is at its lowest permitted value in terms of the DM, they may conclude that the Bank of France and the Bundesbank lack the resources or determination to save the weak currency from an attack. This is what happened in the summer of 1993, and as a result, EMS countries widened the DM/FFr fluctuation band (along with most other bilateral bands) to ± 15 percent.

Because the stability of the EMS and the need for its members to intervene are closely linked to currencies' positions within their bilateral bands, the *Financial Times* publishes every Monday the EMS grid diagram reproduced in Figure 21-1. This diagram is a convenient way to visualize the relative positions of the various currencies in the EMS exchange rate mechanism. To see how the diagram works, however, we first must understand in greater detail how the EMS sets its exchange rate bands.

As mentioned in Chapter 18, the EMS assigns each of its currencies an *ECU central rate,* which is a specified exchange rate against the European Currency Unit. At the end of 1992 the French franc's ECU central rate, for example, was FFr 6.60683 per ECU, while that of the DM was DM 1.96992 per ECU. These two ECU rates, however, define a *bilateral central rate* between the DM and the French franc, which is DM 0.29816 per franc (= DM 1.96992 per ECU ÷ FFr 6.60683 per ECU). This bilateral central rate is the DM/FFr rate around which the EMS fluctuation band for the franc against the DM is defined. The upper margin for this band (where the franc is strongest) is DM 0.30494 per franc, while the lower margin (where the franc is weakest) is DM 0.29153 per franc, implying that the exchange rate may vary by a maximum of DM 0.01341 per franc (= DM 0.30494 per franc − DM 0.29153 per franc). This distance equals 4.5 percent of the bilateral central rate of DM 0.29816 per franc. Because 2.25 is half of 4.5, we see that the old EMS bands allowed the franc to move ± 2.25 percent away from its bilateral central DM rate. This narrow band applied to most EMS currencies, but, as mentioned above, for a few currencies bilateral bands were set to allow exchange rate changes as large as ± 6 percent.

We can now tackle Figure 21-1, starting with panel a, which shows the EMS grid just before currency crisis erupted in September 1992. The chart takes as a benchmark currency the weakest currency with a 2.25 percent fluctuation band, which at the time was the Italian lira. Each heavy black line measures the percent difference between the corresponding currency's price in lire and the central exchange rate of the lira against the currency. As you can see, the DM, the Belgian franc, and the Dutch guilder all were at their maximum values relative to the lira, that is, their lira prices were all 2.25 percent above their central lira prices. The Spanish peseta, while stronger than the lira, was well below its ceiling, which would have been 6 percent above the central lira/peseta rate. Finally, Britain's pound, under heavy speculative pressure, was more than 2 percent *below* its central lira rate, and thus more than 4 percent below its central rates against the strongest EMS currencies.

The last sentence illustates an important feature of the EMS grid diagram. While the grid in Figure 21-1a reports only exchange rates against the lira, we can use it to figure out the positions of *other* bilateral exchange rates relative to their central rates. If the lira/French franc rate is 1 percent above the central lira/French franc rate, for example, while the pound/lira rate is 2 percent above the central pound/lira rate, then the pound/franc rate's distance from the central pound/franc rate is approximately the sum of the pound's distance from its central lira rate *and* the lira's distance from its central franc rate, or 3 percent (= 2 percent + 1 percent).* Thus, for example, we can deduce from Figure 21-1a that the Belgian franc, guilder, and DM, all of which are shown as being 2.25 percent above their central lira values, were trading *against each other* at their bilateral central exchange rates.

Figure 21-1b shows the grid on December 11, 1992. Notice that Britain and Italy are absent, having floated their currencies in September. The Irish punt, Danish krone, and Franch franc all were targets of speculation at the end of 1992 and therefore are shown at or near the bottoms of their bilateral bands against the strong narrow-band currencies, the Belgian franc, the guilder, and the DM. Correspondingly, the three strong currencies were at or near the tops of their bilateral bands against the three weak currencies. Portugal's escudo and Spain's peseta were devalued relative to the ECU on November 22, and, as you see in the figure, on December 11 they both were in the upper portions of their wide bilateral bands.

Figure 21-1 shows two particularly turbulent episodes in EMS history prior to the August 1993 move to wide bands. In more tranquil periods the weakest narrow-band currency would usually have been less than 2.25 percent below its central DM value. Historically, Germany has been the least inflation-prone country in the EMS; as a result, the DM tends to be the system's strongest currency. A configuration placing the DM in the middle of the grid's positive section therefore would normally have been one in which all currencies were safely within their EMS margins.

* If this approximate equality does not hold true, there will be an opportunity for currency *arbitrage,* as discussed in Chapter 14. To see how the formula used in the text is derived, let $E_{£/FFr}$, $E_{£/Lit}$, and $E_{Lit/FFr}$ be the bilateral pound/franc, pound/lira, and lira/franc exchange rates, respectively, and let $E^c_{£/FFr}$, $E^c_{£/Lit}$, and $E^c_{Lit/FFr}$ be the bilateral central rates. Exchange rate arbitrage ensures that

$$E_{£/FFr}/E^c_{£/FFr} = (E_{£/Lit} \times E_{Lit/FFr})/(E^c_{£/Lit} \times E^c_{Lit/FFr}) = (E_{£/Lit}/E^c_{£/Lit}) \times (E_{Lit/FFr}/E^c_{Lit/FFr}).$$

Returning to the numerical example in the text, we see that $E_{£/FFr}/E^c_{£/FFr} = 1.02 \times 1.01 = 1.0302$, so that the pound/franc rate is 3 percent above its central rate.

relative to Germany's, shown in Figure 21-2 for six of the other original EMS members.[7] As the figure shows, inflation rates have gradually converged toward the low German levels. France even managed to bring its inflation rate below Germany's in the early 1990s, something most observers would have thought impossible a decade earlier.[8]

[7] Figure 21-2 does not include the tiny country of Luxembourg because (as noted earlier) that country has a currency union with Belgium and an inflation rate very close to Belgium's.

[8] Those skeptical of the credibility theory of EMS inflation convergence point out that the United States, Britain, and Japan also reduced inflation to low levels over the 1980s, but did so without fixing their exchange rates.

PROBLEMS WITH GERMANY'S DOMINANT POSITION

While lower inflation is a benefit, German monetary dominance has also had costs for its EMS partners. Just as the U.S. government sometimes put its own interests ahead of its broader responsibilities under the Bretton Woods system, Germany has been accused of gearing monetary policy mainly toward its own economic needs. As we see later in this chapter, Germany's economic policies have recently made it harder for EMS countries to live with fixed exchange rates and have encouraged the search for an alternative European currency system in which Germany is less dominant.

THE EC "1992" INITIATIVE

The EC countries have tried to achieve greater internal economic unity not only by fixing mutual exchange rates, but also through direct measures to encourage the free flow of goods, services, and factors of production. Later in this chapter you will learn that the extent of product and factor market integration within Europe helps to determine how fixed exchange rates affect Europe's macroeconomic stability. Europe's efforts to raise *microeconomic* efficiency through direct market liberalization have also increased its preference for mutually fixed exchange rates on *macroeconomic* grounds. The most recent phase of EC market liberalization, an ambitious plan known as the "1992" initiative because all of its goals were supposed to have been met by January 1, 1993, therefore is an important consideration in our discussion of European exchange rate policy.

The process of market unification that began when the original EC members formed their customs union in 1957 was still incomplete thirty years later, as we saw in Chapter 8. In a number of industries, such as automobiles and telecommunications, trade within Europe was discouraged by government-imposed standards and registration requirements; often government licensing or purchasing practices gave domestic producers virtual monopoly positions in domestic markets. Differing national tax structures and health and safety regulations also inhibited trade. For example, countries with high value-added taxes had to post customs officials at EC frontiers to prevent their citizens from shopping in neighboring low-tax countries. Similarly, customs checks were needed to enforce national product standards. Significant barriers to factor movements within Europe also remained.[9]

In June 1985 the EC's executive organ, the European Commission, issued a White Paper containing 300 proposals for "Completing the Internal Market" by the end of 1992, that is, for removing all remaining internal barriers to trade, capital movements, and labor migration. In the Single European Act of 1986 (which amended the founding Treaty of Rome), EC members took the crucial political steps to translate the White Paper's 1992 into reality. Most important, they dropped the Treaty of Rome's requirement of unanimous consent for measures related to market completion, so that one or two self-interested EC members could not block trade liberalization measures as in the past. The Single European Act thus gave the European Community the procedural tools needed to attain its ambitious goal, namely, that "the internal market shall comprise an area without internal frontiers in which the free movement of goods, persons, services and capital is ensured."

By now most of 1992's market integration measures have been implemented or

[9] An excellent discussion of the microeconomic objectives of 1992 is in Harry Flam, "Product Markets and 1992: Full Integration, Large Gains?" *Journal of Economic Perspectives* 6 (Fall 1992), pp. 7–30.

are being phased in. National economic barriers within EC Europe generally are lower than a decade ago, but 1992 has been more effective in some areas than in others. Financial capital, for example, can move quite freely, not only within the European Community, but between the European Community and outside jurisdictions. While a few EC countries still maintain controls over foreign exchange transactions and capital movements, they are scheduled for removal.

Progress has been slower, however, in lowering barriers to the free movement of *people* within the European Community. EC workers are legally free to seek jobs or reside anywhere in the Community, but labor mobility remains limited. Several EC members feared illegal immigration from outside the European Community, however, and as a result the original goal to abolish passport checks at EC members' common borders by January 1, 1993 was not fully met.

The Theory of Optimum Currency Areas

There is little doubt that the EMS has helped advance the *political* goals of its founders by giving the European Community a stronger position in international affairs. The survival and future development of the European monetary experiment depend more heavily, however, on its ability to help countries reach their *economic* goals. Here the picture is less clear because a country's decision to fix its exchange rate can in principle lead to economic sacrifices as well as to benefits.

We saw in Chapter 20 that by changing its exchange rate, a country may succeed in cushioning the disruptive impact of various economic shocks. On the other hand, exchange rate flexibility can have potentially harmful effects, such as making relative prices less predictable or undermining the government's resolve to keep inflation in check. To weigh the economic costs of joining a group of countries with mutually fixed exchange rates against the advantages, we need a framework for thinking systematically about the stabilization powers a country sacrifices and the gains in efficiency and credibility it may reap.

In this section we show that a country's costs and benefits from joining a fixed-exchange rate area such as the EMS depend on how well-integrated its economy is with those of its potential partners. The analysis leading to this conclusion, which is known as the theory of **optimum currency areas,** predicts that fixed exchange rates are most appropriate for areas closely integrated through international trade and factor movements.[10]

ECONOMIC INTEGRATION AND THE BENEFITS OF A FIXED EXCHANGE RATE AREA: THE *GG* SCHEDULE

Consider how an individual country, for example, Finland, might approach the decision of whether to join an area of fixed exchange rates, for example, the EMS. Our goal is to develop a simple diagram that clarifies Finland's choice.

We begin by deriving the first of two elements in the diagram, a schedule called *GG* that shows how the potential gain to Finland from joining the EMS depends on Finland's trading links with the EMS.

[10] The original reference is Robert A. Mundell's classic, "The Theory of Optimum Currency Areas," *American Economic Review* 51 (September 1961), pp. 717–725. Subsequent contributions are summarized in the book by Tower and Willett listed in Further Reading.

A major economic benefit of fixed exchange rates is that they simplify economic calculations and provide a more predictable basis for decisions that involve international transactions than do floating rates. Imagine the time and resources American consumers and businesses would waste every day if each of the fifty United States had its own currency that fluctuated in value against the currencies of all the other states! Finland faces a similar disadvantage in its trade with the EMS when it allows its currency, the markka, to float against EMS currencies. The **monetary efficiency gain** from joining the fixed exchange rate system equals the joiner's savings from avoiding the uncertainty, confusion, and calculation and transaction costs that arise when exchange rates float.

In practice, it may be hard to attach a precise number to the monetary efficiency gain Finland would enjoy as a result of joining the EMS. We can be sure, however, that this gain will be higher if Finland trades a lot with EMS countries. For example, if Finland's trade with the EMS amounts to 60 percent of its GNP while its trade with the United States amounts to only 5 percent of GNP, then, other things equal, a fixed markka/ECU exchange rate clearly yields a greater monetary efficiency gain to Finnish traders than a fixed markka/dollar rate. Similarly, the efficiency gain from a fixed markka/ECU rate is greater when Finland-EMS trade is extensive than when it is small.

The monetary efficiency gain from pegging the markka to EMS currencies will also be higher if factors of production can migrate freely between Finland and the EMS.[11] Finns who invest in EMS countries benefit when the returns on their investments are more predictable. Similarly, Finns who work in EMS countries may benefit if a fixed exchange rate makes their wages more stable relative to Finland's cost of living.

Our conclusion is that *a high degree of economic integration between a country and a fixed exchange rate area magnifies the monetary efficiency gain the country reaps when it fixes its exchange rate against the area's currencies.* The more extensive are cross-border trade and factor movements, the greater is the gain from a fixed cross-border exchange rate.

The upward-sloping curve *GG* in Figure 21-3 shows the relation between a country's degree of economic integration with a fixed exchange rate area and the monetary efficiency gain to the country from joining the area. The figure's horizontal axis measures the extent to which Finland (the joining country in our example) is economically integrated into EMS product and factor markets. The vertical axis measures the monetary efficiency gain to Finland from joining the EMS. *GG*'s positive slope reflects the conclusion that the monetary efficiency gain a country gets by joining a fixed exchange rate area rises as its economic integration with the area increases.

In our example we have implicitly assumed that the larger exchange rate area, the EMS, has a stable and predictable price level. If it does not, the greater variability in Finland's price level that would follow a decision to join the exchange rate area would likely offset any monetary efficiency gain a fixed exchange rate might provide. A different problem arises if Finland's commitment to fix the markka's exchange rate is not fully believed by economic actors. In this situation, some exchange rate uncertainty would remain and Finland would therefore enjoy a smaller monetary efficiency gain. If the EMS price level is stable and Finland's exchange rate commitment is firm, however, the main conclusion follows: when Finland joins the EMS exchange rate mechanism, it gains from the stability of its markka against EMS currencies, and this efficiency gain is greater the more closely tied are Finland's markets with EMS markets.

[11] Chapter 7 discussed the economic causes and effects of international movements of labor and capital.

FIGURE 21-3
The *GG* schedule.
The upward sloping *GG* schedule shows that a country's monetary efficiency gain from joining a fixed exchange rate area rises as the country's economic integration with the area rises.

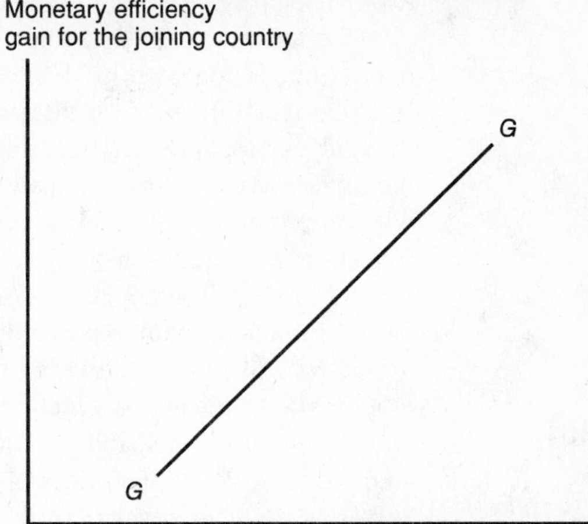

Earlier in this chapter we learned that a country may wish to peg its exchange rate to an area of price stability to import the anti-inflationary resolve of the area's monetary authorities. When the economy of the pegging country is well integrated with that of the low-inflation area, however, low domestic inflation is easier to achieve. The reason is that close economic integration leads to international price convergence and therefore lessens the scope for independent variation in the pegging country's price level. This argument provides another reason why high economic integration with a fixed exchange rate area enhances a country's gain from membership.

ECONOMIC INTEGRATION AND THE COSTS OF A FIXED EXCHANGE RATE AREA: THE *LL* SCHEDULE

Membership in an exchange rate area may involve costs as well as benefits, even when the area has low inflation. These costs arise because a country that joins an exchange rate area gives up its ability to use the exchange rate and monetary policy for the purpose of stabilizing output and employment. This **economic stability loss** from joining, like the country's monetary efficiency gain, is related to the country's economic integration with its exchange rate partners. We can derive a second schedule, the *LL* schedule, that shows the relationship graphically.

In Chapter 20's discussion of the relative merits of fixed and floating exchange rates, we concluded that when the economy is disturbed by a change in the output market (that is, by a shift in the *DD* schedule), a floating exchange rate has an advantage over a fixed rate: it automatically cushions the economy's output and employment by allowing an immediate change in the relative price of domestic and foriegn goods. Furthermore, you will recall from Chapter 18 that when the exchange rate is fixed, purposeful stabilization is more difficult because monetary policy has no power at all to affect domestic output. Given these two conclusions, we would expect changes in the *DD* schedule to have more severe effects on an economy in which the monetary authority is required to fix the exchange rate against a group of foreign currencies. The *extra* instability caused by the fixed exchange rate is the economic stability loss.[12]

To derive the *LL* schedule we must understand how the extent of Finland's economic integration with the EMS will affect the size of this loss in economic stability. Imagine that Finland is in the EMS and there is a fall in the aggregate demand for Finland's output—a leftward shift of Finland's *DD* schedule. If the *DD* schedules of the other EMS countries happen simultaneously to shift to the left, all EMS currencies will simply depreciate jointly against outside currencies, providing the automatic stabilization we studied in the last chapter. Finland has a serious problem only when it *alone* faces a fall in demand—for example, if the world demand for forestry products, one of Finland's main exports, drops.

How will Finland adjust to this shock? Since nothing has happened to budge the other EMS currencies to which Finland is pegged, its markka will remain stable against *all* foreign currencies. Full employment will be restored only after a period of costly slump during which the prices of Finnish goods and the wages of Finnish workers fall.

How does the severity of this slump depend on the level of economic integration between the Finnish economy and those of the other EMS countries? The answer is that greater integration implies a shallower slump, and therefore a less costly adjustment to the adverse shift in *DD*. There are two reasons for this reduction in the cost of adjustment. First, if Finland has close trading links with the EMS, a small reduction in its prices will lead to an increase in EMS demand for Finnish goods that is large relative to Finland's output. Thus, full employment can be restored fairly quickly. Second, if Finland's labor and capital markets are closely meshed with those of its EMS neighbors, unemployed workers can easily move abroad to find work and domestic capital can be shifted to more profitable uses in other countries. The ability of factors to migrate abroad thus reduces the severity of unemployment in Finland and the fall in the rate of return available to investors.[13]

Notice that our conclusions also apply to a situation in which Finland experiences an *increase* in demand for its output (a rightward shift of *DD*). If Finland is tightly

[12] You might think that when Finland unilaterally fixes its exchange rate against the ECU, but leaves the markka free to float against non-EMS currencies, it is able to keep at least some monetary independence. Perhaps surprisingly, this intuition is *wrong*. The reason is that any independent money supply change in Finland would put pressure on markka interest rates and thus on the markka/ECU exchange rate. So by pegging the markka even to a single foreign currency, Finland completely surrenders its domestic monetary control. This result has, however, a positive side for Finland. After Finland unilaterally pegs the markka to the ECU, domestic money market disturbances (shifts in the *AA* schedule) will no longer affect domestic output, despite the continuing float against non-EMS currencies. Why? Because Finland's interest rate must equal the EMS interest rate, any pure shifts in *AA* will (as in Chapter 20) result in immediate reserve inflows or outflows that leave Finland's interest rate unchanged. Thus, a markka/ECU peg alone is enough to provide automatic stability in the face of any monetary shocks that shift the *AA* schedule. This is why the discussion in the text can focus on shifts in the *DD* schedule.

[13] Installed plant and equipment typically is costly to transport abroad or to adapt to new uses. Owners of such relatively immobile Finnish capital therefore will always earn low returns on it after an adverse shift in the demand for Finnish products. If Finland's capital market is integrated with those of its EMS neighbors, however, Finns will invest some of their wealth in other countries, while at the same time part of Finland's capital stock will be owned by foreigners. As a result of this process of international wealth *diversification* (see Chapter 22), unexpected changes in the return to Finland's capital will automatically be shared among investors throughout the EMS. Thus, even owners of capital that cannot be moved can avoid more of the economic stability loss due to fixed exchange rates when Finland's economy is open to capital flows.

When international labor mobility is low or nonexistent, higher international capital mobility may *not* reduce the economic stability loss from fixed exchange rates, as we discuss below in evaluating the European experience.

integrated with other EMS countries, a small increase in Finland's price level, combined with some movement of foreign capital and labor into Finland, quickly eliminates the excess demand for Finnish products.[14]

An additional consideration that we have not yet discussed strengthens the argument that the economic stability loss to Finland from joining the EMS is lower when Finland and the EMS engage in a large volume of trade. Since imports from the EMS make up a large fraction of Finnish workers' consumption in this case, changes in the markka/ECU exchange rate may quickly affect nominal Finnish wages, reducing any impact on employment. A depreciation of the markka against the ECU, for example, causes a sharp fall in Finns' living standards when imports from the EMS countries are substantial; workers are likely to demand higher nominal wages from their employers to compensate them for the loss. In this situation the additional macroeconomic stability Finland gets from a floating exchange rate is small, so the country has little to lose by joining the EMS.

We conclude that *a high degree of economic integration between a country and the fixed exchange rate area that it joins reduces the resulting economic stability loss due to output market disturbances.*

The *LL* schedule shown in Figure 21-4 summarizes this conclusion. The figure's horizontal axis measures the joining country's economic integration with the fixed exchange rate area, the vertical axis the country's economic stability loss. As we have seen, *LL* has a negative slope because the economic stability loss from pegging to the area's currencies falls as the degree of economic interdependence rises.

THE DECISION TO JOIN A CURRENCY AREA: PUTTING THE *GG* AND *LL* SCHEDULES TOGETHER

Figure 21-5 combines the *GG* and *LL* schedules to show how Finland should decide whether to join the EMS. The figure implies that Finland should join if the degree of economic integration between Finnish and markets and those of the EMS is at least equal to θ_1, the integration level determined by the intersection of *GG* and *LL* at point 1.

Let's see why Finland should join the EMS if its degree of economic integration with EMS markets is at least θ_1. Figure 21-5 shows that for levels of economic integration below θ_1 the *GG* schedule lies below the *LL* schedule. Thus, the loss Finland would suffer from greater output and employment instability after joining exceeds the monetary efficiency gain, and the country would do better to stay out.

When the degree of integration is θ_1 or higher, however, the monetary efficiency gain measured by *GG* is greater than the stability sacrifice measured by *LL*, and joining the EMS results in a net gain for Finland. Thus the intersection of *GG* and *LL* determines the minimum integration level (here, θ_1) at which Finland will desire to peg its currency to the ECU.

The *GG*-*LL* framework has important implications about how changes in a country's economic environment affect its willingness to peg its currency to an outside currency area. Consider, for example, an increase in the size and frequency of sudden shifts in the demand for the country's exports. As shown in Figure 21-6, such a change

[14] The preceding reasoning applies to other economic disturbances that fall unequally on Finland's output market and those of its exchange rate partners. A problem at the end of this chapter asks you to think through the effects of an increase in demand for EMS exports other than Finland's.

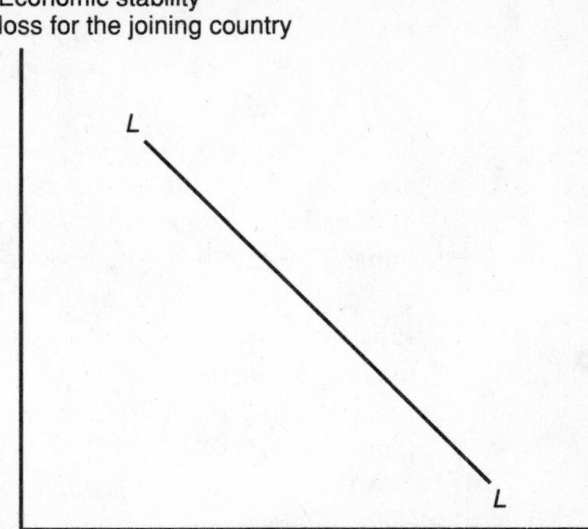

FIGURE 21-4
The *LL* schedule.
The downward sloping *LL* schedule shows that a country's economic stability loss from joining a fixed exchange rate area falls as the country's economic integration with the area rises.

pushes L^1L^1 upward to L^2L^2: at any level of economic integration with the currency area, the extra output and unemployment instability the country suffers by fixing its exchange rate is now greater. As a result, the level of economic integration at which it becomes worthwhile to join the currency area rises to θ_2 (determined by the intersection of *GG* and L^2L^2 at point 2). Other things equal, increased variability in their product markets makes countries less willing to enter fixed exchange rate areas—a prediction that helps explain why the oil price shocks after 1973 made countries unwilling to revive the Bretton Woods system of fixed exchange rates (Chapter 20). As we see later in this chapter, the same reasoning also explains some of the bumps and potholes on the road to European monetary unification.

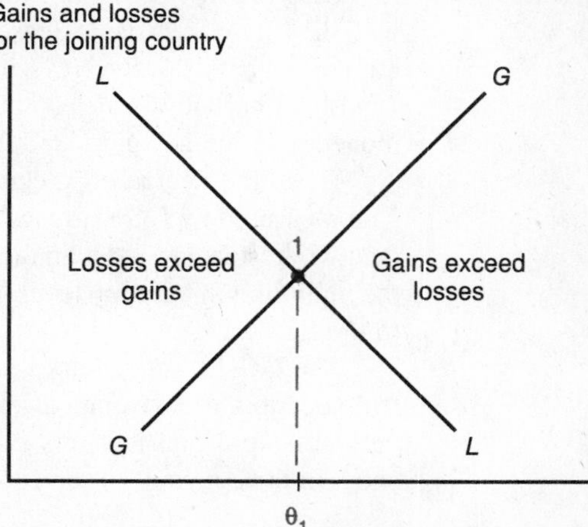

FIGURE 21-5
Deciding when to peg the exchange rate.
The intersection of *GG* and *LL* at point 1 determines a critical level of economic integration θ_1 between a fixed exchange rate area and a country considering whether to join. At any level of integration above θ_1, the decision to join yields positive net economic benefits to the joining country.

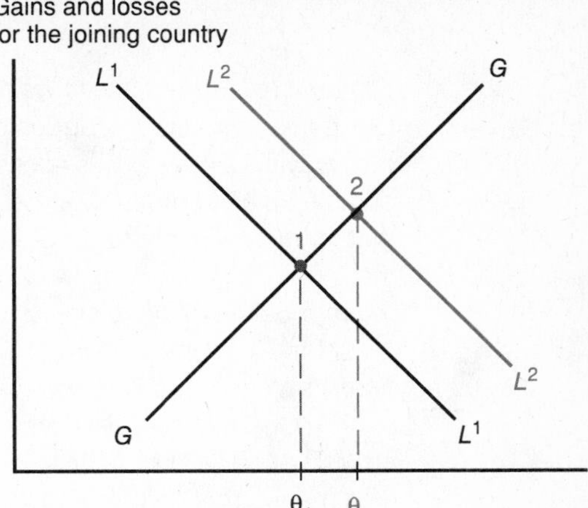

FIGURE 21-6
An increase in output market variability.
A rise in the size and frequency of country-specific disturbances to the joining country's product markets shifts the *LL* schedule upward, because for a given level of economic integration with the fixed exchange rate area the country's economic stability loss from pegging its exchange rate rises. The shift in *LL* raises the critical level of economic integration at which the exchange rate area is joined.

WHAT IS AN OPTIMUM CURRENCY AREA?

The *GG-LL* model we have developed suggests a theory of the optimum currency area. *Optimum currency areas* are groups of regions with economies closely linked by trade in goods and services and by factor mobility. This result follows from our finding that a fixed exchange rate area will best serve the economic interests of each of its members if the degree of output and factor trade among the included economies is high.

This perspective helps us understand, for example, why it may make sense for the United States, Japan, and Europe to allow their mutual exchange rates to float. Even though these regions trade with each other, the extent of that trade is modest compared with regional GNPs and interregional labor mobility is low. In 1990, for example, U.S. merchandise trade with Western Europe (measured as the average of imports and exports) amounted to only about 2 percent of U.S. GNP; U.S. merchandise trade with Japan was even smaller.

The more interesting question, and the critical one for judging the economic success of the EMS, is whether Europe itself makes up an optimum currency area. We take up this topic next.

Case Study

IS EUROPE AN OPTIMUM CURRENCY AREA?

The theory of optimum currency areas gives us a useful framework for thinking about the considerations that determine whether a group of countries will gain or lose by fixing their mutual exchange rates. A nation's gains and losses from pegging its currency to an exchange rate area are hard to measure numerically, but by combining our theory with information on actual economic performance we can evaluate the claim that Europe is an optimum currency area.

The Extent of Intra-European Trade

Our earlier discussion suggested that a country is more likely to benefit from joining a currency area if the area's economy is closely integrated with its own. The overall degree of economic integration can be judged by looking at the integration of product markets, that is, the extent of trade between the joining country and the currency area, and at the integration of factor markets, that is, the ease with which labor and capital can migrate between the joining country and the currency area.

Most EC members export from 10 to 20 percent of their output to other EC members. These numbers are larger than those for EC-U.S. trade, which is only around 2 percent of U.S. GNP and an even smaller percentage of EC GNP, but much smaller than the amount of trade between regions of the United States. If we take trade relative to GNP as a measure economic integration, the *GG-LL* model of the last section suggests that a joint float of Europe's currencies against the rest of the world is a better strategy for EC members than a fixed dollar-ECU exchange rate would be. The extent of intra-European trade is not large enough, however, to give us an overwhelming reason for believing the European Community itself is an optimum currency area.

To some degree intra-EC trade may have been artificially limited until now by trade restrictions that will be removed by the 1992 reforms. Evidence supporting the idea that restrictions seriously limited trade comes from comparisons of prices for similar products sold in different EC countries. As late as the end of 1992, for example, a can of Coca Cola cost twice as much in Ireland as in France, while a box of Kellogg's cornflakes was nearly 2.5 times more expensive in Italy than in Britain.[15] It is still too early to tell how effective the 1992 measures will be in bringing Europe closer to being an optimum currency area.

How Mobile Is Europe's Labor Force?

Earlier we mentioned that the European Community did not succeed in removing internal passport checks by the original deadline of January 1, 1993. The main barriers to labor mobility within Europe are probably not due to border controls, however. Differences in language and culture discourage labor movements between European countries to a greater extent than is true, for example, between regions of the United States. In one econometric study comparing unemployment patterns in U.S. regions with those in EC countries, Barry Eichengreen of the University of California at Berkeley found that differences in regional unemployment rates are smaller and less persistent in the United States than are differences between national unemployment rates in the European Community.[16]

Even *within* European countries labor mobility appears limited, partly because of government regulations. For example, the requirement in some countries that workers

[15] See "Whither the Cross-Border Cornflake?" *Financial Times,* January 4, 1993, p. 7.

[16] See Eichengreen, "One Money for Europe? Lessons of the U.S. Currency Union," *Economic Policy* 10 (April 1990), pp. 118–166. Further study of the U.S. labor market has shown that regional unemployment is eliminated almost entirely by worker migration rather than by changes in regional real wages. This pattern of labor market adjustment is unlikely to be possible in Europe in the near future. See Olivier Jean Blanchard and Lawrence F. Katz, "Regional Evolutions," *Brookings Papers on Economic Activity* 1:1992, pp. 1–75.

TABLE 21-2 **People changing region of residence in 1986 (percent of total population)**

Britain	*France*	*Germany*	*Italy*	*Japan*	*United States*
1.1	1.3	1.1	0.6	2.6	3.0

Source: Organization for Economic Cooperation and Development. *OECD Employment Outlook.* Paris: OECD, July 1990, Table 3.3.

establish residence before receiving unemployment benefits makes it harder for unemployed workers to seek jobs in regions that are far from their current homes. Table 21-2 presents evidence on the frequency of regional labor movement in the largest EC countries, as compared with Japan and the United States. Although these data must be interpreted with caution because the definition of "region" differs from country to country, they do suggest that in a typical year Japanese and Americans were significantly more footloose than Europeans.

Other Considerations

While the *GG-LL* model is useful for organizing our thinking about optimum currency areas, it is not the whole story. At least two other elements affect our evaluation of the EMS currency area's past and prospective performance.

Similarity of Economic Structure. The *GG-LL* model tells us that extensive trade with the EMS makes it easier for a member to adjust to output market disturbances that affect it and its EMS partners differently. But it does not tell us what factors will reduce the frequency and size of member-specific product market shocks.

A key element in minimizing such disturbances is similarity in economic structure, especially in the types of products produced. EMS countries are not entirely dissimilar in manufacturing structure, as evidenced by the very high volume of *intraindustry trade*—trade in similar products—within Europe (see Chapter 6). There are also important differences, however: the countries of northern Europe are better endowed with capital and skilled labor than the countries in Europe's South, and EC products that make intensive use of low-skill labor thus are likely to come from Portugal, Spain, Greece, or southern Italy. It is not yet clear whether completion of the single European market will remove these differences by redistributing capital and labor across Europe or increase them by encouraging regional specialization to exploit economies of scale in production.

Fiscal Federalism. Another consideration in evaluating the EMS is the European Community's ability to transfer economic resources from members with healthy economies to those suffering economic setbacks. In the United States, for example, states faring poorly relative to the rest of the nation automatically receive support from Washington in the form of welfare benefits and other federal transfer payments that ultimately come out of the taxes other states pay. Such **fiscal federalism** can help offset the economic stability loss due to fixed exchange rates, as it does in the United States. Unfortunately,

Can Europe Learn Lessons from America's Fiscal Federalism?

In 1992 the California economy faced an especially deep recession as it was jolted by a series of natural disasters and a fall in the demand for its defense-related products. If California had its own currency, the state government might have devalued it to shift demand from elsewhere in the world onto California output. Because California uses the same greenback as the other forty-nine states, however, it did not have this option. Instead, California suffered a high unemployment rate (over 10 percent by the end of 1992) that led many workers and businesses to leave the state.

California's recent slump is a grim example of the economic stability loss due to membership in a currency area. Yet no one seriously suggested that California might be better off if it left the Union and adopted its own currency. By seceding, California would have given up the benefits of U.S. fiscal federalism, which entitles states to a flow of aid from other states in times of economic distress. Such fiscal flows are omnipresent in the U.S. economy and are an important element behind the workability of the American currency area.

A very visible form of aid to unfortunate states is federal disaster relief. The federal tax and transfer system, however, provides implicit insurance against economic misfortune of other types. For example, when California's income grows more slowly than that of other states, the flow of income and corporate taxes it pays to Washington automatically declines relative to theirs. At the same time, certain transfer payments from Washington to California, for example, welfare and veterans' benefits, are likely to rise. Taxpayers elsewhere in the United States must shoulder the higher fiscal burden implied by this increase in net federal cash flows into California.*

Xavier Sala-i-Martin of Yale University and Jeffrey Sachs of Harvard University studied how this insurance mechanism has worked for nine U.S. regions.** They estimated that over 1970–1988, a $1 decline in a region's income led to a 33 to 37 cent fall in tax payments to Washington and a 1 to 8 cent increase in transfer receipts. Thus, at least a third of a region's bad economic luck is offset by the federal fiscal system.

No comparable scheme has been agreed upon by EC governments, although richer EC members do make limited "structural" payments to poorer members. In fact, such extensive insurance would not currently be feasible in Europe because the total revenue of the central EC institutions is only a small fraction of the EC's combined GNP. Thus, the fiscal federalism that helps the U.S. currency area succeed despite the economic diversity of U.S. regions is nearly absent in the European Community.

* Notice that currency depreciation merely spreads the impact of a negative shock over the entire population by replacing unemployment (which mainly affects those laid off) with a terms of trade deterioration. Actual aid flows, in contrast, are a net income transfer to the depressed region from more fortunate ones.

** See their paper "Fiscal Federalism and Optimum Currency Areas: Evidence for Europe from the United States," in Matthew Canzoneri, Vittorio Grilli, and Paul Masson, eds. *Establishing a Central Bank: Issues in Europe and Lessons from the U.S.* (Cambridge, Eng.: Cambridge University Press, 1992).

its limited taxation powers allow the European Community to practice fiscal federalism only on a very small scale (see the box on p. 620).

Summing Up

How should we judge the EMS in light of the theory of optimum currency areas? On balance, there is little evidence that Europe's product and factor markets are sufficiently unified to make it an optimum currency area. Trade with EC partners typically is less than a quarter of each member's GNP, and while capital moves with little interference, labor mobility is nowhere near the high level countries would need to adjust smoothly to product market disturbances through labor migration.

The recent "1992" drive toward economic liberalization has moved the European Community closer to being an optimum currency area in some respects, but it has done very little to promote labor mobility within Europe. Because labor income makes up around two-thirds of GNP in the European Community and the hardships of unemployment are so severe, the low labor mobility between and within EC countries implies that the economic stability loss from EMS membership is high. Evidence of such losses is provided by the persistently high unemployment rates in some EMS countries (see Table 20-3).

The European Community's current combination of rapid capital migration with limited labor migration may actually *raise* the cost of adjusting to product market shocks without exchange rate changes. If the Netherlands suffers an unfavorable shift in output demand, for example, Dutch capital can flee abroad, leaving even more unemployed Dutch workers behind than if government regulations were to bottle the capital up within national borders. Severe and persistent regional depressions could result, worsened by the likelihood that the relatively few workers who did successfully emigrate would be precisely those who are most skilled, reliable, and enterprising. Given that labor remains relatively immobile within Europe, the European Community's success in liberalizing its capital flows may have worked perversely to worsen the economic stability loss due to fixed EMS exchange rates. This possibility is another example of the *theory of the second best* (Chapter 10), which implies that liberalization of one market (the capital market) can reduce the efficiency of EC economies if another market (the labor market) continues to function poorly.

Despite the possibility of economic stability losses, the macroeconomic performance of EMS members since the mid-1980s has been good in several respects. The gradual convergence of EMS inflation rates toward low levels is a source of monetary efficiency gains (recall Figure 21-2). The European Community's single-market program coincided with an apparent renewal in Europe's ability to generate new jobs and investment. Table 21-3 shows how EC investment and employment growth accelerated sharply after 1985, dropping off only as Europe followed the United States into stagnation in 1991. Unfortunately, it is hard to know how much credit the EMS should get for these favorable developments.

Many European leaders concluded nonetheless that the next step in unifying the European Community's internal market should be to replace the EMS itself with a single European currency issued by a single European central bank. As we discuss below, the desire for a single currency sprang from political in addition to economic motives. Is this visionary program advisable, or even feasible? We examine Europe's plans for a

TABLE 21-3 Growth in investment and employment in EC countries, 1980–1992 (percent per year)

	Investment growth	*Employment growth*
1980	2.6	0.2
1981	−5.4	−1.0
1982	−1.4	−0.9
1983	−0.9	−0.4
1984	2.7	0.2
1985	5.7	0.6
1986	5.5	0.9
1987	8.2	1.1
1988	9.8	1.7
1989	8.2	1.7
1990	4.7	1.7
1991	−0.1	0.3
1992	−3.1	−1.2

Source: Organization for Economic Cooperation and Development. *OECD Economic Outlook* 53 (June 1993), Tables R6 and R17.

single currency in greater detail, and then describe how events upset those plans in 1992 and 1993.

European Monetary Union

Countries can link their currencies together in many ways. We can imagine that the different modes of linkage form a spectrum, with the arrangements at one end requiring little sacrifice of monetary policy independence while those at the other end require independence to be given up entirely.

The early EMS, characterized by frequent currency realignments and widespread government control over capital movements, left significant scope for national monetary policies. In 1989 a committee headed by Jacques Delors, president of the European Commission, recommended a three-stage transition to a goal at the other extreme end of the policy spectrum just described. That goal is a **European Monetary Union (EMU),** a European Community in which national currencies are replaced by a single EC currency managed by a sole central bank that operates on behalf of all EC members.

In stage 1 of the Delors plan all EC members would join the EMS exchange rate mechanism (Greece has never joined, while Britain and Italy suspended their memberships in September 1992). In stage 2 exchange rate margins would be narrowed and certain macroeconomic policy decisions placed under more centralized EC control. Finally, stage 3 of the Delors plan involves the replacement of national currencies by the ECU and the vesting of all monetary policy decisions in a European System of Central Banks, similar to the U.S. Federal Reserve System and headed by a European Central Bank.

On December 10, 1991, the leaders of the EC countries met at the ancient Dutch city of Maastricht and agreed to propose for national ratification far-reaching amendments to the Treaty of Rome. These amendments were meant to place the EC squarely on the road to EMU. Included in the 250-page **Maastricht Treaty** were provisions calling for a start to stage 2 of the Delors plan on January 1, 1994 and a start to stage 3 no later than January 1, 1999. In addition to its *monetary policy* provisions, the Maastricht Treaty included steps toward harmonizing social policy within the European Community (such as workplace safety, consumer protection, and immigration rules) and toward centralizing foreign and defense policy decisions that each EC member currently makes on its own.

These proposals have turned out to be controversial, stirring impassioned debate all over Europe. Why did the European Community's leaders press ahead with EMU even though the European Community doesn't currently appear to meet the requirements of an optimum currency area? Three main motives led them to support EMU:

1. They believed a single EC currency would produce greater monetary efficiency gains than fixed exchange rates by removing the threat of EMS currency realignments and eliminating the costs to traders of converting one EMS currency into another.
2. Some EC leaders thought Germany's management of EMS monetary policy had placed a one-sided emphasis on German macroeconomic goals at the expense of its EMS partners' interests. The European Central Bank that would replace the German Bundesbank under EMU would have to be more considerate of other countries' problems.
3. All of the EC countries' leaders hoped the Maastricht Treaty's provisions would guarantee the *political* stability of western Europe. Beyond its purely economic functions, the single EC currency was intended as a potent symbol of Europe's desire to place cooperation ahead of the national rivalries that often had led to war in the past.

The Maastricht Treaty's critics denied that EMU would have these positive effects and opposed the treaty's provisions for vesting stronger governmental powers with the European Community. To these critics, EMU was symptomatic of a tendency for the European Community's central institutions to ignore local needs, meddle in local affairs, and downgrade prized symbols of national identity (including, of course, national currencies).

Despite the optimistic atmosphere at Maastricht, the treaty soon was in trouble, in large part because of economic developments that led many Europeans to question whether their countries would be wise to sacrifice any more control over national economic policies.

Case Study

HOW EUROPEAN MACROECONOMIC TENSIONS HELPED DERAIL MAASTRICHT

The Maastricht Treaty could not come into force until all twelve EC countries had ratified it through national referendum or parliamentary vote. EC leaders were stunned in June 1992 when the treaty, in its very first electoral test, was narrowly rejected by Danish voters. Prospects for EMU worsened later in 1992. In September EMS parities were hit by speculative attacks that reversed much of the European Community's progress in completing stage 1 of the 1989 Delors plan for monetary unification, on which the treaty was based. In August 1993 speculators forced another retreat, this time to very wide exchange rate bands. How could EMU now go forward?

At the time of writing, the future of EMU is in serious doubt. The economic stresses that produced the EMS's worst speculative crisis and slowed the drive toward European integration were not accidental, however. These stresses were the direct result of two features of the EMS discussed earlier in this chapter: the high economic stability losses members could suffer by holding exchange rates fixed and Germany's dominance over EMS monetary policy.

German Reunification

The reunification of East and West Germany in 1990 was an economic disturbance that the EMS was poorly designed to handle. As we see below, Germany's EMS partners very quickly felt the effects of the internal German policy decisions that accompanied unification.

The East German revolution of 1989—symbolized by the fall of the Berlin Wall—allowed the two parts of Germany, divided since the end of World War II, again to become a single country. Economic reunification commenced on July 1, 1990, when East Germans traded in their holdings of East German currency for DM (recall Chapter 20).

East German wages, initially far below those in the West, jumped upward as East German workers demanded parity with workers elsewhere in the country. This development was surprising because demand for the inferior products manufactured in the East was low and many East German workers lacked the training, diligence, and modern equipment of those in the West. Furthermore, hoped-for flows of private investment to modernize eastern Germany didn't materialize. The result was high unemployment in the East (the measured unemployment rate was around 15 percent in 1992) and a dizzying fall in East Germany's output.[17] The eastern Germans' richer western cousins soon found themselves making massive payments to the East—to support and retrain unemployed workers, to renovate the east's antiquated capital stock, and to clean up its polluted environment.

Helmut Kohl, the German chancellor, had promised voters in the West that reunification would be painless. Instead, by 1991 western Germans were transferring an amount well over 5 percent of their income to the east, a figure that appeared unlikely to decline quickly. Because the German government borrowed much of this sum rather than raising taxes, the public fiscal deficit widened sharply. This fiscal stimulus added to demand pressures that had been building up even before 1990.

Disillusion in the West and resentment in the East contributed to aggressive union wage demands and strikes. Additional inflationary pressure came from the liberal spending of the East Germans, who used many of the DM they received from the West to buy the high-quality consumer durables they had been denied under Communism. To halt

[17] The number cited in the text is an underestimate of actual unemployment, since many workers with jobs (at least 5 percent of the labor force) were on "short time," working fewer hours than they would have liked. For a detailed analysis of the internal economic impact of German reunification, see George A. Akerlof, Andrew K. Rose, Janet L. Yellen, and Helga Hessenius, "East Germany in from the Cold: The Economic Aftermath of Currency Union," *Brookings Papers on Economic Activity* 1:1991, pp. 1–105.

rising prices, Germany's Bundesbank hit its monetary brakes in 1992 and pushed interest rates to historically high levels.

At the time, however, the European economies other than Germany's had been weakening for more than a year. One factor behind this weakness may have been the German aggregate demand expansion itself, which had already raised interest rates in Germany and throughout the EMS. (The appendix to this chapter shows how an increase in aggregate demand in Germany can depress the economies of countries that peg their currencies to the DM.) A second factor behind Europe's plight was the continuing slow economic activity in the U.S. and the resulting real depreciation of the dollar, which shifted world demand away from European goods and toward American goods.

Germany's decision to tighten its monetary policy sharply therefore placed Britain, France, and Germany's other EMS partners in a dilemma: should they tighten their own monetary policies in tandem with Germany's to maintain EMS exchange rates, or should they devalue their currencies against the DM as a way of stimulating international demand for their products? You will recognize this dilemma as exactly the type of situation that imposes economic stability losses in a multiregion currency area. While criticizing Germany's tight monetary policy, its EMS partners allowed their own interest rates to rise in order to resist devaluation. With EMU seemingly within reach, governments wanted to avoid being forced into realignment.

Unfortunately, the defense of EMS exchange parities deepened the European downturn outside of Germany. Germany denied any responsibility for Europe's macroeconomic problems and refused to make substantial policy changes.

Public Opinion and the Maastricht Treaty

The lesson of this policy conflict was not lost on European voters and legislatures. Europeans outside Germany feared that a European central bank would not be much better than the Bundesbank at meeting the monetary policy needs of individual countries; they also feared that a powerful, reunited Germany would have the decisive voice in running EMU. The Germans themselves worried that a European central bank would be less zealous than their own Bundesbank in fighting inflation. With unemployment on the rise everywhere, Europeans became more willing to believe EMU opponents who blamed job losses on the European Community's liberal trade and migration policies. Public disaffection with the Maastricht Treaty increased, and in June 1992 Denmark, the first country to vote on the accord, rejected it by a small margin. The Danish rejection raised a serious legal problem because amendments to the Treaty of Rome require the unanimous approval of all twelve EC members.

As EC lawyers and diplomats searched for a way around this problem, the treaty ran into unexpected trouble in France, where a referendum was scheduled for September 20. Public opinion polls taken in August showed that French voters, angry at their government over its management of the economy, were equally divided between supporters and opponents of the treaty. Rejection by France would have killed the treaty and possibly weakened the determination of EMS countries to maintain their fixed exchange rates.

Black Wednesday

The prospect of a French refusal to ratify the Maastricht Treaty encouraged foreign exchange market participants to gamble that weak currencies would be devalued. The first currencies to be hit by all-out speculative attacks were the Finnish markka and the

Swedish krona. Neither country belonged to the EMS, but both desired EC membership and had pegged their currencies to the ECU to prove they were ready for admission. Finland gave up its fight quickly, letting the markka depreciate steeply against the ECU on September 8. Sweden was temporarily successful in defending the krona, but speculation died down only after its central bank, the Riksbank, allowed interest rates on overnight loans to reach 500 percent per annum (roughly 1.4 percent *per day*). At the same time, the British and Italian governments were struggling to keep their currencies above the floors of their EMS bands.

Pressure on the pound and lira continued during the week. By the evening of Friday, September 11, the Bundesbank had spent DM 24 billion (roughly $16 billion) in following EMS intervention rules and supporting the lira. The Bundesbank was reluctant to spend any more, however, and over the weekend the EMS agreed to let Italy devalue its currency by 7 percent against the ECU. The lira's parity change was the first EMS realignment under market pressure since January 1987, and it signaled to participants in the foreign exchange market that attacks on other EMS currencies might succeed.

On Tuesday, September 15, Bundesbank President Helmut Schlesinger told a German newspaper that a broad currency realignment would be needed to ease existing macroeconomic tensions in the EMS. His careless remark set off the most massive speculative attack yet. On September 16, a day now known as "Black Wednesday" because of the damage done to the EMS, the pound was allowed to float after the Bank of England lost billions of dollars defending it. This action followed repeated pledges by the British government not to realign. Despite having devalued only two days before, Italy took the lira out of the EMS exchange rate mechanism rather than lose more reserves. Spain devalued its peseta and reimposed exchange controls to slow its own reserve losses.

Even the French franc came under attack, despite a French inflation rate lower than Germany's (see Figure 21-1). Heavy and prolonged intervention by the Bank of France and the Bundesbank, coupled with a sharp rise in French interest rates, eventually pried the franc from the bottom of its DM band. After the most turbulent week in EMS history, French voters narrowly approved the Maastricht Treaty on September 20 and thereby gave EMU another chance to stumble ahead.

Continuing Crisis

Currency turmoil continued in Europe through 1992 and into the spring of 1993. Later in 1992 the Portuguese escudo was devalued, the Spanish peseta devalued again, and the Swedish krona and Norwegian krone set afloat. In the first half of 1993, the Irish punt was devalued, the escudo devalued a second time, and the Spanish peseta devalued a third time. The French franc and Danish krone remained under periodic speculative pressure. The backdrop for these events was deepening recession in the EMS economies, coupled with the Bundesbank's insistence on making only gradual cuts in German interest rates.

In the spring of 1993 Denmark held a second referendum on the Maastricht Treaty after other EC countries gave Denmark the right to refuse participation in the common monetary and defense institutions the treaty would create. This time the Danes went along, and Britain's Parliament followed suit by narrowly voting for ratification. By August 1993 all EC members but Germany had approved the Maastricht Treaty.

The plan's vision of monetary union by the end of the century seemed increasingly out of touch, however, with the realities of EMS policy making. At the end of July speculators attacked the French franc and other EMS currencies with unprecedented fury after a new disagreement over interest rates between Germany and other EMS members. On Friday, July 30, alone, the Bundesbank sold DM 50 billion (nearly $30 billion) to help prop up the French franc, while the Bank of France itself used up all of its foreign reserves. The following Monday, August 2, EMS exchange rates (other than the DM/Dutch guilder rate) were floating within drastically widened bands of ±15 percent around the existing central parities. This change in EMS rules was the only scheme EC ministers could find that let France's government avoid a formal devaluation of the franc (a step it had pledged to avoid at all costs) while leaving the Bundesbank free to lower German interest rates slowly.

EC leaders insisted that these setbacks would not alter the Maastricht Treaty's timetable for EMU. To observers, however, it was unclear how long the amended EMS rules would stay in effect and hard to see the route that would lead from monetary disarray to monetary union in little more than five years. The dramatic economic events of 1992 and 1993 convinced many Europeans that the EMS was flawed; many were skeptical that the move to EMU would be an improvement. Maastricht Treaty or no, the economic and political climates in Europe in the mid-1990s make it very unlikely that EMU will be born this century.

Summary

1. European Community countries have three reasons for favoring mutually fixed exchange rates: they believe monetary cooperation will give them a heavier weight in international economic negotiations; they view fixed exchange rates as a complement to EC initiatives aimed at building a common European market; and fixed rates simplify the administration of the European Community's Common Agricultural Policy.

2. The European Moneary System was inaugurated in March 1979 and originally included Belgium, Denmark, France, Germany, Ireland, Italy, Luxembourg, and the Netherlands. Until recently, these countries all maintained their mutual exchange rates within a band of ±2.25 percent. Britain, Portugal, and Spain joined a decade later, but with wider currency bands of ±6 percent. Capital controls were an essential ingredient in maintining the system until the mid-1980s, but since then many controls have been abolished as part of the European Community's wider "1992" program of market unification. During the currency crisis that broke out in September 1992, however, Britain and Italy allowed their currencies to float and several countries reimposed or tightened controls over international payments. In August 1993 most EMS currency bands were widened to ±15 percent in the face of continuing speculative attacks.

3. In practice all EMS currencies are pegged to the DM. As a result Germany is able to set monetary policy for the EMS, just as the United States did in the Bretton Woods system. The *credibility theory of the EMS* holds that participating governments profit from the German Bundesbank's reputation as an inflation fighter when they peg their currencies to the DM. In fact, inflation rates in EMS countries have tended to converge around Germany's generally low inflation rate. Critics of Germany charge, however, that it has abused its dominant position by neglecting the effects its policies have on other EMS countries.

4. The theory of *optimum currency areas* implies that countries will wish to join fixed exchange rate areas closely linked to their own economies through trade and factor mobility. A country's decision to join an exchange rate area is determined by the difference between the *monetary efficiency gain* from joining and the *economic stability loss* from joining. The *GG-LL* diagram relates both of these factors to the degree of economic integration between the joining country and the larger fixed exchange rate zone. Only when economic integration passes a critical level is it beneficial to join.

5. The European Community does not appear to satisfy all of the criteria for an optimum currency area. Although 1992 removed many barriers to market integration within the European Community, intra-EC trade still is not very extensive. In addition, labor mobility between and even within EC countries appears more limited than within other large currency areas, such as the United States. Finally, the level of *fiscal federalism* in the European Community is too small to cushion member countries from adverse economic events. Between 1985 and the early 1990s, however, good economic performance within the EMS allowed EC leaders to seek greater economic and monetary unity without significant voter opposition.

6. EC leaders currently hope to replace the EMS by a *European Monetary Union (EMU).* The EMU would imply a single European currency, the ECU, issued by a European System of Central Banks under a governing European Central Bank. In December 1991 EC heads of state signed the *Maastricht Treaty,* and agreed to seek approval from their electorates for concrete plans that would make EMU a reality by 1999.

7. After public opposition to the Maastricht Treaty grew in the summer of 1992, the EMS was hit by a currency crisis that left its exchange rate mechanism in disarray. By August 1993 all EC members but Germany had nonetheless ratified the treaty. Continuing economic and political tensions in Europe make it unlikely, however, that the ambitious goal of EMU will be reached anytime soon.

Key Terms

credibility theory of the EMS
optimum currency areas
monetary efficiency gain
economic stability loss
fiscal federalism
European Monetary Union (EMU)
Maastricht Treaty

Problems

1. Why might EMS provisions for the extension of central bank credits from strong- to weak-currency members increase the stability of EMS exchange rates?
2. In the EMS before September 1992 the lira/DM exchange rate could fluctuate by up to 2.25 percent up *or* down. Assume that the lira/DM central parity and band are set in this way and cannot be changed. What is the maximum possible difference

between the interest rates on *one-year* lira and DM deposits? What is the maximum possible difference between the interest rates on *six-month* lira and DM deposits? On three-month deposits? Do the answers surprise you? Give an intuitive explanation.

3. Continue with the assumptions of the last question. In Italy the interest rate on five-year government bonds is 11 percent per annum; in Germany the rate on five-year government bonds is 8 percent per annum. What are the implications for the credibility of the current lira/DM exchange parity?

4. Do your answers to the last two questions require an assumption that interest rates and expected exchange rate changes are linked by interest parity? Why or why not?

5. Finland joins the EMS, but soon after the EMS benefits from a favorable shift in the world demand for non-Finnish EMS exports. What happens to the exchange rate of the Finnish markka against non-EMS currencies? How is Finland's output affected? How does the size of this effect depend on the volume of trade between Finland and the other EMS economies?

6. Use the *GG-LL* diagram to show how an increase in the size and frequency of unexpected shifts in a country's money demand function affects the level of economic integration with a currency area at which the country will wish to join.

7. During the speculative pressure on the EMS exchange rate mechanism (ERM) shortly before Britain allowed the pound to float in September 1992, the *Economist,* a London weekly news magazine, opined as follows:

> The [British] government's critics want lower interest rates, and think this would be possible if Britain devalued sterling, leaving the ERM if necessary. They are wrong. Quitting the ERM would soon lead to higher, not lower, interest rates, as British economic management lost the degree of credibility already won through ERM membership. Two years ago British government bonds yielded three percentage points more than German ones. Today the gap is half a point, reflecting investors' belief that British inflation is on its way down—permanently. (See "Crisis? What Crisis?" *Economist,* August 29, 1992, p. 51.)

a. Why might the British government's critics have thought it possible to lower interest rates after taking sterling out of the ERM? (Britain was in a deep recession at the time the article appeared.)

b. Why does the *Economist* think the opposite would occur soon after Britain exited the ERM?

c. In what way might ERM membership have gained credibility for British policy makers? (Britain entered the ERM in October 1990.)

d. Why would a high level of British nominal interest rates relative to German rates have suggested an expectation of high future British inflation? Can you think of other explanations?

e. Suggest two reasons why British interest rates might have been somewhat higher than German rates at the time of writing, despite the alleged "belief that British inflation is on the way down—permanently."

8. Imagine that the EMS becomes a monetary union with a single currency but that it creates no European Central Bank to manage this currency. Instead, the task is left to the various national central banks, each of which is allowed to issue as much of the European currency as it likes, and to conduct open-market operations. What problems could you foresee arising from such a scheme?

9. Why would the failure to create a unified EC labor market be particularly harmful to the prospects for a smoothly functioning EMU?

10. In the model of this chapter's appendix, what happens to Britain's output and interest rate if foreign exchange market participants decide the pound will be devalued against the DM in the future? What is the effect on Germany's economy? You should reach the conclusion that EMS currency crises harm all member countries.

Further Reading

Charles R. Bean. ''Economic and Monetary Union in Europe.'' *Journal of Economic Perspectives* 6 (Fall 1992), pp. 31–52. Overview of the debate over European monetary unification, written just before the currency crisis in the autumn of 1992.

Barry Eichengreen and Charles Wyplosz. ''The Unstable EMS.'' *Brookings Papers on Economic Activity* 1:1993, pp. 51–143. Detailed postmortem on the 1992 EMS currency collapse.

Martin Feldstein. ''Does One Market Require One Money?'' in *Policy Implications of Trade and Currency Zones.* Kansas City: Federal Reserve Bank of Kansas City, 1991, pp. 77–84. A prominent U.S. economist marshals the arguments against EMU.

Francesco Giavazzi and Alberto Giovannini. *Limiting Exchange Rate Flexibility: The European Monetary System.* Cambridge: MIT Press, 1989. A comprehensive and fascinating account of EMS institutions and experience.

Peter B. Kenen. *EMU after Maastricht.* New York: Group of Thirty, 1992. A thorough economic analysis of the Maastricht summit and the Maastricht Treaty's vision of EMU.

David Marsh. *The Bundesbank: The Bank That Rules Europe.* London: Heinemann, 1992. A journalist's account of the German central bank's role in formulating national and European economic policy.

Edward Tower and Thomas D. Willett. *The Theory of Optimal Currency Areas and Exchange Rate Flexibility,* Princeton Special Papers in International Economics 11. International Finance Section, Department of Economics, Princeton University, May 1976. Surveys the theory of optimum currency areas.

Appendix to Chapter 21 ●
How German Reunification May Have Deepened the European Recession of the Early 1990s

The chapter described how the German aggregate demand expansion that followed the country's reunification in 1990 possibly depressed the economies of its EMS partners. It may surprise you that under fixed exchange rates a boom in one country can push its trading partners into a slump. This appendix explains the economic forces that can bring about this result.

To understand the effects of German reunification on the EMS, we must use the *IS-LM* model developed in Appendix I to Chapter 17. The *DD-AA* model is inappropriate for our purpose because it does not take into account the negative effects of higher real interest rates on consumption and investment. As we see below, these interest rate effects on aggregate demand are central to the analysis.

For simplicity imagine that the EMS consists of two countries, Germany and the United Kingdom. Germany has an independent monetary policy, but U.K. monetary policy is devoted completely to maintaining the pound/DM exchange rate at the fixed level $E^0_{£/DM}$. (To avoid unimportant complications we ignore the EMS exchange rate bands.)

The equation for Britain's *IS* curve takes the form

$$Y_{UK} = D_{UK}(E^0_{£/DM}P_G/P_{UK}, Y_{UK} - T_{UK}, Y_G - T_G, R_£ - \pi^e_{UK}, G_{UK}). \qquad \textbf{(21A-1)}$$

As in the two-country model of Chapter 20 (recall equations (20-1) and (20-2)), we recognize that an increase in German disposable income, $Y_G - T_G$, raises the aggregate demand for British goods and services by raising Germany's demand for imports. We also take notice in (21A-1) of the effect of U.K. government purchases on aggregate demand for British output. Germany's *IS* curve has a form similar to Britain's,

$$Y_G = D_G(P_{UK}/E^0_{£/DM}P_G, Y_G - T_G, Y_{UK} - T_{UK}, R_{DM} - \pi^e_G, G_G). \qquad \textbf{(21A-2)}$$

Figure 21A-1 shows both of these *IS* curves as downward-sloping schedules (recall Appendix I to Chapter 17).

The U.K. and German money market equilibrium conditions are $M^s_{UK}/P_{UK} = L_{UK}(Y_{UK}, R_£)$ and $M^s_G/P_G = L_G(Y_G, R_{DM})$. The *LM* curves along which national money markets clear also are shown in Figure 21A-1. The key point to remember about EMS monetary arrangements is that Germany has the power to manage its money supply as it wishes. Because the United Kingdom pegs its currency to the DM, however, it must passively adjust its own money supply to maintain equilibrium in the foreign exchange market.

Assume that participants in the foreign exchange market don't expect the fixed exchange rate $E^0_{£/DM}$ to be changed.[1] Then the nominal sterling interest rate must equal the nominal DM interest rate:

$$R_£ = R_{DM}. \qquad \textbf{(21A-3)}$$

Equation (21A-3) is the equilibrium condition for the foreign exchange market. Britain's intervention to peg the pound/DM exchange rate has the effect of shifting its *LM* curve so that (21A-3) always holds true.

[1] A problem at the end of this chapter asks you to study the effects of expectations that the pound will be devalued.

FIGURE 21A-1
The effects of German reunification on an EMS partner's economy. The rise in German spending and income raises the demand for United Kingdom exports and shifts the U.K.'s *IS* curve to the right. In addition, however, the U.K. must reduce its money supply to match the rise in German interest rates and hold the pound/DM exchange rate steady. This reduction in money supply shifts the U.K. *LM* curve to the left. The net effect on Britain is likely to be a fall in its output.

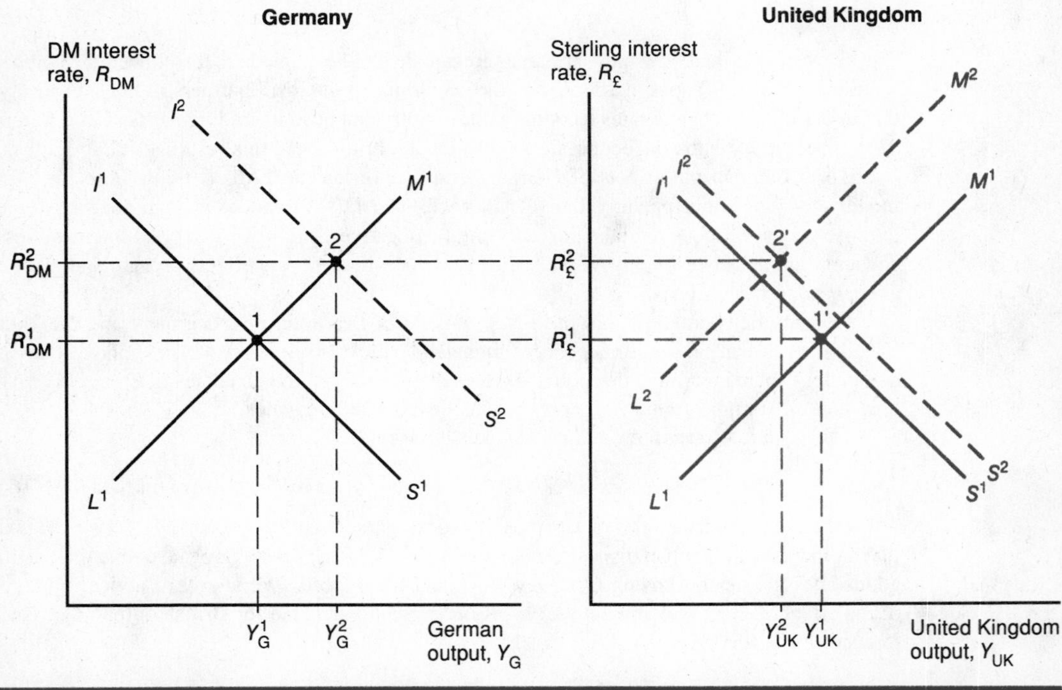

Figure 21A-1 shows that Germany and Britain are initially at points 1 and 1′, respectively, where both countries' output and money markets *and* the foreign exchange market are in equilibrium.

What happens when Germany reunifies and its private and government spending both rise? In Germany the *IS* curve shifts to the right and determines a new equilibrium (point 2) at which German output and interest rates are higher. Germany's *LM* curve does *not* shift because Germany has not changed its money supply. Because the DM is in practice the reserve currency of the EMS, Germany's EMS partners have to adjust their own money supplies to maintain their currencies' DM exchange rates.

This adjustment can be seen by looking at the United Kingdom's position after Germany's economic expansion. As you see in the diagram, two things happen in the United Kingdom:

1. The increase in Germany's income increases German demand for British exports and thereby moves Britain's *IS* curve to the right.
2. To keep its exchange rate fixed despite Germany's higher interest rate, Britain must intervene in the foreign exchange market, buying pounds with DM. The result is a leftward shift in Britain's *LM* curve that maintains equality between British and German interest rates.

As a result of these two shifts, Britain's new equilibrium is at point 2′ and its output there is below its original level.

The result that Britain's output falls is true in Figure 21A-1, but it is not impossible that Y_{UK} rises as a result of Germany's spending increase. To get this alternative outcome, we would simply need a larger rightward shift of Britain's *IS* curve. The fall in British output shown in the figure will occur when trade between Britain and Germany is too limited for German income shifts to have a very strong effect on aggregate demand in Britain. Limited trade between Britain and Germany does not, however, weaken the impact of the German interest rate on the British interest rate and on the British economy. Even when Anglo-German trade is small, Britain must fully match German interest rate changes to maintain the fixed exchange rate of the pound against the DM.

Many economists believe that intra-EC trade is still too limited for German reunification to have produced a positive stimulus for the economies of its larger EMS partners. The argument that German reunification had a depressing effect elsewhere in Europe is not universally accepted, however. The Bundesbank has argued that the positive output effects of Germany's increased import demand outweighed the negative effects of higher interest rates, that is, that German reunification had a net positive effect on output in other EMS countries.[2]

As the chapter discussed, reunification led to inflationary pressures within Germany that the Bundesbank resisted in 1992 through a tighter monetary policy. This change would be shown in Figure 21A-1 as a leftward shift of Germany's *LM* curve, which Britain must match to hold the pound/DM exchange rate fixed. Monetary tightening in Germany worsens the slump in the United Kingdom and, if taken too far, can also throw Germany into recession. This description of German monetary policy and its effects elsewhere in the EMS fits the European Community's predicament at the end of 1992 and in 1993.

[2] See "The Impact of the German Unification Process on Economic Trends in Germany's European Partner Countries," *Monthly Report of the Deutsche Bundesbank* 44 (July 1992), pp. 21–27.

The Global Capital Market: Performance and Policy Problems

Chapter 22

If a financier named Rip van Winkle had gone to sleep in the early 1960s and awakened two decades later, he would have been shocked by changes in both the nature and the scale of international financial activity. In the early 1960s, for example, most banking business was purely domestic, involving the currency and customers of the bank's home country. Two decades later many banks were deriving a large share of their profits from international activities. To his surprise, Rip would have found that he could locate branches of Citibank in São Paulo, Brazil, and branches of Britain's National Westminster Bank in New York. He would also have discovered that by the early 1980s, it had become routine for a branch of an American bank located in London to accept a deposit denominated in Japanese yen from a Swedish corporation, or to lend Swiss francs to a Dutch manufacturer.

The market in which residents of different countries trade assets is called the **international capital market.** The international capital market is not really a single market; it is a group of closely interconnected markets in which asset exchanges with some international dimension take place. International currency trades take place in the foreign exchange market, which is an important part of the international capital market. The main actors in the international capital market are the same as those in the foreign exchange market (Chapter 14): commercial banks, large corporations, nonbank financial institutions, central banks, and other government agencies. And, like the foreign exchange market, the international capital market's activities take place in a network of world financial centers linked by sophisticated communications systems. The assets traded in the international capital market, however, include different countries' stocks and bonds in addition to bank deposits denominated in their currencies.

This chapter discusses three main questions about the international capital market. First, how has this well-oiled global financial network enhanced countries' gains from international trade? Second, what caused the rapid growth in international financial activity that has occurred since the early 1960s? And third, how can policy makers minimize the problems raised by a worldwide capital market without sharply reducing the benefits it provides?

The International Capital Market and the Gains from Trade

In earlier chapters, the discussion of gains from international trade concentrated on exchanges involving goods and services. By providing a worldwide payments system that lowers transaction costs, banks active in the international capital market enlarge the trade gains that result from such exchanges. But most deals that take place in the international capital market result in exchanges of assets between residents of different countries, for example, the exchange of a share of IBM stock for some British government bonds. Although such asset trades are sometimes derided as unproductive "speculation," they do, in fact, lead to gains from trade that can make consumers everywhere better off.

THREE TYPES OF GAIN FROM TRADE

All transactions between the residents of different countries fall into one of three categories: trades of goods or services for goods or services, trades of goods or services for assets, and trades of assets for assets. At any moment, a country is generally carrying out trades in each of these categories. Figure 22-1 (which assumes that there are two countries, Home and Foreign) illustrates the three types of international transaction, each of which involves a different set of possible gains from trade.

So far in this book we have discussed two types of trade gain. Chapters 2 through 6 showed that countries can gain by concentrating on the production activities in which they are most efficient and using some of their output to pay for imports of other products from abroad. This type of trade gain involves the exchange of goods or services for other goods or services. The top horizontal arrow in Figure 22-1 shows exchanges of goods and services between Home and Foreign.

A second set of trade gains results from *intertemporal* trade, which is the exchange of goods and services for claims to future goods and services, that is, for assets (Chapters 7 and 19). When a developing country borrows abroad (that is, sells a bond to foreigners) so that it can import materials for a domestic investment project, it is engaging in intertemporal trade. The borrowing country gains from this trade because it can carry out a project that it could not easily finance out of its domestic savings alone; the lending country gains because it gets an asset that yields a higher return than is available at home. The diagonal arrows in Figure 22-1 indicate trades of goods and services for assets. If Home has a current account deficit with Foreign, for example, it is a net exporter of assets to Foreign and a net importer of goods and services from Foreign.

FIGURE 22-1
The three types of international transaction.
Residents of different countries can trade goods and services for other goods and services, goods and services for assets (that is, for future goods and services), and assets for other assets. All three types of exchange lead to gains from trade.

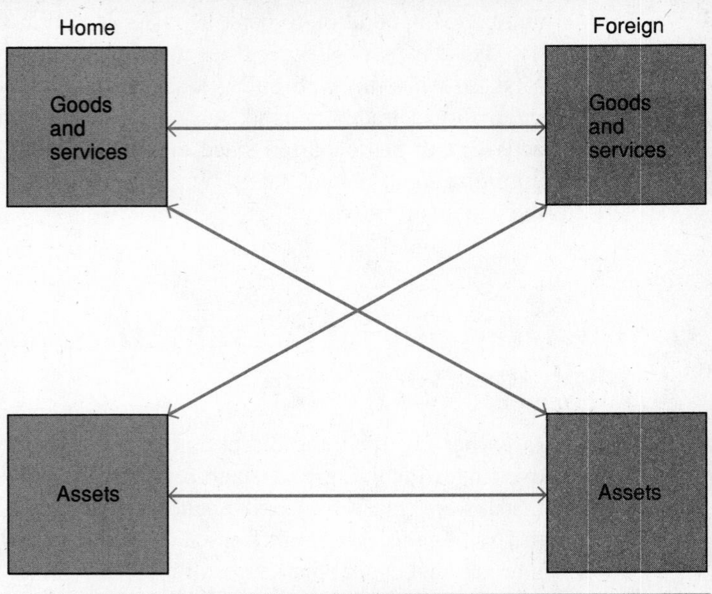

The bottom horizontal arrow in Figure 22-1 represents the last category of international transaction, trades of assets for assets, such as the exchange of real estate located in France for U.S. Treasury bonds. In Table 13-3, which shows the 1991 U.S. balance of payments accounts, you will see under the capital account both a \$62.2 billion purchase of foreign assets by U.S. residents (a capital outflow) and a \$67.0 billion purchase of U.S. assets by foreign residents (a capital inflow). So while the United States could have financed its \$3.7 billion current account deficit for 1991 simply by selling to foreigners \$3.7 billion worth of assets, U.S. and foreign residents also engaged in a considerable volume of pure asset swapping. Such a large volume of trade in assets between countries occurs because international asset trades, like trades involving goods and services, can yield benefits to all the countries involved.

RISK AVERSION

When individuals select assets, an important factor in their decisions is the riskiness of each asset's return (Chapter 14). Other things equal, people dislike risk. Economists call this property of peoples' preferences **risk aversion.** Chapter 18 showed that risk-averse investors in foreign currency assets base their demand for a particular asset on its riskiness (as measured by a risk premium) in addition to its expected return.

An example will make the meaning of risk aversion clearer. Suppose you are offered a gamble in which you win \$1000 half the time but lose \$1000 half the time. Since you are as likely to win as to lose the \$1000, the average payoff on this gamble—its *expected value*—is $(\frac{1}{2}) \times (\$1000) + (\frac{1}{2}) \times (-\$1000) = 0$. If you are risk averse, you will not take the gamble because, for you, the possibility of losing \$1000 outweighs the possibility that you will win, even though both outcomes are equally likely. Although some people (called risk lovers) enjoy taking risks and would take the gamble, there is much evidence that risk-averse behavior is the norm. For example, risk aversion helps explain the profitability of insurance companies, which sell policies that allow people to protect themselves or their families from the financial risks of theft, illness, and other mishaps.

If people are risk averse, they value a collection (or portfolio) of assets not only on the basis of its expected return but also on the basis of the riskiness of that return. Under risk aversion, for example, people may be willing to hold bonds denominated in several different currencies, even if the interest rates they offer are not linked by the interest parity condition, if the resulting portfolio of assets offers a desirable combination of return and risk. In general, a portfolio whose return fluctuates wildly from year to year is less desirable than one that offers the same average return with only mild year-to-year fluctuations. This observation is basic to understanding why countries exchange assets.

PORTFOLIO DIVERSIFICATION AS A MOTIVE FOR INTERNATIONAL ASSET TRADE

International trade in assets can make both parties to the trade better off by allowing them to reduce the riskiness of the return on their wealth. Trade accomplishes this reduction in risk by allowing both parties to diversify their portfolios—to divide their wealth among a wider spectrum of assets and thus reduce the amount of money they have riding on each individual asset. The economist James Tobin of Yale University, an originator of the theory of portfolio choice with risk aversion, has described the idea of **portfolio diversification** as: ''Don't put all your eggs in one basket.'' When an economy is opened to the international capital market, it can reduce the riskiness of its wealth by placing some of its ''eggs'' in additional foreign ''baskets.'' This reduction in risk is the basic motive for asset trade.

A simple two-country example illusrates how countries are made better off by trade in assets. Imagine that there are two countries, Home and Foreign, and that residents of each own only one asset, domestic land yielding an annual harvest of kiwi fruit.

The yield of the land is uncertain, however. Half the time, Home's land yields a harvest of 100 tons of kiwi fruit at the same time as Foreign's land yields a harvest of 50 tons. The other half the time the outcomes are reversed: the Foreign harvest is 100 tons, but the Home harvest is only 50. On average, then, each country has a harvest of $(\frac{1}{2}) \times (100) + (\frac{1}{2}) \times (50) = 75$ tons of kiwi fruit, but its inhabitants never know whether the next year will bring feast or famine.

Now suppose the two countries can trade shares in the ownership of their respective assets. A Home owner of a 10 percent share in Foreign land, for example, receives 10 percent of the annual Foreign kiwi fruit harvest, and a Foreign owner of a 10 percent share in Home land is similarly entitled to 10 percent of the Home harvest. What happens if international trade in these two assets is allowed? Home residents will buy a 50 percent share of Foreign land, and they will pay for it by giving Foreign residents a 50 percent share in Home land.

To understand why this is the outcome, think about the returns to the Home and Foreign portfolios when both are equally divided between titles to Home and Foreign land. When times are good in Home (and therefore bad in Foreign), each country earns the same return on its portfolio: half of the Home harvest (100 tons of kiwi fruit) plus half of the Foreign harvest (50 tons of kiwi fruit), or 75 tons of fruit. In the opposite case—bad times in Home, good times in Foreign—each country *still* earns 75 tons of fruit. If the countries hold portfolios equally divided between the two assets, therefore, each country earns a *certain* return of 75 tons of fruit—the same as the average harvest each faced before intenational asset trade was allowed.

Since the two available assets—Home and Foreign land—have the same return on average, any portfolio consisting of those assets yields an expected (or average) return of 75 tons of fruit. Since people everywhere are risk averse, however, all prefer to hold the 50-50 portfolio described above, which gives a sure return of 75 tons of fruit every year. After trade is opened, therefore, residents of the two countries will swap titles to land until the 50-50 outcome is reached. Because this trade eliminates the risk faced by both countries without changing average returns, both countries are clearly better off as a result of asset trade.

The above example is oversimplified because countries can never really eliminate *all* risk through international asset trade. (Unlike the model's world, the real world is a risky place even in the aggregate!) The example does demonstrate that countries can nonetheless *reduce* the riskiness of their wealth by diversifying their asset portfolios internationally. A major function of the international capital market is to make this diversification possible.[1]

THE MENU OF INTERNATIONAL ASSETS: DEBT VERSUS EQUITY

International asset trades can be exchanges of many different types of assets. Among the many assets traded in the international capital market are bonds and deposits denominated in different currencies, shares of stock, and more complicated financial instruments such as stock or currency options. A purchase of foreign real estate and the direct acquisition of a factory in another country are other ways of diversifying abroad.

In thinking about asset trades it is frequently useful to make a distinction between **debt instruments** and **equity instruments.** Bonds and bank deposits are debt instruments, since they specify that the issuer of the instrument must repay a fixed value (the sum of principal plus interest) regardless of economic circumstances. In contrast, a share of stock is an equity instrument: it is a claim to a firm's profits, rather than to a fixed payment, and its payoff will vary according to circumstance. Similarly, the kiwi fruit shares traded in our example are equity instruments. By choosing how to divide their portfolios between debt and equity instruments, individuals and nations can arrange to stay close to desired consumption and investment levels despite the different eventualities that could occur.

The dividing line between debt and equity is not a neat one in practice. Even if an instrument's money payout is the same in different states of the world, its *real* payout in a particular state will depend on national price levels and exchange rates. In addition, the payments that a given instrument promises to make may not occur in cases of

[1] The Mathematical Postscript to this chapter develops a detailed model of international portfolio diversification. You may have noticed that in our example, countries could reduce risk through transactions other than the asset swap we have described. The high-output country could run a current account surplus and lend to the low-output country, for example, thereby partially evening out the cross-country consumption difference in every state of the world economy. The economic functions of intertemporal trades and of pure asset swaps thus can overlap. To some extent, trade over time can substitute for trade across states of nature, and vice versa, simply because different economic states of the world occur at different points in time.

bankruptcy, government seizure of foreign-owned assets, and so on. Assets like low-grade corporate bonds, which superficially appear to be debt, may in reality be like equity in offering payoffs that depend on the doubtful financial fortunes of the issuer. The same has turned out to be true of the debt of many developing countries, as we will see in Chapter 23.

International Banking and the International Capital Market

The Home-Foreign kiwi fruit example above portrayed an imaginary world with only two assets. Since the number of assets available in the real world is enormous, specialized institutions have sprung up to bring together buyers and sellers of assets located in different countries.

THE STRUCTURE OF THE INTERNATIONAL CAPITAL MARKET

As we noted above, the main actors in the international capital market include commercial banks, corporations, nonbank financial institutions (such as insurance companies and pension funds), central banks, and other government agencies.

1. *Commercial banks.* Commercial banks are at the center of the international capital market, not only because they run the international payments mechanism but because of the broad range of financial activities they undertake. Bank liabilities consist chiefly of deposits of various maturities, while their assets consist largely of loans (to corporations and governments), deposits at other banks (interbank deposits), and bonds. Multinational banks are also heavily involved in other types of asset transaction. For example, banks may *underwrite* issues of corporate stocks and bonds by agreeing, for a fee, to find buyers for those securities at a guaranteed price. One of the key facts about international banking is that banks are often free to pursue activities abroad that they would not be allowed to pursue in their home countries. This type of regulatory asymmetry has spurred the growth of international banking over the last thirty years.

2. *Corporations.* Corporations—particularly those with multinational operations—routinely finance their investments by drawing on foreign sources of funds. To obtain these funds, corporations may sell shares of stock, which give owners an equity claim to the corporation's assets, or they may use debt finance. Debt finance often takes the form of borrowing from and through international banks or other institutional lenders; when longer-term borrowing is desired, firms may sell corporate debt instruments in the international capital market. Corporations frequently denominate their bonds in the currency of the financial center in which the bonds are being offered for sale. Increasingly, however, corporations have been pursuing novel denomination strategies that make their bonds attractive to a wider spectrum of potential buyers. **Eurobonds** are corporate bonds that are *not* denominated in the currency of the financial center in which they are sold, for example, DM bonds sold in London. Dollar-denominated Eurobonds were most important in the late 1960s, but they have lost their predominance since then. Some Eurobonds are not denominated in a single currency but are multicurrency instruments that give the lender the right to request repayment

in one of several currencies. For example, the bond may give its owner the right to be repaid either \$1.50 or £1 five years after the date it is issued if the exchange rate on the issue date is \$1.50 per pound; because this provision gives the lender the option of being paid £1.20 if the pound has depreciated to \$1.25 per pound or \$1.75 if the dollar has depreciated to \$1.75 per pound, he or she is partially protected from exchange risk and therefore may be willing to lend at a lower interest rate. More complicated denomination schemes, called ''currency cocktails,'' are also available. One of these is a Eurobond denominated in IMF Special Drawing Rights, introduced in 1975. Bonds denominated in the European Currency Unit (ECU) of the European Community are gaining in popularity. Corporations sometimes issue *Euronotes* or *Eurocommercial paper* to cover short-term (three to six months) borrowing.

3. *Nonbank financial institutions.* Nonbank institutions such as insurance companies, pension funds, and mutual funds have become important players in the international capital market as they have moved into foreign assets to diversify their portfolios. Of particular importance are *investment banks* such as First Boston Corporation, Goldman Sachs, and Lazard Frères, which are not banks at all but specialize in underwriting sales of stocks and bonds by corporations and (in some cases) governments. In 1933 U.S. commercial banks were barred from investment banking activity within the United States (and from most other domestic transactions involving corporate stocks and bonds), although the U.S. government is in the process of easing some of these barriers. But U.S. commercial banks have long been allowed to participate in investment banking activities overseas, and such banks as Citicorp, Morgan Guaranty, and Bankers Trust have competed vigorously with the more specialized investment banks. Figure 22-2 shows how an international consortium of underwriters announced an offering of short-term Mexican debt in September 1992.

4. *Central banks and other government agencies.* Central banks are routinely involved in the international financial markets through foreign exchange intervention. In addition, other government agencies frequently borrow abroad. For example, foreigners purchase U.S. government bonds, and in the late 1970s the U.S. Treasury sold bonds denominated in foreign currencies (known as ''Carter bonds'') in Europe. Developing country governments and state-owned enterprises have borrowed substantially from foreign commercial banks. Even the governments of some Eastern European countries such as Poland and Hungary, which had Communist regimes until recently, are heavily indebted to Western capitalist bankers.

OFFSHORE BANKING AND OFFSHORE CURRENCY TRADING

One of the most pervasive features of the commercial banking industry in the 1990s is that banking activities have become globalized as banks have branched out from their home countries into foreign financial centers. In 1960, only eight American banks had branches in foreign countries, but now hundreds have such branches. Similarly, the number of foreign bank offices in the United States has risen steadily in recent years.

The term **offshore banking** is used to describe the business that banks' foreign offices conduct outside of their home countries. Banks may conduct foreign business through any of three types of institution:

1. An *agency* office located abroad, which arranges loans and transfers funds but does not accept deposits.

FIGURE 22-2
Advertising an international bond issue.
This September 1992 issue of short-term Mexican debt was underwritten by an international consortium of financial institutions.

2. A *subsidiary* bank located abroad. A subsidiary of a foreign bank differs from a local bank only in that a foreign bank is the controlling owner. Switzerland's Banca del Gottardo, for example, is a subsidiary of Japan's Sumitomo Bank, which bought it in 1984. Subsidiaries are subject to the same regulations as local banks but are not subject to the regulations of the parent bank's country.
3. A foreign *branch,* which is simply an office of the home bank in another country. Branches carry out the same business as local banks and are usually subject to local *and* home banking regulations. Often, however, branches can take advantage of cross-border regulatory differences.

The growth of **offshore currency trading** has gone hand in hand with that of offshore banking. An offshore deposit is simply a bank deposit denominated in a currency other than that of the country in which the bank resides—for example, yen deposits in a London bank or French franc deposits in Zurich. Many of the deposits traded in the foreign exchange market are offshore deposits. Offshore currency deposits are usually referred to as **Eurocurrencies,** something of a misnomer since much Eurocurrency trading occurs in such non-European centers as Singapore and Hong

Kong. Dollar deposits located outside the United States are called **Eurodollars.** Banks that accept deposits denominated in Eurocurrencies (including Eurodollars) are called **Eurobanks.**

One motivation for the rapid growth of offshore banking and currency trading has been the growth of international trade and the increasingly multinational nature of corporate activity. American firms engaged in international trade, for example, require overseas financial services, and American banks have naturally expanded their domestic business with these firms into foreign areas. By offering more rapid clearing of payments and the flexibility and trust established in previous dealings, American banks compete with the foreign banks that could also serve American customers. Eurocurrency trading is another natural outgrowth of expanding world trade in goods and services. British importers of American goods frequently need to hold dollar deposits, for example, and it is natural for banks based in London to woo their business.

World trade growth alone, however, cannot explain the growth of international banking since the 1960s. Ralph Bryant of the Brookings Institution has estimated that between 1964 and 1985, international trade (measured as the total exports of goods and services by all countries outside the Soviet bloc) grew at a compound rate of 12.4 percent per year. In contrast, Bryant's measures of international banking transactions grew at a compound annual rate of around 26 percent per year—just about double the figure for world trade.[2]

Two main factors explain the rapid expansion of international banking beyond what would be required by the growth of world trade. The first is the banks' desire to escape domestic government regulations on financial activity (and sometimes taxes) by shifting some of their operations abroad and into foreign currencies. The second factor is political: the desire by some depositors to hold currencies outside the jurisdictions of the countries that issue them.

Eurodollars and Other Eurocurrencies

The large pool of Eurocurrency deposits is often a cause of alarm. Politicans and the press worry that this ''stateless money,'' beyond the control of any national monetary authority, may foil govenments' efforts to maintain economic stability and may even set off a worldwide inflation. How are Eurocurrency deposits created, and why has Eurocurrency trading expanded so swiftly since the 1960s? Do Eurocurrencies pose a threat to the world's eocnomic health?

HOW BIG IS THE EUROCURRENCY MARKET?

In the early 1990s, the size of the Eurocurrency market stood at around $6 trillion. That number is the total stock of bank deposit liabilities denominated in foreign currencies. Roughly one-fifth of those deposits were held by private nonbanks. The rest

[2] See pages 19–22 in the book by Bryant in Further Reading. As Bryant points out, the complex nature of international banking makes any measure of international banking activity somewhat arbitrary and incomplete. The ones cited in the text are based on Eurocurrency transactions. The conclusion that international banking has grown much more rapidly than world trade would only be reinforced, however, if more comprehensive measures of international banking transactions were used.

were interbank deposits, held by other banks, or were held by official monetary institutions, primarily central banks. The Eurodollar component of the market is by far the largest. Roughly two-thirds of the Eurocurrency market (about $4 trillion) is dollar-denominated. Contrast the market's current size with its size in 1963—just $7 *billion,* of which $5 billion were Eurodollars.

HOW EUROCURRENCIES ARE CREATED

It is easier to understand how Eurocurrency trading came into being once the process of Eurocurrency deposit creation is understood. Discussions of the problems posed by Eurocurrencies are, unfortunately, often clouded by confused notions about the determination of Eurocurrency supplies. As you will see, however, it is misleading to view Eurocurrencies as portions of national currency supplies that have somehow migrated from their countries of origin.

The typical Eurocurrency deposit is a nonnegotiable time deposit with a fixed term to maturity ranging from overnight to five years. The process through which these deposits are created is extremely simple. We deal with the example of Eurodollars, but other Eurocurrencies come into being in exactly the same way.

A Eurodollar Deposit Is Born. Imagine that the German company Daimler-Benz has just sold a car to an American for $40,000. The American pays with a check on an account at Citibank, so Daimler-Benz ends up holding a check for $40,000 and faces a decision about where to put the money. Suppose the company expects that it will need dollars in a month to pay for computer components bought in the United States. It may well decide to hold the dollars for a month, in some interest-earning form, until they are needed to pay for the components.

Two ways Daimler-Benz could hold its $40,000 are by buying U.S. Treasury bills or by buying certificates of deposit issued by American banks. But it could also buy a Eurodollar deposit by depositing the check from the American citizen with a British bank, Barclays Bank, in London. (For reasons to be explained later, this last option is attractive because Barclays will typically be offering a higher interest rate on dollar deposits than that available in the United States.) If Daimler-Benz chooses to deposit the dollars at Barclays, a Eurodollar deposit is born.

The Effect on Bank Balance Sheets. A look at the balance sheets of the banks involved will clarify what has happened. Assume that Barclays has a dollar account with Chase Manhattan in New York, in which it deposits any dollars it acquires. Then the sequence of transactions just described affects three banks' balance sheets. First, Barclays's liabilities rise by the amount of Daimler-Benz's $40,000 deposit, and its assets rise by the amount of the $40,000 increase in its deposits at Chase:

Balance sheet of Barclays Bank, London

Change in assets		*Change in liabilities*	
Deposits at Chase	+$40,000	Customers' deposits (Daimler-Benz account)	+$40,000

Second, Citibank's checking account at the Federal Reserve Bank of New York is debited by $40,000 as the check used to pay Daimler-Benz clears. The funds a private bank deposits with its home central bank are referred to as the private bank's *reserves,* which are part of its assets. (Private bank reserves should not be confused with the central bank's foreign exchange reserves.) Citibank's reserves therefore drop by $40,000, but so do its liabilities to the depositor who bought the car:

Balance sheet of Citibank, New York

Change in assets		*Change in liabilities*	
Reserves at Fed	− $40,000	Customers' deposits (car buyer's account)	− $40,000

Third, the $40,000 in reserves debited from Citibank's account at the New York Fed are credited to Chase's account there. At the same time, Chase's liabilities rise by the $40,000 that Barclays deposits at Chase:

Balance sheet of Chase Manhattan Bank, New York

Change in assets		*Change in liabilities*	
Reserves at Fed	+ $40,000	Customers' deposits (Barclays account)	+ $40,000

Have Any Dollars Escaped Abroad? The $40,000 increase in Barclays Bank's dollar liabilities is the increase in the supply of Eurodollars resulting from Daimler-Benz's decision to hold its dollars in London rather than in the United States. But notice that the company's action has the same effect on the U.S. banking system as would a decision to hold the $40,000 in the form of a deposit at Chase (or some other U.S. bank): a reshuffling of reserves between banks' accounts at the Fed and a corresponding shift in deposits from the bank losing reserves to the one gaining them. In particular, the U.S. *monetary base*—the sum of the banking system's reserves at the Fed and the currency supply—does not change. *Because the U.S. monetary base equals the liabilities side of the Fed's balance sheet (Chapter 18), which has not changed, no reduction in the U.S. money supply has to occur for the Eurodollar supply to rise.*

These observations are important because Eurodollars are often viewed incorrectly as dollars that have somehow "escaped" abroad. In the example, the supply of Eurodollars goes up even though the $40,000 paid to Daimler-Benz is returned to the U.S. banking system when Barclays Bank deposits that sum with Chase.

You may wonder how the picture changes if Barclays does not deposit all of the $40,000 in its Chase account. Indeed, Barclays is likely to have customers who want to borrow dollars; that is why it accepted the dollar deposit from Daimler-Benz in the first place. If Barclays lends part of the $40,000 to customers, the Eurodollar supply can rise by *more* than $40,000, but there is still no migration of dollars from the United States to Europe.

Secondary Eurodollar Deposit Expansion. Let's see how an additional expansion of the Eurodollar pool can come about if Barclays lends part of its new $40,000 deposit. To guard against an unexpected need for dollar liquidity, Barclays is likely to keep some fraction of its new $40,000 deposit—$5000, say—in its Chase account. But it can earn a high return by lending the remaining $35,000 to a Dutch multinational corporation, Philips. Barclays balance sheet now becomes:

Balance sheet of Barclays Bank, London

Change in assets		*Change in liabilities*	
Deposits at Chase	+$5,000	Customers' deposits	+$40,000
Loan to Philips	+$35,000	(Daimler-Benz account)	

After the loan to Philips, the Eurodollar supply is still $40,000 higher than it was before Daimler-Benz deposited its dollars at Barclays.

This may not be the end of the story, however, because Philips has several options for using its newly borrowed $35,000. If Philips spends the money immediately to buy goods from the United States, or if it deposits the money in an onshore U.S. bank, there is no further increase in the Eurodollar supply. The $35,000 is simply shifted from Barclay's account at Chase to some other account in the United States. If Philips does not need to use its loan immediately, it could deposit the $35,000 with Barclays or with some other European bank. Suppose Philips temporarily places the money with the London branch of Deutsche Bank, which in turn deposits Philips's check at Bankers Trust in New York. The balance sheets of Deutsche Bank and Bankers Trust are affected as follows:

Balance sheet of Deutsche Bank, London

Change in assets		*Change in liabilities*	
Deposits at Bankers Trust	+$35,000	Customers' deposits	+$35,000
		(Philips account)	

Balance sheet of Bankers Trust, New York

Change in assets		*Change in liabilities*	
Reserves at Fed	+$35,000	Customers' deposits	+$35,000
		(Deutsche Bank account)	

In this case, the supply of Eurodollars rises by $75,000—the $40,000 deposited at Barclays by Daimler-Benz plus the $35,000 deposited at Deutsche Bank by Philips. As before, the U.S. monetary base is unaffected: the net result of the long chain of transactions is simply a transfer of reserves from Citibank's Fed account (which falls by $40,000) to those of Chase and Bankers Trust (which rise by $5000 and $35,000, respectively). Obviously, the process can continue further if Deutsche Bank lends out part of the $35,000 deposited by Philips rather than holding it all in its Bankers Trust account in New York. The $40,000 paid out by the U.S. auto buyer who initiates all this, however, always finds its way back to the U.S. banking system. Once again, the expansion in the volume of Eurodollars can occur without any dollars ever having to "leave" the United States.[3]

Eurodollars and the U.S. Balance of Payments. Another assertion often made about Eurodollars is that growth in the Eurodollar supply requires continuing U.S. balance of payments deficits. The example shows that this statement is also incorrect. The $40,000 paid to import a car from Germany enters the U.S. current account as a debit. Offsetting this debit is a capital account credit of $40,000, which reflects the $5000 deposit at Chase acquired by Barclays and the $35,000 deposit at Bankers Trust acquired by Deutsche Bank. The net effect on the U.S. balance of payments is nil, even though the Eurodollar supply rises by $75,000.

THE GROWTH OF EUROCURRENCY TRADING

Earlier we outlined the main reasons for the growth of offshore banking activities: (1) the growth of world trade; (2) government financial regulations (including taxes); and (3) political considerations. The growth of Eurocurrency trading illustrates the importance of all three of these factors in the internationalization of banking.

Eurodollars were born in the late 1950s, a response to the needs generated by a growing volume of international trade. European firms involved in trade frequently wished to hold dollar balances or to borrow dollars. In many cases, banks located in the United States could have served these needs, but Europeans often found it cheaper and more convenient to deal with local banks familiar with their circumstances. As currencies other than the dollar became increasingly convertible after the late 1950s, offshore markets for them sprang up also.

While the convenience of dealing with local banks was a key factor inspiring the invention of Eurodollars, the growth of Eurodollar trading was encouraged at an early stage by both of the two other factors we have mentioned: official regulations and political concerns.

In 1957, at the height of a balance of payments crisis, the British government prohibited British banks from lending pounds to finance non-British trade. This lending had been a highly profitable business, and to avoid losing it British banks began financing the same trade by attracting dollar deposits and lending dollars instead of pounds. Because stringent financial regulations prevented the British banks' nonsterling transactions from affecting Britain's domestic asset markets, the government was willing to take a laissez-faire attitude toward foreign currency activities. As a result, London became—and has remained—the leading center of Eurocurrency trading.

[3] There is a slight inaccuracy in the preceding example due to the technicalities of measuring the U.S. money supply. Deposits by foreign banks in U.S. banks are *not* counted by the Fed as part of the U.S. money supply, so when our imaginary American buys his Mercedes, extinguishing his own $40,000 deposit at Citibank and (indirectly) creating a $40,000 deposit at Chase owned by Barclays Bank, the measured U.S. money supply drops by $40,000. However, the monetary base doesn't change, and it is still true that the *second* round of Eurocurrency creation analyzed above (which occurs after Barclays lends $35,000 to Philips) raises the Eurodollar supply by $35,000 with no change in any U.S. monetary aggregate. So it might be more accurate to say that Eurodollar expansion never affects the U.S. monetary base and need not affect the U.S. money supply. The first part of our example shows an instance in which Eurodollar transactions alter the money multipliers linking the base to broader monetary aggregates. We return to this issue in a moment.

The political factor stimulating the Eurodollar market's early growth was a surprising one—the Cold War between the United States and the U.S.S.R. During the 1950s, the Soviet Union acquired dollars (largely through sales of gold and other raw materials) so that it could purchase goods such as grains from the West. The Soviets feared the United States might confiscate dollars placed in American banks if the Cold War were to heat up. So instead, Soviet dollars were placed in European banks, which had the advantage of residing outside America's jurisdiction. Indeed, the folklore of international banking has it that the term *Eurobank* originated as the telex code of a Soviet-controlled Paris bank.

The Eurodollar system mushroomed in the 1960s as a result of new U.S. restrictions on capital outflows and U.S. banking regulations. As America's balance of payments weakened in the 1960s, the Kennedy and Johnson administrations imposed a series of measures to discourage American lending abroad. The first of these was the Interest Equalization Tax of 1963, which discouraged Americans from buying foreign assets by taxing those assets' returns. Next, in 1965, came ''voluntary'' guidelines on the amounts U.S. commercial banks could lend abroad, followed three years later by a set of wide-ranging mandatory controls. All these measures increased the demand for Eurodollar loans by making it harder for would-be dollar borrowers located abroad to obtain the funds they wanted in the United States.

Federal Reserve regulations on U.S. banks also encouraged the creation of Eurodollars—and new Eurobanks—in the 1960s. The Fed's Regulation Q (which was phased out after 1980) placed a ceiling on the interest rates U.S. banks could pay on time deposits. When U.S. monetary policy was tightened at the end of the 1960s to combat rising inflationary pressures (see Chapter 19), market interest rates were driven above the Regulation Q ceiling and American banks found it impossible to attract time deposits for relending. The banks got around the problem by borrowing funds from their European branches, which faced no restriction on the interest they could pay on Eurodollar deposits and were able to attract deposits from investors who might have placed their funds with U.S. banks in the absence of Regulation Q. Many American banks that had previously not had foreign branches established them in the late 1960s so that they could end-run Regulation Q.

With the move to floating exchange rates in 1973, the United States and other countries began to dismantle controls on capital flows across their borders, removing an important impetus to the growth of Eurocurrency markets in earlier years. But at that point, the political factor once again came into play in a big way. Arab members of OPEC accumulated vast wealth as a result of the oil shocks of 1973–1974 and 1979–1980 but were reluctant to place most of their money in American banks for fear of possible confiscation. Instead, these countries placed funds with Eurobanks. (In 1979, Iranian assets in U.S. banks and their European branches were frozen by President Carter in response to the taking of hostages at the American embassy in Teheran. A similar fate befell Iraq's U.S. assets after that country invaded neighboring Kuwait in 1990.)

THE IMPORTANCE OF REGULATORY ASYMMETRIES

The history of Eurocurrencies shows how the growth of world trade, financial regulations, and political considerations all helped form the present system. The major factor behind the continuing profitability of Eurocurrency trading is, however, regulatory: in formulating bank regulations, governments in the main Eurocurrency centers discriminate between deposits denominated in the home currency and those denominated in others and between transactions with domestic customers and those with foreign customers. Domestic currency deposits are heavily regulated as a way of maintaining control over the domestic money supply, while banks are given much more freedom in their dealings in foreign currencies. Domestic currency deposits held by foreign customers may receive special treatment, however, if regulators feel they can insulate the domestic financial system from shifts in foreigners' asset demands.

The example of U.S. *reserve requirements* shows how regulatory asymmetries can operate to enhance the profitability of Eurocurrency trading. Every time a U.S. bank operating onshore accepts a deposit, it must place some fraction of that deposit in a non-interest-bearing account at the Fed as part of its required reserves.[4] The British government imposes reserve requirements on *pound sterling* deposits within its borders, but it does not impose reserve requirements on *dollar* deposits within its borders. Nor are the London branches of U.S. banks subject to U.S. reserve requirements on dollar deposits, provided those deposits are payable only outside the United States. A London Eurobank therefore has a competitive advantage over a bank in New York in attracting dollar deposits: it can pay more interest to its depositors than the New York bank while still covering its operating costs. The Eurobank's competitive advantage comes from its ability to avoid a "tax" (the reserve requirement) that the Fed imposes on domestic banks' dollar deposits.

To understand this competitive advantage, suppose the New York bank faces a 10 percent reserve requirement. If the bank receives a \$100 deposit, it can relend at most \$90 and is obliged to place \$10 in its Fed account, which pays no interest. Suppose the bank has annual operating costs equal to \$1 per \$100 of deposits and the interest rate on bank loans is 10 percent per year. Then the New York bank can offer its depositors an interest rate of at most 8 percent and still cover its costs. At that deposit rate, the bank pays the owner of the \$100 dollar deposit $0.08 \times \$100 = \$8$, while earning $0.10 \times \$90 = \$9$ on the fraction of the deposit it can relend. So the bank is just able to cover its \$1 operating expense out of the difference between what it gets from the borrower and what it pays to the depositor.

In contrast, a Eurobank can offer a higher interest rate on dollar deposits than the New York bank. The Eurobank, which faces no reserve requirement, can lend *all* of a \$100 deposit, and therefore it can earn $0.10 \times \$100 = \$10$ at a loan rate of 10 percent. If the Eurobank pays its depositors interest of 9 percent, the owner of a \$100 deposit gets \$9, and the difference, $\$10 - \$9 = \$1$, just covers the bank's operating cost. Because the Eurobank faces no reserve requirement, it is able to offer its depositors an interest rate that is a full percentage point higher than what the New York bank can offer. Interest rates on Eurodollar deposits are always higher than rates on comparable time deposits located in the United States (in fact as well as in theory), and many depositors have been lured to the Eurocurrency markets by the higher interest rates Eurobanks offer.

Eurobanks can compete with onshore banks on the loan side also by offering lower interest rates to borrowers, but competition in the loan market tends to drive all banks' loan charges to approximate equality. Why are any depositors willing to hold onshore time deposits when they offer lower yields than Eurocurrency deposits? Part of the

[4] Alternatively, the bank could add the same amount to its holdings of vault cash, which also pay no interest. The discussion assumes the bank holds reserves at the Fed.

reason is that the regulations faced by onshore banks make domestic deposits less susceptible to the risk of bank failure. The risk that depositors' claims will not be honored is greater in the unregulated Eurocurrency market, and the higher deposit rates paid there compensate depositors for bearing this risk.

Freedom from reserve requirements is probably the most important regulatory factor that makes Eurocurrency trading attractive to banks and their customers, but there are others. For example, Eurodollar deposits are available in shorter maturities than the corresponding time deposits banks are allowed to issue in the United States. Regulatory asymmetries like these explain why those financial centers whose governments impose the fewest restrictions on foreign currency banking have become the main Eurocurrency centers. London is the leader in this respect, but it has been followed by Luxembourg, Bahrain, Hong Kong, and other countries that have competed for international banking business by lowering restrictions and taxes on foreign bank operations within their borders.

Neither the United States nor Germany has attracted a significant share of the world's Eurocurrency business because both countries apply fairly uniform regulations to all domestic deposits, regardless of their currency of denomination. Recently, however, the U.S. government has tried to help the American banking industry get more of the action. In 1981, the Fed allowed resident banks to set up **international banking facilities (IBFs)** in the United States for the purpose of accepting time deposits and making loans to foreign customers. IBFs are not subject to reserve requirements or interest rate ceilings, and they are exempt from state and local taxes. But an IBF is prohibited from accepting deposits from or lending money to U.S. residents (other than the establishing bank or another IBF). Before 1981, much of the business currently carried out by IBFs was done less efficiently through ''shell'' branch offices located in the Caribbean.

Technically speaking, a dollar deposit in an IBF is not a Eurodollar because the IBF resides physically within the United States. U.S. regulators have imposed rules, however, that fence off IBFs from onshore banks as effectively as if the IBF were overseas. IBFs provide an excellent example of how countries have lured lucrative international banking business to their shores while trying to insulate domestic financial systems from the banks' international activities. Similar international banking enclaves in other countries include the Offshore Banking Units of Bahrain, the Asian Currency Units of Singapore, and the Tokyo Offshore Market.

EUROCURRENCIES AND MACROECONOMIC STABILITY

The large pool of Eurocurrency deposits is often viewed with alarm by macroeconomic policy makers. Two related fears appear to be paramount: (1) The unregulated process of Eurocurrency creation has been producing a vast pool of international liquidity that could set off worldwide inflation. (2) The Eurocurrency system makes it more difficult for national monetary authorities to control their money supplies.

Eurocurrencies and World Inflation. In Chapter 15, we linked a country's inflation rate to the growth of its money supply, defined as the stock of currency and checking deposits. Eurocurrency deposits do not fit easily into this definition of money—which corresponds to the Federal Reserve's money measure M1—because they are relatively illiquid. Instead, Eurocurrency deposits typically are much more like time deposits, and the Fed includes Eurodollar deposits held by nonbank U.S. residents in its broader money-stock measures. But the fact that most Eurocurrency deposits are *near-money* rather than money does not mean their influence on countries' price levels can be ignored. Central banks watch all monetary aggregates, because, to the extent that near-monies substitute for money as mediums of exchange, they can exert an important influence on the price level. Thus, the possibility that creation of Eurocurrencies has had some inflationary effect cannot be dismissed.[5]

There is no clear-cut evidence that the inflationary effect of Eurocurrency creation has been important, but this does not mean the effect could not become important in the future if Eurocurrency growth continues at a rapid clip. Unfortunately, there are few (if any) options individual governments can pursue to limit the growth of offshore deposits of their currencies. If the U.S. government imposed reserve requirements on the dollar liabilities of American banks' foreign branches and subsidiaries, for example, it would succeed only in driving Eurodollar business to banks headquartered in other countries. Eurocurrency growth can be brought under control only if all governments cooperatively impose reserve requirements on the foreign currency operations of banks within their regulatory jurisdictions. But such cooperation, technically complex and politically difficult, is unlikely to occur in the near future. In particular, international agreement on reserve requirements and other financial regulations would be required.

The inflationary dangers of Eurocurrencies, while real, should not be exaggerated. Financial regulation has always induced markets to create unregulated near-monies in the domestic sphere as well as in the international sphere. While such financial innovation causes problems of monetary control in the short run, it has never set off the protracted inflation that some worried observers of the Eurocurrency system seem to fear. The difficulty peculiar to *international* financial innovations like Eurocurrencies is that the creation of near-monies by *offshore* institutions is usually beyond the control of any individual government.

Eurocurrencies and Monetary Control. Because the monetary base equals the central bank's liabilities, a central bank directly controls the monetary base through its transactions in domestic and foreign assets (Chapter 18). The relationship between the base and various monetary aggregates is through *money multipliers* that tell us what size monetary aggregate a given monetary base can support. Reserve requirements on different categories of deposit are of central importance in determining the size of money multipliers, and this implies that one effect of Eurocurrency trading is to make the multipliers less stable. When people shift their money between domestic deposits subject to reserve requirements and Eurobank liabilities that are not, the quantitative link between the monetary base and monetary aggregates is likely shift as well.

To the extent that the existence of Eurocurrencies makes money multipliers less stable, central banks are prevented from controlling monetary aggregates as closely as they might like in the short run. Once again, however, the problem is not intrinsic to Eurocurrencies—purely domestic financial innovations also cause multiplier instability—and the effect of such instability over the longer run need not be large. By reducing

[5] It would be misleading, however, to take the total size of the Eurocurrency market as a measure of the addition to national monetary aggregates from offshore deposit creation. About four-fifths of the measured Eurocurrency market represents interbank deposits. Domestic interbank deposits are not included in measuring domestic monetary aggregates, so interbank Eurocurrency deposits should not be included in monetary aggregates that take account of offshore activities.

Of Samurai and Sushi: Opening Japan's Financial Markets

From the end of World War II to the mid-1970s, Japan's financial system was tightly regulated, both internally and in its relations with foreign capital markets. In the last fifteen years, however, Japanese authorities have promoted the creation of freer domestic financial markets and the introduction of new financial instruments. They also have made rapid progress in integrating Japan's financial markets with the world's.

Starting in the late 1970s the Japanese began to liberalize the capital account by removing restrictions on foreign purchases of domestic assets. In May 1984, under American pressure, the U.S. Treasury and Japanese Ministry of Finance agreed on a long list of further liberalization measures. Specifically, a wider range of direct foreign investments in Japan was sanctioned, Japanese residents were given greater freedom to purchase foreign assets, and restrictions on foreign issues of bonds within Japan were relaxed. In February 1986 the first foreign members of the Tokyo Stock Exchange took their seats. And at the end of 1986 the Japanese opened an offshore banking market in Tokyo, in which Japanese as well as foreign banks can operate as long as they observe a strict separation between their foreign business and any domestic Japanese business.

Closer contact between the Japanese and foreign financial cultures has spawned some colorful terminology. Yen-denominated bonds issued in Japan by nonresidents are called *samurai* bonds. When these bonds are denominated in foreign currencies rather than in yen, they are called *shogun* bonds. Foreign currency bonds issued abroad by Japanese residents are known as *sushi* bonds. Finally, yen bonds issued in the United States by Japanese residents don't have a catchy Japanese name. These obligations, first issued in 1985, are called Yankee yen bonds.

the cost of international asset trades, the Eurocurrency system certainly encourages portfolio shifts that authorities may find undesirable on macroeconomic grounds. But against any macroeconomic disadvantages must be set the fact that the cost savings are to the advantage of consumers, as are the asset exchanges that Eurobanks facilitate.

As we have emphasized above, however, any monetary instability connected with Eurocurrency markets does not extend to the monetary base: that monetary aggregate is firmly under the control of the central bank, which manages the base through its transactions in domestic and foreign assets. When an individual takes dollars out of a time deposit at Citibank in New York and places them in an account at Barclays Bank in London, the Federal Reserve is not involved in the transaction and so no change in its balance sheet need occur. From a balance of payments standpoint, the capital outflow measured when the individual switches funds from New York to London is exactly balanced by the inflow that occurs when Barclays or an ultimate borrower of the dollars uses them to purchase goods and services or assets from the United States. A symmetric argument shows that the U.S. monetary base would not balloon if, for example, a political scare in Europe led to a huge demand shift out of Eurocurrencies and into onshore dollar assets. Thus, the fear that Eurodollars can come "flooding back" into the United States is highly exaggerated.

Regulating International Banking

Increased regulation of international banking may be desirable on grounds that have nothing to do with the effectiveness of month-to-month macroeconomic policy. Many observers believe the largely unregulated nature of global banking activity leaves the world financial system vulnerable to bank failure on a massive scale. Is this a real threat? If so, what measures have governments taken to reduce it?

THE PROBLEM OF BANK FAILURE

A bank fails when it is unable to meet its obligations to its depositors. Banks use depositors' funds to make loans and to purchase other assets, but some of a bank's borrowers may find themselves unable to repay their loans, or the bank's assets may decline in value for some other reason. In these circumstances the bank could find itself unable to pay off its deposits.

A peculiar feature of banking is that a bank's financial health depends on the confidence of depositors in the value of its assets. If depositors come to believe many of the bank's assets have declined in value, each has an incentive to withdraw her funds and place them in another bank. A bank faced with the wholesale loss of deposits is likely to close its doors, however, even if the asset side of its balance sheet is fundamentally sound. The reason is that many bank assets are illiquid and cannot be sold quickly to meet deposit obligations without substantial loss to the bank. If an atmosphere of financial panic develops, therefore, bank failure may not be limited to banks that have mismanaged their assets. It is in the interest of each depositor to withdraw her money from a bank if all other depositors are doing the same, even when the bank's assets are sound.

Bank failures obviously inflict serious financial harm on individual depositors who lose their money. But beyond these individual losses, bank failure can harm the economy's macroeconomic stability. One bank's problems may easily spread to sounder banks if they are suspected of having lent to the bank that is in trouble. Such a general loss of confidence in banks undermines the payments system on which the economy runs. And a rash of bank failures can bring a drastic reduction in the banking system's ability to finance investment and consumer-durable expenditure, thus reducing aggregate demand and throwing the economy into a slump. There is evidence that the string of U.S. bank closings in the early 1930s helped start and worsen the Great Depression.[6]

Because the potential consequences of a banking collapse are so harmful, governments attempt to prevent bank failures through extensive regulation of their domestic banking systems. Well-managed banks themselves take precautions against failure even in the absence of regulation, but because the costs of failure extend far beyond the bank's owners, some banks might be led by their own self-interest to shoulder a level of risk greater than what is socially optimal. In addition, even banks with cautious investment strategies may fail if rumors of financial trouble begin circulating. Many of the precautionary bank regulation measures taken by governments today are a direct result of their countries' experiences during the Great Depression.

In the United States an extensive ''safety net'' has been set up to reduce the risk

[6] For an evaluation, see Ben S. Bernanke, ''Nonmonetary Effects of the Financial Crisis in the Propagation of the Great Depression,'' *American Economic Review* 73 (June 1983), pp. 257–276.

of bank failure; other industrialized countries have taken similar precautions. The main U.S. safeguards are:

1. *Deposit insurance.* The Federal Deposit Insurance Corporation (FDIC) insures bank depositors against losses up to $100,000. Banks are required to make contributions to the FDIC to cover the cost of this insurance. FDIC insurance discourages ''runs'' on banks because small depositors, knowing their losses will be made good by the government, no longer have an incentive to withdraw their money just because others are doing so. Since 1989, the FDIC has also provided insurance for deposits with savings and loan (S&L) associations.[7]

2. *Reserve requirements.* Reserve requirements are central to monetary policy as the main channel through which the central bank influences the relation between the monetary base and monetary aggregates. At the same time, reserve requirements force the bank to hold a portion of its assets in a liquid form easily mobilized to meet sudden deposit outflows.

3. *Capital requirements and asset restrictions.* The difference between a bank's assets and its liabilities, equal to the bank's net worth, is also called its *bank capital.* Bank capital is the equity that the bank's shareholders acquire when they buy the bank's stock, and since it equals the portion of the bank's assets that is *not* owed to depositors it gives the bank an extra margin of safety in case some of its other assets go bad. U.S. bank regulators set minimum required levels of bank capital to reduce the system's vulnerability to failure. Other rules prevent banks from holding assets that are ''too risky,'' such as common stocks, whose prices tend to be volatile. Banks also face rules against lending too large a fraction of their assets to a single private customer or to a single foreign government borrower.

4. *Bank examination.* The Fed, the FDIC, and the Office of the Comptroller of the Currency all have the right to examine a bank's books to ensure compliance with bank capital standards and other regulations. Banks may be forced to sell assets that the examiner deems too risky or to adjust their balance sheets by writing off loans the examiner thinks will not be repaid.

5. *Lender of last resort facilities.* U.S. banks can borrow from the Fed's discount window. While discounting is a tool of monetary management, the Fed can also use discounting to prevent bank panics. Since the Fed has the ability to create currency, it can lend to banks facing massive deposit outflows as much as they need to satisfy their depositors' claims. When the Fed acts in this way, it is acting as a **lender of last resort (LLR)** to the bank. When depositors know the Fed is standing by as the LLR, they have more confidence in the bank's ability to withstand a panic and are therefore less likely to run if financial trouble looms. The administration of LLR facilities is complex, however. If banks think the central bank will *always* bail them out, they will take excessive risks. So the central bank must make access to its LLR services conditional on sound management. To decide when banks in trouble have not brought it on themselves through unwise risk taking, the LLR must be involved in the bank examination process.

[7] Holders of deposits over $100,000 still have an incentive to run if they scent trouble, of course. When rumors began circulating in May 1984 that the Continental Illinois National Bank had made a large number of bad loans, the bank began rapidly to lose its large, uninsured deposits. As part of its rescue effort, the FDIC extended its insurance coverage to all of Continental Illnois's deposits, regardless of size. This and later episodes have convinced people that the FDIC is following a ''too-big-to-fail'' policy of fully protecting all depositors at the largest banks. Officially, however, FDIC insurance still applies automatically only up to the $100,000 limit.

The banking safeguards listed above are interdependent: laxness in one area may cause other safeguards to backfire. Deposit insurance alone, for example, may encourage bankers to make risky loans because depositors no longer have any reason to withdraw their funds even from carelessly managed banks. The recent U.S. S&L crisis is a case in point. In the early 1980s, the U.S. deregulated the S&Ls. Before deregulation, S&Ls had largely been restricted to home mortgage lending; after, they were allowed to make much riskier loans, for example, loans on commercial real estate. At the same time this deregulation was occurring, bank examination was inadequate for the new situation and depositors, lulled by government-provided insurance, had no reason to be vigilant about the possibility that S&L managers might finance foolish ventures. The result was a wave of S&L failures that left taxpayers holding the bill for the insured deposits.

The U.S. commercial bank safety net worked reasonably well until the late 1980s, but as a result of deregulation, the 1990–1991 recession, and a sharp fall in commercial property values, bank closings have risen dramatically of late and the FDIC insurance fund has been depleted. The U.S. government is currently in the process of overhauling its system of banking safeguards. Like the United States, other countries that deregulated domestic banking in the 1980s—including Japan, the Scandinavian countries, the United Kingdom, and even Switzerland—faced serious problems a decade later.

DIFFICULTIES IN REGULATING INTERNATIONAL BANKING

Banking regulations of the type used in the United States and other countries become even less effective in an international environment where banks can shift their business among different regulatory jurisdictions. A good way of seeing why an international banking system is harder to regulate than a national one is to look at how the effectiveness of the U.S. safeguards just described is reduced as a result of offshore banking activities.

1. Deposit insurance is essentially absent in international banking. National deposit insurance systems may protect domestic and foreign depositors alike, but the amount of insurance available is invariably too small to cover the size of deposit usual in international banking. In particular, interbank deposits are unprotected.

2. The absence of reserve requirements has been a major factor in the growth of Eurocurrency trading. While Eurobanks derive a competitive advantage from escaping the required reserve tax, there is a social cost in terms of the reduced stability of the banking system. No country can solve the problem single-handedly by imposing reserve requirements on its own banks' overseas branches. Concerted international action is blocked, however, by the political and technical difficulty of agreeing on an internationally uniform set of regulations and by the reluctance of some countries to drive banking business away by tightening regulations.

3 and 4. Bank examination to enforce capital requirements and asset restrictions becomes more difficult in an international setting. National bank regulators usually monitor the balance sheets of domestic banks and their foreign branches on a consolidated basis. But they are less strict in keeping track of banks' foreign subsidiaries and affiliates, which are more tenuously tied to the parent bank but whose financial fortunes may affect the parent's solvency. Banks have often been able to take advantage of this laxity by shifting risky business that home regulators might question to regulatory jurisdictions where fewer questions are asked. Further, it is often unclear which group of regulators has responsibility for monitoring a given bank's assets. Suppose the

London subsidiary of an Italian bank deals primarily in Eurodollars. Should the subsidiary's assets be the concern of British, Italian, or American regulators?

5. There is uncertainty over which central bank, if any, is responsible for providing LLR assistance in international banking. The problem is similar to the one that arises in allocating responsibility for bank supervision. Let's return to the example of the London subsidiary of an Italian bank. Should the Fed bear responsibility for saving the subsidiary from a sudden drain of dollar deposits? Should the Bank of England step in? Or should the Banca d'Italia bear the ultimate responsibility? When central banks provide LLR assistance they increase their domestic money supplies and may compromise domestic macroeconomic objectives. In an international setting, a central bank may also be providing resources to a bank located abroad whose behavior it is not equipped to monitor. Central banks are therefore reluctant to extend the coverage of their LLR responsibilities. The problems surrounding the 1982 failure of Italy's Banco Ambrosiano, discussed in the box on page 656 illustrate how international banking can lead to gaps in LLR coverage.

INTERNATIONAL REGULATORY COOPERATION

The internationalization of banking has weakened national safeguards against banking collapse, but at the same time it has made the need for effective safeguards more urgent. Offshore banking involves a tremendous volume of interbank deposits—roughly 80 percent of all Eurocurrency deposits, for example, are owned by private banks. A high level of interbank depositing implies that problems affecting a single bank could be highly contagious and could spread quickly to banks with which it is thought to do business. Through this ripple effect, a localized disturbance could, conceivably, set off a banking panic on a global scale.

This nightmarish scenario has haunted central bankers and other government officials since offshore banking began to grow rapidly in the 1960s. Little was done, however, until 1974. In that year a number of banks failed as a result of foreign exchange losses, among them the Franklin National Bank in the United States and Germany's Bankhaus I.D. Herstatt. The failures sent tremors through the international financial markets, and the volume of international lending dropped sharply.

In response to the 1974 banking crises, central bank heads from eleven industrialized countries set up a group called the **Basle Committee** whose job was to achieve "a better co-ordination of the surveillance exercised by national authorities over the international banking system. . . ." (The group was named after Basle, Switzerland, the home of the central bankers' meeting place, the Bank for International Settlements.) The Basle Committee remains the major forum for cooperation among bank regulators from different countries.

In 1975, the Committee reached an agreement, called the Concordat, which allocated responsibility for supervising multinational banking establishments between parent and host countries. (A revised Concordat was issued in 1983.) In addition, the Concordat called for the sharing of information about banks by parent and host regulators and for "the granting of permission for inspections by or on behalf of parent authorities on the territory of the host authority."[8] In further work the Basle Committee has located loopholes in the supervision of multinational banks and brought these to

[8] The Concordat was summarized in these terms by W. P. Cooke of the Bank of England, then chairman of the Basle Committee, in "Developments in Co-operation among Banking Supervisory Authorities," *Bank of England Quarterly Bulletin* 21 (June 1981), pp. 238–244.

The Banco Ambrosiano Collapse

The collapse of Italy's most important private bank in June 1982 is a vivid illustration of how the intricate cross-border links between financial institutions can frustrate bank supervisors and cause financial crises. The Banco Ambrosiano failure is notorious, however, because of the bank president's close connections with a subversive political group and with the Vatican. Roberto Calvi, the president of Banco Ambrosiano, stood at the center of a vast international financial network spanning Europe, the Caribbean, and South America. In 1981, Calvi was convicted of violating Italian foreign exchange regulations. At the same time, government investigators obtained the membership roster of a secret lodge of right-wing freemasons known as Propaganda-2 (or P-2). P-2 numbered Calvi and many other influential Italians among its members, including two cabinet ministers. The government of Prime Minister Arnaldo Forlani was forced to resign, and P-2 was outlawed.

Because Banco Ambrosiano had become the object of such close scrutiny by the government and the press, it soon became known that some of the bank's loans were weak. This revelation led to a deposit run. Italy's central bank, the Banca d'Italia, set up a consortium of Italy's major banks that took over many of Banco Ambrosiano's assets and liabilities and established a new bank, Nuovo Banco Ambrosiano.

The Banca d'Italia exercised its LLR function by ensuring that Nuovo Banco Ambrosiano repaid domestic and foreign residents who had placed deposits with Banco Ambrosiano itself. The central bank did not, however, guarantee the liabilities of Banco Ambrosiano's foreign subsidiaries. Banco Ambrosiano and its subsidiaries allegedly had extensive financial connections with the Catholic Church's Institute for Religious Works (sometimes called the "Vatican bank"). As a result of the many claims raised by Banco Ambrosiano's failure, the Vatican bank's finances came under investigation.

Calvi himself never saw the ramifications of his bank's collapse. In mid-June 1982 he disappeared from Italy. Shortly afterward he was found dead, hanging from Blackfriars Bridge in London, his pockets stuffed with rocks. It has never been determined if he died by suicide or murder.*

* For a lively account of the Banco Ambrosiano scandal and its background, see Rupert Cornwell, *"God's Banker"* (New York: Dodd, Mead & Company, 1984). The 1991 film *The Godfather, Part III* derived part of its plot from the Ambrosiano affair.

the attention of national authorities. The Committee has recommended, for example, that regulatory agencies monitor the assets of banks' foreign subsidiaries as well as their branches. Much of the group's work has been devoted to developing better data on the balance sheets of multinational banks, a prerequisite to more effective supervision.

A major step toward reconciling countries' supervisory practices was taken in January 1988 when the Basle Committee agreed to a set of common standards for assessing bank capital adequacy. These standards require international banks to hold capital equal to at least 8 percent of their risk-weighted assets plus off-balance-sheet commitments. This 8 percent requirement is high by historical standards for some banks (for example, Japan's). But the narrow escape from financial crisis during the worldwide stock market crash of October 1987 presented the Committee with a persuasive case for tough standards.

While the work of the Basle Committee has improved the supervision of multinational banks, little has been done to clarify the division of LLR responsibilities among countries. Following the 1974 bank failures, central bankers discussed the provision of international LLR facilities but declined to announce any definite agreement. There is speculation that such an agreement exists but that central bankers have kept it secret to avoid suggesting an automatic bailout for banks that take unwise risks and get into trouble.

The international activities of nonbank financial institutions are another potential trouble spot. International cooperation in bank supervision has come a long way since the early 1970s, but regulators are just starting to grapple with the problems raised by nonbank financial firms. Their task is, however, an important one. The failure of a major securities house, for example, like the failure of a bank, could seriously disrupt national payments and credit networks. Increasing **securitization** (in which bank assets are repackaged in readily marketable forms) has made it harder for regulators to get an accurate picture of global financial flows by examining bank balance sheets alone. As a result, the need for authorities to collect and pool data on internationally active nonbanks has become acute. In 1992 the European Community moved to impose uniform capital requirements on securities firms and on banks' trading operations.

As we will see in Chapter 23, the world banking system faced a major crisis in the early 1980s as a result of some developing countries' debt-servicing difficulties. Several major banks' holdings of Brazilian or Mexican debt exceeded their capital, and a payments halt would have called into question the ability of those banks to meet deposit obligations. The International Monetary Fund and the central banks of industrialized countries initially played a LLR role in the debt crisis, but with a twist. Rather than lending directly to banks with troubled developing country loans, the IMF and the central banks protected bank solvency by channeling liquidity to the banks' debtors.

Case Study

THE BCCI AFFAIR

The notorious case of the Bank of Credit and Commerce International (BCCI) shows how an unscrupulous multinational bank can exploit regulatory gaps to defraud depositors and stock holders and to bypass national laws.

BCCI operated free of any government's restraint for nearly two decades until it was shut down by regulators from sixty-two countries on July 5, 1991. It was found that the bank had acted as an international conduit for drug and arms money while doctoring its books to conceal the true nature of its financial dealings. Among BCCI's alleged clients were numerous government agencies, such as Peru's central bank, which deposited the country's foreign exchange reserves with BCCI, and the U.S. Central Intelligence Agency. *Time* magazine reported that the bank had a specialized covert division specializing in "bribery, extortion, kidnapping, and even, by some accounts, murder."[9]

Incorporated in Luxembourg and headquartered in London, BCCI was founded in 1972 by a Pakistani businessman who hoped to create an international banking giant geared to the needs of developing countries. A quarter of the new bank's capital was

[9] See "The World's Sleaziest Bank," *Time,* July 29, 1991, pp. 42–47.

put up by California-based Bank of America, which sold its BCCI stock in 1978 after getting wind of some problem loans. In the meantime, BCCI had grown at a dizzying pace: by 1977, the bank had 146 branches in thirty-two countries, including 45 branches in Britain alone. By 1991, the bank was doing business in at least seventy countries.

International banking regulators had suspicions about BCCI's unconventional practices but seemed unable to agree on assigning primary responsibility for overseeing the bank's worldwide activities. In 1986 Luxembourg asked the Bank of England to take on the job, but Britain's central bank declined. Many of the countries in which BCCI did business were incapable of exercising close supervision over its activities. Despite mounting evidence that something was amiss, the Bank of England saw no practical way to police BCCI and pressure it to behave. Besides, the British regulators argued, the Basle Committee's Concordat technically assigned to Luxembourg the main responsibility for overseeing BCCI. Ninety-eight percent of BCCI's business took place outside of Luxembourg, however, and the tiny country's oversight unit, the *Institut Monétaire Luxembourgeois* (IML), simply lacked the resources to supervise BCCI.

In 1987 the IML persuaded seven other countries to join with it in forming a "college of regulators" to oversee BCCI. Even this group was unable to track adequately the bank's far-flung dealings or to see through its falsified financial records. Only in the spring of 1990 did regulators uncover clear evidence of fraud, and it took more than a year longer for them to recognize that BCCI had long been engaged in deception and money laundering on an epic scale. At that point the bank was closed down, depositors in many countries found themselves denied access to their accounts, and the Bank of England faced a storm of criticism for not acting sooner.

Following this scandal, the Basle Committee moved to close the loopholes that had allowed BCCI to flourish. On July 6, 1992, almost the first anniversary of the BCCI shutdown, the Committee announced a new agreement aimed at standardizing the regulation of international banks. The agreement calls for every international bank's global operations to fall under the surveillance of a single home-country regulator, who will have wide-ranging powers to obtain information on the bank's activities. Furthermore, countries have the right to bar banks that are not regulated in this way and to restrict or even close domestic branches of international banks that seem not to be effectively supervised.

Observers fear that even the Basle Committee's latest effort will not prevent future BCCIs. Regulatory agencies lack the resources they would need to keep a close watch over banks' increasingly complex worldwide transactions. For the foreseeable future, determined renegade banks may still be able to find weak links in the chain of international supervision.

How Well Has the International Capital Market Performed?

The present structure of the international capital market involves risks of financial instability that can be reduced only through the close cooperation of bank supervisors in many countries. But the same profit motive that leads multinational financial institutions to innovate their way around national regulations can also provide important gains for consumers. As we have seen, the international capital market allows residents of different countries to diversify their portfolios by trading risky assets. Further, by ensuring a rapid international flow of information about investment opportunities around the world, the market can help allocate the world's savings to their most productive uses. How well has the international capital market performed in these respects?

THE EXTENT OF INTERNATIONAL PORTFOLIO DIVERSIFICATION

Since accurate data on the overall portfolio positions of a country's residents are often impossible to assemble, it is not feasible to gauge the extent of international portfolio diversification by direct observation. Nonetheless, some U.S. data can be used to get a rough idea about changes in international diversification in recent years.

In 1970, the foreign assets held by U.S. residents were equal in value to 6.2 percent of the U.S. capital stock. Foreign claims on the United States amounted to 4.0 percent of its capital stock. By 1989, U.S.-owned assets abroad equaled 11.7 percent of U.S. capital, while foreign assets in the United States had risen to 13.7 percent of U.S. capital.

These percentages seem small; with full international portfolio diversification, we would expect them to reflect the size of the U.S. economy relative to that of the rest of the world. Thus, in a fully diversified world economy, something like 70 percent of the U.S. capital stock would be owned by foreigners, while U.S. residents' claims on foreigners would equal around 70 percent of the value of the U.S. capital stock. What makes the apparently low extent of international portfolio diversification even more puzzling is the presumption most economists would make that the potential gains from diversification are large. An influential study by the French financial economist Bruno Solnik, for example, estimated that a U.S. investor holding only American stocks could more than halve the riskiness of her portfolio by further diversification into stocks from European countries.[10]

The data do show, however, that diversification has increased substantially as a result of the growth of the international capital market since 1970. Further, international asset holdings are large in absolute terms. At the end of 1991, for example, U.S. claims on foreigners were about $2.0 trillion, equal to 34 percent of the U.S. GNP in that year, while foreign claims on the United States were about $2.3 trillion, or 41 percent of U.S. GNP. Stock exchanges around the world are establishing closer communication links, and companies are showing an increasing readiness to sell shares on foreign exchanges. Japan (as noted above) began a gradual but continuing opening of its financial markets in the late 1970s; Britain removed restrictions barring its public from international asset trade in 1979; and the European Community embarked in the late 1980s on a broad program of market unification meant to integrate its financial markets more fully into the global capital market.

The seemingly low extent of international portfolio diversification attained so far is not a strong indictment of the world capital market. The market has certainly contributed to a rise in diversification since the early 1970s, despite some remaining impediments to international capital movement. Further, there is no foolproof measure

[10] See Solnik, "Why Not Diversify Internationally Rather than Domestically?" *Financial Analysts Journal* (July-August 1974), pp. 48–54.

of the socially optimal extent of diversification; in particular, the existence of nontraded products can cut down significantly the gains from international asset trade. What seems certain is that asset trade will continue to expand as barriers to the international flow of capital are progressively dismantled.

THE EXTENT OF INTERTEMPORAL TRADE

An alternative way of evaluating the performance of the world capital market has been suggested by the economists Martin Feldstein and Charles Horioka. Feldstein and Horioka pointed out that a smoothly working international capital market allows countries' domestic investment rates to diverge widely from their saving rates. In such an idealized world, saving seeks out its most productive uses worldwide, regardless of their location; at the same time, domestic investment is not limited by national saving because a global pool of funds is available to finance it.

For many countries, however, differences between national saving and domestic investment rates (that is, current account balances) have not been large since World War II: countries with high saving rates over long periods also have high investment rates. Feldstein and Horioka concluded from this evidence that cross-border capital mobility is low, in the sense that most of any sustained increase in national saving will lead to increased capital accumulation at home. The world capital market, according to this view, does not do a good job of helping countries reap the long-run gains from intertemporal trade.[11]

The main problem with the Feldstein-Horioka argument is that it is impossible to gauge whether the extent of intertemporal trade is deficient without knowing if there are unexploited trade gains, and knowing this requires more knowledge about actual economies than we generally have. For example, a country's saving and investment may usually move together simply because the factors that generate a high saving rate (such as rapid economic growth) also generate a high investment rate. In such cases, the country's gain from intertemporal trade may simply be small. An alternative explanation of high saving-investment correlations is that governments have tried to manage macroeconomic policy to avoid large current account imbalances. In any case, events appear to be overtaking this particular debate. For industrialized countries, the empirical regularity noted by Feldstein and Horioka seems to have weakened recently in the face of the historically high external imbalances of the United States, Germany, and Japan.

ONSHORE-OFFSHORE INTEREST DIFFERENTIALS

A quite different barometer of the international capital market's performance is the relationship between onshore and offshore interest rates on similar assets denominated in the same currency. If the world capital market is doing its job of communicating information about global investment opportunities, these interest rates should move closely together and not differ too greatly. Large interest rate differences would be strong evidence of unrealized gains from trade.

Figure 22-3 shows the interest rate difference between two comparable dollar bank liabilities, three-month Eurodollar deposits and certificates of deposit issued in the United States. As we saw earlier, these rates should differ mainly by the required

[11] See Martin Feldstein and Charles Horioka, "Domestic Savings and International Capital Flows," *Economic Journal* 90 (June 1980), pp. 314–329.

reserve ''tax'' on domestic banks, provided Eurobanks are competitive and efficient. The black line (showing the difference between the offshore and onshore rates) confirms that Eurodollar interest rates are always higher than the corresponding domestic rates, as our theory predicts. The colored line (which adjusts the interest rate difference to account for the required reserve tax) shows that the adjusted differential typically was low after the mid-1970s. Thus, these data provide no indication of large unexploited gains.

Studies of Germany and the Netherlands, countries with open capital markets, also show an approximate equality between onshore and offshore interest rates. The same equality has held for Japan since it completed a major step in its program of phased capital account liberalization in December 1980. France and Italy maintained capital controls until the late 1980s, but onshore and offshore rates, which had tended to move in tandem even before, converged quickly after those countries began dismantling the restrictions.[12]

THE EFFICIENCY OF THE FOREIGN EXCHANGE MARKET

The foreign exchange market is a central component of the international capital market, and the exchange rates it sets help determine the profitability of international transactions of all types. Exchange rates therefore communicate important economic signals to households and firms engaged in international trade and investment. If these signals do not reflect all available information about market opportunities, a misallocation of resources will result. Studies of the foreign exchange market's use of available information are therefore potentially important in judging whether the international capital market is sending the right signals to markets.

Studies Based on Interest Parity. The interest parity condition that was the basis of the discussion of exchange rate determination in Chapter 14 has also been used to study whether market exchange rates incorporate all available information. Recall that interest parity holds when the interest difference between deposits denominated in different currencies is the market's forecast of the percentage by which the exchange rate between those two currencies will change. More formally, if R_t is the date-t interest rate on home currency deposits, R^*_t the interest rate on foreign currency deposits, E_t the exchange rate (defined as the home-currency price of foreign currency), and E^e_{t+1} the exchange rate market participants expect when the deposits paying interest R_t and R^*_t mature, the interest parity condition is

$$R_t - R^*_t = (E^e_{t+1} - E_t)/E_t. \qquad \textbf{(22-1)}$$

Equation (22-1) implies a simple way to test whether the foreign exchange market is doing a good job of using current information to forecast exchange rates. Since the interest difference, $R_t - R^*_t$, is the market's forecast, a comparison of this *predicted*

[12] On the European countries, see Francesco Giavazzi and Marco Pagano, ''Capital Controls and the European Monetary System'' in *Capital Controls and Foreign Exchange Legislation,* Occasional Paper 1. Milan, Italy: Euromobiliare, June 1985, pp. 19–38. The Japanese case is investigated by Takatoshi Ito, ''Capital Controls and Covered Interest Parity,'' *Economic Studies Quarterly* 37 (September 1986), pp. 223–241. A detailed study on the United States is in Lawrence L. Kreicher, ''Eurodollar Arbitrage,'' *Federal Reserve Bank of New York Quarterly Review* 7 (1982), pp. 10–21. An examination of Germany between 1970 and 1974, when capital controls were in effect, found large differences between onshore and offshore DM interest rates. See Michael P. Dooley and Peter Isard, ''Capital Controls, Political Risk, and Deviations from Interest-Rate Parity,'' *Journal of Political Economy* 88 (April 1980), pp. 370–384.

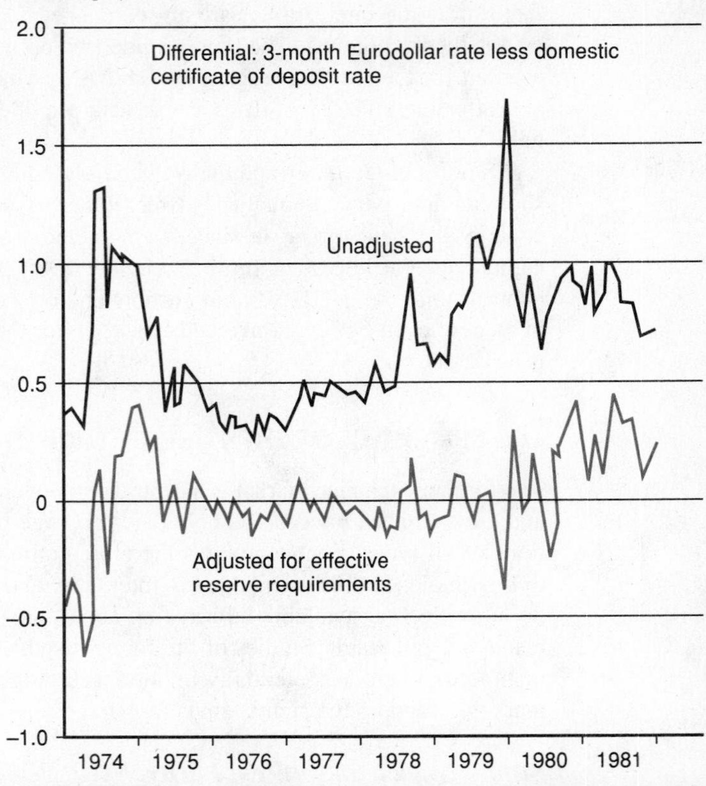

FIGURE 22-3
Comparing Eurodollar and onshore interest rates.
When adjusted for the required reserve "tax," the difference between the Eurodollar interest rate and the domestic U.S. certificate of deposit rate is usually very close to zero.
Source: Edward J. Frydl, "The Eurodollar Conundrum," *Federal Reserve Bank of New York Quarterly Review* 7 (Spring 1982), p. 13.

exchange rate change with the *actual* exchange rate change that subsequently occurs indicates the market's skill in forecasting.[13]

Figure 22-4 shows the relationship between the interest difference and later depreciation rates for four currencies over the period 1980–1988. Clearly the interest difference was a very bad predictor, in the sense that it failed to catch any of the large swings in exchange rates. Even worse, over the period shown, the interest difference was a *biased* predictor; and on average the interest difference even failed to predict correctly the direction in which the spot exchange rate would change. If the interest rate difference were a poor but unbiased predictor, we could argue that the market is setting the exchange rate according to interest parity and doing the best job possible in a rapidly changing world where prediction is inherently difficult. The finding of bias, however, seems at odds with this interpretation of the data.

The interest parity condition also furnishes a test of a second implication of the hypothesis that the market uses all available information in setting exchange rates.

[13] Most studies of exchange market efficiency study how the forward exchange rate premium does as a predictor of subsequent spot exchange rate change. That procedure is equivalent to the one we are following if the covered interest parity condition holds, so that the interest difference $R_t - R^*_t$ equals the forward premium (see the appendix to Chapter 14). As noted in Chapter 14, there is strong evidence that covered interest parity holds when the interest rates being compared apply to deposits in the same financial center—for example, London Eurocurrency rates.

FIGURE 22-4
International interest difference and percentage future spot rate change.
International interest rate differences have been poor and biased predictors of future movements in exchange rates.
Source: Richard M. Levich, "Is the Foreign Exchange Market Efficient?" *Oxford Review of Economic Policy* 5 (1989), pp. 51–52. The interest rates are Eurocurrency rates and their differences (3-month dollar rate less 3-month foreign currency rate) are measured by forward exchange premiums. Exchange rates are dollars per unit of foreign currency. Observations are at 3-month intervals.

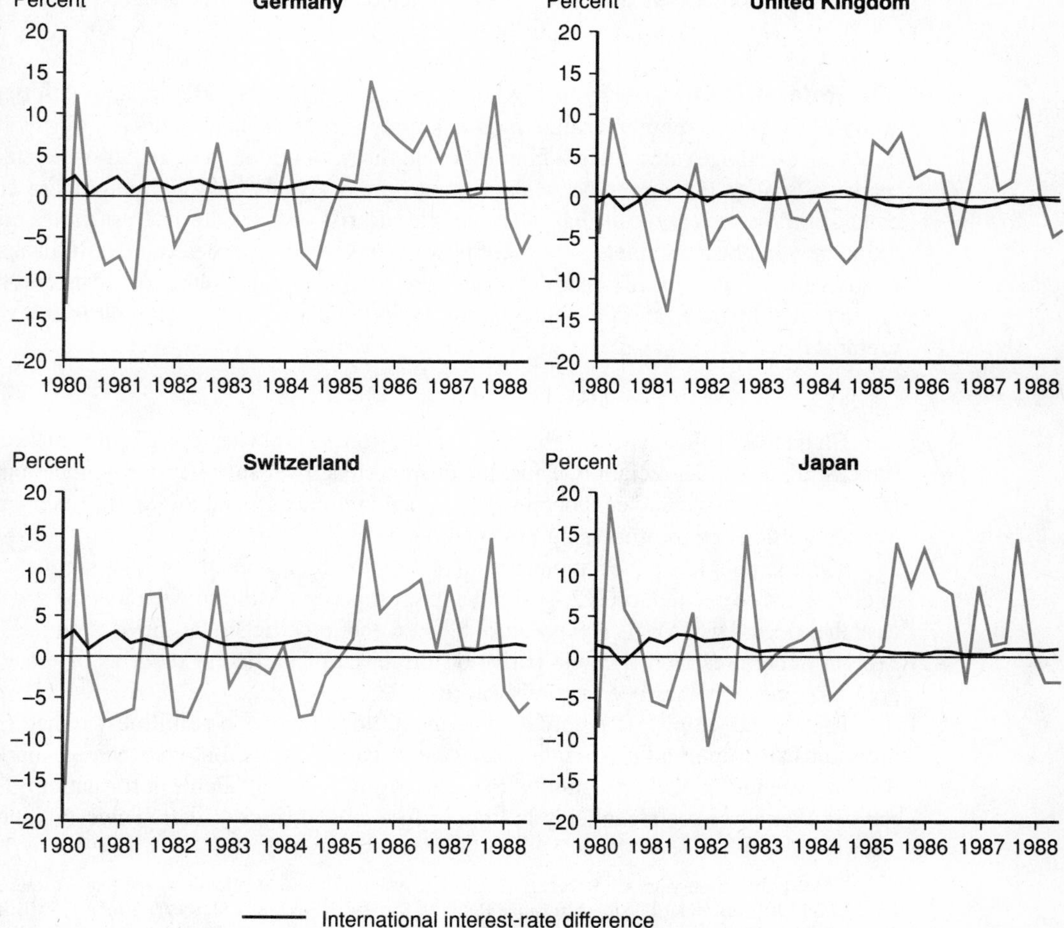

Suppose that E_{t+1} is the actual future exchange rate people are trying to guess; then the forecast error they make in predicting future depreciation, u_{t+1}, can be expressed as actual minus expected depreciation:

$$u_{t+1} = (E_{t+1} - E_t)/E_t - (E^e_{t+1} - E_t)/E_t. \qquad \textbf{(22-2)}$$

If the market is making use of all available information, its forecast error, u_{t+1}, should be statistically unrelated to data known to the market on date *t,* when expectations were formed. In other words, there should be no opportunity for the market to exploit known data to reduce its later forecast errors.

Under interest parity, this hypothesis can be tested by writing u_{t+1} as actual currency depreciation less the international interest difference:

$$u_{t+1} = (E_{t+1} - E_t)/E_t - (R_t - R_t^*). \tag{22-3}$$

Statistical methods can be used to examine whether u_{t+1} is predictable, on average, through use of past information. A number of researchers have found that forecast errors, when defined as above, *can* be predicted. For example, past forecast errors, which are widely known, are useful in predicting future errors.[14]

The Role of Risk Premiums. One explanation of the research results described above is that the foreign exchange market simply ignores easily available information in setting exchange rates. Such a finding would throw doubt on the international capital market's ability to communicate appropriate price signals. Before jumping to this conclusion, however, recall that when people are risk averse, the interest parity condition may *not* be a complete account of how exchange rates are determined. If, instead, bonds denominated in different currencies are *imperfect* substitutes for investors, the international interest rate difference equals expected currency depreciation *plus* a risk premium, ρ_t:

$$R_t - R_t^* = (E_{t+1}^e - E_t)/E_t + \rho_t \tag{22-4}$$

(see Chapter 18). In this case, the interest difference is not necessarily the market's forecast of future depreciation. Thus, under imperfect asset substitutability, the empirical results just discussed cannot be used to draw inferences about the foreign exchange market's efficiency in processing information.

Because people's expectations are inherently unobservable, there is no simple way to decide between equation (22-4) and the interest parity condition, which is the special case that occurs when ρ_t is always zero. Several econometric studies have attempted to explain departures from interest parity on the basis of particular theories of the risk premium, but none has been entirely successful.[15]

The mixed empirical record leaves the following two possibilities: either risk premiums are important in exchange rate determination, or the foreign exchange market has been ignoring the opportunity to profit from easily available information. The second alternative seems unlikely in light of foreign exchange traders' powerful incen-

[14] For further discussion, see Robert E. Cumby and Maurice Obstfeld, "International Interest Rate and Price Level Linkages under Flexible Exchange Rates: A Review of Recent Evidence," in John F. O. Bilson and Richard C. Marston, eds., *Exchange Rate Theory and Practice* (Chicago: University of Chicago Press, 1984), pp. 121–151; and Lars Peter Hansen and Robert J. Hodrick, "Forward Exchange Rates as Optimal Predictors of Future Spot Rates: An Econometric Analysis," *Journal of Political Economy* 88 (October 1980), pp. 829–853.

[15] Among these studies are Lars Peter Hansen and Robert J. Hodrick, "Risk Averse Speculation in the Forward Foreign Exchange Market: An Econometric Analysis of Linear Models," in Jacob A. Frenkel, ed., *Exchange Rates and International Macroeconomics* (Chicago: University of Chicago Press, 1983), pp. 113–142; Jeffrey A. Frankel, "In Search of the Risk Premium: A Six-Currency Test Assuming Mean-Variance Optimization," *Journal of International Money and Finance* 1 (December 1982), pp. 255–274; and Robert E. Cumby, "Is It Risk? Explaining Deviations from Uncovered Interest Parity," *Journal of Monetary Economics* 22 (September 1988), pp. 279–299.

tives to make profits. The first alternative, however, awaits solid statistical confirmation. It is certainly not supported by the evidence reviewed in Chapter 18, which suggests that sterilized foreign exchange intervention has not been an effective tool for exchange rate management. More sophisticated theories show, however, that sterilized intervention may be powerless even under imperfect asset substitutability. Thus, a finding that sterilized intervention is ineffective does not necessarily imply that risk premiums are absent.

Tests for Excessive Volatility. An additional line of research on the foreign exchange market examines whether exchange rates have been excessively volatile, perhaps because the foreign exchange market ''overreacts'' to events. A finding of excessive volatility would prove that the foreign exchange market is sending confusing signals to traders and investors who base their decisions on exchange rates. But how volatile must an exchange rate be before its volatility becomes excessive? As we saw in Chapter 14, exchange rates *should* be volatile, because to send the correct price signals they must move swiftly in response to economic news. It is possible, though, that exchange rates are substantially more volatile than the underlying factors that move them—such as money supplies, national outputs, and fiscal variables. Attempts to compare exchange rates' volatility with those of their underlying determinants have, however, produced inconclusive results.[16] A basic problem underlying tests for excessive volatility is the impossibility of quantifying exactly all the variables that convey relevant news about the economic future. For example, how does one attach a number to a political assassination attempt or a major bank failure?

The Bottom Line. The ambiguous evidence on the foreign exchange market's performance warrants an open-minded view. Such a view is particularly advisable because the statistical methods that have been used to study exchange rates are very imperfect. A judgment that the market is doing its job well would support a laissez-faire attitude by governments and a continuation of the present trend toward increased cross-border financial integration in the industrial world. A judgment of market failure, on the other hand, might imply a need for increased foreign exchange intervention by central banks and a reversal of the trend toward capital account liberalization. The stakes are high, and more research and experience are needed before a firm conclusion can be reached.

Summary

1. When people are *risk averse,* countries can gain through the exchange of risky assets. The gains from trade take the form of a reduction in the riskiness of each country's consumption. International *portfolio diversification* can be carried out through the exchange of *debt instruments* or *equity instruments.*

2. The *international capital market* is the market in which residents of different countries trade assets. One of its important components is the foreign exchange market.

[16] See, for example, Richard A. Meese, ''Testing for Bubbles in Exchange Markets: A Case of Sparkling Rates?'' *Journal of Political Economy* 94 (April 1986), pp. 345–373; and Kenneth D. West ''A Standard Monetary Model and the Variability of the Deutschemark-Dollar Exchange Rate,'' *Journal of International Economics* 23 (August 1987), pp. 57–76.

Banks are at the center of the international capital market, and many operate offshore, that is, outside the countries where their head offices are based.

3. Regulatory and political factors have encouraged *offshore banking*. The same factors have encouraged *offshore currency trading,* that is, trade in bank deposits denominated in currencies of countries other than the one in which the bank is located. Such *Eurocurrency* trading has received a major stimulus from the absence of reserve requirements on deposits in *Eurobanks.*

4. Creation of a Eurocurrency deposit does not occur because that currency leaves its country of origin; all that is required is that a Eurobank accept a deposit liability denominated in the currency. Eurocurrencies therefore pose no threat for central banks' control over their domestic monetary bases. Fears that *Eurodollars,* for example, will some day come ''flooding in'' to the United States are misplaced. Eurocurrency creation can add significantly to the broader monetary aggregates, however, and may complicate central bank monetary management by shifting money multipliers unpredictably.

5. Offshore banking is largely unprotected by the safeguards national governments have imposed to prevent domestic bank failures. In addition, the opportunity banks have to shift operations offshore has undermined the effectiveness of national bank supervision. Since 1974, the *Basle Committee* of industrial country bank supervisors has worked to enhance regulatory cooperation in the international area. That group's 1975 Concordat allocated national responsibility for monitoring banking institutions and provided for information exchange. There is still uncertainty, however, about a central bank's obligations as an international *lender of last resort.* The trend toward *securitization* has increased the need for international cooperation in monitoring and regulating nonbank financial institutions.

6. The international capital market has contributed to an increase in international portfolio diversification since 1970, but the extent of diversification still appears small compared with what economic theory would predict. Similarly, some observers have claimed that the extent of intertemporal trade, as measured by countries' current account balances, has been too small. Such claims are hard to evaluate without more detailed information about the functioning of the world economy than is yet available. Less ambiguous evidence comes from international interest rate comparisons, and this evidence points to a well-functioning market. Rates of return on similar deposits issued in the major financial centers are quite close.

7. The foreign exchange market's record in communicating appropriate price signals to international traders and investors is mixed. Tests based on the interest parity condition seem to suggest that the market ignores readily available information in setting exchange rates, but since the interest parity theory ignores risk aversion and the resulting risk premiums, it may be an oversimplification of reality. Attempts to model risk factors empirically have not, however, been very successful. Tests of excessive exchange rate volatility also yield a mixed verdict on the foreign exchange market's performance.

Key Terms

international capital market
risk aversion
portfolio diversification
debt instrument
equity instrument
Eurobonds

offshore banking
offshore currency trading
Eurocurrencies
Eurodollars
Eurobanks
international banking facilities (IBFs)
lender of last resort (LLR)
Basle Committee
securitization

Problems

1. Which portfolio is better diversified, one that contains stock in a dental supply company and a candy company or one that contains stock in a dental supply company and a dairy product company?
2. Imagine a world of two countries in which the only causes of fluctuations in stock prices are unexpected shifts in monetary policies. Under which exchange rate regime would you expect the gains from international asset trade to be greater, fixed or floating?
3. The text points out that covered interest parity holds quite closely for deposits of differing currency denomination issued in a single financial center. Why might covered interest parity fail to hold when deposits issued in *different* financial centers are compared?
4. When a U.S. bank accepts a deposit from one of its foreign branches, or from its own IBF, that deposit is subject to Fed reserve requirements. Similarly, reserve requirements are imposed on any loan from a U.S. bank's foreign branch to a U.S. resident, or on any asset purchase by the branch bank from its U.S. parent. What do you think is the rationale for these regulations?
5. Show that the competitive advantage of Eurobanks relative to onshore banks rises as domestic interest rates rise. (Hint: Take the example on page 648 in the text and ask what happens when the U.S. loan rate is 15 percent. You will see that while Eurobanks can offer depositors an interest rate of 14 percent, the best that New York banks can do for their depositors is 12.5 percent—a difference of 1.5 percentage points rather than the 1 percentage point we found assuming a 10 percent loan rate.)
6. Figure 22-3 shows that in 1981 there was an upward jump in the difference between Eurodollar interest rates and interest rates on U.S. certificates of deposit, adjusted for the required reserve tax. 1981 was also a year in which Poland encountered severe difficulties in servicing a large debt owed to European banks. Can you suggest a link between the two developments?
7. Suppose an English resident holding a dollar deposit in a London bank decides to switch $10,000 to an account in a New York bank. What are the effects on the supply of Eurodollars, the U.S. balance of payments, the British balance of payments, the U.S. monetary base, and Britain's monetary base?
8. The Swiss economist Alexander Swoboda has argued that the Eurodollar market's early growth was fueled by the desire of banks outside the United States to appropriate some of the revenue the United States was collecting as issuer of the principal reserve currency. (This argument is made in *The Euro-Dollar Market:*

An Interpretation, Princeton Essays in International Finance 64. International Finance Section, Department of Economics, Princeton University, February 1968.) Do you agree with Swoboda's interpretation?

9. After the developing country debt crisis began in 1982, U.S. bank regulators imposed tighter supervisory restrictions on the lending policies of American banks and their subsidiaries. Over the 1980s, the share of U.S. banks in London banking activity declined. Can you suggest a connection between these two developments?
10. Why might growing securitization make it harder for bank supervisors to keep track of risks to the financial system?

Further Reading

Bank for International Settlements. *Recent Innovations in International Banking.* Basle, Switzerland: Bank for International Settlements, April 1986. This document (also known as the Cross Report) is a comprehensive review of international capital markets by a study group representing the central banks of ten industrialized countries.

Ralph C. Bryant. *International Financial Intermediation.* Washington, D.C.: Brookings Institution, 1987. A review of the growth and regulation of the international capital market, with emphasis on the interdependence of different governments' regulatory decisions.

Milton Friedman. ''The Euro-Dollar Market: Some First Principles.'' *Morgan Guaranty Survey* (October 1969), pp. 4–14. A classic account of Eurodollar creation.

Kenneth A. Froot and Richard H. Thaler. ''Anomalies: Foreign Exchange.'' *Journal of Economic Perspectives* 4 (Summer 1990), pp. 179–192. Clear, nontechnical discussion of the foreign exchange market's efficiency.

Edward J. Frydl. ''The Eurodollar Conundrum.'' *Federal Reserve Bank of New York Quarterly Review* 7 (Spring 1982), pp. 11–19. An examination of the Eurodollar market's effect on U.S. monetary policy.

Marvin Goodfriend. ''Eurodollars,'' in Timothy Q. Cook and Timothy D. Rowe, eds. *Instruments of the Money Market.* Richmond, VA: Federal Reserve Bank of Richmond, 1986, pp. 53–64. Describes the Eurodollar market's evolution and functions.

Jack Guttentag and Richard Herring. *The Lender-of-Last-Resort Function in an International Context.* Princeton Essays in International Finance 151. International Finance Section, Department of Economics, Princeton University, May 1983. A study of the need for and the feasibility of an international lender of last resort.

Richard M. Levich. ''Financial Innovations in International Financial Markets,'' in Martin S. Feldstein, ed. *The United States in the World Economy.* Chicago: University of Chicago Press, 1988, pp. 215–257. Concise survey of recent issues related to international financial innovation.

Richard M. Levich. ''Is the Foreign Exchange Market Efficient?'' *Oxford Review of Economic Policy* 5 (1989), pp. 40–60. Valuable survey of research on the efficiency of the foreign exchange market.

Haim Levy and Marshall Sarnat. ''International Portfolio Diversification,'' in Richard J. Herring, ed. *Managing Foreign Exchange Risk.* Cambridge, Eng.: Cambridge University Press, 1983, pp. 115–142. A nice exposition of the logic of international asset diversification.

Warren D. McClam. ''Financial Fragility and Instability: Monetary Authorities as Borrowers and Lenders of Last Resort,'' in Charles P. Kindleberger and Jean-Pierre Laffargue, eds. *Financial Crises: Theory, History, and Policy.* Cambridge, Eng.: Cambridge University

Press, 1982, pp. 256–291. Historical overview of instability in the international capital market.

Maurice Obstfeld. ''International Capital Mobility in the 1990s,'' in Peter B. Kenen, ed. *Understanding Interdependence: The Macroeconomics of the Open Economy*. Princeton, NJ: Princeton University Press, 1994. Advanced discussion of the functions and operations of the world capital market.

Developing Countries: Debt, Stabilization, and Reform

Chapter 23

Until now, we have studied macroeconomic interactions between industrialized market economies like those of the United States, Canada, Japan, and the countries of Europe. Richly endowed with capital and skilled labor, these economies generate high levels of GNP for their populations. And their markets, compared with those of poorer countries, are relatively free of direct government control.

Since the early 1980s, however, the macroeconomic problems of the world's poorer countries have been at the forefront of concerns about the stability and future of the international economy. Over a period of nearly four decades following World War II, trade between developing and industrialized nations expanded, as did developing country borrowing from richer lands. In turn, the more extensive links between the two groups of economies made each group more dependent than before on the economic health of the other. Events in developing countries therefore have a significant impact on welfare and policies in more advanced economies.

This chapter studies the macroeconomic problems of developing countries and the repercussions of those problems on the developed world. Although many of the insights from international macroeconomics gained in previous chapters also apply to developing countries, the structures of poorer economies are sufficiently different from those of the rich industrialized countries to warrant separate discussion. In addition, the lower income levels of developing areas make macroeconomic fluctuations there even more painful than in developed economies, with consequences that may threaten internal political stability.

The chapter also reviews the history of relations between developed and developing countries during the twentieth century. That history culminated in 1982 in a sharp decade-long contraction of rich country lending to poorer countries—an international debt crisis. Below, we apply what we learn about developing country macroeconomics to examine the causes and effects of the debt crisis and the factors that have helped to bring it under control.

Income and Wealth in the World Economy

Compared with industrialized countries, developing countries are poor in the factors of production essential to modern industry: capital and skilled labor. The relative scarcity of these factors contributes to low levels of per capita income and often prevents developing countries from realizing economies of scale from which many richer nations benefit. Political instability and misguided economic policies frequently have made matters worse.

The world's economies can be divided into four main categories according to per capita income levels: low-income economies (including mainland China, India, and much of sub-Saharan Africa); lower-middle-income economies (including the smaller Latin American and Caribbean countries, Argentina, Chile, and most of the remaining African countries); upper-middle-income economies (including most of the largest Latin American countries, Korea, and the poorer European countries); and high-income economies (including the rich industrial market economies and a handful of exceptionally fortunate developing countries such as Singapore and Kuwait). The first three categories consist mainly of countries at a backward stage of development relative to the industrial economies. Table 23-1 shows 1990 average per capita income levels (measured in dollars) for these country groups, together with another indicator of economic well-being, average life expectancy at birth.[1]

Table 23-1 illustrates the sharp disparities in international income levels. Average per capita annual GNP in the richest economies is 56 times that of the poorest developing countries. Even the upper-middle-income countries enjoy only one-sixth of the annual per capita GNP of the industrial group. The life expectancy figures generally reflect international differences in income levels: average life spans fall as relative poverty increases.

Macroeconomic Features of Developing Countries

While there are many economic features that differentiate developing from developed countries, five are particularly important for macroeconomic analysis. These features

[1] Chapter 16 showed that an international comparison of *dollar* incomes will portray relative welfare levels inaccurately because countries' price levels measured in terms of a common currency (here U.S. dollars) generally differ. An additional problem with dollar income comparisons is that some developing countries have multiple exchange rates for current account transactions. A detailed description of how the numbers in Table 23-1 were constructed and adjusted is given in their source, the World Bank's *World Development Report 1992.* More reliable real output estimates are reported by Robert Summers and Alan Heston, "The Penn World Table (Mark 5): An Expanded Set of International Comparisons, 1950–1988," *Quarterly Journal of Economics* 106 (May 1991), pp. 327–368. The alternative estimates, like those in Table 23-1, show that real output per capita differs widely among countries.

TABLE 23-1 Indicators of economic welfare in four groups of countries, 1990

Income group	*GNP per capita (U.S. dollars)*	*Life expectancy (years)*
Low-income	350	55*
Lower-middle-income	1530	65
Upper-middle-income	3410	68
High-income	19,590	77

* Excluding China (average life expectancy, 70) and India (59).
Source: World Bank, *World Development Report 1992.* The ex-Communist countries of Eastern Europe are included with lower- and upper-middle-income developing countries. The table does not cover the former Soviet Union (average life expectancy, 71). The World Bank classifies Hong Kong, Singapore, Kuwait, the United Arab Emirates, and Israel as high-income developing countries.

apply to a majority of developing countries, but not to all, and several are shared by some industrialized economies. Nonetheless, a broad description of a ''typical'' developing economy's structure is essential to understanding macroeconomic relationships between the developed and less-developed parts of the world economy. This description also will help you to understand the steps many developing countries currently are taking to reform their economies.

1. Financial markets in developing countries are limited in extent and subject to heavy official control. Governments often keep interest rates below the level that would equalize demand and supply for loans, so loans tend to be rationed.
2. Direct government involvement in the economy extends beyond the financial markets. Governments own a significant portion of the economy's firms, and government spending is a very high percentage of GNP.
3. The government finances a large fraction of its outlays by printing money. This practice results in high average inflation rates and, sometimes, the indexation of wages, loan contracts, and other money prices to the general price level.
4. Exchange rates are set by the government rather than determined in the foreign exchange market. Private international borrowing and lending are heavily restricted, and the government may allow residents to purchase foreign exchange only for certain purposes. In some countries different exchange rates apply to different categories of transaction.
5. Natural resources or agricultural commodities make up an important share of exports for many developing countries.

UNDEVELOPED FINANCIAL MARKETS

On the whole, developing countries lack the broad and rapidly adjusting financial markets characteristic of the main industrial countries. Stock markets are usually rudimentary or nonexistent, as are markets for long-term debt. Bank lending to businesses and the farm sector is tightly controlled by the government, which often decrees artificially low interest rates.

Developing country governments sometimes exercise direct control over credit markets because it is one way of channeling funds at reduced interest rates to favored industries or sectors of the economy. Governments often find this method of helping selected industries preferable to outright subsidization because subsidies would show up in the government's budget as an increase in its measured deficit. Thus, credit diversion by the government to favored sectors results in an implicit subsidy to those who get artificially cheap loans. At the same time, it results in an implicit tax on the banking system, which could earn higher profits in a less heavily regulated national capital market. Low domestic interest rates also help the government finance its budget deficit.

The absence of the higher-yielding assets available in industrial economies means that the few assets that are available to developing country savers are not very attractive as stores of wealth. Government controls often aim to prevent domestic savers from holding foreign assets, so the main financial assets available are money and time deposits. Partly as a result, saving rates have tended to be low in some developing regions. Much of the private saving flow that is available ends up financing government activities, and fragmented capital markets make it costly to funnel the rest into private corporate investment.

Wealthier savers in developing countries can sometimes get around government controls and acquire high-yielding assets located abroad. Such outflows of domestic savings make it harder to finance domestic investment. *Capital flight*—a flow of private funds into foreign assets, prompted by domestic economic instability—is common, and provides a clear illustration of how developing country residents often try to shield their wealth by moving it abroad and out of the domestic government's reach.

In most developing countries an informal ''curb market'' for loans conducts small-scale lending at market-determined interest rates. The supply side of the curb market includes individual moneylenders, pawnbrokers, merchant trade credit, and private saving associations; the demand side includes households and small farms and businesses. Some developing countries are building on these informal financial markets in broader programs of financial market restructuring.

GOVERNMENT'S PERVASIVE ROLE

To a greater extent than in most industrial countries, developing country governments are involved in the day-to-day management of the economy. Government regulations abound, and many firms are state companies run directly by the government. (Brazil's state companies, for example, produce half the country's recorded GNP.) In recent years there has been more **privatization** in the developing world, with some governments selling state-owned enterprises to trim public deficits. Because underdeveloped financial markets have difficulty pricing and absorbing such government divestments, however, it has not always been easy for governments to sell them to private domestic owners. Successful privatization thus may depend on capital inflows from abroad. Fierce political opposition from those who stand to lose comfortable jobs at inefficient public firms often stalls the privatization process. In a few developing countries privatization efforts have brought a qualitative change in the government's central economic role, but not in most.[2]

[2] For a clear account see Eliana A. Cardoso, ''Privatization Fever in Latin America,'' *Challenge* (September/October 1991), pp. 35–41. Similar but more severe privatization problems have arisen in Eastern Europe and the former Soviet Union, where most or all of the economy must be privatized. See David Lipton and Jeffrey Sachs, ''Privatization in Eastern Europe: The Case of Poland,'' *Brookings Papers on Economic Activity* 2:1990, pp. 293–341. We discuss problems of that region in Chapter 24.

INFLATION AND THE GOVERNMENT BUDGET

When domestic financial markets are underdeveloped, governments find it difficult to finance their deficits through domestic bond issues. This difficulty has resulted in extensive direct government borrowing from foreigners. Developing country governments are also led to rely on an additional instrument of public finance: they run the printing press and use newly created money to purchase goods and services.

The real output that a government obtains by printing money and spending it is called **seigniorage.** Seigniorage is a component of government revenue everywhere, but it is particularly important in the finances of developing country governments.

Money creation leads to inflation, which erodes the real value of nominal money holdings. This ''inflation tax'' paid by moneyholders is one component of the real resources the government obtains by printing money. The inflation rates attained by some developing countries seem spectacular compared with the low (usually less than double-digit) rates seen recently in industrial economies. (See the Case Study on Latin American inflation stabilization efforts, p. 681.) Such rapid rates of price increase reflect continuing attempts by governments to extract seigniorage from their economies by printing money.

As a result of chronically high inflation, nominal wages are sometimes indexed to the price level. When wages are indexed, they are adjusted frequently in response to inflation rather than set, once and for all, until the next contract negotiation. This procedure is meant to prevent the large fluctuations in workers' real wages that would otherwise occur over the life of a labor contract.

Wage indexation has two major drawbacks that have contributed to macroeconomic instability in developing countries. First, changes in real wages are sometimes necessary to maintain full employment, but indexation makes these changes difficult if not impossible to achieve. If real wages do not fall when the terms of trade deteriorate, for example, export industries are forced to lay off workers and shut down plants.

The second problem with indexation is that wages are often linked to *past* price level increases. If a government decides to reduce a rapid inflation rate, for example, real wages may rise for a time as nominal wages continue to be adjusted upward to compensate for earlier inflation. Rising real wages, however, lead to layoffs and put additional upward pressure on product prices. A government that contemplates disinflation may therefore be discouraged by the prospect of a long and painful adjustment to a lower inflation rate. Developing country governments have recently coupled disinflation programs with direct wage controls, but such ''incomes policies'' are politically unpopular and cannot be sustained unless the government's program improves economic conditions very quickly.[3]

PEGGED EXCHANGE RATES, EXCHANGE CONTROLS, AND INCONVERTIBLE CURRENCIES

Most developing countries set exchange rates and strictly control financial transactions involving foreign currencies. Foreign exchange controls prevent residents from legally

[3] Some industrial countries that experienced double-digit inflation, such as Italy, also indexed wages. Developing country governments sometimes index their bonds by adjusting interest and principal payments upward in line with domestic inflation. Once again, some industrial countries (such as Britain) also issue indexed government debt.

purchasing foreign currencies without government permission; at the same time, someone who earns foreign currency abroad may be required to sell it to the government for domestic currency. Foreigners holding a developing country's currency are not generally able to exchange it for foreign currencies with the country's central bank or residents. Thus, developing country currencies are often *inconvertible,* even for current action transactions.

Why do developing countries peg exchange rates and supervise foreign transactions? One main reason is the government's desire to use exchange rate arrangements as a tool of commercial policy. Many developing countries maintain different exchange rates for different types of current account transaction. For example, the government may subsidize investment by selling dollars cheaply to firms that import machinery, while taxing luxury consumption goods by selling dollars at a higher price to individuals who import limousines.[4]

Such multiple exchange rate systems cannot be enforced unless the government itself buys and sells foreign currencies at the rates it wishes to maintain and prevents the private sector from transacting at other rates. Exchange controls also help the central bank prevent sharp reductions in its foreign exchange reserves, which might eventually leave it unable to peg rates. Finally, by preventing the public from holding foreign rather than domestic money, the government can collect more seigniorage by running its printing press.

Even if considerations of commercial and macroeconomic policy did not lead developing countries to peg exchange rates, financial restrictions would make private foreign exchange trading time-consuming and costly under a floating exchange rate. Because they typically are inconvertible, developing country currencies are not traded on a significant scale by financial institutions in the developed world. In addition, financial institutions in less-developed countries face burdensome restrictions that prevent them from trading freely. The actors who normally would be at the center of a market in developing country currencies—domestic and foreign financial institutions—are therefore unable to participate, leaving the developing country's central bank as the main trader in its currency. Transaction costs for the economy are reduced if the central bank fixes the exchange rate and ''makes a market'' at that rate for individuals authorized to trade foreign exchange.

A few countries have tried to combine this official market-making role with greater exchange rate flexibility through government-run auctions of foreign exchange. Bolivia, Ghana, and Jamaica are among the countries that have experimented with foreign exchange auctions.

It is not surprising that strict foreign exchange controls lead to black markets for foreign exchange in most developing countries. In black markets, foreign currencies smuggled into the country generally command a higher domestic currency price than the one offered by the central bank. As a tourist, you can often take advantage of the black market rate simply by selling dollars to one of the dealers stationed in front of your hotel. The dollars you sell will probably be used by a resident to purchase goods or assets abroad without official approval.

Since high inflation makes it impossible to maintain absolutely rigid exchange rates for long, many developing countries have used an exchange rate system called the **crawling peg.** Under a crawling peg, the central bank always fixes the domestic

[4] Chapter 11 examined in detail the commercial policies of developing countries.

How Important Is Seigniorage?

According to some accounts, the use of inflation as a tax on moneyholders was discovered by the ancient Romans, who first hit upon the idea of debasing their coinage to raise revenue. The word *seigniorage* refers to a tax that feudal princes levied for turning nonmonetary gold into coins at their mints.

Seigniorage has remained important in the modern world of paper money. One way to measure real seigniorage revenue is by summing the cash and checks issued by the central bank during the year and dividing the result by the price level.*

Data for a selection of developing countries are shown in the accompanying table. Reported are calculations of period averages for (1) real seigniorage revenue as a fraction of total real output and (2) inflation.

In the table's "high-seigniorage" countries, governments were able to acquire significant shares of national output simply by running their printing presses. It should be no surprise that Bolivia, which on average taxed away more than 6 percent of output through inflation, suffered a hyperinflation. (Later in this chapter we describe how the hyperinflation was stopped.) Low-seigniorage countries tended to have low inflation too. In this group the share of seigniorage revenue in output is less than 1 percent.

How dependent are *developed* countries' governments on seigniorage? As a comparison, the United States had an av-

Seigniorage revenue and inflation, 1980–1985 averages

	Real seigniorage (percent of real output)	*Inflation (percent per year)*
High-seigniorage developing countries		
Argentina	4.0	274
Bolivia	6.2	506
Ghana	2.2	54
Sierra Leone	2.4	43
Moderate-seigniorage developing countries		
Brazil	1.0	147
Israel	1.1	181
Mexico	1.5	58
Peru	1.9	97
Turkey	1.2	46
Low-seigniorage developing countries		
Bangladesh	0.6	12
Colombia	0.8	22
Ivory Coast	0.7	7
Dominican Republic	0.7	15
Korea	0.5	9
Nigeria	0.8	16
Venezuela	0.4	12

Source: World Bank, *World Development Report 1988,* Table 3.1.

erage annual inflation rate of 7 percent over 1980–1985, and its government came away with seigniorage averaging 0.3 percent of GNP. This figure is low compared with those shown in the table.

The somewhat atypical case of Italy provides a counterexample to assertions that developing countries rely more heavily on seigniorage than do developed countries. Italy's inflation averaged 15 percent per year over 1980–1985 and seigniorage averaged 2.3 percent of output. Italy's record thus would place it in the "high-seigniorage" group in the table. Remember, however, that Italy's inflation rate fell after 1980, so that some of the seigniorage it collected was the result of increasing money demand rather than the inflation tax. In countries like Argentina and Bolivia, inflation was on the rise during the period shown.

* This is an oversimplified description of how seigniorage should be measured. In some countries seigniorage is extracted in subtle ways, for example, by requiring private banks to hold government debt that pays below-market interest rates. Furthermore, the government may gain by unexpectedly inflating away some of the real value of its nominal debt. The numbers we report for developing countries (though not for developed) actually understate seigniorage, because they do not cover increases in the reserves of the banking system.

currency price of foreign exchange but allows that price to ''crawl'' upward over time, so that the home currency is being devalued continuously against foreign currencies. The mini-devaluations take place quite frequently, sometimes even daily.

Until the early 1970s, developing countries generally pegged their currencies to a single major industrial country currency—usually the dollar, but sometimes the British pound or French franc. In response to floating dollar exchange rates among the industrialized countries, some countries chose to peg their currencies instead to *baskets* of industrialized country currencies. An example shows that floating rates make it riskier for a country to peg to a single foreign currency. A developing country pegging to the dollar would find itself forced to revalue its currency against nondollar currencies if the dollar appreciated sharply in the foreign exchange market. By pegging to a basket instead, the country can reduce the effect on its international trade of large swings in the values of the individual currencies in the basket.

THE STRUCTURE OF DEVELOPING COUNTRY EXPORTS

Many developing countries draw a large fraction of export earnings from a small number of natural resources or agricultural products. Nigeria depends heavily on oil exports, Chile on copper, Colombia on coffee (and cocaine), and Malaysia on rubber.

Dependence on such exports poses a macroeconomic problem because commodity prices are highly variable relative to those of manufactured goods. In turn, drastic shifts in the prices of a country's most important export goods cause corresponding shifts in real income and the current account. A fall in export prices, for example, could simultaneously cause a slump in the economy and a current account deficit. The government might find it impossible to regain internal and external balance until export prices recover.

Developing country export prices are particularly sensitive to macroeconomic policies adopted in industrialized economies. A reduction in aggregate demand in the industrialized countries is quickly transmitted to the developing world as commodity prices plummet and developing country real incomes fall.

Developing Country Borrowing and Debt

One further feature of developing countries is crucial to understanding their macroeconomic problems: they rely heavily on capital inflows from abroad to finance domestic investment. In the decades after World War II, developing economies borrowed from richer countries and built up a substantial debt to the rest of the world (around $1.4 trillion at the end of 1992). This debt was at the center of the crisis in international lending that preoccupied economic policy makers throughout the world for a decade after 1982.

THE ECONOMICS OF BORROWING BY DEVELOPING COUNTRIES

Many developing countries have borrowed extensively abroad and now carry substantial debts to foreigners. What economic factors lie behind this borrowing?

Recall the identity (analyzed in Chapter 13) that links national saving, S, domestic investment, I, and the current account balance, CA: $S - I = CA$. If national saving falls short of domestic investment, the difference equals the current account deficit. National saving, as we saw earlier, is often low in developing countries, but because these same countries are relatively poor in capital, the opportunities for profitably introducing plant and equipment can be abundant. Such opportunities justify a high level of investment. By running a deficit in its current account balance, a country can obtain resources to invest even if its domestic saving level is low. A deficit in the current account implies, however, that the country is borrowing abroad. In return for being able to import more foreign goods today than it exports today, the country must promise to repay in the future the interest and principal on the loan foreigners are making.

Thus, much developing country borrowing could potentially be explained by the incentives for *intertemporal trade* examined in Chapter 7. Low-income countries generate too little saving of their own to take advantage of all their profitable investment opportunities, so they must borrow abroad. In capital-rich countries, on the other hand, the most productive investment opportunities have been exploited already but saving levels are relatively high. Savers in developed countries can obtain more attractive rates of return, however, by lending to finance investments in the developing world.

Notice that when developing countries borrow to undertake productive investments they would not otherwise undertake, both they and the lenders reap gains from trade. Borrowers gain because they can build up their capital stocks in spite of limited national saving levels. Lenders gain because they earn higher returns on their savings than they could earn at home.

While the reasoning above provides a rationale for developing country external deficits and debt, it does not say that *any* loan from developed to developing countries is justified. Loans made to finance unprofitable investments or imports of consumption goods may result in debts that borrowers cannot repay. In addition, faulty government policies that abnormally depress the national saving rate may lead to excessive foreign borrowing.

Potential gains from international borrowing and lending will not be realized unless lenders are confident they will be repaid. As we see below, a widespread loss of confidence in repayment caused the onset in 1982 of the developing country debt crisis.

ALTERNATIVE FORMS OF CAPITAL INFLOW

When a developing country has a current account deficit, it is selling assets to foreigners to finance the difference between its spending and its income. While we have lumped these asset sales together under the catchall term *borrowing,* the capital inflows that finance developing countries' deficits (and, indeed, any country's deficit) can take several forms. Different types of capital inflow have predominated in different historical periods. Because different types of inflow give rise to different obligations to foreign lenders, an understanding of the macroeconomic scene in developing countries requires a careful analysis of the four major channels through which they have financed external deficits.

1. *Bond finance.* Developing countries have sometimes sold bonds to private foreign citizens to finance their deficits. Bond finance was important in the period up to 1914 and in the interwar years (1918–1939) but has been a relatively small component of developing country external financing since World War II.

2. *Bank loans.* Since the early 1970s, developing countries have increasingly borrowed directly from commercial banks in the developed countries. In 1970, roughly a quarter of developing country external finance was provided by banks; in 1981 banks provided $98.3 billion in loans, an amount roughly equal to the nonoil developing countries' current account deficit for that year.[5] These aggregate figures conceal large differences in the experiences of individual borrowers. Some Latin American countries, for example, became much more dependent on bank finance by the 1980s than average figures indicate. These countries' sharp shift toward bank finance was an important element in the post-1982 debt crisis.

3. *Direct foreign investment.* In direct foreign investment, a firm largely owned by foreign residents acquires or expands a subsidiary firm or factory located domestically (Chapter 7). A loan from IBM to its plant in Mexico, for example, would be a direct investment by the United States in Mexico. Similarly, Japanese stockholders financing the construction of a Toyota development lab in the United States are carrying out direct investment. The first of these direct investments would enter the Mexican balance of payments accounts as a capital inflow (and the U.S. balance of payments accounts as an equal capital outflow); the second would enter Japan's balance of payments accounts as a capital outflow (and the U.S. balance of payments accounts as an equal capital inflow). Direct investment is sometimes the only way for foreigners to acquire substantial direct claims on plant and equipment operating within a developing economy.

[5] See World Bank, *World Development Report 1985,* Table 2.3, p. 21, for 1970 data on developing country external finance. For 1981 data see International Monetary Fund, *World Economic Outlook,* April 1989, Table A40.

Direct investment was an important source of developing country external finance in the twenty-five years after World War II. Over the 1970s, however, direct investment declined in importance as bank lending grew. During the early 1980s direct investment inflows fell even further, from $20 billion in 1982 to a mere $11 billion at the trough of the debt crisis in 1986. Only recently has direct foreign investment in developing countries made an apparent comeback, jumping to $25 billion in 1991.

4. *Official lending.* Developing countries sometimes borrow from international agencies like the International Monetary Fund and the World Bank and from the governments of other countries. Such loans can be made on a ''concessional'' basis—that is, at interest rates below market rates—or on a market basis that allows the lender to earn the market rate of return. Official lending flows to developing nations have shrunk relative to total flows over the post-World War II period.

The four types of finance just described can be classified into two categories: *debt* and *equity* finance (Chapter 22). Bond, bank, and official finance are all forms of debt finance. The debtor must repay the face value of the loan, plus interest, regardless of its own economic circumstances. Direct investment, on the other hand, is a form of equity finance. Foreign owners of a direct investment have a claim to a share of its net return, not a claim to a fixed stream of money payments. Adverse economic events in the host country thus result in an automatic fall in the earnings of direct investments and in the dividends paid to foreigners.

The distinction between debt and equity finance is useful in analyzing how developing country payments to foreigners adjust to unforseen economic disturbances such as recessions and terms of trade changes. When a country's liabilities take the form of debt, its scheduled payments to creditors do not fall if its real income falls. It may then become painful for the country to continue honoring its foreign obligations. Life often is easier, however, with equity finance. In that case, a fall in domestic income automatically reduces the earnings of foreign shareholders without violating any loan agreement. By acquiring equity, foreigners have effectively agreed to share in both the bad and the good times of the economy.

In recent years a new source of equity finance for developing countries has started to grow in importance: the direct purchase of domestic stock shares by foreign portfolio investors. Sometimes these shares are marketed on industrial country stock exchanges, but there has also been increasing foreign interest in the emerging stock markets of the developing countries themselves. Particularly in Asia, but also in Latin American countries such as Mexico, Chile, and Argentina, thriving local stock markets are beginning to attract capital from abroad.

GOVERNMENT AND PUBLICLY GUARANTEED BORROWING

It is important to realize that most developing country debt represents either direct loans to governments and government-owned firms or publicly guaranteed loans to the private sector, that is, loans for which the government agrees to be responsible in case of private nonpayment. In the presence of exchange controls and undeveloped domestic financial markets, governments more or less automatically become involved in any borrowing agreement between domestic residents and foreigners. Because of the government's ultimate responsibility for paying the nation's debts, external payment troubles interact with government budgetary problems and can affect most of a developing country's external debt at the same time.

Case Study

ORTHODOX AND HETERODOX STABILIZATION PROGRAMS IN LATIN AMERICA

In the early 1980s most governments in Latin America ran into severe financial difficulties as the flow of industrial country lending to that part of the developing world all but dried up. We will discuss this debt crisis at length later in this chapter, but we focus here on one of its major consequences: high inflation sometimes crossing the border into hyperinflation.

Two interpretations of the inflation led to different prescriptions for stopping it. An "orthodox" school of economists argued that inflation came from the seignorage governments were using to make up for the foreign lending cut off in the debt crisis. The remedy, they argued, was to raise taxes and cut public spending, thereby eliminating the budget deficits and the excessive money growth needed to finance them. In fact, tax receipts in the inflating economies had actually fallen as taxpayers delayed payment in the hope of reducing the real value of their nominal tax bills. These delays only worsened the public deficits and, according to the orthodox school, led inflation to accelerate over time.

An opposing school of "heterodox" economists identified "inertia" in price and wage setting as the main culprit. They listed indexation of wages to the price level and entrenched expectations of rapid inflation as major causes of this inertia. Not all heterodox economists denied the importance of balancing the government budget, but all did agree that fiscal rectitude itself would not be enough to stop a roaring inflation. Only stiff controls on nominal prices and wages, and on the exchange rate, could shift expectations abruptly and break the accumulated momentum of inflation.

Which school was right? The 1980s provided an uncomfortably large number of national economic crises in which both approaches were tested.

Bolivia, a country without explicit wage indexation, was in the grip of hyperinflation in August 1985 when a newly elected government introduced an orthodox stabilization program that *ended* most existing price controls and decisively cut the government budget deficit. Total tax revenues rose from 1.6 percent of output in the third quarter of 1985 to 11.3 percent in the last. The effects on inflation were dramatic: inflation went from an annual rate of 8170 percent in 1985 to 66 percent in 1986, to only 11 percent in 1987. At the end of the 1980s Bolivia's inflation was still running at around 15 percent per year.

While the Bolivian program succeeded in halting inflation, it was much less successful in restoring robust real economic growth. Critics of the orthodox Bolivian approach claim that it would not have put a stop to inflation elsewhere in Latin America.

Argentina and Brazil, both economies with wage indexation, introduced heterodox anti-inflation programs in June 1985 and February 1986, respectively. Both programs were centered around currency reforms: Argentina's currency, the peso, was replaced by the austral, while Brazil's cruzeiro was replaced by the cruzado. Among the more substantive elements of the stabilization plans were wage-price controls and (at least in Argentina) revenue-enhancing fiscal reforms. Both plans met with apparent initial success, as Argentina's annual inflation rate fell from 385 percent in 1985 to 82 percent in 1986 and Brazil's fell from 249 percent in 1985 to 64 percent in 1986.

Argentina's government budget deficit widened in 1987, however. Brazil had not improved its underlying budgetary situation in 1986, and conditions only deteriorated in 1987. By 1987 inflation had returned to 175 percent per year in Argentina and 321 percent per year in Brazil. Subsequent half-hearted attempts at reform in both countries did not produce happy results. Argentina slipped into hyperinflation: the country's price level increased by 197 percent *in July 1989 alone,* the month President Carlos Menem was inaugurated after street rioting and the virtual breakdown of Argentina's payments system. As Brazil faced its own presidential election in the fall of 1989, its inflation was running at an annual rate of around 1300 percent. Brazil's main producer of electronic calculators reported that in the first nine months of 1989 it had doubled its 1988 sales of handheld models. Evidently, Brazil's consumers needed help in the dizzying task of extracting economic signals from exploding nominal prices.

Brazil's new president, Fernando Collor, announced an ambitious reform program based on budget cuts, aggressive privatization, and the elimination of government graft. Little progress was made on any of these fronts, however. By 1993, Brazilian inflation still stood at about 800 percent per year while Collor himself had resigned from the presidency to avoid impeachment on corruption charges.

Argentina, in contrast, turned to radically orthodox measures in a bid to end its history of hyperinflation. In January 1991 President Menem appointed a new economy minister, Domingo Cavallo, who implemented a broad plan of budgetary, trade, and monetary reform. Under the "Plan Cavallo," import tariffs were dramatically slashed, major state companies, including the national airline, were privatized, and tax reforms increased government revenues. Government expenditures also were cut, so that by 1992 the government budget was nearing balance.

The most daring component of Cavallo's plan, however, was a new law of April 1991 making the Argentine austral fully convertible into U.S. dollars at a *fixed* rate of 10,000 australs per dollar. This law also required the monetary base to be backed entirely by official foreign reserves—gold or foreign currency—so in one stroke it removed the central bank's ability to finance government deficits through continuing money creation. Another provision of the law banned the indexation of wage or financial contracts to the price level. In January 1992 the currency was reformed, with one new peso replacing every 10,000 australs and thus trading at a fixed exchange rate of one peso per dollar.

Backed as it was by genuine fiscal reform, the Cavallo plan had a dramatic effect on inflation, which dropped from 800 percent per year in 1990 to 56 percent in 1991 and to around 20 percent in 1992. Nominal interest rates fell to historically low levels and capital flowed in from abroad. The continuation of inflation despite a fixed exchange rate implied, however, a real appreciation of the peso; with legislative elections looming for 1993, the government, in October 1992, gave in to pressures from manufacturing exporters and introduced a system of export subsidies and import taxes that was equivalent to a 5–10 percent devaluation of the peso. This ominous sign of weakening government resolve set off a foreign exchange crisis. Argentina's bold stabilization plan had met with initial success; but at the end of 1992 it appeared that political pressures might rapidly deprive the government of its painfully earned credibility.

What are the lessons of these recent experiences? Price controls may be helpful (and, arguably, necessary) in the transition to lower inflation, but low inflation cannot be maintained without a permanent and credible tightening of the government budget, which in turn permits a slowing of money supply growth. Factors such as wage indexation and stubborn expectations certainly affect the transmission of money creation to prices. As the orthodox school contends, however, money creation itself seems to be the ultimate cause of the sustained inflation seen recently in Latin America.

Developing Country Borrowing in Historical Perspective

With this background on the general features of developing country macroeconomic structure and the long-run factors behind developing country borrowing, we now turn to the role developing countries have played in the world economy over the last century. From the late nineteenth century to the early 1980s, lending to the developing world first boomed, then disappeared as the world slid into the Great Depression, and finally reappeared and expanded quickly. Events of 1982 led to a sharp contraction in lending to developing debtors and an international debt crisis that crippled the economies of many nations for a decade or more. The events of the pre-1982 period provide valuable historical lessons that help illuminate this recent debt crisis.

CAPITAL FLOWS TO DEVELOPING COUNTRIES BEFORE 1914

The period ending with World War I was one of substantial capital flow from Europe to developing areas, much of it in the form of loans. Between 1870 and 1914, Britain invested on average, more than 5 percent of its GNP abroad. The corresponding numbers for France and Germany, the other two leading foreign lenders, were between 2 and 3 percent. In this period London, the hub of the gold standard system, was the main international financial center. Many developing countries borrowed by selling bonds in London, usually through syndicates of London financial brokers and banks.

From the vantage point of an international economy shattered by World War I, the pre-1914 period appeared to be a paradise for international investors. The international capital market centered in London certainly did thrive up to 1914, but conditions were not as tranquil as nostalgic descriptions penned during the interwar period (and after) might lead you to believe. As we saw in Chapter 19, economic fluctuations were severe under the gold standard, and fluctuations in Europe had a major impact on the prosperity of developing borrowers. Faced with sudden declines in export earnings, debtor countries were sometimes forced to suspend payments of interest and principal on their debt. In addition, domestic economic mismanagement sometimes contributed to the interruption of payments to foreign creditors.

A loan is said to be in **default** whenever the borrower does not make the payments specified in the loan contract. Defaults by less-developed debtors were not at all uncommon before 1914—in fact, several American states defaulted on foreign loans in that period. The losers in cases of default were the individual lenders. Even though a defaulting borrower sometimes resumed payments after its economic circumstances had improved, the immediate effect of default was a sharp fall in the value of its outstanding bonds, and therefore a sharp capital loss for bondholders. Private bondholders generally could do little to prevent developing country governments from defaulting.

Why did international capital flows to developing countries thrive before 1914 despite the very real possibility of default? Three factors appear to have been particularly important:

1. Foreign investment opportunities appeared very profitable. Resource-rich areas were relatively unexploited, and the payoffs expected from building factories, railways, and utilities were immense.

2. Countries like the United States, Canada, Argentina, and Australia, which absorbed most of the funds lent by Europe before 1914, had low population densities and were therefore attracting a large immigration of Europeans, including skilled workers and entrepreneurs. In a famous article, Ragnar Nurkse of Columbia University pointed out that flows of labor and capital from Europe were mutually reinforcing. European lenders felt confident that European immigrants moving to "regions of recent settlement" would successfully transplant the achievements of the Industrial Revolution, and a shared cultural heritage made the negotiation of international loans easier. European countries invested in more densely populated tropical areas too, but largely by acquiring direct investments in mines, plantations, or other resource-based ventures. Unlike bond lending, direct investments run by European managers could be profitable even in the absence of local entrepreneurial talent.[6]

3. Britain's leadership of the world economy played a key role in promoting a hospitable environment for international investment. As a champion of free trade and capital movements, Britain provided a ready source of savings for the rest of the world and a ready market in which developing exporters could earn the money needed to meet foreign debt payments. Because investment opportunities within Britain appeared relatively sparse by the end of the nineteenth century, anywhere from 25 to 40 percent of Britain's savings flowed abroad between 1870 and 1914. London's financial houses therefore had strong incentives to seek investment opportunities overseas, and foreign investment made up a large part of their activities. In addition, British loans to developing countries allowed the borrowers to import machinery and other goods from Britain. Recognizing foreign lending as crucial to domestic prosperity, the British government played an active role in assuring that defaults were settled quickly and did not lead to a breakdown of international lending and trade.

THE INTERWAR PERIOD AND ITS AFTERMATH: 1918–1972

London lost its position as the world's leading financial center after World War I and the United States emerged as the major lender to the less-developed world. Britain and France had incurred large war debts to the United States, while Germany was saddled with reparations. None of these European countries, which had been the main foreign lenders before 1914, was now in a position to play a major role in development lending. To bolster its weak balance of payments, Britain prohibited foreign lending by its residents at several points during the interwar years.

During the 1920s, many developing countries floated bonds in the United States and experienced growing inflows of American direct investment. No developing country governments defaulted in the 1920s, but signs of trouble appeared as the decade

[6] See Nurkse, "International Investment Today in the Light of Nineteenth-Century Experience," *Economic Journal* 64 (1954), pp. 134–150.

drew to a close. After the mid-1920s, world prices for agricultural products, a main source of export revenue in much of the developing world, declined. And after 1928, U.S. lending abroad fell as Americans diverted their savings from foreign investments to the booming New York stock market.

The New York stock market crash of October 1929 and the ensuing worldwide depression caused foreign finance to dry up almost entirely. No longer able to borrow abroad, developing countries were forced to cut imports, a move that accentuated the decline in aggregate demand facing the developed world. As industrialized countries erected higher barriers to imports, it became nearly impossible for international debtors to earn the export revenues needed to meet debt payments. Bolivia defaulted on January 1, 1931, and was followed, within three years, by almost every other country in Latin America. Most of these countries simultaneously left the gold standard, adopted floating exchange rates, and pursued expansionary monetary and fiscal policies to combat the effects of the depression.

The United States was not in a position to avert the worldwide financial collapse, as Britain might have been before 1914. Only a small fraction of U.S. saving was lent abroad and exports were a relatively small part of U.S. GNP. Therefore, the American govenrment and financial community did not perceive a well-functioning international trade and financial system as really crucial to U.S. economic health.

Also in contrast to Britain before 1914, the United States failed to shoulder its responsibility as an international creditor of providing a ready market for debtor exports. As countries throughout the world raised tariffs in the early 1920s to combat recession or protect new industries that had grown up during World War I, the United States, rather than setting an example of free trade, enacted the Fordney-McCumber tariff in 1922. Many economists think the subsequent Smoot-Hawley tariff of 1930 was particularly damaging to the world economy (Chapters 10 and 19). That measure aggravated the plunge in developing country agricultural export prices at the beginning of the Great Depression.

While debt defaults had occurred in the years before 1914, the widespread and synchronized default of the early 1930s was unprecedented. The nearly universal developing country default was accompanied by that of a major developed country, Germany, after Adolf Hitler's accession to power. Under the pressure of these shocks, the flow of international lending that had encouraged world economic growth during the 1920s shrank to a trickle in the 1930s. Before 1914, individual countries in default generally were able to resume borrowing once their economic prospects brightened and their previous foreign debts were settled. After the defaults of the 1930s, however, the international capital market showed no such resilience. The generalized nature of the interwar debt crisis helped deepen the Great Depression. The Depression and the trade restrictions it inspired, in turn, encouraged default and discouraged a return to normal international lending. At the outbreak of World War II, developing countries remained largely shut out of the international capital market; private lending to them on the scale seen before the Depression did not revive until the 1970s.

From 1945 to the early 1970s, most capital flows to developing countries took one of three forms: official lending, short-term trade credit granted by foreign exporters, or direct foreign investment. Many trade-related loans to developing countries became official loans when lender governments guaranteed them as a way of indirectly subsidizing their countries' exports. Because individual borrowers sometimes encountered difficulties in paying their debts during this period, governments and international lending institutions established the **Paris Club** in 1956 as a framework for rescheduling debts to official creditors (see the box below). **Debt rescheduling** occurs when payments on the debt are postponed, subject to the provision that interest is charged on the postponed payments.

Direct investments were subject to a threat different from default: the threat of nationalization (that is, expropriation) by the host government. The period following World War II was one of rising nationalism as former colonial territories became independent. In this environment, some governments did not stop at taxing the profits of foreign-owned firms but instead simply seized their assets. Disputes over compensation for such seizures were resolved on a case-by-case basis, but companies whose assets were seized usually had little power over the outcome. In spite of the risk of nationalization or heavy taxation, direct investment flows to developing countries grew quickly in the 1950s and 1960s, in part because many of them offered abundant supplies of valuable raw materials.

BORROWING AFTER 1973: OIL SHOCKS AND FLOATING INTEREST RATES

The OPEC oil shock of 1973–1974 marked the beginning of a surge in private commercial bank lending to developing countries. Banks in the industrialized world had not previously played a dominant role in such lending, but the huge OPEC current account surplus that followed the rise in oil prices had to be ''recycled'' to finance the current account deficit of the rest of the world. OPEC countries lent their surplus funds

The Paris Club

In 1956, Argentine debt difficulties prompted the formation of the Paris Club, a forum for negotiations on countries' debts to government creditors. The club has no set membership. Instead, the participants in any Paris Club negotiation are the debtor government and its creditors, who traditionally meet under the chairmanship of a senior French treasury official.

An important principle governing Paris Club rescheduling negotiations is the symmetric treatment of all creditors. Prior to the conclusion of an agreement, debtor countries approaching the Paris Club are usually required to conclude an agreement with the International Monetary Fund providing for an IMF loan together with an IMF-approved program of economic policy measures. The IMF adjustment program, an example of Fund conditionality, is typically aimed at restricting aggregate demand in the debtor country and raising its exports. Creditors view the IMF stabilization package as essential for attaining a current account path that allows the debtor to resume payment on its foreign debt.*

Commercial banks faced with the need to reschedule a country's debt to them take their cues from the Paris Club. These private creditors negotiate through a newer institution, the London Club.

* Brazil, which concluded a Paris Club negotiation in 1986 *without* agreeing to an IMF program, is one exception. By early 1987, however, Brazil's domestic economic problems had led it temporarily to suspend interest payments on its foreign commercial bank debt.

to developed countries, and banks in those countries found it profitable to relend the funds to developing borrowers.

Table 23-2 shows the global pattern of current account balances for the period between 1973 and 1986. An immediate effect of the oil price rise was a tenfold increase in the current account surplus of the major oil exporters between 1973 and 1974. These countries could not raise their spending quickly enough in the short run to keep pace with their skyrocketing export earnings, so they ran large but declining surpluses until 1978, when their expenditure finally caught up with their income. As a group, the industrial countries ran a short-lived deficit after the first OPEC shock. In contrast, the current account deficits of the nonoil developing countries rose sharply in 1974 and remained high through 1978. Why did nonoil developing countries fail to adjust their current accounts quickly to the oil shock? As the industrial countries slipped into the recession of 1974–1975, developing country governments adopted and maintained expansionary policies that spurred investment and helped keep their output growth rates high relative to those in the industrialized world. The cost of these measures was a large and persistent deficit: developing countries were borrowing heavily abroad and building up foreign debt to maintain spending levels in excess of their incomes. The total debt of the nonoil developing countries at the end of 1978 ($336 billion) was two and a half times its 1973 level ($130 billion).[7]

[7] See International Monetary Fund, *World Economic Outlook,* 1983, Table 32.

TABLE 23-2 Current account balances of major oil exporters, other developing countries, and industrial countries, 1973–1986 (billions of dollars)

Year	*Major oil exporters*	*Other developing countries*	*Industrial countries*
1973	6.7	−11.3	20.3
1974	68.3	−37.0	−10.8
1975	35.4	−46.3	19.8
1976	40.3	−32.6	0.5
1977	29.4	−29.6	−2.4
1978	−1.3	−33.2	14.6
1979	56.8	−49.7	−25.6
1980	102.4	−74.4	−61.8
1981	45.8	−95.0	−18.9
1982	−17.8	−73.2	−22.2
1983	−18.0	−40.9	−23.0
1984	−10.0	−25.0	−64.2
1985	−5.5	−28.7	−54.2
1986	−37.1	−9.4	−27.1

Source: International Monetary Fund, *World Economic Outlook,* 1983–1991. The current account balances reported above do not include official transfers. The countries included as major oil exporters are those whose oil exports are at least two-thirds of overall exports and at least 100 million barrels per year. Global current accounts may not sum to zero because of errors, omissions, and the exclusion of some countries (for example, members of the former Soviet bloc).

In most of the years between 1974 and 1978, the deficits of the nonoil developing countries shown in Table 23-2 correspond closely to the surpluses of the major oil producers. Oil producers were not lending directly to other developing countries but instead were lending whatever oil earnings they could not spend to industrial countries, whose banks in turn lent these funds to developing borrowers. Why was this recycling necessary? Oil exporters did not want to assume the risks of direct lending to developing countries but preferred to acquire safer assets located in industrial economies. At the same time, banks in developed countries faced interest rates that were low; in fact, when measured in real terms, that is, in terms of output, interest rates in developed countries were negative.[8] It is no wonder that when faced with negative real interest rates at home, developed country banks were eager to lend to developing country borrowers, who were willing to pay somewhat higher rates than the banks' local customers. Even after the addition of a borrowing premium, developing countries faced historically low real interest charges for foreign loans, which naturally encouraged them to borrow abroad.

The second oil shock brought a renewed surge in the current account surpluses of the main oil exporters in 1979; at the same time, it worsened the deficits of other countries. Oil producers' earnings were once again recycled to developing borrowers, but while the industrial countries as a group were closer to current account balance by 1981, the nonoil developing countries borrowed close to $100 billion in that year to finance their overall current account deficit. From a year-end level of $336 billion in 1978, the indebtedness of these countries rose to over $600 billion by the end of 1982. By 1982, however, the oil exporters were themselves running a deficit and therefore were not providing the funds to finance the still large deficit of the other developing countries. As a result, less-developed debtors were encountering increased difficulty in borrowing from developed country banks even before the debt crisis erupted in the second half of 1982.

The severity of the debt crisis is closely tied to a key institutional feature of bank lending to developing countries in the late 1970s: the use of loan contracts with adjustable interest rates, called **floating-rate loan contracts.** Under a floating-rate loan contract, the lender is allowed to change the interest rate the borrower pays on the loan as market interest rates change. As an example, suppose you borrow from a bank for a year at a rate of 5 percentage points above the rate on U.S. Treasury bills, adjustable every six months. If the Treasury bill rate is 5 percent per annum when you take out your loan, you pay interest at a rate of 10 percent during the loan's first six months; but if the Treasury bill rate rises to 9 percent within the first six months, you must pay interest at a rate of 14 percent for the next six months. Typically, the interest charged on floating-rate dollar loans from banks to developing countries was tied to the London Interbank Offered Rate (LIBOR), the interest rate London commercial banks charge each other for dollar loans.

Banks favored the use of floating-rate contracts because adjustable interest rates protected them from being "locked in" to low-interest rate loans when the interest rates they themselves had to pay to depositors rose. By the late 1970s, a large portion

[8] In 1976, for example, the interest rate on three-month U.S. Treasury bills averaged 4.9 percent per year, while the consumer price index rose by 6.7 percent over the same year. These figures tell us that a U.S. bank lending domestically in 1976 would have earned an average real rate of return of 4.9 − 6.7 = −1.8 percent over the year. Econometric studies suggest that *expected* as well as realized U.S. real interest rates were negative in the mid-1970s.

of developing country debt (particularly that of Latin American countries) carried floating interest rates. Heavy borrowing on a floating-rate basis left developing countries exposed to the danger that a sharp rise in U.S. interest rates would increase their interest burden dramatically. Such an increase did occur in the late 1970s, and that increase, together with the events that accompanied it, set the stage for a widespread developing country debt crisis comparable only with that of the 1930s.

Origins of the Developing Country Debt Crisis

In the years 1981–1983, the world economy suffered the worst recession since the 1930s. Just as the Great Depression made it hard for developing countries to make payments on their foreign loans—quickly causing an almost universal default—the great recession of the 1980s also sparked a crisis over developing country debt.

LEADING UP TO THE CRISIS

Chapter 20 described how the U.S. Federal Reserve in 1979 adopted a tough anti-inflation monetary policy that helped push the world economy into recession by 1981. Even before the recession hit, however, the U.S. monetary shift had direct adverse effects on developing countries' real incomes.

Adverse effects came through two principal channels, U.S. interest rates and the dollar's exchange rate. The Fed's monetary changes were followed by sharp rises in dollar interest rates and in the dollar's foreign exchange market value. LIBOR, to which interest rates on many developing country loans are tied, rose sharply in 1979 (Figure 23-1a).[9] This rise in LIBOR made new borrowing more expensive, and because much developing country debt had been contracted at floating interest rates, the interest payments due on previous loans also rose. The developing world's foreign interest burden therefore took an immediate upward jump.

The interest rate effect was reinforced by the behavior of the dollar. Since much developing country debt is denominated in dollars, the dollar's appreciation increased the *real* value of **debt service**—the flow of interest payments and principal to foreign creditors. Table 23-3 shows a measure of the dollar value of developing country debt service payments from 1977 to 1985. In reading this table, keep in mind that the dollar's real appreciation after 1980 caused the real value of these payments to rise by more than their dollar value. Thus, the rise in dollar payments after 1980 understates the increase in the real interest burden of developing countries.

The developing countries' reaction to the adverse movements in interest rates and debt burdens helped set the stage for the crisis to follow. The rise in nonoil developing country borrowing after 1978 (Table 23-2) resulted not only from the oil shock but also from the simultaneous rise in real debt service burdens. Developing countries viewed both setbacks as partially temporary and hoped to soften their impact by borrowing abroad and maintaining domestic demand until better conditions allowed

[9] Through asset market arbitrage, LIBOR is determined mainly by interest rates on dollar assets located in the United States. The shift in U.S. monetary policy in 1979 therefore had a direct and immediate impact on LIBOR.

FIGURE 23-1
LIBOR and developing country nonoil commodity export prices, 1978–1991.
In 1981, dollar interest rates reached a historic high point, worsening developing country debt service burdens. At the same time, the prices of developing country commodity exports (and with them, the terms of trade) plunged. In 1985, the favorable effect of lower dollar interest rates on debt service burdens was offset by another decline in commodity export prices.
Source: (a) International Monetary Fund, *International Financial Statistics,* various issues. (b) International Monetary Fund, *World Economic Outlook,* various issues, Table A29.

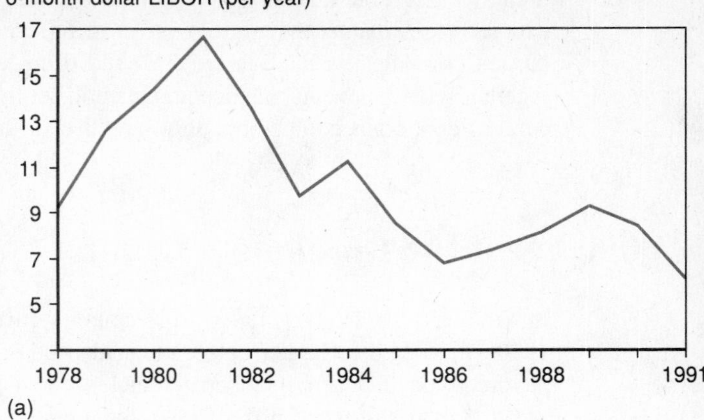

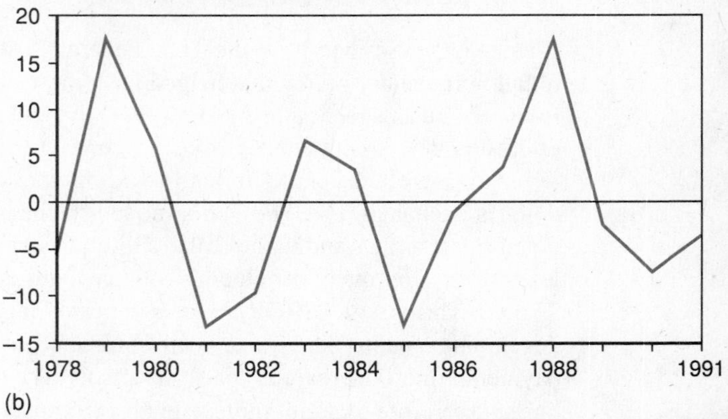

them to repay their loans. Interest rates did not, however, return quickly to pre-1979 levels.

As the world economy slid into recession in 1981, developing countries therefore were carrying an unprecedented external debt burden. U.S. interest rates were at a peak, and these rates were reflected in payments on both new borrowing and older floating-rate debt (Figure 23-1a). Much of the short-term borrowing of the immediately preceding years was coming due, and countries faced the choice of repaying these loans or refinancing them at historically high interest rates. As Table 23-2 shows, the overall current account surplus of the oil exporters turned to a deficit between 1981 and 1982, so the ready supply of "petrodollars" that had financed developing country borrowing in earlier years was disappearing. And with inflation falling throughout the industrialized world (see Table 20-4), commercial banks in the developed countries found they could now earn high real returns by lending at home. As a result, developing debtors were finding it increasingly hard to borrow from the banks that had eagerly financed their earlier current account deficits.

TABLE 23-3 Debt service payments of developing debtors, 1977–1985 (billions of dollars)

1977	*1978*	*1979*	*1980*	*1981*	*1982*	*1983*	*1984*	*1985*
39.5	57.2	83.8	102.6	124.1	135.9	132.5	124.0	129.0

Source: International Monetary Fund, *World Economic Outlook,* 1985–1991. The debt service payments reported here include all interest payments plus principal payments on debt with a maturity exceeding one year. These figures exclude Eastern Europe and the former Soviet Union.

DEVELOPING COUNTRIES IN THE WORLDWIDE RECESSION

The 1981–1983 growth slowdown in industrial countries had two immediate effects on developing country incomes. First, as growth slowed in the industrialized world, developing countries began to face diminished demand for their exports. This fall in aggregate demand directly reduced the growth rate of output in developing countries. Second, the reduction in demand for developing country exports tended to lower their prices. As noted earlier, many less-developed countries depend on exports of agricultural products or raw materials, whose prices are sensitive to demand conditions in world markets. Developing countries' real incomes therefore declined not only because output growth slowed but also because the prices of the primary commodities they export fell relative to the prices of their imports. A further negative factor was increased protectionist pressure in a number of industrialized countries, which made it harder to sell in industrial country markets.

The effect of the world recession on the dollar prices of nonoil primary commodities can be seen in Figure 23-1b. After rising fairly steadily from the mid-1960s to 1980, commodity prices plunged dramatically in 1981 and 1982. The fall in prices was not entirely due to the fall in worldwide aggregate demand. The dollar's appreciation also put downward pressure on dollar commodity prices.[10]

Table 23-4 shows recent output growth rates for developed and developing countries. The table indicates a marked reduction in industrial country growth rates during the early 1980s, with GNP growth actually turning negative in 1982, the low point of the 1981–1983 recession. Developing countries exhibit a similar fall in growth rates during the early 1980s. However, the numbers for developing countries as a group conceal important regional differences.

In Asian countries such as South Korea and Taiwan the recession had little effect on growth, which soon reached levels far exceeding those of the previous decade. Many of these countries (with the notable exception of the Philippines) had relatively low debt levels and had been promoting vigorous manufacturing export sectors for some time.

Countries in Africa and the Western Hemisphere did not fare so well (and their growth rates have generally remained at levels well below those of the 1970s). The

[10] The fall in commodity prices was mirrored in the behavior of the developing countries' terms of trade. The terms of trade of indebted developing countries fell by 3.3 percent in 1981 and by 2.7 percent in 1982. See International Monetary Fund, *World Economic Outlook*, April 1985, Table 27.

TABLE 23-4 Growth rates of output for developed and developing countries, 1971–1980 average and 1981–1992 (percent per year)

Country group	*1971–1980 average*	*1981*	*1982*	*1983*	*1984*	*1985*	*1986*	*1987*	*1988*	*1989*	*1990*	*1991*	*1992*
Industrial countries	3.2	1.5	−0.3	2.8	4.5	3.3	2.8	3.2	4.3	3.4	2.5	0.8	1.7
Developing countries	5.5	1.9	2.2	2.2	4.5	4.4	3.8	4.5	3.9	3.7	3.5	3.3	6.2
Africa	3.8	1.9	2.5	−0.9	1.4	4.1	1.7	0.8	3.6	2.7	0.9	1.4	1.9
Asia	5.3	5.9	5.4	7.8	8.4	6.7	6.7	8.1	8.9	5.3	5.6	5.8	6.9
Middle East	7.2	−1.3	1.3	1.7	0.6	1.4	−1.6	2.4	−1.7	4.7	4.2	0.4	—
Western Hemisphere	5.9	0.3	−0.8	−2.7	3.6	3.4	4.3	2.2	0.7	1.0	−0.1	2.9	2.8

Source: International Monetary Fund, *World Economic Outlook,* 1989–1992. Developing countries exclude Eastern Europe and the former Soviet Union. Growth rates for 1992 are projections.

group of Western Hemisphere developing countries, which includes Latin America, was especially hard hit, with an output growth rate of only 0.3 percent in 1981 and *negative* 0.8 percent in 1982. The staggering −2.7 percent growth rate these countries suffered in 1983 was a direct result of the debt crisis, which started in August 1982.

MEXICO: THE BEGINNING OF THE CRISIS

On August 12, 1982, Mexico notified foreign financial officials that its central bank had nearly run out of reserves and that it could no longer meet previously scheduled payments on its foreign debt. That debt, amounting to more than $80 billion at the time, made Mexico, after Brazil, the world's largest developing debtor. Mexico requested a loan from foreign governments and central banks, a moratorium on payments of principal to commercial banks, and a rescheduling of the principal on debt due to mature in coming months. At the same time, Mexican officials approached the International Monetary Fund with a request for a loan and an IMF-sponsored macroeconomic stabilization plan.

What chain of events had placed Mexico on the brink of default? As was typically the case in countries that experienced debt servicing problems in the 1980s, both adverse external shocks and internal macroeconomic mismanagement were to blame. In the mid-1970s, Mexico had become a major oil exporter (though not a member of OPEC); by the mid-1980s some 60 percent of Mexico's export revenues came from oil. Since the Mexican oil industry is government-owned, the surge in oil revenues accrued directly to the government, which used the funds to finance subsidies, public works, and social programs. Indeed, government spending rose more quickly than oil revenues: some of this spending was financed through seigniorage—that is, the monetary printing press—while some was financed by borrowing abroad. Money creation sparked rapid inflation and a real appreciation of the Mexican peso, whose nominal exchange rate with the dollar was fixed by the Banco de Mexico, Mexico's central bank. But, helped by the fiscal stimulus, Mexico achieved a high rate of economic growth, and with oil prices high and rising, foreign banks, particularly U.S. banks, competed to lend Mexico money.

Mexico's prospects dimmed in 1981 as the worldwide recession began and oil demand fell. The Mexican government committed the major blunder of not immediately lowering the price of its oil in the face of weakening demand, and it had to borrow abroad to make up for the resulting fall in oil revenues. The Banco de Mexico's foreign reserves fell as Mexicans, increasingly nervous about a possible peso devaluation, fled from pesos to dollars.

In early 1982 the recession in the United States deepened. Closely linked to the United States through international trade, Mexico was bound to suffer a large decline in growth as a result of the fall in U.S. demand. Mexico devalued the peso in February 1982 but failed to cut the government budget deficit or adopt other significant expenditure-changing measures that would curb its current account deficit and thus reduce the country's need for additional loans from abroad. The devaluation therefore translated quickly into additional domestic inflation, with little benefit to external balance or employment.

Commercial banks began to question Mexico's ability to repay its substantial debt without politically hazardous cuts in public and private consumption: petroleum prices were weak; demand for Mexican exports was down as a result of the recession; high interest rates and the high dollar had increased the country's debt service burden; and there was no confidence that the government would brake its inflationary fiscal expansion. By the summer of 1982, Mexico found its customary foreign credit lines drying up. Like many other developing countries, Mexico had built up a substantial short-term debt whose principal had to be "rolled over" by the banks—that is, relent to Mexico—or repaid. Any banks still willing to lend to Mexico would now do so only at penalty interest rates that reflected the possibility of default. Anticipating another devaluation, Mexicans had nearly bought out the Banco de Mexico's dollar reserves by mid-August 1982. At that point the Mexican government took the dramatic step of seeking a multilateral international loan package and negotiations with its commercial bank creditors.

THE DEBT CRISIS IN OTHER COUNTRIES

Even as Mexico began its long and complex debt negotiations, other debtors in Latin America, for example, Brazil (with a 1982 debt of close to $88 billion) and Argentina (with a 1982 debt near $40 billion), found themselves unable to take out additional foreign loans or even roll over maturing short-term debt. Bankers saw similarities in the economic circumstances of all the Latin American debtors, and they feared that if Mexico defaulted other countries might follow its example, as happened in the 1930s. Banks scrambled to reduce their risks by refusing to extend new credits or renew old ones. By the end of 1986, more than forty countries in Latin America, Africa, and elsewhere had encountered severe external financing problems. Countries in East Asia (other than the Philippines) maintained high growth rates throughout the recession and avoided the need to reschedule their debts (see Table 23-4).

Much of the debt of African nations was owed to official agencies and governments; the Paris Club therefore provided a ready-made forum for the resolution of African debt issues. A framework for rescheduling Latin America's massive debts to commercial banks, however, did not yet exist. Hundreds of banks around the world had claims on Latin America, and American giants like Citicorp, Bank of America, and Manufacturers Hanover had invested significant portions of their loan portfolios in the region. A widespread Latin American default would have threatened the viability of the large banks and some of the smaller banks, endangering the world financial system. The Fed and foreign central banks therefore viewed the task of averting default, even by a single country, as crucial. A Brazilian default, say, could have set off a chain reaction of bank failures involving many countries. No one wanted a replay of the widespread banking crisis that occurred at the beginning of the Great Depression.

The Economics of Sovereign Default

Management of the debt crisis turned out to be a difficult and changing process involving creditor and debtor governments, the IMF, the World Bank, and the largest private banks with claims on developing countries. To understand how policy toward troubled third-world debts has evolved, however, we must first examine the economic factors behind a government's decision to default.[11] As noted above, most loans extended to a developing country are either taken out or guaranteed by the country's government. This characteristic of lending to developing countries makes the default decision essentially a government decision, not a decision by individual resident borrowers.

A government decision to default on external obligations is called a **sovereign default** because a defaulting government is not subject to the legal remedies that would usually be invoked in cases of private default. Even a sovereign defaulter does, however, incur significant costs. How does a government measure the costs of sovereign default against the benefits in deciding whether to continue meeting its debt-service obligations?

THE COSTS OF SOVEREIGN DEFAULT

When a sovereign borrower defaults on its foreign debt, its creditors cannot penalize it as they would penalize defaulting private borrowers resident in their own countries. If you default on a student loan, for example, the lender can take you to court. A bank cannot take Brazil or Mexico to court if those countries fail to live up to the terms of their loan agreements. Nonetheless, even sovereign borrowers cannot default with impunity. There are three main costs a sovereign borrower must consider in deciding whether to default:

1. *Seizure of assets.* Creditors of a sovereign defaulter may be able to persuade their governments to seize any of the debtor's assets located in their jurisdiction. These could in principle include the foreign reserves of the defaulting country's central bank, foreign assets owned by the defaulting country's private citizens, or even goods in

[11] A pioneering analytical study of developing country default is Jonathan Eaton and Mark Gersovitz, "Debt with Potential Repudiation: Theoretical and Empirical Analysis," *Review of Economic Studies* 48 (April 1981), pp. 289–309. For further developments emphasizing rescheduling, see Jeremy Bulow and Kenneth Rogoff, "A Constant Recontracting Model of Sovereign Debt," *Journal of Political Economy* 97 (February 1989), pp. 155–178.

international trade owned by the debtor and crossing creditors' borders. Seizure of assets is probably a minor deterrent to default, given the magnitude of developing countries' foreign debts, but the possibility does enter governments' calculations. In early 1986, for example, the Peruvian government brought home some $700 million worth of gold and silver it had been holding abroad. The country had fallen into serious arrears in its debt payments, and it feared that its precious metal stocks would be seized by creditors.

2. *Exclusion from future borrowing.* A country that defaulted could be shut out of the international capital market for some time. Once a country has already defaulted on previous debts, prospective lenders will be unwilling to believe promises that it will abide by the terms of new loan contracts. If a sovereign defaulter did succeed in getting a loan abroad, its existing creditors would try to seize the new funds.

The characteristics of developing country borrowing make an exclusion from the international capital market costly. A defaulting country would no longer be able to draw on foreign savings to develop profitable domestic investment opportunities; all domestic investment would have to be financed from the possibly meager supply of domestic savings. Further, the country would lose the flexibility to borrow abroad and maintain consumption and investment in the face of temporary fluctuations in its real income. Sharper booms and busts would impose economic costs and might also threaten the country's political stability.

3. *Reduction of the gains from international trade.* The most serious cost of default is a consequence of the first two: sovereign defaulters could find their ability to engage in international trade severely curtailed. As noted above, debtor country goods involved in international trade would be subject to seizure whenever they crossed a creditor's border. In addition, a defaulter's exclusion from the international capital market might leave it unable to obtain trade credits abroad or even to mainain checking accounts in foreign banks (since these accounts could be seized). Without the ability to make payments in internationally acceptable currencies, a sovereign defaulter could be reduced to barter trade.

Conceivably, a country could default on loans to some banks but not to others, and thus maintain its ability to trade. In practice, however, loans to developing countries have been made by large *syndicates* of banks, and loan agreements require that a country falling into default with respect to one creditor be declared in default by the other creditors.

THE BENEFIT OF SOVEREIGN DEFAULT

The benefit of default is that the debtor escapes the responsibility of paying interest and principal on its foreign debt. The more money a debtor owes, the greater is its gain from defaulting. Factors other than the debt service burden affect the benefit from default, however. The most important of these is the country's income level at the time. If a country's income is high, it can service its foreign debt without painful cuts in domestic consumption and investment, but if the economy is in a slump, continuation of debt service may impose severe hardship on the population and thereby court revolution.

A good indicator of the current burden of servicing an external debt is the net **resource transfer** from creditors to the debtor, that is, the amount of new loans creditors are extending, less the flow interest and principal payments from debtor to creditor, less any other net capital outflows from the debtor. In symbols, we can express this resouce transfer, *RT,* as

$$RT = L - S - O, \tag{23-1}$$

where L stands for new loans to debtors (including rollovers of maturing debt), S stands for total debt service payments to creditors (principal plus interest), and O stands for other net capital outflows from the debtor (including, for example, capital flight by debtor country residents). A positive value of RT means that new loans to debtors exceed debtors' payments to foreigners, so that on balance debtors are receiving resources from abroad. A negative RT, however, means that new loans are insufficient to cover debt service plus other capital outflows, so that there is a net resource flow from debtors to creditors.[12]

WHEN DOES A DEBTOR CHOOSE TO DEFAULT?

A debtor clearly will never default as long as the resource transfer it is receiving from creditors is positive—it always pays to service debts as long as the money to service them is painlessly provided by new capital inflows! Once the resource transfer becomes negative, however, the temptation to default can arise, and it will increase as new loans decline or as debt service payments rise. *A debtor will find it advantageous to default when the benefit of stopping payment on loans exceeds the perceived cost of violating loan agreements.*

Table 23-5 shows how the debt crisis changed the resource transfer from creditors to developing debtors. For the years 1980–1982 you can see the normal pattern of a positive resource transfer from capital-rich creditors to less-developed debtors. In 1983, the first full year of the debt crisis, there is a sharp turnaround as the resource transfer becomes negative, that is, as net new lending falls below debt service payments. By 1984 the *reverse* transfer from debtors to creditors has mushroomed to $41.0 billion.

These numbers make it easy to see why the events of the early 1980s made a generalized developing country default seem imminent. Economic growth in much of the developing world had slowed as a result of the global recession. At the same time, soaring real interest costs coupled with banks' unwillingness to extend new loans and private capital flight imposed a heavy transfer burden on developing debtors. In August 1982, policy makers concerned with the debt crisis faced the immediate task of deflecting debtor countries and creditor banks from their collision course.

Managing the Debt Crisis

By late 1982, individual banks in the industrial world wanted not only to avoid additional lending to developing countries, but also to reduce their overall holdings of those countries' liabilities. A single bank can reduce its holdings of developing country loans

[12] In terms of the balance of payments, the resource transfer from creditors to the debtor is just the debtor's capital account surplus less its net interest payments to creditors. RT thus can be thought of as the *noninterest* portion of the debtor's current account deficit, that is, debtor imports less debtor exports, exclusive of interest payments. This makes intuitive sense: the difference between noninterest imports and noninterest exports is the net flow of real resources into debtor economies. Alternatively, RT equals private consumption plus domestic investment plus government purchases *less* gross domestic product.

TABLE 23-5 Resource transfer to indebted developing countries, 1980–1992 (billions of dollars)

1980	*1981*	*1982*	*1983*	*1984*	*1985*	*1986*	*1987*	*1988*	*1989*	*1990*	*1991*	*1992*
27.9	49.6	38.2	−8.5	−41.0	−38.4	−20.6	−53.8	−51.5	−56.3	−59.1	−43.8	−16.8

Source: International Monetary Fund, *World Economic Outlook*, 1988–1992. Calculated as current account deficit less interest payments abroad. Figure for 1992 is based on projections.

by refusing to renew existing loans or by selling them off; *all* banks can do so at the same time, however, only if developing countries rapidly achieve a current account surplus large enough to reduce substantially their aggregate bank debt. Developing countries generally had current account deficits in 1982 and preferred default to the politically unacceptable fiscal measures that would have been needed to generate the resource transfer banks wanted. The debt crisis has gone through several phases since 1982, but all of them reflect this basic and continuing conflict over the resource transfer between commercial banks and developing debtors.

THE FIRST PHASE: CONCERTED LENDING

The 1982 debt panic raised a coordination problem similar to the one that arises when individual depositors attempt to withdraw deposits during a bank run (Chapter 22). Each individual depositor finds it in her interest to withdraw her money from the bank, even though the joint action of *all* depositors forces the bank to close and prevents *anyone* from getting money out. Similarly, individual banks, in pursuing their own interests, collectively risked causing sovereign defaults that would leave all parties worse off.

Deposit insurance and last-resort lending by central banks discourage panics in domestic banking systems, but no similar institutions back up the obligations of sovereign debtors. The task facing international policy makers was somehow to generate enough new lending to deter immediate default, even though individual banks preferred to reduce their exposure to developing borrowers.

When the Mexican crisis began, Mexico and the United States organized a meeting between Mexican financial officials and representatives of the hundreds of banks with claims on the country. A bank advisory committee of the largest banks was set up to represent all banks and to keep them informed about the progress of negotiations. This advisory committee system turned into a model for the numerous debt problems that arose after the Mexican case. One purpose of the advisory committees was to help coordinate continued lending. The banks on a country advisory committee had lent too much to the country to stop lending without provoking an immediate default; these large banks, joined by industrial country governments and the IMF, provided new credits and coaxed (or pressured) smaller banks into continued lending.

Bank lending under these arrangements is known as **concerted lending,** a polite term for lending that in many cases was involuntary! Under concerted lending, banks are supposed to contribute new funds in proportion to their loan exposure at the beginning of the debt crisis. Continued bank lending to developing countries has taken two forms, rescheduling and extension of new credits. Rescheduling is one way of rolling over maturing debts: principal payments are postponed, but they are due with additional interest, so that short-term debts are changed into longer-term debts. But if lenders roll over or reschedule principal only on maturing debts, a debtor's net foreign liabilities cannot increase. Thus, its current account must be balanced or in surplus and the reverse resource transfer to creditors must equal or exceed the entire interest bill on its debt. Banks initially provided some additional loans to help finance debtors' (much-reduced) current account deficits, but as we will see, this additional finance quickly dried up.

THE ROLE OF THE IMF

IMF lending and conditionality have been more visible during the debt crisis than ever before. Recall that IMF conditionality is the close economic surveillance a country's policy makers may have to accept as a condition for borrowing Fund resources (Chapter 19). Countries rescheduling debts usually borrowed from the IMF as well and agreed to IMF-designed macroeconomic stabilization programs. Even though the amounts lent by the Fund have been small relative to each debtor's needs, the Fund's involvement has been crucial, often signaling to banks that the debtor is taking measures to improve its credit standing.

In addition, IMF involvement has provided some debtor governments with a politically convenient scapegoat. To reduce current account deficits, governments have had to remove subsidies, raise taxes, cut wages in publicly owned industries, and increase the prices of publicly supplied goods and services. Expenditure-switching devaluations often have been a necessary accompaniment. Such measures are naturally unpopular at home. Debtor governments have at times shifted public resentment toward the IMF, which can be blamed for "imposing" restrictive economic measures. In reality, debtor governments cooperating with the IMF have viewed the costs of cooperation as being preferable to the costs of default.

The IMF initially played a central role in coordinating bank lending to debt-ridden countries. Starting with the Mexican case, the IMF made it a rule to hold off approval on its own lending to debtors until banks had agreed on theirs. Since IMF loans and stabilization programs were seen by banks as critical to debtor solvency, this tactic was effective at first in getting banks to come up with new money. The banks' reluctance to provide money grew, however, as the years passed and the debt crisis refused to go away.

THE SECOND PHASE: TRYING TO MUDDLE THROUGH

Policy makers hoped that appropriate adjustments of debtor policies and quicker economic growth in the industrial world would promote an early return to "spontaneous" or voluntary capital flows to developing countries. Concerted lending was intended as a stopgap measure, meant to buy time while banks reduced developing country exposure and while developing countries reduced their debt-output ratios. The hope in official circles was that eventually debtors would be able and willing to repay creditors in full.

The effects of the adjustment measures taken by developing countries after 1982 are clearly visible in Tables 23-2, 23-4, and 23-5. By 1984, the current account deficits of nonoil developing countries had fallen far below their levels of the early 1980s, and developing debtors were making a substantial reverse resource transfer to creditor countries. This reduction in external deficits was not achieved without cost. As Table 23-4 shows, the regions most affected by the crisis had negative output growth rates in 1983. Sharply lowered growth was naturally accompanied by high levels of unemployment, falling real wages, and growing political unrest. Further, low growth in Latin America helped deepen the recession of the early 1980s in the developed world.

The recovery of 1984 had a positive effect on developing country growth and employment. By early 1985, many observers felt that the worst of the debt crisis was over and that the world economy would indeed be able to "muddle through" by simply outgrowing the debt problem. These hopes were shown to be premature later in 1985.

The worldwide recovery slowed down in that year, directly reducing foreign demand for developing countries' exports and contributing to a fall in their terms of trade (see Figure 23-1). Debtors derived some benefit from a decline in U.S. interest rates, which slowed the growth of debt service burdens, but there was no sign that the vigorous developed country growth that had pushed developing countries closer to internal and external balance in 1984 would soon resume. Pressure on public budgets led to accelerating inflation in a number of developing debtors.

Also worrisome was the growing domestic political pressure in some industrialized countries (including the United States) for restrictive trade measures aimed in part at developing country exports. By closing industrialized country markets to developing debtors, protectionist policies, as they had done in the 1930s, risked pushing debtor countries closer to default.

Debts of the Eastern Bloc

Nonmarket economies in Eastern Europe borrowed heavily from Western banks and governments in the years before 1982. Although these countries were not usually classified as "developing," they suffered from generally low living standards and heavy government control of economic activity. Like the developing world, Eastern Europe encountered debt problems in the 1980s.

Poland, for example, owed nearly $40 billion to foreigners in the West at the end of 1989. The country's debt problems began even before 1982, when workers striking under the banner of the Solidarity movement brought production to a standstill. After years of shortages and political repression, Poland took a sudden turn toward democracy in 1989. A new government led by Solidarity began to decentralize the heavily controlled economy and moved Poland's currency, the zloty, toward partial convertibility. The IMF, the World Bank, and Western governments stepped in with substantial loan packages despite Poland's past failure to meet fully its payments to official creditors. Early in 1991, Poland and its government creditors reached a Paris Club agreement canceling half of the country's obligations to them. Commercial bank creditors have, however, been reluctant to extend Poland new credits or to forgive old debts.

Hungary, with a 1990 foreign debt of $21 billion, has so far avoided rescheduling. The country was able to finance its 1990 current account deficit only by submitting to strict IMF conditionality. But in 1991 and 1992 official capital inflows were supplemented by a surge in private direct foreign investment.

One country that took a different approach to the debt crisis was Romania, whose dictatorial leader, Nicolae Ceaucescu, decided to repay rapidly his country's $21 billion foreign debt. Ceaucescu stopped imports and exported food badly needed at home, paying off much of the debt by 1989 but in the process pushing Romania's living standard to the poverty level. The harsh debt repayment strategy, enforced with the help of a ruthless secret police force, had political costs. In the last days of 1989, as other Eastern European nations were moving peacefully toward democracy, Ceaucescu and his regime were swept away by a bloody revolution.

The Soviet Union itself was a heavy borrower from capitalist countries. When the U.S.S.R. broke up into independent states in 1991, Russia offered to take responsibility for all of the former Soviet government's debts, which at year's end totaled $66 billion. (Eastern Europe's total foreign debt was estimated to be $109 billion at the end of 1991.) Disarray in the domestic economy forced Russia to miss debt payments, and promised aid from Western governments was slow to materialize. As Russia's political and economic instability grew worse during the 1992–1993 winter, many Western commentators urged their governments to reduce the beleaguered country's foreign debts.

In an attempt to support Russia's reform-minded president, Boris Yeltsin, Western governments agreed in April 1993 to reschedule $15 billion of the country's $20 billion debt to foreign official creditors. This move opened the way for London Club negotiations between Russia and its private creditors.

By 1986, developing debtors were showing serious signs of ''debt fatigue,'' despite some improvement in their terms of trade. Proposals for some form of **debt relief**—for example, lower interest rates on debt or forgiveness of principal—were heard more frequently. Creditors feared that other countries might follow the example of Peru, which had already announced it would limit debt service payments to 10 percent of its export earnings. Many banks had sold off developing country loans, and these ''securitized'' assets were traded in a growing secondary market at discounted prices reflecting the possibility of nonpayment. Figure 23-2 shows how the growing pessimism over developing country prospects was reflected in a falling secondary market value of developing country debt. In February 1987 Brazil moved abruptly toward default by announcing a unilateral suspension of interest payments on its commercial bank debt. Creditor pressure soon brought Brazil to heel, but the episode made bankers reduce their expectations that developing country loans would be repaid in full.

The American bank Citicorp stunned financial markets in May 1987 by announcing a sharp increase in the reserves it held against possible losses on bad loans. This action, which was followed by other banks with third-world loans, implied large accounting losses because funds added to loan loss reserves (which increase bank capital) reduce profits immediately (as opposed to later when they are used to cover bad loans). The action also was a tacit admission that the banks did not expect full repayment. As Figure 23-2 shows, the average market value of a loan to a heavily indebted developing country plummeted before the year's end to less than half its face value. This price reduction meant that investors expected the average loan to repay less than 50 cents on the dollar.

In the years since 1982, American banks had reduced the fraction of developing country loans in their portfolios and increased the ratio of bank capital to such loans. (See Table 23-6.) With their balance sheets now less vulnerable to default, the banks were signaling their intention to play a tougher game with indebted countries by lending even less than before. The resource transfer to developing countries dropped sharply in 1987 (Table 23-5) and output growth slowed in the problem debt regions (Table 23-

FIGURE 23-2
Value of developing country loans in the secondary market.
Since the end of 1986, the average secondary market value of developing country loans has plummeted.
Source: Salomon Brothers. The plot shows a weighted average of market values (relative to face values) for bank loans to the fifteen most heavily indebted developing countries.

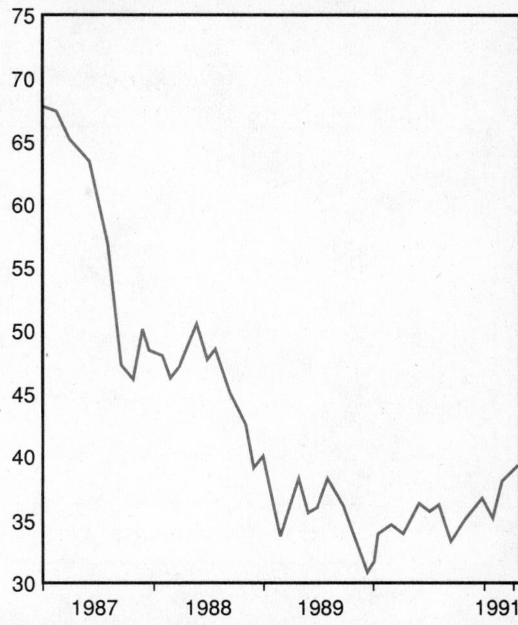

4). Argentina, a major debtor, went deeply into arrears on its debt payments. By early 1989, secondary market prices for developing country loans had reached new lows.

THE BRADY PLAN

The persistence of the debt problem led the U.S. government to advance a new debt initiative, the Brady Plan, in March 1989. In 1985, U.S. Treasury Secretary James A. Baker III had set out an American debt policy based on continuing muddling through and a presumption that debts would eventually be repaid in full. The strategy of his successor, Nicholas Brady, recognized implicitly that full repayment was no longer a reasonable goal. His plan put pressure on banks to concede some form of debt relief, and also called for an expansion in secondary market transactions aimed at debt reduction.

More specifically, the Brady Plan had three major parts:

1. Commercial banks were urged "to work with debtor nations to provide a broader range of alternatives for financial support, including greater efforts to achieve both debt and debt service reduction and to provide new lending." The syndication agreements governing commercial bank lending to debtor countries contain "sharing" and "negative pledge" clauses that prevent individual syndicate members from making mutually advantageous financial deals with the debtor. Brady called for a temporary waiver of the clauses to allow debtors and individual banks to settle debts.

2. The IMF and World Bank were urged to provide funding "for debt or debt

TABLE 23-6 Developing country loans as percentages of assets and capital of U.S. banks, 1979–1990 (percentage points)

Year	External claims on developing countries relative to total assets	External claims on developing countries relative to bank capital
1979	9.8	184.8
1980	10.1	188.7
1981	11.0	204.1
1982	11.3	202.4
1983	10.9	183.2
1984	10.0	152.7
1985	8.4	122.2
1986	7.4	102.1
1987	6.7	84.2
1988	5.6	68.7
1989	4.5	54.3
1990	3.8	46.1

Source: International Monetary Fund.

service reduction purposes.'' In practice, the international institutions might guarantee new bonds issued by a debtor in exchange for existing debt or might provide loans ''to replenish [debtor] reserves following a cash buyback'' of debt on the secondary market.

3. The IMF was urged to modify its practice of delaying its own disbursements to debtors until commercial bank creditors had agreed on their own lending commitments. The original rationale for this IMF practice was the institution's desire to overcome a market coordination problem and push banks into concerted lending, but by 1989 IMF delays had turned into a bargaining chip used by the banks against debtors.

The Brady Plan clearly had features that would seriously reduce the cohesiveness of the banks as a negotiating group. It thus represented a ''tilt'' in U.S. government policy toward the debtors. What had persuaded the United States to get tough on the banks? Most important, the debt crisis seemed to be undermining political stability in Latin America; Mexico's ruling party had been badly mauled in that country's 1988 presidential election, and fledgling democracies in Argentina, Brazil, and elsewhere seemed in danger. In addition, however, banks had strengthened their balance sheets sufficiently over the past seven years that even substantial losses on developing country debt no longer posed the threat to world financial stability they had posed in 1982 (see Table 23-6).

The Brady Plan was vague in describing exactly how its recommendations were to be put into action. One clear message, however, was that **market-based debt reduction**—the reduction of countries' debts through ''voluntary'' market transactions—should be promoted by official agencies. Before describing the impact of the Brady Plan, we therefore examine what economic theory can tell us about the effects of market-based approaches to the debt problem.

Market-Based Debt Reduction

By 1987, loans to problem debtors were trading in the secondary market at prices far below face value (see Figure 23-2). To some observers, these bargain-basement prices suggested easy, market-based ways of reducing developing countries' debt burdens. Most obviously (or so it seemed), countries could achieve significant debt reduction simply by buying back their own debt at the low market prices. In this spirit, the Brady Plan gave strong official backing to market-based debt reduction.

There is, however, reason to be skeptical of claims that market debt buybacks or related transactions will help resolve a country's debt problem. Indeed, a careful examination of exactly what happens when a country uses its own resources to buy back its troubled debt reveals that the country's *creditors* are the only ones who benefit! The country itself is likely to be left worse off than before the buyback. Recent experience with debt repurchases appears to confirm this claim.

Imagine that a country with current debt servicing problems spends $250 million of its own money to buy back $1 billion of its $100 billion foreign debt at a secondary market price of 25 cents on the dollar. How can this transaction possibly hurt the country and benefit its creditors? After all, *if* the country does well enough to be in a position to repay the remainder of its debt ($99 billion) it will pay $1 billion less, and the cost of this $1 billion relief will have been only $250 million.

The problem with the preceding argument is that a country whose debt sells for a low secondary market price is unlikely to do well enough to repay even its reduced debt of $99 billion, or anything close to that sum. The amount that creditors can extract from the country in this case will likely be unaffected by the fact that the face value of the debt is $99 billion rather that $100 billion. In the meantime, the indebted country will have wasted $250 million—in effect, it will have given that sum away to its creditors.

This example is an extreme one, but it illustrates a more general point. A country that uses its resources to buy back its own discounted debt derives a benefit that is less than the amount it spends. The country therefore takes a loss, and its creditors make a corresponding profit.

THIRD-PARTY BUYBACKS

Our example was of a buyback paid out of the debtor's own resources, but it is possible that some third party provides funds for extinguishing part of the debt. Indeed, some observers interpreted the Brady Plan as suggesting that the IMF and World Bank provide money for this purpose.

The case of a self-financed buyback just analyzed is useful for understanding the distribution of gains from externally financed buybacks. We have seen that the benefit to a debtor of a self-financed buyback generally is less than the sum it spends to reduce its debt. Suppose the money for the buyback is provided by an outside benefactor rather than by the debtor country itself. Our earlier analysis then implies that the debtor will derive a benefit that is *less* than the sum of money the benefactor provides. The difference between the benefactor's gift and the benefit to the debtor is, once again, a windfall gain for creditors. Clearly the debtor country would be better off spending its gift on something other than a buyback, for example, additional commodity imports from abroad.

The case of Bolivia provides an example of how a buyback plan meant to help the debtor can degenerate into a large giveaway to creditors. In March 1988 Bolivia got $34 million from an anonymous group of countries to buy back part of its commercial bank debt. Before the buyback was planned. Bolivia's total foreign obligations were valued by the market at $53 million; the price of the country's debt was 7 cents on the dollar. This meant that Bolivia's creditors expected to be paid 7 cents for every dollar Bolivia owed them, with total payments to all creditors summing to $53 million. After the buyback, the remaining debt sold for 12 cents on the dollar and was valued by the market at $43.4 million. Bolivia's benefit from the $34 million gift was the reduction in its total expected debt payments, equal to just $9.6 million (= $53 million − $43.4 million). Creditors walked away with the lion's share of the $34 million gift, $24.4 million.[13]

DEBT FORGIVENESS

A special case of an externally financed buyback is debt forgiveness, in which creditors cancel or forgive part of the debt. In effect, the funds for the "buyback" of the canceled debt are provided by the creditors themselves. Our analysis implies that it would cost creditors *as a group* less than it seems to cancel the debts of problem debtors.

In July 1989, for example, Argentina's debt was traded on the secondary market at a price of only 17.5 cents on the dollar. This low price meant that much of Argentina's debt had very little chance of ever being repaid, so that creditors could forgive at least some of it at virtually no real cost to themselves. Such forgiveness would benefit debtors not only by reducing their expected payments on debt, but also by lowering the costs and penalties due to ongoing friction with creditors.

It is theoretically possible that the economic uncertainty caused by a large stock of overdue foreign debt discourages a borrower's investment and policy-reform efforts to such an extent that debt reduction would actually *raise* its total expected payments to creditors. In the presence of such a strong debt "overhang" effect, creditors as a group *gain* from debt forgiveness: the forgiveness costs them nothing, yet their expected payments from the debtor rise.[14]

Unfortunately, a serious coordination problem stands in the way of debt forgiveness. Even in a case like the one just described, the market price of debt would increase after some debt was forgiven, as in our example above. Thus, each creditor would prefer that other creditors forgive while he holds out and collects a capital gain on his own debt holdings. In these circumstances, no individual creditor will voluntarily step forward to forgive debt. Forgiveness can occur only if it is coordinated by official international agencies or governments.

Is the Debt Crisis Over?

The goal of the Brady Plan was to end the debt crisis, in part by weakening the united front banks had presented to debtors since the onset of Mexico's problems in August 1982. By the summer of 1992, foreign capital was again flowing spontaneously to some

[13] For discussion, see Jeremy Bulow and Kenneth Rogoff, "The Buyback Boondoggle," *Brookings Papers on Economic Activity* 2: 1988, pp. 675–698; and, in the same issue of the journal, pp. 705–713, Jeffrey D. Sachs, "Comprehensive Debt Retirement: The Bolivian Example."

[14] For a discussion of the debt overhang theory, see "Investment and Growth in Heavily Indebted Countries," Supplementary Note 1 in International Monetary Fund, *World Economic Outlook,* April 1989, pp. 61–67.

indebted countries and several financial journals were proclaiming the debt crisis over. In this section we examine the Brady initiative's impact and the prospects for renewed developing country access to world capital markets.

THE EFFECTS OF THE BRADY PLAN

The Brady Plan's authors believed direct negotiations between debtors and individual banks would promote a process of ''voluntary'' debt reduction that might place developing debtors on the path to economic growth. By implication, the United States had served notice that it would not act as a collection agency for the banks: they would now be on their own in reaching some mutually agreeable deal with debtors.

Mexico provided the first test case for the Brady Plan when it asked its commercial bank creditors for debt reduction. In July 1989, after months of negotiation and some coaxing from the U.S. government, an agreement emerged. Each bank had the options of (1) swapping old loans for thirty-year bonds worth 65 percent of the loans' face value but carrying the same interest rate, (2) swapping old loans at par for thirty-year bonds carrying a lower interest rate, or (3) providing new loans equivalent to 25 percent of their existing medium- to long-term loans to Mexico. The IMF, the World Bank, and Japan together put aside $7 billion to help secure the new bonds. Not surprisingly, most banks went for one of the first two options. Under the package eventually offered by the banks in February 1990, the face value of Mexico's debt was reduced by about 12 percent.

Mexico holds special strategic importance for the United States, and it also had been the ''model'' debtor, meeting its rescheduled obligations promptly and moving aggressively to reform its economy by reducing the government's role. Within a year, however, commercial bank debt reduction agreements were negotiated by the Philippines, Costa Rica, Venezuela, Uruguay, and Niger. (Table 23-7 shows IMF estimates of the effective debt reduction achieved in the first six Brady Plan agreements.) When Argentina and Brazil reached preliminary relief agreements with their creditors in 1992, it looked as if all the major debtors, along with a number of smaller countries, had at last put the debt crisis behind them.

RENEWED CAPITAL INFLOWS

The years 1991 and 1992 saw an apparent renewal of private capital flows into some highly indebted countries. According to one estimate, $36 billion of such flows reached Latin American in 1991, with more expected for the following year. As Table 23-5 shows, the negative resource transfer from developed to developing countries also began turning around in those years.

It is unlikely that the Brady Plan itself was the major catalyst for this renewed private lending. As you can see in Table 23-7, the debt relief negotiated in the initial round of Brady deals amounted to a very large fraction of outstanding commercial bank debt only for the tiny nations of Costa Rica and Niger. While the Brady Plan may have removed some uncertainties for investors, its quantitative effects seem too small to have substantially improved the creditworthiness of the larger debtor countries.

More significant was the sharp decline in U.S. interest rates after 1990 (Figure 23-1a), which both lowered debtors' interest burdens and induced American capital to seek higher returns in the developing world.

TABLE 23-7 Debt effects of the first six Brady Plan packages

	Mexico	*Philippines*	*Costa Rica*	*Venezuela*	*Uruguay*	*Niger*
Net effective debt reduction (as a percent of public sector debt to banks)	11.9	4.7	47.1	9.9	18.8	100.0

Source: Alessandro Leipold et al., *International Capital Markets: Developments and Prospects.* Washington, D.C.: International Monetary Fund, May 1991, Table 15.

An additional important factor is the decisive move toward deregulation, privatization, trade liberalization, and inflation stabilization in several developing countries. Mexico, Chile, Venezuela, Argentina, and Colombia are among the Latin American countries engaged in wide-ranging restructuring. In 1987, Mexico made a significant commitment to free trade by entering the GATT. Mexico has been seeking to cement its reform program by joining the United States and Canada in a North American Free Trade Area.[15]

THE ROAD AHEAD

The 1980s were a lost decade in much of the developing world. Per capita income growth went into reverse in many countries, leaving their inhabitants worse off at the decade's end than they had been at its start. In developing countries with debt servicing problems, GNP per person grew at an average annual rate of 2.6 percent per year from 1970 to 1980, but at an average annual rate of *negative* 1.0 percent per year over 1981–1990. Only in the early 1990s did renewed growth start to appear possible.

Is the debt crisis finally over? The world economy will not soon return to the unrestrained bank lending of the 1970s—nor should it, as some of that lending was unwise. But countries offering the most stable and profitable investment environments do seem to have regained some access to world capital markets in the 1990s. An increasing fraction of the capital flow from developed to developing countries is likely to take the form of equity investment, which leaves borrowers less vulnerable to repayment crises than the floating-rate debt contracts that prevailed before 1982.

Developing countries that successfully pursue stabilization and economic reform will find that the savings of industrialized economies are available to them once again. This pattern has reemerged after previous developing country debt crises, and it seems likely to reemerge now. Countries with shaky political systems, or in which progress toward stability and reform is uncertain, will continue to face difficulties in borrowing. The debt crisis illustrates that the theoretical gains from trading commodities across time or across states of the world can be difficult to realize in practice when the legal framework for enforcing international financial contracts is weak. Developing country governments that allow their economies to operate under transparent rules of the game,

[15] On Mexico's reform efforts, see Nora Lustig, *Mexico: The Remaking of an Economy* (Washington, D.C.: Brookings Institution, 1992).

and with a minimum of arbitrary intervention, will also have easiest access to the global capital market.

Unfortunately, relatively few of the countries that suffered through the debt crisis have yet established sufficient stability to attract long-term private capital flows from abroad. Even Venezuela, a leading recipient of capital inflows in the early 1990s, faced jittery foreign investors as a result of two military coup attempts in 1992. Similarly, Argentina saw confidence in its stability recede for a time after it retreated from trade liberalization late in 1992.

In some parts of Latin America and in much of Africa, access to world capital markets remains impaired or nonexistent. As a group, the once Communist countries of Eastern Europe and the former Soviet Union stand in special need of resource transfers from abroad as they try to build market economies under the burden of foreign debts (Chapter 24). For these countries a debt crisis continues. Governments that marshal the political will to reform their economies will ultimately raise national living standards. Industrial country governments can help by organizing debt relief and by removing protectionist barriers that make it harder for debtors to grow or even to service their debts.

Summary

1. Undeveloped financial markets and heavy government intervention characterize the economies of most developing countries. As a result, many developing countries have turned to fixed exchange rates or *crawling pegs,* inflationary finance of government deficits through *seigniorage,* and widespread wage indexation. Heavy dependence on flexible-price primary commodity exports makes developing countries particularly vulnerable to shocks originating in international markets.

2. Because many developing countries offer potentially rich opportunities for investment, it is natural that they have current account deficits and borrow from richer countries. In principle, developing country borrowing from richer countries can lead to gains from intertemporal trade that make all countries better off.

3. Borrowing by developing countries can take a number of forms, including bond finance, bank finance, loans from official entities, and direct foreign investment. Direct foreign investment is a form of equity finance, which differs from debt finance in that the outflows of payments it generates are not contractually prespecified but depend instead on economic conditions in the borrowing country.

4. In the nineteenth and early twentieth centuries, developing countries borrowed heavily from Europe, particularly from Britain. Despite frequent individual episodes of *default* and sharp international business fluctuations, the international capital market thrived until the outbreak of World War I. This was in part a result of London's leadership of the world economy—its commitment to free trade and its flexibility in accommodating the temporary difficulties of less-developed debtors. In the interwar period, most developing country loans originated in the United States. When the Great Depression began, there was no internationally recognized authority prepared to support free trade and ensure a continuing flow of credit to the developing world. As a result, most countries there defaulted on their foreign debts. Private lending to developing countries on the scale of the 1920s did not resume until the early 1970s.

5. Bank lending to developing countries after 1973 was stimulated by negative real interest rates in industrialized countries and the need to recycle OPEC's current account surplus. By borrowing abroad, developing countries were able to sustain high growth rates of spending and output through the 1970s. Heavy borrowing after the second oil shock led to trouble, however, as disinflation in the industrial economies raised interest rates and drove the world into recession. In August 1982, Mexico's announcement that it could no longer meet scheduled payments to creditors sparked a generalized slowdown in lending to developing countries.

6. A country contemplating *sovereign default* faces several potential penalties, the most serious of which is virtual exclusion from international trade. An immediate benefit of default is relief from the burden of *debt service.* Economic theory predicts that a sovereign debtor will choose to default when the benefit exceeds the cost, but not otherwise. The disturbances of the early 1980s created circumstances in which developing countries might well have defaulted had governments, banks, and the IMF not joined to ensure a continuing flow of loans through *debt rescheduling* and *concerted lending*. Coordinated collective action initially prevented the complete halt in lending that might have occurred if each bank, acting in its own self-interest, had attempted to reduce its holdings of loans to developing countries.

7. Developing country attempts to reduce their current account gaps in 1983 (often the result of IMF stabilization programs) contributed to negative output growth rates in some regions, particularly Latin America. Growth improved as exports picked up in the recovery year 1984. More moderate growth in industrial countries and growing protectionist pressures there subsequently dimmed hopes for a ''muddling through'' solution to the debt problem. As the negative *resource transfer* from creditors to debtors grew, secondary market prices of developing country loans plunged.

8. The Brady Plan of March 1989 hoped to encourage *market-based debt reduction* on terms agreeable to debtors and creditors alike. Unfortunately, market solutions appear unlikely to provide debtors with much real help: self-financed debtor buybacks of discounted debt, for example, actually harm the debtor while benefiting creditors. Coordinated *debt relief* following the model of Mexico's July 1989 agreement with creditors seems to have provided a more solid basis for renewed growth in some heavily indebted economies. New private capital flows to developing debtors did accelerate in the early 1990s. A key factor behind this renewed lending is the ability of several countries, notably Chile and Mexico, to mount credible programs of economic liberalization and inflation reduction against a background of political stability. The main elements of the successful reform programs are trade liberalization, extensive *privatization* of state-owned enterprises, market deregulation, moderate monetary growth, and low government budget deficits.

Key Terms

privatization
seigniorage
crawling peg
default
Paris Club
debt rescheduling
floating-rate loan contracts
debt service
sovereign default
resource transfer
concerted lending
debt relief
market-based debt reduction

Problems

1. Can a government always collect more seigniorage simply by letting the money supply grow faster? Explain your answer.
2. Assume that a country's inflation rate was 100 percent per year in both 1980 and 1990 but that inflation was falling in the first year and rising in the second. Other things equal, in which year was seigniorage revenue greater? (Assume that asset holders correctly anticipated the path of inflation.)
3. The table in the box on measuring seigniorage (p. 676) shows that Brazil's government, through an average inflation rate of 147 percent per year, got only 1.0 percent of output as seigniorage, while Sierra Leone's government got 2.4 percent through an inflation rate less than a third as high. Can you think of differences in financial structure that might partially explain this contrast? (Hint: In Sierra Leone the ratio of currency to nominal output averaged 7.7 percent; in Brazil it averaged only 1.4 percent.)
4. How does an artificially low domestic interest rate help a developing country government finance its budget deficit?
5. Suppose an economy open to international capital movements has a crawling peg exchange rate under which its currency is continuously devalued at a rate of 10 percent per year. How would the domestic nominal interest rate be related to the foreign nominal interest rate?
6. In the late 1970s, the countries in Latin America's "Southern Cone" (Argentina, Chile, and Uruguay) all tried to reduce domestic inflation by adopting crawling pegs in which the rate of exchange rate crawl was supposed to fall gradually to zero according to a preannounced schedule. People in those countries believed, however, that the government might deviate from the preannounced schedule at some point and carry out a large surprise devaluation of the domestic currency. How would you expect this belief to affect the behavior of wages and the real exchange rate during the course of disinflation? (Hint: All three countries had massive real currency appreciations as a result of their programs.)
7. The external debt buildup of some developing countries (such as Argentina) is in large part due to (legal or illegal) capital flight in the face of expected currency devaluation. (Governments and central banks borrowed foreign currencies to prop up their exchange rates, and these funds found their way into private hands and into bank accounts in New York and elsewhere.) Since capital flight leaves a government with a large debt but creates an offsetting foreign asset for citizens who take money abroad, the consolidated net debt of the country as a whole does not change. Does this mean that countries whose external government debt is largely the result of capital flight face no debt problem?
8. Much developing country borrowing was carried out by state-owned companies. In some of these countries there have been moves to privatize the economy by selling state companies to private owners. Would the countries have borrowed more or less if their economies had been privatized earlier?
9. How might a developing country's decision to reduce trade restrictions such as import tariffs affect its ability to borrow in the world capital market?
10. Given output, a country can improve its current account by either cutting investment or cutting consumption (private or government). After the debt crisis began,

many developing countries achieved improvements in their current accounts by cutting investment. Is this a sensible strategy?

11. Do you agree that it has been a good idea partially to forgive some developing country debt? What problems might arise from such an approach to resolving the debt crisis?

12. Economist Peter B. Kenen of Princeton University has suggested the creation of a government-sponsored International Debt Discount Corporation (IDDC) that would issue its own long-term bonds to banks in exchange for their loans to developing countries. How might an IDDC facilitate debt relief for developing countries? What problems can you see in operating such a facility? (For a symposium on these and related questions, see the Winter 1990 issue of the *Journal of Economic Perspectives.*)

Further Reading

Bela Balassa. ''Adjustment Policies in Developing Countries: A Reassessment.'' *World Development* 12 (September 1984), pp. 955–972. A review of trade and macroeconomic policies in developing countries after 1973.

Michael Bruno et al., eds. *Inflation Stabilization: The Experience of Israel, Argentina, Brazil, Bolivia, and Mexico.* Cambridge: MIT Press, 1988. A collection of case studies of stabilization programs in developing countries.

Michael Bruno et al., eds. *Lessons of Economic Stabilization and Its Aftermath.* Cambridge: MIT Press, 1991. A valuable sequel to the preceding book.

Susan M. Collins. ''Multiple Exchange Rates, Capital Controls, and Commercial Policy,'' in Rudiger Dornbusch and F. Leslie C. H. Helmers, eds. *The Open Economy: Tools for Policymakers in Developing Countries.* New York: Oxford University Press (for the World Bank), 1988. Describes how developing country governments have regulated trade and capital flows to achieve policy goals.

Carlos F. Díaz-Alejandro. ''Good-bye Financial Repression, Hello Financial Crash.'' *Journal of Development Economics* 19 (September-October 1986), pp. 1–24. Discusses linkages among financial liberalization, macroeconomic policy, and external debt problems.

Sebastian Edwards. *The Order of Liberalization of the External Sector in Developing Economies.* Princeton Essays in International Finance 156. International Finance Section, Department of Economics, Princeton University, December 1984. Examines problems of liberalizing trade and capital movements in developing countries.

Albert Fishlow. ''Lessons from the Past: Capital Markets during the 19th Century and the Interwar Period.'' *International Organization* 39 (Summer 1985), pp. 383–439. Historical review of international borrowing experience, including comparisons with the post-1982 debt crisis.

Miguel A. Kiguel and Nissan Liviatan. ''Inflationary Rigidities and Orthodox Stabilization Policies: Lessons from Latin America.'' *World Bank Economic Review* 2 (September 1988), pp. 273–298. A case for heterodox approaches to stabilization in high-inflation economies.

Ronald I. McKinnon. *The Order of Economic Liberalization: Financial Control in the Transition to a Market Economy.* Baltimore: The Johns Hopkins University Press, 1991. A comparative study of financial problems in reforming developing economies and former Communist countries.

Jeffrey D. Sachs, ed. *Developing Country Debt and the World Economy.* Chicago: University of Chicago Press, 1989. Useful surveys of recent debt problems and individual country experiences.

International Economic Problems of Former Communist Countries

Chapter 24

At the beginning of 1989 more than 400 million people, producing about 12 percent of the world's output, lived in **centrally planned economies**—that is, economies in which decisions about production and employment were made by government officials rather than by private firms. In spite of some efforts at reform, the Soviet Union and the Eastern European governments installed by Soviet forces after World War II still ran their economies mostly by central directive rather than through a decentralized market mechanism.

By the end of 1991, however, the situation had changed dramatically. Communist governments had abdicated or been overthrown throughout the former Soviet Empire, and the Soviet Union itself had broken apart into its separate republics. Most of the Eastern European nations and the largest of the former Soviet republics had launched economic reforms intended to transform themselves into Western-style market economies.

Few economists doubted that in the long run the turn to market economics would raise productivity and living standards. It was widely believed that central planning had proved to be a much less efficient system than a private market economy. Some parts of Eastern Europe, such as the Czech Republic and East Germany, had been advanced industrial regions before falling under Communist rule. When the Iron Curtain lifted they were revealed to have antiquated factories, low quality goods and services, and crippling environmental problems. The return to the market offered the hope of rapid growth in these once-prosperous areas, perhaps even of an "economic miracle" comparable to the recovery of Western Europe after World War II.

But while there were high hopes for economic performance in the long run, the immediate effects of the breakup of the economic system centered on the Soviet Union were far less positive. As Table 24-1 shows, 1990 and 1991 were marked by very large declines in output and soaring inflation in both Eastern Europe and the Soviet Union (which broke up in the summer of 1991), and most observers believed that the economic situation had deteriorated even further during 1992 and 1993, especially in the former Soviet republics.

The causes of the severe economic difficulties in Eastern Europe and the former Soviet Union are complex and a matter of heated dispute. One major reason for these difficulties is, however, clear: the breakdown of traditional trading relations both among the former communist nations and among the republics of the former Soviet Union has had adverse impacts on both supply and demand. On the demand side, the breakdown of the special trading relationships enforced by the Soviet Union has led to sharp falls in exports of Eastern European nations to the Soviet Union and each other, as well as a marked worsening in many countries' terms of trade (the prices of their exports relative to those of their imports). On the supply side, collapsing trade has led to widespread shortages—especially in the former Soviet Union—including shortages of raw materials for industry. Added to all of this have been the special monetary difficulties created when a number of newly sovereign states still share a single currency.

In this chapter we review the trade problems associated with the fall of communism. We begin by describing the trade of the Soviet Union and its allies just before the collapse. We then look at the macroeconomic effects of the breakup of that trading system and the microeconomic disruptions that have so troubled the former Soviet republics. Finally, we describe the monetary difficulties that plague the group of former Soviet republics that still use a common currency.

Trade in Eastern Europe before 1989

After its victory in the Russian Civil War of 1917–1921, the Communist Party of the Soviet Union experimented briefly with a market economy. This experiment was abandoned, however, when Joseph Stalin took power after the death of Lenin. Stalin imposed full-scale central planning, in which factories and farms were required to meet production targets set by government officials, in 1928. Between then and World War II, he followed a strategy of industrialization aimed, among other things, at making the nation highly self-sufficient. After the war, as pro-Soviet governments took power in Eastern Europe, those nations were integrated into the Soviet system. Formally, trade among Soviet-bloc nations was supposed to be governed by a body known as the **Council for Mutual Economic Assistance**; the Soviet-centered economic zone is therefore often referred to as the CMEA. Its members are shown in Figure 24-1.

CMEA TRADE UNDER COMMUNISM

Viewed as a unit, the CMEA was largely shut off from external trade. In 1980, the combined output of the CMEA was estimated at about 50 percent that of either the European Community or the United States. Yet EC exports to the rest of the world

TABLE 24-1 Economic developments in former Communist nations

	Growth in real GDP		*Inflation*	
	1990	*1991*	*1990*	*1991*
Eastern Europe	−7.1	−16.6	149.1	134.7
Bulgaria	−10.6	−25.0	26.3	460.4
Czechslovakia	−0.4	−16.4	10.8	58.7
Hungary	−4.0	−7.5	33.4	33.0
Poland	−11.6	−8.0	585.8	70.3
Romania	−7.4	−12.0	4.7	164.3
Soviet Union	−2.0	−17.0	5.6	86.0
Russia	0.4	−9.0	5.0	90.4

Source: IMF *World Economic Outlook,* May 1992, p. 31.

were $412 billion, compared with only $84 billion for the CMEA. Broadly speaking, the CMEA nations tried to make for themselves anything they could, and their low-quality manufactured goods had little market in the Western world; thus their trade consisted largely of an exchange of raw materials, especially Soviet oil, for sophisticated Western products that they were unable to produce (such as the machinery in the Italian-built factory that in turn manufactured more than half of Soviet automobiles in 1989).

While the CMEA nations traded little with the outside world, however, they traded extensively with each other. Soviet central planners and their Eastern European students believed strongly in the advantages of specialization, especially to achieve economies of scale. Thus they tended to favor geographical concentration of many kinds of industrial production, often building huge plants to supply goods to enormous market areas. For example, most tractors for Eastern Europe were produced at one huge Polish tractor factory, most buses at one large Hungarian plant. The Russian steel plant at Magnetogorsk, with 60,000 employees, produced half the steel the Soviet Union used to fight World War II. Even in 1991, a single plant in Belarus (the world's largest) produced 90 percent of the Soviet Union's polyester and a single plant in Russia produced 58 percent of the Union's automobiles.

As a result of this policy of specialization, trade as a share of national income was quite large for many Eastern European nations. Figure 24-2 illustrates this point. Figure 24-2 shows ratios of exports to GNP for the Eastern European nations (excluding the Soviet Union) and for developing countries elsewhere in the world. The figure shows that in 1984, the typical Eastern European nation exported about 27 percent of its output, compared with only 25 percent for the typical developing market economy. That is, the Eastern European countries were actually somewhat more open to trade until the plunge at the end of the 1980s. The reason is that while the planned economies did very little trade with the West, they made up for it by doing much more than one might have expected with each other.

The high degree of *interdependence* among Eastern European nations was matched or exceeded by the degree of interdependence among the republics of the Soviet Union.

FIGURE 24-1
The former communist nations.
Panel (a): The CMEA in 1988. Until 1989 the Soviet Union and most of Eastern Europe were economically linked as part of the Council for Mutual Economic Assistance. Panel (b): The former CMEA in 1993. By 1993 the CMEA had broken up. In addition, Czechoslovakia had separated into two separate nations, and the Soviet Union had broken up into its constituent republics.

FIGURE 24-2
Exports and output of Eastern European nations.
Until the late 1980s the communist nations of Eastern Europe were at least as export-oriented as developing countries elsewhere in the world.
Source: IMF *World Economic Outlook,* May 1992.

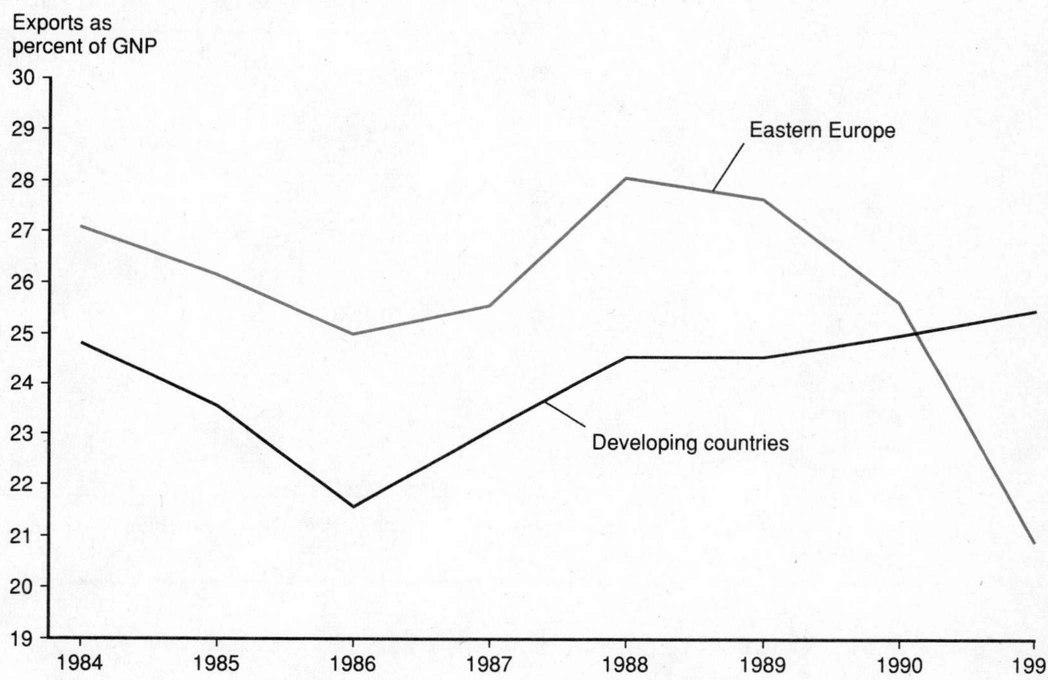

The Soviet constitution in principle gave these republics considerable leeway to run their own affairs, but in practice before 1991 all important decisions were made in Moscow. After a right-wing coup failed in August 1991, however, central authority collapsed and the republics suddenly found themselves sovereign states, free to issue their own currencies and raise their own taxes. Yet their economies remained deeply interconnected. Table 24-2 shows that even Russia, the largest and most self-sufficient of the republics, exported 18 percent of its physical output to other republics in 1989; other republics were far more dependent on trade.[1]

The overall picture of CMEA trade before 1989, then, is one of nations that had closed themselves off from trade with the outside world while becoming highly dependent on one another.

[1] Before the collapse of central planning, most Communist nations did not produce national income accounts along the lines described in Chapter 13. Instead, they measured ''net material product''—a measure that excludes the service sector but fails to make all the corrections that Western nations make to calculate value added in the goods-producing sectors. In principle, net material product could be either smaller or larger than GDP. In practice, it is usually somewhat smaller, so that the trade shares in Table 24-2 are somewhat exaggerated.

TABLE 24-2 Trade of the former Soviet republics, 1989

Republic	*Population (millions)*	*Exports as a percentage of output*	
		To other republics	*To other countries*
Russia	51.4	18.0	8.6
Ukraine	18.0	39.1	6.7
Uzbekistan	6.9	43.2	7.4
Kazakhstan	5.8	30.9	3.0
Belarus	3.6	69.6	6.5
Azerbaijan	2.5	58.7	3.7
Georgia	1.9	53.7	3.9
Tadzhikistan	1.8	41.8	6.9
Moldova	1.5	62.1	3.4
Kirgizia	1.5	50.2	1.2
Lithuania	1.3	60.9	5.9
Turkmenistan	1.2	50.7	4.2
Armenia	1.1	63.7	1.4
Latvia	0.9	64.1	5.7
Estonia	0.5	66.5	7.4

Source: Stanley Fischer, ''Economic Reform in the USS and the Role of Aid.'' *Brookings Papers on Economic Activity* 2:1991, pp. 289–302.

THE MANAGEMENT OF TRADE WITHIN THE SOVIET UNION

How was the large volume of trade within the CMEA managed? In principle, trade flows were decided as part of a coordinated central planning process. In practice, this planning process worked only within the Soviet Union itself—and even there it worked on a somewhat haphazard basis. In the larger CMEA area, trade is best seen as a process of barter deals negotiated among national governments.

Within the Soviet Union, economic management was conducted on an annual basis by the preparation of central economic plans that specified production levels for most commodities. A general plan that determined output targets at the economy-wide level would be handed down to a variety of government agencies. These agencies would break these targets down into specific targets for individual enterprises and factories, together with instructions about to whom they should deliver the output. Implicit in these targets would be a pattern of trade within the Soviet Union.

In practice, the system was far messier. Targets were often unrealistic and would either not be met or would be met by producing goods of inferior quality. At each level of the process, administrators would realize they could not count on receiving the supplies promised by the plan, and as a result there was a drive for self-sufficiency. For example, a steel factory would not trust the mines that were supposed to deliver iron ore or coal; if possible, it would try to establish control over its own iron and coal mines, as well as its own construction enterprises, hospitals, and everything else it could manage to appropriate. Soviet industrial enterprises often came to resemble diversified little economies, with small-scale (and usually inefficient) production across a wide range of activities seemingly unrelated to their primary function.

You might think this drive for self-sufficiency would have reduced the volume of interrepublic trade, but often an enterprise would have branches thousands of miles apart—and would find it easier to procure necessary supplies from a branch in another republic than from a nearby source controlled by another enterprise. When enterprises could not achieve self-sufficiency, they would often negotiate informal barter deals with each other.

The result of this system was a complex pattern of trade between enterprises and across space. The system involved some clear inefficiencies. On one side, factories were often excessively self-sufficient, while on the other there was a good deal of unnecessary long-distance shipping of goods. Until the mid-1980s, however, the Soviet economy got by, largely because the central authority was able to intervene and force enterprises to change their behavior whenever shortages in a particular sector became particularly glaring. After 1985, as the power of the central government began to erode, the system began to collapse. We will examine the nature of this collapse later in this chapter.

THE MANAGEMENT OF TRADE AMONG CMEA NATIONS

Outside the Soviet Union, trade among the CMEA nations was in principle conducted through a process of mutually agreed central planning. In the early years of Soviet domination, the Eastern European nations were in fact largely treated as part of the Soviet economy, with their production dictated by planners in Moscow. These plans often exploited the newly communist nations, requiring them to ship large quantities of goods to the Soviet Union, with little sent in return. During the mid-1950s, however, a series of uprisings occurred in Eastern Europe, driven in part by anger over poor living standards. Although the workers' riots in East Germany and Poland in 1953 and the full-scale revolution in Hungary in 1956 were suppressed, they did lead to a change in Soviet policy. National Communist leaders were given more autonomy and the trade among CMEA nations was put on a more equal footing.

Once Soviet control was weakened, any attempt to plan the economies of the CMEA nations as a unit faded into a pure formality. Trade within the CMEA area began to be determined largely through direct negotiations between countries. These negotiations were made more difficult by the absence of an accepted international medium of exchange among the CMEA countries. If Poland, say, were to deliver tractors to Hungary, it would be paid in rubles,[2] but since there was little if anything it could buy with these rubles, it would insist on receiving real goods, such as buses, in return. The result was that trade among the CMEA nations gradually turned into a form of country-to-country barter.

What determined the terms of this barter? That is, how did Poland and Hungary decide how many buses were equal in value to a tractor? There is no straightforward answer. Sometimes prices would be based on the prices at which equivalent goods were trading on world, which is to say Western, markets. In many cases, however, there were no equivalents. For example, East Germany's tiny, two-cylinder Trabant automobile clearly could not be compared with the far more comfortable cars being produced even at the bottom end of the capitalist world market, yet it was unclear by how much it should be discounted compared with, say, a Ford Escort. (After German

[2] There was a technical distinction between the ordinary rubles used as currency in the Soviet Union and the "transferable rubles" used to settle accounts among CMEA countries; the latter were fictitious accounting units that could not be converted into any circulating currency, even ordinary rubles.

reunification, no attempt was made to keep Trabants in production.) Terms of trade were also highly politicized. Most notably, after world oil prices surged in the 1970s one might have expected the Soviet Union, the supplier of most Eastern European oil, to demand more manufactured goods in return. It did not do so, however, for two reasons. First, the idea that the terms of trade among ''fraternal socialist nations'' should be sharply affected by a rise in the price that Saudi Arabia charged the United States for oil seemed to conflict with the whole ideology of communism, which denounced the arbitrary and unequal distribution of income created by free markets. Second, the Soviet Union was reluctant to impose new economic burdens on its Eastern European allies at a time when the people of these countries were becoming increasingly discontent with communist rule. A foretaste of the 1989 collapse came in 1981, when a Polish austerity program led to a wave of strikes that nearly forced the government to appeal for Soviet help to hold on to power. (The labor movement that emerged in 1981—Solidarity—survived underground and took power in 1989, setting in motion the whole process of Communist collapse.)

The combination of a lack of clear standards for, and the politicization of, trade prices meant that trade between CMEA nations took place at prices that were very different from world market prices. In particular, manufactured goods were generally overvalued given their poor quality, while raw materials—especially oil—were priced well below world levels. In effect, raw material exporters—which included, above all, the Soviet Union itself—were subsidizing the exporters of manufactured goods.

Similar but probably much larger deviations of trading prices from world levels characterized internal trade within the Soviet Union. Regions with relatively advanced manufacturing, such as the Baltic republics of Lithuania, Latvia, and Estonia, had captive markets for their rather shoddy products, while raw materials were made available at very low prices.

In summary, then, the trading system in the CMEA differed from what would have happened under free markets in two main ways:

1. The *direction* of trade was distorted, with CMEA nations trading much more with each other and much less with the West than they would have under a free market system.
2. The *prices* at which trade took place were very far from world prices.

Given the distorted nature of this trading system, it was inevitable that its breakup would be traumatic. In particular, former communist countries faced two kinds of problem. Throughout Eastern Europe, they faced the **problem of adjustment**, that is, of reorienting their economies in the face of new competition for their exports and much higher prices for many of their imports. Within the Soviet Union this problem was compounded by a collapse of **coordination:** the centralized control that enforced at least some rationality in interrepublic trade was gone, but a functioning market system had not yet taken its place.

The Adjustment Problem in Eastern Europe

In 1990 and 1991 several Eastern Europe countries found themselves with a novel set of problems. For more than forty years these had been shortage economies—places where shops were often empty of useful merchandise and where standing on long lines was part of daily experience. On the other hand, they had virtually full employment. As first Poland and then other nations liberalized, the shops began to fill with higher-quality goods and the lines got shorter or disappeared—but so did many of the jobs. For the first time since the 1940s, Eastern Europe found itself in a severe Western-style recession.

While the causes of the Eastern European recession are a matter of considerable dispute, a large part of it can be attributed to the CMEA trading system's breakdown, which adversely affected exports *and* the terms of trade of most Eastern European nations.

THE DECLINE IN INTRA-CMEA EXPORTS

As we pointed out above, before 1989 the CMEA nations engaged in relatively little trade with the outside world but were highly dependent on each other. Once communist rule had collapsed, this special trading relationship broke down. Poland no longer felt obliged to buy Hungarian buses, but was prepared to buy, say, more reliable and fuel-efficient Volvo buses from Sweden instead. Hungary, conversely, might choose to stop buying Polish tractors and instead buy the superior products of America's Caterpillar or Japan's Komatsu.

The problem was that such reasonable decisions by individual countries had a sharply contractionary effect on the Eastern European economy as a whole.

To see why, we can return to the simple analysis of interdependence developed in Chapter 20 (p. 574). In that analysis, we considered two countries, each of whose income depends in part on the value of exports to the other. To think about the Eastern European situation, let us imagine a world of *three* countries: call them Czechoslovakia (C), Hungary (H), and Western Europe (W). Countries C, H, and W all export to each other. Suppose, however, that W's economy is much larger than C's or H's, so that we can treat its output as unaffected by developments in the other two countries.

In the model developed in Chapter 20, we showed how output in two countries can be interdependent. That is, if either country's output rises, it will import more from the other country, which will stimulate output in that country as well. We reproduce that analysis in Figure 24-3, which is essentially the same as Figure 20-4 (p. 576). On the axes of the figure are the outputs of Czechoslovakia and Hungary, Y_C and Y_H, respectively. The curve H^1H^1 shows how Hungarian output is affected by Czech output. It is upward-sloping because an increase in Y_C will lead to an increase in Czech imports from Hungary, which will lead to an expansion of Hungarian output. Similarly, C^1C^1 shows how Czech output is affected by Hungarian output. As explained in Chapter 20, we can normally assume that H^1H^1 is flatter than C^1C^1, implying that point 1 is a stable equilibrium.

Now suppose that after the breakup of the CMEA, each country shifts away from its traditional Eastern European suppliers toward suppliers in the West. This means that at any given level of Hungarian output, Hungary will import less from Czechoslovakia. Because Hungary will be importing less, Czech output will be less than it would otherwise have been. So the curve determining Czech output shifts left, to C^2C^2. Similarly, at any given level of Czech output, Hungarian exports to Czechoslovakia are lower, so the curve determining Hungarian output shifts down to H^2H^2. The equilibrium shifts from point 1 to point 2: each country's decision to buy less from its neighbor and more from the West leads to a fall in output in both countries.

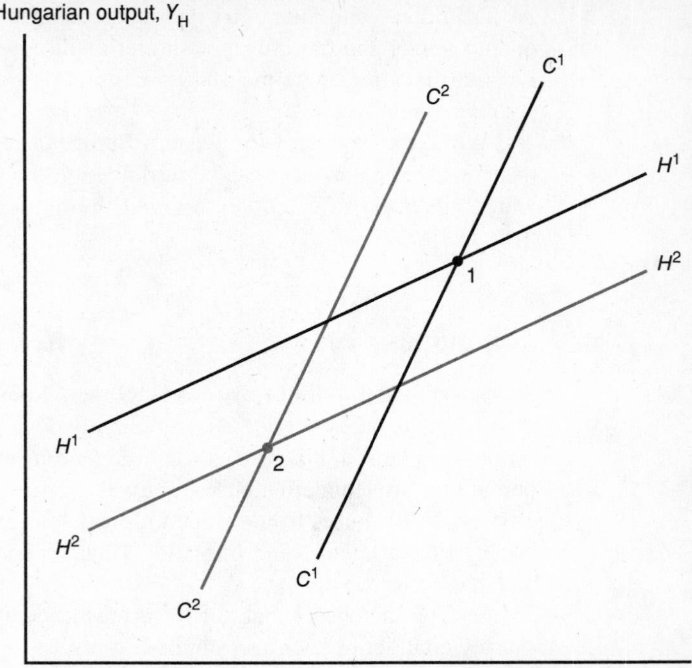

FIGURE 24-3
The adjustment problem when special trading relationships end.
The economies of Czechoslovakia and Hungary are linked by their imports from each other. The higher each country's output is, the higher the other country's exports and output. If each country shifts to buying from other sources, equilibrium moves from 1 to 2: output in both countries falls.

A rough look at the experience of the Eastern European nations suggests that the decline of trade within the CMEA has been a major factor in their output slump. Table 24-3 compares the declines in output for Eastern European countries with the declines in their exports to other CMEA nations. It shows that the declines in traditional trade are very large and could indeed be a significant part of the explanation of output decline.

The decline in trade within the CMEA is only part of the trade story, however. Equally important is the massive terms of trade shock that has occurred as trade within the former Soviet bloc has moved to world prices.

THE TERMS OF TRADE SHOCK

As we learned earlier, the trade that took place under central planning lacked any clear mechanism for determining relative prices. As a result, the de facto prices that Eastern European countries paid and received for traded goods were often very different from those prevailing on the world market. In general, the low-quality manufactured goods that entered into CMEA trade were overpriced, and the raw materials, especially oil, were underpriced.

With the collapse of communism, trade among the former communist nations moved quickly to a ''hard currency'' basis. That is, countries were no longer willing to accept nearly worthless ''transferable rubles'' in exchange for their products; they

TABLE 24-3 Trade and output declines

Country	*Decline in output, 1989–1991 (percent)*	*Change in exports (as percentage of initial output)*
Romania	−19	−10
Czechoslovakia	−17	−9
Hungary	−12	−8
Poland	−20	−4
Soviet Union	−17	−4

Source: Stanley Fischer, ''Stabilization and Economic Reform in Russia.'' *Brookings Papers on Economic Activity* 1:1992, pp. 77–126.

demanded payment in internationally acceptable currencies such as dollars or DM. And as trade moved to a hard currency basis, the prices of goods in Eastern European trade also moved toward world prices. After all, if, say, Russia was going to sell oil to Hungary for dollars, it was hard to justify charging Hungary a price lower than the price oil could fetch on the open world market.

This sudden move to world prices meant huge adverse terms of trade shocks for several Eastern European nations. In particular, the relatively advanced nations like Czechoslovakia and Hungary, which had exported manufactured goods to the Soviet Union and received cheap raw materials in exchange, were very hard hit. Table 24-4 shows calculations of the adverse shift in the terms of trade for major Eastern European countries as a result of the move to trade at world prices.

HOW SEVERE WAS THE SHOCK?

It may be useful to compare the terms of trade shocks that hit the Eastern European nations after 1988 with those that hit the industrialized nations of the West after the 1973 and 1979 oil shocks. Each of those oil price increases imposed a terms of trade loss equal to about 3 percent of the combined GNPs of the industrial nations, equivalent to roughly a 15 percent terms of trade decline for most Western European nations. As we saw in Chapter 20, this was enough in each case to trigger a major global recession, and indeed the recessions following the 1973 and 1979 oil shocks were the two worst slumps since World War II. The terms of trade shocks hitting the advanced Eastern European nations, however, were at least twice as large—and they came at the same time that exports within the former Soviet bloc were declining sharply. At least in retrospect, it is not surprising that the former communist nations found themselves in great economic difficulty.

There is one puzzle in this story, however. A deterioration in one country's terms of trade must have as its counterpart an improvement in another's terms of trade. As advanced Eastern European countries found themselves paying more for raw materials and receiving less for their manufactured goods, the raw material suppliers in the former Soviet bloc—largely the resource-rich areas of the Soviet Union itself—must have

TABLE 24-4 Estimated effects of shift to world prices

Country	*Change in terms of trade (percent)*
Hungary	−36.7
Romania	−31.4
Czechoslovakia	−30.9
Bulgaria	−24.0
Poland	−22.6

Source: Peter B. Kenen, ''Transitional Arrangements for Trade and Payments among the CMEA Countries.'' *International Monetary Fund Staff Papers* 38 (June 1991), pp. 235–267.

experienced a corresponding improvement in their terms of trade. And that is exactly what happened: the Soviet Union's terms of trade improved by approximately 40 percent in 1990 and 1991. Yet as we have seen, output declined in the Soviet Union by an amount similar to the decline in Eastern Europe. Why didn't these raw material exporting areas see an economic boom?

The answer is that any favorable impact of improved terms of trade was more than offset by other unfavorable developments, especially the collapse of internal trade in the Soviet Union. We turn to these developments below. For now, the important point is that the relatively advanced countries of Eastern Europe, which one might have expected to have the best chance of a quick conversion to successful market economies, were hampered by a sudden and massive worsening of their terms of trade.

POLICY OPTIONS

Could anything have been done to alleviate the contractionary effects of the decline in Eastern European trade? A number of partial solutions were proposed, but at least in the first few years after the fall of communism none was implemented.

Perhaps the simplest option would have been for countries to try to offset the loss in exports to their traditional markets with increased exports elsewhere. Such an increase in nontraditional exports could have been promoted by devaluing their currencies relative to those of Western nations, in order to make their products more competitive.

In fact, the major Eastern European nations did devalue their currencies sharply between 1988 and 1992 and in some cases did increase their exports to the West substantially. The potential of this policy response in the short run was limited, however, by two main factors.

First, although nominal devaluations were substantial—by June 1992 the price of a U.S. dollar in Polish zlotys had risen 3000 percent from its 1988 level—real devaluations were much smaller, because of severe inflation problems. Table 24-5 compares the changes in the nominal exchange rates of major Eastern European nations with the increases in consumer prices and nominal wage rates. The table shows that real depreciation was much less than nominal; that is, much of the gain in competitiveness from depreciation was offset by domestic inflation. It also shows why governments were

TABLE 24-5 **Devaluation and inflation in Eastern Europe, 1989–fourth quarter 1991 (percentage changes)**

Country	*Exchange rate*	*Consumer prices*	*Wages*
Bulgaria	na	427	1888
Czech republic	78	42	94
Hungary	na	118	29
Poland	1213	817	745
Romania	na	251	899

na = not available
Source: *Financial Times,* September 28, 1992, p. 5.

reluctant to devalue more aggressively: they feared that more aggressive devaluation would make inflation even worse. In this respect the economic problems of the former communist nations were very similar to the adjustment problems of third-world debtor nations, discussed in Chapter 23. Countries were torn between the desire to devalue to improve their export competitiveness and the desire to stabilize the exchange rate as a brake on inflation.

Furthermore, in the short run the efforts to increase exports to the West were disappointing. Exports did increase, but primarily in product lines in which the Eastern European economies had already established Western markets—for example, Polish exports of basic steel and agricultural goods. Many observers hoped for the establishment of whole new export industries, and in particular for large-scale investment in Eastern Europe by multinational firms. The initial response of foreign investors was, however, cautious, largely because of uncertainty about the political situation.

THE CASE FOR POLICY COORDINATION

Because of the difficulty of increasing exports, it was clear that the adjustment of Eastern European nations to a new trade pattern oriented toward the West was going to be painful and prolonged. This realization then raised the question of whether some coordination of policies among the former members of the CMEA could ease the pain of that adjustment.

There is a case for policy coordination when countries can achieve a better outcome by negotiating common policies than if each country acts independently in its own interest. The situation illustrated in Figure 24-3 appears to fit that description. In the example, it is in the separate self-interests of both Czechoslovakia and Hungary to reduce their imports from the CMEA and turn to Western suppliers instead. Yet when both countries do this, they are both pushed into a recession. One might argue that both would be better off if they could agree, at least on a temporary basis, to continue to buy each others' products. (Over time, as they developed new markets in the West, this agreement could be phased out.) A number of economists have argued that the Eastern European countries could manage their adjustment to market economics better if they could agree on a temporary basis to sustain their special trading relationships.

The problem with this solution is how to achieve it. The special trading relationships of the old CMEA were based on the common economic and political structures of the communist regimes, with pressure from the militarily dominant Soviet Union also helping to keep trade going among its allies. What mechanism could help maintain trade among the former CMEA nations without these ''natural'' forces?

One possible answer would be a special monetary arrangement. The sharp decline in CMEA trade after 1989 was largely due to the governments' insistence on receiving payment in hard currency at a time when hard currency was in short supply. Western European nations had faced somewhat similar, although much milder, problems during the ''dollar shortage'' era that followed World War II. They coped with those problems in part through the formation of the European Payments Union (1950–1958), a special set of credit lines extended by the European nations to each other, which allowed them to settle accounts within Europe without using scarce dollars. In principle the ex-Communist countries could form a similar arrangement that would in effect encourage a continuation of traditional trading patterns during a transitional period. That is, Poland and Hungary might agree to accept IOUs from each other, rather than insist on payment in dollars or marks. This would encourage Poland to keep buying Hungarian buses and Hungary to keep buying Polish tractors for a few years, which would help keep employment up until, say, Sony and Matsushita got around to offering new jobs at their new VCR assembly plants in Krakow and Budapest.

Although a number of proposals have been advanced for an Eastern European Payments Union,[3] however, none has been adopted, primarily because of political problems.

Until August 1991, the most important former member of the CMEA was the Soviet Union; indeed, most Eastern European nations still did more trade with the Soviet Union than with all other Eastern European nations combined. Unfortunately, the Soviet Union could not plausibly be part of a payments union, because it had neither abandoned communism nor embarked on a full-scale economic reform.

After 1991 the Soviet Union itself had ceased to exist, and sheer economic logic would have suggested that many of its former republics would gain from entering a special monetary arrangement with Eastern European nations. The economic and political chaos within the former Soviet Union, however, made such an arrangement impossible. In fact, political tensions were on the rise through much of Eastern Europe. In Romania, for example, the supposedly noncommunist government was dominated by unrepentant ex-communists, and there was severe conflict with newly democratic Hungary over Romania's treatment of ethnic Hungarians. In Czechoslovakia, tensions between Czechs and Slovaks quickly escalated to the point that the Czech and Slovak republics agreed to become separate countries at the beginning of 1993. And the outbreak of vicious civil wars in several former communist states made it difficult to focus on economic coordination.

We saw in Chapters 19 through 21 how hard it has been to achieve monetary cooperation and coordination even among the major democratic capitalist nations. The post-1989 situation in Eastern Europe presented a strong economic case for monetary cooperation, but at the time of writing there seemed to be little chance that such cooperation could be achieved.

[3] The most comprehensive proposal was that of Peter Kenen. See Peter B. Kenen, ''Transitional Arrangements for Trade and Payments among the CMEA Countries,'' *International Monetary Fund Staff Papers* 38 (June 1991), pp. 235–267.

The Coordination Problem in the Soviet Union

One might have expected the Soviet Union to realize significant economic benefits from the collapse of its Eastern European empire. After all, by 1989 the Soviet Union was in effect heavily subsidizing the Eastern European economies by overpaying for their inferior manufactured goods and undercharging for its oil and other raw materials. The end of this system, together with the possibility of reduced military spending as confrontation with the West diminished, should have allowed a significant rise in living standards.

In fact, however, the Soviet economy began a rapid decline in the late 1980s, which continued after the breakup in 1991. And while some Eastern European countries were showing signs of recovery by the end of 1992, the decline in the former Soviet republics showed no indication of ending.

The economic troubles of the former Soviet Union are complex, but many of them can be attributed to one basic problem: the system of central planning has collapsed, but a sufficiently free market to replace that system has not yet been introduced. That is, nobody has the authority to order firms to produce more or less what is needed, but there are still too many controlled prices, and too little private property, to allow market prices to provide a decentralized form of coordination.

The whole problem may be viewed as an extreme case of the problem of the *second best,* introduced in our discussion of the market failure case for trade policy in Chapter 10. As an example, recall that there we showed that allowing free trade between the members of a customs union may reduce welfare instead of increasing it if the members continue to impose tariffs against imports from other countries: the customs union may divert existing trade to expensive sources rather than create new trade. The general insight was that if incentives in some markets are distorted, a move to free other markets may hurt instead of helping.

In the case of the former Soviet Union, the collapse of central planning has left enterprises free to make their own decisions about what to produce and who to sell it to. In a well-functioning market system, such decentralization of decision making is normally a good thing. But the continued existence of price controls and the absence of clear property rights mean that the enterprise managers often lack incentives to deliver goods where they are most needed. Central planning helped make up for the lack of such incentives by simply ordering needed deliveries, and its collapse has therefore made things worse instead of better—at least for the time being.

This general second-best problem is pervasive in the ex-Soviet economies. It is particularly clear-cut and severe, however, in the case of interregional trade.

PRICE CONTROLS, CENTRAL PLANNING, AND INTERREGIONAL TRADE

As we saw in Table 24-2, the republics of the former Soviet Union are highly interdependent economically, primarily because communist planners liked to build huge plants. Before 1991, trade flows between the republics and between regions of the large republics, such as Russia, were not based on the incentives provided by realistic prices. Instead, they were dictated by central planners in Moscow. Now those central planners are gone. To see why this causes problems, let us consider an abstract example.

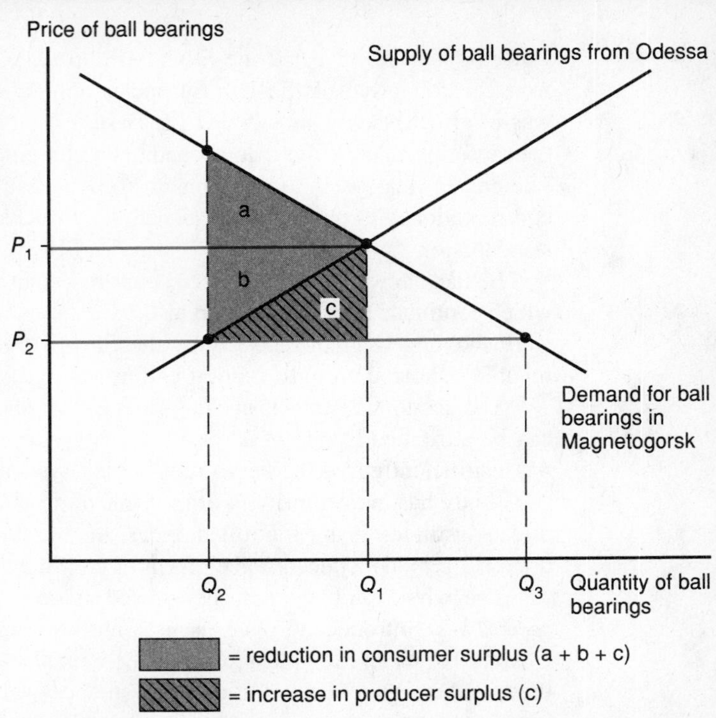

FIGURE 24-4
The problem of coordination in interregional trade.
The price of a good (ball bearings in our example) shipped from Odessa to Magnetogorsk is set at P_2, a price below its market-clearing price, P_1. Under central planning the producer can be ordered to ship as much of the good (Q_1) as it would with a free market. Without central control, however, and with the price remaining at P_2, Odessa will reduce its deliveries to Q_2. The losses to consumers from this reduction in deliveries (the sum of the areas of triangles a, b, and c) greatly exceed the gains to the producer (the area of triangle c).

Suppose there is some product used in Magnetogorsk (in the Russian Republic)—say, ball bearings—that is produced only in Odessa (in Ukraine). In Figure 24-4 we show the demand for bearings in Magnetogorsk and the supply of ball bearings from Odessa, both as functions of the price in rubles.[4]

In a free-market system, the price of bearings would clear the market. Odessa would deliver a quantity Q_1 of bearings to Magnetogorsk, at a price P_1.

Under the central planning system, the price of bearings was unlikely to be anywhere near this market-clearing level. Many prices were well below market-clearing levels, so we might imagine that the price was set at some lower level, P_2.

As long as the central planning was effective, however, the level of the price of bearings was pretty much irrelevant. The factory in Odessa would make what it was told to, and send it where it was supposed to, regardless of profitability.

To make our point, let us give the central planners some undeserved credit for effectiveness, and suppose they were able to reproduce the same outcome that would

[4] In reality, it is unclear whether it even makes sense to imagine normal demand or supply curves in the former Soviet Union. For one thing, most enterprises were still, at the time of writing, officially state-owned, although no longer under effective central control. It was therefore unclear what exactly the objective of their managers was, and whether they would really respond to incentives like higher prices. Furthermore, enterprises often have a great deal of monopoly power, further distorting their response to incentives. These problems only compound the difficulties we stress in this example.

have occurred under a free market. That is, they would order Odessa to send Q_1 bearings to Magnetogorsk.

Now suppose the authority of the central planning agency collapses, so it is no longer able to direct the factory in Odessa. But the market is not entirely freed. Suppose that although there is no longer central control, *the price remains fixed at* P_2. This is more or less what happened increasingly in the Soviet Union after the mid 1980s, as central control grew weak but market prices remained fixed. What is the result of this partial freeing?

The answer is that Odessa will reduce its deliveries of ball bearings to Q_2, the quantity it is willing to supply at price P_2. If the production of ball bearings is now governed by voluntary supply decisions, output delivered to Magnetogorsk will fall to the level Q_2. At the price P_2 consumers would like to buy Q_3 units, which is even more than the amount produced under central planning (Q_1). There would have been shortages, and rationing of some form, even under central planning. With the reduction in output, these shortages will intensify.

Producers in Odessa will benefit from their ability to choose their own level of output. We can measure this benefit by applying the analysis of producer surplus introduced in Chapter 9.[5] The supply curve shows the marginal cost of production, which is equal to the reduction in cost achieved by reducing output by one unit. Meanwhile, the revenue of producers will fall by only P_2 when output falls 1 unit. So as long as the supply curve lies above the market price, a reduction in output will raise profits. It is straightforward to show that reducing output to Q_2 raises producer surplus in Odessa by an amount equal in value to the area of the triangle labeled c (the hatched area).

Unfortunately, this output fall hurts consumers. The demand curve shows the price that consumers would be willing to pay for a marginal unit of bearings. As long as the price lies below that demand curve, that is, as long as there is excess demand, a reduction in supply reduces consumer welfare. Again using the analysis of consumer surplus from Chapter 9, we find that the fall in output from Q_1 to Q_2 reduces consumer surplus by an amount equal to the sums of the areas of the triangles a, b, and c.

There is, then, a net loss to the former Soviet economy from the collapse of central control, equal to the area $a + b$. In this example, Odessa gains while Magnetogorsk loses. But think of this story as taking place simultaneously in many markets, so that in nearly every region the gains from reducing unprofitable sales of exported goods are much more than offset by the losses from reduced supplies of imported goods. That is, there is a nearly universal decline in welfare as interregional trade shrinks.

Moreover, many of the goods that enter into interregional trade are intermediate goods, such as coal, steel, and spare parts, whose consumers are producers rather than households. Shortages of these goods reduce the ability of factories to produce. This worsens shortages of other goods and leads to further output declines. There is thus a vicious circle of shrinking output and shrinking trade, which accounts for much of the economic crisis.

[5] In reality, incentives are so distorted in the former Soviet Union that it is doubtful whether producer and consumer surplus are accurate measures of welfare in any given market. The basic point of our simplified example—that the collapse of central planning in the absence of realistic prices often makes matters worse—does not depend on the exact details.

Monetary Problems within the Former Soviet Union

With the breakup of the Soviet Union, a new set of problems emerged involving monetary relations among the former Soviet republics. Unlike the Eastern European nations, these new countries shared a common currency, the ruble. Given the very large trade among the republics, there were obvious advantages to maintaining that common currency. Yet policy conflicts had the effect of pushing many of the republics toward abandoning the ruble and introducing their own currencies.

The monetary problem within the former Soviet Union arises from two facts. First, most of the republics have large budget deficits and little ability to borrow money on the open market. Second, only one republic—Russia, the largest—has the ability actually to print rubles.

To see why these two facts interact to produce an incentive for introduction of new currencies, let us against consider a stylized example. Imagine an economy—call it the FSU, for former Soviet Union—consisting of two republics, Russia and Ukraine. Each republic has an independent state bank,[6] which accepts deposits and makes loans. The economies of the two republics, however, remain closely integrated, with the combined money supply of the FSU consisting of deposits at the two banks plus ruble bills in circulation. And only the Russian bank can print rubles.

Further suppose that private individuals insist on holding some fraction of their money as cash. This demand must be met with ruble bills, which the Russian bank can print but Ukraine's bank cannot.

Table 24-6 shows hypothetical balance sheets for the two central banks. They look somewhat different. The liabilities of the central bank of Ukraine are the deposits of Ukrainian residents—they are liabilities because depositors have the right to cash them in for rubles. The bank cannot lend all of the money it has on deposit, because it must be able to supply ruble notes to depositors who want cash, so its assets consist of loans plus whatever reserve of rubles it holds.

By contrast, the central bank of Russia can always print rubles. Deposits with that bank can still be regarded as liabilities, although they can easily be met. It is useful to think of cash rubles as also representing a kind of liability, although the only thing the Russian bank is required to supply in exchange for a ruble is another ruble.

Now consider two cases. First, suppose Russia has a budget deficit, which it is unable or unwilling either to eliminate or to finance by borrowing on world markets. Instead, the Russian government simply borrows from the state bank.

This expands the FSU money supply, which raises the price level, and hence the demand for money, in both Russia and Ukraine. In Ukraine, private citizens will increase their holdings of cash. They will also increase their holdings of deposits at the central bank, with the increase in deposits matched by an increase in the central bank's reserves of rubles.

But how does Ukraine acquire more rubles? Since it cannot print them, it can only acquire them by selling Russia something in return—such as wheat or coal. Thus Russia is in effect able to extract real goods in return for paper rubles. To put it another way,

[6] As of 1992, the major republics had established their own central banks. Several had also introduced private commercial banks, which got their money primarily by borrowing from the central bank. The main banking business remained, however, in the hands of the state-controlled institution.

TABLE 24-6 Balance sheets of central banks within former Soviet Union

Central bank of Russia

Assets	*Liabilities*
Loans to Russian government	Deposits of Russian residents Rubles held by Russian residents Rubles held by Ukrainian residents Rubles held by Ukraine central bank

Central bank of Ukraine

Assets	*Liabilities*
Loans to Ukraine government Ruble reserves	Deposits of Ukrainian residents

Russia is able to extract *seigniorage* (see Chapter 23) from the residents of *other* republics.

Can Ukraine play the same game? No. Suppose Ukraine's central bank lends additional money to its government. This money will initially be paid out as deposits in the central bank, but Ukrainian residents will want to turn part of these deposits into cash, so that the central bank will have to pay out some of its limited reserves of rubles. Thus Ukraine is limited in its own ability to pursue an inflationary policy.

This story should look familiar. The position of Russia vis-à-vis the other republics is essentially the same as that of a *reserve currency* country under fixed exchange rates, like the United States before 1973 (see Chapters 18 and 19)—except that the reserve currency is not only held by central banks but also used by the general public as the medium of exchange. As we saw, the asymmetry of a reserve currency system created considerable conflict even among advanced countries with basically healthy economies and budgets. The situation is far worse among the republics of the former Soviet Union. Russia has a huge budget deficit, which it can finance only by money creation; this leads to complaints by all the other republics that Russia is in effect exploiting its ruble monopoly to extract revenue from them. At the same time, most of the republics are in even worse shape and find their own inability to print money a severe limitation.

The result is that there are strong pressures to introduce independent currencies for the different republics, even though doing so will significantly raise the costs of inter-republic trade.

Prospects for the Former Communist Countries

There is a painful irony in the economic difficulties of the former communist nations. Communism fell in large part because of its economic failure—its inability to match the productivity and living standards of Western market economies. Yet the initial consequence of the fall of communism has been a further sharp decline in output and living standards.

The reasons for that economic decline are somewhat different in Eastern Europe and in the former Soviet Union. In Eastern Europe hard economic times can be attributed to a considerable extent to the combination of the breakup of traditional trading relationships and the worsening of their terms of trade following the shift of CMEA trade to world prices. These two adverse shocks have been severe blows to the economies, but they are one-time events. Thus there are reasonable prospects for recovery. In particular, the more advanced Eastern European countries—Hungary, the Czech Republic, and Poland—have rapidly growing private sectors and have started to increase their exports to the West. They have also launched ambitious plans to privatize state-owned industry. There is thus a reasonable prospect that these countries will, over the course of a few years, begin to show convincing growth in output and living standards.

The prospect in the former Soviet Union seems grimmer. The domestic economy is still, at time of writing, unraveling. In most of the republics the economy seems to have the worst of both worlds: neither a working market nor an effective central planning mechanism. Reformers in Russia have tried to push for a rapid freeing of markets and privatization of state enterprises to get the economy out of this unworkable halfway house, but the poor results of the reforms so far have undermined the political consensus for further change.

What happens next is unclear. The one sure thing is that the current situation is not sustainable. Either the republics will finally succeed in moving to a functioning market mechanism, or—what seems increasingly likely—they will move back toward centralized control.

Summary

1. The fall of communism between 1989 and 1991 led to the breakup of a once tightly unified economic zone. Before communism's fall, the Soviet Union and Eastern Europe were joined in the *Council for Mutual Economic Assistance (CMEA),* and the various republics of the Soviet Union were part of a single planning mechanism. The collapse of the CMEA and the breakup of the Soviet Union itself have played a role in creating serious economic difficulties.

2. Before the fall of communism, the CMEA countries formed a largely self-sufficient economic unit, which did little trade with the rest of the world. Because central planners believed strongly in the advantages of specialization, however, the CMEA economies and the Soviet republics did a very large amount of trade with each other. This trade took place at prices very different from those prevailing on world markets, so that most Eastern European countries had artificially favorable terms of trade.

3. After communism's fall, the Eastern European countries plunged into a severe recession. Trade factors played a significant role in this recession, for two reasons. First, as the countries shifted toward importing from the West rather than each other, they experienced a contraction of exports. Second, the move to trade at world prices inflicted a serious loss in their terms of trade.

4. The Soviet Union in general, and the Russian Republic in particular, experienced an improvement in terms of trade after the breakup. This gain was more than offset, however, by the disruption of trade *within* the former Soviet Union. The central planning mechanism that had once more or less coordinated interrepublic trade had broken down, but prices remained far from market-clearing levels; as a result, interrepublic trade contracted sharply, causing serious welfare losses.

5. The use of the ruble as a common currency within the former Soviet Union was also breaking down. The Russian Republic, which maintained a monopoly of the issue of ruble notes, was in effect in the position of a reserve currency country with respect to the other republics. At the same time, all of the republics suffered from large budget deficits that they attempted to finance through money creation. The result was tension both because the republics resented the seigniorage Russia was extracting at their expense and because the republics found that their inability to issue currency constrained their own ability to engage in inflationary finance.

Key Terms

centrally planned economies
Council for Mutual Economic Assistance (CMEA)
adjustment problem
coordination problem

Problems

1. In the text we showed that the CMEA economies as a group were relatively closed to outside trade, but that they did a great deal of trade with each other. To illustrate the effects of the CMEA's inward orientation, imagine a simplified world in which there are only two CMEA economies, Poland and Hungary, and only two goods, buses and tractors. Furthermore, the world is Ricardian: as in the models we studied in Chapter 2, labor is the only factor of production. Each country has 1 million units of labor. We assume that it takes 5 units of either country's labor to produce a tractor, but that it takes either 6 units of Hungarian labor or 8 units of Polish labor to produce a bus.

Suppose initially that both countries operate free-market economies, and that they trade freely on a world market in which both tractors and buses sell for $30,000 each.

a. Describe the pattern of specialization and trade.

b. Determine real wages in each country in terms of both goods.

c. Suppose that each country spends half its income on tractors, the other half on buses. What are the shares of exports in each country's GDP? What is the share of exports to the outside world in the combined GDP of the region?

2. Maintaining the assumptions of problem 1, now suppose that Poland and Hungary cut themselves off from trade with the rest of the world, but maintain trade with each other. Ignore the fact that these are planned economies, and ask what would happen under free markets.

a. Determine the pattern of specialization and trade.

b. What is the share of exports in each country's GDP? Compare with the results under (c) of question 1, and explain.

c. Determine real wages in each country, and compare with the results when the region is open to trade.

3. One country that was never communist has nonetheless suffered serious difficulties as a result of the turmoil among former communist nations. Before 1991 manufactured goods from Finland, a market economy but a politically neutral neighbor of the Soviet Union, had a privileged position in Soviet markets. Finland is now in a severe recession and has devalued its currency, the markka.

Place Finland in the context of the analysis of the adjustment problem in Eastern Europe. How is it the same, how different from the Eastern European nations?

4. Another country that has been battered by political events is Cuba. Before 1991 the Soviet Union bought most of Cuba's sugar crop (its main export) at prices above world market levels, and sold it oil at less than world market prices. It also provided a significant amount of direct aid. Now all of that is gone.

a. Compare the Cuban situation with that of East European nations. Is the *mix* of shocks any different?

b. Suppose that you headed the first post-communist government of Cuba. What international trade strategy might you follow? (There is no single right answer.)

5. One reason why there may have been so much trade between Soviet republics was that under the Soviet system transportation prices were set very low, well below the true costs of shipping goods. Why would low transport charges encourage the construction of very large plants? What would be the economic inefficiency involved in doing so?

6. During the 1970s, there were serious shortages of natural gas in the northern United States. Many economists attributed these shortages to federal regulations on natural gas pipelines, which transport the gas from fields in Texas and Louisiana, limiting the prices pipelines could charge their customers. Discuss the impact of these regulations in terms of the framework presented in Figure 24-4.

7. We have seen how the special monetary role of Russia's central bank has created tensions within the former Soviet Union. In Chapter 21 we saw that the special monetary role of Germany has also created tensions within the European Monetary System. The nature of the tensions has, however, been very different. Why?

Further Reading

Susan M. Collins and Dani Rodrik. *Eastern Europe and the Soviet Union in the World Economy.* Washington, D.C.: Institute for International Economics, 1991. Written just before the Soviet breakup, this study remains useful as an attempt to chart the likely changes in East European trade.

Padma Desai. *Perestroika in Perspective: The Design and Dilemmas of Soviet Reform.* Princeton: Princeton University Press, 1989. Books on the Soviet Union have quickly become out of date, but this volume remains a useful survey of the difficulties that brought the Soviet system down.

Stanley Fischer. ''Economic Reform in the USS and the Role of Aid.'' *Brookings Papers on Economic Activity* 2:1991, pp. 289–302. A good discussion of the economic crisis just following the breakup of the Soviet Union.

Oleh Havrylyshyn and John Williamson. *From Soviet disUnion to Eastern Economic Community?* Washington, D.C.: Institute for International Economics, 1991. A good survey of the case for policy coordination among former Soviet republics and the countries of Eastern Europe.

William Hogan. ''Economic Reforms in the Sovereign States of the Former Soviet Union.'' *Brookings Papers on Economic Activity* 2:1991, pp. 303–319. A survey of the issues involved in moving to a market economy, with emphasis on the case of Ukraine.

William Nordhaus, Merton J. Peck, and Thomas J. Richardson. ''Do Borders Matter? Soviet Economic Reform after the Coup.'' *Brookings Papers on Economic Activity* 2:1991, pp. 321–340. A discussion of the problem of managing interrepublic trade following the end of political union.

Gerlinde Sinn and Hans-Werner Sinn. *Jumpstart: The Economic Unification of Germany.* Cambridge, MA: MIT Press, 1992. Analyzes the special problems of merging a former communist economy with an advanced market economy.

John Williamson, ed. *Currency Convertibility in Eastern Europe.* Washington, D.C.: Institute for International Economics, 1991. Papers from a conference on monetary issues in former communist nations.

Mathematical Postscripts

Postscript to Chapter 3 The Specific Factors Model

In this postscript we set out a formal mathematical treatment for the specific factors model of production explained in Chapter 3. The mathematical treatment is useful in deepening understanding of the model itself, and it also provides an opportunity to develop concepts and techniques that apply to subsequent models. In particular, it is a good place to introduce an extremely useful tool of analysis, the so-called hat algebra.

Factor Prices, Costs, and Factor Demands

The specific factors model has two sectors: manufactures and food. In each sector, two factors of production are employed: capital and labor in manufactures, land and labor in food. Before turning to the full model, let us examine in general how costs and the demand for factors of production are related to the prices of factors when producers employ two factors.

Consider the production of some good that requires capital and labor as factors of production. Provided the good is produced with constant returns to scale, the technology of production may be summarized in terms of the *unit isoquant* (*II* in Figure 3P-1), a curve showing all the combinations of capital and labor that can be used to produce one unit of the good. Curve *II* shows that there is a trade-off between the quantity of

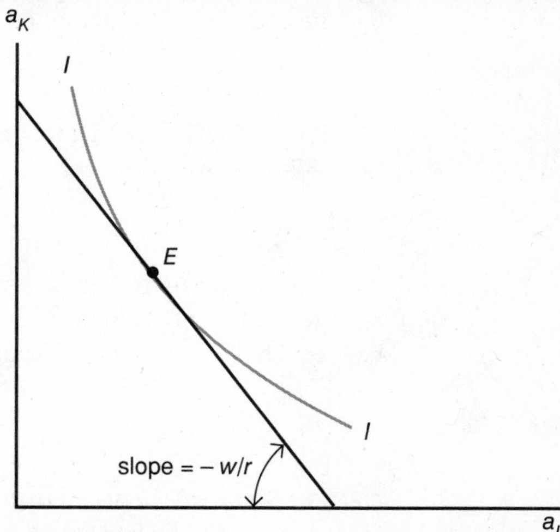

FIGURE 3P-1
Efficient production.
The cost-minimizing capital-labor ratio depends on factor prices.

capital used per unit of output, a_K, and the quantity of labor per unit of output, a_L. The curvature of the unit isoquant reflects the assumption that it becomes increasingly difficult to substitute capital for labor as the capital-labor ratio increases, and conversely.

In a competitive market economy, producers will choose the capital-labor ratio in production that minimizes their cost. Such a cost-minimizing production choice is shown in Figure 3P-1 as point *E*. It is the point at which the unit isoquant *II* is tangent to a line whose slope is equal to minus the ratio of the price of labor, *w*, to the price of capital, *r*.

The actual cost of production is equal to the sum of the cost of capital and labor inputs,

$$C = a_K r + a_L w, \tag{3P-1}$$

where the input coefficients, a_K and a_L have been chosen to minimize *C*.

Because the capital-labor ratio has been chosen to minimize costs, it follows that a change in that ratio cannot reduce costs. Costs cannot be reduced by increasing a_K while reducing a_L, nor conversely. It follows that an infinitesimal change in the capital-labor ratio from the cost-minimizing choice must have no effect on cost. Let da_K, da_L be small changes from the optimal input choices. Then

$$r da_K + w da_L = 0 \tag{3P-2}$$

for any movement along the unit isoquant.

Consider next what happens if the factor prices *r* and *w* change. This alteration will have two effects: it will change the choice of a_K and a_L, and it will change the cost of production.

First, consider the effect on the relative quantities of capital and labor used to produce one unit of output. The cost-minimizing labor-capital ratio depends on the ratio of the price of labor to that of capital:

$$\frac{a_K}{a_L} = \Phi\left(\frac{w}{r}\right). \tag{3P-3}$$

The cost of production will also change. For small changes in factor prices *dr* and *dw*, the change in production cost is

$$dC = a_K dr + a_L dw + r da_K + w da_L. \tag{3P-4}$$

From equation (3P-2), however, we already know that the last two terms of equation (3P-4) sum to zero. Hence the effect of factor prices on cost may be written

$$dC = a_K dr + a_L dw. \tag{3P-4'}$$

It turns out to be very convenient to derive a somewhat different equation from equation (3P-4′). Dividing and multiplying some of the elements of the equation, a new equation can be derived that looks as follows:

$$\frac{dC}{C} = \left(\frac{a_K r}{C}\right)\left(\frac{dr}{r}\right) + \left(\frac{a_L w}{C}\right)\left(\frac{dw}{w}\right). \tag{3P-5}$$

The term dC/C may be interpreted as the *percentage change* in *C*, and may conveniently be designated as $\hat{C}$; similarly, let $dr/r = \hat{r}$ and $dw/w = \hat{w}$. The term

$a_K r/C$ may be interpreted as the *share of capital in total production costs;* it may be conveniently designated θ_K. Thus equation (3P-5) can be compactly written

$$\hat{C} = \theta_K \hat{r} + \theta_L \hat{w}, \tag{3P-5$'$}$$

where

$$\theta_K + \theta_L = 1.$$

This is an example of "hat algebra," an extremely useful way to express mathematical relationships in international economics.

The relationship between factor prices and the capital-labor ratio can also be expressed in hat algebra. A rise in the price of labor relative to the price of capital lowers the ratio of labor to capital; this statement may be written

$$\hat{a}_L - \hat{a}_K = -\sigma(\hat{w} - \hat{r}), \tag{3P-6}$$

where σ is the percentage change in the labor capital ratio that results from a 1 percent change in the ratio of factor prices, and is known as the *elasticity of substitution.*

Factor Price Determination in the Specific Factors Model

The specific factors model has two sectors, each of which is like that just described. Manufactures are produced using capital (the specific factor) and labor:

$$Q_M = Q_M(K, L_M). \tag{3P-7}$$

Food is produced using the specific factor land and labor:

$$Q_F = Q_F(T, L_F). \tag{3P-8}$$

The supplies of capital and land to each sector are simply whatever they are. Labor, however, can be allocated to either sector:

$$L_M + L_F = \bar{L}, \tag{3P-9}$$

where $\bar{L}$ is the economy's total supply of labor.

In a perfectly competitive economy, the price of each good must just equal its cost of production. In manufactures, then,

$$P_M = a_{KM} r_K + a_{LM} w, \tag{3P-10}$$

where r_K is the price of capital, w the wage rate of labor, and a_{KM} and a_{LM} the unit input coefficients. Using the notation introduced in equation (3P-6), it follows that

$$\hat{P}_M = \theta_{KM} \hat{r}_K + \theta_{LM} \hat{w}, \tag{3P-11}$$

or

$$\hat{r}_K = \left(\frac{1}{\theta_{KM}}\right)(\hat{P}_M - \theta_{LM}\hat{w}) = \hat{P}_M + \left(\frac{\theta_{LM}}{\theta_{KM}}\right)(\hat{P}_M - \hat{w}). \tag{3P-12}$$

Similarly, with parallel notation, in the Food sector

$$\hat{r}_T = \left(\frac{1}{\theta_{TF}}\right)(\hat{P}_F - \theta_{LF}\hat{w}) = \hat{P}_F + \left(\frac{\theta_{LF}}{\theta_{TF}}\right)(\hat{P}_F - \hat{w}). \qquad \textbf{(3P-13)}$$

Equations (3P-12) and (3P-13) allow derivation of the change in the prices of capital and land, given the changes in the prices of manufactures, food, and labor. The next step is to derive the change in the wage rate, which we do by examining the demand and supply for labor.

Notice first that

$$K = a_{KM}Q_M \qquad \textbf{(3P-14)}$$

and

$$L_M = a_{LM}Q_M. \qquad \textbf{(3P-15)}$$

It follows that

$$L_M = \left(\frac{a_{LM}}{a_{KM}}\right)K. \qquad \textbf{(3P-16)}$$

Because the supply of the specific factor capital is fixed, employment of labor in the production of manufactures can change only through changes in the capital-labor ratio. Using the hat notation, the following can be derived:

$$\hat{L}_M = \hat{a}_{LM} - \hat{a}_{KM} = -\sigma(\hat{w} - \hat{r}_K). \qquad \textbf{(3P-17)}$$

From equation (3P-12), it can be shown that

$$\hat{r}_K - \hat{w} = \left(\frac{1}{\theta_{KM}}\right)(\hat{P}_M - \hat{w}). \qquad \textbf{(3P-18)}$$

Hence,

$$\hat{L}_M = \sigma_M\left(\frac{1}{\theta_{KM}}\right)(\hat{P}_M - \hat{w}), \qquad \textbf{(3P-19)}$$

where σ_M is the elasticity of substitution in manufactures and, by analogy,

$$\hat{L}_F = \sigma_F\left(\frac{1}{\theta_{TF}}\right)(\hat{P}_F - \hat{w}). \qquad \textbf{(3P-20)}$$

Now turn to the full-employment condition for labor, equation (3P-9). If total employment is to remain unchanged, an increase in one sector's employment must be offset by a decline in the other sector:

$$dL_M + dL_F = 0. \qquad \textbf{(3P-21)}$$

As before, this expression can be transformed into one that uses the hat algebra:

$$\left(\frac{dL_M}{L_M}\right)\left(\frac{L_M}{L}\right) + \left(\frac{dL_F}{L_F}\right)\left(\frac{L_F}{L}\right) = 0 \qquad \textbf{(3P-22)}$$

or

$$\alpha_M\hat{L}_M + \alpha_F\hat{L}_F = 0, \qquad \textbf{(3P-22')}$$

where $\alpha_M = L_M/L$ is the share of the labor employed in manufactures in the economy's total labor supply.

The last step is to substitute the labor-demand equations (3P-19) and (3P-20) into equation (3P-22′):

$$(\alpha_M\sigma_M/\theta_{KM})\hat{P}_M + (\alpha_F\sigma_F/\theta_{TF})\hat{P}_F = [(\alpha_M\sigma_M/\theta_{KM}) + (\alpha_F\sigma_F/\theta_{TF})]\hat{w} \qquad \textbf{(3P-23)}$$

or

$$\hat{w} = \frac{[(\alpha_M\sigma_M/\theta_{KM})\hat{P}_M + (\alpha_F\sigma_F/\theta_{TF})\hat{P}_F]}{[(\alpha_M\sigma_M/\theta_{KM}) + (\alpha_F\sigma_F/\theta_{TF})]}. \qquad \textbf{(3P-23′)}$$

That is, the rise in the wage rate is a weighted average of the increases in the prices of manufactures and food.

Effects of a Change in Relative Prices

Suppose the price of manufactures rises relative to that of food; that is, $\hat{P}_M > \hat{P}_F$. Then, because the change in the wage rate is a weighted average of the change in the two goods prices,

$$\hat{P}_M > \hat{w} > \hat{P}_F.$$

The effect on the allocation of labor is apparent from equations (3P-19) and (3P-20): Because $\hat{P}_M > \hat{w}$, $\hat{L}_M > 0$; since $\hat{P}_F < \hat{w}$, $\hat{L}_F < 0$. Employment in manufactures rises and employment in food falls.

The effects on the prices of capital and land may be seen from equations (3P-12) and (3P-13). Again, because $\hat{P}_M > \hat{w}$, r_K must rise by *more* than P_M, while conversely r_T rises by less than P_F. Thus the overall description of the relation of goods price and factor price changes is

$$\hat{r}_K > \hat{P}_M > \hat{w} > \hat{P}_F > \hat{r}_T. \qquad \textbf{(3P-24)}$$

Because the price of capital rises in terms of both goods, someone who derived his or her income entirely from capital would be unambiguously better off. Because the price of land falls relative to both goods, someone deriving his or her income entirely from land would be unambiguously worse off. Someone deriving income from labor would find that the purchasing power of that income had risen in terms of food and fallen in terms of manufactures.

Postscript to Chapter 4 The Factor Proportions Model

The factor proportions model with flexible coefficients is very similar to the specific factors model: it has two sectors, each of which uses two factors of production. The only difference is that these are the *same* factors of production, so that both labor and the other factor (land in this example) can be allocated across sectors.

The Basic Equations in the Factor-Proportions Model

Suppose a country produces two goods, X and Y, using two factors of production, land and labor. Assume that X is land intensive. The price of each good must equal its production cost:

$$P_X = a_{TX}r + a_{LX}w, \quad \textbf{(4P-1)}$$
$$P_Y = a_{TY}r + a_{LY}w, \quad \textbf{(4P-2)}$$

where $a_{TX}, a_{LX}, a_{TY}, a_{LY}$ are the cost-minimizing input choices given the prices of land r and labor w.

Also, the economy's factors of production must be full employed:

$$a_{TX}Q_X + a_{TY}Q_Y = T, \quad \textbf{(4P-3)}$$
$$a_{LX}Q_X + a_{LY}Q_Y = L, \quad \textbf{(4P-4)}$$

where T, L, are the total supplies of land and labor.

The factor-price equations (4P-1) and (4P-2) imply equations for the rate of change for factor prices, just as in the specific factors model:

$$\hat{P}_X = \theta_{TX}\hat{r} + \theta_{LX}\hat{w}, \quad \textbf{(4P-5)}$$
$$\hat{P}_Y = \theta_{TY}\hat{r} + \theta_{LY}\hat{w}, \quad \textbf{(4P-6)}$$

where θ_{TX} is the share of land in the production cost of X, etc. $\theta_{TX} > \theta_{TY}$, and $\theta_{LX} < \theta_{LY}$, because X is more land-intensive than Y.

The quantity equations (4P-3) and (4P-4) must be treated more carefully. The unit inputs a_{TX}, etc. can change if factor prices change. If goods prices are held constant, however, then factor prices will not change. Thus for *given* prices of X and Y, it is also possible to write hat equations in terms of factor supplies and outputs:

$$\alpha_{TX}\hat{Q}_X + \alpha_{TY}\hat{Q}_Y = \hat{T}, \quad \textbf{(4P-7)}$$
$$\alpha_{LX}\hat{Q}_X + \alpha_{LY}\hat{Q}_Y = \hat{L}, \quad \textbf{(4P-8)}$$

where α_{TX} is the share of the economy's land supply that is used in production of X, etc. $\alpha_{TX} > \alpha_{LX}$, and $\alpha_{TY} < \alpha_{LY}$, because of the greater land intensity of X production.

Goods Prices and Factor Prices

The factor-price equations (4P-5) and (4P-6) may be solved together to express factor prices as the outcome of goods prices (these solutions make use of the fact that $\theta_{LX} = 1 - \theta_{TX}$ and $\theta_{LY} = 1 - \theta_{TY}$):

$$\hat{r} = \left(\frac{1}{D}\right)[(1 - \theta_{TY})\hat{P}_X - \theta_{LX}\hat{P}_Y], \tag{4P-9}$$

$$\hat{w} = \left(\frac{1}{D}\right)[\theta_{TX}\hat{P}_Y - \theta_{TY}\hat{P}_X], \tag{4P-10}$$

where $D = \theta_{TX} - \theta_{TY}$ (implying that $D > 0$). These may be arranged in the form

$$\hat{r} = \hat{P}_X + \left(\frac{\theta_{LX}}{D}\right)(\hat{P}_X - \hat{P}_Y), \tag{4P-9'}$$

$$\hat{w} = \hat{P}_Y - \left(\frac{\theta_{TY}}{D}\right)(\hat{P}_X - \hat{P}_Y). \tag{4P-10'}$$

Suppose that the price of X rises relative to the price of Y, so that $\hat{P}_X > \hat{P}_Y$. Then it follows that

$$\hat{r} > \hat{P}_X > \hat{P}_Y > \hat{w}. \tag{4P-11}$$

That is, the real price of land rises in terms of both goods, while the real price of labor falls in terms of both goods. In particular, if the price of X were to rise with no change in the price of Y, the wage rate would actually fall.

Factor Supplies and Outputs

As long as goods prices may be taken as given, equations (4P-7) and (4P-8) can be solved, using the fact that $\alpha_{TY} = 1 - \alpha_{TX}$ and $\alpha_{LY} = 1 - \alpha_{LX}$, to express the change in output of each good as the outcome of changes in factor supplies:

$$\hat{Q}_X = \left(\frac{1}{\Delta}\right)[\alpha_{LY}\hat{T} - \alpha_{TY}\hat{L}], \tag{4P-12}$$

$$\hat{Q}_Y = \left(\frac{1}{\Delta}\right)[-\alpha_{LX}\hat{T} + \alpha_{TX}\hat{L}], \tag{4P-13}$$

where $\Delta = \alpha_{TX} - \alpha_{LX}$, $\Delta > 0$.

These equations may be rewritten

$$\hat{Q}_X = \hat{T} + \left(\frac{\alpha_{TY}}{\Delta}\right)(\hat{T} - \hat{L}), \tag{4P-12'}$$

$$\hat{Q}_Y = \hat{L} - \left(\frac{\alpha_{LX}}{\Delta}\right)(\hat{T} - \hat{L}). \tag{4P-13'}$$

Suppose that P_X and P_Y remain constant, while the supply of land rises relative to the supply of labor—$\hat{T} > \hat{L}$. Then it is immediately apparent that

$$\hat{Q}_X > \hat{T} > \hat{L} > \hat{Q}_Y. \tag{4P-14}$$

In particular, if T rises with L remaining constant, output of X will rise more than in proportion while output of Y will actually fall.

Postscript to Chapter 5
The Trading World Economy

Supply, Demand, and Equilibrium

WORLD EQUILIBRIUM

Although for graphical purposes it is easiest to express world equilibrium as an equality between relative supply and relative demand, for a mathematical treatment it is preferable to use an alternative formulation. This approach is to focus on the conditions of equality between supply and demand of either one of the two goods cloth and food. It does not matter which good is chosen, because equilibrium in the cloth market implies equilibrium in the food market and vice versa.

To see this condition, let Q_C, Q_C^* be the output of cloth in Home and Foreign respectively, D_C, D_C^* the quantity demanded in each country, and corresponding variables with an F subscript refer to the food market. Also, let p be the price of cloth relative to that of food.

In all cases world expenditure will be equal to world income. World income is the sum of income earned from sales of cloth and sales of food; world expenditure is the sum of purchases of cloth and food. Thus the equality of income and expenditure may be written

$$p(Q_C + Q_C^*) + Q_F + Q_F^* = p(D_C + D_C^*) + D_F + D_F^*. \qquad \textbf{(5P-1)}$$

Now suppose that the world market for cloth is in equilibrium; that is,

$$Q_C + Q_C^* = D_C + D_C^*. \qquad \textbf{(5P-2)}$$

Then from equation (5P-1) it follows that

$$Q_F + Q_F^* = D_F + D_F^*. \qquad \textbf{(5P-3)}$$

That is, the market for food must be in equilibrium as well. Clearly the converse is also true: if the market for food is in equilibrium, so too is the market for cloth.

It is therefore sufficient to focus on the market for cloth to determine the equilibrium relative price.

PRODUCTION AND INCOME

Each country has a production possibility frontier along which it can trade off between producing cloth and food. The economy chooses the point on that frontier which maximizes the value of output at the given relative price of cloth. This value may be written

$$V = pQ_C + Q_F. \qquad \textbf{(5P-4)}$$

As in the cost-minimization cases described in earlier postscripts, the fact that the output mix chosen maximizes value implies that a small shift in production along the production possibility frontier away from the optimal mix has no effect on the value of output:

$$pdQ_C + dQ_F = 0. \tag{5P-5}$$

A change in the relative price of cloth will lead to both a change in the output mix and a change in the value of output. The change in the value of output is

$$dV = Q_C dp + pdQ_C + dQ_F; \tag{5P-6}$$

however, because the last two terms are, by equation (5P-5), equal to zero, this expression reduces to

$$dV = Q_C dp. \tag{5P-6$'$}$$

Similarly, in Foreign,

$$dV^* = Q_C^* dp. \tag{5P-7}$$

INCOME, PRICES, AND UTILITY

Each country is treated as if it were one individual. The tastes of the country can be represented by a utility function depending on consumption of cloth and food:

$$U = U(D_C, D_F). \tag{5P-8}$$

Suppose a country has an income I in terms of food. Its total expenditure must be equal to this income, so that

$$pD_C + D_F = I. \tag{5P-9}$$

Consumers will maximize utility given their income and the prices they face. Let MU_C, MU_F be the marginal utility that consumers derive from cloth and food; then the change in utility that results from any change in consumption is

$$dU = MU_C dD_C + MU_F dD_F. \tag{5P-10}$$

Because consumers are maximizing utility given income and prices, there cannot be any affordable change in consumption that makes them better off. This condition implies that at the optimum,

$$\frac{MU_C}{MU_F} = p. \tag{5P-11}$$

Now consider the effect on utility of changing income and prices. Differentiating equation (5P-9) yields

$$pdD_C + dD_F = dI - D_C dp. \tag{5P-12}$$

But from equations (5P-10) and (5P-11),

$$dU = MU_F[pdD_C + dD_F]. \tag{5P-13}$$

Thus

$$dU = MU_F[dI - D_C dp]. \tag{5P-14}$$

It is convenient to introduce now a new definition: the change in utility divided by the marginal utility of food, which is the commodity in which income is measured, may be defined as the change in *real income,* and indicated by the symbol dy:

$$dy = \frac{dU}{MU_F} = dI - D_C dp. \tag{5P-15}$$

For the economy as a whole, income equals the value of output: $I = V$. Thus the effect of a change in the relative price of cloth on the economy's real income is

$$dy = [Q_C - D_C]dp. \tag{5P-16}$$

The quantity $Q_C - D_C$ is the economy's exports of cloth. A rise in the relative price of cloth, then, will benefit an economy that exports cloth; it is an improvement in that economy's terms of trade. It is instructive to restate this idea in a slightly different way:

$$dy = [p(Q_C - D_C)]\left(\frac{dp}{p}\right). \tag{5P-17}$$

The term in brackets is the value of exports; the term in parentheses is the percentage change in the terms of trade. The expression therefore says that the real income gain from a given percentage in terms of trade change is equal to the percentage change in the terms of trade multiplied by the initial value of exports. If a country is initially exporting $100 billion and its terms of trade improve by 10 percent, the gain is equivalent to a gain in national income of $10 billion.

Supply, Demand, and the Stability of Equilibrium

In the market for cloth, a change in the relative price will induce changes in both supply and demand.

On the supply side, a rise in p will lead both Home and Foreign to produce more cloth. We will denote this supply response as s, s^* in Home and Foreign respectively, so that

$$dQ_C = s\,dp, \tag{5P-18}$$
$$dQ_C^* = s^*\,dp, \tag{5P-19}$$

The demand side is more complex. A change in p will lead to both *income* and *substitution* effects. These effects are illustrated in Figure 5P-1. The figure shows an economy that initially faces a relative price indicated by the slope of the line V^0V^0. Given this relative price, the economy produces at point Q^0 and consumes at point D^0. Now suppose the relative price of cloth rises to the level indicated by the slope of V^2V^2. If there were no increase in utility, consumption would shift to D^1, which would involve an unambiguous fall in consumption of cloth. There is also, however, a change in the economy's real income; in this case, because the economy is initially a net exporter of cloth, real income rises. This change leads to consumption at D^2 rather than D^1, and this income effect tends to raise consumption of cloth. Analyzing the effect of change in p on demand requires taking account of both the substitution effect, which is the change in consumption that would take place if real income were held constant, and the income effect, which is the additional change in consumption that is the consequence of the fact that real income changes.

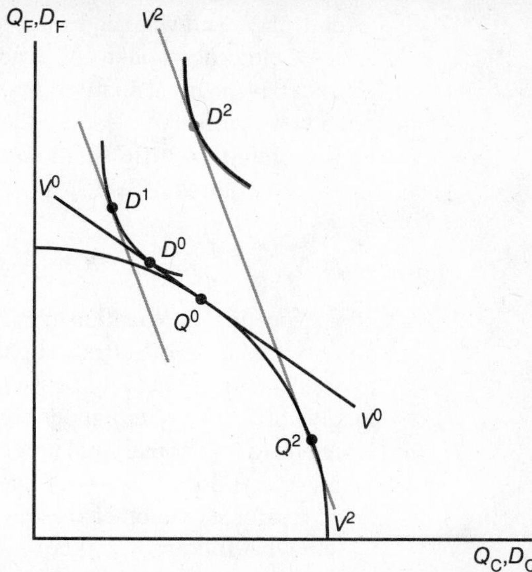

FIGURE 5P-1
Consumption effects of a price change.
A change in relative prices produces both income and substitution effects.

Let the substitution effect be denoted by $-e\,dp$; it is always negative. Also, let the income effect be denoted by $n\,dy$; as long as cloth is a normal good, for which demand rises with real income, it is positive if the country is a net exporter of cloth, negative if it is a net importer.[1] Then the total effect of a change in p on Home's demand for cloth is

$$\begin{aligned} dD_C &= -e\,dp + n\,dy \\ &= [-e + n(Q_C - D_C)]dp. \end{aligned} \quad \textbf{(5P-20)}$$

The effect on Foreign's demand similarly is

$$dD_C^* = [-e^* + n^*(Q_C^* - D_C^*)]dp. \quad \textbf{(5P-21)}$$

Because $Q_C^* - D_C^*$ is negative, the income effect in Foreign is negative.

The demand and supply effect can now be put together to get the overall effect of a change in p on the market for cloth. The *excess supply* of cloth is the difference between desired world production and consumption:

$$ES_C = Q_C + Q_C^* - D_C - D_C^*. \quad \textbf{(5P-22)}$$

The effect of a change in p on world excess supply is

$$dES_C = [s + s^* + e + e^* - n(Q_C - D_C) - n^*(Q_C^* - D_C^*)]dp. \quad \textbf{(5P-23)}$$

If the market is initially in equilibrium, however, Home's exports equal Foreign's imports, so that $Q_C^* - D_C^* = -(Q_C - D_C)$; the effect of p on excess supply may therefore be written

$$dES_C = [s + s^* + e + e^* - (n - n^*)(Q_C - D_C)]dp. \quad \textbf{(5P-23')}$$

[1] If food is also a normal good, n must be less than $1/p$. To see this effect, notice that if I were to rise by dI without any change in p, spending on cloth would rise by $np\,dI$. Unless $n < 1/p$, then, more than 100 percent of the increase in income would be spent on cloth.

Suppose the relative price of cloth were initially a little higher than its equilibrium level. If the result were an excess supply of cloth, market forces would push the relative price of cloth down and thus lead to restoration of equilibrium. On the other hand, if an excessively high relative price of cloth leads to an excess *demand* for cloth, the price will rise further, leading the economy away from equilibrium. Thus equilibrium will be *stable* only if a small increase in the relative price of cloth leads to an excess supply of cloth; that is, if

$$\frac{dES_C}{dp} > 0. \tag{5P-24}$$

Inspection of equation (5P-23′) reveals the factors determining whether or not equilibrium is stable. Both supply effects and substitution effects in demand work toward stability. The only possible source of instability lies in income effects. The net income effect is of ambiguous sign: it depends on whether $n > n^*$; that is, on whether Home has a higher marginal propensity to consume cloth when its real income increases than Foreign does. If $n > n^*$, the income effect works against stability, while if $n < n^*$, it reinforces the other reasons for stability.

In what follows it will be assumed that equation (5P-24) holds, so that the equilibrium of the world economy is in fact stable.

Effects of Changes in Supply and Demand

THE METHOD OF COMPARATIVE STATICS

To evaluate the effects of changes in the world economy, a method known as *comparative statics* is applied. In each of the cases considered in the text, the world economy is subjected to some change, which will lead to a change in the world relative price of cloth. The first step in the method of comparative statics is to calculate the effect of the change in the world economy on the excess supply of cloth *at the original p*. This change is denoted by $dES|_p$. Then the change in the relative price needed to restore equilibrium is calculated by

$$dp = \frac{-dES|_p}{(dES/dp)}, \tag{5P-25}$$

where dES/dp reflects the supply, income, and substitution effects described earlier.

The effects of a given change on national welfare can be calculated in two stages. First there is whatever direct effect the change has on real income, which we can denote by $dy|_p$; then there is the indirect effect of the resulting change in the terms of trade, which can be calculated using equation (5P-16). Thus the total effect on welfare is

$$dy = dy|_p + (Q_C - D_C)dp. \tag{5P-26}$$

Economic Growth

Consider the effect of growth in the Home economy. As pointed out in the text, by growth we mean an outward shift in the production possibility frontier. This change will lead to changes in both cloth and food output at the initial relative price p; let dQ_C, dQ_F be these changes in output. If growth is strongly biased, one or the other of these changes may be negative, but because production possibilities have expanded, the value of output at the initial p must rise:

$$dV = p\,dQ_C + dQ_F = dy|_p > 0. \qquad \textbf{(5P-27)}$$

At the initial p the supply of cloth will rise by the amount dQ_C. The demand for cloth will also rise, by an amount $n\,dy|_p$. The net effect on world excess supply of cloth will therefore be

$$dES|_p = dQ_C - n(p\,dQ_C + dQ_F). \qquad \textbf{(5P-28)}$$

This expression can have either sign. Suppose first that growth is biased toward cloth, so that while $dQ_C > 0$, $dQ_F \le 0$. Then demand for cloth will rise by

$$dD_C = n(p\,dQ_C + dQ_F) \le np\,dQ_C < dQ_C.$$

(See footnote 1).

Thus the overall effect on excess supply will be

$$dES|_p = dQ_C - dD_C > 0.$$

As a result, $dp = -dES|_p/(dES/dp) < 0$: Home's terms of trade worsen.

On the other hand, suppose that growth is strongly biased toward food, so that $dQ_C \le 0$, $dQ_F > 0$. Then the effect on the supply of cloth at the initial p is negative, but the effect on the demand for cloth remains positive. It follows that

$$dES|_p = dQ_C - dD_C < 0,$$

so that $dp > 0$. Home's terms of trade improve.

Growth that is less strongly biased can move p either way, depending on the strength of the bias compared with the way Home divides its income at the margin.

Turning next to the welfare effects, the effect on Foreign depends only on the terms of trade. The effect on Home, however, depends on the combination of the initial income change and the subsequent change in the terms of trade, as shown in equation (5P-26). If growth turns the terms of trade against Home, this condition will oppose the immediate favorable effect of growth.

But can growth worsen the terms of trade sufficiently to make the growing country actually worse off? To see that it can, consider first the case of a country that experiences a biased shift in its production possibilities that raises Q_C and lowers Q_F while leaving the value of its output unchanged at initial relative prices. (This change would not necessarily be considered growth, because it violates the assumption of equation (5P-27), but it is a useful reference point). Then there would be no change in demand at the initial p, while the supply of cloth rises; hence p must fall. The change in real income is $dI|_p - (Q_C - D_C)dp$; by construction, however, this is a case in which $dI|_p = 0$, so dy is certainly negative.

Now this country did not grow, in the usual sense, because the value of output at initial prices did not rise. By allowing the output of either good to rise slightly more, however, we would have a case in which the definition of growth is satisfied. If the extra growth is sufficiently small, however, it will not outweigh the welfare loss from the fall in p. Therefore, sufficiently biased growth can leave the growing country worse off.

The Transfer Problem

Suppose Home makes a transfer of some of its income to Foreign, say as foreign aid. Let the amount of the transfer, measured in terms of food, be da. What effect does this alteration have?

At unchanged relative prices there is no effect on supply. The only effect is on demand. Home's income is reduced by da, while Foreign's is raised by the same amount. This adjustment leads to a decline in D_C by $-n\, da$, while D_C^* rises by a n^*da. Thus

$$dES|_p = (n - n^*)da \qquad \textbf{(5P-29)}$$

and the change in the terms of trade is

$$dp = -da\frac{(n - n^*)}{(dES/dp)}. \qquad \textbf{(5P-30)}$$

Home's terms of trade will worsen if $n > n^*$, which is widely regarded as the normal case; they will, however, improve if $n^* > n$.

The effect on Home's real income combines a direct negative effect from the transfer and an indirect terms of trade effect that can go either way. Is it possible for a favorable terms of trade effect to outweigh the income loss? In this model it is not.

To see the reason, notice that

$$\begin{aligned} dy &= dy|_p + (Q_C - D_C)dp \\ &= -da + (Q_C - D_C)dp \qquad \textbf{(5P-31)} \\ &= -da\left\{1 + \frac{(n - n^*)(Q_C - D_C)}{s + s^* + e + e^* - (n - n^*)(Q_C - D_C)}\right\} \\ &= -da\frac{(s + s^* + e + e^*)}{[s + s^* + e + e^* - (n - n^*)(Q_C - D_C)]} < 0. \end{aligned}$$

Similar algebra will reveal correspondingly that a transfer cannot make the recipient worse off.

An intuitive explanation of this result is the following. Suppose p were to rise sufficiently to leave Home as well off as it would be if it made no transfer and to leave Foreign no better off as a result of the transfer. Then there would be no income effects on demand in the world economy. But the rise in price would produce both increased output of cloth and substitution in demand away from cloth, leading to an excess supply that would drive down the price. This result demonstrates that a p sufficiently high to reverse the direct welfare effects of a transfer is above the equilibrium p.

In the text we mention that recent work shows how perverse effects of a transfer are nonetheless possible. This work depends on relaxing the assumptions of this model, either by breaking the assumption that each country may be treated as if it were one individual or by introducing more than two countries.

A Tariff

Suppose Home places a tariff on imports, imposing a tax equal to the fraction t of the price. Then for a given world relative price of cloth p, Home consumers and producers will face an internal relative price $\bar{p} = p/(1 + t)$. If the tariff is sufficiently small, the internal relative price will be approximately equal to

$$\bar{p} = p - pt. \quad \textbf{(5P-32)}$$

In addition to affecting p, a tariff will raise revenue, which will be assumed to be redistributed to the rest of the economy.

At the initial terms of trade, a tariff will influence the excess supply of cloth in two ways. First, the fall in the relative price of cloth inside Home will lower production of cloth and induce consumers to substitute away from food toward cloth. Second, the tariff may affect Home's real income, with resulting income effects on demand. If Home starts with no tariff and imposes a small tariff, however, the problem may be simplified, because the tariff will have a negligible effect on real income. To see this relation, recall that

$$dy = p\, dD_C + dD_F.$$

The value of output and the value of consumption must always be equal at world prices, so that

$$p\, dD_C + dD_F = p\, dQ_C + dQ_F$$

at the initial terms of trade. But because the economy was maximizing the value of output before the tariff was imposed,

$$p\, dQ_C + dQ_F = 0.$$

Because there is no income effect, only the substitution effect is left. The fall in the internal relative price $\bar{p}$ induces a decline in production and a rise in consumption:

$$dQ_C = -sp\, dt, \quad \textbf{(5P-33)}$$
$$dD_C = ep\, dt, \quad \textbf{(5P-34)}$$

where dt is the tariff increase. Hence

$$dES|_p = -(s + e)p\, dt < 0, \quad \textbf{(5P-35)}$$

implying

$$\begin{aligned} dp &= \frac{-dES|_p}{(dES/dp)} \\ &= \frac{p\, dt(s + e)}{[s + s^* + e + e^* - (n - n^*)(Q_c - D_c)]} > 0. \end{aligned} \quad \textbf{(5P-36)}$$

This expression shows that a tariff unambiguously improves the terms of trade of the country that imposes it.

Can a tariff actually improve the terms of trade so much that the internal relative price of the imported good falls and the internal price of the exported good rises? The change in $\bar{p}$ is

$$d\bar{p} = dp - p\, dt, \quad \textbf{(5P-37)}$$

so that this paradoxical result will occur if $dp > p\, dt$.

By inspecting equation (5P-36) it can be seen that this result, the famous Metzler paradox, is indeed possible. If $s^* + e^* - (n - n^*)(Q_c - D_c) < 0$, there will be a Metzler paradox; this need not imply instability, because the extra terms s and e help give the denominator a positive sign.

Postscript to Chapter 6
The Monopolistic Competition Model

We want to consider the effects of changes in the size of the market on equilibrium in a monopolistically competitive industry. Each firm has the total cost relationship

$$C = F + cX, \tag{6P-1}$$

where c is marginal cost, F a fixed cost, and X the firm's output. This implies an average cost curve of the form

$$AC = C/X = F/X + c. \tag{6P-2}$$

Also, each firm faces a demand curve of the form

$$X = S[1/n - b(P - \overline{P})], \tag{6P-3}$$

where S is total industry sales (taken as given), n is the number of firms, and $\overline{P}$ is the average price charged by other firms (which each firm is assumed to take as given).

Each firm chooses its price to maximize profits. Profits of a typical firm are

$$\pi = PX - C = PS[1/n - b(P - \overline{P})] - F - cS[1/n - b(P - \overline{P})]. \tag{6P-4}$$

To maximize profits, a firm sets the derivative $d\pi/dP = 0$. This implies

$$X - SbP + Sbc = 0. \tag{6P-5}$$

Since all firms are symmetric, however, in equilibrium $P = \overline{P}$ and $X = S/n$. Thus (6P-5) implies

$$P = 1/bn + c, \tag{6P-6}$$

which is the relationship derived in the text.

Since $X = S/n$, average cost is a function of S and n,

$$AC = Fn/S + c. \tag{6P-7}$$

In zero-profit equilibrium, however, the price charged by a typical firm must also equal its average cost. So we must have

$$1/bn + c = Fn/S + c, \tag{6P-8}$$

which in turn implies

$$n = \sqrt{S/bF}. \tag{6P-9}$$

This shows that an increase in the size of the market, S, will lead to an increase in the number of firms, n, but not in proportion—for example, a doubling of the size of the market will increase the number of firms by a factor of approximately 1.4.

The price charged by the representative firm is

$$P = 1/bn + c = c + \sqrt{F/Sb}, \qquad \textbf{(6P-10)}$$

which shows that an increase in the size of the market leads to lower prices.

Finally, notice that the sales per firm, X, equal

$$X = S/n = \sqrt{SbF}. \qquad \textbf{(6P-11)}$$

This shows that the scale of each individual firm also increases with the size of the market.

Postscript to Chapter 22 Risk Aversion and International Portfolio Diversification

This postscript develops a model of international portfolio diversification by risk-averse investors. The model shows that investors generally care about the risk as well as the return of their portfolios. In particular, people may hold assets whose expected returns are smaller than those of other assets if this strategy reduces the overall riskiness of their wealth.

A representative investor can divide her real wealth, W, between a Home asset and a Foreign asset. Two possible states of nature can occur in the future, and it is impossible to predict in advance which one it will be. In state 1, which occurs with probability q, a unit of wealth invested in the Home asset pays out H_1 units of output and a unit of wealth invested in the Foreign asset pays out F_1 units of output. In state 2, which occurs with probability $1 - q$, the payoffs to unit investments in the Home and Foreign assets are H_2 and F_2, respectively.

Let α be the share of wealth invested in the Home asset and $1 - \alpha$ the share invested in the Foreign asset. Then if state 1 occurs, the investor will be able to consume the weighted average of her two assets' values,

$$C_1 = [\alpha H_1 + (1 - \alpha)F_1] \times W. \quad \textbf{(22P-1)}$$

Similarly, consumption in state 2 is

$$C_2 = [\alpha H_2 + (1 - \alpha)F_2] \times W. \quad \textbf{(22P-2)}$$

In any state, the investor derives utility $U(C)$ from a consumption level of C. Since the investor does not know beforehand which state will occur, she makes the portfolio decision to maximize the average or *expected* utility from future consumption,

$$qU(C_1) + (1 - q)U(C_2).$$

An Analytical Derivation of the Optimal Portfolio

After the state 1 and 2 consumption levels given by (22P-1) and (22P-2) are substituted into the expected utility function above, the investor's decision problem can be expressed as follows: choose the portfolio share α to maximize expected utility,

$$qU\{[\alpha H_1 + (1 - \alpha)F_1] \times W\} + (1 - q)U\{[\alpha H_2 + (1 - \alpha)F_2] \times W\}.$$

This problem is solved (as usual) by differentiating the expected utility above with respect to α and setting the resulting derivative equal to 0.

Let $U'(C)$ be the derivative of the utility function $U(C)$ with respect to C; that is, $U'(C)$ is the *marginal utility* of consumption. Then α maximizes expected utility if

$$\frac{H_1 - F_1}{H_2 - F_2} = -\frac{(1 - q)U'\{[\alpha H_2 + (1 - \alpha)F_2] \times W\}}{qU'\{[\alpha H_1 + (1 - \alpha)F_1] \times W\}}. \qquad \textbf{(22P-3)}$$

This equation can be solved for α, the optimal portfolio share.

For a risk-averse investor, the marginal utility of consumption, $U'(C)$, falls as consumption rises. Declining marginal utility explains why someone who is risk averse will not take a gamble with an expected payoff of zero: the extra consumption made possible by a win yields less utility than the utility sacrificed if the gamble is lost. If the marginal utility of consumption does not change as consumption changes, we say the investor is *risk neutral* rather than risk averse. A risk neutral investor is willing to take gambles with a zero expected payoff.

If the investor is risk neutral, so that $U'(C)$ is constant for all C, however, equation (22P-3) becomes

$$qH_1 + (1 - q)H_2 = qF_1 + (1 - q)F_2,$$

which states that *the expected rates of return on Home and Foreign assets are equal.* This result is the basis for the assertion in Chapter 14 that all assets must yield the same expected return in equilibrium when considerations of risk (and liquidity) are ignored. Thus, the interest parity condition of Chapter 14 is valid under risk-neutral behavior, but not, in general, under risk aversion.

For the analysis above to make sense, neither of the assets can yield a higher return than the other in *both* states of nature. If one asset did dominate the other in this way, the left-hand side of equation (22P-3) would be positive while its right-hand side would be negative (because the marginal utility of consumption is usually assumed to be positive). Thus, (22P-3) would have no solution. Intuitively, no one would want to hold a particular asset if another asset that *always* did better were available. Indeed, if anyone did, other investors would be able to make riskless arbitrage profits by issuing the low-return asset and using the proceeds to purchase the high-return asset.

To be definite, we therefore assume that $H_1 > F_1$ and $H_2 < F_2$, so that the Home asset does better in state 1 but does worse in state 2. This assumption is now used to develop a diagrammatic analysis that helps illustrate additional implications of the model.

A Diagrammatic Derivation of the Optimal Portfolio

Figure 22P-1 shows indifference curves for the expected utility function $qU(C_1) + (1 - q)U(C_2)$. The points in the diagram should be thought of as contingency plans showing the level of consumption that will occur in each state of nature. The preferences represented apply to these contingent consumption plans rather than to consumption of different goods in a single state of nature. As with standard indifference curves, however, each curve in the figure represents a set of contingency plans for consumption with which the investor is equally satisfied.

FIGURE 22P-1
Indifference curves and budget line for the portfolio-selection problem.
The indifference curves are sets of state-contingent consumption plans with which the individual is equally happy. The budget line describes the trade-off between state 1 and state 2 consumption that results from portfolio shifts between Home and Foreign assets.

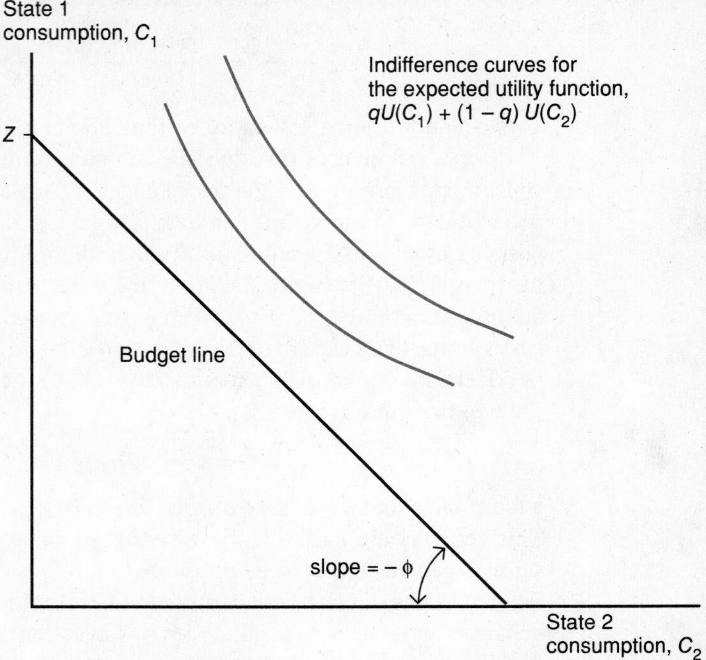

To compensate the investor for a reduction of consumption in state 1 (C_1), consumption in state 2 (C_2) must rise. The indifference curves therefore slope downward. Each curve becomes flatter however, as C_1 falls and C_2 rises. This property of the curves reflects the property of $U(C)$ that the marginal utility of consumption declines when C rises. As C_1 falls, the investor can be kept on her original indifference curve only by successively greater increments in C_2: additions to C_2 are becoming less enjoyable at the same time as subtractions from C_1 are becoming more painful.

Equations (22P-1) and (22P-2) imply that by choosing the portfolio division given by α, the investor also chooses her consumption levels in the two states of nature. Thus, the problem of choosing an optimal portfolio is equivalent to one of optimally choosing the contingent consumption levels C_1 and C_2. Accordingly, the indifference curves in Figure 22P-1 can be used to determine the optimal portfolio for the investor. All that is needed to complete the analysis is a budget line showing the trade-off between state 1 consumption and state 2 consumption that the market makes available.

This trade-off is given by equations (22P-1) and (22P-2). If equation (22P-2) is solved for α, the result is

$$\alpha = \frac{F_2W - C_2}{F_2W - H_2W}.$$

After substitution of this expression for α in (22P-1), the latter equation becomes

$$C_1 + \phi C_2 = Z, \qquad \textbf{(22P-4)}$$

where $\phi = (H_1 - F_1)/(F_2 - H_2)$ and $Z = W \times (H_1F_2 - H_2F_1)/(F_2 - H_2)$. Notice that because $H_1 > F_1$ and $H_2 < F_2$, both ϕ and Z are positive. Thus, equation (22P-4) looks like the budget line that appears in the usual analysis of consumer choice, with ϕ playing the role of a relative price and Z the role of income measured in terms of state 1 consumption. This budget line is graphed in Figure 22P-1 as a straight line with slope $-\phi$ intersecting the vertical axis at Z.

To interpret ϕ as the market trade-off between state 2 and state 1 consumption (that is, as the price of state 2 consumption in terms of state 1 consumption), suppose the investor shifts one unit of her wealth from the Home to the Foreign asset. Since the Home asset has the higher payoff in state 1, her net loss of state 1 consumption is H_1 *less* the Foreign asset's state 1 payoff, F_1. Similarly, her net gain in state 2 consumption is $F_2 - H_2$. To obtain additional state 2 consumption of $F_2 - H_2$, the investor therefore must sacrifice $H_1 - F_1$ in state 1. The price of a unit of C_2 in terms of C_1 is therefore $H_1 - F_1$ divided by $F_2 - H_2$, which equals ϕ, the absolute value of the slope of budget line (22P-4).

Figure 22P-2 shows how the choices of C_1 and C_2—and, by implication, the choice of the portfolio share α—are determined. As usual, the investor picks the consumption levels given by point 1, where the budget line just touches the highest attainable indifference curve, I_1I_1. Given the optimal choices of C_1 and C_2, α can be calculated using equation (22P-1) or (22P-2). As we move downward and to the right along the budget constraint, the Home asset's portfolio share, α, falls. (Why?)

For some values of C_1 and C_2, α may be negative or greater than 1. These possibilities raise no conceptual problems. A negative α, for example, means that the investor has "gone short" in the Home asset, that is, issued some quantity of state-contingent claims that promise to pay their holders H_1 units of output in state 1 and H_2 units in state 2. The proceeds of this borrowing are used to increase the Foreign asset's portfolio share, $1 - \alpha$, above 1.

Figure 22P-3 shows the points on the investor's budget constraint at which $\alpha =$

FIGURE 22P-2
Solving the international investor's problem.
To maximize expected utility, the investor makes the state-contingent consumption choices shown at point 1, where the budget line is tangent to the highest attainable indifference curve, I_1I_1. The optimal portfolio share, α, can be calculated as $(F_2W - C_2^1) \div (F_2W - H_2W)$.

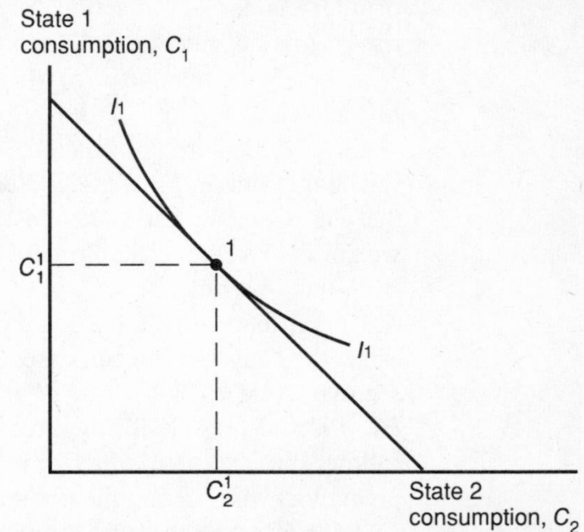

FIGURE 22P-3
Nondiversified portfolios.
When $\alpha = 1$, the investor holds all her wealth in the Home asset. When $\alpha = 0$ she holds all her wealth in the Foreign asset. Moves along the budget constraint upward and to the left from $\alpha = 1$ correspond to short sales of the Foreign asset, which raise α above 1. Moves downward and to the right from $\alpha = 0$ correspond to short sales of the Home asset, which push α below 0.

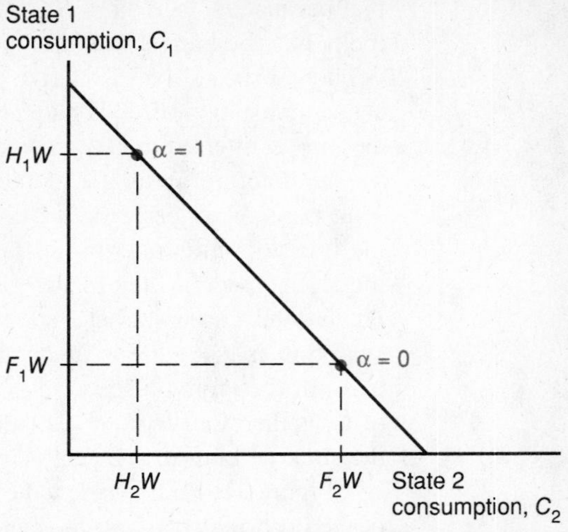

1 (so that $C_1 = H_1W$, $C_2 = H_2W$) and $\alpha = 0$ (so that $C_1 = F_1W$, $C_2 = F_2W$). Starting from $\alpha = 1$, the investor can move upward and to the left along the constraint by going short in the Foreign asset (thereby making α greater than 1 and $1 - \alpha$ negative). She can move downward and to the right from $\alpha = 0$ by going short in the Home asset.

The Effects of Changing Rates of Return

The diagram we have developed can be used to illustrate the effect of changes in rates of return under risk aversion. Suppose, for example, the Home asset's state 1 payoff rises while all other payoffs and the investor's wealth, W, stay the same. The rise in H_1 raises ϕ, the relative price of state 2 consumption, and therefore steepens the budget line shown in Figure 22P-3.

We need more information, however, to describe completely how the position of the budget line in Figure 22P-3 changes when H_1 rises. The following reasoning fills the gap. Consider the portfolio allocation $\alpha = 0$ in Figure 22P-3, under which all wealth is invested in the Foreign asset. The contingent consumption levels that result from this investment strategy, $C_1 = F_1W$, $C_2 = F_2W$, do not change as a result of a rise in H_1, because the portfolio we are considering does not involve the Home asset. Since the consumption pair associated with $\alpha = 0$ does not change when H_1 rises, we see that $C_1 = F_1W$, $C_2 = F_2W$ is a point on the new budget constraint: after a rise in H_1, it is still feasible for the investor to put all of her wealth into the Foreign asset. It follows that the effect of a rise in H_1 is to make the budget constraint in Figure 22P-3 pivot clockwise around the point $\alpha = 0$.

The effect on the investor of a rise in H_1 is shown in Figure 22P-4, which assumes that initially $\alpha > 0$ (that is, the investor initially owns a positive amount of the Home

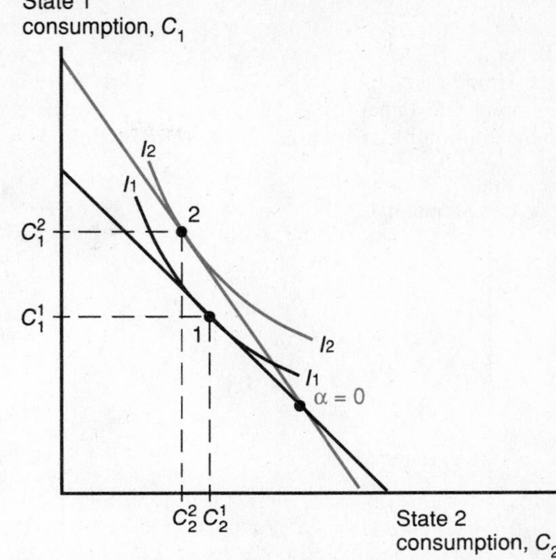

FIGURE 22P-4
Effects of a rise in H_1.
A rise in H_1 causes the budget line to pivot clockwise around $\alpha = 0$, and the investor's optimum shifts to point 2. State 1 consumption always rises; in the case shown, state 2 consumption falls.

asset).[1] As usual, both a "substitution" and an "income" effect influence the shift of the investor's contingent consumption plan from point 1 to point 2. The substitution effect is a tendency to demand more C_1, whose relative price has fallen, and less C_2, whose relative price has risen. The income effect of the rise in H_1, however, pushes the entire budget line outward and tends to raise consumption in *both* states (as long as $\alpha > 0$ initially). Because the investor will be richer in state 1, she can afford to shift some of her wealth toward the Foreign asset (which has the higher payoff in state 2) and thereby even out her consumption in the two states of nature. Risk aversion explains the investor's desire to avoid large consumption fluctuations across states. As Figure 22P-4 suggests, C_1 definitely rises while C_2 may rise or fall. (In the case illustrated, the substitution effect is stronger than the income effect and C_2 falls.)

Corresponding to this ambiguity is an ambiguity concerning the effect of the rise in H_1 on the portfolio share, α. Figure 22P-5 illustrates the two possibilities. The key to understanding this figure is the observation that if the investor does *not* change α in response to the rise in H_1, her consumption choices are given by point 1′, which lies on the new budget constraint vertically above the initial consumption point 1. Why is this the case? Equation (22P-2) implies that $C_2^1 = [\alpha H_2 + (1 - \alpha)F_2] \times W$ doesn't change if α doesn't change; the new, higher value of state 1 consumption corresponding to the original portfolio choice is then given by the point on the new budget constraint directly above C_2^1. In both panels of Figure 22P-5, the slope of the ray *OR* connecting the origin and point 1′ shows the ratio C_1/C_2 implied by the initial portfolio composition after the rise in H_1.

It is now clear, however, that to shift to a lower value of C_2 the investor must raise α above its initial value, that is, shift the portfolio toward the Home asset. To raise C_2

[1] The case in which $\alpha < 0$ initially is left as an exercise.

FIGURE 22P-5
Effects of a rise in H_1 on portfolio shares.
Panel (a): If the investor is not too risk averse, she shifts her portfolio toward the Home asset, picking a C_1/C_2 ratio greater than the one indicated by the slope of *OR*. Panel (b): A very risk-averse investor might increase state 2 consumption by shifting her portfolio toward the Foreign asset.

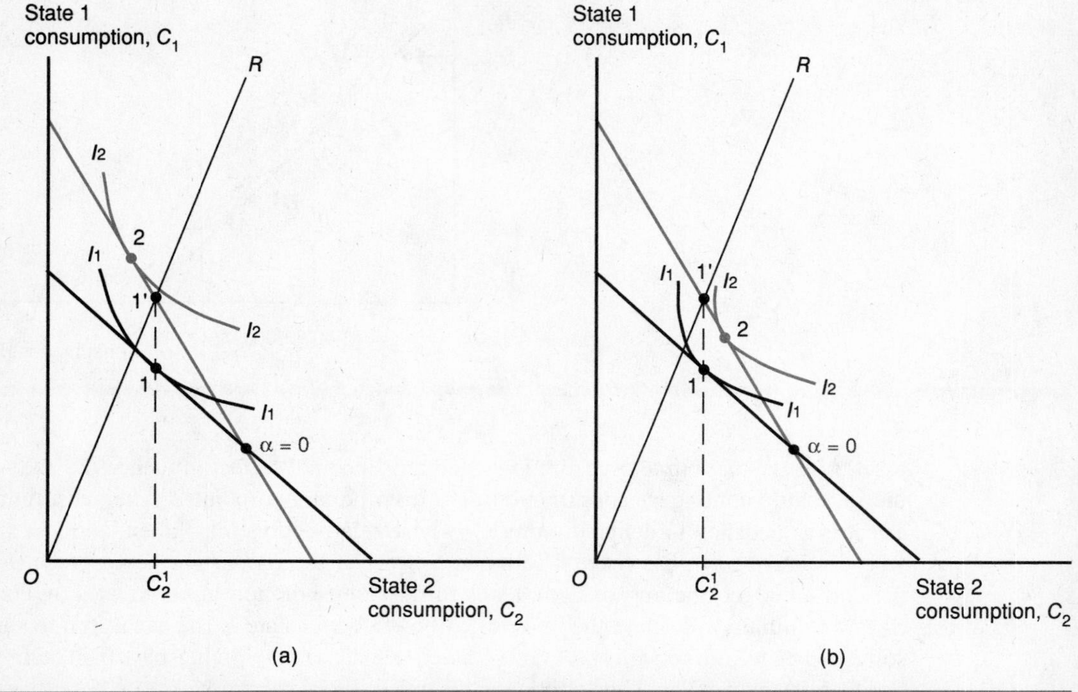

she must lower α, that is, shift toward the Foreign asset. Figure 22P-5a shows again the case in which the substitution effect outweighs the income effect. In that case, C_2 falls as the investor shifts her portfolio toward the Home asset, whose expected rate of return has risen relative to that on the Foreign asset. This case corresponds to those we studied in the text, in which the portfolio share of an asset rises as its relative expected rate of return rises.

Figure 22P-5b shows the opposite case, in which C_2 rises and α falls, implying a portfolio shift toward the Foreign asset. You can see that the factor giving rise to this possibility is the sharper curvature of the indifference curves *II* in Figure 22P-5b. This curvature is precisely what economists mean by the term *risk aversion.* An investor who becomes more risk averse regards consumptions in different states of nature as poorer substitutes, and thus requires a larger increase in state 1 consumption to compensate her for a fall in state 2 consumption (and vice versa). Note that the paradoxical case shown in Figure 22P-5b, in which a rise in an asset's expected rate of return can cause investors to demand *less* of it, is unlikely in the real world. For example, an increase in the interest rate a currency offers, other things equal, raises the expected rate of return on deposits of that currency in all states of nature, not just in one. The portfolio substitution effect in favor of the currency therefore is much stronger.

The results we have found are quite different from those that would occur if the investor were risk neutral. A risk-neutral investor would shift all of her wealth into the asset with the higher expected return, paying no attention to the riskiness of this move.[2] The greater the degree of risk aversion, however, the greater the concern with the riskiness of the overall portfolio of assets.

[2] In fact, a risk-neutral investor would always like to take the maximum possible short position in the low-return asset and, correspondingly, the maximum possible long position in the high-return asset. It is this behavior that gives rise to the interest parity condition.

Index

Page numbers followed by **t** and **f** denote tables and figures, respectively.